P9-AGC-809

ABNORMAL PSYCHOLOGY
Second Edition

David L. Rosenhan
STANFORD UNIVERSITY

Martin E. P. Seligman
UNIVERSITY OF PENNSYLVANIA

ABNORMAL PSYCHOLOGY
Second Edition

W. W. NORTON AND COMPANY
New York   London

For Mollie and Mandy

Copyright © 1989, 1984, by W. W. Norton & Company, Inc.

All rights reserved.

Printed in the United States of America.

Library of Congress Cataloging-in-Publication Data

Rosenhan, David L.
  Abnormal psychology/David L. Rosenhan, Martin E. P. Seligman.—2nd ed.
    p.   cm.
  Includes index.
    1. Psychology, Pathological.   2. Psychotherapy—Case studies.
I. Seligman, Martin E. P.   II. Title.
RC454.R578 1989   616.89—dc 19   88-28908
ISBN 0-393-95696-2

The text of this book is composed in Times Roman, with display type set in Times Roman.
Composition by New England Typographic Service, Inc.
Manufacturing by Hawkins/Arcata

Cover illustration: *Composition: "City People"* by Abraham Rattner. Collection of Charles E. Curry. Photograph courtesy of Kennedy Galleries, Inc., New York.

Acknowledgments and copyrights appear on pages 762–66, which constitute a continuation of the copyright page.

W. W. Norton & Company, Inc., 500 Fifth Avenue, New York, N.Y. 10110
W. W. Norton & Company, Ltd., 10 Coptic Street, London WC1A 1PU

5 6 7 8 9 0

Contents in Brief

PART 1   The Nature and History of Abnormality

    1 THE MEANINGS OF ABNORMALITY
    2 ABNORMALITY ACROSS TIME AND PLACE

PART 2   Models and Treatments of Abnormality

    3 THE BIOMEDICAL MODEL
    4 PSYCHODYNAMIC AND EXISTENTIAL APPROACHES
    5 THE ENVIRONMENTALIST MODEL: BEHAVIORAL AND COGNITIVE
      APPROACHES

PART 3   Investigating and Diagnosing Abnormality

    6 INVESTIGATING ABNORMALITY
    7 PSYCHOLOGICAL ASSESSMENT AND CLASSIFICATION

PART 4   Anxiety and Psychosomatic Disorders

    8 FEAR AND PHOBIA: ANXIETY FELT
    9 OBSESSION, HYSTERIA, AND DISSOCIATION: ANXIETY INFERRED
   10 HEALTH PSYCHOLOGY AND PSYCHOSOMATIC DISORDERS

PART 5   Depression and the Schizophrenias

   11 DEPRESSION AND SUICIDE
   12 THE SCHIZOPHRENIAS

PART 6   Social and Interpersonal Disorders

13 SEXUAL BEHAVIOR, DYSFUNCTION, AND DISORDER
14 PSYCHOACTIVE SUBSTANCE USE DISORDERS
15 PERSONALITY DISORDERS

PART 7   Abnormality across the Lifespan

16 CHILDHOOD DISORDERS AND MENTAL RETARDATION
17 DISORDERS OF THE NERVOUS SYSTEM AND PSYCHOPATHOLOGY

PART 8   Abnormality, the Law, and Choosing a Psychotherapy

18 THE LAW AND POLITICS OF ABNORMALITY
19 A CONSUMER'S GUIDE TO PSYCHOLOGICAL TREATMENT

APPENDIX   THE DIAGNOSTIC AND STATISTICAL MANUAL OF MENTAL
DISORDERS, REVISED (DSM-III-R)

Contents

PREFACE xvii

PART 1   The Nature and History of Abnormality

1 THE MEANINGS OF ABNORMALITY   3

Abnormality 5 *Why Can't Abnormality Be Easily Defined?* 6

The Elements of Abnormality 7 *Suffering* 7
Maladaptiveness 8 *Irrationality and Incomprehensibility* 9
Unpredictability and Loss of Control 10 *Vividness and
Unconventionality* 10 *Observer Discomfort* 11 *Violation of
Moral and Ideal Standards* 12

Abnormality as a Social Judgment 12

Applying the Elements of Abnormality 13 *Using the Family
Resemblance Approach* 13 *Abnormality and Psychological
Diagnosis* 15

Normality 17 *Positives and Negatives: The Meaning of
Meaning* 18

Beyond Normality: Living Optimally 18 *Some Elements of
Optimal Living* 19 *The Hazards of Self-Diagnosis* 21

Summary 22

2 ABNORMALITY ACROSS TIME AND PLACE   23

The Perceived Causes of Abnormal Behavior 24 *Animistic
Origins: Possession* 24 *Physical Causes* 28 *Psychogenic
Origins* 30

vii

Treatment of the Mentally Distressed 34 *Treating Demonic Possession* 34 *Treating Physical Causes* 35 *The Rise of Psychogenic Treatments* 35

The Rise of the Psychiatric Hospital 36 *Institutionalizing the Poor* 36 *Segregating the Insane* 37 *The Growth of Humane Treatment* 39

Summary 43

PART 2 Models and Treatments of Abnormality

3 THE BIOMEDICAL MODEL 47

Models of Abnormality 48

Assumptions of the Biomedical Model 49 *Germs as Etiology: Syphilis and General Paresis* 50 *Genetics as Etiology: Twins and Schizophrenia* 53 *Biochemistry as Etiology: Dopamine and Schizophrenia* 54 *Neuroanatomy as Etiology: The Disordered Brain* 55 *Genetics and Biochemistry as Etiology: Manic-Depression among the Amish* 56

Treatment 58

Evaluating the Biomedical Model 59 *Strengths* 59 *Weaknesses* 60

Reductionism: An Ongoing Debate 60

Summary 61

4 PSYCHODYNAMIC AND EXISTENTIAL APPROACHES 62

Freud and Psychoanalytic Theory 62 *The Development of Personality* 63 *The Three Processes of Personality* 67 *Unconscious Ideas and Impulses* 69 *Anxiety* 70 *Faults of Early Psychoanalytic Theory* 71

The Neo-Freudians 71

Modern Psychodynamic Theory 73 *The Self and Self-Theory* 74 *Defenses and Consciousness* 77 *Growth and Existential Theories* 88

Psychodynamic Treatment 93 *Brief Psychotherapy* 93 *Client-Centered Therapy* 98 *Gestalt Therapy* 99 *Logotherapy* 100

Evaluating Psychodynamic Theory 101 *Strengths of Psychodynamic Theories* 101 *Shortcomings of Psychodynamic Theories* 101

Summary 103

5 THE ENVIRONMENTALIST MODEL: BEHAVIORAL AND COGNITIVE APPROACHES   105

History and Assumptions of the Environmentalist Model 105   *Empiricism and Associations* 105 *Behaviorism* 106

Behavioral Psychology: Principles and Therapies 107 *Pavlovian Conditioning* 107   *Operant Conditioning* 112 *Avoidance Learning* 117

Cognitive Psychology: Principles and Applications 118 *Assumptions of the Cognitive View* 118   *Cognitive Therapy* 119 *Cognitive-Behavioral Therapy* 125

Combining Cognitive-Behavior Therapy and Psychodynamics 126

Evaluating the Behavioral and Cognitive Models 127

Summary 128

PART 3   Investigating and Diagnosing Abnormality

6 INVESTIGATING ABNORMALITY   133

The Clinical Case History 134   *A Clinical Case History* 134 *Evaluating the Clinical Case History* 135

Scientific Experimentation 137   *An Experiment* 138 *Experimental Confounds* 140   *Statistical Inference* 142 *Experiments with a Single Subject* 144   *Evaluation of the Experimental Method* 146

Correlation 147   *Correlation Coefficients* 149   *Correlation and Causality* 149   *Evaluation of the Correlational Method* 150

Experiments of Nature 150   *Evaluation of Experiments of Nature* 151

The Laboratory Model 152   *Evaluation of the Laboratory Model* 153

Combining Several Methods: A Woven Fabric   153

Summary 154

7 PSYCHOLOGICAL ASSESSMENT AND CLASSIFICATION   156

Psychological Assessment 157   *Reliability* 157   *The Clinical Interview* 159   *Psychological Testing* 161   *Observations* 170

Diagnosis 173   *Reasons for Diagnosis* 174   *Historical Origins* 174   *The Diagnostic and Statistical Manuals (DSM-III and DSM-III-R)* 175   *Conditions That Bias Diagnosis* 181 *Evaluating Psychological Diagnoses* 184

Summary 185

PART 4   Anxiety and Psychosomatic Disorders

8 FEAR AND PHOBIA: ANXIETY FELT   189

Fear and Anxiety 189 *Fear* 190 *Anxiety* 195

Phobia 196 *Phobia Defined* 196 *Prevalence of Phobias* 198
Kinds of Phobias 198 *The Psychoanalytic Account of
Phobias* 204 *The Behavioral Account of Phobias* 206
Therapies for Phobias 209 *Evaluation of the Behavioral
Account* 214

Post-Traumatic Stress Disorder 217 *Naturally Occurring
Disasters* 218 *Manmade Catastrophes* 220 *Rape Trauma
Syndrome* 221 *Course of Post-Traumatic Stress Disorder* 222
Treatment and Prevention 225

Panic Disorder and Generalized Anxiety Disorder 228
Panic Disorder 228 *Generalized Anxiety Disorder* 231

Summary 232

9 OBSESSION, HYSTERIA, AND DISSOCIATION: ANXIETY INFERRED   235

Obsessions and Compulsions 236 *Obsessions and the Social
Context* 237 *Anxiety, Depression, and Obsessions* 238
Vulnerability to Obsessive-Compulsive Disorder 239 *Theories
of Obsessive-Compulsive Disorder* 241 *Treatment for
Obsessive-Compulsive Disorder* 245 *Obsessive-Compulsive
Disorder: Anxiety Revisited* 246

Somatoform Disorders 247 *The Types of Somatoform
Disorders* 248 *Diagnosing Somatoform Disorder* 250
Vulnerability to Somatoform Disorders 252 *Course of
Somatoform Disorders* 253 *The Etiology of Somatoform
Disorders* 253 *Treatment of Somatoform Disorder* 257

Dissociative Disorders 258 *Psychogenic Amnesia* 259
Multiple Personality 261

DSM-III-R and the Neuroses 268

Summary 269

10 HEALTH PSYCHOLOGY AND PSYCHOSOMATIC DISORDERS   271

Stigmata 271

An Overview of Psychosomatic Disorders 272

Peptic Ulcers 273 *Symptoms of Peptic Ulcer* 274 *Physiological
Development of an Ulcer* 275 *Who Is Susceptible to
Ulcers?* 275 *Psychological Factors Influencing Peptic
Ulcers* 276 *Treatment of Peptic Ulcers* 281

Coronary Heart Disease and the Type A Personality 282
Defining the Type A Personality 283 *Type A's at Risk for
Coronary Heart Disease* 283 *Type A Dissected* 284

Psychoneuroimmunology (PNI) 289 *The Mind-Body Problem* 289 *Immunocompetence and Psychological States* 292 *The Mind-Body Problem Re-examined* 294

Theories of Psychosomatic Illness 295 *The Biomedical Model of Psychosomatic Disorders* 295 *The Psychodynamic Model* 298 *Behavioral and Cognitive Models* 298

Summary 302

PART 5   Depression and the Schizophrenias

11 DEPRESSION AND SUICIDE   307

Normal versus Clinical Depression 307
Unipolar Depression 308 *Symptoms of Unipolar Depression* 308 *Classifying Depression* 315 *Vulnerability to Depression* 317 *The Course of Depression* 323

Theories and Therapies of Unipolar Depression 324 *The Biological Model of Depression* 325 *The Psychodynamic Model of Depression* 329 *Cognitive Models of Depression* 332 *Integration of Theories and Therapies for Unipolar Depression* 347

Bipolar Depression (Manic-Depression) 348 *Symptoms of Mania* 349 *Course and Characteristics of Manic-Depression* 350 *Cause of Manic-Depression* 352 *Treatment* 353 *Seasonal Affective Disorder (SAD)* 354

Suicide 355 *Who Is at Risk for Suicide?* 356 *The Motivation for Suicide* 360 *Prevention of Suicide and Treatment of the Suicidal Person* 362

Summary 362

12 THE SCHIZOPHRENIAS   364

History and Background 364 *Some Myths about Schizophrenia* 364 *Evolving Views of Schizophrenia* 366 *Schizophrenia Defined* 367 *Incidence and Prevalence of Schizophrenia* 369

Types of Schizophrenia 370 *Paranoid Schizophrenia* 370 *Disorganized Schizophrenia* 370 *Catatonic Schizophrenia* 371 *Residual Schizophrenia* 371 *Undifferentiated Schizophrenia* 372

The Symptoms of Schizophrenia 372 *Perceptual Difficulties* 372 *Thought Disorders* 373 *Affective Disturbances* 380 *Meaning in Schizophrenia* 381

The Dimensions of Schizophrenia 382 *Acute and Chronic* 382 *Type I and Type II* 383

The Causes of the Schizophrenias 384 *The Genetics of Schizophrenia* 384 *The Biology of the Schizophrenias* 392

The Schizophrenogenic Family 395 *Society and Schizophrenia* 398

The Treatment of Schizophrenia 400 *Drug Therapy* 401
Full Treatment: Milieu and Therapeutic Communities 404

Summary 406

PART 6   Social and Interpersonal Disorders

13 SEXUAL BEHAVIOR, DYSFUNCTION, AND DISORDER   411

The Scientific Study of Sexual Behavior 412

Sexual Function 413 *The Physiology of the Human Sexual Response* 414

Sexual Dysfunction: The Sexual Inabilities 415 *The Impairment of Erotic Desire and Excitement* 416 *Orgasmic Dysfunction* 418 *The Causes of Sexual Dysfunction* 419
Treatment of Sexual Dysfunctions 422 *Evaluation of Sexual Therapy* 424

Sexual Order and Disorder 424 *Attitudes toward Human Sexuality* 425 *Sexual Identity* 427

Sexual Disorders: The Paraphilias 428 *Types of Paraphilias* 428 *The Causes of Paraphilias* 436 *The Treatment of the Paraphilias* 438 *Ego-Dystonic Homosexuality* 439

Sexual Disorders: Transsexualism 443 *The Etiology of Transsexualism* 445 *Therapy of Transsexualism: Sex-Change Operations* 448

Summary 449

14 PSYCHOACTIVE SUBSTANCE USE DISORDERS   450
Joseph Volpicelli, M.D., PH.D.

Diagnosing Drug Abuse 451 *Cultural Variations* 451
DSM-III-R Criteria 451

Substance Dependence 454 *Vulnerability Factors* 454
Basic Effects of Drugs 455

Alcohol 461 *Theories of Alcohol Dependence* 461 *Medical and Social Complications* 466 *Treatment* 468 *AIDS and Alcohol* 470

Narcotics 471 *Psychopharmacology of Opiates* 472 *Medical and Social Complications* 473 *Treatment of Narcotic Dependence* 473

Stimulants 475 *Psychopharmacology of Stimulants* 475
Medical and Social Complications 477 *Treatment* 478

Hallucinogens (Marijuana, PCP, LSD) 478
Psychopharmacology 480 *Medical and Social
Complications* 481

Cigarette Smoking and Nicotine 481
Psychopharmacology 482 *Medical and Social
Consequences* 484 *Treatment* 484

Sedatives-Tranquilizers (Barbiturates,
Benzodiazepines) 485

Prognosis for Ending Drug Abuse 486 *Drug
Availability* 487 *Education* 488 *Treatment* 489
Our Society and Drug Use and Abuse 489

Summary 490

15 PERSONALITY DISORDERS 492

The Antisocial Personality Disorder 493 *Disorders of
Will* 493 *Characterizing the Antisocial Personality
Disorder* 494 *The Sources of Sociopathy* 496 *The Antisocial
Personality Disorder: An Overview* 504

Other Personality Disorders 505 *Paranoid Personality
Disorder* 505 *Histrionic Personality Disorder* 505 *Narcissistic
Personality Disorder* 506 *Avoidant Personality Disorder* 507
Dependent Personality Disorder 508 *Obsessive-Compulsive
Personality Disorder* 508 *Passive-Aggressive Personality
Disorder* 509 *Schizoid Personality Disorder* 510 *Schizotypal
Personality Disorder* 510 *Borderline Personality Disorder* 511

The Personality Disorders: An Evaluation 513 *Alternative
View of the Personality Disorders* 513

Summary 515

PART 7   Abnormality across the Lifespan

16 CHILDHOOD DISORDERS AND MENTAL RETARDATION 519
revised by Susan Nolen-Hoeksema

Classifying Children's Disorders 521

Disruptive Behavior Disorders 522 *Conduct Disorders* 523
Attention-Deficit Hyperactivity Disorder(ADHD) 527

Emotional Disorders 530 *Separation Anxiety Disorder* 530
Phobias 531

Habit Disorders and Eating Disorders 534 *Enuresis* 534
Stuttering 535 *Anorexia Nervosa* 536 *Bulimia Nervosa: The
Gorge/Purge Cycle* 538 *Obesity* 539

Developmental Disorders 541   *Mental Retardation* 541
  Specific Developmental Disorders 546 *Pervasive Developmental
  Disorders: Autism* 547

Areas for Further Consideration 556

Summary 557

17 DISORDERS OF THE NERVOUS SYSTEM AND PSYCHOPATHOLOGY   558
    Morris Moscovitch and Paul Rozin

The Organization of the Nervous System in Relation to
  Organic Disorders 560   *Structural and Functional Units:
  Neurons, Glia, Synapses, and Neurotransmitters* 560 *The
  Biochemical Organization of the Brain* 562   *The Spatial
  Organization of the Brain: Localization of Function* 562

General Aspects of Diseases of the Nervous System 569
  Agents of Damage to the Nervous System 569 *The Expression
  of Damage in the Nervous System* 570 *Susceptibility to
  Damage: Vulnerable Systems* 570 *Resistance to Damage:
  Redundancy in the Nervous System* 571 *The Neurological
  Diagnosis* 572

Some Selected Diseases of the Nervous System 575
  Disorders of Language: The Aphasias 575 *Dyslexia* 579 *A
  Disorder of Memory: The Amnesic Syndrome* 581
  Dementia 589

The Treatment of Diseases of the Nervous System 593

The Virtues and Limitations of the Neurological
  Approach 595

Summary 598

PART 8   Abnormality, the Law, and Choosing a Psychotherapy

18 THE LAW AND POLITICS OF ABNORMALITY   603

INVOLUNTARY COMMITMENT AND TREATMENT 604   *Procedures to
  Commit* 605 *The Patients' Rights Movement* 616
  Abolish Involuntary Hospitalization? 616

Criminal Commitment 618   *The Insanity Defense* 618
  Competence to Stand Trial 624

The Social and Political Abuse of Abnormal
  Psychology 626   *Abuse by State* 627 *Abuse by Society* 630

Summary 631

19 A CONSUMER'S GUIDE TO PSYCHOLOGICAL TREATMENT   633

Who Treats? 634

The Common Ingredients of Therapy 638 *Free Choice and Treatment* 638 *Hopes and Expectations* 639 *Characteristics of Therapist-Client Interactions* 641 *Therapeutic Effectiveness* 646

The Variety of Treatment 647 *Specific vs. Global Therapies* 648 *Specific Therapies* 648 *Global Therapies* 652

The Choice of Treatment 656 *Specific Treatments* 656 *Global Treatments* 665

Outreach and Prevention: The Hopes of Community Psychology 667 *Prevention* 667 *Containment* 669 *Rehabilitation* 673

Summary 675

APPENDIX: THE DIAGNOSTIC AND STATISTICAL MANUAL OF MENTAL DISORDERS, REVISED (DSM-III-R) 676

GLOSSARY 685

REFERENCES 698

NAME INDEX 735

SUBJECT INDEX 747

Preface

Although it was written for courses in abnormal psychology, this book was conceived in, of all places, a mental hospital. One of us, David Rosenhan, was engaged in a study in which a diverse group of "normal" people went into mental hospitals pretending to have a single symptom: they heard voices that said "empty," "meaningless," and "thud." From the start, these "pseudopatients" acted the way "normal" people did. But they were labeled as "crazy" and treated as such, for reasons that will become clear when you read this book. Martin Seligman heard about the study and wrote Rosenhan a fan letter expressing his admiration for the courage it involved. To his surprise, Seligman received a phone call several days later inviting him to enter a hospital with Rosenhan. So it came about that in October 1973 both of us assumed false names—you figure out why—and wound up in the locked men's ward of a state mental hospital.

One can hardly think of better places for two psychologists to become fast friends than in such trenches. In the hours and days that followed, discussions ranged over an enormous variety of topics: how we and our fellow patients were being treated; our personal and academic lives; and to such issues as the legal rights of mental patients, how to choose a therapist, the dehumanizing effects of labeling, the diagnosis of schizophrenia (more often, its misdiagnosis), depression and suicide, and finally teaching itself —how the experience of psychopathology, of hospitalization, of therapy, of diagnosis, and the range of psychological miseries, could be communicated to students. We left the hospital good friends, and with the hope that we might some day attempt to do something to improve the teaching of abnormal psychology.

This book, now in its second edition, is the result of more than fifteen years of collaboration, research, clinical experience, delving into a vast literature, writing and rewriting, and teaching abnormal psychology to undergraduates.

The work, though occasionally overwhelming, has been simply exhilarating. We have no regrets. During the last quarter century, the progress that has been made in understanding and treating psychological disorders has been extraordinary. Disorders that were once wholly mysterious and untreatable, like the schizophrenias, depression, the anxiety disorders, and the sexual dysfunctions, can now be treated, often with considerable success. They are not yet fully understood, but neither are they completely shrouded in mystery. Indeed, we not only understand them better than ever before, but we are enormously optimistic about the immediate future. If the last twenty-five years were highly informative, the next twenty-five promise exciting discovery.

THE EXCITEMENT OF THE PAST HALF DECADE

Just consider the new advances and emphases in abnormal psychology since the first edition of this book was published—barely half a decade ago. The latest diagnostic technology in medicine—the PET and CAT scans, as well as regional cerebral blood flow (rCBF)—has been used successfully in the study of schizophrenia, a disorder that was once held to be *hopelessly* complicated. The roles of cognitive therapy and of interpersonal therapy in the treatment of depression have been greatly elucidated. Remarkable advances have been achieved in psychoneuroimmunology, and they have changed our understandings about the development of cancer. A psychological treatment has been implemented that cures panic disorder in virtually 100 percent of the cases. Our knowledge about the action of neurotransmitters in depression and schizophrenia has deepened. Our understanding of the genetics of bipolar (manic) depression has grown immeasurably as the result of a classic study of that disorder among the Amish.

The second edition of *Abnormal Psychology* incorporates these findings, as well as new research on the psychodynamics of cognition, the outcome of specific psychotherapies for certain disorders, the epidemiology of psychological disorder, the lasting effects of loss and of post-traumatic stress, the psychobiology of panic, and the effects of seasonal changes on depression. New understandings about the relationship between sleep and depression, Type A behavior, teenage suicide, depression in children, psychological aspects of AIDS, and sexual apathy have been assimilated into the revision. And of course, all of these findings have been informed by the latest revision of the increasingly controversial *Diagnostic and Statistical Manual of the Mental Disorders,* DSM-III-R.

PSYCHOLOGICAL THEORY AND TREATMENT THAT BEST FITS THE DISORDER

The revision continues the strong emphasis on theory that marked the book in its first edition. Rather than viewing all of psychopathology through a single theoretical lens, we continue to choose the theory that best illuminates a particular disorder. But the applicability of theories to disorders and treatments itself changes over time. New theories, particularly those that emphasize the role of *self* and the nature of *systems,* are introduced for their utility in understanding the personality disorders, as well as forming the basis of couple and family therapies.

Abnormal Psychology, in text and in substance, is inherently interesting to anyone who is concerned with people and with what makes them "tick." We have tried to augment that interest by using richly described case histories that convey the immediacy and drama of pscyhopathology. We hope, too, that we have sustained the reader's interest by writing clearly and directly, by treating research findings in a coherent manner, by avoiding shotgun citations and by avoiding technical jargon. The book is written for the intelligent reader, most likely, but not invariably, an undergraduate who has a quarter or a semester to give to this effort. For that effort, we expect the reader not only to have gained an intelligent grasp of, and sympathy for, the issues in abnormal psychology but also to be able to evaluate and appreciate the significance of new research that will have emerged after the course was completed.

TWIN EMPHASES: PEOPLE AND SCIENCE

One final point: This book emphasizes the science of abnormal psychology, and it stresses equally the human suffering that abnormality spawns and its social costs. We want to be clear about that joint emphasis. As we take up each disorder and the scientific theories and therapies used to explain and treat them, we have spared little effort to convey the human side of this ongoing endeavor. Scientific explorations into diagnosis and treatment promise wholesale amelioration of human misery. Nothing else does with any degree of reliability. But the "science" of abnormality has no meaning unless human suffering is kept centrally in mind.

THE PLAN OF THE BOOK

This book is designed to be used in one-semester or one-quarter courses in abnormal psychology. The definitions, history, and major schools of thought and treatment of abnormality are presented first. Then, each of the major disorders—their description, their causes, and their treatments—is laid out in light of the competing schools of thought.

The book opens with two chapters on abnormality across time and place (Part 1). In Chapter 1, the notion of abnormality is defined. We argue that there is no one element that all cases of abnormality have; rather several important elements combine to yield the judgment of abnormality. Chapter 2 examines how the view of madness had changed across history. It emphasizes a notion that is now considered "common sense"—that the origins of madness may be either physical or psychological—a view that was not accepted until the twentieth century.

Part 2 describes the prominent schools of thought and their approaches to and treatments of abnormality. Chapter 3, the biomedical model, looks at abnormality as a disease of the body. It examines the role of germs, of genes, and of biochemistry in the production of abnormality. Chapter 4 takes up both the psychodynamic model of abnormality, from the towering work of Sigmund Freud to more modern views and the existential approach to abnormality. Chapter 5 presents the environmentalist model, incorporating the behavioral school of thought, which emphasizes the role of classical conditioning and of instrumental learning as potential causes and treatments of abnormality, and the cognitive school, which holds that psychological abnormality is produced by disordered thinking, and that changing disordered thinking produces cure.

Having outlined the major schools of thought of abnormality, Part 3 turns to how abnormality is investigated and how it is diagnosed. Chapter 6 investigates the role of different methods of assessment for illuminating the cause and cure of abnormality. Case histories, laboratory experiments, correlational studies, experiments of nature, and experimental models are all examined and compared. We conclude that each method contributes to our knowledge of abnormality, and we describe how they do so. This section ends with Chapter 7, which discusses the diagnosis and assessment of abnormality. DSM-III-R is fully described and evaluated, and part of it is reprinted as an appendix at the end of the book. Varieties of psychological tests, which help to diagnose abnormality, are examined.

In Part 4, which covers anxiety and the psychosomatic disorders, we provide a detailed examination of psychopathology. The three chapters on anxiety and psychosomatic disorders are organized around the degree to which anxiety is apparent in the disorder itself. Chapter 8 discusses those anxiety disorders in which the sufferer actually feels fear and anxiety: phobia, post-traumatic stress disorder, panic disorder, and generalized anxiety disorder. Chapter 9 turns to those disorders in which the existence of anxiety is inferred rather than apparent: obsessive-compulsive disorders, hysterical conversion (now called a somatoform disorder), dissociative disorders, and multiple personality. Chapter 10 looks at health psychology and psychosomatic disorders, those disorders in which physical illness is influenced, and in the strongest case, caused by psychological factors. We examine in detail psychosomatic principles and illustrate these principles through discussing the disorders of stomach ulcers, coronary heart disease and the Type A personality, and sudden death. We also have a detailed discussion of the new field of psychoneuroimmunology.

Part 5 turns to the major depressive disorders and the schizophrenias. Chapter 11 deals with depression and suicide. It describes the symptoms of depression, the distinguishing features of manic-depressive disorder and unipolar depression, and it provides a description of the three major competing theories and therapies of depression. We propose an integrative theory of depression, and then discuss the most tragic consequence of depression, suicide. Chapter 12 describes schizophrenia and its symptoms, illustrating the disorder with rich case history material. We conclude the section with an evaluation of competing psychological, biochemical, and societal theories of schizophrenia and a discussion of the prospects of treatment and rehabilitation of people with this devastating disorder.

In Part 6, we look at social and interpersonal disorders. Chapter 13, on sexual disorders, begins with an examination of human sexuality. We first examine sexual function and dysfunction. We then look at sexual order and disorder, examining the paraphilias and then transsexuality. Finally, we present an integrative theory of the origin of sexual disorders. In Chapter 14, we examine psychoactive substance abuse disorders. We look at each of the major abused drugs, from alcohol, narcotics, and stimulants, to cigarette smoking and sedatives, as well as the underlying psychological and biological phenomena. In Chapter 15, we discuss the personality disorders, that is, disorders in which a person's entire character structure presents a problem for the individual or for society. We focus particularly on the antisocial personality disorder.

In Part 7, we take up abnormality through the lifespan. In Chapter 16, we look at the disorders of childhood. In many respects, children and adults suffer similar problems: fears, phobias, eating disorders, and the like. In Chapter 17, we concentrate on disorders of the nervous system. We differentiate here between psychological problems and neurological problems, and we describe assessment techniques by which neurological damage is detected. Finally, we examine the major disorders of the nervous system, including one that afflicts older people, Alzheimer's disease (the disorder of senility).

The final section of the book—Part 8—considers the legal issues related to psychological abnormality, and the issues associated with choosing a psychotherapy. In Chapter 18, we look at society's institutionalized reaction to abnormality and our laws about commitment—voluntary versus involuntary commitment. We then examine the insanity defense and ask: When, if ever, is insanity an excuse for a criminal action? In the final chapter, Chapter 19, we ask, "How can one use the information in this book to best choose an appropriate psychotherapy?" We review the specificity of different schools of thought and their therapies for different disorders. We make suggestions about what therapies are apt to be most effective for what particular disorders. We then examine the general characteristics of psychotherapists and psychotherapy, which enable individuals to grow.

ACKNOWLEDGMENTS

Over the years of writing this book, we have accumulated intellectual and personal debts to many colleagues, students, friends, and family. Many people have been more generous with time and criticism than we had a right to anticipate. Chief among these is Paul Rozin of the University of Pennsylvania, our friend and colleague and Norton's editorial adviser. He encouraged us when we flagged. He raised pointed questions in every draft of every chapter of the second edition, as he did with the first.

Writing such a text is a challenging undertaking, and there were three areas, psychoactive substance use disorders, child psychopathology, and disorders of the nervous system, where we felt others, more expert in these areas, might best take up the role of author. We particularly thank Susan Nolen-Hoeksema of Stanford University, for thoroughly revising Chapter 16, Childhood Disorders and Mental Retardation; Joseph Volpicelli of the Veterans Administration, Philadelphia, for writing a completely new Chapter 14, Psychoactive Substance Use Disorders; and Paul Rozin, again, and Morris Moscovitch of the University of Toronto, for writing Chapter 17, Disorders of the Nervous System and Psychopathology.

From other specialists, we received comments on specific chapters in the book. For their time and thoughtful advice, which we, at times, ran the risk of not taking, we thank the following:

Thomas M. Achenbach
The University of Vermont

Julian Davidson
Stanford University

I.I. Gottesman
University of Virginia

Margo Horn
Stanford University

Mardi J. Horowitz
University of California

Robert Howell
Brigham Young University

Lester Luborsky
University of Pennsylvania

Stephen Matthysse
McLean Hospital

Gary P. Melton
University of Nebraska

Douglas Mook
University of Virginia

Tibor Palfai
Syracuse University

Myrna Schwartz
*Moss Rehabilitation Center,
Philadelphia*

Varda Shoham-Salomon
University of Arizona

Richard A. Shweder
University of Chicago

Shepard Siegel
McMaster University

John Teasdale
Medical Research Council, UK

Joseph R. Volpicelli
*Veterans Administration,
Philadelphia*

Ingrid Waldron
University of Pennsylvania

Myrna M. Weissman
Yale University

We also thank (and pay tribute to) those teachers of abnormal psychology courses on whom we came to rely for suggestions and changes for the second edition based on their experience in the classroom, among them:

Cole Barton
Davidson College

Sarah A. Burnett
Rice University

Nancy G. Caine
Bucknell University

Nancy Campbell-Goymer
Birmingham-Southern College

James F. Carruth
West Virginia University

Thomas F. Cash
Old Dominion University

Jean E. Dumas
The University of Western Ontario

Joseph D. Eubanks
San Antonio College

Norman Finkel
Georgetown University

Stephen E. Finn
The University of Texas at Austin

Roy Fontaine
Williamsport Area Community College

Frederick P. Gault
Western Michigan University

Anne E. Harris
Arizona State University

Laurie Heatherington
Williams College

Rick Ingram
San Diego State University

John B. Knowles
Queen's University

Tim Kochems
Boston College

Gregory J. Neimeyer

James November
Jacksonville University

Philip L. Rice
Moorhead State University

Rosemary A. Robbins
Private Practice, Cherry Hill, N.J.

David G. Sequin
James Community College

Thomas E. Shipley, Jr.
Temple University

Jane Ellen Smith
University of New Mexico

Leonard Solomon

The second edition of this book benefited enormously from the research assistance of Sally Davis, Joseph Firschheim, Bruce Hamilton, Shelli Irwin, Jane Penaz, Pam Schaffer, and Pat Tansey. Administrative and supportive assistance came from Chris Beck, Shannon Temple, and Mary Tye. Our debt to these people is great.

Finally, we thank those at Norton with whom we have worked for better than a decade across two editions of *Abnormal Psychology*. We are especially grateful to Donald Fusting, our editor, who guided both editions. No mere acquiring editor he, Don criticized each and every chapter, offering conceptual, organizational, and editorial suggestions. We learned to ignore those suggestions at the book's peril. Next we thank Sandra Lifland, whose efforts on this book defy brief description. Like Don, she took a collegial role in this revision, raising theoretical questions and pressing relentlessly for answers. She ferreted out many instances—every one of them, we now believe—of awkward and inelegant prose and made handsome remedial suggestions. Much of what is *visually* attractive about the book came about through her hard work. And all of her work was done with the incredible gentleness that evokes admiration, respect and gratitude. We also thank other members of the Norton team, Ruth Dworkin, Ruth Mandel, Ben Gamit, Roberta Flechner, Elizabeth Garrigue, and Rachel Lee, who contributed in many ways to the book and its timely publication.

D.L.R.
M.E.P.S.
November, 1988

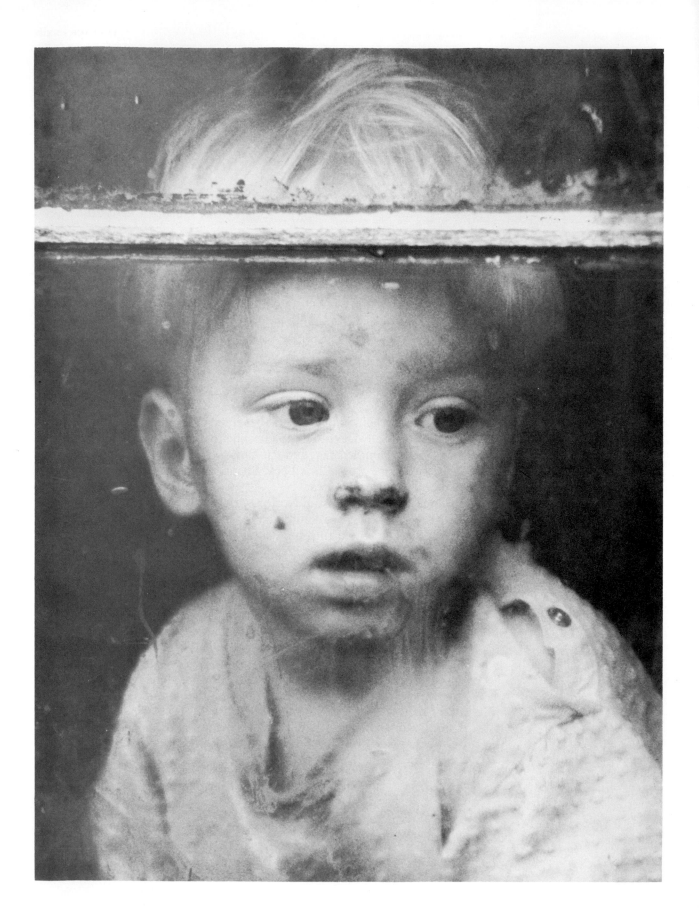

Part 1

THE NATURE AND HISTORY OF ABNORMALITY

CHAPTER

1

The Meanings of Abnormality

W HAT does it mean to say that someone is "abnormal"? How do we *know* that person is abnormal? If we are right that the person is abnormal, how did he become that way? How can he be changed? By any means possible? Does he have any rights in this matter? These are the issues that concern this book. And they are not minor matters.

The case of
Joyce Brown

Joyce Brown* lived in one of the wealthiest neighborhoods in the United States —New York City's Upper East Side, 65th Street and Second Avenue. The neighborhood is so wealthy that people pay as much as $50 a week to have their dog walked, and $450 a month to park their car. Dinner for two in a local restaurant can easily set you back a couple hundred dollars, and then only if you order cheap wine!

Joyce Brown lived over the hot air vent in front of a restaurant and ice cream parlor, right next door to a major bank, literally on the ground floor, the pavement. If you don't live in a big city, it may surprise you to learn that some people live, fall and winter, over hot air vents, and right on the street at other times. But they do. And Joyce Brown was one of them.

In the fall of 1987, the City of New York instituted a new program aimed at helping the homeless. Greatly encouraged by Mayor Edward Koch, teams of social workers and medical technicians were organized, equipped with mobile units, and sent out onto the city streets. Their purpose was to find the homeless, attend to any immediate health problems, and then, if it seemed warranted, take them to a hospital or mental health facility for evaluation and treatment.

By ironic coincidence, the first person picked up was Joyce Brown. Ultimately, her case proved to be an ambiguous one. But from her manner and from eyewitness reports, she *appeared* deranged. She was homeless, and she was not a pretty

---

* Joyce Brown is her real name. We use it because her plight has been prominently discussed in the news media. The identities of other people whose difficulties are described in this book have been carefully camouflaged.

Left: Joyce Brown on the street before she was picked up and taken to Bellevue Hospital. *Right:* Joyce Brown during a television interview after she was released from Bellevue.

sight. According to some observers, she smelled. She soiled herself. She occasionally burned paper money that was doled out to her. And she frequently muttered angry imprecations at innocent passersby.

And so, she was taken to Bellevue Hospital and its mental health ward. There, she was evaluated by a team of psychiatrists who diagnosed her as paranoid schizophrenic. They began treatment. But Joyce Brown protested against both the hospitalization and the treatment. An investigation was initiated by the American Civil Liberties Union (ACLU), which felt that her civil rights might have been violated. Lawyers from the ACLU retained their own psychiatric team which, contrary to the City's psychiatrists, did not find Joyce Brown to be schizophrenic.

The battle that began there was accompanied by much media hoopla. A televised debate pitted the Mayor against an articulate Joyce Brown. The Mayor, relying on the City's psychiatrists, insisted that she was mentally ill. "Both morally and legally we have an obligation to help those who can't or won't help themselves," he said.* "I decided . . . that it is terrible to see these people who are lying in their own feces, who are clearly gross mental cases, who if they were your mother or your sister or a family relative you would want to pick up and take to a hospital right away, even if they resisted, because they are mentally incompetent to make such a judgment."[†]

Ms. Brown objected. "This is the United States of America," she pointed out. "If that's . . . the way the person wants to live their life . . . who am I to say that they can't do that? . . . If they're just sitting on the street, dirty and nasty, that's not a crime. And as far as using the pavement as a toilet, I didn't have access to a bathroom. There were times when I'd go to restaurants and ask them, could I use their bathroom, and they would say, no you can't. . . ."[‡]

Insisting that she was not mentally ill, Ms. Brown said about where she lived and her life-style, "It's my choice, my life, and my body, and I'll live it as I see fit."

Is Joyce Brown normal, or is she "mentally ill"? The answer is difficult to find and has powerful implications.

* *New York Times,* August 29, 1987.
[†] *Sixty Minutes,* January 24, 1988.
[‡] Ibid.

Implications of
diagnosing
abnormality

• How much agreement is there about what constitutes normality and abnormality? Can we really spot abnormal people when we see them? We take up this issue in this chapter.

• Can mental health professionals agree on the diagnosis of the mentally disordered? How are such matters determined in the first place (see Chapter 7)?

• Joyce Brown was thought to be schizophrenic. How treatable are schizophrenics? And how long do the cures last (see Chapters 12 and 19)? Surely, if someone is thought to be schizophrenic and is brought to a psychiatric hospital, there ought to be some hope of helping, of curing them. Is there?

• Finally, is the state justified in using the instruments and insights of abnormal psychology to make social and political policy, i.e., removing unsightly people from the streets of an elegant neighborhood? How can individuals be protected against potential abuse by the state (see Chapter 18)?

If Joyce Brown is "normal" (and if she is not breaking any laws), the Mayor has no right to interfere with her life. It is, as she says, her life, her body, and her choice to live as she sees fit. But if she is "mentally ill," and if in addition she is likely to harm herself or others, then most reasonable people would agree with the Mayor that the only decent thing to do is to hospitalize and treat her regardless of whether she consents.

These questions, about Joyce Brown or anyone else, have no easy answers. But before we begin to search for answers, we need to understand what is normal and what is abnormal.

There are no clear-cut definitions of abnormality, and no infallible way to recognize abnormality. Many of us will have suspected as much from our own experience. Recall your descent from innocence when, after periods of special distress, you asked yourself "Am I normal?" or "Is she normal?" Those were difficult questions whose answers were not immediately forthcoming. And they were often questions that were quickly abandoned, lest they lead to uncharted areas in ourselves or others that were more difficult and distressing than the behaviors we were trying to understand in the first place.

ABNORMALITY

Disagreement on
what is abnormal

If abnormality cannot be defined simply and clearly, does that mean that there is no such thing as abnormal behavior? Far from it. Abnormality is recognized everywhere, in every culture, by nearly everyone. Sometimes the impression of abnormality comes through clearly and unambiguously. At other times, reasonable people will disagree as to whether a particular person, action, or thought is or is not abnormal. The following clinical vignettes make this clear.

• Don is viewed by nearly everyone as a quiet mild-mannered executive. But one day, gripped by a sudden seizure in the temporal lobe of the brain, he picks up his sales manager, chair and all, and hurls her to death through the eleventh floor window of an office building.

Reasonable people will disagree as to whether a particular person is abnormal. This boy with a punk haircut attracts the stares of passersby.

• Vanessa, a teenage girl, eats nothing at all for several days, then gorges herself on eight hot-fudge sundaes within two hours, vomits explosively, and then eats nothing more for three days.

• Carla's religious principles forbid her from wearing makeup or drinking liquor. Her college friends do both. She is continually anxious when she is with them.

Of these cases, two things can be said immediately. First, they involve different behaviors, which arise from sources as diverse as brain pathology and religious beliefs. And second, while some people will be quite confident that all of these instances represent abnormality, not everyone will agree. Everyone will judge the first case abnormal. Nearly everyone will judge the second case abnormal. But there will be vigorous debate about the third.

WHY CAN'T ABNORMALITY BE EASILY DEFINED?

Necessary and sufficient conditions

The act of defining the word "abnormal" suggests that there is some single property that these three cases of abnormality, and all others, must share. This shared property is called a *necessary* condition for abnormality. But these is no common element among these three cases, for what is it that temporal lobe seizures, gorging oneself on hot-fudge sundaes, and conflict between religious conviction and social acceptance have in common? Moreover, the definition of "abnormal" requires that there be at least one distinguishing element that only cases of abnormality share and that no cases of "normality" share. This is called a *sufficient* condition of abnormality. But is there any one feature that separates all cases of abnormality from all those that we would call normal? Not any that we can find. In fact, as we will shortly see, there is no single element shared by all cases of abnormality, and no single element that distinguishes abnormality from normality.

In short, the word "abnormal" cannot be defined precisely. Indeed, few of the words we commonly use, and especially those that are used socially, are precisely defined, for the use of language often depends on flexible meanings. But the fact that abnormality cannot be defined "tightly" does not mean that abnormality doesn't exist or that it can't be recognized at all. It does exist, and it is recognized in much the same way that families are recognized. How do we know, for example, that Ed Smith is the *biological* offspring of Bill and Jane Smith? Well, he *looks* like them. He has Bill's blue eyes and sandy hair, and Jane's upturned nose and easy smile. Even though Ed is six inches taller than his father and has a rounder face than his mother, we sense a ***family resemblance*** among them because they have many significant elements in common. (But careful now: Ed might just be the *adopted* son of Bill and Jane Smith. Such are the hazards of family resemblances!)

Abnormality is recognized in the same way, by determining whether the behavior, thought, or person bears a family resemblance to the behaviors, thoughts, and people we would all recognize as abnormal. That determination is made by spelling out the properties of abnormality, the various *elements* that count toward defining a behavior as abnormal. The more such elements there are and the more clearly each one is present, the more likely it is that the behavior, thought, or person will be judged abnormal. Let's examine those elements.

THE ELEMENTS OF ABNORMALITY

The seven elements of abnormality

We will look at seven properties or elements that count toward deciding whether an action or a person is abnormal. Our analysis describes the way ordinary people and well-trained psychologists actually use the word. These elements or properties of abnormality are:

- Suffering
- Maladaptiveness
- Irrationality and incomprehensibility
- Unpredictability and loss of control
- Vividness and unconventionality
- Observer discomfort
- Violation of moral and ideal standards.

The more of these elements that are present, and the more clearly they can be seen, the more certain we are that the behavior or person is abnormal. At least one of these elements *must* be present for abnormality to exist. But no one particular element must always be present, and only rarely will all of the elements be present. Let us examine these elements in greater detail.

SUFFERING

Abnormality hurts. A depressed housewife feels miserable. For her, the prospect of going through another day seems unbearable.

We are likely to call people abnormal if they are suffering psychologically, and the more they suffer, the more certain we are. But suffering is not a *necessary* condition of abnormality: it does not have to be present for us to label a behavior as abnormal. Someone who phones the President in the middle

Suffering. The person in this painting is obviously suffering, but the decision about the abnormality of her suffering would depend on whether other elements of abnormality are present. (Painting by Edgar Degas, 1834–1917)

of the night, certain that the Chief Executive wants to hear all about his latest disarmament plan, can feel exuberant, cheerful, and full of hope. Nevertheless, such a person is viewed as abnormal, as the other elements of abnormality override the absence of suffering and convince us that his behavior is abnormal.

Suffering, moreover, is not a *sufficient* condition for abnormality because suffering is commonplace in the normal course of life. A child will grieve for a dead pet, for example, much as all of us mourn the loss of loved ones. If no other elements of abnormality are present, however, grief and suffering will not be judged as abnormal.

Suffering, then, is an element that counts toward the perception of abnormality. But it is neither necessary nor sufficient. The context in which the suffering occurs counts heavily toward whether it is seen as abnormal.

MALADAPTIVENESS

Whether a behavior is functional and adaptive—how well it enables the individual to achieve certain goals—is a fundamental element in deciding whether the behavior is normal or abnormal. In biology, the fundamental scientific yardstick of adaptiveness is applied to the three important questions: Does it promote survival of the species? Does it promote the well-being of the individual? And does it promote the well-being of society? Psychologists tend most strongly to ask the last two questions: How well does the behavior foster individual well-being? And how well does it foster the well-being of society? Behaviors that strongly interfere with individual or social well-being are maladaptive and would count as factors in assessing abnormality.

By *individual well-being,* we mean the ability to work and the ability to conduct satisfying relations with other people. Depression and anxiety interfere with love and work and, almost always, with an individual's sense of well-being. A fear of going out (agoraphobia) can be so strong that it keeps the sufferer locked inside an apartment, unable to fulfill any of the individual's goals. Such a fear grossly interferes with the enjoyment of life, the ability to work, and relations with others. The more there is such interference, the clearer the abnormality.

It is abnormal to interfere strongly with the *well-being of society.* Murderers and arsonists are often called psychopaths, indicating society's judgment that their actions are abnormal. But are those actions truly abnormal? Are there enough elements of abnormality in these actions to make the family resemblance plausible? Or are these actions merely wrong or illegal? A "psychopathic" mobster may go about his work well, arranging theft and murder without the slightest pang of conscience. But he may also be an attentive husband, devoted father, and a lover of the good life. His behavior is maladaptive for the group, causing a negative social judgment of his behavior. But whether his behavior is ultimately held to be *abnormal* will depend on how many of the other elements of abnormality are present.

Maladaptiveness. Depression and anxiety interfere with love and work, and almost always with an individual's sense of well-being.

IRRATIONALITY AND INCOMPREHENSIBILITY

When a person's behavior seems to have no rational meaning, we are inclined to call that behavior and that person abnormal. People who, like Vanessa, alternately gorge themselves and vomit, who speak earnest gibberish, who somehow ensure that they will be disliked by precisely those from whom they most desire affection—these people exhibit incomprehensible and irrational behaviors that are elements of abnormality.

One kind of incomprehensibility that counts very strongly for the designation of abnormality is *thought disorder,* a major symptom of schizophrenia. Beliefs that are patently absurd and bizarre, perceptions that have no basis in objective reality, and mental processes that ramble from one idea to another unrelated one constitute thought disorders. A memorable example of such thought disorganization occurred during a formal experiment. The patient's task consisted of sorting colored blocks of various shapes and colors into a number of groups. The patient was cooperative and earnest. But he also exhibited an irresistible tendency to sort objects on the desk and on the experimenter's person, as well as parts of the room, things he pulled from his pockets, and even the experimenter himself, whom the patient recommended be remade of wood and cut into blocks. Here is what he said:

> I've got to pick it out of the whole room. I can't confine myself to this game . . . Three blues [test blocks] . . . now, how about that green blotter? Put it there too. Green peas you eat. You can't eat them unless you write on it (pointing to green blotter). Like that wristwatch (on the experimenter's wrist, a foot from the subject)—don't see three meals coming off that watch . . . To do this trick *you'd* have to be made of wood. You've got a white shirt on—and the white blocks. You have to have them cut out of *you!* You've got a white shirt on—this (white hexagonal block) will hold you and never let you go. I've got a blue shirt on, but it can't be a blue shirt and still go together. And the room's got to be the same . . . (Excerpted from Cameron, 1947, p. 59.)

UNPREDICTABILITY AND LOSS OF CONTROL

We expect people to be consistent from time to time, predictable from one occasion to the next, and very much in control of themselves. To be loved one day and hated the next is troubling. One hardly knows how to respond or what to expect. Our need to control our environment (Rotter, 1966: Seligman, 1975; Rothbaum, Weisz, and Snyder, 1982) and to retain our own freedom (Brehm and Brehm, 1981) require that other people be predictable. In a predictable world, there is consistency and control. In an unpredictable one, we feel vulnerable and threatened. Don, the mild-mannered executive who hurled his sales manager out the window, is frightening in much the same way that Dr. Jekyll's alter ego, Mr. Hyde, is: both are unpredictable and out of control.

The judgment that behavior is out of control will be made under two conditions. The first occurs when the ordinary guides and inhibitors of behavior suddenly break down. Don exemplifies this judgment. The second condition occurs when we do not know what causes an action. Imagine coming upon someone who is angry—raging and screaming in the streets. There may be good and socially acceptable reasons for such an anger. But if we do not know those reasons and are unable to elicit them at the time, we are likely to consider that the person is out of control and to designate those actions as abnormal.

Not all instances of loss of control, however, are abnormal. *Flexible control,* the ability to retain control or give it up as the self and situation require, is a hallmark of good psychological functioning (London and Rosenhan, 1968). The inability to relinquish control during sexual intercourse, for example, is likely to breed problems rather than reflect them.

VIVIDNESS AND UNCONVENTIONALITY

Generally, people recognize as acceptable and conventional those actions that they themselves are willing to do. Those who accede to a request to walk around campus wearing a sandwich board that reads "EAT AT JOE'S" are likely to estimate that a healthy majority of their peers would make the same choice. On the other hand, those who are unwilling to wear such a sign estimate that relatively *few* people would be willing. Thus, with the exception of behaviors that require great skill or daring, we tend to judge the abnormality of others' behavior by our own. Would *you* spend the winter in New York over a hot air vent on the Upper East Side? If you would, you would judge such behavior as conventional and normal. If you wouldn't, such behavior would stand out vividly as unconventional and abnormal (Ross, Greene, and House, 1977).

What is conventional and acceptable in any society is always changing. Those who are on the leading edge of that change are very visible compared to the rest of us (whose behavior is still conventional), and they run the risk of being labeled as deviants, and therefore as abnormal. Thirty years ago, for example, beards were rare. Those who wore them stood out in the crowd and were perceived as deviant and abnormal. Today, of course, those same beards would hardly be noticed.

Vividness. We tend to judge the abnormality of others' behavior by our own. Would you paint yourself with spots and go out in public?

The element of vividness is affected by whether an action is rare. Behaviors that are rare *and* undesirable are very likely to seem quite vivid, and hence to be considered abnormal. It hardly matters whether the behavior actually *is* rare, so long as it is *perceived* to be rare. Thus, there are many varieties of sexual and aggressive fantasies that are quite common but that are perceived to be rare and therefore abnormal. Nor is rareness itself a necessary condition for abnormality. Depression is a common disorder, as are anxiety states, and both are considered to be abnormal. But behavior that is both rare and socially undesirable is seen as abnormal. A rare behavior that is socially desirable, would be considered a "gift" and only abnormal in the statistical sense. Genius is rare. So is high moral character. But if they are abnormal, they are abnormalities to which most of us aspire.

OBSERVER DISCOMFORT

People who are very dependent on others, or ingratiating, or hostile, create discomfort in observers. Their behaviors often enable them to feel more comfortable, but the psychological conflicts they create are painful for others. In some ways, they are like people who are becoming gradually deaf and who turn up the volume on their radio to compensate. Suddenly, they can hear perfectly well again, but the noise that is created is intolerable to others.

We are most likely to experience vague observer discomfort when someone violates unwritten or ***residual rules*** of behavior (Scheff, 1966). Residual rules are rules that no one ever teaches but that we nonetheless know intuitively and use to guide our behavior. Violation of those rules creates the kind of discomfort that leads to the designation "abnormal."

For example, in some cultures, there is an unwritten rule which states that, except when angry or making love, one's face should be at least ten inches away from that of one's partner. Should that invisible boundary be overstepped, a residual rule will be violated, and the partner will feel uncomfortable. Similarly, there are unwritten rules about speech fluency (that one ought not to stutter) and about clothing one's genital area which, when

Violation of standards. At times, behavior is assessed against idealized norms about how people should properly behave. This woman is holding an open umbrella although it is not raining. She has all her life's possessions beside her on this sidewalk rather than in her home. Is she abnormal?

violated, contribute to the impression that the person is abnormal. Joyce Brown violated residual rules about where one ought to live and where one ought to defecate, thereby creating considerable observer discomfort in the Mayor of New York and others.

VIOLATION OF MORAL AND IDEAL STANDARDS

There are times when behavior is assessed, not against our judgments of what is common and conventional, but against moral standards and idealized norms that are believed to characterize all right-thinking and right-acting people. This view starts with the notion that people *ought* to behave in a certain way, whether they really do or not, and it concludes with the view that it is normal to behave in the way one ought, and abnormal to fail to behave properly. Thus, it is normal to work, and abnormal not to do so (unless wealth, the unavailability of job openings, or illness exonerate one). It is normal to love, to be loyal, and to be supportive, and abnormal not to —regardless of the fact that evidence for these dispositions is not widely found in modern society. It is abnormal to be too aggressive or too restrained, too shy or too forward, too ambitious or not sufficiently ambitious. It is abnormal to believe in the devil and abnormal *not* to believe in a good supernatural being. As far as ideal standards are concerned, abnormality becomes another word for all manner of behaviors that range from that which is down-right wicked to that which is best done without.

ABNORMALITY AS A SOCIAL JUDGMENT

Unlike the judgment of temperature, the judgment of abnormality is a social one. Look again at some of the elements: observer discomfort, vividness and unconventionality, and violation of moral and ideal standards. These all require the presence of other people, while the remaining elements of abnormality can also easily be interpreted socially. Social judgments can easily

Susceptibility to social abuse

be abused, and because the judgment of abnormality is so heavily social, it is even more susceptible to social abuse. At times, those who have worked for social change, as well as political dissenters, have been labeled as abnormal. We might well wish that this were not the case and that abnormality were a more objective judgment. But our present wishes are beside the point, though eventually abnormality may be assessed with considerably greater objectivity. We are not endorsing the way abnormality is presently judged. Nor are we prescribing how the word "abnormal" should be used. Rather, we are merely describing how the word is actually used by laymen and professionals alike.

APPLYING THE ELEMENTS OF ABNORMALITY

The family resemblance approach

Family members resemble each other across a fixed number of dimensions, such as height, hair and eye color, and shape of nose, mouth, and ears. Similarly, abnormality is assessed according to the match between an individual's characteristics and the seven elements of abnormality.

USING THE FAMILY RESEMBLANCE APPROACH

Examine the following case study with a view toward determining the "family resemblance" between the individual and the elements of abnormality.

Ralph, the seventeen-year-old son of a physician and a pharmacist, moved with his family from a small farming town to a large suburban community during the middle of his junior year in high school. The move was sudden: both his parents were offered jobs that were simply too good to turn down. The abruptness of the move generated no complaint from Ralph, nor did he acknowledge any difficulty. Nevertheless, he seemed to withdraw. At the outset, his family hardly noticed, but once the family settled down, his distant behavior became apparent. He made no friends in his new school, and when the summer came, he seemed to withdraw even further. He spent a good deal of the summer in his room, emerging only to take extended walks around the house. He often seemed preoccupied, and occasionally seemed to be listening to sounds that only he could hear.

Autumn approached and with it the time for Ralph to return to his senior year of high school. Ralph became even more withdrawn. He had difficulty sleeping, and he paced inside and outside the house. Shortly after he returned to school, his behavior deteriorated further. Sometimes, he seemed not to hear when called upon in class, while at other times his answers bore no relation to the questions. Both behaviors generated a good deal of mocking laughter in his classes, and his classmates actively avoided him. One day, he marched into class, stood up, and began to speak absolute gibberish. School authorities notified his parents, who came immediately to pick him up. When he saw them, he grimaced and began to roll a lock of hair between his fingers. He said nothing as he was brought to a psychiatric clinic. (Adapted from DSM-III Training Guide, 1981.)

Is Ralph abnormal according to the preceding criteria? Even this brief vignette, which fails to describe fully the richness of Ralph's problem, leaves us convinced that Ralph is suffering some kind of psychological abnormality. Let us return to the elements of abnormality, and examine the extent to which Ralph's actions reflect those elements.

• *Suffering.*   We have no information about whether, or to what degree, Ralph is suffering. His withdrawal from his family *might* reflect subjective distress. But then again, it might not.

• *Maladaptiveness.*   Ralph's behavior is highly dysfunctional. Not only does he needlessly draw negative attention to himself, but he obviously fails to respond to the demands of school. Such behavior neither serves his own needs nor those of society.

• *Incomprehensibility and irrationality.*   There can be little doubt that Ralph's behavior is incomprehensible to observers, and that his verbalizations seem irrational to them.

• *Unpredictability and loss of control.*   There is little evidence for loss of control in the vignette, but Ralph's parents would presumably find his behavior unpredictable. So too might his schoolmates.

• *Vividness.*   Ralph's behavior is quite vivid. His silent withdrawal stands out noticeably and his speeches in class make him the center of undesirable attention.

• *Observer discomfort.*   It is not clear from the vignette whether *all* observers are made uncomfortable by Ralph's behavior, but it is a fair guess that his schoolmates are avoiding him because they feel uncomfortable.

• *Violation of moral and ideal standards.*   There is no evidence that Ralph's behavior violates widely held moral standards.

In the main, then, Ralph's behavior is dysfunctional and incomprehensible. These elements alone would have qualified his behavior as abnormal in most people's judgment. Additionally, there is some evidence that his behavior is unpredictable, vivid, and creates discomfort in observers. These

In the film *One Flew over the Cuckoo's Nest*, based on a novel by Ken Kesey, it is ambiguous whether the main character is abnormal or not.

elements lend additional strength to the judgment that his behavior is abnormal.

What is the locus of Ralph's abnormality? His behavior is abnormal. His thought is abnormal. And because these problems of behavior and thought last for such a long time and occur across so many different situations, we come to call Ralph himself abnormal. This is the convention; it invites us to generalize from the actions and thoughts of an individual to the individual himself. This linguistic convention is not without costs, however, for we can easily be misled into believing that a particular pattern of behavior or thought is much more disabling and pervasive than it really is. It is tragic enough that Ralph has the problems he is afflicted with. But it adds considerably to his tragedy to somehow infer that Ralph himself is flawed, rather than merely realizing that *sometimes* and in *some* situations Ralph's *behaviors and thoughts* are abnormal.

Abnormality and Psychological Diagnosis

Abnormality is a global term. It serves only to indicate that something is judged to be wrong psychologically with a person's behavior or personality. But once the judgment is made that a person's behavior is abnormal, the question arises: How is it abnormal?

DSM-III-R AND DIAGNOSIS

DSM-III-R

The specific ways in which people are judged to be abnormal are described in the revised *Diagnostic and Statistical Manual of Mental Disorders* (Third Edition), commonly called DSM-III-R, which was published by the American Psychiatric Association in 1987. This catalog of psychological distress is large and all-embracing, and we will describe it at some length in Chapter 7. For the present, however, it is important to know that arriving at a specific disorder or diagnosis in DSM-III-R itself amounts to using family resemblances. DSM-III-R describes the elements that are said to characterize a particular disorder. Moreover, it describes the criteria for recognizing whether a particular element is present. The better the match between an individual's behavior and the elements offered for the disorder, the more confident we can be of the diagnosis (Cantor, Smith, French, and Mezzich, 1980).

"FAMILY RESEMBLANCE" APPROACH AND ITS HAZARDS

Family resemblance approach

The virtue of a family resemblance approach to abnormality arises from the fact that, much as there is no *single* way in which all sons resemble all fathers, neither is there a *single* way in which all abnormal behaviors resemble each other. The notion that all abnormality must involve psychological suffering, or vividness, or observer discomfort is simply false, as we have seen. No single element exists that binds the behaviors of, say, a person who is deeply depressed, a person who is afraid to be alone, and a person who gorges herself and then vomits. Yet, we regard each of these people to be suffering an abnormality because their behaviors are members of the family of characteristics that we have come to regard as abnormal.

But there are some hazards to the family resemblance approach to abnormality. Let's look at three of these hazards: society's error, disagreement between observers, and disagreement between actor and observer.

Hazards of the family resemblance approach

□ SOCIETY MAY ERR IN WHOM IT CALLS ABNORMAL.   The notion of abnormality can easily and erroneously be applied to all manner of behavior that society presently finds objectionable. As we indicated earlier, those who wore beards thirty years ago were seen as abnormal because they "stood out in the crowd." Their behavior matched one of the elements of abnormality, and they were, therefore, erroneously termed abnormal.

But it is not merely vivid behavior that can trigger allegations of abnormality. Behavior that creates discomfort in observers, for whatever reason, risks triggering those allegations. The student who refuses to haze when his fraternity brothers are doing so, or the person who, for deeply philosophic reasons, refuses to fight in any war, and therefore refuses to register for the draft—these people march to their own drummers, and they create discomfort in the observers who disagree with them. Similarly, those who violate the ideal standards of others in the course of maintaining their *own* ideal standards risk being termed abnormal.

□ OBSERVERS WILL DISAGREE ABOUT PARTICULAR BEHAVIORS OR INDIVIDUALS.   A family resemblance approach to abnormality is bound to generate some disagreements about whether or not a behavior qualifies as abnormal. Two observers might disagree that any given element was present. Moreover, they might disagree about whether enough elements were present, or whether they were present with sufficient intensity to constitute a clear case of abnormality.

In a study that will be more fully described in Chapter 7 (pp. 181–82), daily visitors came to large psychiatric hospitals to visit "pseudopatients," that is, people who were in the hospital to study it, not to be treated. These visitors quickly learned that they had to leave the hospital before the next staff shift came to work. Otherwise, they would be faced with the difficult task of proving that they, the visitors, were not patients. After all, they shared at least two visible elements with true patients: Like true patients, they had no keys! And like many of them, the visitors insisted that they did not belong there. That common family resemblance was occasionally strong enough to create some difficult moments for the visitors.

Such an approach generates disagreement for the further reason that the elements of abnormality are neither so precise nor so quantifiable that everyone will agree that a behavior or person fits the category. The more dramatic the behaviors and the longer they are sustained, the more agreement there will be among observers. The problem of observer disagreement is a serious one. As we shall see in Chapter 7, the problem is dealt with, to some extent, by stipulating as clearly as one can, the kinds of behaviors that are associated with each element of abnormality. When this is done, wider agreement occurs.

□ OBSERVERS AND ACTORS WILL OCCASIONALLY DISAGREE.   There will occasionally be different opinions as to whether a behavior or person should be judged as abnormal, according to who is doing the judging: the individ-

To many of his peers, this protester was behaving in accord with ideal standards. These soldiers and many other members of society, however, had a different view.

uals who are generating the behaviors in question—we call them actors—or those who observe the behaviors. Generally, actors will be less inclined to judge their own behaviors as abnormal for three reasons: First, they have much more information available to them about their own behaviors than do observers. What seems unpredictable or incomprehensible to an observer may seem quite predictable and comprehensible to an actor, and what generates discomfort in an observer may, as we indicated, generate none in the actor. Second, people who are psychologically distressed are not distressed all the time. Distress comes and goes. People, therefore, may be "crazy" at one time, but not crazy at another. Actors are uniquely positioned to recognize changes in themselves. Observers, however, often assume a continuity of psychological state that does not exist. Third, people generally are inclined to see themselves in a more favorable light than observers see them. As a result, actors will tend to see themselves and their behaviors more favorably, and hence more normally, than observers. Such differences in the perspectives of actors and observers could alone account for the differing viewpoints of Joyce Brown and the Mayor of New York.

NORMALITY

What is normality?

We have dealt at length with the meaning of abnormality and the elements that are associated with it, but it will not take us as long to define normality. *Normality is simply the absence of abnormality.* It means nothing beyond that. If abnormality is a matter of judgment and social perspective, so is normality. If abnormality is much more a matter of degree than of kind, so too is normality. And if there are enormous gray areas associated with the judgment of abnormality, such that we often don't really know whether a behavior or person is abnormal, those same gray areas will apply to the question of normality.

POSITIVES AND NEGATIVES: THE MEANING OF MEANING

Words can be stated in positive and negative forms. Usually, the positive form is well-defined, while the negative form is merely the opposite of the positive one. We know what "embarrassed" means, and it follows that "unembarrassed" means not embarrassed. The positive word is the primary member of the opposing pair and the "un" word gets its meaning only by negating the positive word. If we did not already know the meaning of the positive word, we would not understand its negation.

Normal as not abnormal

But this is not always the case. Sometimes the primary meaning resides in the *negative* case, and the positive word only makes sense as a negation of the negative word. The logic of "normal-abnormal" reflects the primacy of the negative case. Abnormal is the concept that makes primary sense. *Normal means nothing over and above "not abnormal."* To decide whether a person or an action is normal, we merely ask about the absence of the elements of abnormality. Are only a few of the elements of abnormality present, and those not intensely? Once we decide that actions or persons are *not* abnormal, we have simultaneously decided that they *are* normal. Normality has no meaning beyond the absence of abnormality.

We are occasionally uneasy about our own normality because of the logic of abnormality. Many things that we do have one or two elements of abnormality in them. While this is not enough for our actions to be termed abnormal, it is enough to make us uneasy about our own normality, particularly if we persist in the belief that normality is a state that has meaning beyond the absence of abnormality. Consider masturbation as a case in point. A fifteen-year-old boy who masturbates every day may wonder if he is normal. But if we examine that action against the elements of abnormality, we find very little to be concerned about. Is his masturbation *irrational?* Not at all. Is it *dysfunctional?* Not in any obvious way. Does he *suffer?* Quite the contrary (though worrying about it gives some pain). Does it produce *observer discomfort?* No, there are no observers. Is it *visible and unconventional?* No, over 90 percent of males acknowledge masturbation at one time or another, and adolescents who masturbate as often as three times a day are not uncommon. Is the behavior unacceptable because it *violates moral standards?* Marginally, with enormous variation from subculture to subculture. Overall, then, masturbation is somewhat unacceptable from some moral viewpoints, but it shares in no other element of abnormality. Why, then, would anyone be concerned about whether masturbation is normal? Because of that marginal unacceptability to some subcultures. The fact that it taps into one (and only one) element of abnormality is sufficient to make some people worry about its normality.

BEYOND NORMALITY: LIVING OPTIMALLY

To be normal is not necessarily to live well, for there is more to living than being normal and avoiding abnormality. There are pleasures, maturities, insights, achievements, and wisdoms—the joys of life. They are mentioned

Positive aspects of living constitute a good defense against abnormality.

Eleanor Roosevelt devoted herself to human rights and to helping the poor, oppressed, and dispossessed. "The important thing," she said, just before she died, "was that you never let down doing the best that you were able to do . . ."

here because without them, our conceptions of psychological life can become so oriented around abnormality that we fail to attend sufficiently to the positive aspects of living. These positive aspects constitute a good defense against abnormality itself (Rosenhan, 1969, 1970), if only because it is difficult for suffering and irrationality to exist simultaneously with joy and wisdom.

There is really no satisfactory psychological term to describe the positive side of life, nor any psychological theory to tell us how to achieve it. Some writers call it "self-actualization," a term, unfortunately, that describes a happy sadist and a happy homemaker equally well (Goldstein, 1939; Rogers, 1961; Maslow, 1971). Others (Jahoda, 1958) call it "positive mental health," stressing its medical, and implicitly, its disease aspects. We call it *optimal living.*

SOME ELEMENTS OF OPTIMAL LIVING

Like abnormality, optimal living is more a matter of degree than of kind. One doesn't live optimally all the time, any more than one is abnormal all the time. Rather, optimality is a goal that, on some days and under some conditions we feel more of, and at other times and conditions, less. No one lives optimally all the time.

There are six areas in which optimality can be recognized (Jahoda, 1958). They are:

• Positive attitudes toward self
• Growth and development
• Autonomy
• Accurate perception of reality
• Environmental competence
• Positive interpersonal relations.

POSITIVE ATTITUDES TOWARD SELF

The phrase *self-acceptance* has many connotations, but generally it implies knowing ourselves, accepting rather than denying what we know, and feeling good about that knowledge. "Self-acceptance implies that a person has learned to live with himself, accepting both the limitations and possibilities he may find in himself" (Jahoda, 1958, p. 24). This does not mean we are thinking about ourselves all the time; rather, much of the time we take ourselves for granted. But when we do think about ourselves, we accept and like what we see.

GROWTH AND DEVELOPMENT

Living optimally involves a desire to utilize one's abilities instead of stagnating, to devote oneself to a mission or vocation, and to establish long-range goals (Maslow, 1954). At its best, this kind of growth involves a full investment in living, a capacity to get out of one's skin and to lose oneself in work, thought, sport, or other people (Allport, 1937).

AUTONOMY

Optimal living both requires and generates a degree of emotional freedom from the demands of the immediate social environment and greater responsiveness to one's own internal standards. Increasingly, *self*-regard—the approval of oneself by oneself—rather than the approval of others, becomes the mark of this kind of maturity. Often, it is the exercise of one's own standards that brings about such self-rewarded independence.

ACCURATE PERCEPTION OF REALITY

When we dislike someone, we prefer to believe that they are thoroughly unpleasant, rather than finding that in many ways they are really nice. If the latter perception is more accurate, however, it is also more constructive because it leads us to investigate the conditions that led to the difficulties in the first place. Is it possible that we misunderstood? Could her awful behavior have been accidental? In short, testing our perceptions against reality involves some risk that we may have been wrong, but also the greater gain that we can do something about it.

Closely related to that concern for accurately assessing reality is the ability to tolerate realities that are simply ambiguous without prematurely casting them into present molds. The ability to say "I don't know," to live with ignorance, to wait for information that is accurate—these abilities strongly influence our capacity to perceive reality accurately.

ENVIRONMENTAL COMPETENCE

Being competent in life's tasks—in work, love, and play—contributes enormously to the sense of living optimally. The reasons for this are obvious: competence brings with it not only external gratifications but also internal ones. Coping with the requirements of one's environment and meeting one's own standards of performance contribute to one's sense of efficacy (Bandura, 1977a).

POSITIVE INTERPERSONAL RELATIONS

The final area of optimal living involves positive interpersonal relations— the ability to enjoy the company of others, to empathize with them, to give

Positive interpersonal relations with family and friends help us avoid emotional misery, alienation, and serious psychological disorders.

and receive support, to respect others regardless of their status, and the capacity to love and be loved—all of these are implied in the notion of positive interpersonal relations. Some theorists believe that the absence of such relations is a major source of emotional misery, resulting in alienation, loss of sense of community, and finally fear of one another (May, 1953).

THE HAZARDS OF SELF-DIAGNOSIS

There is almost no one who has not harbored secret doubts about his or her normality, "Do I cry too easily?" "Am I too afraid of speaking up in class?" "Do other people occasionally have fantasies about their parents dying in violent accidents?"

Interns' syndrome

Related to our concern about our normality is a phenomenon called "interns' syndrome." In the course of early training, the fledgling medical student finds in himself symptoms of almost every disease he studies.

> I remember going to the British Museum one day to read up the treatment for some slight ailment of which I had a touch—hay fever, I fancy it was. I got down the book, and read all I came to read; and then, in an unthinking moment, I idly turned the leaves, and began to indolently study diseases, generally. I forgot which was the first distemper I plunged into—some fearful, devastating scourge. I know —and, before I had glanced half down the list of "premonitory symptoms," it was borne in upon me that I had fairly got it.
>
> I sat for a while frozen with horror, and then in the listlessness of dispair, I again turned over the pages. I came to typhoid fever—read the symptoms—discovered that I had typhoid fever, must have had it for months without knowing it—wondered what else I had got; turned up St. Vitus's Dance—found, as I expected, that I had that too—began to get interested in my case, and determined to sift it to the bottom, and so started alphabetically—looked up ague, and learnt that I was sickening for it, and that the acute stage would commence in about another fortnight. Bright's disease, I was relieved to find, I had only in a modified form, and, so far as that was concerned, I might live for years. Cholera I had, with severe complications; and diptheria I seemed to have been born with. I plodded conscientiously through the twenty-six letters, and the only malady I could conclude I had not got was housemaid's knee.
>
> I felt rather hurt about this at first; it seemed somehow to be a sort of slight. Why hadn't I got housemaid's knee? Why this invidious reservation? After a while, however, less grasping feelings prevailed. I reflected that I had every other known malady in the pharmacology, and I grew less selfish, and determined to do without housemaid's knee. Gout, in its most malignant stage, it would appear, had seized me without my being aware of it; and zymosis I had evidently been suffering with from boyhood. There were no more diseases after zymosis, so I concluded there was nothing else the matter with me . . . I had walked into that reading-room a happy healthy man. I crawled out a decrepit wreck." (Jerome, 1880)

As you read this book, you too will encounter symptoms in yourself that will make you think you have each disorder in turn. Be forewarned: It is a very unpleasant experience and one about which neither authors nor readers can really do much. In part, it arises from the privacy that surrounds our lives. Many of our thoughts, and some of our actions, strike us as private, if not secret—things about which no one should know. If they did know, people, even (perhaps particularly) friends, might think less of us, or be offended, or both. One consequence of this privacy is the development of an exaggerated sense of the uniqueness of our forbidden thoughts and behaviors. Seeing them suddenly alluded to on these pages and associated with certain syndromes (commonly in contexts that are quite different from the contexts of our own behaviors—but we don't notice that) makes us believe that we have fallen prey to that problem too.

There are two things that can be done to combat the distress you may experience from reading this book and going to lectures. First, read carefully. You may, for example, be concerned when you read about depression: "Yes, I'm blue. I cry now more than I used to." But as you inquire deeply into the symptoms of depression, you will find that the absence of suicidal thoughts, your continued interest in sex or sports, your optimism about the future, all count against the diagnosis of depression.

Second, talk with your friends. Sometimes, merely mentioning that "when I read Chapter so-and-so, I get the feeling they're talking about me. Do you ever get that feeling?" will bring forth a chorus of "you bets," and relief for all of you.

SUMMARY

1. There are no hard and fast definitions of normality and abnormality, for there is no single element that all instances of abnormality share, nor any single property that distinguishes normality from abnormality.

2. *Abnormality* is recognized the way members of a family are recognized: because they share a *family resemblance* in that they have many significant elements in common.

3. With regard to abnormality, there are seven properties or elements that count toward deciding whether a person or an action is abnormal: suffering, maladaptiveness, irrationality and incomprehensibility, unpredictability and loss of control, vividness and unconventionality, observer discomfort, and violation of moral and ideal standards. The more of these elements that are present, and the more visible each element is, the more likely are we to judge the person or the action as abnormal.

4. Because the judgment of abnormality is a *social judgment,* there is sometimes disagreement about who is abnormal, and about which thoughts and actions qualify as being considered abnormal. Society occasionally errs about whom it calls abnormal, as sometimes do observers, even those who are qualified diagnosticians. But the absence of complete agreement should not be taken to mean that abnormality is always or frequently a matter of dispute.

5 *Normality* is simply the absence of abnormality, nothing more. To be normal is to possess so few of the elements of abnormality, and those at such a minimal degree, that no qualified observer would make the judgment of abnormality. But to be normal is not necessarily to live happily or well.

6. *Optimal living* requires some quite positive capacities, among them: positive attitudes toward oneself, capacity for growth and development, autonomy, an accurate perception of reality, social and vocational competence, and positive interpersonal relationships.

2

Abnormality across Time and Place

T HROUGHOUT human history, there have been many different notions about what behaviors can be defined as madness. This is only to be expected, for as the elements of abnormality change relative to historical context, so must the notions of what is normal and abnormal. Behaviors that have been revered in one time or place may have been defined as clear examples of madness in others. The ancient Hebrews and the ancient Greeks held in awe those who claimed to be prophets and had "the gift of tongues." Yet in the modern world, those who claim to see into the future generate suspicion, and those who speak in unknown words and rhythms are often classified as schizophrenics.

So too have there been different and contradictory theories about the causes of abnormal behavior. Shakespeare portrayed Ophelia as driven "mad" by Hamlet's cruel rejection, implying to his Elizabethan audiences that Ophelia's withdrawal and eventual suicide were products of the social influences in her immediate environment. Yet, during the same period in history, other "mad" women were accused of having willfully made pacts with Satan. Clearly, a society's definitions of madness and perceptions of its causes have played significant roles in how the abnormal have been viewed: they have influenced whether the mad were revered, feared, pitied, or simply accepted. In turn, these perceptions have determined the ways in which the mad have been treated: whether they were honored for their unique powers or incarcerated, treated, or abandoned for their madness.*

---

* Curiously, even the forms of abnormal behavior have been different in different ages and cultures. For example, hysteria, identified for more than two thousand years as a discrete syndrome, was especially prevalent at certain times. It was rife in the nineteenth century, if the historian is to judge by the notebooks of physicians and the guest registries of hostels like those in Lourdes. Yet, hysteria seems to have all but disappeared in the present century.

The history of abnormality, like the history of most other human phenomena, is not linear and logical but meandering and inconsistent. In this chapter, we will examine two significant issues in the history of madness: (1) theories of cause, and (2) methods of treatment and care. Remember that notions of abnormality change when values change, for notions of normality and abnormality are guided by the predominant values of a culture. We take it for granted, for example, that wearing a bikini to the pool is acceptable behavior today. But we know it would have been scandalous a hundred years ago. Why? Because our view of what is modest and immodest has undergone enormous change during the past century. So, too, has our view of abnormality.

THE PERCEIVED CAUSES OF ABNORMAL BEHAVIOR

There is very little about abnormality that tells what caused it, or that even provides clues about where to look for causes. Yet, because treatment and cure depend upon perceived cause—a complex relationship to which we will return many times in later chapters—people find it difficult to resist attributing causes to abnormality. Thus, there were times when abnormality was attributed to the wrath of the gods or to possession by demons. At other times and in other places, earthquakes and tides, germs and illness, interpersonal conflict and bad blood were separately and together used to explain the origins of abnormality. Notions about abnormality arise from the culture's world-view. If the culture has a theory of natural law that is animistic, abnormality will be viewed in animistic terms. If it is scientific and materialistic, as it is today, abnormality will be viewed in scientific terms. How our understanding of abnormality is articulated, therefore, depends distinctly on the beliefs that dominate in a culture and epoch. We will present three general explanations of abnormality, discussing in turn: animistic causes, physical causes, and psychogenic origins.

ANIMISTIC ORIGINS: POSSESSION

In a remote cave in the French Pyrenees, there is a twenty-thousand-year-old painting that portrays a dancer disguised as an animal with massive branching horns. The figure is thought to represent a sorcerer (Cohn, 1975). The belief that the natural world is inhabited by spirits and demons has pervaded history. With it, too, has come the conviction that such spirits and demons can be controlled through supernatural means. Such beliefs prevail today in many cultures.

ANIMISTIC FORCES

In premodern societies, the belief in *animism*—that everyone and everything has a "soul"—was widespread, and mental disturbance was often ascribed to *animistic* causes. One of the most common explanations of madness was that evil spirits had taken *possession* of an individual and controlled that person's behavior. Much as a parasitic tapeworm lives in and weakens the body, so could a parasitic spirit inhabit and weaken the mind.

This Paleolithic cave drawing portrays a dancer disguised as an animal, and is thought to represent a sorcerer.

The belief in animism

Paleolithic cave dwellers are believed to have produced these holes in the skulls of those who were "possessed" by evil spirits. This method, which is called *trephining*, freed the possessed from the presence of evil spirits.

Some skulls of Paleolithic cave dwellers have characteristic holes, called **trephines,** that appear to have been chipped out by stone instruments. It is thought that trephining was performed to provide an exit for demons or evil spirits trapped within the skull.

People could be possessed by many different kinds of spirits. The spirits of ancestors, animals, gods, and heroes, and of victims whose wrongs had not been redressed, were among those who could wreak madness. These spirits could enter a person through their own cunning, through the work of an evildoer with magical powers, or through a lack of faith on the part of the possessed individual. Not surprisingly, because possession was a result of invisible forces, freeing the possessed individual from these spirits required special techniques. Across time and place, there has been the widespread belief in the power of some individuals to use magic both to induce evil and to expel it; shamans, witch doctors, sorcerers, and witches were all believed to be able to influence animistic forces (Douglas, 1970). In medieval Europe, for example, individuals from all levels of society resorted to sorcerers and witches for spells, potents, and prophecies. Although they were often feared, witches were generally left alone unless they were thought to have murdered or to have destroyed property. But even then, they were prosecuted by secular, not religious, authorities (Currie, 1968).

Much of what is presently understood as originating from psychological distress was earlier attributed to animistic causes. Dancing **manias,** for example, often involved hundreds of people, who danced for days on end until they succumbed to exhaustion. These manias spread like an epidemic throughout much of Western Europe. **Tarantism,** a form of the dancing mania that occurred in Italy, was thought to have been brought on by the tarantula. Episodes of **lycanthropy,** in which groups of people believed they were wolves and acted accordingly, were common in rural areas. In these examples, **animal possession** was the dominant motif. In many other cases, individuals were thought to be possessed by evil spirits (Ellenberger, 1970).

Attitude towards
witches

SATANISTIC FORCES

By the middle of the fifteenth century, tolerance for bizarre behavior became strained. The perception of witches and the response to them changed radically, and for nearly three hundred years thereafter, Europe was caught up in a frenzied fear of witches—a fear that caused thousands to be led to their death. For modern students of abnormal psychology, these witch hunts provide a fascinating look at how animistic forces were used to explain madness and why it was such a convincing theory at the time.

Such changed attitudes toward witches arose out of the great social and intellectual upheavals prevailing during the late fifteenth century and the sixteenth century (McFarlane, 1970). With the rise of capitalism, individual values were replacing communal ones, towns were replacing rural communities, and the structure of the medieval family and village was being disturbed (Midelfort, 1972). Traditional authority was weakening. The Church itself was rife with schism as the Protestant Reformation plunged much of Europe into religious civil wars that further upset social equilibrium (Trevor-Roper, 1970).

It was within this context of extensive social instability that a belief in witches flourished in Europe. Witches were those who made pacts with Satan and who took delight in harming others. A Biblical injunction, hardly used until that time, was recalled vividly and implemented:

*Any man or woman among you who calls up ghosts or spirits
shall be put to death.*

MALLEVS
MALEFICARVM.
IN TRES DIVISVS
PARTES,

The frontispiece of one of the many editions of the *Malleus Maleficarum*, by Heinrich Kraemer and Johann Sprenger.

The Church had earlier considered witchcraft mere "illusion" to be dealt with by secular authorities. Now it was heresy, treason against God, to be suppressed by the Church of Rome through its investigative agency, the Holy Inquisition. Two Dominican monks, Heinrich Kraemer and Johann Sprenger, wrote the *Malleus Maleficarum,* or *The Witches' Hammer,* a 1486 manual for hunting and disposing of witches. Printed on the recently invented printing press, the *Malleus Maleficarum* was widely distributed. Its official stamp and easy availability made it enormously popular, and more than thirty editions were published in the next hundred years (Summers, 1971). But it was not the only such treatise. Scores of "handbooks" on detecting the presence of witches flooded Europe.

Who were the witches? Overwhelmingly, they were women. "All witchcraft comes from carnal lust," the *Malleus Maleficarum* states, "which is in women insatiable." The association of evil with women's sexuality, and the fear of women's sexuality from which it arose, was probably widespread then, much as it is widespread today (see Gregor, 1985, for example). The most heinous crimes of which witches were accused were linked to reproduction: robbing men of their sexual potency, murdering born and unborn babies, and wanton lust. Men were protected from this heinous crime because Jesus was a man. The *Malleus Maleficarum,* then, was a religious document that reflected a strong fear of women's sexuality. Profoundly misogynist, it legitimized the persecution, torture, and death of women.

The occurrence of inexplicable events led one to suspect witchcraft. A sudden and dramatic illness in an otherwise healthy person might generate such suspicions. Or a roof that had collapsed on an unsuspecting bystander might lead one to ask why it had collapsed on *him?* That question, impermissible by modern scientific standards, was one that was especially inter-

This title page from a 1613 text on witches depicts a common test for witchcraft: throwing the suspect into water. If the woman floated, she was guilty; if she sank, innocent.

esting in those times. The answer was sought in the following way: A collapsing roof is a rare event, and the fact that it had collapsed on this particular individual might well have made it rarer. Witchcraft too was rare, and if witches were present and active in this matter, they would have left other improbable traces. It was the presence of *other improbable facts* that lent credence to the view that witches had brought about this particular disaster.

Tests for witches

There were a variety of ingenious tests for the presence of witches. One might hold molten lead over a sick person and then pour the lead into a bowl of water. If the lead condensed into an image, one might conclude that the sickness was due to witchcraft. Or one might lacerate a suspected witch. If there was no bleeding, one's suspicion would grow firmer. Or one might weight a suspect and throw her into a lake. If she floated inexplicably, she might well be a witch.

These were *strong* tests of witchcraft, and if they had been the only ones used, very few witches would have been discovered. But the belief in witchcraft was as strong as the fear of women's sexuality, and the presence of witchcraft was considered so widespread that two less reliable sorts of evidence were called upon. The first was the presence of *body marks* on the suspect. Any birthmark, scar, or mole on the woman's body indicated that she had entered into a pact with Satan. But because body marks are common in the first place, and more common among people who do manual labor, the test was likely to generate a substantial number of "false positives," that is, people who had body marks but were not witches.

The second indicator of witchcraft was *confession.* An individual's confession that she was a witch was held to be ideal. "Common justice demands that a witch should not be condemned to death unless she is convicted of her own confession." But because notions of "due process" were not highly developed then, confession could often be suggested or extracted. Again, false positives—people who were alleged to be witches on the basis of shaky evidence—were probably very common.

It was believed that there was no "cure" for witchcraft, except for the physical destruction of the witch. On the continent, the confessed witch was burned by the secular authorities. In England and the colonies, witches were hanged. Conservatively, between the middle of the fifteenth and seven-

Box 2-1   EVIDENCE AT THE SALEM WITCH TRIALS

The famous Salem Witch Trials, and the witchcraft mania that grew up in that town, evidently arose from the antics of children. A group of young girls used to play imaginary games at the village minister's house. Ghosts, devils, witches, and the whole invisible world were the subjects of their games, borrowed in the manner that children today borrow space explorations from the adult world that surrounds them. Their games of imagination, however, came to the attention of the village elders who solemnly concluded that these children were "bewitched." The children, perhaps stimulated by the attention they were receiving and the excitement they had caused, became more involved in their imaginings, feeding the concern of the elders.

Pressed by the elders to name those who had been casting evil spells over them, they named one person, then another, then still others, until it appeared that nearly half the people in the village had signed their souls over to the devil. Neighbors hurled wild accusations against each other. These accusations resulted in the arrest and trial of 250 persons in one year (1691–1692), of whom 50 were condemned, 19 executed, 2 died in prison, and 1 of torture.

It is important to remember that the elders of the community were "sane," sober, and intelligent people. Cotton Mather was a leading colonial figure, son of the president of Harvard University, and a founder of Yale. Deeply religious, he wanted to protect the community against dangers that, for him, were real. And precisely because he and the other elders were so deeply convinced of the dangers, they were remarkably credulous in weighing the evidence. An example of their gullibility is seen in the interrogation of Sarah Carrier, age eight, whose mother, Martha, was subsequently hanged as a witch.

"How long hast thou been a witch?"
"Ever since I was six years old."
"How old are you now?"
"Nearly eight years old."
"Who made you a witch?"
"My mother. She made me set my hand to the book."
"You said you saw a cat once. What did the cat say to you?"
"It said it would tear me to pieces if I would not set my hand to the book."
(Sarah is speaking here of the *Devil's Book*.)
"How did you know that it was your mother?"
"The cat told me so, that she was my mother."

SOURCE: Upham, 1867, cited in Deutsch, 1949, p. 35.

teenth century, more than 100,000 people (mostly women) in Europe and in the American colonies died as a result of the witch trials (see Box 2-1) (Deutsch, 1949). Witch hunting was not the monopoly of the Church of Rome. With the Reformation, many Protestant sects also mounted zealous campaigns against the lustful consorts of Satan. Not surprisingly, charges of witchcraft were often hurled at members of rival religions (Thomas, 1971).

PHYSICAL CAUSES

While animistic beliefs served to explain psychological distress for centuries, an approach to abnormality that emphasizes *physical* causes can also be traced back to the ancient world. In fact, it is possible that the prehistoric peoples who practiced trephining were employing a primitive surgical technique to relieve the pain of severe headaches. One of the first psychological disorders that was thought to have arisen from physical causes was *hysteria.*

Papyri from early Egypt, as well as the writings of Greek physicians, record a remarkable disorder that was found mainly among women who were virgins or widows. Its symptoms included such complaints as epileptic-like fits, pains of all sorts in various parts of the body, aphonia (loss of voice), headaches, dizziness, paralysis, blindness, lameness, listlessness, and melancholia. The Greeks believed that all of these difficulties arose from a single source: a roaming uterus.

The Greeks believed that the uterus was an animated organ that had somehow dislodged itself from its normal place to rove around the body, perhaps in search of water and nourishment, but often enough, for no good reason. In the course of its wanderings, it would attach itself here or there and create havoc. If it attached itself to the liver, for instance, the person would lose her voice, grind her teeth, and her complexion would turn ashen. Lodged in the chest cavity, this roaming uterus would produce convulsions similar to epilepsy, and at the heart it would produce anxiety, oppression, and vomiting. The Greek word for uterus is *hystera,* and the Greeks believed so deeply that the uterus was responsible for these difficulties that they named the entire disorder after it—hysteria (Veith, 1965).

The Greek physician Galen (circa 130–201 A.D.) was an early theorist who believed that some apparently physical disorders were psychological in origin.

This view of hysteria prevailed until the second century A.D., when it was challenged by Soranus and Galen, physicians who recognized that the uterus was not a living animal. Soranus wrote, ". . . the uterus does not issue forth like a wild animal from the lair, delighted by fragrant odors and fleeing bad odors; rather it is drawn together because of stricture caused by inflammation" (Veith, 1965, pp. 30–31). This new view of hysteria led to entirely different views of its origins and treatment. Since the *hystera* was not a roaming animal but rather a malfunctioning sexual organ, might there be a similar organ in men which, when malfunctioning, could cause them to have similar symptoms? Galen believed there was. He had observed that both men and women suffer similar symptoms following periods of sexual abstinence. He, therefore, argued that hysteria has a sexual basis, a view that is widely accepted today.

Attributing psychological distress to physical causes took a peculiar twist hundreds of years later with the belief in *animalism.* This belief asserted that there were remarkable similarities between animals and mad people. Like animals, the mad could not control themselves and therefore needed to be severely controlled. Like animals, the insane were capable of violence, often suddenly and without provocation. Like animals, they could live without protest in miserable conditions, conditions under which normal people simply could not exist (see Box 2-2). One proponent of this view pointed to

The ease with which certain of the insane of both sexes bear the most rigorous and prolonged cold. . . . On certain days when the thermometer indicated . . . as many as 16 degrees below freezing, a madman . . . could not endure his wool blanket, and remained sitting on the icy floor of his cell. In the morning, one no sooner opened his door than he ran in his shirt into the inner court, taking ice and snow by the fistful, applying it to his breast and letting it melt with a sort of delectation. (Foucault, 1965, pp. 74–75)

Box 2-2   **A PATIENT'S COMPLAINT**

James Carkesse, who was a clerk to the English diarist Samuel Pepys (1633–1703), became deranged and was institutionalized in London. He described in verse the experience from a patient's viewpoint.

> . . . I'll tell you his way of Proceeding,
> All you, that here shall enter;
> *Purges, Vomits and Bleeding,*
> are his method of Cure, at a Venture . . .
> I laid him in Straw for a Bed,
> Lest *Feathers should make him light-headed*
> That there his wild Oats he might shed,
> and gain to his Wits be wedded.
> Without either Shirt, or Cloaths,
> I lodg'd my merry mad Youth;
> For of Kin we may well suppose,
> The *Sober to Naked-Truth* . . .
> I order'd his *Keeper*, at Large,
> On occasion to ply him with Blows,
> That what *Jugular* did not discharge,
> The mad *Blood* might come out at his *Nose* . . .

SOURCE: Carkesse, cited in Hunter and Macalpine, 1963, p. 215.

The relatively primitive notions of physical cause that are captured in the early Greek views of hysteria, or in animalism, gradually yielded to more sophisticated approaches. With the development of modern medicine, many physicians came to consider madness to be a form of illness amenable to the same kinds of treatment as physical illness. Purges, bleeding, and forced vomiting were choice medical remedies of the seventeenth and eighteenth centuries, and these were administered to the infirm and the insane alike. Gradually, these views and treatments were replaced by the kinds of approaches that characterize present-day medicine, in particular, surgery and pharmacology (see Chapter 3).

PSYCHOGENIC ORIGINS

Psychological causes of abnormality

The quest for understanding psychological abnormality was pursued down still another path by the ancient Greeks and Romans, this time to its ***psychological*** origins. In addition to his observations about hysteria, Galen contributed important insights into the psychological causes of abnormality. In a particularly striking instance, Galen examined a woman who complained of sleeplessness, listlessness, and general malaise. He could find no direct evidence of physical illness and ultimately narrowed his inferences to two possibilities. Either she was suffering from melancholy, which was a physical disorder of one of the four body "humors," or fluids, "or else she was troubled about something she was unwilling to confess," a psychological explanation. He concluded:

After I had diagnosed that there was no bodily trouble, and that the woman was suffering from some mental uneasiness, it happened that at the very time I was examining her, this was confirmed. Somebody came from the theatre and said he had seen Pylades dancing. Then both her expression and the colour of her face changed. Seeing this, I applied my hand to her wrist, and noticed that her pulse had suddenly become extremely irregular. This kind of pulse indicates that the mind is disturbed; thus it occurs also in people who are disputing over any subject. So on the next day I said to one of my followers that, when I paid my visit to the woman, he was to come a little later and announce to me, "Morphus is dancing today." When he said this, I found that the pulse was unaffected. Similarly also on the next day, when I had an announcement made about the third member of the troupe, the pulse remained unchanged as before. On the fourth evening I kept very careful watch when it was announced the Pylades was dancing, and noticed that the pulse was very much disturbed. Thus I found out that the woman was in love with Pylades, and by careful watch on the succeeding days my discovery was confirmed. (Galen, cited in Veith, 1965, p. 36)

Galen's assessment of possible cause is the hallmark of the scientific method that was eventually to advance our understanding and treatment of psychological disorders. Rather than leaping to a conclusion, Galen tested two alternative hypotheses and decided which was correct according to the evidence. In this case, the evidence favored the hypothesis that stressed psychological experience rather than physiology.

Galen's observations on the psychological origins of abnormality were forgotten for centuries. Thus, until the middle of the eighteenth century, hysteria was believed to be a female neurological disorder that had its origins in genital illness. The recognition that mental disorders were psychological in origin and could be treated by psychological means did not arise again until the middle of the eighteenth century. To understand how this view arose, we first need to look at one of the most colorful people in the history of abnormal psychology, Franz Anton Mesmer (1734–1815).

MESMERISM

Mesmer is not only one of the most colorful, but surely one of the most maligned characters in the history of abnormal psychology. Variously called a genius and a charlatan, he proposed that many diseases, from epilepsy to

Franz Anton Mesmer (1734–1815) and his patients around the *banquet*. The banquet was supposed to concentrate a patient's magnetic fluid and induce a crisis, which would eventually restore the body's equilibrium, and the patient's health.

*Mesmer and
animal magnetism*

hysteria, develop from the obstruction of the flow of an invisible and impalpable entity that he first called "universal magnetic fluid" and later ***animal magnetism.*** Very much a man of the Enlightenment, Mesmer was influenced by contemporary discoveries in electricity and proposed the existence of a physical magnetic fluid which, when unequally distributed, causes disease in the body. He theorized that magnetic fluid was influenced by the lunar cycle, the tides, the planets, and the stars. Mesmer believed that health could be restored by using certain techniques which induced "crises" in the body. These crises would be provoked again and again, but each time would be experienced as less severe by the patient, until they disappeared and the body was back in equilibrium.

Mesmer went to Paris from Vienna in 1778. He opened a clinic where patients suffering from the various symptoms of hysteria were seen in groups. In a heavily curtained room, patients were arranged around a large wooden tub, or baquet, which was filled with water and magnetized iron filings. Iron rods protruded from the tub and were pointed by the patients to their ailing parts. The baquet was supposed to concentrate the magnetic fluid and induce the patient's crisis. Mesmer, dressed in a lavender cape, would pass among the patients to the accompaniment of gentle music, fixing his eye on them, and touching each with his iron wand. One patient would experience strange sensations, including trembling and convulsions. After the first succumbed, others were not long in having similar experiences, though there were always a few who were unaffected (Pattie, 1967).

*Discrediting
Mesmer's theory*

Mesmer had departed from Vienna under a cloud: he had been accused of charlatanry. And, despite his therapeutic successes, it was not long before similar accusations were leveled against him in Paris. So heated and acrimonious were the charges and countercharges, that in 1783, Louis XVI appointed a Royal Commission to investigate animal magnetism. Its eminent members included the chemist Lavoisier, the astronomer Bailly, and Benjamin Franklin, who was then serving as U.S. ambassador to France. The Commission heard evidence, deliberated for five months, and concluded that there was no such thing as animal magnetism. Interestingly, the Commission did not question Mesmer's success in curing patients of their ills; rather, it addressed his theory that the ills themselves were the result of the imbalance of magnetic fluid in the body. The Commission found that there was no physical proof for the existence of this fluid. Thus, they concluded that Mesmer's cures were entirely due to "imagination." Crushingly defeated, Mesmer, a proud man, vanished into obscurity. But the *reality* of his "cures" remained. People in distress continued to seek this kind of help, and to benefit from it, so much so that animal magnetism came to be called ***mesmerism.***

HYPNOTISM

*Survival of
techniques of
mesmerism*

The findings of the Royal Commission were deadly to the scientific theory of mesmerism, but the techniques themselves survived. Underground in France, but publicly in the United States and in Germany, mesmerism continued to be practiced and studied. (Indeed, one of the most famous patients to be treated by this method in America was Mary Baker Eddy, the founder of Christian Science.) While the quest for finding the elusive magnetic fluid led to a dead end and was finally abandoned, the cures that derived from

Jean Martin Charcot (1825–1893) demonstrating hypnosis to a class of medical students.

Charcot and hypnotism

After studying with Charcot, Sigmund Freud (1856–1939) went on to articulate a theory whose influence continues to be felt in modern psychology and psychiatry.

mesmerism continued to excite interest. The process that had been called mesmerism underwent a name change and came to be known as *hypnotism.*

A major figure in the scientific study of hypnosis was Jean Martin Charcot (1825–1893), Medical Director of one of the largest sections at La Salpêtrière and Professor of Diseases of the Nervous System at the University of Paris. Charcot was widely regarded as a first-rate scientist, the most eminent neurologist of the nineteenth century, and an awesome and much-feared teacher. The latter characteristic, we shall see, was his scientific undoing.

While Charcot was at La Salpêtrière, one of the wards in his charge housed women patients who suffered from convulsions. Charcot sought to distinguish hysterical convulsions from those brought on by epilepsy. In order to distinguish hysteria from other neurological disorders, Charcot employed hypnosis. If, for example, a patient who suffered a paralyzed arm was able to move her arm under hypnosis, then the diagnosis of hysteria could be given; otherwise, the appropriate diagnosis was a neurological disorder. Charcot extended his study to male patients as well, demonstrating that the symptoms of traumatic paralysis in men were the same as those of hysterical paralysis (Ellenberger, 1970).

Hypnosis fascinated Charcot, and he quickly generated a neurological theory about it. His students, ever eager to please, tested his views and brought back confirmatory evidence. But Charcot himself never hypnotized his patients. Rather, his students "worked them up" and taught them how to perform, after which Charcot unwittingly used them as demonstration subjects. Other scientists, particularly Hyppolyte Bernheim in Nancy, were unable to replicate Charcot's findings, and quickly located the source of error. Once again, a theory of hypnosis fell into disrepute, though the fact that hypnosis could be used to cure was unquestioned.

Charcot trained a large number of neurologists and psychiatrists, among them Sigmund Freud, the father of psychoanalysis. Freud proposed psychogenic causes as the root of madness. His contribution to the psychological approach to abnormality is so great, however, that we will take it up separately in Chapter 4.

TREATMENT OF THE MENTALLY DISTRESSED

How a psychological disorder is treated depends heavily on how it is understood. When mental disturbance was deemed to be the result of animistic causes, supernatural means were often needed to rid the individual of the distress. Similarly, when its origins were believed to be physical or psychological, treatment tended to rely on those means.

TREATING DEMONIC POSSESSION

Exorcism as treatment

Possession by animistic forces—demons, spirits, and the like—was most commonly treated by *exorcism,* a ceremonial ritual during which the demons were expelled from the victim's bodies. Exhausting and often time-consuming, exorcism rituals generally involved a cooperative relationship between the *shaman* or priest, and the afflicted. Together they tried to make the alien spirits identify themselves and then to cajole, threaten, and overwhelm the intruders so that they would leave the poor unfortunates. The belief that mental distress is the result of possession by evil spirits has been a persistent one. While they are rare and commonly frowned upon, exorcism rituals are performed even today in the United States.

Ostracism as treatment

If exorcism failed, *ostracism*—casting out the person as well as his or her demons—might be used. It was with regard to ostracism that the myth of *narrenschiffen* arose (Foucault, 1965). These were thought to be ships full of "fools," quite possibly manned by madmen, which went from harbor to harbor, seeking but not finding safe port. While it is unlikely that such *narrenschiffen* ever existed—no such ship records have been found, and who after all, would entrust an expensive ship to a crew of madmen?—the myth conveys unequivocally the degree to which the mad were rejected (Maher and Maher, 1982).

This sixteenth-century woodcut depicts a demon being exorcised from a woman. The exorcism is being performed by a bishop in front of the altar in a cathedral.

TREATING PHYSICAL CAUSES

Treating a
wandering uterus

When hysteria was thought to result from a wandering uterus, there were a prodigious number of proposed cures. The Egyptians and Greeks based most of them on the pull-push principle: Draw the uterus back to its proper place with pleasant experiences and aromatic substances, and drive it away from its current attachment with fetid fumigations. Perfumes and gentle massage played a therapeutic role in pulling the uterus back to where it was supposed to be; garlic and burning dung were applied to the aching areas in order to drive the prodigal uterus away. Later, in the Middle Ages, human attempts to keep the uterus in its place appear to have been abandoned in favor of divine intercession, as in this tenth-century prayer: "I conjure thee, O womb . . . not to harm that maid of God, N., not to occupy her head, throat, neck, chest, . . . but to lie down quietly in the place which God chose for thee, so that this maid of God, N., be restored to health. . . . (From Zilboorg, 1941, pp. 131–32).

THE RISE OF PSYCHOGENIC TREATMENTS

By the eighteenth century, the explanations that stressed animistic causes, while never completely abandoned, no longer commanded respect among serious thinkers, who emphasized rational rather than supernatural explanations. Thus, emphasis turned to two explanations, both of which, as we have seen, were first proposed in ancient times. One, following notions of physical cause, defined psychological distress as fundamentally *illness,* not different in kind from other physical illnesses. The other held that psychological disorder was fundamentally *psychological,* and *very* different in kind from physical illness. These theories continue to dominate our thinking today. Both views command considerable supportive evidence. We will examine the biological or medical view of psychological distress and its implications for treatment in the next chapter. Now, we focus on the treatments that grew out of psychogenic theories of madness.

Psychological vs.
biological views

Much of the excitement that was generated by the psychogenic viewpoint came about, as we have seen, through the study of hysteria. With its paralyses, anesthesias, and convulsions, its loss of voice, sight, or hearing, and occasional loss of consciousness, hysteria seemed patently a *physical* disorder. It was on the basis of his physical theory of animal magnetism that Mesmer developed the technique which came to be called hypnosis. Charcot, in his path-breaking work, was subsequently able to use hypnosis to distinguish between symptoms that had an organic cause and symptoms that were hysterical in nature. Subsequent theorists suggested that the therapeutic effects of hypnosis resulted from psychological suggestion (Bernheim, 1886, cited in Pattie, 1967). Thus, "psychotherapeutics" became an accepted treatment for the mentally disturbed.

Technique of
hypnosis

By the end of the nineteenth century, hypnosis was widely used in Europe and in the United States for treating hysterical disorders. It formed the basis for the development of modern forms of psychotherapy, and it was a significant milestone in the psychogenic approach to mental disorders.

One of the people who used hypnosis in his treatment of patients was Josef Breuer (1842–1925), a distinguished Viennese internist whose prac-

Josef Breuer (1842–1925) collaborated with Sigmund Freud in writing *Studies in Hysteria* (1895).

tice included a large number of hysterical patients. Breuer's treatment often consisted of inducing these patients to talk about their problems and fantasies under hypnosis. Frequently patients would become emotional under hypnosis, reliving painful experiences, experiencing a deep *emotional catharsis,* and emerging from the hypnotic trance feeling much better. The patients, of course, were unaware of a relationship between what they discussed under hypnosis, how emotional they had become, and how they felt subsequently. But Breuer believed that because his patients had experienced a catharsis under hypnosis, their symptoms disappeared.

Just as Breuer was making these discoveries, Sigmund Freud, then a neurologist, returned to Vienna. Freud had just completed his studies with Charcot and began to work with Breuer. Together they utilized Breuer's "cathartic method," encouraging patients to report their experiences and fantasies under hypnosis. Freud, however, noticed that similar therapeutic effects could be obtained *without* hypnosis, so long as the patient reported everything that came to mind and experienced emotional catharsis. It was this discovery that led Freud to the theory and therapeutic technique called *psychoanalysis,* which is described in detail in Chapter 4.

THE RISE OF THE PSYCHIATRIC HOSPITAL

There is no precise date to mark the beginning of modern treatments for madness. In fact, beliefs in animistic causes persisted into the twentieth century in some parts of the West. Nonetheless, most observers date the beginning of the modern psychological era with the establishment of the psychiatric hospital, an institution that itself has a rather special history.

INSTITUTIONALIZING THE POOR

The word "hospital" has only recently acquired its strong medical connotation. Even as late as the early twentieth century, it meant something quite different: an asylum for the underprivileged. Even today, Webster's primary definition of hospital is "a charitable institution for the needy, aged, infirm or young."

The early hospitals

The medical hospital and surely the psychiatric one are relatively modern inventions. Both evolved in the seventeenth century from institutions that were created to house and confine the poor, the homeless, the unemployed, and among them, the insane. Throughout the sixteenth and seventeenth centuries, poverty was widespread. War and economic depression had dislocated large numbers of people and reduced them to begging and petty crime. In 1532, in Paris, these problems were so severe that beggars were arrested and forced to work in pairs in the city's sewers. Two years later, a new decree forced "poor scholars and indigents" to leave the city. All to no avail, for at the beginning of the seventeenth century, Paris, which had a population of fewer than 100,000 people, had more than 30,000 beggars! In 1606, it was decreed that beggars should be publicly whipped, branded, shorn, and driven from the city. And a year later, in 1607, an ordinance established companies of archers who were located at the gates of the city—their sole task to forbid the return of these indigents.

The Hôpital
Général

It was in this social and economic climate that, in 1656, the Hôpital Général of Paris was founded for the poor "of both sexes, of all ages, and from all localities, of whatever breeding and birth, in whatever state they may be, able-bodied or invalid, sick or convalescent, curable or incurable" (Edict of 1656, cited in Foucault, 1965, p. 39). From a strictly humane point of view, the Hôpital Général, which included La Salpêtrière, La Pitie, and La Bicêtre—institutions that later became famous in their own right—was surely an improvement over the conditions that preceded it. For the first time in France, the government took responsibility for feeding and housing its "undesirables." But in return, those undesirables—the poor, the homeless, the mad—yielded up the privilege of roaming the streets. Personal liberty was traded for room and board. It was not a voluntary trade; shortly after the decree was proclaimed, the militia scoured the city, hunting and herding beggars into the various buildings of the Hôpital. Within four years, the Hôpital housed 1 percent of Paris's population.

Unemployment as
moral failure

Paris was not alone in its concern to confine undesirables. During the same period, all over France and throughout Europe, similar institutions were being established. To the modern mind, it seems inconceivable that the poor, the mad, the aged, the infirm, and even the petty criminal could somehow be lumped together and signed over to the same institution. Yet, a compelling commonality bound these people together. *They were not gainfully employed.* Unemployment was viewed, not as the result of economic depression, technological change, or bad luck, but as a personal, indeed a moral, failure. Simple indolence was its accepted name. The task of the Hôpital Général was a moral one: to prevent "mendicancy and idleness as the source of all disorders" (Edict of 1656, cited in Foucault, 1965, p. 47). Whatever restrictions were imposed, whatever behaviors required, and whatever punishments meted out, all were justified by the moral mission of the Hôpital Général.

The hospital as
workplace

The hospital was a place of confinement during periods of economic depression. But during economic growth, the hospital was easily and justifiably converted into a workhouse. It required that its residents work (but it paid them a mere fraction of what they would ordinarily make). With increasing industrialization in England, for example, many such workhouses were established in industrial centers, providing cheap, forced labor to growing industries.

SEGREGATING THE INSANE

Brutal care of the
insane

While governments failed to distinguish the insane from the other unfortunates, within the hospital such distinctions were quickly made and were ultimately institutionalized. The insane were given much worse care than other residents of the hospital, and were subjected to brutal physical abuse. At the end of the eighteenth century, one visitor to La Bicêtre described the miserable condition in which he found one mad inmate:

> The unfortunate whose entire furniture consisted of this straw pallet, lying with his head, feet, and body pressed against the wall, could not enjoy sleep without being soaked by the water that trickled from that mass of stone. (Desportes, cited in Foucault, 1965, pp. 70–71)

The same reporter said of La Salpêtrière that what made the place more miserable, and often more fatal, was that in winter, "when the waters of the Seine rose, those cells situated at the level of the sewers became not only more unhealthy, but worse still, a refuge for a swarm of huge rats, which during the night attacked the unfortunates confined there and bit them wherever they could reach them; madwomen have been found with feet, hands, and face torn by bites which are often dangerous and from which several have died" (Desportes, cited in Foucault, 1965, pp. 70–71).

Paris was not unique. In the London hospital, St. Mary's of Bethlehem (which soon became known as Bedlam), patients were chained to the walls or kept on long leashes. Nearby, in Bethnal Green, patients were bound hand and foot, and confined in filthy quarters.

The United States established its first hospital, the Pennsylvania Hospital, in 1756. At the urging of Benjamin Franklin, the government set aside a section for "lunatics." They were consigned to the cellar and

> Their scalps were shaved and blistered; they were bled to the point of syncope; purged until the alimentary canal failed to yield anything but mucus, and in the intervals, they were chained by the waist or the ankle to the cell wall . . . It was not considered unusual or improper for the keeper to carry a whip and use it freely. (Morton, 1897, cited in Deutsch, 1949, p. 600)

Madness as resulting from animalism and loss of reason

Clearly, to the modern mind, such treatment is cruel and inhumane. That judgment arises because, in the modern view, the insane are entitled to compassion and kindness. But it is not the case that our predecessors were less concerned with the treatment of the insane, or necessarily, morally obtuse. Rather, they had a different theory of insanity; they believed that madness resulted from animalism, that the insane had lost the one capacity that distinguished humans from beasts: *reason.* Because they had lost that capacity, their behavior was disordered, unruly, and wild. The first mandate of treatment, then, was to restore reason. *Fear* was believed to be the emotion that was best suited to restoring the disordered mind. The eminent

A day at the lunatic asylum was a popular excursion in the eighteenth century, much as a day at the zoo is today. To judge by the gate receipts, visits to La Salpetrière in Paris, Bedlam in London, and the Pennsylvania Hospital in Philadelphia were popular attractions. This engraving by the eighteenth century painter William Hogarth shows visitors touring Bedlam.

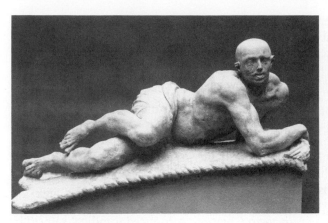 

The sculptured figures above the gates to St. Mary's of Bethlehem Hospital (formerly referred to as "Bedlam") in London. When the hospital was first built, patients were chained to the walls or kept on long leashes.

physician William Cullen wrote that it was "necessary to employ a very constant impression of fear . . . awe and dread." Such emotions should be aroused by "all restraints that may occasionally be proper . . . even by stripes and blows" (Cullen, 1808, cited in Scull, 1981). Clearly, some unscrupulous madhouse operators took advantage of this view to abuse those in their care. But even the most eminent patients received similar treatment. King George III of England was a clear case in point. As Countess Harcourt later described his situation, "the unhappy patient . . . was no longer treated as a human being. His body was immediately encased in a machine which left it no liberty of motion. He was sometimes chained to a stake. He was frequently beaten and starved, and at best he was kept in subjection by menacing and violent language." (Jones, 1955, cited in Bynum, 1981). In addition, he was bled, blistered, given emetics and various other drugs of the day. Again, such treatment arose from the belief that the insane did not have the physical sensitivities of human beings but rather were like animals in their lack of sensitivity to pain, temperature, and other external stimuli.

THE GROWTH OF HUMANE TREATMENT

Changing views of insane and treatment

By the end of the eighteenth century, the idea that the incarcerated insane should be treated as animals was under attack. No degree of intellectual or theological rationalization could conceal the torment that these punitive treatments imposed on patients. From a variety of respected sources, protest grew over the conditions of confinement, and especially over the shackles, the chains, the dungeons, and the whippings. Other models for treatment were sought. One was found at Gheel, a Belgian community that had been accepting the insane for quite some time. New ones were found through courageous experiments in Italy, France, England, and the United States.

GHEEL

As the site of a religious shrine in Belgium, the small town of Gheel had been a recuperative center for the insane since the Middle Ages. There, consistent with a religious ethos, "cure" was achieved through prayer and in the "laying on of the hands." Those who prayed were treated in a special, and for the time, unusual way. The deeply troubled were shown habitual kindness, courtesy, and gentleness. The insane lived in the community and, apart from being forbidden alcohol, suffered few restrictions. They took rooms in

William Norris was erroneously confined for fourteen years in Bedlam before coming to the attention of members of Parliament. He had been confined by a "stout iron ring, rivotted round his neck," which was attached to a twelve-inch chain, which in turn was attached to the wall. He was therefore unable to move more than twelve inches from the wall and could not even turn over in his bed because of the shortness of the chain.

people's homes, where they were treated as guests. Gheel's reputation grew, and so did the number of people who went there. It provided a model of treatment that stressed sympathy, respect, and concern.

STRIKING PATIENTS' CHAINS

Gheel was not a hospital, but rather a refuge for those who were fortunate enough to make their way there. Although some of the insane were tolerated within their own communities, most of them were impoverished, abandoned, or simply unlucky. They filled the public institutions, which were cruel beyond the telling. But late in the eighteenth century, things began to change. The first hospital to remove the chains from psychiatric patients was St. Boniface in Florence, Italy. There, in 1774, by allowing patients freedom of movement, Vincenzo Chiarugi introduced a radical reform in patient care. It took hold. Later, in 1787, Joseph Dacquin initiated similar reforms in the Insane Department of the hospital at Chambéry, France. And in 1792, during the French Revolution, Philippe Pinel, the newly appointed director of La Bicêtre, unshackled the patients of the Hôpital Général of Paris from their chains, moved them from the cellar dungeons into sunny and airy rooms, and allowed them freedom of the hospital grounds. Pinel was not applying the dicta of liberty and equality to psychiatric patients. Indeed, he believed in the need for control and coercion in psychiatric care. But, he insisted that for coercion to be effective, it needed to be *psychological* rather than physical. The control exerted by shackles and chains would be ended just as soon as the patient was discharged. What was required was internalized control that would endure after the patient left the hospital grounds.

His was not an easy decision. There was little public support for Pinel's views. Not only did the view that the insane were like animals linger on, but more important, the belief that they were "dangerous animals" also remained. Moreover, the political consequences of his decision were potentially disastrous. The function of La Bicêtre and its sister institutions was

The eighteenth-century French reformer Philippe Pinel shown ordering the removal of chains from mental patients.

Function of
hospitals to
confine madmen

confinement. Most people believed that the hospitals existed in order to protect the civilized citizens of France from the dangerous and disturbing excesses of madmen. "Liberty, equality, and fraternity" were not meant to apply to the mentally deranged! An interchange between Pinel and Couthon, an aide to one of the Revolution's most radical leaders, reveals how foolhardy Pinel's reforms were thought to be. Couthon, after having been insulted and cursed by La Bicêtre's patients, had turned to Pinel and said:

"Now citizen, are you mad yourself to seek to unchain such beasts?"

Pinel replied calmly: "I am convinced that these madmen are so intractable only because they have been deprived of air and liberty."

"Well, do as you like with them, but I fear you may become the victim of your own presumption."

(Foucault, 1965, p. 242)

It is not difficult to appreciate Couthon's position in this debate. Abnormal behavior makes other people fearful and defensive. They worry much more about possible consequences than about causes. Couthon was concerned about what these people might do, and he failed to see, as Pinel had seen, that violent behavior might, at least partially, be a *result* of the cruel confinement.

RELIGIOUS REFORMS IN ENGLAND

Reforms in
England develop
from religious
concerns

Reforms in France were undertaken by secular authorities, but those in England developed from religious concerns. In 1791, Hannah Mills, a Quaker, was admitted to the Lunatick Asylum at York, one of the two major institutions for the insane in England (the other being Bedlam in London). Mills's friends came to visit her but were denied entry on the grounds that she was in no condition to see visitors. A few weeks later, Mills was dead. Her friends suspected that the treatment she had received at York caused or at least contributed to her death. Their suspicions were not entirely groundless, for the conditions in England's institutions for the insane were widely known to be horrible, even by the standards of those days.

Among Mills's friends was William Tuke who, moved by her death, urged the Yorkshire Society of Friends to establish a humanitarian institution for the insane. Despite stiff opposition, similar to the opposition Pinel faced in France, the Retreat at York was established in 1796. It was called a retreat in order to avoid the stigma of such words as "madhouse," "insane asylum," and "lunatickhouse." The name conveyed "the idea of what such an institution should be, namely, a place in which the unhappy might obtain a refuge; a quiet haven in which the shattered bark might find the means of reparation and safety." The kind of treatment that had originated at Gheel —long established, successful, but ignored—was finally being implemented elsewhere (Hunt, 1932, cited in Deutsch, 1949, p. 93).

From the outset, the Retreat's approach to care was dramatically different from practices elsewhere in England. Patients were guests, not "prisoners," as they were called at both Bedlam and the Lunatick Asylum at York. The cornerstones of care were kindness, consideration, courtesy, and dignity. To

A sketch of the English reformer William Tuke.

The need for
esteem and the
value of work

the extent that treatment principles were defined at the Retreat, two dominated: the need for esteem and the value of work, especially physical work.
This emphasis on the therapeutic value of work was unique to the Retreat.
The moral virtue of work is deeply embedded in Quaker philosophy. It was
consistent with the widely held work ethic of the day and its concomitant
distaste for unemployment and the unemployed. The need for esteem was
an even more highly valued principle. Treatment took the form of encouraging the insane to acquire social skills, to utilize them, and to gain rewards
for meeting the requirements of everyday social interaction. Thus, in the
manner of the English during those times, the staff of the Retreat would regularly invite the guests to tea (Foucault, 1965, p. 249).

The effects of the Retreat upon some of its guests were dramatic. Samuel
Tuke, the founder's grandson, tells of a guest who was brought to the Retreat
in such a violent condition that even though he was chained and shackled,
his escorts were afraid of him. Immediately upon entering the Retreat, however, his chains were removed. He was invited to dine with the staff and then
was courteously shown to his room. So long as he was considerate of the
needs of others, he was told, there would be no need for restraint. (Restraint
was not entirely abolished. In emergencies, patients were bound in broad
leather belts that left the arms free. In extreme circumstances, straitjackets
were used). The patient promised to restrain himself. When, however, he
became agitated, he was reminded of the agreements he had made on his
first day. After four months, he was able to leave the Retreat.

MORAL TREATMENT IN THE UNITED STATES

Kind treatment
and virtues of
work

The ideas that led to the founding and success of Tuke's Retreat at York
spread quickly to the United States. The essence of this form of treatment,
called *moral treatment,* was enunciated by Dr. Romeyn Beck, of New York,
in 1811. He wrote:

> . . . The rules most proper to be observed are the following: Convince the lunatics
> that the power of the physician and keeper is absolute; have humane attendants,
> who shall act as servants to them; never threaten but execute; offer no indignities
> to them, as they have a high sense of honour; punish disobedience pre-emptorily,
> in the presence of other maniacs; if unruly, forbid them the company of others,
> use the strait waistcoats, confine them in a dark and quiet room, order spare
> diet. . . .; tolerate noisy ejaculations; . . . Let their fears and resentments be
> soothed without unnecessary opposition; thus acting, the patient will "minister to
> himself." (Beck, 1811, cited in Deutsch, 1949, pp. 91–92)

In 1817, the Friends Asylum at Frankford, Pennsylvania, was established.
Shortly thereafter, in 1821, the Bloomingdale Asylum was founded through
the efforts of Thomas Eddy, a Quaker businessman who had been much influenced by Samuel Tuke. The Bloomingdale Asylum, located on the site of
the present campus of Columbia University in New York City, stressed the
two features that were the hallmarks of humane care: kind treatment and
the virtues of work. For the first time, moreover, records were kept of patients' progress in the hospital as well as of their condition before entering
it. The efforts at the Bloomingdale Asylum served as the model for several
later hospitals, including the Hartford Retreat and the McLean Hospital
(Tourney, 1967; Rothman, 1971; Scull, 1981). Although not yet especially

effective, treatment became increasingly humane. And that was a very important improvement over the past.

SUMMARY

1. The times and culture in which individuals live and the general way in which they perceive the world influence how abnormality is understood and treated.

2. When the world is perceived in animistic terms, abnormality is likely to be viewed as a *supernatural* phenomenon. Prehistoric people attributed abnormality to possession by spirits trapped in the head and chipped *trephines* in the skull to let the spirits out.

3. Some Greeks and Romans attributed abnormality to *physical* causes. For example, they believed that *hysteria* was caused by a wandering uterus that created discomfort wherever it settled. They treated it by trying to draw the uterus back to its proper place. Galen challenged this idea and said that hysteria was caused by a malfunctioning sexual organ. Furthermore, Galen also contributed important insights into *psychological* causes of abnormality.

4. In medieval Europe, some behaviors that might seem bizarre today were esteemed as being evidence of piety and holiness. Other behaviors, equally bizarre from a modern perspective, were held to be the result of *possession.* Individuals so possessed were subjected to rites of exorcism and were sometimes ostracized from their communities entirely.

5. During the Middle Ages and Renaissance, those suffering from psychological distress were often viewed as possessed, or accused of practicing witchcraft and causing others to be possessed. Tens of thousands of people were accused of being witches and were hanged or burned during this period, as there was no known "cure" for witchcraft.

6. In the seventeenth century, hospitals grew out of institutions that were originally created to house and confine the poor, lame, dispossessed, and insane. The insane, however, were segregated from the other residents of the hospital and were subjected to brutal physical abuse. Treatment in the early insane asylum was predicated on the view that the insane lacked *reason* and displayed the characteristics of animals and could therefore be treated like animals.

7. In the middle of the eighteenth century, it gradually was recognized that mental disorders were *psychological* in origin and could be treated by psychological means. Mesmer tried to induce crises to restore the flow of *animal magnetism.* Charcot treated mental disorders by *hypnosis,* after distinguishing hysterical convulsions from symptoms with an organic cause. Both Breuer and Freud used hypnosis to induce *catharsis* in hysterical patients.

8. By the end of the eighteenth century, new and more humane treatments for the insane were found. The best hospitals began to stress the need for *moral treatment,* for patient dignity and work, and they began to keep records of patients' condition, both before they entered the hospital and while they were being treated.

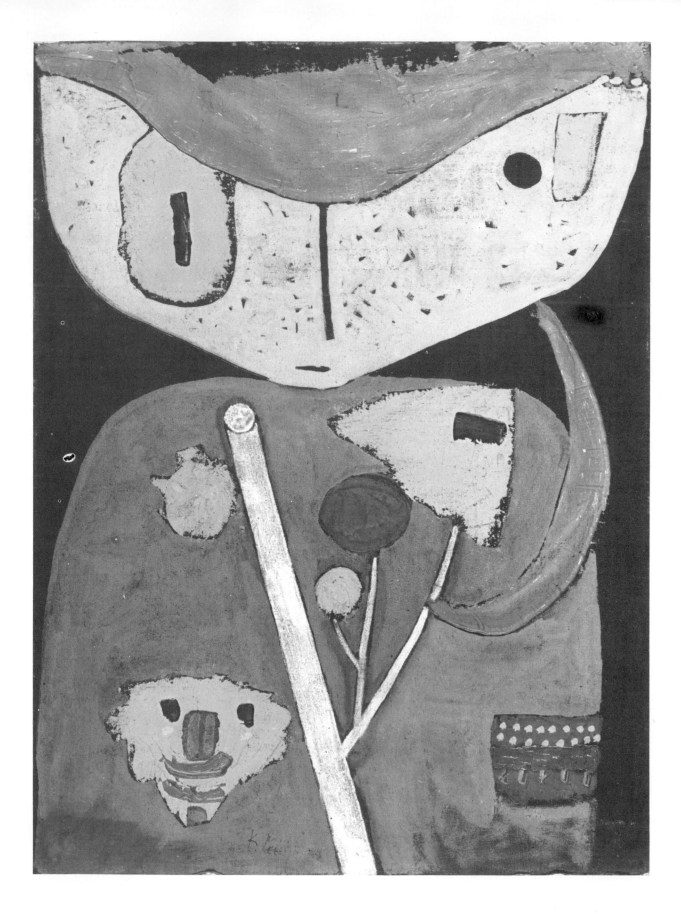

Part 2

MODELS AND TREATMENTS OF ABNORMALITY

The Biomedical Model

W HEN anthropologists try to study the development of culture, they seek out existing "primitive" peoples untouched by modern society and technology. Anthropologists have had to travel to remote places of the world to do so. For genetic researchers, the challenge of studying the causes of mental illness has been even greater. Pure strains of white mice have often been their experimental subjects. But how can we best study human disorders, like manic-depression (bipolar depression)? A few years ago, a group of researchers started to answer this question. They traveled to Lancaster County, Pennsylvania, not a remote area geographically, but certainly culturally. There, they studied as pure a strain of humans as any geneticist would want to find in the laboratory—the Amish. The story of this study and its major contribution to our understanding of human misery is told later in this chapter.

How one defines abnormality has been the subject of the previous two chapters. Chapter 1 presented the problem, and Chapter 2 discussed the different historical approaches to its definition. In this chapter, we begin our discussion of modern-day models of abnormality.

Abnormality as physical illness

The biomedical model explains abnormality as a physical malfunction, such as a chemical or anatomical defect. Thus, it explains such symptoms as memory loss for recent events, language disorders, inability to deal with new situations, loss of personal skills and abilities, and neglect of bodily functions in an older person as physical malfunctions. It emphasizes the problems resulting from an abnormality in the synthesis of the neurotransmitter acetylcholine rather than considering poor adaptation to change or demoralization arising out of retirement and reduced income. Similarly it explains depression by concentrating on those symptoms of the depressive that are related to the depressive's biological processes rather than emphasizing distorted thinking or poor interpersonal relations. Thus, a biomedical scientist

The biomedical model uses tools such as the PET scan to study how the chemistry of a depressive's brain differs from that of a normal's brain. The person pictured here is having a PET scan to determine opiate receptor activity; the image on the left shows the distribution of these receptors in the brain of a normal, which will later be compared to a PET scan of a depressive's brain.

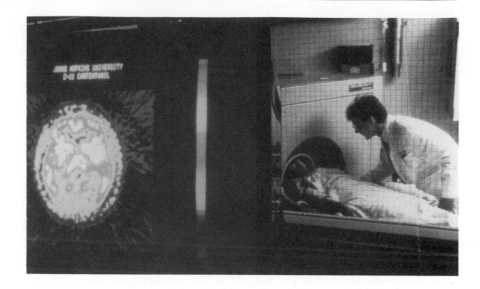

investigates the evidence that the chemistry of a depressive's brain changes when he is depressed. The biomedical scientist will experiment with these biochemical factors in order to see if they are the cause, or etiology, of the depression. Also, in an attempt to alleviate the disorder, the biomedical investigator will be more likely to develop chemical therapies or drugs that will counteract biochemical factors.

MODELS OF ABNORMALITY

Approaches to abnormality

What model we follow and how we define the causes of abnormality help to determine how we will treat abnormality. Each approach to abnormality can be considered a *model* of abnormality. At present, there are three major models, which are sometimes complementary and often competing in their attempt to understand and cure abnormality. The *biomedical model,* discussed in this chapter, holds that abnormality is an illness of the body. The *psychodynamic model,* discussed in Chapter 4, holds that abnormality is driven by hidden conflicts within our personality. (Besides classical psychoanalysis, Chapter 4 discusses self theory and existential theory, which deals with questions of life's meaning, human potential, responsibility, and will.) The *environmentalist model,* discussed in Chapter 5, includes the behavioral approach, which holds that we learn to be abnormal through conditioning and that we can unlearn these maladaptive ways of behaving, and the cognitive approach, which holds that abnormality springs from disordered conscious thought about oneself and the world.

Problems with following one model

Following a particular model of abnormality is a matter of choice, and the choice always involves risk. For example, an investigator might believe that early childhood experiences are the primary influence on adult psychopathology. He could spend years studying his manic-depressive patient's past history and never cure him, for it might turn out that manic-depression is caused by a biological problem and cured by a chemical. His strict adherence to a particular model would have blinded him to this other possibility

—in this case, a biological explanation of manic-depression. In sum, there is a danger inherent in following any particular model of abnormality. By concentrating on one level of evidence, we might neglect some of the other, more crucial evidence. The kinds of abnormality vary so much that we do not believe that one particular model of abnormality will explain all mental disorders.

We now turn to our first model of abnormality, the biomedical model. We review the landmark experiments that showed that physical illness could cause psychopathology.

ASSUMPTIONS OF THE BIOMEDICAL MODEL

Syndrome
↓
etiology
↓
treatment

Those who advocate the biomedical model typically approach abnormality as medical researchers approach an illness: They will group diverse, but co-occurring, symptoms together into a coherent **syndrome.** Then they will search for the **etiology,** or cause, of the syndrome, examining four possible causes: First, looking for a *germ.* Second, studying the patient's relatives to see if the person's *genes* might be causing the disorder. Third, examining the *biochemistry* of the patient's brain. Fourth, looking at the patient's *neuro-anatomy.* Once an etiology has been discovered, some biological **treatment** that attacks the cause, usually a drug, will be sought to alleviate the abnormality.

The idea that psychological disorders have physical etiologies is both ancient and venerable. We saw in the last chapter that the ancients believed that hysteria resulted from a wandering uterus. The Egyptians, Greeks, and Romans sought to cure this psychological abnormality by physical means: assaulting the body of the sufferer with a great variety of drugs, massages, fumigations, and so on. Behind all these treatments lay the belief that the cause of the psychological disorder was a physical disorder. It was not until the latter half of the nineteenth century, however, that anyone convincingly

The view that mental illness was a disorder of the body reached its most concrete stage with the Stone of Folly. Here in Jan Sanders van Hemessen's painting (c. 1530), early ''physicians'' attempt to remove one such stone from a bound patient possessed with madness. This appears crude in its execution, but we now have far more sophisticated methods for removing, not the Stone of Folly, but rather tumors—growths in the brain that sometimes bring about abnormality.

demonstrated that any form of psychological disorder was caused by organic illness. At that time, it was found that syphilis caused general paresis. This story illustrates how the isolation of a syndrome led to the discovery of an etiology, which in turn led to the discovery of a therapy. In addition, it illustrates how a mental disorder can be caused by a germ (one of the biomedical model's four possible causes of abnormality). This proved to be one of the great sagas in the history of biomedical science.

GERMS AS ETIOLOGY: SYPHILIS AND GENERAL PARESIS

The syndrome of general paresis

There was an enormous upsurge in the incidence of a particular kind of mental illness during the sixteenth century, after Columbus discovered the New World. We have come to call this disorder *general paresis.* In the sixteenth century, its symptoms seemed to be mainly delusions of grandeur: the false notion that one is rather more important than the objective facts indicate. Such delusions presumably existed before the sixteenth century, and the newly deluded seemed no different, except in number, from those who had preceded them.

As early as 1672, Thomas Willis (1621–1675), an English anatomist, observed that some of these patients exhibited dullness of the mind and forgetfulness that seemed to develop into downright stupidity and foolishness. Later in life, these same people would fall into paralysis. This was not a precise observation. Rather, it served loosely to differentiate one group of madmen from others, based on signs of developing stupidity and paralysis. In 1805, the French physician, Jean Esquirol (1772–1840), added another significant observation: the mental deterioration and paralysis observed in this group of patients quickly culminated in the death of the patients.

There the matter stood until 1826, when Esquirol's student, A. L. J. Bayle, undertook the first major step necessary for a disorder to be understood as biomedical: organization of symptoms into a syndrome, which allowed precise description and diagnosis of the illness. He formalized the diagnosis by giving a complete and exact description of the physical and psychological symptoms, and arguing strongly that these constituted a separate disease, a different madness, if you will, from all others then known. He argued that mental deterioration, paralysis, and subsequent death, among others, were a group of symptoms that clustered together and formed the distinct syndrome of general paresis.

The etiology of general paresis

Bayle's rigorous definition of the disorder led to considerable speculation about its etiology. Quite early, there had been some suspicion that it was caused by syphilis. But at the time, Wilhelm Greisinger (1817–1868), an eminent psychiatric authority of physiological bent, had dismissed that view on the seemingly sound basis that paresis occurred among people in whom no trace of syphilitic infection could be found. Reports of cases in which paretics were known to have had syphilis were clearly not sufficient, since these were contradicted by the paretics who adamantly denied they had ever had syphilis and who showed no evidence of syphilis.

Despite Greisinger's opinion and the support of his colleagues, evidence gradually emerged that syphilis was somehow implicated in general paresis. But that evidence was difficult to accumulate for three reasons. First, and perhaps most important, syphilis precedes paresis by as many as thirty years. The connection between the one and the other was difficult to see. Second, syphilis was then, as now, a disease about which there was considerable shame. People were often unable to admit to themselves, and surely not to others, that they had contracted the disease. Third, the diagnosis of syphilis was itself not an exact science. In the early part of the nineteenth century, techniques were still not available for ascertaining that someone had syphilis, because the overt symptoms that occur immediately after contracting it soon disappear. Not until there were improvements in microscopy, was it ascertained that syphilitic organisms (spirochetes) remain in the body long after the overt symptoms vanish.

The evidence, then, accumulated slowly. By about 1860, it was possible to demonstrate that there was enormous destruction in the neural tissue of the brains of people who had died from general paresis. Later, in 1869, D. M. Argyll (1837–1909), a Scottish eye surgeon, demonstrated that the central nervous system was implicated in syphilis by showing that the eyes of syphilitics failed to show the standard pupillary reflex—the narrowing of the pupil to bright light. In 1884, Alfred Fournier (1832–1914), a French physician, provided highly suggestive *epidemiological* evidence (that is, evidence from many individuals) on the relation between syphilis and general paresis: some 65 percent of paretics has a demonstrable history of syphilis, compared to only 10 percent of nonparetics. That evidence, of course, was merely suggestive: it did not demonstrate cause since it did not show that 100 percent of paretics had prior histories of syphilis. But it added significantly to the mounting tide of data, turning belief away from Greisinger's view that strong spirits and cigars were the culprits, toward the syphilis-paresis link.

The overt symptoms of syphilis—the sores (chancres) on the genitals—may disappear in a few weeks, but the disease does not. It goes underground, attacking the central nervous system. Cures for syphilis were unknown then. Thus, not only was it true that if you had the disease you couldn't get rid of it, but it was equally true and also known that *like measles, if you contracted syphilis once, you couldn't get it again.* More bluntly, if someone who has already become syphilitic (a paretic) comes in contact with another syphilitic germ, he will not develop sores on his genitals.

Consider the situation of those who believed that this psychological disorder (general paresis) was caused by the syphilitic germ. On the one hand, there was evidence that many paretics had syphilis. But some paretics claimed never to have contracted syphilis. The investigators had a hypothesis: perhaps those paretics who claimed not to have had syphilis actually had had the disease and did not know it or were too ashamed to admit it. If indeed these paretics were ignorant or not telling the truth, then the case for a biological cause of general paresis would be convincing. There was one means, but a risky one, of finding out by way of an experiment if these paretics had previously had syphilis. The investigators reasoned that if you inject these paretics with the syphilitic germ, one startling result would come about. The paretics would not contract the disease since you cannot get syphilis twice. Betting on this outcome, the German neurologist Richard von Krafft-Ebing (1840–1902) performed this critical experiment. In 1897, he innoculated nine paretics who had denied ever having had syphilis, with material from syphilitic sores. None developed sores themselves, leading to

The German neurologist Richard von Krafft-Ebing (1840–1902), an unsung hero of the biomedical model, performed the crucial experiment that forged the link between syphilis and general paresis.

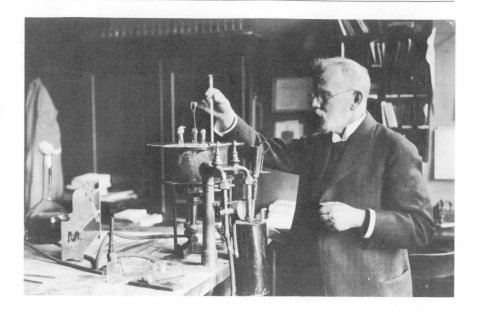

The German bacteriologist Paul Ehrlich (1854–1915), shown in his laboratory, discovered "606," an arsenic compound that was the first effective cure of syphilis. The compound was so named because it was discovered after 605 failures. 606 acts by killing the syphilis germs in the bloodstream. In the 1940s, penicillin, which arrests syphilis at any point in its development, replaced 606 as the preferred treatment.

the conclusion that they must have already been infected. The link between syphilis and general paresis was forged.

It is worth pondering for a moment whether you would have done that experiment, or permitted it to be done. Consider the facts. The year is 1897, nearly three-quarters of a century after Bayle defined the syndrome. General paresis is now a raging disorder, perhaps the most widespread of the psychoses, affecting the great (Henry VIII and Randolph Churchill, Winston's father, were probably both paretics) and the ordinary alike. There is no question that if a direct connection between paresis and syphilis can be demonstrated, there will be an enormous leap forward in the direction of understanding and therefore conquering the disease. But in 1897, the relationship between syphilis and paresis is still speculative: a good hunch, but only a hunch. What if the hunch is wrong? Syphilis is still incurable. If the hunch is wrong, you will be taking people whose lives are already burdened by paresis and adding incurable syphilis to their misery. Can such an experiment be justified? Would you carry out such an experiment?

We suspect that such an experiment could not be done in our society today. The risks are now deemed too large, regardless of the possibility that the gain may be overwhelming. But such a judgment is not an easy one to make. Many would argue that the benefits to each of us from huge advances in medicine are such that we are, each of us, obligated to contribute to those advances (Eisenberg, 1977).

Krafft-Ebing's was a crucial experiment, but had he not conducted it, a similar link might have been forged less dangerously within a decade. In 1906, a German physician and bacteriologist, August von Wassermann (1866–1925), developed a blood test for detecting the presence of syphilis. More than 90 percent of paretics responded positively to the test. The causal connection between the syphilis germ and paresis, a mental disorder, was now understood.

Once the syndrome of paresis was isolated and its etiology understood, it was only a matter of time before investigators developed a treatment for

The treatment of general paresis

general paresis. In 1909, a German bacteriologist, Paul Ehrlich (1854–1915), discovered "606," an arsenic compound that was given that name because it followed after 605 failures! Arsphenamine, the first effective cure of syphilis, acted by killing the syphilis germs in the bloodstream. By curing syphilis it prevented the occurrence of paresis. It was not until the 1940s that penicillin, a drug that arrests syphilis almost at any point in its development, replaced "606" as the preferred treatment.

Thus was general paresis, a psychological disorder characterized by stupidity and delusions of grandeur, understood and eradicated. These early advocates of the biomedical model found it to be caused by a germ in much the same way that germs cause pneumonia. Moreover, it was successfully treated in the way one might treat any physical illness. The magnitude of the success needs to be understood before the implications of the method can be appreciated. Paresis was perhaps the most widespread psychological disorder of that time. Yet today, it is common to meet psychologists and psychiatrists who have *never* seen a case of general paresis, so rare is it now.

GENETICS AS ETIOLOGY: TWINS AND SCHIZOPHRENIA

Genetic origins of schizophrenia

Genetics is the second biomedical etiology that may lead researchers to consider a psychological disorder as being a physical illness. Schizophrenia is a severe psychotic condition that strikes approximately 1 percent of the population the world over. Usually beginning in adolescence or early adulthood, it results in highly disordered thinking, perception, and language. Schizophrenic individuals function poorly in complex and primitive societies alike. What causes schizophrenia? The biomedical model holds that it is an illness passed on genetically. Investigators have approached schizophrenia by studying twins.

There are two kinds of twins: identical and fraternal. Identical twins have all the same genes, whereas fraternal twins have only half of their genes in common—exactly the same proportion of common genetic material as any two siblings share. Twins are an exquisite research tool for those who advocate the biomedical model because twins usually share very similar environ-

Genetic studies provide a means to study disorders. Twin researchers study the heritability of various traits and characteristics, as well as predispositions to mental disorders. In the Minnesota twin family studies, twins separated at birth and reared apart have been studied by Dr. Thomas J. Bouchard, Jr., and his colleagues. When these twins are reunited, many discover each other to have similar personalities, mannerisms, likes and dislikes, as did these two brothers, both of whom were fire chiefs, had the same mustache, sideburns, eyeglasses, drank the same beer, and used the same gestures.

Concordance for
schizophrenia

ments (same age, same social class, same food, similar social circles, etc.), while they differ systematically on how many genes they share.

If there are genes that determine whether one will be schizophrenic or not, and if one twin becomes schizophrenic, what is the probability that the other twin will also be schizophrenic? (Assume, for the sake of the argument, that diagnosis of schizophrenia is infallible and environment has no influence.) Since identical twins share all of their genes, if one identical twin is schizophrenic, then the other *must* also be schizophrenic. This is not so with fraternal twins, since they share only half their genes. Depending on the nature of the alleged gene, the prediction would be 50 percent or 25 percent for fraternal twins (McGue, Gottesman, and Rao, 1985). Those who hold the biomedical view use this method of observing identical and fraternal twins. If they find that one twin is schizophrenic, they will then find out if the other twin is also schizophrenic. When both twins are schizophrenic, they are called **concordant** for schizophrenia; when only one is schizophrenic, they are called **discordant.**

About ten studies from Europe, Japan, and the U.S.A. have looked at about 400 pairs of twins in this way. Overall, identical twins have a concordance rate for schizophrenia of about 50 percent, while fraternal twins have a concordance of about 10 percent. Keep in mind that the rate of schizophrenia in the population as a whole is about 1 percent. So when one of the identical twins is schizophrenic, the other is five times more likely to be schizophrenic than the fraternal twin of a schizophrenic, who is in turn ten times more likely than the average to be schizophrenic. This suggests a causal influence of genes, but not genetic determination, since concordance for identical twins is only 50 percent, not 100 percent. And since the concordance for identical twins is less than 100 percent, genes cannot be the whole etiological story. Environment also must have an influence on the cause of schizophrenia. This issue, the inheritance of schizophrenia, remains hotly debated. We will take it up more fully in Chapter 12. In this section, however, we have emphasized how adherents of the biomedical model have approached this disorder.

BIOCHEMISTRY AS ETIOLOGY: DOPAMINE AND SCHIZOPHRENIA

As we mentioned earlier, those believing in the biomedical model may also look for the cause of a disorder in a third category; irregularities in an individual's biochemistry. One hypothesis about schizophrenia is that it is caused by an unbalanced biochemistry. The "dopamine hypothesis," as it is called, states that schizophrenic behavior is caused by too much dopamine in the brain. Dopamine is a chemical in the brain that allows "messages" to be relayed from one neuron to another. There is a considerable amount of evidence in favor of this hypothesis. But all of it is rather indirect, since it is still technically impossible to look into the brain of a living person and count how much of a given chemical is there. The most important evidence comes from the fact that drugs which usually relieve the symptoms of schizophrenia also lower the amount of usable dopamine in the brain. Such drugs do not completely cure schizophrenia, but they do reduce hallucinations and delusions, improve concentration, and make schizophrenic symptoms less bizarre. This action is called dopamine "blocking," and these

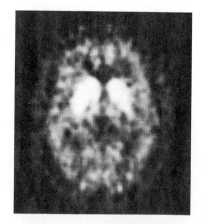

The "dopamine hypothesis" states that schizophrenia may be caused by excess dopamine in the brain. Here is a PET (positron emission tomography) scan of a human brain after it has been injected with a drug that enables researchers to visualize the distribution of dopamine receptors in the brain.

Box 3-1   NUCLEAR MEDICINE AND SCHIZOPHRENIA

Modern techniques of nuclear medicine are beginning to tell us about the anatomical and chemical structures of the brains of schizophrenics. One technique measures regional cerebral blood flow (rCBF) by having patients inhale air with minute (and harmless) traces of radioactive xenon in it. The more blood flowing to any part of the brain, the more active is that part; the path and amount of blood flowing can be tracked by watching where the radioactivity goes. As the xenon courses through the blood supply in the brain, detectors of radioactivity placed on the scalp monitor how much is absorbed and how fast it is cleared from the brain. The more blood goes to a given part of the brain, the more xenon will be detected in that part. So the more active a part of the brain is, the more xenon it will absorb, and the faster the brain will get rid of it.

A group of researchers at the University of Pennsylvania have isolated an important pattern of blood flow in schizophrenics using the rCBF technique (Gur, Gur, Skolnick, Caroff, Obrist, Resnick, and Reivich, 1985). They studied nineteen schizophrenic patients and nineteen controls, matched for sex and age. After subjects inhaled xenon, the researchers looked at the amount of resting activity in the two hemispheres of the brain. They found a striking difference: Schizophrenic patients had more blood flowing to the left hemisphere than to the right hemisphere. The more severe the schizophrenia, the more blood flowed to the left hemisphere. Antipsychotic drugs, moreover, appeared to reduce the flow to the left hemisphere.

This work suggests that one cause of schizophrenia may be subtle damage to the left hemisphere of the brain. The increased blood flow might be the body's attempt to compensate for the damage. Since verbal thought and language seem to be controlled by the left hemisphere, and since thought and language are disrupted in schizophrenia, the rCBF data can explain some of the central symptoms of schizophrenia. The future of nuclear medicine may bring further insights, leading to the early identification and perhaps the alleviation of schizophrenia.

Disorders in
biochemistry
causing
schizophrenia

drugs block dopamine by binding themselves to the nerve cells in the brain that receive dopamine, thus preventing naturally occurring dopamine from getting to these receptors. And the more dopamine that can be blocked by various drugs, the greater the ability of the drugs to relieve schizophrenic symptoms (Matthysse, 1973). Some investigators conclude that since these drugs decrease dopamine, an increase of dopamine causes schizophrenia.

Such evidence argues that the symptoms of schizophrenia are caused by too much dopamine in the brain. From the viewpoint of the biomedical school, evidence which shows that altering the biochemistry of the brain alters the symptoms of a disorder (for better or worse), suggests that the disorder is an illness, just as does evidence that the disorder is caused by a germ and is relieved by killing that germ, or that a disorder can be transmitted genetically.

NEUROANATOMY AS ETIOLOGY: THE DISORDERED BRAIN

Those who believe in the biomedical model also consider disorders in the anatomy of the brain as an explanation for psychopathology. Brain disorders may result from malfunctioning of specific areas of the brain. For example, the brain is organized in a hierarchy from bottom to top, with the higher levels generally controlling more abstract, cognitive, and voluntary functions. These higher areas are more fragile. So the sequence of symptoms of senility—problems in coping with new situations, confusion about when events occurred, intermittent memory loss, loss of personal skills, abilities, and social habits, and eventually failures in ability to perform basic bodily functions—can be explained by the biomedical model, which says that higher levels of brain function will malfunction first, followed by malfunctioning of the lower systems.

Malfunctions in neuroanatomy

Loss of other functions can also be explained by the biomedical model. Some functions of the brain are more vulnerable to damage than others; all parts of the brain are not equally resilient. A group of neurons may be more vulnerable because it has a relatively poor blood supply or because it has a higher requirement for oxygen or nutrients. Long-term memories, for example, are particularly vulnerable; they may be selectively damaged by general trauma, such as blows to the head, or by Vitamin B1 deficiency.

GENETICS ALONG WITH BIOCHEMISTRY AS ETIOLOGY: MANIC-DEPRESSION AMONG THE AMISH

The Old Order Amish

A disordered biochemistry of the brain might be linked with a genetic etiology, for it could well be that biochemical irregularity is inherited. New work on manic-depression and the Amish documents this possibility. The Old Order Amish of Lancaster County, Pennsylvania, are an ultraconservative Protestant sect numbering about 12,000 people. They are all descended from about thirty pacifist couples who came to Pennsylvania from Germany between 1720 and 1750, fleeing the wars ravaging Europe. They have created a prosperous farming community without the use of electricity or automobiles. During two and a half centuries, few people have left and even fewer have entered the community.

The Amish are ideal for the study of the genetic transmission of mental illness for several reasons: First, the geneology of any person with a mental illness can be traced exactly, because marital fidelity is very strong and parental lineage is thus known with certainty. Second, alcohol and drugs are forbidden, and violence (other than suicide) is unknown. This is ideal for tracing the lineage of manic-depression, because alcoholism, drugs, and violence can mask its diagnosis. Third, the Amish have been extraordinarily cooperative with researchers on mental illness, because they believe that it is a terrible scourge on the well-being of humanity. Their cooperation has resulted in a pioneering study linking a specific molecular genetic defect with the occurrence of manic-depression and suggesting a biochemical cause.

Manic-depression

Manic-depression, also known as bipolar depression (see pp. 348–54), is one of the most ruinous forms of mental illness. It afflicts between one and two million Americans, producing extreme mood swings. During the manic phase, the victim is euphoric and engages in such poorly judged behavioral excesses that catastrophic economic and social consequences frequently follow. (For example, the victim spends three years trying to pay off the debt for the three sports cars he bought during this manic episode, and the rest of his life trying to live down his reputation for foolishness.) During the depressive phase, the victim suffers such extreme sadness and hopelessness

The Amish retain old customs and modes of dress in the midst of our fast-changing modern world. They believe that mental illness is one of God's most terrible scourges and have therefore been very cooperative in epidemiological research. Because they are highly inbred, they have been studied to understand the genetic component of manic-depression.

that, before the advent of lithium therapy, 15 percent of manic-depressives ended their lives in suicide.

Manic-depression and chromosome 11

It has long been suspected that manic-depression was heritable, because identical twins were much more concordant for it than fraternal twins (Allen, 1976); in addition, among adopted persons with the disorder, only 2 percent of their adoptive parents had the disorder, but 30 percent of their biological parents had it (Gershon, 1983). The study of the Amish demonstrates convincingly that the disorder is heritable and what the defective chromosome may be while at the same time suggesting the biochemical defect that is responsible. In the study, Janice Egeland and her co-workers chose one extended family (Pedigree 110) for blood studies because, of its eighty-one members over several generations, eleven were diagnosed as having manic-depressive illness, and sixty-two others had no disorders at all. How did these eleven manic-depressives differ in their genetic structure from the unaffected sixty-two members of the family? The researchers examined white blood cells from the affected members for genetic markers that distinguished the genetic structure of their blood cells from those of individuals without the disorder. Part of chromosome 11 (humans have forty-six chromosomes) looked different for affected people: They had two marker genes at the tip of the short arm of this chromosome. The association was not perfect, but it was strong; 63 percent of the members of Pedigree 110 who had these markers had manic-depressive illness, but 37 percent did not (this is called "incomplete penetrance," or "63 percent penetrance" of the gene). Further, this defect is absent in two other non-Amish samples of people who are manic-depressive. Nonetheless, the study does establish convincingly that some defect on chromosome 11 can put people at risk for manic-depression (Egeland, Gerhard, Pauls, Sussex, Kidd, Allen, Hostetter, and Housman, 1987).

How might such a genetic defect go about producing manic-depressive illness? One way might be by producing an abnormal biochemistry of the brain. As we shall see in Chapter 11, depression may be partly caused by inadequacies in certain brain chemicals that aid in the neural transmission of messages from one brain cell to the next. A lack of some of these neurotransmitters, called catecholamines, may be the culprit here. Near the newly discovered marker genes on chromosome 11 is a gene that controls the production of the catecholamines by encoding the enzyme tyrosine hydroxylase. If tyrosine hydroxylase is inadequate, insufficiency of catecholamines in the brain would be expected, and a depressive disorder might result. Researchers are now examining the tyrosine hydroxylase of the affected Amish to determine if it is the key to abnormality.

So, for the first time, molecular genetics has entered the arena of mental illness in a convincing way. And it holds real promise. In this study, it allows us to locate the site of the genetic defect that produces manic-depression and to test how the defect might work biochemically. Genes do not completely determine the disorder—there is only 63 percent penetrance, and even among the 63 percent who are affected, they are only disordered for a small fraction of their lives. But this study indicates that we can identify people at risk and perhaps find protective environmental factors as well as the factors that trigger manic and depressive episodes.

TREATMENT

Correcting brain function

The biomedical model views mental disorders as physical illnesses, with biochemical malfunctioning of the brain as the most common cause. The nature of the therapy follows directly from this model: Correct the brain function by changing its biochemistry with drugs and other agents. Drugs have been used, with considerable but not unalloyed success, to treat such disorders as schizophrenia, unipolar depression, manic-depression, panic attacks, anxiety, and phobia. In searching for appropriate drug treatments, researchers have had to discover the areas of the brain that are the site of the malfunction, as well as establishing how much of the drug will correct the biochemical imbalances without overcorrecting and causing new problems.

Serendipitous discovery of drugs

Often the effects of drugs on mental disorders have been discovered when treating individuals for other, unrelated disorders. Thus, while John Cade was seeking a cure for tuberculosis, he serendipitously discovered a treatment for manic-depression. Noticing that lithium made guinea pigs lethargic, he experimentally used it to treat manic patients and found that it did indeed end severe manic attacks. Similarly, while synthesizing new drugs to treat asthmatics, researchers noticed that these drugs had strong calming effects on those being treated. Consequently, Jean Delay and Pierre Daniker used one of these drugs, chlorpromazine, to treat patients with various mental disorders; those with schizophrenia improved appreciably.

Side effects

Although certain drugs have successfully treated symptoms caused by biochemical imbalances, they have also often had other, unwanted side effects. The body is a complex, chemically interacting system, and since it is often not known why particular drugs work or what their mode of action is, they may correct some biochemical imbalances while at the same time causing others. Thus, lithium, for example, will cause full or partial alleviation of manic-depressive symptoms in 80 percent of manic-depressives and will prevent manic-depressive relapses in vulnerable individuals (Depue, 1979), but it also may have serious cardiovascular, digestive, and central nervous system effects. The minor tranquilizers, the benzodiazepines, will alleviate anxiety by reducing tension, sedating, and relaxing muscles, but

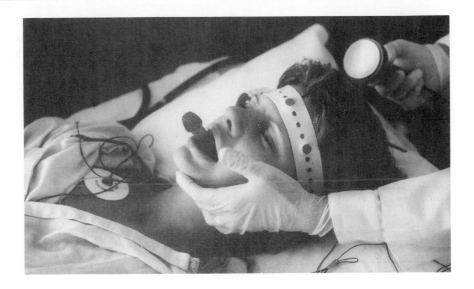

Here a patient is being prepared for electroconvulsive shock treatment. The object in her mouth is to prevent her from swallowing her tongue when the electric current passes through her body.

they may also cause drowsiness and lethargy. The major tranquilizers, including chlorpromazine and haloperidol, will calm schizophrenics and alleviate thought disorders, hallucinations, affect, and withdrawal, but they also may cause such unpleasant side effects as dryness of the mouth and throat, drowsiness, visual disturbances, weight gain or loss, tremors at the extremeties and spasms of limbs and body, or sucking, lip-smacking, and tongue movements (Klein and Davis, 1969).

Electroconvulsive shock treatment

Another biomedical treatment is electroconvulsive shock treatment (ECT). This is a controversial but often successful treatment for severe unipolar depression. In its less-refined forms, it can have serious side effects, such as memory loss and motivational changes, yet it often succeeds in ending depressive episodes in patients who have not otherwise been treatable.

Overall, then, somatic therapies are often effective for several specific disorders. But like most useful agents, they have drawbacks. Each can produce unwanted side effects, some of them crippling. And when used unwisely, some may produce dependence. Perhaps most importantly, when you take a drug you come to depend on an external agent for your well-being, rather than your own skills and abilities.

As we discuss the various mental disorders in subsequent chapters, we will also take a closer look at particular biomedical treatments for these disorders. We will look at their underlying mechanisms (where they are known), we will examine their clinical use with patients, and we will discuss any side effects that are also produced by their use.

EVALUATING THE BIOMEDICAL MODEL

STRENGTHS

Measurable and objective concepts

The biomedical model is grounded in mature sciences. Its basic concepts, such as dopamine, heritability, and the central nervous system, seem measurable and objective. It has a well-defined sequence of methods: syndrome, etiology, and treatment. One hundred years of biomedical research, highlighted by such stunning successes as the eradication of smallpox and of general paresis, make it clear that its hypotheses are testable and, when correct, applicable. The pursuit of the biological bases of abnormality is so extensive that all of Chapter 17 is devoted to it. There, we take up in detail the boundary between neurologically based disorders and psychologically based ones.

WEAKNESSES

Problems with the model

With all this, why don't we stop our search for models right here? Because the model also has several problems. First, psychological events sometimes cause psychopathology, and changing these events—without directly changing anything about the body—can indeed cure. Eliminating a phobic's fear of cats by behavioral procedures and changing a depressive's belief that he is useless by cognitive means, can greatly help these patients. Second, biomedical treatments sometimes produce nasty side effects. For example, drugs that relieve the symptoms of schizophrenia can produce tardive dyskinesia, the loss of muscular control we discussed under "side effects" above. Because of such effects, many patients cannot tolerate biomedical treatments. Finally, some disorders may indeed be illnesses of the body, but others are **problems in living** (Szasz, 1961). General paresis is a disease, the consequence of syphilitic spirochetes. But marital discord, fear of public speaking, and depression following the death of one's child are not. These are psychological problems that can best be alleviated by psychological means.

REDUCTIONISM: AN ONGOING DEBATE

Reductionists vs. anti-reductionists

The thoroughgoing adherent of the biomedical model is a **reductionist.** A reductionist believes that *all psychological phenomena can be explained by and reduced to biological phenomena.* A reductionist points to *pellagra psychosis* as a clear example of a seemingly psychological disorder that can be wholly reduced to a biological disorder. In pellagra psychosis, formerly healthy individuals are stricken with confusion, inappropriate emotion (e.g., smiling and laughing at tragic events), hallucinations, and delirium (Ishii and Nishihara, 1985). On the surface, they appear to be schizophrenic. But there proves to be an underlying biological disorder: When people are deprived of niacin (a vitamin), either naturally or by taking an anti-tuberculosis drug (isoniazid), the skin lesions and intestinal problems of the vitamin deficiency disease, pellagra, follow along with psychosis.

The **anti-reductionist** holds that *there are at least some psychological phenomena that cannot be reduced to biological phenomena.* The anti-reductionist points to the example of "deprivation dwarfism" (Foster and Wilson, 1985) to illustrate a biological phenomenon that is caused by a psychological rather than a physical state. In deprivation dwarfism a child living in a stressful environment, such as an abusive home, does not grow. The child may show no output of growth hormones and appears to have a malfunctioning pituitary gland. When the child is removed from the abusive home and placed in a foster home, however, pituitary hormones become normal and a growth spurt begins. This indicates that an underlying psychological state produces the biological changes in growth hormone.

The battle between reductionists and anti-reductionists is still very much alive. It has important implications for the biomedical model: Proponents of this model can take great comfort in such phenomena as chromosome 11 abnormalities controlling manic-depression, paresis and syphilis, and pellagra psychosis. They must think seriously, however, about the challenge presented by instances in which psychological events precede the biological changes, such as deprivation dwarfism, stigmata, and psychoneuroimmunology (see Chapter 10). At this stage of knowledge, we believe that the most that can be concluded is that biological and psychological forces *interact* to produce mental illness.

SUMMARY

1. The *biomedical model* holds that psychological disorders are illnesses of the body.

2. The biomedical school of thought dictates an ideal procedure for isolating a psychological disorder as an illness: grouping the symptoms into a coherent *syndrome* that can be diagnosed reliably; searching for an *etiology,* or cause, of the syndrome; and finding a *treatment* and *prevention* that follow from knowing the cause.

3. Four sorts of evidence about etiology of a disorder point toward a psychological disorder being considered a physical illness: discovery of a *germ* causing the illness, *genetic transmission* of the disorder, a disordered *biochemistry* or *neuroanatomy of the brain* producing the disorder, or a combined *genetic and biochemical* etiology.

4. We discussed examples of each of these etiologies. The eradication of general paresis by the discovery that it was caused by the spirochete that caused syphilis exemplified the germ etiology. The evidence that schizophrenia is partly transmitted genetically exemplified the genetic etiology. The relationship between the blocking of dopamine and the alleviation of schizophrenia exemplified the biochemical etiology. The malfunctioning of higher and then lower levels of brain function illustrated the neuroanatomical etiology. The inheritance of manic-depression and a defect on chromosome 11 illustrated the linkage between genetic and biochemical etiologies.

5. Biomedical therapy tries to correct disordered brain function by drugs and other agents. But these drugs may also have serious side effects.

6. The main strengths of the biomedical model are that it is grounded in well-established biological sciences, and that physical treatments are often able to bring relief.

7. The main weaknesses of the biomedical model are that psychological treatments also are able to bring relief to individuals with psychological problems, that some psychopathological problems are *problems in living,* and that there are side effects to some biomedical treatments.

Psychodynamic and Existential Approaches

THE psychodynamic theories of personality and abnormality are concerned with the psychological forces that—consciously or unconsciously—influence the mind. These inner forces, these desires and motives, often conflict. When these conflicts are well-resolved, they produce growth, vigor. But when they are poorly resolved, or remain unresolved, conflicts generate anxiety and unhappiness, against which people try to defend themselves. In this chapter we examine some of the causes and consequences of conflict and the conditions that lead to its resolution, for better or for worse.

Psychodynamic approaches to personality and abnormality begin with the work of a single towering genius—a Viennese physician named Sigmund Freud. Freud's views were modified and elaborated by a group of clinicians who are commonly called *Neo-Freudians.* Finally, modern psychodynamic approaches culminate in the ideas of a large number of clinicians and scientists, whose observations and research have greatly revised Freud's original assertions about the nature of human development and the origins of psychological misery. We consider each in turn.

FREUD AND PSYCHOANALYTIC THEORY

Sigmund Freud (1856–1939) in 1909.

Psychic energy

Born in 1856, Freud produced some twenty-four volumes of theoretical observations and case histories before he died in 1939. His own methods of studying and changing personality, as well as those of his students, are called *psychoanalysis.*

Throughout his life, Freud's consuming intellectual and clinical passion was with *psychic energy.* The natural scientists of his time were having a heyday with physical energy. Electricity had been harnessed during Freud's youth, and engines invented. In the spirit of the times, Freud turned his attention to the energies that fuel psychological life. People are endowed with a fixed amount of psychic energy, he assumed. Why is it, then, that sometimes people seem to be vigorous and full of life, while at others they seem listless? How is it that some people devote their energies to love and work, while others are largely concerned with their aches and pains? How is psychic energy used at the very beginning of life, and how do those uses become transformed as a person matures?

We begin our examination of psychoanalytic theories with the last question: How is psychic energy used very early in life, and how are its uses changed as a result of maturation? Conflict, anxiety, and defense play large roles here, and not only negative ones, for these matters play constructive as well as destructive roles in psychological development.

The Development of Personality

Psychosexual development

From birth to maturity, people go through five overlapping stages of psychosexual development: the oral, anal, phallic, latency, and genital stages. Psychoanalysts call this kind of maturation *psychosexual* because it underscores the relationship between mind and pleasure. Sexuality, in Freudian usage, is not restricted to sexual intercourse, or even to the fantasies and behaviors that precede it. Rather, sexual energy is one important form of pleasurable psychic energy. Long before sexuality takes its adult form, sexual energy exists as *libido* (from the Latin, meaning desire or lust). Libido, then, is psychic energy that can become associated with a host of pleasurable activities. Early in life, during the oral stage, for example, those pleasures are associated with the gratification of biological needs. Later on, libido becomes attached to social and psychological needs.

ORAL STAGE

The first psychosexual stage, the *oral stage,* develops out of the central biological activity of very young infants: feeding. Their sucking response is instinctive, and it is through this behavior that a basic need is gratified. But quite independent of biological need, sucking provides pleasure of its own. The mouth and tongue are early pleasure centers: Freud called them *erogenous zones.* Sucking itself, then, engenders bliss.

Like all of the psychosexual stages, the oral stage is richly endowed with the capacity to permanently disfigure development. For many infants, it can be the stage of pleasurable dependency. Those who find this stage very gratifying and therefore become fixated here, develop *oral character traits,* which are enduring dispositions to react in the dependent ways of infants and young children. Like infants, they remain heavily dependent on others and overwhelmingly disposed to receive rather than give. On the other hand, those who experience intense conflict at the oral stage may well develop lifelong incapacities to trust others, perhaps especially to trust them to satisfy their needs.

ANAL STAGE

As infants begin to overcome their dependence, and as they become more autonomous and exploratory, they are confronted with social control. So-

The oral stage is the first psychosexual stage. Through nursing, this two-week-old infant is simultaneously satisfying his basic need for food and deriving pleasure.

During the anal stage, toilet training provides an outlet for pleasurable energy as well as an area of potential conflict between parent and child.

cial control takes many familiar forms, nearly all of them preceded by "don't." "Don't throw your food," "Don't go into the closet," "Don't play in the street"—these are the parental dicta to children in the "terrible two's." But a particular kind of parental control has been of interest to psychoanalysts because it centers on the body and provides yet another outlet for pleasurable energy as well as opportunity for conflict and defense. This is the control involved in toilet training.

From a parental perspective, toilet training is merely a way of controlling a child's mess. To the extent that parents speak of it at all, they speak of the gradual disappearance of diapers and the occasional occurrence of "accidents." From the child's viewpoint, toilet training may be an opportunity to savor the joys of increasing self-control, to please parents, and to be lavished with praise. Or it may be an opportunity to rebel, to pit a growing will against that of adults. But regardless of how the child views toilet training, one thing is certain from the psychoanalytic viewpoint: parental concern with toilet training makes the child attend to the anal area, to the sensations that arise there, and the body products that are eliminated. The anal region can now be stimulated through the voluntary retention and expulsion of feces as well as through manual stimulation. Thus, libido—pleasurable energy—is now associated with the anal area.

Opportunities for conflict and for fixation are rife in this stage. Early on, conflict may arise between children's natural inclination to eliminate when and where they will, and parental insistence that elimination occur in a particular place, and often at a particular time. If that conflict is not resolved, children may later manifest the remnants of that experience in character traits of messiness, disorderliness, and even rebelliousness. But even greater opportunities for conflict come later in the anal stage, when children have already learned to control their bowel movement. Then, a particularly strict

The anal character

toilet training will make children especially careful, or orderly, about their wastes. Moreover, because parents applaud their timely eliminations, they may come to consider their body wastes as especially valuable, and they may resist giving them up. Fixation can therefore generate enduring ***anal character traits*** of orderliness, stinginess, and stubbornness—a triad of traits that will persist into later life.

By the time children are approximately three years old, they will have traversed the anal stage more or less successfully. Now relatively autonomous and exploratory, they are ready to discover the pleasures of the third stage of psychosexual development. These pleasures lie in the genital area.

PHALLIC STAGE

The phallic stage is different from the stages that precede it in one important sense. In the oral stage, libido was associated with a biological process, feeding. In the anal stage, it was again associated with biological processes, defecation and urination, and also with social control. But phallic pleasures are self-initiated ones, arising from curiosity, first about one's own body, and gradually from curiosity about other people's bodies. At first, the idea that children stimulate themselves genitally horrified Freud's Victorian contemporaries. Gradually, the notion took hold, such that it is now commonly accepted that young children, from the ages of about three through six or

 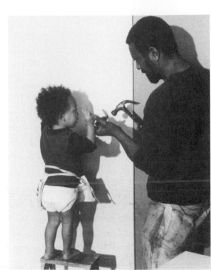

Psychoanalysts consider that, by identifying with the same-sex parent, the child is able to resolve the Oedipal conflict.

seven, engage in pleasurable genital stimulation that is the rudimentary form of adult sexuality.

Adult sexual adjustment is often crucially determined at this stage by the outcome of what Freud called the ***Oedipus complex.*** That conflict takes its name from a Greek legend that is now more than 2500 years old, in which Oedipus killed Laius the king of Thebes and married the queen, Jocasta, only later to find that the king was his father, and that he had therefore married his mother. Appalled by his unintentional crime, Oedipus gouged his eyes out. That legend symbolized for Freud the desire that all young children have: to do away with the parent of the same sex, and take possession of the parent of the opposite sex. That desire is often captured in the commonplace remarks of little boys—"when I grow up I'm going to marry you, mommy"—as well as in their fantasies.

What prevents young children from acting vigorously on their desire to take the opposite-sex parent for themselves and to do away with the same-sex one? Fear. The very curiosity that guided their interest in the opposite-sex parent teaches them quickly that the same-sex parent is bigger and stronger than they, and that that parent will resist their attempted conquest. Boys, especially, are vulnerable to this fear. During their childish explorations, sooner or later they come to know that women do not have a penis. Assuming that women once had a penis like themselves, they infer that their penis must have been cut off. The fear that they, too, will be castrated by their father if they persist in such longings is sufficient to dampen those desires considerably. ***Castration anxiety,*** then, terminates incestuous desire in boys.

For girls, the matter is more complicated and, in psychoanalytic theory, less well resolved. The young girl, too, sees the absence of a penis as a lack and may be angry with her mother for having created her incomplete and inferior. She continues to experience ***penis envy,*** which results in her further desire for her father, even in the desire to have a child by him and thereby to symbolically acquire a penis. Only the mother's greater strength, as well as her father's resistance to the idea, restrains the impulse to take him. These

The Oedipus complex

During latency, there is a decline in sexual interest, and the child attempts to master social and cognitive skills.

factors are less effective in terminating the Oedipal conflict in girls than is castration anxiety in boys.

Identification

The outcome of this intense conflict is not merely withdrawal. It is ***identification*** with the same-sex parent: becoming that person in a psychological sense, such that the adult's values, attitudes, standards, sexual orientation, and even mannerisms become the child's own. Identification is a defense that we will discuss later in the chapter. It resolves the Oedipal conflict because the child internalizes the very values that prohibit incest.

LATENCY STAGE

Decline of sexual interest

The Oedipal conflict is exhausting and frightening, and it is not surprising that by the age of six or seven when it is over, sexual interest declines. Sexuality is repressed, that is, deflected from consciousness. This decline of sexual interest marks the beginning of the latency period. During latency, the child is relatively asexual. Attention is directed toward mastering social and cognitive skills.

GENITAL STAGE

Sexual interest reawakens in socialized form

The final stage of psychosexual development comes with the onset of puberty. Sexual impulse reawakens, but now in a more mature and socialized form. Earlier sexuality was fundamentally narcissistic, concerned nearly entirely with self-gratification. The developing adolescent is much more socialized than the child was, and adolescent sexual energies are channeled to reflect that growth. In the heterosexual sphere, others now are valued in their own right, and not merely as adjuncts for self-gratification. Love becomes possible and pleasurable, and altruism—the concern for another's welfare, independent of one's own—becomes possible too. Additionally, some sexual energy is channeled into work. Competence and efficacy in the workplace become rewarding in themselves, independent of the riches they bring.

Full-fledged genitality involves the capacities to love and to work, the two capacities that Freud felt were most significant for maturity. Psychoanalysts use the term *sublimation* to denote the transfer of libidinal energies from relatively narcissistic gratifications to those—like love and work—that gratify others and are highly socialized.

THE THREE PROCESSES OF PERSONALITY

Id, ego, and superego

According to Freud, human personality is structured by three kinds of forces: the id, ego, and superego. These are neither objects nor places in the mind. Rather, they are dynamic and interactive *processes,* with their own origins and specific roles. The word *id* originates from the German "es," literally meaning "it," and connotes processes that seem to lie outside of an individual's control. *Ego,* in German, means "ich" or "I," and designates those capacities that enable a person to cope with reality, while *superego* (in German "Uberich" or "over I") describes those processes that are "above the self"—conscience, ideals, and morals.

THE ID

The id designates the mental representation of processes that are fundamentally biological in origin. In the newborn infant, nearly all psychic energy is devoted to such biological processes. And over the course of development, id processes continue to fuel personality, providing the energy for the diverse pursuits that are associated with psychological growth as well as biological survival.

Biological drives are raw and urgent. They create desires that clamor for immediate gratification, tensions that seek instantaneous relief. They are dominated by the *pleasure principle,* which demands immediate impulse gratification and tension reduction. The id is like a spoiled child. It wants

The id is dominated by the pleasure principle. It demands immediate gratification of biological needs such as eating *(left)*. Where delay of gratification is necessary, however, it is like a spoiled child—pouting and petulant, as here *(right)*.

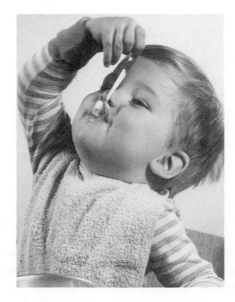

what it wants when it wants it. When they seek external gratification, id drives know nothing of appropriateness, or even danger. Were people wholly dominated by id processes they would, like the spoiled child, eat any food when they were hungry, regardless of whether it was theirs, healthy, or even still alive.

THE EGO

Whereas the id seeks pleasure, the ego seeks reality. One function of the ego is to express and gratify the desires of the id in accordance with the requirements of reality. While the id operates on the pleasure principle, the ego utilizes the *reality principle.* It tests reality to determine whether the expression of an impulse is safe or dangerous. It delays the impulses of the id until the time is right, and may even divert those impulses toward appropriate targets. Freud describes the relations between ego and id this way:

> The ego's relation to the id might be compared with that of a rider to his horse. The horse supplies the locomotive energy, while the rider has the privilege of deciding on the goal and of guiding the powerful animal's movement. But only too often there arises between the ego and the id the not precisely ideal situation of the rider being obliged to guide the horse along the path by which it [the id] itself wants to go. (Freud, 1923, p. 77)

The ego's success in enabling impulses to be realistically and safely gratified depends on its ability to use thought processes, like reasoning, remembering, evaluating, and planning. The ego is the executive of the personality, carrying out the demands of the id in such a way as to minimize negative consequences.

THE SUPEREGO

Those processes of mind that comprise both conscience and idealistic striving are termed superego processes. Conscience is acquired through parents. It arises from the forceful resolution of the Oedipal conflict, and it results in the internalization of society's views of which thoughts, impulses, and behaviors are permissible and forbidden, as well as which goals and ideals should be pursued.

Superego processes are just as irrational as id processes; neither cares or knows much about reality. Conscience can also be overly harsh, suppressing not only permissible behaviors, but even the very thought of those behaviors. Whereas the person whose id processes are relatively uncontrolled seems impulse-ridden, the person who is overly dominated by his or her superego seems wooden and moralistic, unable to be comfortable with pleasure and overly sensitive to "Thou shalt not . . ."

Through the superego, the child internalizes society's views of what behaviors are permissible and which are forbidden. Here this child is scolding her doll, saying, "Bad girl! Didn't I tell you to keep out of the dirt? Now what shall I do with you?"

The processes that regulate normal personality and development are identical to those that regulate abnormal personality. What distinguishes normal from abnormal personality is the manner in which psychic energy is distributed between the three components of personality. In normal personality, psychic energy is strongly invested in ego processes, as well as those of the id and superego. In abnormal personality, psychic energy is distributed improperly, with the result that either the id or the superego is too strong, and ego processes are unable to control desire or conscience.

Id, ego, and superego regularly interact and often conflict. Sexual desires that arise in a classroom, for example, may be delayed by ego processes until a more permissible place is found. But even in such a place, they may be blocked by superego processes which proclaim that sex is sinful, or that the time might better be spent studying. As the executive, the ego is supposed to mediate these conflicts. But how does the ego do this? And what happens to desires that are blocked? The answers to these questions become clear when we examine additional ideas that have become central to psychodynamic thinking: unconscious ideas and impulses, and anxiety.

Unconscious Ideas and Impulses

Three levels of consciousness

Freud (1923) proposed that there are three levels of consciousness. The first is ***perceptual consciousness,*** consisting of the very small number of mental events to which the individual is presently attending. Being aware of reading a book and of the meaning of a passage would exemplify this kind of consciousness.

The second level of consciousness is ***pre-conscious.*** It consists of information and impulses that are not at the center of attention but that can be retrieved more or less easily. Though not now part of one's central awareness, last night's dinner can be recalled with little difficulty.

The large mass of memory, experience, and impulse lies at the third level of consciousness: the ***unconscious.*** Two kinds of memories become unconscious: (1) those that are forgotten, and (2) those that, because of conflict are ***repressed,*** or actively barred from consciousness. Ordinary forgotten events, such as the cost of a loaf of bread last year, gradually decay and exert no subsequent influence on personality. But repressed events live on, and all the more vigorously, because they are not subject to rational control. They reveal their potent identities in normal fantasies and dreams, in slips of the tongue and "motivated" forgetting, under hypnosis and in a variety of abnormal psychological conditions. By far, unconscious forces are the dominant ones in personality.

> Ann was in love with two men, Michael and Jules. Both wanted to marry her, and she could not decide between them. Finally, after more than six months, she decided for Michael. The next night, she had the following dream:
>
> "I was climbing the fire-escape outside my dormitory. It was a dark and rainy night, and I was carrying a big box under my raincoat. I came to the fifth floor, opened the door silently, and tiptoed quickly to my room. Once inside, I double-locked the door, and put this box—it's a treasure chest—on my bed. I opened it and it was full of diamonds and rubies and emeralds."
>
> In Ann's dream, "diamonds and rubies and emeralds"=jewels=Jules. Her dream reveals her continuing attachment to her former lover, and quite possibly her desire to maintain the relationship secretly. The mind's extraordinary capacity to play on Jules's name and to transform it into visual symbols is revealed in this dream.

Certain personality processes operate more at the unconscious level than do others. Id impulses are entirely unconscious, as are many superego proceses. In contrast, ego processes, because they must mediate between desire, conscience, and reality, are often pre-conscious or conscious.

ANXIETY

Anxiety as signal of conflict

Conflicts among the various personality processes regularly give rise to a kind of psychic pain that Freud termed **anxiety.** Anxiety can be conscious or unconscious, and its presence is always a signal that conflict is at hand. When the conflict causes the person to feel overwhelmed, helpless, and unable to cope, anxiety arises. The degree of experienced anxiety depends on the anticipated consequences to self.

Freud distinguished three kinds of anxiety, each of which arises from a different source of perceived danger. **Realistic anxiety** arises from the expectation that real-world events may be harmful to the self. Ordinarily, this is what is meant by fear. A person who slips while crossing the street may experience realistic anxiety as moving traffic approaches. **Neurotic anxiety** arises from the possibility that one will be overwhelmed by one's impulses, especially unconscious sexual and aggressive ones. The unconscious desire to vanquish someone who controls an important destiny—say, a father, employer, or lover—may breed neurotic anxiety. Finally, **conscience** or **moral anxiety** arises when one anticipates that one's behavior will violate one's personal standards, or when that behavior has, in fact, violated those standards. The legend of Oedipus (described earlier) contains a classic instance of moral anxiety. Having learned that he has murdered his father and married his mother, Oedipus is overwhelmed with guilt, shame, and revulsion and, as a result, gouges out his eyes.

The experience of anxiety, even the anticipation of anxiety, is an uncomfortable experience that people try to relieve immediately. Humans are particularly well-endowed with strategies for alleviating anxiety. Beyond "overcoming fear" as we do when we learn to ride a bicycle, or "fleeing the

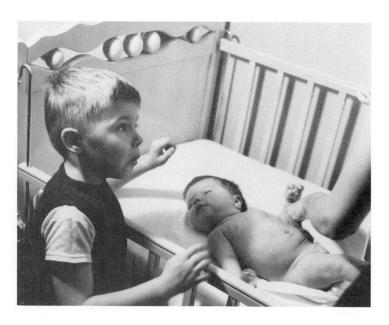

Neurotic anxiety may arise from the possibility that aggressive impulses may overwhelm one. Here this boy displays anxiety over his unexpressed wish to hurt his new baby brother.

field" when pursued by strong enemies, humans can, in their own minds, alter the very meaning and significance of troublesome drives and impulses. They perform these alterations by using coping strategies, or defenses. The more common of these include such defenses as repression and projection, as well as identification and rationalization, to name but a few. We discuss each in turn later in the chapter.

FAULTS OF EARLY PSYCHOANALYTIC THEORY

Nonverifiable
nature of
concepts

Early psychoanalytic theory suffered two major faults. First, it was simply nonverifiable. However interesting or compelling it might have been, there seemed no way at all to subject these notions to any kind of scientific test (Grunbaum, 1984). How does one test whether oral fixation really exists? How does one determine whether castration anxiety really leads to identification with the same-sex parent and thereby the resolution of the Oedipal conflict? Indeed, it seemed to some observers that it was the *belief* that present troubles are embedded in the deep past that led psychoanalytic thinkers to invent childhood *metaphors* that might make the present more cogent (Stern, 1985). Moreover, it became increasingly clear that modern evidence strongly disputed Freud's assertions about infancy and childhood (Flavell, 1977; Clarke-Stewart, 1973; Erdelyi, 1985). Freud, it should be remembered, had spent little time with infants and children (other than his own, presumably); as a result, his theories about childhood development could not have been much more than intelligent speculation. What would have greatly informed these speculations, and what might very well have altered them, was patient observation of, and experimentation with, infants and children.

Observation of
individual clients

Second, nearly all of psychoanalytic theory arose from carefully observing *individual clients* who had come for treatment. The virtue of this theory lay precisely in the fact that it arose from very detailed examination of individual personalities. But that was also its liability. Freud's clients, for example, were mainly Viennese women, in early and middle adulthood, who suffered a fairly restricted range of psychological symptoms. Yet his experience with such people led him to generalize to children as well as adults, to men as well as women, to normals as well as clients, and to the rest of the world as well as Vienna. His restricted experience, it has often been said (Eysenck, 1961; Mischel, 1968; Hall and Lindzey, 1970; Lamiell, 1987), hardly provided a basis for generalization, and many of his generalizations simply have proven to be wrong.

THE NEO-FREUDIANS

Differences
between Freud
and
Neo-Freudians

Though they were rejected at first, Freud's ideas later came to attract a number of highly original thinkers who elaborated on his views and often disagreed with them. In some cases, the disagreements led to a break with Freud. Such was the case with Carl Jung (1875–1961) and Alfred Adler (1870–1937).

What were the differences between Freud and the other thinkers? First, some theorists differed with Freud regarding the origins of motivation.

Carl Jung (1875–1961).

Alfred Adler (1870–1937).

Left: Karen Horney (1885–1952). *Right*: Harry Stack Sullivan (1892–1949)

Granting that motivation was mainly unconscious, these thinkers believed that Freud held much too narrow a view of *what* was unconscious. For example, Jung felt that there was also a ***collective unconscious,*** consisting of the memory traces of the experience of past generations and not just memories of early childhood as Freud thought. In Jung's view, we are born wiser than we think, already afraid of darkness and fire because our ancestors were, and already knowing of death because past generations have died. Jung called these universal ideas with which we are born ***archetypes.*** For Jung, these archetypes form the basis of personality, accounting for why people are not merely driven by their past experiences but also strive to grow and become something better. In essence, Jung saw the self as striving for wholeness.

Freud's emphasis on biological urges—the id impulses—as determinants of behavior is the basis of a second major dispute, particularly with Alfred Adler. In Freud's view, human activity serves fundamental sexual and aggressive needs arising from the id and mediated by the ego. But according to Alfred Adler, the self serves a more meaningful purpose. The self enables us to fulfill our life-style, to become more than the genes with which we are endowed and the environment that presses on us. The self creates something new, something unique, something that is not wholly determined by biological impulse or cultural press (Ansbacher and Ansbacher, 1956). As we will show, Adler's concerns foreshadowed the modern emphasis on self.

There is considerable difference in a third area, that of psycho*sexual* versus psycho*social* development. Fundamentally, that difference reduces to whether people are fundamentally biological or social animals. For example, Karen Horney (1885–1952) saw basic anxiety as a social rather than simply a biological experience. For her, that basic anxiety consisted of "the feeling a child has of being isolated and helpless in a potentially hostile world" (Horney, 1945, p. 41). That anxiety may lead children to develop one of three modes of coping. They may become hostile, seeking revenge against those who rejected them. Or they may become submissive, hoping thereby to regain the lost love. Or they may simply withdraw, giving up the quest entirely. These three strategies—moving against, moving toward, and moving away—are social responses to a fundamentally social anxiety.

Similarly, Harry Stack Sullivan (1892–1949) held that the very notion of personality is itself an illusion that cannot be separated from the social context in which it is seen and operates. According to Sullivan, psychological problems do not merely originate in faulty social development, they *consist* of faulty social relationships and need to be examined and treated as such. Sullivan's concerns are mirrored in the modern emphasis on the social context in which personality operates (Nisbett and Ross, 1980; Gergen, 1982).

Erik Erikson (1902–) has provided a broader theory of development, one that stresses the psycho*social* nature of people and the interrelations between individuals and society. Unlike Freud, who believed that the foundations of personality were essentially completed in childhood, Erikson sees human personality as developing and changing throughout life, from infancy on through adulthood and old age. Moreover, Erikson's eight stages of man, even where they overlap with Freud's stages during early childhood, emphasize the social aspects of development.

Erich Fromm (1900–1980) saw personality as fundamentally social. At birth and with development, humans find themselves increasingly isolated from others. That isolation—the fundamental human condition—is painful, and however much people cherish their freedom, they also seek to terminate their isolation. They can do this either through love and shared work—a constructive mode—or through conformity and submission to authority, a very destructive mode.

MODERN PSYCHODYNAMIC THEORY

As a group, the Neo-Freudians brought refinements to basic Freudian theory. Other theorists and practitioners have proposed further modifications to this theory. But these modern psychodynamic theorists still take as the basis for their work the approaches of Freud and the Neo-Freudians.

Today, there really is no single coherent theory of personality dynamics. Rather, the work that goes on in many clinics and laboratories sheds light on *aspects* of personality and human development, and it greatly revises Freud's notions and those of his immediate followers. The core of that revision has to do with the nature of the *self*—the processes and crises that shape it, the role of the defenses in shaping consciousness, and those aspects of the self that contribute to growth.

Left: Erik Erikson (1902–).
Right: Erich Fromm (1900–1980).

Heinz Kohut (1913–   )

THE SELF AND SELF THEORY

Let us grant, as Freud held, that personality is composed of the id, ego, and superego. But what gives personality its unity? What leads individuals to believe that they are the same person across time and place, that they are not fractured and fragmented psychologically? How is it that even though they are *doing* different things at different times with different people, they remain the very same person? For some, these questions have little meaning: they *are* the same person physically, and therefore psychologically. For others, however, especially those who have had a "shaky" self, or who see themselves as having undergone great change, such that they can say that "I am not the person that I was five years ago," these questions are significant and worth pursuing.

THE SELF

Modern psychodynamic theory is concerned with the **introcosm** (Jaynes, 1977), the vast subjective psychological space that is the storehouse of personal experience within each of us. Central to its theoretical formulations is the *self* in all its senses, and especially the ways in which it *emerges,* is *experienced,* and often becomes embattled and *defended* (Winnicott, 1971; Kohut, 1971, 1977; Mahler, 1979; Stern, 1985). There are three aspects of self that arise sequentially and are especially important in psychodynamic theory: the core self, the subjective self, and the verbal self.

The core self arises when the infant becomes aware that he and his caretaker are physically separate. This four-month-old baby recognizes himself in a mirror.

☐ THE CORE SELF.   The "first self" arises sometime between the second and sixth months of an infant's life, when he becomes aware that he and his caretaker are *physically separate.* The physical or **core self** that arises in this way is the "body self" and is pretty much taken for granted. Usually, people are unaware of their core selves. Nevertheless, it serves a very important function. The core self gives each person his sense of separateness, coherence, and identity. Moreover, it is the core self that enables individuals to confer coherence and identity on *others.*

The core self has four especially important features. First, it embraces a sense of *agency,* that we are the authors and controllers of our own actions (cf. Yalom, 1980) and correspondingly, we are *not* the controllers of other people's actions (nor they of ours). Daniel Stern (1985) describes a dramatic experiment that he and his colleagues conducted with a pair of "Siamese twins," Alice and Betty, young infants who were attached in such a way that they always faced each other. When Alice was sucking her own fingers and the experimenters tried to remove them from her mouth, they could sense resistance in Alice's arm, but no straining forward of her head. But when they tried to remove Betty's fingers from Alice's mouth, there was no resistance in Alice's arm, but her head strained forward. Clearly Alice knew whether she had her own or her sister's fingers in her mouth, and moreover, she understood best how she could control whether they remained in her mouth.

Second, the core self fosters and is promoted by a sense of *self-coherence,* that one is a physical unity. Third, the sense that the *emotions* one experi-

The subjective self is the self in relation to others. This baby is communicating with her older brother.

ences are part of oneself contributes to the growth and maintenance of the core self. And finally, the core self promotes the sense of *self-history,* the perception of our continuity in time, despite the fact that we are not the same people we once were.

So long as these features of the core self remain strong, personality remains strong. But if there is a breakdown in say, the sense of agency and control, if one develops the sense that "things are happening to me outside of my control" or that "I can control other people's minds," there is also fertile ground for disruption.

☐ THE SUBJECTIVE SELF. At about seven to nine months of age, a second sense of self emerges. It is the ***subjective self,*** and it encourages the development of ***intersubjectivity***—the sense that we understand each others' intentions and feelings, as well as the sharing of experiences about things and events. At that age, children begin to draw their parents' attention to things, sharing that attention. They communicate intentions. And they share affective states. The result is meaningful exchanges between the infant and her caretakers, exchanges that are characterized by empathy and a sense of common understanding, exchanges that are distinctly human.

Disturbances in the subjective self may result in difficulties in feeling connected to other people and in empathizing with them or with oneself. The sense of being out of touch with self and others is what may arise when there are disturbances in the subjective self.

☐ THE VERBAL SELF. At about fifteen to eighteen months of age, children begin to develop the third sense of self: the self as a storehouse of knowledge and experience. That ***verbal self*** develops by using symbols and language.

The verbal self develops by using symbols and language.

The use of language, of course, opens a world of infinite variety and action for the infant. It permits rapid and direct communication, often about issues that are not behaviorally obvious. "Give me milk" is a precise request that might, without language, be misunderstood and very drawn out. Moreover, because the infant begins to use words such as "I" or "me" or "you," he can soon objectify the self, often seeing the self as others might.

But language has a special down side, for it can distort the same reality that it might otherwise extend and enrich. Imagine a child who is visibly bored or tired, and whose parent says, "My! Aren't we having a wonderful time!" Indeed, language has been implicated in the development of the "false self," the self that is a semantic construction of disavowed experiences and beliefs.

SELFOBJECTS

The various selves are not sturdy and wholly independent structures. Much as they are formed by interactions between caretakers and infant, so they require support and sustenance from others throughout life. Those centrally important people who provide support for personality cohesiveness are called *selfobjects,* people and things that each of us requires to keep our personalities functioning at their optimum level (Kohut, 1977). The notion of selfobjects underscores the importance of the environment for optimal personality functioning. It shows that we are, none of us, islands unto ourselves, free and independent of the contexts in which we are found. As we will see, selfobject disturbances, in particular, are held to be important in the borderline personality disorders.

Selfobjects are people and things that provide support and sustenance to the self throughout life, be they mothers or friends.

THE SIGNIFICANCE OF SELF

Changing world
of private
experience

The notion of self is central to understanding the private world of experience. According to Carl Rogers (1902–1987), who was a leading theorist about the self, each person lives in a "continually changing world of experience of which he is the center." No one can understand a person's private world as well as that person does. But neither are we wholly barred from the private experience of others. *Empathy* is the gift and tool that enables us to understand others (Rogers, 1961; Kohut, 1978).

Introjected values

The self is the aspect of personality that embodies a person's perceptions and values. There are two kinds of values: those that are acquired from the experience of the subjective self, and those that are introjected or acquired from others, perhaps through the verbal self. Values that arise from experience are the ones that most commonly contribute to personal growth and self-knowledge. Values that are introjected, on the other hand, may be a source of confusion, for they often require that a person deny his or her own feelings in order to conform to the desires of another. Thus, when children are told that it is bad to be angry with a sibling, they may gradually come to avoid labeling their feelings toward siblings as anger in order to preserve parental affection. Their subjective self may be out of tune with their verbal self, and that may produce tension and conflict, particularly when they are with those siblings.

DEFENSES AND CONSCIOUSNESS

Consciousness may be shaped by defenses against anxiety. An individual may turn to a variety of mechanisms to avoid and alter the psychological reality of consciousness. Modern psychodynamic theorists describe these mechanisms much as did Freud. But they depart from Freudian theory in that modern theorists organize these strategies in a hierarchy according to their level of maturity. First we will describe the various mechanisms, then we will discuss the hierarchical ordering of defenses as formulated by such theorists as George Vaillant, and finally we will describe how the defensive process can shape consciousness.

THE COPING STRATEGIES OF EVERYDAY LIFE

Defense
mechanisms to
reduce anxiety

As we discussed earlier, Freud described anxiety as the psychic pain arising out of conflict. "The mind is its own place," the poet John Milton tells us. "It can make a heaven of hell or a hell of heaven." This is especially the case when the mind is experiencing conflict and anxiety. Then, the mind becomes enormously creative, finding all sorts of ways to reduce anxiety. The ways in which the mind accomplishes this are often automatic and unconscious, occurring outside the willful control of the individual. Sometimes it can be achieved in a direct and conscious effort to mitigate conflict and minimize psychic pain. We call the ways in which the mind alters painful psychological events *coping strategies* or *defense mechanisms.*

☐ REPRESSION.   The most fundamental and widely used means for altering psychological realities is repression. In *Notes from Underground,* the Russian novelist Fyodor Dostoyevsky describes why repression is used and the role it plays. He writes:

> Every man has reminiscences which he would not tell to every one, but only to his friends. He has other matters in his mind which he would not reveal even to his friends, but only to himself, and that in secret. But there are other things which a man is afraid to tell even to himself, and every decent man has a number of such things stored away in his mind. The more decent he is, the greater the number of such things in his mind. (Dostoyevsky, 1864, pp. 57–59)

Repression is a defense by which the individual unconsciously forces unwanted thoughts or prohibited desires out of mind. Memories that evoke shame, guilt, humiliation, or self-deprecation—in short, affective memories (Davis and Schwartz, 1987)—are often repressed.

Not all painful memories are repressed nor, for that matter, are all repressed memories objectively painful. Whether repression occurs depends, at least partly, on the degree to which an experience or memory conflicts with self-image. People who think little of themselves and their abilities may well repress memories of the praise they received for a job well done. Such repression stabilizes their self-image and reduces anxiety that might arise from discrepant information.

Processes of repression

Two processes facilitate repression: ***mental inhibition*** and ***attention withdrawal.*** Mental inhibition occurs when images or memories are blocked. Blocking can be either intentional and conscious (under which condition it is sometimes called suppression), or automatic and unconscious. Young children, for example, are frequently and uncomfortably concerned with dying. They may try to put those thoughts out of their mind. But putting thoughts out of mind is difficult. Because thinking about death is painful, the entire blocking process may become unconscious and automatic, relieving the child of the difficult burden of repressing consciously.

Repression can also occur through withdrawing attention and redirecting it. If thinking about sex makes people feel guilty, for example, they can think about success and achievement instead, which makes them feel good. If repression is successful, each sexual impulse will be replaced by fantasies of fame and success.

Repression can be nearly complete, or it can be partial. When an idea or memory is partially repressed, some aspects may be consciously available, while others are not. For example, a person who had had a difficult relationship with a parent, may recall crying at that parent's funeral but may not recall what he or she cried about or anything else about the event. The available evidence also suggests that it is *partially* repressed conflicts and memories that play a significant role in abnormal behavior (Perkins and Reyher, 1971; Reyher and Smyth, 1971; Burns and Reyher, 1976; Silverman, 1976). In *multiple personality,* for example, an individual has two or more personalities that are alien to each other. When one personality is dominant, the others are repressed.

Mind as editor

The capacity of the mind to be "its own place" is not limited merely to its ability to repress, to reject images and memories from consciousness, as important as that ability is. Rather, the mind is an editor, deleting whole chapters of experience and reorganizing others. Ordinarily, even in the absence of conflict, both perception and memory are reconstructive (Ander-

Young children are frequently concerned with dying. In order to reduce the pain of thinking about death, they may engage in mental inhibition and ultimately repress these thoughts.

© 1982 Jules Feiffer. Reprinted with permission of United Press Syndicate. All rights reserved.

son and Bower, 1973). This is to say that minds take direct experience, edit, and make something "new" of it, by adding to, or subtracting from perception, by embellishing memory in ways that range from innocent decoration to filling memorial gaps with new "memories." It is no surprise, therefore, that these enlivening capacities of the mind should be used in the coping process, when anxiety is experienced or when conflict occurs between self-image and impulse or behavior. Here, sometimes consciously, but more often unconsciously, editing processes are invoked to enable the individual to cope by making perception and memory more pleasant. A description of some of the more significant coping strategies follows.

Attributing private understandings to others

☐ **PROJECTION.** Fundamentally, projection consists of attributing private understandings and meanings to others, of substituting "you" for "I." It is the bedrock upon which language comprehension rests. Consider the sentence "I love Mary." Anyone reading that sentence will have little difficulty comprehending it because she will ***project*** her own notion of love onto the speaker's phrase and mind. Generally, when someone says that "she hurt my feelings" or "I'm worried about that exam," we feel we understand what she is saying, even though in another context, we would readily grant that our own "hurt" might feel different from hers, and our "worry" different, too. We call this ***assimilative projection*** because it is an attribution to another of something that we are quite aware of feeling ourselves. It is part of the general process of quickly assigning meanings to events. Such attributions can be correct or incorrect, and they can obviously lead to a host of wrong predictions and misunderstandings (Nisbett and Ross, 1980).

Attributing to others feelings we deny

Another kind of projection, called ***disowning projection,*** is more common in the coping process. It consists in attributing to others those feelings and experiences that we personally *deny* having and that we usually repress. Think of the preacher who sees and decries sin everywhere but denies hav-

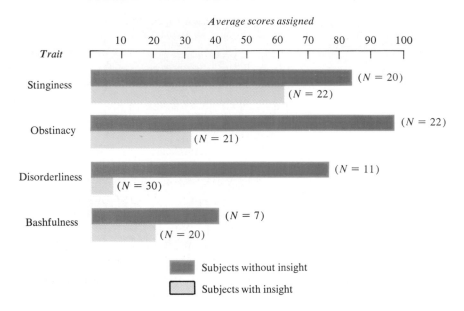

Figure 4-1
Average scores on four traits that were assigned to others by people who were themselves high scorers on those traits, and who either had or did not have insight into themselves on those dimensions. (Source: Based on data from R. Sears, 1936)

ing a sinful impulse himself. That's disowning projection. Robert R. Sears (1936), in the first experimental validation of disowning projection, asked students in a dormitory to rate themselves and their fraternity brothers on four traits: stinginess, obstinacy, disorderliness, and bashfulness. The extent to which individuals actually possessed each trait was estimated from the average of the ratings assigned to them by their fraternity brothers. When that average departed significantly from the rating the person gave himself, it was assumed that the person lacked self-awareness and, as a result, it was predicted that he would project more of that trait onto his fraternity brothers. And indeed he did, as Figure 4-1 indicates. Similarly, people who deny or repress their own sexual impulses have been shown to project them on others and to rate others as more lustful than in fact they are (Halpern, 1977).

Double role of projection

Psychodynamic thinkers point out that projection plays a double role in psychological distress. First, it reduces distress by allowing a person to attribute an anxiety-provoking impulse to another person, rather than the self. Thus, if anger makes us feel anxious, then the anxiety that anger creates can be reduced by attributing that anger to someone else. Second, projection allows us to do something about anger, for when someone is angry at us, are we not permitted to take aggressive or retaliative action in our own defense? Thus, projection can provide the rationale for engaging in the behavior that would have been forbidden in the first place.

☐ REACTION FORMATION. In the process of editing experience, we can delete a verb and substitute its opposite. Sometimes we say, "I hate her," when in fact we really mean "I love her." Such an editorial process is called ***reaction formation,*** because an opposite reaction is formed to the initial impulse.

Feeling substitution

Reaction formation, in fact, is a special case of a more generalized ***feeling substitution,*** which is easy to accomplish because feelings are often so ephemeral and difficult to label. For example, people in whom feelings of dependency are especially stressful may unwittingly experience and express anger each time they are in a situation that would ordinarily evoke dependency.

Reaction formation may be especially significant in **mania.** There, individuals behave as if they are full of joy and boundless energy, but one senses that their fundamental experience is one of sadness and depression, against which a reaction has been formed. Reaction formation is also seen in **counterphobia,** where individuals pursue precisely those activities that they deeply fear.

But if the mind can so easily revise experience and substitute a real feeling for its opposite, how can one tell the real feeling from its false opposite? When someone says "I love you!" how do we know he or she is not "really" feeling hatred? And conversely, if someone says "I can't stand you" should we not take that as a frank declaration of affection? Psychodynamic theorists offer two clues. First, because the conditions for experiencing and expressing the "real feeling" are not present in the reaction formation, the latter expressions of feeling tend to be thin, shallow, and seemingly wooden. Fabricated affections and genuine feelings are expressed in quite different ways. Second, the reaction formation is inflexible. Precisely because a stated fondness is formed, say, in reaction to hot anger, the anger must be avoided at all costs. Yet, anyone who has really liked someone knows that we are all occasionally annoyed or angry with people we truly care for. And we say so. Those who engage in reaction formation rarely are angry and rarely say so.

☐ DISPLACEMENT.   When the strategy of **displacement** is used, the individual edits the target of his or her emotions by replacing the true object with one that is more innocent and less threatening. People who are angry and frustrated at work, but who cannot vent those feelings at work, are unconsciously using displacement strategies when they return home and vent their feelings on innocent spouses and children.

☐ IDENTIFICATION.   **Identification** describes the process by which we internalize the characteristics of others—their ideas, values, mannerisms, status, and power. Identification is the opposite of projection. It is a fairly common strategy for overcoming fear and inadequacy.

People identify with those who have power and status, and they try to do many of the things that those they identify with do. Thus, some people are willing to spend considerably more money for a house in a "proper" neighborhood, than they would spend for the identical house at a less fashionable address, feeling that if their home is in a better neighborhood, they must perforce be "better" people. Similarly, people often rate themselves and each other by the college they attended, where they buy their clothes, or by the car they drive, even though we are, all of us, precisely what we are, no more and no less, regardless of the neighborhood we live in, the status of our college, where we buy our clothes, or the car we drive.

Identification relies heavily on people's sensitivity to context. Much as the perceived color of gray is changed according to whether it is seen against a black or white background, so are the perceived qualities of people altered by whether they are seen in an attractive or unattractive context.

There seems to be considerable clinical evidence for a special form of identification: identification with the aggressor. Bruno Bettelheim, a Jewish psychoanalyst who was interned at two notoriously cruel Nazi concentra-

---

(margin notes)

Differentiating real feelings from false opposites

Venting feelings on innocent objects

Internalizing characteristics of others

tion camps during World War II, observed how people coped with concentration camp conditions. One of his most striking descriptions concerns how some of the old prisoners—those who had been in the camps more than three years—identified with their Nazi jailers. They used the language of the Gestapo, adopted its mannerisms and even its carriage. Occasionally, they wore scraps of discarded Nazi uniforms or altered their own clothing to resemble Nazi uniforms. At times, they appeared to use the same patterns of cruelty as the Gestapo used toward other prisoners. When it became necessary to kill another inmate, they would do so in a manner that was strikingly similar to that used by the Gestapo. Bettelheim sensed that the only way these prisoners could allay their own fears of the Gestapo was by identifying with the Gestapo and pretending to have its power (Bettelheim, 1943).

Identification is a particularly useful strategy for coping with fear. Anna Freud tells of a little girl who was afraid to cross the hall in the dark lest she meet a ghost. She handled this fear by making peculiar gestures as she crossed the hall. "There's no need to be afraid in the hall," she explained to her little brother, "you just have to pretend that you're the ghost who might meet you" (A. Freud, 1936, p. 119). Incidentally, this example points out what has been stressed previously: coping strategies need not be unconscious.

Identification plays an especially large role in psychodynamic views of depression. People who are depressed, as we shall see in Chapter 11, often suffer enormously from self-deprecation, feelings of worthlessness, and suicidal impulses. Such feelings arise from the combined action of mourning and identification. When people suffer a loss, either through death or rejection, they go through a period of mourning. That much is quite normal. Often, however, people identify with these lost objects, unwittingly merging these objects with themselves. Because they feel a good deal of unconscious anger toward these objects for having abandoned or rejected them, that anger now comes to be experienced toward the self, and they become depressed. An examination of their feelings of self-deprecation and worthlessness would reveal, in the psychoanalytic view, that these feelings are more properly directed toward those who have died or rejected them.

Doing away with distressing external facts

□ DENIAL.   If repression obliterates inner facts, **denial** does away with distressing external ones. Denial commonly occurs when our sense of security and of being loved is threatened. The fact that people generally find it difficult to accurately perceive negative feelings directed toward themselves suggests that the denial process is widespread (Taguiri, Bruner, and Blake, 1958). Denial is often used when people are threatened by death. The parents of a fatally ill child, much as the fatally ill themselves, often deny that anything is wrong, even though they have the diagnosis and prognosis in hand.

Repressing affective components of experience

□ ISOLATION.   Whereas in repression and denial, both the affective and informational components of experience are deleted, in **isolation** only the affective ones (which, after all, are the sources of distress) are repressed, while information is retained. People who have suffered great brutality and humiliation, such as those in the German death camps during World War II, or

The parent who responsibly reprimands a child must isolate himself from the child's hurt feelings, else the reprimand will fail.

those who have been raped, may utilize isolation. They may be able to recount their experience precisely and in copious detail but be unable to recall the accompanying intense feelings. The very experiences that would ordinarily bring tears to a teller's eyes or make a listener wince in empathic pain, may be related blandly, suggesting that the feelings that were originally associated with the experience have been isolated.

Isolation can also be a constructive strategy. The parent who responsibly reprimands a child cannot be too sensitive to the hurt feelings the reprimand engenders, else the reprimand will fail. Neither can a surgeon allow herself to be overly sensitive to the fact that the tissue she is cutting is human flesh. Isolation constructively permits these emotional concerns to be withheld from consciousness.

Repressing and restating experience in abstract terms

☐ INTELLECTUALIZATION.   Related to denial and isolation, *intellectualization* consists of repressing the emotional component of experience, and restating the experience as an abstract intellectual analysis. Unable to deal with a particularly intense feeling, we sometimes seek to read all about it and to produce elaborate self-analyses that are all but devoid of feeling.

Assigning socially desirable motives to behavior

☐ RATIONALIZATION.   In recalling experiences and accounting for them, people commonly edit not only the facts of the experience but the motives as well. The process of assigning to behavior socially desirable motives that an impartial analysis would not substantiate is called *rationalization.* Late to a party that they didn't want to attend in the first place, some people will offer socially desirable excuses: the car broke down, or their watch stopped. Those excuses are rationalizations.

The process of rationalization is beautifully illustrated in experiments involving posthypnotic suggestion (Hilgard, 1965). A person is hypnotized and told that upon awakening, he should attend carefully to the handkerchief in the hypnotist's pocket. When that handkerchief is removed, the subject is instructed to open the window. The subject is further given a posthypnotic amnesia, that is, he is instructed to forget that the hypnotist ever told him to open the window. He is then aroused from the hypnotic trance.

He circulates among the people in the room, all the while keeping a careful eye on the hypnotist. The hypnotist removes his handkerchief. The subject hesitates: after all, one simply does not go around opening windows for no reason at all. "Isn't it a bit stuffy in here?" he finally asks—and then, having found a proper rationalization for his behavior, proceeds to raise the window.

Hypochondriasis

Rationalization plays a dramatic role in the development of **hypochondriasis,** which is the conviction in the absence of medical evidence that one is ill or about to become ill. "I can't do the job, not because I fear failure or because I fear it won't be done as well as the next guy, but because I'm not feeling well." Because illness evokes concern from others, the seemingly ill are encouraged to abandon the job and given a good measure of comfort to boot. Thus, the tendency to rationalize is often supported by the positive reactions it evokes from others.

Rechanneling psychic energies

□ SUBLIMATION. *Sublimation* is the process of rechanneling psychic energies from socially undesirable goals to constructive and socially desirable ones. As we have seen, capacities for love, work, altruism, and even humor involve such rechanneling of raw sexual and aggressive impulses. According to Freud, love is an especially powerful form of sublimation because it allows people also to achieve sexual gratification in a socially acceptable context. Simultaneously, however, loving leaves one vulnerable to rejection or the death of a loved one. Thus, the gratifications of loving and working are often matched by the anxieties to which they give rise. Sublimation, in Freud's view, is therefore as fragile as it is constructive.

THE ORGANIZATION OF COPING STRATEGIES

Maturational hierarchy of strategies

Everyone uses coping strategies. But are some strategies better—more effective, more adaptive, more useful—than others? Psychodynamic theorists believe that some defenses are primitive and immature in the sense that they grossly distort reality; they believe that other defenses do less violence to reality and are therefore more mature. These strategies can be organized into a **maturational hierarchy** that has four levels (Vaillant, 1986). *Level I* is the least mature and involves strategies wherein the cloth of reality is either wholly invented or entirely discarded. Denial or outright distortion of external reality as well as delusional projection are included here. *Level II* strategies are somewhat more mature. They include projection as well as the strategies that result in hypochondriasis and passive-aggressive behavior. They also include **acting out,** the direct expression of unconscious impulses (without being aware of those impulses), as well as **dissociation,** the temporary but drastic modification of one's sense of self or character in order to avoid emotional distress. At *Level III,* one finds the mechanisms of intellectualization, isolation, repression, and displacement—strategies that are awfully common, although somewhat debilitating for all of us. The most mature strategies—*Level IV*—are the ones we all strive for. They include dealing with anxiety through sublimation, and with it, the mechanisms of altruism, humor, conscious suppression, and impulse delay.

Several longitudinal studies have provided evidence that supports this notion of a maturational hierarchy of coping strategies. A group of men who graduated Harvard College between 1939 and 1944 were studied then, and for thirty years subsequently. Initially selected because they were quite independent, there was, even in this highly qualified group, considerable variability in the maturity of their coping strategies. Thirty years after they were first studied, the following question was asked: Did differences in the way they coped as undergraduates result in differences in the quality of their lives some thirty years later? Indeed they did, and dramatically so, as can be seen in Table 4-1.

A similar study examined the psychological health of a vastly different group (Vaillant, Bond, and Vaillant, 1986). In this study, a group of inner-city men who had first been interviewed between 1940 and 1945 were interviewed and rated again more than thirty years later, in 1977. The maturity of their defenses was established from the early interviews, when these men were in junior high school, while the adequacy of their present

Table 4-1 A COMPARISON BETWEEN MEN WHO USED MATURE ADAPTIVE MECHANISMS AND THOSE WHO USED IMMATURE ADAPTIVE MECHANISMS

| | Adaptive Strategies | | |
	Mature *n = 25*	*Immature* *n = 31*	*Statistical Significance of Difference*
Overall Adjustment			
1) Top third in adult adjustment	60%	0%	***
2) Bottom third in adult adjustment	4%	61%	***
3) "Happiness" (top third)	68%	16%	***
Career Adjustment			
1) Income over $20,000/year	88%	48%	**
2) Job meets ambition for self	92%	58%	***
3) Active public service outside job	56%	29%	*
Social Adjustment			
1) Rich friendship pattern	64%	6%	***
2) Marriage in least harmonious quartile or divorced	28%	61%	**
3) Barren friendship pattern	4%	52%	***
4) No competitive sports (ages 40–50)	24%	77%	***
Psychological Adjustment			
1) 10 + psychiatric visits	0%	45%	**
2) Ever diagnosed mentally ill	0%	55%	***
3) Emotional problems in childhood	20%	45%	*
4) Worst childhood environment (bottom fourth)	12%	39%	*
5) Fails to take full vacation	28%	61%	*
6) Able to be aggressive with other (top fourth)	36%	6%	*
Medical Adjustment			
1) Four or more adult hospitalizations	8%	26%	
2) 5 + days sick leave/year	0%	23%	*
3) Recent health poor by objective exam	0%	36%	*
4) Subjective health consistently judged "excellent" since college	68%	48%	*

*** Very significant difference (p < .001—a difference that would occur by chance only one time in a thousand)

** Significant difference (p < .01)—a difference that would occur by chance one time in a hundred.

* Probably significant difference (p < .05)

SOURCE: Adapted from Vaillant, 1977, p. 88.

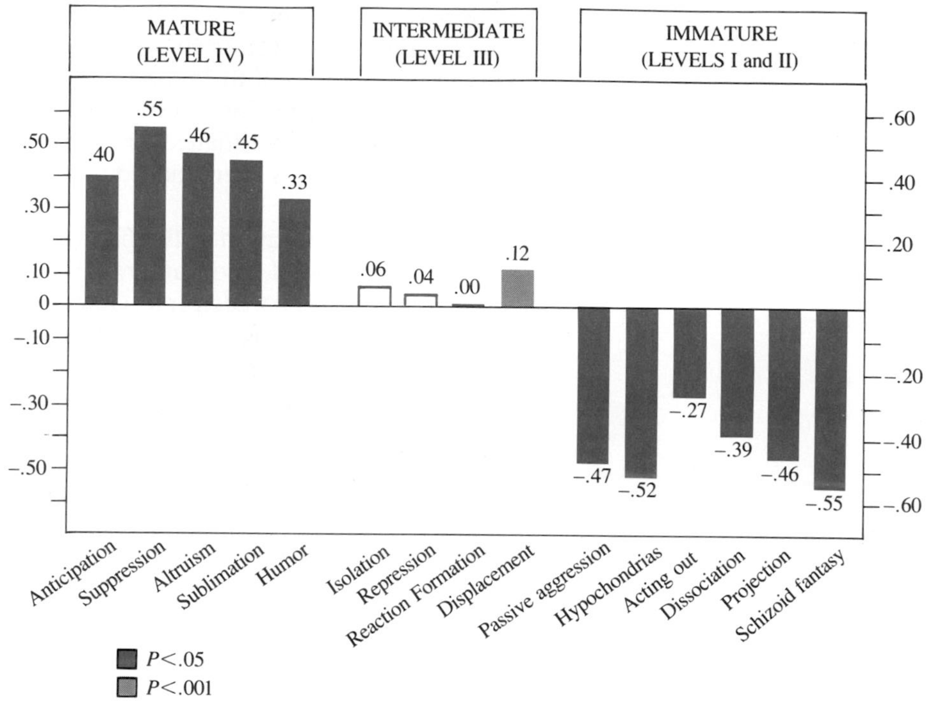

Figure 4-2
Adaptive style and personal adequacy. The bars represent correlations of adaptive styles with global measures of personal adequacy. (Source: Adapted from Vaillant, Bond, and Vaillant, 1986)

functioning was rated from the later interviews. The findings, once again, are remarkable, and are shown in Figure 4-2. Those men whose defenses can be characterized as mature functioned far better than those whose defenses were less mature.

Not only does the maturity of coping strategies affect overall psychological and social adjustment subsequently, but even *medical* adjustment is dramatically affected. People whose coping strategies were relatively immature tended later to be objectively in poorer health and to feel worse than those who coped more maturely.

THE SHAPING OF CONSCIOUS EXPERIENCE

Choice of defenses and strength of coping

Fueled by anxiety, the defenses shape conscious experience in dramatic ways. And the choice of defense, as well as its maturity, dictates the nature of subjective experience and the strength of coping. Consider the following case vignette (adapted from Vaillant, 1986):

Married at the age of thirty, Mary Walt had one miscarriage and then tried for seven years to have children. When she was thirty-eight, a cervical biopsy examination revealed an early cancer. She immediately underwent surgery to remove her uterus.

It was an awful blow. Both she and her husband had desperately wanted kids. Moreover, Mary had always felt inadequate in comparison to her younger sister, who already had four children and had been the one in the family who had won praise for being good with kids. Below are a number of possible responses that Mary could have had to this crisis, each of which illustrates the use of a different defense.

Level IV:

Altruism. A month after surgery, Mary organized a group of other women who had breast and uterine surgery to visit and counsel patients who were now undergoing such surgery. From their own experience, these women gave information, counsel, and comfort, trying to answer questions and allay the fears that such surgery always engenders.

Sublimation. Mary took great pleasure from the get-well cards she received from her sister's children. She agreed to teach a Sunday School class for preschoolers. And she had a poem published in her local newspaper on the bittersweet joys of the maiden aunt.

Humor. The *Playboy* definition of a hysterectomy—"throwing out the baby carriage, but keeping the playpen"—made her laugh so hard that tears came to her eyes and her ribs ached.

Level III:

Repression. Mary found herself unable to remember the name of the operation. In addition, she forgot her first follow-up visit to the physician. And upon returning home, she burst into tears upon breaking an inexpensive vase. She had no idea why.

Intellectualization. She read a lot about uterine cancer, and asked the physician numerous questions. She concerned herself with the details of preventing postoperative infection.

Reaction Formation. She renewed an early interest in planned parenthood, and urged younger friends to limit their families. Moreover, she remembered that she had always been afraid of the pain of childbirth, and remarked to others that she was lucky to be spared that burden.

Level II:

Projection. Following a slight postoperative infection, she wrote long and angry letters blaming the hospital for unsanitary conditions. In addition, she blamed her doctor for not doing a Pap smear earlier, threatening to institute malpractice proceedings.

Hypochondriasis. Mary worried that the cancer might have spread to her lymph nodes, and could not be reassured by careful physical examination. She belabored her visitors with accounts of tiny lumps in her neck and groin.

Passive Aggression. While inserting her IV, the medical intern missed the vein. Mary smiled, told him not to worry, and said, "When you're *just* a medical student, it must be hard to get things right." Later, unable to sleep, Mary watched her IV run dry. At 4 A.M., the night nurse had to call the intern to restart the IV. Cheerfully, she told him that she had not rung for the nurse because she knew how busy everyone in the hospital was.

Level I:

Denial. Less than twenty-four hours after surgery, Mary ordered nurses to move her upstairs to the maternity ward. She then wandered about the hospital looking for *her* baby. She experienced no postoperative pain.

Delusional Projection. Mary complained that the hospital was being run by racists who were trying to sterilize her. She attempted to phone the FBI to report the hospital for genocide. She refused pain medication, claiming it was an experimental drug for thought control.

These defenses describe the variety of ways in which people cope with trauma. People characteristically use defenses from one or two adjacent levels. No one uses all of them.

GROWTH AND EXISTENTIAL THEORIES

Recently, psychodynamically oriented theorists have sought to examine what it is that is especially human in human experience, and particularly those aspects of human experience that contribute to growth or to abnormality. These existential theorists find three issues that are particularly important: fear of dying, personal responsibility, and will.

THE FUNDAMENTAL ANXIETY: DEATH AND LIFE

Fear of dying as central human fear

Existential psychologists assert that the central human fear and the one from which most psychopathology develops is the ***fear of dying.*** Anxiety about death is most prominent in, and best recalled from childhood. Perhaps because children are vulnerable, and because their worst imaginings are barely informed by reality, their fears are stark, vivid, and memorable. For them, the idea of death does not involve mere biological process. It is terrifyingly full of awful meanings. Death means being forgotten, being left out. Death means helplessness, aloneness, finiteness. In short, the idea of death is so awful that children and adults nearly universally employ coping strategies for dealing with it.

How does one deal with the fear of nonbeing? Broadly speaking, there are two kinds of strategies: by coming to believe oneself special, and by fusion. (Yalom, 1980).

Specialness as protection from death

□ SPECIALNESS.   One way through which some people protect themselves from death fears is by cultivating in themselves the notion that they are special. It is a peculiar notion in that it holds that the laws of nature apply to all mortals except oneself. The ***notion of specialness*** manifests itself in many ways. For example, the terminally ill simply cannot believe that it is they who are dying. They understand the laws of nature fully well, but they believe themselves somehow to be exempt from them. Similarly, people who smoke heavily, overeat, or fail to exercise sufficiently may also believe that somehow they are exempt from nature's laws.

People sometimes try to protect themselves from death by cultivating a notion of specialness. Motorcycle daredevil Evel Knievel may have attempted stunts like jumping over these fourteen cars because he believed that he was exempt from the laws of nature.

People may attempt to protect themselves against nonbeing by fusing with others. These five people had plastic surgery so that they would look like famous rock stars (Jim Croce, Linda Ronstadt, Kenny Rogers, Elvis Presley, and Buddy Holly). By so doing, they merged their identities with those of their favorite stars.

The notion of specialness underlies many valued character traits. Physical courage may result from the belief that one is inviolable. So too may ambition and striving, and especially striving for power and control. But at the extreme, the unconscious belief in one's specialness may also lead to a spectrum of behavior disorders. The workaholic who compulsively strives to achieve success and power may also harbor the delusion that achieving that one kind of specialness may confer the other, immortal kind. Narcissistic people who devote enormous attention to themselves and are correspondingly insensitive to the requirements of others may believe that only that kind of self-nourishment will protect them from death and its associated anxieties.

Fusing with others as protection from death

□ FUSION.   Protection against the fear of death or nonbeing can also be achieved by fusing with others. *Fusion* is an especially useful strategy for those whose death fears take the form of loneliness. By attaching themselves to, and making themselves indistinguishable from others, they hope that their lot is cast with them. They believe that much as these others continue to live, so will they. They also develop a fear of standing apart, as they believe that if they do stand apart, they will no longer be protected from death.

The fear of standing apart has socially valuable features. Why else would we marry and have children if not to create fusions? Why else would we form clubs, communities, and organizations? Such attachments protect against loneliness, against being separated from the flow of life. At the extreme, however, fusion is responsible for much unhappiness. Children who have grown up in brutal homes may be unwilling to leave them, not because they have nowhere else to go, but because they have established a fusion with their powerful parents and are afraid to destroy it. Similarly, spouses whose marriages have long ceased providing them satisfaction often find it difficult to separate lest in their old age, they find themselves alone. One example of an individual's need for fusion in order to ward off his fears of death is as follows:

A well-trained, enormously presentable business executive had held seven positions in as many years, and he was now finding it difficult to gain employment.

Each of his employers had been impressed both by his credentials and his industriousness. He was moved gradually into positions of greater responsibility. Oddly, however, just as he had begun to inspire faith in others, he would "foul up." His errors were as costly as they were inexcusable, and they led quickly to termination from the job. In the course of treatment with an existential therapist, it was found that success had a powerfully unconscious meaning for him. He feared success, for it meant isolation, standing apart from others. For him, success was analogous to death, in that it destroyed fusion. He unconsciously felt that it was better to be indistinguishable from the mass of people than to stand alone, even successfully.

False modes of behaving

□ AUTHENTICITY AND INAUTHENTICITY. The desire for either specialness or fusion can lead to *inauthentic,* or false, modes of behavior. These ways of acting are false in that they are designed to achieve unattainable goals. Consider someone who tries to avoid the fear of nonbeing by fusing with others. He may say things to others that he hopes will please them, but that he does not really mean. For example, he may conform his opinions to theirs, bend his behaviors to suit them, do the things they do, even though his mind and body would rather believe and do something else. Gradually, he comes to lose sight of what it is he wants to do, while finding his conformity to others' opinions and behaviors only a pale pleasure. He has paid for a tenuous security against the fear of death by sacrificing his own authenticity.

The fear of death, then, promotes a host of irrational behaviors, according to existential thinkers. But that is not the only source of human irrationality. Whether one believes that one is fully responsible for one's life plays an equal role in determining human happiness or misery.

RESPONSIBILITY

Existentialists believe that we are responsible for the way we perceive the world and for the way we react to those perceptions. This includes taking responsibility for those who are close to us when they are too young or old to be able to help themselves.

The assumption of personal *responsibility* is central to existential thinking, for responsibility means authorship. It says that we are responsible for the way we perceive the world and for the way we react to those perceptions. To be responsible "is to be aware that one has created one's own self, destiny, life, predicament, feelings and, if such be the case, one's own suffering" (Yalom, 1980).

Existential psychologists generally pay careful attention to language; they are especially sensitive to the use of such words as "can't" and "it." People often say, "I just can't study" or "I can't get up in the morning," implying that the behavior is somehow removed from their control. What they really mean is, "I won't do it." They bury an act over which they have control beneath the appearance of disability. Young children who break something are inclined to say, "it broke," not "I broke it." Similarly, for adults to say that "something happened" or "it happened" is to imply that one is passively influenced by a capricious world. In short, they do not want to be held responsible. Generally, the use of the passive rather than the active voice, the avoidance of first person pronouns, as well as the attributions of the causes of current events to historical sources (i.e., my upbringing, my parents, the things I did as a child), are seen as signs of responsibility avoidance.

Responsibility avoidance is occasionally achieved by losing control. More accurately, it is achieved by *appearing* to lose control, by *seeming* to go out of one's mind, by *making it appear* that forbidden actions were taken because one was drunk or crazy. But behavior that is "out of control" is never really so. Otherwise, it could hardly be so purposive. For what is remarkable about "crazy" anger is the accuracy with which it is targeted: the blows fall, not on any random person, but precisely on the person toward whom the anger was experienced.

> Robert, age twenty-two, had just had an enormous fight with his father, and he was still furious. He went to his room and drank heavily. Inflamed, he took his bottle and went out for a drive—not in his own car, but in his father's sports car. At the end of the driveway, he turned too hard and accidentally dented the car's fender on a large oak tree.

> Sara had been married for many years to a brutal and insensitive man who, without notice, one day asked for a divorce. She went "crazy." She followed him around town, repeatedly vandalized his apartment, and created wild scenes while he was dining with friends in a restaurant. Her crazy behavior defeated him. At first, he sought police protection, then he required emergency psychiatric hospitalization. Once he was hospitalized, she suddenly "regained her sanity." (Adapted from Yalom, 1980)

Because people can see themselves as responsible for their experiences and because they can plan for the future as well as live in the present, they are capable of *will,* which is a further theme in existential psychology.

WILLING

The capacity to will is as central a feature of existential views as are freedom and responsibility. Yet, despite its centrality, will is difficult to define unambiguously. Will is used psychologically in at least two senses. First, there is will as in willpower: the will of gritted teeth, clenched jaw, and tensed muscle. This is **exhortative will.** It can be useful at times, as when we force ourselves to work when we would rather play.

A second and more significant kind of will is associated with future goals. It is called **goal-directed will.** Much as memory is the organ of the past, goal-directed will has been called "the organ of the future" (Arendt, 1978). It is quite different from exhortative will, for it develops out of hope, expec-

Goal-directed will develops out of hope, expectation, and competence. It is enabling this runner to push herself to her limits in order to win this race.

tation, and competence. Unlike exhortative will, it is not urged upon us but is rather a freely chosen arousal in the service of a future that is willingly embraced. This kind of will cannot be created: it can only be unleashed or disinhibited.

> Susan was bright enough to do well in college but nevertheless was having a struggle. It was difficult for her to get up in the morning, difficult to crack the books, and difficult to put away the temptations that deflected her from achievement. She had no sense of what she wanted to study in college and, therefore, little motivation to work in her courses. After her midyear grades were posted, she went to the counseling center to "try to get myself down to work." During several counseling sessions, she realized that although she had plenty of intelligence, she lacked confidence in her ability to do well in college and, as a result, found it difficult to commit herself to any career. She had had a difficult start in the primary grades, and those bruises had remained with her. During one significant counseling session, she realized that grade school was far behind her and that, moreover, she had achieved a good deal since those experiences. Nearly simultaneously, a long-buried desire surfaced: to be a doctor.
>
> At the next session, she reported that "her life had come together during the past week." No longer did she find it difficult to get up in the morning or to resist going to the movies. It was easy to study now, and indeed, she bounded out of bed and headed for the books effortlessly. "Now that I know what I want to do, everything else has fallen into place. I no longer have to force myself."

Disorders of will

Disorders of will are found among people who know what they should do, what they ought to do, and what they must do, but who have no notion of what they want to do. Lacking that knowledge of what they *want,* their goals seem apparently lusterless, and movement toward them is correspondingly difficult. People may fail to know what they want for three reasons. First, they may simply fear wanting. Wanting makes them vulnerable to failure and hurt, and that is especially difficult for those who wish to appear strong. Second, they may fail to know what they want because they fear rejection. They long ago learned that if their wishes departed from those of their friends or family, their wishes would infuriate and drive others away. Finally, they may fail to know what they wish because they want others, magically, to discover their silent wishes and fulfill them.

> Most graduate students complete a dissertation before receiving their doctoral degree, and the dissertation is often viewed by them as a significant hurdle in their graduate career. For some, however, that final hurdle is insurmountable. Such seemed to be the case for Cathy. She had done well until that point. Her course grades were excellent, and the research that she had completed while in graduate school had been quite interesting. But somehow she found it difficult to get down to the dissertation. In fact, she had begun three separate studies and had dropped each of them for no particular reason other than that she had lost interest. The fact of the matter was that she viewed the dissertation as a major undertaking, much bigger than anything she had undertaken before, and much beyond her abilities. Her fear of being criticized by her teachers or, worse, of failing her oral examination prevented her from finding a study that she really wanted to do.

For existential psychologists, then, goal-directed willing is more than just forcing oneself to do something (exhortative will). Rather, it is going through the pain and risk of finding what one really wants and then doing it.

PSYCHODYNAMIC TREATMENT

Modes of treatment generated by theory

Freud's own views and those of his disciples and descendants find expression in the modes of treatment that they have generated. Here, theory and practice come together. For it was from the clinic that Freud's most interesting ideas developed. We therefore turn to psychodynamic treatment in order to examine those views in practice. Much as psychoanalytic theory spawned a variety of psychodynamic theories, so did psychoanalysis, as a mode of treatment, give birth to numerous and varied treatment modes. Among these are a variety of brief psychoanalytically "inspired" treatments that alter classical treatment in a variety of important ways; existential therapies that focus on the meaning of thoughts and actions; psychodynamic family and couple therapies that focus on ameliorating the problems that arise among people who are significant to each other. We take up these forms of treatment in greater detail later in the book.

BRIEF PSYCHOTHERAPY

Altering thought and behavior

Brief psychoanalytically inspired treatments have much in common with classical psychoanalysis. Both seek to alter thought and behavior. Both do so by examining early conflicts in the context of present relationships, and by making conscious that which is repressed. Both examine free associations, dreams, and resistances. In so doing, psychic energy is freed for more constructive purposes, and the individual is able to find more constructive resolutions for conflict. Anxiety is reduced because impulses now find "safe" methods of expression. And coping strategies, where they are required, are now more mature. These matters become much clearer when we examine an actual case of psychodynamic psychotherapy.

An example of
brief
psychotherapy

It had been more than two years since Patty had had a moment's peace. Her problems were in her head, quite literally. There, continually pounding headaches kept her in bed all day every day, unable to sleep, unable to rise, clawing at the sheets.

The headaches themselves were not unusual. What was unusual was the simultaneous presence of three of them, and their intensity. One was a drilling headache. "It's as if someone were drilling from the top of my head to the center of my brain." The second pulsed at the back of her head and felt as if someone were ripping the two lobes of her brain apart. And the third was a fairly common headache, one that felt as if there were a steel band around her head which was getting tighter and tighter.

Patty had sought help for these headaches for well over a year. She had had several medical and neurological work-ups. She had seen two allergists in the hope that they could find whether something she was ingesting was harmful to her. "In the hope . . ." is the appropriate phrase here, for, after searching for so long, anything that remotely promised an answer, however difficult, was more comforting than the perpetual pain.

She finally requested neurosurgery in the hope that the severing of nerve endings would alleviate the pain. Informed that nothing could be done surgically, she became exceedingly depressed. The situation by now seemed entirely hopeless to her. A burden to her husband, useless to her young children, there seemed little to do but end it all. It was then that she was referred for psychodynamic therapy.

The early part of her first meeting was spent describing the problem. With great pain, she described her headaches but quickly ran out of things to say. She didn't think that the problem was psychological, nor that anyone in their right mind would feel as she did under the circumstances. There being nothing more to say, she turned to the therapist and asked "What should I talk about now?"

Psychodynamically oriented psychotherapists seek to understand the present by relating it to the past. Having acquired as full an account of the patient's current status as possible, they enquire about the past. Therefore, in response to Patty's question, the therapist said, "Tell me about your childhood."

She began slowly and then with growing animation to describe her father. (Indeed, during the remainder of that very long interview, Patty alluded to her mother only in passing.) Her father had come originally from a stretch of land that borders Greece and Turkey. He was a man of violent passions and frustrations, a man who had once angrily left his family for four years, only to return as suddenly as he had gone. In her earliest memory of him, he threatened to take a train to a far off place, never to return.

He was, in her description, a drunk, a womanizer, an erratic supporter of the family, a man who often beat her mother. Despite this, Patty retained a hidden fount of fondness for him, one that was particularly evident (so it seemed to her therapist) in her description of the times he used to take her with him to the neighborhood saloon. He would put her up on the bar, and she would dance while everyone else clapped. It was a particularly warm memory in an otherwise distressing relationship.

"Did you ever go to bed with your father?" The question came suddenly, without warning.* Patty paled. "How did you know?" she asked. And then, not waiting for the answer, she burst into tears.

"Yes, it was him. And I still hate him. He's an old man now. And I still hate him. On Sunday morning, my mother would clean the house. All of us, except my mother, slept late on Sunday. When she cleaned my room, I went into her bed. I

---

* Such questions are not usually asked so directly or so early in psychodynamic treatment. In this case, however, Patty's depression seemed so overwhelming that the therapist felt he had to quicken the therapeutic pace.

would get under the covers, close my eyes, and go back to sleep. My father was there. He would touch me . . . rub . . . the rat. How could he do that to his own daughter?"

In anger, in sadness, and in shame, she cried as she tore furiously into incidents that had occurred more than a quarter century ago, when she was eight years old.

Suddenly, she stopped crying, even talking. Then smiling in disbelief, she said "They're gone. The headaches are gone." She rose slowly and walked around the office, moving her head from side to side. For the first time in more than two years, she felt normal.

Before the session was over, those headaches would return again. But regardless, a connection had been made between her present suffering and her early memories of her father.

During subsequent sessions, Patty was able to retrieve from memory more experiences with her father. Her father, it appeared, had had another family, which he had left behind in Greece when he came to America and married her mother. Patty felt it was her responsibility to keep him in America by making him so happy that he would not want to return. The fear of abandonment ran deep in both Patty and her mother.

She could not recall what her father had done to her in bed, but she knew that it was bad and that even *he* must have thought so. Once, after an outing with a group of friends, her father spotted her on a subway platform. He pulled her roughly aside from her schoolmates, slapped her hard across the face, and called her "Whore."

Those recaptured events—relived, remembered, re-experienced during therapy—brought relief over longer and longer periods. But certain experiences and even thoughts brought on headaches suddenly and fiercely, as when:

- she was shopping for a brassiere;
- Phil, her husband, was bouncing their young daughters on his lap, and the three of them were laughing;
- friends suggested that they go to a movie;
- she had gone with the family to a Greek wedding celebration, and all the young people were dancing; and
- she was washing the children's laundry.

All of these scenes vaguely connoted sexuality and therefore brought pain. Talking about them was difficult. There was a tension between exploring the psychodynamics of her situation and risking disturbing a trouble-free day. But she pushed on, pursuing her mental and emotional associations to early experiences and memories, not only about father and mother, but also about husband, children, friends, and later even about the therapist.

Severe sexual conflicts

To a psychodynamic therapist, this search into Patty's past suggested that her headaches resulted from severe sexual conflicts that appeared to arise during the phallic stage. These conflicts paralyzed her, rendering her unable to even initiate caretaking activities on behalf of her husband, children, and increasingly, even herself.

The three headaches were themselves testimony to the power of the conflicts as well as the coping strategies. Those headaches—the drilling one, the one that felt as if the lobes of her brain were being torn apart, and the steel band that somehow refused to yield—symbolically suggested a conflict about rape. But since the conflict was going on in Patty's own mind, it suggested, too, a conflict about her *own* sexual desires. By some process which is not yet understood, these conflicting desires were repressed and displaced, not outward to other people, but upward to her head.

Patty clearly projected much of this conflict onto her husband and even her children. Their horseplay was seen, not as an innocent rumpus, but as a highly sexualized event. Shopping for underclothes, weddings, Greek dancing, and the weekly laundry were all similarly sexualized. Ego processes that normally differentiate these events and allow people to share social perceptions of them were clearly defective here. The defects, psychodynamic therapists hold, arose because of the intense and poorly contained pressure that was generated from Patty's own sexual conflicts.

Catharsis

It was ***catharsis,*** the uncovering and reliving of early traumatic conflicts, that mainly enabled Patty to rapidly remit her symptoms. But in psychodynamic theory, symptom remission is only part of the treatment, often the smallest part. Much more significant is the fact that enduring patterns of perceiving and reacting in adults are laid down in childhood and pervade all adult activities. They need to be altered because they are transferred from the people and impulses that originally stimulated the conflict to other significant people in one's life. Psychodynamic therapy seeks, therefore, not merely to relieve symptoms, but to alter personality—the very attitudes, perceptions, and behaviors that were misshaped by early experience.

Transference

How does psychodynamic treatment achieve personality changes? In practice, psychodynamic therapists must be nonreactive. They must listen calmly and intensely, but they must not be shocked by the clients' revelations, nor should they commonly offer opinions or judgments. They should act as blank screens, onto which clients can project their own expectations, imaginings, and attributions. Over time, therapists themselves become central in the lives of their clients. This centrality is of such therapeutic importance that it is given a technical name in psychodynamic theory: ***transference.*** Transference describes the fact that during psychodynamic therapy, clients come to transfer emotions, conflicts, and expectations from the diverse sources from which they were acquired, onto their therapists. Therapists become mother, father, son, daughter, spouse, lover, and even

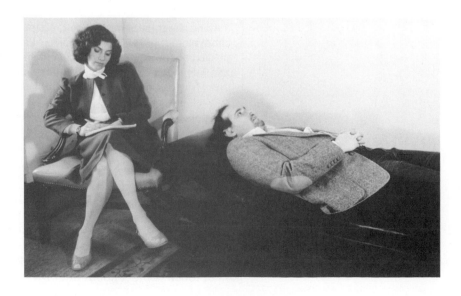

In psychodynamic therapy, clients are encouraged to free associate to emotionally charged ideas while the therapist listens without offering opinions or judgments.

employer or stranger, to their clients. In this emotional climate, clients are encouraged to speak frankly, to let their minds ramble, to freely associate to emotionally charged ideas, even if the resulting ideas seem silly, embarrassing, or meaningless. Under these conditions, what was formerly repressed and distorted becomes available to consciousness and therefore more controllable by ego processes, as can be seen from further examination of Patty's case.

In less than three months, Patty's symptoms had abated. Her attention turned away from her headaches to other matters. Her mother, for example, was a "pain." She had always been melancholy and merely obedient, surely no fun to live with. Patty quickly related the impression that "she was no fun to live with" to her own relationship with her father. He had already abandoned a family in Greece. Had she been trying to keep him in the family? Might he not abandon them? More important, could her own sexual involvement with her father have been little more than an attempt to keep him at home? That possibility cast her memories in a much more positive light, relieving her of the guilt that the memories evoked. Shortly thereafter, she could observe her husband and children playing together, without suffering from headaches and guilt.

Gradually, attention turned from her parents, even from her husband and children, to the therapist himself. His lack of reacting now provoked discomfort; his occasional lateness caused her to feel anxiety; and when her therapist took a week-long vacation, she experienced dread. In turn, these feelings led to long, blocked silences during the therapy sessions. What thoughts lay behind these silences? It was difficult for her to say, and nearly impossible for her to free associate. But finally, she was able to allude to the embarrassing sexual fantasies that attended these events, fantasies now about the therapist himself. This was transference, for it shortly became clear that she interpreted his silences, lateness, and absences as abandonment, and she was unconsciously motivated to do what she had wanted to do in the past to retain the affections of significant others. She was, of course, initially unaware of the unconscious connection between abandonment and sexuality, and she was therefore deeply embarrassed by the thoughts that assailed her. Once she understood the reasons for those thoughts, however, she was able to see her relationship to the therapist in more objective terms, to recognize that an occasional lateness or absence is not the same as abandonment, and to find less self-demeaning and guilt-provoking ways to express her affections.

At about this time, and seemingly for no good reason, Patty began to explore an entirely new matter: what to do with her life. Upon graduating high school, she had considered going to college, but had given up that idea as "simply ridiculous." She had also been attracted to dance, but had not acted on that interest either. Now both ideas returned, as well as the desire to take a job again, and she began to explore those ideas with great enthusiasm. In Freud's view, energies that had once been bound up in repression and other defensive maneuvers, were now freed for other activities. Erik Erikson would point out that having resolved many of the guilts that were associated with sexuality, she was now free to take initiatives on her own behalf, to do something with her life.

Ultimately, over a period of a year, many of Patty's conflicts were resolved. She no longer felt that she had to be different from her mother, more sexual, more "fun to live with." Nor did she continue to feel that sexual behaviors were the only ones that would make her attractive and enable her to retain prized relationships. One result of these explorations was that her personal identity underwent considerable change. She had been an ineffectual, guilt-ridden person, dominated by forbidden impulses. She became an actively initiating and exploring person who trusted much more in others and took her own worth increasingly for granted.

Her stronger and more mature identity resulted from the greater understanding she had of herself and the greater control over impulses that this understanding brought. And it had one further result. The more Patty probed, the less clear it became that she had actually had a sexual relationship with her father. Eventually, that "memory" came to be seen as a false one, reflecting her own desire to retain his affections, rather than his actual behavior. In this, Patty repeated the experience of many of Freud's clients, for the mind, Freud observed, is a powerfully inventive place in which even "memories" can arise from desires, conflicts, and defenses.

CLIENT-CENTERED THERAPY

Assumptions of client-centered therapy

Client-centered therapy rests on two fundamental assumptions (Rogers, 1951, 1961, 1977). The first is that therapy proceeds best when the client experiences the therapist's ***unconditional positive regard.*** That regard arises from the therapist's belief that people are fundamentally good even when they are doing "bad" things. Indeed, they do "bad" things precisely because they have not experienced such unconditional respect. Thus, clients who are rude, boorish, liars, thieves, and brutes are both entitled to and needy of such unconditional regard. Without it, all people simply become defensive and when they are defensive, the process of change is retarded.

The second hallmark of client-centered therapy resides in the therapist's attempt to achieve ***empathy*** with the client, to see the world as he or she does. Client-centered therapists listen carefully to what the client says and then reflect or mirror their understanding back to the client. This procedure enables clients to clarify and properly label their own experiences, and eventually to accept them.

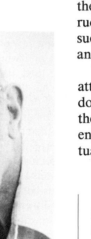

Carl Rogers (1902–   ) developed client-centered therapy, which emphasizes unconditional positive regard and therapist empathy.

CLIENT: Well, I made a very remarkable discovery. I know it's—*(laughs)* I found out that you actually *care* how this thing goes. *(Both laugh.)* It gave me the feeling, it's sort of well—"maybe I'll let you get in the act," sort of thing. It's—again you see, on an examination sheet, I would have had the correct answer. I mean—but it suddenly dawned on me that in the—client-counselor kind of thing, you *actually care* what happens to this thing. And it was a revelation, a—not that . . . That doesn't describe it. It was a—well, the closest I can come to it is a kind of relaxation, a—not letting down, but a *(pause)* more of a straightening out without tension if that means anything. I don't know.
THERAPIST: Sounds as though it isn't as though this was a new idea, but it was a new *experience* of really *feeling* that I did care and if I get the rest of that, sort of willingness on your part to let me care.
CLIENT: Yes.

Because the client feels accepted and because he or she senses that the therapist is trying to understand, the client feels free to examine the host of feelings that lie just beneath surface behavior and that have been suppressed. That emphasis on feeling is one of the significant features of this therapy.

CLIENT: You know over in this area of, of sexual disturbance, I have a feeling that I'm beginning to discover that it's pretty bad, pretty bad. I'm finding out that, that I'm bitter, really. Damn bitter. I—and I'm not turning it back in, into myself. . . I think what I probably feel is a certain element of "I've been cheated." *(Her voice is very tight and her throat chokes up.)* And I've covered up very nicely, to the point of consciously not caring. But I'm, I'm sort of amazed to find that in this practice of, what shall I call it, a kind of sublimation that right under it—again words—there's a, a kind of passive force that's, it's pas—it's very passive, but at the same time it's just kind of *murderous.*

THERAPIST: So there's the feeling, "I've really been cheated. I've covered that up and seem not to care and yet underneath that there's a kind of a, a latent but very much present *bitterness* that is very, very strong."

CLIENT: It's very strong. I—that I know. It's terribly powerful.

THERAPIST: Almost a dominating kind of force.

CLIENT: Of which I am rarely conscious. Almost never. . . . Well, the only way I can describe it, it's a kind of murderous thing, but without violence. . . . It's more like a feeling of wanting to get even. . . . And of course, I won't pay back, but I'd like to. I really would like to.

In the above excerpt, the feelings of bitterness and the desire for revenge begin to surface as a result of the therapist's patient understanding and reflection. Client-centered techniques, however, are not the only ones available for reaching a patient's feelings. Gestalt therapists, to which we now turn, utilize a different approach to the same issue.

GESTALT THERAPY

Acting out
conflicts

Trained in Europe as a physician and psychoanalyst, Frederick (Fritz) Perls (1893–1970) repudiated large portions of psychoanalytic theory, while using some other aspects of that theory as part of his Gestalt therapy (1970). Gestalt therapists have little interest in the past except as it impacts on the immediate present. When it does, then Gestalt therapists seize upon it, open it up, and make it extraordinarily vivid. If, for example, a young woman is still rankling over the way her mother treated her when she was eight, then a Gestalt therapist will take the mother's role and ask the client to act out the conflict. In this way, the vivid experience of those times will be re-experienced and confronted, perhaps even resolved. Gestalt clients are urged to re-experience these emotions as vividly and as violently as is necessary. They are encouraged to swear, kick, and scream, all in the service of teaching people that they can know, control, and be responsible for their feelings, rather than allowing their feelings to control them.

One of the techniques that Perls carried over from psychoanalysis to Gestalt therapy was dream analysis. But rather than have the therapist and client merely interpret dreams, Perls encouraged them to act out the dreams, as the following excerpt indicates:

Frederick (Fritz) Perls (1893–1970) developed Gestalt therapy.

In a large group therapy session, Jane has just described a dream in which she has returned to her parents' home. She opens the door to the large house, but the house is dark. She calls out to her mother and father, but there is no answer, and so she goes from room to room looking for them. Finally, "I get into the bedroom and my mother and father are in bed but they're, they're just, they're not my m— they're skeletons. They don't have any skin. They're not, they don't talk . . . they don't say anything. And I shake—This dream happens over and over and lately I've gotten brave enough to shake them." At one point during the analysis of this dream, Perls asked Jane to "resurrect" the skeletons, and to talk to them.

PERLS: Talk to them.

JANE: Wake up! (Perls: Again.)

JANE *(loudly):* Wake up! (Perls: Again.)
JANE *(loudly): Wake up!* (Perls: Again.)
JANE *(loudly):* Wake up! *(loudly, almost crying)* You can't hear me! Why can't you hear me? . . . *(sighs)* And they don't answer. They don't say anything.

The analysis of the dream continues, and Perls tells Jane to talk to her parents again.

PERLS: Tell them that you still need them.
JANE: I still need you.
PERLS: Tell them in more detail what you need.
JANE: I still need my mother to hold me.
PERLS: Tell this to her.
JANE: I still need you to hold me. *(crying)* I want to be a little girl, sometimes— forget the "sometimes."
PERLS: You're not talking to her yet.
JANE *(sobbing):* O.K. Mother, you think I'm very grown up. . . . And I think I'm very grown up. But there's a part of me that isn't away from you and I can't, I can't let go of.

Confronting feelings is the first step in accepting and taking responsibility for them. It is, moreover, a way of understanding how the emotional experiences of the past directly affect the present, the here and now.

LOGOTHERAPY

Endowing life with meaning

Learning about one's feelings and especially about personal values—the meaning that life has—is a central feature of existential therapies. Viktor Frankl (1905–   ), a leading existential analyst, was imprisoned in Nazi concentration camps during World War II. Even under those conditions of unbearable suffering, however, Frankl found that life can be made meaningful. For example, he found meaning by helping others rather than concentrating merely on self-preservation and his own personal suffering. Though physically imprisoned under harsh circumstances, he believed that people were still free to give meaning to their lives.

Logotherapists (and their existential counterparts) use a variety of techniques to communicate that individuals are free to control their lives and to endow them with meaning. Two techniques especially should be noted here. The first is ***dereflection,*** which involves turning clients' attention from their symptoms and pointing out how much they could be doing, becoming, and enjoying if they were not so preoccupied with themselves. The second is termed ***paradoxical intention,*** which encourages clients to indulge and even exaggerate their symptoms. Clients who claim that they cannot control their desires for, say, ice cream, are encouraged to eat it by the gallon, while those who need to wash their hands twenty times a day are told to double or triple their ablutions. In that way, clients quickly learn that they have considerable control over their symptoms and not vice versa. Moreover, they can then consider whether the values that are represented by, say, self-indulgence or excessive cleanliness are values that they would freely choose for themselves.

Viktor Frankl (1905–   ) uses techniques of dereflection and paradoxical intention to communicate that individuals are free to control their lives and to endow them with meaning.

EVALUATING PSYCHODYNAMIC THEORY

STRENGTHS OF PSYCHODYNAMIC THEORIES

Comprehensive description of human personality

Psychodynamic theory is nothing less than a comprehensive description of human personality. This theory describes personality's development, the way personality functions, and every aspect of human thought, emotion, experience, and judgment—from dreams through slips of the tongue to normal and abnormal behavior.

Because of this, Freud is considered, along with Marx and Darwin, one of the great geniuses of the century. Perhaps the most important of his ideas is the view that the psychological processes that underlie normal and abnormal behaviors are fundamentally the same. Neither conflict, nor anxiety, nor defense, nor unconscious processes are the sole property of abnormal people. Rather, the *outcome* of conflict and the *nature* of defense will determine whether behavior will be normal or abnormal.

A method of investigation

In addition, Freud developed a method for investigating psychodynamic processes and treating psychological distress. This was important for several reasons. First, his methods of investigation shed light on abnormal processes and thus demystified them. By accounting for why they behaved as they did, Freud "rehumanized" the distressed, making their suffering more comprehensible to the rest of humankind. Second, by providing a method of treatment, Freud encouraged an optimism regarding psychological distress that had been sorely lacking before him. Finally, while Freudian psychoanalysis must be distinguished sharply from modern psychodynamic therapies, the former was the progenitor of the modern efforts, and the modern therapies have been found to be quite effective (Smith, Glass, and Miller, 1980).

SHORTCOMINGS OF PSYCHODYNAMIC THEORIES

Any theory that aspires to be as comprehensive as psychodynamic theory inevitably has faults, and Freud's theories and those of his successors have been no exception. We have already seen that not long after they were first enunciated, Freud's theories were attacked for several broad reasons (Gay, 1988). Over time, these deficiencies were remedied. But there are further

Further criticisms

criticisms of psychodynamic theory and therapy that have been more difficult to remedy: (1) the theory is simply too difficult to prove or disprove; (2) when studies have been conducted, psychodynamic theories have often failed to be supported; and (3) in emphasizing the role of the person, these theories neglect the situation. We will examine each of these criticisms in this section.

DIFFICULTIES OF PROOF

Overdetermined behaviors

Psychodynamic theories are difficult to support or disprove. Some of the difficulty arises because they take complex views of personality and behavior. Many behaviors are held to be **overdetermined,** that is, determined by more than one force and with more than the required psychic energy. Altering a particular psychological force—for example, by recovering a crucial early memory—may have no visible effect on a particular trait or behavior because the latter are supported and sustained by many interrelated psychological forces.

Nevertheless, problems of proof are serious. Only rarely is it possible to confirm, for example, that a particular unconscious motive is really operating. Precisely because the motive is unconscious, it is invisible to the client and only *inferred* by the therapist. Even in Patty's case, where seeming confirmation was obtained because the headaches gradually disappeared, can we be sure that these changes were due to her increasing awareness of sexual motives and fears of abandonment? Might not the cure have arisen, with equal plausibility, from the fact that she had finally found someone whom she trusted and in whom she could confide?

LACK OF SCIENTIFIC EVIDENCE

Failure to confirm theories

Psychodynamic theories have been subjected to a variety of ingenious studies, many of which have failed to confirm the theories. Consider the Oedipus conflict, for example. The notion that boys desire to replace their fathers as their mothers' lovers has failed to find support in a variety of studies (Fisher and Greenberg, 1977). Similarly, the universality of castration anxiety remains to be demonstrated. Moreover, the idea that females, because they lack a penis, feel inferior to males has not been demonstrated either. Also, studies have not been able to prove Freud's notion that unresolved conflicts that occur during the oral stage of development are responsible for adult dependency. In short, many aspects of psychodynamic theories have yet to accrue sufficient scientific support to merit belief.

PERSON VERSUS SITUATION

Underestimating the role of situation and context

Psychodynamic theories overwhelmingly emphasize the impact of traits and dispositions, those stable constellations of attitude and experience that are held to influence behavior. But what of situations? Because psychodynamic theories are derived mainly from information conveyed by clients during treatment, and because clients are encouraged to talk about their own reactions rather than the situation in which they find themselves, psychodynamic theory underestimates the role of situation and context. For example, it is much easier to infer that a person's continuing irritation with his employer results from unconscious and unresolved conflicts about authority when the employer's behavior has not been observed directly than when it has been. Similarly, it is easier to construe marriage conflicts in terms of the traits of the spouse who has sought consultation precisely because one has no first-hand experience with that spouse's marital situation.

Freud's disciples, as well as modern psychodynamic theorists, have built on Freud's foundation. Many of his teachings have been found to be universally true. At the least, psychodynamic theory accords with everyday notions of personality. Most people believe, for example, that there is such a thing as the self, and they reflect that belief in their ordinary language when they say such things as "myself," "yourself," and "ourselves." They behave as if they and others are responsible, as if they are free to do what they will, as if their lives have meaning. Our laws reflect what each of us believes: that people act freely, for better or for worse, and that they are accountable for their actions. Rightly or wrongly, the modern psychodynamic perspective reflects a good deal of common sense.

SUMMARY

1. Psychodynamic theories are centrally concerned with conflict, anxiety, and defense. *Conflict* arises when desires cannot find immediate gratification because such gratification is not permitted by reality or conscience. Conflict generates *anxiety,* a form of psychic pain that arises when individuals feel they cannot cope. Anxiety can be either conscious or unconscious and gives rise to *defense mechanisms,* which are the mind's flexible editing mechanisms that allow individuals to alter or entirely obliterate painful stimuli that arise from either desire or reality.

2. From birth to maturity, people move through five psychosexual stages, in which the use of *psychic energy* changes. The first is the *oral stage,* during which sensual pleasure is located around the mouth. Subsequently, they move through the *anal stage,* when pleasure is focused on the anus, and then the *phallic stage,* when pleasure is centered on the genitals. The *latency period* follows, during which time sexual instincts lie dormant. Individuals then emerge into the final stage of development, the *genital stage,* which marks the beginning of adult sexual functioning.

3. Adult sexual adjustment necessitates the child's resolution of the *Oedipal conflict.* Children desire to do away with the parent of the same sex and to take possession of the opposite-sex parent. *Castration anxiety* terminates the incestuous desire in boys. *Penis envy* is experienced by girls, who must also overcome their desire for the opposite-sex parent. *Identification* with the same-sex parent enables the child to resolve the Oedipus conflict.

4. Freud divided the personality into three kinds of processes: id, ego, and superego. The *id* is concerned with sexual and aggressive desires and is dominated by the *pleasure principle.* The *ego* is concerned with the individual's safety, allows desire to be expressed only when aversive consequences from other sources are minimal, and is dominated by the *reality principle.* The *superego* consists of the individual's conscience and ideals, and regardless of what reality permits, it either forbids individuals from expressing desires, or urges them toward the achievement of higher goals.

5. Freud proposed three levels of consciousness: perceptual consciousness, the pre-conscious, and the unconscious. The large mass of memory, experience, and impulse lies in the unconscious, which includes forgotten memories and repressed memories. Repressed memories live on because they are not subject to rational control; they are the dominant forces in personality.

6. There are three kinds of anxiety: realistic anxiety, neurotic anxiety, and moral anxiety. To relieve anxiety, individuals use such coping strategies as repression, projection, reaction formation, displacement, identification, denial, isolation, intellectualization, rationalization, and sublimation. Psychodynamic theorists believe that there is a maturational hierarchy of coping strategies and classify the strategies into four levels of maturity. Those that do less violence to reality are considered to be more mature strategies.

7.   Jung asserted that the unconscious is not merely a concealed store-house of sexual and aggressive desires, but that it contains a rich variety of attributes. Among these are the *collective unconscious,* which contains the memory traces of the experiences of past generations in the form of *archetypes,* or universal ideas.

8.   Adler, Horney, Sullivan, Erikson, and Fromm stressed the impact of *social* relationships on psychological development, as well as the central role of ego processes in personality. According to these later theorists, ego processes have energies of their own which generate goals that are neither sexual nor aggressive.

9.   Modern psychodynamic theorists stress the importance of the *self* as the repository of values and the source of continuity across time and place. There are at least three significant aspects of self: the physical self, the subjective self, and the objective self. Selfobjects are aspects of the environment—people and things—that are especially important for maintaining the self.

10.   Existentialists believe that the fundamental anxiety is *fear of death.* Psychologically, death means nonbeing. Because the fear of death is so threatening, people attempt to endow themselves with immortality by becoming *special* or by *fusion* with others, which may lead to *inauthentic,* or false, modes of behavior.

11.   Existential theorists hold that we are the authors of our experience. We determine what we perceive and what we experience; we are *responsible* for how we behave. Freedom and responsibility, however, may create anxiety. Responsibility avoidance is occasionally achieved through denying ownership of behavior and thought. In extreme form, that denial appears as "craziness" or drunkenness, which are purposeful behaviors designed to make it seem that we are not responsible.

12.   Existentialists often posit two kinds of will: *exhortative will* forces us to do what we know we should do, and *goal-directed will* is unleashed when we have freely chosen our goals and want to pursue and achieve them.

13.   Psychodynamic therapies seek to make conscious that which is unconscious through encouraging the client to *free associate* and to examine dreams, resistances, and the *transference* that occurs between the client and therapist. Psychodynamic treatment aims to enable the client to reduce the amount of psychic energy that is invested in defensive maneuvers, and to achieve greater control over impulse expression.

14.   *Client-centered therapy* stresses the role of *unconditional positive regard* and therapist empathy and warmth in enabling people to overcome their defensiveness and to begin to clarify and accept their own experiences.

15.   *Gestalt therapy* stresses conscious experience and feelings, dealing with the past only insofar as it has implications for the present. Gestalt therapists are particularly concerned to re-evoke and resolve conflictual feelings. Patients are encouraged to act out feelings, roles, dreams, and events.

16.   *Logotherapists* stress the meanings that symptoms have for an individual's life, as well as the individual's freedom to alter those meanings. They use two techniques to do this: *dereflection* and *paradoxical intention.*

17.   Psychodynamic theories have demystified psychological processes and have offered the possibility of overcoming psychological distress. But critics cite difficulties of proof, their indifference to the scientific method and scientific proof, and their disregard of the situation.

The Environmentalist Model: Behavioral and Cognitive Approaches

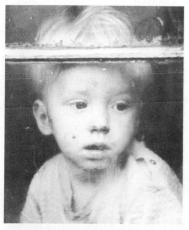

The child's development is affected by the environment. If that environment changes, the whole course of the child's life may be changed. When applied to social sciences, behaviorism claims that crime, prejudice, and stupidity can be overcome respectively by spreading wealth, learning, and environmental enrichment.

Is schizophrenia the result of conflicts over mother, or is it an inherited malady? Are phobias learned, or are they merely innate fears rekindled by environmental trauma? Is mental retardation acquired, or is it inherited from one's parents? Questions of this type bring to the forefront one of the major debates in psychology: the nature-nurture issue. Is our behavior determined by heredity or by our environment? The environmentalist model takes a clear stand on these issues. It asserts that mental life and mental illness are a product of environmental learning and can be changed by changing the environment. This model includes both behavioral and cognitive theory. After discussing the common roots of these two arms of the environmentalist model, we will discuss behavior therapy in the first half of this chapter, and then cognitive therapy.

HISTORY AND ASSUMPTIONS OF THE ENVIRONMENTALIST MODEL

EMPIRICISM AND ASSOCIATIONS

The seventeenth-century French philosopher, René Descartes (1596–1650), founded a movement called rationalism. Its adherents believed that many of the basic ideas that human beings hold—the ideas of self, of God, of space, of time, of causality—are inborn. This was called the *doctrine of innate ideas.* In contrast, the British empiricists believed that all knowledge comes from the senses, that all that we know and all that we are result from our experiences. John Locke (1632–1704), one of the founders of empiric-

Knowledge from experience and associations

ism claimed that at birth the mind of the child is a *tabula rasa,* a blank slate, on which experience "writes." A child's development is determined by what gets "written." If a certain child had had a wholly different set of experiences, he would be a wholly different person. But how does this child learn about the world? The empiricists answer "through associations." Associations between ideas are the mental glue holding the future to the present. David Hume (1711–1776), the most influential of the empiricists, claimed that the connections we make between ideas reduce to two simple principles: resemblance and contiguity. Through **resemblance,** the idea of a portrait of any individual makes us think of the real individual. Through the principle of **contiguity,** or conjunction in time or place, imagining one part of a face will call up images of the rest of the face. For Hume, causality reduces to contiguity: we believe that A causes B, when each A is followed by a B. Since all knowledge consists only of ideas derived from the senses, and associations between ideas come only from our experience, it follows that we are creations of our environment, of our past. It was out of this empiricist tradition that behaviorism grew. And out of behaviorism that both behavior therapy and then cognitive therapy grew.

BEHAVIORISM

First assumption: environmentalism

A single movement—**behaviorism**—dominated academic psychology in the United States and Soviet Russia for almost fifty years, roughly from 1920 until the mid-1960s. Behaviorism is an ambitious effort to discover in the laboratory the general laws of human and animal learning and to apply these laws to the classroom, the workplace, the penitentiary, and to society as a whole. Thus, behaviorism is not only a model for the study of abnormal behavior, it is a world view. Its first assumption is **environmentalism,** which states that all organisms, including humans, are shaped by the environment. We learn about the future through the associations of the past. This is why our behavior is subject to rewards and punishments. If our employers paid us twice as much per hour for working one Saturday, we would be more likely to work on future Saturdays. If a child were denied T.V. for not eating her vegetables, her plate would be cleaned more often in the future.

Second assumption: experimentalism

The second assumption of behaviorism is **experimentalism,** which states that through an experiment, we can find out what aspect of the environment caused our behavior and how we can change it. What causes us to work on Saturdays? If the crucial element is withheld, the present characteristic will disappear. If the crucial element is reinstated, the characteristic will reappear. Remove double-time pay, and work on Saturday will stop. Reinstate double-time pay, and work on Saturday will resume. This is the heart of the experimental method. From the experimental method, we can determine what causes people, in general, to forget, to be anxious, to fight, and we can then apply these general laws to individual cases. This is in contrast to the clinical method, which pervades the psychodynamic model. For this model, the individual case must first be understood, and general laws then extrapolated. For the environmentalist it is the other way around.

Third assumption: optimism

The third assumption of behaviorism is **optimism** concerning change. If an individual is a product of the environment and if those parts of the environment that have molded him can be known by experimentation, he will be changed when the environment is changed. When applied to social problems, behaviorism claims that crime is caused by poverty and other environmental circumstances and that it can be overcome by spreading wealth, that prejudice is caused by ignorance and can be overcome by learning, that stupidity is caused by deprivation and can be overcome by environmental enrichment, and so on.

These first three assumptions of behaviorism apply directly to abnormal psychology. First, abnormal as well as normal behavior is learned from past experiences. Psychopathology consists of acquired habits that are maladaptive. Second, we can find out by experiment what aspects of the environment cause abnormal behavior. Third, if we change these aspects of the environment the individual will unlearn his old, maladaptive habits and will learn new, adaptive habits.

Fourth
assumption:
anti-mentalism

There is also a fourth assumption of behaviorism: anti-mentalism, which is a view that mental events, feelings, and thoughts are not valid objects of scientific inquiry. While the environmentalism, experimentation, and optimism of behaviorism can all be traced directly to British empiricism, the disdain for mental events is behaviorism's very own. The empiricists were thoroughgoing mentalists; they believed that the building blocks of knowledge were mental ideas subject to introspection. (In fact, cognitive psychology, which we will discuss in the latter part of this chapter as the other pillar of the environmentalist model, is a science of mental events directly traceable to the empiricists.) The behaviorists, however, led in the 1920s by John B. Watson, reacted against the idea that an objective science could be built on an analysis of consciousness carried out by introspection. Consciousness, Watson argued, is not a material object, and the objects of science must be material. He believed that mental events do not cause behavior, and he further argued that introspection was not an objective method. Thoughts and feelings are essentially private and unverifiable. In contrast, behavior is material, and the study of behavior must be public and verifiable.

Behaviorism was founded on these four premises and it reigned supreme in academic psychology for fifty years. We now turn to the principles of behavioral psychology and to behavior therapy.

BEHAVIORAL PSYCHOLOGY: PRINCIPLES AND THERAPIES

How do we learn and what is it we learn? For the behavioral psychologist, two basic learning processes exist, and it is from these two that all behaviors, both normal and abnormal, derive. We can learn what goes with what through *Pavlovian* or *classical conditioning.* And we can learn what to do to obtain what we want and rid ourselves of what we do not want through *instrumental* or *operant conditioning.*

PAVLOVIAN CONDITIONING

Just after the turn of the century, the Russian physiologist, Ivan Pavlov (1849–1936) began work on a phenomenon that would change the nature of psychology. Pavlov was studying the digestive system of dogs, specifically

Ivan Pavlov (1849–1936).

the salivary reflex. He received the Nobel Prize in 1904 for his studies of digestive physiology. During his experiments, he would put food powder in the dog's mouth, and he would then measure the drops of saliva by way of a tube surgically inserted into the dog's mouth. But in the course of his work, Pavlov noticed dogs began to salivate merely when he walked into the room. This salivation could not be a reflex since it did not occur the first few times Pavlov walked in; it only occurred once the dog had learned that Pavlov's appearance signaled food. That is, Pavlov's appearance became associated with a future event: food. He called this a psychic reflex, or a conditional reflex, since it was conditional upon past experience. It has come to be

The conditioned response

called, through mistranslation, a ***conditioned response,*** or ***CR.*** A typical Pavlovian conditioning experiment goes as follows: we know that food (unconditioned stimulus, US) produces salivation (unconditioned response, UR)

$$\text{US (food)} \longrightarrow \text{UR (salivation)}$$

We present a tone just prior to presenting the food. Because the tone itself does not produce salivation, it is a neutral stimulus. But after pairing the tone with the food several times we discover that salivation will occur upon presentation of the tone. The tone can now be called a conditioned stimulus (CS) because it produces salivation, the conditioned response (CR). In short:

$$\text{CS (tone)} \longrightarrow \text{US (food)} \longrightarrow \text{UR (salivation)}$$

After several pairings of CS and US:

$$\text{CS (tone)} \longrightarrow \text{CR (salivation)}$$

This kind of experiment has been carried out using may species (Siamese fighting fish, rats, dogs, and humans), conditioned stimuli (tones, lights, tastes), and unconditioned responses (salivation, fear, nausea). It can be used in therapeutic situations to eliminate unsatisfactory behaviors. For example, Pavlovian conditioning may be used to cure alcoholism (Baker and Cannon, 1979). The following case illustrates how the conditioning would proceed when curing alcoholism.

Steven drinks a quart of vodka daily and has done so for several months. His drunkenness interferes greatly with his work, his marriage is falling apart, and he has been arrested twice for drunken driving. He has sought out a dramatic form of therapy: Pavlovian aversion therapy.

In the therapist's office, Steven gulps down a shot of his favorite vodka. He then drinks ipecac, a drug that causes him to become nauseated within a few minutes. He vomits. A week later, the same procedure is repeated. The taste of vodka (CS) is paired with the ipecac (the US). The ipecac produces nausea and vomiting (the UR). After several such sessions, a major change in Steven's preferences has occurred. Vodka now tastes terrible to him (CR). Merely thinking about alcohol makes him nauseated. And, most importantly, he no longer drinks liquor.

THE BASIC PAVLOVIAN PHENOMENA

There are two processes in Pavlovian conditioning that occur time and time again, regardless of what species, which kind of CS or US, or what kind of a response is tested. Pavlov discovered both: acquisition and extinction.

Acquisition is the learning of a response based on the contingency between a CS and US. Depending on the response to be learned, acquisition usually takes from three to fifteen pairings. *Extinction* is the loss of the CS's power to produce the formerly acquired response. This is brought about by presenting the CS, and no longer following it with the US. For example, it is possible to condition fear in humans. Fear can be measured by increased heart rate, perspiration, and muscle tension. When mild shocks (US) are given to humans, these measures become evident, that is, pain (UR) is produced. After several pairings of tone (CS) and shock (US), the tone (CS) alone begins to elicit fear (CR). That is what we call acquisition. But if we now repeatedly present the tone (CS) no longer followed with the shock (US), the individual no longer shows signs of fear. The tone (CS) no longer signals a shock (US). We call this process extinction.

In addition, there are two phenomena concerned with the stimulus properties of the CS. If the person has the CS of a high tone paired with shock, and then hears a lower-pitched tone, he may show a modified conditioned response to this new, but similar tone. This is called *stimulus generalization,* or the tendency of a response that has been conditioned to one stimulus to occur to similar stimuli. The more dissimilar the new stimulus from the original, the weaker will be the CR. Steven, for example, after becoming conditioned to vodka paired with ipecac, may show stimulus generalization to gin, and become nauseated when tasting gin.

If a person has experienced the CS of a high tone paired with shock and a low tone repeatedly followed by no shock, he will give a CR to the high tone, but learn to give no CR to the low tone. This is *discrimination,* or showing a CR to a CS that has been paired with a US while showing no CR to similar stimuli that have been paired with the absence of the US. So if Steven had ipecac after drinking hard liquor, but no ipecac after tasting wine, he will discriminate the two, showing nausea following vodka and gin, but no nausea when he tastes Chardonnay.

(margin note: Acquisition and extinction)

(margin note: Stimulus generalization)

(margin note: Stimulus discrimination)

PAVLOVIAN CONDITIONING, EMOTIONS, AND PSYCHOPATHOLOGY

There are situations in the world that arouse strong emotions in us. Some of these arouse the emotion *unconditionally,* or from our very first encounter with them: a loud clap of thunder startles us the very first time we hear it.

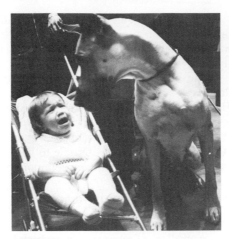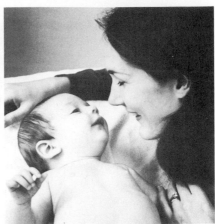

Pavlovian conditioning provides a powerful account of how objects take on emotional significance. The sight of all dogs may produce dread in this child due to this early frightening encounter with a large dog. Conversely, the sight of its mother's face will produce a sense of well-being in a baby due to the pairing of the mother's face with the baby's sense of contentment.

Acquired emotional states

Other objects acquire emotional significance: the face of a person we love produces a sense of well-being; seeing a stranger in a dark alleyway arouses dread. Pavlovian conditioning provides a powerful account of how objects take on emotional significance; it is this account that makes conditioning of great interest to the student of abnormality.

According to the behavioral account, the basic mechanism for all acquired emotional states is the pairing of a neutral object (CS) with an unconditioned emotional state (US). With enough pairings, the neutral object will lose its neutrality, become a CS, and all by itself produce the emotional state (CR). Consider the case of a child who is continually beaten with a tan hairbrush by his father. Before the beatings, the child had no feelings about the brush whatsoever. But, after several beatings (US), the brush becomes a CS and merely seeing the tan brush produces fear (CR).

Acquired emotional disorders

If normal emotions are acquired in this way, the same should be true of acquired emotional disorders. Several of the psychopathological disorders explored in the following chapters involve the acquisition of an exaggerated or unusual emotional state in regard to inappropriate objects. For example, phobias are said to be a result of Pavlovian conditioning. A *phobia* is a fear greatly out of proportion to how dangerous the phobic object actually is. For example, a cat phobic had a history of cats (CS) paired with painful events such as being scratched (US). As a result, cats became terrifying to the phobic individual, despite the fact that cats generally are not dangerous.

Here we can contrast the behavioral view of what causes emotional disorders with the biomedical model and the psychodynamic model. According to the behavioral view, the symptom of the disorder *is* the disorder. In the case above, the phobic individual's fear of cats is the disorder. There is no underlying pathological state that produces the symptoms. For the biomedical model, an underlying pathology such as a "virus," a disordered biochemistry, or a dysfunctional organ causes the symptoms. For the psychodynamic view, an intrapsychic conflict, usually sexual or aggressive in nature and stemming from childhood fixations, causes the symptoms.

Removing symptoms by extinction

The therapeutic optimism of the behavioral view follows directly from its view of the cause of the disorder. If the disorders are the symptoms and do not reflect an underlying pathology, eliminating the symptoms will cure the disorder. Since the symptoms of emotional disorders are emotional responses acquired by Pavlovian conditioning, it follows that those techniques which have been found experimentally to extinguish conditioned emotional responses will cure emotional disorders. This contrasts with the biomedical and psychodynamic stance on therapy: for these models, getting rid of the symptoms is only cosmetic; cure consists of removing the underlying disorder. For example, treating the symptoms of general paresis instead of attacking the syphilitic spirochete would not help much, for the underlying pathological process would remain intact. A strong test, then, of the behavioral view as opposed to the biomedical and psychodynamic views of emotional disorders would be whether the symptoms can be removed by extinction procedures, and whether other emotional problems will then occur, reflecting an uncured underlying pathology, after behavior therapy has removed one set of symptoms (see Chapter 8).

THE PAVLOVIAN THERAPIES

In the chapters on phobias and sexual dysfunction, we will look in detail at the therapies involving Pavlovian extinction of emotional disorders. But, some of the specific therapies should be briefly mentioned now.

Two Pavlovian therapies involving extinction have been applied to phobias and other anxiety disorders. In *flooding,* the phobic patient is immersed in the phobic situation (either real or imagined) for several consecutive hours. For example, a claustrophobic (who is terrified of being in small enclosed places) would be placed in a closet (CS); the original trauma (US) would not occur, and the fear of being enclosed would dimin-

In this mild form of flooding, a child who has acquired a fear of dogs is gently prodded toward one. Upon learning that the dog no longer presents danger, the child's fear of dogs disappears.

Edward L. Thorndike (1874–1949) studied animal intelligence and formulated the "law of effect."

B. F. Skinner (1904–   ) formulated the basic concepts of operant conditioning.

ish (Stampfl and Levis, 1967; Marks, 1969). In *systematic desensitization* (developed by Joseph Wolpe, then a South African psychiatrist), the phobic patient would imagine a set of gradually more frightening scenes involving the phobic object (CS), at the same time as he would be making a response incompatible with fear. Pavlovian extinction would occur with this exposure to the CS (thoughts about and eventually the actual phobic object) without the US (original trauma) and the UR (terror) (Wolpe, 1969).

Pavlovian conditioning, then, provides a theory of how we normally learn to feel a given emotion toward a given object. By applying its basic phenomena to emotional disorders, we can arrive at a theory of how emotional disorders come about, and we can deduce a set of therapies that should undo abnormal emotional responses.

OPERANT CONDITIONING

At about the same time as Pavlov discovered an objective way of studying how we learn "what goes with what," Edward L. Thorndike (1874–1949) began to objectively study how we learn "what to do to get what we want." Thorndike was studying animal intelligence. In one series of experiments he put hungry cats in puzzle boxes and observed how they learned to escape confinement and get food. He designed various boxes—some had levers to push, others had strings to pull, and some had shelves to jump on—and he left food—often fish—outside the box. The cat would have to make the correct response to escape from the puzzle box.

Thorndike's first major discovery was that learning what to do was gradual, not insightful. That is, the cat proceeded by trial and error. On the first few trials, the time to escape was very long; but with repeated success, the time gradually shortened to a few seconds. To explain his findings, Thorndike formulated the "law of effect." Still a major principle, this holds that when, in a given stimulus situation, a response is made and followed by positive consequences, the response will tend to be repeated; when followed by negative consequences, it will tend not to be repeated. Thorndike's work, like Pavlov's, was an objective way of studying the properties of learning.

This tradition was refined, popularized, and applied to a range of real-life settings by B. F. Skinner (1904–   ), who worked largely with rats pressing levers for food and with pigeons pecking lighted discs for grain. It was Skinner who formulated the basic concepts of operant conditioning.

THE CONCEPTS OF OPERANT CONDITIONING

Through his basic concepts, Skinner defined the elements of the law of effect rigorously. His three basic concepts consist of the reinforcer (both positive and negative), the operant, and the discriminative stimulus.

A *positive reinforcer* is an event whose onset increases the probability that a response preceding it will occur again. In effect, a positive reinforcer rewards behavior. A *negative reinforcer* is an event whose removal increases the probability of recurrence of a response that precedes it. *Punishers,* on the other hand, are events whose onset will decrease the probability of recurrence of a response that precedes it. The same stimulus whose onset acts as a punisher will usually act as a negative reinforcer when removed.

Winning at cards is a positive reinforcer for this little girl. She will probably play cards with the boys again in the future.

Operants and discriminative stimuli

An *operant* is a response whose probability can either be increased by positive reinforcement or decreased by negative reinforcement. If a mother reinforces her twelve-month-old child with a hug every time he says "Daddy," the probability that he will say it again is increased. In this case, the operant is "saying Daddy." If the mother hugs the child for saying Daddy only when the child's father is in sight, and does not hug him for saying Daddy when the father is not around, she is teaching the child to respond to a discriminative stimulus. In this case, the father being in sight is the *discriminative stimulus,* a signal that means that reinforcement is available if the operant is made.

THE OPERANT PHENOMENA

Acquisition and extinction

□ ACQUISITION AND EXTINCTION. The phenomena of *acquisition* and *extinction* in the operant conditioning of voluntary responses parallel the Pavlovian conditioning of involuntary responses. Consider a typical operant paradigm. A hungry rat is placed inside an operant chamber. The desired operant is the pressing of a lever. Each time the rat presses a lever, food is delivered down a chute. During this acquisition procedure, learning to lever press proceeds gradually, as shown in Figure 5-1. It takes about ten sessions

Figure 5-1

Acquisition and extinction of lever pressing. This curve depicts the growth in the frequency of lever pressing over the course of a number of experimental sessions, followed by its extinction when reinforcement is discontinued. (Source: Schwartz, 1983)

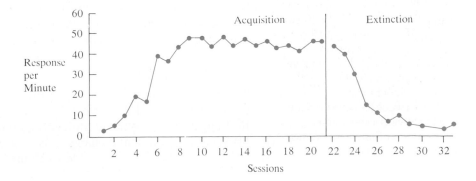

for the rat to learn to press at a high and constant rate. Extinction is then begun (in session 22), and the reinforcer (food) is no longer delivered when the rat presses the lever. As a result, responding gradually diminishes back to zero.

Schedules of reinforcement

□ **PARTIAL REINFORCEMENT AND SCHEDULES OF REINFORCEMENT.** An operant experimenter can arrange a rich variety of contingencies between the responses that his subjects make and the reinforcers they receive. In the simplest contingency, each and every time a subject makes a response a reinforcer is delivered. This is called *continuous reinforcement (CRF).* For example, every time the rat presses a lever, a food pellet arrives. In the real world, however, reinforcements do not usually come with such high consistency. More often, reinforcements only occur for some of the responses that are made, and many responses are in vain. To capture this, the experimenter arranges the contingencies such that reinforcement is delivered for only some of the responses that the subject makes. This is called a *partial* or *intermittent reinforcement* schedule. So, for example, the rat might receive one food pellet only when he has pressed the bar fifty times, rather than for each press.

Partial reinforcement

Partial reinforcement schedules make initial learning slower, but these schedules have two other properties that are important for engineering human behavior. In the first place, a great deal of work can be produced for very little payoff. So, for one small food pellet, a rat or a person can be made to emit hundreds of responses. The second property has to do with extinction and is called the *partial reinforcement extinction effect.* After a subject has been partially reinforced for a response, and extinction (consisting of no reinforcement at all) has begun, a surprisingly large number of responses will occur before the subject gives up. A rat who had responded on a partial reinforcement schedule in which it pressed the lever fifty times in order to get one reinforcement will respond hundreds of times during extinction before it quits. In contrast, a rat who has had continuous reinforcement and whose behavior is then extinguished will stop pressing after only five to ten attempts.

Maladaptive human behavior in the real world is often highly resistant to extinction in the same way that partially reinforced operant behavior is in the laboratory. For example, a compulsive "checker" who fears that she left the gas in the stove on may check the stove hundreds of times a day. She is reinforced very little; that is, she almost never checks and finds that the gas is on. Most of her responding is in vain. The operant explanation of her behavior is partial reinforcement. Because once every several hundred times she was reinforced by finding the gas on, she will now check thousands of times in order to get one reinforcer (Rachman and Hodgson, 1980).

This boy doesn't want to go to bed. He may be trying to manipulate his mother by throwing a tantrum because in the past she occasionally has given in to his crying and allowed him to stay up. Due to the partial reinforcement extinction effect, it will be difficult to extinguish the child's crying if the mother doesn't consistently ignore his tantrums at bedtime.

THE OPERANT THERAPIES

The operant therapist uses these principles in asking three essential questions: (1) What undesirable behavior or maladaptive operants does the patient engage in? (2) What reinforcers maintain these maladaptive responses? (3) What environmental changes, usually reinforcement or discriminative stimulus changes, can be made to change the maladaptive behavior into

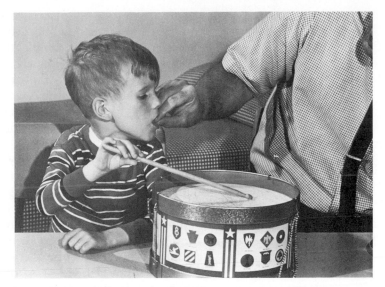

Selective positive reinforcement. This autistic boy is being fed each time he hits the drum with his stick. Thus, one of his symptoms—lack of social interaction—is targeted for change into adaptive behavior through the reinforcement of being fed.

adaptive behavior? (Ullmann and Krasner, 1965). A variety of operant therapies have been employed for a variety of forms of psychopathology. We will look at a selection of them now and others will be discussed in more detail in the chapters that involve the specific disorders that these therapies treat.

□ SELECTIVE POSITIVE REINFORCEMENT.   In the technique of selective positive reinforcement, the therapist selects a *target behavior* or adaptive behavior that is to be increased in probability. By the systematic delivery of positive reinforcement contingent on the occurrence of the target behavior, this behavior becomes more frequent.

Anorexia nervosa is a life-threatening disorder that, for the most part, afflicts women in their teens and early twenties. They literally starve themselves to death. By engaging in bizarre eating habits, such as eating only three Cheerios a day, an anorexic will lose 25 to 30 percent of her body weight within a couple of months. When they are hospitalized, the first problem with these patients (who may weigh as little as seventy-five pounds) is not curing them, but just saving their lives. Such patients usually do not cooperate with regimes that attempt to force them to eat. One highly effective way of saving the life of an anorexic woman is to selectively reinforce her for eating by using a reinforcer that is more highly desired than is eating. But, if you ask her what would be a reward that would induce her to eat, she will probably not tell you. In order to discover what is positively reinforcing, a therapist will look for a behavior that the patient engages in frequently and will only give her the opportunity to perform it if she first eats (Premack, 1959). If we observe and time what an anorexic does during the day, we might find, for example, that she watches television for an hour and a half, spends forty-five minutes talking with fellow patients, and spends an hour pacing the halls. An operant therapist would then set up a regime such that in order to be allowed to do any one of these three activities, the anorexic would have to first eat a fixed amount. For example, if she

Pop singer Karen Carpenter died of complications of anorexia nervosa.

first ate a tablespoon of custard, she would then be allowed to watch television for ten minutes; if she ate all of her steak, she would then be allowed to pace the halls for twenty minutes (Stunkard, 1976).

During thirty years of research, selective positive reinforcement has been shown to be an effective technique across a very wide range of behavioral disorders. When a discrete and specifiable instrumental response is missing from the adaptive repertoire of an individual, application of selective positive reinforcement will generally produce and maintain that response.

□ SELECTIVE PUNISHMENT.   In *selective punishment,* or selective negative reinforcement procedures, the therapist selects a target behavior that is maladaptive. By applying an aversive event when this target behavior occurs, the therapist causes its probability of occurrence to decrease.

Treating autism

Although we are not sure why, some autistic children engage in self-mutilation.* This maladaptive behavior is persistent, and most attempts at intervention on the part of a therapist will produce no or only temporary effects. In some of these cases, operant therapists have applied selective punishment. In one particular case, whenever the autistic child hit himself, a shock was delivered to him. The child soon learned that his behavior brought punishment, and he engaged less often in self-mutilation (Lovaas and Simmons, 1969; Dorsey, Iwata, Ong, and McSween, 1980). This procedure did not cure the child's autism, but it did stop his maladaptive behavior.

Punishment in the form of pinches, spanks, and cold water is now widely used to curtail the self-destructive behavior of autistic children. Punishment in this form strikes some people as cruel, and the Office for Children of the State of Massachusetts barred the use of such punishments in a school for autistic children in 1986. The children promptly regressed to their self-destructive behavior, and their parents went to court to overturn the ban, claiming that this was the only effective treatment their children had ever received. The court overturned the ban, charging that, out of sentimentalism, the Office for Children had played "Russian Roulette with the lives and safety of the students" by banning selective punishment (*New York Times,* June 5, 1986).

Eliminating behavior by extinction

□ EXTINCTION.   Punishment involves imposing some noxious event on the patient, such as a loud noise, an electric shock, or a nauseating drug. Even though such stimuli can be highly effective in removing unwanted behaviors, there are obvious undesirable aspects to such therapy. For example, patients may come to find the entire therapeutic setting aversive. Or many therapists, quite understandably, may feel uncomfortable with shocking, nauseating, and otherwise scaring fellow human beings, particularly those already burdened with psychological problems. Extinction is sometimes an alternative strategy: one can eliminate a behavior by merely omitting some highly desired event whenever the target behavior occurs.

The most common use of extinction in behavior therapy is when the therapist suspects that some maladaptive target behavior is being performed in order to get some positive reinforcement. The therapist then arranges the

* Autism, a psychotic disorder, is characterized by severe social withdrawal (see Chapter 16).

contingencies so that this behavior no longer produces the reinforcement. If the behavior decreases in frequency, extinction has been successful. For example, there was a case of a female psychotic patient who would make numerous disruptive visits to the nurses' office on the ward. An operant therapist believed that the attention the patient received from the nurses when she barged into their office was a positive reinforcer that maintained the disruptive behavior. So the therapist instructed the nurses to ignore the patient completely when the patient entered their office, thereby eliminating what was believed to be positive reinforcement. After seven weeks of treatment, the patient's visits dropped from an average of sixteen per day to two per day (Ayllon and Michel, 1959).

AVOIDANCE LEARNING

Avoiding aversive events

As we have seen, learning theorists regard human beings as capable of learning two sorts of relationships: the Pavlovian relationship—what goes with what—and the operant relationship—what to do in order to get what you want. There are many situations in which both sorts of learning go on at the same time. Prominent among such situations is learning to avoid aversive events. In an ***avoidance situation,*** two relationships have to be learned: (1) what predicts the aversive event, and (2) how to get away. The avoidance situation combines both a Pavlovian relationship and an operant relationship. To investigate avoidance, behavior theorists typically place a rat in a two-compartment chamber called a shuttlebox. After a while, a tone is turned on. Ten seconds after the tone has gone on, an electric shock is delivered through the floor of the apparatus. If the rat runs to the other side of the shuttlebox before the shock comes on, the tone terminates and the shock is prevented from occurring. Rats, dogs, and people usually learn to avoid shock altogether in these circumstances. In order to avoid the shock, the subject must learn two relationships (Mowrer, 1948; Rescorla and Solomon, 1967): (1) He must learn that the tone predicts shock, and he must become afraid of the tone. This is a Pavlovian relationship in which the CS is tone, the US is shock, and the CR is fear. (2) Having learned to fear the tone,

Avoidance learning may be overcome if a person is placed in the aversive situation and prevented from escaping. When nothing aversive occurs after all, the situation will no longer be avoided in the future.

he must learn what to do about it. He must learn that running to the other side of the shuttlebox terminates the fearful tone and prevents the shock from occurring. This is an operant relationship in which the discriminative stimulus is the tone, the operant is running to the other side of the shuttlebox, and the reinforcer is the termination of fear and the omission of shock.

Compulsions explained by avoidance learning

An understanding of avoidance learning helps in the treatment of certain psychopathologies. The behavioral view of obsessive-compulsive disorders, for example, involves the concept of avoidance learning. According to this view, the obsessive-compulsive checker believes that by engaging in the compulsive behavior of checking the stove several hundred times a day, she can prevent disaster from befalling her family. In this case, the occurrence and persistence of the compulsion may be explained by avoidance learning.

Behavior therapists often use both operant and Pavlovian relationships. Recall Steven, the chronic alcoholic who came to hate the taste of vodka after he received vomit-inducing ipecac. Whenever Steven made the operant response of reaching for vodka, he felt queasy and withdrew his hand. By Pavlovian conditioning, the taste of vodka had become nauseating. By operant conditioning, Steve had learned that withdrawing his hand from the bottle of vodka would reduce his queasiness.

COGNITIVE PSYCHOLOGY: PRINCIPLES AND APPLICATIONS

Cognitive school a reaction to behaviorism

The cognitive school is a modern outgrowth from, and reaction to, behaviorism. Implicit in the behavioral view is the assumption that the connection between the environment and behavior is direct. But over time, behaviorism has been challenged on this point, particularly by cognitive psychologists, who hold that behavior is influenced by more than just this direct relation between environment and response. Rather, cognitive psychologists contend that what a person thinks, believes, expects, attends to —in short, his or her mental life—influences how he or she behaves. Behaviorists, when pressed, frequently admit that mental life exists (Skinner, 1971). But they deny that such cognitions play a causal role in behavior. Rather, they dismiss cognitive processes, calling them ***epiphenomena.*** An epiphenomenon is a process that, while not causal, reflects the underlying process that is causal. A behaviorist who admits that mental processes exist likens them to the speedometer of an automobile. While a speedometer reflects how fast the automobile is going, it does not itself influence the speed.

ASSUMPTIONS OF THE COGNITIVE VIEW

The importance of thoughts

The cognitive psychologist, as opposed to the behaviorist, believes tht mental events are not mere epiphenomena, that cognitive processes influence behavior. Specifically, the cognitive psychologist contends that disordered cognitive processes cause some psychological disorders and that by changing these cognitions, the disorder can be alleviated and perhaps even cured.

The following case demonstrates the difference in emphasis between those holding the behavioral view and those holding the cognitive view:

An artist's depiction of the fear of speaking in public. (Drawing by John Vassos.)

Two individuals have the same speaking skills, but one is very anxious when giving a public speech, and the other speaks with ease in public. On different occasions, each gives a public speech and, as is common during the course of almost any speech, a few members of the audience walk out of the room during each speech. When these two people record what they were thinking when a member of the audience walked out, a very different pattern emerges. The anxious individual thinks, " I must be boring. How much longer do I have to speak? This speech is going to be a failure." In contrast, the low-anxiety person says to herself, "The person walking out must have a class to make. Gee, that's too bad, he will miss the best part of my talk." The same environmental event—people walking out of the room during the speech—produces a very different set of thoughts: the high-anxiety individual has depressing and tension-inducing thoughts, whereas the low-anxiety individual does not. (Meichenbaum, 1977)

How do the behavioral and cognitive therapists look at this? On the one hand, the behaviorist will focus on the particular environmental event—people walking out during a speech—and how this affects behavior. (In this example the environmental event is the same, but the consequences are different.) The cognitive therapist, on the other hand, will focus on the difference in the *thoughts* of the two speakers, on how he or she *interprets* the event. For the cognitive therapist, a person's thoughts are of primary importance.

COGNITIVE THERAPY

Therapy to change thoughts

Underlying the cognitive model is the view that mental events—that is, expectations, beliefs, memories, and so on—can cause behavior. If these mental events are changed, behavior change will follow. Believing this, the cognitive therapist looks for the cause, or etiology, of psychological disorders in disordered mental events. For example, if someone is depressed, the cognitive therapist will look for the cause of the individual's depression in her beliefs or thoughts. Perhaps she believes that she has no control over the events of her life. Thinking that she has no control, the individual may well become passive, sad, and eventually clinically depressed. Successful therapy for such disorders will consist of changing these thoughts. In the

If an individual expects that he will have no control over the events of his life, he may become passive, sad, and eventually clinically depressed.

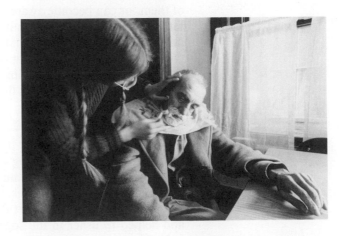

case of the depressive, a cognitive therapist will draw out, analyze, and then change the individual's thoughts, hoping to discover, and then reverse the thoughts that caused the depressive's feeling of hopelessness.

To understand what a cognitive therapist does, let us return to the case study of the two speech givers. What if the high-anxiety speaker becomes increasingly depressed when he sees members of the audience walking out? He may label the speech, and himself, a failure. Perhaps he gets so depressed that he can no longer give a good speech, or worse, refuses to speak before an audience. Because of this problem, he may enter therapy. What will a cognitive therapist do?

Because a cognitive therapist is concerned primarily with what a person thinks and believes, he or she will inquire about the anxious speaker's thoughts. Upon finding out that the speaker thinks that he is boring his audience, the therapist will pursue two hypotheses. First, there is the hypothesis that the speaker in reality is boring. If, however, in the course of the therapy, the therapist learns that the person's speeches have in the past been received very well and that some have even been reprinted, the therapist will conclude that the first hypothesis is wrong.

After discarding the hypothesis that the speaker really is boring, the therapist will turn to the hypothesis that the speaker's thoughts are distorting reality. According to this hypothesis, the speaker is selecting negative evidence by focusing too narrowly on one event: he is thinking too much about those members of the audience who walked out. He believes that they think he is boring, that they dislike him, and so on. Here, the therapist gets the client to point out the contrary evidence. First, he has a fine speaking record. Second, only a very small number of people walked out; some probably had important appointments to catch and were glad to have heard at least part of the speech. Perhaps some of them were bored. But third, and most important, he minimized the fact that almost all of the audience remained, and he paid no attention to the fact that the audience applauded enthusiastically. The therapist's job is to draw out all of the distorted negative thoughts, to have the client confront the contrary evidence, and then to get the client to change these thoughts.

Short-term and long-term cognitive processes

What kinds of mental events do cognitive therapists deal with? For the purposes of therapy, cognitive processes can be divided into short-term and long-term processes. The short-term processes are conscious. We are aware of them, or can become aware of them with practice. These include expectations, appraisals, and attributions. The long-term cognitive processes are not, generally speaking, available to consciousness. They are hypothetical constructs or dispositions that show themselves in the way they govern the short-term processes. One long-term process involves beliefs. We will discuss the short-term processes first.

OVERCOMING SELF-DEFEATING EXPECTATIONS

Expectations are cognitions that explicitly anticipate future events. The speech giver who, upon seeing a few people walk out, thought "this is going to be a failure" is reporting an expectation. He anticipates future consequences, in this case, bad ones.

In his seminal work, Albert Bandura analyzed the notion of expectation and helped to usher in the cognitive school of therapy. In his early work,

Left: This boy's behavior reflects his expectation that he will complete his project. *Right:* The behavior of these twin girls reflects two different efficacy expectations. The twin on the left believes that she can successfully execute the response that will solve the puzzle. The twin on the right believes that she cannot execute the response, and therefore she gives up.

Outcome and efficacy expectations

Bandura showed that people learned not only by direct reinforcement but also by observing others being reinforced. He concluded that the behavioral principles of reinforcement were insufficient and that such "vicarious learning" must involve the learning of expectations (Rotter, 1954; Bandura and Walters, 1959; Bandura, 1977a, 1978). For Bandura, a person in therapy has two kinds of expectancies: an *outcome expectation* is a person's estimate that a given behavior will lead to a desired outcome, and an *efficacy expectation* is the belief that he can successfully execute the behavior that produces the desired outcome. Outcome and efficacy expectations are different because a person may be certain that a particular course of action will produce a given outcome, but he may doubt that he can perform this action. For example, he may realize that touching a snake will reduce his snake phobia, but he may still be unable to touch the snake. Bandura believes that the success of systematic desensitization and modeling therapies in curing phobias (Chapter 8) is attributable to changes in self-efficacy expectations. In both situations, the patient learns that he can make those responses—relaxation and approach—which will overcome the phobia. A "micro-analysis" of efficacy expectations and behavioral change in snake phobics has confirmed this speculation. Successful therapy created high efficacy expectations for approaching a boa constrictor. The higher the level of efficacy expectations at the end of treatment, the better was the approach behavior to the snake (Bandura, 1977a, 1982; Bandura and Adams, 1977; Staats, 1978; Biran and Wilson, 1981).

MODIFYING NEGATIVE APPRAISALS

Automatic thoughts

We are constantly appraising and evaluating both what happens to us and what we do. These *appraisals* and evaluations are sometimes very obvious to us, but at other times we are unaware of them. For cognitive therapists, such automatic thoughts often precede and cause emotion (Beck, 1976). The speech giver becomes anxious and depressed once he thinks, "This is going to be a failure." He is not only expecting future consequences, he is also appraising his actions. He judges them to be failures, and this appraisal causes his negative emotions. This appraisal process is automatic. After a lifetime of practice, it occurs habitually and rapidly. The individual in therapy must be trained to slow down his thought process to become aware of such thoughts. Automatic thoughts are not vague and ill-formed, rather they are specific and discrete sentences. In addition, while they may seem implausible to the objective observer, they seem highly reasonable to the person who has them (see also Lazarus, 1976; Kanfer and Karoly, 1972; Mahoney and Thoresen, 1974; Rehm, 1978).

Test-anxious individuals are often found to make self-defeating appraisals. A student, for example, taking an examination may say to himself, "Look at that other student. She just left the room. She's much smarter than I am. My going so slowly means I will surely fail." In therapy, this person is taught to reappraise the situation: in short, to test his original appraisal of the event. "She left the room early because she didn't bother to check her answers. Chances are I probably won't fail. And even if I do people probably won't think I'm stupid. And even if they do that doesn't mean I *am* stupid." The goal of the therapist here is to get the client to catch hold of his self-defeating thoughts as they come about, criticize them, control them, and thereby avoid the occurrence of anxiety (Goldfried, Decenteceo, and Wineburg, 1974; Goldfried, Linehan, and Smith, 1978; see also Langer, Janis, and Wolfer, 1975; Meichenbaum, 1977).

One instrument for discovering the frequency of automatic thoughts is the *Automatic Thoughts Questionnaire* (Hollon and Kendall, 1980). In answering its questions, clients record the frequency with which they make the following sorts of automatic appraisals of themselves, "I'm no good," "I'm so weak," "My life is a mess," "No one understands me," "It's just not worth it." The results show that when people are depressed, they have many more frequent negative automatic thoughts than when they are not depressed, and further, that these thoughts are specific to depressives. Schizophrenics, substance abusers, and people with anxiety disorders do not record having frequent negative thoughts about themselves unless they are also depressed (Hollon, Kendall, and Lumry, 1986).

A major proponent of cognitive therapy, A. T. Beck (1976) argues that specific emotions are *always* preceded by discrete thoughts. Sadness is preceded by the thought "something of value has been lost." Anxiety is preceded by the thought "a threat of harm exists," and anger is preceded by the thought "my personal domain is being trespassed against." This is a sweeping and simple formulation of emotional life: the essence of sadness, anxiety, and anger consists of appraisals of loss, threat, and trespass, respectively. Thus, for cognitive therapists, modifying those thoughts will alter the emotion.

CHANGING ATTRIBUTIONS

Another kind of short-term mental event that cognitive therapists try to modify is attribution. An **attribution** is an individual's conception of *why* an event has befallen him. When a student fails an examination, he asks himself, "Why did I fail?" Depending on the causal analysis he makes, different consequences ensue. The student might make an **external** or **internal attribution** (Rotter, 1966). He might believe that the examination was unfair, an external cause. Alternatively, he might believe that he is stupid, an internal cause. A second dimension along which attributions for failure are made is **stable** or **unstable** (Weiner, 1974). A stable cause is one that persists

Top: If an athlete believes that his team is losing because of his actions, he is making an internal attribution. *Bottom:* Alternatively, if an athlete believes that it is the referee's fault that his team is losing, he is making an external attribution.

Table 5-1 CHARACTERISTICS OF ATTRIBUTIONS OF STUDENTS WHO DO POORLY ON THE GRADUATE RECORD EXAMINATION

	Internal		External	
	Stable	Unstable	Stable	Unstable
Global	Lack of intelligence	Exhaustion	ETS gives unfair tests.	Today is Friday the 13th.
	(Laziness)	(Having a cold makes me stupid.)	(People are usually unlucky on the GRE.)	(ETS gave experimental tests this time that were too hard for everyone.)
Specific	Lack of mathematical ability	Fed up with math problems	ETS gives unfair math tests.	The math test was form No. 13.
	(Math always bores me.)	(Having a cold ruins my arithmetic.)	(People are usually unlucky on math tests.)	(Everyone's copy of the math test was blurred.)

NOTE: ETS = Educational Testing Service, the maker of graduate record examinations (GRE)
SOURCE: Abramson, Seligman, and Teasdale, 1978.

Dimensions of attributions

in time; an unstable cause is one that is transient. For example, the student might believe that he failed because he did not get a good night's sleep, an unstable cause (which is also internal). Alternatively, the student might believe that he has no mathematical ability, a stable cause (which is also internal). Finally, an attribution for failure can be **global** or **specific** (Abramson, Seligman, and Teasdale, 1978). An attribution to global factors means that failure must occur on many different tasks, and an attribution to specific factors means that failure must occur only on this task. For example, the student who fails might believe that he failed because he is stupid, a global cause (which is also stable and internal). Or he might believe that he failed because the form number of the test was 13, an unlucky number. This latter is a specific attribution (which is also external and stable). Table 5-1 presents these alternative attributions (Heider, 1958; Kelley, 1967; Weiner, 1972).

Cognitive therapists try to change an individual's attributions. For example, women with low self-esteem usually make internal attributions when they fail. They believe that they have failed because they are stupid, incompetent, and unlovable. To deal with this attribution, each week, the therapist has them record five different bad events that have occurred during each week and then he has them write down *external* attributions for the events. For example, one woman might write, "my boyfriend criticized my behavior at a party last night, not because I am socially unskilled, but rather because he was in a bad mood." The goal is to get the woman to shift from internal to external what she believes to be the causes of bad events. After a few weeks, clients begin to see that there are alternative causes for their failures, and the low self-esteem and depression brought about by the internal attributions begin to lift (Ickes and Leyden, 1978; Beck et al., 1979).

LONG-TERM COGNITIVE PROCESSES

Abandoning irrational beliefs

The short-term mental events that we have examined—expectations, appraisals, and attributions—are available to consciousness. Long-term cognitive processes are different. They are hypothetical constructs, inferred dispositions that govern the mental events now in consciousness. One of these long-term cognitive processes is *beliefs.*

Albert Ellis, the founder of rational-emotive therapy, argues that psychological disorder stems largely from irrational beliefs. He gives an example of a client who, over the course of a lifetime, had had a set of destructive beliefs instilled in him by his parents and by society. Among these are the ideas that: (1) it is a dire necessity for an adult human being to be loved or approved by virtually every significant other person in his community; (2) one should be thoroughly competent, adequate, and achieving in all possible respects in order to be worthwhile; (3) it is awful and catastrophic when things are not the way one would very much like them to be; (4) human unhappiness is externally caused, and we have little or no ability to control our own sorrows; (5) our past history is an all-important determinant of our present behavior; if something once strongly affected our life, it should always have a similar effect; and (6) there is invariably a right, precise, and perfect solution to human problems, and it is catastrophic if this perfect solution is not found (Ellis, 1962).

Ridding the individual of the tyranny of should's

These irrational and illogical beliefs shape the short-term distorted expectations, appraisals, and attributions that produce psychological disorder. The client is afflicted with a "tyranny of should's," and the job of the therapist is to break the hold of these "should's." Once the patient abandons the above beliefs, it is impossible for him to remain disturbed. The job of the therapist is to rid the individual of these beliefs. The therapy is an aggressive one. It makes a concerted attack on the client's beliefs in two ways: (1) the therapist is a frank counter-propagandist who contradicts superstitions and self-defeating propaganda embodied in the irrational beliefs of the patient, and (2) the therapist encourages, persuades, cajoles, and occasionally insists that the patient engage in behavior that will itself be forceful counter-propaganda against the irrational beliefs (Ellis, 1962).

This particular brand of cognitive therapy is called rational-emotive therapy, and it is among the most active and aggressive of psychotherapeutic procedures. The following case illustrates the force of therapeutic persuasion:

During his therapy session, a twenty-three-year-old man said that he was very depressed and did not know why. A little questioning showed that this severely neurotic patient, whose main presenting problem was that he had been doing too much drinking during the last two years, had been putting off the inventory keeping he was required to do as part of his job as an apprentice glass-staining artist.

PATIENT: I know that I should do the inventory before it piles up to enormous proportions, but I just keep putting it off. To be honest, I guess it's because I resent doing it so much.

Albert Ellis, founder of rational-emotive therapy, argues that psychological disorder stems largely from irrational beliefs.

THERAPIST: But why do you resent it so much?

PATIENT: It's boring. I just don't like it.

THERAPIST: So it's boring. That's a good reason for disliking this work, but is it an equally good reason for resenting it?

PATIENT: Aren't the two the same thing?

THERAPIST: By no means. Dislike equals the sentence, "I don't enjoy doing this thing, and therefore I don't want to do it." And that's a perfectly sane sentence in most instances. But resentment is the sentence, "*Because* I dislike doing this thing, I shouldn't *have* to do it." And that's invariably a very crazy sentence.

PATIENT: Why is it so crazy to resent something that you don't like to do?

THERAPIST: There are several reasons. First of all, from a purely logical stand-point, it just makes no sense at all to say to yourself, "Because I dislike doing this thing, I shouldn't *have* to do it." The second part of this sentence just doesn't follow in any way from the first part. Your reasoning goes something like this: "Because *I* dislike doing this thing, *other people* and the *universe* should be so considerate of me that they should never make me do what I dislike." But, of course, this doesn't make any sense. Why *should* other people and the universe be that considerate of you? If might be nice if they were. But why the devil *should* they be? In order for your reasoning to be true, the entire universe, and all the people in it, would really have to revolve around and be uniquely considerate of you. (Ellis, 1962)

Here the therapist directly attacks the client's belief, arguing that it is irrational. This is an important distinction between cognitive therapists, on the one hand, and behavioral or dynamic therapists on the other. Behavioral and dynamic therapists point out that a client's actions and beliefs are maladaptive and self-defeating. Cognitive therapists emphasize that, in addition, the beliefs are irrational and illogical.

COGNITIVE-BEHAVIORAL THERAPY

Combining therapies

Cognitive therapists, then, believe that distorted thinking causes disordered behavior and that correcting the distorted thinking will alleviate and even cure the disordered behavior. Behavior therapists, in contrast, view disordered behavior as learned from past experience, and they attempt to alleviate the disorders by training new, more adaptive habits. These two positions are not incompatible, and many therapists try both to correct distorted cognitions and to train new habits. When therapists combine both techniques, it is called cognitive-behavioral therapy (Ellis, 1962; Mahoney, 1974; Meichenbaum, 1977; Beck et al., 1979).

Lazarus and multi-modal therapy

Arnold Lazarus is one of the therapists who integrates cognitive and behavioral techniques in therapy. Lazarus argues that disorder occurs in the same patient at seven different levels, and that there are levels of therapy appropriate to each level of disorder. The mnemonic device for these seven levels is BASIC ID, where B is behavior, A affect, S sensation, I imagery, C cognition, I interpersonal relations, D drugs. The job of the therapist using such *multi-modal therapy* is to separate the disorder into its different levels and to choose appropriate techniques for each level. Lazarus is willing to use cognitive techniques, behavioral techniques, and even psychoanalytic procedures. Table 5-2 shows the variety of treatments used in the course of the thirteen-month therapy for Mary Ann, a twenty-four-year-old woman diagnosed as a chronic undifferentiated schizophrenic with a very poor

Table 5-2 BASIC ID TECHNIQUES

Modality	Problem	Proposed Treatment
Behavior	Inappropriate withdrawal responses Frequent crying Excessive eating	Assertiveness training Nonreinforcement Low-calorie regimen
Affect	Unable to express overt anger Frequent anxiety Absence of enthusiasm and spontaneous joy	Role playing Relaxation training and reassurance Positive imagery procedures
Sensation	Stomach spasms Out of touch with most sensual pleasures Tension in jaw and neck	Abdominal breathing and relaxing Sensate focus method Differential relaxation
Imagery	Distressing scenes of sister's funeral Recurring dreams about airplane bombings	Desensitization Eidetic imagery invoking feelings of being safe
Cognition	Irrational self-talk: "I am evil." "I must suffer." "Sex is dirty." "I am inferior." Syllogistic reasoning and overgeneralization	Deliberate rational disputation and corrective self-talk Parsing of irrational sentences
Interpersonal relationships	Childlike dependence Easily exploited and submissive Manipulative tendencies	Specific self-sufficiency assignments Assertiveness training Training in direct and confrontative behaviors
Drugs	Disordered biochemistry	Antipsychotic drugs

SOURCE: Adapted from Lazarus, 1976.

prognosis. She was overweight, apathetic, and withdrawn. She had been heavily medicated but with little effect. By the end of thirteen months of the techniques shown in Table 5-2, she was functioning well and engaged to be married.

COMBINING COGNITIVE-BEHAVIORAL THERAPY AND PSYCHODYNAMICS

CCRT There has been a movement among psychodynamically oriented therapists that augurs well for a fruitful combination of cognitively oriented concepts and psychodynamic therapy. Lester Luborsky (1984) argues that what a patient consciously thinks about in three spheres of life reveals the underlying, and often unconscious, core conflictual relationship theme (CCRT). The three spheres are: (1) current in-treatment relationship (the relationship with the therapist), (2) current out-of-treatment relationships, and (3) past relationships. Common cognitions about these spheres, their recurrent overlap, point to the CCRT.

Ms. N. thinks, "I am trying to do well in my work," a thought about her current out-of-treatment relationships. She tells this to the therapist, and she begins to cry. The therapist then remarks, "You get tearful and cry when I refer to your attractiveness," a result of her thoughts about the in-treatment relationship. Ms. N. then spontaneously thinks about her past, "Father could never stand my being attractive." The content of these three conscious spheres reflects the main unconscious CCRT. By disentangling the cognitions involved in the three spheres, the therapist can discover the client's *wish:* "I wish I could find a suitable man to provide me with the physical and emotional support I need." The therapist can also discover (and attempt to alter) the negative *consequence,* or automatic thoughts, that follow from the wish: "But I shouldn't because I am independent, and I can't because I will be rejected, and the man will not be able to provide that kind of support."

Wish and consequence

By attending to the conscious automatic thoughts that cognitive therapists emphasize, psychodynamically oriented therapists are beginning to bring these two disparate models closer together. The future will likely lead to more of such creative integrations across models.

EVALUATING THE BEHAVIORAL AND COGNITIVE MODELS

Strengths of behavioral and cognitive therapy

There are several virtues of behavior therapy and cognitive therapy: they are effective in a number of discrete disorders; therapy is generally brief and inexpensive; they seem to be based on a science of behavioral and cognitive psychology; and their units of analysis, stimuli, responses, reinforcers, expectations, and attributions can be measured. Behavior and cognitive therapies, however, are not without problems. Perhaps the most serious allegation is that they are superficial.

Shortcomings of behavioral and cognitive therapy

Are humans more than just behavior and cognition? Are psychological disorders more than disordered action and disordered thinking? Must therapy, in order to be successful, do more than merely provide more adaptive actions and more rational ways of thinking? Because behavior therapists and cognitive therapists restrict themselves to an analysis of the discrete behaviors and cognitions of the human being, they miss the essence: that individuals are wholes, that individuals are free to choose. A phobic patient is more than a machine who happens to be afraid of cats. He is an individual whose symptoms are deeply rooted in his personality and psychodynamics. Alternatively, he is an individual who has made bad choices but who can still choose health. An autistic child who treats other human beings as if they were pieces of furniture may be taught by behaviorists to hug other people in order to receive food or to escape from shock. But in the end, all we have is an autistic child who hugs people. Merely changing how one behaves fails to change the underlying disorder.

Those who object to the behavioral and cognitive views feel that there are deeper disorders that produce symptoms. Because of this, seemingly superficial behavioral change may be short-lived, as in the case of what had been highly successful behavioral treatments of obesity. After one year and three years, obese individuals who had undergone behavior therapy had kept their weight down. But after five years, their weight returned (Stunkard and Penick, 1979). Although behavior therapy had led to change by removing the symptom of obesity, the underlying problem remained and ultimately sabotaged the therapy.

How might behavioral and cognitive therapists respond to these charges of superficiality? A militant response might be to deny the concept of the "whole person." To radical behaviorists such a concept is romantic; it makes sense in literature and in poetry, but not for human beings in distress and in need of relief. We would make a less militant reply. Removing symptoms—either behavioral or cognitive—at least helps. Symptom substitution has rarely, if ever, followed successful behavioral or cognitive therapy. Some disorders are highly specific, peripheral to the heart of an individual's being and amenable to behavioral and cognitive therapies. Phobias, obsessions, stuttering, and some sexual problems are such disorders. On the other hand, there may be deeper disorders left untouched by behavior and cognitive therapy: schizophrenia and psychopathy, perhaps. For these disorders, change of personality, uncovering dynamics, and drugs are probably necessary.

We believe that human misery, including problems of psychological disorder, is sometimes, but not always, produced by an unfortunate set of environmental circumstances or by distorted cognition. To counteract such circumstances by applying behavioral and cognitive laws does not diminish or devalue human wholeness or freedom, but rather enlarges it. An individual who is so crippled by a phobia of leaving his apartment that he cannot work or see those he loves, is not free. By applying behavioral and cognitive therapy to such an individual, one can remove this phobia. Such an individual will then be free to lead a rational life.

SUMMARY

1. The behavioral school of abnormality grows out of British empiricism, the view that knowledge is caused by experience and that *resemblance* and *contiguity* between ideas are the two simple principles that are the mental glue of experience.

2. The behavioral model sees the cause of abnormality as the *learning of maladaptive habits.* It aims to discover, by laboratory experiment, what aspect of the environment produced this learning, and it sees successful therapy as learning new and more adaptive ways of behaving.

3. Two kinds of basic learning processes exist: *Pavlovian* and *operant conditioning.* These have each generated a set of behavior therapies.

4. Pavlovian therapies begin with the assumption that emotional habits have been acquired by the contingency between a *conditioned stimulus* and an *unconditioned stimulus.* The formerly neutral conditioned stimulus now produces a *conditioned response,* which is the acquired emotion. Two Pavlovian therapies, *systematic desensitization* and *flooding,* extinguish some maladaptive emotional habits quite successfully.

5. Operant conditioning is based on three concepts: reinforcer, operant, and discriminative stimulus. Operant therapies are based on the assumption that people acquire voluntary habits by positive reinforcement and punishment. Operant therapies provide new and more adaptive repertoires of voluntary responses and extinguish maladaptive voluntary responses. Among such therapies are *selective positive reinforcement, selective punishment,* and *extinction.* These have been applied with some success to such disorders as *anorexia nervosa* and *autism.*

6. The understanding of *avoidance learning* combines operant and Pavlovian theory, and helps in the treatment of obsessive-compulsive disorders.

7. The cognitive school is an outgrowth and reaction to the behavioral school.

8. In contrast to the behaviorists, the cognitive school holds that mental events are not *epiphenomena,* rather they cause behavior. More particularly, disordered cognitions cause disordered behavior, and changing these disordered cognitions will alleviate and sometimes cure psychopathology.

9. Cognitive therapy is carried out by attempting to change different sorts of mental events, which can be divided into short-term mental events and long-term mental events.

10. Short-term mental events consist of expectations, including *outcome and efficacy expectations, appraisals,* or mental evaluations of our experience, and *attributions,* the designation of causes concerning our experience.

11. Long-term mental events include *beliefs,* some of which are irrational and illogical. A prominent example is a set of beliefs called the "tyranny of should's," which has been viewed as a cause of depression.

12. Many therapists practice both cognitive and behavioral therapy and are called *cognitive-behavioral therapists. Multi-modal therapy* is an example of the use of cognitive and behavioral techniques along with techniques from the other models.

13. The cognitive and behavioral models have been seriously criticized. The most important criticisms argue that human beings are more than their behaviors and cognitions, and that it is superficial to treat only the symptoms rather than the whole person. The cognitive and behavioral schools reply by arguing that many times it is helpful to the client merely to remove the symptoms and that the disorder *is* often just the symptoms.

Part 3

INVESTIGATING AND DIAGNOSING ABNORMALITY

Investigating Abnormality

Methods of
investigating
abnormality

Tʜᴇ chapters later in this book describe many individuals' abnormal behaviors. Some people are terrified at the thought of entering an elevator; some seem to act in a way that seems totally inappropriate, like laughing
at a close friend's funeral. Others complain of physical ailments that have
no biological basis. Why do they act this way? What can one do to treat these
individuals?

These two questions arise from the human fascination with scientific
phenomena. We take notice of various phenomena, and then we seek understanding of them. We ask "Why?" What is the cause or *etiology* of the
phenomena? When we find the etiology, we seek a way of applying our
newly found knowledge. Physicists and engineers developed nuclear power
plants after they studied the whys of the atom. Psychologists and psychiatrists developed therapies after studying abnormal (and sometimes, normal)
behavior. This chapter is devoted to examining the ways, or methods, in
which we investigate abnormality. We will look closely at the two principal
methods: clinical case histories and experimental studies.

We will begin with *clinical case histories,* which provide the major source
of hypotheses and intuitions about the causes and cures of abnormality.
While case histories provide rich hypotheses, however, they cannot isolate
the causal elements. *Experimental studies,* which manipulate possible
causes in order to isolate the crucial elements, are our next concern. Often,
however, for ethical or practical reasons, experiments cannot be carried out
on people who have problems of psychopathology. Three alternate methods
are therefore available to the scientist: *correlational studies, experiments of
nature,* and *laboratory models of psychopathology.* It is most satisfying when
several or all of the methods converge to form a woven fabric of evidence.

Before we begin our examination of method, a warning is in order. Sound
method is a means, not an end. The end is becoming justifiably convinced
that *A* is the cause of *B;* where *A* is a past event and *B* a form of abnormality,

Methods as a means to understanding

or where *A* is a therapy and *B* the relief of abnormality. Understanding can be arrived at by any of the methods discussed here; no one of them is the only road to truth. It is easy to become a slave to method, and to forget that the study of method describes how scientists or clinicians have attained understanding in the past. The study of method does not prescribe how this must be done in the future. Great thinkers have often developed (sometimes by accident) new methods at the same time as they discovered new truths.

THE CLINICAL CASE HISTORY

Recording the life of an individual

If we keep in mind that the end point of any method is the discovery of evidence about cause, we will see that each of the methods we examine can lead toward this end. The first, the ***clinical case history,*** is the record of part of the life of an individual as seen during therapy. In developing his theories of personality, Sigmund Freud made extensive use of clinical case histories. For example, much of what we know about hysteria today came out of Freud's hypotheses based on his patients' case histories. After seeing a number of patients with hysterical symptoms, Freud hypothesized that repressed wishes were the cause of their hysteria. The clinician who is observing and recording the case history can not only make hypotheses, but sometimes he or she can test them and discover compelling evidence as to whether he or she is right or wrong. The following case of hysterical "anniversary blindness" is such an instance.

The clinical case history of Bertha Pappenheim, known as Anna O. in *Studies on Hysteria,* helped Sigmund Freud to formulate his hypotheses on hysteria.

A CLINICAL CASE HISTORY

At age fifty, Jack went completely blind. For three months, he had been unable even to distinguish light from dark. His symptoms had begun, rather suddenly, at Christmas time. An exhaustive series of eye tests revealed nothing wrong physically. A variety of medications and several types of psychotherapy had been tried, all to no avail.

Jack was conscious of no incident that might have precipitated the blindness, and nothing in Jack's narration of his life provided a clue. At this point, his therapist formulated an hypothesis: hysterical blindness. This was indicated by the total absence of physical cause plus the absence of psychological insight (almost to the point of indifference) concerning precipitating events. If this were classical hysteria, then some event, so traumatic that it had been driven out of the patient's consciousness and repressed, should be responsible. If this were so, Jack might have access to the event under hypnosis, and reliving the trauma might bring about a cure. The therapist therefore decided to hypnotize Jack. Under hypnosis, he instructed Jack to go back to any period of his life that he could not remember when he was awake. Jack then relived an astonishing event.

Twenty-five years ago, Jack had been deeply in love. Both he and an acquaintance, Ronald, were courting Sarah in open competition. One day—it was Christmas—she confronted Jack with bad news: she was in love with Ronald and would no longer see Jack. In a state of wild jealousy, he went to Ronald and told him a tragic lie: Sarah, Jack said, was not in love with either of them, but with a third party. Ronald became extremely upset, jumped into his car, and drove off at high speed. In a frenzy of rage, he tried to race a train to a crossing, but his car was hit, and he was killed. Sarah found out soon afterward that Ronald had been killed, and she suspected that Jack was involved. Sarah made Jack come with her to the scene of the accident, and as they arrived, the wreckage was being cleared and Ronald's mangled body was being taken away by ambulance. Sarah accused Jack of being directly responsible for Ronald's death. The whole incident was described under hypnosis with extreme emotion, and Jack climaxed the narrative by sobbing out, "She made me go up and *see* what I had done; that I had killed him!"

This was the buried trauma that the therapist had guessed was there. At this point, he reassured Jack that although he had some responsibility, he had not foreseen or intended Ronald's death, that it was an accident.

At this point yet another revelation occurred: every Christmas, Sarah, who had married someone else, called Jack to remind him of what he had done. This last Christmas had been the twenty-fifth anniversary and shortly after the call, the blindness had begun. The therapist inferred that Jack could no longer bear to *see* what he had done, and the memory of both the calls and the initial trauma had been repressed.

With the trauma relived under hypnosis, the therapist told Jack that upon waking, if he wanted to see, his sight would gradually return in the next few days, which, in fact, it did. (Stinnett, 1978)

Here then is an exemplary case history. A skilled therapist is presented with a syndrome: blindness with no physical cause. He then hypothesizes that it is hysterical blindness. Drawing on his knowledge of past case histories, theory, and therapeutic technique, he tests his hypothesis by finding under hypnosis a precipitating trauma of tragic proportions. Once the trauma is relived, the blindness disappears. Under hypnosis, two missing pieces—the accident and the anniversary phone calls—fall into place, and the etiology of the blindness becomes clear.

In a lifetime, a therapist may come across only a handful of such dramatic encounters in which the causal chain is so clear. No experiment and no personality test could bolster our certainty about the origin of Jack's blindness. Much more common, however, are those cases in which painstaking work on the part of the therapist and patient results in only gradual understanding of the complex network of cause and in only gradual symptom relief. But in all cases, whether they be dramatic or more commonplace, the method is the same: with the aid of a therapist, the patient comes to grips with past events and their influences, on his present problems. Based on a patient's history, a therapist will hypothesize about possible causes and then help the patient overcome his past.

EVALUATING THE CLINICAL CASE HISTORY

Advantages of
the case history

As a method of inquiry, the study of the clinical case history has four advantages. First, it is not artificial. The investigation is working with an actual person who has an actual problem. The reader can easily empathize with a well-reported case and understand the connection between past events and present problems, and between therapeutic actions and the patient's improvement. As we will see later, methods involving laboratory experiments and statistical surveys are more artificial in nature.

Second, the clinical case history can document a phenomenon so rare or bizarre that it probably could not be explored by other standard forms of investigation. The origin of Jack's blindness is such a phenomenon.

Third, the clinical case history is a major source of hypotheses about the etiology and cure of abnormality. At the present state of knowledge, no other method equals it in the generation of ideas and insights that can then be tested in the laboratory and the clinic. Finally, a convincing clinical case history can provide disconfirming evidence against a generally accepted hypothesis.

But there are also four major disadvantages to clinical case histories: selectivity of memory, lack of repeatability, lack of generality, and insufficient evidence for causality.

SELECTIVITY

Disadvantages of the case history

The reported "evidence" may be distorted. Clinical reports are almost always *retrospective;* they deal with incidents in the past, often in the distant past. The patient may have an axe to grind; he may, for example, want to absolve himself of blame or, conversely, emphasize his guilt. To accomplish this, he may select the evidence that serves these purposes. While talking to his therapist, he may magnify trivial events and ignore important ones. Commonly, he has his own explanation about what happened, and he will remember and report the evidence that best fits this explanation.

Sometimes it is the therapist, not the patient, who has the axe to grind. A therapist might believe in a particular theory, which may influence what evidence she considers relevant and what evidence she ignores. If the therapist is an orthodox Freudian, she may seek and emphasize evidence about early life events, while ignoring evidence about present events. If the therapist is an orthodox behavior therapist, she may focus on ways to change the patient's present behavior, while neglecting childhood events. Although such selectivity does not invalidate the insights gained through the single case, we must keep in mind that this method is particularly susceptible to bias by patient and therapist.

LACK OF REPEATABILITY

Case histories, because they are part of the flow of real life, are not repeatable. If we could repeat an observation exactly, we could look carefully at the details, making certain that it happened the way it was reported to us. If an observation could be repeated, we would have a better chance of determining what caused it, for we could vary one and only one element and see if the observation changed. But this is not the case with clinical case histories; they each differ in one respect or another from one another.

LACK OF GENERALITY

Even a convincing case history, like Jack's, is specific to one person. Does *all* hysterical blindness begin with an unconscious wish not to see, and conversely, do *all* such wishes result in hysterical blindness? How many people have unconsciously not wanted to see something yet have not become hysterically blind? We simply do not know, and a single case history can, at best, tell us only that one such case of hysterical blindness began in this way. By studying several case histories of hysterical blindness, we might find that each individual had an unconscious motivation not to see; this would indicate that such a desire is general to hysterical blindness. But we would still be ignorant about whether individuals who are not hysterically blind lack such a desire. And this is just what is needed to infer cause.

INSUFFICIENT EVIDENCE FOR CAUSALITY

Single clinical case histories only rarely convince us about etiology. In cases like Jack's, the cause was clear, but usually cause is more ambiguous. In most cases, there are several incidents, each of which might be the cause, or there is no obvious incident at all. This is the most serious problem with clinical case histories. In order to know that *A* causes *B,* we must at least know that every time *A* occurs, *B* follows, If we collect many cases of *B,* we could determine if, in general, *B*'s are preceded by *A*'s. But here the causal question is the converse: When *A* occurs, does *B* always follow? Are unconscious wishes not to see followed, in general, by hysterical blindness? To determine this, we would have to look at many cases of people who are not hysterically blind and find that they lack the unconscious wish. The case history method, however, investigates only people with the disorder, not those without the disorder, and therefore it usually cannot isolate the cause.

Clinical case histories provide the richest source of hypotheses about the cause and cure of abnormality. Usually case histories generate several possible causes that cannot be unraveled even by adding further similar cases. The search for the cause among several possible causes is the theme of this chapter. This search provides the central rationale for us to move from examining the clinical case to discussing the experiment.

SCIENTIFIC EXPERIMENTATION

The experimental method

The grand ambition of all scientific experiments is to provide understanding by answering the question of cause. The basic experimental method is simple: (1) you make a guess (hypothesis) at the cause of an event; (2) you remove the suspected cause, and see if the event fails to occur; (3) you put the suspected cause back in and see if the event now reoccurs.

An experiment, then, consists of a procedure in which the hypothesized cause is manipulated and the occurrence of the effect is measured. The hypothesized cause, which the experimenter manipulates, is called the ***independent variable.*** The effect, which the experimenter measures, is called the ***dependent variable,*** because its occurrence depends on whether the cause precedes it. Both independent and dependent variables are operationally defined. An ***operational definition*** is the set of measurable conditions under which a phenomenon is said to occur. So, for example, obesity can be operationally defined as being 15 percent or more above the normal weights for a given height as given in a table of weights, or depression can be defined as having greater than a given score on a checklist of depressive symptoms. When manipulating an independent variable produces changes in a dependent variable, an ***experimental effect*** has been obtained.

Clinical case histories, you will recall, usually cannot answer the causal question definitively. While multiple similar cases can establish that hysterical blindness is generally preceded by unconscious wishes, they cannot establish whether such wishes are generally followed by the symptom in question. In principle, a well-done experiment can answer this question by imposing the wish (independent variable) on individuals and see if hysterical blindness follows (dependent variable). There are a variety of ethical and practical reasons, however, why this experiment would never be done. We will now turn to an actual experiment designed to test the effectiveness of a novel therapy for depression.

AN EXPERIMENT

Relieving depression by dream deprivation

Several clinical case histories about sleep deprivation recently came to the attention of researchers looking for cures of depression. It appeared that, in a few instances, depressed individuals who for one reason or another missed several whole nights of sleep surprisingly became less depressed. Putting this together with the fact that two antidepressant drugs, tricyclics and MAO inhibitors, incidentally reduce the amount of dreaming, investigators hypothesized that dream deprivation itself might relieve depression (Vogel, 1975).

When we dream, our eyes move rapidly back and forth beneath our closed lids; the muscles from the neck down lose their tone; and in males, the penis becomes erect. Since we can monitor when an individual is dreaming, we can deprive him of dreams by waking him up every time these signs appear. Such dream deprivation, carried out in a sleep laboratory for several nights running, was the independent variable that was manipulated in this experiment. Individuals who had been hospitalized for depression were the subjects, and the dependent variables were changes in ratings of the severity of depression on a variety of symptoms. The investigators obtained the expected experimental effect: when the depressed people were deprived of dreaming over a period of three weeks, they became markedly less depressed. But not all the depressed people improved. Only the subgroup who suffered from a specific kind of depression (called endogenous depression, see Chapter 11) showed signs of improvement.

Can we now conclude that dream deprivation causes relief from depression? Not yet. Perhaps it was not the dream deprivation that was effective, but some other aspect of what was done to the depressed patients. For example, the patients had electrodes strapped on them, got less total sleep than normal, and slept in a laboratory. Any one of these might have been effec-

In the sleep laboratory, studies of dream deprivation are carried out by using electrical signals which detect rapid eye movements to turn on an alarm clock, waking up the subject.

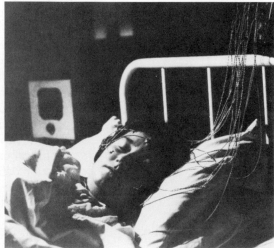

tive, rather than the specific manipulation of preventing them from dreaming.

Control groups to
eliminate
confounds

Factors other than the independent variable which might produce an experimental effect and which occur along with the independent variable are called *confounds.* In order to eliminate such confounds, experimenters use control procedures, the most typical of which is the *control group.* In principle, a control group is a group of subjects similar to those in the experimental group, who experience just the confounded factors that the experimental group had, but who do not experience the hypothesized cause. In contrast, the *experimental group* experiences both the confounds and the hypothesized cause. In general, whenever there is reason to suspect that some factor confounded with the independent variable might produce the effect, groups that control for that confounding factor must be run.

In this study, the investigators ran an appropriate control group, which controlled for a number of confounds. Other depressed patients were put through exactly the same procedure as above. They spent three weeks sleeping in the laboratory, electrodes were taped on them, and they were awakened the same number of times during each night as were those in the experimental group. But there was one crucial difference: the awakenings occurred, not when the patients were dreaming, but during non-dreaming phases of sleep. The patients in the control group did not become less depressed. This study is a good example of a *therapy outcome study,* in which the effects of a therapy are observed as it attempts to alleviate a disorder. Such experiments allow us to determine which therapies are effective. Here we can conclude that dream deprivation alleviates depression in endogenously depressed patients.

META-ANALYSIS

Meta-analysis to
integrate large
numbers of
conflicting studies

Any single therapy outcome study can be hard to evaluate and even harder to generalize even to similar therapies. So, for example, if the therapy works on severely depressed young students, we cannot be sure it will work with middle-aged adults who are mildly depressed. If the therapy worked and the therapists were very experienced, is it likely to work even if the therapists are less experienced? These are important questions, since what therapy choices the public makes can depend on being able to generalize from such studies. To solve this dilemma the technique of *meta-analysis* of therapy outcome studies has arisen.

In meta-analysis, the analyst looks at a large number of therapy outcome studies, which may differ in many of their particulars, and attempts to integrate them statistically by concluding whether the therapy works and how large an effect it has. Consider the question of whether psychotherapy works at all. To answer this, Smith and Glass (1977) meta-analyzed 375 studies of psychotherapy involving 25,000 clients and 25,000 control subjects. These studies differed on many dimensions: age of clients, experience of therapists, type of disorder, duration of therapy, kind of therapy, and measure of outcome. But they were all similar in that each had a treated (experimental) group and a control condition. The analysts asked whether the experimental group benefited from therapy more than did the control group. In this meta-analysis, the average client under treatment does better than 75 percent of the untreated controls. So we can conclude that, in general, psychotherapy produces robust benefits relative to not being treated.

The meta-analyst can then ask about specific forms of therapy or about specific kinds of problems. So, for example, clients undergoing systematic desensitization for phobias (Chapter 5) do better on average than 82 percent of untreated controls, and those undergoing psychodynamic therapy for interpersonal conflicts (Chapter 4) do better than 72 percent of untreated controls.

EXPERIMENTAL CONFOUNDS

A well-done experiment can allow us to determine whether *A* causes *B*. Experimenters, however, must be on their guard against a variety of subtle confounds, which might actually produce the experimental effect. Common among these are nonrandom assignment, experimenter bias, subject bias, and demand characteristics.

NONRANDOM ASSIGNMENT

Mistaken inferences based on nonrandom assignment

In an experiment that includes an experimental group and a control group, it is important that subjects be assigned to groups on a random basis. Such **random assignment** means that each subject should have had an equal chance of being assigned to each group. If subjects are not assigned by random selection, disastrously mistaken inferences, like the following example, can occur.

Who gets more stomach ulcers, individuals with a great deal of responsibility or individuals who have little responsibility? To decide this, four "executive" monkeys learned to lever press in order to avoid shock both for themselves and for their four yoked partners (Brady et al., 1958). In a *yoking* procedure, both experimental and control groups receive exactly the same physical events (shocks), but only the experimental group influences these events by its responses. In the case of the executive monkeys, those in the experimental group could avoid the shocks by pressing a lever. The yoked control group, on the other hand, received exactly the same shock but had no responsibility for turning it off; they were helpless since no response they made enabled them to avoid shock. The study showed that the "executives" developed stomach ulcers and died, while their helpless partners remained healthy. Many readers drew the conclusion that executives run a higher risk of psychosomatic illness than more powerless individuals. Only years later did other scientists notice that the monkeys had not been randomly selected to the two groups. When the experiment began, all eight of the monkeys were shocked, and the first four to start pressing the lever were assigned to the "executive" group. We now realize that the more emotional the monkey was or the more the shock hurt him, the sooner he started banging at the lever. As it turned out, the four most emotionally reactive monkeys became the executives and the four most stolid became the yoked controls. Not surprisingly, the emotional "executives" died with ulcers, and the stolid but helpless monkeys stayed healthy. When the experiment was repeated thirteen years later, this time with randomly assigned subjects, the helpless animals developed more ulcers than the executives (Weiss, 1971).

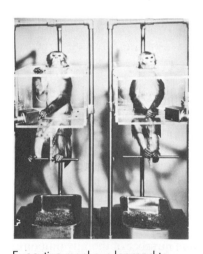

Executive monkeys learned to lever press to avoid shock for themselves and their yoked partners. Nonrandom assignment of subjects to the "executive group," however, may have confounded the results of this experiment and produced more ulcers in the executive group.

EXPERIMENTER AND SUBJECT BIAS

Expectations as
influencing results

Another source of mistaken inference from experiments comes from *experimenter bias.* If an experimenter wants or expects a particular result, he can subtly influence his subjects to produce that result, sometimes without being aware of it. If the experimenter merely nods his head agreeably at the crucial time he might be able to produce the experimental result spuriously (Greenspoon, 1955). An even bigger problem than experimenter bias is **subject bias.** Human subjects routinely form beliefs about what they are expected to do. When someone believes that a drug that is actually useless is going to help him, he may still sometimes get better after taking the drug. For example, following major surgery, pain is frequent and severe. Yet, about 35 percent of patients report marked relief after taking a useless drug, or **placebo** (Beecher, 1959). Morphine, even in large doses, relieves pain only 75 percent of the time. We can conclude from this that suggestion probably provides much of the pain-killing benefits of morphine (Melzack, 1973). To deal with subject bias, investigators use an experimental group that receives a real drug and a control group that is given a placebo. Both groups are given identical instructions. The mere belief on the part of all subjects that any pill should work has powerful effects. For it to be considered effective, the investigators must then find the real drug to be more potent than the placebo alone.

If neither the experimenter nor the subject knows whether the subject is in the experimental or the placebo control group, the results cannot be affected by either experimenter or subject bias. This elegant design in which both subject and experimenter are "blind" as to which subjects have received a drug or placebo is called a **double-blind experiment.** An experiment in which only the subject does not know whether he is receiving a drug or placebo is called a **single-blind experiment.** The design in which only the experimenter is blind and the subject is not is an **experimenter-blind design.**

DEMAND CHARACTERISTICS

Subjects
hypothesizing
how they should
behave

Most subjects want to be good subjects and to confirm the experimenter's hypothesis. Frequently at the end of an experiment, subjects ask, "I hope I didn't ruin the experiment?" A few subjects want to be bad subjects and try to undermine the experiment. Both need, first, to figure out what the experimenter's hypothesis is and then to act accordingly. Campus scuttlebutt, the advertisement to get subjects, the personality of the experimenter, the explicit statement of the instructions, implicit suggestions in the instructions, and the setting of the laboratory all constitute a set of **demand characteristics** that may induce a subject to invent a hypothesis about how he should behave.

The demand characteristics can be powerful cues, which lead to grossly mistaken inferences. In the 1950s, the topic of sensory deprivation was fashionable. In studies of this phenomenon, college students were paid $20 for a twenty-four-hour day of lying on cots in darkened, sound-deadened rooms. They wore translucent goggles that made sight impossible, gloves and cuffs that made feeling impossible, and they listened to masking noise that blocked hearing (Bexton, Heron, and Scott, 1954). The investigators found that the subjects had hallucinations: first they saw simple patterns, later they

Demand characteristics can provide powerful clues to how a subject should behave. Here, a subject is participating in a sensory deprivation experiment. Will he have stress-induced hallucinations during isolation because of the sensory deprivation or because he *believes* he should be having hallucinations during such an experience?

saw complex, moving figures. They also felt highly stressed, nauseous, agitated, and fatigued. It was concluded that removing vision, touch, and hearing for normal human subjects produced stress-induced hallucinations.

But in reviewing these sensory deprivation experiments, Martin Orne and his associates noticed something fishy about their design. There seemed to be some powerful demand characteristics: subjects were first greeted by a doctor in a white coat; a sign "Sensory Deprivation Laboratory" was on the door; the subjects had to sign awesome release forms absolving the experimenter of responsibility should anything untoward happen; and they had a panic button that would release them from the experiment if "anything undesirable should happen." Could it be that these trappings communicated to the subject that he was expected to be stressed and perhaps to have hallucinations? This would mean that it was not the sensory deprivation but the demand characteristics that produced the experimental effect.

To test this, subjects were led into a room labeled "Memory Deprivation Laboratory," and they were greeted by a doctor in a white coat with a stethoscope. Awesome release forms were signed. Subjects were told that if the experiment proved to be too much for them, they could use the red panic button conspicuously installed in the wall of the experimental room. *No sensory deprivation whatsoever was imposed on the subjects.* Rather, they sat in a well-lighted room with two comfortable chairs, they were provided with ice water and sandwiches, and they were also given an optional task of adding numbers. In this situation, the subjects also reported stress-induced hallucinations, indicating that the demand characteristics and not the sensory deprivation may have caused the hallucinations (Orne, 1962).

STATISTICAL INFERENCE

Frequently there is room for doubt about whether an experimental manipulation really worked, even when experimental confounds have been ruled out. This is particularly true when there is an experimental and control group, each made up of several subjects. What happens when most, but not all subjects in the experimental group show an effect, and few, but not many subjects in the control group do not? How do we decide whether an effect is real, rather than due to chance?

Statistical inferences are the procedures we use to decide whether the ***sample,*** or particular observations we made, truly represents the ***population,*** or the entire set of potential observations we might have made.

Statistics to determine if sample represents the population

Let us say we try out a new drug therapy on a sample of ten schizophrenics, and at the end of a year, six of them recover from schizophrenia. Did the drug cure the disorder? To begin with, we need to compare the drug therapy group to a control group of schizophrenics who were given placebos. Let's say we have an excellent control group: there is a control group consisting of 100 other wards in which each of the ten schizophrenic individuals is untreated, that is, merely given a placebo. On the average, for all of these wards, three out of ten schizophrenics have recovered by the end of the year. Is the difference between six out of ten recoveries with the drug and an average of three out of ten recoveries with the placebo, real? Or, could as many as six out of ten of the patients have recovered, untreated, by chance alone? If this were so, the new drug would be worthless. It is vital to decide this, for unless we can, we will not know if it is worthwhile to use the drug for the population of schizophrenics as a whole.

To decide if the difference between six out of ten and three out of ten could have occurred by chance, we need to know the ***frequency distribution*** of recoveries from ward to ward. A frequency distribution is the number of occurrences in each given class observed; in this case, the number of wards showing no recoveries, one recovery, two recoveries, and so on. This frequency distribution shows how different numbers of recoveries among the wards are distributed. We know that the ***mean,*** or total number of recoveries divided by the total number of schizophrenics, is three out of ten, but for how many of the other wards did six (or more) out of ten schizophrenics recover? With a mean of three out of ten, six could be a very infrequent occurrence. For example, if exactly three out of ten recovered in each and every ward, then six out of ten would be very unlikely to occur by chance. With a different distribution, it could be a very frequent occurrence, for example, if for 50 of the wards, six out of ten recovered, but for the other 50 wards, zero out of ten recovered. In the first case, we could be very confident that the drug produced a real effect; in the second case, we would have very little confidence that the drug worked, and we would assume that six out of ten recoveries was just a chance fluctuation in the recovery rate.

Statistically significant results

Let us say we know the distribution of recovery for the 100 placebo wards (see Figure 6-1). In only 5 wards (noted by color) did six (or more) schizophrenics recover without treatment. This means that only 5 percent of the time (i.e., in 5 out of 100 placebo wards) will chance fluctuation produce recovery in as many as six out of ten cases. Scientists are generally quite conservative about making claims, and by convention, a real effect will be claimed only with at least 95 percent confidence that chance did not produce the result. When effects exceed this conventional confidence level, they are called ***statistically significant.***

Misses and false alarms

Making inferences in this way, however, can result in two kinds of mistakes: ***misses*** (saying x is false when it is true) and ***false alarms*** (saying x is

Figure 6-1
Frequency distribution for spontaneous recovery of schizophrenics. The bar graph shows the number of schizophrenic patients recovering without drug treatment out of ten in a given ward. The bars in color show the wards in which six or more patients recovered without treatment.

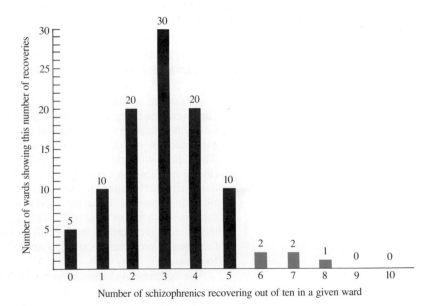

true when it is false). A miss can occur when, for example, confidence does not reach the 5 percent level: say we are only confident at the 10 percent level that the number of drug recoveries was not due to chance and so we reject the hypothesis that the drug causes recovery, and yet the drug really does cure schizophrenia. We have missed a real cure by our conservative procedure. On the other hand, a false alarm can occur when confidence does reach the 5 percent level: say we accept the hypothesis that the drug causes recovery, but this turns out to be one of the 5 percent of the wards in which six people would have recovered without treatment and the drug really does nothing. Here not being conservative enough caused us to adopt a therapy which was really ineffective.

These two kinds of mistakes have both occurred many times in science; in fact, they are inversely related, they stand in a trade-off relationship to each other. The choice of a confidence level is always a difficult and sometimes a life or death decision. If we require a very conservative level of confidence before we accept a new therapy, say 1 percent, then we will have very few false alarms. As a consequence, we will incorrectly believe a therapy works when it does not, only 1 percent of the time. But the cost of this is that we will miss many therapies that really are effective. On the other hand, if we set a much less conservative level—say 20 percent—we will not miss many real therapies, but we will believe that certain therapies work quite often when they are actually ineffective.

EXPERIMENTS WITH A SINGLE SUBJECT

Experiments with many subjects

Most experiments involve an experimental group and a control group, each with several subjects. Several subjects, as opposed to one, increase our confidence in the causal inference made in an experiment because of two factors: (1) *repeatability*—the experimental manipulation is repeated and has its effect on several individuals; and (2) *generality*—several randomly chosen individuals, not just one, are affected, and this increases our confidence that any new individual, randomly chosen, would also be so affected.

Experiments with one subject

But useful experiments can be carried out with just one subject, and a well-designed ***single-subject experiment*** can accomplish the goal of demonstrating repeatability. The demonstration of generality, however, always requires several subjects. An example of a single-subject experiment follows:

Walter was a retarded ten-year-old, whose outbursts in his special education class were contagious, and therefore particularly disruptive. His teacher, in conjunction with several experimental and clinical psychologists, hypothesized that his outbursts, or "talk outs" were maintained by the teacher's attention to him when she reprimanded him, and that by ignoring the talk outs and giving attention to him for more constructive actions, the talk outs would extinguish. They designed what is called an "A-B-A-B" experiment to test this. In such a design untreated, or baseline, behavior is measured (A_1), then treatment is instituted (B_1), then there is a return to no treatment (A_2), then treatment is reinstituted (B_2). (You may notice, incidentally, that a clinical case history, like the case of Jack in which a therapeutic procedure is tried, is an A-B design: A_1, untreated, followed by B_1, treatment).

The experiment to change Walter's behavior was divided into four phases, during each of which the number of talk outs was counted. In the first five-day phase (A₁-untreated) the teacher handled the talk outs as she normally did, by reprimanding him. In the second five-day phase (B₁-treatment₁), the teacher ignored the talk outs and paid attention to Walter whenever he did anything constructive. The third phase (A₂-untreated₂) repeated the first phase: talk outs were again reprimanded. Finally, the fourth five-day phase (B₂-treatment₂) repeated the second phase: the talk outs were ignored, and the teacher only paid attention to him for constructive actions.

As you can see from Figure 6-2, the hypothesis proved correct. During A₁, there were about four outbursts in each session, but when contingent attention was instituted (B₁), Walter rapidly learned to produce no outbursts. The most important and convincing part of the experiments, however, were the repeated procedures, A₂ and B₂. These phases gave us evidence of repeatability. By reinstituting reprimands and showing that talk outs again increased, the experimenters showed that the decrease in talk outs during treatment was unlikely to have been caused by chance; rather the high rate of outbursts probably was caused by the reprimands. Then, by reinstituting treatment and showing fewer outbursts once again, we can infer that treatment probably caused his quieter behavior rather than chance. In addition, since the two conditions (each repeated) differed only in the direction of the teacher's attention—to bad behavior or to constructive behavior—cause is isolated in the same way that a control group isolates cause in a multi-subject experiment. The control condition occurs within the same subject and therefore does not require a separate control *group.*

It could be, however, that only Walter in particular, rather than misbehaving, retarded boys in general, would improve with attention to constructive behavior. Only repeating the procedure with several subjects would show generality. When there is only one subject available, however, as in a rare disorder or unique therapy, single-subject designs are the only way of determining causality.

Figure 6-2
A record of talking-out behavior of a retarded student. A₁ untreated—before experimental conditions. B₂ treatment—systematic ignoring of talking out and increased teacher attention to appropriate behavior. A₂ untreated—reinstatement of teacher attention to talking-out behavior. B₂ treatment—return to systematic ignoring of talking out and increased attention to appropriate behavior. (Source: Hall et al., 1971)

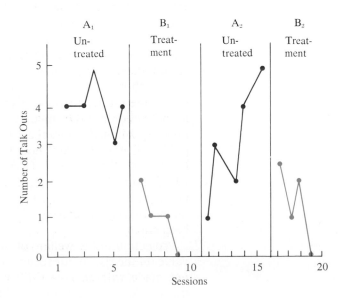

EVALUATION OF THE EXPERIMENTAL METHOD

Strengths and weaknesses

The experimental method has three strengths and three weaknesses. The first strength is that it is the foremost method for isolating causal elements. Second, it is general to the population sampled, when group—as opposed to single-subject—experiments are done. Third, it is repeatable. The first weakness is that an experiment is artificial; it does not capture the full reality of a disorder. Second, inferences made are probabilistic, not certain. Finally, performing certain experiments sometimes may be unethical or impractical. We now turn to a discussion of this last point: the practical and ethical difficulties of experimentation.

Practical problems

Often the road to experimental inquiry is completely blocked, and an alternate method must be used to attempt to investigate etiology. The reason an experiment cannot be done is often practical. It may be too expensive or time consuming. For example, will changing the child-rearing practices of schizophrenic parents lower the chances that their children will eventually become schizophrenic? An experiment may require more subjects than can be practically obtained. For example, "Will anti-anxiety drugs prevent hysterical blindness, which is a rare disorder?" The right technology may not yet exist. For example, "Will stimulating single brain cells related to satiation reduce obesity in humans?"

Ethical problems

Very often we do not experiment for ethical reasons. In 1920, an experiment was performed on a healthy nine-month-old infant, Little Albert (see Chapter 8). Investigators experimentally instilled in him a phobia of small animals by pairing a startling loud noise with his playing with a white rat (Watson and Rayner, 1920). There are two sides to this ethical issue. Look at the experiment from Little Albert's point of view. An innocent and healthy child, with no say in the matter, was caused to be terrified of small, furry creatures. Should he have had to endure this suffering? Further, Albert was taken from the hospital by his mother, who was a wet nurse there, before curative procedures could be tried out, and he was never heard from again. Was he victimized by a lifelong phobia of rats? The moral climate has changed, and this is an experiment that could not be undertaken today.

But now look at the Little Albert experiment from a real phobic's point of view. Forget, for a moment, Albert's suffering and the possibility that he became a phobic. As we shall see in the fear and phobia chapter, as a direct result of the Little Albert experiment, curative procedures were tried out in fearful children, experimental models of phobias were developed and refined in animals and then applied to human adults, and a cure for many phobias is now known. Thousands of phobic individuals today are free to lead normal lives because of a line of experimentation that began with Little Albert's suffering. There is a clear conflict of interest here, and it is very difficult to decide whose rights are more important: one innocent Albert made phobic through no choice of his own versus thousands of phobics who have been cured.

Protection of the welfare of human (and animal) subjects is presently a value on the rise in our society. But deciding to increase such protection is not made without cost (Miller, 1985). There is an unavoidable consequence: some research that might have benefited troubled people is left undone. There is, however, one set of values that investigators of abnormality generally do agree on: the less drastic experiment is preferable to the more drastic, less shock to more shock, less deceptive experiments to more deceptive ones, using animals to using humans. But even here there are costs, since we must infer that the results found with less drastic conditions are valid for more drastic conditions, or that the finding is general beyond the species investigated.

There are a variety of ethical and practical reasons why the road to experimentation is often blocked in the study of abnormal psychology. The most frequent reason is that we value the right of the subjects in experiments to be treated humanely more than the right of humanity to possible experimental knowledge about cure and cause of abnormality. When the relevant experiment cannot be done, three other methods have been devised to provide information about etiology and cure: correlation, experiments of nature, and laboratory models.

CORRELATION

In an experiment, the experimenter manipulates the independent variable in order to discover cause. He or she imposes the independent variable on the subjects in the experimental group, but withholds it from subjects in the control group. If the experimental group but not the control group shows the effect, the experimenter infers causation. For ethical and practical reasons, such manipulation cannot be done in many settings of abnormality, so correlation is a widely used investigative technique. *Correlation* is pure observation, without manipulation. An observer performing a correlation measures two classes of events and records the relationship between them. There are three possible relationships: (1) As one increases, so does the other. This is called a *positive correlation.* Height, for example, correlates positively with weight, for the taller a person is, generally the more he weighs. This correlation is shown graphically in Figure 6-3A. (2) As one increases, the other decreases. This is called a *negative correlation.* Studying is, in general, negatively correlated with failure, for the more we study, the less likely we are to fail (Figure 6-3B). (3) As one changes, the other does not change in any systematic way. Two such events are said to be *uncorrelated.* Hair length is uncorrelated with failure on algebra exams, for how long our hair is, in general, makes no difference as to whether or not we fail (Figure 6-3C). The central point here is that in correlational studies, we are observers of the variables; we do not manipulate weight, height, hair length, studying, or failure. Instead, we look at the relationships among variables.

Let us now see how correlation can be applied to burning issues of abnormal psychology by working through an example of a negative correlation. One investigator proposed an elegantly simple theory of human depression: that depression is caused by having too few rewards in daily life (Lewinsohn, 1975). Experimentation on this is limited by ethical considerations; we cannot take nondepressed people and withhold rewards in their daily lives to see if depression results. But we can perform relevant correlations: Does depth of depression correlate with the number of pleasant activities that different individuals engage in? The experimenter predicted a negative cor-

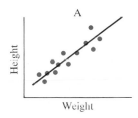

A

Height

Weight

B

Hours of Study

Number of
Failures

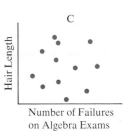

C

Hair Length

Number of Failures
on Algebra Exams

Figure 6-3
Correlations. Here are three scatterplots illustrating a positive correlation (A), a negative correlation (B), and a lack of correlation (C). The positive correlation indicates that taller individuals tend to weigh more. The negative correlation indicates that individuals who study less tend to fail more. The lack of correlation indicates no relationship between hair length and failure on algebra exams.

Table 6-1 NEGATIVE CORRELATION BETWEEN DEPRESSION AND NUMBER OF PLEASANT ACTIVITIES

Name	Degree of Depression (the higher the score, the more depression)	Number of Pleasant Activities (in the past week)
Adam	30	1
Minerva	24	4
Davey	19	2
Elmo	11	4
John	7	7
Alphonso	6	9
Lynn	3	6
Lauren	2	11
Sarah	0	13
Amy	0	10

relation: as pleasant activities decrease, the degree of depression increases. Both variables can be operationally defined: degree of depression by a self-report test (Beck Depression Inventory), which totals up the number and severity of mood, thought, motivational, and physical symptoms that an individual reports; and a Pleasant Events Scale, which totals up the number of good events, such as going on a date, listening to music, watching TV, dancing, that the individual has recently engaged in. The predicted negative correlation has been found: the higher the degree of depression, the fewer pleasant events that have been engaged in.

Consider the following hypothetical, but representative data, showing a negative correlation between depression and pleasant events in ten individuals (Table 6-1). The data show a strong negative correlation between depression and pleasant activities. Adam, who is far and away the most depressed, engaged in only one pleasant activity in the past week: watching TV. Sarah and Amy, who are not at all depressed, did many enjoyable things. In general, among the other seven individuals, the more the depression, the fewer pleasant activities they engaged in. The correlation is strong, but less than a perfect negative correlation, since, for example, Minerva was considerably more depressed than Davey (24 vs. 19) but engaged in more pleasant activities (4 vs. 2), although both were near the low end of activity.

This negative correlation can be seen graphically in Figure 6-4. Each person is represented by a point. A straight line is "fitted" to the points and the

Figure 6-4
Graph of the negative correlation between depression and number of pleasant events documented in Table 6-1. As pleasant events increase, severity of depression decreases.

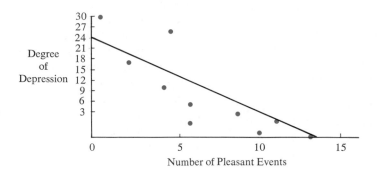

negative correlation is indicated by the descending line: the more depression, the fewer activities. If the correlation had turned out positive (the more depression, the more activities), the best fitting line would have been ascending.

CORRELATION COEFFICIENTS

Determining level of confidence

The strength of the relationship between two classes of events can be expressed by a ***correlation coefficient,*** the symbol for which is r (representing the Pearson Product Moment Correlation Coefficient, which is named after its inventor, Karl Pearson). The range for r is as follows: r can be as great as $+ 1.00$, for a perfect positive correlation; it can vary through 0.00, meaning no relationship at all; and it can go down to $- 1.00$ for a perfect negative correlation. The r for our depression scores and pleasant activities turns out to be $- .87$, a strong negative correlation. The level of confidence that the relation did not occur by chance, or its ***statistical significance,*** can be determined for r, by using logic similar to that used for deciding whether or not two groups really differ. In general, the farther the correlation coefficient is from .00, in either the positive or negative direction, and the more observations there are that contribute to the correlation, the higher is our confidence that the relationship did not occur by chance. Conventionally, the 95 percent level of confidence is chosen as statistically significant.

CORRELATION AND CAUSALITY

Determining causes

Given the strong negative correlation in our example, can we conclude that a life with few rewards *causes* depression? The answer is no. And herein lies the main disadvantage of the correlational method compared to the experimental method. There are really three causal possibilities and not just one: (1) engaging in only a few pleasant activities might cause depression; (2) depression itself might cause people to engage in fewer pleasant activities; for example, perhaps depression blunts the desire to be social; and (3) both depression and lower activity could be caused by some unobserved third variable, such as some biochemical imbalance. In general, whether there is a correlation between X and Y, it can be either that X causes Y, that Y causes X, or that Z causes both X and Y.

Narrowing down possible causes

Carrying out correlation studies, then, does not always lead us to discover cause. But there are ways of narrowing down the possible causes. One way is to perform an experiment. For example, an experiment has actually been done to test causation for the depression example above. In this experiment, depressed students were induced to increase the number of pleasant events they engaged in each day. Depressed students who increased their activities did not become any less depressed than the control group of depressed students, who did not change their activity level; rather they became more depressed (Hammen and Glass, 1975). So the fact that activity and depression correlate negatively does not seem to reflect a causal relationship. Having few rewards probably does not cause depression, rather depression either causes individuals to engage in fewer rewarding activities, or both are caused by an unobserved third variable. We infer this because the number of pleasant activities has been experimentally manipulated, yet depression has not been alleviated.

Doing the relevant experiment is one way of determining the direction of causality that has been suggested, but not proven, by a correlation. A second way has to do with the order in which the variables occur in time. For example, positive correlations have been found between illness and the number of major life events, such as divorce and job loss, in the year preceding illness; the more life events before, the more illnesses after (Holmes and Rahe, 1967). Here, temporal sequence narrows the possibilities of cause from three to two: a hassled life could produce illness, or some third variable, like unstable personality, could produce both more illness and more life events, but the hypothesis that the illness causes the increases in life events is ruled out.

EVALUATION OF THE CORRELATIONAL METHOD

Advantages and disadvantage of correlation

There are several advantages, and one major disadvantage, to correlational studies of abnormality. The use of correlations allows a quantitative and rigorous observation of relation between variables. Also, because the observations are on natural phenomenon, correlations do not have the artificiality of laboratory studies. Further, correlational studies are an option when performing an experiment is not a possibility, whether for practical or for ethical reasons. Lastly, correlations are repeatable. On the negative side, the major disadvantage in performing correlational studies is that the cause of a particular phenomenon usually cannot be isolated. One can move closer to discovering the cause, but other methods, such as experimental tests, are needed to determine causation more definitively.

EXPERIMENTS OF NATURE

Inferences of causes of unusual natural events

Nature sometimes performs the experimental manipulation that scientists themselves could not do because of ethical or practical considerations. Sometimes a striking event occurs that changes the lives of individuals. An alert investigator can use such accidents to make inferences about what causes and cures abnormality. Because the accident is usually so striking, it is reasonable to suppose that *it,* and not some other extraneous event that happens to occur at the same time, is the cause. Such a strategy is an ***experiment of nature,*** in short, a study in which the experimenter observes the effects of an unusual natural event.

An act of nature may permit us to study the effects of trauma on human behavior. We can go into villages to find survivors of earthquakes, volcano eruptions and so on, and we can observe their behavior. Ethical considerations (if not practical ones) prevent scientists from intentionally subjecting humans to traumatic stress. But because knowledge about the effects of trauma is so important to the study of abnormality, scientists will occasionally visit the scenes of natural disasters to observe the effects of such experiments of nature. One such study was of the survivors of a flood in the Buffalo Creek area of Appalachia. For many months following the trauma, the survivors showed symptoms of terror, disturbed sleep, guilt over surviving, and reliving of the events (Erikson, 1976). These observations helped to give rise to a new category of anxiety disorder called "post-traumatic stress disorder" (see Chapter 8).

Victims of disasters are often observed and studied by psychologists. One victim of the Buffalo Creek flood related, ''I have good new neighbors, but it's not the same . . . The day the flood came, the people of Buffalo Creek started running, and they are still running inside their minds. They don't have time to stand and talk.''

Longitudinal
studies

An experiment of nature is usually *retrospective,* with systematic observation beginning only after the precipitating event. But experiments of nature can also be *prospective,* with observation beginning before an expected outcome occurs. When prospective studies are *longitudinal* as well, that is looking at the same subjects on the same variables at different points over their lifetime, they are particularly powerful methods of investigation (Baltes, Reese, and Lipsitt, 1980). Consider the following prospective, longitudinal study of children vulnerable to schizophrenia by virtue of being born to a mother who was schizophrenic (Mednick, Parnas, and Schulsinger, 1987). In this Copenhagen study, 207 children of schizophrenic mothers and 104 controls have been followed from 1962 until now. By 1972, 8.6 percent of the high-risk children had become schizophrenic, but only 1 percent of the children of normal mothers. Which of the vulnerable children became schizophrenic? Two factors emerge from this longitudinal study: (1) those high-risk children who had more traumatic births and birth complications tended to become schizophrenic, and (2) those high-risk children who had more unstable parenting tended to become schizophrenic. As more prospective, longitudinal studies are carried out, we will learn a great deal more about what environmental factors trigger psychopathology in individuals who are genetically vulnerable.

EVALUATION OF EXPERIMENTS OF NATURE

Strengths and
weaknesses

Experiments of nature have three strengths as a method of inquiry: (1) like a case history, they document an actual happening and lack the artificiality of the laboratory experiment or the abstractness of a correlation; (2) no unethical manipulation is performed by the investigator since he merely observes an event produced by nature; and (3) the gross cause can be determined, in fact, the gross cause defines the investigation as an experiment of nature. However, the method also has three weaknesses: (1) we cannot isolate the elements in the gross cause that are active from those that are inactive; for example, we cannot know which aspects—the suddenness of the disaster or seeing others die or the uprooting of the community—of the Buffalo Creek Flood produced the stress disorder; (2) experiments of nature, as they are rare and conspicuous events, are not repeatable; and (3) like case histories, this method is also subject to retrospective bias by both victim and investigator.

THE LABORATORY MODEL

Correlations and experiments of nature are both used by investigators of abnormality when the road to experimentation is blocked. The final technique for getting around the impossibility of direct experimentation is the *laboratory model.* In the last decade, scientists have made considerable strides in understanding psychopathology by using such laboratory models.

Producing symptoms to test hypotheses

A laboratory model is in essence the production, under controlled conditions, of phenomena analogous to naturally occurring mental disorders. That is, a particular symptom or constellation of symptoms is produced in miniature to test hypotheses about cause and cure. Confirmed hypotheses can then be further tested in situations outside the laboratory. Both human or animal subjects are utilized in laboratory models.

As an example, let us see how scientists have created an animal model of unipolar depression. About twenty-five years ago, investigators noticed that animals who received electric shock that was *uncontrollable*—that went on and off regardless of what the animal was doing—later became very passive. Later on in a different situation, they failed to even try to escape shock that was actually escapable. They just sat and took the shock (Seligman and Maier, 1967; Maier and Seligman, 1976). Evidence soon began to accumulate that such "learned helplessness" had many of the same symptoms as depression in humans.

Learned helplessness as a model for depression

Learned helplessness has been systematically evaluated to find if it is a valid model of depression (Weiss, Simson, Ambrose, Webster, and Hoffman, 1985). For a person to meet the DSM-III-R criteria for diagnosis of depression, at least five of these *nine* symptoms must be present: (1) loss of interest in usual activities, (2) weight loss and poor appetite, (3) insomnia, (4) psychomotor alterations, (5) fatigue or loss of energy, (6) diminished ability to think or attend, (7) depressed mood, (8) feelings of worthlessness, and (9) suicidal thoughts.

Animals who have experienced uncontrollable events show each of the first six symptoms. They would receive a diagnosis of depression if they were human. The last three symptoms (depressed mood, feelings of worthlessness, and suicidal thoughts cannot be displayed by animals. But the argument can be carried further. When humans are given uncontrollable noise, they display depressed mood and feelings of worthlessness in addition to the hallmark symptoms above (Hiroto and Seligman, 1975; Abramson, 1978). This means that eight of the nine symptoms of depression can be produced in the laboratory by uncontrollable events. The ninth, suicidal thoughts, cannot be produced, but probably because the intensity of the uncontrollable events in the laboratory is very mild.

This mapping of symptoms has inspired investigators to look for the biochemical basis of learned helplessness and to discover drug treatments that cure learned helplessness in animals. The brain chemistry of those suffering from learned helplessness has been explored and looks quite similar to what is known about the brain chemistry of those suffering from depression (Weiss et al., 1985). In addition, the drugs that break up helplessness in animals also alleviate depression in humans (Sherman and Petty, 1980).

All of this seems to argue that learned helplessness in animals is a convincing laboratory model of depression in humans. This model may help us to understand the brain chemistry of human depression, to understand how drugs can relieve depression, and to find new treatments for depression. The brain chemistry and experimental drug treatment of depression cannot be ethically carried out in humans, but such animal models enable us to understand and relieve human suffering with experimental rigor and to do so with fewer ethical dilemmas (Miller, 1985).

EVALUATION OF THE LABORATORY MODEL

Strengths and weaknesses

Laboratory models have three strengths: (1) as experiments, they can isolate the cause of the disorder; (2) they are repeatable; (3) they minimize unethical manipulation. Like all other methods, they also have several weaknesses: (1) as laboratory creations, they are not the natural phenomenon, only a *model* of it. Thus, they are *analogous* to but not identical with the real disorder itself; (2) since observers often use animal subjects in laboratory models, they must infer that humans and the species being investigated are similarly susceptible to the disorder.

As similarity of symptoms, cause, physiology, cure, and prevention mount, we become more convinced that the model is the actual disorder. In later chapters, we will see examples of models that have given insight into the cause and cure of such disorders as depression, stomach ulcers, and phobias. Sophisticated laboratory modeling is a new development in the field of abnormality. The verdict is not entirely in on any one model, but the technique promises to add to our understanding of abnormality.

COMBINING SEVERAL METHODS: A WOVEN FABRIC

Using several methods to gain understanding

There is no single, most convincing way to understand abnormality. Each method has strengths and weaknesses (Table 6-2). But clinical case histories, experimental studies, correlational studies, experiments of nature, and laboratory models all can provide some insight. Each by itself can, on occasion, provide conclusive understanding. But most of the time, each taken in isolation resembles blind men groping at an elephant: one has hold of the tail, another the trunk, another a foot. Each captures only one aspect of being an elephant, but none captures the whole thing. Similarly, the clinical case, well done, best conveys the reality of a disorder, but it usually fails to isolate the cause. The experiment, well done, isolates the cause, but it remains artificial. The correlation, well done, picks out crucial relationships, but not necessarily causal ones. But when the methods together converge on a theory, a fabric of understanding is woven. In the particular disorders that we are close to understanding, case history evidence, experimental studies, correlations, experiments of nature, and laboratory models all play a role. A

Table 6-2 STRENGTHS AND WEAKNESSES OF VARIOUS METHODS

Method	Strengths	Weaknesses
Single Clinical Case	1. Is not artificial. 2. Documents rare events. 3. Generates causal hypotheses.	1. Is selective and susceptible to retrospective bias. 2. Is not repeatable. 3. Is not general. 4. Does not isolate causal elements.
Experiments	1. Isolate causal elements. 2. Are general to population sampled (not true of single-subject experiments). 3. Are repeatable.	1. Are artificial; don't capture full reality of the disorder. 2. Inferences are probabilistic or statistical, rather than certain. 3. It is unethical or impractical to manipulate many crucial variables.
Correlations	1. Quantify and observe relationships. 2. Are not artificial. 3. Are repeatable.	1. Do not isolate causal elements.
Experiments of Nature	1. Are not artificial. 2. There is no unethical manipulation. 3. Isolate gross cause.	1. Do not isolate active elements of the cause. 2. Are not repeatable. 3. Are susceptible to retrospective bias.
Experimental Models	1. Isolate causal elements. 2. Are repeatable. 3. Minimize unethical manipulation.	1. Are analogous to but not identical with the real disorder. 2. Make cross-species inferences (with animal models).

worthy scientific fabric of converging evidence has already been woven for phobias, for the genetics of schizophrenia, for depression, for certain kinds of brain damage, and for sexual identity. For some of the specific disorders that we will discuss in the ensuing chapters, the reader when done, will probably feel bewildered, at sea. For most others, the reader probably will feel that he or she understands them partially but that pieces of the puzzle are still missing. But for several others, the reader should feel the pleasure and excitement of discovery and understanding, because these are examples of the woven fabric.

SUMMARY

1. The *clinical case history* is the record of part of the life of an individual as seen during therapy. Based on the patient's case history, the therapist will hypothesize about possible causes of a problem and then help the patient overcome his past.

2. A *scientific experiment* consists of a procedure in which the hypothesized cause (the *independent variable*) is manipulated and the occurrence of the effect (the *dependent variable*) is measured. Both independent and dependent variables are operationally defined. An *operational definition* is the set of measurable conditions under which a phenomenon is said to occur.

When manipulating an independent variable produces changes in a dependent variable, an *experimental effect* has been obtained.

3. *Confounds* are factors other than the independent variable that might produce an experimental effect. An *experimental group* experiences both the confounds and the hypothesized cause. The *control group* is similar to the experimental group, but the control group only experiences the confounds. Subtle confounds that might produce the experimental effect include nonrandom assignment, experimenter bias, subject bias, and demand characteristics.

4. *Statistical inferences* are the procedures used to determine whether the *sample* (the particular observations) truly represents the *population* (the entire set of potential observations). When effects exceed a conventional confidence level, they are called *statistically significant*.

5. If an hypothesis is rejected but it is really true, the mistake is called a *miss*. If an hypothesis is accepted but it is really false, the mistake is called a *false alarm*. Misses and false alarms stand in a trade-off relationship to each other; when there are many misses, there are few false alarms; when there are many false alarms, there are few misses.

6. *Correlation* is pure observation without manipulation. In a correlation, two classes of events are measured and the relationship between them is recorded. In a *positive correlation,* as one variable increases, the other does too. In a *negative correlation,* as one variable increases, the other decreases. Events are *uncorrelated* when, as one variable changes, the other does not change in any systematic way.

7. A relationship is *statistically significant* if it is unlikely to have occurred by chance. Generally, the farther the correlation is from .00 in either the positive or negative direction and the more observations that are made, the higher the level of confidence and the greater the likelihood that the relationship did not occur by chance.

8. *Experiments of nature* are studies in which the experimenter observes the effects of an unusual natural event. *Prospective, longitudinal* studies are a powerful means of assessing the effects of events on the development of psychopathology.

9. In a *laboratory model,* investigators produce, under controlled conditions, phenomena that are analogous to naturally occurring mental disorders. This is done to test hypotheses about biological and psychological causes and cures of symptoms.

10. No one method alone will provide complete understanding of psychopathology. But each method may lead us to an understanding of various aspects of abnormality. When all these methods converge in confirmation of a theory, we can say that a fabric of understanding has been woven.

CHAPTER
7

Psychological Assessment and Classification

ONE does not observe a group of people for very long without being struck by the differences among them. There are tall people and short ones, thin people and stout ones, redheads and brunettes. Such physical differences among people are obviously useful—they allow us to classify people according to their height or weight or hair color. But differences are useful in a more subtle way—they allow us to ask important questions about people. For example, we might want to know whether tall people are more successful than short ones, whether thin people live longer than fat ones, or whether redheads are more temperamental than brunettes. Being able to classify people according to certain physical characteristics may enable us to explore other significant questions.

People differ psychologically too. There are shy people and outgoing ones, industrious people and lazy ones, depressed people and happy ones. This observation too is a commonplace, but it leads to some very important ideas. Psychological classification permits us to group people according to their similarities, to ask how they came to be that way and how they can be changed. Without classification, there can be no science, no understanding of how things came to be and how they will evolve.

Psychological diagnosis

In this chapter, we take up the assessment and classification of abnormal psychological conditions. Because such classification often arises in a medical context and is modeled after medicine itself, it is often called psychological or psychiatric diagnosis. You know from the biological approach to abnormality (Chapter 3) that psychological diagnosis has already been a beneficial enterprise, for without it medical research could not have eliminated a disorder called general paresis. Those useful insights occurred nearly a century ago, however; here we will concern ourselves with modern psychological assessment and diagnosis. What kinds of assessment techniques promise reliable understanding of human misery and lead to useful diagnosis? What diagnostic categories seem most promising for understanding and treating psychological distress? Indeed, how do we assess whether an assessment procedure or diagnostic category is useful or promising?

Psychologists seek to understand individuals through a variety of procedures. They talk to people, administer psychological tests, and assess their behavior in real life situations. The first theme of this chapter consists of the contribution of these assessment techniques to the process of classification. The second theme concerns diagnosis itself: the reliability and usefulness of current diagnostic schemes.

PSYCHOLOGICAL ASSESSMENT

Assessment is undertaken to achieve a deep understanding of the client. That understanding may result in a diagnosis, but it commonly also results in much more. Commonly, assessment yields a sense of a person's individuality, the forces that generate his or her uniqueness. Often, it will give a sense of why a person is in difficulty, and occasionally a clue as to how the difficulty can be resolved.

Reliability and validity

In order for an assessment device to generate meaningful understandings about people, it must possess two characteristics. First, it must be *reliable,* that is, it must generate the same findings on repeated use; it must be stable. Much as a rubber yardstick has limited utility for measuring a room, a psychological test that yields different findings on different occasions has limited usefulness for understanding people. Second, it must be *valid.* It must be useful for the purposes for which it is intended. Even a good thermometer is useless for measuring a room. Similarly, a psychological test can be useful for one purpose and thoroughly invalid for others. Before examining specific assessment techniques, it is particularly important to have a good grasp of what is meant by reliability. The discussion of validity will be delayed until we take up psychological classification.

RELIABILITY

Developing reliable tests

Imagine a physical universe in which yardsticks are made of rubber. Each time you would measure something, you would come up with different answers simply because of the nature of the measuring instrument, for rubber stretches. Such an instrument would be *un*reliable, which is to say you could not depend on it to come up with the same measurement each time it was used. Though we don't often think about it, reliability is basic to all kinds of measurement, including the psychological measurement of people. In order to diagnose a problem, psychologists have developed certain measures, or tests, that aid in the assessment of people. The major challenge is to develop tests that are reliable. Do two psychologists arrive at the same impression on the basis of test or interview evidence? If they do, this is held to be evidence of *inter-judge reliability.* To what extent will a test administered today yield the same results when given a week or a month from now *(test-retest reliability* or *test stability)*? Reliability refers to the extent to which an instru-

Figure 7-1
These diagrams depict various levels of reliability. Notice that even if reliability is relatively high, such as .67, there is considerable difference between say, the scores on Variable X and those on Variable Y that are supposed to measure the same thing.

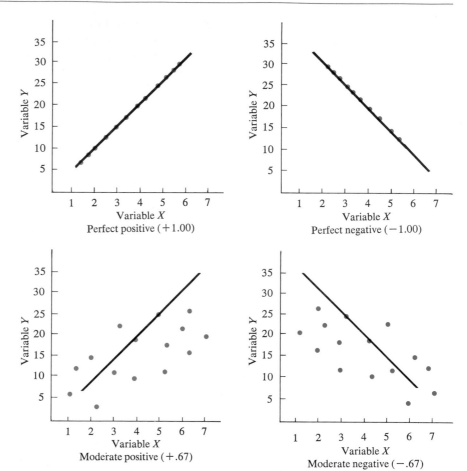

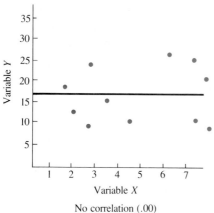

Reliability and use of instruments

ment—be it a test or an observer—yields the same result in repeated trials or with different observers. When a group of psychologists examines a patient, and all arrive at the same conclusion, that conclusion is said to have ***high reliability.*** When, however, they cannot agree, each proffered viewpoint is considered to have ***low reliability.*** Figure 7-1 describes reliability graphically. When two observers or tests are in complete agreement, their reliability is said to be 1.00. When they arrive at diametrically opposite conclusions, reliability is said to be −1.00. And when there seems to be no relationship between their conclusions, the reliability of those conclusions is 0.00.

As anyone who has tried to measure a floor knows, even using physical yardsticks, one rarely gets a reliability of 1.00. There are tiny measurement differences. Depending upon the purpose of the measurement, such differences may mean a great deal or nothing at all. A difference of an eighth of an inch means little to the height of an oak, but a lot to the diameter of a diamond. So it is with psychological measurement. How reliable an instrument needs to be depends upon many things, among them the purposes for which it is being used and the consequences of small and large errors (Cronbach et al., 1972). Generally, a high degree of reliability is required when individuals are being assessed, especially when the findings are to be used for individual care and treatment rather than, say, research. The human consequences of error in diagnosis and treatment are harsh: nothing less than individual well-being is at stake. Therefore, the reliability standards are stringent. A research diagnosis, however, is tentative until it is proven useful. Little harm is done with such diagnoses (Rosenhan, 1975). One cannot specify a degree of reliability that will be acceptable for all occasions of measurement and for all uses to which a measure will be put. But conservatively, a measure or observation whose reliability is below .80 should not be used for purposes of individual assessment or care, while one whose reliability descends below .60 is unreliable for research purposes.

Several factors influence both inter-judge reliability and test-retest reliability. Reliability coefficients calculated after separate interviews (test-retest reliability) are commonly lower than those from joint interviews (inter-judge reliability). These differences may arise from several sources: actual changes in the patient's condition between the interviews (occasion variance); different information obtained by each interviewer (information variance); and the absence of cues that are sometimes inadvertently provided by one observer to another in joint interview situations (Robins, 1985; Williams, Barefoot, and Shekelle, 1985).

The Kappa statistic

Reliability is also influenced by chance agreement between interviewers. The Kappa statistic *(K)* was developed to deal with this problem. The formula for K is:

$$K = \frac{P_o - P_c}{1 - P_c},$$

where P_o is the observed proportion of agreement, and P_c is the agreement expected by chance alone from the sample that is being studied. Kappa, therefore, indicates the proportion of agreement obtained over that which would have been expected to occur by chance in a particular sample. Kappa yields an index that ranges from $+1.00$ for perfect agreement to -1.00 for perfect disagreement. Technically, there are occasions when a low value of Kappa is satisfactory (Blashfield, 1984; Carey and Gottesman, 1978; Meehl, 1986). But generally, values of Kappa greater than 0.75 indicate chance-corrected agreement that is satisfactory, while values between roughly 0.40 and 0.74 indicate fair agreement. Values below 0.40 evidence poor agreement (Spitzer and Fleiss, 1974; Hasin and Grant, 1987).

THE CLINICAL INTERVIEW

Assessment techniques are divided into three processes: interviewing, testing, and observing. The first of these, the ***clinical interview,*** is the favorite instrument of clinical psychologists and psychiatrists, reflecting the widespread view that we don't know someone well until we've met and talked with him. Good interviewers get information, not only from what people say, but from how they say it: their manner, tone of voice, body postures, and degree of eye contact (Exline and Winters, 1965; Ellsworth and Carlsmith, 1968; Ekman, Friesen, and Ellsworth, 1972). Of course, in order to get this information, there must be a good rapport between the client and interviewer. One should not expect people to be honest if they feel that their statements are going to incriminate them or lead to aversive decisions about

For a client to open up to a therapist during a clinical interview, the client must perceive the interviewer to be nonthreatening, supportive, and encouraging of self-disclosure.

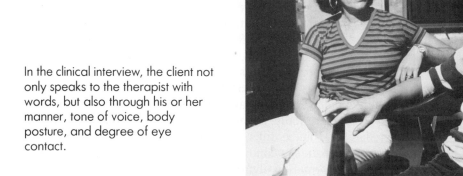

In the clinical interview, the client not only speaks to the therapist with words, but also through his or her manner, tone of voice, body posture, and degree of eye contact.

their future. For an interview to be maximally informative, the client needs to perceive the interviewer as being nonthreatening, supportive, and encouraging of self-disclosure (Jourard, 1974).

Unstructured interview

The clinical interview may range from an unstructured conversation to a quite structured encounter. Fundamentally, an ***unstructured interview*** allows the interviewer to take advantage of the exigencies of the moment. The client may want to talk about a particular problem, and right now, rather than later. The unstructured interview permits that. Similarly, the interviewer may want to inquire into a particular issue. The unstructured interview, therefore, is very flexible, but it "pays a price" for that flexibility. Because they are unstructured, no two of these interviews are the same. They elicit different information and, therefore, the reliability and validity of the information that is elicited may be reduced (Fisher, Epstein, and Harris, 1967).

Although the unstructured interview may seem like a rambling event, it is not random. The kind of information interviewers attempt to elicit is heavily determined by their own orientation, by the theory that guides their own understanding of human behavior. For example, interviewers with a psychoanalytic orientation will often concentrate on early childhood experiences, sexual experiences, and dreams because such data enable them to form a psychoanalytic impression of personality. Behaviorists, on the other hand, tend to concentrate on current events, on behavior that is presently distressing and the events and experiences that surround it, again because these experiences are especially meaningful within their theoretical framework.

Structured interview

The fact that different interviewers pursue different issues and, therefore, often arrive at varying conclusions, has led increasingly to the use of ***structured interviews*** in which all of the interviewer's questions are prepared in an ***interview schedule*** and may, in fact, be read. The structured interview standardizes the questions that are asked by each interviewer. The amount of clinical judgment required in these interviews is substantially reduced, since the answers to the specific questions and probes lead automatically to the scoring of the symptoms, which can be processed by a computer. Such interview schedules remove much of the unreliability that is introduced by differences in the way clinicians elicit information in diagnostic interviews (Matarazzo, 1983) and make it possible for even lay interviewers to gather psychological information and make diagnoses.

Several structured interview schedules have been developed in recent years. The Schedule of Affective Disorders and Schizophrenia (SADS, 1978), the Diagnostic Interview Schedule (DIS, 1981), and the Renard Diagnostic Interview (RDI, 1981) are among the most widely used.

The SADS   The Schedule of Affective Disorders and Schizophrenia (SADS) was designed to elicit information about a person's symptoms and current level of functioning, as well as providing data that would lead to a diagnosis. Part I of SADS yields a detailed description of the person's current episode or condition, as well as her functioning during the week preceding the interview. It is unique in that the items are used to describe features of the current episode when they were most severe. Part II collects data on previous psychological disturbances. It provides a progression of questions and criteria that systematically rule in or out specific diagnoses (Endicott and Spitzer, 1978). For example, if a clinician is using SADS to assess whether a person is a schizophrenic, she will direct the questioning around the symptoms of schizophrenia. Since schizophrenics hallucinate and sometimes hear voices, the clinician will ask:

• Has there been anything unusual about the way things looked, or sounded, or smelled?

• Have you heard voices or other things that weren't there or that other people couldn't hear, or seen things that were not there?

• The (sounds, voices) that you said you heard, did you hear them outside your head, through your ears, or did they come from inside your head?

• Could you hear what the voice was saying?

• Did you hear anything else? What about noises?

The RDI and the DIS   The Renard Diagnostic Interview (RDI) and Diagnostic Interview Schedule (DIS) provide standardized interview formats that can be used by lay interviewers as well as professionals. Both are accompanied by a set of computer programs that enable one to arrive at a diagnosis utilizing a variety of criteria while minimizing the amount of clinical judgment required (Robins, Helzer, Croughan, and Ratcliff, 1981; Robins, 1985; Robins and Helzer, 1986). Lay interviewers have successfully used the DIS to estimate the prevalence of specific mental disorders and to study health care (Anthony, Folstein, Romanoski, Von Korff, Nestadt, Chahal, Merchant, Brown, Shapiro, Kramer, and Gruenberg, 1985).

PSYCHOLOGICAL TESTING

Additional psychological information about the nature of an individual's problems and disabilities comes from psychological testing. Personality assessment is a subject that fascinates many people, so much so that there are thousands of personality tests, and hundreds of books written about them.

Psychological testing may be projective, requiring the person to draw a series of designs or to put together a figure.

Some tests are focal, designed to illuminate a single personality attribute, such as anxiety or depression, or to uncover a particular kind of brain damage. Others are omnibus, seeking to describe a larger portion of personality and abnormality. Many tests are unstructured or projective, requiring the client to draw a person or persons or a series of designs, to determine abnormality through careful interviewing, while others aspire to the same goal through formal, structured examinations.

Most psychological testing procedures are relatively standardized. That important fact increases the likelihood that different examiners will obtain similar information from the client: that is, that the test will be reliable. If several examiners give the Wechsler Adult Intelligence Scale to the same client, for example, then the client's score should be approximately the same from one examination to the next.

Psychological tests fall into three categories: psychological inventories, "projective" tests, and intelligence tests.

PSYCHOLOGICAL INVENTORIES

Nearly everyone has taken a ***psychological inventory*** at one time or another for vocational guidance, or personal counseling, or in connection with a job. These tests are highly structured and contain a variety of statements that can be answered "true" or "false." The client is asked to indicate whether or not each statement applies to her. Inventories have enormous advantages: they are commonly highly reliable; they can often be given to several people simultaneously and are therefore relatively inexpensive to administer and score; and by providing statistical norms, they allow comparative judgments to be made. The inventory that is used most widely is the Minnesota Multiphasic Personality Inventory. Less widely used, but very useful for certain purposes, are the Q-sort and the Rep Test.

The MMPI and forming a profile

□ MINNESOTA MULTIPHASIC PERSONALITY INVENTORY (MMPI). By far, the most widely used and studied personality inventory in clinical assessment is the ***Minnesota Multiphasic Personality Inventory*** or the ***MMPI*** (Hathaway and McKinley, 1943). The MMPI consists of 550 test items that inquire into a wide array of behaviors, thoughts, and feelings. Although each item can be administered separately to individual clients, the MMPI is most often administered to small groups of people. All respondents are usually given the same test items, but the meaning of those items may not be identical for each respondent. Thus, a college student who responds "yes" to the statement, "I usually feel fine," obviously means something quite different from the hospitalized person who responded "yes" without reading the statement. As a consequence, the meanings of the MMPI items are by no means self-evident, and they have had to be ascertained by empirical research. Scales have been constructed by examining the responses of people with known characteristics, such as depressed versus nondepressed persons, manic versus non-manic, introverted versus extraverted. All in all, the MMPI provides scores for the ten categories shown in Table 7-1. These categories have been validated against diagnostic judgments that arose from psychiatric interviews and other tests (Wrobel and Lochar, 1982).

Any paper-and-pencil inventory is subject to a variety of distortions, and the MMPI is no exception. One can simply lie. One can be evasive. Or one

Table 7-1 PERSONALITY CHARACTERISTICS ASSOCIATED WITH ELEVATIONS ON THE BASIC MMPI SCALES

Scale	Characteristics
1 (Hs), Hypochondriasis	High scorers are described as cynical, defeatist, preoccupied with self, complaining, hostile, and presenting numerous physical problems.
2 (D), Depression	High scorers are described as moody, shy, despondent, pessimistic, and distressed. This scale is one of the most frequently elevated in clinical patients.
3 (Hy), Hysteria	High scorers tend to be repressed, dependent, naive, outgoing, and to have multiple physical complaints. Expression of psychological conflict through vague and unbased physical complaints.
4 (Pd), Psychopathic Deviate	High scorers often are rebellious, impulsive, hedonistic, and antisocial. They often have difficulty in marital or family relationships and trouble with the law or authority in general.
5 (MF), Masculinity-Femininity	High-scoring males are described as sensitive, aesthetic, passive, or feminine. High-scoring females are described as aggressive, rebellious, and unrealistic.
6 (Pa), Paranoia	Elevations on this scale are often associated with being suspicious, aloof, shrewd, guarded, worrisome, and overly sensitive. High scorers may project or externalize blame.
7 (Pt), Psychasthenia	High scorers are tense, anxious, ruminative, preoccupied, obsessional, phobic, rigid. They frequently are self-condemning and feel inferior and inadequate.
8 (Sc), Schizophrenia	High scorers are often withdrawn, shy, unusual, or strange and have peculiar thoughts or ideas. They may have poor reality contact and in severe cases bizarre sensory experiences—delusions and hallucinations.
9 (Ma), Mania	High scorers are called sociable, outgoing, impulsive, overly energetic, optimistic, and in some cases amoral, flighty, confused, disoriented.
0 (Si), Social Introversion-Extraversion	High scorers tend to be modest, shy, withdrawn, self-effacing, inhibited. Low scorers are outgoing, spontaneous, sociable, confident.

SOURCE: Butcher, 1969.

can try to put oneself in the best possible social light. And one can do these things intentionally or unintentionally. However, the MMPI contains four "validity" scales that are designed to alert the diagnostician to such distortions. Thus, if a person were to respond "yes" to the following items: "I never tell lies," and "I read the newspaper editorials every day," it might be reasonable to surmise that the test-taker is trying to present herself as favorably as she can—since it is a rare person who never tells lies and who reads the editorials daily. Notice that these judgments about social desirability and lying are *not* absolutely foolproof. Rather they are "best guesses." Most (but not all) people who respond positively to the above items will be, willingly or unwittingly, trying to improve their image. For all we know, however, there may well be some people who read every editorial every day and who never tell lies (bless 'em!).

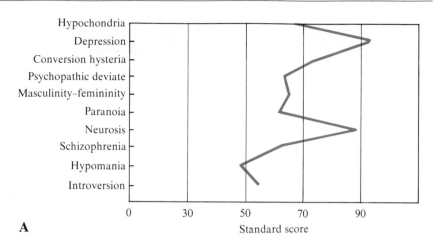

Figure 7-2

(A) An example of a Minnesota Multiphasic Personality Inventory (MMPI) profile. (B) An "automated" interpretation provided by a computer. The computer prints out statements that have been found to have some validity for other individuals with similar profiles. (Sources: Gleitman, 1981; NCS Interpretive Scoring Systems)

Assessment can be approached from a variety of angles. Some inventories examine thought. Others focus on behavior. Some concentrate on context and situation, others on traits. The content of the MMPI items has been compared to other personality inventories. The MMPI was found to have the highest percent of items dealing with the *cognitive* area of functioning, and the lowest percent dealing with *behavioral acts.* It was also lowest in terms of the proportion of items that referred to a situation, rather than a personal characteristic or trait (Werner and Pervin, 1986).

The results of the MMPI are recorded in the form of a profile (Figure 7-2A). The profile tells a clinician more than the individual scores would. By utilizing an MMPI atlas (e.g., Gilberstadt and Duker, 1965), the profile of a particular person can be compared with similar profiles obtained from individuals about whom a great deal is known (Figure 7-2B). The resulting personality assessment is more than the sum of the individual's MMPI scores. This larger assessment can then be examined against inferences from other sources of information that the clinician has obtained, with the goal of noting consistencies and reconciling inconsistencies (Korchin, 1976).

The Q-sort and subjective experience

☐ Q-SORT.   Many psychologists are considerably less interested in diagnostic categories and personality traits than they are in the individual's subjective experience. They ask such questions as: How does this person perceive himself now? What kind of person would he like to become? Quite apart from predicting the individual's behavior or response to treatment, the answers to these questions are of intrinsic interest. They provide a basis for comparing the individual's *real* and *ideal* self, as well as the degree to which he is dissatisfied with himself. Data for these impressions arise from tests such as the Q-sort.

The ***Q-sort*** consists of a large number of cards, each of which contains a statement like "is an assertive person," "evades responsibility," or "is sensitive." The client is asked to place each statement in one of nine piles, according to whether the statement is more or less characteristic of him. Moreover, in order to forestall the possibility that clients would only use extreme or center categories in describing themselves, the number of items allowed in each of the nine categories is ranged in accord with the bell-shaped normal distribution. Fewer items are permitted at the extremes, and more in the center. (This enhances the Q-sort as a research instrument as well.) Clients may also be asked to rearrange these cards to reflect the kind of person they would like to be—their "ideal" selves. Some therapists have demonstrated that, as treatment progresses, the discrepancy between the real and the ideal self described by the Q-sort test declines (Rogers, 1959).

The Rep Test and eliciting constructs

☐ ROLE CONSTRUCT REPERTORY TEST (REP TEST).   Another psychological test that is favored by behavioral psychologists is the ***Role Construct Repertory Test*** or the ***Rep Test,*** as it is commonly called (Kelly, 1955). This test proceeds from the assumption that all events are subject to varying interpretations or constructions. It attempts to elicit the particular constructs that each client uses in interpreting significant events. A construct is deduced by examining the ways in which two things are alike but different from a third. To begin with, the client lists the important people in his life, such as his mother, father, roommate(s), girlfriend, etc. When he has completed the list, he examines these people in groups of three, and he indicates the ways in which two of them are similar to each other and different from the third person. In this way, we see the subjective constructs used by an individual to determine similarity and difference. For example, after examining all of the ways in which the client perceives two people to be similar to each other and different from a third, one might notice that the similar people are all perceived as angry, and they are seen as differing from the other people who are calm. "Angry vs. calm" would therefore be an underlying construct for this person, a primary way in which his psychological world is organized. Further examination of similarities and differences might reveal other significant constructs. Indeed, simply appraising the number of constructs used by an individual would suggest something about the richness and variety of his experiential life.

PROJECTIVE TESTS

Assessing unconscious forces

For many psychologists, and especially those who are psychodynamically oriented, the focus of assessment is on unconscious conflicts, latent fears, sexual and aggressive impulses, and hidden anxieties. Structured inventories, because they inquire about *conscious* experience and feelings, obscure these deeper dynamics. But because **projective tests** utilize meaningless stimuli, such as inkblot forms, they minimize reality constraints, encourage imaginative processes, and maximize the opportunity for conflictual or unconscious concerns to emerge (Murray, 1951). Two of the most widely used projective tests are the Roschach Test and the Thematic Apperception Test.

□ THE RORSCHACH TEST.   Invented by Hermann Rorschach (1884–1922), a Swiss psychiatrist, the **Rorschach Test** consists of ten bilaterally symmetrical "inkblots," some in color, some in black, gray, and white, and each on an individual card. The respondent is shown each card separately and asked to tell the examiner everything she sees on the card, that is, everything the inkblot could resemble. Figure 7-3 shows two inkblots that are similar to such cards.

Here are the responses made by one person to the card on the left (Exner, 1978, p. 170):

> PATIENT: I think it could be a woman standing in the middle there . . . Should I try to find something else?
>
> EXAMINER: Most people see more than one thing.
>
> PATIENT: I suppose the entire thing could be a butterfly. . . . I don't see anything else.

Scoring responses to Rorschach inkblots

Responses to these inkblots are scored in several ways. First, they are scored for the nature and quality of what has been seen. In this instance, the woman and the butterfly are well-formed percepts, indicative of someone whose view of the world is relatively clear. Second, whether the percept is commonly seen by others, or relatively rare (and if rare, whether creative or bizarre) is scored. Seeing a woman and a butterfly on this blot is a common occurrence. It suggests that this person is capable of seeing the world as others do. Additional scoring will examine whether the entire blot or only

Figure 7-3
Facsimiles of Rorschach Test cards. These projective instruments are composed of stimuli that seem like inkblots and that allow the respondent to project impressions of what those inkblots might be. (Source: Based on Gleitman, 1981, p. 635)

A psychologist uses the Rorschach test to assess a client's feelings and conflicts.

part of it was used, and whether color is used and integrated into the percept. These scores, as well as what is seen in the blot, are integrated to give an overall picture of the vitality of the respondent's inner life, his conflicts, the degree to which he can control sexual and aggressive urges, and the like.

Rorschach interpretation

Perusal of the inkblot on the left in Figure 7-3 will give some sense of the thinking that goes into Rorschach interpretation. Imagine someone who has responded to the bits of ink that surround the central percept, but who failed to respond to the main part of the blot. You might hypothesize (and it is *only* a hypothesis) that this individual has difficulty confronting "central" realities and perhaps, as a result, turns her attention to trivia, as if *they* were central. Using the responses to a single blot, of course, would be merely one of any number of hypotheses you might entertain. There might, for example, be something about the central percept of this particular card that the respondent finds aversive. If so, the response would indicate little about generalized tendencies to avoid centralities. If, however, such responses were forthcoming on several cards—if on each of them the respondent "missed" the central percept and puttered about at the edges, an examiner might feel that the hunch was well-substantiated. This is the kind of thinking that is used to examine the use of color, of forms, of the popularity of the percept, and so on. A test record that reveals only commonly given percepts might be judged to be behaviorally conformist and cognitively banal, especially if all other indices were consistent with that view.

Interpreting the Rorschach requires enormous skill. It is a fascinating and complex process, whose full richness is not given by the above examples. But it is not without its hazards. Precisely because the interpretative logic is so compelling, there is a strong tendency to believe in it without validation, and to disregard contrary evidence. Indeed, the interpretation of Rorschach protocols turns out to be a place to examine the attributional errors that the intuitive mind makes (Ross, 1977; Nisbett and Ross, 1980). For example, clinicians might be asked to assess which of the following sets of responses given by a male respondent to the card on the right in Figure 7-3 indicates the presence of homosexual tendencies:

Protocol 1: The whole thing looks ominous. There are violent monsters here. You can see them clawing at each other. I don't know what kind they are, but they sure are scary. . . . In fact, the entire blot looks like an angry centaur, rearing on its hind legs. You can see the human face and the animal body, and the arms there, the horse here.

Protocol 2: Well, these in the center seem like sex organs. Male sex organs. . . . And over here, this looks like a dress and a bra. Kind of a padded bra, it looks like. . . . Here's someone's butt. Kind of a child's butt—you can even see the err . . . uh, rectum I think. . . . And this is—what do you call them—someone who is part man and part woman. The bottom part looks like it's a man, but when you look up, it's a woman.

Clinicians who examined many such protocols were emphatic in interpreting responses of the kind given in Protocol 2 as indicative of homosexuality, while responses like those in Protocol 1 were given much less weight (Chapman and Chapman, 1969). In fact, the responses shown in Protocol 2 are *entirely invalid* as indices of homosexual interest or behavior, having no research support whatsoever. Those in Protocol 1, however, though seemingly removed from homosexuality at the intuitive level, are moderately well-supported in validation studies as signs of homosexuality.

The conflict between intuition (or common sense) on the one hand and validated data on the other pervades assessment, as it pervades psychological judgment in general. Time and again, it will seem to clinicians that a certain sign makes sense as an indicator of a larger behavior, so much so that it hardly seems worth the effort to assess the validity of the sign empirically. And time and again, when that assessment *is* made, it will be found that the correlation between sign and indicator is *illusory* (Chapman and Chapman, 1969), being based merely on a commonly held view and not on reality.

Low reliability and validity

As might be expected with an instrument that is so complex and that is predicated on ambiguity, neither the reliability nor the validity of the Rorschach have been high. Reliability of scoring is low despite the variety of manuals that are available to assist the clinician (e.g., Exner, 1974, 1978; Aronow and Reznikoff, 1976). One attempt to objectify and standardize scoring has resulted in a new set of inkblots (Holtzman, 1961; Hill, 1972), which mainly has been used in research rather than in clinical practice.

Tests that purport to reveal "underlying psychodynamics" are particularly difficult to validate because such dynamics are inferred. Technically, they are *hypothetical* constructs, assumed to be there for theoretical reasons since they cannot be directly examined nor directly verified. When, however, interpretations from the Rorschach have been susceptible to verification (as when the indices point to homosexuality or predict suicide), validation studies have been conducted. And in those studies, the evidence in the main has gone against the Rorschach (Zubin, Eron, and Schumer, 1965; Mischel, 1968, 1976; Peterson, 1978; see Weiner, 1986, for a more optimistic position).

Using the TAT to explore motives

□ THEMATIC APPERCEPTION TEST.   Another commonly used instrument is the ***Thematic Apperception Test,*** or the ***TAT.*** It consists of a series of pictures that are not as ambiguous as Rorschach cards, but not as clear as photographs either. Respondents are asked to look at each picture and to make up a story about it. They are told to tell how the story began, what is happening now, and how it will end. As with the Rorschach, it is assumed that because

The psychologist is administering the TAT to a client. Each TAT picture is designed to be sufficiently vague to allow respondents to project their own meaningful story onto it.

the pictures are ambiguous, the stories will reflect the respondent's proclivity to see situations in a particular way. If a respondent repeatedly uses the same theme to describe several different pictures, this is considered especially indicative of underlying dynamics.

The TAT has been used extensively as a research instrument to explore a variety of motives, particularly the need for achievement (McClelland et al., 1953; Atkinson, 1958). Its use in that context has been fruitful and provocative. But its use as a clinical instrument for assessing individual personality is prey to the same problems that beset the Rorschach. Although reliability of scoring is adequate (Harrison, 1965), the interpretations of TAT protocols by different clinicians is quite diverse (Murstein, 1965).

INTELLIGENCE TESTS

Perhaps the most reliable and, for many purposes, the most valid of all psychological tests are those that measure intelligence. Originally designed by Alfred Binet to differentiate backward school children from those who are mentally retarded, the test underwent many revisions, culminating in the Stanford-Binet Intelligence Test for Children. Somewhat later, David Wechsler standardized individually administered intelligence tests for both adults and children. These tests include the Wechsler Adult Intelligence WAIS Scale (WAIS), the Wechsler Intelligence Scale for Children (WISC), and the Wechsler Preschool and Primary Scale of Intelligence (WPPSI). The WAIS was revised and restandardized as the Wechsler Adult Intelligence Scale— Revised (WAIS-R) in 1981 to eliminate or modify items that were considered unfair to minority groups (Mishra and Brown, 1983), to update the test content, and to provide new norms. While there are high correlations between the WAIS and the WAIS-R, the overall scores on the latter tend to be substantially *lower* than those on the former (Urbina, Golden, and Ariel, 1982; Lippold and Claiborn, 1983; Mishra and Brown, 1983).

The Wechsler Scales provide a total IQ (Intelligence Quotient) which is composed of two subscores: Verbal IQ and Performance IQ. Verbal IQ comprises such matters as vocabulary, ability to comprehend verbal statements and problems, and general information. Performance IQ measures intelligence in ways that are less dependent upon verbal ability, such as the ability to copy designs and to associate symbols with numbers.

Intelligence tests are routinely administered to school children and may help to determine the kind of education they will receive. Here, the psychologist is timing the child's responses to questions from the interview schedule that makes up this intelligence test.

Intelligence tests play an important role in assessing mental retardation and brain damage. Moreover, they are the only psychological tests that are routinely administered to school children and that determine, in some measure, the kind of education that children will obtain. It is important, therefore, to understand what intelligence tests actually measure.

Intelligence itself is not directly knowable. It can only be inferred from behavior, and it is inferred best from behavior on standardized tasks. Intelligence tests sample certain behaviors, particularly those that predict success in school. Other behaviors, like the ability to make it "on the street" or the ability to appreciate classical music, are simply not measured. For that reason, intelligence has often been defined as what an intelligence test measures. That is not quite a satisfying definition, but it is accurate. If one's working definition of intelligence differs from the one that is implicit in a particular intelligence test, one should not be surprised that the test score fails to meet expectations. An intelligence test that measures verbal facility will not predict well ability on psychomotor tasks.

OBSERVATIONS

The assessment techniques reviewed so far—the interview, the standardized and projective tests, the intelligence test—have had one thing in common: all of them are verbal and all of them use words to portray psychological assets and liabilities. But words are often imprecise. Often they overstate the matter. Depressed people are wont to say that "My life is just miserable all the time," an expression that conveys the full sense of their feelings right now, but no sense at all of what the problem is, how often it occurs, and how to begin working on it. In marital conflict, for example, the following complaints are not uncommon.

> HE: She never has a meal on the table on time.
> SHE: He never takes me out.

Observing actual behavior

Both clearly believe what they are saying and their beliefs amplify their anger with each other. The beliefs, however, are false. When they begin to take notice of actual behavior, rather than accusations, they find that most (but not all) of the meals are on the table on time, and they go out with some frequency (but not as often as she would like). Already the gap between them has narrowed, creating a smaller disagreement out of what seemed to be a major conflict.

More than a quarter century ago, Wendell Johnson (1946; cited in Goldfried and Davison, 1976) captured the significance of behavioral assessment for treatment:

> To say that Henry is mean implies that he has some sort of inherent trait, but it tells us nothing about what Henry has done. Consequently, it fails to suggest any specific means of improving Henry. If, on the other hand, it is said that Henry snatched Billy's cap and threw it in the bonfire, the situation is rendered somewhat more clear and actually more hopeful. You might never eliminate "meanness," but there are fairly definite steps to be taken in order to remove Henry's incentives or opportunities for throwing caps in bonfires . . . (What needs to be done) . . . is to get the person to tell him not what he *is* or what he *has,* but what he *does,* and the conditions under which he does it.

BEHAVIORAL ASSESSMENT

Behavioral assessment is commonly used in conjunction with treatment itself: to define the problem, to narrow it, to provide a record of what needs to be changed, and subsequently, of what progress has been made. The assessment does not stand apart from the treatment, nor is it an evaluation of the client for the therapist's use only. It is rather, part and parcel of the treatment, a procedure of interest to both client and therapist, and one in which they fully share.

Functional analysis

Behavioral assessment consists in keeping as accurate a record as possible of the behaviors and thoughts one wishes to change: when they occur (incidence), how long they last (duration), and where possible, how intense they are. When the assessment includes, not only the behaviors, but also the stimuli that are presumed either to increase or decrease the incidence of those behaviors, the assessment is called a ***functional analysis.***

A person might report, for example, that she becomes nervous when she has to speak in public. If a fairly precise measure of how nervous she becomes were required, she could be asked to deliver a speech publicly (Paul, 1966). One could then record, in good detail, not only how anxious she was —in blocks of thirty seconds throughout her speech—but what forms the anxiety took, utilizing the assessment form shown in Figure 7-4. Moreover, the overall degree of anxiety could be assessed by summing the scores on each of the twenty variables.

Behavioral assessment can also be done by clients themselves. People who desire to give up smoking are commonly asked to begin by recording when and under what conditions they smoke each cigarette. People who desire to lose weight are asked to record when, where, how much, and under what conditions they eat. Assessments by clients are not only useful for overt behaviors, but for private thoughts as well. Mahoney (1971), for example, asked a client to record each time she had a self-critical thought. Her record became the basis for evaluating whether subsequent interventions had any effect.

Sometimes behavioral assessment reveals causes for distress of which the respondent was unaware and that were not elicited in the interview. Metcalfe (1956; cited in Mischel, 1976) asked a patient who was hospitalized for asthma, but free to take leave from the hospital, to keep a careful record of the incidence, duration, and the events surrounding her asthma attacks. Attacks occurred on fifteen of the eighty-five days during which records were kept. Nine of the attacks occurred after contact with her mother. Moreover, on 80 percent of the days in which she had no asthma attacks, she also had had no contact with her mother. But while "contact with mother" seemed to be a source of the attacks, attempts to induce an attack by *discussing* her mother during an interview, or by presenting the patient with mother-relevant TAT cards, were unsuccessful. Because words, as symbols of experience, sometimes do not elicit the behaviors that the direct experiences themselves produce, interviews that rely heavily on words often fail to be fully diagnostic.

While behavioral assessment has clear advantages, it cannot be used with every psychological problem. Sometimes, tracking behavior in the required detail is simply too costly or time-consuming. Often, when the tracking is

Figure 7-4
Behavior assessment form. This behavior rating form permits assessment of speech anxiety. Each time period is thirty seconds long. Evidence of any of the twenty anxiety-relevant behaviors during each time period is indicated by a (✔) in the relevant boxes. (Source: Paul, 1966)

Behavior observed	Time period								
	1	2	3	4	5	6	7	8	Σ
1. Paces									
2. Sways									
3. Shuffles feet									
4. Knees tremble									
5. Extraneous arm and hand movement (swings, scratches, toys, etc.)									
6. Arms rigid									
7. Hands restrained (in pockets, behind back, clasped)									
8. Hand tremors									
9. No eye contact									
10. Face muscles tense (drawn, tics, grimaces)									
11. Face "deadpan"									
12. Face pale									
13. Face flushed (blushes)									
14. Moistens lips									
15. Swallows									
16. Clears throat									
17. Breathes heavily									
18. Perspires (face, hands, armpits)									
19. Voice quivers									
20. Speech blocks or stammers									

done by the client alone, the assessment fails for lack of motivation or precision. Finally, there are situations in which behavioral assessment may not work well: covert behaviors such as thoughts and feelings are not as amenable to reliable assessments as are overt behaviors.

PSYCHOPHYSIOLOGICAL ASSESSMENT

Some abnormal psychological states are reflected in physiological ones, while others grow directly out of physiological disorder. Careful diagnosis and treatment of abnormality therefore often requires psychophysiological assessment, which has become increasingly sophisticated during the past decade. The treatment of both physical tension and some sexual disorders has been enhanced by using psychophysiological assessment.

Biofeedback

Anxiety, fear, and tension often have physiological correlates. When people are anxious, they may feel it in their muscles or in the way they breathe or perspire. Psychophysiological assessment not only confirms whether there is a physiological component to the anxiety, but how intense that component is, and whether treatment affects it. Indeed, some treatments can ac-

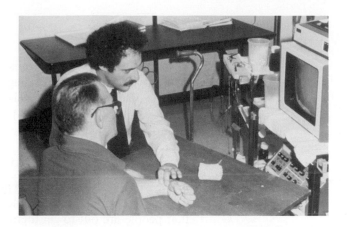

This client is being alerted to psychophysiological changes through the use of an electromyagraph.

tually be pegged to psychophysiological changes. Biofeedback proceeds by alerting the client to small psychophysiological changes, and to the psychological states that bring them about. Tension headaches often arise from contraction of frontalis muscles. Those contractions can be directly measured through the use of an ***electromyagraph*** (EMG) and communicated to the client. As the client is trained to relax, he can immediately see the effects of that relaxation on the EMG, and he can gradually eliminate muscle tension and headache by using the techniques he has learned (Budzynski, Stoyva, Adler, and Mullaney, 1973).

Physiological difficulties commonly accompany sexual disorders, too. Among men, the inability to become sexually aroused is often manifested in the failure of the penis to become engorged with blood and therefore to become erect. In women, absence of sexual excitement is evidenced in the failure of the vaginal walls to become engorged. In both men and women, these conditions can be measured with considerable precision with devices that are called ***genital plethysmographs.*** A penile plethysmograph consists of a thin circular tube that contains a small amount of mercury. The tube is placed around the penis. As the penis becomes engorged, the pressure on the tube increases. The vaginal plethysmograph is shaped like a tampon and has a light at the upper end. The light reflects from the vaginal walls and provides a measure of the degree to which the walls are engorged. Increases in sexual arousal due to treatment can easily be detected on these psychophysiological instruments.

DIAGNOSIS

The first hallmark of a good assessment instrument—whether it is a structured or unstructured interview, an objective or projective test, or a behavioral rating system—is its ***reliability.*** Will two skilled users obtain the same findings? And provided nothing changes, will the test impressions obtained at one time be similar to those obtained at a later date? These are the first issues with which one is concerned. But they are not the only issues. Equally important are the purposes for which the test is being used. The purpose of assessment is to understand people, and one form of understanding is categorization, or ***diagnosis.*** We turn now to an examination of the reasons for, and nature of, diagnosis.

REASONS FOR DIAGNOSIS

Reasons for
making a
diagnosis

Properly executed, diagnosis is a long and complicated procedure. What does one gain from careful diagnosis? There are four important reasons to make a diagnosis: (1) diagnosis is a communication shorthand, (2) it tells something about treatment, (3) it may communicate etiology, and (4) it aids scientific investigations.

COMMUNICATION SHORTHAND

As we will shortly see, troubled people often have a host of symptoms. They may, for example, have trouble keeping their thoughts straight, often feel that people are out to get them, be unable to go to work, feel tense all the time, and have visual hallucinations. And they may be troubled by each of these symptoms simultaneously. A single diagnosis, in this case paranoid schizophrenia, incorporates all of these symptoms. Rather than going down an endless list of troubles, the diagnostician can merely indicate the *syndrome* (that is, the collection of symptoms that run together) in the single phrase: paranoid schizophrenia.

TREATMENT POSSIBILITIES

There is an ever-increasing fund of treatments available for psychological distress, and most are specific to certain disorders. Diagnosis enables the clinician to concentrate on the handful of treatments that might be useful in particular situations. Paranoid schizophrenia, for example, does not yield readily to verbal psychotherapies, nor is it effectively treated by Valium. But paranoid schizophrenics often respond well to a drug called chlorpromazine. A good diagnosis, then, suggests a small number of treatments that might alleviate the symptoms.

ETIOLOGY

People's problems arise from an infinity of sources, but certain problems are more reliably associated with particular causes or etiologies. For example, psychodynamic theorists believe that anxiety arises from poorly repressed conflicts and wishes. Knowing the diagnosis may tell something about the underlying cause.

AID TO SCIENTIFIC INVESTIGATIONS

Abnormal psychology and psychiatry are developing sciences that have yet to discover all the causes and cures of human misery. By collecting together people with like symptoms, diagnosis allows psychological investigators to learn what those symptoms have in common by way of etiology and treatment. Indeed, for a developing science, this may be the single most important function of diagnosis.

HISTORICAL ORIGINS

The psychological diagnosis of personality has a long and interesting history. The Greeks, for example, recognized such diagnoses as senility (a disorder of aging), alcoholism, mania, melancholia (or depression), and paranoia. Many of these early diagnoses are still used today. Later, during the Middle Ages, it was widely believed that psychological disorders were caused by demons, and many different demonic "diagnoses" were described in such books as *The Witches' Hammer* (see Chapter 2).

Pinel's classification system

The formal classification of human abnormalities, modeled upon biological classification of plants and animals, began with Philippe Pinel (1745–1826), the psychiatric reformer. He divided psychological disorders into melancholia, mania with and without delirium, dementia, and idiotism—a classification system that was to undergo many revisions and refinements during the next two centuries.

Kraepelin's classification system

The first comprehensive system of classification of psychological disorders was created in 1896 by Emil Kraepelin (1856–1926). He believed that mental disorders have the same basis as physical ones and that the same diagnostic criteria and procedures should be applied to them. Above all, he insisted that diagnosis of mental disorders ought to be based on *symptoms* in much the sense that diagnosis of physical disorders proceeds from a careful assessment of physical symptoms. He might have stressed alternative bases for diagnosis such as drives, social deviance, level of adjustment, or social efficacy. But those bases were either merely inferred or social rather than physical. Inspired by the notion that there was a purely *physical* basis to psychological disorder, he proceeded to give psychological diagnosis the flavor of medical diagnosis, a flavor it still retains today.

Emil Kraepelin (1856–1926) created the first comprehensive system of classification of psychological disorders.

Kraepelin's was not the only diagnostic system used for mental disorders. Early in the twentieth century, other clinicians, among them Eugen Bleuler, Adolf Meyer, and Ernst Kretschmer suggested other systems. Each of these systems enjoyed some popularity, with the result that different languages of diagnosis were invented and often used simultaneously. But because one basic function of diagnosis is communication, it is important to have a single and widely accepted language. This need for communication led to the creation, in 1952, of the first *Diagnostic and Statistical Manual of Mental Disorders* (DSM). Approved by the American Psychiatric Association, it was refined and ultimately replaced by DSM-II in 1968. DSM-II, however, was plagued by low reliability. When asked to diagnose a troubled person, diagnosticians had great difficulty agreeing with each other, and often they agreed no more than they would have by chance (Beck et al., 1962; Rosenhan, 1975; Spitzer, 1975). Those problems alone dictated the need for a new diagnostic system, one that took quite a different approach to diagnosis than did the one that originated with Kraepelin. The results of this new approach were published in 1980, in what is called DSM-III (more formally, *Diagnostic and Statistical Manual of Mental Disorders,* Third Edition), and revised in 1987 as DSM-III-R.

DSM-III-R

THE DIAGNOSTIC AND STATISTICAL MANUALS (DSM-III AND DSM-III-R)

Defining mental disorder in DSM-III-R

In DSM-III-R a **mental disorder** is defined as a behavioral or psychological pattern that either has *caused* the individual distress or *disabled* the individual in one or more significant areas of functioning. One must be able to infer that there is a genuine **dysfunction,** and not merely a disturbance between the individual and society. The latter is social deviance, and social

---

Box 7-1 THE DEFINITION OF MENTAL DISORDER IN DSM-III-R

In DSM-III-R each of the mental disorders is conceptualized as a clinically significant behavioral or psychological syndrome or pattern that occurs in a person and that is associated with present distress (a painful symptom) or disability (impairment in one or more important areas of functioning) or with significantly increased risk of suffering death, pain, disability, or an important loss of freedom. In addition, this syndrome or pattern must not be merely an expectable response to a particular event, e.g., the death of a loved one. Whatever its original cause, it must currently be considered a manifestation of a behavioral, psychological, or biological dysfunction in the person. Neither deviant behavior, e.g., political, religious, or sexual, nor conflicts that are primarily between the individual and society are mental disorders unless the deviance or condition is a symptom of a dysfunction in the person, as described above. (DSM-III-R, 1987, p. xxii)

---

deviance is not a mental disorder. The full definition of mental disorder is given in Box 7-1.

Diagnostic criteria for each disorder

Beyond defining mental disorder, DSM-III-R seeks to provide specific and operational diagnostic criteria for each mental disorder. In large measure, the unreliability of previous diagnostic systems, especially DSM-II, arose from the fact that its definitions were vague and imprecise. For example, DSM-II described a depressive episode, but left it to the diagnostician to determine what precisely an "episode" consisted of. The definition left unresolved such practical questions as: Would a one-hour depressive experience qualify? Would depression that continued for a month be considered more than a single episode? The new diagnostic system takes much of the guesswork out of diagnosis by offering sharper definitions. With regard to a major depressive episode, for example, DSM-III-R states that "At least five of the following symptoms have been present during the same two-week period . . . at least one of the symptoms is either (1) depressed mood or (2) loss of interest or pleasure . . . ," and it lists nine different symptoms. It was hoped that the use of functional definitions would contribute to the reliability of diagnosis.

Multidimensional diagnostic guides

In DSM-III and DSM-III-R, diagnosis is not a single classifying statement, but rather it consists of multidimensional diagnostic guides. All told, there are five dimensions or axes that should be used, not only to classify a disorder, but to help plan treatment and predict outcome (see Appendix for Axes I and II categories and codes). This is an advance over former diagnostic systems that were used merely to classify individuals. DSM-III and DSM-III-R provide useful information for functional diagnoses on the following axes:

• *Axis I—Clinical Syndromes.* The florid and fairly traditional clinical labels are included here, among them such familiar diagnostic terms as paranoid schizophrenia, major depression, and the various anxiety disorders. Also included on this axis are conditions that are *not* mental disorders as defined in DSM-III and DSM-III-R but that may nevertheless require treatment. Among the latter are school, marital, and occupational problems that do not arise from psychological sources.

• Axis II—*Developmental Disorders and Personality Disorders.* Here are included disorders that are not listed on Axis I but that often accompany Axis I disorders, among them: mental retardation, the personality disorders, and the developmental disorders. The Axis II disorders generally begin in childhood or adolescence and persist in stable form into adulthood. Often, such disorders are overlooked by the diagnostician. Listing them as a separate axis ensures that they will be attended to. Axis I and II, then, comprise all of the psychological diagnoses.

• *Axis III—Physical Disorders and Conditions.* All medical problems that may be relevant to the psychological ones are listed here.

• *Axis IV—Psychosocial Stressors.* Included here are sources of difficulty during the past year, or anticipated difficulties such as retirement, which may be contributing to the individual's present difficulties.

• *Axis V—Global Assessment of Functioning at Present and during the Past Year.* The level of adaptive functioning has powerful prognostic significance, since individuals commonly return to their highest level of functioning when their psychological difficulties become less intense. The assessment on Axis V considers three areas: social relations with family and friends, occupational functioning, and use of leisure time, and is noted on a scale that runs from 1 (very low) to 90.

Information gathered along all five axes can yield greater understanding about a person's difficulty than can a simple descriptive diagnosis based on Axis I. Here is an example of the way a DSM-III-R diagnosis would look using the multiple axes approach (DSM-III-R, p. 21):

Axis I:	296.23	Major Depression, Single Episode, severe without psychotic features.
	303.90	Alcohol Dependence
Axis II:	301.60	Dependent Personality Disorder (Provisional, rule out Borderline Personality Disorder)
Axis III:		Alcoholic cirrhosis of liver
Axis IV:		Psychosocial stressors: anticipated retirement and change in residence with loss of contact with friends
		Severity: 4—Moderate (predominantly enduring circumstances)
Axis V:		Current GAF (Global Assessment of Functioning) 44 (i.e., serious symptoms)
		Highest GAF past year: 55 (i.e., moderate symptoms)

THE RELIABILITY OF DSM-III AND DSM-III-R

Problems of reliability

Earlier *Diagnostic and Statistical Manuals* were badly flawed by problems of reliability. Experienced diagnosticians using DSM-II, for example, found they could not agree with each other. In some instances, inter-judge reliability was so low as to make a diagnostic category functionally useless. Indeed, Spitzer and Fleiss (1974), in a review of all of the reliability studies of DSM-II, found that only three broad categories were sufficiently reliable to be clinically useful: mental retardation, alcoholism, and organic brain syndrome. These are fairly broad categories, and when diagnosticians attempted to use finer categories—to distinguish the different kinds of alcoholism or brain damage, for example—diagnostic reliability fell further.

Attempts to increase reliability

The compilers of DSM-III hoped to change all that, as we have seen, by making the categories much more specific and precise, and by having criteria for both including and excluding behaviors. Even more important, however, was the intention of conducting reliability studies *before* DSM-III was issued (rather than afterwards, as was the case with DSM-II) in order to minimize reliability errors. Reliability studies were in fact conducted, but they did not turn out quite as well as one might have hoped. Practicing clinicians were asked to examine the same patients and to arrive at independent diagnoses. They were asked not to confer before arriving at a diagnosis and to submit their findings to the research committee even if they later learned that they had disagreed. Unfortunately, there was no mechanism to prevent collaborative discussion after they had arrived at different diagnoses. In addition, it is impossible to know whether they sent in their discrepant diagnoses as consistently as their nondiscrepant ones.

Reliabilities for clusters of diagnoses

DSM-III encourages clinicians to use multiple diagnoses, both within Axis I and Axis II and between these axes. But multiple diagnoses, of course, increase the likelihood of agreement between clinicians. If clinician A makes six diagnoses and clinician B makes five, the likelihood that they will agree on one of them is much higher than if each had only made a single diagnosis. Even so, the reliabilities of DSM-III for adults are quite low, as seen in Table 7-2. Notice, first of all, that the reliabilities given are for *clusters* or classes of diagnosis, not for specific diagnoses. Thus, if two clinicians arrived at quite different diagnoses—if one found "agoraphobia with panic attacks" and the other "obsessive-compulsive disorder"—diagnostic agreement would be considered "perfect" because the diagnoses were in the same class, even though there was no agreement on the specific diagnoses (Kutchins and Kirk, 1986)! In fact, Axis I, *Clinical Syndromes,* provides nearly 200 specific diagnoses subsumed under seventeen major classes or clusters. DSM-III provides reliabilities on only 16 of these specific diagnoses. For the remaining specific diagnoses on Axis I, no reliability information is presented.

In the field trials, over half the adults and a quarter of the children received a diagnosis on Axis II, *Personality Disorders and Specific Developmental Disorders* (called *Developmental Disorders and Personality Disorders* in DSM-III-R). Nevertheless, no data on the reliability of the specific diagnoses have been published by the compilers of DSM-III. Moreover, as can be seen in Table 7-2, the reliability of the cluster diagnoses is disappointing. Subsequent studies (e.g., Mellsop and Varghese, 1983; Werry, Methven, Fitzpatrick, and Dixon, 1983) have confirmed the poor reliability of Axis II.

Although the compilers of DSM-III report collecting data on all five axes, no reliability data are presented from Axis III, *Physical Disorders.* The reliability of Axis IV, *Psychosocial Stressors* (Table 7-2), is modest at best. The reliability of Axis V, *Highest Level of Adaptive Functioning in the Past Year* (called *Global Assessment of Functioning at Present and during the Past Year* in DSM-III-R), is quite good. That axis, however, has been greatly revised for DSM-III-R. No reliability data for any of the DSM-III-R categories are presently available.

Table 7-2 AGREEMENT COEFFICIENTS (KAPPA) FOR CLUSTER AND SPECIFIC DIAGNOSES FOR ADULTS AND CHILDREN

	Study I		Study II	
	Adults	Children	Adults	Children
Axis I				
Disorders usually first evident in infancy, childhood, or adolescence	.65	.69	.73	.63
Mental retardation	.80	1.0	.83	
Attention-deficit hyperactivity disorder		.58		.50
Conduct disorder		.61		.61
Anxiety disorders of childhood and adolescence		.25		.44
Other disorders of infancy, childhood, or adolescence		.79		.73
Eating disorders	.59			
Organic mental disorders	.79		.76	
Disorders of the senium and presenium	.85		.91	
Substance induced	.63		.58	
Other	.66		.65	
Substance use disorders	.86		.80	.54
Schizophrenic disorders	.81		.81	
Psychotic disorders not elsewhere classified	.64		.69	
Affective disorders	.69	.53	.83	.30
Major affective disorders	.68	.36	.80	
Other specific affective disorders	.49		.69	
Atypical affective disorders	.29		.49	
Anxiety disorders	.63		.72	
Somatoform disorders	.54		.42	
Psychosexual disorders	.92		.75	
Disorders of impulse control not elsewhere classified	.28		.80	
Adjustment disorder	.67	.66	.68	.36
Axis II				
Specific developmental disorders		.77		.51
Personality disorders	.56	.56	.65	.61

* Cluster diagnoses in bold type. Subcluster and specific diagnoses in ordinary type. Numbers on the *left* in each category are Kappas for cluster diagnoses; numbers on the *right* are Kappas for subcluster and specific diagnoses. Only categories that include more than five diagnostic observations are included. Kappas of .75 and greater indicate satisfactory agreement; Kappas between .40 and .74 indicate fair agreement; values below .40 indicate poor agreement. (Source: Data from DSM-III-R)

In sum, the reliabilities of DSM-III are disappointing. They may well be a substantial improvement over the reliabilities of earlier diagnostic manuals, but they are still too low for credible clinical use.

THE VALIDITY OF PSYCHOLOGICAL DIAGNOSIS

The validity of an instrument is a measure of its ultimate usefulness, whether it does what it is supposed to do. People who obtain high scores on a good test of clerical ability, for example, should perform better in clerical

Descriptive and
predictive validity

tasks than those who obtain low scores. With regard to systems of diagnosis such as DSM-III, we want to know whether the diagnostic categories satisfy the central functions of clinical diagnosis. Do they facilitate communication by describing patients, and particularly by differentiating patients in one category from those in another? This is called *descriptive validity.* Do diagnostic categories enable one to predict the course and especially the outcome of treatment? This is called *outcome* or *predictive validity* (Blashfield and Draguns, 1976). Of course, low reliability, as we have seen, undermines validity. To the extent that clinicians cannot agree about how the diagnostic categories should be applied, the usefulness of the diagnostic system is curtailed.

Problems with
clinical categories

□ DESCRIPTIVE VALIDITY.   To the extent that DSM-III and DSM-III-R resemble their forebears, DSM-I and DSM-II, their descriptive validity is problematic. Most clinicians, when told that a patient is schizophrenic, for example, do not seem to get a rich sense of how that person will think, feel, and act. This failure has less to do with their imaginativeness and much more to do with the way clinical categories are used. A study by Zigler and Phillips (1961) exemplifies this problem. They investigated the relationship between the symptoms that patients presented to diagnosticians and the diagnoses that were made. In all, 793 patients were diagnosed in four broad categories: neurotic, manic-depressive, character disorder, and schizophrenic. Then the symptoms that these patients experienced were examined. A person whose symptom was "depressed" was likely to be diagnosed "manic-depressive." But he or she was also just as likely to be diagnosed "neurotic." Even of those diagnosed schizophrenic, better than one-quarter were likely to be depressed. Thus, the evidence from this study strongly suggests that diagnosis does not convey the kind of information about symptoms that might allow one to differentiate one patient from the other, or to have a reliable sense of what symptoms that patient has.

Patterns of
symptoms

Perhaps that is the way it should be. After all, diagnosis does not proceed by simply listing symptoms and hoping they will *add* up to a particular diagnosis. Rather, a diagnosis emerges from a *pattern* of symptoms and from the current state of scientific understanding of abnormality. In the realm of physical disorder, "fever" yields a different diagnosis according to whether it is accompanied by a stuffed nose, swollen glands, or acute stomach pains. Similarly, symptoms such as "depressed" and "tense" mean different things when they are accompanied by other symptoms and form different patterns. Of course, this view of the diagnostic process only underscores the fact that summary diagnoses, such as schizophrenia and personality disorder, do not convey much information about a person.

□ PREDICTIVE VALIDITY.   Predictive validity—demonstrating that the predictions that derive from a diagnosis are borne out by subsequent events —is especially crucial since it bears directly on the kind of treatment that is selected (Robins and Helzer, 1986). A diagnostic system with good outcome or predictive validity should also tell something about the future course of the disorder, and about what gave rise to the disorder. The validity of a system depends on the questions that are asked: Will the problem respond to particular kinds of treatment? Will the affected individual be violent or suicidal? What kinds of early childhood experiences are likely to bring about the disorder? These are the kinds of questions that can be answered if a diagnostic system has high predictive validity.

Predictive validity and treatment

Predictive validity is high when a diagnosis can lead to an effective treatment for a disorder. For example, the predictive validity for "Bipolar Affective Disorder" is quite high when the disorder is treated with a drug called lithium. Here, the diagnosis performs a fine predictive function, in that a specific treatment is mandated. So, too, does "Premature Ejaculation," in that the disorder responds well to specific behavioral and social learning treatments. In these instances, the diagnosis indicates a treatment that has a high probability of succeeding. Unfortunately, in most diagnostic situations merely having a diagnosis is of limited use. Often, the diagnosis does not dictate a particular course of treatment, nor can the outcome of particular treatments be predicted. Moreover, the diagnosis does not say much about the causes of the disorder. When much more is learned about the nature of particular forms of abnormality, we may be able to say that a particular diagnostic scheme is valid. But right now, the predictive validity of many diagnostic categories of the DSM-III and DSM-III-R is still an open question.

CONDITIONS THAT BIAS DIAGNOSES

Influences on diagnosis

Psychological diagnoses are not at all like medical diagnoses. In the latter, there are physical data to support the final judgment. These include fever, X-ray results, and palpation. Often surgery and laboratory reports back up the diagnosis. Psychological diagnosis is quite different. No evidence of psychological disorder can be found in feces, or blood, or on X rays. You cannot palpate psychological disorder or see its physical presence. The evidence for psychological disorder is always transient, and highly subject to a variety of social psychological considerations. Three of the most important influences on diagnoses are context, expectation, and source credibility.

CONTEXT

Hospital context

The context in which a behavior is observed can dramatically affect the meaning that is ascribed to it (Asch, 1951; Gergen, 1982). In one study, a group of people who were free from major psychological symptoms *simulated* a particularly idiosyncratic symptom to the admitting doctors at general psychiatric hospitals. The "patients" alleged that they heard a voice—nothing particularly idiosyncratic about that—and that the voice said "dull," "empty," and "thud." Now *those* particular verbalizations were quite idiosyncratic, but nothing else about these people was unusual. Indeed, they had been carefully instructed to behave as they commonly behave, and to give truthful answers to all questions, except those that dealt with their auditory hallucinations. Had they been outside of the hospital context, their simulation would have been detected, or at least suspected. Surely someone would have indicated that this single symptom with no accompanying symptoms was strange indeed. But that did not happen in the hospitals in which these patients sought admission. Rather, they were admitted mainly with the diagnosis of schizophrenia, and they were discharged with the diagnosis of schizophrenia in remission. The fact that most patients in hospitals who hallucinate are schizophrenics created a compelling context for these "pseudopatients" to be considered schizophrenics. Although their symptoms were not those of schizophrenia, the context of the symptoms mattered more in the diagnosis than did the symptoms themselves (Rosenhan, 1973).

Diagnoses constituting contexts

Not only hospital settings, but the diagnoses themselves can constitute contexts that admit certain kinds of information and interpretations, bias other kinds, and disallow still others. For example, once the pseudopatients were admitted to the hospital, they of course began to observe their surroundings carefully and to take copious notes on their observations. Patients asked them what they were writing. Soon the patients concluded that the writers were not patients at all, but rather were journalists or college professors doing a study of the hospital. It was not an especially ingenious inference for the patients to make, since the pseudopatients did in fact behave quite differently than many of the real patients did. But the staff, on the other hand, made no such inference. They too noted that the pseudopatients often wrote. "Patient engages in writing behavior," the staff recorded about a particular patient. But they interpreted his writing within the context of the diagnosis itself, viewed the writing as yet another confirming bit of psychopathology, and closed off any explanation that lay outside of the diagnostic context.

Similar findings about the effects of contexts are demonstrated in a study in which clinicians were shown a videotape of a young man talking to an older, bearded man about his feelings and experiences in various jobs (Langer and Abelson, 1974). Some of the mental health professionals were told that the young man was a job applicant, while the others were told that he was a clinical patient. After seeing the videotape, all were asked for their observations about the young man. Those who saw the "job applicant" found him "attractive and conventional looking," "candid and innovative," an "upstanding middle-class citizen type." Those who saw the "patient" described him as a "tight, defensive person," "dependent, passive-aggressive," and "frightened of his own aggressive impulses."

In this study, the different labels—"job applicant" and "patient"—created not only a context for perceiving the person but also for explaining his behavior. The therapists were asked: "What do you think might explain Mr. Smith's outlook on life? Do you think he is realistic?" Those who saw the "patient" offered such observations as "Doesn't seem to be realistic because he seems to use denial (and rationalization and intellectualization) to center his problems in situations and other people," "seems afraid of his own drives, motives . . . outlook not based on realities of "objective world." But those who saw the "job applicant" explained the identical behavior in a quite different way. "His attitudes are consistent with a large subculture in the U.S. . . . the silent majority," "he seems fairly realistic, fairly reality oriented; recognizes injustices of large systems but doesn't seem to think that he can individually do anything to change them."

The descriptive comments that were made by the clinicians were subsequently quantified by raters who had no knowledge about either the experimental conditions (patient or job applicant) or the hypotheses that guided this study. These raters were simply asked to score the comments on a scale that ranged from 1 (very disturbed) to 10 (very well adjusted). The data are provided in Figure 7-5. Context clearly affected the evaluations of adjustment, as well as the perception of the causes of the behavior.

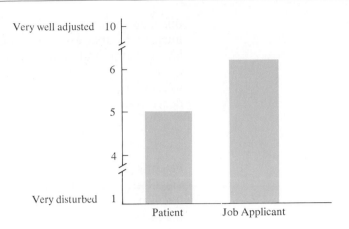

Figure 7-5
Overall adjustment ratings of
"job applicant" and "patient"

EXPECTATION

Expectations of
diagnosticians

Whether a diagnostician is expecting to see a person in distress or a normal person may heavily influence diagnostic judgment. For example, one hospital administrator, having heard how easily the pseudopatients described earlier had been diagnosed as schizophrenic and had gained admission to a hospital, insisted that "it can't happen here." As a result, a simple study was devised (Rosenhan, 1973). The hospital was informed that sometime during the following three months, one or more pseudopatients would appear at the admissions office. During this period, each staff member—attendants, nurses, psychiatrists, and psychologists—was asked to rate each patient who sought admission or who was already on the ward, using a scale that indicated how likely it was that the patient was, in fact, a pseudopatient. More than 20 percent of the patients who were admitted for psychiatric treatment were judged, with high confidence, to be pseudopatients by at least one staff member, and nearly 10 percent were thought to be pseudopatients by two staff members. Set in the direction of finding a pseudopatient, they found many. In fact, not a single pseudopatient ever presented himself for admission—at least not from this study!

SOURCE CREDIBILITY

Influence of
unimpeachable
authorities

Psychological diagnosis is particularly vulnerable to suggestions from "unimpeachable authorities." That vulnerability is demonstrated in a study in which groups of diagnosticians heard a taped interview of a man who seemed to be going through an especially happy and vigorous period in his life (Temerlin, 1970). His work was rewarding and going well, his relationships with others were cordial and gratifying, and he was happily married and enjoyed sexual relations. He was also entirely free of the symptoms that commonly generate a psychiatric diagnosis: depression, anxiety, psychosomatic symptoms, suspiciousness, hostility, and thought disturbance. After listening to the interview, one group of diagnosticians heard a respected authority say that the man seemed neurotic but was actually "quite psychotic." Other diagnosticians heard the same authority say that the person was quite healthy. Yet others heard someone on the tape say that it was an interview for a job. The results of this study are quite dramatic. Psychologically trained diagnosticians—psychiatrists, psychologists, and clinical psychology graduate students—were highly influenced by the assertions that this man might be quite disturbed. Indeed, they were somewhat more influenced by that assertion than were untrained diagnosticians, including law students and undergraduates. Correspondingly, when a composite group of diagnosticians (including both trained and untrained ones) was told that the individual was "healthy," their diagnoses mentioned no evidence of disturbance.

EVALUATING PSYCHOLOGICAL DIAGNOSES

Patently, there is a good deal that needs to be improved about psychological diagnosis. It is often unreliable: equally expert diagnosticians arrive at different diagnoses of the same individual. This is, of course, a problem in medicine too, but it is much more prevalent in psychological diagnosis since, as we mentioned earlier, there are few physical guideposts to support the psychological diagnostic effort. Psychological diagnosis, moreover, is not always valid, for it often fails to suggest a clear-cut and useful treatment, and to communicate a known cause of the disorder. And, as we have said, psychological diagnosis is vulnerable to context, expectation, and source credibility effects.

Need for categorization and diagnosis

But can we do without diagnosis? Absolutely not. In the first place, seeing itself involves categorization. As we read these words, we may be aware that we are reading words (a categorization) rather than merely black ink (a categorization) on white paper (another categorization). And diagnosis is just another word for categorization, one that arises from a medical model. Second, and more important, there can be no science and no advance in understanding abnormality, without somehow segregating one kind of abnormality from another. That you recall, is what initiated the understanding and, subsequently, the cure for general paresis (Chapter 3). Diagnosing general paresis as something quite different from other mental disorders ultimately made the treatment breakthrough possible. Without diagnosis, that advance would not have been possible. On the other hand, Jacqueline Persons (1986) criticizes diagnostic systems such as DSM-III precisely because they do not lend themselves sufficiently to scientific advance. She urges a closer examination of the symptoms of distress themselves, rather than the more global diagnosis. Such an approach has a number of attractive features, not the least of which is that it is likely to augment the reliability of classification, allowing us to study important phenomena that are buried in traditional classification.

Utility of research diagnoses

We cannot live without diagnosis, but this does not mean that every diagnosis is accurate, or that every diagnostic term in DSM-III-R truly reflects illness or mental disorder. The accuracy and utility of any diagnosis needs to be demonstrated. Indeed, as scientific understanding progresses, we come to understand which diagnoses are useful and which are not. Some diagnoses already have proven usefulness and precision. They are already reliable and valid. Most, however, are promising at best. Eventually, they may shed light on the nature and treatment of particular kinds of psychological distress. Meanwhile, however, they are necessary if research is to proceed, with their utility mainly residing in their promise as *research diagnoses* (i.e., hunches that may prove useful in communicating about people and in treating them). The difference between a research and clinical diagnosis is very important; it rests on the reliability and validity of the diagnosis (Rosenhan, 1975). The remaining chapters of the book describe what is known about disorders for which we have fairly reliable research information.

SUMMARY

1. Personality assessment techniques may be divided into three processes: interviewing, testing, and observing. Assessment devices must be reliable and valid. *Reliability* refers to the stability of a measure, whether it yields the same findings with repeated use. *Validity* refers to how useful the device is, whether it can be used for the purposes for which it is intended.

2. When two psychologists arrive at the same assessment of a patient, there is said to be inter-judge *reliability.*

3. The clinical interview may be structured and have questions prepared in an *interview schedule,* or it may be unstructured and therefore more flexible.

4. Psychological tests fall into three categories: *psychological inventories,* including the MMPI, the Q-sort, and the Rep Test; *projective tests,* including the Rorschach and the TAT; and *intelligence tests,* including the WAIS and the WISC. All of these are verbal tests and use words to portray psychological assets and liabilities.

5. *Behavioral assessment* is used in conjunction with treatment. It consists of a record of the patient's behavior and thoughts—their incidence, duration, and intensity. A *functional analysis* assesses the behavior and the stimuli affecting that behavior.

6. *Psychophysiological assessment* confirms whether there is a physiological component to abnormal psychological states—how intense it is and whether treatment affects it.

7. *Diagnosis* is the categorization of psychological disorders according to behavioral or psychological patterns. To be useful, or valid, the diagnosis should describe the patient's status, predict the course of the difficulty (with or without treatment), or aid in deepening our understanding of abnormality.

8. DSM-III-R is a multidimensional diagnostic guide. It seeks to provide specific and operational diagnostic criteria for each mental disorder. Within DSM-III-R, there are five dimensions, or axes, to classify a disorder and to help plan treatment and predict outcome. The overall reliability of DSM-III-R is unknown. The reliability of its immediate predecessor, DSM-III, is only fair.

9. *Descriptive validity* refers to whether a diagnosis successfully differentiates patients in one category from those in another. *Outcome* or *predictive validity* refers to whether the diagnosis tells something about the future course of the disorder, what gave rise to the disorder, and whether the disorder will respond to treatment.

10. The accuracy and usefulness of a diagnosis may be compromised by the *context* in which it occurs and by the *expectations* and *credibility* of the diagnosticians and their informants.

11. Diagnosis and assessment are fundamental to treatment and necessary for scientific advancement. However, that does not mean that every assessment is useful or necessary.

Part 4

ANXIETY AND
PSYCHOSOMATIC
DISORDERS

Fear and Phobia:
Anxiety Felt

W E now begin our discussion of the psychological disorders themselves. In this chapter and Chapter 9, we discuss the disorders that
used to be called "neuroses." In this chapter, we consider the disorders in
which anxiety is actually felt by the victim. In Chapter 9, we will deal with
disorders in which anxiety generally is not felt, although its existence can be
inferred from the patient's symptoms. In Chapter 10, we will consider the
psychosomatic disorders, in which an organic problem can be exacerbated
or even started by anxiety and other psychological events.

FEAR AND ANXIETY

Distinguishing
fear from anxiety

There are four disorders in which fear and anxiety are actually felt by the individual, and these divide into two classes: the fear disorders and the anxiety
disorders. Fear is distinguished from anxiety by the presence of a specific,
dangerous object. Phobias and post-traumatic stress disorders constitute the
fear disorders; in these disorders, a specific object causes the anxiety. In
phobic disorders, the individual shows fear of an object (such as cats) which
is out of all proportion to the reality of the danger that object presents. In
post-traumatic stress disorders, the individual experiences anxiety, depression, numbing, and constant reliving of the trauma after experiencing some
catastrophe beyond the normal range of human suffering. For example, an
undergraduate who was raped in her dormitory may subsequently relive the
trauma repeatedly in memory and in her dreams, becoming numb to the
world around her and experiencing intense anxiety whenever she is alone
with a man.

189

Panic disorder and generalized anxiety disorder are the anxiety disorders. In these two disorders, no specific danger or object threatens the individual, yet he or she still feels very anxious. In *panic disorder,* an individual is suddenly overwhelmed with brief attacks of anxiety, apprehension, and then terror. *Generalized anxiety disorder,* on the other hand, consists of chronic anxiety that can be more or less continually present for months on end.

All four of these disorders share in common an exaggerated version of the normal and adaptive fear that each of us has felt on many occasions. We begin our discussion of these disorders by examining what fear and anxiety are.

Fear

Normal fear and anxiety

All of us have experienced fear. The degree of danger we encounter has to do in large part with our job, where we live, and so on. Being a member of a team responsible for constructing an oil rig in the wintry North Sea opens one up to more danger than being an accountant. But an accountant living in New York City may experience more danger than one working in De Kalb, Illinois. When the oilman experiences fear, it is directly related to the danger of his situation; his reactions will be appropriate and normal. Similarly, the accountant's heart has every reason to beat rapidly upon hearing a noise at the window at three o'clock in the morning. Normal fear and anxiety, unlike the disorders we will discuss in this chapter, are in keeping with the reality of the danger.

ELEMENTS OF FEAR

The fear response

When we experience danger, we undergo the various somatic and emotional changes that make up the fear response. There are four elements to the fear response: (1) cognitive elements—expectations of impending harm; (2) somatic elements—the body's emergency reaction to danger, as well as changes in our appearance; (3) emotional elements—feelings of dread and

The degree of danger we encounter has to do in large part with the realities of our job. Workers of the sort shown here may experience considerable fear because the work is highly dangerous.

Table 8-1 ELEMENTS OF FEAR

Cognitive
Thoughts of impending harm
Exaggerating the actual amount of danger

Somatic	
Paleness of skin	Liver releases carbohydrates
Goosebumps	Bronchioles widen
Tension of muscles	Pupils dilate
Face of fear	Sweat glands secrete
Heart rate increases	Coagulants and lymphocytes increase in blood
Spleen contracts	Adrenaline is secreted from adrenal medulla
Respiration accelerates	Stomach acid is inhibited
Respiration deepens	Loss of bladder and anal sphincter control
Peripheral vessels dilate	Salivation decreases

Emotional-Subjective	
Feelings of dread, terror, panic	Tight stomach
Queasiness and butterflies	Creeping sensations

Behavioral	
Appetitive responding decreases	Avoidance
Aversive responding increases	Freezing
Escape	Aggression

terror and panic; and (4) behavioral elements—fleeing and fighting (Lang, 1967; Rachman, 1978). These four elements of the fear response are summarized in Table 8-1.

Fear may take several forms, and different elements may be involved. No two individuals need display the same elements of fear when they are afraid. Nor is there any particular element that must be present. Fear is diagnosed according to the following logic: (1) all of the elements need not be present; (2) some of the elements must be present, although there need not be the same combination every time; (3) no one element must be present; (4) the more intense any element and the more elements present, the more confident are we in labeling the state as "fear." What are each of these elements of fear?

Cognitive elements of fear

The **cognitive elements** of fear are expectations of specific impending harm, usually in the immediate future. A large doberman growls menacingly at you. You think, "He's going to bite me," and you feel a surge of fear. On a dark and lonely street, you sense a sudden movement behind you. You think, "It's a mugger," and you freeze. You are unprepared at a recitation, and the teacher calls on you. You break into a cold sweat as you think, "I'm going to be humiliated." Notice that mental representations evoke the bodily reactions of fear (Lang, 1979; Foa and Kozak, 1986).

Somatic elements of fear

Somatic or bodily reactions also occur when we are afraid. There are two classes of bodily changes: external changes and internal changes. Like the octopus, who changes from green to red when afraid, human appearance changes, often dramatically, when we are afraid. A keen observer will notice the changes in bodily surface: our skin becomes pale, goosebumps may form, beads of sweat appear on our forehead, the palms of our hands become clammy, our lips tremble and shiver, and our muscles tense. But, most salient of all, fear can be seen in our face and those changes in the face can, by themselves, increase fear reactions elsewhere in the body (Lanzetta and Orr, 1980; see Figure 8-1). In addition to the changes in appearance, there are internal changes within the body. In a matter of seconds after we perceive danger, our body's resources are mobilized in the **emergency reaction;** these internal changes are the physiological elements of fear (see Box 8-1).

Box 8-1

THE CHAIN OF COMMAND OF THE EMERGENCY REACTION

When faced with a potential attacker, a person may have certain thoughts or cognitions about what is going to happen. Terror or other emotions may overcome him. He may react or behave in several ways: by running or by attacking the assailant. He may begin breathing heavily, his muscles may tense up, and any number of other somatic changes may occur.

The somatic changes that begin in a few seconds after a person perceives danger constitute the emergency reaction, in which the body mobilizes to maximize its chances for survival. These internal changes are directly caused by our **autonomic nervous system** and our **adrenal glands,** which are in turn controlled by our **central nervous system** (CNS).

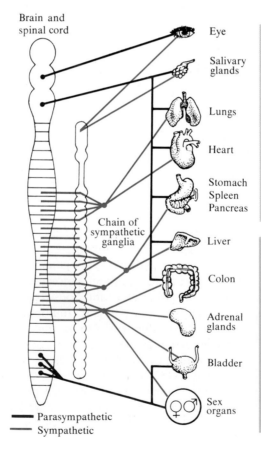

PARASYMPATHETIC SYSTEM

Constriction of pupil

Secretion of tear glands

Salivation

Inhibition of heart action

Constriction of respiratory passages

Stomach contraction: secretion of digestive fluids

Intestinal peristalsis

Contraction of bladder

Erection

SYMPATHETIC SYSTEM

Dilation of pupil

Inhibition of tear glands

Inhibition of salivation

Acceleration of heart action

Opens respiratory passages

Inhibits stomach contractions and digestive secretion

Inhibits intestinal peristalsis

Relaxes bladder

Inhibits erection

SOURCE: Gleitman, 1981, p. 66.

Emotional
elements of fear

Fear is also accompanied by the following strong *emotional elements:* dread, terror, queasiness, the chills, creeping sensations, a lump in the pit of the stomach. These elements are familiar to us because we talk about them when describing our feelings of fear. We are also more conscious of the emotional elements, whereas we generally do not stop to reflect on our cog-

First, the danger registers, and this perception is transmitted from the sense organs and the higher centers of the brain (cortex) to the **hypothalamus** by wholly unknown processes. The hypothalamus is a brain structure about the size of a walnut, which lies under the cortex. (Roughly, if you follow the line of your nostrils up into your brain, you soon come to the hypothalamus.) The hypothalamus greatly influences eating, drinking, and sexual behavior, and is involved in regulating fundamental bodily processes, including metabolism and water balance. In times of emergency, it sends out messages of alarm.

The message from the hypothalamus activates the **sympathetic nervous system** (SNS) and, via this route, the **adrenal medulla,** the central part of the adrenal glands. These two systems then produce bodily changes by sending out adrenaline (epinephrine) and noradrenaline (norepinephrine) as their chemical messengers. The SNS releases norepinephrine from its neurons at the juncture with the neurons that excite the organ in question. The adrenal medulla amplifies the action of the SNS by releasing its chemical message into the blood, from where it diffuses into the organ tissues.

The chemicals released by the SNS and the adrenal medulla race throughout the body, producing the internal changes that constitute the emergency reaction. The heart beats faster and blood is pumped in greater volume. Peripheral blood vessels widen so that more oxygen will be pumped more rapidly around the body, and blood is redistributed from the skin and gut to the muscles and the brain. The spleen contracts, releasing stores of red blood cells to carry more oxygen. Breathing becomes deeper, and the air passages widen to take in more oxygen. The liver releases sugar for use by the muscles. Sweating increases to allow rapid cooling of the muscles and perhaps to increase tactile sensitivity. The content of the blood changes so that coagulation to seal possible wounds will occur more rapidly and lymphocyte cells that repair damage will increase in number.

The emergency reaction can be counteracted by the **parasympathetic nervous system** (PNS), which is responsible for producing a relaxation response. The PNS and the SNS generally oppose each other; together they make up the autonomic nervous system (ANS), which controls the organs that regulate the internal environment of the body, including the heart, stomach, adrenals, and intestines. Thus, when the PNS is excited, the heart slows down, whereas when the SNS is excited, the heart speeds up; while the PNS turns stomach acid secretions on, the SNS inhibits the secretion of acids. The SNS is an **adrenergic** system, using adrenaline and noradrenaline as the chemical messengers to produce an emergency reaction. The PNS is a **cholinergic** system, which uses the chemical transmitter acetylcholine to produce the relaxation reaction.

The completed mobilization of the body during the emergency reaction will increase the oxygen and energy resources that are available to the tissues, will increase circulation so that these resources can be moved through the body more quickly, will provide for waste product release, tactile sensitivity, surface protection, and quick repair of tissue damage. This will enable the individual to react to danger adaptively, so that he is able to run from an assailant or other fear-provoking situations. When the danger has passed, there will be a relaxation response, with a slowing down of the heart and breathing and a reduction in blood pressure.

In Alfred Hitchcock's film *Psycho,* Vera Miles displayed the emergency reaction when she feared she would be killed.

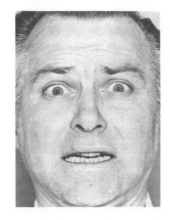

Figure 8-1
The faces of fear. When individuals are afraid, their eyebrows are raised and drawn together, wrinkles appear in the center of their forehead, eyes are wide, and their mouth will open with the lips stretched and tense. (Source: Ekman and Friesen, 1975, p. 62)

Behavioral elements of fear

nitions, nor are we particularly aware of the inner physiological workings set off by fear.

The ***behavior*** we engage in when afraid constitutes the fourth and final element of fear. There are two kinds of fear behavior: ***classically conditioned*** fear responses, which are involuntary reactions to being afraid, and ***instrumental*** responses, which are voluntary attempts to do something about the object we are afraid of.

In the world of elementary school children, bullies sometimes pick on a hapless child on his way home from school, perhaps in what was once a safe alley. After this occurs a few times, the youth will become afraid when approaching the alley. He will display a number of involuntary fear reactions, like sweating and faster heartbeat. This is an example of classical conditioning of fear. From Chapter 5, we know that classical fear conditioning takes place when a previously neutral signal is paired with a traumatic event. As a result of this pairing, the signal itself will cause fear reactions. In this case, the signal is the conditioned stimulus (CS), the trauma is the unconditioned stimulus (US), and fear is the conditioned response (CR) (see Table 8-2). Once conditioning has occurred, the signal alone causes the physiological emergency reaction to occur, profoundly changing other voluntary behavior. In our example, when the hapless youth sees the alley, he will stop munching on potato chips and will cease reading his comic book.

Fleeing and fighting are the main instrumental behaviors in response to fear. There are two types of flight responses: escape and avoidance. In ***escape***

Table 8-2 FEAR AND CLASSICAL CONDITIONING. FEAR IS CONDITIONED IN A CHILD WHEN A NEUTRAL STIMULUS, AN ALLEY, IS PAIRED WITH REPEATED UNPLEASANT ENCOUNTERS WITH BULLIES. AFTER A FEW PAIRINGS, THE ALLEY ITSELF ELICITS FEAR IN THE CHILD.

Neutral CS	Fear Conditioning Trial	Test
CS (alley) ↓ No CR (no fear response)	CS (alley) ↓ US (encounter with bullies) ↓ UR (Pain and fear reaction)	CS (alley) ↓ CR (fear reaction)

responding, the harmful event actually occurs and the subject leaves the scene. For example, the child while being beaten up by his schoolmates will run out of the alley if given the chance. Similarly, a rat will jump across a hurdle to escape from and terminate an electric shock. In contrast, in *avoidance responding,* the subject will leave *before* the harmful event occurs. A signal will herald the bad event: the alley is a signal that some bullies might await the child, just as a tone might signal shock to a rat. The child will run out of the alley and take another route home, even if no bullies are beating him up. Responding to the tone, a rat will avoid the shock before it comes on, thereby preventing the shock from occurring at all. The signal, because of its previous pairing with shock (in early trials, in which the subject failed to make the avoidance response, shock occurred), produces fear, and the subject responds during the signal to remove itself from fear.

DEGREE OF FEAR

Range of fear
responses

The degree of fear varies in different people and in different situations. Some people actually like to step inside a cage with a chair and whip to teach lions tricks. Lion tamers probably experience some fear, whereas most of us would be terrified. Hence, we do not go into cages. Instead, we go to the circus or the zoo. This is considered normal behavior.

There is a range of dangerous situations, as well as a range of fear responses. We accept our fear response when it is in proportion to the degree of danger in the situation. But when the fear response is out of proportion to the amount of danger, we label it abnormal, in short, a phobia. While fear is normal and a phobia is abnormal, they are both on the same continuum; they differ in degree, not in kind (see Figure 8-2).

ANXIETY

Difference
between anxiety
and fear

Anxiety has the same four components as fear but with one crucial difference: the cognitive component of fear is the expectation of a clear and specific danger, whereas the cognitive component of anxiety is the expectation of a much more diffuse danger. "Something terrible might happen!" is the essential thought in a panic disorder or generalized anxiety disorder, whereas in phobic and post-traumatic stress disorders the typical expectation might be, "A dog might bite me" or "There are clouds in the sky; it might flood again." The somatic component of anxiety is the same as that of fear: the elements of the emergency reaction. The emotional elements of anxiety are also the same as those of fear: dread, terror, apprehension, a lump in the pit of the stomach. Finally, the behavioral components of anxiety are also the same as those of fear: flight or fight is elicited. But the object that the afflicted individual should escape or avoid, or against which he should aggress, is shapeless. Thus, fear is based in reality, on an exaggeration of a real danger, whereas anxiety is based on the irrational, on a formless danger.

We now turn to the specific disorders themselves. First, we will examine the two fear disorders: phobia and post-traumatic stress disorder. Then, we will discuss the two anxiety disorders: panic disorder and generalized anxiety disorder. We begin with the phobias.

Figure 8-2
Phobia versus normal fear. This figure gives us a schematic way of distinguishing normal fear from a phobia. It plots the degree of the reality of the danger (as measured by societal consensus) against the degree of accompanying fear (as measured by the strength of the emergency reaction). The 45 degree line indicates normal fear. The area in color shows the phobic range. *A* plots an accountant at work, *B* plots an oil rig construction worker in the wintry North Sea. He probably feels more fear, but the level of fear is in proportion to what he should feel compared to an accountant. *C*, however, plots a phobic, whose reaction to the feared object is far out of proportion to the real danger. *D* plots decorated bomb disposers, who when placed in laboratory fear tasks, show a lack of reaction (Cox, Hallam, O'Connor, and Rachman, 1983). Although these courageous individuals are in dangerous situations that would cause a high level of fear in most individuals, the bomb disposers display only a minimal emergency reaction.

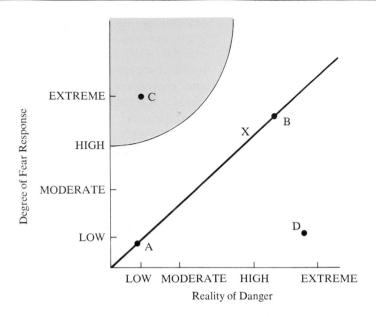

PHOBIA

We begin our discussion with phobia for several reasons: (1) phobia is an unusually well-defined phenomenon, and there is little trouble diagnosing it correctly; and (2) it is a disorder about which much is known concerning its cause and cure. Until three decades ago, phobias were a mysterious disorder from which there was no escape—unless you were one of the lucky individuals whose phobia disappeared just as inexplicably as it arrived. Today, most phobias can be successfully treated, and of all psychological disorders, phobias are perhaps the best understood.

This section narrates the story of the conquest of phobia. We begin by defining phobia and then proceed to discuss what kinds of phobias exist. We discuss two rival theories of phobias: the psychoanalytic and the behavioral, and then we discuss the four therapies that seem to work on phobias. Finally, we present an integrated theory of phobia, which seems to account quite adequately for symptoms, cause, and treatment.

Phobia Defined

Phobia as fear reaction

A ***phobia*** is a persistent fear reaction that is strongly out of proportion to the reality of the danger. For example, there are some people who, out of exaggerated fear, will not go the circus or the zoo. In fact, a cat phobic cannot even be in the same room with a house cat because of her extreme fear of cats. Although we can repeatedly tell the cat phobic that house cats rarely attack humans, the fear will persist nonetheless.

A fear reaction may interfere with a phobic's entire life. Consider the following case in which fear is so great that the woman is even afraid to leave her home:

Anna was housebound. Six months ago, the house next door had become vacant and the grass had begun to grow long. Soon, the garden had become a ren-

Pictured here are a girl about to ride a bronco, a construction worker, and a bomb disposer. Where on the graph of Figure 8-2 would we plot these individuals?

dezvous for the local cats. Now Anna was terrified that if she left her house, a cat would spring on her and attack her. Her fear of cats was of thirty years' status, having begun at age four when she remembered watching in horror as her father drowned a kitten. In spite of saying that she believed it was unlikely that her father actually did such a thing, she was haunted by the fear. At the sight of a cat, she would panic and sometimes be completely overwhelmed with terror. She could think of nothing else but her fear of cats. She interpreted any unexpected movement, shadow, or noise as a cat.

Anna is housebound because she is afraid that she might be attacked by a cat if she goes outside. Her fear is greatly out of proportion to the reality of the danger of actually being injured by a cat. The real danger is near zero, but her fear is extreme and irrational. Her problem is more than fear; it is a phobia. Very intense fear, however, does not constitute a phobia unless the actual danger is slight. For example, all of us would be housebound upon hearing about an approaching tornado. Here, the danger is great; the behavior is rational.

There is little trouble diagnosing a phobia when it is present, since its symptoms are unambiguous: (1) persistent fear of a specific situation out of proportion to the reality of the danger, (2) compelling desire to avoid and escape the situation, (3) recognition that the fear is unreasonably excessive, and (4) symptoms that are not due to another disorder, such as schizophrenia, depression, or obsessive-compulsive disorder. Finally, with the exception of agoraphobics (who fear crowds and open spaces), a phobic's psychological problems are quite isolated; typically, the only problem is the phobia itself, and phobics function well in most other areas of their life (Marks, 1969).

Role of society in labeling phobias

We must recognize that what we label a phobia is, by definition, partly a societal judgment. If the consensus of a society is that cats are extremely dangerous, it would not be considered a phobia to avoid them at all costs. Some superstitious societies attributed certain powers to animate and inanimate objects. Reacting to such objects with extreme fear would not constitute a phobia. For members of that society, such reactions made good rational sense.

There is no question that phobias cause one to suffer. They are maladaptive, since the individual's activities are greatly restricted; they are irrational, since the sense of danger is out of proportion to the reality of the danger. Phobics make others uncomfortable, and their behavior is considered socially unacceptable. Phobias are out of the individual's control, and phobics want to be rid of their fear. Thus, phobias are clearly abnormal.

PREVALENCE OF PHOBIAS

Who has phobias?

The most recent estimate of the prevalence of phobias puts the rate at between 7 and 20 percent of the population with some phobic symptoms and about 1 percent of the population with severe phobias—phobias so strong that they might, for example, keep the phobic housebound (Robins et al., 1984; Marks, 1986a). *Prevalence* is defined as the percentage of population having a disorder at any given time and is contrasted with *incidence,* which is the rate of new cases of a disorder in a given time period. So mild phobias are a widespread disorder, although crippling phobias are uncommon. In clinical practice, about 5 to 10 percent of all psychiatric patients have phobias. Moreover, there may be a genetic predisposition to phobias. In seven of eight pairs of identical twins, both of the twins had phobic features, but in only five of thirteen fraternal twins both had phobic features (Carey and Gottesman, 1981; Marks, 1986a).

KINDS OF PHOBIAS

Classifying phobias

While there are reports of such unusual phobias as fear of flowers (anthophobia), the number 13 (triskaedekophobia), and snow (blanchophobia), these are very rare. The most common phobias in our society are fear of places of assembly and open spaces (agoraphobia), social phobias, and three classes of specific phobias: (1) fear of particular animals, usually cats, dogs, birds (most commonly pigeons), rats, snakes, and insects; (2) inanimate object phobias, including dirt, heights, closed spaces, darkness, and travel; and (3) fear of illness, injury, or death (see Table 8-3).

AGORAPHOBIA

Prevalence of agoraphobia

The most common phobia is *agoraphobia,* literally "fear of the marketplace." Approximately half of all phobics treated in clinics are agoraphobics, although only 10 percent of mild phobics are agoraphobic. Agoraphobia is not a particularly apt term, since these unfortunate individuals are beset not only with a terror of being in the marketplace, but also of open spaces, crowds, traveling, and streets. Typically, agoraphobics believe that some disaster, most typically a panic attack, will befall them when they are away from the security of their home, and that no one will help them. They then go to great lengths to avoid such places. Agoraphobia is the most crippling of the common phobias because many agoraphobics are unable to leave their home. Here is the account of an agoraphobic who experienced a phobic attack in the snows of Vermont:

Table 8-3 THE COMMON PHOBIAS

		Approximate Percent of All Phobias	Sex Difference	Typical Age of Onset
Agoraphobias (fear of places of assembly, crowds, open spaces)		10-50%	large majority are women	early adulthood
Social Phobias (fear of being observed doing something humiliating)		10%	majority are women	adolescence
The Specific Phobias				
Animals		5-15%	vast majority are women	childhood
Cats (ailurophobia)	Birds (avisophobia)			
Dogs (cynophobia)	Horses (equinophobia)			
Insects (insectophobia)	Snakes (ophidiophobia)			
Spiders (arachnophobia)	Rodents (rodentophobia)			
Inanimate Objects Phobias		20%	none	any age
Dirt (mysophobia)	Darkness (nyctophobia)			
Storms (brontophobia)	Closed spaces (claustrophobia)			
Heights (acrophobia)				
Illness-Injury (nosophobia)		15-25%	none	middle age
Death phobia (thanatophobia)				
Cancer (cancerophobia)				
Venereal disease (venerophobia)				

SOURCE: Marks, 1969.

As a cold wind hit the hill, she stood holding her chin, looking back at the house in the distance. Her friends heard her mutter something—that she had snow in her boot, or needed the bathroom—some such lie. Then she began to run, looking down at the snow. She couldn't look at the house, it seemed too far away. She started to sweat and her legs went soft. She could not feel her feet, but they were running. Her heart was pounding, her face flushed. She began to pant. She felt as though she were coming apart, as if she had been running forever through the syrupy snow of a nightmare. Six Miltowns rattled against four Valiums in her pocket. The sweat on her body tripped triggers in her brain, the adrenaline signaled the nerves to further panic. "What if I die?" she thought. "Oh, my God, I'm going crazy." Then she was at the house, the "safe" place. But she had added more fears to an already long list. She was afraid of snow. She was afraid of hills. And, above all, she was afraid of ever again feeling the way she did running from that snowy hill in Vermont. (Baumgold, 1977)

Fear of open spaces

Notice her fear of open spaces, and the panic that occurs when she fears that she may not easily reach the safety of a contained space—the house. Agoraphobics dread a variety of objects connected with open space: smooth bodies of water, bleak landscapes, the street, train travel on clear days. These objects are much less terrifying when the space is more comfortably circumscribed as by a snowstorm or trees, or when an enclosed space is easily within reach.

Agoraphobics and panic attacks

The great majority of agoraphobics are women, and their phobia begins in early adulthood with a panic attack, as in the following typical onset:

A girl of nineteen suddenly came home from her work as a shop assistant and screamed that she was going to die. While standing at her counter, she had experienced the worst sensations in her life. Her heart began to pound like a jackhammer, she could not catch her breath, she was gripped by panic and dread, she felt the ground underneath her was about to give way, and she was convinced she was having a stroke or a heart attack. She spent the next two weeks in bed and, thereafter, she refused to walk beyond the front gate. She did not improve after four months as a psychiatric in-patient. After her discharge, she left her home only twice in the following seven years.

Agoraphobics are prone to panic attacks even when they are not in the agoraphobic situation. Moreover, they have more psychological problems —other than their phobia—than the other types of phobics. In addition to their phobic symptoms, these patients are often highly anxious and generally depressed. Seventy percent of fifty-five patients with agoraphobia and panic also suffer depression as well (Breier, Charney, and Heninger, 1986). Obsessive-compulsive disorders occasionally accompany agoraphobia as well, and the relatives of agoraphobics are at greater risk for the range of anxiety disorders (Harris, Noyes, Crowe, and Chaudry, 1983). Untreated, agoraphobia will sometimes remit spontaneously, and then return mysteriously, or it may be unabating (Marks, 1969; Zitrin, Klein, Woerner, and Ross, 1983).

SOCIAL PHOBIAS

All of us are, at times, anxious in social situations. *Social phobias* are exaggerations of such fears. In the 4th century B.C., Hippocrates, the Greek physician, described a classic social phobic who

> . . .will not be seen abroad: loves darkness as life, and cannot endure the light, or to sit in lightsome places; his hat still in his eyes, he will neither see, nor be seen by his good will. He dare not come in company for fear he should be misused, disgraced, overshoot himself in gesture or speeches, or be sick, he thinks every man observes him. . . . (Burton, 1621, p. 272, quoted in Marks, 1969)

Social phobics fear being seen or observed. They are terrified of speaking, or eating and drinking in front of other people. They may be unable to eat in a restaurant for fear they will vomit and be humiliated. A student may stop writing during an exam when watched by a teacher for fear of shaking violently. A factory worker may stop going to work lest he be unable to tie packages when observed. An actor may be terrified that he will begin to stutter or forget his lines when on stage. The fears are almost always unrealistic: individuals who fear they *might* shake, do not shake, nor do those who fear vomiting in public actually vomit in public.

Social phobias usually begin in adolescence, and only rarely in childhood. Both agoraphobics and social phobics are afraid of crowds, but for different reasons. The agoraphobic fears being crushed or suffocated by the mass, or he fears that no one will come to his aid if he is in need of help. The social phobic, on the other hand, fears that some individuals in the crowd will look at him and observe him doing something embarrassing. Social phobias usually begin gradually. For example, while brooding about whether the groom is really good enough for her, a bride may begin to fear that she will tremble when she walks down the aisle with her father and that the guests will see how nervous she is. Thereafter, being observed by others in public

This boy may be shy and avoiding the group on the bench because he is embarrassed to talk to them. A social phobia may begin gradually in adolescence out of fear of doing something embarrassing or it may be precipitated by a dramatic incidence in which something very embarrassing actually does occur.

may become more and more frightening for her. But sometimes a particularly dramatic incident will cause a social phobia. For example, a young man may actually vomit at a dance before making it to the toilet. This may so greatly embarrass him that he will no longer interact socially.

These phobias make up about 10 percent of all phobic cases, and they are reported somewhat more frequently by women than by men. Unlike in agoraphobics, in social phobics the phobia itself is generally their only psychological problem.

THE SPECIFIC PHOBIAS

Animal phobias

There are three classes of *specific phobias:* animal phobias, phobias of inanimate objects, and illness and injury phobias. The first of these, ***animal phobias,*** such as Anna's cat phobia, contrasts with agoraphobia. Animal phobias uniformly begin in early childhood, almost never beginning after puberty. While common in childhood, most animal phobias are outgrown by adulthood.

Animal phobias are highly focused: Anna may be terrified of cats, but she is rather fond of dogs and birds. Agoraphobic problems, in contrast, are diffuse, ranging over a great variety of situations. Untreated animal phobias can persist for decades with no period of remission, while untreated agoraphobia fluctuates from remissions to relapses.

Only about 5 percent of all crippling phobias and perhaps 15 percent of milder phobias are of specific animals. The vast majority (95 percent) of animal phobias are reported by women; unlike agoraphobics, they are rather healthy individuals and the phobia is apt to be their only psychological problem (Marks, 1969).

Animal phobics sometimes can describe a specific childhood incident that they believe set the phobia off. Anna seemed to recall that her father had drowned a kitten. Dog phobias may begin with a dog bite; a bird phobia may begin if a bird lands on a child's shoulder. Overall, about 60 percent of phobic patients can describe a clear precipitating trauma. But for the remaining 40 percent, no clear incident, only vague clues extracted from the

A specific childhood incident may set off a phobia. This child may grow up to be a dog phobic.

An artist's conception of the fear of animals. Such a phobic could not even be in the same room as a house cat. (Drawing by John Vassos)

mists of childhood memory can be isolated (Öst and Hugdahl, 1981). One child seemed to have developed a phobia by reading about a warrior dog in a fairy tale, and then hearing that a boy down the street had been bitten by a dog. Another child, already somewhat apprehensive about birds, was teased mercilessly with feathers by her playmates. In each case, there are a number of events, often several accumulating over time, that might contribute to the phobia. But uncovering the essential events, if such exist, can be enormously difficult. Usually animal phobias are outgrown, but for unknown reasons, a few remain robust and persist into adulthood.

Inanimate object phobias share many of the same characteristics as animal phobias. Heights, closed spaces, storms, dirt, darkness, running water, travel, flying in airplanes, and wind make up the majority of these phobias. As in animal phobias, the symptoms are focused on one object, and the individuals are otherwise psychologically normal. Onset is sometimes embedded in a traumatic incident. For example, a nineteen-year-old develops an airplane phobia after a plane he has just gotten off crashes at its next stop. An eight-year-old girl, who saw a boy hit by lightning and killed, develops a phobia of thunder and lightning. These phobias are somewhat more common than animal phobias, and they occur about equally in women and men. Unlike animal phobias, they can begin at any age.

Hilda's case illustrates how a traumatic incident can bring about a phobia. It is unusual in that the trauma occurred when she was eleven years old, but the phobia went underground for twenty years and then reemerged during an adult stress. The trauma, in reality, was life-threatening; the abnormal aspect was how widely her fear generalized, showing that even a very specific phobia can disrupt one's entire life.

A delayed onset phobia

Hilda, a thirty-two-year-old married woman, came into therapy because of an unusual type of phobia: a fear of snow.

This phobia was her major presenting feature and had become increasingly handicapping and troublesome. As one consequence of her husband's business success, they had moved to the suburbs, where there was likely to be ever more snow than in the city. More travel was required—at times through snow during wintertime—to get to the store or to any other place; and in the last several winters, there had been a great deal of snow in her particular metropolitan area.

It is hard to picture adequately the extent of fear: this woman's fear of snow petrified her. She could not stand to go out in it; she could not stand to see it; in winter she could not listen to weather reports because someone might make some reference to snow! Any reference to snow, or even subjective thoughts about it, would make her uncomfortable, frightened, and tense. The many, many ways in which this phobia could affect her day-to-day living were almost incredible. The effects were pervasive and thereby profound.

In this instance, we were most fortunate eventually to uncover what proved to have been the major precipitating event in the onset of the phobia. This was a traumatic experience dating from when the patient was eleven years old. This experience had lain completely out of sight, hidden in her unconscious, for twenty-one years—repressed, but hardly dormant.

In the winter of her eleventh year, she had accompanied an aunt and an uncle to a ski lodge in Vermont. One afternoon, she wandered off by herself, into a small ravine that lay parallel to, but considerably below an old logging road. She played and gradually waded her way through the snow for several hundred yards down the ravine. Looking up at this point, she could see some people on the road far above her. There was some banter exchanged between them. A few snowballs or stones were thrown in her direction. A large chunk of snow either came loose or was started toward her. To her intense horror, it quickly gathered speed and volume. Suddenly she found herself in the path of a miniature avalanche. She was helpless to move out of the way in time, and was engulfed. She was literally buried alive, and was unable to move or to extricate herself. Somehow, however, she managed to maintain, or was fortunate enough to have, a channel so that she could continue breathing. The people on the road above simply disappeared, either not knowing what had transpired, or perhaps in a guilty attempt to dissociate themselves from tragedy.

The little girl remained there, absolutely petrified with fear, for an indeterminate period of time, until discovered through most fortuitous circumstances by her worried uncle. It had seemed an eternity.

Her complete repression of this episode was believed to be caused by its unbearable horror, plus her certainty of death. This may have also been encouraged a bit by her fear of having her parents ever learn about her near tragedy. Each would feel in some measure responsible and subject to censure. Any possibility of future excursions would, in addition, become extremely unlikely. (Adapted from Laughlin, 1967.)

Illness and injury phobias

Illness and injury phobias (nosophobias) are the final class of specific phobias. Phobias of illness, injury, and death make up between 15 percent and 25 percent of all phobias. A person with such a phobia fears having one specific illness, although the kind of illness feared has changed throughout the centuries. In the nineteenth century, nosophobics feared they had tuberculosis or perhaps syphilis and other venereal diseases. More recently, cancer, heart disease, stroke and AIDS have been the terrors.

A nosophobic is usually perfectly healthy, but he worries endlessly that he may have or will soon contract a particular disease. He searches his body for the slightest sign of the disease, and since fear itself produces symptoms like tightness in the chest and stomach pain, he interprets these symptoms as further evidence that the disease is upon him. And so it spirals to more stomach or chest pain and to more certainty that he has the dreaded disease.

There are no sex differences in overall reports of nosophobia, although cancer phobias tend to occur more in females and phobias of venereal disease almost always occur in males. Other psychological problems accompany the disorder frequently, and it usually arises in middle age. Nosophobics often know someone who has the feared disease.

Strangely enough, contracting the disease may cure the phobia. A man was admitted to a hospital, beside himself with syphilophobia. After discharge, he actually caught syphilis. The phobia disappeared at once, and the patient happily had his syphilis cured by medical treatment (Rogerson, 1951, cited in Marks, 1969).

Distinguishing nosophobia from hypochondriasis

Nosophobia is distinguished from **hypochondriasis.** Hypochondriacs have three attitudes: (1) They are convinced they have a serious disease that is undetected. (2) They are highly anxious and vigilant about a variety of illnesses in various parts of the body, unlike the phobic who is concerned with one specific illness in one organ. (3) They are preoccupied with their body, its physiological functioning, and its appearance (Barsky, Wyshak, and Klerman, 1986). Today hypochondriasis is not regarded as a phobia. Rather it seems to be associated with several disorders, although it was originally believed to be a discrete disorder of a nonexistent organ, the *hypochondria,* located in the abdomen.

We have now described the characteristics of the various kinds of phobias. How do phobias come about, and how can they be treated? There are two schools of thought that present comprehensive theories about phobias: the psychoanalytic and the behavioral. We now turn to these contrasting theories, and then to the therapies that work successfully on phobias.

THE PSYCHOANALYTIC ACCOUNT OF PHOBIAS

Freud's interpretation of phobia

The psychoanalytic account of phobias was put forward in 1909 by Sigmund Freud in the famous Little Hans case. To this day, psychodynamic accounts of phobia rely heavily on the logic of this case (Odier, 1956; Arieti, 1979). Freud's interpretation of a phobia consists of several steps: (1) the phobic (if he is male) is in love with and wants to seduce his mother; (2) he jealously hates his father, and wishes to kill him (these first two steps constitute the Oedipus complex); (3) the phobic fears that, in retaliation, his father will castrate him; (4) this conflict produces enormous anxiety in the phobic; because the wishes are unacceptable to the conscious mind, the anxiety is displaced onto an innocent object (the phobic object), which symbolizes the conflict and is a more acceptable receptacle for fear; (5) the phobia is cured when the phobic gains insight into the nature of the underlying conflict.

THE LITTLE HANS CASE

The Little Hans case

Hans was a five-year-old boy who developed a fear of horses intense enough to keep him indoors. When he was four, he saw a horse fall down in the street and then thrash its legs violently in an apparent attempt to get up. Hans was very upset by this and thereafter was reluctant to leave the house, lest he be bitten by a horse who had fallen in the street. After extensive conversation with his father who had been guided by Freud, Little Hans's phobia gradually weakened.

Freud weaved an enchanting story, and in the 150-page case history, marshaled evidence for each of the five premises of phobic origin. For example, he related how Hans had shown a desire to seduce his mother.

Hans had shown an active interest in widdlers (penises) from an early age, and was an affectionate and physical child toward his parents and playmates. When he was four-and-a-quarter years old, a scene of considerable sexual interest occurred. That morning, Hans was given his usual daily bath by his mother, and afterward, he was dried and powdered. As his mother was powdering around his penis and taking care not to touch it, Hans said, "Why don't you put your finger there?"

MOTHER: Because that'd be piggish.
HANS: What's that? Piggish? Why?
MOTHER: Because it's not proper.
HANS: *(laughing)* But it's great fun.

Freud also believed that Hans wanted to kill his father and replace him as his mother's lover. Hans had the following conversation with hs father:

FATHER: Did you often get into bed with Mummy at Gmünden?

HANS: Yes.

FATHER: And you used to think to yourself you were Daddy?

HANS: Yes.

FATHER: And then you felt afraid of Daddy?

HANS: *You know everything; I didn't know anything.*

FATHER: When Fritzl fell down, you thought, "If only Daddy would fall down like that!" and when the lamb butted you, you thought, "If only it would butt Daddy!" Can you remember the funeral at Gmünden?

HANS: Yes. What about it?

FATHER: You thought then that, if only Daddy would die, you'd be Daddy.

HANS: Yes.

As the phobia waned, Freud told how Hans had the fantasy of a plumber giving him a new and bigger widdler, and that with this fantasy, Hans overcame his fear of castration and identified with his father (Freud, 1909).

EVALUATION OF THE PSYCHOANALYTIC ACCOUNT

Shortcomings of psychoanalytic account

The psychoanalytic account of phobias is not compelling. There are three grounds for skepticism: (1) the account is based almost entirely on case history material, and the theoretical inferences from this material are loose; (2) psychoanalytic therapy for phobias works only infrequently, and then only with years of therapy; (3) there exists a viable alternative account—the behavioral analysis—which is based on both experimental evidence and case histories and which is associated with therapies that treat most phobias successfully within a few months.

First, we will consider the looseness of inference from the case history evidence. Did Hans really secretly wish to seduce his mother? The only evidence for this is based on Hans's primitive attempt to get his mother to touch his penis. It is a large leap of inference from such a common expression of sexual interest to a desire to possess the mother and replace the father. At most, we have evidence of some sexual interest, not very well disguised at that.

Did Hans really wish to kill and to replace his father? Hans never expressed fear or hatred for his father. He was told by Freud—who saw Hans only once—that he hated his father. Later, he was asked by his father about this, in a series of leading questions. First, Hans denied that it was so, and eventually he answered with a single "yes."

FATHER: Are you fond of Daddy?

HANS: Oh yes.

FATHER: Or perhaps not. . . . You're a little vexed with Daddy because Mummy's fond of him.

HANS: No.

FATHER: Then why do you always cry whenever Mummy gives me a kiss? It's because you're jealous.

HANS: Jealous, yes.

Hans's phobic improvement seems to be smooth and gradual through this period, not a sudden remission following his "insights." It has since been documented that children between the ages of two and six suddenly develop strong fears of animals, which decline gradually on their own with no therapy (Holmes, 1935; MacFarland, Allen, and Honzik, 1954). Hans is well within the age in which fear spontaneously declines; this speculation is more consistent with the gradual elimination of his phobia than with the interpretation that his Oedipal conflict was suddenly resolved.

Would any evidence "count" as a disconfirmation of the theory? Hans's denial that he is vexed with his father does not count—in fact, it can be construed as confirmatory, by showing that Hans is defending himself against realizing his unacceptable hatred of his father. The theory is built in such a way that both denying and accepting an interpretation confirm that theory. This makes the theory difficult to test.

Psychoanalytic therapy for phobias

The success of a therapy can sometimes be relevant evidence for the theory from which the therapy is derived. What is the psychoanalytic therapy for phobias, and how does it fare? The psychoanalytic therapy for phobia follows from the theory that phobic fear is the displacement of anxiety generated by unacceptable intrapsychic conflict onto some innocent object. The therapist must help the patient to bring the unconscious conflict to light, and to gain insight into the repressed traumatic incident that generated the phobia. In addition, some analysts recommend that the patient's attention should be focused away from the phobic object, but that as the patient comes to recognize the unconscious conflict, he should be encouraged to re-experience the phobic situation while learning that the fear is not intolerable. Psychoanalysts recognize that the prognosis for phobics under this regime is not good (Laughlin, 1967; Arieti, 1979).

> One must anticipate that many, many sessions will be required. A great deal of time and effort is generally required on the part of both doctor and patient alike.
> Further, no guarantee as to the results can be given. . . . It may be a strenuous job, taking hundreds of therapeutic sessions over some years. The end result can be worth far more than the considerable investment of time, effort and money required. (Laughlin, 1967, p. 601)

Overall, then, the Little Hans case history provides unsatisfactory evidence for the psychoanalytic view of phobias. The interpretations are large, uncompelling leaps. This alone would not necessarily be fatal to the theory if there existed experimental evidence to support the interpretation, or if psychoanalysis cured phobias. There is no such evidence, however, and psychoanalytic therapy is of doubtful value for overcoming phobias. Moreover, there exists an alternate account that is consistent with case history material and experimental evidence, and that is of considerable therapeutic value: the behavioral account.

THE BEHAVIORAL ACCOUNT OF PHOBIAS

The behavioral analysis of phobias begins by assuming that normal fear and phobia are learned in the same way. According to this view, both fear and phobia arise when a neutral signal happens to be around at the same time as a bad event. If the bad event is mild, the neutral signal becomes mildly fear provoking. If, however, the bad event is particularly traumatic, the signal becomes terrifying, and the phobia develops. Phobic conditioning is simply an instance of classical fear being conditioned by a particularly traumatic unconditioned stimulus.

CLASSICAL CONDITIONING OF FEAR

Recall that classical conditioning consists of a procedure in which a conditioned stimulus (CS)—or signal—happens to occur at the same time as an unconditioned stimulus (US)—or traumatic event in the case of fear conditioning—which evokes a strong unconditioned reaction (UR). Thereafter, the previously neutral CS produces a conditioned response (CR) that resembles the UR. The CR is the phobic response and the CS is the phobic object. Hans's experience fits this description. Hans himself asserted that his phobia began suddenly when he saw a horse fall down in the street and violently thrash its legs. This gave him an awful fright. The sight of a horse, once not fearful, is a neutral CS. As he looks at the horse, it falls down and thrashes about (US) which evokes fear (UR). Thereafter, the CS of seeing a horse produces a CR of fear. Hans has been classically conditioned to fear horses; we need not postulate deeper fears or lusts. According to this analysis, Hans was not afraid of castration by his father; he was afraid of horses (Wolpe and Rachman, 1960). The precipitating trauma, when it occurs in phobic cases, can be well described by classical fear conditioning. Table 8-4 details the classical fear conditioning analysis of several of our phobic case histories.

In addition to fitting many case histories, a substantial body of experimental evidence supports the hypothesis that pairing a neutral object with a frightening situation produces strong fear of the neutral object. In 1920, John B. Watson and Rosalie Rayner performed the first experiment on this topic. Little Albert B. was a normal, healthy eleven-month-old who, from birth, had been reared in the hospital in which his mother worked as a wet

This child who is crying on Santa's lap may develop a classically conditioned fear of men with white beards. The US is being separated from his mother and put on Santa's lap. The UR is terror. The CS is fear of men with white beards.

Table 8-4 THE BEHAVIORAL ACCOUNT OF PHOBIAS. WHEN THE SIGNAL (CS) IS PAIRED IN TIME WITH THE TRAUMATIC EVENT (US), THIS ELICITS A REACTION (UR). LATER WHEN THE CS AGAIN OCCURS, IT PRODUCES A PHOBIA (CR).

Case	Signal (CS)	Traumatic Event (US)	Reaction (UR)	Phobia (CR)
Little Hans	Horse	Sight of horse falling down thrashing violently	Fright	Horse phobia
Anna	Kitten	Sight of kitten being drowned by father	Horror, fright	Cat phobia
Hilda	Snow	Being buried alive by avalanche	Fear of death, freezing, panic, helplessness	Snow phobia
Social Phobic	Party	Vomiting in public before reaching toilet	Humiliation	Phobia of social gatherings
Little Albert	Rat	Hearing a loud noise	Crying, being startled	Fear of rats, rabbits, fur

John B. Watson (1878–1958).

nurse. On the whole, he was big, stolid, and unemotional. One day, Albert was presented with a white rat, and he eagerly began to reach for it. Just as his hand touched the rat, the experimenters struck a metal bar suspended above Albert's head with a hammer. This produced such a loud and startling sound that Albert jerked violently, burying his head in the mattress, and whimpered. This pairing of the rat and the sound was repeated several times. When Albert was shown the rat later, he began to cry. He fell over on his side, and began to crawl away as rapidly as he could. A phobia had been conditioned.

This experiment was a primitive, but pioneering study. We will discuss below some of the flaws (Harris, 1979; Seligman, 1980). Nonetheless, since the Little Albert experiment, literally hundreds of studies of classically conditioned fear in animals and several in humans have been published. It is now well established that pairing a neutral CS with a traumatic US produces strong acquired fear to the CS. So classical conditioning of fear provides a potential experimental model of phobias because it fits many case histories and seems to be a sufficient condition for learning strong fear.

THE PERSISTENCE OF PHOBIAS

Phobias as resistant to extinction

Can the behavioral analysis also offer an account of persistence, a defining feature of phobias? After fear is classically conditioned in the laboratory by pairing a tone a few times with shock, extinction will occur rapidly when the tone is presented without the shock. Within ten or twenty presentations of the tone without shock, fear will always disappear. Even when shock is extremely painful, fear of the tone will extinguish in no more than forty trials (Annau and Kamin, 1961). Phobias, on the other hand, are very robust. They seem to resist extinction; some persist for a lifetime. How can a model based on an ephemeral phenomenon, classical fear conditioning, capture phobias that last and last?

An *extinction trial* in fear conditioning occurs when the fear-evoking signal is presented to the subject, but the traumatic event no longer follows. For example, a rat is put into the box in which it has received shocks. A fear-evoking tone that has been paired with shock comes on but no shock is presented. The rat can do nothing to escape the tone and is exposed to the fact that the tone no longer predicts shock. Because the rat cannot escape, it *reality tests* and find out that the trauma no longer follows the signal. Under these conditions, fear extinguishes rapidly.

In contrast, phobics rarely test the reality of their fears. When the phobic object is around, they rarely sit there waiting to be passively exposed to an extinction trial. Rather, they run away as quickly as possible. For example, Anna would avoid cats as best she could, but if she did happen across a cat, she would flee as fast as she could. She would not reality test by staying in the presence of the cat and finding out what would happen.

Avoidance and escape from phobic object

Since phobias involve avoidance and escape from the phobic object, does fear of a signal that has been paired with trauma extinguish under the parallel laboratory conditions when the subject avoids the trauma by fleeing from the signal as soon as he is permitted to do so? Consider a rat in an avoidance procedure: a tone comes on, and at the end of ten seconds shock occurs. Remember that the tone equals the phobic object, and the shock

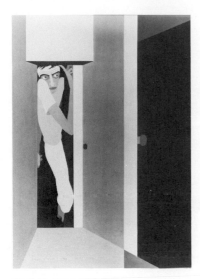

Phobics rarely test the reality of their fears. Claustrophobia is the fear of enclosed spaces; a claustrophobic would avoid or flee from any situation in which he or she would be put into an enclosed space, and would therefore not reality test to find out that no harm would come to him or her in such a space. (Drawing by John Vassos)

equals the traumatic event that originally conditioned the phobia. If the rat jumps onto a platform before the ten seconds are up, the tone will go off and shock will not occur. Soon the rat learns to jump up, and does so in less than two seconds on every trial. When extinction begins, the shock is disconnected (the phobic object no longer signals trauma). Now the rat undergoes one hundred trials in which he jumps up after two seconds of tone, the tone goes off promptly, but shock never occurs. If the rat's fear of the two-second tone is measured behaviorally or physiologically, fear has extinguished. But is the rat still afraid of the longer ten-second tone? Remember that he has not reality tested: he has *not* remained on the grid floor for ten seconds and has not found out that shock is no longer delivered. When tested with the full ten-second tone, the rat shows great fear. Escaping the signal and avoiding the trauma has protected the fear of the signal from extinction (Rescorla and Solomon, 1967; Baum, 1969; Seligman and Johnston, 1973).

Now consider the social phobic who no longer goes to parties because he was humiliated when he once vomited at a party. He avoids parties altogether, and if he must attend one, he escapes as quickly as he can. He is afraid that if he finds himself at a party (CS—the signal), he will again throw up (US—the trauma) and be publicly humiliated (UR—the reaction). His fear does not extinguish because he does not allow himself to be exposed to extinction trials—being at a party and finding out that he does not throw up and is not humiliated. He does not test the reality of the fact that parties (CS) no longer lead to vomiting (US) and humiliation (UR). The ability to avoid and escape the phobic object protects fear of the phobic object from being extinguished, just as allowing a rat to avoid reality testing protects fear from extinguishing.

The behavioral analysis can thus account for the persistence of phobias. Most importantly, it makes direct predictions about therapy; those procedures that extinguish fear conditioning in the laboratory should also cure phobias.

THERAPIES FOR PHOBIAS

There are three therapies that have proven highly effective against phobias: systematic desensitization, flooding, and modeling. All three were developed within the framework of the behavioral analysis. Historically, the first is systematic desensitization.

SYSTEMATIC DESENSITIZATION

In the 1950s, Joseph Wolpe, a South African psychiatrist, classically conditioned cats to fear a chamber in which they had been shocked. Using this animal model of phobias, Wolpe developed the therapy of *systematic desensitization*. First he cured his cats of their acquired fear, and then he successfully applied the therapy to human phobias.

Phases of systematic desensitization

Systematic desensitization is effective and brief, usually lasting at most a few months. It involves three phases: training in relaxation, hierarchy construction, and counterconditioning. First the therapist trains the phobic patient in deep muscle relaxation, a technique in which the subject sits or lies with eyes closed, with all his muscles completely relaxed. This state of relax-

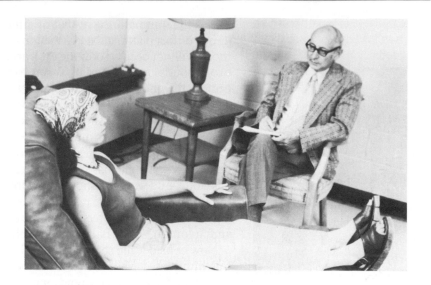

Psychiatrist Joseph Wolpe is conducting systematic desensitization with a patient. The patient is imagining a fear-evoking scene while engaged in deep muscle relaxation. If fear becomes unbearable, she will signal this by lifting her left forefinger.

ation will be used in the third phase to neutralize fear, since it is believed that individuals cannot be deeply relaxed and afraid at the same time (that is, fear and relaxation are incompatible responses). Second, with the aid of the therapist, the patient constructs a hierarchy of frightening situations, in which the most dreaded possible scene is on the highest rung and a scene evoking some, but minimal, fear is on the lowest rung. For example, a hierarchy constructed by a woman with a phobia of physical deformity (from Wolpe, 1969) might be as follows (from minimally feared situations to maximally feared situations):

1. Ambulances (minimally feared)
2. Hospitals
3. Wheelchairs
4. Nurses in uniform
5. Automobile accidents
6. The sight of somebody who is seriously ill
7. The sight of bleeding
8. Someone in pain
9. The sight of physical deformity (maximally feared)

The third phase removes the fear of the phobic object by gradual counterconditioning; that is, causing a response that is incompatible with fear to occur at the same time as the feared CS. The patient goes into deep relaxation, and simultaneously imagines the first, least-arousing scene in the hierarchy. This serves two purposes. First, it pairs the CS, ambulances, with the absence of the original traumatic US. (You will recall that presenting the CS without the original US is an extinction procedure that will weaken the fear response to the CS.) Second, a new response, relaxation, which neutralizes the old response of fear, occurs in the presence of the CS. This is repeated until the patient can imagine scene 1 of the hierarchy without any fear at all. Then scene 2, which provokes a slightly greater fear than scene 1, is paired with relaxation. And so the patient progresses up the hierarchy by the graded extinction procedure until she reaches the most terrifying scene. Here the patient again relaxes and visualizes the final scene. When she can do this with no fear at all, the patient may be tested in real life by being confronted with an actual instance of something at the top of her hierarchy—in this case, with a real physical deformity. Therapy is considered successful when the patient can tolerate being in the actual presence of the most terrifying item on the hierarchy.

Improvement with systematic desensitization

Eighty to ninety percent of specific phobias improve greatly with such treatment. These gains are usually maintained over follow-ups of a year or two. Follow-up studies universally report that new symptoms rarely, if ever, develop to replace the phobia. (For a sample of such studies, see Paul, 1967; Kazdin and Wilcoxon, 1976.) This absence of "symptom substitution" argues that Freud's theory of phobias, as anxiety displaced from deep intrapsychic conflict onto an innocent object, is mistaken: characteristically, the psychoanalytic view of phobias claims that the phobia is merely a superficial symptom of a deeper, unresolved conflict, which is the genuine disorder. The psychoanalytic view maintains that removing the symptoms by desensitizing the phobic object cannot resolve the underlying conflict, and that therefore a new phobia or some other disorder will arise to bind the anxiety that can now no longer be displaced onto the newly desensitized object. This has not been shown to be the case.

Through flooding, a child who is afraid of the water would be put in the water and thereby forced to reality test and see that no catastrophe would occur in the water.

FLOODING

Recall that behaviorists believe that phobias persist because phobics will avoid the phobic object if at all possible, and if forced into its presence, they will escape rapidly. This failure to find out that the phobic object no longer predicts the original traumatic event will protect the phobia from extinction.

What happens when a phobic is forced or volunteers to be in the presence of a phobic object? What happens when rats, who are avoiding shock by escaping the tone in two seconds, are forced to sit repeatedly through the ten-second tone and find out that shock no longer occurs? Such a *flooding* or reality-testing procedure in rats reliably brings reduced amount of fear and eliminates future avoidance (Baum, 1969; Tryon, 1976). The success of eliminating fear in animals by a flooding procedure encouraged behavior therapists to try, with caution, flooding in real phobic patients (Stampfl and Levis, 1967).

Procedure of flooding

In a flooding procedure, the phobic patient agrees, usually with great apprehension, to imagine the phobic situation or to stay in its presence, without attempting to escape for a long period. For example, a claustrophobic will be put in a closet for four hours, or an individual with a fear of flying (aviaphobia) will take a course including a real, aborted jet takeoff and a real flight (Serling, 1986). When done in imagination, for example, an agoraphobic will listen to a long and vivid tape recording that describes his going to a shopping center, falling down, being trampled by crowds, hearing them laugh as they observe him vomiting all over himself. Usually the phobic is terrified for the first hour or two of flooding, and then gradually the terror will subside. When he is then taken to a shopping center, he will usually be greatly improved, and the phobia may be gone.

Improvement with
flooding

In general, flooding has proven to be equal, and sometimes even superior, to systematic desensitization in its therapeutic effects. This has been particularly true of treatment for agoraphobia, which sometimes resists desensitization but is effectively treated by flooding. Treatment gains are maintained: four years after flooding, 75 percent of a group of seventy agoraphobics remained improved (Marks, Boulougouris, and Marset, 1971; Crowe, Marks, Agras, and Leitenberg, 1972; Emmelkamp and Kuipers, 1979). By forcing a patient to reality test and to stay in the phobic situation, and thereby find out that catastrophe does not ensue, extinction of the phobia can usually be accomplished. This directly confirms the hypothesis that phobias are so persistent because the object is avoided in real life and therefore not extinguished by the discovery that they are harmless.

MODELING

Observing a
model

The third effective therapy for phobias is modeling. In a typical modeling procedure, the phobic watches someone who is not phobic perform the behavior that the phobic is unable to do himself. For example, a snake phobic will repeatedly watch a nonfearful model approach, pick up, and fondle a real snake (Bandura, Adams, and Beyer, 1977; Bandura, 1986). Seeing that the other person is not harmed, the phobic may become less fearful of the situation. However, if the phobic thinks that the model is endowed with special powers to deal with a snake, he may continue to fear the situation. In order to change this belief about the model, the therapist will attempt to find a model who resembles the phobic. Then, the therapist will gradually involve the phobic in the exercises. First, the phobic may be asked to describe aloud what he sees, then to approach the snake, and finally to touch it. The procedure will be repeated until the phobia diminishes.

Overall, modeling, when used in therapy, seems to work about as well as both desensitization and flooding in curing both mild and severe clinical phobias (Rachman, 1976). This therapy brings about cognitive change, as well as behavioral change. Once a patient has observed a model, the single best predictor of therapeutic progress is the extent to which he now expects that he will be able to perform the actions he formerly was unable to do (Bandura, Adams, and Beyer, 1977).

By watching others handle snakes, those formerly fearful of them learn to do so themselves, and by doing so, lose their fear of snakes. Such "modeling" is a form of therapy used to overcome phobias.

Process of extinction

A single underlying process—extinction—seems to be the operative element in all three effective therapies for phobias. In all three treatments, the patient is exposed, repeatedly and enduringly, to the phobic object in the absence of the original traumatic event. Each technique keeps the phobic in the presence of the phobic object by a different tactic so that extinction can take place: desensitization by having the patient relax and imagine the object, flooding by forcibly keeping the phobic in the phobic situation, and modeling by encouraging the phobic to approach the phobic object as the model has done. The fact that each of these three therapies works and employs classical fear extinction supports the view that the phobia was originally acquired by classical fear conditioning.

Classical fear extinction can be described in alternative, cognitive language (see Chapter 5, p. 120). In order for permanent fear reduction to occur, two conditions must be met: First, information about the feared situation must be acquired forcefully enough to activate the entire fear memory, which consists of the fear response as well as the stimulus. Second, new information must be absorbed that is incompatible with the old fear memory, so that a new fear memory can be formed. Fear reduction occurs when this new information is integrated with the old memory (Lang, 1977; Foa and Kozak, 1986).

DRUGS

Antidepressant and anti-anxiety drugs may be very helpful in alleviating phobias, either alone or when given in concert with behavior therapy and supportive therapy (Marks, Gray, Cohen, Hill, Mawson, Ramm, and Stern, 1983; Zitrin, Klein, Woerner, and Ross, 1983; Charney and Heninger, 1985; Ballenger, 1986; Mavissakalian, Perel, Bowler, and Dealy, 1987). But there is an important distinction between the phobics who will benefit from antidepressant medication and those who will not. The distinction is between phobics who do and who do not have ***spontaneous panic attacks***. As we mentioned earlier, agoraphobics typically have spontaneous panic attacks in which their heart pounds, they believe the ground is trembling beneath them, and they think they are going to die. Agoraphobia often develops in early adulthood following such a panic attack.

Reducing or removing panic with drugs

The behavioral model suggests the following analysis of the acquisition of agoraphobia for those people whose condition begins with a panic attack. The CS is the agora (or any stimulus complex in which panic might occur and help not come), the US is the first panic attack, the UR is the panic response, so the CR is fear and avoidance of the agora. Based on this analysis, one way to cure agoraphobia would be to remove the possibility of panic attacks by drugs and to show the agoraphobic that panic no longer occurs. In fact, it appears that the antidepressant imipramine reduces and removes panic. Groups that receive both imipramine and exposure therapy show improvement, in that they experience less panic and tend to avoid the agora less. In contrast, groups that receive only exposure therapy show no less panic and only partial improvement in avoidance of the agora (Klein, Ross, and Cohen, 1987). This suggests that imipramine works by quelling the agoraphobic's spontaneous panic attacks. Once the panic attack is so controlled, the agoraphobic need no longer fear going into the street because the panic attack had been the traumatic event (the US) that he had feared and that he now knows will no longer occur. If this is so, the effectiveness of the antidepressants in curing agoraphobia also provides us with a fourth type of therapy that works because fear of the CS—fear of the phobic object—is extinguished by learning that the dreaded US will not occur.

EVALUATION OF THE BEHAVIORAL ACCOUNT

Problems with the behavioral account

The behavioral model of phobias appears to be adequate—in fact, it is as good a model of a form of abnormality as any we know. It is consistent with case history material; it has generated three effective therapies based on classical fear extinction; and it is supported by a good deal of laboratory evidence. However, there are three main problems with this account: selectivity, irrationality, and lack of traumatic conditioning. We will now examine these three problems and will look at the theory that has been used to account for them: prepared classical conditioning.

SELECTIVITY OF PHOBIAS

Restricted set of phobic objects

Phobias occur almost entirely to a highly restricted set of objects, whereas ordinary classical conditioning of fear occurs to any object that happens to be around at the same time as trauma. Why are phobias of the dark so common but phobias of pillows are nonexistent, although both are paired with nighttime trauma? Why are phobias of knives so rare even though knives are often paired with injury? Why have we never heard of a phobia of electric outlets? Why are there rat, horse, dog, and spider phobias, but not lamb or kitten phobias?

Although Watson and Raynor had found it simple to condition Little Albert to fear rats, E. L. Thorndike (1874–1949), the American learning theorist, had difficulty trying to train his children to stay away from sharp objects and to stay out of the street, even though such trespasses were paired with spankings. In consequence, Thorndike decided to study this phenomenon experimentally. He brought young children to his laboratory and presented them with objects like curtains and wooden ducks which, unlike rats, do not contort and move themselves. These objects were paired with traumatic noise. No fear conditioning resulted, even after many pairings (Valentine, 1930; Bregman, 1934). Phobic conditioning, both in and out of the laboratory, is highly selective. Can the behavioral analysis accommodate this observation?

Prepared classical conditioning

Yes, with some modification of its basic principles (Seligman, 1970; Eysenck, 1979; Mineka, 1985). Although ordinarily laboratory conditioning may be nonselective (as Pavlov claimed), there is a kind of classical conditioning that is highly selective: **prepared classical conditioning**, such as the conditioning of taste aversions. In an experiment by John Garcia, rats received sweet-tasting water at the same time as being subjected to light and noise, all signaling radiation sickness. They learned to hate the sweet taste in one trial, but the light and noise did not become at all aversive. Rats who received the same compound signals paired several times with shock, rather than stomach illness learned to fear the light and noise, but they continued to love the sweet taste (Garcia and Koelling, 1966). Evolution seems to have selected rats who learn aversions very readily when taste is paired with stom-

Prepared classical conditioning may account for a fear of spiders. This girl is afraid of the tarantula crawling up her arm.

Phobias of the dark are very common, but phobias of pajamas do not exist. This may be due to prepared classical conditioning.

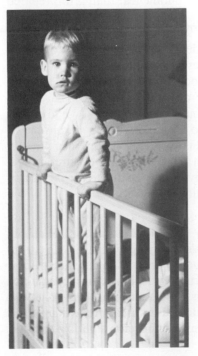

ach illness, but who learn to fear noise and light only when it is paired with shock.

The great majority of common phobias are of objects that were once actually dangerous to pre-technological man (De Silva, Rachman, and Seligman, 1977; Zafiropoulou and McPherson, 1986). Natural selection probably favored those of our ancestors who, once they had minimal exposure to trauma paired with such signals, were highly prepared to learn that strangers, crowds, heights, insects, large animals, and dirt were dangerous. Such primates would have had a clear reproductive and survival edge over others who learned only gradually about such real dangers. Thus, evolution seems to have selected a certain set of objects, all once dangerous to man, that are readily conditionable to trauma, and it seems to have left out other objects that are much more difficult to condition to fear (such as lambs, electric outlets, knives), either because they were never dangerous or because their origin is too recent to have been subject to natural selection. One theory suggests that prepared phobic fear may reside in lower neural systems that are rekindled under adult stress (Jacobs and Nadel, 1985).

In an important series of experiments, Arne Öhman, Kenneth Hugdahl, and their collaborators at the University of Uppsala in Sweden, created what appears to be a close laboratory model of phobias (Öhman, Fredrikson, Hugdahl, and Rimmo, 1976). Fear was conditioned in student volunteers using a variety of prepared—once dangerous to Homo sapiens—or unprepared fear CSs: pictures of snakes or spiders (prepared) versus pictures of houses, faces, or flowers (unprepared). In a typical experiment, in the "prepared" group, the pictures of snakes signaled that brief, painful electric shock would occur ten seconds later. In the "unprepared" group, pictures of houses signaled shock. Fear conditioning, as measured by galvanic skin response (akin to sweating), occurred much more rapidly to prepared signals than to unprepared ones when each was paired with shock. In fact, conditioning took place in one pairing with snakes or spiders, but it took four or five pairings with shock for fear of unprepared signals to be conditioned.

This study demonstrates that humans seem more prepared to learn to be afraid of certain objects than of others. Consider guns, therefore, as a potentially phobic object. Guns are too recent to have been prepared for fear conditioning by evolution, but guns have had voluminous cultural preparation: stories, TV shows, parental warnings. Does the fear conditioned to pictures of guns have the properties of snakes and spiders, or of houses and flowers? Guns turn out to resemble houses and flowers, not spiders and snakes in their conditioning properties. This indicates that the preparedness of spiders and snakes is biological, not cultural.

The behavioral reply to the selectivity of phobias is to assert that phobias are not instances of ordinary classical conditioning, but rather they are instances of *prepared classical conditioning* (C. F. McNally, 1987): certain evolutionarily dangerous objects are prepared to become phobic objects when paired with trauma, but others are not and require much more extensive and traumatic conditioning to become phobic objects. Phobias to snow, knives, lambs, and the like may be conditioned, but more trials and more intense trauma must occur. Thus, such unprepared phobias are very rare.

One researcher tells the story of a four-year-old girl who saw a snake while walking through a park in England. She found the snake interesting, but she was not greatly frightened by it. A short time later, she returned to the family car, and her hand was smashed in the car door. She developed a lifelong phobia, not of cars or doors but of snakes (Marks, 1977). So we see that phobias are selective, both in the laboratory and in real life.

IRRATIONALITY OF PHOBIAS

Phobic behavior irrational as is prepared classical conditioning

Laboratory fear conditioning seems very rational. When a signal predicts shock, the subject learns to expect shock and fear develops. When the signal predicts no shock (extinction or "inhibition"), the subject gradually learns to expect no shock, and fear accordingly is eliminated. When a signal is redundant and tells the subject no more than she already knows about when the shock will occur, no learning occurs (Rescorla and Wagner, 1972). Phobias, in contrast, are not so rational. The elevator phobic, when far away from the elevator, may believe that the probability of the cable snapping is negligible. But, as she approaches and gets on, in her mind the probability grows to 1/100, then to 1/2, then to certainty and panic sets in.

How can theories like the behavioral theory of fear conditioning, calling on the rationality of human beings, explain phobias? A phobic's life may be so impoverished by avoiding the phobic object that she cannot even leave her house. Why doesn't she merely give up the avoidance behavior and change her beliefs so that they match the realities of the danger?

Unprepared classical conditioning may be rational, but prepared classical conditioning is not. Taste aversions do not seem to be phenomena that accurately reflect the actual probability of danger. Once an aversion to Sauce Béarnaise is learned—based on vomiting after eating the sauce—merely knowing that a stomach virus rather than the Sauce Béarnaise caused the vomiting will not change the acquired distaste for Sauce Béarnaise. Instead, taste aversions are better seen as examples of blind, irrational conditioning (Garcia and Koelling, 1966; Rozin and Kalat, 1971; Seligman and Hager, 1972). If prepared conditioning is more like phobic fear than is unprepared fear conditioning, phobias should be irrational.

Kenneth Hugdahl and Arne Öhman (1977) have provided the relevant evidence for this conclusion. Swedish students were conditioned to fear either snakes and spiders or houses and faces by pairing each CS with shock. At the end of the conditioning, the electrodes were removed, and the subjects were told that shock would not be delivered anymore. Fear extinguished immediately to houses and faces, but remained full-blown to snakes and spiders. Similarly, it is utterly futile to try to convince a cat phobic by arguing that cats aren't dangerous, while it is quite easy to convince the very same phobic that the building he works in has been effectively fireproofed. In general, the irrationality of phobic behavior may be due to the fact that it is prepared, rather than unprepared, learning (Eysenck, 1979).

NONTRAUMATIC PHOBIAS

Nontraumatically induced phobias

Classical fear conditioning requires an explicit pairing of the CS with a traumatic event. Sometimes phobias have such a history (e.g., Hilda's snow phobia), but frequently they do not (Lazarus, 1971). For example, a phobia may develop gradually with minor impetus: the phobic's mother was always afraid of birds; when the patient was a child she saw a film in which people were attacked by flocks of birds, and she came to develop a phobia to birds.

Can the behavioral analysis based on traumatic conditioning also account for nontraumatically induced phobias? It turns out that prepared fear conditioning, unlike unprepared, can occur with minimal relations between CS and US. In fact, this is the definition of prepared conditioning. Rhesus monkeys become phobic of snakes after merely observing their parents behave fearfully in the presence of a toy snake (Mineka, Davidson, Cook, and Keir, 1984). Even if six-hour delays occur between taste and illness, the taste aversion will still form (Garcia, Ervin, and Koelling, 1967).

Arne Öhman and his collaborators have also provided the direct evidence that prepared fear conditioning can occur without the experience of trauma paired with the signal. Verbal threat of shock alone produced robust fear conditioning following prepared signals, but fear conditioning did not follow unprepared signals (Hygge and Öhman, 1978). In addition, social modeling alone (without threat of shock) was more effective in producing robust fear conditioning to pictures of snakes and spiders than to flowers, mushrooms, and berries (Bandura, 1969; Hygge and Öhman, 1978).

SUSCEPTIBILITY TO PHOBIAS

Phobias as heritable

One large mystery remains to be solved: Who becomes phobic and who doesn't? Some evidence indicates that phobias may be heritable (Carey, 1982). Although many people are exposed as children and young adults to potentially phobic signals paired with traumatic or subtraumatic events (they are bitten by large dogs, they are involved in auto accidents, they throw up in public), only a few develop phobias. Most show a transient disturbance that dissipates in time. The behavioral account does not now provide us with a way of telling in advance if a disturbance will become a phobia. A complete explanation of phobias will need to account for such individual differences as preparedness and proneness to spontaneous panic attacks (see McNally, 1987, for a critique of this theory).

POST-TRAUMATIC STRESS DISORDER

Phobia, as we saw, is a disorder in which fear is triggered by a specific object. There is a second emotional disorder that is also precipitated by a specific event: *post-traumatic stress disorder.* The following case shows an individual who is suffering from a delayed onset post-traumatic stress disorder.

Case of post-traumatic stress disorder

Mr. A was raised as a Quaker until he was thirteen. In 1943 he was drafted into the Army and served as a machine gunner until the end of the war. A giant of a man, he could carry his fifty-five pound gun on his shoulder and run at full tilt. He was frequently in the center of combat and killed many enemy soldiers, often at close range. After the Battle of the Bulge, his sergeant and his assistant gunner were killed. For three days, he wandered the battlefield in a daze and crying, not noticing his own shrapnel wounds. There was one incident during the war of which he was ashamed. After machine-gunning a group of German attackers, he looked at the bodies and saw that many were teenage boys with imitation rifles. At the end of the war, only four of his original forty comrades remained alive, and Mr. A was awarded several of the nation's highest decorations for valor.

Mr. A went on to become a very successful architect and remained in excellent health for the next twenty years. Aside from avoiding war movies, he seemed to

Fire or earthquake victims may suffer post-traumatic stress disorder following their ordeal, especially if others close to them have not survived.

show no immediate traces of his combat traumas. By 1975, thirty years after the war, because of diabetes and visual problems, he was forced to retire. At this point, he began to suffer nightmares about the war. In one recurring nightmare, his troop charged at and machine-gunned German teenagers, and he saw that they included his grandsons. When he revisited the battlefield as a guest of the German government in 1979, he broke down, distraught with anxiety about not being able to find the graves of his two comrades. He began to take many drugs to try to relieve his anxieties. (Van Dyke, Zilberg, and McKinnon, 1985)

Catastrophic event as precipitant

In phobia, the objects or events that set off the phobia are quite commonplace; for example, crowds, embarrassment, cats, and illness. But the precipitant of a post-traumatic stress disorder, in contrast, is a catastrophic event beyond the normal range of human suffering; for example, an earthquake, a rape, combat, or imprisonment in a concentration camp. Three symptoms that result from the catastrophe define the disorder: (1) the person *relives* the trauma recurrently, in dreams, in flashbacks, and in reverie; (2) the person becomes *numb* to the world, and avoids stimuli that remind him of the trauma; and (3) the person experiences symptoms of *anxiety* and arousal that were not present before the trauma (DSM-III-R). The anxiety symptoms include over-alertness, trouble concentrating, memory impairment, irritability, and outbursts of anger. In addition, the individual may be wracked with guilt about surviving the catastrophe when others did not.

NATURALLY OCCURRING DISASTERS

Buffalo Creek Flood of 1972

The Buffalo Creek Flood of 1972 produced devastation and death in a small West Virginia community, setting off many cases of post-traumatic stress disorder among its survivors (Erikson, 1976; Gleser, Green, and Winget, 1981). In the early morning of February 26, 1972, the dam on Buffalo Creek in the coal region of West Virginia collapsed, and within a few seconds, 132 million gallons of the sludge-filled black water roared down upon the residents of the mountain hollows below. Wilbur, his wife Deborah, and their four children managed to survive. What happened to them is described below.

Reactions to
Buffalo Creek
disaster

For some reason, I opened the inside door and looked up the road—and there it came. Just a big black cloud. It looked like 12 or 15 foot of water . . .

Well, my neighbor's house was coming right up to where we live, coming down the creek . . . It was coming slow, but my wife was still asleep with the baby—she was about seven years old at the time—and the other kids were still asleep upstairs. I screamed for my wife in a bad tone of voice so I could get her attention real quick . . . I don't know how she got the girls downstairs so fast, but she run up there in her sliptail and she got the children out of bed and downstairs . . .

We headed up the road . . . My wife and some of the children went up between the gons [railway gondonas]; me and my baby went under them because we didn't have much time . . . I looked around and our house was done gone. It didn't wash plumb away. It washed down about four or five house lots from where it was setting, tore all to pieces.

Anxiety
symptoms

Two years after the disaster, Wilbur and Deborah describe their psychological scars, the defining symptoms of a post-traumatic stress disorder. First, Wilbur experiences symptoms of *anxiety,* including hyper-alertness and phobic reactions to events that remind him of the flood, such as rain and impending bad weather:

. . . I listen to the news, and if there is a storm warning out, why I don't go to bed that night. I sit up. I tell my wife, "Don't undress our little girls; just let them lay down like they are and go to bed and go to sleep and then if I see anything going to happen, I'll wake you in plenty of time to get you out of the house." I don't go to bed. I stay up.

My nerves is a problem. Every time it rains, every time it storms, I just can't take it. I walk the floor. I get so nervous I break out in a rash. I am taking shots for it now . . .

Second, Wilbur *relives* the trauma repeatedly in his dreams:

What I went through on Buffalo Creek is the cause of my problem. The whole thing happens over to me even in my dreams, when I retire for the night. In my dreams, I run from water all the time, all the time. The whole thing just happens over and over in my dreams . . .

Third, Wilbur and Deborah have become *numb* psychologically. Affect is blunted and they are emotionally anesthetized to the sorrows and joys of the world around them. Wilbur says:

I didn't even go to the cemetary when my father died (about a year after the flood). It didn't dawn on me that he was gone forever. And those people that dies around me now, it don't bother me like it did before the disaster . . . It just didn't bother me that my dad was dead and never would be back. I don't have the feeling I used to have about something like death. It just don't affect me like it used to.

And Deborah says:

I am neglecting my children. I just simply quit cooking. I don't do no housework. I just won't do nothing. Can't sleep. Can't eat. Just want to take me a lot of pills and just go to bed and go to sleep and not wake up. I enjoyed my home and my family, but outside of them to me, everything else in life that I had any interest in is destroyed. I loved to cook. I loved to sew. I loved to keep house. I was all the time working in making improvements in my home. But now I just got to the point where it don't mean a thing in the world to me. I haven't cooked a hot meal and put it on the table for my children in almost three weeks.

Wilbur also suffers from ***survival guilt:***

> At that time, why, I heard somebody holler at me, and I looked around and saw Mrs. Constable. She had a little baby in her arms and she was hollering, "Hey, Wilbur, come and help me; if you can't help me, come get my baby," But I didn't give it a thought to go back and help her. I blame myself a whole lot for that yet. She had her baby in her arms and looked as though she were going to throw it to me. Well, I never thought to go help that lady. I was thinking about my own family. They all six got drowned in that house. She was standing in water up to her waist, and they all got drowned.

A similar naturally occurring disaster was the 1980 eruption of Mount St. Helens. Three years after the disaster survivors were interviewed to see if they had symptoms of psychological stress. Those interviewed included 138 individuals who had high exposure (either death of a family member or substantial financial loss) to the disaster, 410 who had low exposure (merely lived in the affected area), and 477 control subjects. Eleven percent of the men in the high-exposure group had either post-traumatic stress disorder, depression, or anxiety disorders; 2.5 percent of the low-exposure group had these disorders; and 1 percent of the control group (see Figure 8-3). Women had double these rates in all groups (Shore, Tatum, and Vollmer, 1986). Similar findings occurred after the Three Mile Island Nuclear disaster (Davidson and Baum, 1986).

MANMADE CATASTROPHES

The catastrophe that brings about a post-traumatic stress reaction need not be a naturally occurring one like the Buffalo Creek Flood. Human beings have made a hell of the lives of other human beings since time immemorial; concentration camps, war, and torture ruin the lives of their victims long

This man lived in the area affected by the eruption of Mount St. Helens. Here, he is taking a break from trying to dig his car out of the ash that spread over the roads during the eruption. If he lost a family member or suffered substantial financial loss, he is at greater risk for post-traumatic stress disorder.

Figure 8-3
Lifetime prevalence of single-episode depression, generalized anxiety disorder, and post-traumatic stress disorder in men and women before and after the Mount St. Helens disaster. (Source: Shore, Tatum, and Vollmer, 1986, p. 592)

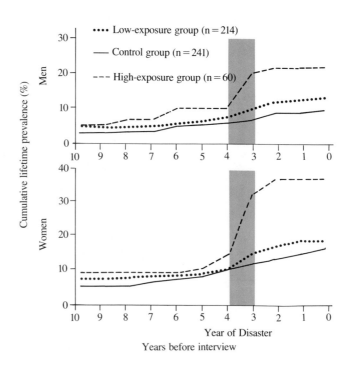

These Jews in the Warsaw Ghetto are being rounded up by German soldiers who will send them to concentration camps. Many survivors of the concentration camps still suffer the psychological effects of one of the most deliberately evil acts of this century.

after the victims have ceased to experience the original trauma. Unfortunately, the disorders following these catastrophes may be even more severe and long-lasting than those following natural disasters; it may be easier for us to deal with the "acts of God" than with the acts of men.

Reactions of concentration camp survivors

The survivors of the Nazi concentration camps illustrate how long-lasting and severe the post-traumatic stress reaction can be. In a study of 149 camp survivors, 142 (or 97 percent) were still troubled with anxiety twenty years after they were freed from the camps (Krystal, 1968). Phobic symptoms were marked: 31 percent were troubled with fears that something terrible would happen to their mates or their children whenever they were out of sight. Many of them were phobic about certain people whose appearance or behavior reminded them of their jailors; for example, the sight of a uniformed policeman or the inquisitive behavior of a doctor might be enough to set off panic. Seven percent had such severe panic attacks that the individual became confused and disoriented, entering a dreamlike state in which he believed himself to be back in the concentration camp.

The survivors relived the trauma in dreams for twenty years; 71 percent of these patients had anxiety dreams and nightmares, with 41 percent having severe ones. These nightmares were usually reruns of their persecution. Particularly terrifying were dreams in which only one detail was changed from the reality; for example, dreaming that their children who had not yet been born at the time of the camps, had been imprisoned with them in the camps.

Eighty percent of the patients suffered survivor guilt, depression, and crying spells. Survival guilt was especially strong when the patient's children had been killed; those who were the most severely depressed had lost an only child or had lost all of their children, with no children being born since. Ninety-two percent expressed self-reproach for failing to save their relatives, and 14 percent wished they had been killed instead of their relatives (Krystal, 1968).

RAPE TRAUMA SYNDROME

The catastrophe that brings about a post-traumatic stress disorder need not be experienced en masse, as in flood, war, and concentration camp; it can be solitary. Rape is, perhaps, the most common such catastrophe in modern American society. A woman's reaction to rape looks very much like the post-traumatic stress syndrome and has been called the ***rape trauma syndrome*** (Burgess and Holmstrom, 1979).

The reactions can be divided into two phases: the acute (disorganization) and the long-term (reorganization). In one study, researchers found that immediately following rape, a roughly equal number of women exhibited one of two emotional styles; expressive—showing fear, anger, anxiety, crying, sobbing, and tenseness, or controlled—masking feelings and showing a calm exterior. There soon followed symptoms that strongly resemble reactions to floods, combat, and concentration camps, particularly anxiety and reliving of the rape. Physical symptoms also appeared: sleep disturbances with inability to get to sleep or sudden awakening, stomach pains, genitourinary disturbances, and tension headache. Women who had been suddenly awakened by the rapist found that they would awake each night, at about the same time the attack had occurred, screaming from rape nightmares. Dreams and nightmares of the rape continued for a long time, with one-third of the victims reporting terrifying rape dreams.

Like flood victims, they startled easily in response to even minor episodes, such as being alone. In addition, fear, depression, humiliation, embarassment, anger, and self-blame became dominant emotions, particularly fear of violence and death. Like the victims of floods and concentration camps, these women sometimes developed phobias. Women who had been attacked indoors developed phobias of the indoors, and women who had been attacked outdoors developed phobias of the outdoors. Sexual fears were fairly common after rape, and some women were unable to resume normal sexual activity. Five months after being raped, a woman said, "There are times I get hysterical with my boyfriend. I don't want him near me; I get panicked. Sex is okay, but I still feel like screaming." According to another study, depressive symptoms seemed to disappear in most rape victims within about four months (Resick and Ellis, 1982).

After being raped, a woman may experience symptoms of the rape trauma syndrome.

In the long-term process of reorganization, most women took action to ensure safety. Many changed their telephone numbers, and half of the women made special trips home to seek support from family members. Half of the victims moved. One victim who couldn't afford to move first stayed with relatives, and then she rearranged her home. The rape had occurred in her bedroom, and here is what she did: "Wouldn't sleep in my own bed. Stayed with friends for a while. Changed my bedroom around, and got a new bedroom set." Many of the victims began to read about rape and to write about their experience. Some became active in rape crisis centers and assisted other victims, and of these, 70 percent recovered in a few months. When contacted four to six years after the rape, three-quarters of the victims felt that they had recovered, half of these within a few months and the other half within several years. One-quarter of the women, however, felt that they still had not recovered (Burgess and Holmstrom, 1979; Meyer and Taylor, 1986).

COURSE OF POST-TRAUMATIC STRESS DISORDER

Not much is known about the specific course of the post-traumatic stress disorder. Sometimes the symptoms disappear within a few months, resembling recovery from a depressive disorder (see Chapter 11). But overall, the prognosis is probably bleak, particularly for the victims of very severe trauma. As we saw, a high percentage of concentration camp victims are still troubled with anxiety and guilt twenty years later, and people who lose a child or spouse in a motor accident are still more depressed and anxious four to seven years later (Lehman, Wortman, and Williams, 1987). This also seems to be true of some veterans of combat. Sixty-two veterans of World War II who suffered chronic "combat fatigue," with symptoms of exaggerated jumpiness, recurrent nightmares, and irritability, were examined twenty years later. Irritability, depression, restlessness, difficulties in concentration and memory, blackouts, wakefulness, fatigability, and jumpiness persisted for twenty years. These symptoms were more prominent in the veterans suffering from combat fatigue than in noncombat patients or in healthy combat veterans. Combat fatigue victims still jumped when they heard noises of jets and firecrackers. Three-quarters of these men reported that their symptoms interfered with providing for their family. Half reported their sex lives were unsatisfactory, and that they were unduly irritable with their children. A third of the men were unemployed. Figure 8-4 presents the incidence of symptoms of World War II combat fatigue victims compared to control groups twenty years later (Archibald and Tuddenham, 1965).

Similar long-lasting symptoms are found among prisoners-of-war. Forty years after World War II, a random sample of Australian soldiers who were held in Japanese prison camps were compared to non-POW soldiers. The POWs were more depressed forty years later and had more stomach ulcers, but they did not have increased anxiety or alcohol problems (Tennant, Goulston, and Dent, 1986). Of 188 former World War II American POWs, about one-third had fully recovered, one-third still had mild post-traumatic stress symptoms, and one-third still had moderate to severe symptoms forty years later (Kluznik, Speed, Van Valkenberg, and Magraw, 1986).

Vietnam veterans are also now reporting post-traumatic stress disorders, particularly those who saw buddies killed in action. Those who saw, and particularly those who participated in atrocities, are at severe risk for post-traumatic stress disorder (Breslau and Davis, 1987). These extreme stressors

Reactions of World War II combat veterans

POW reactions

Vietnam veterans' reactions

Men who have been through combat, such as these American soldiers in Vietnam, may later suffer symptoms of chronic "combat fatigue," which may last for years following their combat experiences.

Figure 8-4
Post-traumatic stress disorder in veterans. The bars indicate the percentage of incidence of symptoms twenty years after World War II in veterans who suffered combat fatigue in comparison to healthy combat veterans and noncombat patients. (Source: Archibald and Tuddenham, 1965, p. 478)

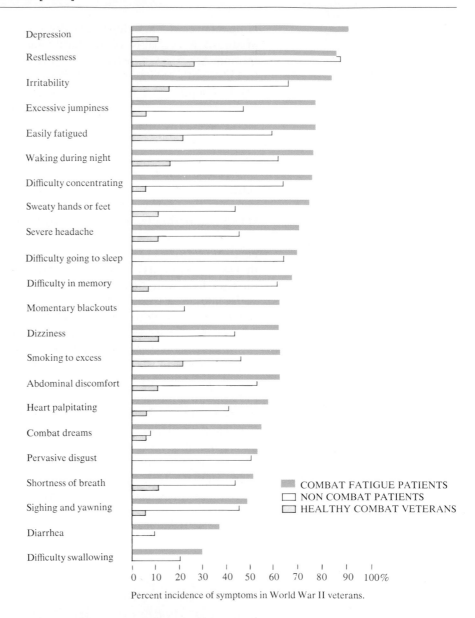

Percent incidence of symptoms in World War II veterans.

seem to produce post-traumatic stress disorder specifically, since the risk for panic and depression is not elevated.

One caveat, which may sound hard-hearted, is in order, however. Post-traumatic stress disorder became an official disorder with the advent of DSM-III in 1980. It is now reimbursable under disability claims, and large lawsuits against the government and against private companies have been instituted. The lawyers for the victims of Buffalo Creek sued the Pittston Company, who owned the dam that burst, for enormous sums. We can no longer be sure that duration and severity of symptoms following disasters are disinterestedly reported, and future epidemiologists would do well to compare symptoms under reimbursable and nonreimbursable conditions to arrive at accurate severity and prevalence figures. But pre-DSM-III data make it look as if post-traumatic stress disorder is both real and long-lasting.

Lawsuits

TREATMENT AND PREVENTION

Vulnerable individuals; secondary gain

In spite of the fact that so many of our fellow human beings are victims of extraordinary traumas, almost nothing is known about how to alleviate or prevent post-traumatic stress reactions. Relatives, friends, and therapists are inclined to tell the victims of catastrophe to try to "forget it," but it should be apparent that such painful memories cannot be easily blotted out. Only small improvement has been reported by either drug therapy or psychotherapy among victims of trauma. Two important caveats are in order, however. First, it is difficult to find out what the individuals who suffer stress reactions to trauma were like before. It is possible that those individuals whose symptoms persist for years and years also had poor adjustment before the trauma, whereas those individuals who were in good psychological shape before the trauma were less hurt by it and therefore didn't show up for long-term follow-up. We cannot tell if the trauma itself, or the combination of trauma and a vulnerable individual, produces the reactions that are so devastating and often permanent. Second, there is the problem of *secondary gain:* victims occasionally have some incentive for staying ill for a long time. As noted earlier, the Buffalo Creek victims, for example, were in the process of suing the Pittston Company (the owner of the dam that collapsed) for millions of dollars. Only careful longitudinal work will tell us who is most vulnerable to post-traumatic stress reactions, how long such reactions last, and what therapy can work. These studies have not yet been done (Chodoff, 1963; Leopold and Dillon, 1963; Archibald and Tuddenham, 1965; Merbaum, 1971).

PREVENTING POST-TRAUMATIC STRESS REACTIONS

Although we know almost nothing about how to treat post-traumatic stress disorder once it has set in, some steps have been taken to prevent the reaction once a trauma has been experienced. When a tornado strikes a town or when soldiers return from combat, therapists have an excellent opportunity to use preventative procedures. Thus, therapists can try to prevent a stress reaction from occurring in victims of a trauma. They can try to prevent the onset of three symptoms—anxiety, numbness, and reliving—in the victims, or the therapists can attempt to minimize the symptoms before they take hold. Such an attempt was made by therapists who worked with the victims of the takeover of the B'nai B'rith national headquarters in Washington, D.C., after the victims had been freed by their terrorist captors.

From March 9 to March 11, 1977, more than one hundred persons had been held hostage by members of the Hanafi Muslim sect in a B'nai B'rith headquarters. During the thirty-nine hours of their captivity, they had been exposed to physical violence, verbal abuse, threats, severe physical restraints, hunger, humiliation, and the continual threat of imminent death. What happened to Shirley is shown in the following case:

Shirley is a forty-two-year-old, white, married, Jewish female who was working as an administrative assistant for the B'nai B'rith on March 9, 1977. She was at her desk when several Hanafis burst into her work area. She was herded together with all her colleagues on the floor, and was pushed into the stairwell to be marched up

Here one of the hostages of the Hanafi Muslims' takeover of B'nai B'rith headquarters recounts how gunmen broke into her office. Psychologists may attempt to prevent post-traumatic stress disorder by intervening just after the trauma.

to the eighth floor conference room that was to serve as their prison for thirty ter-ror-filled hours. Shirley did not see the actual stabbing of another employee, but she did hear the screams and did see the bloodied machete of her Hanafi captor. She remembers her body aching from the damp cold of the concrete floor and her head aching from repeated crying spells. She recalls vividly the men being sepa-rated from the women and being roughly bound. She also remembers the humili-ation heaped on several of the men because one wept, another wet himself, and still another behaved too effeminately.

She remembers many moments of overwhelming fear—the worst seemed to coincide with appearances of Khaalis, the Hanafi leader, who repeatedly threat-ened grisly death to specific individuals and then the entire group. She recalls images of bodies pressed against each other for comfort and protection and her annoyance at the petty grumbling about the sharing of food and floor space for sleeping. . . .

Shirley's ordeal was not over, however, once she was released by the Hanafis. For several months she experienced a number of symptoms related to the extreme stress she had undergone while held prisoner. Shirley had great difficulty return-ing to work; she found herself crying without explanation and intolerant of others. She felt considerable anxiety and mild, persistent depression. She associated this emotional state with a sense of being exhausted much of the time, as if she "had mononucleosis." Shirley slept poorly at first, reliving scenes of the building take-over, bloodied faces and clothes. (Sank, 1982)

Treating victims with behavioral and cognitive techniques

The Health Maintenance Organization of Washington decided to seek the victims out and offer care immediately, rather than wait for calls for help from the victims well after their release. The idea was to *prevent* post-traumatic stress disorder which, as we have seen, frequently occurs in the weeks and months following extraordinary stress. The treatment format was short term and used a variety of techniques, both behavioral and cognitive, to treat neurotic problems (Lazarus, 1976). Therapy sessions were held in the building that had served as the work site of the victims and as their prison, and approximately half of the B'nai B'rith hostages came to therapy. Systematic desensitization was used to curb phobic reactions; group sharing of the experience was used to counteract numbness. Substituting calming imagery for fantasies of the takeover was used to prevent and counteract re-living the trauma repeatedly. Table 8-5 shows the different forms of behav-ioral and cognitive therapy for dealing with the symptoms that the victims already had or for symptoms that the therapists believed would arise in the victims in the future.

No systematic follow-up of the victims was carried out, but a few anecdo-tal reports show that some were doing quite well in 1982, but others still had trauma-related problems (Sank, 1982). Without such follow-up, we cannot know if this treatment prevented post-traumatic stress reactions, but it is a unique and exemplary use of preventative procedures for fear disorders.

DRUG TREATMENT FOR POST-TRAUMATIC STRESS DISORDER

Drugs as successful treatment

A group of twelve survivors of Cambodian concentration camps were diag-nosed as having post-traumatic stress disorder and were treated with anti-depressant and anti-anxiety drugs for one year. These victims had been severely traumatized. They had been starved, tortured, forced to witness the execution of family members, and given four years of forced labor. Five im-

Table 8–5 HOSTAGES' MULTI-MODAL PROFILE

Modality of Symptom	Problem	Treatment
Behavior	Avoidance (of stairwells, taxis, elevators, being alone, the work site)	*In vivo* and systematic desensitization
	Crying	Deep Muscle Relaxation (DMR)
	Fear of isolation	Writing and sharing experience with others
Affect	Numbness	Group sharing of the experience and writing about feelings
	Mild depression	Planning rewarding activities and reassurance
	Anxiety attacks	DMR, coping imagery, assertiveness training
	Anger	Assertiveness training
Sensation	Sleep disturbance	DMR, scheduling relaxing activities, exercise, coping imagery
	Headaches	DMR with concentration on muscles of the face, neck, and shoulders
Imagery	Reliving of takeover and holocaust fantasies	Substituting calming imagery
	Being vulnerable in all life situations	Assertiveness imagery
Cognitions	"I'll never get over this." "The Hanafis know my name and address and will come to kill me later." "No place is safe anymore."	Rational-Emotive Therapy (behavioral and cognitive therapy)
	Isolation	Group sharing, therapists providing information about the human reactions to stress
Interpersonal	Suspicious of strangers	Take more realistic precautions (lock car and home, etc.), *in vivo* desensitization
Drugs	Increased use of tranquilizers, sleeping medications, alcohol	Substitution of DMR, exercise, coping imagery, limited use of drugs
	Somatic disturbances	Medical check after release and before rejoining families, medical follow-ups of new complaints or old ones exacerbated by stress

SOURCE: Adapted from Sank, 1979, pp. 334–38.

proved; they experienced fewer nightmares and less startle. Shame, guilt, and avoidance of Cambodia-related stimuli improved least (Kinzie, Fredrickson, Ben, Fleck, and Karls, 1984; Boehnlein, Kinzie, Ben, and Fleck, 1985). So, drugs may benefit at least some of the victims of post-traumatic stress disorder in some ways.

PANIC DISORDER AND GENERALIZED ANXIETY DISORDER

Anxiety not focused

In our discussion so far, we have focused on phobia and post-traumatic stress disorders, which we consider *fear disorders.* Both are problems in which anxiety is felt. Also, the individual afflicted by either of them experiences the four elements of fear: expectations of danger (the cognitive element); the emergency reaction (the somatic element); feelings of terror, apprehension, and dread (the emotional element); and avoidance and escape (the behavioral element). Phobia and post-traumatic stress disorder are similar in that they both stem from dread of a specific object: the phobic object (cat, etc.) in the case of phobias, and the precipitating situation (flood, etc.) in the cases of post-traumatic stress disorder. In contrast, in the *anxiety disorders,* panic disorder and generalized anxiety disorder, although anxiety is also felt, there is no specific object that is feared. In these disorders, the anxiety felt by the individual is not focused on a clear and specific object. We will now consider the two anxiety disorders. Panic attacks are acute experiences of anxiety, whereas generalized anxiety disorder is the chronic experience of anxiety.

PANIC DISORDER

Recurrent panic attacks

How many of us have at some time been suddenly overwhelmed by intense apprehension? Physically, we feel jumpy and tense. Cognitively, we expect that something bad—we don't know what—is going to happen. Such an attack comes out of nowhere; no specific object or event sets it off, and the attack gradually subsides. But some people have more severe attacks, and have them frequently. These people suffer from *panic disorder.* Panic disorder consists of recurrent panic attacks, at least four within a month (DSM-III-R).

SYMPTOMS OF A PANIC ATTACK

A panic attack consists of the four elements of fear, with the emotional and physical elements most salient.

Emotional symptoms

Emotionally the individual is overwhelmed with intense apprehension, terror, or depersonalization.

> It was just like I was petrified with fear. If I were to meet a lion face to face, I couldn't be more scared. Everything got black, and I felt I would faint; but I didn't. I thought I won't be able to hold on"... (Laughlin, 1967, p. 92)

Physical symptoms

Physically, a panic attack consists of an acute emergency reaction (including shortness of breath, dizziness, racing heart, trembling, chills, or chest pains).

Many of us have felt at times a sudden and overwhelming sense of apprehension or anxiety. Those who have frequent and severe attacks of anxiety are said to suffer from panic disorder.

My heart was beating so hard and fast it would jump out and hit my hand. I felt like I couldn't stand up—that my legs wouldn't support me. My hands got icy and my feet stung. There were horrible shooting pains in my forehead. My head felt tight, like someone had pulled the skin down too tight and I wanted to pull it away . . .

I couldn't breathe, I was short of breath. I literally got out of breath and panted like I had run up and down the stairs. I felt like I had run an eight-mile race. I couldn't do anything. I felt all in; weak, no strength. I can't even dial a telephone. . . . (Laughlin, 1967, p. 92)

Cognitive symptoms

Cognitively, the individual thinks he might die, go crazy, or lose control.

Even then I can't be still when I am like this. I am restless and I pace up and down. I feel like I am just not responsible. I don't know what I'll do. These things are terrible. I can go along real calmly for awhile. Then, without any warning, this happens. I just blow my top. (Laughlin, 1967, p. 92)

Prevalence of panic attacks

Such an attack usually lasts for a matter of minutes, subsiding rather gradually. What distinguishes a panic attack from a phobic disorder is that a panic attack comes out of nowhere, rather than in response to a specific threatening situation. As we mentioned earlier, some phobics, particularly agoraphobics, are often subject to panic attacks before their phobic disorder develops, and the agoraphobia may in fact begin with a panic attack. An occasional panic attack is quite common, with about 20 percent of students and about 5 percent of senior citizens reporting one episode of panic in the preceding week (Barlow, 1987). Panic disorder and agoraphobia with panic attacks together have a prevalence rate of 4 to 7 percent. Both are diagnosed more frequently in women (Myers et al., 1984; Robins et al., 1984), and samples of patients in clinics indicate about a 2:1 ratio of women to men. The first attack typically occurs in the mid-twenties (Barlow, 1987, 1988).

ETIOLOGY AND THERAPY: BIOMEDICAL VERSUS COGNITIVE VIEWS

Recently, both the biomedical school and the cognitive school have produced important new results about the cause and cure of panic disorder, and the two schools are now locked in an important confrontation.

Panic as a
disease of the
body

□ BIOMEDICAL APPROACH.   Four pieces of interlocking evidence indicate that panic disorder may be a disease of the body: heritability, chemical induction of panic, neurochemical abnormalities in panic patients, and drug relief of panic.

First, panic disorder may have a genetic origin. If one of two identical twins has panic disorder or agoraphobia with panic, 31 percent of the co-twins will also have the disorder. This compares to a zero percent concordance for this disorder in fraternal twins (Torgersen, 1983). This suggests some heritability. Second, panic attacks can be induced chemically in patients who suffer them frequently. The most common way of inducing an attack in the laboratory is with sodium lactate infusions. Between 60 to 90 percent of panic disorder patients, but only 0 to 20 percent of nonpatients or patients with other anxiety disorders will experience an attack when taking lactate (Liebowitz, Gorman, Fyer, Levitt, Dillon, Levy, Appleby, Anderson, Palij, Davies, and Klein, 1985; but cf. Margraf, Ehlers, and Roth, 1986). This suggest that the trigger of a panic attack in nature might be an excess of sodium lactate.

Third, there is some evidence that panic patients may have a specific neurochemical abnormality. The efficiency of adrenergic transmission in the brain may be impaired in such a way as to cause poor damping of the emergency reaction (Charney, Breier, and Heninger, 1984; Nesse, Cameron, Curtis, McCann, and Huber-Smith, 1984). This may mean that the spontaneous emergency reactions that panic patients experience may come from a brain chemistry deficit in adrenergic receptors.

The final piece of evidence for the biomedical view of panic comes from drug therapy. Antidepressant drugs and some anti-anxiety drugs appear to be useful in the treatment of panic and of agoraphobia with panic (Klein, 1984; Sheehan, 1985). Both may act by dampening the panic per se.

So by demonstrating some heritability, by chemically inducing panic, by finding chemical abnormalities in the brain, and by relieving panic with drugs, a strong case can be made to view panic disorder as a disease of the body. This view is uncomfortable with the data that panic disorder is frequently precipitated by major life events, such as moving to a new city (Roy-Byrne, Geraci, and Uhde, 1986).

□ COGNITIVE APPROACH.   The cognitive school has challenged the biomedical view, claiming that the evidence can all be viewed as cognitive abnormality, and creating a therapy that appears to work well.

Cognitive therapists claim that panic disorder results from catastrophic misinterpretations of bodily sensations (Beck and Emery, 1985; Clark, 1988). The panic disorder patient misinterprets normal anxiety responses, such as heart racing, breathlessness, and dizziness as indicating impending disaster. Palpitations are interpreted as meaning a heart attack is about to occur; dizziness as meaning insanity and loss of control. Here is how the cognitive view reinterprets the four pieces of evidence for the biomedical view: (1) What is inherited is the tendency toward salient palpitations or dizziness, which can easily be misinterpreted catastrophically. (2) Sodium lactate induces these bodily sensations, which then get misinterpreted. (3) The failure of the adrenergic system to dampen is a consequence, not a cause, of the misinterpretation of impending doom. (4) The drugs dampen the bodily sensations.

A new therapy

So far then, it is a tie. Both schools can adequately explain the four sets of evidence. But the cognitive school claims to have a unique prediction about therapy that the biomedical view does not deduce: Teach panic disorder patients to correctly reinterpret their bodily sensations and the disorder will be cured. Both David Clark at Oxford and Aaron Beck of the University of Pennsylvania have reported dramatic improvement in panic disorder patients who have undergone such a therapy (Clark, 1988; Beck, 1988). In this therapy, patients overbreathe (hyperventilate) into a bag in the clinic. At first, this will usually induce an immediate panic attack by producing shortness of breath. The patient is then taught to recognize that the bodily sensations that usually induce panic for her are produced by overbreathing. The patient then comes to see that she is suffering from stress-induced hyperventilation when she panics outside the clinic. She then learns to reattribute those sensations to stress, rather than to impending doom. Both Clark and Beck have reported 100 percent reduction in panic attacks in almost all patients, with no relapse.

In summary, both the biomedical and the cognitive schools have made major contributions to the understanding of panic disorder. Both have produced therapies that appear to relieve panic, as well as theories of how it is caused. But the cognitive approach seems, at the moment, to explain all of the biomedical evidence and to have created a therapy that the biomedical view cannot account for.

GENERALIZED ANXIETY DISORDER

Chronic nature of generalized anxiety disorder

In contrast to a panic attack, which is sudden and acute, generalized anxiety is chronic, and may last for months on end, with the elements of anxiety more or less continually present (see Box 8-2). Emotionally, the individual feels jittery and tense, vigilant, and constantly on edge.

> I feel tense and fearful much of the time. I don't know what it is. I can't put my finger on it. . . . I just get all nervous inside. . . . I act like I'm scared to death of something. I guess maybe I am. (Laughlin, 1967, p. 107)

Cognitively, as in panic attacks, the individual expects something awful, but doesn't know what.

> I am frightened, but don't know what I fear. I keep expecting something bad to happen. . . . I have thought I could tie it to definite things, but this isn't true. It varies, and is unpredictable. I can't tell when it will come on. If I could just put my finger on what it is. . . . (Laughlin, 1967, p. 107)

Physically, the individual experiences a mild chronic emergency reaction: he sweats, his heart races, his stomach is usually upset, he feels cold, light-headed, and his hands usually feel clammy.

Behaviorally, he is always ready to run away, flee, or hide.

> For the past week or so I don't want to get away from the house. I fear I might go all to pieces, maybe become hysterical . . .
> Sometimes I get fearful and tense when I am talking to people and I just want to run away. (Laughlin, 1967, p. 107)

Box 8-2   **ANXIETY: STATE VERSUS TRAIT**

As we have seen, some individuals have acute attacks of anxiety and do not have them again for some time (panic disorder); others seem to feel anxious all of the time (generalized anxiety disorder). Some have suggested that there is a **state** versus **trait** distinction that may explain this observation. That is, many of us at one time or another may feel panic whether or not we understand what it was in the situation that brought it on. In short, we fall into a state of anxiety. But others, those who feel anxious all of the time, may have a predisposition to anxiety. They are always ready to feel anxiety; they are chronically anxious. We say that they have a trait of anxiety.

Various paper and pencil tests have been designed to determine whether one is in a state of anxiety, whether one has a trait for anxiety, or if neither measure applies. Among the most widely used are Janet Taylor Spence's Manifest Anxiety Scale (Taylor, 1951, 1953), Marvin Zuckerman's Affect Adjective Checklist (Zuckerman and Lubin, 1965), and Charles Spielberger's State-Trait Anxiety Inventory (Spielberger, Gorsuch, and Lushene, 1970). These questionnaires ask about the four elements of anxiety.

An anxiety *state* questionnaire asks how the individual feels right now, whereas an anxiety *trait* questionnaire focuses on an individual's dispositions to display the elements of anxiety across time and across different situations. For example, the following questions might be asked: "Are you a steady person?" "Do unimportant thoughts run through your mind and bother you?" "Do you worry too much over something that really doesn't matter?" Affirmative answers to such questions point toward a trait of anxiety-proneness. Some sample items that seek to find state anxiety are shown on p. xxx. This questionnaire was developed by Norman Endler and his colleagues at York University (Endler, Magnusson, Ekehammar, and Okada, 1975). The questions ask how the individual feels at the time that he or she is taking the test.

Generalized anxiety disorder is usually found in individuals who have major depressive disorders as well (Breier, Charney, and Heninger, 1985). There is no evidence that it is heritable. While the symptoms of generalized anxiety disorder are quite clear, its causes remain a mystery (Wolpe and Lazarus, 1969; Klein, 1980). Unfortunately, little is known abut how to treat it, although drug therapy, particularly with tranquilizers, sometimes helps.

SUMMARY

1. Phobias and post-traumatic stress disorder are both disorders in which fear is felt and there exist specific objects or events that set them off. Panic disorder and generalized anxiety disorder are both anxiety disorders in that the individual feels very anxious although no specific danger is anticipated.

Anxiety State Questionnaire

Please circle a number from 1 to 5 for each of the items in response to the question: "HOW DO YOU FEEL AT THIS PARTICULAR MOMENT?"

		Very Much				Not at All
Cognitive	1. Self-Confident	1	2	3	4	5
		Able to Focus				Unable to Focus
	2. Able to focus my thoughts	1	2	3	4	5
		Very Calm				Not at All
Emotional	3. Calm	1	2	3	4	5
		Not at All				Very Nervous
	4. Nervous	1	2	3	4	5
		Not at All				Very Uneasy
	5. Uneasy	1	2	3	4	5
		Not at All				Very Moist
	6. Hands Moist	1	2	3	4	5
Somatic		Not at All				Very Irregular
	7. Breathing is irregular	1	2	3	4	5
		Not at All				Very Tense
	8. Tense in my stomach	1	2	3	4	5
		Not at All				Very Much
Behavioral	9. Want to avoid this situation	1	2	3	4	5

SOURCE: Adapted from Endler, Magnusson, Ekehammar, and Okoda, 1975.

2. The state of fear consists of four elements: *cognitively,* the individual expects danger; *somatically,* the individual experiences the emergency reaction; *emotionally,* the individual feels apprehension, terror, or dread; and *behaviorally,* the individual tries to flee the feared situation. The elements of anxiety are identical to those of fear except for the cognitive element; the anxious individual does not expect a specific danger but simply that *something* bad will happen.

3. A *phobia* is a persistent fear of a specific object in which the fear is greatly out of proportion to the amount of danger actually present. There are five types of phobias: agoraphobia (fear of the marketplace), social phobias, phobias of animals and insects, phobias of specific inanimate objects, and phobias of illness and injury (nosophobia).

4. The psychoanalytic school holds that phobias occur when anxiety stemming from an intrapsychic conflict is displaced onto an innocent object.

5. The behavioral school holds that phobias are merely instances of the

normal classical conditioning of fear to an innocent object that happened to be around when a traumatic event occurred. The behavioral model is consistent with case histories and laboratory evidence, and it has generated three effective therapies based on classical fear extinction: systematic desensitization, flooding, and modeling. Moreover, there is reason to believe that antidepressant drugs may be helpful in treating agoraphobia because these drugs prevent the spontaneous panic attacks that agoraphobics often have.

6. The three problems with the behavioral model—selectivity of phobias, irrationality of phobias, and nontraumatic phobias—can be accounted for by the theory of *prepared classical conditioning,* which states that humans seem more prepared to learn to be afraid of certain objects than of others.

7. *Post-traumatic stress disorder* is a fear disorder that resembles phobias in that it is set off by a specific event. In this case, the specific event is a catastrophic happening beyond the normal range of human suffering. Natural disasters, rape, combat, and imprisonment in a concentration camp may all set off post-traumatic stress disorder. Following the event, symptoms of fear, reliving the event in dreams and waking, and numbness toward the external world may develop. Also, the individual may experience survivor guilt. The symptoms may last a lifetime; very little is known about how to cure or prevent them.

8. *Panic attacks* come out of the blue, with no specific event or object setting them off. They last for only a few minutes and consist of the four elements of the anxiety reaction. *Panic disorder* consists of recurrent panic attacks. Panic disorders can be relieved by drugs and perhaps cured by learning to reinterpret frightening bodily sensations as resulting from stress and not impending doom. Both the biomedical and cognitive approaches have recently contributed to an understanding of panic.

9. *Generalized anxiety disorder* is similar to panic disorder in that there is no specific event that sets it off. However, in generalized anxiety disorder, the anxiety is milder and is chronic, with the elements of anxiety more or less continually present for weeks or months on end.

Obsession, Hysteria, and
Dissociation: Anxiety Inferred

Underlying
anxiety inferred
as cause of
symptoms

W E have divided anxiety disorders into two classes: those in which anxiety is actually experienced by the sufferer, and those in which anxiety is not experienced but is inferred to explain the various symptoms. In the last chapter, we discussed those disorders in which anxiety is manifest: phobia, post-traumatic stress disorder, panic disorder, and generalized anxiety disorder. In this chapter, we will discuss those disorders in which underlying anxiety has often been inferred to be the cause of the symptoms.

We will discuss three types of disorders. First are the ***obsessive-compulsive disorders*** in which the individual is plagued with uncontrollable, repulsive thoughts and engages in seemingly senseless rituals. An obsessive-compulsive may think that he left the gas stove on and get out of bed to check it twenty times during the night, or he may have continual thoughts of killing his children and keep all knives and sharp objects out of his own reach. The second disorder is the somatoform disorder that is sometimes called ***hysterical conversion***. This disorder is characterized by a loss of physical functioning not due to any physical disorder but apparently resulting from psychological conflict. An individual may, for no biological reason, suddenly become blind, deaf, paralyzed, or suffer excruciating pain as a result of psychological stress. The third kind of disorder consists of the ***dissociative disorders***, in which the individual's very identity is fragmented. Among these are ***amnesia***, in which an individual suddenly loses the memory of who he is and ***multiple personality***, in which more than one personality exists in the same individual, each with a relatively rich and stable life of its own.

In contrast to the disorders in the last chapter, anxiety is not usually felt by the victims of these three types of disorders. Obsessive-compulsives sometimes feel anxiety, but if their compulsion is frequent and fast enough they can ward off anxiety altogether. Individuals with somatoform and dissociative disorders usually feel little anxiety. In fact, they may be surprisingly indifferent to their symptoms. But when psychoanalytic clinicians and researchers look at the conflicts that precede these disorders, they often infer that the symptoms are an attempt to harness underlying anxiety that otherwise threatens to overwhelm the individual. For example, a man who believes he caused the paralysis of his friend may himself unconsciously assume the symptoms of paralysis; or a teenager who is plagued with unresolvable troubles at home and in school may forget who he is, wander to a new city, and assume a new identity. We begin our discussion of these disorders with obsessions and compulsions.

OBSESSIONS AND COMPULSIONS

All of us at least occasionally have distasteful and unacceptable thoughts. Most people at one time or another have had the following thoughts: "Might I do violence to someone I love?" "Am I absolutely sure that I've locked all the doors and windows?" "Have I left the gas in the stove on?" Most of us pay little attention to these thoughts when they occur or if we do, we soon dismiss them. Such is not the case in individuals with obsessive-compulsive disorders. An example of such an individual follows:

> A thirty-eight-year-old mother of one child had been obsessed by fears of contamination during her entire adult life. Literally hundreds of times a day, thoughts of being infected by germs would occur to her. Once she began to think that either she or her child might become infected, she could not dismiss the thought. This constant concern about infection resulted in a series of washing and cleaning rituals that took up most of her day. Her child was confined to one room only, which the woman tried to keep entirely free of germs by scrubbing it—floor to ceiling—several times a day. Moreover, she opened and closed all doors with her feet, in order to avoid contaminating her own hands. (Rachman and Hodgson, 1980)

Obsessions and compulsions

Obsessive-compulsive disorder consists of the two components from which we derive its name: obsessions and compulsions. ***Obsessions*** are repetitive thoughts, images, or impulses that invade consciousness, are often abhorrent, and are very difficult to dismiss or control. In the case above, the mother is occupied with repulsive thoughts and images of disease and infection, which she cannot turn off. ***Compulsions*** are the behavioral responses to obsessive thoughts. A compulsion is a repetitive, stereotyped, and unwanted action that can be resisted only with difficulty. The mother above reacts to her thoughts of germs by compulsively scrubbing her child's room. Generally, individuals who are afflicted with obsessions also suffer from compulsions (Rachman, 1978; Rachman and Hodgson, 1980). Some writers use the terms "obsessive" and "compulsive" interchangeably, but essentially they refer to two distinct events: obsessions are thoughts, compulsions are actions. The two are often found together though.

Three hallmarks of clinical obsessions

What distinguishes obsessions of clinical proportions from more harmless recurring thoughts? There are three hallmarks: (1) obsessions are *unwelcome* and *intrude* on consciousness; an obsessive complains, "The thought that I might strangle a child keeps returning and prevents me from concentrating on my work," whereas mere recurring thoughts do not interfere with work; (2) obsessions arise *from within,* not from an external situation; and (3) obsessions are very *difficult to control.* Someone with merely recurring thoughts can readily distract himself and think of something else; someone with an obsession, in contrast, complains, "I can't help myself—I keep saying the numbers over and over again."

OBSESSIONS AND THE SOCIAL CONTEXT

Historical trends
of obsessions

The content of obsessions changes over time. In past centuries in the Western world, obsessions were often religious and sexual. John Bunyan, seventeenth-century author of *A Pilgrim's Progress,* was "fiercely assaulted" with the wicked suggestion to "sell Christ" running in his mind. " 'Sell him, sell him, sell him, sell him,' as fast as a man could speak. Against which also in my mind I answered, 'No, no, not for thousands, thousands, thousands,' at least twenty times together." Other famous religious personalities believed they suffered from "pollution of the mind" with "naughty and blasphemous thoughts" of committing sexual sins "revolving in a restless circle." Today, obsessions about religion and sex have become somewhat rarer; obsessions about dirt and contamination, violence, and orderliness are more common (Hunter and MacAlpine, 1963; Akhtar, Wig, Varma, Pershard, and Verma, 1975; Rachman, 1978; Rachman and Hodgson, 1980). One patient embodied this historical trend in the course of her thirty-five-year-long disorder. For the first ten years, she was obsessed with contracting syphilis. She repeatedly scrubbed and disinfected herself, and took extraordinary care to avoid walking on used condoms in public places. The syphilis fear disappeared and gave way to obsessions about being infected with cancer, and she continued to wash and disinfect herself many times. Obsessions about contamination are perhaps the most common kind of obsession today. Here is a description of a striking case:

Pictured here is Howard Hughes, who in the last half of his life, was afflicted with a severe obsessive-compulsive disorder about germs.

> Howard Hughes was one of America's richest and most colorful tycoons. During at least the last half of his life, Hughes was apparently afflicted with a severe obsessive-compulsive disorder about infection. He lived as a recluse, but unlike most obsessives, he was rich enough to be able to hire a retinue of servants to carry out his rituals for him, rather than doing them himself. Hughes's fear of germs and contamination dominated his life. He wrote numerous memos in which he explained in detail what he wanted done to prevent the "back transmission" of germs to him. For example, in a three-page memo, he explained how he wanted a can of fruit opened to prevent "fallout" of germs. He required that special equipment be used to open the can, writing, "The equipment used in connection with this operation will consist of the following items: 1 unopened newspaper, 1 sterile can opener; 1 large sterile plate; 1 sterile fork; 1 sterile spoon; 2 sterile brushes; 2 bars of soap; sterile paper towels." The ritual he devised for opening the can had nine steps: "preparing a table, procuring of fruit can, washing of can, drying the can, processing the hands, opening the can, removing fruit from can, fallout rules while around can, and conclusion of operation." He worked out complicated procedures for each step of the operation; for example, to wash the can, he wrote:

> The man in charge then turns the valve in the bathtub on, using his bare hands to do so. He also adjusts the water temperature so that it is not too hot nor too cold. He then takes one of the brushes, and, using one of the bars of soap, creates a good lather, and then scrubs the can from a point two inches below the

top of the can. He should first soak and remove the label, and then brush the cylindrical part of the can over and over until all particles of dust, pieces of paper label, and, in general, all sources of contamination have been removed. Holding the can in the center at all times, he then processes the bottom of the can in the same manner, being very sure that all the bristles of the brush have thoroughly cleaned all the small indentations on the perimeter of the bottom of the can. He then rinses the soap from the cylindrical sides and the bottom of the can. (Barlett and Steele, 1979, p. 233)

Hughes's persistent fear of contamination led to a series of compulsive rituals that increasingly dominated his daily life. He eventually became a prisoner of his obsessions, confined to his "sterile" rooms, and seeing only his selected servants. He hired servants to wave newspapers to scare away imaginary flies, to wash everything in sight, and to open doors only with their feet (Fowler, 1986). Hughes's compulsive rituals bore a rational relationship to the obsession—if there really was rampant danger of infection from germs around food, the compulsion might have cut down the risk—but it was his obsession that germs were rampant that was irrational. The ritual to control contamination need not be so rational, as this next case illustrates.

A twenty-seven-year-old veterinarian described his severe compulsive ritual. His compulsion required him to flush the toilet a multiple of three times whenever he entered a bathroom. Sometimes he was "satisfied" with three times only; but on other occasions, nine, twenty-seven, or even more were needed. He was at a loss to control his compulsive ritual which had sometimes embarrassed him socially and was professionally handicapping. (Laughlin, 1967, p. 351)

ANXIETY, DEPRESSION, AND OBSESSIONS

Neutralizing anxiety

What motivates an obsessive-compulsive to perform such strange actions as flushing a toilet in multiples of three? How does he feel when he has obsessive thoughts and performs his compulsive rituals? The thoughts (the obsessive component) are very disturbing. Typically, the individual suffers considerable internal distress. A mild emergency reaction of the type described in the previous chapter is often present; he feels foreboding and dread. If the ritual is performed frequently and fast enough in response to the thoughts, he can reduce or even ward off the ensuing anxiety. This is why obsession-compulsion is put in the anxiety-inferred category. The obsessive finds ways of dealing with the anxiety—by acting out his compulsions. But if his compulsive ritual is prevented, he will first feel tension similar to what we would feel if someone prevented us from answering a ringing telephone. If the barrier persists, intense distress will sweep over the patient. Here, of course, the anxiety will be felt. The individual's distress then can only be alleviated by carrying out the compulsion, thereby neutralizing the anxiety evoked by the obsessive thoughts and images. The next case illustrates this.

A middle-aged woman complained of an obsession concerning colors and heat, "The main problem is colors. I cannot look at any of the colors that are in the fire, red, orange or pink."
She believed the colors blue, green, brown, white, and gray were neutral, and she used these colors to "neutralize" the fiery colors. "If I happen to see a fire

color, I've got to immediately look at some other color to cancel it out. I've got to look at a tree or flowers out on the grounds, something brown or white, to neutralize it." She used to walk around with a small piece of green carpet in order to neutralize the effects of any orange colors she might happen upon and see or imagine.

She described the traumatic feelings that images of colored stimuli (or hot stimuli) evoked:

> It starts in my mind, and when I look at the color, I start to tremble, and I go hot all over, just as though I'm on fire. I cannot stand up; I've got to sit down or else I'll fall. I feel sick, and all I can say is that it is a traumatic feeling, that's the only word I can think of to describe it. If it is the last color I look at before I get into bed, I just won't sleep all night. . . .
>
> I try to fight it, and get into bed and tell myself it is ridiculous. I know it can't hurt me physically, although it does harm me mentally. I lie there and this hot feeling comes over me, and I start to tremble. If that happens, I have to get up, put all my clothes on again and start once more, as though I am getting into bed. Sometimes I have to do this four or five times before finally getting to sleep. (Rachman and Hodgson, 1980)

Link between obsessions and depression

Anxiety is in some way always there. And it is not the only negative affect associated with obsessions. Depression bears an intimate relationship as well. Obsessions and clinical depression appear frequently together; in fact, from 10 to 35 percent of depressed patients may have obsessions as well (Gittleson, 1966; Sakai, 1967; Beech and Vaughan, 1979). During their periods of depression, the incidence of obsessions triples over the rate before and after the depression (Videnbech, 1975). Not only do depressed patients tend to develop obsessions, but obsessional patients are prone to develop depression (Wilner, Reich, Robins, Fishman, and Van Doren, 1976; Teasdale and Rezin, 1978).

VULNERABILITY TO OBSESSIVE-COMPULSIVE DISORDER

Prevalence of obsessive-compulsive disorders

Obsessive-compulsive disorders are not uncommon. Between 2 and 3 percent of adults are diagnosed as obsessive-compulsive. Women are probably more vulnerable than men (Robins et al., 1984). The problem may be somewhat heritable, since identical twins show higher concordance than fraternal twins (Carey and Gottesman, 1981). The disorder usually comes on gradually beginning in adolescence or early adulthood. Our patient with color obsession describes the typically vague and gradual onset of her disorder:

> It is hard to say exactly when the obsession started. It was gradual. My obsession about colors must have been coming on for a couple of years very, very gradually. I only noticed it fully during the past twelve years when it got worse and worse. I can't look at certain colors, can't bathe, can't do any cooking, have to repeat many activities over and over again. . . .
>
> I think it all began some years ago when I had a sort of nervous breakdown. At the onset, I went very hot; it seemed to happen overnight somehow. I was in bed, and woke up feeling very hot. It was connected with an obsession that I had about my ailing mother at the time. I feared for her safety, and when I got a horrible thought that she might have an accident or a serious illness, this horrible hot feeling came over me. (Rachman and Hodgson, 1980)

Felix Ungar in the *Odd Couple* had an obsessive-compulsive personality. He was methodical, paid close attention to detail, and disliked dirt. He did not, however, have an obsessive-compulsive disorder, as he was proud of his meticulousness and love of detail.

The obsessive-compulsive personality

Is there a specific type of personality that is vulnerable to an obsessive-compulsive disorder? Based on case histories, psychodynamic theorists focus on the ***obsessive-compulsive personality,*** and this notion has crept into ordinary language. The person with an obsessive-compulsive personality is methodical and leads a very well-ordered life. He is always on time. He is meticulous in how he dresses and what he says. He pays exasperatingly close attention to detail, and he strongly dislikes dirt. He may have a distinct cognitive style, showing intellectual rigidity and focusing on details. He is deliberate in thought and action, and highly moralistic about himself and others (Sandler and Hazari, 1960; Shapiro, 1965; Pollack, 1979; DSM-III-R).

Obsessive-compulsive personality not a precursor to obsessive-compulsive disorder

What is the relationship between having an obsessive-compulsive *personality* and having an obsessive-compulsive *disorder?* One hypothesis is that when an individual with an obsessive-compulsive personality is under stress, he reacts by developing an obsessive-compulsive disorder (Shapiro, 1965). This is an important hypothesis, because if true, it would give us a way of predicting in advance who might be especially at risk for this disorder. Unfortunately, the evidence for this hypothesis is unconvincing. The crucial difference between having an obsessive-compulsive personality and having an obsessive-compulsive disorder has to do with how much the person *likes* having the symptoms. An obsessive-compulsive person views his meticulousness and love of detail with pride and self-esteem. For an individual with an obsession-compulsive disorder, however, these characteristics are abhorrent, unwanted, and tormenting. They are "ego-alien."

When one actually looks at the personality of individuals with obsessive-compulsive disorders, little evidence emerges showing that they also have an obsessive-compulsive personality. To test this, S. J. Rachman and Ray Hodgson of the Maudsley Hospital in London developed a questionnaire that distinguishes between patients with obsessive-compulsive disorders and patients with other anxiety disorders. Table 9-1 presents some of the questions from the Maudsley Obsessive-Compulsive Disorder Inventory. The questionnaire isolates three major components of obsessive-compulsive disorders: cleaning, checking, and doubting. Patients who had either an obsessive-compulsive disorder or some other anxiety disorder took both this inventory and an inventory that measured obsessive-compulsive personality by focusing on orderliness, perseverance, and rigidity. While there were

Table 9-1 SAMPLE QUESTIONS FROM THE MAUDSLEY OBSESSIVE-COMPULSIVE DISORDER INVENTORY

Components of Obsessive-Compulsive Disorder	Obsessive-Compulsive Disorder Answer
Cleaning	
1. I am not excessively concerned about cleanliness.	False
2. I avoid using public telephones because of possible contamination.	True
3. I can use well-kept toilets without any hesitation.	False
4. I take a rather long time to complete my washing in the morning.	True
Checking	
1. I frequently have to check things (gas or water taps, doors) more than once.	True
2. I do not check letters over and over again before mailing them.	False
3. I frequently get nasty thoughts and have difficulty getting rid of them.	True
Doubting-Conscience	
1. I have a very strict conscience.	True
2. I usually have serious doubts about the simple everyday things I do.	True
3. Neither of my parents was very strict during my childhood.	False

SOURCE: RACHMAN AND HODGSON, 1980.

extreme differences between patients with obsessive-compulsive disorders and those with other anxiety disorders on the Obsessive-Compulsive Disorder Inventory, there were no differences between these two groups on obsessive-compulsive personality measures. These results suggest that the obsessive-compulsive personality is not a precursor of obsessive-compulsive disorders, and that individuals who are meticulous and lead a well-ordered life are no more likely to develop an obsessive-compulsive disorder than any other individuals (Sandler and Hazari, 1960; Shapiro, 1965; Rosenberg, 1967; Rack, 1977; Pollack, 1979; Rachman and Hodgson, 1980).

Abnormal brain characteristics

While there may not be a personality style that predisposes to obsessive-compulsive disorder, there may well be abnormal brain characteristics (Turner, Beidel, and Nathan, 1985). Measuring by PET scan, the brain metabolism of fourteen obsessive-compulsive patients was compared to that in depressed and normal controls. Two areas of the brain showed consistently higher activity in the obsessive-compulsives: a part of the cortex called the orbital gyrus (particularly on the left side) and a part of the basal ganglia system called the caudate nuclei (Baxter, Phelps, Mazziotta, Guze, Schwartz, and Selin, 1987). Overactivity in these particular areas is suggestive because the orbital gyri may be related to the filtering out of interfering stimuli and the caudate nuclei may be related to perseveration of behavior. Inability to turn off distracting thoughts and perseveration of behavior seem like central problems in obsessions and in compulsions. One puzzling aspect of this study, however, is that eight of the patients responded well to drug treatment, but they continued to show abnormally elevated metabolism in these two brain areas.

THEORIES OF OBSESSIVE-COMPULSIVE DISORDER

What causes an obsessive-compulsive disorder? There are two major theoretical views: cognitive-behavioral and psychoanalytic. Their strengths complement each other well. The psychoanalytic view wrestles with the question of the genesis of the obsession—who gets it and why it takes a particular form—but is less illuminating about why it persists for years once it has started. The cognitive-behavioral view illuminates its persistence, but leaves us in the dark as to who gets it and what its content will be.

COGNITIVE-BEHAVIORAL VIEW OF THE OBSESSIVE-COMPULSIVE DISORDER

Inability to ignore abhorrent thoughts

S. J. Rachman and Ray Hodgson have formulated the most comprehensive cognitive-behavioral theory of obsessions (Rachman, 1978; Rachman and Hodgson, 1980). The theory begins with the assumption that we all experience obsessional thoughts occasionally. The thought "Step on a crack and you'll break your mother's back" followed by an avoidance of sidewalk cracks is a common obsessive-compulsive ritual in children. For others, memories of radio jingles often intrude, unbidden, into consciousness. But most of us outgrow the sidewalk ritual, and we easily are able to distract ourselves from and habituate to the radio jingles. We can also dismiss the more abhorrent thoughts that occasionally run through our heads. Individuals with obsessive-compulsive disorders, however, differ from the rest of us in that they are unable to habituate, dismiss, and distract themselves from abhorrent thoughts.

The more anxiety-provoking and depressing the content of the obsession, the more difficult it is for anyone—obsessive or non-obsessive—to dismiss the thought or distract himself from it. When normal individuals are shown a brief but stressful film, most of them have intrusive and repetitive thoughts. For example, a stressful film depicting a gruesome woodshop accident brought about anxiety and repetitive thoughts about the accident. The more emotionally upset an individual was made by the film, the more intrusive and repetitive the thoughts (Horowitz, 1975). Furthermore, anxious individuals find threatening words more intrusive than normal controls (Mathews and MacLeod, 1986). This supports two of the assumptions of the cognitive-behavioral view of obsessions: (1) we all have unwanted and repetitive thoughts; and (2) the more stressed we are, the more frequent and intense are these thoughts.

S. J. Rachman has formulated a comprehensive cognitive-behaviora theory of obsessions.

Recall now the link between depression and obsession. To the extent that an individual is depressed beforehand, obsessive thoughts will be more disturbing and therefore more difficult to dismiss. In addition, as we will see in Chapter 11, depressed individuals display more helplessness (Seligman, 1975). This means that they are less able to initiate voluntary responses to relieve their own distress. The act of distracting oneself is a voluntary cognitive response, and like other such responses, it will be weakened by depression. A background of depression is therefore fertile soil for an obsessive-compulsive disorder.

Chain of events leading to obsessions and compulsions

Here, then, is the chain of events that distinguishes an obsessive-compulsive from a non-obsessive, according to the cognitive-behavioral view. For a non-obsessive, some initiating event, either internal or external, leads to a disturbing image or thought. A non-obsessive person may find this thought unacceptable but will not be made anxious by it. If he is not in a state of depression, he will easily dismiss the thought or distract himself from it. In contrast, the obsessive-compulsive will be made anxious by the thought, and the anxiety and depression will reduce his ability to dismiss it. The

Drawing by W. Miller
© 1982 The New Yorker Magazine, Inc.

thought will persist, and the obsessive-compulsive's inability to turn the thought off will lead to further anxiety, helplessness, and depression, which will increase his susceptibility to the intrusive thought.

Cognitive explanations for compulsive rituals

The cognitive-behavioral view also attempts to explain compulsive rituals. The rituals are reinforced by the temporary relief from anxiety that they bring. Since the obsessive-compulsive cannot remove the thoughts by the distraction and dismissal techniques that the rest of us readily use, he resorts to other tactics. He attempts to neutralize the bad thought, often by substituting a good thought. The fiery color obsessive-compulsive neutralized the color orange by looking at a swatch of green carpet. Alternatively, he attempts to neutralize the bad thoughts by an action that ensures safety. So, in an attempt to allay his fear of germs, the late millionaire Howard Hughes, saw to it that his servants did not cough on the fruit he ate. Individuals who are obsessively afraid that their doors are not locked check them dozens of times a night. These compulsive rituals produce temporary relief, but they also produce a stronger tendency to check, wash, or seek reassurance, since they are followed by anxiety reduction and therefore strengthened. But the rituals can only be cosmetic, and the relief they provide is temporary. They leave the obsessions intact; they continue to return with frequency and intensity. Each time a thought recurs, the ritual must be performed in order to produce any relief.

The strength of the cognitive-behavioral view is that it provides an account of why obsessions and compulsions, once started, might be maintained. But what are their origins? There are two questions about their origins that the cognitive-behavioral account leaves unanswered. The first has to do with the *content* of the obsessive thought and the compulsive act. Why this particular thought and this particular ritual? The second has to do with *individual susceptibility.* Since we all have intrusive thoughts, why are so few people afflicted with obsessive-compulsive disorders? Why are particular individuals deficient in their ability to dismiss, distract, and habituate to abhorrent thoughts? Complementing the cognitive-behavioral view of obsessive-compulsive disorders, the psychoanalytic view focuses on these questions.

THE PSYCHODYNAMICS OF THE OBSESSIVE-COMPULSIVE DISORDER

Obsessive thoughts as defenses against anxiety

The questions "Who will get an obsessive-compulsive disorder?" and "What form will it take?" lie at the heart of the psychoanalytic view of obsessive thoughts. According to this view, an obsessive thought is seen as a *defense* against an even more unwelcome and unconscious thought. This defensive process involves *displacement* and *substitution* (see Chapter 4). What happens is that an unconscious dangerous thought, such as "my mother might die of a fever," threatens to break into the individual's consciousness. This arouses anxiety. To defend against this anxiety, the individual unconsciously displaces this anxiety from the original terrifying thought onto a less unwelcome substitute, like hot and fiery colors. The defense has a powerful internal logic, and the thoughts that are substituted for the underlying thought are not arbitrary. Fiery and hot colors symbolize the fever that her ailing mother might die of.

Freud's original case of obsessional neurosis, the "Rat Man," illustrates the logic of obsessional defenses (Freud, 1909/1976):

The case of the Rat Man

The Rat Man, whose name derives from his obsessional images of rats chewing their way into anuses, was plagued with a host of other obsessional thoughts, often of a violent nature. While a young man, the Rat Man lost some weeks of study, because he was distressed about his girlfriend's absence. She had left him to nurse her seriously ill grandmother. While trying to study, an obsessional thought intruded—"If you were commanded to cut your throat with a razor, what then?" Freud interpreted this as caused by an unconscious rage that was even more threatening and more unacceptable: "I should like to go and kill that old woman for robbing me of my love!" The moral and high-minded Rat Man, with this horrendous thought knocking on the doors of consciousness, substitutes a more acceptable command "Kill yourself" and this is a fitting punishment for his savage and murderous passion. (Freud, 1909/1976, pp. 187–98)

Susceptibility to particular content of obsession

Psychoanalytic theory explains *who* will develop an obsession in response to underlying conflict-arousing anxiety, and *what content* the obsession will take on to symbolize the underlying conflict. The following case of obsession about infanticide illustrates why the particular individual would be susceptible to the particular form of obsession she developed:

A thirty-two-year-old mother of two had obsessional thoughts of injuring and murdering her children and more infrequently, her husband. These thoughts were almost as threatening and as guilt-provoking as the very act itself. Therapy uncovered even more threatening impulses from her childhood which had been displaced onto her children. She had been the eldest of three siblings and while very young had been given undue responsibility for their care. She felt deprived of affection from her parents and was greatly resentful of her younger sister and brother. She entertained murderous fantasies about them, which were accompanied by tremendous guilt and anxiety. As a result, these fantasies had been completely driven from consciousness. When she became an adult, her children symbolically stood for her siblings, whose destruction would make her the sole object of parental love and relieve her of her childhood burden. Her own mother's occasional visits triggered the obsessions. She was particularly susceptible because she had unresolved and anxiety-provoking resentment against her own parents and siblings. Her obsession had the content of death as it symbolized the death of her siblings, which would have solved her childhood problem. (Adapted from Laughlin, 1967, pp. 324–26.)

Thus, the psychodynamic view of obsessions claims that powerful, abhorrent wishes and conflicts that have been repressed and threaten to break into consciousness put an individual at risk for obsessions, and that adopting the defense of displacement and substitution provides the immediate mechanism for relief. In addition, the particular content of the obsessions these individuals acquire will be a symbol for the underlying conflict.

TREATMENT FOR OBSESSIVE-COMPULSIVE DISORDER

Prognosis for improvement not promising by ordinary therapy

The prognosis of obsessive-compulsive disorders, either untreated or treated with the therapies (other than behavior therapy) used over the last forty years is not particularly promising. Electroconvulsive shock, antidepressant drugs, supportive psychotherapy, and surgical removal of part of the brain (lobotomy) have all been tried frequently. Overall, five years after treatment, roughly half of obsessive-compulsives are unchanged or worse, with only 20 to 40 percent markedly improved. Roughly the same outcome is found ten years after treatment (Pollit, 1960; Grimshaw, 1964; Kringlen, 1965). Are there any therapies that can improve on this prognosis? How do the psychoanalytic and behavior therapies fare?

Psychoanalytic therapy

In psychoanalytic therapy for obsessions, the central issue is to enable the patient to recognize the underlying conflict by undoing repression of this unconscious conflict. The mother with thoughts of infanticide must gain insight into her impulses to do away with her siblings during childhood and understand the connection of this conflict to her present problems. The psychodynamic treatment of the obsessive-compulsive patient involves a thorough analysis of the obsessive-compulsive's defenses and can be expected to take several years (Fenichel, 1945; Laughlin, 1967). Because there has been no controlled study of psychoanalytic treatment of obsessive-compulsive disorders, we can conclude little about its effectiveness.

Behavior therapies

In contrast, behavior therapies for obsessive-compulsive disorders have been explored in several controlled studies (Marks and Rachman, 1978). The results have been promising but are not conclusive. A combination of the three basic techniques of behavior therapy—response prevention, flooding, and modeling—are used in treating obsessive-compulsive disorders. These three procedures all encourage and persuade but do not force the patient to endure the disturbing situations that set off obsessions without engaging in compulsive rituals to undo the thoughts. For example, one patient had obsessive thoughts that he might be contaminated with germs. He spent four hours a day washing himself. In therapy, he first watched the therapist contaminate herself with dirt (modeling). He then was urged to rub dirt and dust all over himself (flooding) and endure it without washing it off (response prevention). After about a dozen sessions of covering himself with dirt and just sitting there without washing it off, the thoughts of contamination diminished and the washing rituals no longer occurred in his daily life.

Flooding and
response
prevention

In this case, flooding the patient and preventing him from washing off the dirt cured the compulsion. In addition to such case histories, there have been six controlled studies of response prevention, flooding, and modeling in obsessive-compulsive patients. These indicate marked improvement in about two-thirds of the patients; follow-up for as long as two years indicates that improvement is maintained (Rachman, Hodgson, and Marks, 1971; Hodgson, Rachman, and Marks, 1972; Rachman, Marks, and Hodgson, 1973; Roper, Rachman, and Marks, 1975; Marks and Rachman, 1978; Salzman and Thaler, 1981). The behavior therapies are specific in their effects: obsessive thoughts, compulsive rituals, and anxiety all decrease, but depression, sexual adjustment, and family harmony are not clearly helped. These results are not conclusive, however, since very few patients lose all their symptoms completely or are functioning well in all areas of life at follow-up. In addition, roughly 20 to 30 percent fail to improve at all (Meyer, 1966; Hackmann and McLean, 1975; Rabavilos, Boulougouris, and Stefanis, 1976; Beech and Vaughan, 1979; Rachman, Cobb, Grey, MacDonald, Mawson, Sartory, and Stern, 1979).

Why do flooding, response prevention, and modeling work, and what are their critical elements? Recall that in the laboratory, flooding and response prevention reliably extinguish avoidance responding. If a rat is prevented from making his habitual avoidance responses by a barrier interposed between him and safety (response prevention) while sitting and hearing a signal that used to predict shock (flooding), avoidance behavior extinguishes. On future trials, even when the animal is free to flee, he will sit still during the signal. Response prevention has forcibly exposed the rat to the fact that the signal is no longer followed by shock and that he does not have to make the response in order to be safe (Seligman and Johnston, 1973).

Reconsider the man who washed himself for four hours a day. He had the obsession that some terrible illness would strike him if he did not wash. When he was persuaded to endure being dirty without washing, his obsessive thoughts of illness waned, and his compulsive rituals of washing vanished. What had he learned during flooding and response prevention? By covering himself with dirt and then not washing, his fear that dirt would lead to illness extinguished. The CS was the dirt, and the anticipated US was illness. He received stark exposure to being dirty without getting sick, and Pavlovian extinction occurred. In addition, he learned that illness did not happen even though he did not wash. This was an instrumental extinction procedure for the compulsive ritual of washing. So flooding and response prevention may work for two reasons: (1) by showing the patient that the dreaded event does not occur in the feared situation (Pavlovian extinction), and (2) by showing the patient that no dreaded event occurs even though the compulsive ritual is not performed (instrumental extinction of the compulsion).

OBSESSIVE-COMPULSIVE DISORDER: ANXIETY REVISITED

This chapter deals with those disorders in which anxiety is not directly felt by the afflicted individual. But we have assumed that anxiety underlies these disorders, specifically the obsessive-compulsive disorder. What is the evidence for this? There are four clues that anxiety underlies obsessive-

Clues for
existence of
underlying
anxiety

compulsive disorder. First of all, the fact that flooding and response prevention seem to work suggest that obsessive-compulsive disorders are basically anxiety disorders. Since it is known from the laboratory that flooding and response prevention are techniques that produce extinction of conditioned fear and anxiety, we infer from the fact that they work that the obsessive suffered anxiety that is then extinguished in therapy.

The second clue relates to the integral relationship between the obsessive thought and the compulsive act. An obsessive-compulsive who continually thinks that he left the gas on will compulsively check the kitchen stove. In observing him we probably would not see him as particularly anxious. But what if we do not allow him to perform his checking ritual? In this case, the obsessive-compulsive may be overcome with anxiety, and think that his house will blow up as a result of the gas leak. This suggests that the function of the ritual is to ward off underlying anxiety. In short, when the compulsive symptoms are successful, they prevent anxiety from being experienced.

The third clue is that some obsessive-compulsives actually do experience some anxiety during the obsession but lose it when the compulsion is performed. The color obsessive-compulsive felt traumatized when she saw the color orange, and felt her anxiety turn off when she looked at the swatch of green carpet.

The fourth clue is the most intriguing of all. The content of the obsession can often be seen as a symbol of an underlying, unresolved conflict which when recognized provokes great anxiety. The mother with the infanticide obsession may have displaced her anxiety and guilt over wanting to murder her siblings onto a less unwelcome thought. During therapy, when she realized that she had done that even unconsciously, she felt very anxious.

Overall then there is reason to suspect that anxiety underlies obsessive-compulsive disorders. Sometimes the anxiety can actually be observed, as it is in phobias and panic attacks; but at most other times, the role of anxiety is inferred from clues about the patient's past, or by arranging special conditions such as response blocking to bring anxiety to the surface. In the next section, we will examine a set of disorders in which anxiety is almost never observed. In fact, it is the absence of anxiety that is often remarkable. These are the somatoform disorders, in which psychological factors cause the loss of some bodily function. We will look principally at hysterical conversions.

SOMATOFORM DISORDERS

As we learned in Chapter 2, Professor Jean Martin Charcot (1825–1893), a great French neurologist in Paris working at La Salpêtrière, saw a large number of female patients who had such symptoms as convulsive fits and muscular paralysis, although he could not find any clear organic basis for them. These symptoms characterized disorders that were called *hysterical conversions,* and Charcot believed that they were produced by psychological events. To show this, he hypnotized normal women and, by suggestion, produced in them symptoms identical to hysterical paralysis and hysterical convulsions. In addition, he hypnotized patients who had these symptoms and, by hypnotic suggestion, he was able to remove the symptoms. Charcot's demonstration that hysterical conversion, a somatoform disorder,

The French neurologist Jean Martin Charcot (1825–1893) believed the symptoms of hysterical conversions were produced by psychological events.

could be induced and removed merely by influencing the mind formed the basis of the theories of anxiety disorders put forth by Pierre Janet (1859–1947), Josef Breuer (1842–1925), and most importantly, by Sigmund Freud himself (1856–1939).

THE TYPES OF SOMATOFORM DISORDERS

Symptoms of somatoform disorders

What is a *somatoform disorder?* There are five factors to consider. First, there is lost or altered physical functioning. One may, for example, become deaf or paralyzed. Second, the symptom cannot be explained by a known physical condition. There is no evidence of neurological damage to produce the deafness or the paralysis. Third, there is positive evidence that psychological factors have caused the symptom. Fourth, the patient is often, but not always, indifferent to the physical loss. More specifically, he or she does not feel anxiety. Finally, the symptoms are not under voluntary control. Conversion, somatization disorder, and somatoform pain disorder are all considered somatoform disorders by DSM-III-R.

CONVERSION

Before DSM-III and DSM-III-R, *conversion* was called "hysterical conversion." It was renamed by DSM-III to remove the suggestion that it affects only women. "Hysteria," is derived from the Greek word *hystera,* which means womb, implying that the disorder is confined to women only. We now know this to be false, as men also suffer from the somatoform disorders (Veith, 1965; Chodoff, 1974, 1982). The case below illustrates a conversion disorder, where psychological stress has been converted into physical symptoms:

A case of conversion disorder

Bear was a burly twenty-five-year-old construction worker who was paralyzed from the waist down—totally without movement or feeling—and had been so for three weeks. What's more, he was not particularly upset by his paralysis; that is, he was a bit concerned that he could not walk, but he was not emotional nor excessively anxious.

After three days of tests that failed to show anything, the neurologist examining Bear had decided that there was nothing wrong with him physically and had sent him to Psychiatry.

In Psychiatry, there was the same frustration as that experienced by the neurologist. Bear's recent life seemed uneventful to him, and he recalled no precipitating incident. He had used drugs occasionally, and he drank a bit, but he had no previous psychiatric history. Mystified, groping for any lead, one of the residents asked him if he knew anybody else who was paralyzed. At first, Bear couldn't think of anyone, but after a minute or so, he mumbled, without any show of emotion:

"Yeah, come to think of it, Tom, a good friend of mine, is paralyzed from the waist down. Broke his neck."

"How did that happen?"

"It was really sad, and, you know, I guess it was pretty much my fault. Tom's a virgin, like in every way possible. Doesn't even drink or smoke. Well, we were together at a party about a month ago, and I was riding him. I thought he should live a little, try some LSD. I guess he couldn't take it, so he gave in.

"Well, we downed a couple of tabs, and within a few minutes he was flying. Seeing all sorts of weird things. He ran out of the apartment, and I followed, a little

> afraid for him. God, it was awful! He was running away from something in his head. Next thing I knew, he jumped off the bridge. You know, the one over the tracks at 30th Street Station. He was still alive when the rescue squad got him down from the high tension lines. They say he'll never walk, or anything, again."
>
> "Bear, tell me again when your problem started."
>
> "Out of nowhere. About three weeks ago. I was at work, driving my forklift down at the station. As I crossed over the tracks under the high tension lines, suddenly I was all dead down there. I shouted for help, and my buddies took me off to. . . . Oh, my God! Don't you see what I've done!"
>
> And within a few days, Bear walked home. (Stinnett, 1978)

Bear's paralysis has the five symptoms of somatoform disorder. First, he has lost physical functioning: he is paralyzed. Second, physical damage cannot explain the paralysis, since he is neurologically sound, and the paralysis is not under voluntary control. Third, Bear seems remarkably indifferent to his paralysis. Fourth, he feels no anxiety. And fifth, there is good evidence that psychological factors caused the symptoms: (1) he has a friend with paralysis caused partly by his actions; (2) the paralysis began at the same site that his friend's paralysis occurred; (3) Bear did not easily remember the incident when his friend was paralyzed, nor did he relate it to his own paralysis; and (4) Bear could not control his paralysis, but when he gained insight into this, his paralysis remitted.

SOMATIZATION DISORDER (BRIQUET'S SYNDROME)

Multiple and recurrent bodily complaints

In *somatization disorder (Briquet's syndrome),* the individual will have a dramatic and complicated medical history for most of her adult life (Mai and Mersky, 1980). She will receive extensive medical care from a variety of physicians for multiple and recurrent bodily complaints in many organs, although these are not physically caused. The symptoms may include headaches, fatigue, fainting, nausea, vomiting, stomach pains, allergies, menstrual and sexual difficulties, as well as one or more specific conversion symptoms. Unnecessary surgery addiction to prescription medicines, depression, and attempted suicide are common complications of this syndrome. The fundamental difference between somatization and conversion is that the somatizer will suffer from many physical problems; the conversion patient generally has only one complaint.

There may be two distinct kinds of somatization disorders. The first is called "high frequency" and the second "diversiform." Individuals with high-frequency disorder have frequent stomach and back pains, along with psychiatric problems. These individuals have an extraordinarily large number of sick leaves, and they tend to abuse alcohol ten times as frequently as those in the normal population. Those with diversiform disorder have fewer back problems; instead, their complaints cover the rest of the body, although they also are prone to alcohol abuse. In a study of a Swedish population, the prevalence of these problems ran as high as 11 percent of all adult women (Cloninger, Sigvardsson, von Knorring, and Bohman, 1984).

SOMATOFORM PAIN DISORDER (PSYCHALGIA)

In *somatoform pain disorder (psychalgia),* there is pain that is not attributed to physical cause. Statistically, it may be the most frequent of the somatoform disorders today (Watson and Buranen, 1979; Drossman, 1982). The following case illustrates an individual suffering from psychalgia:

A case of
somatoform pain
disorder

> Harry, a forty-one-year-old man, suffered a sudden onset of severe abdominal pain. Emergency surgery was about to be performed, but there was no elevated white cell count, and other physical symptoms were normal. In addition, Harry seemed emotionally indifferent to the pain and the fact of impending surgery. He was obviously in pain, but not anxious about it.
>
> Upon consultation, it was decided to abandon urgent preparations for surgery, and to explore for a possible psychological basis. It emerged that Harry had had a childhood that predisposed him to psychalgia. His parents had been materially wealthy, but they had given him very little love and affection. The one break in this emotional barrenness in his childhood had been his appendectomy. The love he had received during this period was meaningful, real, and what he had "always longed for."
>
> The present abdominal pain was set off by an incident of domestic deceit. His wife had become infatuated with another man and had threatened to go off with him. At this very point, the abdominal pain had begun. (Adapted from Laughlin, 1967, pp. 667–68.)

The hypothesis in Harry's case is that whenever he is under serious stress, Harry will suffer pain in his abdomen. This pain becomes a somatic excuse for not suffering the anxiety brought on by the stressful events.

DIAGNOSING SOMATOFORM DISORDER

A somatoform disorder is one of the most difficult disorders to diagnose correctly. In the case study discussed earlier, how can we tell if Bear was faking paralysis or if he had some obscure physical illness that was as yet undiagnosed?

Distinguishing
somatoform
disorders from
malingering

In an attempt to make diagnosis clearer, let us distinguish somatoform disorders from four other disorders with which it can be confused, sometimes tragically. These disorders are malingering, psychosomatic disorders, factitious disorders, and undiagnosed physical illness. In principle, there are two differences between *malingering* (faking) and an authentic somatoform disorder—neither of which is easy to pin down in practice. First, the symptoms of a malingerer are under his voluntary control, whereas they are not under the voluntary control of an individual with a somatoform disorder. A malingerer can turn the paralysis on and off, although it may be difficult indeed to induce him to display this voluntary control for you. The individual suffering conversion cannot. For example, even if we had offered Bear an irresistibly large amount of money to get up out of his wheelchair and walk away, he would not have been able to do so. Second, the malingerer acquires an obvious environmental goal as a result of his symptom (e.g., getting out of the army by feigning paralysis), whereas an individual with a conversion disorder does not necessarily achieve anything obvious by his symptom.

Malingering itself should be distinguished from *secondary gain.* Secondary gain consists of deriving benefits from one's environment as a consequence of having abnormal symptoms. Individuals with somatoform disorders frequently get secondary gains. So, for example, a person with so-

© 1982 Jules Feiffer. Reprinted with permission of Universal Press Syndicate. All rights reserved.

matoform pain disorder may get more love and attention from his family when he is in pain. The use of secondary gain seems to be part of the universal human trait of making the best of a bad situation. A person with a somatoform disorder, who derives secondary gain, differs from a malingerer. The malingerer is faking the initial symptoms and then may, in addition, use them to benefit. The individual with the somatoform disorder, in contrast, is not faking the symptoms but may well derive benefit from having them.

Distinguishing somatoform disorders from psychosomatic disorders

The second disorder that resembles somatoform disorders are ***psychosomatic disorders,*** which are the subject of the next chapter. What distinguishes psychosomatic disorders from somatoform disorders is the existence of a physical basis that can explain the symptom. Although some individuals who have a peptic ulcer or high blood pressure may have these conditions exaggerated or even initiated by psychological factors, the ulcers and hypertension are actually being caused by specific known physical mechanisms. In contrast, ***glove anesthesia,*** a conversion symptom in which nothing can be felt in the hand and fingers, but in which sensation is intact from the wrist up, cannot be induced by any known pattern of damage to the nerves innervating the hand.

Distinguishing somatoform disorders from factitious disorder

The third disorder from which somatoform disorder must be distinguished is ***factitious disorder,*** also called "Münchhausen syndrome." This disorder is characterized by multiple hospitalizations and operations in which the individual voluntarily produces the signs of illness, not through underlying anxiety, but by physiological tampering (Pope, Jonas, and Jones, 1982). He might, for example, take anticoagulent drugs, then seek treatment for his bleeding. There was one documented case of a thirty-four-year-old man who, over a decade, had made 200 visits to physicians under

Table 9-2 CRITERIA FOR DIFFERENTIAL DIAGNOSIS OF SYMPTOMS SUGGESTING PHYSICAL ILLNESS

Classification	Can a known physical mechanism explain the symptom?	Are the symptoms linked to psychological causes?	Is the symptom under voluntary control?	Is there an obvious goal?
Conversion	Never	Always	Never	Sometimes
Malingering	Sometimes	Sometimes	Always	Always
Psychosomatic Disorders	Always	Always	Never	Sometimes
Factitious Disorders	Sometimes	Always	Always	Never (other than medical attention)
Undiagnosed Physical Illness	Sometimes	Sometimes	Never	Never

SOURCE: Based on Hyler and Spitzer, 1978.

dozens of aliases at more than sixty-eight hospitals and who had cost Britain's health service $2,000,000. In contrast to malingering, a factitious disorder has no obvious goal other than gaining medical attention. It is crucially different from somatoform disorders because the symptoms are voluntarily produced by the person who has them and they are physically based.

Distinguishing somatoform disorders from undiagnosed physical illness

Finally, a somatoform disorder may be misdiagnosed and actually result from an ***undiagnosed physical illness.*** The diagnosis of a somatoform disorder is for many people degrading, as the patient and his family are told that the disease is in his mind, not in his body. Current medical diagnosis is far from perfect, and occasionally an individual who has been labeled "hysteric" will eventually develop a full-blown physical disease, such as multiple sclerosis, which in fact had caused the earlier "hysterical" symptoms. This is one reason the diagnosis must be made with caution.

Table 9-2 summarizes the distinctions among conversion, malingering, psychosomatic disorders, factitious disorders, and undiagnosed physical illness.

VULNERABILITY TO SOMATOFORM DISORDERS

Who gets conversion disorders?

Conversion disorders are not particularly common. Estimates vary widely, but probably not more than 5 percent of all nonpsychotic patients (or much less than 1 percent of the entire American population) have conversion disorders (Laughlin, 1967; Woodruff, Clayton, and Guze, 1971). Initially, conversion symptoms usually are displayed from late adolescence to middle adulthood; they occur in children and old people, but rarely (Kotsopoulos and Snow, 1986). Because conversion disorders were long regarded as hysteria, and hysteria (a wandering womb) was by definition a disorder of women, conversion disorders in men were somehow overlooked. This is the basis of the myth that conversion afflicts only women. On the contrary, contemporary studies indicate that between 20 and 40 percent of conversion disorders occur in men (Ziegler, Imboden, and Meyer, 1960; Chodoff, 1974).

Who gets
somatization
disorders?

Somatization disorder, in which the patient has a complicated medical history before the age of thirty-five, with a large number of symptoms ranging across many organ systems, and with no known medical explanations, is more common. As many as 2 to 10 percent of all adult women may display this disorder, and it is rarely diagnosed in men (Woodruff, Clayton, and Guze, 1971; Cloninger et al., 1984).

There is marginal evidence that somatoform disorders may run in families (Torgersen, 1986). Somatization disorder probably does run in families. The sisters, mothers, and daughters of women with this disorder are ten times more likely to develop it than women in the general population (Woodruff, Clayton, and Guze, 1971). Nothing is presently known about family patterns of somatoform pain disorder.

COURSE OF SOMATOFORM DISORDERS

Onset and
remission of
somatoform
disorders

What is the course of these disorders once they appear? Surprisingly, there has not been a single useful longitudinal study of conversion disorders, and our knowledge is based only on clinical impressions. Conversion disorders come on suddenly, and they remit suddenly and spontaneously. They probably do not last very long, and it has been estimated that 50 percent spontaneously disappear within two years (Rachman and Wilson, 1979). Somatization disorder is much more insidious. Seventy percent of women who develop it probably will still have it fifteen years later, and as many as one-third of them will then be diagnosed as psychotic (Ziegler and Paul, 1954; Perley and Guze, 1962; Woodruff, Clayton and Guze, 1971; Coryell and Norten, 1981).

THE ETIOLOGY OF SOMATOFORM DISORDERS

What causes the loss of the function of a bodily organ in the absence of any underlying physiological basis? This remains one of the great questions of psychopathology.

THE PSYCHOANALYTIC VIEW

Psychoanalytic
explanations

The psychoanalytic view was put forth by Sigmund Freud in 1894. Freud believed that the physical symptom was a defense that absorbed and neutralized the anxiety generated by an unacceptable unconscious conflict. (Freud, 1894/1976, p. 63). Today, the psychodynamic explanation of conversion still revolves around this notion, and postulates three distinct processes: First, the individual is made anxious by some unacceptable idea, and the conversion is a defense against this anxiety. Second, psychic energy is transmuted into a somatic loss. The anxiety is detached from the idea, rendering it neutral. Because anxiety is psychic energy it must go some place, and in this case it is used to debilitate a physical organ. Third, the particular somatic loss symbolizes the underlying conflict. For Bear, the three processes seem to play a role: Bear is unconsciously anxious and guilty about causing Tom's paralysis, and he walls off these feelings from consciousness by transmuting the guilt and anxiety into his own paralysis. The particular symptom—paralysis—obviously symbolizes the real paralysis suffered by his friend.

"La belle indifference"

This theory is just about the only idea that can explain one of the strangest symptoms of conversion: "la belle indifference." Unlike patients with actual physical loss due to injury, conversion patients are often strangely indifferent to their physical symptoms. For example, a patient with conversion paralysis may show much more concern over a minor skin irritation on his legs than with the fact that he cannot move them (Laughlin, 1967, pp. 673–74). In the psychoanalytic view, a conversion symptom may absorb anxiety so well by transmuting it into a physical loss that the patient can actually be calm about being crippled, blind, deaf, or insensate.

While no complete behavioral view of somatoform disorders has been put forward, the psychoanalytic view gives a hint of what the behavioral view might look like. If conversion symptoms do, in fact, absorb anxiety, anxiety reduction reinforces the patient for having a symptom.

The concept of anxiety has exerted a mighty hold on theories about psychopathology for the last hundred years. For Freud and for the diagnostic systems prior to DSM-III, anxiety was the most important emotion we experienced. All the disorders discussed in Chapter 8 and in this chapter were said to be caused by the process of defending against anxiety. In phobias and panic attacks, in which anxiety was observed, the patient felt dread and displayed an emergency reaction; so its role could not be denied. But in others, such as conversion, in which anxiety was not observed, its existence was inferred to explain the symptom.

An age of anxiety

Why did anxiety play such a central role in psychoanalytic theory? Part of the answer might have to do with the circumstances of Sigmund Freud's life. Freud grew up in Vienna in the declining days of the Hapsburg empire, in the last half of the nineteenth century, and much of his theorizing took place while his society was collapsing around him. The dissolution of the fixed order, with the attendant uncertainty about the future and about values, may have made anxiety a dominant emotion among the patients that Freud saw. The turn of the century in Vienna may truly have been the "age of anxiety."

THE COMMUNICATIVE VIEW

Communicating distress through physical symptoms

There are negative emotions other than anxiety: sadness, anger, guilt, awe, bewilderment, and shame are all elements of the human experience. Phobics and obsessive-compulsives experience these emotions as well as anxiety, particularly sadness and anger. Moreover, patients with conversions—if they are defending at all—might not be defending against anxiety but against depression, guilt, or anger. This possibility has spawned another theory of conversion, which emphasizes the *communicative*, rather than the defensive, function of the symptom. The communicative model claims that the patient uses the disorder to deal with a variety of distressing emotions—not only anxiety—and to negotiate difficult interpersonal transactions. He expresses his underlying distress to himself in terms of physical illness, thereby distracting himself from his distress. He then communicates the fact that he is distressed to others with his physical loss. He unconsciously chooses his symptoms according to his own conception of a physical illness —which will derive in part from the illnesses that important people in his life have had—and according to what in his time does and doesn't count as an illness. His particular symptoms will then simulate physical illness either expertly or crudely, depending on how much he knows (Ziegler and Imboden, 1962).

Symptoms to express feelings

The communicative model views the case study of Bear in the following way: Bear is depressed, anxious, and guilty over his role in paralyzing his friend. In addition, he cannot *talk* about his distress because he is not verbal about his troubles. By paralyzing himself he is able to distract himself from these emotions, so he *shows* his distress to others by his paralysis. Bear's particular symptom derives directly from identification with his friend's paralysis. Bear is alexithymic. The term ***alexithymia*** (literally, no words for feelings) has been coined to categorize such people who cannot easily express their feelings (Sifneos, 1973). When asked about how they feel about highly charged events, such as the death of a spouse, they describe their physical symptoms or simply fail to understand the question. For example, they may say, "My headaches got worse . . . it was like a band around my head . . . that's all I felt" (Lesser, 1985). Alexithymic people are particularly susceptible to somatoform disorders and the psychosomatic problems discussed in the next chapter.

Experiencing a trauma but not talking about it may precede physical health problems. In a survey of 2020 respondents, 367 reported having at one time experienced a sexual trauma. These people had higher rates of virtually all physical diseases inquired about than did those who had not experienced a trauma (Rubenstein, 1982; Pennebaker, 1985). In another study, 115 students were classified into a group that had not experienced a trauma, that had experienced a trauma but had confided in others, and a group that had experienced a trauma but had not told anybody. The trauma/no confide group had more diseases, symptoms, and took more medication. Finally, among nineteen people whose spouses had died by accident or suicide, the illness rate was substantially greater in those who did not talk to their friends about the death (Pennebaker, 1985). While these studies are not definitive, the possibility that silence hurts is intriguing and important. The mechanism by which silence hurts may be rumination; the less people talk to others about tragedy, the more they ruminate, and there may be some as yet unknown way in which rumination undermines physical health (Rachman and Hodgson, 1980). We will return to this idea in the next chapter.

The communicative model explains the odd fact that the kinds of physical losses produced by conversion have changed over the last hundred years, and that they vary with education. For Charcot in Paris in the 1880s, convulsions with frenzied, uncoordinated movements were the most common hysterical conversion. By the turn of the century in Vienna, Freud and his contemporaries saw in their upper-middle-class patients fewer convulsions and more paralysis, "glove" anesthesia, "stocking" anesthesia, blindness, and deafness. At the time of World War I, *clavus*—the painful sensation of a nail being driven into the head—and a severe low back pain producing a forwardly bent back were common. Today in urban America, pain, dizziness, headache, loss of sensation, and weakness are the most common conversion reactions; whereas in backwoods America, conversion reactions of the type Freud saw still predominate (Laughlin, 1967; Watson and Buranen, 1979; Chodoff, 1974; Woodruff, Goodwin, and Guze, 1974).

Conversion reactions as a cry for help

The communicative model holds that conversion reactions "talk." They are a cry for help, particularly among individuals who are reluctant or unable to *talk* about their emotional distress. Such people may be forced to rely on physical symptoms to tell the people they love and their physicians that all is not well in their emotional lives. The physical losses that such individuals generate will correspond to what they know about illness. Once an age or a social class discovers that glove anesthesia is physically impossible, it is no longer a "plausible" symptom to communicate with. Pain, paralysis, and deafness are still plausible somatic symptoms in sophisticated, urban America, and so they are still seen as symptoms in conversion disorders.

THE PERCEPT BLOCKING VIEW

Blocking perceptions from conscious awareness

There is a third view of somatoform disorders compatible with either the psychoanalytic or communicative views. It focuses on how a perception can be blocked from conscious experience. This view is best illustrated by hysterical blindness, a conversion disorder in which blindness is the physical loss. Surprisingly, in spite of the claim that he is aware of no visual input at all, the behavior of a hysterically blind person is often controlled by visual input. Such individuals usually avoid walking in front of cars and tripping over furniture, even though they report no awareness of actually seeing anything. In the laboratory, they also give evidence that some visual material is getting through. When given discrimination tasks that can only be solved by visual cues, such as "pick the side—left or right—that has the square, as opposed to the circle, on it," they perform significantly *below* chance. They do worse than if they were guessing at random, and they systematically pick the side that has the circle. In order to be so wrong, the patient must be right—the square of which he is not aware must register at some level of his mind, and then be reacted to by choosing the circle (Theodor and Mandelcorn, 1978; see also Brady and Lind, 1961; Gross and Zimmerman, 1965).

What are we to make of this? If we assume that the hysterically blind individual is not lying when he says he is not aware of anything visual, then we are led to the following model: visual input can register in the sensory system and directly affect behavior (hence the avoidance of furniture and below-chance performance), while being blocked from conscious awareness (hence the report "I see nothing"). The conversion process consists in the blocking of the percept from awareness (Hilgard, 1977; Sackeim, Nordlie, and Gur, 1979). This is compatible with both the psychoanalytic and communicative models since it makes no claims about what motivations can cause blocking—a need to defend against anxiety or a desire to distract oneself from inner distress. This model is also physiologically possible. When some parts of the brain that control vision are destroyed, individuals report that they can see nothing at all in specific regions of their visual field. But in spite of consistent reports of blindness, such patients perform above chance on visual discrimination problems. When confronted with this fact, the patients, like the hysterically blind, insist they saw nothing at all and were merely guessing (Weiskrantz, Warrington, Sanders, and Marshall, 1974). So we conclude that the mechanism of hysterical blindness may be the blocking of a visual percept from awareness. The blocking could be motivated either by anxiety (as Freud held), by a need to communicate distress, or it might be reinforced by anxiety reduction (as a behaviorist would hold).

TREATMENT OF SOMATOFORM DISORDER

There is an ancient Persian legend about a physician named Rhazes who was called into the palace for the purpose of diagnosing and treating a young prince. Apparently, the prince could not walk. After the usual examination of the day, Rhazes determined that there was nothing wrong with the prince's legs, at least not physically. With little more than a hunch, Rhazes set out to treat what may be the first recorded case of conversion. In doing so, he took a risk: Rhazes unexpectedly walked into the prince's bathroom brandishing a dagger and threatened to kill him. Upon seeing him, "the startled prince abruptly fled, leaving his clothes, his dignity, his symptom, and undoubtedly part of his self-esteem behind" (Laughlin, 1967, p. 678).

Confrontation

Modern clinicians tend to approach their "princes" brandishing a less drastic technology. They will sometimes confront a conversion patient and try to force him out of his symptom. For example, therapists may tell hysterically blind patients that they are performing significantly below or above chance on visual tasks in spite of seeing nothing, which may cause visual awareness to gradually return in the patient (Brady and Lind, 1961; but see also Gross and Zimmerman, 1965). But these recoveries are usually temporary, and they may produce conflict and loss of self-esteem in the patient. They also may make the patient feel that the therapist is unsympathetic, and so they may ultimately undermine therapy.

SUGGESTION

Suggestibility

Simple suggestion, merely telling a patient in a convincing manner that the symptoms will go away, may fare somewhat better than confrontation does. Conversion patients are particularly suggestible, and certain therapists have found improvement by directly telling the patient, in an authoritative sounding way, that the symptom will go away. In an account of 100 cases of patients with conversion symptoms, one investigator found that following strong suggestion 75 percent of the patients were either symptom-free or much improved four to six years later (Carter, 1949). But since there was no comparison group that might have controlled for the spontaneous disappearance of conversion without suggestion, we cannot be sure that suggestion had any real effect (Bird, 1979).

INSIGHT

Recognizing the underlying conflict

Insight, or coming to recognize the underlying conflict producing the physical loss, is psychoanalysts' therapy of choice for conversion disorders. According to these therapists, when the patient comes to see, and emotionally appreciate, that there is an underlying conflict that is producing a conversion disorder, the symptom should disappear. A number of dramatic case histories confirm this. For example, when Bear realized that his paralysis expressed his guilt over his friend's paralysis, the symptom remitted. Unfortunately, there does not exist a well-controlled study that tests whether psychoanalytic insight has any effect over and above suggestion, confrontation, spontaneous remission, or the mere formation of a therapeutic alliance.

Somatoform disorders still remain a great challenge for students of abnormality. These disorders are a real phenomenon—hysterically blind or paralyzed individuals are not feigning their symptoms. When Charcot showed that the symptoms could be produced by hypnotic suggestion and removed by hypnosis, he convinced most of the world that conversion disorders were psychological in origin. Thereupon Freud proposed that the symptoms defended against anxiety. More recent theorists have proposed that the symptoms are meant to communicate more global distress by individuals who find it impossible to talk about their problems. But we have not come much farther since Charcot. The theories of somatoform disorders have yet to be tested in a definitive way, and their cure remains a mystery.

DISSOCIATIVE DISORDERS

Depersonal-
ization

All of us have at one time or another awakened in the middle of the night and being somewhat befuddled, wondered, "Where am I?" Sometimes the disorientation is more profound. "Who is the person sleeping next to me?" "Who am I, anyway?" When such *depersonalization* happens—most commonly following fatigue, travel, or drinking—it usually wears off in a few seconds or minutes, and knowledge of our identity returns. But for others it is different. Such a loss of memory about identity sometimes occurs in people who have suffered a strong psychological trauma. It is then more profound, extends over a longer time, and is at the heart of the *dissociative disorders.* They are called "dissociative" because some area of memory is split off or dissociated from conscious awareness.

The dissociative disorders have much in common with our last topic, the somatoform disorders, particularly conversion. In conversion disorders, anxiety is not experienced by the victim; in fact, complete indifference is common. Rather, the symptom can be seen as a way to prevent underlying

In Alfred Hitchcock's film *Spellbound*, Gregory Peck plays an amnesic in the fugue state. He lost memory of his identity as a defense aganst unbearable guilt and anxiety.

anxiety from surfacing. So it is with dissociative disorders. For example, when an individual suddenly loses his memory following an unbearable trauma, he is not necessarily overtly anxious. Rather, theorists infer that the loss of memory allows him to escape from intolerable anxiety brought on by the trauma.

We will discuss two dissociative disorders: *psychogenic amnesia,* a sudden loss of memory caused by severe trauma, such as the death of a child or the dashing of a career; and *multiple personality,* in which two or more distinct personalities exist within the same individual and each leads a rather full life.

PSYCHOGENIC AMNESIA

A case of amnesia

Timmy was fifteen years old and attending high school in upstate New York. He was teased mercilessly by his fellow students and was doing poorly in his schoolwork. In addition, he fought constantly with his parents. He was very upset about his problems, and it seemed to him that they had become absolutely insoluble. One spring afternoon, he went home from school extremely distressed and threw his books down on the porch in disgust.

At that moment, Timmy became a victim of amnesia. This was his last memory for a year, and we will never know exactly what happened next. The next thing we know with certainty is that a year later, a young soldier was admitted to an army hospital after a year of military service. He had severe stomach cramps and convulsions of no apparent physical origin. The following morning, he was better, calm and mentally clear. Astonishingly, he was at a total loss to explain where he was or how he got there. He asked how he came to be in the hospital, what town he was in, and who the people around him were. He was Timmy, all right, awake and in a military hospital with his last memory that of throwing his books down on the porch in disgust. Timmy's father was phoned, and he corroborated the story. At his father's request, Timmy was discharged from the service as underage. (Adapted from Laughlin, 1967, pp. 862–63.)

Timmy was the victim of amnesia (the loss of memory of one's identity). As in many cases of amnesia, Timmy wandered and took up a new life by joining the army. Such unexpected travel away from home during amnesia is called a *fugue state,* from the Latin *fuga,* meaning flight. Timmy's loss of memory and fugue are understandable as a flight from intolerable anxiety caused by his problems at home and at school. Timmy adopted the most extreme defense against a painful situation: he became amnesic, not only for the situation, but for his very identity, and he took up a new identity. By becoming amnesic, he was able to escape from his anxiety. During his army life he remembered nothing about his previous painful life and following recovery of his earlier memories, he was totally amnesic for his year in the army.

KINDS OF PSYCHOGENIC AMNESIA

Kinds of amnesia

What happened to Timmy was a *global* or *generalized amnesia:* all the details of his personal life had vanished when he joined the army. Amnesia can be less global than this. *Retrograde amnesia* is a more localized amnesia, in which all events immediately before some trauma are forgotten. For example, an uninjured survivor of an automobile accident may be unable to re-call anything that happened during the twenty-four hours up to and including the accident that killed the rest of her family. Somewhat rarer is *anterograde amnesia,* in which all events *after* the trauma are forgotten. Fi-nally, there exists *selective* or *categorical amnesia,* in which only events re-lated to a particular theme vanish (Hirst, 1982).

PSYCHOGENIC VERSUS ORGANIC AMNESIA

Distinguishing
psychogenic from
organic amnesia

Amnesia can also be caused by physical trauma, such as a blow to the head or a gunshot wound to the brain, alcoholism, Alzheimer's disease, and stroke (see Chapter 17). Such organically caused amnesia should be distin-guished from psychogenic amnesia. Aside from its physical basis, organic amnesia differs from psychogenic amnesia in several ways. First, a psycho-genic amnesic is usually sorely troubled by marital, financial, or career stress before the amnesia, whereas an individual who suffers organic amne-sia need not be. Second, psychogenic amnesia resembles glove anesthesia—it does not result from any known neural damage.

Pattern of
memory loss

A psychogenic amnesic shows a four-fold pattern of memory loss that no organic amnesic has ever shown. First, a psychogenic amnesic loses his past, both recent and remote—he cannot remember how many brothers and sis-ters he has; he cannot remember a well-learned fact from the distant past, nor can he remember the recent episode of what he had for breakfast right before the amnesia started. Organic amnesics, on the other hand, remember the distant past well—after a blow on the head, they can tell you perfectly well who taught them Sunday school when they were six years old, or the starting lineup of the 1948 Dodgers—but they remember the recent past poorly. Second, an individual with psychogenic amnesia loses his personal identity—name, address, occupation, and the like—but his store of general knowledge remains intact. He still remembers who the President is, what the date is, and what the capital of Saskatchewan is (Regina). Organic am-nesics, in contrast, tend to lose both personal and general knowledge.

Third, psychogenic amnesics have no anterograde loss; they remember well events that happen after the moment amnesia starts. In contrast, or-ganic amnesics have severe anterograde amnesia and this is their primary symptom; they remember very little about episodes that happen after the organic damage (like the name of the doctor treating them for the blow on the head). Finally, psychogenic amnesia often reverses abruptly. Psycho-genic amnesia often ends within a few hours or days, and within twenty-four hours of the return of his memory the individual may even recall the trau-matic episode that set off the memory loss. In organic amnesia, memory only gradually returns for retrograde memories and hardly ever returns for anterograde memories following organic treatment, and memory of trauma is never revived (Suarez and Pittlick, 1976).

VULNERABILITY AND CAUSES OF PSYCHOGENIC AMNESIA

Only a few other facts about psychogenic amnesia are known, and they tell us a bit more about vulnerability to this disorder. Psychogenic amnesia and fugue states are rare disorders in peacetime, but in times of war and natural disaster they are much more common. They apparently occur in men more than in women and in younger people more than in old people.

Causes of
psychogenic
amnesia

The cause of psychogenic amnesia is a mystery, more shrouded even than the causes of the somatoform disorders, which it resembles. We can speculate on how it might be caused, however. If we take the symptoms of conversion at face value, we assume that the mind sometimes can deal with emotionally distressing conflicts by producing physical losses. So, Bear, anxious and guilty about causing his friend's paralysis, converts his distress into his own paralysis. We do not know the mechanism of this conversion, but whatever it is, it might also be working in the amnesic. What happens when a vulnerable individual faces an even more traumatic conflict, such as occurs during war? What happens when one's physical existence is suddenly threatened, or when one's entire life plans are shattered? Enormous anxiety should be generated. Perhaps we have one ultimate psychological escape hatch—to forget who we are and thereby neutralize our anxiety about our death, our shattered future, or our insoluble problems. Both the psychoanalytic model and behavioral model are compatible with this explanation. For the psychoanalyst, the painful memory of who we are is repressed, and this defends successfully against anxiety. For the behaviorist, anxiety reduction reinforces the symptom of taking on a new identity. In short, amnesia may be the most global of defenses against anxiety produced by very traumatic and unacceptable circumstances.

We will now take up the final disorder in this chapter, multiple personality, in which amnesia plays a major role. Here it will be quite clear that the multiple personalities and their attendant amnesia for each other function to minimize unbearable anxiety.

MULTIPLE PERSONALITY

Defining multiple
personality

Multiple personality is defined as the occurrence of two or more personalities in the same individual, each of which is sufficiently integrated to have a relatively stable life of its own and to recurrently take full control of the person's behavior (Taylor and Martin, 1944; DSM-III-R). It is as astonishing a form of psychopathology as exists. Multiple personality used to be thought of as a very rare disorder—only 200 cases had been reported—but now that clinicians are looking for it, much more of it seems to be around. One researcher, Eugene Bliss, has seen 14 cases of it in the recent past, just in Utah (Bliss, 1980; Bliss and Jeppsen, 1985), and 100 recent cases have been reviewed by one group (Putnam, Guroff, and Silberman et al., 1986).

Bliss's first introduction to multiple personality occurred in 1978 when he received a call from a distressed supervisor of nurses at a Salt Lake City hospital. The supervisor suspected that one of her nurses had been secretly injecting herself with Demerol. The supervisor and Bliss called the nurse into the office and accused her of improper conduct. They asked the nurse to roll up her sleeves because they wanted to examine her arms for needlemarks. The nurse complied, and the telltale marks were there. But in the process of complying, the nurse underwent a remarkable transformation. Her facial expression, her manner, and her voice all changed, claiming that she was not Lois, the demure nurse, but Lucy, the brazen drug addict. Almost everyone has heard of other famous multiple personalities, as in "The Three Faces of Eve" (Thigpen and Cleckley, 1954), Sybil (Schreiber, 1974), or Dr. Jekyll and Mr. Hyde. Among the more recent cases is that of Julie-Jenny-Jerrie (Davis and Osherson, 1977):

Chris Sizemore, on whose life the film *The Three Faces of Eve* is based, is a well-known multiple personality. Here the real Chris Sizemore is shown next to her own painting that shows the coexistence of her three personalities.

A case of multiple personality

Julie came to therapy through her son, Adam, age nine, who had been referred for counseling because of very poor school performance, poor relations with peers, and aggressive behavior at home. Eventually it was decided to see his thirty-six-year-old mother, Julie, in hope that she could help in the therapeutic process.

Julie was highly cooperative, sophisticated, and concerned about Adam. She seemed to have a good understanding of herself, and her general style of solving interpersonal problems was discussion and compromise. She felt that she had trouble setting limits for her son, and she worried that she sometimes behaved too rigidly toward him.

During a session in the sixth week of discussions with Julie, she suddenly announced that she wanted to introduce someone to the therapist. The therapist assumed there was someone out in the waiting room, but to his astonishment he witnessed the following: Julie closed her eyes for a few seconds, frowned, and then raised her eyelids slowly. Putting out her cigarette, she said, "I wish Julie would stop smoking. I hate the taste of tobacco." She intoduced herself as Jerrie, and later in the hour and in the same way, she introduced Jenny, yet a third personality.

Jenny revealed that she was the original personality and said that she created Jerrie at age three and subsequently created Julie at age eight. Both times Jenny created the new personalities to cope with her disturbed family life. Jerrie emerged as the outer personality when Jenny was recovering from a severe case of measles, and Jerrie became a buffer who allowed Jenny to keep her distance from seven rejecting siblings and two frightening parents. Jenny said that observing Jerrie was like observing a character in a play.

Between the ages of three and eight, Jenny remembers that her physical welfare was neglected, that she was sexually molested by a neighbor, and was given away for permanent adoption at age eight, with her parents telling her she was "incorrigible." At this time, Jenny created Julie, a gentle personality who was better able to cope with rejection and not as vulnerable to cruelty as either Jerrie or Jenny. Remarkably, while Julie was allowed to know about Jenny, the original personality, Julie was kept unaware of the existence of Jerrie. Julie did not find out about Jerrie until age thirty-four, two years before therapy began.

At age eighteen, Julie-Jenny-Jerrie left home for good. Jerrie and Julie by this time were always the alternating outer personalities, and Jenny was always inside. In fact, Jenny had been "out" only twice since age seven. At age twenty-six, Jerrie married, and the couple adopted Adam, who was the husband's son by a woman with whom he was having an affair while he and Jerrie were married. Jerrie soon divorced him, but she kept Adam.

The three personalities were strikingly different. Jenny—the original—was a frightened person, very shy and vulnerable. She was the most insecure and child-like of the three and felt "exposed" whenever she was out. Jenny felt she had created two Frankensteins who were now out of her control. She liked Julie better, but she was put off by Julie's stubbornness and strong individuality. She felt Jerrie was tougher than Julie and better able to cope with the world, but she didn't like her as well. Jenny's main hope in therapy was that Julie and Jerrie would come to get along better with each other and therefore be better mothers to Adam.

Julie seemed to be the most integrated of the three personalities. Julie was heterosexual, and emotionally invested in being a good mother—this in spite of the fact that it was Jerrie who had adopted Adam.

Jerrie was the opposite of Julie. Jerrie was homosexual, dressed in masculine fashion, sophisticated, and sure of herself. She was accomplished and proficient in the business world, and she enjoyed it. Jerrie didn't smoke, whereas Julie was a heavy smoker, and Jerrie's blood pressure was a consistent twenty points higher than Julie's.

Jerrie had known about Julie since Julie was "born" at age eight, but she had been in touch with her only in the past two years. She wanted to have nothing to do with Julie because she was afraid Julie would have a mental breakdown. Julie and Jerrie did not get along. When one of them was out and having a good time, she would resist relinquishing her position. But when a crisis was at hand, the personality who was out would duck in, leaving the inner personality to face the problem. For example, Julie took LSD and then let Jerrie out so that Jerrie would be the victim of the hallucinations.

Ultimately Jerrie was able to tell Adam that there were two personalities who had been contributing to his misery, and Adam's immediate response was amusement and curiosity. He was able to accept the explanation that "Mother is two people who keep going in and out, but both of them love me." Adam appeared relieved rather than disturbed. Soon thereafter, Jerrie terminated therapy. Julie, in a suicidal depression, had gotten herself admitted to a state hospital against Jerrie's will, but Jerrie had gained control and talked her way out of the hospital. Julie wrote the therapist that she wanted to come to therapy, but Jerrie would not allow it and refused to come anymore. And this was the last that was seen of Julie-Jenny-Jerrie. (Adapted from Davis and Osherson, 1977.)

Parts of the day missing

This fascinating case exemplifies much of what is known about multiple personality. Amnesia of some kind or other almost always exists. It is common for one of the personalities to be aware of the experience of the other personalities (Jenny knew of both Julie and Jerrie, and Jerrie knew of Julie), and for one of the personalities to be amnesic about the others (Julie did not know of Jerrie). The presence of unexplained amnesia—hours or days each week that are missing—is a clue to the undetected presence of multiple personality.

There is a personality who says, "I just have fun. I go out with the kids and drink beer." The patient, who had been instructed to listen, comments, "So that is the reason why I wake up drunk in the morning with terrible headaches." (Bliss, 1980)

Differences
among the
various
personalities

In the history of multiple personalities, the several personalities within an individual—like Julie-Jenny-Jerrie—differ along many dimensions. Not only do they differ in their memories, but also in their wishes, attitudes, interests, learning ability, knowledge, morals, sexual orientation, age, rate of speech, personality test scores, and physiological indices such as heart rate, blood pressure, and EEG (Lester, 1977). Remarkably, women with multiple personality report that they menstruate much of the month because each personality has her own cycle (Jens and Evans, 1983). For unknown reasons, most cases of multiple personality are women.

The personalities also differ in psychological health. Often, the dominant personality is the healthier personality. One patient, a proper Southern lady, was publicly accused of wanton sexuality, including sexual intercourse with strangers. She made a clumsy attempt at a self-induced abortion, but she could not remember it. Her submerged personality said, "I did it because I suspected a pregnancy. I took a sharp stick and shoved it inside, then I started to bleed badly" (Bliss, 1980). The dominant personality, however, is not always the healthiest, and the submerged personality may actually sympathize with the unhealthy dominant personality and try to help. In one case, the submerged personality wrote to the dominant personality giving her helpful information to try to make her healthier (Taylor and Martin, 1944).

MULTIPLE PERSONALITY AND SCHIZOPHRENIA

Multiple
personality not
schizophrenia

Multiple personality is commonly confused with schizophrenia by the layperson. This is because "schizophrenia" is mistakenly thought to refer to a "split personality." Schizophrenia actually refers to one mental process, such as emotion, being split off from another, such as judgment, rather than to the splitting of one entire personality from another. Schizophrenia, as we will see in Chapter 12, is characterized by incoherence of speech and thought, hallucinations, delusions, and blunted or inappropriate emotion, along with deterioration in work, social relationships, and self-care. The individual with multiple personalities, on the other hand, may show none of these symptoms. Multiple personality is diagnosed merely by the existence of two or more coherent and well-developed personalities in the same person. While some schizophrenics may have multiple personalities as well, and some individuals with multiple personality may be schizophrenic, the two disorders are distinct.

THE ETIOLOGY OF MULTIPLE PERSONALITY

Early trauma,
susceptibility to
self-hypnosis,
escape from
emotional
problems

Where does multiple personality come from? The fourteen cases of multiple personality, all seen by Bliss, share some important common features, and provide us with some clues as to how multiple personality begins and how it develops. Bliss's hypothesis about how multiple personality proceeds has three steps. First, an individual between ages four and six experiences a traumatic emotional problem. Indeed, multiple personality has much in common with post-traumatic stress disorder (Spiegel, 1984), and the rate of child abuse experienced by those who develop multiple personalities may be as high as 97 percent (Putnam, Guroff, and Silberman et al., 1986). She copes with the trauma by creating another personality to take the brunt of the problem. Second, the individual is particularly vulnerable because she is

A sample of the handwriting of a patient with multiple personality. When one of the person's personalities dominates the individual's consciousness, the handwriting changes. Here each of seventeen personalities, as identified by their names, has written a message in a different handwriting.

highly susceptible to self-hypnosis, a process by which one is able to put oneself at will into trance states that have the properties of formal hypnotic inductions. Third, the individual finds out that creating another personality by self-hypnosis relieves her of her emotional burden, so that in the future, when she confronts other emotional problems, she creates new personalities to take the brunt.

There is some evidence for each of these three steps. First, all fourteen of the patients that Bliss saw did, in fact, create their first alternative personality between the ages of four and six, and each seemed to be created in order to cope with very difficult emotional circumstances. Roberta, for example, created the first of her eighteen personalities when her mother held her under water and tried to drown her. This personality had the purpose of controlling and feeling Roberta's anger and of handling Roberta's homicidal rage without Roberta's having to do so. Another patient was molested at age four by an adult man; she created her first alternative personality in order to handle the molestation and thereafter used this personality to handle all sexual encounters.

Second, there is evidence that these patients are extraordinarily good at self-hypnosis. All fourteen of Bliss's patients were excellent hypnotic subjects. When Bliss hypnotized them, they went rapidly into a trance on the first induction. During the hypnosis, when he instructed them to have amnesia for what happened during hypnosis, they did this as well. In addition, when these patients reported the way in which they created the personalities, they described a process that sounds like hypnotic induction. One of the personalities of a patient said, "She creates personalities by blocking everything from her head, mentally relaxes, concentrates very hard and wishes." Another said, "She lies down, but can do it sitting up, concentrates very hard, clears her mind, blocks everything out and then wishes for the person, but she isn't aware of what she is doing." Once these patients were introduced to formal hypnosis in therapy, most reported that this experience was identical to experiences they had had dating back to their childhood, and that an inordinate amount of their lives had been spent in this altered state of consciousness. One patient said, "I spent an awful lot of time in hypnosis when I was young. . . . I've always lived in a dream world. Now that I know what hypnosis is, I can say that I was in a trance often. There was a little place where I could sit, close my eyes and imagine, until I felt very relaxed, just like hypnosis—and it could be very deep."

Third, patients used new personalities to defend against distress later in life. Jenny, you will recall, created Julie, a gentle personality, to cope with her parents' putting her up for adoption at age eight. Most of the patients reported instances in which they created new personalities to cope with new stresses even when they were adults.

In short, multiple personality may come about in the following way: An individual, who is particularly good at self-hypnosis, confronts a serious trauma while a young child. She copes with this by producing a second personality to endure the trauma, rather than enduring it herself. She finds out that this tactic relieves her of emotional stress and, in the future, when she confronts new problems, she creates new personalities to bear them.

PSYCHOTHERAPY FOR MULTIPLE PERSONALITY

Confronting the problem

As in the case of Julie-Jenny-Jerrie, the treatment of patients with multiple personalities is difficult and frustrating. The first step is to make the patient aware of the problem. Although she may have lived in this strange state for many years, had amnesias, and been told by others about her bizarre behavior, she may not yet have confronted the fact of other personalities.

Under hypnosis, the therapist calls up the alter-egos and allows them to speak freely. In addition, the patient herself is asked to listen and then is introduced to some of these personalities. She is told to remember the experience when she emerges from hypnosis. Enormous distress and turmoil often follow this discovery, but it is important for her to keep hold of the facts of many personalities. At this point, she may display one of the most troublesome problems for therapy—dodging back into a self-hypnotic state and so avoiding the unpleasant reality. The therapist may then try to enlist the aid of various personalities (Kluft, 1987).

After the patient is made fully aware of her many personalities, the therapist explains to her that they are products of self-hypnosis induced at an early age and without any conscious or malicious intent. The patient is told

Improvement with therapy

that now she is an adult, strong and capable, and that if she has the courage, she can flush these specters out and defeat them. The other personalities may object, or want to continue their own life, but she is the only real person here. There is only one body and one head, and the other personalities are her creations. She will have the privilege of deciding what aspects of the personalities she will retain. In a study of thirty-four patients treated by an experienced therapist, 94 percent apparently showed strong improvement, with a two-year follow-up (Kluft, 1987).

Overall, the, multiple personality, like somatoform disorders and amnesia, can be seen as an attempt to defend against intolerable emotional distress. A child of four to six who is unusually capable of self-hypnosis creates a new personality—an imaginary companion and ally—to help her deal with the anxiety generated by a traumatic experience. This innocent, childhood ploy inadvertently becomes an adult disaster as the patient repeatedly uses this technique to cope with the stresses she encounters as she grows up.

FAKING MULTIPLE PERSONALITY: THE HILLSIDE STRANGLER

As much as there is evidence for the existence and treatment of multiple personality, there can also be abuses of and faking of the symptoms of this disorder. Consider the case of the Hillside Strangler.

> Ten attractive young females were murdered, and some of their bodies were left conspicuously displayed on Los Angeles hillsides during the winter of 1977–78. A year later, two similar murders took place in Bellingham, Washington, and Kenneth Bianchi was arrested. Bianchi claimed that he was totally ignorant of what had happened, and he insisted he was innocent. During the next six weeks, he reported a number of alibis, which could not be confirmed. Upon psychiatric examination, it was suggested that hypnosis be used to break through his "shell" of defenses.
>
> Under hypnosis, a new personality, Steve, appeared. Steve took credit for the murders and described them in detail. Steve displayed pleasure in "fixing" Ken and showed no remorse. Ken claimed to be ignorant of Steve's existence.

Was Bianchi really a multiple personality, and therefore perhaps not guilty of murder by reason of insanity (see Chapter 18)? Or had Bianchi made up Steve in an attempt to fake multiple personality?

Leading experts on the dissociative disorders and hypnosis were brought in, among them Martin Orne of the University of Pennsylvania. They argued that Bianchi was faking, on four grounds: (1) Steve's personality changed over time. Early on Steve was polite, passive, and unaggressive. Later he became abusive and aggressive. Multiples, it was argued, show stable patterns, particularly when the personality has existed for nineteen years. (2) When it was suggested to Ken that "real" multiples have three or more personalities, not just two, a new one, nine-year-old "Billy" appeared. (3) When real multiple personality exists, it is noticed by many others and for a long time. Adam, Julie-Jenny-Jerrie's son, could have corroborated the existence of two distinct personalities in his mother. But there was no external corroboration of Steve's existence. (4) Most interestingly, it appeared that Bianchi was simulating hypnosis, rather than being in a deep trance. There are some striking differences between simulators and those in a trance, and Bianchi had the characteristics of a simulator. For example,

Kenneth Bianchi, known as the Hillside Strangler, was determined by experts to be faking multiple personality.

Bianchi shook hands with a hallucination that he was induced to have, and he did not engage in trance logic during hypnotically induced anesthesia.

The experts argued that Bianchi was simulating multiple personality, but that he did warrant the diagnosis of antisocial personality disorder with sexual sadism, a diagnosis that does not excuse crime in the state of California. The court agreed (after Orne, Dinges, and Orne, 1984; Spanos, Weekes, and Bertrand, 1985).

DSM-III-R AND THE NEUROSES

Relation of "neuroses" and DSM-III-R categories

In this chapter and Chapter 8, we have examined disorders that appear, on the surface, to be quite varied: phobia, post-traumatic stress disorder, panic disorder, generalized anxiety disorder, obsessions, somatoform disorders, amnesia, and multiple personality. In the past, these disorders looked more like a coherent whole than they do today. Historically, they were all viewed as "neuroses," and all were thought to involve anxiety as the central process. In the case of phobia and post-traumatic stress disorder, fear is on the surface; in panic disorder and generalized anxiety disorder, anxiety (fear without a specific object) is also on the surface. The individual with one of these problems feels anxiety, apprehension, fear, terror, and dread in his daily life. In obsessive-compulsive disorders, on the other hand, anxiety is sometimes felt, but not if the compulsion is frequent and effective. In contrast, in the somatoform disorders and the dissociative disorders, anxiety is not usually observed. But in order to explain the bizarre symptoms of these disorders, theorists have inferred that, with his symptoms, the individual is defending against underlying anxiety. To the extent that the defense is successful, the symptoms will appear, and anxiety will not be felt.

The last fifteen years have witnessed a sea change in the field of psychopathology: our categories have become more descriptive and less theoretical. DSM-III-R disavows a common process—defending against anxiety—as the mechanism of these disorders. The dissociative disorders and somatoform disorders no longer fall under the larger class "Anxiety Disorders" in DSM-III-R, which includes as anxiety disorders only those disorders in which anxiety is observed: phobia, panic disorder, generalized anxiety disorder, post-traumatic stress disorder, and obsessive-compulsive disorder. Descriptively it makes good sense to segregate those disorders in which anxiety is observed from those in which anxiety is only inferred by a theory. But at a theoretical level, these disorders cry out for a common explanation.

For phobia and post-traumatic stress disorder, theories that come out of behavioral models seem appropriate, as in both of these disorders we can postulate a trauma that imbued parts of the environment with terror, and the symptoms, the course, and the therapies roughly follow known behavioral laws. Obsessive-compulsive disorder is not as easy to handle in this way. How obsessions stay around once they have been acquired fits reasonably well within behavioral views, as do therapies that alleviate obsessions. But this is only part of the story. The questions of who is vulnerable to obsessions and what content obsessions will take are not answered by the behavioral school, nor is there even a useful theory from this tradition. These questions may be best viewed within a psychodynamic tradition, in which emotional distress lurks beneath the surface. Finally, we have somatoform disorders, psychogenic amnesia, and multiple personality. Here theories of surface anxiety are useless, nor does there exist an adequate behavioral theory of these three disorders. Anxiety, or some other dysphoric emotion that lies beneath the surface and is being defended against, seems to make more sense of the symptoms of these disorders, but the details of their etiology and which therapy is best for them remain a mystery.

Overall, then, we find that when fear and anxiety are on the surface, behavioral models serve us well. As fear and anxiety tend to disappear from the surface, however, we find ourselves in need of models to attempt to explain what we do observe. It seems likely that for the present we still need, at least for disorders like conversion, amnesia, and multiple personality, theories such as the psychodynamic model, which postulates deep, unobserved emotional conflict and psychological defenses that are so rich as to still inspire awe in those who study these disorders closely.

SUMMARY

1. This chapter examined the disorders in which anxiety is inferred to exist as opposed to being observed. Three kinds of disorders were considered: obsessive-compulsive disorders, somatoform disorders, and dissociative disorders.

2. *Obsessive-compulsive disorders* consist of *obsessions,* which are repetitive thoughts, images, or impulses that invade consciousness, are often abhorrent, and are very difficult to dismiss or control. In addition, most obsessions are associated with *compulsions,* which are repetitive, stereotyped, and unwanted actions to undo the obsession. Compulsions can be resisted only with difficulty.

3. The content of obsessions has changed over history. In past centuries, they were mostly religious and sexual; now they are concerned mostly with dirt and contamination, violence, and orderliness.

4. An obsessive-compulsive individual displays anxiety when his or her rituals are blocked. In addition, depression is associated with this disorder. When such an individual is depressed, obsessions occur much more frequently. Moreover, such individuals are more prone to depression than the normal population. There is no personality type that seems predisposed to obsessive-compulsive disorders, but the brain metabolism of people with obsessive-compulsive disorders may be disturbed in specific areas. Individuals who are obsessive-compulsive in their daily life and concerned with order are not more vulnerable to the obsessive-compulsive disorder. What distinguishes these individuals from individuals with the disorder is that individuals with the obsessive-compulsive personality are proud of their meticulousness and love of detail, whereas individuals who have the disorder are tormented by their symptoms.

5. Cognitive-behavioral theory explains why the disorder and its rituals are maintained. The theory claims that individuals with the disorder are unable to habituate, dismiss, and distract themselves from disturbing thoughts. Behavior therapies for obsessive-compulsive disorders include

flooding, forcing the patient to endure the aversive situation, *response blocking,* preventing the individual from engaging in the ritual, and *modeling,* watching another person refrain from the ritual. These therapies bring about marked improvement in about two-thirds of the patients with obsessive-compulsive disorders.

6. Psychoanalytic theory explains who is vulnerable to the disorder and why it has the particular content it does. It claims that the obsessive thought is a *defense* against an even more unwelcome unconscious thought. The anxiety the unconscious thought arouses is displaced onto a less unwelcome substitute, which symbolically stands for the underlying conflict.

7. The *somatoform disorders* have five symptoms: (1) lost or altered physical functioning, (2) the absence of a known physical cause, (3) positive evidence that psychological factors have caused the symptom, (4) indifference to the physical loss, and (5) the absence of voluntary control over the symptom.

8. The three kinds of somatoform disorders are (1) *conversion,* in which one physical function is lost or altered, (2) *somatization disorder,* in which there is a dramatic and complicated medical history for multiple and recurrent bodily complaints in many organs, although the symptoms are not physically caused, and (3) *somatoform pain disorder,* in which pain is not attributed to physical cause, and which is the most common somatoform disorder today. Somatoform disorders should be distinguished from malingering, secondary gain, psychosomatic disorders, and undiagnosed physical illness.

9. Psychoanalytic theory holds that somatoform disorders are a defense against anxiety, that psychic energy is transmuted into somatic loss, and that the particular somatic loss symbolizes the underlying conflict.

10. The *dissociative disorders* involve the symptoms of *depersonalization* and a *loss of memory* about identity. In these disorders, some area of memory is split off or dissociated from conscious awareness.

11. *Psychogenic amnesia* is a sudden loss of memory caused by unbearable trauma and can either be general or highly specific. *Retrograde amnesia* is a specific amnesia in which events immediately *before* some trauma are forgotten. *Anterograde amnesia* is an amnesia in which events *after* a trauma are forgotten.

12. *Multiple personality* is the existence of two or more personalities in the same individual, each personality being sufficiently integrated to have a relatively stable life of its own and recurrently to take full control over the person's behavior. This disorder is more frequent than previously believed and seems to involve individuals who are highly susceptible to self-hypnosis, who experience a serious emotional problem between ages four and six, and who use the creation of alternative personalities to bear this trauma, which they are unable to cope with in any other way.

Health Psychology and Psychosomatic Disorders

DOES what we think and what we feel change our physical well-being? We have learned from our discussion of emotion in the last two chapters that our thoughts and emotions can modify how our body reacts. One of our bodily reactions is, of course, disease, and we do not usually think of physical disease—stomach ulcers, coronary heart disease, cancer, tuberculosis, asthma—as reactions that can be influenced by thoughts and feelings. But there is a good deal of evidence that the course, and perhaps the very occurrence, of such illnesses can be influenced by the psychological states of their victims. Such a disorder is called a ***psychosomatic disorder*** and is defined as a disorder of the body (the soma) that is influenced by, or in the strongest case, caused by the mind (the psyche). The field that deals with these disorders stands at the border of psychology and medicine, and is now called **health psychology** (Stone, Weiss, Matarazzo, Miller, Rodin, Belar, Follick, and Singer, 1987).

Psychosomatic disorders defined

We will present an overview of psychosomatic disorders, followed by a close look at two such problems: peptic ulcers and coronary heart disease. We will then look at a newly emerging field, ***psychoneuroimmunology (PNI),*** which investigates how mental state and behavior influence the immune system and disease. Finally, we will distill the principles used to analyze these examples by discussing various theoretical approaches to psychosomatics. We begin with a striking example of psychosomatic phenomenon on the skin: stigmata.

STIGMATA

One of the most dramatic examples of psychosomatic disorder is the rare phenomenon of ***stigmata.*** Stigmata are marks on the skin—usually bleeding or bruises—often of high religious or personal significance, brought on by an emotional state. About 300 instances of stigmata, many of them called miracles, have been reported in the last 2,000 years. Most are found in religious histories, but only a handful of these are documented well enough to take seriously scientifically. This handful provides the quintessential demonstration of a psychosomatic phenomenon: a mental state causing the body to react in a way usually thought of as being purely physical. Consider the following case history:

A case of stigmata

Since childhood, Steven had suffered from nightmares and sleepwalking. His sleepwalking became a particular problem when, in 1935, he was hospitalized because of an infection. To prevent him from sleepwalking about the ward in the middle of the night, he was restrained physically while he slept; his hands were tightly bound behind his back when he went to sleep. On one such occasion he awoke, and in a half-conscious state, found himself tied down. Although he could not untie his hands, he was still able to evade his bodyguard and escape into the surrounding countryside, from which he returned a few hours later.

Some ten years later, at age thirty-five, Steven was again admitted to a hospital —this time in an attempt to cure his recurrent sleepwalking. One evening at about midnight the nurse saw him struggling violently on his bed, apparently having a nightmare. He was holding his hands behind his back and seemed to be trying to free them from some imaginary bond. After carrying on in this way for about an hour, he crept out of bed still holding his hands behind his back, and disappeared into the hospital grounds. He returned twenty minutes later in a state of normal consciousness. As the nurse put him into bed, she noted deep weals like rope marks on each arm, but until then Steven seemed unaware of their presence. The next day the marks were still visible and were observed by the hospital staff. Three nights later the marks had disappeared.

His physician believed that the marks were stigmata caused by reliving the traumatic event of a decade earlier. To test this, he caused Steven to relive the experience of ten years before under a hypnotic drug. While reliving the experience, Steven writhed violently on the couch for about three-quarters of an hour. After a few minutes weals appeared on both forearms. Gradually these became deeply indented and finally blood appeared along their course. Next morning the marks were still clearly visible (see Figure 10-1). (Moody, 1946)

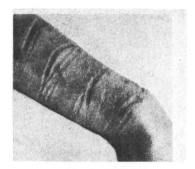

Figure 10-1
Steven's right forearm shows indented weals, resembling rope marks. They appeared in the course of reliving an earlier traumatic experience, which occurred while Steven was under an hypnotic drug. (Source: Moody, 1946)

Here is a clear example of an essentially psychosomatic phenomenon. A process that we usually believe to be strictly physical—the appearance of rope marks and bleeding—is induced by the mental state of recalling a traumatic incident with high emotion. The patient was carefully observed during the development of the rope marks, and there is no ready explanation other than an emotional state influencing a physical state.

AN OVERVIEW OF PSYCHOSOMATIC DISORDERS

It is already clear that psychosomatic illness may take a bizarre form. In the case of Steven, there is little doubt of the existence of a psychosomatic disorder. But what about those cases where there is less dramatic evidence? Many believe that some ulcers, heart attacks, and other physical problems are partly caused by an adverse psychological state. But how does a clinician know this, and when there is evidence, how does he or she classify it?

Criteria for
diagnosing
psychosomatic
disorders

The diagnosis of psychosomatic disorder is made if (1) there is a disorder of known physical pathology present, *and* (2) psychologically meaningful events preceded and are judged to contribute to the onset or worsening of the disorder. The diagnosis is contained in DSM-III-R's name for these disorders "psychological factors affecting physical condition."

The first criterion distinguishes psychosomatic disorders from somatoform disorders. Conversion, psychogenic amnesia, and the like have no known physical basis, whereas psychosomatic disorders do. Bear's paralysis was not accompanied by any physical damage to his nerves or spinal cord, whereas an individual whose peptic ulcer flares up every time he is criticized by his boss (which meets the second criterion) has actual physical damage to the lining of his gastrointestinal system. By these criteria, Steven's forearm weals are a clear case of psychosomatic disorder, since symptoms of known physical pathology are present—rope marks and bleeding—and a psychologically traumatic incident—being bound while asleep—preceded these symptoms.

The diathesis-
stress model

These two defining criteria of psychosomatic disorder have been incorporated into a particular model: *the diathesis-stress model.* "Diathesis" refers to the constitutional weakness that underlies the physical pathology, and "stress" to the psychological reaction to meaningful events. According to this model, an individual develops a psychosomatic disorder when he both has some physical vulnerability (diathesis) and experiences psychological disturbance (stress). If an individual is extremely weak constitutionally, very little stress will be needed to trigger the illness; if, on the other hand, extreme stress occurs, even individuals who are constitutionally strong may fall ill. In effect, the model suggests that individuals who develop peptic ulcers are both constitutionally vulnerable to gastrointestinal problems and experience sufficient stress to trigger the pathology.

Psychological factors can affect many physical conditions in a large number of organ systems: the skin, the skeletal-musculature, the respiratory, the cardiovascular, the blood and lymphatic, the gastrointestinal, the genito-urinary, the endocrine systems, or the sense organs (Looncy, Lipp, and Spitzer, 1978). There is no evidence, however, that the process causing psychosomatic effects is different for each different organ, although any given individual may be especially vulnerable to psychosomatic influence in only one organ system. Some of us react to stress with the stomach, others by sweating, some by muscle tension, and still others with a racing heart.

PEPTIC ULCERS

A *peptic ulcer* is a circumscribed erosion of the mucous membrane of the stomach or of the duodenum, the upper portion of the small intestine. Such ulcers are called "peptic" because it is commonly thought that they are at least partially caused by pepsin, which is contained in the acidic juices normally secreted by the stomach. There are two sorts of peptic ulcers named by their location: a stomach (gastric) ulcer and a duodenal ulcer.

Roughly two million people in the United States today have a peptic ulcer, and about five thousand people die of peptic ulcer each year in the

United States (Center for Disease Control, 1982). We begin our discussion of psychosomatic disorders with the peptic ulcers because they are so widespread and because much is known, both about the physical pathology underlying ulcers and about psychological influence on their development and course. Carlos's gastrointestinal problems illustrate the ways in which environmental stress influences peptic ulcers.

A case of peptic ulcer

Carlos has had an ulcer for the last seventeen years. Until recently he had it under control; for whenever he experienced gastric pain, drinking a quart of milk or eating eggs would relieve it. Three years ago he was promoted to manager of a major department store and moved from his home town to a distant city. Since he took on this increased responsibility, he has experienced severe ulcer pain.

He had been born and raised in a small New England town. His father was wealthy and the head of a chain of department stores. Although his father was in general dominating and intolerant (and also had an ulcer), he was kind and generous to Carlos. After graduation from college Carlos entered the department store business and even now, at age forty-one, he feels incapable of holding a job without his father's intervention, influence, and support.

As soon as Carlos took over the management of the store, he became tense and anxious and began to brood over trivial details. He was afraid the store would catch fire; he was afraid that there would be bookkeeping errors that he might not catch; he was afraid the store would not make a big profit. Convinced he was a complete failure, and plagued with severe pains from his duodenal ulcer, he entered psychotherapy. During these sessions, Carlos and his therapist learned how much the psychological factors in his life contributed to the worsening of the ulcer. The following three incidents particularly illustrate this.

First, on a day when the store was full of people a large ventilating fan broke. The store began to shake as the customers rushed to the street, and Carlos went into a panic. As soon as the excitement subsided and his panic diminished, severe ulcer pains started.

Second, Carlos's mother had for many years complained of a "heart condition." While his mother's physician had never isolated a physical cause, Carlos nevertheless worried about it. One day Carlos saw a hearse pass in front of the store. Immediately he thought that his mother had died and in panic ran several miles to her home finding her quite alive. As he started to run the stomach pains broke out, and these pains remained until he saw his mother was not ill.

Third, one night Carlos's store burned to the ground. He was highly anxious that he would be found negligent during the ensuing insurance investigation. As he awaited the results of the inquiry, his wife called and told him that his daughter had broken a leg. He ran home and found his wife in tears, and he immediately developed severe stomach pains.

Before he had become manager of the store he had occasionally had stomach pains while on the job, but he had found a technique for reliably and immediately alleviating them: he would go to an older person for comfort. Upon being reassured by an authority figure, his ulcer pain would disappear. In his new job, however, he was the authority figure, there was no one to turn to, and his ulcer pains persisted, unrelieved. (Adapted from Weisman, 1956.)

Symptoms of Peptic Ulcer

Abdominal pain as main symptom

Carlos suffered the main symptom of peptic ulcer: abdominal pain. Such abdominal pain can vary from mild discomfort to severe and penetrating, extreme pain. Pain may be steady, aching, and gnawing, or it may be sharp and cramp-like. Pain is usually not present before breakfast; it generally starts from one to four hours after meals. Bland foods and antacids usually alleviate the pain and peppery food, alcohol, and aspirin usually intensify it (Lachman, 1972; Weiner, 1977). Peptic ulcers that become very serious sometimes perforate or bleed. Without well-timed surgery, a perforated ulcer can lead to death from internal bleeding.

PHYSIOLOGICAL DEVELOPMENT OF AN ULCER

How an ulcer is formed

In order to understand how these symptoms come to be, we must first take a brief look at the actions of the digestive system. Digestion breaks down food in the stomach so that when the food passes through the intestines, the appropriate materials can be absorbed for use by the body. In order to digest food, the stomach secretes two highly corrosive juices: hydrochloric acid, which breaks food down, and pepsin, which decomposes protein. Why, you might wonder, does the stomach not digest itself? Fortunately, the stomach and the small intestine are lined with a mucous membrane that protects them from corrosion by the hydrochloric acid the stomach secretes. In addition, gastric juices are normally secreted only when there is food in the stomach to absorb most of the corrosive acid. But sometimes the system develops a problem. A break may occur in the mucous coating of the stomach or duodenum. Such a break may occur when some of the thin lining is worn away in the normal course of digestion. It may also occur when an overdose of aspirin, particularly in combination with alcohol, is ingested, or when naturally secreted bile attacks the membrane. If a break occurs in the absence of too much gastric juice, it will repair itself and no ulcer will form, since cell growth completely renews the stomach lining every three days (Davenport, 1972). If an excess of hydrochloric acid or pepsin is around, however, particularly when food is not in the stomach, the abrasion will worsen and an ulcer will form.

WHO IS SUSCEPTIBLE TO ULCERS?

Constitutional weakness for ulcers

The way an ulcer develops gives us clues about what diathesis, or constitutional weakness, makes ulcers more likely. Individuals who secrete excess hydrochloric acid or pepsin, individuals with an especially weak mucous defense against acid, and individuals whose stomach lining regenerates slowly may generally be more susceptible to ulcers. This condition may be genetically inherited.

The prevalence of peptic ulcer varies widely from country to country, and from decade to decade. Today, approximately 1 percent of the adult American population has an ulcer, and almost four hundred thousand Americans are hospitalized yearly for peptic ulcers. The frequency of peptic ulcers has, for unexplained reasons, declined by about 25 percent over the last decade in the U.S. and Europe (McConnell, 1966; Lachman, 1972; Weiner, 1977; Elashoff and Grossman, 1980).

Ulcers in men and women

The susceptibility of women versus men seems to have undergone a major change over the past 100 years. Before 1900, peptic ulcers occurred more frequently in women than in men, but in the beginning of the twentieth century a shift occurred, with men becoming considerably more ulcer prone. By the late 1950s, men had 3.5 times as many duodenal ulcers as women (Watkins, 1960). In recent years the male/female ratio has been changing (Elashoff and Grossman, 1980). By 1978, men had only 1.2 times as many peptic ulcers as women in America. Ulcers in men had become less frequent and ulcers in women had either stayed the same or slightly increased (Sturdevant, 1976).

Ulcers and social class

Social class also influences the incidence of ulcers. For a time it was commonly believed that highly pressured, upwardly mobile and professionally successful individuals develop the most ulcers. But in fact many patients with peptic ulcer are now poor and wholly unsuccessful, and those presently at highest risk for peptic ulcer are in the lower classes (Susser, 1967; Langman, 1974).

Age does not make much of a difference beyond the age of twenty. Children probably have ulcers less frequently than adults. Among children, girls have peptic ulcers about twice as frequently as boys (Christodoulou, Gergoulas, Paploukas, Marinopoulou, and Sideris, 1977; Medley, 1978).

Genetic basis for ulcers

Ulcers clearly run in families. The relatives of patients with duodenal and gastric ulcers are about three times as likely to have an ulcer as those in the general population (McConnell, 1966). Further, healthy individuals who have relatives with peptic ulcers secrete more gastric juice than individuals without relatives with ulcers (Fodor, Vestea, and Urcan, 1968). This increased susceptibility in families could either be genetic or environmental, since family members share many of the same stresses, as well as genes. But twin data suggest it is genetic. If one of two identical twins has a peptic ulcer, the chances are 54 out of 100 that the co-twin will also have a peptic ulcer; whereas if one of two fraternal twins has a peptic ulcer, there is only a 17 percent chance that the co-twin will also have peptic ulcer (Eberhard, 1968).

Here then is the foundation of the diathesis in the diathesis-stress model of peptic ulcers. How much acid and pepsin the stomach secretes contributes to the formation of an ulcer. High acid and pepsin secretion runs in families and may be the constitutional weakness that makes individuals more susceptible to ulcers (Mirsky, 1958).

PSYCHOLOGICAL FACTORS INFLUENCING PEPTIC ULCERS

Stress and ulcers

To what extent does stress influence the development or worsening of peptic ulcers? When individuals who have a constitutional weakness of the intestinal system—such as hereditary oversecretion of acid—encounter certain kinds of stress, peptic ulcers may result. By "stress" researchers refer to the reaction of an individual to disturbing events in the environment. A stress reaction can either be a short-term emotional reaction induced by a specific situation, or it can be a long-term pattern of such emotional reactions, adding up to an ulcer-prone personality. We turn first to the evidence that emotional states influence peptic ulcer, and then we examine the possibility that individuals who have a certain personality pattern of reacting to stress are ulcer prone.

GASTRIC SECRETION, PEPTIC ULCER, AND EMOTIONAL STATES

Emotions and gastric secretions

Let us now take a look at the evidence that emotional states affect gastric secretion. Two researchers were afforded a rare opportunity to study directly the effects of anxiety and depression on digestion when they discov-

Anxiety on the job, such as overwork, may influence the development of peptic ulcers.

ered a man who, because of a childhood experience, was forced to feed himself through a hole in his stomach.

> Tom was a fifty-seven-year-old workman who at age seven swallowed some very hot soup, which so burnt his esophagus that it had to be surgically sealed off. After many unsuccessful attempts at corrective surgery, Tom had to resort to feeding himself by chewing his food (to satisfy his taste) and then depositing the food directly into his stomach using a funnel and a rubber tube. He was secretive about this for many years, but when he was in his fifties, Tom allowed himself to be experimented upon. Investigators directly examined his gastric secretions under different emotional conditions. When Tom was anxious, angry, or resentful, gastric secretions increased. When he was sad, his gastric secretions decreased. (Wolff, 1965)

In another study, thirteen patients with ulcers and thirteen normal subjects were interviewed under emotion-provoking conditions. The patients with ulcers showed a greater secretion of hydrochloric acid in the stomach and more stomach motility than the patients without ulcers (Mittelmann, Wolff, and Scharf, 1942). Findings with normal individuals under hypnosis also confirmed that gastric secretions are influenced by emotion. Hypnotically induced thoughts of anger and anxiety produced high gastric secretion, while thoughts of depression, helplessness, and hopelessness produced low secretion (Kehoe and Ironside, 1963).

High-anxiety occupations and ulcers

High rates of peptic ulcers were found in people in occupations that produce high anxiety. For example, air traffic controllers have twice the ulcer rate of matched control groups, and those controllers who work at towers with much traffic have twice the ulcer rate of those who work at towers with less traffic (Cobb and Rose, 1973). We must be cautious, however, about this correlation between occupation and ulcers. It could be that ulcer-prone individuals, for some reason, choose anxiety-provoking jobs. If this is the case, it need not be the anxiety of the job that causes the ulcer.

The evidence presented above does suggest that emotional states like anxiety and anger cause excess stomach acid; this in turn, contributes to the development of peptic ulcers. Also, certain anxiety-producing occupations

Air traffic controllers have a high incidence of peptic ulcers.

may lead to more employees with stomach ulcers. Here again, greater anxiety produces excess acid in the stomach. This latter point fits in with Carlos's story narrated earlier. Like many individuals with ulcers, Carlos's ulcer worsened and caused more pain after emotional crises. When he was anxious, needed reassurance, and felt excessive demands for responsibility, his ulcer flared up. When he allowed himself to be dependent, his ulcer was inactive.

ANIMAL MODELS OF PEPTIC ULCER

Some investigators have shed light on the relation between emotional states and ulcers by studying animals. In doing so, they have put animals in conditions that change the emotional state of the animal. We will look at three such situations: conflict, unpredictability, and uncontrollability. All of these factors increase anxiety.

Avoidance-approach conflict and ulcers

□ CONFLICT. Can "conflict" be aroused in a rat in order to find out whether or not conflict produces ulcers? One way to bring about conflict is to make a hungry rat run through shock in order to get food. This is called an "avoidance-approach" conflict. In one experiment, one group of rats was required to cross a shock grid in order to obtain food and water for forty-seven out of forty-eight hour cycles. During one hour, the grid was not electrified so that the animals could have sufficient water and food. Six of nine rats in this group developed ulcers, whereas none of the comparison group rats did. Control groups with shock alone, food and water deprivation alone, or nothing got fewer ulcers. So avoidance-approach conflict is more likely to produce stomach ulcers than is electric shock, hunger, or thirst without conflict (Sawrey, Conger, and Turrell, 1956; Sawrey and Weiss, 1956). Therefore conflict, a psychological state that produces anxiety, can engender ulcers in rats.

□ UNPREDICTABILITY. When noxious events are experienced by an individual, they can either be signaled, and therefore predictable, or unsignaled, and therefore unpredictable. For example, the rockets that fell on London in World War II were signaled by an air raid siren. But when a concentration camp guard arbitrarily singled out a prisoner for a beating, this was entirely unsignaled. There is considerable evidence, both in rats and humans, that when noxious events are signaled, individuals are terrified during the signal. But they also learn that when the signal is not on, the noxious event does not occur, so they are safe and can relax. Also if something can be done, a signal allows a person to prepare for the bad event. In contrast, when the identical noxious event occurs without a signal, individuals are afraid all the time because they have no signal of safety that tells them they can relax (Seligman and Binik, 1977). Since oversecretion of gastric juices occurs during anxiety and more anxiety occurs with unpredictability, we might expect that more ulcers would occur as well. It has been found that they do.

In one study, investigators took two groups of rats and deprived them of food. Each group received occasional brief electric shocks. For one group, the shocks were predictable: each shock was preceded by a tone or a light. Another group of rats received exactly the same shocks and at the same times, but they had no signal to tell them when shock would occur and

This farmer may lose his farm if he cannot pay his mortgage because the drought has affected his harvest. The unpredictability and uncontrollability of the weather and rain may make him prone to ulcers, particularly if he has a constitutional vulnerability.

Those who work on the Mercantile Exchange may feel that there is little they can do to protect their jobs if economic panic sets in; they too may be prone to ulcers particularly if they have a constitutional vulnerability.

therefore no absence of signal to tell them when they were safe. More of the rats who received unpredictable shock formed ulcers, and the ulcers they formed were larger than those in the predictable shock group. Being in the presence of chronic anxiety—as produced by unpredictable shock—causes ulcers in rats (Seligman, 1968; Weiss, 1968).

□ UNCONTROLLABILITY.   When noxious events occur, sometimes you can do something about them, but at other times you are helpless. So, for example, being a victim of lung cancer is at least partly controllable; you can take action to avoid lung cancer by not smoking cigarettes. Losing your job during a national depression, however, is quite uncontrollable. There is very little you can do to protect your job once economic panic has set in and most of your colleagues are being fired. More precisely, an event is *uncontrollable* when no response an individual can make will change the probability of the event. An event is *controllable* when at least one response the individual has in his repertoire can change the probability of the event. Which produces more ulcers, controllable or uncontrollable dangers?

The executive monkey study

In 1958, a study now known as the "executive monkey" study was performed. (See Chapter 6, where we discussed this study in the context of the confound of nonrandom assignment). Eight monkeys were given occasional electric shocks. Four of them could avoid the shocks by pressing a lever. The other four received exactly the same shocks as their four executive partners, but they were helpless; no response that they made would affect whether or not they were shocked; only their executive partners' actions made any difference. The monkeys could not see or hear each other. The executives in each of the four pairs developed duodenal ulcers and died; their helpless partners remained healthy (Brady, 1958). The conclusion from this study was that having control over threat would cause ulcers. The moral was that executives, or others in a position of great responsibility, would be more prone to ulcers than their employees.

This study was widely publicized, and for years many believed it was valid. It is, however, an artifact. When experimenters in the 1960s had trouble replicating it, the details of the procedure were scrutinized. As it turned out, the eight monkeys had not been randomly assigned to the executive group. The four monkeys who probably had been the most emotionally

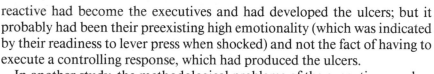

Table 10-1 MEDIAN NUMBER OF ULCERS AND WHEEL TURNS

	Ulcers	Wheel Turns
Escape Groups		
Signaled	2.0	3,717
Unsignaled	3.5	13,992
Yoked, Inescapable Groups		
Signaled	3.5	1,404
Unsignaled	6.0	4,357
No Shock Groups		
Signaled	1.0	60
Unsignaled	1.0	51

SOURCE: Adapted from Weiss, 1971.

Uncontrollable life events like losing one's job can be a factor in the development of psychosomatic problems. This automobile worker was laid off during a recession through no fault of his own.

Uncontrollability, inescapable shock, and ulcers

reactive had become the executives and had developed the ulcers; but it probably had been their preexisting high emotionality (which was indicated by their readiness to lever press when shocked) and not the fact of having to execute a controlling response, which had produced the ulcers.

In another study, the methodological problems of the executive monkey study were avoided and the opposite results were obtained. Rats were divided into six groups. Two of the groups received escapable shock, shock they could turn off by rotating a wheel in front of them. Two of the groups were "yoked." They received exactly the same pattern of shock, but it was inescapable—no response they made affected the shock; it went on and off for them at the same time as for their "executive" partners in the "escapable" group. Two of the groups received no shock. Within each of these groups, shock was either signaled or unsignaled. In this experiment, then, both the controllability and predictability of the shock were varied. The rats were assigned to these six groups randomly, thereby distributing any preexisting emotionality equally among the groups (Weiss, 1971).

As can be seen from Table 10-1, two basic findings emerged. First, unpredictability leads to ulcers—the rats developed more ulcers when they were subjected to unsignaled than to signaled shock, whether or not they could escape it. Second, uncontrollability leads to ulcers—rats who received inescapable shock developed more ulcers than rats who could escape shock, whether or not the shock was signaled.

What are we to conclude from this and other animal studies? First of all, it seems clear that the "executives" were actually less likely to develop ulcers. Second, this and other studies set up three conditions—conflict, unpredictability, and uncontrollability—that produce anxiety, and eventually a greater number of ulcers. Research on how humans react in parallel situations continues. Indeed our environment may well be constructed in a way to produce ulcers in some individuals. Other researchers, however, have looked elsewhere for the cause of ulcers, to the dynamics of personality.

PERSONALITY AND SUSCEPTIBILITY TO PEPTIC ULCER

In 1950, the psychoanalyst Franz Alexander formulated the most influential statement of the ulcer-prone personality (Alexander, 1950). Based on his observations of his ulcer patients, mostly men from upper-middle-class backgrounds, Alexander postulated that an unconscious conflict of dependence versus independence predisposes an individual to ulcers. He claimed that the ulcer patient has a deep-seated wish to be loved and nurtured like an infant. But at the same time, these motives give rise to shame and guilt and are rejected by the adult ego. To avoid displaying the oral motives of an infant, which he considers shameful, the ulcer-prone person puts on a mask of exaggerated self-sufficiency and "pseudoindependence." He is characterized by driving ambition and inappropriate displays of strength. When his dependency wishes are rearoused, the conflict is intensified with gastric hypersecretion worsening the symptoms. For example, Alexander would consider Carlos, from our earlier case study, as having an ulcer-prone personality, for when the fire breaks out in Carlos's store, his need for nurturance by his father is evoked and his ulcer pain is exacerbated.

Alexander's formulation contains three parts: (1) the predisposition—pseudoindependent defenses against the need to be dependent, (2) the conditions for exacerbation—the rearousal of the oral-dependency conflict, and (3) a physiological mechanism—gastric hypersecretion brought on by this conflict (Alexander, 1950; Weiner, 1977).

This formulation has received some experimental support. A group of specialists in internal medicine and a group of psychoanalysts were asked to diagnose which psychosomatic illnesses were suffered by a group of patients. The judges had to do this on the basis only of edited interviews that omitted all reference to the patients' psychosomatic symptoms. Each of the eighty-three patients had one of the seven "classic" psychosomatic illnesses (arthritis, ulcer, high blood pressure, dermatitis, ulcerative colitis, asthma, and thyroid oversecretion). The judges were asked to pick out which ones had the ulcers using Alexander's characterization of the ulcer-prone personality. Eighteen of the patients actually had ulcers. The group of psychoanalysts correctly picked out 50 percent of the men but only 16 percent of the women who had ulcers. The group specializing in internal medicine made a successful diagnosis of 40 percent of the men and 10 percent of the women. Chance guessing would have gotten 14 percent (one out of seven) right. This indicates that Alexander's formulations may separate the ulcer-prone man from men who have other psychosomatic disorders but that his theory does not work for women (Alexander, French, and Pollack, 1968). So far, these remain tentative findings, for more studies are needed to clarify exactly what might be an ulcer-prone personality.

TREATMENT OF PEPTIC ULCERS

In times past, peptic ulcers were treated primarily by giving patients antacid drugs in an attempt to lower stomach acidity. In addition, bland diets that restricted intake of foods that stimulate hydrochloric acid secretion were recommended to patients. Smoking, drinking alcohol, and drinking coffee or tea were also restricted. About half of the ulcers usually healed under such a regimen. In the late 1970s, a new drug—cimetidine—came into use. Cimetidine reduces stomach acid by about two-thirds, and it produces healing in 70 to 95 percent of patients with peptic ulcers in a few months. It is now clearly the treatment of choice for peptic ulcer (Bardhan, 1980).

Psychological treatments of ulcers are less well charted. Rest, relaxation, anxiety management, and removal from the external sources of psychological stress are often prescribed for ulcer patients, and there is at least strong

Conflict of dependence vs. independence

Cimetidine as treatment

Psychological treatment

clinical evidence that these are effective. Psychoanalytic therapy has been reported to be effective with ulcer patients, but the appropriate controlled studies have yet to be done (Orgel, 1985).

Biofeedback

Some individuals without ulcers can learn to control their level of gastric acid secretion voluntarily by using biofeedback about their gastric acid secretion (Welgan, 1974). But it has yet to be demonstrated that patients who actually have ulcers can learn voluntary control over gastric acid secretion or that this will alleviate their peptic ulcers.

To summarize, peptic ulcers are best viewed within a diathesis-stress model. A peptic ulcer is caused when gastric juice that is naturally secreted in the stomach eats a hole into the protective mucous membrane of the stomach or the duodenum. This erosion is the ulcer. Three kinds of constitutional weaknesses or "diatheses," can make an individual prone to ulcers: (1) an oversecretion of gastric juices, which may be genetically inherited; (2) a weak mucous membrane; and (3) a stomach lining that regenerates slowly. Psychological factors can also influence the formation of a peptic ulcer in individuals who have such a diathesis. There is evidence that emotional states, particularly anxiety, cause oversecretion of acid in the stomach. In addition, there is further experimental evidence that rats who experience anxiety when placed in conflict, in the presence of unpredictable stressors, or in the presence of uncontrollable stressors develop peptic ulcers. This suggests that chronic or frequent anxiety may cause oversecretion of stomach acid which, in turn, may produce ulcers in individuals whose gastrointestinal system is genetically vulnerable.

CORONARY HEART DISEASE AND THE TYPE A PERSONALITY

In the last century, Sir William Osler (1849–1919), a famous Canadian physician, prefigured what was to be learned in our century about personality and heart attacks:

> A man who has early risen and late taken rest, who has eaten the bread of carefulness, striving for success in commercial, professional, or political life, after twenty-five or thirty years of incessant toil, reaches the point where he can say, perhaps with just satisfaction, "Soul, thou has much goods laid up for many years; take thine ease," all unconscious that the fell sergeant has already issued the warrant. (Osler, 1897)

Coronary heart disease (CHD) kills more people than any other disease in the Western world. In the United States, over half the deaths of individuals over forty-five are caused by some form of heart or circulatory problem (Lachman, 1972; Weiner, 1977). The underlying condition in most instances of heart attack and sudden death is *arteriosclerosis*, a building up of fat on the inner walls of the coronary arteries. Such clogging blocks blood from reaching heart muscle; heart attack and sudden death can result (Diamond, 1982).

Risk factors for CHD

Epidemiologists have thoroughly studied risk factors for CHD. There are six major physical risk factors: (1) growing old, (2) being male, (3) smoking cigarettes, (4) having high blood pressure, (5) having high serum cholesterol, and (6) physical inactivity. A psychological risk factor now joins the list: the Type A personality, which we will consider here.

DEFINING THE TYPE A PERSONALITY

Type A vs. Type B personalities

Type A personality was said to have been discovered by an upholsterer. When he came to reupholster the chairs in the office of a physician who specialized in seeing patients who had had heart attacks, he noticed that the chairs were worn in the front of the seat, not the back. Coronary-prone individuals, Type A's, sit on the edge of their chair (see Figure 10-2). They are defined by (1) an exaggerated sense of time urgency—deadlines are always with them, (2) competitiveness and ambition, and (3) aggressiveness and hostility, particularly when things get in their way. They contrast to ***Type B persons***, who are relaxed, serene, and have no sense of time urgency. When Type A's miss a bus, they become upset. When Type B's miss a bus, they say to themselves, "Why worry? There will always be another bus coming along." The Type A sees the environment as threatening, and seems to be engaged in prolonged emergency reactions. Type A characteristics may begin as early as three or four years old (Steinberg, 1986).

Figure 10-2
The Type A logo. A clenched fist holding a stopwatch indicates the Type A's exaggerated sense of time urgency.

Classifying individuals into Type A's and Type B's is done either by a standard stress interview or by a self-administered questionnaire (Jenkins, Rosenman, and Friedman, 1967; Glass, 1977). Typical questions are:

1. "Has your spouse or friend ever told you that you eat too fast?" Type A's say, "yes, often." Type B's say, "yes, once or twice" or "no."

2. "How would your spouse (or best friend) rate your general level of activity?" Type A's say, "too active, need to slow down." Type B's say, "too slow, should be more active."

3. "Do you ever set deadlines or quotas for yourself at work or at home?" Type A's say, "yes, once a week or more often." Type B's say, "no" or "only occasionally."

4. "When you are in the midst of doing a job and someone (not your boss) interrupts you, how do you feel inside?" Type A's say, "I really feel irritated because most such interruptions are unnecessary." Type B's say, "I feel O.K. because I work better after an occasional break."

TYPE A'S AT RISK FOR CHD

Studies of Type A's and CHD

Several excellent prospective studies exist of the Type A personality as a risk factor for CHD in the population at large:

• *The Western Collaborative Study.* Beginning in 1960, 3200 working men who had no history of CHD were followed for eight and a half years. Men who had been judged Type A by the structured interview had 2.2 times as much CHD as Type B's. When the physical risk factors were statistically controlled, Type A's still had double the risk for CHD (Rosenman, Brand, Jenkins, Friedman, Straus, and Wurm, 1975).

• *The Framingham Heart Study.* More than 1600 men and women, who were classified Type A or B by a questionnaire and who were free of any

CHD, were followed for eight years. White-collar Type A men had almost three times the risk for CHD as white-collar Type B's, and female Type A's had twice the risk as female Type B's (Haynes, Feinleib, and Kannel, 1980).

• *The Belgian Heart Disease Prevention Trial.* Two thousand men, having demonstrated good health by passing a strenuous exercise test, were rated along the Type A–B continuum and followed for five years. The upper third had 1.9 times the risk for CHD as the lower third (Kittel, Kornitzer, deBacker, and Dramaix, 1982).

Challenges to
Type A as risk for
CHD

The conclusion that Type A is a risk factor for CHD has not gone unchallenged. When the population at large is studied, as above, the relationship holds; but when the population is selected to be at high risk already or at low risk already, Type A does not predict CHD. In the Honolulu Heart Program study, 2200 Japanese-Americans, a low-risk group, were followed for eight years; this sample had only about half the incidence of heart attacks as a Caucasian sample. Type A did not predict increased risk here (Cohen and Reed, 1985). In the MRFIT (Multiple Risk Factor Intervention Trial), a very high-risk group was followed for seven years. These men were selected because they scored in the top 10 percent for risk, based on smoking, cholesterol, and blood pressure. Here, also, being Type A did not confer extra risk for CHD (Shekelle, Hulley, and Neaton et al., 1985).

TYPE A DISSECTED

Which factors of
Type A confer
risk for CHD

Type A confers extra risk for CHD in the general population. But Type A is a global and heterogeneous concept, including as it does hostility, aggressiveness, time urgency, competitiveness, and ambitiousness. In addition to these defining components, there are many factors that correlate with these components: People who are time urgent and ambitious might have more encounters with defeat, failure, and helplessness. People who are hostile and competitive might spend more time in the emergency reaction. Could it be that only one of the components, or a correlated factor, is the killer? We will examine two possibilities—hostility and helplessness—and then propose a third—more total emergency reaction—that seems to integrate the evidence.

HOSTILITY AND THE TYPE A

Hostility and
hypertension

Hostility and anger may be the killing components of Type A. It has long been suspected that high blood pressure, also called ***hypertension***, may be intimately related to hostility and to how we deal with our anger (Diamond, 1982). Psychodynamic theorists believe that dammed-up hostility underlies the hypertensive personality. Franz Alexander theorized that individuals with high blood pressure were struggling against their own aggressive impulses (Alexander, French, and Pollack, 1968). Later studies also suggested that hypertensives are particularly sensitive to hostility and respond with blood pressure elevation to threat in general and anger toward the threat in particular (Wolf, Cardon, Shepard, and Wolff, 1955; Kaplan, Gottschalk, Magliocco, Rohobit, and Ross, 1960). Other studies showed that opportunities to vent hostility lower blood pressure, and the failure to release hostility may keep blood pressure high (Hokanson, 1961; Hokanson and Burgess,

Hostility and anger may lead to hypertension, although the opportunity to vent hostility may lower blood pressure.

Hostility and CHD

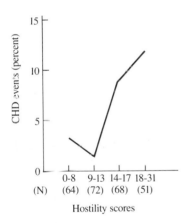

Figure 10-3
Hostility and coronary heart disease incidence (myocardial infarction or cardiac death) over a 25-year follow-up period in 255 physicians who took the MMPI during medical school. (Source: Barefoot et al., 1983)

1962; Hokanson, Willers, and Koropsak, 1968; Dimsdale, Pierce, Schoenfeld, Brown, Zusman, and Graham, 1986).

Two recent studies, both very long term, directly relate hostility to CHD. Two hundred and fifty-five physicians were given the MMPI in medical school and were followed for twenty-five years (see Figure 10-3). One component of the MMPI is the Cook-Medley hostility score (Cook and Medley, 1954). High hostility scores strongly predicted CHD (Barefoot, Dahlstrom, and Williams, 1983; Williams, Barefoot, and Shekelle, 1985). This relationship was replicated in the Western Electric Study of 1877 men followed for ten years; the high-hostility men had five times the incidence of CHD (Shekelle, Gale, Ostfeld, and Paul, 1983).

Similarly, the studies of the Type A personality seem to indicate that where hostility and anger exist and are not released in Type A's, there is more likelihood of CHD and heart attacks. In two of the prospective studies of Type A and CHD, separate analyses were done for different components of Type A. In the Western Collaborative Study, those men who had heart attacks had been judged at the outset to have had significantly more "potential for anger," more explosive voices, more irritation when waiting, and frequent outwardly directed anger. In the Framingham Study, Type A white-collar men who did not outwardly express anger and Type A women who did not discuss their anger had more CHD (Matthews and Haynes, 1986).

HELPLESSNESS AND THE TYPE A

Helplessness is not one of the defining components of the Type A personality, but it may correlate highly with it. People who are ambitious, competitive, and time urgent may get themselves into more situations that produce more frustration, failure, and helplessness, and they may react more strongly to helplessness than do Type B's.

The struggle for control

Type A individuals seem to be engaged in a lifelong struggle to control a world they see as threatening. David Glass suggests that it is this struggle for control that crucially distinguishes a Type A from a Type B personality.

The Type A personality is time urgent and dislikes being in such an uncontrollable situation as a traffic jam.

Inhibited need for power

Glass postulates that a cycle of desperate efforts to control the environment, alternating with giving up when the environment proves uncontrollable, is repeated over and over again during the lifetime of the Type A individual. This struggle may result in high blood pressure and other physiological changes that in turn cause heart attacks.

Glass has demonstrated that Type A's and Type B's show a different reaction to helplessness and that it is this reaction that may predispose them to CHD (see Chapter 11). Both Type A and Type B subjects are presented with cognitive problems that are unsolvable, and failure is made highly salient. Type A's response to this uncontrollable and highly stressful situation is twofold: (1) they respond to salient and stressful threats to their sense of control with desperate efforts to keep control, and (2) when they are forced into the recognition that they are helpless, their giving up is profound, and they fail to solve cognitive problems given later in the experiment. Type B individuals do not give up in such a profound way, and they end up solving more easily the solvable problems given later. This confirms Glass's suggestion that a life of attempting to control, then giving up, then trying all over again, may characterize Type A individuals and predispose them to CHD.

A second line of evidence comes from a study of "inhibited need for power" and hypertension. Seventy-eight Harvard juniors were tested in the late 1930s and early 1940s for high blood pressure and various personality characteristics. Ten years later, these individuals were given a projective test in which they told stores about five pictures from the TAT (see Chapter 7). The themes of the stories they told were used as indications of what their personality was like. Twenty years later, in the early 1970s, these men were tested for high blood pressure. The findings are remarkable.

The expression of need for power and need for affiliation was judged from their TAT stories. A person was scored as having a high need for power if his story contained a reference to having an impact on others by aggression, persuasion, and prestige. A person was scored as having a high need for affiliation if his story included being friendly with other people. Finally, a person was judged for the amount of "inhibition of the need for power" by the number of times the word "not" appeared in his stories. Those of particular theoretical interest were the men who had a high need for power (which was greater than their need for affiliation), but who showed high inhibition in their stories. Twenty-three of the men fell into this group at approximately age thirty. By the time these men were in their fifties, 61 percent had shown definite signs of hypertensive pathology, whereas only 23 percent of the remaining forty-seven men showed hypertensive pathology. These findings become even more remarkable when we realize that they are unrelated to the blood pressure of these men when they were in their thirties. In other words, at age thirty the need for power combined with its inhibition predicted that individuals would be at risk for severe high blood pressure at age fifty, irrespective of what their blood pressure was when they were thirty years old (McClelland, 1979). We can view the inhibited need for power as a sign of the repeated helplessness in these individuals' lives.

THE EMERGENCY REACTION AND TYPE A

There is one simple way to view the evidence on Type A, CHD, and hypertension. Consider the heart as a glorified pump. As a pump breaks after

Nursing might be considered a demanding and hectic job that has a low amount of choice; nurses may therefore be at increased risk for CHD.

Exercise lowers risk for CHD

some fixed number of uses, so the heart fails after it has exceeded its genetically allotted number of beats. The more beats you use up, the earlier your heart will fail. Being a Type A, continually viewing the world as a hostile and threatening place, will lead to the beats being used up earlier. We saw in Chapter 8 that when we are threatened we go into an emergency reaction that involves increased heart rate and increased blood pressure (Southard, Coates, Kolodner, Parker, Padgett, and Kennedy, 1986). Continuing threat leads to a **continual emergency reaction**. Perhaps the Type A views the world as a more threatening place than does the Type B. Such a view may lead the Type A to experience a sustained emergency reaction, which on average will use up his allotted beats more quickly.

Data on **overload** at work is compatible with this simple hypothesis (Jenkins, 1982). In the Western Collaborative Study, men who carried two jobs were at greater risk for CHD. In a particularly elegant analysis, job demand and decision latitude were related to CHD (Karasek, Baker, Marxer, Ahlbom, and Theorell, 1981). Among over 1500 Swedish workers, a hectic and demanding job increased the risk for CHD, as did low amount of choice (see Figure 10-4). We might infer from this that workers whose jobs create the most frequent emergency reactions (high demand, low choice) use up their beats faster than those with other kinds of jobs, and such workers are at greater CHD risk.

Finally, it is of considerable importance that physical activity and exercise lower the risk for CHD. In a review of forty-three studies, inactivity presented a consistent risk for CHD of about the same size as high blood pressure, smoking, or high cholesterol (Powell, Thompson, Caspersen, and Kendrick, 1987). The practical importance of this study is that in prevention programs, regular exercise should be promoted strongly. The theoretical importance concerns the emergency reaction: While vigorous exercise increases heart rate and blood pressure when you are engaged in it, its long-term consequences are to lower resting heart rate and blood pressure, thereby conserving the pump.

Figure 10-4
Prevalence of coronary heart disease. The risk for coronary heart disease is increased where job characteristics include high demands and low decision latitude. The vertical bars indicate the percent of people developing CHD according to whether their job characteristics include high, medium, or low job demands and high, medium, or low decision latitude. There was a grand total of 1621 men who at the beginning of the study in 1968 did not have CHD. The numbers in parentheses are the number of people in each subgroup, and the percentage is the percent of those people in the subgroup who developed symptoms of CHD over the six-year course of the study. (Adapted from Karasek, Baker, Marxer, Ahlbom, and Theorell, 1981)

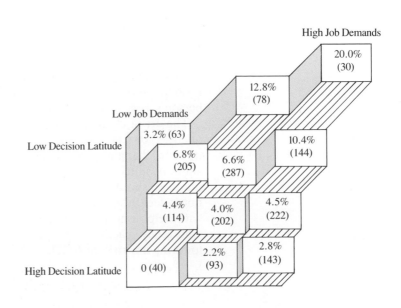

CHANGING TYPE A BEHAVIOR

There have been substantial developments in the understanding and treatment of cardiovascular diseases in the last twenty years: open heart surgery, heart transplants, anti-hypertensive drugs, and the like. But it is possible that scientific technology has reached an upper limit on what it can do to save our lives once we have developed CHD. Even if no further technological breakthroughs occur, vastly better health is still possible. We may be able to reduce our chances of dying from heart attack and stroke by making certain choices about how we live our lives, including not smoking cigarettes, exercising regularly, and changing Type A behavior.

Counseling to reduce Type A behavior

Can the Type A personality be changed? And if it is changed, will this lower the person's risk of heart disease? The answer to the first question is Yes. It has been shown that a person can exert voluntary control over Type A behavior. Eight hundred and sixty-two patients who had had a heart attack volunteered to be randomly assigned into one of two treatment groups: (1) a Type A counseling group of 592, and (2) a control group of 270 who received only group cardiological counseling. After three years, those in the Type A counseling group were engaged in fewer Type A behaviors (Friedman, Thoresen, and Gill et al., 1984). In a similar study, 118 senior officers of the U.S. Army were assigned to either Type A counseling or no counseling. At the end of nine months, a marked reduction in Type A behavior was seen in only 9 percent of the controls, but such behavior was markedly reduced in 42 percent of those expressly counseled (Gill, Price, Friedman Thoresen et al., 1985).

So a reduction of Type A behavior can be learned. But does it have an effect on CHD? The answer is a tentative "yes." In the first of the two studies above, the rate of recurrence of CHD in the Type A counseled group was 7 percent, significantly less than the rate of recurrence of 13 percent in the control group. Among the senior Army officers, cholesterol levels were lower for those who reduced their Type A behavior. The study was too brief to find any CHD differences.

Should a person try to change his Type A behavior? It is likely that Type A behavior has benefits, as well as costs. Being time urgent, competitive, and ambitious may well produce professional success in our society, and changing may produce better health but less success. Type A children get better grades than less competitive children (Matthews, Stoney, Rakaczky, and Jamison, 1986). But if being Type A causes coronary disease, then changing a person's Type A life-style may lower his risk of heart attack.

Lowering risk for CHD

The art of changing Type A behavior is at its beginning, and its consequences for CHD are still highly tentative. The present therapies concentrate on changing time urgency and competitiveness. But if the evidence about hostility, helplessness, and the emergency reaction is correct, changing these should become important parts of Type A counseling. Learning not to feel threatened by mildly provocative stimuli, learning how to cope with helplessness or better how to avoid it, and learning to turn off our emergency reactions when they are not adaptive may be central parts of lowering our risk for CHD.

PSYCHONEUROIMMUNOLOGY (PNI)

Psychological factors and the immune system

Psychological factors, in particular hostility and competitiveness, can thus increase the risk of coronary heart disease. Can psychological factors increase the risk of infectious disease, allergy, auto-immune disease, cancer, and even death? There is a new and rapidly expanding field of health psychology, called *psychoneuroimmunology (PNI),* which studies how psychological factors change the immune system and ultimately increase the risk for these immune-related diseases. The basic findings in this field are that personality, behavior, emotion, and cognition can all change the body's immune response, and thereby change risk for these diseases. The hope of this field is that psychotherapy can be used to prevent, and perhaps even to cure, such physical illnesses.

THE MIND-BODY PROBLEM

Sudden death

Researchers have hypothesized that psychological states can have profound effects on the body. An early example of this link between mind and body can be found when one examines the phenomenon of *sudden death,* in which the individual perceives the environment as threatening, but rather than mobilizing against the danger gives up.

This is the apparatus used by Curt Richter in his experiments on the phenomenon of sudden death. Richter found that the rats drowned within a few minutes of being placed in this apparatus, apparently of "hopelessness."

> In 1967 a distraught woman, pleading for help, entered the Baltimore City Hospital a few days before her 23rd birthday. She and two other girls, had been born of different mothers assisted by the same midwife in the Okefenokee Swamp on a Friday the 13th. The midwife cursed all three babies, saying one would die before her 16th birthday, another before her 21st birthday, and the third before her 23rd birthday. The first had died in a car crash during her 15th year; the second was accidentally shot to death in a nightclub fight on the evening of her 21st birthday. Now she, the third, waited in terror for her own death. The hospital somewhat skeptically admitted her for observation. The next morning two days before her 23rd birthday, she was found dead in her hospital bed—physical cause unknown. (Seligman, 1975, p. 5)

One sequence of events that could produce sudden death seems to be the following: (1) perceiving a strong threat to life followed by giving up and accepting one's fate, (2) a depressed, quiescent state; and (3) death.

THE EFFECTS OF HOPELESSNESS AND HELPLESSNESS

Carl Richter, an American psychologist, studied the phenomenon of sudden death in animals. Richter found that, on occasion, when he held a wild rat tightly it would die—right there, in his hand (Richter, 1957b). He hypothesized that when animals gave up in the face of threat and entered a state of hopelessness, they would die. To test this, he took wild rats and held them in his (chain-mailed) gloved hand until they stopped struggling. Then he put them in a vat of water three feet deep with a jet of water playing down on them to stop them from floating. The rats would swim for three to five minutes, then dive to the bottom and drown. In contrast, wild rats who had not been restrained in the experimenter's hand until they gave up would swim from sixty to eighty hours—vigorously trying to survive.

There were two findings that led Richter to believe that these were deaths from hopelessness. The first was that if he took the rat and held it in his hand until it stopped struggling, then released the rat "showing the rat there was hope," held the rat in his hand again, released it, then held it until it stopped struggling, and finally put it in the vat, the rat would swim for between sixty and eighty hours. Second, if he restrained the rat in his hand until it gave up, then put the rat in the water and waited three to five minutes until the rat started to go down, plucked it out, released it—again "showing it there was hope"—and then repeated the process several times, when the rat was finally placed in the water it would swim for sixty to eighty hours.

Two prospective studies indicate human susceptibility to pathogens following experiences of hopelessness and depression. Six months before an influenza epidemic swept an Army base, 600 employees had been given a battery of personality inventories. Twenty-six individuals came down with the flu during the epidemic; of these, 12 still had the flu three weeks later. These 12 individuals had been significantly more depressed six months earlier than the rest of the population, and as we shall see in Chapter 11, depression is intimately related to helplessness induced by giving up.

One of the most insidious of all illnesses influenced by psychological factors is cancer. There is mounting evidence that hopelessness may play a role in susceptibility to cancer. Fifty-one women who entered a Rochester, New York, clinic for a cancer test were interviewed upon arriving. Each of these women had previously shown suspicious cells in her cervix which might indicate cancer, but which could not definitely be diagnosed as cancer without further testing. The investigators found that eighteen of these fifty-one women had experienced significant losses in the last six months to which they reacted with feelings of hopelessness and helplessness. The others had experienced no such life event. Of the eighteen who had experienced hopelessness, eleven were found to have cancer. Of the other thirty-three, only eight had cancer. The difference between the two groups was statistically significant (Schmale and Iker, 1966). Similarly, lack of meaning in one's life, job instability, and no plans for the future predict who has lung cancer better than does the amount of smoking (Horne and Picard, 1979). Conversely, breast cancer patients who responded with a fighting spirit rather than stoic acceptance had a better chance of recurrence-free survival five years later (Greer, Morris, and Pettingale, 1979).

Loss of one's spouse by death can be an experience that engenders profound hopelessness. Following the death of their wives, 4,500 British widowers fifty-five years or older were identified from British records. During the first six months of their bereavement, 213 of them died. This is 40 percent more than the expected mortality for men of this age. Susceptibility to death during bereavement seems to be concentrated in the first six months, since the death rate returns to normal thereafter. Most of these men died from cardiac problems (Parkes, Benjamin, and Fitzgerald, 1969; Helsing, Szklo, and Comstock, 1981).

The structure of some institutions may promote helplessness and hopelessness on a massive scale. Consider patient care in nursing homes. When

Hopelessness increases human susceptibility to pathogens

Hopelessness and cancer

Individuals who lose what is most important to them may experience feelings of hopelessness and depression that may make them more susceptible to illnesses or environmental pathogens.

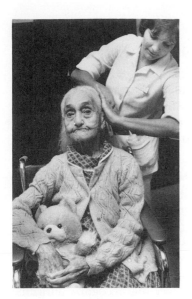

Those in a nursing home who have no choice or control over their life may give up and die.

we arrange care for the elderly, there is sometimes a tendency to try to do everything for them. On the one hand, this seems benevolent, but on the other hand, we end up taking all of their control away. By treating them as total patients, we undermine self-care (Bandura, 1982).

When we remove the last vestiges of control over the environment from human beings already weakened by age, we put them in a helpless situation, one without purpose. Some give up and die. Conversely, if we bring choice and control into geriatric wards, we may be able to prolong life. Ellen Langer and Judith Rodin divided nursing home residents of equal health into two groups. One group was given enhanced choice and control over small things at the nursing home. They were encouraged to decide how they would spend their own time, they were given the choice of what night to attend a movie, and they were given the opportunity to select a plant for their room and to take care of it themselves. Those in the comparison group were told about all the good things that were available to them, they were told on what day they would see a movie, and they were given a plant (no choice) and told that the nurse would care for it. The comparison group was treated very much like ordinary geriatric patients. Although they experienced some positive events, they exerted little or no control over their life. Eighteen months later, 30 percent of the comparison group (thirteen out of forty-four patients) had died, while only 15 percent (seven of forty-four patients) of the group that had control and responsibility had died. These differences were statistically significant (Langer and Rodin, 1976; Rodin and Langer, 1977).

THE EFFECT OF A PESSIMISTIC EXPLANATORY STYLE

*Pessimistic
explanatory style
and illness*

You will recall from Chapter 5 (pp. 122–24) that individuals who habitually see the causes of bad events as internal, stable, and global ("it's me," "it's going to last forever," "it's going to undermine everything") are said to have a pessimistic explanatory style. These individuals are at greater risk for helplessness and depression when they confront uncontrollable events, for their pessimistic explanatory style may amplify negative psychological states and increase risk for illness and death. What is the risk of having such a style for illness?

Infectious illness and number of doctor visits were counted for undergraduates who had either optimistic or pessimistic explanatory style. In the year following the test for explanatory style, pessimists had about twice as many infectious illnesses and made about twice as many visits to doctors as optimists (Peterson and Seligman, 1987). Survival from cancer may follow the same regularity. Thirty-four women who came to the National Cancer Institute with a second recurrence of breast cancer were followed for five years. The pessimists died sooner than the optimists, and their survival time was shorter even when the physical severity of the disease was controlled (Levy, Morrow, Bagley, and Lippman, 1989).

Taken over a lifetime, pessimists may suffer more illness and die younger. One new study points in this direction (Peterson, Seligman, and Vaillant, 1988). Five percent of the Harvard classes of 1939–1944 have been followed since leaving college. At age twenty-five, when they came back from World War II, they filled out open-ended questionnaires from which their explanatory style was determined. They have physical checkups every five years and are now in their late sixties. Pessimism at age twenty-five predicts poorer health beginning about age forty-five. The optimists remain in better health through middle age.

IMMUNOCOMPETENCE AND PSYCHOLOGICAL STATES

Given that the body is affected by psychological states, how can we explain the mind's effect on illness? Recent work postulates that the immune system is changed by psychological states. First, we will examine how the immune system works under optimal conditions, then we will go into the mechanisms whereby the immune system breaks down.

THE IMMUNE SYSTEM

The two tasks of the immune system

The immune system has two basic tasks. First it must recognize foreign invaders, called antigens, and then it must inactivate them and remove them from the body (Maier, Laudenslager, and Ryan, 1985; Borysenko, 1987). A group of cells, called lymphocytes, recognizes foreign cells. There are three main types of lymphocytes: B-cells (which come from bone marrow), T-cells (which come from the thymus gland), and Natural Killer (NK) cells. B-cells and T-cells have receptors on their surface that recognize antigens. This recognition is very specific, and any given lymphocyte recognizes only a small number of foreign invaders, so that at any time there are a large number of different lymphocytes surveying the body for different antigens.

What happens when antigens are spotted? They are destroyed in four main ways: First, the B-cells that are specific to that antigen multiply and produce antibodies. Antigens often simply bind to the antibody and form a complex that is inactive and can do no further harm. Second, some T-cells, once activated by recognizing their specific antigen, multiply rapidly and can directly kill their antigen by lysing (breaking down) the cell membrane of the target. Third, some T-cells attract macrophages (big eaters) and neutrophils. Macrophages eat the antigens, and neutrophils eat the antigen-antibody complexes. Fourth, when the antigen is a tumor, Natural Killer cells rapidly lyse the cells of the tumor.

It is important that the second time the body is challenged by a specific invader, the immune system does a better job of destroying it than it did the first time. This is called *immunologic memory.* The T-cells and B-cells that took on the antigen the first time will multiply more rapidly the second time this antigen is spotted. This memory is responsible for *immunization. Immunocompetence,* the degree to which these events proceed efficiently to protect the organism, is measured in several ways: assessing the amount of immunoglobulin (antibodies formed after immunization) in the blood or saliva, assessing the amount of T-cell multiplication when antigens are challenged, assessing the ability of Natural Killer cells to kill tumors, and measuring how much the skin reddens and swells when injected with an antigen (the greater the reaction, the better the immune system is working) through the delayed hypersensitivity test.

Measuring immuno-competence

LOWERED IMMUNOCOMPETENCE IN ANIMALS

Some of the most convincing evidence that psychological states can influence the immune system and illness comes from the animal laboratory. This

Animal models of
worsened immune
function

evidence suggests that experience with helplessness and hopelessness may weaken the immune system, making it less able to fight off illnesses successfully. Animal models of helplessness and hopelessness may allow us to investigate the way in which these experiences make us more susceptible to illness. Rats were implanted with tumors, and on the following day, they were divided into three groups. One group was given escapable shock—electric shock that the rats could turn off by bar pressing. A second group received exactly the same pattern of electric shock, but it went on and off independently of all the rats' actions; those in this group were helpless to turn off the shock. The third group was not shocked at all. How did such experience with helplessness affect the rejection of tumors? Fifty-five percent of the animals who were not shocked rejected the tumor, and 65 percent of the animals that received experience mastering electric shock rejected the tumor. Only 27 percent of the animals who received helplessness experience, however, rejected the tumor.

How might the state of helplessness make tumors grow faster and be rejected less? One possibility is that helplessness changes immunocompetence. When the T-cells taken from the blood of helpless rats are exposed to foreign substances, they multiply at a slower rate than T-cells from rats who had escapable shock or no shock at all. When Natural Killer cells from rats that had inescapable shock are set loose on tumor cells, they do not lyse the tumor cells as well as the NK cells from rats that had escapable shock or no shock (Sklar and Anisman, 1979; Visintainer, Volpicelli, and Seligman, 1982; Laudenslager, Ryan, Drugan, Hyson, and Maier, 1983; Maier, Laudenslager, and Ryan, 1985; Shavit and Martin, 1987).

LOWERED IMMUNOCOMPETENCE IN HUMANS

Human examples
of worsened
immune function

Evidence is accumulating that psychological states related to those that produce immune and disease changes in animals have similar effects in humans. Pessimistic explanatory style may lower immunocompetence as well as increasing helplessness in the face of bad events. The combination of a poorly functioning immune system and passivity (e.g., not seeking out medical care, not getting social support, allowing bad life events to overwhelm you) may lead to more illness.

There are several examples of how depression, helplessness, hopelessness, and stressful life events seem linked to immune change in people. Twenty-six spouses, whose mates had died, were followed for six weeks after the death of their spouses; the bereaved group showed depressed T-cell multiplication to antigens (Bartrop, Luckhurst, Lazarus, Kiloh, and Penny, 1977). The T-cells of senior citizens whose explanatory style had been assessed were challenged with antigens. Pessimists had poorer T-cell function than optimists (Kamen, Rodin, Seligman and Dwyer, 1988).

Natural Killer cell activity was lower in women who had recently experienced major life events like the death of their spouse; the more depressed the woman, the more both NK and T-cell functions were impaired (Irwin, Daniels, Bloom, Smith, and Weiner, 1987). Blood was drawn twice from seventy-five first-year medical students, one month before and then on the first day of final exams. NK activity was lower just at finals time; the more loneliness and the more stressful life events reported, the lower the NK activity (Kiecolt-Glaser, Garner, Speicher, Penn, Holliday, and Glaser, 1984; Kiecolt-Glaser and Glaser, 1987).

One hundred and thirty-three male prisoners were assessed for how strong their need for power was. The more stressful the life events they had experienced and the higher their need for power, the lower was the concentration of immunoglobulin in their saliva. These men also reported the most illnesses (McClelland, Alexander, and Marks, 1982).

Human immune changes in the laboratory

These studies indicate that depression, helplessness, hopelessness, and stressful life events can lower immunocompetence. Efforts are now underway in the laboratory to show that learned helplessness directly produces disruption in immune function in human volunteers. The prediction is that inescapable noise will lower the functioning of T-cells and heighten susceptibility to virally induced illness.

THE MIND-BODY PROBLEM RE-EXAMINED

The chain of events for lowered immuno-competence

At the beginning of this chapter we wondered how psychological states could influence physical illness. At this point, for at least one chain of events, we have arrived at a plausible route (see Figure 10-5). Consider how the experience of a loss might bring about cancer: (1) The individual whose husband has died perceives that she has lost something valuable. (2) She believes she is helpless to do anything about it, and if she has a pessimistic explanatory style she becomes severely depressed. (3) Depression and helplessness, as we will see in Chapter 11, are accompanied by depletion of catecholamines, a group of neurotransmitters in the brain, as well as an increase in endorphins, internal morphine-like substances that block pain. (4) The immune system has receptors for endorphins that may then lower immunocompetence. (5) If there are pathogens in the body, say the beginnings of a tumor in the uterus, NK cells and T-cells may be too inactivated to kill it. (6) A tumor that would ordinarily have been lysed in its early stages can now grow to life-threatening size.

Figure 10-5
The chain of events, leading from loss to cancer.

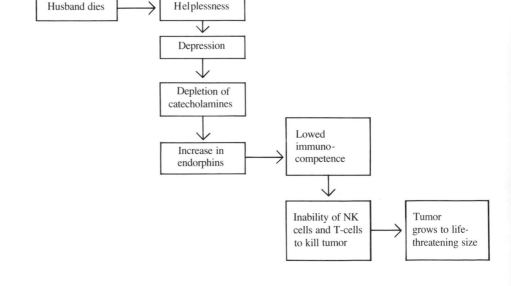

Implications for
prevention and
therapy

We do not know if this schema is correct, but there is now evidence for each stage of this chain. If such a chain illuminates how tragedy can make us physically ill, there are important implications for prevention and therapy. Procedures that intervene at each of the steps might prevent or even reverse such illnesses. So, for example, cognitive therapy might be used to prevent the perception of helplessness or the depressive response, thereby interrupting the chain. Or drug therapy that breaks the catecholamine-endorphin link or blocks the immune receptors to endorphin stimulation might also interrupt the chain. We believe the final decade of this century will see major advances in this area.

THEORIES OF PSYCHOSOMATIC ILLNESS

Four theories of
psychosomatic
illness

We have now had a detailed look at two physical problems that are influenced by psychological factors: stomach ulcers and coronary heart disease. In addition to these two, many other diseases are often thought to have psychosomatic components: migraine headaches, arthritis, chronic pain, and asthma, among others (see Box 10-1).

Let us now look at the different principles that recur through explanations of the cause and the alleviation of these psychosomatic disorders. There are four theories, and they correspond to four of the schools of abnormality: biomedical, psychodynamic, behavioral, and cognitive. All are compatible with the diathesis-stress perspective.

THE BIOMEDICAL MODEL OF PSYCHOSOMATIC DISORDERS

The biomedical model emphasizes the diathesis underlying psychosomatic illness. There are four components that fall under the biomedical view: genetic, specific organ vulnerability, evolutionary selection, and the general adaptation syndrome. These components do not all exclude one another, and most biomedical theorists emphasize more than one of them when explaining psychosomatic disorders.

GENETIC

High
concordance in
identical twins for
disorders

Is the predisposition to psychosomatic disorders genetically inherited? We have seen evidence that this is so for ulcers. If one identical twin has ulcers, then his co-twin is more likely to have ulcers than is the case between fraternal twins. All the genes of two identical twins are the same, but only half the genes of fraternal twins are the same. The higher concordance of identical twins is most likely explained by genetics, since the environment fraternal twins share is probably almost as similar as that of identical twins. Thus, similar oversecretion of gastric juices or weakness of the mucous membrane of the stomach, each producing similar vulnerability to ulcers, is probably what is inherited.

SPECIFIC ORGAN VULNERABILITY

Specific organ
reacts to stress

A variant of the genetic view holds that it is weakness in a specific organ that is inherited. That is, when an individual is stressed, the weakest link in his bodily chain snaps. The hypothesis that oversecretion of stomach acid is an

Box 10–1   ASTHMA IN CHILDREN AND FAMILY SEPARATION

Asthma is a condition in which the air passages of the bronchia narrow, swell, and secrete excess fluid to a variety of stimuli. This results in wheezing, which in its worst form can be severe and can produce a convulsive struggle for breath. Asthma can be caused by infection, by allergy, or by psychological factors. It has been estimated that each of these plays the dominant role in about a third of the cases (Weiner, 1977). Put differently, asthma stems from psychological sources in only a minority of cases. In this minority, the personal relations between parents and the asthmatic child have long been suspected to be the major source of psychological disturbance.

Anecdotes indicated that when European children with asthma were sent off by their parents to spas "to take the waters" they cheerfully ignored their parents' long lists of instructions, showed few signs of asthma, and seemed to be psychologically improved as well. To test the possibility that separation from parents might alleviate asthma, Dennis Purcell and his colleagues chose twenty-five chronically asthmatic school children who lived with their families (Purcell, Brady, Chai, Muser, Molk, Gordon, and Means, 1969). They divided these children into two groups —those in whom emotional factors had usually preceded past attacks of asthma at home, and those in whom emotional factors seemed irrelevant to the onset of past attacks. The first group was expected to benefit from separation, but not the second.

The parents and siblings were removed from the home and sent to a motel for two weeks, while the child continued to live in his home environment. A surrogate parent was provided, and the child continued normal attendance at school and normal play activities. After two weeks of not seeing their child, the parents returned to the home and life went on as usual.

As predicted, the effects were beneficial for the group suspected of emotionally induced asthma. Their medication during separation was reduced by half during daily physician checks, and on top of this the number of asthma attacks and amount of wheezing was reduced by half as well. When the parents returned, wheezing, number of attacks, and amount of necessary medication all increased. Beneficial effects of separation on asthma did not appear for the group in which emotional factors had been judged unimportant.

So, for some children, emotional factors are probably irrelevant to asthma. For others, however, family stresses may set off or worsen asthmatic attacks. In these cases, if the family members learn more effective and less stressful ways of dealing with each other, the child's asthma may get better.

---

inherited cause of ulcers is an instance of the specific organ vulnerability hypothesis. Organ specificity is confirmed by the fact that individuals tend to react to stress with one characteristic part of the body. Some of us usually react to stress with a queasy stomach, others with headache, others with sweating, and still others with a racing heart. Patients with ulcers react with gastric secretion, and patients with recurrent headaches tend to react with increased muscle tension (Malmo and Shagass, 1949; Lacey, 1950).

Progression of locus of symptoms

More recent evidence challenges the view that there are target organs for stress that remain stable across the lifespan. Ninety-five men were followed for thirty years. Men who reported one pattern of physical symptoms under stress at one time in their lives reported different patterns later. There did seem to be a natural progression of locus of symptoms over the life-span, however. People who as adolescents reported experiencing stress with many

Canadian researcher Hans Selye believed that when a person or animal is stressed, the general adaptation syndrome will ensue.

Figure 10-6
Characteristic symptoms of the general adaptation syndrome. Note the enlarged adrenals (A), the shrunken thymus (B) and the shrunken lymph nodes (C). (Source: Selye, 1956)

Normal   Alarmed

physical symptoms—hay fever, diarrhea, asthma, palpitations—as adults experienced stress with mental symptoms—headache, insomnia, irritability (Vaillant, 1978).

EVOLUTION

Evolution may have actually favored the development of certain psychosomatic disorders. Consider the emergency reaction for which evolution has clearly selected. In a generally threatening environment, individuals who tended to perceive the world as hostile and responded crisply with elevation of blood pressure, muscle tension, and the like would be those most likely to survive and reproduce. Only under modern conditions, in which the level of physical threat has been reduced from the days of the cave and the jungle, is hypertension considered a disorder rather than a strength. Notice that hypertension does not kill young persons; it is deadly to individuals who are many years past the prime age of reproduction. This seems to suggest that tendencies to various psychosomatic disorders are inherited because at one time in history these "diseases" actually favored survival and reproduction.

STRESS AND THE GENERAL ADAPTATION SYNDROME

Hans Selye (1907–1983) integrated the emergency reaction of the sympathetic nervous system into the major theory of reaction to stress. He emphasized the stress side of the diathesis-stress model. Selye believed that the general adaptation syndrome is nonspecific, that one and the same stress reaction will occur to the whole gamut of disturbing events. He held that when a human being or an animal is stressed, a sequence of three stages called the *general adaptation syndrome* ensues. The first stage is the *alarm reaction.* After an initial phase of lowered resistance, the system goes into *counter shock*—the pituitary gland releases ACTH (adrenocorticotrophic hormone) into the bloodstream, which stimulates the adrenal cortex. This throws the organism into the emergency reaction. If the alarm reaction stage is successful, it restores bodily balance. The alarm reaction is followed by a second stage—the stage of *resistance,* in which defense and adaptation are sustained and optimal. If the stressor persists, the final stage, *exhaustion,* ensues, and adaptive responding ceases. Illness and, in some cases, death may follow (Selye, 1956).

The reaction of rats to long-term cold stress illustrates the general adaptation syndrome. Rats were placed in a refrigerated room where the temperature was near freezing. During the first forty-eight hours, the rats showed the alarm reaction. They developed stomach ulcers, had swollen adrenals, and showed the changes of the thymus gland illustrated in Figure 10-6. The rats continued to live in this environment for many weeks. After five weeks, they had apparently entered the stage of resistance, for when these animals were placed in a still colder chamber they survived temperatures that animals who had not become adapted could not withstand. Finally, the stage of exhaustion was demonstrated. After several months in the cold room, these rats could not survive a change to cold temperature that normal rats could survive.

From the point of view of this theory, symptoms such as high blood pressure and stomach ulcer may indicate that the individual is in an alarm reaction to stress. The theory postulates that psychosomatic symptoms are general stress reactions underlying the general adaptation syndrome (Selye, 1975; but see Mason, 1971, 1975).

THE PSYCHODYNAMIC MODEL

Role of
personality and
psychodynamics

Diathesis and other biological considerations play a large role in the predisposition to psychosomatic disorders, but there is also evidence that personality and psychodynamics play a role as well. These factors contribute to the stress side of the diathesis-stress model.

Franz Alexander (1950) is the most influential psychoanalytic theorist of psychosomatic disorders. His view integrates genetic organ vulnerability, personality factors, and life stress. A person who is genetically vulnerable in a specific organ and has specific psychodynamic conflicts will develop disease of that organ when the stress of living arouses his psychodynamic conflicts and he is no longer able to defend against them. All three factors—a vulnerable organ system, an underlying dynamic conflict, and a precipitating life situation—interact to produce the disorder. The essence of the personality constellation for an individual who will develop peptic ulcer is conflict over dependent needs versus independent self-assertion. Alexander postulates other conflicts for asthma, arthritis, and skin disorders.

As we have seen, some evidence supports this theory: from the psychological profile alone, researchers have been able to pick out which male patients have ulcer well beyond the level of chance. Further, gastric secretion occurs when the relevant emotions are aroused in individuals who have ulcers. Some evidence contradicts this theory as well, however. In Vaillant's thirty-year longitudinal study of ninety-five men, fifty developed one of the classic psychosomatic illnesses. But the locus of physical symptoms under stress did not predict which psychosomatic illness would develop. So the eleven men who eventually developed ulcers were not the same men who had earlier reported abdominal pain under stress (Vaillant, 1978).

BEHAVIORAL AND COGNITIVE MODELS

Theories that stem from behavioral and cognitive views hold that learning or cognition produces psychosomatic disorders, and they emphasize the stress side of diathesis-stress. The stress can be produced by conditioning, by cognitions, or by life events.

CONDITIONING

Symptoms as a
conditioned
response

The conditioning view of psychosomatic disorders maintains that the symptoms are a conditioned response acquired when a neutral stimulus was paired with an unconditioned stimulus that produced the disorder. For example, asthma has been conditioned in the laboratory:

> A thirty-seven-year-old shop assistant suffered from severe bronchial asthma that could be reliably set off by house dust. In the laboratory, she was sprayed with an aerosol having a neutral solvent; the aerosol was to be the conditioned stimulus. Following being sprayed with the aerosol, she inhaled house dust (unconditioned stimulus), and an asthma attack (unconditioned response) followed. Thereafter, upon inhaling from the aerosol, asthma attacks ensued. (Dekker, Pelse, and Groen, 1957)

Table 10-2 COGNITIONS AND PSYCHOSOMATIC DISORDERS

Illness	Cognition	Examples of thoughts during illness-producing event
1. Hives	Perception of mistreatment.	"My fiance knocked me down and walked all over me, but what could I do?"
2. Eczema	Being prevented from doing something and helpless to deal with the frustration.	"I want to make my mother understand but I can't."
3. Asthma	Wishing the situation would go away or someone else would take over the responsibility for it.	"I just couldn't face it."
4. Diarrhea	Wishing to be done with the situation and have it over with.	"If the war was only over with."
5. Constipation	Grim determination to carry on even faced with an unsolvable problem.	"This marriage is never going to be any better but I won't quit."
6. Ulcer	Revenge seeking.	"He hurt me, so I wanted to hurt him."
7. Migraine headache	Engaged in an intense effort to carry out a definite plan.	"I had a million things to do before lunch."

SOURCE: Based on Grace and Graham, 1952.

Since individuals who suffer from asthma sometimes have attacks following exposure to highly specific events, such as experiencing a family argument or other emotional conflicts, this is an appealing model of psychosomatic illness (see again Box 10-1). It has, however, only been demonstrated under limited laboratory conditions and only some patients can be so conditioned.

COGNITIONS AND PSYCHOSOMATIC DISORDERS

Specific thoughts associated with specific illnesses

Could it be that specific thoughts set off physical symptoms? William Grace and David Graham argue that an individual's perception of the world and what he thinks about threat predicts what psychosomatic disorder will develop. This argument antedates, but is wholly compatible with the cognitive model of abnormality. Grace and Graham interviewed 128 patients with a variety of diseases to find out what situations immediately preceded the onset of the symptoms and how the individual perceived what was happening to him. They found specific thoughts associated with specific illnesses. For example, individuals with high blood pressure were in a state of constant preparation to meet all threats, and when confronted with threat they thought, "Nobody is ever going to beat me. I'm ready for everything." Table 10-2 lists other illnesses that have specific thoughts associated with them (Grace and Graham, 1952). The modern cognitive school has yet to put forward a more articulate, research-supported view.

LIFE EVENTS

Another behavioral theory of psychological influence on illness involves life stressors. It holds that stressful life events set off disease. If our reaction to

Stressful life events may make us susceptible to physical disease. The death of a close relative, losing a job, or a move or eviction all constitute stressful life events.

stress makes us susceptible to physical disease, then frequent stressful life events should correlate with frequent disease. In the early pioneering research on this question, Thomas Holmes and Richard Rahe devised a life events scale, the Social Readjustment Rating Scale, by having individuals rank the amount of stress different life events would cause them. Based on these rankings, Holmes and Rahe assigned a number to each stressful event (see Table 10-3). Death of a spouse was the most stressful life event; divorce and separation were near the top; taking a new job in the middle; holidays, vacations; minor violations of the law were considered the least stressful.

The more life events an individual experiences, the more likely is he or she to get sick from a variety of disorders. For example, individuals who had heart attacks had more total significant life events in the six months prior to their heart attack than in the year before. Similarly, individuals who became depressed had a larger number of life events, particularly losses, than those who did not (Holmes and Rahe, 1967; Paykel, Meyers, Dienelt, Klerman, Lindenthal, and Peffer, 1969; Theorell and Rahe, 1971).

Since the construction of the Social Readjustment Rating Scale, investigators have taken a closer look at the nature of the life events themselves. First of all, some of the life events listed by Holmes and Rahe could themselves reflect the fact of ongoing illness. An individual might be forced to retire (item 10) because he had high blood pressure, as opposed to getting high blood pressure as a consequence of retiring. Investigations of life events now distinguish between events that are confounded with illness and those that might contribute to it (Dohrenwend and Dohrenwend, 1974).

Second, some of the life events are positive *entrances,* such as item 25, outstanding personal achievement, while others are negative *exits,* like item 1, the death of a spouse. Losses or exits seem to produce more problems than do entrances (Paykel, 1974a, 1974b).

Third, repetitive, daily hassles of life may be better predictors of illness than major life events. Losing your wallet, a price rise in the weekly food bill, and the breaking of a window may ultimately push health around more than deaths, divorces, and pregnancies (Kanner, Coyne, Schaefer, and Lazarus, 1981; Dohrenwend and Shrout, 1985). The gradual chipping away at an individual by stresses may wear him down to a point where susceptibility to illness jumps dramatically (Depue and Monroe, 1986).

□ CONTROLLABLE VERSUS UNCONTROLLABLE LIFE EVENTS. Another development in life events research concerns control over one's life. David Glass predicted that it is not life events themselves but **uncontrollable life events** that precede heart attacks, especially among Type A's. He differentiates between uncontrollable and controllable life events, categorizing death of a close family member, death of a best friend, and being laid off from work as uncontrollable losses, but divorce, separation, and changes in eating habits as controllable life events (Dohrenwend and Martin, 1978). Glass identified three groups of patients who had experienced the same total number of life events in the preceding year. Those who had had heart attacks (who tended to be Type A's) and those who had been hospitalized for noncoronary illnesses experienced more helplessness-inducing life events than did the healthy controls, indicating that a combination of being a Type A and experiencing uncontrollable life events—as opposed to a large number of life events per se—may be a formula for heart attack (Glass, 1977).

Table 10-3 SOCIAL READJUSTMENT RATING SCALE

Rank	Life event	Mean value
1	Death of spouse	100
2	Divorce	73
3	Marital separation	65
4	Jail term	63
5	Death of close family member	63
6	Personal injury or illness	53
7	Marriage	50
8	Fired at work	47
9	Marital reconciliation	45
10	Retirement	45
11	Change in health of family member	44
12	Pregnancy	40
13	Sex difficulties	39
14	Gain of new family member	39
15	Business readjustment	39
16	Change in financial state	38
17	Death of close friend	37
18	Change to different line of work	36
19	Change in number of arguments with spouse	35
20	Mortgage over $10,000	31
21	Foreclosure of mortgage or loan	30
22	Change in responsibilities at work	29
23	Son or daughter leaving home	29
24	Trouble with in-laws	29
25	Outstanding personal achievement	28
26	Wife begins or stops work	26
27	Begin or end school	26
28	Change in living conditions	25
29	Revision of personal habits	24
30	Trouble with boss	23
31	Change in work hours or conditions	20
32	Change in residence	20
33	Change in schools	20
34	Change in recreation	19
35	Change in church activities	19
36	Change in social activities	18
37	Mortgage or loan less than $10,000	17
38	Change in sleeping habits	16
39	Change in number of family get-togethers	15
40	Change in eating habits	15
41	Vacation	13
42	Christmas	12
43	Minor violations of the law	11

SOURCE: Holmes and Rahe, 1967.

☐ LIFE EVENTS, PERSONALITY, AND LIFE-STYLE. Partly because of how easily the instrument in Table 10-3 can be given, investigators of life events have regarded such events as an independent and deep explanation of illness. In contrast, we regard the fact that many hassles or life events predict illness to be superficial, itself in need of deeper explanation. Perhaps it is personality and life-style that cause both the illness frequency and the number of life events.

Heroin addicts and alcoholics experience many life changes. In contrast, those who are aging experience fewer life events. What is causal here? It would be foolish to say that many life events cause the substance abuse or that the dearth of life changes causes aging. Here life events are caused by personality, by life-style, and by the normal changes of the life course; these factors may be the risk or protective factors for illness (Kasl, 1983). Personality can modify what the response to life events is. In one study, two groups of executives had comparable numbers of life events over the previous three years, but only one group tended to become ill. The *hardy* group, characterized by a strong sense of self, a strong sense of meaning, and vigor resisted illness (Garrity, Somes, and Marx, 1977; Kobasa, 1979). Social support can similarly buffer the effects of life events. Individuals who are isolated from friends and relatives are at higher risk for illness and death (Berkman, 1984; 1986).

Hardiness

VOLUNTARY BEHAVIOR

The role of choice

Most of the classic work on psychosomatic disorders from the psychodynamic and biomedical models focused on behaviors over which we have little or no voluntary control. Specific organ vulnerability, unconscious conflicts, and release of ACTH happen to us, we do not make them happen. The behavioral and cognitive models have shifted the focus onto behaviors that we can control voluntarily. A major part of health psychology emphasizes that we choose life-styles and particular actions that can produce illness, and that by knowing this we can choose to lead healthier lives.

In our discussion of CHD, we emphasized that some of the risk factors are chosen: lack of exercise, eating cholesterol-laden foods, and smoking. We can choose not to engage in these behaviors. Others, like the time urgency component of the Type A personality, we can learn to change with counseling. In our discussion of psychoneuroimmunology (PNI), we saw that pessimists may be at risk for more chronic illness and early death. One source of this may be their belief that they are helpless, that they will not be able to lose weight through dieting, that if they see a doctor their lump will still not go away. The failure to seek out and follow medical advice is part of a life-style that can be voluntarily changed by knowledge and by counseling.

Smoking: frailty or addiction?

Why would some individuals voluntarily continue to smoke even though they know smoking is a risk factor for CHD? Is it because smoking is an addiction that cannot be changed or because it is a human frailty that is maintained by the contingencies of the environment? There is evidence that nicotine rapidly, but temporarily, improves performance and affect. Smokers may use cigarettes as a coping response to do better or feel better during the demands of daily living. Such choices may contribute to smoking above and beyond addiction, the avoidance of nicotine withdrawal (Pomerleau and Pomerleau, 1984). From the behavioral and cognitive point of view, a major part of the cause, the cure, and the prevention of psychosomatic disorders comes from the choices we make every day about how we will lead our lives.

SUMMARY

1. Psychological factors can influence the course, and even the beginning, of a physical illness. *Psychosomatic disorders* are defined as physical

illnesses whose course or onset can be influenced by such psychological factors, and health psychology is the field that studies those phenomena.

2. Psychosomatic disorders can be viewed within a *diathesis-stress model.* In this view, psychosomatic disorder occurs when an individual is both constitutionally vulnerable to a particular physical problem and experiences life stress.

3. *Peptic ulcers* occur when the naturally secreted hydrochloric acid of the stomach erodes the protective mucous membrane of the stomach or duodenum. Emotional states, particularly anxiety, can cause an oversecretion of hydrochloric acid in the stomach.

4. Coronary heart disease (CHD) is the leading cause of death in the Western world. The Type A personality—characterized by hostility, time urgency, and competitiveness—is a risk factor for CHD.

5. Hostility may be the active, insidious component of Type A. People high in hostility and anger have more CHD than those who are low in hostility and anger. More helplessness in the face of uncontrollable events might also be an insidious component of the Type A personality. Frequent engagement in the emergency reaction may be the process by which Type A's, hostile people, and overloaded people are at greater risk for CHD.

6. Type A behavior can be changed by counseling, and risk for CHD may decrease accordingly.

7. The immune system recognizes and destroys antigens and its activity can be influenced by psychological states. Psychoneuroimmunology is the field that studies this process.

8. Depression, stressful life events, and helplessness decrease immunocompetence and increase immune-related diseases in both animals and humans.

9. Individuals with pessimistic explanatory style may suffer more illness and die earlier than optimists. One chain of events by which pessimism might produce immune-related illness may go from the occurrence of loss, to depression, followed by catecholamine depletion and endorphin increase, leading to immunosuppression, resulting in failure of the immune system to destroy threatening pathogens.

10. Biomedical, psychodynamic, behavioral, and cognitive models have all shed light on the causes and treatment of psychosomatic disorders. All are compatible with the diathesis-stress perspective.

11. The biomedical view emphasizes the "diathesis" of the diathesis-stress model, and it argues that genetic inheritance and vulnerability in a specific organ contribute to psychosomatic disorders.

12. The psychodynamic view emphasizes the personality types in whom underlying dynamic conflicts, a vulnerable organ system, and a precipitating life situation interact to produce psychosomatic disorders.

13. The behavioral and cognitive views emphasize the "stress" of the diathesis-stress model. They hold that the way individuals learn to cope with threat, think about threat, and the actual stressful and uncontrollable life events that they experience play the major role in the way psychological factors cause and aggravate physical illness. They emphasize that choice and voluntary behavior are central to the cause and prevention of psychosomatic disorders.

Part 5

DEPRESSION AND THE SCHIZOPHRENIAS

Depression and Suicide

DEPRESSION is the most widespread psychological disorder. And it has been strongly on the rise recently. If you were born after 1960, you are ten times more likely to become depressed than were your grandparents. Depression is the common cold of mental illness. Almost everyone has felt depression, at least in its mild forms. Feeling blue, low, sad, downhearted, discouraged, and unhappy are all common depressive experiences. But familiarity does not produce understanding; for it is only in the last two decades that major advances have been made. Today the great majority of individuals suffering from severe depressions can be helped. We also now know a great deal about its causes.

NORMAL VERSUS CLINICAL DEPRESSION

Depressed symptoms in normals

Loss and pain are inevitable parts of growing up and growing older. Sometimes people we care for reject us, we write bad papers, our stocks go down, we fail to get the job we want, people we love die. When these losses occur we go into mourning, and then emerge, our lives poorer, but with hope for the future. Almost everyone reacts to loss with some of the symptoms of depression. We become sad and discouraged, apathetic and passive, the future looks bleak, some of the zest goes out of living. Such a reaction is normal—and we have repeatedly found that at any given moment 25 to 30 percent of college undergraduates will have such symptoms, at least to some extent (Seligman, unpublished). Nancy's depression is mild and within the normal range of reaction to loss.

> Within a two-day period, Nancy got a C on her Abnormal Psychology midterm and found out that the boy she had loved in her home town during high school had become engaged. The week that followed was awful: her future looked empty

since she believed she would now not get into graduate school in clinical psychology and that she would never find anyone she could deeply love again. She blamed herself for these failures in the two most important arenas of her life. For the first few days she had trouble getting out of bed to go to class. She burst into tears over dinner one evening and had to leave the table. Missing dinner didn't much matter anyway since she wasn't hungry. After one week, the world started to look better. The instructor said that because the grades were so low on the midterm, everyone had the option of writing a paper to cancel out their midterm grade, and Nancy found herself looking forward to a blind date that her roommate had arranged for the weekend. Her usual bounce and enthusiasm for life began to return, and with it her appetite. She thought, "It will be an uphill battle, but I'm basically O.K. and I think I may find love and success."

Kinds of depression

How does such "normal" depression relate to the more serious depressive disorders? There are two kinds of depressive disorders, **unipolar depression** in which the individual suffers only depressive symptoms without ever experiencing mania, and **bipolar depression** (or **manic-depression**) in which both depression and mania occur. **Mania** is defined by excessive elation, expansiveness, irritability, talkativeness, inflated self-esteem, and flight of ideas. The existence of two mood disorders, which go in apparently opposite directions, has given rise to the name **affective disorders** to embrace unipolar depression, bipolar depression, and mania. Normal depression differs in degree from unipolar depression; both have the same kinds of symptoms, but the unipolar depressive has more symptoms, more severely, more frequently, and for a longer time. The line between a "normal" depressive disturbance and a clinically significant depressive disorder is blurry.

Bipolar depressions, on the other hand, are clearly distinguishable from normal and unipolar depressions. They involve swings between episodes of mania and episodes of depression, and as we shall see, they probably have a genetic component. Bipolar depression develops at a younger age, and is often more crippling to the individual. Fortunately, a specific drug, lithium carbonate, seems to help considerably.

For many years, all depression was viewed as part of manic-depression. In the last decade, it has become clear that the large majority of depressions are unipolar and unrelated to manic-depression. Depression usually occurs in people who have never had mania, and mania may occur in people who have never been depressed. For this reason, we shall first discuss unipolar depression. We will then take up bipolar depression (manic-depression). We conclude by examining the most catastrophic outcome of both unipolar and bipolar depression: suicide.

Sorrow by Vincent Van Gogh

UNIPOLAR DEPRESSION

SYMPTOMS OF UNIPOLAR DEPRESSION

Four sets of symptoms

Depression is widely regarded as a disorder of mood, but this is an oversimplification. There are actually four sets of symptoms in depression. In addition to mood or emotional symptoms, there are thought or cognitive symptoms, motivational symptoms, and physical or somatic symptoms. An individual does not have to have all these symptoms to be correctly diag-

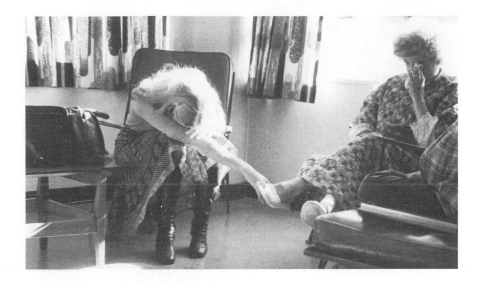

Sadness is the most salient emotional symptom in depression. A depressive may be so sad that she cries continuously during the day.

nosed as "depressed," but the more symptoms he or she has and the more intense is each set, the more confident we can be that the individual is suffering from depression.

EMOTIONAL SYMPTOMS

When a depressed patient is asked how she feels, the most common adjectives she uses are: "sad, blue, miserable, helpless, hopeless, lonely, unhappy, downhearted, worthless, humiliated, ashamed, worried, useless, guilty."

Sadness most salient symptom

Sadness is the most salient and widespread emotional symptom in depression. One person's life was so dominated by sadness that she cried during almost all her waking hours. She was unable to carry on a social conversation because of excessive crying. This occurred even in therapy to such an extent that almost no therapy was taking place (Beck et al., 1979). This melancholic mood varies with time of day. Most commonly, depressed people feel worse in the morning, and the mood seems to lighten a bit as the day goes on. Along with feelings of sadness, feelings of anxiety are very often present in depression (Fowles and Gersh, 1979).

Loss of interest and pleasure

Almost as pervasive as sadness in depression is loss of gratification, the numbing of the joy of living. Activities that used to bring satisfaction feel dull and flat. Loss of interest usually starts in only a few activities, such as work. But as depression increases in severity, it spreads through practically everything the individual does. The pleasure derived from hobbies, recreation, and family diminishes. Gregarious individuals who used to enjoy partygoing avoid social gatherings. Finally, even biological functions, such as eating and sex, lose their appeal. Ninety-two percent of depressed patients no longer derive gratification from some major interests in their life, and 64 percent of depressed patients lose their feeling for other people (Beck, 1967).

COGNITIVE SYMPTOMS

A depressed person thinks of himself in a very negative light. He has low self-esteem and views the future as being hopeless.

Box 11-1   DEPRESSION AND THE PERCEPTION OF REALITY

Depressed people clearly have more negative beliefs about themselves and their future than nondepressed people. But who is accurate? Sometimes the distortion from reality is in the mind of the depressive as in the example of the man who believed his wallpaper job was a failure because a couple of the panels weren't perfect. But is it possible that depressed individuals are sometimes more in touch with reality about their abilities than are nondepressed individuals? Perhaps it is nondepressed individuals who are making optimistic distortions? Lauren Alloy and Lyn Abramson (1979) conducted a study in which depressed and nondepressed college students performed a task where they pushed a button on some trials and refrained from button pushing on other trials. When the button was pushed, a green light sometimes went on. They were asked to judge how much control they had. For one group (75–0), the green light went on 75 percent of the time they pressed the button, and never went on when they didn't press the button. Their actual control was 75. For another group (75–50), the green light went on 75 percent of the time they pressed the button, but also went on 50 percent of the time when they didn't press the button, resulting in actual control of 25. In the most interesting group (75–75), the green light went on 75 percent of the time, whether or not they pressed the button. In this condition, actual control was zero since the green light went on regardless of whether they pressed the button.

The figure below shows the surprising results. Depressed people accurately judge how much control they have. When they exert control, they judge the contingency correctly. When they do not have control, they say that they do not. There *is* a net difference between depressed and nondepressed individuals, but the distortion resides in nondepressed individuals who believe they have control even when they do not. Alloy and Abramson speculated that depressed people are sadder, but wiser. What needs explaining on this account is not why people are sometimes depressed, but how nondepressed people successfully defend themselves from a grim reality (Alloy and Abramson, 1979).

This conclusion has been borne out in studies of perception of social ability. Depressed patients' assessment of their social skills is closer to the assessment of their

Low self-esteem

□ NEGATIVE VIEW OF THE SELF.   A depressed individual often has low self-esteem. He believes he has failed and that he is the cause of his own failures. He believes he is inferior, inadequate, and incompetent. He believes that he lacks the qualities necessary to succeed in those areas of his life that are important to him, be they intelligence, attractiveness, wealth, health, or talent (see Box 11-1). These views of failure and incompetence are often distortions.

One patient managed to wallpaper a kitchen although very depressed. Here is how he distorted this achievement into a failure:

> THERAPIST: Why didn't you rate wallpapering the kitchen as a mastery experience?
> PATIENT: Because the flowers didn't line up.
> THERAPIST: You did in fact complete the job?
> PATIENT: Yes.
> THERAPIST: Your kitchen?
> PATIENT: No. I helped a neighbor do his kitchen.
> THERAPIST: Did he do most of the work?

skills by a panel of judges than is the assessment of nondepressed patients to the assessment of the judges. The nondepressed patients tend to believe that they are more socially skilled than the judges believe they are (Lewinsohn, Mischel, Chaplin, and Barton, 1980). Depressed people have low self-esteem, but this low self-evaluation may not always be a distortion; sometimes it may be merely a sober and accurate assessment of reality, which contrasts to that of others who may overinflate their view of themselves.

Judgment of control in depressed and nondepressed students. Depressed students accurately judge that they exert control over a green light when they in fact have control (75–0, 75–50), and they are also accurate in judging that they do not have control when the light comes on 75 percent of the time, whether or not they button press (75–75). Nondepressed students judge that they exert control even when they do not. (Source: Alloy and Abramson, 1979)

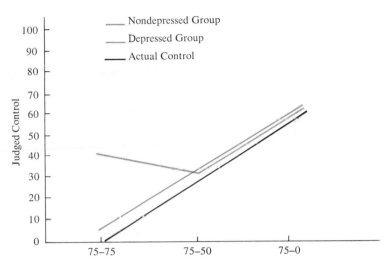

The probability of the green light going on when a response is made versus the probability of the green light going on when a response is not made. At point 75–75, the green light goes on 75% of the time whether or not a response is made. At point 75–50, the green light goes on 75% of the time when a response is made, but only 50% of the time when a response is not made. At 75–0, the green light goes on 75% of the time when a response is made, but never comes on when a response is not made.

PATIENT: No, I really did almost all of it. He hadn't wallpapered before.
THERAPIST: Did anything else go wrong? Did you spill the paste all over? Ruin a lot of wallpaper? Leave a big mess?
PATIENT: No, no, the only problem was that the flowers did not line up.
THERAPIST: So, since it was not perfect, you get no credit at all.
PATIENT: Well . . . yes.
THERAPIST: Just how far off was the alignment of the flowers?
PATIENT: (holds out fingers about 1/8 of an inch apart) About that much.
THERAPIST: On each strip of paper?
PATIENT: No . . . on two or three pieces.
THERAPIST: Out of how many?
PATIENT: About 20–25.
THERAPIST: Did anyone else notice it?
PATIENT: No. In fact, my neighbor thought it was great.
THERAPIST: Did your wife see it?
PATIENT: Yeah, she admired the job.
THERAPIST: Could you see the defect when you stood back and looked at the whole wall?
PATIENT: Well . . . not really.

> THERAPIST: So you've selectively attended to a real but very small flaw in your effort to wallpaper. Is it logical that such a small defect should entirely cancel the credit you deserve?
> PATIENT: Well, it wasn't as good as it should have been.
> THERAPIST: If your neighbor had done the same quality job in your kitchen, what would you say?
> PATIENT: . . . pretty good job!

(Beck et al., 1979)

Blame self for troubles

Depressed people not only have low self-esteem, but they blame themselves and feel guilty for the troubles that afflict them. When failure occurs, depressed individuals tend to take the responsibility on themselves.

When failure has not yet occurred, they imagine that it will soon and that it will be caused by them. Those who are the most severely depressed may even believe that they are responsible for the violence and suffering of the world and that they should be greatly punished for their sins.

Pessimism about future

□ BELIEF IN A HOPELESS FUTURE.   In addition to negative beliefs and guilt about the self, the depressed individual almost always views the future with great pessimism and hopelessness. A depressed individual believes that his actions, even if he could undertake them, are doomed. For example, when a middle-aged, depressed woman was told by her therapist that it would be a good idea for her to get a job, she replied, "I just couldn't possibly do it. How would I find the number of an employment agency? Even if I found the phone number, no one would want to hire me because I'm unqualified." Upon being reminded that she held a Ph.D. she replied, "Well, they might hire me, but they will surely fire me because I'm incompetent; and even if they kept me on it wouldn't be because of competence, but only because I'm so pathetic" (Seligman, unpublished). The depressed individual is equipped with a host of reasons for future failure, and no reasons at all for why success might occur.

Small obstacles in the path of a depressive seem insuperable barriers. One patient wanted to go swimming but was overwhelmed by the difficulties she saw in her way:

> PATIENT: There is nowhere I could go swimming.
> THERAPIST: How could you find a place?
> PATIENT: There is a YWCA if I could get there . . . I'd get my hair wet and get a cold.
> THERAPIST: How could you get there?
> PATIENT: My husband would take me.
> THERAPIST: How about your wet hair?
> PATIENT: I couldn't take a hair dryer; someone would steal it.
> THERAPIST: Could you do something about that?
> PATIENT: They don't have lockers.
> THERAPIST: How do you know?
> PATIENT: I just don't think they do.

(Beck et al., 1979)

The depressive's belief that future action will be ineffective has been demonstrated experimentally. Hospitalized depressives worked on a task of skill and a task of chance. When they succeeded at the task of skill, their expectancies for future success did not go up, and when they failed, their expectancies that they would succeed did not go down. Unlike nondepressed individuals and unlike schizophrenics (either depressed or nondepressed), whose expectancies rise when they succeed and lower when they fail, depressed patients did not seem to believe that their responses could make any difference to future success (Abramson, Garber, Edwards, and Seligman, 1978).

MOTIVATIONAL SYMPTOMS

People vary as to how motivated they are. Most of us, however, are able to get up in the morning, go to work, find ways of entertaining ourselves and others, and so on. But depressed individuals have great trouble getting started. This passivity or lack of response initiation undermines working and loving. An advertising executive loses his initiative in planning a major sales campaign; a college professor cannot bring herself to prepare her lectures; a student loses the desire to study.

Lack of response initiation

One depressed man who was hospitalized after a suicide attempt merely sat motionless day after day in the lounge. His therapist decided to prepare a schedule of activities to get the patient engaged:

> THERAPIST: I understand that you spend most of your day in the lounge. Is that true?
>
> PATIENT: Yes, being quiet gives me the peace of mind I need.
>
> THERAPIST: When you sit here, how's your mood?
>
> PATIENT: I feel awful all the time. I just wish I could fall in a hole somewhere and die.
>
> THERAPIST: Do you feel better after sitting for two or three hours?
>
> PATIENT: No, the same.
>
> THERAPIST: So you're sitting in the hope that you'll find peace of mind, but it doesn't sound like your depression improves.
>
> PATIENT: I get so bored.
>
> THERAPIST: Would you consider being more active? There are a number of reasons why I think increasing your activity level might help.
>
> PATIENT: There's nothing to do around here.
>
> THERAPIST: Would you consider trying some activities if I could come up with a list?
>
> PATIENT: If you think it will help, but I think you're wasting your time. I don't have any interests.
>
> (Beck et al., 1979)

Depressed individuals may have trouble motivating themselves to get up in the morning to go to work or study. Depressive problems are usually worse in the morning.

In extreme form, lack of response initiation is "paralysis of the will." Such a patient cannot bring himself to do even those things that are necessary to life. He has to be pushed and prodded out of bed, clothed, and fed. In severe depression, there may be ***psychomotor retardation*** in which movements slow down and the patient walks and talks excruciatingly slowly.

Lack of response initiation in depression has been seen clearly in the laboratory. Depressed college students fail to escape loud noise when performing tasks in which all that is required to turn off the noise is moving the hand two feet. This lack of response initiation occurs not only in instrumental motor behavior but also in cognitive tasks as well. Depressed students and depressed patients fail to solve anagrams that nondepressed individuals

Box 11-2   MEASURING DEPRESSIVE SYMPTOMS

Aaron T. Beck of the University of Pennsylvania has developed the most widely used inventory of depressive symptoms. Each of the questions describes one of the symptoms of depression, and each question provides a severity score of 0 through 3 for that symptom. The person circles the answer that best describes how he or she feels right now. The symptoms divide into mood, thought, motivational, and physical sets. The statements below show responses to eight of the twenty-one in the short form of the Beck Depression Inventory.

This test is designed, not as a way of diagnosing depression, but as a way of knowing how many symptoms are present and how severe they are once depression is clinically diagnosed. A high score alone is not diagnostic of clinical depression or mental illness. Generally speaking, research has shown that the average score (for the total of the numbers from the eight questions) in a North American college population is about 3 or 4, and students who score below this can be considered nondepressed. Mildly depressed students typically have scores from about 5 to 9, and scores of 10 or higher suggest moderate to severe depression. If an individual scores 10 or more for a period of one or two weeks, it would probably be in his best interest to seek help. If he has serious or persistent thoughts of suicide, regardless of his total score, it is imperative that he seek aid.

Beck Depression Inventory

Mood A (Sadness)
0   I do not feel sad.
1   I feel blue or sad.
2a   I am blue or sad all the time and I can't snap out of it.
2b   I am so sad or unhappy that it is quite painful.
3   I am so sad or unhappy that I can't stand it.

Mood B (Interest in others)
0   I have not lost interest in other people.
1   I am less interested in other people now than I used to be.
2   I have lost most of my interest in other people and have little feeling for them.
3   I have lost all my interest in other people and don't care about them at all.

Thought C (Pessimism)
0   I am not particularly pessimistic or discouraged about the future.
1   I feel discouraged about the future.
2a   I feel I have nothing to look forward to.
2b   I feel that I won't ever get over my troubles.
3   I feel that the future is hopeless and that things cannot improve.

Thought D (Failure)
0   I do not feel like a failure.
1   I feel I have failed more than the average person.
2   I feel I have accomplished very little that is worthwhile or that means anything.
3   I feel I am a complete failure as a person (parent, husband, wife).

Motivation E (Work initiation)
0   I can work about as well as before.
1a   It takes extra effort to get started at doing something.
1b   I don't work as well as I used to.
2   I have to push myself very hard to do anything.
3   I can't do any work at all.

Motivation F (Suicide)
0   I don't have any thoughts of harming myself.
1   I have thoughts of harming myself but I would not carry them out.
2a   I feel I would be better off dead.
2b   I feel my family would be better off if I were dead.
3a   I have definite plans about committing suicide.
3b   I would kill myself if I could.

Physical G (Appetite)
0   My appetite is no worse than usual.
1   My appetite is not as good as it used to be.
2   My appetite is much worse now.
3   I have no appetite at all any more.

Physical H (Sleep loss)
0   I can sleep as well as usual.
1   I wake up more tired in the morning than I used to.
2   I wake up 1–2 hours earlier than usual and find it hard to get back to sleep.
3   I wake up early every day and can't get more than 5 hours of sleep.

SOURCE: Beck, 1967.

solve readily. The more depressed an individual is, the more severe are these deficits (Miller and Seligman, 1975, 1976; Price, Tryon, and Raps, 1978).

Difficulty making decisions

Difficulty in making a decision also seems to be a common symptom of depression (Hammen and Padesky, 1977). The following case illustrates how indecisiveness can overwhelm a depressed individual:

> Sylvia is a very bright college student whose life is being ruined by her depression. She finds it increasingly difficult to get on with routine studying because she can't take the initial steps. Now a major life decision has paralyzed her for the last three weeks. She has been accepted to two good graduate schools and has to make up her mind which to accept. One school offers a large scholarship, the other is more prestigious. She constantly ruminates over being selfish if she chooses the prestigious one without money, versus the cowardliness of giving in to her parents by choosing the other. Sylvia has managed to turn a can't-lose situation into a can't-win situation. (After Beck et al., 1979)

For a depressed individual, making a decision may be overwhelming and frightening. Every decision seems momentous, of make or break significance, and the fear of the wrong decision can be paralyzing.

Somatic Symptoms

Perhaps the most insidious set of symptoms in depression are the physical changes. As depression worsens, every biological and psychological joy that makes life worth living is eroded.

Loss of appetite and sleep disturbance

Loss of appetite is common. A gourmet finds that food does not taste good to her anymore. Weight loss occurs in moderate and severe depression, although in mild depression weight gain sometimes occurs. Sleep disturbance occurs as well. Depressed individuals may experience trouble getting to sleep at night, or they may experience early morning awakening, with great difficulty getting back to sleep for the rest of the night. Sleep disturbance and weight loss both lead to weakness and fatigue. A depressed individual also may lose interest in sex. Erectile difficulties in men and lack of arousal in women are common side effects of depression.

A depressed individual is often self-absorbed and focused on the present. His body absorbs his attention, and increased worry about aches and pains can occur. In addition to more worrying about health, depressed individuals may, in fact, be more susceptible to physical illness, since depression, as it becomes severe, may erode basic biological drives. For example, when a flu swept through an Army base, those individuals who had been depressed took significantly longer to recover (Imboden, Cantor, and Cluff, 1961).

Classifying Depression

Episodic vs. chronic depression

Depression of all kinds produces emotional, cognitive, motivational, and somatic deficits. What kinds of depression exist? DSM-III-R uses the most reliable and basic distinction in depression: the unipolar-bipolar distinction, which we defined above. In addition to the bipolar-unipolar distinction, however, DSM-III-R also distinguishes between *episodic* and *chronic* depressions. In chronic depression, **dysthymia,** the individual has been depressed for at least two solid years without having had a remission to normality of at least two months in duration. An episodic depression, which is much more common, is of less than two years' duration and has a clear onset, which distinguishes it from previous nondepressed functioning.

ENDOGENOUS V. EXOGENOUS DEPRESSION

Separating
biologically
based from
psychologically
based
depressions

The endogenous vs. exogenous distinction in depression, which DSM-III-R calls depression with melancholia vs. depression without melancholia, is an attempt to separate biologically based from psychologically based depressions. (*Melancholia* is characterized chiefly by loss of pleasure in all activities and general lack of reaction to pleasurable events.) The word *endogenous* (biological—with melancholia) means "coming from within the body," and *exogenous* (psychological—without melancholia) means "coming from outside the body"; the implication of these terms is that an exogenous depression is precipitated by a life stressor, while an endogenous depression arises from a disordered biology. This distinction is associated with two fairly reliable symptom clusters: endogenous depressions involve psychomotor retardation, more severe symptoms, the lack of reaction to environmental changes during the depression, loss of interest in life, and somatic symptoms, while exogenous depressions show fewer of these characteristics. In addition, early morning awakening, guilt, and suicidal behavior may be more associated with endogenous than exogenous depressions (Mendels and Cochran, 1968).

Different
treatment for
endogenous and
exogenous
depression

The usefulness of the endogenous-exogenous distinction is compromised, however, by a lack of difference in precipitating events. Endogenous depressions have been found to have no fewer precipitating events than exogenous depressions (Paykel, Meyers, Dienelt, Klerman, Lindenthal, and Pfefer, 1969; Leff, Roatch, and Bunney, 1970). But while there is no difference in precipitating events, there may be different treatment implications: endogenous depressions, identified by the endogenous symptom cluster may respond better to antidepressant drugs and electroconvulsive shock, while exogenous depressions may fare better with psychotherapy alone. The results of differential treatment studies have not been uniform, however, and the distinction must be viewed with caution (Fowles and Gersh, 1979).

Another finding that compromises the usefulness of the endogenous-exogenous distinction comes from a major family study of depression (Andreasen, Scheftner, Reich, Hirschfeld, Endicott, and Keller, 1986). Three thousand first-degree relatives (immediate family) of 566 individuals with major depressive disorders were themselves diagnosed. Since endogenous depression is assumed to be genetic, a noticeably higher rate of depression was expected in relatives of endogenous depressives. But the rate of depression (of all subtypes) was the same for relatives of the endogenous and of the non-endogenous depressives.

Finally, there is also a good possibility that the distinction between mild and severe may be the basis of the endogenous-exogenous continuum, with the endogenous depressions merely being more severe. This would mean that there is only one type of unipolar depression but that there are important differences in intensity.

VULNERABILITY TO DEPRESSION

How specific can we be about this "common cold of mental illness"? At the very moment about one out of twenty Americans is severely depressed, and chances are one in ten of having a depressive episode of clinical proportions at least once in your lifetime (Myers et al., 1984; Robins et al., 1984).

Who, among our population, is vulnerable to depression? Everyone. No group—not blacks or whites, not women or men, not young or old, not rich or poor—is wholly spared. While depression is found among all segments of mankind, some groups, however, are more susceptible than others.

MODERNITY AND DEPRESSION: AN AGE OF MELANCHOLY?

There is growing evidence that we now live in an Age of Melancholy. Three lines of evidence point this way: (1) epidemiological studies of large groups of Americans, randomly sampled, showing that people born earlier in this century have experienced less depression in their lifetimes than people born later; (2) diagnostic studies of relatives of people who have clinically severe depression, with older relatives less susceptible than younger relatives; (3) a study of a premodern culture, the Old Order Amish of Lancaster County, Pennsylvania, living surrounded by modern America, but having a rate of unipolar depression much lower than ours.

☐ THE EPIDEMIOLOGICAL CATCHMENT AREA (ECA) STUDY   The lifetime prevalence of a disorder is the percent of a population that has had the disorder at least once in their lifetime. Because this is a cumulative statistic, if the disorder has the same risk across historical time, older people will have a higher lifetime prevalence than younger people, simply because older people have had more years in which to get the disorder. The occurrence of a major depressive disorder was ascertained by asking 10,000 adults, sampled randomly across New Haven, Baltimore, and St. Louis, if enough symptoms of depression had occurred at any time of life, and Table 11-1 shows the lifetime prevalence of different age groups across the three sites.

Young people at risk for depression

These data are remarkable. They suggest that if you were born around 1910, you have only a 1.3 percent chance of having a major depressive episode, even though you have had at least sixty-five years of opportunity to get it. In contrast, if you were born after 1960, you have already had a 5.3 per-

Table 11-1 LIFETIME PREVALENCE OF MAJOR DEPRESSIVE EPISODES BY AGE (PERCENTAGE)

	18–24 years born c. 1960 n = 1397	*25–44 years c. 1945 n = 3722*	*45–64 years c. 1925 n = 2351*	*over 65 c. 1910 n = 1654*
New Haven	7.5	10.4	4.2	1.8
Baltimore	4.1	7.5	4.2	1.4
St. Louis	4.5	8.0	5.2	0.8

SOURCE: Adapted from Robins et al., 1984.

cent chance, even though you have only had twenty years of opportunity. These are whopping differences, suggesting a roughly tenfold increase in risk for depression across two generations (Robins et al, 1984).

Young relatives at risk more

□ BIRTH COHORT STUDY OF RELATIVES OF UNIPOLAR DEPRESSIVES.   Relatives of individuals with major depressive disorders are themselves at heightened risk for depression, probably for genetic reasons. Do the same trends for groups of people born within the same period hold with relatives at risk?

To ask this question, 2289 relatives of 523 people with affective disorders were given the structured diagnostic interview probing for their lifetime prevalence of major depressive disorder. Figure 11-1 plots the percentage of relatives who have had at least one episode against their age. Men and women are plotted separately (Klerman, Lavori, Rice et al., 1985).

Again the effects of historical time are enormous—about one order of magnitude. Consider, for example, women born in 1950 versus women born before 1910. By age thirty about 65 percent of the women born in 1950 had had one depressive episode, whereas fewer than 5 percent of women in the 1910 cohort had had such an episode by the time they were thirty. At almost all corresponding points, a more recent year of birth confers more and earlier risk for major depressive disorder. Overall, we can again estimate a risk increase of roughly tenfold across two generations.

Risk for unipolar depression less in ultraconservative Amish

□ THE OLD ORDER AMISH.   During just the period of these two studies, the rate of depression among the 12,500 Amish living in Lancaster County, Pennsylvania, was assessed using a parallel diagnostic interview (see Chapter 3). As we have said, the Amish are an ultraconservative Protestant sect. No electricity is permitted in their homes, horses and buggies are used for transportation, alcoholism and crime are unknown, and pacifism is absolute. They are a closed population, descended entirely from thirty eighteenth-century progenitors.

For the five-year period from 1976–1980, forty-one active cases of major depressive disorder were found; this is a five-year prevalence of about 0.5 percent (there are 8186 adult Amish). If we compare this rate to the parallel figures from the ECA studies, we can roughly estimate that the Amish have about one-fifth to one-tenth the risk for unipolar depression as their neigh-

Figure 11-1
Increases in depression over the twentieth century. (A) Cumulative probability of diagnosable major depressive disorder in male relatives by birth cohort. (B) Cumulative probability of diagnosable major depressive disorder in female relatives by birth cohort. (Source: Klerman, Lavori, Rice et al., 1985)

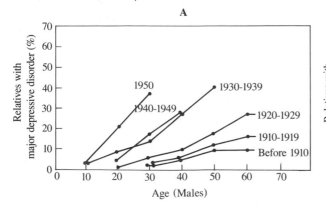

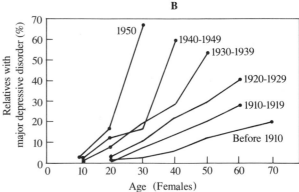

boring Americans from modern culture. Importantly the rate of bipolar depression is the same as for modern Americans. (Egeland and Hostetter, 1983).

SEX DIFFERENCES IN DEPRESSION

Women more at risk than men

Women seem to have twice the risk for depression as men (Nolen-Hoeksema, 1988). Methodologically strong studies of depression (those that use standardized assessment procedures, large sample sizes, and diagnostic systems that separate out unipolar and bipolar depression) can be divided into treated cases (people undergoing therapy) and community samples (in which the researchers go door-to-door). In seven of the eight studies of treated cases in the United States, females were significantly more depressed than males, with a mean ratio of 2:1. In the ten studies of treated cases outside the United States, nine showed more females than males with depression, with a mean ratio of 2.3:1. Treated cases may not reveal underlying sex differences in depression, however, because women might be more likely to seek out treatment than men. To get around this problem, a large number of community studies have been conducted; most of these studies show a preponderance of depression in females over males, with a mean ratio slightly under 2:1.

Overall, the preponderance of depression among women is clearly established. Why this is so is much less clear. Several hypotheses have been advanced to account for this sex difference in depression. First, women may be more willing to express depressive symptoms than men are in our society. When they confront loss, women are more reinforced for passivity and crying, while men are more reinforced for anger or indifference (Weissman and Paykel, 1974). Second, biological hypotheses suggest that chemical enzyme activity, genetic proneness, and a monthly bout of premenstrual depression influence vulnerability in women. Also there is the possibility that female carriers of a depressive gene become depressed, whereas male carriers of the same gene become alcoholic (Robinson, Davis, Nies, Ravaris, and Sylvester, 1971; Winokur, 1972). A third hypothesis grows out of the learned helplessness theory of depression (see pp. 336–39). If depression is related to helplessness, then to the extent that women learn to be more helpless than men, depression will appear more frequently in women than in men. A society that rewards women for brooding and becoming passive in the face of loss while rewarding men for active coping attempts may pay a heavy price in later female depression (Radloff, 1975). Fourth, women are *more state-oriented* than men, and so are inclined to worry about and explain bad life events (foremost among them, depression itself), whereas men are inclined to more *action* and less thought (Nolen-Hoeksema, 1988). State-orientation about depression will amplify depression (Zullow and Seligman, 1985); whereas action-orientation may dampen a depressive mood and bring about the resolution of the life problems.

Premenstrual depression

One possible artifact in the findings that women show more depression than men concerns premenstrual mood changes. In any survey, 25 percent of adult women will be within one week of menstruating, but zero percent of the men will be. If there is a valid phenomenon of *premenstrual depression,* its occurrence would inflate the amount of female depression. Does premenstrual depression exist?

Women may be more willing to express sadness, and ultimately depressive symptoms, than are men in our society.

This is a controversial topic, so much so that DSM-III-R relegates its category, "late luteal phase dysphoric disorder," to a section at the back of the book called "proposed diagnostic categories needing further study." Characterizing this disorder are: (1) in most cycles in the last year emotional changes have occurred before menses which remit with the onset of menses; (2) the presence of at least five symptoms, including emotional lability, anger, tension, depression, low interest, fatigability, difficulty concentrating, appetite changes, sleep changes, or physical symptoms; and (3) the serious impairing of work or social functioning by these symptoms.

Overall at least 40 percent of adult women experience some of these symptoms premenstrually. Most of these women rate the symptoms as mild and are not impaired by them, but about 2 to 10 percent rate them as severe. This group may be significantly impaired by them (Logue and Moos, 1986; Nolen-Hoeksema, 1988; McMillan and Pihl, 1987). Depression is a prominent symptom in this cluster; one major study of 335 women found that 145 met criteria for premenstrual increases in depressive symptoms (Halbreich, Endicott, and Nee, 1983).

AGE AND DEPRESSION

Anaclitic depression

No age group is exempt from depression. Comparison of the frequency of depression across age is controversial since depression may have different manifestations at different times of life, and a cohort effect clearly exists, with people born early in this century reporting much less depression than people born midway and later through the century.

The earliest psychological state that may be related to depression was described by the American psychiatrist Rene Spitz in 1946 and was called *anaclitic depression*. Spitz observed that when infants between the ages of six and eighteen months were separated from their mothers for prolonged periods of time, a state of unresponsive apathy, listlessness, weight loss, increased susceptibility to serious childhood illness, and even death occurred. The mothers' return, or the substitution of a different, permanent mother, reversed these effects (Spitz, 1946). Similar effects have been observed when infant rhesus monkeys are separated from their mothers. A regular sequence of the reaction to the separation—first protest, then despair, then reattachment—has been documented (Bowlby, 1960; Kaufman and Rosenblum, 1967; McKinney, Suomi, and Harlow, 1972).

Childhood depression

Childhood depression is a controversial issue (Schulterbrand and Raven, 1977). Until recently, it was alleged that depression in childhood with the core symptoms of passivity, negative cognitions, resigned behavior, sadness, and inhibition in working and loving, was relatively rare. Instead, reaction to loss was thought to take other forms, such as hyperactivity, aggression, and delinquency (Cytryn and McKnew, 1972). More sensitive tests of depression in childhood have recently been developed and have revealed as high a rate of depressive symptoms in children as among adults, along with accompanying intellectual deficits (Kovacs and Beck, 1977; Kaslow, Tanenbaum, Abramson, Peterson, and Seligman, 1983; Blumberg and Izard, 1985).

The loss of a parent by divorce may precipitate depression among children, as illustrated by the following case:

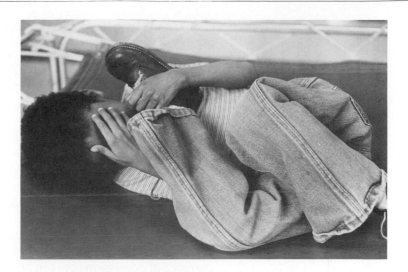

Children show as high a rate of depressive symptoms as do adults.

> Peter, age nine, had not seen his father, who lived nearby, more than once every two to three months. We expected that he would be troubled, but we were entirely unprepared for the extent of this child's misery. The interviewer observed: "I asked Peter when he had last seen his dad. The child looked at me blankly and his thinking became confused, his speech halting. Just then, a police car went by with its siren screaming. The child stared into space and seemed lost in reverie. As this continued for a few minutes, I gently suggested that the police car had reminded him of his father, a police officer. Peter began to cry and sobbed without stopping for 35 minutes (Wallerstein and Kelly, 1980).

Adolescent depression

In adolescents, depression has all the symptoms that we saw for depression in adults. In addition to the core symptoms of depression, depressed adolescents, particularly boys, are commonly negativistic and even antisocial. Restlessness, grouchiness, aggression, and strong desire to leave home are also common symptoms; and sulkiness, uncooperativeness in family activities, school difficulties, alcohol and drug abuse can also be symptoms of adolescent depression.

Depression among aged less than among young

Depression among adults does not increase in frequency and in severity with age as used to be believed (Myers et al., 1984; Robins et al., 1984). Although in old age, depression is compounded by the helplessness induced by increasing physical and mental incapacities, as a visit to any old-age home will dramatically confirm, the frequency of depression among old people is at present much lower than among younger people.

RACE AND SOCIAL CLASS

Race and social class make little difference

There are no strong or consistent differences in the incidence of depression according to race or social class. For many years, depression was thought to be uncommon among North American blacks, but recent research does not bear this out. In the largest study to date, race and social class made little difference in incidence of depression among 159 black and 555 white patients. There was a tendency for the blacks to be more negativistic, more angry, and to attempt suicide more often than whites. In addition, the blacks were younger and had more rapid onset of symptoms (Raskin,

Crook, and Herman, 1975). Caution should be used, however, in interpreting any study of cross-racial, cross-age, cross-sex, or cross-cultural psychological disorders. Since diagnosis is, for the most part, made by middle-class white psychiatrists and psychologists, insensitivity to symptoms of depression within another culture or elicitation of greater hostility among the patients may easily contaminate the results (Tonks, Paykel, and Klerman, 1970).

No strong differences occur in depression among social classes. Unlike schizophrenia, which is less frequent in middle and upper classes, depression is democratic. Again, however, it is possible that depression may have different manifestations according to the patient's social class: lower-class patients may show more feelings of powerlessness and hopelessness, middle-class patients stronger feelings of loneliness and rejection, and upper-class patients greater pessimism and social withdrawal (Schwab, Bialow, Holzer, Brown, and Stevenson, 1967). At any rate, the similarities in the occurrence of depression between black people and white people and between rich people and poor people, far outweigh the differences.

EFFECTS OF LIFE EVENTS

Stressful life events increase risk for depression

Are the lives of depressed people, before the onset of their depression, different from the lives of people who do not become depressed? Depressed individuals have experienced more early childhood losses than nondepressed individuals and more frequent stressful losses within a year or two before the onset of depression. Yet, many individuals suffer both early childhood loss and recent loss without becoming depressed, and a substantial number of depressed individuals do not suffer early childhood loss or recent loss. So we are far from saying that such life events *cause* depression, but some events do seem to increase the risk of depression.

Effect of early loss of mother

□ EARLY CHILDHOOD LOSS.   The death of a person's mother before the child is eleven years old may predispose an individual to depression in adulthood. In a study of depression in its natural setting, the English sociologists George W. Brown and Tirril Harris interviewed women door-to-door in the working class borough of Camberwell in London. They found that an alarmingly high percentage—15 to 20 percent—were moderately to severely depressed and that these women were not receiving treatment for their depression. The rate of depression was almost three times higher among women who, before age eleven, had lost their mother and who also had experienced a severe recent loss than among women who, before age eleven, had not lost their mother but who had experienced a similar recent loss. Death of the mother after the child reached age eleven had no effect on risk for depression according to this study (Brown and Harris, 1978). Death of the father while the child is young is also probably associated with later depression (Barnes and Prosin, 1985).

Effect of recent loss

□ RECENT LOSS.   Most depressions are preceded by a recent stressful loss. Failure at work, marital separation, failure at school, loss of a job, rejection by a loved one, death of a child, illness of a family member, and physical illness are common precipitants of depression. Individuals who become de-

If a woman has more than three children still at home, she may be more vulnerable to depressive symptoms after experiencing a recent stressful loss.

pressed show more such losses preceding their depression than matched controls (Leff, Roatch and Bunney, 1970; Paykel, 1973; Brown and Harris, 1978; Littlefield and Rushton, 1986; Breslau and Davis, 1986).

Invulnerability factors

But such losses do not always bring on depressions, by any means. Only about 10 percent of those persons who experience losses equivalent in severity to those of an average depressed person, themselves become depressed. Why is it that the other 90 percent do *not* become depressed? Brown and Harris proposed that there are four invulnerability factors that can help prevent depression from occurring, even in the presence of the predisposing factors and recent loss. Only half the women who, before age eleven, had lost their mother and who also had suffered a recent loss became depressed. What about the other half? The invulnerable women had either (1) an intimate relationship with a spouse or a lover, or (2) a part-time or full-time job away from home, or (3) fewer than three children still at home, or (4) a serious religious commitment. So intimacy, employment, a life not overburdened by child care, and strong religious belief may protect against depression. Perhaps what these four invulnerability factors have in common is that they contribute self-esteem and a sense of mastery, while undercutting the formation of an outlook pervaded by hopelessness. All of these, in effect, help to ward off depression.

THE COURSE OF DEPRESSION

Depression dissipates with time

When a vulnerable individual becomes depressed, what is likely to happen if the individual fails to seek out treatment? If anything good about depression can be said, it is that it usually dissipates in time. After the initial attack, which comes on suddenly about three-quarters of the time, depression seems to last an average of about three months in outpatients. Among inpatients, who are usually more severely depressed, it lasts about six months on the average. At first, the depression gets progressively worse, eventually reaching the bottom, but then the depressed individual begins to recover gradually to the state that existed before the onset (Beck, 1967; Robins and Guze, 1972). What our grandmothers told us about our own personal tragedies—time heals all wounds—is certainly true for depression. The mind, or the body, seems incapable of sustaining a dark mood forever, and unknown homeostatic mechanisms take over and, in time, correct the disorder.

The time that a depressive episode lasts, however, is painfully long, and to an individual suffering from it, it seems like forever. For this reason, a therapist will always emphasize that the depressive episode will go away in time. Without minimizing the suffering the patient is feeling now, the therapist should tell the patient that complete recovery from the episode occurs in 70 to 95 percent of the cases. For some, this ray of hope may speed the time when the depression will lift.

Three patterns of depression

Once a depressive episode has occurred, one of three patterns may develop. The first is *recovery without recurrence.* About half the patients who have had a depressive episode will not have another one, at least during the following ten years. Generally, the more stable a person is before the episode, the less likely depression will recur. On the other hand, half of depressed individuals will show the second pattern: *recovery with recurrence.* The second depressive episode, if it occurs, will tend to be of about the same duration as the first attack. On the average, however, most individuals who have recurrent episodes of depression can expect an average symptom-free interval of more than three years before the next episode. But the interval between episodes in recurrent depression tends to become shorter over the years. The period of greatest risk for recurrence is in the first six months after recovery. And substance abuse increases the risk for recurrence (NIMH, 1984). For some individuals, the third pattern will develop: *chronic depression.* Roughly 10 percent of those individuals who have a major depressive episode will not recover and will remain chronically depressed (Perris, 1968; Kerr, Roth, Schapira, and Gurney, 1972; Schuyler, 1974). Therapy for depression usually attempts to make the current episode shorter or to postpone the time at which another episode might strike. The therapies for depression derive from three different theories, and it is to these theories and therapies that we now turn.

THEORIES AND THERAPIES OF UNIPOLAR DEPRESSION

Three main theories of depression

What causes depression, and how is depression most effectively treated? In the last twenty years, we have moved out of the dark ages in our understanding of depression. Substantial strides have been made in the understanding and treatment of the disorder. Between 80 and 90 percent of severe depressions can now be markedly alleviated with a brief course of therapy. Although several theories, with substantial research support, have emerged to explain the origins of depression, we still cannot say with certainty what the cause of depression is or how it can best be treated. We can, however, make highly educated guesses. There are three main theories and therapies for depression: the biological model, the psychodynamic model, and the cognitive model. These theories overlap, and there is also a good deal of overlap in the therapies each recommends, but each tends to focus on one aspect of depression. At the end of this section, we will attempt a synthesis of these models.

THE BIOLOGICAL MODEL OF DEPRESSION

Depression and
the body

According to the biological model, depression is a disorder of the body. While in principle, depression could be caused by a problem in any bodily organ, speculation has centered almost entirely on the brain, and in particular on depletion of a class of substances (biogenic amines) that help transmit nerve impulses across the gaps (synapses) between nerve cells (neurons). There are four clues that the body is intimately involved in depression (Schuyler, 1974). First of all, depression occurs with some frequency following periods of natural physiological change in women: after giving birth to a child, at menopause, and just before menstruation. Second, there is considerable similarity of symptoms across cultures, sexes, ages, and races, indicating an underlying biological process. Third, somatic therapies, in particular drugs like tricyclic antidepressants and MAO inhibitors, and electroconvulsive shock, are effective treatments of depression. Fourth, depression is occasionally induced in normal individuals as a side effect of medications; in particular depression may be induced by reserpine, a high-blood-pressure-reducing drug (Schuyler, 1974). These clues have fueled the search for a biological basis of depression.

GENETICS AND UNIPOLAR DEPRESSION

First-degree relatives of unipolar depressives have between two and five times the risk for depression above the risk for those in the normal population (Weissman, Kidd, and Prusoff, 1982; Keller, Beardslee, Dorer, Lavori, Samuelson, and Klerman, 1986). If the depressive is alcoholic as well, the risk for both depression and alcoholism increases; but if the relative is not alcoholic, there is increased risk for only depression (Merikangas, Leckman, Prusoff, Pauls, and Weissman, 1985). Is this increased risk genetic?

Evidence for
weak inheritance
of unipolar
depression

While there is evidence that bipolar depression can be strongly inherited, unipolar depression is only weakly inherited. Only 28 percent of identical twins are discordant for bipolar depression, but at least 60 percent of identical twins are discordant for unipolar depression (Allen, 1976). The most recent twin study does not find evidence for concordance for unipolar depression (Torgersen, 1986a). Better evidence comes from studies of adoptive versus biological relatives of depressed patients. Biological relatives had an eightfold increased risk for unipolar depression relative to adoptive relatives (Wender, Kety, Rosenthal, Schulsinger, Ortmann, and Lunde, 1986). Overall it is clear that having a depressed family member confers risk for depression, but whether this risk is genetic awaits more evidence. Thus, the genetic evidence gives marginal support for a biomedical approach to unipolar depression. The drug and biochemical evidence, however, is stronger.

THE NEUROCHEMICAL BASIS OF DEPRESSION

Insufficiencies of
biogenic amines

The biological model holds that depression is a disorder of motivation caused by insufficiencies of the biogenic amines. The *biogenic amines* are neurochemicals that facilitate neural transmission. They divide into two groups with different chemical structures: the *catecholamines*, which in-

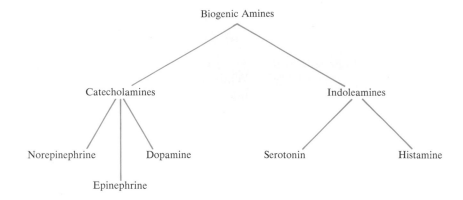

Figure 11-2
The biogenic amines.

clude norepinephrine, epinephrine, and dopamine; and the ***indoleamines***, which include serotonin and histamine (see Figure 11-2).

The biogenic amines play significant roles in neural transmission in the medial forebrain bundle (MFB) and the periventricular system (PVS). The MFB and PVS are two major pathways that run through lower centers of the brain. Research with animals indicates that the MFB and PVS may be the neuroanatomical basis of reward and punishment respectively (Stein, 1968). Electrical stimulation of the MFB is highly reinforcing to rats, and electrical stimulation of the periventricular system is very punishing. The MFB may function as a "go" system that facilitates active behavior, whereas the PVS may act as a "stop" system. When the biogenic amines are depleted, the functioning of these systems is reduced and depression, with its loss of motivation, may ensue. Speculation about the neurochemical basis of depression has centered primarily around decreased availability of one of the catecholamines, ***norepinephrine (NE)*** (Schildkraut, 1965), and one of the indoleamines, ***serotonin*** (Maas, 1975; McNeal and Cimbolic, 1986).

Figure 11-3 depicts the hypothesized mode of action of norepinephrine in transmission of a nerve impulse from one neuron across the synapse to a second neuron in the brain. When a nerve impulse occurs in neuron 1, norepinephrine is discharged into the synapse (the gap between neuron 1 and neuron 2). This stimulates neuron 2 to fire when the NE makes contact with

Figure 11-3
Schematized action of norepinephrine (NE) in neural transmission. NE produced in nerve cell 1 is discharged into the synapse, where it stimulates nerve cell 2 to fire. In order to stop the NE from stimulating nerve cell 2, NE can be inactivated either by being reabsorbed back into nerve cell 1 (reuptake) or by being broken down and excreted out of the synapse (breakdown). Antidepressant drugs keep NE available in the synapse by blocking its reuptake (tricyclics) or slowing its breakdown (MAO inhibitors).

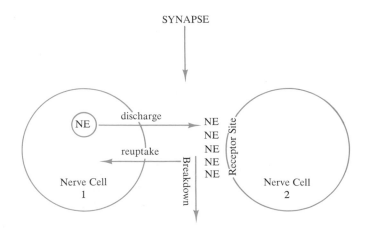

the receptors on the membrane of neuron 2. Norepinephrine is now sitting in the synapse and on the membrane of neuron 2. Neuron 2 will continue to fire until the NE is inactivated. There are two relevant ways that norepinephrine can now be inactivated. The first way is by *reuptake*, in which neuron 1 reabsorbs norepinephrine, thereby decreasing the amount of norepinephrine at the receptors. The second is by *breakdown*. This is facilitated by the enzyme monoamine oxidase (MAO) among others. This enzyme breaks down the norepinephrine chemically and renders it inactive. As we said above, norepinephrine is a catecholamine, which is one of two classes of biogenic amines. The biogenic amines affect our motivation. And when we decrease the amount of biogenic amines (in this case, norepinephrine), we will have less motivation. The catecholamine hypothesis claims that when reuptake and/or breakdown are doing their job too well, our norepinephrine level drops too low, and we become highly unmotivated, in short, depressed.

Two groups of drugs are used to treat depression: tricyclic antidepressants and MAO inhibitors. Each affects the availability of NE in the brain. It was a serendipitous finding that led to their use as antidepressants. Individuals with tuberculosis, who are frequently depressed, were tested with a new drug, iproniazid. It turned out that the drug didn't help cure their tuberculosis, but it did produce a much brighter mood in the patients, and they became less depressed. Why did this happen? The drug, iproniazid, is an MAO inhibitor. As we have seen, the enzyme MAO facilitates breakdown, thereby making less norepinephrine available for neural transmission. So this drug, iproniazid, inhibited the enzyme MAO in the patients with tuberculosis, and in part prevented breakdown of NE. The catecholamine hypothesis claims that, as a result, more norepinephrine was available, and with more NE available, the tuberculosis patients became less depressed. Since then, MAO inhibitors have been successfully used in treating depression, thereby rendering support for the biological model, specifically the catecholamine hypothesis.

Also discovered by accident, the tricyclic antidepressants affect the availability of NE. These drugs block the process of reuptake. As we saw above, reuptake occurs when the neuron that released NE absorbs it back. If reuptake is blocked, then less NE is absorbed, and more will be available. As a result of more NE, the patient will become less depressed. This provides further evidence for the catecholamine hypothesis.

Further evidence of this hypothesis has come from reserpine-induced depression. Reserpine is a powerful sedative given to high blood pressure patients. Physicians discovered that it produces an unwanted side effect, depression with suicidal tendencies, in about 15 percent of the people who take it. It turns out that reserpine, among other actions, depletes norepinephrine. With less NE, these high blood pressure patients became depressed.

Despite the favorable evidence supporting the catecholamine hypothesis based on the action of these drugs, advocates of the hypothesis are appropriately cautious. The reason is that reserpine, the tricyclics, and the MAO inhibitors all have a large number of effects other than their effect on norepinephrine. Because of this, it is very possible that their effects might be due to some other properties of the drugs and not necessarily to their effect on norepinephrine.

Tricyclic antidepressants and MAO inhibitors

THE NEUROANATOMICAL BASIS OF DEPRESSION

Right frontal lobe
and depression

There is also an anatomical theory of depression that claims that overactivity of the right frontal lobes in the brain produces depression. Subjects express more negativity about pictures of faces presented to the right hemisphere (left visual field) than about pictures presented to the left hemisphere (right visual field). This is particularly accentuated in depressed people (Davidson, Schaffer, and Saron, 1985). Brain damage to the left hemisphere due to stroke (oxygen starvation in part of the brain) more often results in depression than does damage to the right hemisphere (Sackheim, Greenberg et al., 1982).

SOMATIC THERAPIES FOR DEPRESSION

Advocates of the biological model approach the treatment of unipolar depression, particularly when it is severe, in two ways. The first is to treat the patient with drugs like the tricyclics and the MAO inhibitors. The second approach is to administer electroconvulsive shock.

Drug treatment

□ DRUG TREATMENT.   Tricyclic antidepressants, you will recall, block the reuptake of norepinephrine. As a result, less NE is absorbed, more NE is available, and the patient becomes less depressed. On the average, between 63 and 75 percent of depressed patients given tricyclics show significant clinical improvement (Beck, 1973). Further, maintaining a patient with recurrent depression on tricyclics or lithium between attacks reduces recurrence (Gelenberg and Klerman, 1978; NIMH, 1984).

The MAO inhibitors prevent the breakdown of norepinephrine by inhibiting the enzyme MAO. With more NE available, the patient becomes less depressed. But MAO inhibitors are now prescribed much less often than tricyclic antidepressants, largely because the MAO inhibitors can have lethal side effects. When combined with cheese, alcohol, pickled herring, narcotics, or high blood-pressure-reducing drugs, MAO inhibitors can be fatal. Most studies show MAO inhibitors to be superior to placebos in alleviating depression, however, and if tricyclics fail, the MAO inhibitors should be tried.

ECT

□ ELECTROCONVULSIVE SHOCK (ECT).   Electroconvulsive shock is, to the layman, the scariest of the antidepressant treatments. In the two decades following ECT's discovery as a psychotherapeutic treatment in 1938, enthusiasm was high, and it was promiscuously prescribed for a very broad range of disorders. The treatment, particularly in its less refined forms, can have very serious side effects, however, and it has come to be regarded by the general public as "barbaric" and "punitive." But strong evidence exists that ECT, when given to severely depressed unipolar depressive patients, is a highly effective antidepressant therapy. Modern techniques have greatly reduced the common and severe side effects of yesteryear (Fink, 1979; Malitz and Sackheim, 1984).

Typically, ECT is administered by a medical team consisting of a psychiatrist, anesthesiologist, and a nurse. Metal electrodes are taped to either side of the patient's forehead, and the patient is anesthetized. The patient is given drugs to induce muscular relaxation in order to prevent the breaking

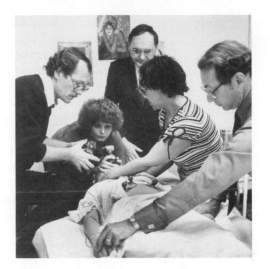

Electroconvulsive shock treatment has been found to be highly effective as treatment for those suffering from severe unipolar depression. It often has untoward side effects, however.

of bones during the convulsion. A high current is then passed through the brain for approximately a half second. This is followed by convulsions that last for almost one minute. As the anesthetic wears off, the patient wakens and will not remember the period of treatment. Within twenty minutes, the patient is functioning reasonably well and has little, if any, physical discomfort. A course of ECT usually consists of a half dozen treatments, one every other day (Schuyler, 1974).

ECT administered unilaterally

Electroconvulsive shock is today often administered unilaterally, that is, to only half of the brain. Producing the convulsion on the side of the brain that does not contain the speech centers (in the nondominant hemisphere, see Chapter 17) greatly reduces the possibility of the side effect of impaired speech following ECT. Unilateral ECT is an effective antidepressant, but it probably is not as effective as bilateral ECT (Scovern and Killman, 1980; Abrams, Taylor, Faber, Ts'o, Williams, and Almy, 1983).

ECT probably increases available norepinephrine and other biogenic amines, but it is such a gross technique—shocking the entire brain—and has so many other effects, including memory loss and motivational changes, that isolation of the effective ingredient in ECT is quite difficult (Squire, 1986).

THE PSYCHODYNAMIC MODEL OF DEPRESSION

Psychodynamic theorists have stressed three causes of depression: anger turned against the self, excessive dependence on others for self-esteem, and helplessness at achieving one's goals.

ANGER TURNED UPON THE SELF

Anger turned inward

The first contributions of the psychodynamic model to the understanding of depression came from the early psychoanalysts. Karl Abraham (1911) and Sigmund Freud (1917) in his classic paper, "Mourning and Melancholia," both stressed the importance of anger turned inward upon the self in producing depression.

On the surface, depressed individuals may seem drained of anger, but their anger may be bound up inside them.

On the surface, depressed individuals often seem drained of anger, and this leads to the suspicion that their anger may be bound up inside them. For Freud, the main clue to their inner state came from the difference between normal bereavement (mourning) and depression (melancholia). The normal individual and the depressive have two strikingly different reactions to the loss of a person they love. For the mourner, the world now seems empty, but his self-esteem is not threatened. The mourner will survive the loss. In contrast, according to Freud, the depressive will begin to feel a powerful sense of worthlessness and self-blame. He will feel rotten and guilty; he will accuse himself of being a failure. This self-reproach is usually moral, grossly unjustified, and most remarkable, publicly and shamelessly declared. It provides the clue that anger turned against the self is actively motivated and generates the low self-esteem of depression.

How could it come about that some individuals react to loss or rejection by turning their fury against themselves? For Freud, such a motivation for self-punishment follows from events in the depressive's childhood. During childhood, the future depressive forms an intense love that is undermined by disappointment with the other person. The depressive feels rage at having been disappointed. The libidinal energy underlying love is freed, but it does not become attached to any other person. Instead, the ego identifies with or "incorporates" the lost person, and the released libido attaches to this part of the ego. The rage originally felt for the person now is directed against the self.

Subsequent losses and rejection reactivate the primal loss and cause the depressive's rage to be turned again toward the original traitorous person, who has now been fused with the depressive's own ego. Such turning of anger in upon the self is the crucial step in producing the symptoms of low self-esteem, public accusation, the need for punishment, and in the most extreme cases, suicide. Depression ends either when the rage has spent itself or when the new loss is devalued—ends, that is, until a new loss starts the depressive sequence yet again.

The incorporation of a lost love object and anger turned inward upon the self producing depression is well illustrated by the following case:

Debby was a nineteen-year-old who was hospitalized because of strong suicidal impulses. During her hospitalization, she made a number of unsuccessful suicide attempts, and in addition, she engaged in a bizarre form of self-mutilation: clawing terribly at a particular spot on her left arm. These actions and impulses frightened her because she experienced them as originating outside of herself. On the other hand, however, she saw them as justified because she wanted to atone for her own worthlessness and promiscuity.

Debby's depression seemed to be closely related to her feelings about her mother, who had died a few years earlier under compromising circumstances; she had been murdered by a soldier with whom she had been spending the night. The body was so badly battered that it was identified only by a large distinctive birthmark on the left arm.

After her mother's death, Debby felt more warmth toward her mother than ever before. She became her mother's staunchest defender. When her mother was accused of ruining the family's reputation, Debby maintained that her mother had been badly misunderstood and ill treated by the family, and that this had caused her to carry on with other men. At the same time, however, Debby began to drop her former friends and to take up new friendships with people who had "bad reputations." She began to think of herself as a "bad person." As if to satisfy her new self-image, she began for the first time to behave promiscuously.

Debby's promiscuity seemed to result from identification with her mother, for this new part of herself provided the perfect target for the rage that her mother's death provoked. Debby's genuine feelings were mixed: both love and anger. We do not easily condemn the dead in our society, so instead Debby vented her anger by hating the part of herself that had become her mother. This was expressed most concretely through her self-mutilation. The specific part of her arm that she scratched so terribly was the exact location of her mother's birthmark. By mutilating herself, she was simultaneously able to *identify* with her mother by creating an ugly disfigurement on her left arm and to express her anger toward her mother.

Once Debby began to acknowledge her feelings of anger toward her mother consciously during therapy, her depression began to lift. The crisis and resolution came violently, when Debby smashed every pane of glass in a door with her fist. During this experience she believed she was hitting not a door but an image of her mother. The conscious acknowledgment of this rage removed the need for indirect and symbolic expression, and Debby's feelings of worthlessness and self-hatred began to disappear. (Adapted from Fancher, 1973.)

THE DEPRESSIVE PERSONALITY

Excessive dependence on others for self-esteem

Psychodynamic theorists since Freud have emphasized a personality style that may make individuals especially vulnerable to depression: the depressive depends excessively on others for his self-esteem. The depressive desperately needs to be showered with love and admiration. He goes through the world in a state of perpetual greediness for love, and when his need for love is not satisfied, his self-esteem plummets. When he is disappointed he has difficulty tolerating frustration, and even trivial losses upset his self-regard and result in immediate and frantic efforts to relieve discomfort. So depressives are seen as love addicts, who have become exquisitely skilled at producing demonstrations of love from others and who insist on a constant flow of love. Beyond receiving such love, however, the depressive cares little for the actual personality of the person he loves (Rado, 1928; Fenichel, 1945; Arieti and Bemporad, 1978).

HELPLESSNESS AT ACHIEVING ONE'S GOALS

Helplessness at achieving goals

The third major strand in psychodynamic theorizing about depression comes from the psychoanalyst Edward Bibring's (1953) claim that depression results when the ego feels helpless before its aspirations. Perceived helplessness at achieving the ego's high goals produces loss of self-esteem, the central feature in depression. The depression-prone individual has extremely high standards, and this increases his vulnerability to feeling helpless in the face of his goals. The combination of strongly held goals to be worthy, to be strong, and to be good, along with the ego's acute awareness of its helplessness and incapacity to live up to these goals, is for Bibring the mechanism of all depression.

PSYCHODYNAMIC THERAPY FOR DEPRESSION

Therapeutic strategies

In general, psychodynamic theory emphasizes the long-term predisposition to depression, rather than the losses that happen to set it off in the short term. Psychodynamic therapies similarly are directed toward long-term change, rather than short-term alleviation of depression. Several therapeutic strategies follow from the three strands of psychodynamic theorizing about depression. First, psychodynamic therapists inclined toward the anger-turned-inward theory of depression will (as in Debby's case) attempt to make the patient conscious of his misdirected anger and the early conflicts that produced it. Learning to come to terms with the anger that loss and rejection produce and to direct it toward more appropriate objects should prevent and relieve depression. Second, psychodynamic therapists who deal with the depressive's strong dependence on others for self-esteem will attempt to get the patient to discover and then resolve the conflicts that make him perpetually greedy for love and esteem from others. Such a patient must learn that true self-esteem comes only from within. And third, therapists who work within Bibring's helplessness approach try to end the patient's depression by getting him to again perceive his goals as being within reach, to modify his goals so that they can now be realized, or to give up these goals altogether.

COGNITIVE MODELS OF DEPRESSION

Thoughts that lead to depression

The two cognitive models of depression view particular thoughts as the crucial cause of depressive symptoms. The first, developed by Aaron T. Beck, derives mainly from extensive therapeutic experience with depressed patients, and it views depression as caused by negative thoughts about the self, about ongoing experience, and about the future. The second, developed by Martin E. P. Seligman, derives mainly from experiments with dogs, rats, and mildly depressed people, and it views depression as caused by the expectation of future helplessness. A depressed person expects bad events to occur and believes that there is nothing he can do to prevent them from occurring.

BECK'S COGNITIVE THEORY OF DEPRESSION

Aaron T. Beck has devised cognitive treatments for depression.

Aaron T. Beck (along with Albert Ellis) founded a new type of therapy, called cognitive therapy, which we reviewed in Chapter 5. For Beck, two mechanisms, the *cognitive triad* and *errors in logic,* produce depression.

Negative thoughts

□ THE COGNITIVE TRIAD.   The cognitive triad consists of negative thoughts about the self, about ongoing experience, and about the future. The negative thoughts about the self consist of the depressive's belief that he is defective, worthless, and inadequate. The symptom of low self-esteem derives from his belief that he is defective. When he has unpleasant experiences, he attributes them to personal unworthiness. Since he believes he is defective, he believes that he will never attain happiness.

The depressive's negative thoughts about experience consist in his interpretation that what happens to him is bad. He misinterprets neutral interaction with people around him as meaning defeat. He misinterprets small obstacles as impassable barriers. Even when there are more plausible positive views of his experience, he is drawn to the most negative possible interpretation of what has happened to him. Finally, the depressive's negative view of the future is one of hopelessness. When he thinks of the future, he believes that the negative things that are happening to him now will continue unabated because of his personal defects. The following case illustrates how a depressive person may negatively interpret her experiences:

> Stella, a thirty-six-year-old depressed woman, had withdrawn from the tennis games she had previously enjoyed. Instead, her daily behavior pattern consisted of "sleeping and trying to do the housework I've neglected." Stella firmly believed that she was unable to engage in activities as "strenuous" as tennis and that she had become so poor at tennis that no one would ever want to play with her. Her husband arranged for a private tennis lesson in an attempt to help his wife overcome her depression. She reluctantly attended the lesson and appeared to be "a different person" in the eyes of her husband. She stroked the ball well and was agile in following instructions. Despite her good performance during the lesson, Stella concluded that her skills had "deteriorated" beyond the point at which lessons would do any good. She misinterpreted her husband's positive response to her lesson as an indication of how bad her game had become because in her view, "He thinks I'm so hopeless that the only time I can hit the ball is when I'm taking a lesson." She rejected the obvious reason for her husband's enthusiasm in favor of an explanation derived from her negative image of herself. She also stated that she didn't enjoy the tennis session because she wasn't "deserving" of any recreation time. (Adapted from Beck et al., 1979.)

Stella's depression exemplifies the negative triad: (1) She believed that her tennis abilities had deteriorated (negative view of self), (2) she misinterpreted her husband's praise as indication of how poor her game was (negative view of experience), and (3) she believed that no one would ever want to play with her again (negative view of the future). Her motivational and cognitive symptoms stemmed from her negative cognitive triad. Her passivity (giving up tennis for sleeping and housework) resulted from her hopelessness about her abilities. Her cognitive symptoms were the direct expressions of her negative views of herself, her experience, and her future. Beck also claims that the other two classes of depressive symptoms—emotional and physical—result from the depressive's belief that he is doomed to failure.

Systematic errors in logic

□ ERRORS IN LOGIC.   Beck believes that systematic errors in logic are the second mechanism of depression. According to Beck, the depressive makes five different logical errors in thinking, and each of these darkens his experiences: arbitrary inference, selective abstraction, overgeneralization, magnification and minimization, and personalization.

Arbitrary inference refers to drawing a conclusion when there is little or no evidence to support it. For example, an intern became discouraged when she received an announcement which said that in the future all patients worked on by interns would be reexamined by residents. She thought, incorrectly, "The chief doesn't have any faith in my work." *Selective abstraction* consists of focusing on one insignificant detail while ignoring the more important features of a situation. In one case, an employer praised an employee at length about his secretarial work. Midway through the conversation, the boss suggested that he need not make extra carbon copies of her letters anymore. The employee's selective abstraction was, "The boss is dissatisfied with my work." In spite of all the good things said, only this was remembered.

Overgeneralization refers to drawing global conclusions about worth, ability, or performance on the basis of a single fact. Consider a man who fails to fix a leaky faucet in his house. Most husbands would call a plumber and then forget it. But the depressive will overgeneralize and may go so far as to believe that he is a poor husband. *Magnification and minimization* are gross errors of evaluation, in which small bad events are magnified and large good events are minimized. The inability to find the right color shirt is considered a disaster, but a large raise and praise for his good work are considered trivial. And lastly, *personalization* refers to incorrectly taking responsibility for bad events in the world. A neighbor slips and falls on her own icy walk, but the depressed next-door neighbor blames himself unremittingly for not having alerted her to her icy walk and for not insisting that she shovel it.

COGNITIVE THERAPY

Countering negative thoughts and errors in logic

Beck's cognitive theory of depression considers that depression is caused by negative thoughts of self, ongoing experience, and future, and by errors in logic. Cognitive therapy for depression attempts to counter these cognitions (Beck, 1967; Beck, Rush, Shaw, and Emery, 1979). Its aim is to identify and correct the distorted thinking and dysfunctional assumptions underlying depression (Rehm, 1977; Beck et al., 1979). In addition, the patient is taught to conquer problems and master situations that he previously believed were insuperable. Cognitive therapy differs from most other forms of psychotherapy. In contrast to the psychoanalyst, the cognitive therapist actively guides the patient into reorganizing his thinking and his actions. The cognitive therapist talks a lot and is directive. She argues with the patient. She persuades; she cajoles; she leads. Beck claims that nondirective classical psychoanalytic techniques, such as free association, cause depressives to "dissolve in the morass of their negative thinking." Cognitive therapy also contrasts with psychoanalysis by being centered in the present. Childhood problems are rarely discussed, rather the major focus is the patient's current thoughts and feelings. One of the central foci is not to be depressed about depression itself (Teasdale, 1985).

Behavioral techniques as tools for changing thoughts

Cognitive therapy uses such behavioral therapy techniques as activity raising (rewarding the depressive for participating in more activities), graded task assignment (reinforcing the depressive for taking one small step at a time, and gradually increasing the difficulty of these steps), and assertiveness training against depressive symptoms. But in cognitive therapy, these techniques for changing behavioral symptoms are just tools for changing thoughts and assumptions that are seen as the underlying causes of depressed behavior. So, for example, the cognitive therapist believes that teaching a depressive to behave assertively works only insofar as it changes what the depressive believes about his own abilities and his future.

We discuss four specific cognitive therapy techniques: detecting automatic thoughts, reality testing automatic thoughts, reattribution training, and changing depressogenic assumptions.

☐ DETECTION OF AUTOMATIC THOUGHTS. Beck argues that there are discrete, negative sentences that depressed patients say to themselves quickly and habitually. These automatic thoughts maintain depression. Cognitive therapy helps patients to identify such automatic thoughts. Here is a case in which the patient had been unaware of her automatic thoughts:

> A mother of three found that her depression was at its worst from seven to nine in the morning when she prepared breakfast for her children. She was unable to explain this until she was taught to record her thoughts in writing as they occurred. As a result, she discovered she consistently compared herself with her mother, whom she remembered as irritable and argumentative in the morning. When her children misbehaved or made unreasonable requests, the patient often thought, "Don't get angry, or they'll resent you," with the result that she typically ignored them. With increasing frequency, however, she "exploded" at the children and then thought, "I'm worse than my mother ever was. I'm not fit to care for my children. They'd be better off if I were dead." (Beck et al., 1979)

Criticizing automatic negative thoughts

□ **REALITY TESTING AUTOMATIC THOUGHTS.** Once the patient has learned to identify such thoughts, the cognitive therapist engages in a dialogue with the patient in which evidence for and against the thoughts is scrutinized. This is not an attempt to induce spurious optimism, rather to encourage the patient to use the reasonable standards of self-evaluation that nondepressed people use. The mother who thought she was unfit would be encouraged to remember that her children were flourishing in school, partly as a result of her tutoring them. Similarly a young student despondent over the belief that she would not get into a particular college was taught to criticize her automatic negative thoughts.

> THERAPIST: Why do you think you won't be able to get into the university of your choice?
> PATIENT: Because my grades were really not so hot.
> THERAPIST: Well, what was your grade average?
> PATIENT: Well, pretty good up until the last semester in high school.
> THERAPIST: What was your grade average in general?
> PATIENT: A's and B's.
> THERAPIST: Well, how many of each?
> PATIENT: Well, I guess almost all of my grades were A's, but I got terrible grades in my last semester.
> THERAPIST: What were your grades then?
> PATIENT: I got two A's and two B's.
> THERAPIST: So your grade average would seem to me to come to almost all A's. Why don't you think you'll be able to get into the university?
> PATIENT: Because of competition being so tough.
> THERAPIST: Have you found out what the average grades are for admission to the college?
> PATIENT: Well, somebody told me that a B+ average should suffice.
> THERAPIST: Isn't your average better than that?
> PATIENT: I guess so.
>
> (Beck et al., 1979)

By learning to scrutinize and criticize her automatic thoughts and marshaling evidence against them, the patient undermines her negative automatic thoughts, and they wane.

□ **REATTRIBUTION TRAINING.** Depressed patients tend to blame themselves for bad events for which they are not, in fact, responsible. To counteract such irrational blame, the therapist and the patient review the events, applying the standards of nondepressed individuals in order to come up with an assignment of blame. The point here is not to absolve the patient of blame, but rather to let him see that there may be other factors besides his own incompetence that contribute to a bad event.

A fifty-one-year-old bank manager in a state of deep depression believed he was ineffective in his job. His therapy session proceeded as follows:

PATIENT: I can't tell you how much of a mess I've made of things. I made another major error in judgment which should cost me my job.
THERAPIST: Tell me what the error in judgment was.
PATIENT: I approved a loan which fell through completely. I made a very poor decision.
THERAPIST: Can you recall the specifics about the decision?
PATIENT: Yes. I remember it looked good on paper, good collateral, good credit rating, but I should have known that there was going to be a problem.
THERAPIST: Did you have all the pertinent information at the time of your decision?
PATIENT: Not at the time, but I sure found out six weeks later. I'm paid to make profitable decisions, not to give the bank's money away.
THERAPIST: I understand your position. But I'd like to review the information which you had at the time your decision was required, not six weeks after the decision had been made.

When the patient and the therapist reviewed this information, they concluded that the patient had made his judgment on sound banking principles. He recalled that he had even made an intensive check into the client's financial background, which he had forgotten. (Beck et al., 1979)

Such reattribution training enables patients to find sources of blame other than themselves, and it thereby raises their low self-esteem.

Changing depressogenic assumptions

□ CHANGING DEPRESSOGENIC ASSUMPTIONS. The final technique of cognitive therapy is the explicit change of depressogenic assumptions (Ellis, 1962). Beck outlines six assumptions that depressed individuals base their life upon, thereby predisposing themselves to sadness, despair, and disappointment: (1) in order to be happy, I have to be successful in whatever I undertake; (2) to be happy, I must be accepted by all people at all times; (3) if I make a mistake, it means I am inept; (4) I can't live without love; (5) if somebody disagrees with me, it means he doesn't like me; and (6) my value as a person depends on what others think of me. When the patient and therapist identify one of these assumptions, it is vigorously attacked. The validity of the assumption is examined, counterarguments are marshaled, plausible alternative assumptions are presented, and the disastrous consequences of holding the assumption are exposed.

THE LEARNED HELPLESSNESS MODEL OF DEPRESSION

The second cognitive model of depression is the *learned helplessness model.* It is cognitive because it holds that the basic cause of depression is an expectation: the individual expects that bad events will occur to him and that there is nothing he can do to prevent their occurrence. We will discuss the phenomenon and theory of learned helplessness, and then we will discuss the relationship between learned helplessness and depression.

Laboratory model of learned helplessness

□ **EXPERIMENTAL DISCOVERY OF LEARNED HELPLESSNESS.** Learned helplessness was discovered quite by accident. In the course of experiments on the effects of prior Pavlovian conditioning on later instrumental learning, Steven Maier, Bruce Overmier, and Martin Seligman found that dogs first given Pavlovian conditioning with inescapable shock became profoundly passive later on when they were given escapable shock. In the latter condition, although they had the opportunity to flee the shock, they *did not* even attempt to escape.

Here is the basic phenomenon: a dog is strapped into a hammock and given between sixty and eighty five-second inescapable shocks. The shocks are moderately painful, but not physically damaging. The shock is uncontrollable: no response the dog makes during this session will affect the shock, since the shock is programmed to go on and off at a particular moment, independently of all responses. Twenty-four hours later, this dog is placed in a two-compartment shuttlebox from which it is possible to escape shock.

Passivity

When shock is turned on, the dog engages in about thirty seconds of frantic activity, but then it lies down during the shock and does not move, not even attempting to escape shock. This passivity continues trial after trial. This is the basic motivational deficit in learned helplessness: a failure to initiate voluntary responses to escape following a previous experience with uncontrollable events. This behavior is in marked contrast to the behavior of two other groups of dogs who first received escapable shock or who received no shock when strapped into the hammock. These dogs respond readily later on in the shuttlebox, jumping back and forth across the barrier, and learning to escape and avoid shock. This use of these three groups (the triadic design) tells us it is not shock *per se,* but the uncontrollability of the shock that produces the motivational deficits (see Figure 11-4).

There is another basic deficit of learned helplessness found in dogs, rats, and people. This is the failure to learn that responding can be successful, even once a response is made and it succeeds in controlling the outcome. Dogs and rats, who first had inescapable shock, when later placed in the shuttlebox, often sit for three or four trials and fail to escape shock. On the fifth trial, the animal may stand up, cross the barrier, and successfully ter-

Figure 11-4
The effects of matched escapable and inescapable shocks on later escape learning. This figure shows the escape latencies in the shuttle box for three groups of dogs: (a) those given escape training in the shuttle box as naive subjects, (b) those given prior escape training in a different situation, and (c) those given prior inescapable shocks, but matched in duration and temporal distribution to the shocks for the escape-training group. (Source: Maier, Seligman, and Solomon, 1969)

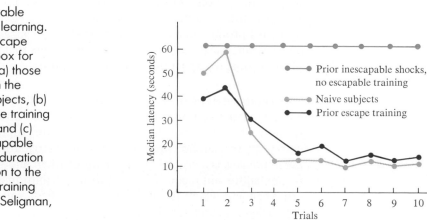

Failure to learn

minate shock. Such an animal, surprisingly, often does not catch on: during later trials it will revert to sitting and taking the shock, even though it has made a successful response. This is, again, in marked contrast to other animals that have had prior escapable shock or no shock. Once these other animals make a response that works, they catch on (Overmier and Seligman, 1967; Maier and Seligman, 1976).

□ LEARNED HELPLESSNESS IN HUMANS. Following the exploration of learned helplessness in animals, it became important for investigators to find out whether or not learned helplessness occurred in normal human beings. It does. In the basic procedure that produces learned helplessness in humans, the triadic design is used with nondepressed volunteers who receive loud noise delivered through earphones. For the first group, the noise is *inescapable;* it is preprogrammed to go on and off independently of what they do. The second group can *escape* noise by pressing a series of buttons in front of them. The third group receives *no noise.* Then all three groups are taken to a human shuttlebox, and noise goes on. If they move their hand from one side of the shuttlebox to the other, the noise goes off. The results parallel those in animals. Individuals who have received inescapable noise sit there passively and fail to escape, but those who have previously learned to escape noise, escape it readily in the shuttlebox (Hiroto, 1974).

The deficits produced by learned helplessness in humans are quite general. Experience with inescapable noise produces deficits at later noise escape, deficits in cognitive tasks such as the solution of anagrams, deficits in seeing patterns in anagrams, and lowered expectancy change following success and failure in skilled tasks. The inducing events for helplessness in man need not be aversive. Not only do inescapable noise and shock produce the phenomenon, but also unsolvable cognitive problems produce it.

Expectation that future responding will be futile

Learned helplessness theory argues that the basic cause of all the deficits observed in helpless animals and humans after uncontrollable events occur is the expectation of future noncontingency between responding and outcomes. This expectation that future responding will be futile causes the two helplessness deficits: (1) it produces deficits in responding by undermining the motivation to respond, and (2) it produces later difficulty in seeing that outcomes are contingent upon responding when they are. The three-group design is the basic evidence for this hypothesis. Recall that just the experience of shock, noise, or problems in themselves does not produce the motivational and cognitive deficits, only *uncontrollable* shock, noise, and problems produce these deficits. This strongly suggests that both animals and humans learn during uncontrollable events that their responding is futile and come to expect this in future situations.

Insidious explanatory style

□ ATTRIBUTIONS IN HUMAN HELPLESSNESS. When a human being experiences inescapable noise or unsolvable problems and perceives that his responding is ineffective, he goes on to ask an important question: What causes my present helplessness? The causal attribution (explanation) that a person makes is a crucial determinant of when and where expectancies for future failure will recur. There are three attributional dimensions that govern when and where future helplessness deficits will be displayed (Abramson, Seligman, and Teasdale, 1978).

The first dimension is the ***internal-external dimension.*** Consider an individual who has received unsolvable problems in an experiment. When he discovers that responding is ineffective, he can either decide that he is stupid but the problem is solvable, or that the problems are rigged to be unsolvable and he is not stupid. The first explanation for this failure is internal (stupidity) and the second is external (unsolvable problem). Evidence suggests that when individuals fail at important tasks and make internal explanations for their failure, passivity appears and self-esteem drops markedly. When individuals make external explanations for failure, passivity ensues but self-esteem stays high (Abramson, 1978).

In addition to deciding whether or not the cause of failure is internal or external, an individual who has failed also scans the dimension of ***stability:*** "Is the cause of my failure something permanent or transient?" An individual who has failed may decide that the cause of the failure is stable and that it will persist into the future. Examples of such stable factors are stupidity (which is internal as well as stable), or the difficulty of the task (which is stable but external). In contrast, an individual may decide that the cause of his failure is unstable. An individual who has failed an exam can believe that the cause was his bad night's sleep the night before, an unstable cause that is internal. Alternatively, he might decide that he failed because it was an unlucky day, an unstable cause that is external. The attributional theory of helplessness postulates that when the cause of failure is attributed to a stable factor, the helplessness deficits will persist in time. Conversely, if the individual believes that the cause of his failure is unstable, he will not necessarily fail again when he encounters the task months hence. According to the attributional model of learned helplessness, stable explanations lead to permanent deficits, and unstable explanations to transient deficits.

The third and final dimension is ***global-specific.*** When an individual finds that he has failed, he must ask himself whether or not the cause of his failure is global—a factor that will produce failure in a wide variety of circumstances—or specific—a factor that will produce failure only in similar circumstances. For example, an individual who has failed to solve a laboratory problem may decide that he is unskilled at solving laboratory problems and probably unskilled at other tasks as well. In this instance, being unskilled is global and the expectation of futility will recur in a wide variety of other situations. It is also a stable and internal factor. Alternatively, he might decide that these particular laboratory problems are too hard. The difficulty of laboratory problems is a specific factor, since it will only produce the expectation that future responding will be ineffective in other laboratory problems and not in real life. This factor, aside from being specific, is stable and external. The attributional model of helplessness holds that when individuals make global explanations for their failure, helplessness deficits will occur in a wide variety of situations. When individuals believe that specific factors cause their failures, the expectation of response ineffectiveness will be narrow, and only a narrow band of situations will produce helplessness.

EVIDENCE FOR EXPLANATORY STYLE AND DEPRESSION

The helplessness model suggests that an insidious explanatory or attributional style (attributing failure to internal, global, and stable factors; attributing success to external, unstable, and specific factors) predisposes an individual to depression. Three types of recent evidence confirm this: longitudinal studies, experiments of nature, and therapy studies.

□ LONGITUDINAL STUDIES.   Longitudinal studies look at the same individual across time, taking the same set of measurements at each point in time. This allows us to find out if explanatory style at an earlier time influences susceptibility to depression later, *over and above how depressed the individual was at the earlier time.* A five-year longitudinal study of 350 third-graders and their parents is attempting to predict depression and poor school achievement from explanatory style. The researchers predict which of these children will become depressed based on the pessimistic explanatory style, bad life events, and lack of popularity of these children as third-graders. Each of these factors makes a separate contribution to predicting which third-graders will experience depression by the end of fourth grade (Nolen-Hoeksema, Girgus, and Seligman, 1987). Parallel questions have been asked of college students by Zullow and Seligman (1985). One hundred and fifty-four students took the ASQ (Attributional Style Questionnaire) and the BDI (Beck Depression Inventory) in three waves over three months. Again depressive explanatory style predicted later depression over and above earlier depression. More specifically, it was the severe end of depression that was particularly affected by their explanatory style. "Keepers and Gainers" were defined as individuals who either *became depressed* or stayed depressed (BDI stayed above sixteen). Of the thirteen Keepers and Gainers, ten came from the quartile that had the most depressive explanatory style.

The last longitudinal study is an unusual one because it involved only one patient. It made, however, a very accurate prediction of his behavior. The subject was a patient, Mr. Q, who demonstrated precipitous shifts in mood during psychotherapy sessions conducted over four years. Three types of sessions were analyzed: those in which Mr. Q became more depressed, those in which he became less depressed, and those in which no shift at all occurred. Explanations for bad events were extracted from these sessions before and after the mood swings, and were rated for internality, stability, and globality. Explanations for bad events were extracted from the 400 words (spoken by Mr. Q) before the swing and from the 400 words following the swing. For comparison purposes, causal explanations were also extracted from randomly chosen 800-word segments of three sessions in which no swing occurred. Means for the different types of sessions are shown in Figure 11-5. The differences predicted were present before swings in mood. Highly internal, stable, and global causal explanations preceded increased depression, whereas much more external, unstable, and specific statements preceded decreased depression. *There was no overlap between the ratings of causal explanations before swings to more versus less depression* (Peterson, Luborsky and Seligman, 1983).

□ EXPERIMENTS OF NATURE.   The ideal way to test the helplessness reformulation is to measure the explanatory style of individuals and then to randomly choose from among them half of those who have experienced some naturally occurring bad event. The most severe depression is predicted to ensue for subjects with the preexisting depressive explanatory style who also then experienced the bad event.

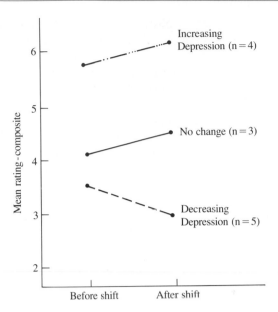

Figure 11-5
Shifts in depression predicted by explanatory style. Means of internal, stable, and global ratings of explanations before and after mood shifts for the different types of sessions. (Numbers of sessions on which means are based are in parentheses.) (Source: Peterson, Luborsky, and Seligman, 1983)

In one study, the naturally occurring bad event was a poor grade on a midterm exam. The participants were undergraduates in an introductory psychology course. At Time 1, they took the ASQ and filled out a questionnaire about the midterm grades with which they would be happy and unhappy. Just prior to the midterm examination, at Time 2, students' level of depressed mood was assessed with a mood checklist. At Time 3, immediately following receipt of the midterm grade, students again completed the mood checklist.

Explanatory style predicted the particular explanation for the midterm failure. The particular explanation in turn predicted depressive reaction. Students who made stable and global explanations for their poor grade became depressed (Metalsky, Halberstadt, and Abramson, 1987). Explanatory style, however, had no effect on depressive reaction over and above its effect on the particular explanation for the poor grade.

□ THERAPY STUDIES. Sixty-four unipolar depressed patients were randomly assigned to either tricyclic therapy, cognitive therapy, or both, and they were given twelve weeks of treatment (Hollon, DuRubeis, and Evans et al., 1988). Each treatment produced strong relief from depression. Explanatory style was measured by the ASQ at the beginning, middle, and end of therapy. What was the relation between relief from depression and change for the better in explanatory style? In the tricyclic group, the correlation was negative and nonsignificant. In the group getting both cognitive therapy and tricyclics, the relation was strongly positive. In the cognitive therapy group, the relationship was very strong. Thus, as patients' explanatory style changed for the better during cognitive therapy, they became less depressed. But with drug therapy, improving explanatory style was unrelated to improvement. This suggests that cognitive therapy and drug therapy break up depression by different means. Perhaps drug therapy merely activates patients, but cognitive therapy changes the way they look at causes. Evidence suggests that those patients whose explanatory style did not change for the better tended to relapse over the next two years (Hollon, DuRubeis, and

Evans et al., 1988). Drug therapy may result in a higher relapse rate because it does not improve explanatory style.

In summary, we have described three interlocking types of research investigating attributional style in the helplessness model of depression. A characteristic way of explaining bad events with internal, stable, and global causes co-occurs with depressive symptoms. The longitudinal studies showed that this explanatory style preceded the development of depressive symptoms. The experiment of nature indicated that this style resulted in depression once bad events were encountered. The study of therapy suggested that changing explanatory style for the better relieves depression.

PARALLELS BETWEEN DEPRESSION AND LEARNED HELPLESSNESS

We have now examined the basic learned helplessness phenomena in animals and humans and the theory behind it. Learned helplessness has been suggested as a model for depression. Table 11-2 outlines the similarity in symptoms, cause, cure, prevention, and predisposition between learned helplessness in the laboratory and unipolar depression as it occurs in real life (Seligman, 1975; Weiss, Simson et al., 1985).

Passivity deficit

☐ SYMPTOMS.   The failure to escape noise and to solve problems after experience with uncontrollable events is the basic *passivity deficit* of learned helplessness. This passivity seems similar to the motivational deficits of depression. Failure to initiate responses by depressed individuals has been systematically demonstrated in the laboratory: depressed students and patients fail to escape noise and fail to solve anagrams. The more depressed they are,

Table 11-2 SIMILARITY OF LEARNED HELPLESSNESS AND DEPRESSION

	Learned Helplessness	*Depression*
Symptoms	Passivity Cognitive deficits Self-esteem deficits Sadness, hostility, anxiety Loss of appetite Loss of aggression Sleep loss Norepinephrine and serotonin depletion	Passivity Negative cognitive triad Low self-esteem Sadness, hostility, anxiety Loss of appetite Loss of aggression Sleep loss NE and serotonin depletion
Cause	Learned belief that responding is independent of important outcomes (plus attributions to internal, global, and stable factors)	Generalized belief that responding will be ineffective
Therapy	Change belief in response futility to belief in response effectiveness ECT, MAO-I, Tricyclics REM deprivation Time	Cognitive and behavioral antidepressant therapy ECT, MAO-I, Tricyclics REM deprivation Time
Prevention	Immunization	Invulnerability factors
Predisposition	Insidious explanatory style	Insidious explanatory style

the more severe is this deficit (Miller and Seligman, 1975, 1976; Price, Tryon, and Raps, 1978).

Cognitive deficit

Nondepressed individuals given inescapable noise or unsolvable problems show the *cognitive deficit* of learned helplessness: they have difficulty learning that responding is successful, even when it is. Depressed individuals show exactly the same deficit. Nondepressed human beings made helpless fail to see patterns in anagrams and fail to change expectancy for future success when they succeed and fail in skill tasks. Depressed students and patients show these same deficits in the laboratory (Miller and Seligman, 1975, 1976; Abramson, Garber, Edwards, and Seligman, 1978). These results suggest that the cognitive deficit both in learned helplessness and depression may be produced by the expectation that future responding will be ineffective, and this expectation seems central to the negative beliefs about self, ongoing experience, and about the future, which cognitive therapists like Beck postulate as the central cause of depression.

Self-esteem deficits

When individuals are made helpless by inescapable noise and attribute their failure to their own shortcomings as opposed to external causes, not only are the motivational and cognitive deficits of helplessness and depression observed, but *self-esteem* drops as well. In contrast, when helpless subjects are led to make external attributions and blame the task difficulty for their failure, the motivational and cognitive deficits are observed but self-esteem deficits are not. This parallels the low self-esteem that occurs in depressives, particularly among individuals who blame themselves for their troubles (Abramson, 1978).

Mood changes

Parallel *mood changes* occur both in learned helplessness and depression. When nondepressed subjects are made helpless by inescapable noise or unsolvable problems, they become sadder, more hostile, and more anxious. These reports parallel the emotional changes in depression: more sadness, anxiety, and perhaps more hostility.

Somatic changes

In the laboratory, rats who receive inescapable shock eat less food, lose more weight, aggress less against other rats, and lose out in competition for food with rats who had received either escapable shock or no shock. This *loss of appetite* and *loss of aggression* produced by helplessness in the laboratory parallel the somatic symptoms of depressives: they lose weight, eat less, lose sleep, their social desires and status drop, and they become less aggressive.

Norepinephrine depletion

Finally, learned helplessness in the rat is accompanied by *norepinephrine depletion.* In an exciting series of studies over the last decade, Jay Weiss at Rockefeller University has demonstrated that the brains of rats who have received inescapable shock have less available norepinephrine than the brains of animals who receive no shock or escapable shock. Weiss argues that it is the norepinephrine depletion and not the expectation of response-outcome independence that causes learned helplessness. While the evidence is not yet in on whether it is the norepinephrine depletion, the expectancies of response-outcome independence, or both that are fundamental in learned helplessness, it is important that norepinephrine depletion is probably a correlate of depression in humans (Weiss, Glazer, and Pohoresky, 1976).

In summary, there are several parallel symptoms in laboratory-created learned helplessness and depression as found in nature. In both conditions, the four basic symptoms of depression are displayed: motivational deficits, cognitive deficits, emotional deficits, and somatic deficits. Since these four deficits were created in the laboratory by a known factor—by imposing the expectation that future responses and important outcomes will be independent—could it be that when we observe the same four symptoms in nature and call the condition depression, that the same cause—a belief in the futility of responding—is at work?

□ CAUSE.   The learned helplessness hypothesis says that depressive deficits, which parallel the learned helplessness deficits, are produced when an individual expects that bad events may occur and that they will be independent of his responding. When this is attributed to internal factors, self-esteem will drop; to stable factors, the depression will be long-lived; and to global factors, the depression will be general. Recent evidence confirms this. This insidious attributional style has been found in depressed students, children, and patients. Depressed patients, moreover, believe that the important goals in their life are less under their control than do other psychiatric patients (Eidelson, 1977; Seligman et al., 1979; Raps, Reinhard, and Seligman, 1980). Most important, individuals who have this explanatory style but are not depressed, become depressed when they later encounter bad events (Peterson and Seligman, 1984).

□ THERAPY.   Since the cause of learned helplessness and depression is hypothesized to be the expectation that responding will be ineffective in controlling future events, the basic therapeutic theme should be to change this belief to one in which the individual believes that responding will be effective and anticipated bad events will be avoided. The attributional theory of learned helplessness suggests some basic strategies for doing this. So, for example, learned helplessness theory suggests that therapies such as teaching social skills and assertiveness training should be antidepressive because they teach the individual that he can control affection and the esteem of other people by his own actions. Further tactics such as criticizing automatic thoughts (it's not that I'm an unfit mother, rather I'm grouchy at 7 A.M.) help alleviate depression because they change attributions for failure from internal, stable, and global (unfit mother) to external, unstable, and specific (7 A.M.). Notice how similar these strategies are to the techniques of cognitive and behavioral therapies that we have just reviewed.

In addition to cognitive and behavior therapy parallels, there are *somatic therapy* parallels as well. Four kinds of somatic therapy appear to break up learned helplessness in animals: electroconvulsive shock, MAO inhibitors, tricyclics, and dream deprivation (Dorworth, 1971; Porsolt et al., 1978; Brett, Burling, and Pavlik, 1981). These are the four somatic therapies that also can break up unipolar depression. In summary, there is reason to believe that the somatic and cognitive therapies that reverse learned helplessness also reverse depression.

□ PREVENTION AND PREDISPOSITION.   Learned helplessness in animals is prevented by prior experience with mastery and immunization. If an animal first controls important events, such as shock and food, then later helplessness never occurs. In effect, it is prevented. Such immunization seems to

Depressed patients have a particular explanatory style. They tend to believe that bad events are caused by internal factors (it's me), by stable factors (it's going to last forever), and by global factors (it's going to undermine everything I do).

Therapy to change learned helplessness

Invulnerability factors

An insidious explanatory style would make an individual prone to depression. If this man believes that he is alone, no longer in control over the events in his life, and that this will not change, he may be predisposed to depression.

be lifelong: rats who learn to escape shock as weanlings do not become help-less when as adults they are given inescapable shock. Conversely, lifelong vulnerability to helplessness is produced by early experience with inescap-able shock: rats who receive inescapable shock as weanlings become helpless adults (Hannum, Rosellini, and Seligman, 1976). This parallels the data on the prevention of and vulnerability to depression. Individuals whose mother dies before the child is eleven years old are more vulnerable to de-pression than those whose mother does not. There are, however, invulnera-bility factors that prevent depression from occurring in such individuals: a job, an intimate relationship with a spouse or lover, not having life bur-dened with child care, and religious belief (Brown and Harris, 1978). These invulnerability factors may all increase the expectation of future control, and vitiate the expectations of future helplessness.

□ EXPLANATORY STYLE AS A PREDISPOSITION. The final parallel in the predisposition to helplessness and depression is that depressed individuals have an insidious explanatory style. As we said above, when they fail, they tend to attribute their failure to internal, global, and stable factors; but when they succeed, they attribute their success to external, unstable, and specific factors (Seligman, Abramson, Semmel, and von Baeyer, 1979; Sweeney, Anderson, and Bailey, 1986). This is a style that maximizes the expectation that responding will be ineffective in the future. The helplessness model suggests that it is this explanatory style that predisposes an individual to de-pression, and as we have seen, recent evidence confirms this.

THE OUTCOME OF COGNITIVE THERAPY

Study on effectiveness of cognitive therapy and interpersonal therapy

The National Institutes of Mental Health (NIMH) sponsored a landmark study on the effectiveness of cognitive therapy, interpersonal therapy (IPT), and tricyclic antidepressants for overcoming unipolar depression (Elkin, Shea, Imber, Pilkonis, Sotsky, Glass, Watkins, Leber, and Collins, 1986). This study is the most extensive and thorough trial of any psychotherapy ever done.

Two hundred and fifty unipolar patients were randomly assigned to one of four groups, and the design was carried out at three different treatment centers. The patients were moderately to severely depressed, and 70 percent were female. Twenty-eight trained therapists were used. Cognitive therapy focused on detecting and changing negative thoughts and assumptions. IPT focused on interpersonal problems; these therapists taught depressives bet-ter techniques for resolving conflicts with others (Klerman, Weissman, and Rousaville, 1984). The drug group was given tricyclic antidepressant drugs, and a fourth group was given a placebo. Therapy was brief: sixteen weeks. Recovery from depression was carefully assessed by a battery of tests and interviews.

More than 50 percent of the patients recovered in the two psychotherapy groups and in the drug group. Only 29 percent recovered in the placebo group. The drug treatment produced faster improvement, but by the end of the sixteen weeks patients in the two psychotherapies had caught up.

We do not yet know about relapse rates in the NIMH study. But there is evidence from other studies which suggests that patients in cognitive therapy have learned a skill to cope with depression that the drugged patients have not, and that this results in lower relapse of those treated with cognitive therapy. For example, in one study, forty-four depressed outpatients were randomly assigned either to individual cognitive therapy or to therapy with tricyclic antidepressants for twelve weeks (Rush, Beck, Kovacs, and Hollon, 1977; Kovacs, Rush, Beck, and Hollon, 1981). Their depressions were quite severe: on the average, the current episode of depression had lasted for twelve months, and patients had already seen two previous therapists unsuccessfully. During the course of therapy, the patients in the cognitive therapy group had a maximum of twenty sessions, and the patients in the drug group were given a tricyclic daily, plus twelve brief sessions with the therapist who had prescribed the drugs.

By the end of treatment, both groups had improved according to both self-report and therapist ratings of depression. Only one of the nineteen patients assigned to cognitive therapy had dropped out, whereas eight of the twenty-five assigned to drug therapy had dropped out. This is not surprising since there is usually notable attrition due to side effects and reluctance to take drugs in drug treatment. Of the cognitive therapy patients, 79 percent showed marked improvement or complete remission, but only 20 percent of the drug patients showed such a strong response. Follow-up at three months, six months, and twelve months after treatment indicated that both groups maintained their improvement. The group that had received cognitive therapy, however, continued to be less depressed than the group that had received drug therapy. In addition, the cognitive group had half the relapse rate of the drug group (see also Reynolds and Coats, 1986).

Overall then it is clear that two systematic psychotherapies—cognitive therapy and interpersonal therapy—work as well as tricyclic antidepressant drugs against unipolar depression. And all three treatments work better than placebos. Tricyclics work faster, but the psychotherapies may produce more lasting relief.

PROBLEMS OF THE COGNITIVE MODEL OF DEPRESSION

Problems of
cognitive model

The cognitive model of depression has three main problems. First, it is vague on what kind of depression is modeled (Depue and Monroe, 1978). It is probably not an especially good model of the subclasses of unipolar depression that are "biological" and "endogenous." Biological depressions may be better treated by somatic therapy than by cognitive-behavioral therapies, although this has yet to be tested.

Second, cognitive theory is weak in accounting for the somatic symptoms of depression; these seem better explained by the biological model. Similarly, although the cognitive model does not predict that somatic therapy would be effective, the effective somatic therapies do succeed in breaking up learned helplessness in animals, as well as depression in humans.

Third, experimental controversy still rages over many of the major points of the learned helplessness model of depression. Some critics doubt whether learned helplessness in animals is produced by an expectation, believing it to be either learned inactivity or norepinephrine depletion (Glazer and Weiss, 1976; Weiss, Glazer, and Pohoresky, 1976, Anisman, 1978). Others have argued that the learned helplessness deficits seen in human beings do not follow closely from the theory (Buchwald, Coyne, and Cole, 1978; Costello, 1978). There also has been difficulty in replicating some of the basic human phenomena (McNitt and Thornton, 1978; Willis and Blaney, 1978). Finally, it is still controversial whether helplessness and depressive explanatory style are consequences or causes of depression (Peterson and Seligman, 1984).

INTEGRATION OF THEORIES AND THERAPIES FOR UNIPOLAR DEPRESSION

Compatibility
of different
theories of
depression

No one theory of depression—not the biological, not the psychodynamic, and not the cognitive—explain all the phenomena of depression. But each of them seems to have a piece of the truth and most important of all, the theories are not, by and large, incompatible. Depression is, in fact, a disorder that occurs on at least three levels. There are clear cognitive deficits—hopelessness and worthlessness being the most prominent; there are clear biological deficits—the somatic symptoms and their biogenic amine correlates; and there may well be psychodynamic predispositions—the dependent and helpless personality style. Cognitive, biological, and psychodynamic factors all may play a role in accounting for the predisposition, the symptoms, the causal mediation, and in producing success in therapy (Akiskal and McKinney, 1973, 1975).

PREDISPOSITION

Predisposition to become depressed and invulnerability from depression may have determinants at all levels of analysis. Biological evidence suggests that individuals who are predisposed to alterations in functional level of biogenic amines may be more vulnerable to depression. At the psychodynamic level, individuals who are heavily dependent on other people and who set such high standards that they frequently find themselves helpless before these standards may also be more vulnerable. At the cognitive level, individuals who have had early experience with loss and who have developed a pessimistic explanatory style in which loss is construed as internal, global, and stable may be more vulnerable to depression.

SYMPTOMS

The symptoms of depression can be described at the cognitive and biological levels of analysis. Cognitive symptoms, motivational symptoms, emotional symptoms, and somatic symptoms all make up depression. The duration and generality of these symptoms may be governed by the attributions an individual makes about loss, with those losses that stem from internal, stable, and global causes producing the most sweeping and long-lasting symptoms.

PRECIPITATING INCIDENTS

Cognitive theory explains precipitating incidents well: the expectation of loss or threat of loss seems to set off most depressions, at least those in which precipitants can be identified. The biomedical model gives the depletion of biogenic amines as a possible explanation for why depression begins when no obvious loss has occurred. The evidence is not in about which of these causes is primary, but we suspect that neither is the sole cause and that either taken alone will produce many of the symptoms of depression.

THERAPY

All three theories have contributed insights into therapy for depression although none of them has yet adequately accounted for the episodic rather than permanent nature of depression. An episode of depression, even severe depression, is no longer cause for despair. A combination of the biological treatments and the cognitive treatments of depression can probably alleviate severe depression roughly 90 percent of the time. In addition, to the extent that there is a depressive personality, dependent and inclined to helplessness, psychodynamic therapies may help to prevent the recurrence of depression.

Thus, biological, psychodynamic, and cognitive views can all be usefully brought to bear on depression. By taking the best from each, a woven fabric may be created in which the predisposition, the symptoms, and the precipitating incidents may be understandable. Ultimately any complete theory must tell us not only how depression starts and how to cure it, but also why it will, in and of itself, usually stop. In the meanwhile, however, what is most important of all is that depression can now be effectively treated.

BIPOLAR DEPRESSION (MANIC-DEPRESSION)

We have now explored the great majority of depressions: 80 to 95 percent of depressions are unipolar and occur without mania. This leaves between 5 and 20 percent of depressions that occur as part of *manic-depression*. These are called *bipolar depressions*.

Kinds of bipolar depression

We classify bipolar depressions in the following way: Given the presence of manic symptoms, an individual is judged to be manic-depressive if he has had one or more depressive episodes in the past. On the other hand, he is diagnosed as having experienced only a *manic episode* if he has never had a depressive episode. Mania itself can occur without depression, although this is very rare. Usually, a depressive episode will occur eventually, once a manic episode has happened. A chronic form of mania is called *chronic hypomanic disorder* or *hypomanic personality*. This diagnosis is made when an individual has experienced an unbroken two-year-long manic state. Finally, when depression is regularly set off by the approach of winter, it is characterized as seasonal affective disorder (SAD).

Since the depressive component of manic-depression is highly similar to what we have described for unipolar depression, we need only describe mania here in order to have a clear picture of bipolar depression. Here is what it feels like to be in the manic state of a manic-depressive disorder.

When I start going into a high, I no longer feel like an ordinary housewife. Instead, I feel organized and accomplished, and I begin to feel I am my most creative self. I can write poetry easily. I can compose melodies without effort. I can paint. My mind feels facile and absorbs everything. I have countless ideas about improving the conditions of mentally retarded children, how a hospital for these children should be run, what they should have around them to keep them happy and calm and unafraid. I see myself as being able to accomplish a great deal for the good of people. I have countless ideas about how the environmental problem could inspire a crusade for the health and betterment of everyone. I feel able to accomplish a great deal for the good of my family and others. I feel pleasure, a sense of euphoria or elation. I want it to last forever. I don't seem to need much sleep. I've lost weight and feel healthy, and I like myself. I've just bought six new dresses, in fact, and they look quite good on me. I feel sexy and men stare at me. Maybe I'll have an affair, or perhaps several. I feel capable of speaking and doing good in politics. I would like to help people with problems similar to mine so they won't feel hopeless. (Fieve, 1975, p. 17)

SYMPTOMS OF MANIA

The onset of a manic episode usually occurs fairly suddenly, and the euphoric mood, racing thoughts, frenetic acts, and the resulting insomnia stand in marked contrast to the person's usual functioning. Mania presents four sets of symptoms: emotional, cognitive, motivational, and somatic symptoms.

MOOD OR EMOTIONAL SYMPTOMS

Euphoric symptoms

The mood of an individual in a manic state is euphoric, expansive, and elevated. A highly successful manic artist describes his mood:

I feel no sense of restriction or censorship whatsoever. I'm afraid of nothing and no one. During this elated state, when no inhibition is present, I feel I can race a car with my foot on the floorboard, fly a plane when I have never flown a plane before, and speak languages I hardly know. Above all, as an artist, I feel I can write poems and paint paintings that I could never dream of when just my normal self. I don't want others to restrict me during this period of complete and utter freedom. (Fieve, 1975)

Grandiose euphoria is not universal in mania, however. Often the dominant mood is irritability, and this is particularly so when a manic individual is thwarted in his ambitions. Manics, even when high, are peculiarly close to tears, and when frustrated may burst out crying. This is one reason to believe that mania is not wholly the opposite state of depression, but that a strong depressive element coexists with it.

THOUGHT OR COGNITIVE SYMPTOMS

Grandiose cognitions

The manic cognitions are appropriate to the mood. They are grandiose. The manic does not believe in limits to his ability, and worse he does not recognize the painful consequences that will ensue when he carries out his plans. A manic who spends $100,000 buying three automobiles in a week does not recognize that he will have a great deal of trouble trying to pay for them over the coming years; a manic who calls the President in the middle of the night to tell him about her latest disarmament proposal does not recognize that this call may bring the police down on her; the manic who enters one sexual affair after another does not realize the permanent damage to his reputation that may ensue.

A manic may have thoughts or ideas racing through his mind faster than he can write them down or say them. This *flight of ideas* easily becomes derailed because the manic is highly distractible. In some extreme cases, the manic has delusional ideas about himself: he may believe that he is a special messenger of God; he may believe that he is an intimate friend of famous political and show business figures. The manic's thinking about other people is black and white: the individuals he knows are either all good or all bad; they are his best friends or his sworn enemies.

MOTIVATIONAL SYMPTOMS

Hyperactive behavior

Manic behavior is hyperactive. The manic engages in frenetic activity, be it in his occupation, in political or religious circles, in sexual relationships, or elsewhere. Describing the mania of a woman, one author wrote:

> Her friends noticed that she was going out every night, dating many new men, attending church meetings, language classes, and dances, and showing a rather frenetic emotional state. Her seductiveness at the office resulted in her going to bed with two of the available married men, who didn't realize that she was ill. She burst into tears on several occasions without provocation and told risqué jokes that were quite out of character. She became more talkative and restless, stopped eating and didn't seem to need any sleep. She began to talk with religious feeling about being in contact with God and insisted that several things were now necessary to carry out God's wishes. This included giving herself sexually to all who needed her. When she was admitted to the hospital, she asked the resident psychiatrist on call to kiss her. Because he refused to do so, she became suddenly silent. Later, she talked incessantly, accusing the doctor of trying to seduce her and began to talk about how God knew every sexual thought that she or the doctor might have. (Fieve, 1975, pp. 22–23)

The activity of the manic has an intrusive, demanding, and domineering quality to it. Manics sometimes make us uncomfortable because of this. It is difficult to spend much time with an individual who delivers a rapid succession of thoughts and who behaves in a frenetic way almost in disregard of those around him. Other behaviors that commonly occur during mania are compulsive gambling, reckless driving, poor financial investments, and flamboyant dress and makeup.

PHYSICAL OR SOMATIC SYMPTOMS

Lessened need for sleep

With all this flurry of activity comes a greatly lessened need for sleep. Such hyposomnia virtually always occurs during mania. After a couple of days of this, exhaustion inevitably sets in and the mania slows down.

COURSE AND CHARACTERISTICS OF MANIC-DEPRESSION

Between .6 and 1.1 percent of the population of the United States will have manic-depression in their lifetime (Robins et al., 1984). Unlike unipolar depression, which affects more women than men, manic-depression affects both sexes equally. The onset of manic-depression is sudden, usually a matter of hours or days, and typically no precipitating event is obvious. The first episode is usually manic, not depressive, and it generally appears between the ages of twenty and thirty. This first attack occurs somewhat earlier than a first attack in unipolar depression. Ninety percent of manic-depressives will have had their first attack before they are fifty years old. Manic-depressive illness tends to recur, and each episode lasts from several days to several months. Over the first ten years of the disorder, the frequency and intensity of the episodes tend to worsen. Surprisingly, however, not many episodes occur twenty years after the initial onset. Both manic and depressive episodes occur in the disorder, but regular cycling (e.g., three months manic, followed by three months depressive, and so on) is rare. The depressive component of manic-depressive illness is similar in kind to that of unipolar depression, but it is often more severe (Angst, Baastrup, Grof, Hippius, Poldinger, and Weiss, 1973; Depue and Monroe, 1978; Loranger and Levine, 1978).

Hardships due to manic-depression

Manic-depressive illness is not a benign, remitting disorder. For some, extreme manic episodes may bring about much hardship. Their hyperactivity and bizarre behavior may be self-defeating. Employers may become annoyed at their behavior, and some manic-depressives may then find themselves without a job. For others, entire careers may be lost. In addition, manic-depressives' social relationships also tend to break down. The manic person is hard to deal with. A much higher percentage of married manic-depressives divorce than do married unipolar depressives. Alcohol abuse, either in attempted self-medication or due to poor judgment and impulsiveness, is very high in manic-depression. The more severe the mania, the more frequent the alcoholism. In all, between 20 and 50 percent of manic-depressives suffer chronic social and occupational impairment. In most extreme cases, hospitalization is required. And for a few, suicide is a constant threat. The rate of attempted and successful suicides is also higher in bipolar than in unipolar depressions. As many as 15 percent of manic-depressives may end their life by suicide (Brodie and Leff, 1971; Carlson, Kotin, Davenport, and Adland, 1974; Reich, Davies, and Himmelhoch, 1974; Dunner, Gershom, and Goodwin, 1976).

Success through controlled manic-depression

When the mania is more moderate and the depressions are not too debilitating, however, the manic-depressive's ambition, hyperactivity, talkativeness, and grandiosity may lead to great achievements. This behavior is

There is evidence that Theodore Roosevelt was a manic-depressive, and that the mania may have contributed to his political success.

conducive to success in our society. It is no surprise that many creative people, leaders of industry, entertainment, politics, and religion may have been able to use and control their manic-depression. Abraham Lincoln, Winston Churchill, and Theodore Roosevelt probably all were manic-depressives. Today, among forty-seven top British writers and artists, one-third suffer from severe mood swings; among fifteen writers at Iowa's prestigious Writers' Workshop, almost all reported manic and hypomanic states. Finally, another study indicates that first-degree relatives of manic-depressives have also been judged to be significantly higher in creativity than normals (Holden, 1986a). It is probably the mania, and not the depression, that contributes to bursts of creativity.

CAUSE OF MANIC-DEPRESSION

Mania as defense against depression

The cause of manic-depressive illness is unknown. On the surface, with its euphoria and hyperactivity, it looks like the opposite state of depression. But as we have seen, feelings of depression are close at hand during the mania. The bipolar individual, when manic, is close to tears; he voices more hopelessness and has more suicidal thoughts than normal individuals. This has led some theorists to believe that mania is a defense against an underlying depression, with a brittle euphoria warding off more fundamental sadness.

Switching process from mania to depression

Other theorists believe that manic-depression results from homeostatic biological processes that have become ungoverned. When a normal individual becomes depressed, the depression is allegedly ended by switching in an opposite, euphoric state that cancels it out. Conversely, when a normal individual becomes euphoric, this state is kept from spiraling out of bounds by switching in a depressive state that neutralizes the euphoria. Investigations of the biochemistry of this switching process seem to indicate that a disturbance in the balance of mania and depression, with the reaction to either overshooting its mark, may be responsible for the manic-depressive disorder (see Figure 11-6). Investigations of the biochemistry of the switching process from mania to depression may illuminate the biological underpinnings of the disorder in the future, and it has recently been proposed that sleep reduction may be the trigger of the switching process (Bunney, Murphy, Goodwin, and Borge, 1972; Solomon and Corbit, 1974; Wehr, Sack, and Rosenthal, 1987).

Genetic vulnerability to manic-depression

Individuals are genetically vulnerable to manic-depressive illness. Manic-depressive individuals are more often found in families in which successive generations have experienced depression or manic-depression. Relatives of manic-depressives have five times the normal 1 percent risk for developing the disorder (Rice, Reich, Andreasen, Endicott, Van Eerdewegh, Fishman, Hirschfeld, and Klerman, 1987). Identical twins have five times the concordance for manic-depressive disorder than do fraternal twins. Thus, the familial risk is probably genetic, at least in part (Allen, 1976). New data have pioneered the exploration of which chromosome might carry the manic-depressive gene (see Chapter 3). Among one extended Amish family, eleven of eighty-one members had manic-depression. Their blood was studied, and two marker genes at the tip of chromosome 11 seemed to be defective in most of those members who were manic-depressive. These genes are, importantly, located near the genes that control the production of catechol-

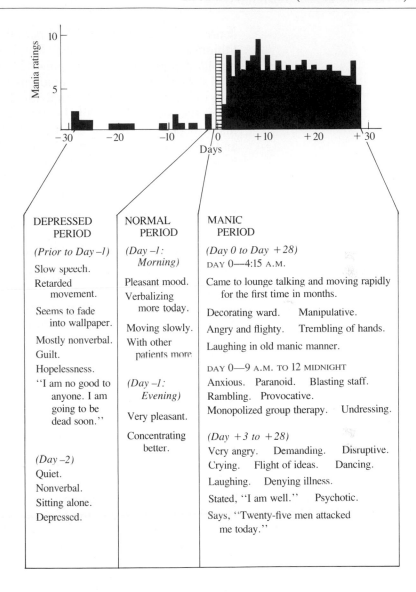

Figure 11-6
The switch process in manic-depression. This illustrates the striking changes in behavior as a bipolar patient switches from depression to mania. (Source: Bunney and Murphy, 1974)

amines (Egeland et al., 1987). Taken together, this strongly suggests that the disorder is partly hereditary. The next decade may see the genetic mechanism of this formerly mysterious disorder explained.

TREATMENT

Treatment with lithium

By and large, manic-depressive illness can be successfully contained by lithium salts. Lithium was originally used as a table salt substitute. In 1949, John Cade, an Australian physician, having found that lithium made guinea pigs lethargic, tried it to dampen mania in humans and found that lithium ended severe manic attacks. Since that time, lithium carbonate has been used extensively with manic-depression. Over the last thirty years, lithium has been shown to be an effective treament both for mania and for the depressive aspects of manic-depression. Approximately 80 percent of manic-depressives will show a full or partial alleviation of symptoms during lithium administration. It is also clear, however, that the other 20 percent of bipolar depressives do not respond (Depue, 1979). Lithium has also been used as a preventative treatment for manic-depression, and repeated dosage with lithium in a vulnerable individual may prevent manic-depressive relapses (Depue, 1979). While lithium can be viewed as a miracle drug for manic-depression, its side effects, particularly its cardiovascular, digestive, and central nervous system effects can be quite serious. Close medical supervision should always accompany the administration of lithium. Both the evidence on the effectiveness of lithium and the evidence on genetic vulnerability suggest that manic-depression is best understood within the framework of the biological model.

SEASONAL AFFECTIVE DISORDER (SAD)

Characteristics of SAD

The most recent addition to the bipolar family has been dubbed ***seasonal affective disorder (SAD).*** For millennia, human activity in the temperate zones has been strongly influenced by the seasons, with highly active behavior occurring during spring and summer, and withdrawal from the frenzy of life tending to occur during fall and winter. This may be the evolutionary basis for SAD.

SAD is characterized by depression beginning each year in October or November and fully remitting, sometimes switching toward mania, when the days start to lengthen (March and April). Patients complain of fatigue, oversleeping, and carbohydrate craving as well as the more typical symptoms of depression. Women outnumber men fourfold. Young children show the problem as well. In one of the first major studies, twenty-nine SAD patients reported their clinical history of depression by month. The remarkable data shown in Figure 11-7 documents how depressive episodes are yoked to the sunlight and temperature of each month. Not only is depression governed by the amount of sunlight where these patients live, but when they travel the depression changes. When they travel south in the winter, depression remits in a few days and when they travel north in the winter it

Figure 11-7
Depression and length of daylight. (A) Percentage of patients depressed per month (based on history) compared with (B) mean minutes of daylight (39°) in Rockville, Maryland (Smithsonian Radiation Biology Laboratory). (Source: Rosenthal et al., 1984)

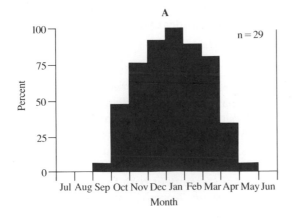

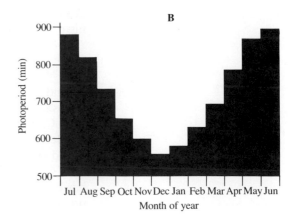

tends to worsen (Rosenthal, Sack, and Gillin, et al., 1984; Rosenthal, Carpenter, and James et al., 1986).

These findings led to the use of artificial light as therapy. Bright "grow-lights" are strategically located in the homes of the patients and come on very early in the morning and after sunset to artificially lengthen daylight hours. Prompt relief of depressive symptoms, particularly with the morning lights, has been reported, and relapse has been reported when light is withdrawn (Hellekson, Kline, and Rosenthal, 1986; Lewy, Sack, Miller, and Hoban, 1987). This is still a new category, but it may illuminate the means by which our evolutionary history still governs our daily mood.

SUICIDE

Suicide a consequence of depression

Suicide is the most disastrous consequence of depression, bipolar or unipolar. Depression is the precursor of a vast majority of suicides. Death only rarely results directly from other psychological disorders: the anorexic patient who refuses food; the hallucinating schizophrenic, who believing he is Christ, attempts to walk on water; the heroin addict who administers an overdose. But it is depression that most frequently results in irreversible harm: death by suicide.

Suicide is the second most frequent cause of death after accidents, among high school and college students (U.S. Department of Health and Human Services, 1987). Further, it is on the rise in this age group. The death of a young person, because of all his unfulfilled promise, is a keenly felt tragedy. As a young man before composing his second symphony, Beethoven almost took his own life. What held him back was the thought that he had not yet produced the best that might be inside him.

Suicide is an act that most societies forbid. Many religions regard it as a sin; and it is, astonishingly, a crime in several states. No act leaves such a bitter and lasting legacy among friends and relatives. It leaves in its wake bewilderment, guilt, shame, and stigma that relatives may carry to their own graves.

Suicide is occasionally an act of high rationality. Seneca, the first century Roman stoic, said:

Depression is the precursor of a vast majority of suicides. Police reach out to grab this suicidal man.

> Living is not good, but living well. The wise man, therefore, lives as well as he should, not as long as he can . . . He will always think of life in terms of quality, not quantity . . . Dying early or late is of no relevance, dying well or ill is . . . Even if it is true that while there is life, there is hope, life is not to be bought at any cost. (Seneca Epistle #70)

More often, however, even though the decision seems rational to the individual who takes his life, he is usually strongly ambivalent about the decision. One vote can tip the balance, as in a declaration of war (see Table 11–3). For example, when a physician canceled an appointment with a patient, this last straw in a series of disappointments tipped the balance toward suicidal death.

The ethical quandaries of suicide are immensely difficult. Does an individual have a right to take his own life, not interfered with by others, just as he has a right to dispose, unimpeded, of his own property? (Szasz, 1974).

Table 11–3 FABLES AND FACTS ABOUT SUICIDE

Fable	Fact
Individuals who talk about killing themselves do not kill themselves.	Of every ten persons who have killed themselves, eight gave definite warnings of their intentions.
Suicidal individuals have made a clear decision to die.	Most are undecided about living or dying. They often gamble with death, leaving it to others to save them.
Once an individual is suicidal, he is forever suicidal.	Usually individuals who wish to kill themselves are suicidal only for a limited period. Suicidal wishes are often linked to depression, and depression usually dissipates in time.
The suicidal risk is over when improvement occurs following a suicidal crisis.	Most suicides occur while the individual is still depressed, but within about three months after the beginning of "improvement." It is at that time that the individual has better access to weapons and more energy to put his suicidal plans into effect than when he is in the hospital or at the nadir of his depression.
Suicide occurs more often among the rich.	Suicide is equally frequent at all levels of society.
The suicidal act is the act of a sick person.	While the suicidal person is almost always extremely unhappy, he is not necessarily "mentally ill." Suicide can be a rational act.

SOURCE: Adapted from Shneidman, 1976.

Jim Jones and his People's Temple followers committed mass suicide in Guyana by drinking poisoned fruit juice after Congressman Leo Ryan was killed.

WHO IS AT RISK FOR SUICIDE?

The list of famous suicides is very long: Marilyn Monroe, Samson, Ernest Hemingway, Cleopatra, Sid Vicious, Virginia Woolf, Jack London, Modigliani, Adolph Hitler, Jim Jones and his People's Temple victims, to name a very few. At the very least, 25,000 people end their lives by suicide every year in the United States. There are also estimated to be at least ten times as many suicide attempts as successful suicides, and it has been estimated that in the United States today, five million people are alive who have attempted suicide.

The estimate of 25,000 suicidal deaths per year in the United States is highly conservative, and the real number is probably between 50,000 and 100,000. There are several reasons for the underreporting of suicide. Such stigma attaches to the act that the influential can often get coroners to label a relative's death as an accident rather than a suicide, and there is often family pressure on physicians not to report deaths as suicides. Many one-car accidents on clear roads are suicides, but they are usually labeled accidental death. Some life insurance policies do not cover death by suicide. Those individuals who flirt with death by high-risk hobbies or occupations, by adopting lethal habits such as heavy smoking, drinking, and drugs, as well as the physically ill who terminate their own life by discontinuing medication are not counted as suicidal deaths. In subcultures in which suicide is seen as feminine and passive, but murder is seen as active and masculine, "victim-induced homicide"—for example, an adolescent provoking a policeman to kill him—is not counted as a suicide (Schuyler, 1974; Diggory, 1976; Linden and Breed, 1976).

Suicide as heritable

Suicide may run in families, and to the extent that the depressive disorders are heritable, suicide itself may be heritable. All twenty-six suicides among the Amish of Lancaster County, Pennsylvania, over the last hundred years, were analyzed. Twenty-four of these individuals had had major affective disorders; 16 percent of the families accounted for 73 percent of the suicides (Egeland and Sussex, 1985).

Suicide and low serotonin levels

Suicide may even have a biochemistry. Among sixty-eight depressed patients, suicide attempts were most frequent in those having low serotonin levels, and when low-serotonin patients attempted suicide, they used more violent means (Asberg, Traskman, and Thoren, 1976).

DEPRESSION AND SUICIDE

Depression as predisposing factor to suicide

Depressed individuals are the single group most at risk for suicide. While suicide occasionally occurs in the absence of depression and the large majority of depressed people do not commit suicide, depression is a strong predisposing factor to suicide. An estimated 80 percent of suicidal patients are significantly depressed. Depressed patients ultimately commit suicide at a rate that is at least twenty-five times as high as control populations (Pokorny,1964; Flood and Seager, 1968; Robins and Guze, 1972).

SEX DIFFERENCES AND SUICIDE

Suicide in men vs. women

Women make roughly three times as many suicide attempts as men, but men actually succeed in killing themselves three times more often than women. These discrepancies seem to have diminished a bit over the last few years. The greater rate of suicide attempts in women is probably related to the fact that more depression occurs in women, whereas the greater completed suicide rate in men probably has to do with choice of methods: women tend to choose less lethal means, such as cutting their wrists and

Men who wish to commit suicide succeed in killing themselves three times more often than do suicidal women, as men tend to choose more lethal means of suicide, such as jumping off buildings or shooting themselves, as here.

overdosing on sleeping pills; whereas men tend to shoot themselves and jump off buildings. The suicide rate for both men and women is higher among individuals who have been divorced and widowed; loneliness as well as a sense of failure in interpersonal affairs surely contributes to this statistic. Men who kill themselves tend to be motivated by failure at work, and women who kill themselves tend to be motivated by failure at love (Mendels, 1970; Linden and Breed, 1976; Shneidman, 1976). As one female patient who tried to find surcease in suicide after being rejected by her lover said, "There's no sense in living. There's nothing here for me. I need love and I don't have it anymore. I can't be happy without love—only miserable. It will just be the same misery, day in and day out. It's senseless to go on" (Beck, 1976).

CULTURAL DIFFERENCES AND SUICIDE

Race, religion, and nationality contribute somewhat to vulnerability to suicide. The suicide rate of young black and white men is approximately the same (Hendin, 1969; Linden and Breed, 1976), but black women and older black men probably kill themselves less often than whites (Swanson and Breed, 1976). There is some evidence that American Indians may have a higher suicide rate than the rest of the population (Frederick, 1978). Religion, at least in the United States, does not offer any protection against suicide in spite of varyingly strong strictures against it. Also, the rate of suicide is roughly the same whether the individual is nonreligious, or Catholic, Protestant, or Jewish.

Suicide and different cultures

Suicide occurs in all cultures, even primitive ones, but it seems to be more common in industrialized countries. At the present time, the countries of central Europe (Hungary, Austria, and Czechoslovakia) and northern Europe (Finland and Denmark) seem to have the highest suicide rate. Ireland and Egypt have very low suicide rates, perhaps because suicide is considered a mortal sin in these cultures. The United States has, on the world scale, an average suicide rate. Sweden has a middling high rate of suicide. Some have blamed this on the lack of incentive provided by its social welfare system, but its suicide rate has remained the same since about 1910, before the introduction of social welfare (Shneidman, 1976; Department of International Economic and Social Affairs, 1985).

AGE AND SUICIDE

Suicide among children

Among children, suicide is rare, with probably fewer than 200 suicides committed in a year in the United States by children who are under the age of fourteen (see Figure 11-8). But among those preschoolers who are suicidal, they tend to be more impulsive and hyperactive, show less pain and crying when hurt, and have parents who abuse and neglect them (Rosenthal and Rosenthal, 1984).

Discussing her wish to die, Michelle, age nine, talks with Joaquim Puig-Antich, a leading expert on childhood depression:

> JOAQUIM PUIG-ANTICH: Do you feel you should be punished?
> MICHELLE: Yes.
> JPA: Why?
> M: I don't know.

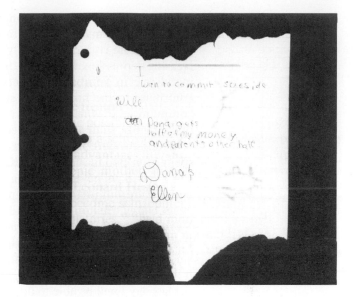

Figure 11-8
The ''will'' of a suicidal 8-year-old girl (name blocked out) was found by her parents, who subsequently arranged to have the child receive psychiatric care. (Source: Jerome, 1979)

JPA: Have you ever had the thought that you might want to hurt yourself?
M: Yes.
JPA: How would you hurt yourself?
M: By drinking a lot of alcohol, or jumping off the balcony.
JPA: Have you ever tried to jump?
M: I once stood on the edge of the terrace and put one leg over the railing, but my mother caught me.
JPA: Did you really want to jump?
M: Yes.
JPA: What would have happened if you had jumped?
M: I would have killed myself.
JPA: Did you want to get killed?
M: Uh-huh.
JPA: Why?
M: Because I don't like the life I live.
JPA: What kind of life do you live?
M: A sad and miserable life.

(Jerome, 1979)

Suicide among young people

Suicide among young people is on the rise. In the past thirty years, the suicide rate among college-age groups has tripled. Males between the ages of twenty and twenty-four are hardest hit, with a rate of about 28 per 100,000 compared to a rate of 12 per 100,000 in the general population. Two studies of the psychological "autopsies" of young suicides have strongly implicated substance abuse and untreated depression as precursors.

In one study, Mohammad Shafi examined the lives of 21 youths who killed themselves in the University of Kentucky area from 1980 to 1983. Seventy percent of them had been drug or alcohol abusers, and 76 percent had been diagnosed as depressed. They strongly exceeded matched controls in substance abuse and depression. In the other study, David Shaffer of Columbia University analyzed 160 youths who killed themselves in New York from 1984–1986. He found the same preponderance of substance abuse, but less depressive disorder. Males made up the bulk of these suicides, but

Suicide among
old people

choice of a more lethal weapon, rather than the number of attempts, accounted for the male preponderance (Holden, 1986b).

Suicide rate rises dramatically through middle age and into old age. Increasing depression, loneliness, moving to a strange setting, loss of a meaningful role in family and society, and loss of people they love all surely contribute to the high rate of suicide among old people. In cultures and communities in which the aged are revered and remain important in the life of the family, suicide is infrequent.

Within two years of the death of her beloved husband with whom she had spent fifty joyous years, Mrs. K. committed suicide. "Alan," she told her son a few days before, "I wasn't made to sleep alone." Percy Bridgman, Nobel Prize winner in physics and famous American positivist, shot himself at age eighty. He had cancer and was in great pain. The day before he killed himself, he mailed the index for his collected works to Harvard University Press. He had repeatedly asked for euthanasia and had been refused. His suicide note was published in the *Bulletin of the Atomic Scientists* (1962): "It is indecent for Society to make a man do this thing himself. Probably this is the last day I will be able to do it myself. PWB" (Shneidman, 1976).

THE MOTIVATION FOR SUICIDE

In the first major modern study of suicide, the French sociologist Émile Durkheim (1858–1917) distinguished three motivations for suicide, all of them intimately related to the way an individual sees his place in society. He called these motives anomic, egoistic, and altruistic. *Anomic suicide* is precipitated by a shattering break in an individual's relationship to his society: the loss of a job, economic depression, even sudden wealth. *Egoistic suicide* occurs when the individual has too few ties to his fellow humans. Societal demands, principal among them the demand to live, do not reach the egoistic individual. Finally, *altruistic suicide* is required by the society. The individual takes his own life in order to benefit his community. Hara-kiri is an altruistic suicide. The Buddhist monks who burned themselves to death to protest the injustices of the Vietnam War are recent reminders of individuals who committed altruistic suicide.

Modern thinkers see two more fundamental motivations for suicide: *surcease* and *manipulation.* Those who wish surcease have simply given up. Their emotional distress is intolerable, and they see no alternative solution. In death, they see an end to their problems, sleep, or nothingness. Fifty-six percent of the suicide attempts observed in a systematic study were classified as individuals trying to achieve surcease. These suicide attempts involved more depression, more hopelessness, and they tended to be more lethal than the remaining suicide attempts (Beck, 1976).

The other motivation for suicide is the wish to manipulate other people by a suicide attempt. Some wish to manipulate the world that remains by dying: to have the final word in an argument, revenge on a rejecting lover, to ruin the life of another person. More commonly in manipulative suicide, the individual intends to remain alive, but by showing the seriousness of his dilemma, he is crying for help from those who are important to him. Trying to prevent a lover from leaving, getting into the hospital and having a temporary respite from problems, and being taken seriously are all manipulative motives for suicide with intent to live.

Buddhist monks in Vietnam burned themselves to death in order to protest the injustices of their governmemnt.

Thirteen percent of suicide attempts were found to be manipulative; these involved less depression, less hopelessness, and less lethal means than did the surcease attempts (Beck, 1976). Those suicides that are manipulative are clearly cries for help, but it should be apparent that all suicides are not cries for help (see Box 11-3). The individual who wishes to escape because life is

---

Box 11-3　　　　　　　　　　**SUICIDE NOTES**

About one-sixth of those individuals who die by their own hand leave suicide notes. A romantic view would lead us to expect that these final words, like those that are supposed to be uttered on the deathbed, would be masterful summaries of a life that preceded them and of the reasons for dying. Only occasionally are they:

"There should be little sadness, and no searching for who is at fault; for the act and result are not sad, and no one is at fault.

"My only sorrow is for my parents who will not easily be able to accept that this is so much better for me. Please, folks, it's all right, really it is.

"I wanted to be too many things, and greatness besides—it was a hopeless task. I never managed to really love another person—only to make the sounds of it. I never could believe what my society taught me to believe, yet I could never manage to quite find the truth.

"Two-fifteen p.m.—I'm about to will myself to stop my heartbeat and respiration. This is a very mystical experience. I have no fear. That surprises me. I thought I would be terrified. Soon I will know what death is like—how many people out there can say that?"

But much more often the notes are commonplace. Creative, unique, and expansive pieces of writing are rare in suicide notes. The individual is usually constricted, his field of consciousness has narrowed, and he is in despair. This is not a state conducive to creativity.

"Dearest darling I want you to know that you are the only one in my life I love you so much I could not do without you please forgive me I drove myself sick honey please believe me I love you you again and the baby honey don't be mean with me please I've lived 50 years since I met you, I love you—I love you. Dearest darling I love you, I love you. Please don't discriminate me darling I know that I will die don't be mean with me please I love you more than you will ever know. Darling please and honey, Tom, I don't tell Tom why his daddy said goodbye honey. Can't stand it anymore. Darling I love you. Darling I love you."

A good number of suicide notes merely contain instructions and directions:

"Dear Mary. I am writing you, as our divorce is not final, and will not be til next month, so the way things stand now you are still my wife, which makes you entitled to the things which belong to me, and I want you to have them. Don't let anyone take them from you as they are yours. Please see a lawyer and get them as soon as you can. I am listing some of the things, they are: a blue davenport and chair, a Magic Chef Stove, a large mattress, and electrolux cleaner, a 9 × 12 rug, reddish flower design and pad. All the things listed above are almost new. Then there is my 30-30 rifle, books, typewriter, tools and a hand contract for a house in Chicago, a savings account in Boston, Massachusetts. Your husband."

And some are simple and starkly practical. A workman before hanging himself in an abandoned house chalked his suicide note on the wall outside.

"Sorry about this. There's a corpse in here. Inform police."

SOURCE: Adapted from Shneidman, 1976.

not worth living is not crying out for help, but for an end to his troubles. The remaining 31 percent of suicide attempts combine surcease and manipulative motivation. Here the individual is not at all sure whether he wishes to live or die, whether he wishes surcease or a change in the world. In this undecided group, the more hopeless and the more depressed the individual is, the stronger are the surcease reasons for the suicide attempt (Beck, Rush, Shaw, and Emery, 1979).

PREVENTION OF SUICIDE AND TREATMENT OF THE SUICIDAL PERSON

Suicide prevention centers

In the initial therapeutic interview with a depressed individual, suicide is the overriding question in the back of the therapist's mind. If clear suicidal intent and hopelessness are pervading themes, crisis intervention, close observation, and hospitalization will probably ensue. If they are not, therapy will proceed at a somewhat more leisurely pace, directed toward careful understanding of the other depressive problems.

In the late 1960s, a network of more than 300 suicide prevention centers was established in the United States to deal with suicidal crises. In addition, hospitals and outpatient units set up hot-lines to deal with the crises of acutely suicidal individuals. It was believed that if someone was available for the suicidal individual to talk to, the suicide could be prevented.

In terms of prevention of suicide, once the suicidal person makes contact with a telephone hot-line volunteer, a psychologist, a psychiatrist, a family physician, a pastor, or emergency room doctor, evaluation of the suicidal risk takes first priority. Does the individual have a clear plan? Does he have access to the weapon? Does he have a past history of suicidal acts? Does he live alone? Once suicidal risk in a crisis is assessed, a treatment decision must be hastily made: home visit, hospitalization, medication, the police, or outpatient psychotherapy. In some cases, merely holding the person on the phone may be appropriate action. Long-term follow-up and after-care must then occur.

Success of the suicide prevention centers is uncertain. Whereas the suicide rate seems to have dropped in Britain in the areas in which centers exist, no differences in suicide rate have yet been reported in the United States in cities with or without prevention centers (Weiner, 1969, Schuyler, 1974; Fox, 1976).

In addition to suicide prevention, psychological intervention in the lives of the surviving relatives is also important. As we have seen, the survivors are themselves more vulnerable to later depression and suicide. They are faced with shame, guilt, bewilderment, and stigma. This is a group that has been neglected and that might benefit greatly from systematic care.

SUMMARY

1. The *affective disorders* consist of three types: unipolar depression, bipolar depression, and mania.

2. *Unipolar depression* consists of depressive symptoms only and involves no symptoms of mania. It is by far the most common of the depressive disorders, and has become much more frequent since World War II.

3. *Bipolar depression* occurs in individuals who have both periods of depression and periods of mania as well.

4. *Mania* consists of four sets of symptoms: euphoric mood, grandiose thoughts, overactivity, and lack of sleep.

5. There are four basic symptoms of unipolar depression: emotional symptoms, largely sadness; motivational symptoms, largely passivity; cognitive symptoms, largely hopelessness and pessimism; and somatic symptoms, including loss of weight and loss of appetite. Untreated, these symptoms will usually dissipate within about three months.

6. Women are more at risk than men for depression.

7. Three theories—biological, psychodynamic, and cognitive—have all shed light on unipolar depression.

8. Biological models have generated three effective therapies; *tricyclic antidepressant drugs, MAO inhibitors,* and *electroconvulsive therapy* (ECT). The biomedical school holds that depression is due to depletions in certain central nervous system neurotransmitters, most usually *norepinephrine.*

9. Psychodynamic theories concentrate on the personality that predisposes one to depression. These theories hold that depression stems from *anger turned upon the self,* and that individuals who are predisposed to depression are overdependent on other people for their self-esteem and that they feel helpless to achieve their goals.

10. Cognitive models concentrate on particular ways of thinking and how these cause and sustain depression. There are two prominent cognitive models: the view of Aaron Beck, which holds that depression stems from a *negative cognitive triad,* and the *learned helplessness model* of depression. Cognitive therapy and interpersonal therapy relieve depression as effectively as tricyclic antidepressant drugs.

11. A pessimistic explanatory style predicts risk for depression. Changing this attribution style to optimistic, as in cognitive therapy, may reverse depression.

12. Unipolar depression can now be effectively treated: nine out of ten people who suffer a severe unipolar depressive episode can be markedly helped either by drugs, ECT, cognitive therapy, or interpersonal therapy.

13. Bipolar depression, or *manic-depressive illness,* is the most crippling of the affective disorders. It results in ruined marriages, irreparable damage to reputation, and not uncommonly suicide. Eighty percent of bipolar depressions can now be greatly helped by *lithium.* This disorder is best viewed within the biomedical model.

14. *Seasonal affective disorder* is characterized by depression that begins each year in October or November and ends in the early spring.

15. *Suicide* is the most disastrous consequence of bipolar and unipolar depression. Its frequency is rising among young people, and it is the second most frequent cause of death among college students. Women make more suicide attempts than men, but men actually succeed in killing themselves more often than women. There are two fundamental motivations for suicide: *surcease,* or desire to end it all, and *manipulation,* or desire to change the world or other individuals by a suicide attempt.

The Schizophrenias

Society's view of the schizophrenic as dangerous, unpredictable, and out of control is
reflected in this illustration by
Charles Bell. In fact, this myth of
the ''raving maniac'' reflects the
non-schizophrenics' fear and
ignorance more than the actual
nature of the schizophrenic.

SCHIZOPHRENIA is the most puzzling and profound of the psychological
disorders. Many theories try to account for it, but a complete understanding of this complex disorder continues to elude us. Briefly, *schizophrenia* is a disorder of thinking from which flows troubled behavior and
troubled mood. This thought disorder is manifested by difficulties in maintaining and focusing attention and in forming concepts. It can result in false
perceptions and expectations, in enormous difficulties in understanding reality, and in corresponding difficulties with language and expression.

"Schizophrenia" is a term that is used for a group of psychoses. As such,
we often refer to these disorders as "the schizophrenias." We will try to understand the schizophrenic disorders by examining the symptoms that are
part of them, and the psychological and biological determinants that promote them. Then we will examine the various treatments that are available
for the schizophrenias. But before doing any of this, it is important to dispel
the myths associated with these disorders, and to sketch out a general picture of the history, prevalence, and dimensions of the schizophrenias.

HISTORY AND BACKGROUND

SOME MYTHS ABOUT SCHIZOPHRENIA

Schizophrenics have been called lunatics, madmen, raving maniacs, un-
hinged, deranged, demented. These words suggest that schizophrenics are
dangerous, unpredictable, impossible to understand, and completely out of

control. These notions, however, say more about non-schizophrenics' fear and ignorance than they do about the nature of schizophrenia itself.

ARE SCHIZOPHRENICS DANGEROUS?

Schizophrenics mirror their treatment

Rather than being raving maniacs on the rampage, schizophrenics are often withdrawn and preoccupied with their own problems. Sometimes they yell and scream, and occasionally they strike someone. But it is by no means clear whether these behaviors arise from the actual disorder, or from the way schizophrenics are treated. Like others, schizophrenics often mirror their treatment. When the treatment is civilized, so are the patients. The mistaken notion that criminals are less dangerous than schizophrenics, and that one would be better off living near a prison than near a hospital, rests squarely on ignorance and fear.

DO SCHIZOPHRENICS HAVE SPLIT PERSONALITIES?

Another common misconception about schizophrenia is that it involves a split personality of the Dr. Jekyll and Mr. Hyde sort, with its attendant unpredictability and potential for violence. This error arises from the origins of the word schizophrenia: *schizo* = split, *phreno* = mind. When the Swiss psychiatrist Eugen Bleuler (1857–1939) coined the term in 1911, he intended to suggest that certain psychological *functions,* ordinarily joined in normal people, are somehow divided in schizophrenics. When non-schizophrenics perceive, say, a horrifying incident, they immediately have an emotional reaction that corresponds to their perception. But according to Bleuler, this does not happen to schizophrenics, for whom thought and emotion are split. Bleuler never meant to imply that there were two or more alternating personalities residing in the schizophrenic. And although Bleuler's view is no longer as widely believed now as it was in 1911, the misconception that arose from his view continues to exist.

Eugen Bleuler (1857–1939).

ONCE A SCHIZOPHRENIC, ALWAYS A SCHIZOPHRENIC?

The schizophrenic disorders are not necessarily durable, and surely not lifelong for all schizophrenics. Often, a single episode will occur and then disappear, never to recur. Sometimes, after a long period in which the individual has been symptom-free, another episode may occur. Much as one may suffer several colds during a lifetime and yet not always have a runny nose, so too can a person suffer several schizophrenic episodes during a lifetime, and be quite sane in between. Many people who have suffered a schizophrenic disorder engage in athletics, read newspapers and novels, watch television, eat their meals, and relate to their friends and families in much the same way that others do. Long stretches of time can pass without evidence of their distress. We do not know why a schizophrenic episode occurs any more than we understand why we come down with a cold. As when the symptoms of a cold are absent and the individual is considered healthy, so when the symptoms of schizophrenia are absent the individual is considered sane. Finally, it goes without saying that schizophrenics are as human as the rest of us.

EVOLVING VIEWS OF SCHIZOPHRENIA

Until about 1880, little progress was made in differentiating one form of disorder from another. There was a *sense* that there were different kinds of madness, but no shared view of what those differences might be. The first widely accepted classificatory system for severe psychological disorders was advanced by the German psychiatrist, Emil Kraepelin (1856–1926). One of the disorders he described in 1896 was ***dementia praecox,*** literally, early or premature deterioration.

Kraepelin and dementia praecox

For Kraepelin, the diagnosis of *dementia praecox* was indicated when individuals displayed certain unusual symptoms. Included among these were inappropriate emotional responses, such as laughter at a funeral or crying at a joke; stereotyped motor behavior, such as bowing repeatedly before entering a room, or clapping five times before putting head to pillow; attentional difficulties, such as being unable to get to work on time because of distractions en route, or being unable to read because of shifting shadows; sensory experiences in the absence of appropriate stimuli, such as seeing people when none are present, or smelling sulphur in a jasmine garden; and beliefs sustained in spite of overwhelming contrary evidence, such as insisting that one is an historical personage like Napoleon, or that one is held together by wire. Kraepelin's views powerfully influenced succeeding generations of psychiatrists, and are important historically for distinguishing and classifying the various forms of madness.

Bleuler and schizophrenia

As we mentioned earlier, the term "schizophrenia" was coined by Eugen Bleuler. Bleuler believed that the disorder was part of one's biological makeup and was likely to recur. He felt that schizophrenia could first occur at any time during a person's life, and while he recognized that schizophrenia was undoubtedly serious, and in many cases chronic, Bleuler asserted that recovery was possible.

Both Kraepelin and Bleuler were convinced that the causes of schizophrenia were biological and that the ultimate cure would be biomedical. Kraepelin hypothesized that a chemical imbalance was produced by malfunctioning sex glands and somehow interfered with the nervous system. Bleuler was convinced that brain disease caused schizophrenia, and he continually resorted to hypothetical brain pathology to account for schizophrenic symptoms. The search for a biological basis for schizophrenia was begun by these two pioneering scientists.

A completely different approach to understanding the origins and cure of schizophrenia was propounded by a contemporary of Kraepelin and Bleuler, Adolf Meyer (1866–1950). Meyer, an American brain pathologist, later became recognized as the dean of American psychiatry. He maintained that there were no fundamental biological differences between schizophrenics and normals, and that there were not any fundamental differences in their respective psychological processes. Rather, he believed that the cognitive and behavioral disorganization that was associated with schizophrenia arose from inadequate early learning, and reflected "adjustive insufficiency" and habit deterioration, and that individual maladjustment rather than biological malfunction lay at the root of the disorder. Meyer's approach mandated research in a wholly different area than did Bleuler's or Kraepelin's. While Bleuler and Kraepelin strengthened the biological tradi-

Adolf Meyer (1866–1950).

tion of research in schizophrenia, Meyer gave impetus to a tradition that focused on learning and biosocial processes. Let us consider some of the modern views of this disorder.

SCHIZOPHRENIA DEFINED

DSM-III-R's
definition

The definition of schizophrenia, as well as who is and who is not schizophrenic has generated heated debate ever since Kraepelin described the symptoms of *dementia praecox* in his *Psychiatrie* in 1896. The most recent definition was offered in 1987 in DSM-III-R. In order to be diagnosed as a schizophrenic now, the onset of the disorder must occur before age forty-five, the symptoms must last for at least six months, and those symptoms must have induced a marked deterioration from the individual's previous level of functioning at work, in social relations, and in self-care. Those are the *temporal* criteria.

Impairment in
reality testing

There are also two *substantive* criteria for the diagnosis: (1) There must be a gross impairment of reality testing, that is, the individual must evaluate the accuracy of his or her thoughts incorrectly and, as a consequence, must make grossly incorrect inferences about reality. Such an impairment in real-

Entitled "Holy Sweat Miracle on the Insole," this drawing was done by a patient with a systematic delusion of poisoning and murder culminating in a miracle of the Holy Ghost. According to the patient, it was a "miracle in the insole of the victim ruthlessly sacrificed, disinherited, declared dead, by the secret violent poisoning and brain crushing of assassins possessed by Satan and mentally disturbed . . ."

ity testing is called a ***psychosis.*** Psychoses reflect major disruptions of reality testing. Minor impairments, such as a tendency to undervalue one's abilities or attractiveness, do not qualify. (2) The disturbance typically must affect several psychological processes, including thought, perception, emotion, communication, and psychomotor behavior. Disturbances of thought characteristically take the form of delusions and hallucinations.

Delusions and hallucinations

Delusions are false beliefs that resist all argument and are sustained in the face of evidence that normally would be sufficient to destroy them. An individual who believes that he has drunk of the Fountain of Youth and is therefore immortal suffers a delusion. And the individual who believes that he not only has knowledge of these legendary waters but also that others are conspiring to pry his secret knowledge from him, is probably suffering from several delusions.

Hallucinations are false sensory perceptions that have a compelling sense of reality, even in the absence of stimuli that ordinarily provoke such perceptions. In schizophrenia, hallucinations are commonly auditory, consisting either of a voice that maintains a running commentary on the individual's behavior, or two or more voices conversing with each other. But they can also be visual or implicate other sense organs, such as taste and smell. An individual who is convinced that she has seen, shook hands with, and had dinner with a minotaur has had an hallucination.

The examples of delusion and hallucination that were just given have their roots in colorful myths. But when real, these disturbances and others that we will examine later are considerably more painful, as the following case (first discussed in Chapter 8) illustrates:

> Carl was twenty-seven years old when he was first admitted to a psychiatric facility. Gangling and intensely shy, he was so incommunicative at the outset that his family had to supply initial information about him. They, it seemed, had been unhappy and uncomfortable with him for quite some time. His father dated the trouble from "sometime in high school." He reported, "Carl turned inward, spent a lot of time alone, had no friends and did no schoolwork." His mother was especially troubled about his untidiness. "He was really an embarrassment to us then, and things haven't improved since. You could never take him anywhere without an argument about washing up. And once he was there, he wouldn't say anything to anyone." His twin sisters, six years younger than Carl, said very little during the family interview, but rather passively agreed with their parents.
>
> One would hardly have guessed from their report that Carl graduated high school in the upper quarter of his class, and had gone on to college where he studied engineering for three years. Though he had always been shy, he had had one close friend, John Winters, throughout high school and college. John had been killed in a car accident a year earlier. (Asked about Winters, his father said, "Oh, him. We don't consider him much of anything at all. He didn't go to church either. And he didn't do any schoolwork.")
>
> Carl and John were unusually close. They went through high school together, served in the army at the same time and when discharged, began college together and roomed in the same house. Both left college before graduating, much to the chagrin of Carl's parents, took jobs as machinists in the same firm, and moved into a nearby apartment.
>
> They lived together for three years until John was killed. Two months later the company for which they worked went out of business. John's death left Carl enor-

"I am an unreal person. I am made of stone . . ." Painting by Magritte entitled, *The Song of the Violet.*

mously distraught. When the company closed, he found himself without the energy and motivation to look for a job. He moved back home. Disagreements between Carl and his family became more frequent and intense. He became more reclusive, as well as sloppy and bizarre; they, more irritable and isolating. Finally they could bear his behavior no longer and took him to the hospital. He went without any resistance.

After ten days in the hospital, Carl told the psychologist who was working with him: "I am an unreal person. I am made of stone, or else I am made of glass. I am wired precisely wrong, precisely. But you will not find my key. I have tried to lose the key to me. You can look at me closely if you wish, but you see more from far away."

Shortly thereafter, the psychologist noted that Carl ". . . smiles when he is uncomfortable, and smiles more when in pain. He cries during television comedies. He seems angry when justice is done, frightened when someone compliments him, and roars with laughter on reading that a young child was burned in a tragic fire. He grimaces often. He eats very little but always carries food away."

After two weeks, the psychologist said to him: "You hide a lot. As you say, you are wired precisely wrong. But why won't you let me see the diagram?"

Carl answered: "Never, ever will you find the lever, the eternalever that will sever me forever with my real, scal, deal, heel. It is not on my shoe, not even on the sole. It walks away."

INCIDENCE AND PREVALENCE OF SCHIZOPHRENIA

Prevalence of schizophrenia

Schizophrenia is one of the most prevalent of the severe psychological disorders. The various types are conservatively estimated to occur in less than 1 percent of the U.S. population (Dohrenwend and Dohrenwend, 1974; DSM-III, 1980), although some national estimates run as high as 3 or 4 percent (Heston, 1970). Moreover, among certain populations, such as college students, some estimates go as high as 18 percent (Koh and Peterson, 1974). These latter estimates are probably exaggerated, but even the conservative estimates mark the schizophrenias as a distressingly prevalent disorder.

First occurrence

The first occurrence of schizophrenia occurs mainly among people who are under forty-five. There are substantial sex differences in the time it occurs: men are at risk for schizophrenia before age twenty-five, with peak incidence occurring at age twenty-four. Women are at risk after age twenty-five (Lewine, 1981; Zigler and Levine, 1981, Sartorius, Jablensky, Korten, Ernberg, Anker, Coaper, and Day, 1986). It afflicts the poor, especially the urban poor. The overall incidence of the schizophrenias (the rate at which new cases develop) is about 150 per 100,000 population (Crocetti and Lemkau, 1967). But compared to incidence among the wealthy, the incidence of the schizophrenias among the poor is three times greater, while its prevalence (the proportion of schizophrenics in the population at any one time) is eight times as high.

At the time of admission to a hospital or day treatment center, the typical schizophrenic is relatively young and relatively poor. Occasionally, schizophrenics come for treatment on their own, but more commonly their family or the police bring them to a treatment center. Often a disturbing incident triggers painful behavioral anomalies that are stressful for family and friends, and that leads to the decision to seek treatment.

TYPES OF SCHIZOPHRENIA

Although we speak of schizophrenia and schizophrenics as if this is a unitary disorder, the differences between the various types of schizophrenia overwhelm their similarities. So much is this the case, that (as we have seen) it is increasingly common to speak of "the schizophrenias" in order to underscore that diversity. We will focus on five subtypes of schizophrenia: paranoid, disorganized, catatonic, residual, and undifferentiated.

PARANOID SCHIZOPHRENIA

Delusions of persecution or grandeur

The presences of systematized delusions or extensive auditory hallucinations marks this subtype. The ***paranoid schizophrenic*** suffers delusions of persecution or grandeur which are remarkably systematized and complex, often like the plots of dark mysteries. This complexity renders his experiences comprehensible to the schizophrenic—a matter of no small importance to which we will return—while simultaneously making it impenetrable to the outsider.

Beyond experiencing delusions of persecution and/or grandeur, paranoid schizophrenics may also experience delusional jealousy, the deep belief that their sexual partner is unfaithful. But despite the intensity of their feelings, paranoid schizophrenics rarely display severely disorganized behavior, incoherence, or loose associations. Nor do they experience flat or inappropriate emotion. Rather, their demeanor tends to be extremely formal or quite intense.

DISORGANIZED SCHIZOPHRENIA

Silliness and incoherence

Formerly called hebephrenic schizophrenia, the most striking behavioral characteristic of ***disorganized schizophrenics*** is apparent silliness and incoherence. Nearly as common is the absence of affect or the presence of inappropriate affect. They burst into laughter, grimaces, or giggles without an appropriate stimulus. Their behavior is jovial, but quite bizarre and absurd, suggesting extreme sensitivity to internal cues and extreme insensitivity to external ones. Correspondingly, they are voluble, bursting into meaningless conversation for long periods of time.

Disorganized schizophrenics may experience delusions and hallucinations, but not systematized ones. Rather, theirs tend to be more disorganized and diffused than those experienced by paranoid schizophrenics, and they often center on their own bodies. For example, disorganized schizophrenics may complain that their intestines are congealed or that their brains have been removed. Sometimes the delusions may be quite pleasant and contribute to the silliness of their behavior.

Disorganized schizophrenics often disregard bathing and grooming. They may not only become incontinent but also frequently eat their own body products, as well as other dirt. Again, a marked insensitivity is found here, similar to their insensitivity to social surroundings.

Catatonic schizophrenics may be entirely immobile, sometimes maintaining uncomfortable postures for hours.

CATATONIC SCHIZOPHRENIA

Excited or frozen behavior

The salient feature of ***catatonic schizophrenia*** is motor behavior that is either enormously excited or strikingly frozen, and that may occasionally alternate between the two states. The onset of the disorder is sudden. When behavior is excited, the individual may seem quite agitated, even wild, vigorously resisting all attempts at control. Affect is quite inappropriate, while agitation is enormously energetic and surprisingly prolonged, commonly yielding only to strong sedation.

Stuporous or frozen behavior is also quite striking in this subtype of schizophrenia. Individuals may be entirely immobile, often adopting quite uncomfortable postures and maintaining them for long periods. If someone moves them, they will freeze in a new position. A kind of statuesque "waxy flexibility" is characteristic. After emerging from such a stuporous episode, patients sometimes report that they had been experiencing hallucinations or delusions. These sometimes center on death and destruction, conveying the sense that any movement will provoke an enormous catastrophe.

Negativism—the apparently motiveless resistance to all instructions or attempts to be moved—is a common characteristic of catatonic schizophrenia so much so that, in addition to the excited and stuporous behaviors, some theorists take negativism to define the category (Maher, 1966). Forbidden to sit, the catatonic will sit. Told to sit, the catatonic will insist on standing. Today this subtype is becoming rare, possibly because the behavior is being controlled with antipsychotic drugs.

RESIDUAL SCHIZOPHRENIA

Absence of prominent symptoms

This form of schizophrenia is characterized by the *absence* of prominent symptoms, such as delusions, hallucinations, incoherence, or grossly disorganized behavior. Rather, continuing evidence of the disorder is indicated by the presence of two or more symptoms which, though they are *relatively* minor, are nevertheless very distressing. These symptoms include: (a) marked social isolation or withdrawal; (b) marked impairment in role functioning; (c) very peculiar behavior; (d) serious impairment of personal hygiene and grooming; (e) blunt, flat, or inappropriate emotional expression; (f) odd, magical, or bizarre thinking; (g) unusual perceptual experiences; or (h) apathy or lack of initiative (DSM-III-R, 1987).

UNDIFFERENTIATED SCHIZOPHRENIA

This designation is used to categorize individuals who do not otherwise fit neatly into other classifications. It is a diagnosis for disturbed individuals who present evidence of thought disorder, as well as behavioral and affective anomalies, but who are not classifiable under the other subtypes.

THE SYMPTOMS OF SCHIZOPHRENIA

In the case history presented earlier, Carl exhibited many of the characteristics associated with schizophrenia: lack of interest in life, withdrawal from social activity, seemingly bizarre behavior, incomprehensible communications, and increasing preoccupation with private matters. These symptoms, like many of the others that are common in schizophrenia, involve three areas of psychological functioning: perception, thought, and emotion.

PERCEPTUAL DIFFICULTIES

Perceptual difficulties

Perceptual anomalies often accompany schizophrenia. Patients sometimes report spatial distortions, such that a room may seem much smaller and more constricting than it really is, or objects may seem farther away. Controlled laboratory studies indicate that compared to non-schizophrenics, schizophrenics are less able to discriminate faces and, more interesting, less able to decode the emotions that are being facially communicated (Feinberg, Rifkin, Schaffer, and Walker, 1986). Moreover, they are less able to estimate sizes accurately (Strauss, Foureman, and Parwatikar, 1974) and less able to judge the passage of time (Petzel and Johnson, 1972).

Generally, upon admission to a hospital, schizophrenics report a great number of perceptual difficulties, such as difficulties in understanding others' speech or identifying them, or overly acute auditory perception. These perceptual difficulties may provide a fertile soil for hallucinations, which are discussed below. Other people, as well as the self, may be described and apparently experienced as hollow, flat, or two-dimensional. Carl, for example, feels that he is made of steel or of glass.

HALLUCINATIONS

Visual hallucinations

As we noted earlier, hallucinations are false sensory experiences that have a compelling sense of reality. Hallucinations are often gripping, and they are sometimes terrifying. Everyone knows what a visual hallucination is because everyone dreams. But for most people, dreams occur only during a certain portion of sleep, called "rapid eye movement," or REM sleep. They do not occur when we are awake, presumably because there is a neurotransmitter-mediated mechanism that inhibits them. Some researchers believe

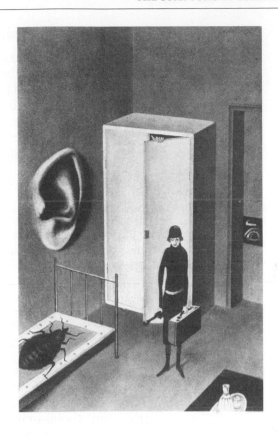

A schizophrenic may have visual and auditory hallucinations that have a compelling sense of reality. (*Das Hotelzimmer* by Anton Machet)

that this mechanism has failed in schizophrenics who hallucinate (Assad and Shapiro, 1986).

Auditory hallucinations

Auditory hallucinations are the most common hallucinations in schizophrenia (Malitz, Wilkens, and Escover, 1962). One finds their origins in ordinary thought, where it is common enough to conduct a private dialogue by imagining oneself talking to others and others talking back. And it is quite common for people to actually talk to themselves, or to talk with deities whose presence can only be presumed. (The psychiatrist Thomas Szasz [1970] observes that it is quite normal to talk with God, and that when we do so it is called prayer. Only when God responds is it called an hallucination!) Of course, the non-schizophrenic has considerably greater control over the internal dialogue than does the schizophrenic. The latter, when experiencing an auditory hallucination, does not believe that the voices originate within the self, or that she has the ability to begin or end the talk. The inability to distinguish between external and internal, real and imagined, controllable and imposed, is central to the schizophrenic experience.

THOUGHT DISORDERS

Insofar as schizophrenics' speech reflects their thought, schizophrenics' thought can be disordered in a variety of ways. Sometimes the *process* of thinking is disordered, and sometimes it is the *content* of thought that is peculiar.

THE DISORDERED PROCESS OF THOUGHT

Neologisms
When the process of thinking is disturbed, the train of thought seems moved by the *sound* of words rather than by their meaning. ***Clang associations***, that is, associations produced by the rhyme of words, such as ". . . my real, seal, deal, heel," abound. Schizophrenics like Carl may also come up with ***neologisms***, new words like "eternalever" that have only private meaning. Some of the most interesting evidence about schizophrenic thought arises from studies of attention and distractibility.

☐ ATTENTIONAL DEFICITS.   Everyone at one time or another has had trouble paying attention or concentrating, in spite of trying hard to do both. Tired or upset, we find our attention roaming, and we cannot direct it. What we have experienced briefly and in microcosm, acute schizophrenics experience profoundly. One patient explains his problem with attention in this way:

> I can't concentrate. It's diversion of attention that troubles me . . . The sounds are coming through to me, but I feel my mind cannot cope with everything. It's difficult to concentrate on any one sound. It's like trying to do two or three different things at one time. (McGhie and Chapman, 1961, p. 104)

Consider for a moment what normal attention involves. We are continuously bombarded by an enormous number of stimuli, many more than our limited channel capacity can absorb. So we need some mechanism for sorting out stimuli to determine which ones will be admitted and which ones barred. That mechanism has been referred to metaphorically as a ***cognitive*** or ***selective filter*** (Broadbent, 1958). Normally, that filter is flexible, sensitive, and sturdy. Sometimes it permits several different stimuli to enter simultaneously, and other times it bars some of those same stimuli. When you drive a car on a clear road, for example, you usually can conduct a conversation with a passenger, often while listening to background music. But when the roads are treacherous, and below you is a several hundred foot drop, attention narrows: it now becomes impossible to conduct a conversation and what was formerly soothing music is now quite an irritant. All of the mind's energy, as it were, is directed to one thing and one thing only: driving safely. Everything else is filtered out.

Breakdown of the attentional filter
Among schizophrenics, something seems wrong with the attentional filter, so wrong, in fact, that attentional deficits have long been thought to be at the heart of the thought disorder that characterizes schizophrenia (Kraepelin, 1919; Bleuler, 1924; Chapman and Chapman, 1973; Garmezy, 1977b; Place and Gilmore, 1980). The sense that there is a breakdown of the filter, that the world's hodgepodge has simply invaded the mind, that one cannot control one's attention and therefore one's thoughts or speech, that it is difficult to focus the mind or sustain that focus once it is achieved—all of these experiences are said to be central to schizophrenia. A former patient puts it well:

> Each of us is capable of coping with a large number of stimuli, invading our being through any one of the senses. We could hear every sound within earshot and see every object, line and colour within the field of vision, and so on. It's obvious that we would be incapable of carrying on any of our daily activities if even one-hun-

Among schizophrenics the attentional filter appears to have broken down, so that the schizophrenic's mind is invaded by stimuli. The person shown in the sketch seems to be beseiged by a multitude of motifs and patterns.

dredth of all these available stimuli invade us at once. So the mind must have a filter which functions without our conscious thought, sorting stimuli and allowing only those which are relevant to the situation in hand to disturb consciousness. And this filter must be working at maximum efficiency at all times, particularly when a high degree of concentration is required. What happened to me . . . was a breakdown in the filter, and a hodge-podge of unrelated stimuli were distracting me from things which should have had my undivided attention. (MacDonald, 1960, p. 218)

Some schizophrenics seem to suffer generalized attentional deficits; they seem not to be attending to anything at all. Others pay too much attention to some stimuli, and not enough to others. For example, someone who is experiencing hallucinations is likely to be hyper-attentive to the hallucinations and correspondingly insensitive to external social stimuli.

Overinclusiveness

☐ OVERINCLUSIVENESS. Another possibility, which has received strong support from a variety of studies, is that schizophrenic thinking generally tends to be overinclusive (Cameron, 1938, 1947; Chapman and Taylor, 1957; Payne, 1966; Yates, 1966). *Overinclusiveness* refers to the tendency to form concepts from both relevant and irrelevant information. This thought defect arises from an impaired capacity to resist distracting information, and it strongly suggests a defect in cognitive filtering.

Generally, then, schizophrenics may be processing much more information than normals, by virtue of overinclusiveness. Evidence from other research indicates that psychotic states generally tax and deplete information processing, slowing and straining a system that is already quite limited, and impairing performance for tasks that require full use of processing capabilities (Braff and Saccuzzo, 1985; Grove and Andreason, 1985; Ohman, Nordby, and d'Elia, 1986; Patterson, Spohn, Bogia, and Hayes, 1986; Saccuzzo and Braff, 1986).

□ COGNITIVE DISTRACTIBILITY.   The notion of a defective filter that gives rise to overinclusiveness in schizophrenic thinking merits further examination. Are there rules that determine what is relevant information and what irrelevant? Of course not. Very likely all of us differ with regard to the kind of information that we attend to and exclude, even on so simple a task as the reaction time task. In what ways, then, may the thought and attentional processes of schizophrenics be different from normals?

Chains of associations

The difference between schizophrenic and normal thinking is unlikely to be a qualitative one, since all of us have associations to a stimulus which may or may not prove to be relevant. The difference lies in the number of associative intrusions, the context in which they arise, and in how they are integrated conceptually. Imagine yourself writing a New Year's greeting to a friend. You wish her a happy and healthy year and then refer to the pleasures and sadnesses of the previous year. Compare your greeting to that written by one of Eugen Bleuler's patients:

> I wish you then a good, happy, joyful, healthy, blessed and fruitful year, and many good wine-years to come, as well as a healthy and good apple-year, and sauerkraut and cabbage and squash and seed year. (Bleuler, 1950, cited in Martin, 1977)

Here, there are many more associations than are found in normal greetings. These associations, moreover, arise in chains that appear to be generated by specific words that seem to distract the patient from his ultimate goal and impair the overall meaning of the greeting. The word fruitful seems to evoke associations to wine, apple, sauerkraut, cabbage, squash, and the like. Moreover, in this context, wine and sauerkraut are not normally the dominant associations of the word fruitful: abundance is. But the patient seems to have centered on "fruit" and to have generated associations that are appropriate for that word but not for "fruitfulness."

Hospitalized in a mental asylum and labeled a schizophrenic, August Klotz spent his time drawing such pictures as this. Here he depicts a person's hair as a combination of worms, fingers with nails, and heads of caterpillars, describing the drawing through free association: "Worm holes (bath faces), worm paths (pianomusicstickteeth), worm strings (spitbathlife of the archlyregallery-tin-timeler-reflections: ad mothersugarmoon in the sevensaltnose water. . . ."

Sensitivity to
dominant
associations

Many words have a variety of meanings, connotations, and associations. And all of us, schizophrenics and normals alike, are sensitive to those meanings and associations. But schizophrenics seem especially sensitive to the dominant associations of words, and are less influenced by the contexts in which they are used. In the following test item:

Pool means the same as
1. puddle
2. notebook
3. swim
4. none of the above.

The correct answer is "puddle." Many schizophrenics as well as some normals, however, will err and offer "swim" as the correct answer. The difference between normal and schizophrenic thought processes in items of this sort is a quantitative rather than a qualitative one (Chapman and Chapman, 1973; Rattan and Chapman, 1973).

THE DISORDERED CONTENT OF THOUGHT

Evidence for disordered thought is as commonly found in the content as the process of thinking. Sometimes the schizophrenic person develops the belief that certain events and people have special significance for him—that television newscasters are speaking to him, for example, or that strangers in the street are looking at him. These beliefs are called *ideas of reference*. When such beliefs become organized into a larger and coherent framework, they are called delusions.

Four kinds of
delusions

□ KINDS OF DELUSIONS. Earlier we noted that a *delusion* is a private theory, deeply held, that often persists despite sound contradictory evidence, and that often does not fit with the individual's level of knowledge or cultural group. These beliefs are so deeply held that psychological lore tells of a delusional patient who was once wired to a lie detector and asked if she were the Virgin Mary. "No," she replied. But the detector indicated that she was lying!

There are four prominent kinds of delusions: delusions of grandeur, delusions of control, delusions of persecution, and delusions of reference. *Delusions of grandeur* consist of convictions that one is especially important. The belief that one is Jesus Christ or fourth in line to the throne of Denmark would indicate a delusion of grandeur.

Delusions of control are characterized by beliefs that one's thoughts or behaviors are being controlled from without. The patient attributes the source of angry, sexual, or otherwise sinful thoughts to external agents. For example, someone who believes that beings from another universe are giving him instructions is suffering from a delusion of control.

Delusions of persecution consist of fears that individuals, groups, or the government have malevolent intentions and are "out to get me." The focus of the delusion may be quite specific: a neighbor, one's boss, the FBI, or a rather vague "they." When these delusions combine with hallucinations so that the subject "sees" and "hears" evidence of a plot, they can induce continual panic. Confirmation for these imaginings can often be found in misinterpretations of everyday experience, as shown in the following case:

Systematized delusions of persecution are a symptom of a schizophrenic's disordered thought. The motif of the eyes as shown in this painting may indicate the delusion of being continuously watched by others who are "out to get him."

Arthur, who had been insecure and shy for as long as he could remember, took a job in a large office. Unsure of his clerical abilities, he worked long and hard at his job, rejecting invitations to have lunch or coffee with his colleagues. Gradually they stopped inviting him, going off merrily by themselves, and returning full of laughter and cheer.

One day Arthur's supervisor found a substantial error in his work. Although it was his first error and the supervisor would easily have forgiven it, Arthur simply could not forget it. It seemed to underscore his own perception of his abilities, a perception that he was quite anxious to conceal. He came to believe that his supervisor knew of other mistakes he had made, and that his colleagues and supervisor were collaboratively examining his work daily. He "knew" that they were excluding him and talking about him, and that their lunchtime laughter was entirely at his expense. Moreover, he felt that their interest in his performance gradually overflowed into an interest in his personal life. When he encountered his co-workers after hours or on the weekend he felt certain that they were following him.

Six weeks after his error had been discovered, he began to "sense" that people had been through his drawers, both at home and in the office. Moreover, certain papers that were necessary for his work were missing, leading him to believe that others were now actively plotting his vocational downfall. Their failure to invite him to lunch was taken as further evidence of the plot.

He became very fearful and disorganized. Continually preoccupied with his troubles, he found it difficult to sleep, eat, or concentrate. His work deteriorated both in quality and in output. When his supervisor finally asked him what was wrong, he blurted out, "You know what's wrong. You and they have made it wrong ever since I came here." He then ran out of the office, never to return. Within the year, Arthur's behavior had so deteriorated that he was hospitalized with the diagnosis of paranoid schizophrenia.

Arthur's sense that others were actively seeking his errors and taking his papers constituted a delusion of persecution. But the continual misinterpretation of others' laughter, as well as their failure to invite him to lunch, constituted the fourth kind of delusion: a ***delusion of reference***. Such delusions rest on the incorrect assumption that the casual remarks or behaviors of others apply to oneself, and can extend to how others act in the street or subway, as well as to the behavior of actors on television. Depending on what they refer to, referential delusions can make a person miserably unhappy, as in the above instance, or quite joyful.

□ DELUSIONS: A NORMAL COGNITIVE ACTIVITY? Delusions are among the most striking symptoms of schizophrenia. To the observer, the content of a delusion seems so bizarre that it automatically suggests the thought disorder that is characteristic of schizophrenia. How else does one explain the feeling that one is being intensely persecuted, or that one is infinitely superior to ordinary mortals, all in the absence of confirming evidence? Indeed, it is the flowering of a delusion in the absence of confirmation, and its resistance to ordinary persuasion, that leads us to believe that the thought processes that are implicated in delusional activity are different from our own.

Before we consider the delusions from the schizophrenic's own vantage point, we might first look for analogies to delusional activity. These, of course, are only analogies, and likely rude analogies at that, but they give us some basis for understanding schizophrenic delusions.

Imagine that you have experienced a partial loss of hearing, and that you are unaware of that loss. You are with two other people who are talking, laughing, making funny faces, and looking at you. All three of you have to work together, but it seems that those two are doing a better job of it than you are. What are you likely to think? Remember that you can't *hear* what's going on very well, so you don't really *know* why they are laughing and looking at you. But that doesn't stop you from trying to make sense of the peculiar situation. One very real possibility is that you will infer that they are talking about *you* and laughing at *you*.

Such an experiment was in fact conducted among normal people who were highly hypnotizable and in whom partial deafness was induced. Subjects who were unaware that they were deaf were rated by judges (who had no knowledge of the subjects' hearing status) as being more agitated, irritated, hostile, and confused than either nondeaf subjects or subjects who were aware of the source of their deafness. Moreover, the experimental subjects rated themselves in very much the same way. Finally, formal measures of psychopathology, such as the Minnesota Multiphasic Personality Inventory (MMPI) and the Thematic Apperception Test (TAT), revealed much higher paranoia scores among subjects who were deaf and unaware of it (Zimbardo, Andersen, and Kabat, 1981).

While the sources of our feelings and perceptions are not always available to us, we do, in fact, develop theories to account for our experiences. These theories arise from the causal attributions we make about our experiences (Nisbett and Ross, 1980). In this sense, we behave like ordinary scientists: given a set of facts or experiences, we seek to explain them (Maher, 1974).

Vivid sensory quality of perceptual experience

A similar process may occur with schizophrenics. Like the normal person, the schizophrenic asks: What is happening? How is it happening? And why is it happening to me and not to others? Because their attention is overinclusive, schizophrenics will frequently "see" aspects of their environment that they are at a loss to explain, and be inundated by stimuli that they cannot control (Venables, 1964). Moreover, there is growing evidence that schizophrenics actually suffer impairments of a physical sort. The sensory quality of their perceptual experience may be more vivid, intense, or defective than in normals (Cooper, Garside, and Kay, 1976; Cooper and Porter, 1976). Much as it is common for older people whose hearing is fading to believe that people are whispering about them, so it may be that schizophrenics' delusions derive from actual perceptual deficits. Such deficits and the experiences to which they give rise are genuine. But they lead schizophrenics to experience their world differently than the rest of us do.

Schizophrenics know that their own experiences are *real*. When others deny the reality of those experiences, schizophrenics have two alternative explanations: either the others are lying, or they are telling the truth. If schizophrenics decide that the others are lying, they feel victimized, and they suffer delusions of persecution. If schizophrenics decide that the others are telling the truth, then they feel privileged because of their special ability to perceive "realities" that are unavailable to others, and they suffer delusions of grandiosity.

"But why me and not others?," the schizophrenic asks. It is in explaining his special fate that the personal history of the schizophrenic may become relevant. If, for example, he harbors a guilty secret in his past, he may conclude that this is why he is being so terribly punished now. If he has done something that he views as especially praiseworthy, he may now see himself as anointed from above. The variety of possible explanations is limited only by the variety of life histories that exist among schizophrenics, while the regularity with which certain explanations occur derives from the common life experiences that a culture provides.

Finally, it is schizophrenics' persistence in maintaining their delusions despite contrary evidence that requires explanation. Reality is not a solid, concrete thing. It can and has been used by normal people to arrive at conclusions that other normals find tenuous. All theories about how the world operates, including scientific ones, are overthrown only when a more satisfactory theory can be found to replace it. Because schizophrenics' theories often rest on invisible agencies, what seems ridiculous to the observer provides schizophrenics with a cohesive and satisfactory account of their situation. On those occasions when it is contradicted by particular kinds of data, the theory (i.e., the delusion) becomes more elaborate and comprehensive to account for the seeming contradiction, much as scientific theories do when they must account for anomalies. For example, if a schizophrenic believes that he is being poisoned and he encounters a nurse who seems particularly kind, he may expand his delusion to include people who seem kind, but who are really poisoners. This occurs not because the schizophrenic fails to test reality, but because he has no more satisfactory explanations.

AFFECTIVE DISTURBANCES

Flat or restricted affect

Emotions, or affects, are jointly a function of perception, cognition, and physiological arousal. *Perceiving* a mad dog quickly generates some worrisome *cognitions* (or thoughts) that in turn generate an *emotion,* fear. Because schizophrenia arises from disorders of perception and cognition, it follows that there should be affective disturbances also.

For some schizophrenics, affect is characteristically flat or bland. They seem entirely unresponsive emotionally. So much is this the case that flat or restricted affect is still considered a diagnostic hallmark of the schizophrenic disturbance (Carpenter, Strauss, and Bartko, 1974). The apparent inability of some schizophrenics to display affect should not, however, be mistaken for absence of *any* affective experience. Schizophrenics are deeply emotional and deeply responsive to cognitions (Arieti, 1974). But the cognitions that affect them are not the ones that are evocative for most of us, and vice versa. In one respect, the schizophrenic experience is like our own when we visit unfamiliar places. For example, American guests at a Thai wedding, not knowing what all of the symbols mean, would hardly know how to act or what to feel. Shared symbolic meanings allow feelings to arise, be expressed, and be understood by others. Because schizophrenics have lost contact with the socially shared domain of symbols and meanings, their affective responses to those stimuli are likely to be blunted.

Inappropriate affect

Sometimes, schizophrenic affect is best characterized as inappropriate. Carl's affect seemed to take that form:

> He smiles when he is uncomfortable, and smiles more when in pain. He cries during television comedies. He seems angry when justice is done . . . and roars with laughter on reading that a young child was burned in a tragic fire.

Affective disturbance can take yet another form: intense ambivalence. A person or situation may arouse opposite feelings simultaneously. Such ambivalence may lead to behavioral paralysis, or to seemingly bizarre attempts to resolve the situation by expressing one affect overwhelmingly and suppressing the other entirely.

MEANING IN SCHIZOPHRENIA

Lack of understandable communication

Most people who read Carl's words are struck and upset by their incomprehensibility. "I am made of stone," he says, "or else I am made of glass. I am wired precisely wrong, precisely . . ." Neurotic communications evoke understanding. If you are told "I'm afraid to go outside" or "I can't stop daydreaming," you have little difficulty comprehending the communication, even empathizing with the speaker. But schizophrenic communications often seem to be gibberish; they seem to result in word salads and syllabic stews. Ideas are not transmitted. Unable to understand, people often turn away from schizophrenics, treating what schizophrenics say as part of the symptomatology of the disorder, and not as communication.

Do schizophrenics attempt to communicate? Is what they say gibberish? Was Carl saying anything that was meaningful? It appears that he was. But from the listener's viewpoint, it was difficult to find the communication in the thicket of strange verbalization.

> I am an unreal person. . . . I am wired precisely wrong, precisely. But you will not find my key. . . . You can look at me closely if you wish, but you see more from far away.

Fear of exposure

Carl is hiding. That is, he is trying "precisely" to mislead his observers. When angry, he pretends friendship; when sad, happiness. He wants to maintain privacy, and he may also feel in danger of being exposed. He is, therefore, all the more in need of concealment. When hiding by means of transparent opposites fails—as when he is asked an intrusive question—he hides more energetically. Or, he hides in more bizarre ways: by generating

The schizophrenic may avoid social contacts, withdrawing behind a blank mask to protect himself from what he perceives to be external hostile influences.

neologisms, by using clang associations to speak—in short, by talking a lot and saying little, by conveying his need to hide in his talk.

The divided self

The divided self is a self that operates at two levels (Laing, 1965b). On one level, there is the silent self—clearly active but vulnerable and afraid to emerge. There is also a smoke-screen self, a mask, a disguise, designed to conceal and protect that silent self. There is no strong evidence for this two-self view, but many psychologists and psychiatrists who have worked with schizophrenics find merit in it. For example, later in his treatment, when his need to hide had abated, Carl had this to say of himself:

> When it's all over, it's hard to remember what you said and how you said it. I wouldn't want to talk that way now even if I could. I was putting people off almost consciously by talking that way. It would have been impossible for me to let on how I really felt. It's still hard . . . But at the same time, while I was putting you off, I really wanted you to know. But I couldn't come out with it—that was too risky. Sometimes I would say things in a special way, hoping you'd take special notice. When I said I'm not angry . . . I wagged my hand back and forth, making a "no" sign—telling but not saying that I'm angry. I don't know why I wanted someone to know. After all, I was hiding. But it was a prison I had made for myself. I didn't know how to get out myself. So I kept throwing out little keys, hoping someone would get at the lock.

THE DIMENSIONS OF SCHIZOPHRENIA

In DSM-III-R, schizophrenics are categorized according to their symptoms. But they can also be categorized according to the onset of schizophrenia, the way the symptoms develop, and the ways in which they respond to treatment. The most common clinical dimension for categorizing schizophrenia is acute versus chronic, while an increasingly significant research mode of characterizing this set of disorders is Type I versus Type II.

ACUTE AND CHRONIC

Acute vs. chronic schizophrenia

The distinction between acute and chronic conditions is based on how quickly the symptoms have developed and how long they have been present. *Acute schizophrenics* are characterized by rapid and sudden onset of very florid symptoms. Quite frequently, one can point to a specific precipitating incident that led to the difficulties: a *reactive* crisis that was precipitated by a severe social or emotional upset, often an upset from which the individual perceives no escape (Zigler and Phillips, 1961; Arieti, 1974). For some schizophrenics, that crisis may involve leaving home, leaving school for a job, their first sexual experience, the loss of a parent or sibling, or marriage. Prior to that upset, their history seems well within normal bounds.

In contrast, *chronic schizophrenics* seem to manifest a rather gradual and prolonged history of withdrawal. No single crisis or identifiable stresses trigger the disorder. Rather, early history gives evidence of familial and peer rejection, inferior school and social adjustment, and intense shyness and social withdrawal, such that peer relations are impaired over a long period of time.

In clinical practice, the acute-chronic distinction rests on how many episodes a person has had and how long she has been hospitalized. First epi-

This patient suffered an acute onset of schizophrenic symptoms after having been sexually approached. The incident made him doubt his own sexuality, and he subsequently hallucinated that God had spoken to him about it. The eye shown in the painting probably indicates the patient's terror of God's omnipresence.

sodes that result in hospitalization for less than a year, or several episodes that lead to a series of very brief hospitalizations, qualify a person for an acute designation. Hospitalization that extends for more than two years invariably results in a chronic classification. When a person has been hospitalized from roughly eighteen to twenty-eight months, it is difficult to distinguish between acute and chronic conditions. That fact alone largely accounts for the low reliability of the classification.

TYPE I AND TYPE II

Type I vs. Type II schizophrenia

The dimensions of the schizophrenias can be examined not only from the precipitants, but rather from the symptoms that are generated, the response to certain kinds of treatment, and the long-term outcome. *Type I* schizophrenia is characterized by such symptoms as delusions, hallucinations, and prominent thought disorder. These are called "positive symptoms" because they reflect marked departures from ordinary cognition. Such positive symptoms are reversible. They are thought to arise from a disturbance in brain chemistry, specifically the neurotransmission of dopamine, an important matter that we will examine shortly. And they are thought to be responsive to a class of medications called *neuroleptics*, which alter brain chemistry.

The *Type II* syndrome is characterized by such symptoms as flat affect, poverty of speech, and loss of volition. These "negative symptoms" are more difficult to define because they reflect the absence or diminution of normal everyday functions. They seem much more difficult to reverse, and are more closely associated with poor long-term outcome. The symptoms are unrelated to dopamine transmission, but may well be associated with structural changes in the brain, as well as intellectual impairment. Type II symptoms have a much graver prognosis.

Type I and Type II syndromes are believed to reflect relatively independent processes that can coexist in the same individual but that follow different time courses. And perhaps because they can coexist simultaneously, they do not quite map on to the acute and chronic dimensions. Paranoid schizophrenia, however, reflects a chronic Type I syndrome, while disorganized schizophrenia includes a strong component of the Type II syndrome (Crow, 1980, 1982, 1985).

THE CAUSES OF THE SCHIZOPHRENIAS

While the schizophrenias have been studied for more than a century, progress in understanding them has been painfully slow. We know less about the origins and treatment of the schizophrenias than we do about some other disorders. In the following sections, we will outline the dominant approaches currently used in the search for the causes and treatment of the schizophrenias.

Knowledge about the origins of schizophrenia is concentrated in four major areas: genetics, neurochemistry, the role of the family, and the role of society. Research on the schizophrenias, like that on other psychological questions, is two-pronged, involving both biological and social questions. Some consider schizophrenia to be rooted in nature; others say that it is the product of social experience. Still others are convinced that nature-nurture interactions are involved, and that these interactions of genetic, biochemical, familial, and social factors predispose a person to schizophrenia (Zubin and Spring, 1977).

THE GENETICS OF SCHIZOPHRENIA

Genetic component of schizophrenia

Various researchers have examined the notion of a genetic vulnerability to schizophrenia. Both twin studies and family studies have demonstrated a strong basis for the genetic component in schizophrenia.

CONCORDANCE FOR SCHIZOPHRENIA IN TWINS

□ MZ AND DZ TWINS.   We can best understand human genetics by examining the similarities and differences between twins. As we discussed in Chapter 3, twins are of two kinds: identical and fraternal. Both kinds descend from the zygote, the fertilized egg from which all life begins. Identical twins are *monozygotic* (MZ), which means that both individuals developed from a single fertilized egg, which divided and produced two individuals. Because all of the cells of these two individuals derived from a single egg, the genes and chromosomes—in short, the heredity—of these individuals is identical. They will, of course, have the identical physical makeup: genes, blood type, eye color, and fingerprints will be the same. There may be differences between them, but such differences will be entirely attributable to different life experiences: one may be thinner because of nutritional differences, or the other may limp because of an accident.

Fraternal, or *dizygotic* (DZ) twins develop from two different eggs. Except for the fact that they are born at the same time, DZ twins are like ordinary siblings. Their hereditary makeup is quite different. They may be of

Separated at birth, the Mallifert twins meet accidentally.

Drawing by Chas. Addams: © 1981, The New Yorker Magazine, Inc.

different gender; they may have different eye color. They have different fingerprints. They can be accurately distinguished from MZ twins on the basis of these characteristics alone, and certainty can be increased by examining blood type.

The logic of a genetic study is really quite simple: if all other things are equal, the more similar people are in their genetic makeup, the more traits they will have in common if those traits are genetically influenced. MZ twins should resemble each other more than DZ twins or ordinary siblings. And DZ twins and siblings should have more in common than unrelated individuals. If both members of a twin set have a trait in common, we say that that twin set is *concordant* for that particular trait. If, however, one member has the trait and one does not, we call the twin set *discordant* for the trait.

MZ twins are wholly identical in their genes and chromosomes. If the traits that subsequently develop are entirely determined by their genetic makeup, there should be 100 percent concordance. If one twin has the trait, the other should have it too. Anything less than 100 percent concordance (but more than the percentage found in DZ twins) will suggest that heredity *influences,* but does not actually determine, the presence of the trait. What is more, that influence depends on the assumption that all other possible influences, such as nutrition, physical health, and psychosocial environment, are themselves about the same. If one twin's physical and social environment differs from the other's, that difference could explain any difference between the pair.

□ LINKING GENETICS AND SCHIZOPHRENIA. Although genetic studies of schizophrenia have been conducted for over fifty years, Irving Gottesman and James Shields (1972) conducted one of the very few studies that were planned in advance. From 1948 through 1964, every patient admitted for treatment to the psychiatric unit at the Maudsley and Bethlem Royal Hospital in London was routinely asked if he or she was a twin. Over these sixteen years, the investigators located 55 patients (out of more than 45,000 admitted) who were twins and whose twin could be located and would cooperate in the study. For analytic purposes, the twin who was first seen at the psychiatric clinic is called the **index case** or **proband**. The other twin, who will be examined for the presence or absence of schizophrenia, is called the **co-twin**.

Of these fifty-five sets of twins, it was determined that twenty-two were MZ twins and thirty-three were DZ twins. The twins ranged in age from nineteen to sixty-four, with a median age of thirty-seven. Concordance for schizophrenia, where it was already present in the co-twin at the time the proband was admitted to the hospital, could, of course, be determined immediately. Discordant pairs were followed for at least three and as long as sixteen years to determine if schizophrenia subsequently developed in the co-twin.

Such a lengthy study examines more than simple diagnosis. In analyzing an enormous variety of psychological, medical, and social data for each twin

Table 12–1 CONCORDANCE RATES FOR SCHIZOPHRENIA IN STUDIES OF TWINS

	Number of Pairs		Concordance Percentages	
	MZ	DZ	MZ	DZ
Luxenburger (1929), Germany	19	13	58	0
Rosanoff et al. (1934), United States and Canada	41	53	61	13
Essen-Moller (1941), Sweden	11	27	64	15
Kallman (1953), New York State	174	296	69	11
Slater (1953), England	37	58	65	14
Inouye (1961), Japan	58	59	20	15
Kringlen (1967), Norway	55	90	25-38	4-10
Pollin, Allen, Hoffer, and Stubeneau (1969), United States	95	125	14-27	4-8
Tienari (1971), Finland	17	20	0-36	5-14
Gottesman and Shields (1972), England	22	33	40-50	9-19
Fischer (1973), Denmark	21	41	24-48	10-19

SOURCE: Adapted and modified from Gottesman and Shields, 1982. The concordance ranges arise from varying "breadth" in the spectrum of behaviors that give rise to the diagnosis of schizophrenia.

pair, Gottesman and Shields observed two findings of special relevance to our own investigation into the genetic causes of schizophrenia. First, they found strict concordance when the proband's co-twin had been hospitalized and diagnosed schizophrenic: 50 percent of MZ twins and 9 percent of DZ twins were concordant for schizophrenia, a ratio of roughly 4:1. Despite the small sample, this is a very significant finding, one consistent with other genetic studies of schizophrenia.

Higher concordance for schizophrenia in MZ than in DZ twins

Second, using length of hospitalization to indicate severity of schizophrenia, Gottesman and Shields found substantial concordance differences between MZ twins whose probands had been hospitalized for more than two years and those whose probands had been hospitalized for less than two years. Hospitalization for more than two years is critical to a diagnosis of chronic schizophrenia. It is therefore of enormous interest that concordance rates rose to 77 percent in this sample. For those who were hospitalized less than two years (very likely the acute, reactive schizophrenias), the concordance rate was only 27 percent (Gottesman and Shields, 1972).

The evidence from the many studies summarized in Table 12-1 is strong: concordance rates for MZ twins are higher than they are for DZ twins; concordance rates for DZ twins are, with one exception, higher than the rate for unrelated persons in the general population (about 1 percent). Concordance, however, is never 100 percent because the genetic component of schizophrenia does not guarantee occurrence. Genetics only makes one vulnerable to schizophrenia: it does not guarantee that it will occur.

CONCORDANCE FOR SCHIZOPHRENIA IN FAMILIES

Genetic vulnerability for schizophrenia

Family studies begin from the same premise as twin studies: individuals who have a similar heredity are more likely to both possess a particular trait than are those who are unrelated. Parents and siblings of a schizophrenic proband should be more likely to be or become schizophrenic than remote relatives, who in turn are more prone to schizophrenia than are those who are not related. The data from more than a dozen studies support this conclusion (Rosenthal, 1970a). As can be seen in Figure 12-1, the likelihood that

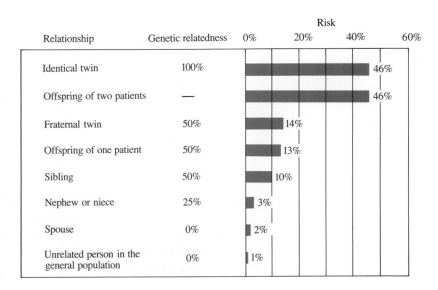

Figure 12-1
Risk estimates for schizophrenia as a function of relationship to schizophrenic proband. (Source: Nicol and Gottesman, 1983, p. 399.)

ordinary siblings of a proband will also be schizophrenic is about 10 per-cent—much higher than the 1 percent one finds among the general popula-tion, but much lower than the 46 percent we find among identical twins. Similarly, the child of two schizophrenic parents, has about a 46 percent chance of becoming schizophrenic. The evidence clearly supports genetic vulnerability—but only vulnerability. In no study do concordance and risk rise to 100 percent. It takes more than genetic vulnerability to produce schizophrenia.

BUT IS IT REALLY GENETIC?

The role of the environment

We have assumed that if all other things are equal, the more similar people are in their genetic makeup, the more traits they will have in common if those traits are genetically influenced. But are all other things equal? Con-sider the finding that children of two schizophrenic parents stand a 46 per-cent chance of becoming schizophrenic themselves. Is that because they share a common gene pool, or is it because schizophrenic parents may be terrible parents, fully capable of inducing schizophrenia in their children, regardless of their common gene pool? Or consider again the twin studies. We know that MZ twins share a unique environment with each other. They tend to mature and to develop language more slowly than other children. They tend to be mistaken for one another and therefore to suffer identity problems of indeterminate magnitude. Could not these environmental problems, rather than genetics, be a major factor in their eventual schizophrenia?

Behavior geneticists have responded to these questions in three ways. First, they have tried to locate probands and co-siblings who have been reared apart. Studies of this kind are called *adoption studies*. Second, they have conducted studies of people who are presumed to be at risk for schizo-phrenia because other members of their families are schizophrenic. These high-risk studies seek to map the development of behavior before schizo-phrenia occurs, in the hope of relating causative, correlative, and especially preventive factors. Finally, there are studies of non-schizophrenic twins which bear on this question.

Adoption studies indicate a strong genetic component

□ ADOPTION STUDIES. Leonard Heston (1966) studied forty-seven chil-dren of schizophrenic mothers who had been placed in adoptive or foster homes less than one month after birth. He compared them to fifty control offspring who had been reared in the same foster homes as the children of schizophrenic mothers. Thus, the environments for both groups were the same, and they were not environments produced by the schizophrenic mothers. All forty-seven children took intelligence tests and psychological tests. Each was interviewed by a psychiatrist. Then two other psychiatrists not previously involved in the experiment came in to evaluate the children's dossiers and, if necessary, to diagnose the children. Neither psychiatrist knew the children's origins, or the nature of the mothers' illness. Even so, the two evaluating psychiatrists diagnosed five of the children of schizo-phrenic mothers as schizophrenic. None of the children from the control group were so diagnosed. Moreover, thirty-seven of the forty-seven children of schizophrenic mothers were given some kind of psychiatric diagnosis, as compared with nine of the fifty children from the control group. Considering that the environments were identical for both groups and the very early age at which the children were placed, the much higher incidence of disordered behavior among the children of schizophrenic mothers points to a strong genetic component in the origins of schizophrenia.

Seymour Kety, David Rosenthal, Paul Wender, and Fini Schulsinger (1968) examined the records of all children born between 1924 and 1947 in Copenhagen, Denmark, who were adopted when quite young. From this large group, they selected those adoptees who were subsequently admitted to a psychiatric hospital and diagnosed as schizophrenic. Thirty-three such probands were compared to a control group drawn from the same population but lacking any psychiatric history. The family histories of biological (but not adoptive) relatives of the schizophrenic index cases revealed a higher incidence of disturbance (which included schizophrenia, uncertain schizophrenia, and inadequate personality) than did those of the controls (8.7 percent to 1.9 percent), providing further evidence for a genetic vulnerability to schizophrenia.

Because these two studies have measured the separate influences of genetics and of environment, and because both have documented the persistence of the genetic link, their combined impact is clear. When environmental and genetic factors are compared for their effect on rates of schizophrenia in relatives of probands, heredity has more influence than does environment. It is important, however, to state this case precisely, and not to overstate it. Genes contribute to vulnerability to schizophrenia, but they do not in themselves completely explain its presence.

At-risk studies of children

☐ CHILDREN AT RISK FOR SCHIZOPHRENIA.   At-risk studies are important because they can identify those children who are most likely to develop schizophrenia, and the investigators can then observe the effects of specific influences on such children in order to reduce the incidence of schizophrenia. At-risk children are more vulnerable to schizophrenia than are other children. Their vulnerability may derive from several factors. Often, at-risk children are defined as those whose parents or siblings are schizophrenic. As we will see later, other factors also make children vulnerable; these are factors that relate to environment and to social class: poverty, broken homes, families where the **double-bind** reigns. (This latter hypothesis, formulated by Gregory Bateson, refers to two mutually exclusive messages from one person, which can neither be satisfied nor avoided.) All of these sources contribute to a child's vulnerability, or high risk for schizophrenia, and all can be studied in an at-risk program (Watt, Anthony, Wynne, and Rolf, 1984).

Perhaps the most extensive at-risk study of schizophrenia was a Danish study begun in 1962 by Sarnoff Mednick and Fini Schulsinger (Mednick, Cudeck, Griffith, Talovic, and Schulsinger, 1984). These investigators isolated 207 subjects who were at significant risk for schizophrenia, and 104 low-risk people who were matched on such variables as age, gender, years of education, father's occupation, and place of residence. When the study began, the average age of the subjects was about fifteen years, and none of them was schizophrenic. Ten years later, 17 of the high-risk (and only 1 of the low-risk) people were diagnosed schizophrenic. The mothers of these schizophrenics were distinguished from the rest of the sample on a variety of characteristics. Most striking among these were the facts that the mothers' own psychotic episodes were precipitated by the childbirth, and that more generally, the mothers were unstable in their relations with men, and were not emotionally attached to the father when pregnancy occurred. Moreover, the fathers themselves were unstable at work and often addicted to drugs or alcohol (Talovic, Mednick, Schulsinger, and Falloon, 1980). The mothers of these disturbed offspring, moreover, were quite temperamental and tended to direct their emotions outwards in highly aggressive forms (Mednick, 1973).

In another study of those at high risk for schizophrenia, investigators from the United States and Israel studied a group of preadolescent children who were born to a schizophrenic parent and who were raised either on a kibbutz or in a town. These index children were matched to kibbutz or town controls. These children were first examined when they were eleven, and again at sixteen and at twenty-five. The first two examinations found the index group to be more impaired on such indices as severity of psychopathology (Nagler and Glueck, 1985), on psychophysiological measures (Kugelmass, Marcus, and Schmueli, 1985), and in the quality of their social and school adjustment (Sohlberg and Yaniv, 1985). But no differences between kibbutz and town child-rearing were found, suggesting that the impairment was due wholly to the genetic predisposition. But the third examination at age twenty-five reversed all that and revealed that children of the kibbutz had the highest incidence of psychological disorder (Mirsky, Silberman, Latz, and Nagler, 1985; and see Kaffman, 1986, for a different interpretation). Why such a difference should occur, especially when the kibbutz has been viewed as a *benign* place in which to raise children, is not clear. Perhaps because the kibbutz is a relatively small community, it provides fewer opportunities for privacy and for familial peculiarities to be forgotten. It may provide many fewer opportunities for self-fulfilling prophecies to be forgotten than exist in towns and cities (Mirsky and Duncan-Johnson, 1984).

Influence of nongenetic factors

Although the Danish and Israeli at-risk studies confirm the genetic hypothesis, their primary importance resides in understanding the influence of nongenetic factors—nutrition, psychophysiology, family, social and academic history, personal skills and liabilities—on the development of schizophrenia. Ultimately, it is hoped that at-risk studies will suggest biological and social interventions that can break the chain that leads to schizophrenia.

□ NON-SCHIZOPHRENIC TWINS.   MZ twins grow up sharing a common environment that often treats them as if they were a single person. They are often dressed alike, confused for one another, compared to one another, and generally scrutinized more closely than are DZ twins or mere siblings. These experiences collectively create a distinct environment for MZ twins in addition to their identical genetic makeup. Could that environment account for the greater probability of schizophrenia in the co-twin when the proband is schizophrenic? Probably not. If the special environmental and psychological factors common to MZ twins were the factors that produced schizophrenia, then the rate of schizophrenia among MZ twins would be higher than that of the general population. But that is not the case. MZ twins are not more likely to become schizophrenic than are non-twins. A co-twin is more likely to become schizophrenic if, and only if, the proband is schizophrenic, and not otherwise (Rosenthal, 1970b). Thus, the identical environment in which MZ twins develop has no bearing on whether the twins become schizophrenic.

ANOTHER SIDE OF SCHIZOPHRENIA: CREATIVITY

Connection between creativity and schizophrenia

Any comprehensive treatment of the role of genetics in schizophrenia must take into account the possible relationship between schizophrenia and creativity. Being related to a schizophrenic may not be all bad. In fact, it may have some distinct advantages. Reporting on a follow-up study of children born to schizophrenic mothers and placed in adoptive or foster homes shortly after birth, Leonard Heston and Duane Denney note that the children who did not become schizophrenic were more "spontaneous," "had more colorful life histories," "held more creative jobs," and "followed the more imaginative hobbies . . . ." than normals (Heston and Denney, 1968, p. 371). Indeed, one study reports that non-paranoid schizophrenics score higher on a test of creativity than either paranoid schizophrenics or non-paranoid controls (Keefe and Magaro, 1980; Magaro, 1981).

A study of genetics and schizophrenia in Iceland by Karlsson (1972) further supports the connection between creativity and schizophrenia. Karlsson observes that the "genetic carriers" of schizophrenia often exhibit "unusual ability" and display "a superior capacity for associative thinking" (Karlsson, 1972, p. 61). Fascinated by this finding, Karlsson proposes that society may even depend upon "persons with a schizophrenic constitution" for its social and scientific progress. He remarks that a disproportionate number of the most creative people in philosophy, physics, music, literature, mathematics, and the fine arts often developed psychiatric disorders. *Superphrenic* is Karlsson's term for these people who are both related to schizophrenics and recognizably outstanding in politics, science, and the arts.

From this discussion of the genetic connection in schizophrenia, it is clear

Representations of irrationality. *Left*: Plate from *Urizen* by William Blake; *right*: *Bacchanalian Scene* by Richard Dadd, a nineteenth-century artist, who was declared schizophrenic and hospitalized in Bedlam after having killed his father.

that a link exists. Although it does not embrace every important influence leading to schizophrenia, it does constitute one such influence. As David Rosenthal observed (1970b), "genetic factors do contribute appreciably and beyond a reasonable doubt" to the development of schizophrenia.

THE BIOLOGY OF THE SCHIZOPHRENIAS

Over the past decade, enormous progress has been made in understanding the biology of the schizophrenias. Two lines of research have been particularly illuminating. The first has looked at irregularities in the neurochemistry of the schizophrenias, the second at differences in brain structure between schizophrenics and normals. Both lines of investigation have important consequences for understanding Type I and Type II schizophrenia.

THE NEUROCHEMISTRY OF THE SCHIZOPHRENIAS: THE DOPAMINE HYPOTHESIS

The idea that there may be biochemical antecedents to schizophrenia is not new. Researchers have frequently tried to find the biochemical differences between schizophrenics and normals, but with little luck. Reports of vast differences in the chemistry of blood or urine of normals as opposed to hospitalized schizophrenics have turned out merely to reflect differences in the diets of hospitalized and non-hospitalized people, or bad lab technique, or the absence of control groups, or experimenter bias.

The dopamine hypothesis

More recently, the strategy has shifted. Instead of looking for biochemical substances that differentiate schizophrenics from normals, scientists are now searching for abnormalities in neurophysiological functioning. Specifically, they are looking at special chemicals in the brain, called **neurotransmitters.** The way these chemicals function, and how increases or decreases in the available quantities of neurotransmitters affect behavior and perhaps influence the development of schizophrenia—these are presently the dominant research concerns. By focusing on these chemicals and by drawing connections between schizophrenia, the amphetamine psychosis, and Parkinson's disease, scientists have constructed what is now called the **dopamine hypothesis** (as we first mentioned in Chapter 3).

Similarities between symptoms of schizophrenia and effects of amphetamines

First, consider the similarities between the symptoms of schizophrenia and the effects of the amphetamines, or "speed." Large doses of amphetamines can create a psychosis with symptoms indistinguishable from those of acute paranoid schizophrenia. Patients suffering amphetamine psychosis have, in fact, been wrongly diagnosed as schizophrenics (Snyder, 1974b) (see Chapter 14). What is more, a very low dose of a drug related to the amphetamines, methylphenidate, will exacerbate a schizophrenic's symptoms almost immediately: paranoid schizophrenics, for example, become increasingly paranoid. Finally, the drugs most helpful in treating the symptoms of schizophrenia—the neuroleptics—are also the best antidotes for amphetamine psychosis and for the exacerbated schizophrenic symptoms induced by amphetamines (Snyder et al., 1974).

These neuroleptics produce varying effects on schizophrenia. One class of neuroleptic, the phenothiazines, blocks the brain's receptors for a neurotransmitter called dopamine. Neurotransmitters are chemicals that facili-

Effects of the
phenothiazines

tate the transmission of electrical impulses between the brain's nerve endings. There are perhaps twenty different neurotransmitters, of which dopamine is particularly important. Since the phenothiazines both decrease the amount of available dopamine and also relieve the symptoms of schizophrenia, it seems to follow that schizophrenia results from excess dopamine. These findings have opened the door for the dopamine hypothesis, with the connection between Parkinson's disease and dopamine offering more support for the hypothesis.

L-DOPA and
Parkinson's
disease

Characterized by growing stiffness in the arms and legs, Parkinson's disease is particularly noticeable because it renders facial expressions flat and dull, and causes tremors, especially in the hands. It happens that the main pathway in the brain for dopamine is the corpus striatum—an area that helps coordinate motor activity. This pathway deteriorates in Parkinson's disease, thus explaining the patient's inability to move and tendency to shake. When victims of Parkinson's disease are treated with L-DOPA, a drug that increases the amount of dopamine available in the brain, their symptoms are relieved. Curiously, when individuals suffering from schizophrenia are treated with heavy doses of phenothiazines for a prolonged period of time, they display symptoms very much like those associated with Parkinson's disease. They, too, develop motor difficulties: they have tremors in their extremities and problems in controlling their body movements in general. While there is no direct proof of a connection, is it possible that the neurotransmitter, dopamine, is involved in schizophrenia? In Parkinson's disease, L-DOPA is given to overcome the insufficiency of dopamine. In schizophrenia, the phenothiazines seem to calm disordered behavior by reducing the amount of dopamine available in the brain. Over time, however, they seem to cause an insufficiency of dopamine, and bring about symptoms of Parkinson's disease. That an excess of dopamine is one of the roots of schizophrenia is shown in the PET (Positron Emission Tomography) scan of the live brains of two twenty-four-year-old men. In Figure 12-2, the picture on the left is of a normal subject when dopamine receptors were blocked with haloperidol, an antipsychotic drug. The picture

Figure 12-2
PET scans showing differing effects of a dose of haloperidol on a normal person and a patient with schizophrenia. The dopamine receptors were blocked in the normal person but not in the schizophrenic, indicating increased dopamine receptor density in schizophrenics. (Source: Dr. Henry N. Wagner, Johns Hopkins Medical Institutions/Divisions of Nuclear Medicine and Radiation Sciences)

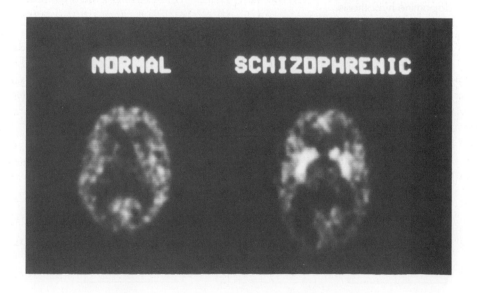

on the right is of a schizophrenic patient's brain after a dose of haloperidol; in this case, the dopamine receptors were not blocked. These results show that there is increased dopamine receptor density in a schizophrenic's brain, and they suggest that an excess of cells that are sensitive to dopamine may be the crucial biochemical deficit in schizophrenia.

Let us summarize the evidence that supports the dopamine hypothesis thus far. First, the symptoms of acute paranoid schizophrenia and of amphetamine psychosis are nearly indistinguishable. Amphetamine psychosis seems to result from an overproduction of dopamine. Is it not reasonable to assure a similar mechanism for schizophrenia (Snyder, 1981)?

Further evidence comes from animal research, where it has been shown that the phenothiazines block dopamine receptors specifically, and not other neurotransmitters. In addition, the more potent the phenothiazine, the more powerfully it blocks dopamine receptors in animals.

Excess dopamine and attention

The combined evidence suggests that dopamine overload, that is, excess dopamine at the synapse, produces many of the symptoms of acute schizophrenia (see Figure 12-3). Consider the attentional difficulties that are so characteristic of schizophrenia. When the **substantia nigra**, a bundle of nerves that go from the brain stem to the **corpus striatum** (an area of high dopamine concentration), is destroyed on one side of the brain, rats stop attending to stimulation on the other side of their bodies (Understedt, 1971). (The left brain controls the right side of the body; the right brain, the left.) It is not that the rats lose their sensory perception. It seems rather that they fail to attend. Phenothiazines may have a similar effect: by blocking dopamine receptors, attention may be diminished.

There is now mounting evidence that confirms the dopamine hypothesis. Post-mortem examination of the brains of schizophrenics confirms what PET scans reveal: a marked increase in the number of dopamine receptor sites. While the precise cause of this increase is not yet known, it is clearly *not* the result of drug treatment. Patients who had been drug-free for at least a year before death also showed a greater number of dopamine receptors (Crow, 1980, 1982; Mackay, 1980).

Figure 12-3
Evidence for the dopamine hypothesis. This analysis of the effects of increasing or decreasing the availability of dopamine offers some support for the dopamine hypothesis.

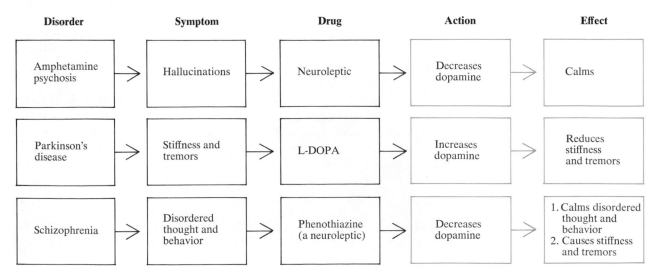

Disorder	Symptom	Drug	Action	Effect
Amphetamine psychosis	Hallucinations	Neuroleptic	Decreases dopamine	Calms
Parkinson's disease	Stiffness and tremors	L-DOPA	Increases dopamine	Reduces stiffness and tremors
Schizophrenia	Disordered thought and behavior	Phenothiazine (a neuroleptic)	Decreases dopamine	1. Calms disordered thought and behavior 2. Causes stiffness and tremors

Dopamine hypothesis limited to Type I schizophrenia

Increased production of dopamine was once thought to be characteristic of all forms of schizophrenia. But recent thinking limits the dopamine hypothesis to Type I schizophrenia (see the discussion of Types I and II on p. 383). Type I is associated with the dramatic positive symptoms of the disorder: delusions, hallucinations, and thought disorder. Those are the symptoms that are alleviated by the phenothiazines, which decrease the amount of dopamine in the brain (see Figure 12-2). Type II schizophrenia is characterized by the "negative" or deficit symptoms of the disorder, such as flat affect, loss of motivation, and poverty of speech. Those symptoms seem unrelated to dopamine and are unaffected by the phenothiazines. They seem rather to arise from a wholly different source—peculiarly abnormal structures in the brain.

BRAIN STRUCTURE IN SCHIZOPHRENICS

Brain abnormalities and Type II schizophrenia

There is mounting evidence that the group of schizophrenics who manifest Type II symptoms—particularly flat emotion, loss of motivation, and poverty of speech—may be suffering from one or several abnormalities in the structure of the brain. So far, three kinds of abnormalities seem to have been located. The first relates to the size and proportion of the brain ventricles. Ventricles are cavities in the brain, spaces that are filled with fluids (see Figure 12-2). The ventricles of schizophrenics are substantially larger than those of normal people. Moreover, those on the left side of the schizophrenic brain appear to be substantially larger than those on the right side (Losonczy, 1986). Ventricular enlargement suggests a process of deterioration or atrophy in brain tissue whose precise effects can only be speculated upon (Brown, Colter, Corsellis, Crow, Frith, Jagoe, Johnstone, and Marsh, 1986).

A second type of abnormality indicates that Type II schizophrenics may have smaller frontal lobes, as well as smaller cerebrums and craniums, than do normals (Andreasen, Nasrallah, Dunn, Olsen, Grove, Ehrhardt, Coffman, and Crossett, 1986).

Finally, there is mounting evidence of neuronal degeneration, especially in the cortex of schizophrenics (Benes, Davidson, and Bird, 1986), as well as evidence for decreased blood flow in that region (Weinberger, Berman, and Zec, 1986).

While the evidence for differences in brain structure mounts daily, just how those differences are related to schizophrenic symptoms—especially Type II symptoms—remains unclear. But the emerging picture seems to support the view that there are at least two forms of schizophrenia. Type I results from difficulties in *neurotransmission,* and particularly from an overabundance of dopamine receptors. That form of schizophrenia seems to be quite responsive to neuroleptic medications. Type II schizophrenia, on the other hand, results from abnormalities in *brain structure,* and is largely unaffected by neuroleptic treatment.

THE SCHIZOPHRENOGENIC FAMILY

The above evidence convinces us that heredity and biology play a role in the development of schizophrenia. But other factors—family and society— contribute in as yet unknown ways and proportions to one's vulnerability to

The schizo-
phrenogenic
family

schizophrenia. Heredity tells us about a biological component of schizophrenia. It can suggest, perhaps, that an individual will be prone to attentional difficulties, to overinclusive thinking, to delusions, and to hallucinations. But heredity does not assure that a propensity will become a certainty. Nor does heredity specify the content of disordered thought and the social reaction it will elicit. In all likelihood, the family plays some role in the development of schizophrenia, although establishing the nature of its contribution with precision is difficult. Families that seem to foster the emergence of schizophrenia in one or more family members are called *schizophrenogenic families.* Such families may themselves be disordered in the way they communicate and in the family structure itself.

Communication
within the family

Since schizophrenia is centrally marked by a thought disorder and since we are examining the families from which schizophrenics come, it follows that we should look at communication within the family as a correlate or cause of such thought disorder. Many researchers believe that the parents of schizophrenics distort their children's perceptions in two principal ways: by encouraging them to doubt their own feelings, perceptions, and experiences (a process that is called *mystification*), and by catching them in double-binds (Bateson, Jackson, Haley, and Weakland, 1956; Laing and Esterson, 1964). Whatever one calls it, this "effort to drive the other person crazy" (Searles, 1959) involves distorting the child's reality both verbally and non-verbally.

There are two characteristics of family communication that seem to bear striking relationships to the development of schizophrenia, particularly among those who are genetically predisposed to such symptoms. Those characteristics are expressed emotion and communication deviance. *Expressed emotion* refers to the ways in which emotions are expressed in the family. When the key elements of such expressions are criticism, overinvolvement, and hostility directed at the offspring, the offspring is more likely to develop the spectrum of symptoms associated with schizophrenia (Rodnick, Goldstein, Lewis, and Doane, 1984).

Communication deviance arises when a parent is unable to establish and maintain a shared arena of attention with a child. There are often deviances in conversations with others, as when one person wants to talk about a movie and the other about a friend. But those deviances quickly become consonances. When a parent regularly is unable to focus attention on the same issue that commands a child's attention, however, the child is likely to develop symptoms that are on the "spectrum" of schizophrenia (Rodnick, Goldstein, Lewis, and Doane, 1984). Not surprisingly, high expressed emotion is correlated with communication deviance (Miklowitz, Strachan, Goldstein, Doane, Snyder, Hogarty, and Falloon, 1986).

Three processes occurring within the families of schizophrenics seem to influence thought disorders: injection of meaning, concealment of meaning, and denial of meaning. Although all three are clearly connected, each of these processes has particular manifestations (Wynne, Singer, Bartko, and Toohey, 1977).

Injection of meaning involves denying the clear meaning of another's message and substituting another meaning. The person who sent the original message can, with a persistent injector around, be left with two different meanings rather than one, with confusion rather than clarity, and with considerable self-doubt about perceiving reality accurately. An incident that occurred during a counseling session illustrates how the injection of meaning can easily lead to confusion.

> Mr. A entered the room quietly and sat down with a benign, attentive expression and posture directed toward his wife. Mrs. A was sputtering with rage: "I'm so furious I can't stand it." She then let loose with a stream of invectives at her husband and concluded with a threat of murdering him. After a few minutes, the husband leaned toward her, patted her arm and said, "You're not angry. You're feeling hurt. I'd like to help you with your pain." With that, the wife screamed: "I don't feel in pain. I feel like killing you." Then to the therapist: "In eight years of marriage that son of a bitch has never once believed that I could really be mad at him." Mrs. A went on to assert that behind her husband's virtuous facade, he was sadistic and murderous. She claimed that on the way to this therapy session, he had deliberately driven carelessly, endangering both their lives, but with the knowledge that she was much more nervous than he about automobile accidents. He stoutly denied that he had had any feeling of maliciousness and said that he had been simply inattentive and preoccupied with other matters. He added that her accusation was part of her "paranoia" and the mental illness for which she needed help. At this point she collapsed in confusion and tears. When he again solicitously "comforted" her, she now no longer protested and by then her experience seemed to fit the "pain" that he had attributed to her—or, as I would say, had injected into her. (Wynne, 1972, p. 436)

Clearly, the husband first denies his wife's anger and its cause. He patiently, virtuously insists on his own explanation and holds his ground. When his wife explains her anger by detailing its causes, the husband only intensifies his denial. By now, the wife is uncertain. Confused, she breaks down, acting hurt, showing that she needs help. In fact, her behavior suggests that the injected meaning has become the reality, at least for the moment. She is still angry, however, and eventually she will experience that anger again, only to be met with another denial, another substitution.

Concealing clear meaning is another form of communication distortion within the schizophrenic family. A person may hide information when it is clear that the information exists. Or the person may simply remain silent, failing to acknowledge a patent fact or sending blurred vague or fragmented messages. These tactics serve to conceal meanings and distort facts.

Denial of meaning takes several forms (Laing and Esterson, 1964; Lidz, 1975). The denial can be a deliberate lie, consciously told. Or it can involve some automatic denial, automatically presented. Or it can be the result of a thought disorder in the parents themselves, one that is so encompassing that they do not even realize that they are denying anything. One patient, for example, felt that his parents were "somehow talking" about him. They denied it. Yet, when the entire family gathered together, it was clear that the parents surreptitiously nodded and winked to one another, as if they could not be seen. They were oblivious to the fact that their communication was visible. More important, they were oblivious to the fact that their winking and nodding was a form of "talking." They denied its reality.

Injecting, concealing, and denying all serve to either block access to consensual reality, or to distort it. Worse, they insidiously undermine the individual's faith in her own capacity to perceive reality. Thus, all of these tactics relate directly to the essential characteristics of schizophrenia: misperceived reality and disordered thought.

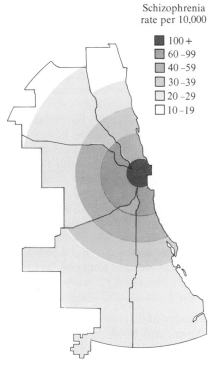

Schizophrenia rate per 10,000

◼ 100 +
▨ 60 –99
▨ 40 –59
▢ 30 –39
▢ 20 –29
▢ 10 –19

Figure 12-4

The prevalence of schizophrenia in a city. In this map of Chicago in 1934, the center zone is the business and amusement section, which is uninhabited, except for transients and vagabonds. Surrounding the center, there is a slum area, largely made up of unskilled workers of low socioeconomic status, and having the highest rate of schizophrenia. The next circle is occupied by skilled workers and has a lower rate of schizophrenia than the slum. The next zone is inhabited by middle-class and upper-middle-class people. The last circle is populated by upper-middle-class commuters and shows the lowest rate of schizophrenia. (Source: Gleitman, 1981, based on data from Faris and Dunham, 1939)

SOCIETY AND SCHIZOPHRENIA

Whether we are schizophrenic or non-schizophrenic, we are all members of a society that, in many ways, exerts its influence upon us. In approaching any mental disorder, scientists will take society into account.

SCHIZOPHRENIA AND SOCIAL CLASS

It happens that, particularly in large urban areas, rates of mental disturbance, and especially of schizophrenia, are significantly and inversely related to social class: the lower the class, the higher the rate of schizophrenia (see Figure 12-4). In the United States, the highest rates of schizophrenia occur in the centers of cities that, in turn, are inhabited by people of lower socioeconomic status (Faris and Dunham, 1939; Hollingshead and Redlich, 1958; Srole, Langner, Michael, Opler, and Rennie, 1962). Similar findings relate to occupation: rates of schizophrenia are highest in the lowest status occupations (Clark, 1948). The larger the city, the more powerful the relationship; in small cities, the relationship between schizophrenia and social class disappears (Clausen and Kohn, 1959).

The problem of sorting out the relationship of class and schizophrenia is similar to the problem encountered in trying to understand the relationship between the family and schizophrenia. Are people who are already members of the lower class likely to become schizophrenics? Or is it more accurate, and more revealing, to say that some people who are schizophrenics find themselves drifting into the lower class? The resolution of this problem is no mere academic matter, because the rate of schizophrenia is eight times as high in the lower class as it is in the middle or upper social classes.

One logical way to resolve the question would be to examine the occupational status of the fathers of schizophrenics. If schizophrenics' fathers were at the lowest occupational rung, it would be likely that the schizophrenic was born into the lower class, and that class therefore preceded psychosis. Such a finding would strengthen the view that social class produces schizophrenia. If on the other hand, schizophrenics' fathers had higher occupational status, it would be likely that the schizophrenics were not born into the lower class, and that psychosis therefore precedes social class. This would support the view that schizophrenics drift into the lower class.

A survey of an entire county in New York State found support for both positions. The incidence of treatment for schizophrenia was remarkably high for people in the lowest occupational group, confirming the relationship between social class and schizophrenia. But the data regarding fathers' occupation was ambiguous, in that it was equally high for those whose fathers were in the lowest occupational group as it was for those whose fathers were employed in the highest occupational group. Although those schizophrenics whose fathers had been in the lowest occupational group had risen above their fathers' occupational level, they and the high occupational group stood at occupational levels lower than those of the general population (Turner and Wagenfeld, 1967).

Membership in the lower class carries with it a host of psychological as well as economic disadvantages that may well increase an individual's vulnerability to schizophrenia. For example, one researcher observed that

Conforming person more vulnerable to schizophrenia

lower-class people attach greater value to conformity to authority than do members of the middle class (Kohn, 1973). When such lower-class people find themselves confronted with personal crises, they are less able to cope than are people who have been more self-directed and less conforming. Solving personal problems has more to do with confronting internal pressures than it has to do with conforming to external demands. The defensive posture of the conforming person often invites attack, so the habit of conformity does little to alleviate tension. With stress unabated, the conforming person may also be more vulnerable to schizophrenia.

THE STRESSES OF MODERN LIVING

Social contradictions

Society's values are often contradictory and many people find those contradictions difficult, even impossible, to live with. Searching for some meaningful purpose in life, people are often confronted with meaninglessness on every level, from the personal to the global. They find themselves running in place so as not to fall behind, working at unfulfilling jobs, often for minimal pay, simply to keep up with the body's demands for food, clothing, and shelter. Even as astrophysicists meet the challenges of space travel, earthbound political leaders draw up moon treaties and calculate military capabilities in space. A rich nation is riddled with unemployment, inflation, and other economic ills. Many are precluded from enjoying material comforts, yet materialist dreams are instilled in all.

Some theorists argue that those who are well-integrated into such an insane society are truly mad, while those who remain alienated are the most sane. Many cope with social contradictions by adjusting to them and accepting them. Others, however, may be too sensitive to the pressures and contradictions of society to cope with them at all. These people may be especially vulnerable to the meaninglessness that pervades our world. Many of them, it has been hypothesized, become schizophrenics.

Schizophrenia as a response to a stressful environment

The hypothesis that schizophrenia is a response to a stressful environment has been expounded by numerous theorists, and is particularly central to the thinking of the Scottish psychiatrist, R. D. Laing (1927–   ). Laing's argument is more speculative than other analyses of schizophrenia. He maintains that the schizophrenic experience arises from a person's sense that the situation can neither be lived with nor evaded. The only way to escape the contradictions and impossibilities of reality is to withdraw from the world and take refuge in schizophrenia. The schizophrenic experience, Laing argues, is potentially beneficial to those who undergo it. He writes:

> Perhaps we will learn to accord to so-called schizophrenics who have come back to us, perhaps after years, no less respect than the often no-less-lost explorers of the Renaissance. If the human race survives, future men will, I suspect, look back on our enlightened epoch as a veritable Age of Darkness. They will presumably be able to savor the irony of this situation with more amusement than we can extract from it. The laugh's on us. They will see that what we call "schizophrenia" was one of the forms in which, often through quite ordinary people, the light began to break through the cracks in our all-too-closed minds. (Laing, 1967, p. 129)

All of the theories about the causes of schizophrenia that we have surveyed are fascinating but unsatisfactory in that they provide only part of the explanation for the emergence of schizophrenia in any one individual. Studies of twins lend credence to a fundamental *genetic* propensity to schizophrenia. But since perfect concordance does not exist even among MZ twins, it is likely that additional variables, particularly overproduction of neurotransmitters like *dopamine* and peculiarities of brain structure, play a role in vulnerability to schizophrenia. Moreover, an individual's vulnerability to schizophrenia may be heightened by social and environmental factors. While schizophrenia may "run in the family" because of a common genetic background, some families (called schizophrenogenic families) may also create a stressful and disordered environment that may induce schizophrenia among the vulnerable (Lewis, Rodnick, and Goldstein, 1981; Roff and Knight, 1981). Similarly, very poor people whose lives are filled with the stress of maintaining a marginal subsistence and who live in the impersonal squalor of the inner cities may be particularly vulnerable to schizophrenia.

Conditions predicting outcome

Nowhere is the interrelation between symptoms, biology, and family more clear than it is in a recent study of the conditions that predict the outcome of an episode of schizophrenia. For the first decade after the episode, premorbid functioning—that is, the individual's capacity to cope with his or her life stresses before succumbing to schizophrenia—was the most influential predictor. In the second decade, family functioning was as important as premorbid coping. Long-term outcome—twenty or more years after the episode—was best predicted by family genetics (McGlashan, 1986a).

THE TREATMENT OF SCHIZOPHRENIA

Until the mid-1950s, treatment of schizophrenia was primarily custodial. Patients were warehoused for long periods of time in environments that were both boring and hopeless. Often their disorder and the hospital environment interacted to bring about behavior that required physical restraint. In 1952, however, a lucky accident changed this bleak situation, and led to a revolution in the treatment of schizophrenia.

Until chlorpromazine enabled the treatment of schizophrenics and their subsequent release from hospitals, treatment was primarily custodial and patients were both bored and hopeless about their condition.

DRUG THERAPY

Treatment with chlorpromazine

While synthesizing new drugs called ***antihistamines*** that benefit asthmatics and those with allergies, researchers noticed the strong calming effects of these drugs. In fact, one of the drugs, promethazine, was so tranquilizing that the French surgeon Henri Laborit gave it to his patients as a prelude to anesthesia. Using a close relative of promethazine with even stronger sedative effects, French psychiatrists Jean Delay and Pierre Deniker treated various mentally disordered patients with varying results. Those who improved had a common diagnosis: schizophrenia. The drug they took was chlorpromazine. Now a prominent member of a class of drugs variously called ***neuroleptics, psychotropics,*** or ***tranquilizing agents,*** chlorpromazine revolutionized the treatment of schizophrenia. In 1955, there were about 560,000 patients in American psychiatric hospitals. One out of every two hospital beds was devoted to psychiatric care. It was then estimated that by 1971, 750,000 beds would be required to care for growing psychiatric populations. In fact, there were only 308,000 patients in psychiatric hospitals in 1971, less than half the projected estimate, and about 40 percent fewer than were hospitalized in 1955. And by 1977, the patient census had declined to less than 160,000 (Witkin, 1981). Such is the power of the major tranquilizers (see Figure 12-5).

Figure 12-5
Distribution of inpatient and outpatient care in mental health facilities, by type of facility: United States, 1955 and 1973. Note the enormous shift from inpatient to outpatient facilities. (Source: Modified from Keith et al., 1976, p. 571)

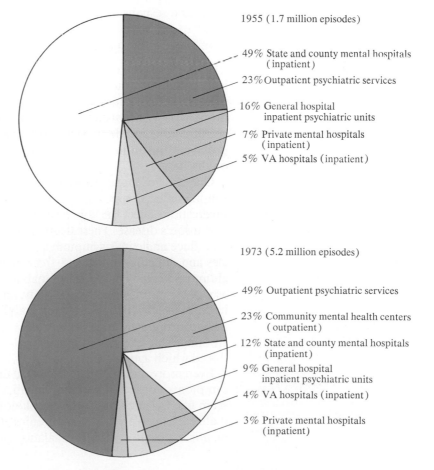

1955 (1.7 million episodes)

49% State and county mental hospitals (inpatient)

23% Outpatient psychiatric services

16% General hospital inpatient psychiatric units

7% Private mental hospitals (inpatient)

5% VA hospitals (inpatient)

1973 (5.2 million episodes)

49% Outpatient psychiatric services

23% Community mental health centers (outpatient)

12% State and county mental hospitals (inpatient)

9% General hospital inpatient psychiatric units

4% VA hospitals (inpatient)

3% Private mental hospitals (inpatient)

ANTIPSYCHOTIC EFFECTS OF DRUG THERAPY

Effects on Type I symptoms

Of the major tranquilizers, chlorpromazine and haloperidol are two of the most commonly used. Their most striking effect is the degree to which they "tranquilize," make peaceful, even sedate. Could it be that these phenothiazines are no different from barbiturates, whose sedative action produces no greater improvements for schizophrenics than placebos? Some evidence suggests that this is not the case. Beyond their sedative effects and even beyond their impact on anxiety, the phenothiazines seem to have specific ameliorating effects on the symptoms of Type I schizophrenia. Thought disorder and hallucinations are particularly affected by the phenothiazines. Equally important, these drugs have virtually no effect on psychiatric symptoms that are not associated with Type I schizophrenia (Casey, Bennett, Lindley, Hollister, Gordon, and Springer, 1960; Crow, 1985). Subjective emotional experiences, such as guilt and depression, continue unabated despite a course of drug treatment.

Blocking dopamine

The chief mode of action of the neuroleptic drugs is in binding to dopamine receptors, thereby preventing dopamine itself from binding to those receptors. Once the dopamine is blocked, the positive symptoms of schizophrenia are also blocked, resulting in marked cognitive and behavioral improvement. So much is this the case that the average hospital stay for a schizophrenic patient has declined to fewer than thirteen days, when formerly it was months, years, even a lifetime. Phenothiazines, nearly alone, have been responsible for a revolution in psychiatric care.

SIDE EFFECTS OF DRUG THERAPY

The antipsychotic drugs have a variety of unpleasant side effects that often lead patients to discontinue using them. Side effects of chlorpromazine (Thorazine), for example, frequently include dryness of mouth and throat, drowsiness, visual disturbances, weight gain or loss, menstrual disturbances, constipation, and depression. For most patients, these are relatively minor problems, but annoying enough to induce them to discontinue medications on discharge.

Parkinson-like side effects

One class of more serious side effects, called extra-pyramidal or Parkinson-like effects, appears to arise because, as we have seen, antipsychotic medications affect the dopamine receptors, which are in turn implicated in Parkinson's disease. These drugs do not cause Parkinson's disease, but they do induce analogous symptoms. These symptoms include stiffness of muscles and difficulty in moving, freezing of facial muscles, which results in a glum or sour look as well as an inability to smile, tremors at the extremities as well as spasms of limbs and body, and *akathesia*—a peculiar "itchiness" in the muscles which results in an inability to sit still, and an urge to pace the halls continuously and energetically (Snyder, 1974a). Other drugs can control these side effects, but interestingly, no phenothiazine has yet been produced which avoids them.

Tardive dyskinesia

Even more serious is a neurological disorder called *tardive dyskinesia*. Its symptoms consist of sucking, lip-smacking, and tongue movements that seem like fly-catching. Tardive dyskinesia is not reversible. Conservatively, it affects 24 percent of schizophrenics after seven years of cumulative neuroleptic exposure (Wegner, Catalano, Gibralter, and Kane, 1985). The prevalence and severity of tardive dyskinesia increases with age. And there may well be a relationship between the severity of a person's *negative* symptoms of schizophrenia (i.e., the symptoms that are not particularly responsive to neuroleptics in the first place) and the risk of developing tardive dyskinesia (Barnes and Braude, 1985).

THE REVOLVING DOOR PHENOMENON

Readmission to hospitals

The widespread use of psychotropic drugs promised a virtual revolution in the treatment of schizophrenia. Even if the disorder could not be cured, it seemed certain that it could be contained. No longer would thousands spend their lives in back wards. No longer would families and society be deprived of their contribution. And no longer would massive economic resources be wasted on custodial care. But the pharmaceutical revolution fell short of its promise. For, while the hospital population of schizophrenics has declined radically since 1955, the readmission rates for schizophrenics have soared. In 1972, for example, 72 percent of the schizophrenics admitted to hospitals had been there before (Taube, 1976). And a more recent study finds a 79 percent relapse rate within two years of discharge (Hogarty, Anderson, Reiss, Kornblith, Greenwald, Javna, and Madonia, 1986). One likely reason for rehospitalization is that only 15 to 40 percent of them are able to work or care for themselves (Keith, Gunderson, Reifman, Buchsbaum, and Mosher, 1976). Another is that they return to aversive environments (Leff, 1976), and to communities that are less than welcoming. Third, they lack work skills (Gunderson and Mosher, 1975) and social skills. Indeed, when patients were given social skills training, and their families were trained to become more proficient in "family problem solving," the relapse rate among such patients declined markedly—though it did not disappear by any means (Hogarty et al., 1986). Finally, they often stop taking medications on discharge because of the drugs' aversive side effects.

One can interpret this "revolving-door" aspect of psychiatric hospitals both negatively and positively. On the negative side, the readmission rates are discouraging; they suggest that the attempt to treat schizophrenics is futile. But on the positive side, is it not better for a patient to be readmitted,

Many of those released into the community from mental hospitals are unable to work or care for themselves. Were these "bag ladies" formerly mental patients? Will they be rehospitalized as a result of the "revolving door phenomenon"?

than never to have been discharged at all? This latter situation characterized the plight of many patients before the advent of the phenothiazines.

Even if one opts for the more positive response to the high readmission rate, the task of understanding its cause and of eventually reducing it remains. One thing is clear: antipsychotic drugs help ameliorate the symptoms of schizophrenia, but the symptoms of schizophrenia are by no means the entire problem. Indeed, the very fact that these drugs alter symptoms and only symptoms raises profound questions about what is meant by treatment, recovery, and cure.

FULL TREATMENT: MILIEU AND THERAPEUTIC COMMUNITIES

Supportive environments

Because schizophrenia appears between the ages of eighteen and thirty-five, it disrupts educational and vocational training, social skills, friendships, and marriages. In addition, because the seeds of the disorder are sown before the disorder appears, both in the individual and in the family, it is a safe bet that there are problems in communication and self-esteem—in short, *psychological problems*—that the antipsychotic drugs simply do not touch. Given that these psychological problems exist and that drugs do not alleviate them, what, other than drugs, can help the schizophrenic live in the outside world? Part of the answer may lie in milieu therapy, which creates a supportive environment, and in the therapeutic communities, which illustrate milieu therapy's principles.

A study of readmission rates underscores the continued importance of considering psychological problems when treating schizophrenic disorders. Patients who relapsed did not differ on their discharge examination from those who did not relapse. Apart from whether they continued their medications, two additional factors featured strongly in determining relapse rates: the emotional quality of the home, and how much time the patient spent there (Leff, 1976).

Emotional quality of home environment

In this study, four considerations went into rating the emotional quality of the home environment: the family's hostility, overinvolvement with the patient, comments that were critical of the patient, and the family's wealth. Patients who came from families that had highly charged emotional environments had a 51 percent relapse rate. Those whose family environment was relatively uncharged had a dramatically lower relapse rate—13 percent. Moreover, for the patients from highly charged environments, the relapse rate was affected by how much time they were spending at home. Those who spent less than thirty-five hours at home—which is to say, those who had jobs or went to a day center—were much less likely to relapse than those who were at home more of the time (see Figure 12-6).

Milieu therapy

What can be done to reduce the relapse rate? For one thing, hospitals have been undergoing enormous changes: from being merely custodial warehouses to becoming centers with a variety of programs designed to increase social skills. Under the broad label of ***milieu therapy***, patients are provided with training in social communication, in work, and in recreation (Hogarty et al., 1986; Liberman, Mueser, and Wallace, 1986). Hospitals that have incorporated such milieu treatments have successfully decreased their relapse rate. Moreover, families who have been trained to cope better with stress through greater understanding of the schizophrenic's problems and more

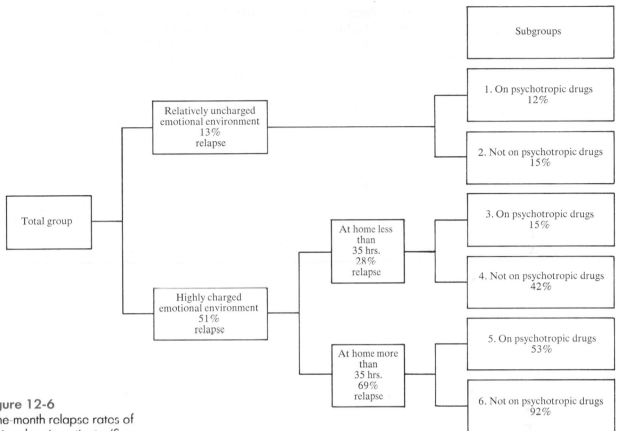

	Subgroups

Figure 12-6
Nine-month relapse rates of schizophrenic patients. (Source: Adapted from Vaughn and Leff, 1976)

The Lodge

efficacious family problem solving appear to improve the emotional quality of the home environment and to reduce the rate of relapse once patients have left hospitals (Vaughn, Snyder, Jones, Freeman, and Falloon, 1984; Doane, Falloon, Goldstein, and Mintz, 1985).

In the late sixties and the seventies, several promising methods were developed for treating schizophrenia. One was organized by George Fairweather and his colleagues (1969). The project began after Fairweather noticed that chronically hospitalized patients who were organized into groups and given tasks to perform were discharged from the hospital much more quickly than patients who did not participate in task-oriented groups. But once discharged, many of these patients relapsed. Since they had improved in the hospital, Fairweather concluded that something must be wrong outside the hospital, that something being the lack of opportunity for task-oriented group experience. Fairweather and his colleagues established the Lodge, a special residence for newly discharged patients. The Lodge's residents had major responsibilities in running the household, shopping, and finding employment for each other. Over time, more and more responsibility was given to patients until finally the Lodge was taken over entirely by former patients. The effectiveness of this program was evaluated. The seventy-five patients who volunteered for it were compared to a matched group who did not volunteer and who received the hospital's routine discharge (which included patient psychotherapy, community assistance, and foster-home placement). After six months, some 65 percent of the Lodge members, but only 27 percent of the comparison group, remained outside the hospital. Fifty percent of the Lodge's members and only 3 percent of the controls were employed full time during this period. These findings held up over the next three and a half years. Clearly, the Lodge experience was a beneficial one for those involved.

Therapeutic communities

Some programs seek alternatives to hospitalization altogether. They may use nonprofessionals to treat patients, rather than doctors, nurses, and psychologists (Kiesler, 1980). Soteria House was one of these **therapeutic communities** (Mosher, Menn, and Matthews, 1975). A community-based residential treatment center, it provided a home for people who were diagnosed as schizophrenics. The staff were selected for their ability to accept and relate to people undergoing an acute schizophrenic crisis. Schizophrenic episodes were viewed as valid, if often terrifying, experiences that have strong potential for individual growth and integration. Antipsychotic drugs were not provided at Soteria House, except in emergencies.

In a study comparing hospitalized patients and patients living in Soteria House, there were no differences between those who were assigned to Soteria House and the controls who had been assigned to a good psychiatric hospital. Residents lived at Soteria House an average of five to six months, while controls remained hospitalized for less than two months. Despite the near-absence of antipsychotic medications in the Soteria sample, both groups manifested the same degree of symptom remission. The intense interpersonal milieu at Soteria House effectively reduced the need for medications. Finally, six months after discharge, 60 percent of Soteria House's residents were able to live independently, while only 4 percent of the controls could live apart from their families.

How does one integrate the remarkable nondrug outcomes from such places as Fairweather's Lodge and Soteria House with the equally remarkable evidence from hospitals that *do* employ drugs? On the one hand, drugs have shortened the length of stay in psychiatric hospitals and have reduced the number of beds that are required for treatment. Yet, on the other hand, they seem responsible for the "revolving-door" phenomenon. It seems clear now that drugs alone cannot provide a full treatment for schizophrenia. The ideal treatment for schizophrenia involves carefully monitored psychopharmacological interventions that are combined with psychological ones.

SUMMARY

1. The schizophrenias are marked by a *thought disorder* that is often combined with affective and behavioral anomalies. There are five subtypes of schizophrenia: *paranoid, disorganized, catatonic, residual,* and *undifferentiated.* Schizophrenics can be differentiated according to whether their condition is *acute* or *chronic.* They can also be differentiated according to the kinds of symptoms they present. *Type I schizophrenia* is associated with the *positive* symptoms of the disorder, such as hallucinations, delusions, and bizarre thoughts. *Type II schizophrenia* is identified with the *negative* symptoms of the syndrome, such as withdrawal, blunted affect, and reduced motivation.

2. The schizophrenic's subjective experience is often one of being invaded by the world's stimuli, crowded by them, and unable to process them. We find this experience rooted in what appears to be a defective *cognitive filter,* itself related to serious *attentional difficulties.* The incapacity to focus attention, as well as the sense that too many stimuli are invading and capturing attention, is characteristic of many schizophrenics' experience.

3. In the cognitive domain, schizophrenics make the same errors of association that normals make, but they make many more of them. They seem especially attracted to the *dominant associations* or connotations of words, regardless of the context in which they are found. Often, their attentional difficulties seem to distract them from the ultimate goal of thought and speech. Thinking may therefore be *overinclusive,* and speech dotted with *clang associations* and *neologisms.*

4. Many schizophrenics appear to experience flattened or restricted emotion, which may make it difficult for them to meaningfully experience reality.

5. Schizophrenics seem to experience perceptual intensities or deficits that lead them to experience the world differently from others. Delusional, hallucinatory, or other cognitive experiences often bring grief or a sense of uniqueness, which they attempt to account for by constructing theories which, in form, are no different from the theories normals construct about their experiences.

6. Vulnerability to schizophrenia is a highly individual matter, but there seem to be four significant factors that promote it. First, there seems little doubt that the schizophrenias are in part a *genetic* disorder. The schizophrenias occur much more often among MZ than DZ twins, and among natural than adoptive families. Second, there is reason to believe that the schizophrenias are *biological* disorders. Type I schizophrenics appear to be suffering a *neurotransmission* disorder, especially involving *dopamine.* Type II schizophrenics seem to have *structural brain deficits*, including enlarged ventricles, a smaller cortex, and reduced cortical blood flow. Third, faulty communications within the *family* may well promote the development of schizophrenia. Finally, schizophrenia is a disorder that afflicts the *poor* more than the rich, and it may be associated with the stresses of society.

7. Treatment of the schizophrenias has been revolutionized by the invention of strong *tranquilizers* that seem to work directly on symptoms of schizophrenia. Hospitalization has become briefer, and there is a greater probability that the schizophrenic person will return to society. The effectiveness of the antipsychotic drugs, however, is limited.

8. Because schizophrenia is a psychological, as well as a biological, disorder there have been increasing attempts to discover nondrug methods for treating the schizophrenias. Among these are *therapeutic communities* that emphasize the positive aspects of the schizophrenic experience and that attempt to directly train the schizophrenic for social living.

Part 6

SOCIAL AND INTERPERSONAL DISORDERS

Sexual Behavior, Dysfunction, and Disorder

Evolving notions
of what is
sexually normal

Notions of what is sexually normal and what is sexually abnormal have changed with time and place. What one society has labeled as deviant may well be labeled as normal by another. Although in the past, premarital sex, masturbation, oral sex, and homosexuality were all condemned by our Puritan society, today most people consider these sexual behaviors to be quite normal.

In the past, what constituted "normal sexual order" and "normal sexual function" was clearer than it is today. Ordinary sexual practices among men and women in our society seem to be more diverse today than they were in the past. And so, our concept of what sexual order is has broadened and our concept of what sexual disorder and dysfunction are has narrowed. We now believe there are three basic classes of sexual problems: sexual dysfunctions, the paraphilias, and transsexualism.

In this chapter, we will discuss the scientific study of sexual behavior. We will explain what has been learned about normal sexual functioning—the sexual response of arousal, excitement, and orgasm. Then we will discuss sexual problems. Despite changing attitudes and more permissiveness in our society, we still find many instances of sexual problems, both in the form of sexual dysfunction and sexual disorder. The sexual dysfunctions are problems of low desire, low arousal, or orgasm. The sexual disorders are problems of sexual object choice and sexual identity. Disordered sexual object choice manifests itself through sexual arousal to the unusual or bizarre, such as fetishes for panties, masochism, and exhibitionism. These are the paraphilias. Disorders of sexual identity can be seen in transsexualism, in which a man believes he is a woman trapped in the body of a man, or a woman believes she is a man trapped in the body of a woman. Both the sex-

411

ual dysfunctions and the sexual disorders grossly impair affectionate, erotic relations between human beings, and as such, are considered abnormal.*

We begin our discussion of human sexuality with material on the scientific study of sexual behavior. The data from these studies have helped us to learn about normal sexual function and normal sexual order. This in turn has enabled us, by contrast, to identify sexual dysfunction and sexual disorder.

THE SCIENTIFIC STUDY OF SEXUAL BEHAVIOR

Dr. Alfred Kinsey interviewing a woman about her sexual practices.

The first major contribution to the scientific understanding of human sexual behavior came from the work of Alfred Kinsey and his colleagues (Kinsey et al., 1948, 1953). Acting in the face of societal taboos, they interviewed over 20,000 adult men and women, asking them explicit questions about their sexual practices. They gathered data on sexual intercourse in marriage, homosexuality, masturbation, premarital intercourse, oral sex, and other sexual activities. They looked at patterns of sex at different times of life, and broke these down by gender, education, religion, and other sociological factors. For example, Kinsey found that masturbation to orgasm was almost universal among men, becoming less frequent with age. He found that women, on the other hand, masturbate less often than men, but that as they become older, they masturbate more frequently than when they were younger.

Kinsey gave us a glimpse into American sexuality. In 1951, Clellan Ford, an anthropologist, and Frank Beach, a psychologist, broadened our knowledge by comparing the sexual behavior of some 190 cultures spread across the world. In addition, they compared cross-cultural human sexual practices to sexual behavior in animals, looking for what was universal and what was specific to a particular culture or species. So, for example, foreplay before intercourse occurs in all cultures and all mammals, but what kind— kissing, fondling, oral caresses—varies from culture to culture and species to species (Ford and Beach, 1951).

More recent data on sexual practices and attitudes among Americans have come from a variety of surveys, similar to those pioneered by Kinsey. Among these are Morton Hunt's (1974) study of 2,000 sexually liberal and sexually active American men and women,and Paul Rozin's (1978, 1981) surveys of sexual practices of several hundred University of Pennsylvania introductory psychology students over several years in the early 1970s.

Basic problems of surveys of sexual practices

Although all of these studies have told us much about what people do and how people feel about what they do, they all share some basic problems. First, consider the nature of the subject. One's sexual behavior is usually a very private matter. Many individuals are unwilling to participate in studies of sexual attitudes and behavior. Because of this, we only know about those who are willing to talk openly. In effect, therefore, these studies were not

---

* There have been long-standing controversies about what to call these sexual behaviors. Some prefer to call them "variations"; others label them "deviations," or even "diseases." We will adopt the term "dysfunction" to refer to the first class of problems, the sexual inabilities. We will adopt the term "disorder" to refer to the second and third problems, the paraphilias and transsexualism.

William Masters and Virginia Johnson brought the study of sexual behavior into the laboratory.

based on a random sample. Second, the results of these surveys are based on self-reporting about a topic that for some people is private, but for others, offers an opportunity for boasting. Many individuals will be candid about their sexuality; others may distort, suppress, or even lie outright about their sexual behavior. As a result, we only know from these surveys what a selected sample of people are willing to say about their sexual practices and attitudes.

Work of Masters and Johnson

While others were collecting data by way of surveys, two researchers, William Masters and Virginia Johnson (1970), were taking a different tack. They brought the study of sexual behavior into the laboratory just as one might study other aspects of behavior. In their work, they observed and recorded at least 15,000 sexual acts. They observed sexual acts under a wide variety of conditions: between married couples, between strangers, between couples with a variety of sexual and interpersonal problems, and under self-stimulation. A picture of the physiology of human sexual response has emerged from their observations. In addition, Masters and Johnson have spent much of their efforts discovering both the nature of sexual dysfunction and its possible treatment. As was the case with the surveys, however, these data come from a selected group of volunteer subjects who allowed themselves to be watched. We can be quite certain that Masters and Johnson's physiological findings are general to human adults, but we cannot always be certain that either their therapeutic outcomes or the subjective reports are general to the entire population of adult men and women. Even so, the scientific study of sexual behavior has brought us much closer today to understanding the nature of sexual behavior, its physiology, and its frequency than was possible in the past.

SEXUAL FUNCTION

To label an individual's sexual practice as a "dysfunction" implies that we know something about what normal sexual functioning is, or should be. In this section, we will discuss the physiology of the normal human sexual re-

Auguste Rodin's *Eternal Springtime*.

sponse, and then we will discuss sexual dysfunction—what it is, what causes it, and how it can be treated.

THE PHYSIOLOGY OF THE HUMAN SEXUAL RESPONSE

In both men and women, the sexual response consists of three phases: the first is ***erotic desire and arousal,*** in which a variety of stimuli—tactile, visual, and more subtle ones such as fantasy—produce arousal. The second phase, ***physical excitement,*** consists of penile erection in the male and of vaginal lubrication and swelling in the genital area of the female. The third phase is ***orgasm.*** We shall review these phases in some detail because sexual dysfunction can disrupt any of them.

Erotic arousal in men

In men, erotic arousal results from a wide variety of events. Being touched on the genitals or looking at and touching a sexually responsive partner are probably the most compelling stimuli. In addition, visual stimuli, smells, a seductive voice, and erotic fantasies, among many others, all produce arousal.

Sexual excitement in men

The second phase of excitement is intertwined with the first phase of erotic arousal. In the male, it consists of penile erection. Sexual excitement stimulates parasympathetic nerves in the spinal cord, and these nerves control the blood vessels of the penis. These vessels widen dramatically and blood streams in, producing erection. The blood is prevented from leaving by a system of valves in the veins. When the parasympathetic fibers are inhibited, the vessels empty, and rapid loss of erection occurs.

Orgasm in men

Orgasm in men consists of two stages that follow each other very rapidly —emission and ejaculation. Unlike arousal and erection, orgasm is controlled by the sympathetic nervous system, as opposed to the parasympathetic nervous system. When sufficient rhythmic pressure on the head and shaft of the penis occur, the stage of orgasmic inevitability is reached and orgasm arrives. Orgasm is engineered to deposit sperm deep into the vagina near the head of the uterus, maximizing the possibility of fertilization. Emission (the discharge of semen) occurs when the reproductive organs all contract. This is followed very rapidly by ejaculation, in which powerful muscles at the base of the penis contract vigorously, ejecting sperm from the penis. During ejaculation, these muscles contract by reflex at intervals of 0.8 seconds. This phase of orgasm is accompanied by intense pleasure. After orgasm has occurred, a man unlike a woman, is "refractory," or unresponsive to further sexual stimulation for some interval. This interval varies from a few minutes to a few hours, and it lengthens as the man gets older.

Erotic arousal in women

The sexual response of a woman transforms the normally tight and dry vagina into a lubricated, perfectly fitting receptacle for the erect penis. The stimuli that produce arousal in women are similar to those that produce arousal in men. Kissing and caressing, visual stimuli, and a whole host of subtle cues are usually effective as sexually arousing stimuli. In our culture, at least, there appear to be some gender differences in what is arousing, with subtle stimuli and gentle touch more initially arousing to women than direct stimulation.

Sexual excitement in women

With arousal, the excitement or "lubrication-swelling" phase begins in the woman. When at rest, the vagina is collapsed, pale in color, and rather dry. When arousal occurs, the vagina balloons exactly enough to "glove" an erect penis, regardless of its size. At the same time, the clitoris, a small knob of tissue located forward of the vagina, swells and lubrication occurs on the walls of the vagina, making penile insertion easier. As excitement continues, the walls of the uterus fill with blood, and the uterus enlarges. This engorgement of blood and swelling greatly add to erotic pleasure and set the stage for orgasm.

Orgasm in women

Orgasm in women consists of a series of reflexive contractions of the muscles surrounding the vagina. These contract rhythmically at 0.8 second intervals against the engorged tissue around the vagina, producing the ecstatic sensation of orgasm. Both the clitoris and the vagina itself play a role: orgasm is triggered by stimulation of the clitoris, and then expressed by contraction of the vagina.

Thus, the sexual response of both men and women is quite similar. Similar stimuli produce erotic arousal in both sexes. Blood flow under the control of the parasympathetic nervous system produces physical excitement and both penile erection and the lubrication and swelling phases of the vagina. Orgasm consists of powerful muscular contractions at 0.8 second intervals, produced by rhythmic pressure on the head and shaft of the penis in the man and of the clitoris of the woman. These parallels are lovely and deep. Before they were known, it was easy to fall prey to the belief that chasms separated the experience of sex between men and women. To learn that one's partner is probably experiencing the same kind of joys that you are is powerful and binding knowledge.

SEXUAL DYSFUNCTION: THE SEXUAL INABILITIES

Impairment of sexual response

In order to function normally, an individual must be capable of sexual desire, sexual arousal, and orgasm. When the mechanism of desire, arousal, or orgasm goes awry, we say an individual suffers a sexual dysfunction.

Dysfunction can occur in any or all of these three areas of sexual response: (1) *desire:* fantasies about and interest in sexual activity may be low or non-existent, and thus erotic arousal may be dysfunctional; (2) *excitement:* when in an appropriate sexual situation, failure to have or maintain an erection in men and lack of vaginal lubrication and genital swelling in women may occur; (3) *orgasm:* in women, orgasm may fail to occur altogether; in men, ejaculation may be premature, occurring within the first few seconds of intercourse, or retarded, occurring only after a half hour of intercourse, if at all.

Impairment may occur in only one of these three areas of sexuality, or in all three in the same individual. The impairment may be lifelong or acquired, it may be limited to only one situation or occur in all situations, and it may occur infrequently or all the time. For example, the failure to maintain an erection can develop after years of satisfactory intercourse, or it can occur from the very first attempt at sexual intercourse. It can occur only with one partner or with all women. It can occur only once in a while or it can occur every time the individual tries to have intercourse.

THE IMPAIRMENT OF EROTIC DESIRE AND EXCITEMENT

Sexual
unresponsiveness
in women

Because erotic desire and physical excitement are so intertwined, we will treat them together. In women, lack of sexual desire and impairment of physical excitement in appropriate situations is called ***sexual unresponsiveness*** (formerly "frigidity"). Some of the symptoms are subjective: the woman may not have sexual fantasies, she may not enjoy sexual intercourse or stimulation, and she may consider sex an ordeal. Other symptoms are physiological: when she is sexually stimulated, her vagina does not lubricate, her clitoris does not enlarge, her uterus does not swell, and her nipples do not become erect. Frequently, she becomes a spectator rather than losing herself in the erotic act. When she finds herself unstimulated, she begins to worry about her own sexual adequacy and what her partner is thinking about her. She thinks, "He must think I'm frigid." "Is he getting pleasure?" "Will I climax?" She remains outside the act, observing and studying how she and her partner are reacting. Fear of failure, scanning for cues of failure, and presiding as a judge at one's lovemaking can diminish pleasurable sex and worsen the problems of arousal and of orgasm. The woman may be unresponsive in all situations or only in specific ones. For example, if the problem is situational, she may be enraged or nauseated by the sexual advances of her husband, but she may feel instantly aroused and may lubricate when an attractive, unavailable man touches her hand. Such a woman may have problems with orgasm as well, but it is not uncommon for a "sexually unresponsive" woman—whose arousal and excitement are impaired—to have orgasm easily once intercourse takes place.

Women's reaction to this problem varies. Some patiently endure nonexciting sexual intercourse, using their bodies mechanically and hoping that their partner will ejaculate quickly. But this is often a formula for resentment. Watching her husband derive great pleasure from sex over and over, while she feels little pleasure may be frustrating and alienating for the woman. And eventually some women will attempt to avoid sex, pleading illness or deliberately provoking a quarrel before bedtime (Kaplan, 1974).

The partner's reaction to the woman's sexual unresponsiveness also varies. Some men accept it and indeed may expect it, based on a false belief that women don't or aren't supposed to enjoy sex. Other men attribute their mate's lack of arousal to inadequate performance on their part and feel that they are poor lovers. Still others will pressure their wife to perform anyway and this, of course, only makes her more unresponsive. Many other couples seem to have good marriages in spite of this and spend a lifetime together without the woman ever responding to her husband sexually.

Erectile dysfunction in men

In men, global impairment of desire is rarer than in women. Rather, the most common dysfunction is one of excitement, called *erectile dysfunction* (formerly "impotence"). It is defined as a recurrent inability to have or maintain an erection for intercourse. This condition can be humiliating, frustrating, and devastating since male self-esteem across most cultures involves good sexual performance. When erection fails, feelings of worthlessness and depression often ensue.

Here, as with the other sexual dysfunctions, the man becomes a spectator during sex. He mentally steps back and thinks, "Will I fail to get an erection this time too?" "She probably thinks I'm not really a man." "Is she really getting pleasure or just pretending?" These fears make it even more difficult for him to maintain an erection.

Like sexual unresponsiveness in females, erectile dysfunction in the male can be either primary or secondary, situation specific or global. Men who have had *primary erectile dysfunction* have never been able to achieve or maintain an erection sufficient for intercourse; whereas men who have *secondary erectile dysfunction* have lost this ability. When the dysfunction is *situation specific,* a man may be able to maintain an erection with one partner, but not with another. Some men can become erect during foreplay, but not during intercourse. When the dysfunction is *global,* a man cannot achieve an erection with any partner under any circumstances. It is important and reassuring for a man to know that a single failure in no way implies "erectile dysfunction," which is by definition, recurrent. Virtually every man on one occasion or another—particularly when upset or fatigued—cannot get an erection or keep it long enough for intercourse.

Here is a case of primary impotence that begins with a particularly sordid circumstance surrounding the man's first attempt at intercourse:

Sheldon was nineteen when his teammates from the freshman football team dragged him along to visit a prostitute. The prostitute's bedroom was squalid; she seemed to be in her mid-fifties, had an unattractive face and a fat body, and foul-smelling breath. He was to be the last of a group of five friends scheduled to perform with her. Sheldon had never had intercourse before and had been anxious to begin with. His anxiety increased as his teammates returned one by one to describe in detail their heroic successes. When his turn arrived, the other four decided to watch and cheer him on, and Sheldon could not get an erection. His teammates shouted that he should hurry up and the prostitute was obviously impatient. He was pressured beyond any ability to perform and ran out of the room.

After this incident, he avoided all erotic contact with women for five years, fearing that he would fail again. At age twenty-four, when his fiancée pressured him to have sex, he was overwhelmed with fears that he would fail, remembering his humiliating failure with the prostitute. In fact, he failed again. This brought Sheldon into therapy for primary erectile dysfunction. (Adapted from Masters and Johnson, 1970.)

BYPASSING AND LACK OF DESIRE

Bypassing

Sexual apathy may result from bypassing, which is the act of tuning out what turns you off and focusing on fantasy.

One source of sexual apathy may be **bypassing,** which is the act of tuning out what turns you off and focusing on fantasy (Apfelbaum,1983). Our culture tells us that sex is supposed to go smoothly. Sex partners work hard at being mutually reassuring, encouraging, and flattering to each other. Sex talk is often mindlessly positive, like infield chatter. But what happens when a discordant note intrudes? You become aware of an unpleasant odor from her, or he touches you in a way that hurts. Many people deliberately narrow their consciousness to sensation or fantasy when their partners turn them off.

> One patient, Ann, says: "Fantasize, or allow myself to be more relaxed, if I force myself to stop thinking . . . of why Tom is acting the way he is. I can sometimes force my mind onto maybe a visual image of past really good sexual experiences we've had or, you know, to do something to focus in another area." (Apfelbaum, 1985)

The good bypasser overlooks the effect on the partner. Ann had no idea that her ability to ignore it, and get turned on anyway, when Tom touched her in ways she didn't like was contributing to Tom's loss of sexual interest in her. She probably thought that her getting turned on anyway would be a potent aphrodisiac. But Tom knew he was being bypassed. He felt left out and ignored, and feeling left out in this way may be a very common sexual experience. Tom's feeling left out, and feeling he could not tell her this, was central to his loss of desire for Ann.

ORGASMIC DYSFUNCTION

Orgasmic dysfunction in women

Some women and some men do not achieve the third phase of sexual response: orgasm. How easily different women can achieve orgasm lies on a continuum. At one extreme are the rare women who can have an orgasm merely by having an intense erotic fantasy, without any physical stimulation at all. Then there are women who climax merely from intense foreplay, women who have orgasm during intercourse, and women who need long and intense clitoral stimulation in order to climax. At the other extreme are approximately 10 percent of adult women who have never had an orgasm in spite of having been exposed to a reasonable amount of stimulation.

Nonorgasmic women frequently have a strong sexual drive (Andersen, 1983). They may enjoy foreplay, lubricate copiously, and love the sensation of phallic penetration. But as they approach climax, the woman may become self-conscious; she may stand apart and judge herself. She may ask herself, "I wonder if I'll climax." "This is taking too long; he's getting sick of it." Frustration, resentment, and the persistent erosion of a couple's erotic and affectionate relationship bring nonorgasmic women into therapy (Kaplan, 1974; McCary, 1978).

Failure to have an orgasm may be primary, with orgasm never having occurred, or secondary, with loss of orgasm. It may be situation specific, with orgasm occurring, for example, in masturbation when alone but not in intercourse, or it may be global.

In men, there are two kinds of orgasmic difficulties and they are opposite problems: premature ejaculation and retarded ejaculation.

PREMATURE EJACULATION

Premature ejaculation

Most men have ejaculated occasionally more quickly than their partner would like, but this is not equivalent to premature ejaculation. Premature ejaculation is the recurrent inability to exert any control over ejaculation such that once sexually aroused, the man reaches orgasm very quickly. This is probably the most common of male sexual problems.

Premature ejaculation can wreak havoc with a couple's sex life. A man who is worried that if he becomes aroused he will ejaculate right away can not be a sensitive and responsive lover. His partner expects him to be better. Not being so, he becomes more self-conscious, and she commonly feels rejected, sometimes perceiving him as cold and insensitive. Not uncommonly, secondary erectile dysfunction follows untreated premature ejaculation.

RETARDED EJACULATION

Retarded ejaculation

Retarded ejaculation, which is less common than premature ejaculation is defined by great difficulty reaching orgasm during sexual intercourse. Frequently, the man may be able to ejaculate easily during masturbation or foreplay, but intercourse may last for an hour or more with no ejaculation. Contrary to myth, the staying power of the retarded ejaculator does not place him in an enviable sexual position. His partner may feel rejected and unskilled, he may feign orgasm, and he may have high anxiety accompanied by self-conscious thoughts like, "She must think something is wrong with me." The retarded ejaculator finds his own touch most arousing; he can be numb to his partner's touch on his penis. His psychological arousal does not keep pace with his physiological, erectile arousal (Apfelbaum, 1985). Secondary erectile dysfunction sometimes follows.

It is unwise to attach time numbers to both retarded ejaculation and premature ejaculation, saying, for example, that premature ejaculation occurs whenever ejaculation persistently takes less than thirty seconds and retarded ejaculation occurs whenever ejaculation persistently takes more than half an hour. This misses the important point that the definition of the sexual problem, both orgasmic and arousal, is always relative to one's partner's expectations. Many couples are able to work out quite satisfactory erotic relationships even when one partner climaxes very quickly or very slowly, and it would be inappropriate to label these individuals as having sexual dysfunction.

THE CAUSES OF SEXUAL DYSFUNCTION

PHYSICAL CAUSES

Physical causes of male sexual dysfunctions

Impairment of sexual desire in both men and women can stem from aging, drug use that antagonizes sexual hormones (e.g., alcohol, barbiturates, narcotics, and marijuana), and prescription drugs (e.g., antihypertensives, major and minor tranquilizers, MAO inhibitors, and antihistamines) (Schiavi et al., 1984). But for men and women, physical causes probably account for a small minority of the problems of sexual dysfunction. Injuries, physical anomalies of the genitals, hormonal imbalances, neurological disorders, and inflammations can all interfere with a woman's capacity for sexual arousal (Kaplan, 1974; McCary, 1978). Male sexual dysfunctions may be caused by excessive alcohol or drugs, circulatory problems, aging, exhaustion, or anatomical defect. Low testosterone may be responsible for some erectile dysfunction problems. Out of 105 patients, 35 percent had disorders of the pituitary-hypothalamic-gonadal axis, and 90 percent of these had potency restored with biological therapy (Spark, White, and Connolly, 1980).

There is a useful way of distinguishing between which men are physically and which men are psychologically unable to get erections. All of us dream approximately 100 minutes a night, and in the male dreaming is almost invariably accompanied by an erection (in the female by vaginal lubrication). We are not certain why this occurs, but it does tell us if a man is physically capable of erection. If a man who is otherwise "impotent" gets erections during dreaming or has an erection upon waking in the morning, the problem is of psychological, not physical, origin.

PSYCHOLOGICAL CAUSES

Psychological problems probably cause the great majority of the sexual dysfunctions. There is general clinical agreement that negative emotional states impair sexual responsiveness. Earlier, we spoke of the sensitive interplay of physiological and psychological factors. The physiological part of the sexual response is autonomic and visceral; essentially it is produced by increased blood flow to the genitals under the control of the autonomic nervous system. Certain autonomic responses, sexual arousal among them, are inhibited by negative emotions. If a woman is frightened or angry during sex, visceral responding will be impaired. Similarly if a man is frightened or feeling pressured during sex, there may not be sufficient blood flow to cause erection.

The psychoanalytic view

What are the sources of the anxiety and anger that women feel which might cause sexual unresponsiveness? From a psychoanalytic point of view, one cause may be unresolved unconscious conflict: a woman unconsciously hostile toward her husband might express her hostility by withholding her sexual response, just as a consciously hostile woman would.

Psychoanalysts also express a view about male sexual dysfunctions. They claim that erectile dysfunction is a defense against castration anxiety. According to Freud, a boy between the ages of three and five wishes to possess his mother and, in his own mind, becomes a hated rival to his father. He fears that his father will castrate him in retaliation. When this Oedipal conflict is unresolved, erectile dysfunction may later ensue. By failing to have an erection, he wards off the anxiety of castration. That is, he will not commit the act with his "mother" and thereby not be castrated by his "father."

These psychoanalytic formulations have not been tested in the laboratory and indeed are quite difficult to test. But in cases of erectile dysfunction, clinical experience suggests substantial unresolved conflicts over the man's mother and father (Masters and Johnson, 1970; Kaplan, 1974). Alternatively, erectile dysfunction can be understood dynamically not as a defense to ward off anxiety but as a physiological response to anxiety that may be coming from any source. When an individual's defenses fail to prevent anxiety, erection will not occur.

There are other, less complex sources of anxiety and anger, all of which interfere with sexual arousal in men and women. A woman may fear that she will not reach orgasm. A woman may feel helpless or exploited. Some men and women may feel shame and guilt, or they may believe that sex is a sin; they may have grown up in situations where sex was seen as dirty and bad, and they may have trouble ridding themselves of feelings of shame and guilt even in the shelter of marriage. Some women may expect physical pain in intercourse and therefore dread it. Many men fear rejection and become self-conscious, thereby inhibiting an otherwise normal physiological potential. And often there is the fear of pregnancy.

Negative emotions arising in relationships must not be overlooked either. Relationships do not always progress well. People change, sometimes developing different living habits and preferences. Their partner may not change accordingly, and conflict may then ensue, bringing about negative feelings between the couple. Understandably, it is often difficult to discard these feelings when the couple enters the bedroom. In such cases, one or both partners might develop a sexual dysfunction, probably specific in nature.

The behavioral view

The behavioral school offers an explanation of the causes of sexual dysfunction based on learning theory. For men, erectile dysfunction may result from an early sexual experience. A particularly traumatic first sexual experience will condition strong fear to sexual encounters. Recall Sheldon's first and formative sexual encounter. Heterosexual activity was the conditioned stimulus (CS), which resulted in a humiliating, public failure to have an erection (US) and an unconditioned response (UR) of ensuing shame and anxiety. Future exposures to the CS of sexual encounters produced the conditioned response (CR) of anxiety, which in turn blocked erection. This formulation fits many of the instances in which there is an early traumatic experience, and it also explains the success of direct sexual therapy with erectile dysfunction. It fails to account for those cases in which no traumatic experience can be discovered, and it also does not account for why certain individuals are more susceptible to sexual traumatic experiences than others. For every individual who undergoes an initial sexual experience that is a failure (such as Sheldon's) and develops erectile dysfunctions, there are many who encounter similar initial failures but do not.

The cognitive view

In addition to psychodynamic and behavioral accounts of sexual dysfunctions, the cognitive view suggests other important considerations as well. We saw that for both the orgasmic and the arousal dysfunctions, what an individual thinks can greatly interfere with performance. Men and women with orgasm difficulties become "orgasm watchers." They may say to themselves, "I wonder if I'll climax this time." "This is taking much too long; he must think I'm frigid." Men and women who have arousal dysfunctions may say to themselves, "If I don't get an erection, she'll laugh at me." "I'm not going to get aroused this time either." These thoughts produce anxiety, which in turn blocks the parasympathetic responding that is the basis of the human sexual response. Such thoughts get in the way of abandoning oneself to erotic feelings. Thus, therapy for the sexual dysfunctions can deal with problems at four levels: physical, behavioral, psychodynamic, and cognitive, for difficulties at any of these levels can produce human sexual dysfunction.

TREATMENT OF SEXUAL DYSFUNCTIONS

It has been estimated that half of American marriages are flawed by some kind of sexual problem (Masters and Johnson, 1970; Frank, Anderson, and Rubenstein, 1978). Sexual problems usually occur in the whole context of a relationship between two human beings. When sex goes badly, many other aspects of the relationship may go badly, and vice versa. Sex—often, but not always—mirrors the way two people feel about and act toward each other overall. Sex therapists often find that underneath the sexual problem are more basic problems of a relationship—love, tenderness, respect, honesty —and that when these are overcome, a fuller sexual relationship may follow.

In the last fifteen years, substantial progress has been made in treating those problems of arousal and orgasm which stem from psychological causes. Overall, only about 25 percent of individuals with these problems fail to improve with a brief course of therapy. Let's look closely at one case:

> When they came to therapy, Carol, age twenty-nine, and Ed, age thirty-eight, had been married for three-and-a-half years and had one child. When they were first married, Carol had achieved orgasm almost every time they made love, but now orgasm was rare for her. She was feeling more and more reluctant to have intercourse with Ed. Ed had a strong sex drive and wanted to have intercourse every day. But Carol had made rules about sex, stating what Ed could and could not do.
>
> As time went on, Carol found it more and more difficult to keep her part of the bargain. Carol's headaches, fatigue, and quarrels deterred Ed's effective initiation of lovemaking. When he did make love to her, Carol would complain about his lovemaking technique. This effectively ended the encounter.
>
> When they first sought out sexual therapy, they were having intercourse once every two weeks, but Carol was becoming progressively more reluctant and intercourse was becoming even more of a dreaded ordeal for her. (Adapted from Kaplan, 1974, case 22.)

DIRECT SEXUAL THERAPY

Direct sexual
therapy

Masters and Johnson founded ***direct sexual therapy*** with sexually dysfunctional patients like Ed and Carol. Such therapy differs in three important ways from previous sexual therapy. First, it defines the problem differently: sexual problems are not labeled as "neuroses" or "diseases" but rather as "limited dysfunctions." A woman like Carol is not labeled as "hysterical," defending against deep intrapsychic conflicts by "freezing" her sexual response, as psychodynamic therapists claim. Rather, she is said to suffer from "inhibition of arousal." Second, and most dramatic, through direct sexual therapy, the clients explicitly practice sexual behavior with the systematic guidance of the therapists. A couple like Carol and Ed first receives education and instruction about their problem, then an authoritative prescription from Masters and Johnson about how to solve it, and most importantly, accompanying sexual practice sessions together. Their third major departure is that people are treated not as individual patients but as couples. In treating individuals, Masters and Johnson had often found that sexual problems do not reside in one individual but in the interaction of the couple. Carol's lack of interest in sex is not only her problem. Her husband's increasing demands, rage, and frustration contribute to her waning interest in sex. By treating the couple together, Ed and Carol's deteriorating sexual interaction could be reversed.

Sensate focus is the major strategy of direct sexual therapy for impaired excitement in females and erectile dysfunction in males. The basic premise of sensate focus is that anxiety occurring during intercourse blocks sexual excitement and pleasure. In the female, anxiety blocks the lubrication and swelling phase; in the male, it blocks erection. The overriding objectives of treatment are to reduce this anxiety and to restore confidence. The immediate goal is to bring about one successful experience with intercourse. This is accomplished, however, in a way in which the demands associated with arousal and orgasm are minimized. Sensate focus has three phases: "pleasuring," genital stimulation, and nondemand intercourse (Masters and Johnson, 1970; Kaplan, 1974). Let us look at the sensate focus treatment for Carol and Ed.

In the "pleasuring" phase, Carol and Ed were instructed not to have sexual intercourse and not to have orgasm during these exercises. Erotic activity was limited to gently touching and caressing each other's body. Carol was instructed to caress Ed first, and then the roles were to be reversed and Ed was to stroke Carol. This was done to permit Carol to concentrate on the sensations later evoked by Ed's caresses without being distracted by guilt over her own selfishness. It also allowed her to relax knowing that intercourse was not going to be demanded of her.

After three sessions of pleasuring, Carol's response was quite dramatic. She felt freed from pressure to have an orgasm and to serve her husband, and she experienced deeply erotic sensations for the first time in her life. Further, she felt that she had taken responsibility for her own pleasure, and she discovered that she was not rejected by her husband when she asserted herself. They then went on to phase two of sensate focus—"genital stimulation." In this phase, light and teasing genital play is added to pleasuring, but the husband is cautioned not to make orgasm-oriented caresses. Orgasm and intercourse are still forbidden. The woman sets the pace of the exercises and directs the husband both verbally and nonverbally, and then the roles are reversed.

The couple's response was also very positive here. Both felt deep pleasure and were aroused and eager to go on to the next step, "nondemand intercourse." In this final phase, after Carol had reached high arousal through pleasuring and genital stimulation, she was instructed to initiate intercourse. Ed and Carol were further instructed that there was to be no pressure for Carol to have an orgasm.

In spite of—or because of—the instruction, Carol had her first orgasm in months. At this point, Ed and Carol were able to work out a mutually arousing and satisfactory style of lovemaking. Carol and Ed's improvement was typical: only about 25 percent of patients fail to improve with sensate focus for female sexual unresponsiveness or for male erectile dysfunction (Masters and Johnson, 1970; Kaplan, 1974; McCary, 1978).

COUNTERBYPASSING

Counterbypassing is a sexual therapy designed to broaden rather than narrow awareness during sexual arousal, by increasing the awareness of sup-

Counterbypassing

pressed negative thoughts and encouraging partners to talk to each other about them (Apfelbaum, 1983). When one partner feels turned off by something, silence about it during sex is the rule. Tom did not tell Ann in the middle of intercourse that this wasn't doing anything for him. Rather he merely suffered his increasing apathy in silence. In counterbypassing, partners are made aware that all is not strongly positive during sex and that it is all right to tell your partner when you don't like something: "I don't like the way you are touching my breasts right now." "Your toes smell." "Stop, I can't stand it."

Pressure to always respond affirmatively can produce sexual apathy. When you feel allowed to complain as well as flatter, guilt about not being turned on starts to evaporate, and the pressure to always be positively responsive can be alleviated. Apathy will disappear, and desire will begin to return.

EVALUATION OF SEXUAL THERAPY

Cautions in evaluating direct therapy

Direct sexual therapy seems to be quite effective in alleviating the dysfunctions of arousal and orgasm in both men and women (Marks, 1981; Heiman and LoPiccolo, 1983). In addition to good success with erectile dysfunction and female unresponsiveness, failure to improve occurs only in 2 percent of cases of premature ejaculation, and in 20 percent of the remaining orgasmic disorders. Moreover, systematic desensitization may also be effective in enhancing desire and orgasm, particularly in women with sexual anxiety (Andersen, 1983). Caution is required in two respects, however. First, the Masters and Johnson reports of success are not as well documented as many would like. Masters and Johnson do not report percentages of *successes,* but rather they report percentages of *failures.* So, for example, they report that only 24 percent of females "failed to improve" following sensate focus training for arousal dysfunction. This is not equivalent to a 75 percent *cure* rate. What "failure to improve" means is not well defined. Moreover, the percentage of patients showing only mild improvement, great improvement, or complete cure is not reported. While direct sex therapy techniques are far superior to what preceded them, well-controlled replications with explicit criteria for sampling and for improvement will be needed before they can be considered definitive (Zilbergeld and Evans, 1980).

The second caution is that while the therapeutic techniques seem effective, the reasons for their good effects are not wholly clear. As has often been the case in psychology and in medicine, effective cure often precedes understanding, and this seems to be the case for sexual dysfunctions as well.

We now turn from the sexual dysfunctions, in which arousal and orgasm are inadequate, to those sexual problems in which arousal and orgasm are adequate, but in which they occur to unusual and bizarre objects. These are the sexual disorders.

SEXUAL ORDER AND DISORDER

Sexual order is largely determined by one's biology and by society's attitudes toward sexuality. Sexual disorder is what society considers to be abnormal sexual identity, behavior, and object choices. What is considered normal sexual behavior has undergone sweeping changes as society has changed.

ATTITUDES TOWARD HUMAN SEXUALITY

Attitudes have changed with time

Attitudes toward sexuality have changed with time. Surveys have found that sexual behavior is by no means restricted to intercourse during marriage (Kinsey et al., 1948, 1953; Hunt, 1974; Rozin, 1978). Sexual behavior in general has increased, in part probably due to the birth control pill, but also due to society's greater permissiveness. Particular sexual practices have become more frequent, mostly as a result of society's attitudes toward these practices. Moreover, a greater variety of sexual behaviors are generally considered normal today, including masturbation, premarital sex, oral sex, homosexuality, and bisexuality. Society's attitudes also have an influence on the frequency of sexual behavior and on kinds of sexual behavior engaged in, or at least on how an individual may feel about his or her behavior. Let us consider a few of these formerly forbidden sexual practices.

MASTURBATION

Depending on age, subculture, religion, and so on, about 95 percent of males and from 50 to 90 percent of females masturbate, or stimulate their own genitals, to orgasm. Indeed, roughly two-thirds of boys have their first orgasm while masturbating (Kinsey et al., 1948; McCary, 1978). In the 1980s, we accept this data without question. But our attitude toward masturbation is very different from attitudes in years past. This practice was long regarded as a disorder by psychiatrists. At the turn of the century, one might well have found oneself hospitalized as a mental patient for frequent masturbation. J. H. Kellogg's now famous cereals were part of his crusade to reduce masturbation with bland foods (*Parade,* 1981). Various religions have also condemned the practice. Whether these negative attitudes resulted in much less frequent masturbation in years past is not clearly known, but they probably brought about much more anxiety and guilt in those who engaged in the practice or who considered doing so.

CHAP. I.

Of the Heinous Sin of Self-Pollution.

Elf-Pollution is that unnatural Practice, by which Persons of either Sex may defile their own Bodies, without the Affistance of others, whilst yielding to filthy Imaginations, they endeavour to imitate and procure to themfelves that Senfation, which God has ordered to attend the carnal Commerce of the two Sexes for the Continuance of our Species.

It is almoft impoffible to treat of this Subject, fo as to be underftood by the meaneft Capacities, without trefpaffing at the fame time a-gainft the Rules of Decency, and making Ufe of Words and Expreffions which Modefty forbids us to utter. But as my great Aim is to promote Virtue and Chriftian Purity, and to difcourage Vice and Uncleannefs, without giving Offence to any, I fhall chufe rather to be lefs intelligible to fome, and leave feveral things
B   to

In the past, masturbation was condemned by society. Pictured here is an early tract against "self-pollution," or masturbation.

PREMARITAL INTERCOURSE

In the 1970s, more than 75 percent of college students believed that virginity was unimportant in the person they marry, and more than three-fifths of Americans believed that premarital intercourse was acceptable if the couple was sufficiently involved emotionally (Gallup Poll, 1970; Hunt, 1974; McCary, 1978; Rozin, 1978). Even being cautious about the findings of the surveys, we can see that there was a high frequency of sexual intercourse prior to marriage. But years ago, attitudes were different. Our grandfathers warned our fathers against premarital intercourse, usually for three reasons: (1) there was the possibility of contracting venereal disease (VD)—syphilis or gonorrhea; (2) there was a greater risk of pregnancy, and the possibility of being forced to marry; and (3) many worried that their children would get involved with someone from a different social sphere. A combination of technology and social opportunity in our culture caused all three of these barriers to become less formidable, and premarital intercourse to increase. In the 1940s, penicillin was introduced to cure syphilis; in the 1960s, the birth control pill promised fewer unwanted pregnancies; and the greater social mobility of the 1950s and 1960s weakened social stratification. In the 1980s, however, there has been a retrenchment in this increase. Young people who take sex education courses are less likely to have sexual intercourse than those who do not take them (Furstenberg, Moore, and Peterson, 1986). Moreover, recently, the AIDS epidemic has markedly reduced premarital intercourse.

Looking at other cultures, anthropologists have found that when one or more of the barriers discussed above are eliminated, more premarital intercourse is likely to occur. For example, in some cultures VD is rare and as a result we find more premarital intercourse. But society can make the barrier even stronger, as in cultures where who marries whom is of the utmost importance. In such tightly stratified societies, there is less premarital intercourse (Ford and Beach, 1951; Whiting and Whiting, 1974).

HOMOSEXUALITY AND BISEXUALITY

Changing attitudes toward homosexuality

More than one-third of all men and one-fifth of all women have had at least one orgasm with a member of the same sex. Figures are lower in the college population, with about 15 percent of men and fewer than 10 percent of women having been involved in at least one homosexual act. Among Rozin's introductory psychology students (1978), almost none of the women reported homosexual experience.

A single homosexual act is far more common and should be distinguished from *exclusive homosexuality,* which is an enduring pattern of sexual acts and fantasies involving only members of one's own sex. About 4 percent of men in the United States are exclusively homosexual and about 4 percent are mostly homosexual (Kinsey et al., 1948, 1953; Gagnon, 1977; Bell and Weinberg, 1978; McCary, 1978; Rozin, 1978).

Homosexuality has usually been deplored in our society. It is a crime in some states, and in past psychiatric classifications it has been called a "disorder." In 1986, the U.S. Supreme Court upheld, by a five to four vote, a Georgia law banning homosexual relations. American attitudes toward homosexuality have shifted over the years. During the 1970s, around 50 percent of Americans believed that homosexuality should not be a crime, with white-collar workers more approving than blue-collar workers, and young people more approving than older people. More than 60 percent of introductory college students approved of homosexual activity (Rozin, 1978). At that time, DSM-III eliminated the classification of homosexuality as a disorder. Only *ego-dystonic homosexuality,* or homosexuality in which the sexual preference is unwanted and a source of strong distress, was classified as a sexual "disorder" by DSM-III. The category was eliminated entirely in DSM-III-R. Popular attitudes continue to shift. The 1980s AIDS epidemic has probably caused a backlash of anti-homosexual attitudes.

Individuals who are neither exclusively heterosexual nor exclusively homosexual are called *bisexual.* The number of American bisexuals is large: about 15 percent of men and 10 percent of women. Among bisexuals, the preference for partners of their own sex varies in all possible ways. Some bisexuals have sex with members of their own sex about as often as with mem-

The Embrace by Auguste Rodin pictures a lesbian couple.

bers of the opposite sex, others have relations with members of their own sex the vast majority of the time, but the majority have sex with members of their own sex only a small percentage of the time (McCary, 1978).

Masturbation and premarital intercourse, as well as oral sex and extramarital intercourse, are common practices in our society. Homosexuality, while not nearly as common, is widespread, and the absolute number of homosexuals is large indeed. One major criterion for calling a practice "abnormal" is rarity, and none of these forms of sexuality is rare today. What seems to have made these sexual behaviors unacceptable in the past was society's attitude about them, and not any physiological or psychological anomaly.

Sexual Identity

The rearing of a child includes the passing on to the child of a sense of sexual identity and a notion of what is acceptable sexual behavior in today's world. Sexual identity has three aspects: object choice, gender identity, and gender role. *Gender identity* is the awareness of being male or female. *Gender role* is the public expression of gender identity, what an individual says or does to indicate that he is a man or she is a woman. *Sexual object choice* consists of the types of persons, parts of the body, and situations that are the objects of sexual fantasies, arousal, and sexual preferences.

Gender role   How does *gender role* come about? By age two, children are able to distinguish between males and females. By three, they can identify gender differences, and they understand that certain behaviors are appropriate to their gender role. By school age, they understand that a person's gender will not change, even if aspects of the person's appearance or behavior do change. Because parents and others in society respond differently to girls and boys from birth onward, taking on a gender role begins immediately.

Gender identity   The process of taking on a *gender identity*—feeling like a boy or a girl—is more mysterious than the process of taking on a gender role. Identification and internalization and imitation of parents probably all play some role. Fear of the same-sex parent or desire for the parent's resources or emotional bonding with the same-sex parent all lead to identification with the same-sex parent, and they lead the young child to imitate the parent's behavior and attitudes, including the parent's sexual behavior and attitudes. The child will then internalize these behaviors and attitudes. Biological processes are important as well; for example, the balance of hormones the fetus is bathed with *in utero* contributes to sexual identity (Money and Ehrhardt, 1972; Ellis and Ames, 1987). However it is accomplished, the process of taking on a gender identity is complete by age two, at which time the child feels like a male or female: this identity will almost never change (Imperato-McGinley, Peterson, Gautier, and Sturla, 1979).

Sexual object choices   Sometime in the first fifteen years of life, individuals acquire their *sexual object choices,* and this preference is likely to stay with them for the rest of their life. For most men, the objects of sexual choice are women; for most women, the objects of sexual choice are men. There is a very large range of situations that men and women find sexually arousing: holding a member of the opposite sex in their arms, dancing, seductive conversation, being caressed by a member of the opposite sex, seeing a member of the opposite sex naked, and the like. Being aroused in real life and in fantasy by these sexual object choices facilitates affectionate sexual activity between human beings.

SEXUAL DISORDERS: THE PARAPHILIAS

Defining paraphilias

When sexual object choice is so disordered that it impairs the capacity for affectionate erotic relations between human beings, the sexual object is called a *paraphilia* (from the Greek "love of [philia] what is beyond [para]"). The paraphilias comprise an array of unusual objects and situations that are sexually arousing to some individuals. Among the more common paraphilias are female underwear, shoes, inflicting or receiving pain, and "peeping." Among the more bizarre paraphilias are human feces, dead bodies, and amputated limbs.

TYPES OF PARAPHILIAS

The paraphilias divide into three categories: (1) sexual arousal and preference for nonhuman objects, including fetishes and transvestism; (2) sexual arousal and preference for situations that involve suffering and humiliation, including sadism and masochism; and (3) sexual arousal and preference for nonconsenting partners, including exhibitionism, voyeurism, and child molesting.

FETISHES

Defining fetishes

To have a *fetish* is to be sexually aroused by a nonliving object. In many cases, it may be harmless. For example, women's panties are sexually arousing to many men. When a man fantasizes and talks erotically about panties during sexual intercourse with a mutually consenting partner, the paraphilia may be playful and lead to heightened arousal. More typically, however, his partner feels excluded; when the underwear a woman wears displaces the woman, and her partner cannot be sexually aroused unless she is wearing it, the object is no longer a means to arousal but the end of arousal. And when it becomes the preferred or exclusive mode of sexual arousal it becomes pathological. At this point it is of clinical interest. The most common fetishes are for female underwear, shoes, boots, various textures such as rubber, fur, silk, and velvet, parts of the female body such as feet, hair, ears, and eyes. Rarer fetishes include human feces (coprophilia), human urine (urophilia), dirt (mysophilia), animals (zoophilia), and even dead bodies (necrophilia). Here is an example of a fetish, specifically a foot fetish:

> At the age of seven Leo was taught to masturbate by his older half sister. In the course of the lesson she accidentally touched his penis with her slipper. From that time on, the mere sight of a woman's shoe was enough to induce sexual excitement and erection. Now twenty-four, virtually all his masturbation occurred while looking at women's shoes or fantasizing about them. When he was at school he was unable to keep himself from grasping his teacher's shoes and in spite of punishment continued to attack her shoes. He found an acceptable way of adapting his life to his fetish. When he was eighteen, he took a job in a shop which sold

ladies' shoes and was excited sexually by fitting shoes onto his customers. He was absolutely unable to have intercourse with his pretty wife unless he was looking at, touching, or thinking about her shoes at the same time. (Krafft-Ebing, 1931, case 114)

Fetish acquired during childhood

It is typical that a fetish is acquired during childhood. The object that will become the fetish accompanies early erotic play. The fetish grows in strength when it is repeatedly fantasized about and rehearsed, especially during masturbation. A fetish may reveal itself when adult interpersonal relationships are unsatisfactory. At this point, one's childhood experience may take over and the fetishist may seek comfort in the simpler sexual pleasures of childhood instead of dealing with the complexity of another human being.

Fetishes and men

Interestingly, virtually all cases of fetishes and the vast majority of all paraphilias occur among men. Such a man is usually full of shame and guilt about his fetish, which isolates him from sexual activity with other people. Erectile dysfunction is the regular consequence of fetishism when the fetish is absent. Depression, anxiety, and loneliness often accompany the fetish. In addition to such individual problems, fetishists are occasionally in trouble with the law. They may steal objects of the fetish, lunge for the objects in public, and they may masturbate on the objects. Some will frequently acquire a collection of the objects. One young shoe fetishist was discovered with a collection of 15,000 to 20,000 pictures of shoes.

TRANSVESTISM

Defining transvestism

Transvestism occurs when a man persistently dresses in clothes of a woman in order to achieve sexual arousal. It is usually carried on in secret, although a transvestite's wife may share the secret and cooperate by having intercourse with him when he is dressed as a woman. The secrecy of the act makes its prevalence difficult to estimate, but it is probably rare—occurring in fewer than one percent of adult men. There have been virtually no reports of transvestism in women.

Transvestism usually begins with cross-dressing in childhood, as shown in the following case of Sam:

Transvestism occurs when a man persistently dresses in a woman's clothes to achieve sexual arousal.

At about the age of fourteen, I discovered in my dad's photo album a photo he had taken of me at five-and-a-half just before having my long (bobbed) hair cut off. My mother had dressed me in girls' clothes to see what I would have looked like if I had been a daughter, which is what she had wanted first. When I saw the photo I recalled the incident clearly and the sight of the photo thoroughly "shook" me, for it appeared to be a rather pretty young girl.

The emotional result was twofold. It aroused my first interest in girls and also an interest in girls' clothes. I found myself compelled to go back to look at the photos again and again.

One winter my wife and I were living alone. Our marital relations were good. We were spending New Year's Eve entirely alone and for some reason my wife, not knowing of my mere leanings (at the time) toward transvestism (a word I did not know then), decided to put one of her dresses on me and make up my face just as a sort of New Year's Eve prank. When she finished we sat around for a while and she asked me how I liked it. When I answered in the affirmative she became resentful and very anxious for me to take off the clothes she had put on me voluntarily. (From Stoller, 1969, subject 3).

This painting is of Edward Hyde, Lord Cornbury, governor of the colonies of New York and New Jersey. Hyde, a man, is shown here dressed as a woman.

When cross-dressing begins, only one or two items of clothing, such as panties, may be used. This item of clothing may become a fetish habitually used in masturbation and in intercourse with a cooperating partner. Such a man may wear these panties under his daily masculine garb. Cross-dressing usually progresses from a single item to a total costume. When dressed as a woman, the transvestite feels considerable pleasure and relaxation; he is intensely frustrated if circumstances block his cross-dressing. A transvestite may believe he has two personalities: one male, which dominates his daily life, and the other female, which comes out when he is dressed up. In other respects, the transvestite is unremarkably masculine in appearance and conventional in his behavior.

Transvestism is often mistakenly confused with homosexuality on the one hand and with transsexuality on the other. Transvestites are decidedly not homosexual: almost three-quarters of them are married and have children, and on the average they have had less homosexual experience than the average American man (Benjamin, 1966; McCary, 1978). Further, a transvestite is aroused by his fetish, whereas a homosexual is obviously aroused by another person. While a male homosexual will occasionally dress in female clothes in order to attract another man, a homosexual, unlike a transvestite, is not sexually aroused by the fact that he is in "drag."

Since most transvestites merely want to be left alone in order to pursue their habit secretly, we must ask why it is considered a problem. Depression, anxiety, shame, and guilt often occur in transvestites; and while sexual arousal is intense during cross-dressing, affectionate sexuality is often impaired by transvestism. A transvestite will commonly be impotent unless he is wearing some female clothing, and this is often not possible when his partner objects.

SADOMASOCHISM

The second class of paraphilias involves inflicting or receiving suffering as a means to sexual excitement, and it consists of two distinct disorders that complement each other. In *sadism* the individual becomes sexually aroused by inflicting physical and psychological suffering or humiliation on another human being, while in *masochism* the individual becomes sexually aroused by having suffering or humiliation inflicted on him. These terms are greatly overused in ordinary language. We often hear individuals who cheerfully put up with suffering or hardship called masochists, and individuals who are aggressive and domineering called sadists. Much more than this is required for sadism or masochism. A sadist *repeatedly* and *intentionally* inflicts suffering on his partner, sometimes a nonconsenting partner, in order to produce sexual excitement. And a masochist repeatedly and intentionally participates in activity in which he is physically harmed, his life is threatened, or he is otherwise made to suffer in order to feel sexual excitement. Not uncommonly, the masochist and sadist will seek each other out and marry, in order to engage in mutually desirable sadomasochism. Both disorders are accompanied by persistent and insistent fantasies in which torture, beating, binding, and raping are common themes producing high sexual arousal.

Many individuals who are neither sadists nor masochists have occasional sexual fantasies about humiliation and suffering. Kinsey found that about

20 percent of men and 12 percent of women reported sexual arousal when they were told stories about rape, bondage, chains, whips, and discipline. But such fantasies are hardly necessary for sexual arousal or orgasm in the great majority of individuals, and this differentiates them from sadomasochists (Gagnon, 1977; McCary, 1978). In addition to fantasies, overt acts involving suffering and humiliation in order to produce arousal must occur for sadism or masochism to be diagnosed. Nor are all overt acts that produce pain during sex play considered sadomasochistic: lightly biting a partner's earlobe, leaving scratch marks on a partner's back, or bruises whose origin is unknown are common elements of sex play. The true sadist or masochist both has the relevant fantasies and engages in acts that sexually arouse him, causing more than minimal pain. Biting, whipping, pinching, and slapping are typical physical acts of the sadist; bullying, threatening, using sarcasm, and belittling are common psychological acts.

Sadism takes its name from the Marquis de Sade (1740–1814), whose descriptions of sadomasochism in his novels are among the most vivid in literature.

> He has harshly ordered me to be silent. I strive to melt him . . . but in vain, he strikes out savagely at my now unprotected bosom: terrible bruises are immediately writ out in black and blue; blood appears as his battering continues, my suffering wrings tears from me, they fall upon the vestiges left by the monster's rage, and render, says he, yet a thousand times more interesting . . . He kisses those marks, he devours them and now and again returns to my mouth, to my eyes whose tears he licks up with lewd delight. (Sade, 1791/1965, pp. 596–98)

Masochism derives its name from Leopold Sacher-Masoch (1836–1895), a very popular German novelist of the nineteenth century, whose male characters were often sexually degraded by women. Below is a description of a typical sadomasochistic interaction:

> Thomas, a masochist, and his wife enact a periodic sadomasochistic ritual, in which about once every six weeks Thomas has himself beaten by his wife. She punishes him for his "weak" and "feminine" behavior. In his daily life he is an aggressive and controlling executive, but underneath he deeply longs to be controlled. He feels he should be punished because it is wrong for him to have feelings of needing to be dominated, and so he has his wife tie him to a rack in their cellar and beat him. (Adapted from Gagnon, 1977.)

Severe cases of sadism and masochism are rare, although mild forms of it occur rather frequently. About 5 percent of the men and 2 percent of the women in one survey of liberal and sexually active individuals at one time or another had gotten sexual pleasure from inflicting pain (Hunt, 1974). The incidence was greater among younger people than older people, and much greater among single men than married men. The great majority of sadists and, contrary to popular belief, masochists as well, are men; but both phenomena appear in women as well.

EXHIBITIONISM, VOYEURISM, AND PEDOPHILIA

The final category of paraphilias involves sexual arousal with nonconsenting partners. Unlike the foregoing, all of these paraphilias are crimes in our society. The criminal aspect derives from the fact that they violate the freedom of others to make unconstrained sexual decisions. *Exhibitionism* involves exposing the genitals to unwitting, and usually unwilling, strangers. *Voyeurism* involves observing the naked body, the disrobing, or the sexual activity of an unsuspecting victim, and *pedophilia* involves sexual relations with children below the age at which we consider it reasonable for them to give mature consent.

Rape not a paraphilia

Rape—the sexual violation of one person by another—is the most heinous instance of sex involving nonconsenting partners. We shall *not* discuss rape in this section for two reasons: First, it is not clearly a paraphilia. To be a paraphilia, the act must be the individual's exclusive, or vastly preferred, mode of sexual release. The shoe fetishist does not become erect or have an orgasm unless he is fantasizing about, seeing, or touching shoes. In contrast, the vast majority of rapists, most of the time, can and do become sexually aroused and achieve sexual release in activities other than rape. While fetishism and sadism may play some role in rape, the coercive violence involved is not usually necessary for sexual arousal by the rapist. Second, rape is a major crime, an act for which it is imperative that society hold the individual responsible, punishing him accordingly. If we were to include rape as a *disorder* in the nosology of paraphilias, there would be some tendency to excuse the act and lighten the burden of the rapist's individual responsibility—even if there was not a shred of evidence other than the rape itself that indicated psychological abnormality. The acts of murder, assault, and theft are not automatically thought of as psychological disorders unless there is additional evidence of abnormality, and we believe rape should be thought of in the same way. The expression "Only a crazy man could have done that," when applied to rape or murder seems to us deeply and insidiously confused. The concepts of "evil" and "insane" are deeply entrenched in our language and our moral codes. Distinguishing between them is time-honored and central to being able to occasionally excuse people for bad actions when they are not responsible by reason of insanity (see Chapter 18). We must not blur this distinction any further.

☐ EXHIBITIONISM. *Exhibitionism* consists of exposing the genitals to an unwitting stranger, on repeated occasions, in order to produce sexual excitement. The exposure itself is the final sexual act, and the exhibitionist does not go on to attempt sexual relations with his victim after exhibiting himself. A "flasher," or "flagwaver" as they are called in prison slang, typically approaches a woman with his genitals exposed. He usually has an erection, but sometimes he is flaccid. Sometimes he will ejaculate while exhibiting himself or more commonly, he will masturbate when he is alone afterwards (Katchadourian and Lunde, 1972).

Exhibitionism most common sexual crime

Exhibitionism is the most common sexual crime in the United States, with roughly one-third of sexual offenders arrested for it. Surprisingly enough, exhibitionism is very rare outside the United States and Europe and nonexistent in cultures such as India and Burma. Almost half of convicted exhibitionists have had four or more prior convictions for this offense (Gebhard, Gagnon, Pomeroy, and Christenson, 1965).

Exhibiting one's genitals or naked body in a public place is viewed quite differently by our society, depending on whether it is done by a man or by a woman. When a man undresses before a female stranger, he is the exhibitionist and she is the victim. When a woman undresses before a male stranger, he is the voyeur and she is again the victim. As Katchadourian and Lunde (1972) put it, "However badly females fare in other areas of sexual behavior, when it comes to voyeurism and exhibitionism the law is on their side." For this reason, exhibitionism and voyeurism are disorders mostly of men.

Exhibitionist's victims

The exhibitionist has a favorite type of victim and will expose himself exclusively to female adults or exclusively to children. He wishes to shock and horrify his victim, and this is essential for the act to be gratifying. A woman who acts calmly when confronted with an exhibitionist and placidly suggests to him that he needs psychological help will usually foil the act.

Exhibitionists are usually not dangerous. The act usually takes place six to sixty feet away from the victim; very rarely is the victim touched or molested. The exhibitionist is more of a nuisance than a menace, and it is much more common for child molesters to become exhibitionists than for exhibitionists to become child molesters (Gagnon, 1977; McCary, 1978).

Exhibitionist's settings

The settings in which exhibitionists perform vary. The most common are in front of girls' schools or churches, in crowds, and in parks; and in these settings, the exhibitionist may pretend he is urinating. Among the more imaginative scenarios are wearing only a raincoat in a department store, taking out a whistle and blowing it, and as the female shoppers look in the direction of the whistler, opening the raincoat; rapping on the window of a house with one's erect penis; sitting down near women in darkened movie theaters and masturbating. All these situations have one important element in common: they are public and it is very unlikely that sexual intercourse could possibly take place. These points provide clues to the dynamics of an exhibitionist. The exhibitionist needs to display his masculinity without the threat of having to perform in an adequate sexual role (Kaplan, 1974).

Personality of typical exhibitionist

What is the personality of the typical exhibitionist like? He is a quiet and timid man with feelings of inadequacy and insecurity. Most exhibitionists are married, but there is conflicting evidence about whether or not their sexual relationships with their wives are poor or good (Maletzky, 1974; Rooth and Marks, 1974; McCary, 1978). He is usually between the ages of thirteen and forty, with the peak being about twenty-five. Exhibitionism may begin any time from preadolescence to about age forty. When an onset occurs after age forty, it is usually associated with another more severe condition like senility. Exhibitionism may be an impulsive response to a transitory stress like being slighted by a woman, or it may be compulsive, insistent, and ritualistic. Overall, however, the one word that best characterizes exhibitionists is "immature."

☐ VOYEURISM. In the eleventh century Leofric, the Lord of Coventry, agreed to lower taxes if his wife, Lady Godiva, would ride unclothed on a white horse through the town. As a friend of the poor, Lady Godiva consented, and everyone in town shuttered their windows and hid their eyes out of respect and gratitude. Only Tom, the tailor, peeked; and he went blind, becoming our legendary peeping Tom, the "original" voyeur.

Voyeurs are individuals who repeatedly seek out situations in which they can look at unsuspecting women who are either naked, disrobing, or en-

Defining
voyeurism

gaged in sexual activity. The acts of a peeping Tom are secret. The voyeur will masturbate during these acts and while fantasizing about the memory of these encounters. Watching an unsuspecting stranger is the final act, and the voyeur almost never approaches his victim for sexual contact. Visual stimulation is commonly erotic both to men and women, but merely being aroused by seeing a naked woman or a sexual act is not equivalent to voyeurism. In normal individuals, visual stimulation is usually a prelude to further sexual activity. In contrast to voyeurs, normal men do not need to watch an unsuspecting stranger in order to become aroused.

Almost all information about voyeurs comes from those cases in which they are caught. The act is a crime, and many of the problems—such as shame and danger to reputation—that it produces come only in the aftermath of the arrest and exposure. In addition to shame, voyeurs sometimes fall off window ledges, are shot as burglars, and are assaulted by couples who catch them peeping.

Personality of
typical voyeur

What is the personality of the typical voyeur? The data on this must be viewed with caution, since we know only a selected sample—those who have been caught and convicted by the court. These data may reflect the difference between the caught and the uncaught as much as the difference between voyeurs and nonvoyeurs. (The same caveat holds for exhibitionists and pedophiles as well.) Typically the voyeur is a man, although recent FBI reports indicate that one out of nine individuals arrested for voyeurism are women (McCary, 1978). He is usually the youngest child or an only child, and only rarely does he come from an all-female home. Through adolescence, he had fewer girlfriends and was slower to begin premarital intercourse than his peers. He is shy, and voyeurism enables him to receive gratification and feel sexual power without having to go through the task of approaching and getting to know a woman and thereby risking rejection. Between one-third and one-half of voyeurs are married, and the quality of their marriages does not differ strikingly from the quality of the marriages of the rest of the male population. Finally, 30 percent of convicted voyeurs had also been convicted as juveniles of a variety of nonsexual minor offenses,

In Alfred Hitchcock's *Rear Window*, a man with a broken leg is confined to his apartment, where he watches his neighbors through a telescopic lens. In a line from the movie, a character says, ''We've become a race of peeping Toms . . .''

more than any other group of sexual offenders (Gebhard, Gagnon, Pomeroy, and Christenson, 1965).

Peter Lorre plays a pedophile in Fritz Lang's film *M*.

☐ PEDOPHILIA. The *pedophile*, sometimes called the child molester, prefers sexual activity with prepubertal children and acts out his preference repeatedly. Society feels a special sense of horror and reserves special fury for the child molester. Pedophilia is the most heavily punished crime of the paraphilias. About 30 percent of all convictions for sex offenses are for child molesting, but it is probably even more common than generally supposed. Between one-quarter and one third of all adults report that when they were children they had been approached sexually by an adult (Kinsey et al., 1948; McConaghy, 1969; McCary, 1978). There are probably two reasons society consigns pedophiles to a special hell. First, we do not consider a child capable of consenting to sexual activity in the same way a mature adult can, and so the child's freedom is seen as being grossly violated in such circumstances. Second, there is a common belief in sexual imprinting; the child's attitude toward future sexuality may be warped by these early sexual contacts.

In spite of the fact that the child molester is so despised, physical violence probably occurs in no more than 3 percent of all cases of child molesting, and in only about 15 percent of all cases does threat or coercion occur. Provocation and active participation by the victim may occur in about 10 percent of the cases (Swanson, 1968; McCary, 1978).

The molested child is twice as likely to be a girl as a boy. Typically the pedophile exposes himself to the child, or he has the child sit on his lap and he manipulates her genitals. Penetration probably occurs in only about 10 percent of the cases of child molestation. Generally, after being molested, the child is emotionally upset and frightened but usually less so than are her parents. The intense reaction of parents and other adults to the incident may even amplify the trauma of the molested child.

Society's image of the child molester as a dirty stranger lurking in the shadows is far from the truth. Most acts of convicted pedophiles take place between the child and a family acquaintance, neighbor, or relative. The acts usually occur in the child's own home or during a voluntary visit of the child to the home of the pedophile. The relationship is not usually particularly intimate, nor is it prolonged: it typically ends when the child begins to protest or reports it to the parents. As with exhibitionism and voyeurism, however, our picture of the pedophile comes from those who have been caught and convicted, and therefore it may not accurately represent those who have successfully evaded capture.

While some convicted molesters are mentally retarded, senile, or schizophrenic, the vast majority are not. The convicted molester is typically older than those in any other class of sex offenders, with the average age being thirty-seven. The majority of those convicted are married. Older offenders seek out younger children in the eight- to ten-year-old age range whereas younger offenders seek out preadolescents of ten to twelve years old. Convicted pedophiles are highly Victorian and rigid in their own sexual attitudes. They generally believe in the double standard and, quite surprisingly, are often highly religious. They see themselves as devout, they read the Bible regularly, and they pray often for cure of their pedophilia. They are often

Who is the child molester?

beset with conflicts about religious piety versus sexuality, are guilt-ridden, and feel doomed. They lack ordinary, adult social skills (Overholser and Beck, 1986). Thus, they are usually uneasy in adult social and sexual relations and feel more comfortable with children than adults. Occasionally an isolated act of pedophilia will be precipitated by a stressor, most commonly finding out that one's wife or girlfriend has been unfaithful. In other cases, child molesters may be substituting child contact for adult contact that they have been unable to get (Gagnon, 1977).

THE CAUSES OF PARAPHILIAS

Objects of sexual choice as ends in themselves

There are some objects that we treat as means to certain ends that merely symbolize other more important objects. Money, for example, stands for the things it can buy and the pleasures it can bring. Similarly, some of our acquaintances are merely contacts we value not for themselves but because of what they do for us. Other objects serve no other master and become an end in themselves: stamps for the stamp collector, work for a "workaholic," power for some politicians. Above all, the objects of sexual choice become ends in themselves: women for most men, shoes for a shoe fetishist, inflicting suffering for a sadist, shocking an unsuspecting woman for the exhibitionist. This is the stuff out of which human passion is made. Where does it begin and how do these processes go awry to produce the paraphilias? Two schools of thought, the psychodynamic and the behavioral, have wrestled with the problem of the origin of paraphilias. While neither has been completely successful, both have contributed to our understanding.

THE PSYCHODYNAMIC VIEW OF PARAPHILIAS

Cathexis

According to Freud, the concepts of "fixation," "object-cathexis," and "sexual object choice" are attempts to describe and explain how certain objects become imbued with erotic attraction for certain individuals as they grow up. *Cathexis* refers to the charging of a neutral object with psychical energy, either positive or negative. In the case of a "positive cathexis" the libido, or the sexual drive, attaches to the object, and it becomes loved. In the case of a "negative cathexis," the object becomes feared.

Freud described the case of the typical foot fetishist who recalled that when he was six, his governess, wearing a velvet slipper, stretched her foot out on a cushion. Although it was decently concealed, this kind of foot, thin and scraggy as it was, thereafter became his only sexual interest (Freud, 1917/1976, p. 348). The fetishist had cathected onto this kind of foot. Freud considered this cathexis to be a concentration of very high psychical energy, bounded and protected by a shield of dead layers. This protection against external stimuli allowed the cathected object to retain its erotic power through life, and only traumatic experiences could breach the protective gates.

Cathected paraphilias have the same three properties as other objects of sexual interest: (1) they have their beginnings in childhood experience; (2) they resist change, particularly rational change; and (3) they last and last—usually remaining for a lifetime. Thus, for example, a foot fetish begins in childhood; telling a foot fetishist that feet don't ordinarily signal sexual pleasure does not diminish their attractiveness; and generally a foot fetish will endure for a lifetime.

While the concept of cathexis is useful descriptively, it is not a satisfactory explanation, for as Freud acknowledged, it is unknown why it strikes one individual rather than another. And this is the main question that concerns us here. The psychodynamic view is content to *describe* the origins of passion for the fetishist, the transvestite, the sadist, the masochist, the exhibitionist, the voyeur, and the pedophile as an acquired cathexis. But it only describes the fact that for all of these individuals their sexual object choice is not a means to an end but an end in itself, that it is persistent, and that it does not yield to reason. Cathexis does not explain how this happens.

THE BEHAVIORAL VIEW OF PARAPHILIAS

Pavlovian account of paraphilias

The learning theories, too, have wrestled with the problem of erotic attachment. The most common account is Pavlovian. Recall the case of Leo, whose foot fetish began when, as a seven-year-old, his half sister's slipper touched his penis. The conditioned stimulus (CS) here is the sight of the slipper. It is paired with the unconditioned stimulus (US) of genital stimulation and the unconditioned response (UR) of sexual pleasure. As a result, future slippers come to produce the conditioned response (CR) of sexual arousal. Such an account explains how cathexis might occur to odd objects in childhood, and it supplements the Freudian account by providing a mechanism.

Persistence of paraphilias

But this account leaves unanswered the question: Why do paraphilias persist? Recall that the Pavlovian account of phobias had the same problem (see Chapter 8, pp. 208–209). Once a conditioned stimulus has been paired with an unconditioned stimulus, it usually extinguishes readily when it occurs without the original unconditioned stimulus. When the shoe no longer signals that his sister will touch his penis, Leo should once again come to find shoes uninteresting—just as the dog, who used to have the clicking sound paired with food but who no longer experiences food following the clicking, will stop salivating to the click. To explain the persistence of phobias, we could make the following argument: once the phobic object became fearful, it was avoided so completely that the phobic never found out that the phobic object was no longer paired with the original trauma. The phobic object remained frightening because it was untested behind its protective wall. But the paraphilic does not avoid the newly erotic object. On the contrary, he continues to seek it, embraces it, fantasizes about it, *and he masturbates to it.*

This latter fact explains the persistence of the paraphilia, once conditioned. Once the fetishistic object has been paired with erotic stimulation and the paraphilic masturbates in the presence of the fantasy of the object or in the presence of the very object itself, he may provide himself with additional Pavlovian conditioning trials, thereby greatly strengthening the connection between the object and the unconditioned response of sexual pleasure. So an adolescent who experienced the sight of panties originally paired with sexual teasing by the girl next door may greatly strengthen his attachment to panties when he masturbates to orgasm while fantasizing about panties (McGuire, Carlisle, and Young, 1965; Storms, 1981).

Laboratory
evidence for
Pavlovian
conditioning of
paraphilias

There is a bit of laboratory evidence to supplement the case histories, which suggests that Pavlovian conditioning may be at the origin of paraphilias. S. J. Rachman and Ray Hodgson of Maudsley Hospital, University of London, attempted to condition a fetish. Pictures of boots (CS) were paired in time with pictures of naked women (US)—the latter causing their male subjects to have erections (UR). After several dozen pairings, the pictures of the boots (CS) themselves caused erections (CR). So a previously neutral object became erotic following Pavlovian sexual conditioning. But the erotic arousal to boots quickly extinguished when boots were no longer followed by the pornographic pictures—in all but one of the six subjects. Perhaps if the subjects had repeatedly masturbated to boots in fantasy the fetish might have resisted extinction (Rachman and Hodgson, 1968).

Prepared erotic
objects

There is another factor, **preparedness**, which was brought up in explaining phobias and which might also help to account for the irrationality and resistance to extinction of fetishes. Phobias are not arbitrary—only several dozen human phobias exist (see Chapter 8). There are no lamb phobias, no tree phobias. Evolution seems to have allowed only a certain class of objects that were actually dangerous at one time or another in evolutionary history to become potentially phobic. A parallel argument may hold for fetishes. There are a limited set of objects that actually become paraphilic. Why are fetishes about parts of the body and about dominance and submission common, but fetishes about windows, pillows, or yellow walls nonexistent despite the fact that such objects are often paired with sexual stimulation in childhood? If there are a special class of objects that are *prepared* to take on an erotic character once they have been paired with unconditioned sexual stimuli—then the other properties of preparedness should follow. Such objects, once conditioned, should be irrational, robust, and learned about readily. These facts describe both the paraphilias and phobias.

Thus, both psychodynamic thinking and learning theory may contribute to the explanation of paraphilias. Pairing of certain objects with actual sexual stimulation in childhood eroticizes these objects. They can be described as "cathected" because they are irrational and they resist extinction. The process by which they become cathected may be explained by Pavlovian conditioning, in which a prepared object is paired with an erotic object. Paraphilias and normal sexual object choices will resist extinction because fantasies (CS) about them are paired repeatedly with sexual arousal and orgasm (US) produced by masturbation and by wet dreams. Such an account of cathexis is compatible with the undoing—or therapy— for the paraphilias, to which we now turn.

THE TREATMENT OF THE PARAPHILIAS

Aversion therapy

Behavior therapists have reported some favorable results in changing the paraphilias, but the success rate is far from perfect (Maletzky, 1974; Rooth and Marks, 1974; Blair and Lanyon, 1981). If paraphilias arise by conditioning during fantasy and masturbation, it might be sufficient for aversion therapy to concentrate on fantasy. The use of imagined sexual stimuli followed by aversive US's is called **covert sensitization** (Cautela, 1967; LaMontagne and LeSage, 1986). For example, the following regime should be effective in changing paraphilias (McGuire et al., 1965). During voluntary

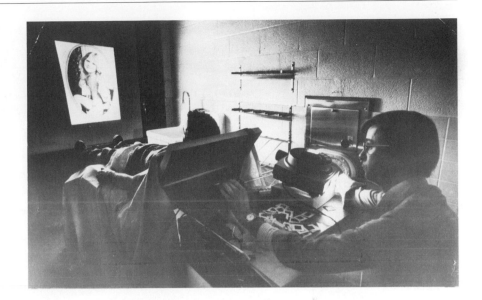

Behavioral therapy for a pedophile. The patient views slides of children, and when he becomes aroused, he receives an electric shock. This helps to extinguish his paraphilia.

therapy, a paraphilic is instructed to imagine a highly sexually stimulating fantasy involving his paraphilia. While engaged in this fantasy, an aversive stimulus, such as a strong electric shock or a nausea-inducing agent, is presented. When the aversive event goes off and relief is experienced, he is told to imagine conventional heterosexual fantasies. This procedure should produce conditioned aversion to the paraphilic fantasy and conditioned excitement to the nonparaphilic fantasy. Behavior therapists also use desensitization and reconditioning to appropriate sexual stimuli, social skills training, and imagery stopping techniques to modify paraphilias. Although some success has been reported using these techniques with exhibitionists (Maletsky, 1974), these procedures have also been known to fail (McConaghy, 1969).

Ego-Dystonic Homosexuality

Up to only a few years ago, the topic of *homosexuality* was listed in textbooks as a paraphilia or a "sexual deviation." We now believe that there is good reason for homosexuality not to be classified as a disorder. Sexual disorders used to be defined as conditions that grossly impaired affectionate sexual relations between a man and a woman, and homosexuality qualified, by definition, as a disorder. We view sexual disorders as conditions that grossly impair affectionate sexual relations between two *human beings*. Homosexuality, while it may impair such relations between men and women, does not, of course, impair them between a man and a man, or a woman and a woman.

Ego-dystonic homosexuality

    The underlying justification for excluding homosexuality as a disorder distinguishes between ego-syntonic and ego-dystonic homosexuality. ***Ego-dystonic homosexuality*** is defined as a sustained pattern of homosexuality which is a source of distress and which is accompanied by the desire to acquire or increase heterosexuality. ***Ego-syntonic homosexuality***, in contrast, is not a source of distress and is *not* marked by a desire to change sexual pref-

Ego-syntonic homosexuality is not a source of distress to a homosexual and is not accompanied by the desire to change sexual preference. These homosexual men attended the Gay National Rodeo in Reno, Nevada. Embracing publicly, it is clear they are not distressed by their sexual orientation.

erence. When we compare ego-dystonic homosexuality to ego-syntonic homosexuality, we see that the former involves suffering and a desire to change, while the latter does not. Since these two elements count strongly toward calling a behavior disordered, we believe that ego-syntonic homosexuality is legitimately excluded from the catalogue of psychological disorders. In contrast, we believe that ego-dystonic homosexuality could be considered a paraphilia, and so treated.

The crux of the matter is that a significant proportion of homosexuals are satisfied with their sexual orientation, do not show signs of psychopathology, and function quite effectively at love and at work. Ego-dystonic homosexuals, on the other hand, are dissatisfied and distressed by their sexual orientation. They are depressed, anxious, ashamed, guilty, and lonely. They are also manifestly impaired in their capacity to love. On the one hand, they feel ashamed of their attraction to members of their own sex, but on the other, they are not sexually aroused by members of the opposite sex.

Because ego-dystonic homosexuality is a new category, not much is known about its prevalence, its male to female ratio, its predisposing factors, and its course. Typically, an ego-dystonic homosexual will have attempted heterosexual relations unsuccessfully. But merely knowing that he was unaroused by females, or she by males, may have prevented heterosexual attempts altogether. Because there is a highly supportive homosexual subculture in many parts of the United States today, some ego-dystonic homosexuals accept their sexual orientation and give up the yearning to become heterosexual. Spontaneous occurrences of satisfactory heterosexual relations in individuals who have been exclusively homosexual are rare (Acosta, 1975).

THE ETIOLOGY OF EGO-DYSTONIC HOMOSEXUALITY

There are two different questions about the causes of ego-dystonic homosexuality: Where does one's dissatisfaction with one's homosexuality come from and where does one's sexual preference, one's homosexuality, come from?

Causes of distress at homosexuality

□ SOURCES OF EGO-DYSTONICITY.   Part of the dissatisfaction or dystonicity stems from the desire to have children and a conventional family life. Another source of dissatisfaction comes from pressures that our society puts on individuals to conform to its sexual norms. Even though American attitudes toward homosexuality are changing, 70 percent of Americans still believe that homosexuals are "sexually abnormal," 50 percent believe they are "perverted," and 40 percent believe they are "mentally ill" (Weinberg and Williams, 1974). Against this sort of disapproval, it would be difficult to retain one's equanimity day in and day out. A major source of the distress felt by ego-dystonic homosexuals stems from rejection and disapproval by their families, their acquaintances, their co-workers. Moreover, they also feel distress because of their own images of "normality."

Some writers believe that the suffering that society's oppression inflicts on homosexuals raises serious ethical questions about whether a therapist should ever consent to treat homosexuality. When an ego-dystonic homosexual comes into therapy with a request that the therapist help him to change his sexual orientation, these writers believe that the therapist should refuse. They believe that because the self-loathing and the desire to become heterosexual are products of the oppression of homosexuals by society, the desire of the ego-dystonic homosexual to change his orientation has been coerced and is not "voluntary," and so should be disregarded (Davison, 1976, 1978). Others disagree. They believe that individual suffering is often the product of societal disapproval and rejection. Exactly how the suffering comes about is theoretical and speculative, but what is not speculative is that another human being comes into the therapist's office and voices a desire to change. The expressed desire to change is, for some, the bottom line of therapeutic decision. The therapist is first and foremost an agent of the patient. When a patient, in obvious distress, asks for help, the patient has called on the therapist's primary duties. The bottom line of interaction between patient and therapist, just as between any two human beings, is that the expression of desires are taken seriously and, if possible, acted upon.

Theories of origin of homosexuality

□ CAUSES OF HOMOSEXUALITY.   Locating the cause of the distress is a simpler question than discovering the cause of the homosexuality. Many of the same considerations that apply to sexual learning in both normal heterosexuality and in the paraphilias, also apply to homosexuality. Prepared Pavlovian conditioning, masturbatory fantasies, nocturnal emission leading to cathexis, all probably play a role in the acquisition of a homosexual orientation. One recent theory proposes that the timing of the maturation of sex drive is critical. If most of your social group are the same sex as you when sex drive matures, you will tend to become homosexual. If opposite sexed, you will tend toward heterosexuality. This theory predicts that early maturing males and individuals with same-sex siblings will have a higher rate of homosexuality, and this may be so (Storms, 1981).

Another major theory of the origin of homosexuality holds that the tendency is laid down before birth by a combination of genetic, hormonal, and neurological processes, and then this orientation is activated by hormonal

Fetal disruption

changes at the onset of puberty (Ellis and Ames, 1987). Learning only alters how, when, and where homosexuality will be expressed. According to the Ellis-Ames theory, the crucial neurochemical events that control masculinization occur during the second to fourth months of pregnancy. This sequence of events is delicate and exquisitely timed and if they are disrupted, incomplete masculinization of the fetus will occur. This disruption will produce neurological feminization in a male fetus, as well as producing genital deformities in extreme cases. At puberty, this feminization will express itself behaviorally and psychologically as homosexuality. Among the causes of fetal disruption are: (1) genetic-hormonal problems, such as the *androgen-insensitivity syndrome*, in which the fetus lacks the receptors for the sex hormone, androgen; (2) taking progesterone-containing drugs during pregnancy to prevent miscarriage; (3) maternal stress early in pregnancy. Mothers of male homosexuals recall more stressful events (deaths, divorces, traumatic sexual and financial events) compared to mothers of bisexuals and heterosexuals (Dorner, Schenk, Schmiedel, and Ahrens, 1983).

Several deductions follow from the Ellis-Ames theory that they claim are supported by recent data: (1) homosexuality should be primarily a male phenomenon in both humans and animals (Davenport, 1965; Gadpaille, 1972); (2) the tendency toward effeminate mannerisms, which is the stereotype of male homosexuals, has a neurochemical basis (Bell, Weinberg, and Hammersmith, 1981); (3) homosexuality should be partially heritable (Cooper, 1978); (4) exclusive homosexuality (as opposed to bisexuality) should not be alterable after birth.

THE TREATMENT OF EGO-DYSTONIC HOMOSEXUALITY

Since ego-dystonic homosexuality is a new category, little is known about its treatment. There are two aspects, either of which might be treated: the ego-dystonicity and/or the homosexuality. The anxiety, depression, guilt, shame, and loneliness that make up the ego-dystonicity may be amenable to the treatments for anxiety and depression outlined in the anxiety and depression chapters. Cognitive therapy, assumption challenging, and progressive relaxation (see Chapter 5) should each allay the sadness and fears that make up the distress.

Homosexuality itself may be changeable if the individual strongly wants to change it. Traditional psychotherapy does not seem to hold much promise for changes of sexual orientation, but behavior therapy may help. In two controlled studies involving seventy-one male homosexuals, a group of British behavior therapists found that sexual orientation could be changed in nearly 60 percent of the cases by using aversion therapy of the sort described for the paraphilias. They defined "change" as the absence of homosexual behavior, plus only occasional homosexual fantasy, plus strong heterosexual fantasy, and some overt heterosexual behavior one year after treatment.

Exclusive homosexuality not changeable by therapy

The theory of Ellis and Ames (1987) claims that exclusive homosexuality should be unchangeable by therapy, since it has its origins before birth. The data are consistent with this view, since individuals who had had some heterosexual experience before therapy showed more change than exclusive homosexuals who had had no prior pleasurable heterosexual history (Mendelsohn and Ross, 1959; Feldman and MacCulloch, 1971; Marciano, 1982; Schwartz and Masters, 1984). When treatment concentrates on additional targets, such as intimacy and social skills, more change occurs (Adams and Sturgis, 1977).

SEXUAL DISORDERS: TRANSSEXUALISM

Disorders of
sexual identity

There are different levels of depth of psychological disorder, and each level may have a level of therapy appropriate to it. Some problems are relatively superficial, such as simple cases of psychogenic impotence. In order to cure —in the full sense of cure—such a problem, only the behavior needs to be changed. The backup machinery is all there: desire and sexual identity are intact; all that is missing is working peripheral machinery, and behavior therapy works well to cure this problem. Other disorders are at a moderate level of depth, such as sadism. Here the peripheral machinery is working, but what is disordered is the desire. A sadist is passionate only when inflicting suffering on another human being; his cognitions and cathexes are disordered. On the other hand, the sadist's sexual identity is still ordered, for the sadist knows he is a man, or she a woman. Any cure of sadism would not simply be a matter of getting peripheral machinery to work, but it would consist of a radical change in what the sadist is passionate about. Deepest of all disorders are the disorders of sexual identity. Few things are more basic to what we are than our sense of what sex we are, and it this sense that has gone awry in transsexualism. The therapy for most sexual disorders is psychologically based, but the therapy for transsexualism does not consist of changing the psychosexual identity. Here it is a matter of actually changing the body to conform to the otherwise unchangeable psychosexual identity.

Defining the
transsexual

A male-to-female transsexual is a man who feels as if he is a woman trapped in a man's body, wants to be rid of his genitals, and wants to live as a woman; or a female-to-male transsexual is a woman who feels that she is a man trapped in a woman's body, wants to acquire male genitals, and wants to live as a man. Transsexuals feel, from early in life, that by some cosmic

Dr. Richard Raskin (*left*) in a tennis match before the transsexual operation that enabled him to become a woman. His name is now Renee Richards (*right*).

mistake they were given the wrong kind of body. This body often disgusts them and the prospect of having to remain in it all their days makes them hopeless, depressed, and sometimes suicidal. By their early twenties, many transsexuals will masquerade in the clothes of the opposite sex. In effect, transsexuals often do everything they can to pass for members of the opposite sex. Unlike transvestites, such actions, particularly the cross-dressing, are not sexually exciting to them but are the means of leading the life compatible with what they perceive to be their sexual identity. Transvestites are decidedly not transsexual and would be horrified at the idea of having a sex-change operation.

Before this century, transsexuals were doomed to live out their lives in a body that repelled them. In the last twenty-five years, medical procedures have developed—although they have not been perfected—which allow transsexuals to acquire the anatomy they desire. The case of Allen-Allison shows the transsexual's problems with sexual identity:

> For the last four years, Allen has been passing by all who know him, as a female, but he is in reality an anatomically normal twenty-three-year-old male. Six months ago, he had his first operation: plastic surgery to enlarge his breasts. He takes female hormones, has had his facial and chest hair removed, and expects in the next two years to undergo the surgery to remove his penis and replace it by a vagina.
>
> Allen says that "As early as I can recall I never had any normal interests and wanted to become a girl and change my name to Allison." He loved to dress in his mother's clothes and always preferred to play with "feminine" things. On one occasion, when he was given a fire engine, he threw a tantrum insisting that he wanted a doll. From about kindergarten on, he demanded acceptance from his parents as a girl and this made for constant conflict. Finally in the fourth grade, he persuaded his parents to allow him to "be" a girl at home, except that he had to wear boys' clothes to school. For the next few years he led a double life, attending school dressed as a boy and then returning home to dress and live as a girl. By eighth grade, he began to feel very uncomfortable around people. The boys teased him mercilessly for being effeminate and the girls would not accept him. He began to avoid school and spent a great deal of time alone.
>
> At fifteen, both school life and family life had become unbearable, and he ran away to San Francisco, where he experimented with homosexuality. He found he could not tolerate homosexual males and left after only a month. While he was attracted to men as sexual partners, only those normal heterosexual men who had accepted him as a female aroused him sexually. Soon, thereafter, he began the odyssey of physical transformation. Allen is now becoming Allison. (Adapted from Pauly, 1969)

Childhood
behavior of
transsexuals

Allen-Allison's history is typical of the adult male transsexual. By age three or four his identity as a female is well on its way to being fixed. Before puberty, most transsexual boys will play almost exclusively with girls, will act like girls, prefer to play with dolls, sew and embroider, and help their mothers with housework. They refuse to climb trees, play cowboys and Indians, or roughhouse. By puberty, they feel completely like females, they want to be accepted by society as females, and when they come to know sex-change operations exist they desperately want one. This desire is so intense that in some cases, male transsexuals actually try to cut their own genitals off (Walinder, 1967; Pauly, 1969; Stoller, 1969; Money and Ehrhardt, 1972).

This transsexual couple married and had a child. However, both felt that they were born with "wrong bodies." Subsequently, each had an operation to change their gender.

Male transsexuals have three kinds of sexual histories: homosexual, heterosexual, and asexual. The *homosexual transsexual* is aroused by other males, but denies that this is "homosexual" since he feels like a woman. In other words, he wants what he considers "heterosexual" contact only, since his identity is female. In a study of seventy-two transsexuals seen at the University Clinic in Manchester, England, three-quarters had exclusively homosexual fantasies and roughly one-third of them engaged in homosexual behavior (Hoenig and Kenna, 1974; Green, 1985). In this study, 15 percent of the sample were *heterosexual transsexuals.* Their sexual fantasies were exclusively about women. Finally, *asexual transsexuals* denied ever having any strong sexual desires, and were preoccupied merely with the desire to live as woman and to get rid of their male genitals. They had had little or no sexual experience.

Transsexualism is chronic and rare

Transsexual is chronic. Once it has developed, there is not a single case on record in which it has spontaneously disappeared. A man who feels like a woman trapped in a man's body, or a woman who feels like a man trapped in a woman's body, will retain this belief for the rest of his or her life.

Transsexualism is rare. The most recent estimate is that about 1 in 100,000 people is transsexual (Walinder, 1967; Pauly, 1974). There are probably more male transsexuals than female transsexuals, and the best estimate of the ratio seems to be about 1.5 or 2 to 1 (Pauly, 1974). The life history of the typical female transsexual parallels that of the typical male transsexual.

THE ETIOLOGY OF TRANSSEXUALISM

Where does such a deep disorder come from? What sorts of events must conspire in order for a physically normal girl to be convinced that she is really a boy or a boy to feel that he is a girl? The answers are very speculative but there are two sets of factors that might disrupt sexual identity, and both of these occur very early in life.

FETAL HORMONES

In the course of a normal pregnancy, the fetus is bathed in a variety of hormones. These hormones modulate physical growth, bodily differentiation, and psychological growth as well. Fetal hormones may influence the way we think and act, and evidence for this comes from the rare, but theoretically important, phenomenon of hermaphroditism.

Pseudo-hermaphrodites are chromosomally female (46XX). But if hormonally masculinized as a fetus, they are born with ambiguous-looking genitals. Either because of genetic defect or because of drugs taken by the mother during pregnancy, some fetuses receive too much *androgen* while they are in the uterus. Hormonal androgenization is principally responsible for the masculinized development of the external genitals in the male. When a female is fetally androgenized, upon birth her clitoris is enlarged and penis-like, and her vagina may be partially sealed off. When the diagnosis is promptly made the vaginal opening is brought to the exterior, and the clitoris is surgically feminized in early infancy. Such females are raised as girls. If the external masculinization is complete, with a penis in an empty scrotum, such a baby may be raised as a boy. Subsequently, circumstances may conspire, and such a child may, on rare occasions, request sex reassignment. Figure 13-1 shows a desperate note from a twelve-year-old child to his doctor expressing the realization of a need for a sex reassignment.

John Money, one of America's leading sex researchers, intensively studied thirty fetally androgenized hermaphrodites, raised in the female role, as children and as adolescents. He found that when compared to girls matched for IQ, race, and class, these girls differed psychologically along several stereotyped dimensions of masculinity and femininity. They expressed more dissatisfaction with the female sex role, they had more athletic interest and skills, they preferred male companions, and they wore slacks, rather than dresses, more often than the controls. These findings lead us to conclude that some stereotyped sex-role behavior may be determined in the uterus by fetal hormones (Money and Ehrhardt, 1972; Money, Schwartz, and Lewis,

Hormonal androgenization

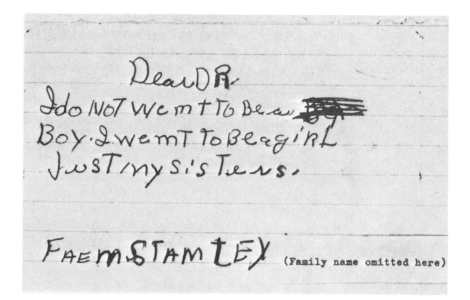

Figure 13-1
The note written by a twelve-year-old boy who wished to have a sex change. (Money and Ehrhardt, 1972)

1983). None of these girls believed they were boys, but some researchers have speculated that in the prenatal history of transsexuals a hormonal or related biochemical error affecting sexual pathways in the brain must have occurred. But no proof has yet been forthcoming.

REARING PRACTICES

Effect of parents on child's sexual identity

How parents treat a young child affects the sexual identity of the child. What would happen to a male child who was given a girl's name, dressed as a girl, and introduced to friends, relatives, and other children as a girl? Parents of a pre-transsexual child are usually ambivalent about what to do. They put off decisions and ultimately panic when the gender disorder doesn't go away. But whether this is a cause or a consequence of the child's transsexualism is unknown. The accidental loss of a penis by one of two identical twins in early childhood provides some evidence that how a child is raised by his or her parents may influence sexual identity. The rearing of this child is described below:

> A terrible accident took place in the life of one of two identical twins when he was seven months old. As he was being circumcised, his entire penis was burned off by a faulty electrical device. After medical and psychological advice, the parents decided to rear the child as a girl, starting at seventeen months of age. But would his sexual identity change? Would he, in spite of his male internal organs, male hormones *in utero*, and seventeen months of being treated as a boy, ever come to feel, act, and have the sexual desires of a girl? At twenty-one months, plastic surgery was undertaken and the appearance of a vagina constructed. The parents, in consultation with the surgeon and psychiatrists, decided to rear the child in the most female-stereotyped way: clothes and hairdo were feminized, and the child was given pink shirts, frilly blouses, bracelets, and hair ribbons. Within a year the little child clearly preferred dresses over slacks, and was proud of her long hair. She became much neater and daintier than her twin brother. Her mother taught her to squat while urinating, unlike her brother who stood. For the next few years, the mother began to prepare the child to become a wife and housekeeper, and the child began to imitate her mother in the housekeeping role. The little girl now preferred dolls and mother roles in play, while her male identical twin preferred toy cars and father roles in play.
>
> By the time the twins were almost six, they had a different vision of their future. "I found that my son chose very masculine things, like a fireman or policeman, or something like that. He wanted to do what Daddy does, work where Daddy does, and carry a lunch kit, and drive a car. And she didn't want any of those things. I asked her, and she said she wanted to be a doctor or a teacher. And I asked her, 'Well, did she have any plans that maybe someday she'd get married, like Mommy?' She'll get married someday—she wasn't too worried about that. She didn't think about that too much but she wants to be a doctor. But none of the things that she ever wanted to be were like a policeman or a fireman, and that sort of thing never appealed to her." (Money and Ehrhardt, 1972)
>
> The twins are now in adolescence and the indications are that the female twin, in spite of being genetically a male—shows some, but not all, the aspects of female role and identity. (Williams and Smith, 1980)

Unfortunately, the twins have been lost to follow-up because of media intrusiveness (Money, personal communication, July 15, 1987). But it is possible, but unproven, that rearing conditions, particularly while the child is very young, and in individuals who are predisposed—perhaps by fetal hormones—may influence sexual identity. The future may hold a way of identifying hormonally vulnerable children and then paying special attention to appropriate rearing conditions. Since we know that transsexualism, once acquired, is very difficult to reverse, the need for a preventative technique of this sort is acute.

THERAPY OF TRANSSEXUALISM: SEX-CHANGE OPERATIONS

Sex-change operations

Transsexualism does not spontaneously change in the lifetime of the transsexual. Also conventional therapies have only very rarely been able to reverse it (see Barlow, Abel, and Blanchard, 1979, for the single report of reversal of transsexualism—by exorcism). In spite of this, there is some hope for transsexuals today. Sex-change operations, while still imperfect, allow transsexuals to get the genitals they desire and to marry. As we have seen normal sexual identity is shaped both by biological conditions, such as what hormones we are exposed to in the womb, and by environmental conditions, such as people reacting to us as male or female. Therapy for transsexuals consists of changing the external reproductive organs by surgery; in addition, this change is supported by social, vocational, domestic, and bodily changes in an attempt to shore up the new gender status.

Therapists treating a transsexual who is a candidate for sex-change surgery often require that the person first live for two years in the new gender role. If after two years of passing for and being treated as a female or male, the individual still wants surgery, the psychological hazards of the surgery are probably lessened. Those who are schizophrenic, delusional, or otherwise emotionally disordered should probably not undertake it (Money and Ambinder, 1978).

Hormonal treatment and surgery

Bodily changes are prerequisite to sex-change surgery. In male-to-female sex changes, there is a combination of hormonal treatment to make the breasts grow and make facial hair disappear, and surgery to remove the penis and transform it into a vagina. Because the skin of the penis is used to line the vagina, sexual intercourse—when the surgery is successful—is erotically pleasurable. Orgasm is a warm, sometimes spasmodic, glow through the body.

In female-to-male sex-change operations, the surgery is much more complicated and extensive. It involves multiple operations that take place over several years. First, hormonal treatment suppresses menstruation, deepens the voice, and causes growth of facial and body hair. Then surgery is performed to remove the breasts, the ovaries, and rarely to construct a penis. The capacity of orgasm is always retained, but such a penis cannot become erect, and a prosthetic device has to be used for sexual intercourse.

Follow-up after sex-change operations

There has not been a massive and well-controlled follow-up of patients who have undergone sex-change operations. In one eight-year follow-up of seventeen male transsexuals after sex-change surgery, modest gains in working and interpersonal relationships occurred, as well as larger gains in sexual satisfaction. Level of psychological disturbance did not change, however (Hunt and Hampson, 1980).

Some clinicians claim that when the two-year trial period in the role of the desired sex precedes the operations, patients always benefit from the surgery, both in their sense of well-being and in their ability to love. Job status improves, sexual relationships tend to be more stable, and patients indicate that if they had to do it over again—even though the surgical outcome may have been disappointing—they would do so (Money and Ambinder, 1978).

But there is disagreement about this. In a follow-up of fourteen patients operated on at UCLA, almost all of the patients had had surgical complications. Urination was frequently difficult and sexual intercourse often proved impossible. One patient committed suicide after surgery, and some of the others became depressed and apathetic (Stoller, 1976).

On balance, sex-change operations seem to provide the best—indeed the only—hope, at present, for transsexuals. As surgical techniques improve, the operation is apt to become more satisfactory, although even then the transsexual must cope with other problems of adjustment. But because there seems to be no alternative but despair, sex-change operations seem to be the therapy of choice.

SUMMARY

1. There are three basic classes of sexual problems: the *sexual dysfunctions,* the *paraphilias,* and *transsexualism.*

2. The scientific study of sexual behavior has illuminated both how the body works during sexual arousal and what the frequency of a variety of sexual acts is.

3. The human sexual response is similar in both men and women and consists of three phases: *erotic desire and arousal; excitement,* which consists of penile erection or vaginal lubrication; and *orgasm.* Any or all of these three phases of sexual response can be disordered.

4. The *sexual dysfunctions* consist of impairment of desire, excitement, or orgasm. In women, these are manifested by insufficient desire, lack of excitement in sexual intercourse, and infrequent or absent orgasm. In men, there is lack of erection, *premature ejaculation,* and *retarded ejaculation.*

5. There is hope for all these conditions, and the work of Masters and Johnson, using *direct sexual therapy* and *sensate focus,* suggests that many, if not most of these sexual dysfunctions, may be curable or greatly improved in a short period of time.

6. The *paraphilias* consist of sexual desires for unusual and bizarre objects. They include sexual arousal to nonhuman objects, most commonly *fetishes,* and *transvestism.* They also include *sadomasochism*—sexual arousal in situations that produce suffering and humiliation—and *exhibitionism, voyeurism,* and *child molesting*—sexual arousal with nonconsenting partners.

7. The paraphilias are often lifelong, and they may have their origin in *cathexes,* or emotional binding, which is then reinforced and potentiated by masturbatory fantasies about the object.

8. It is difficult to change the paraphilias in therapy, but recent behavior therapy techniques have had some success.

9. *Transsexualism* is a disorder of men who believe they are really women trapped in men's bodies and of women who feel that they are really men trapped in women's bodies. These individuals want to get rid of their genitals and live in the opposite sex role. Sex-change operations provide some relief for this most distressing condition.

Psychoactive Substance Use Disorders

Joseph R. Volpicelli, M.D., PH.D.

Joseph R. Volpicelli, M.D., PH.D.

S UBSTANCE abuse is the leading health problem in the United States. This problem is aggravated by the fact that most substance abusers do not receive treatment for their disorder and many are not even aware that they have a serious health problem. A major source of this contradiction no doubt reflects the denial that many substance abusers show, a denial eased by the tacit sanction by society of drug use. For example, although alcohol dependence decreases one's life expectancy by twelve years, the media positively represents drinking by showing young, healthy participants.

Emotional and
financial costs of
substance abuse

Not only does substance abuse cause severe health problems for the individual, but the behavioral consequences of substance abuse lead to emotional and financial difficulties for the family and society. Alcohol dependence alone costs $120 billion a year in health costs, lost hours of work, and legal consequences. About half of all suicides occur when the person is intoxicated, and over half of all fatal car accidents occur when one of the drivers is impaired by alcohol or other drugs. The spread of AIDS into the heterosexual community is largely a result of the transmission of the AIDS virus from IV drug use. What is it about drugs that makes people risk their life to use these substances and society blind to its problems? In this chapter we will begin to understand the powerful motivating properties of drugs from a biobehavioral perspective. We will discuss *pharmacology*, which is the study of drugs, their actions on cells, and physiological processes and *psychopharmacology*, which is that part of pharmacology that studies drug effects on the cells of the brain. We will see that *psychoactive drugs* act on the brain to produce changes in mood, perceptions, or behavior, and that in general, psychoactive drugs interact with brain *neurotransmitters*, substances released by nerve cells to communicate with other nerve cells. We begin with a discussion of what is considered to be drug abuse.

DIAGNOSING DRUG ABUSE

The use of psychoactive drugs is common in our society and not necessarily considered maladaptive. For example, most adults drink alcohol at social functions, and many finish off a meal with a cigarette. Drugs have been used since recorded history as part of religious functions. Psychoactive drugs are used medically to treat depression, anxiety, and pain. Most of us would not quarrel that the above examples do not constitute substance abuse, so when does the use of drugs become a disorder?

The use of psychoactive drugs is common in our society; most adults drink alcohol at social functions.

CULTURAL VARIATIONS

There are wide cultural variations in what is considered the maladaptive use of drugs. For example, in some cultures a glass of wine at dinner is considered a natural way to enjoy dinner but any displays of drunkenness are considered socially inappropriate. Other cultures forbid the use of any psychoactive drug. Still others, encourage the use of illegal drugs as an important part of a sacred, mystical experience. A common joke in the medical profession is that an alcoholic is "someone who drinks more alcohol than his doctor."

The incidence of drug abuse differs widely across different cultures. For example, alcohol dependence is particularly high among the northern Europeans and Irish but less prevalent among the Mediterranean cultures, particularly among the Jews. There are several theories to explain this cultural variability. While the use of alcohol is not discouraged among the Jews, the uncontrolled drinking of alcohol carries negative social sanctions. In contrast, other cultures celebrate the use of alcohol to console hurt feelings and may encourage drunkenness in folk songs. Finally, people in some cultures may be protected against alcohol dependence because they lack a form of the enzyme that breaks down alcohol. Many Orientals, for example, will develop facial flushing and an unpleasant reaction when they drink alcohol because of this enzyme defect.

DSM-III-R CRITERIA

Historically defining substance abuse

Historically, clinicians and researchers who have studied substance abuse have also found it difficult to define substance abuse. Terms such as "psychological" and "physical dependence" tried to differentiate people who had lost control of their drug use and developed psychosocial problems (drug abuse), from individuals who depended on the drug to overcome physical withdrawal symptoms (drug addiction). Since drugs such as cocaine did not appear to have physical withdrawal symptoms, by this definition one could not have a cocaine addiction. But since people using cocaine appeared to have many of the same problems as people dependent on other drugs it made little sense to say cocaine could not cause dependence. Therefore, in 1987 a committee of substance abuse experts revised the old DSM-III definitions of substance use disorders to broaden the range of drug dependence. The presence of physical withdrawal symptoms or the demonstration of physical tolerance was no longer necessary to qualify for a diagnosis of drug dependence. Also, the term "drug abuse" was reserved as a residual category for patients with episodic problems associated with substance use. According to the DSM-III-R classification, ***drug dependence*** is defined by the regular use of drugs that act on the brain and that lead to maladaptive behavioral changes that would be seen as maladaptive in any culture. The nine criteria are presented in Box 14-1, and can generally be broken down into three criteria: (1) a person has lost control over his use of the substance; (2) drug use is associated with impairment in occupational, social, physical, or emotional functioning; and (3) there is evidence of affective or physical adaptation to the drug.

DSM-III-R criteria

The manifestation of loss of control over one's drug use is given by the first three criteria presented in Box 14-1. For example, people who have lost control over drug use will often walk into a bar, planning to have just one drink after work, but they do not leave the bar until five or six drinks are taken. Thus, larger amounts of the drug are taken than intended. Another characteristic of drug abuse is that the person recognizes the maladaptive consequences of his drug use, but he is unable to cut down for substantial periods of time. Finally, loss of control over drug use is manifested by over-involvement with the drug, such that much of the day is occupied with efforts to obtain the drug or recover from the ill effects of the drug.

As one might expect, with loss of control over drug use, this maladaptive behavior will lead to interference with occupational, social, physical, or emotional functioning. This is often associated with interference with job, school, or home responsibilities because of drug intoxication or withdrawal symptoms. For example, a student may miss class on Mondays because of recovering from the cocaine crash. A person may decide to give up job, social, or recreational activities because of preoccupation with drug use. A person may also continue to use the drug despite knowledge that drug use is interfering with emotional or physical health or social relations. Thus, someone may continue to smoke cigarettes despite warnings from his doctor that the cigarettes contribute to asthma symptoms.

Loss of control over drug or alcohol use may lead to interference with occupational, social, physical, or emotional functioning.

Box 14-1   NEW RULES FOR DRUG DEPENDENCE

The 1987 version of the *Diagnostic and Statistical Manual of Mental Disorders* (DSM-III-R), published by the American Psychiatric Association, lists diagnostic criteria for psychoactive substance dependence, which includes dependence on alcohol, cocaine, and other drugs. The new measures are less rigid than those given in the 1980 version of the manual and are as follows.

A. At least three of the following:

(1) substance often taken in larger amounts or over a longer period than the person intended

(2) persistent desire or one or more unsuccessful efforts to cut down or control substance use

(3) a great deal of time spent in activities necessary to get the substance (e.g., theft), taking the substance (e.g., chain smoking), or recovering from its effects

(4) frequent intoxication or withdrawal symptoms when expected to fulfill major role obligations at work, school, or home (e.g., does not go to work because hung over, goes to work or school "high," intoxicated while taking care of his or her children), or when substance use is physically hazardous (e.g., drives when intoxicated)

(5) important social, occupational, or recreational activities given up or reduced because of substance use

(6) continued substance use despite knowledge of having a persistent or recurrent social, psychological, or physical problem that is caused or exacerbated by the use of the substance (e.g., keeps using heroin despite family arguments about it, cocaine-induced depression, or having an ulcer made worse by drinking)

(7) Marked tolerance: need for markedly increased amounts of the substance (i.e., at least a 50 percent increase) in order to achieve intoxication or desired effect, or markedly diminished effect with continued use of the same amount

Note: The following items may not apply to cannabis, hallucinogens, or phencyclidine (PCP):

(8) characteristic withdrawal symptoms (see specific withdrawal symptoms under Psychoactive Substance-induced Organic Mental Disorders)

(9) substance often taken to relieve or avoid withdrawal symptoms

B. Some symptoms of the disturbance have persisted for at least one month, or have occurred repeatedly over a longer period of time.

Source: DSM-III-R, 1987.

Finally, regular drug use can lead to affective or physical adaptation to the drug. This is shown by evidence of drug tolerance, withdrawal, or the use of drugs to decrease or prevent withdrawal symptoms. **Drug tolerance** refers to the need to use increased amounts of the drug to get the desired effect. Drug tolerance can occur not only to the physical effects of the drug, such as incoordination following alcohol use, but also to the subjective effects of the drug such as the "high" from narcotics. For some people, tolerance to the drug "high" occurs before tolerance to the physical effects of the drug, and this can lead to a dangerous escalation of drug use. **Drug withdrawal** refers to characteristic affective and physical symptoms that follow drug use. The cocaine crash and alcohol hangover are examples of withdrawal symptoms. Some people may not experience withdrawal symptoms because they redose on the drug to avoid or decrease the withdrawal symptoms. Many cigarette smokers fail to experience significant withdrawal symptoms because they redose at frequent intervals. It is important to note that according to the DSM-III-R criteria, it is possible that people may have both physical tolerance and withdrawal symptoms and still not meet the criteria for substance dependence. An example of this occurs when a person has been chronically treated with narcotics for pain but has no desire to redose when the drug is being withdrawn.

SUBSTANCE DEPENDENCE

Why drug abuse?

How is it that people go from psychoactive drug use to drug abuse? Clearly, substance abuse is associated with severe physical, emotional, financial, and social problems. Why then do people abuse drugs? This question can be broken down into two complementary approaches to understanding drug dependence: (1) What unique components of a person's physiological and psychological makeup make him vulnerable to drug dependency? (2) Is there something about psychoactive drugs that makes people dependent on them? We will now examine each of these questions.

VULNERABILITY FACTORS

While the psychopharmacologists have taught us a great deal about the interactions of drugs with the brain's neurochemistry, it is important to realize that drugs interact with whole persons. One's cultural and personal beliefs help determine if and how we will be exposed to drugs. Drug effects are superimposed on one's preexisting personality and biochemical makeup.

PERSONALITY FACTORS

Disproving the oral-dependent personality

The search for common factors among substance-abusing individuals has conflicting and inconclusive results. It was formerly thought that substance abusers had some personality flaw that made them prone to become dependent on just about any drug. The concept of oral-dependent personality was developed. These individuals presumably were quite emotionally immature, chronically lonely, dependent on their mothers, and ambivalent to authority figures. These people apparently reduced anxiety by oral stimulation and were prone to become dependent on alcohol, cigarettes, and caffeine. This personality was thought to be caused by a lack of appropriate maternal bonding at an early developmental stage. Empirical attempts to predict vulnerable people from this model have not been reliable.

Antisocial personality

More recently, links between antisocial personality in adolescence and later drug use, especially alcohol abuse, have been established (Nathan, 1988). In general, behaviors such as rejection of rules, poor impulse control, hyperactivity, and poor regard for established institutions predict later substance abuse. Yet, these antisocial behaviors may not reflect an enduring personality flaw that causes people to be more vulnerable to dependence.

Rather, people with these behaviors are more likely to be exposed to drugs and to sample their use. We are still left with the problem of why only a small fraction of people who experiment with drugs become substance abusers.

BIOLOGICAL VULNERABILITY

Genetics and biological vulnerability

People may also be at risk for abusing substances because of some biological vulnerability transmitted genetically. Alcohol dependence, for example, is four times more likely in the offspring of alcohol-dependent parents. This relationship holds up even when the biological children of alcohol-dependent parents are adopted into families that are not alcohol dependent. Also, children without a biological parent who is alcohol dependent do *not* have an increased incidence of alcohol dependence when adopted into homes with alcohol-dependent parents. Thus, increased risk follows from one's biological makeup not from the environment. It is not clear how biological factors may make one more likely to become dependent. It may be that much of substance abuse is a form of self-medication. Someone born with a deficiency in some neurotransmitter may find that psychoactive drugs compensate for this biological defect. For example, one patient claimed that only when she used PCP did she become "normal" and able to talk with friends and family. Now let us turn to the second approach to explaining substance dependence: the properties of the drugs.

Basic Effects of Drugs

What is it about psychoactive drugs that makes people dependent on them? Different psychoactive drugs have different properties and effects. Nonetheless, certain mechanisms are the same across all classes of drugs. Before discussing each drug in turn we will consider certain basic effects, which occur regardless of which drug is ingested.

DRUG EFFECTIVENESS AND POTENCY

The relative effectiveness and potency of all psychoactive drugs depend on three properties: (1) the route of administration, (2) the ability of the drug to enter the brain, and (3) the rate at which a drug is deactivated.

In order to interact with the brain nerve cells, it is necessary for drugs to get to the brain. The speed and amount of drug that gets to the brain depends on the route of drug administration. For example, drugs taken by mouth must first be absorbed by the gut and then must pass the liver before reaching the brain. Since the liver can break down drugs, much of the drug may not make it to the brain. In contrast, inhaled drugs are quickly absorbed by the lungs and transported directly from the heart to the brain before passing the liver. Thus, the drug more effectively reaches the brain and produces a faster psychoactive effect. Drugs that cannot be inhaled can also be efficiently taken by nasal inhalation (*snorting*) or by direct injection into the vein (*mainlining*).

Once the drug gets to the brain, it must still cross the *blood-brain barrier*, a protective device that keeps many chemicals from going from the bloodstream to brain cells. Thus, the more easily a drug passes the blood-brain

Inhaled drugs (such as the nicotine in tobacco) are quickly absorbed in the lungs and transported to the brain.

barrier, the more potent and faster acting its psychoactive effect. For example, both heroin and morphine have similar psychoactive effects, but heroin more easily crosses the blood-brain barrier. Heroin, therefore, produces a quicker, more intense high when given in the same dose as morphine.

Rate of
deactivation of
drug

The duration of a drug effect depends on the *rate of deactivation*—the time it takes for the drug to be broken down. The speed of deactivation is usually expressed as a drug's *half-life*, that is, the time it takes the body to deactivate 50 percent of the drug. In general, drugs with a short half-life lead to many peaks and valleys in their psychoactive effects and, therefore, lead to more problems with frequent periods of intoxication and withdrawal. Heroin, with its short half-life, must be used four to six times per day to prevent withdrawal symptoms, whereas methadone, with its long half-life, can be taken just once a day.

Fat solubility of
drug

Another property that determines the duration of drug effect is the ability of the drug to be stored in fat cells, its *fat solubility*. A drug such as THC (the active chemical in marijuana) is stored in fat cells and released so slowly that traces of the drug can be measured in the blood thirty days after the drug was used.

INTERACTION OF DRUGS AND BRAIN REWARD MECHANISMS

The search for
endorphins

Presumably there is some biochemical basis for the underlying psychoactive effects of drugs. Psychopharmacologists have discovered that psychoactive substances mimic the action of the brain's endogenous (naturally produced) compounds that produce pleasure. For example, in 1973, it was discovered that the brains of mammals contain receptors for opiates. Why do the brains of mammals contain receptors for a compound that comes from a plant? It was hypothesized that endogenous morphine-like substances were produced in animals and that their receptors actually exist for these substances. Thus, a search for endogenous morphine (*endorphins*) began. A year later, several labs simultaneously reported the existence of endogenous opioids (opiate-like compounds). There are several types of endogenous opioids ranging in size from small five amino acid compounds termed *enkephalins* to large proteins such as *beta-endorphins*.

Endorphins and
uncontrollable
stress

The reason why animal brains produce endorphins is still being investigated. The pharmacological effect of opiates on emotional and physical pain and the observation that endorphins are released during uncontrollable stress suggest one mechanism. In Chapter 11, we discussed the learned helplessness phenomena (see pp. 336–39). Organisms exposed to uncontrollable events exhibit a range of affective, behavioral, and physiological changes brought about from the cognition that they have no control over some bad event. One of the important physiological changes is the release of endorphins. Just as the release of certain chemicals (e.g., ACTH and corticosteroids) is thought to prepare the organism for the "fight or flight" response, the release of endorphins gives the animal "no pain from bites." That is, if injured, the organism is not so incapacitated that it is unable to defend itself. This stress-induced analgesia is also apparent in humans. Many anecdotal reports have shown that wartime or sports injuries often go unnoticed during the stress of battle. Only the following day does one realize the pain of the injury.

Opioid receptors
in the brain

The use of opiates appears to mimic the affective and physiological effects of endorphins by attaching to opioid receptors in the brain that normally bind with endorphins. The psychoactive effects of opiates is a function of activity at the opioid receptor. For example, the intensity and duration of a high from a drug like heroin is a direct function of the concentration and half-life of the drug at the opioid receptor. If the receptor is blocked by an opiate antagonist such as naloxone or naltrexone, the affective and physical effects produced by opiates are also blocked. Other psychoactive drugs also interact with brain receptors by either directly stimulating the receptor as do opiates and nicotine (found in tobacco) or by stimulating the release of endogenous neurotransmitters as does amphetamine. It appears that all psychoactive drugs have an intimate relationship with one or more neurotransmitter systems, which in turn affects our mood, perceptions, or behavior.

ACQUIRED MOTIVATION

Motivation to use
drugs increases
with use

The phenomena of dependence are illustrated by a common experience with corn chips. While the first corn chip tastes good, the motivation to eat subsequent corn chips *increases* after one eats them (it's hard to open a bag of corn chips and eat just one). In contrast, for other types of pleasurable foods, grapes for example, the motivation to eat the food *decreases* over time. Consider the awkward state of affairs if you consistently became more hungry as you ate dinner. Psychoactive drugs (and for some people, corn chips), however, have exactly this effect. Once rats learn to bar press for cocaine, they will continue to bar press to the exclusion of sleeping, sex, food, and water. Indeed, rats will eventually die if the cocaine remains available. This increase in desire to use the drug (or eat corn chips) is acquired in the sense that one is not born craving drugs, but rather the motivation to use drugs increases as one uses the drug.

This property of increased motivation to use a drug with continued use can be understood by the ***opponent-process model of addiction.*** This model,

The opponent-process model assumes that a drug will produce affective pleasure (that is, in the case of heroin, calm euphoria, pictured on the left), affective tolerance, and affective withdrawal (panicky, unpleasant feelings, pictured on the right).

Three common
properties of
drugs that
produce
dependence

developed by Richard Solomon (Solomon, 1977), assumes that all drugs that produce dependence have three common properties. First, for each drug, the initial pharmacological effect produced by the drug is a pleasant emotional state, or *affective pleasure.* The affective pleasure differs across the various classes of drugs. For example, the initial effects of narcotics such as heroin are subjective feelings of calm euphoria. In contrast, cocaine produces an emotional rush characterized by increased self-esteem and energy. In both cases, however, the initial pharmacological effects are pleasurable.

A second common property of addictive drugs is *affective tolerance.* With continued use, the drug tends to lose its affective pleasure. Often people with drug abuse problems will attempt to compensate for tolerance by increasing the dose of the drug to maintain the same pleasurable feeling they had when they initially took the drug. Although at first an individual may have needed only two or three drinks to feel high, after many years of abusing alcohol he may need eight to twelve drinks to get the same effect. In the case of cocaine, some individuals report that it is impossible to duplicate the high of the first-time rush. Thus, tolerance can be manifested by either diminished affective pleasure to the same dose of drug or the use of higher doses of the drug to achieve the same effect.

The third common property of drugs of abuse, *affective withdrawal,* is related to tolerance. As the initial effect of narcotics produces a calm euphoria, the sudden termination of narcotics often produces the opposite affective state: dysphoria (panicky, unpleasant feelings). Not only does chronic drug use lead to decreased affective pleasure, but it also results in increased withdrawal reactions. Since a narcotic-abusing individual may develop severe physical and emotional symptoms when narcotics are no longer available, with time the motivation to use drugs may switch from obtaining a pleasurable high to removing the withdrawal symptoms. Of course, different drugs have different withdrawal symptoms. But in general, the withdrawal symptoms are opposite to the initial effects of the drug. For example, if one experiences a pleasurable cocaine rush from the initial use of cocaine, then a cocaine crash, consisting of decreased energy and depression, is the predicted (and observed) withdrawal reaction.

The opponent-
process model

Solomon proposes that the three properties outlined above can be modeled by a negative feedforward opponent-process system. Initially, all psychoactive drugs activate some primary affective process (Process A). The dose and duration of action of the psychoactive drug affects the strength and duration of Process A. Thus, drugs that are slowly broken down by the body are associated with a correspondingly long Process A. Similarly, a higher dose of drug produces a correspondingly larger Process A. Process A in turn stimulates an opposing compensatory process (Process B), which produces affective states opposite to those of Process A.

When one takes an addictive drug, Process A and Process B summate, (see Figure 14-1). Typically, during the initial encounter with the drug, the summation produces a pleasurable affective experience (State A). This occurs because Process A quickly reaches its peak and then diminishes as the drug is broken down by the body. But if we look at the drug effect over time, we see a gradual rising of Process B as it sluggishly tracks the response of Process A. At some point, the dominant process in summation will be

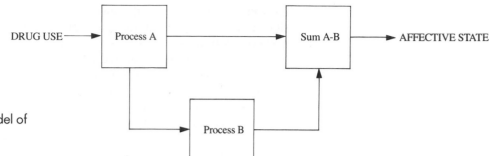

Figure 14-1
The opponent-process model of addiction

Process B, resulting in an unpleasant B-State. Minute by minute, as the two processes continue to add up, the affective experience of the drug taker at any given time will be the result of whichever process is winning out (see Figure 14-2). This model also assumes that with continued drug use, Process B gets stronger. In this way, the drug gradually loses its ability to produce pleasure, and affective tolerance is observed. This adaptation phase continues as long as the individual continues to use the drug. When the individual stops the drug, Process A quickly dies out, and Process B, which is now unopposed, is observed. This rebound after-reaction quickly reaches a peak and then gradually fades. The after-reaction accounts for the affective withdrawal observed with substance dependence.

Pleasure followed by withdrawal craving

From this model, we can see how psychoactive drugs can produce the "corn chip effect." After one eats a corn chip, the initial affective state is pleasure followed by a period of withdrawal craving. While the first corn chip may have been innocently eaten to obtain a small amount of pleasure, subsequent corn chips are eaten to remove the withdrawal craving. The more corn chips one eats, the more intense the withdrawal craving. In this way, one is locked into a vicious cycle. Usually, the only way to stop the pattern is when the chips are all gone. The temporal dynamics differ greatly with different addictive substances. Thus, it may only take ten minutes to

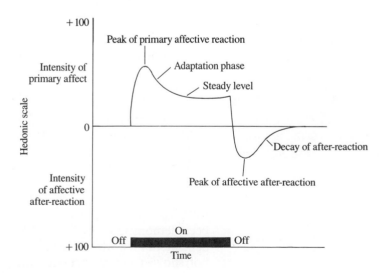

Figure 14-2
Standard pattern of affective dynamics

recover from the chip "withdrawal," but days to recover from alcohol withdrawal. This pattern of abuse, however, appears to be present in virtually all addictive substances.

The additive cycle

The phenomenon of acquired motivation comes about not because the drug feels good, but because the opposing compensatory process feels bad when the drug is no longer present. Once a person learns that the bad feeling can be overcome by taking the drug again, an addictive cycle is created. This addictive cycle accounts for the loss of control over drug use and the neglect of psychosocial responsibilities one observes in drug-dependent individuals. From this model we would predict that drugs with relatively short half-lives and more intense drug withdrawals (B-States) will make it easy to acquire drug dependence.

CONDITIONED CRAVING

If the addictive cycle described above was the only explanation for addictions, then it would be a simple matter to treat substance dependence. We would simply withhold the substance until Process B craving ran its course. Unfortunately, as we know from treating patients with substance dependence, the task is not so simple. Just as one may get corn chip craving when passing the store where corn chips are usually purchased, relapse to other substances often occurs in settings formerly associated with using the substance.

Drug reminder cues

Abraham Wikler (1948) first observed that drug-dependent patients would often have increased drug craving and opiate withdrawal symptoms (e.g., runny nose, sweating, stomach cramps) during group therapy when one of the members described in vivid detail the setting associated with drug use. Wikler suggested that learned associations (drug cues) between the environment and drug use continue to elicit craving for drugs, long after drug detoxification. These drug reminder cues set the occasion for drug relapse. For example, while in-patient treatment of narcotic dependence often effectively reduces the patients' craving for narcotics, when these patients are back in their old neighborhood, they again experience drug craving. In contrast to the difficulty of remaining free from narcotics when returning to a familiar environment, most of the men who used drugs in Vietnam stopped when they returned home. Only 5 percent continued heavy narcotic use.

Situations associated with drug use can elicit compensatory opponent processes, which explains conditioned craving. In situations in which a person expects to receive a drug, the body apparently acts to counter the drug's primary effect (see Figure 14-3). For example, if an alcohol-dependent person walks into a bar, the setting may elicit a conditioned withdrawal (Process B) and increased craving for alcohol.

Experiments in humans and animals clearly demonstrate these conditioned craving and withdrawal reactions for a variety of psychoactive substances. Shepard Segal (1977) has demonstrated that rats injected with morphine in an environment associated with drug injections will be tolerant to morphine's pain-relieving effects. Conditioned craving for alcohol has been demonstrated by Richard Kaplan and his colleagues (1985). Alcohol-dependent men who observed a beer can or consumed near beer (0% alcohol) showed increased craving and physiological arousal. These conditioned craving responses are greater as one becomes dependent on alcohol and less

When recovered drug addicts return to their old neighborhood, they often again experience drug craving due to learned associations between the environment and drug use.

S (stimulus) —————————▶ R (response)

Drug   Pleasure

S + CS (conditioned stimulus)—————————▶ R + OP (opposing response)

Drug + Drug Cues   Mild Pleasure

CS —————————▶ OP

Drug Cues   Craving/Withdrawal

Figure 14-3
Conditioned craving

in problem drinkers. Charles O'Brien and his colleagues (1977) have demonstrated conditioned drug craving for narcotic reminder cues. Furthermore, by presenting these reminder cues over and over, the craving decreases. This procedure is similar to desensitization observed in treatment of phobias, and it may help prevent drug relapse. Now let us turn to specific substances of abuse.

ALCOHOL

Alcohol has been by far the most commonly used psychoactive substance throughout human history and in virtually every society. Not only is alcohol drinking a part of the religious customs of the Judeo-Christian culture, but it is also a part of the customs of cultures that have not had contact with other cultures for thousands of years. We toast the New Year with champagne and celebrate weddings with wine. Bars are an important gathering place for social interactions. Although alcohol drinking has decreased in recent years, two-thirds of all adults drink, and about one-third of high school seniors report having drunk heavily in the previous two weeks. In this section, we will consider why some people become dependent on alcohol, the important medical and social complications from alcohol dependence, and the treatment of alcohol dependence.

THEORIES OF ALCOHOL DEPENDENCE

Before we begin our discussion of theories of alcohol dependence it is important to note that alcohol abuse disorders represent a wide spectrum of degrees of abuse. For example, some alcohol-dependent individuals are binge drinkers and will go on drinking sprees perhaps only once a week, whereas other drinkers will use alcohol consistently throughout the day. Also, alcohol dependence may be associated with psychopathology such as antisocial personality disorder. Thus, theories of alcohol dependence may apply to only a particular subgroup of a heterogeneous group of disorders of which only alcohol abuse is the final result.

GENETICS AND ALCOHOL DRINKING

Alcohol dependence is familial. Adoption studies in Denmark have shown that sons of biological parents who are alcohol dependent have a four times

Bars are an important gathering place for social interactions; two-thirds of all adults drink.

Role of genetics

increased risk of alcohol dependence. In contrast, children adopted into homes in which one of the foster parents is dependent on alcohol do not have an increased risk of alcohol dependence (Goodwin, Schulsinger, Hermansen, Guze, and Winokur, 1973). This observation suggests that alcohol dependence is a genetic, inherited disorder and that environmental influences play little role in its development. This study defined alcohol dependence very narrowly, however, and when the spectrum of less severe forms of alcohol dependence (problem drinkers) is included, a different pattern of results is observed.

More recent adoption studies by Robert Cloninger and his colleagues (1985) suggest that there are two types of alcohol dependence characterized by different genetic factors. The first type is the "milieu-limited" form. It affects both men and women and involves an interaction between mild alcohol dependence in the parents and an impoverished home environment. The second type is "male-limited" alcohol dependence and as its name implies affects only males; this type does not seem to be influenced by environmental variables. This class is similar to the type of alcoholics studied by Donald Goodwin and his colleagues (1973). Cloninger further suggests that daughters of men with "male-limited" or "antisocial" types of alcohol dependence may have many physical complaints and a low pain threshold. These daughters often meet the criteria for somatization disorder.

Biological factors associated with alcohol dependence

Attempts to find what biological factor is associated with alcohol dependence have yielded several provocative findings. People who are at high risk for alcohol dependence because of alcohol dependence in a biological parent exhibit: (1) abnormal brain wave activity, suggesting poor attention (Begleiter, Porjesz, Bihari, and Kisson, 1984), and an increase in alpha wave activity after a moderate dose of alcohol (Propping, Kruger, and Mark, 1981); (2) normal overall IQ test scores, but poor performance on verbal subscales and attention (Tarter et al., 1984); and (3) delayed language development in the four-year-old sons of alcoholics (Tarter, Alterman, and Edwards, 1985). Thus, one risk factor for alcohol abuse may be a disorder in attentional/language abilities.

Genetic risk for alcohol dependence may be due to some neurological instability that is balanced by alcohol (see Tarter, Alterman, and Edwards, 1985, for a review). For example, the sons of alcohol-dependent fathers have increased body sway compared to nonalcoholic fathers when sober (Hegedus et al., 1984) but decreased body sway when intoxicated (Schuckit, 1987). Patients with an inherited disorder in which their hands shake, familial essential tremor, will have less tremor when drinking and a higher prevalence of alcohol dependence (Nasrallah, Schroeder, and Petty, 1982). Finally, while alcohol-dependent people do not have higher levels of arousal at baseline, when stressed they become more aroused as measured by heart rate and are slower to return to baseline (Coopersmith and Woodrow, 1967). Together these data suggest that people at risk for alcohol dependence inherit an impaired neurological homeostasis and that this neurological defect can be corrected in part by alcohol.

Genetic risk studies also suggest that people predisposed to become dependent on alcohol are more sensitive to the pleasure-producing effects of alcohol. The first drink in genetically high-risk individuals produces more profound euphoria (Nagoshi and Wilson, 1987), and alcohol drinking in early alcohol-dependent people produces more analgesia (Brown and Cutter, 1977). Also, the sons of alcohol-dependent fathers have increased levels of acetaldehyde after being given alcohol (Schuckit, 1987). Since acetaldehyde can combine with brain neurotransmitters to produce opiate-like compounds, this finding suggests a link between alcohol and opiates.

Interaction of genes and environment

While these high-risk and adoption studies demonstrate that genetic factors may be important in the etiology of alcohol dependence, it is also clear that much of the variability cannot be accounted for by genetic factors. John Searles (1988) has suggested that important genetic-environmental interactions need to be studied further since, unlike other genetic disorders, the expression of a genetic basis for alcohol dependence must include a learned behavior, that is, alcohol drinking. How one learns to use alcohol in a maladaptive way is addressed in the following theories of alcohol dependence.

TENSION REDUCTION HYPOTHESIS

One reason people may drink alcohol is to reduce tension. After a few experiences with alcohol, people learn that drinking reduces anxiety, and so they continue to drink and some begin to abuse alcohol. This notion has much intuitive appeal, and there are many clinical, epidemiological, and experimental studies that seem to support this theory. Let's look at a few of these.

Alcohol drinking to reduce anxiety and stress

First, clinical observations reveal a high association between alcoholism and anxiety. This association suggests anxious people drink alcohol to reduce anxiety. So, for example, anxiety symptoms often predate alcohol drinking, and phobic patients often report that they use alcohol as a means of coping with their phobia (Mullaney and Trippet, 1982). Also, clinicians often report that alcoholics often relapse after negative life events (Marlatt and Gordon, 1980).

Second, epidemiological studies reveal an association between alcohol drinking and cultural stress. One such study, using macro measures of life stress such as the number of divorces, births, etc., across the fifty states in the United States, found positive associations between life events and alcohol drinking (Linsky, Straus, and Colby, 1985).

Finally, experimental studies suggest that alcohol will dampen the effects of a stressful stimulus (see Levenson, Sher, Grossman, Newman, and Newlin, 1980). For example, experienced male drinkers treated with electric shock or social evaluation exhibited less anxiety, as measured by subjective and physiological indices, when they drank alcohol relative to placebo drinks.

People may drink alcohol to reduce tension, or alternatively, they may drink alcohol following stress, to compensate for reduced endorphin activity.

The experimental studies have also pointed out problems with the tension reduction hypothesis. If tension reduction is the primary reason people drink alcohol, then we would expect that people will increase their alcohol drinking when expecting or during tension-arousing situations. In contrast to this prediction of the tension reduction hypothesis, however, alcohol drinking increases *after* uncontrollable stress (the "weekend is made for Michelob" effect) and during conditions of relief from fear. For example, Volpicelli, Tiven, and Kimmel (1982) found that rats increase their alcohol preference *following* experiences with uncontrollable stress, and rats that live in a fearful environment drink less alcohol than rats returned to their home and a relaxing environment. Similarly, in a human experiment, subjects were given unsolvable problems. Half the subjects were told they did poorly and scored in the lower 15 percent of the class, whereas the other half were told they did well and scored in the upper 85 percent of their class. Subjects were then given the opportunity to drink alcohol. Subjects who thought they had performed well (tension relief condition) drank more alcohol than the other subjects. These studies suggest that it is not tension that increases alcohol drinking, but rather something about relief from tension that increases alcohol drinking.

Recent papers have attempted to revise the tension reduction hypothesis to account for these inconsistencies (see Sher, 1985). Perhaps, alcohol reduces tension only in certain situations (i.e., when there is social stress but not intrapersonal tension), at particular doses (i.e., low doses but not high doses), in a particular context (naturalistic but not experimental situations), and depending on the subject's expectations about alcohol's effect. Clearly, given the ad hoc explanations for the tension reduction hypothesis to predict alcohol's effect on tension or situations in which alcohol drinking increases, this model has lost much of its clinical utility. In contrast, several researchers suggest a new model of alcohol drinking based on alcohol's interaction with the opioid system.

ENDORPHIN COMPENSATION HYPOTHESIS

The endorphin compensation hypothesis, proposed by Volpicelli (1987), assumes that alcohol drinking increases endogenous opioid activity and that the desire to drink alcohol increases during conditions of deficiencies in endorphin activity. This model can explain why organisms increase alcohol drinking following stress. As previously discussed, uncontrollable stress stimulates the release of endorphins. If alcohol drinking compensates for deficiencies in endorphin activity, then organisms should not increase alcohol drinking during stress. As stress continues, however, compensatory opponent-process mechanisms are elicited, and a rebound deficiency in opiate receptor activity may occur. This may lead to increases in alcohol drinking to compensate for the reduction in endorphin activity (Volpicelli, 1987).

As discussed earlier in this chapter, our bodies produce endogenous opioids that bind to opiate receptors. These endogenous opioids produce an emotional "high" or reduce emotional and physical pain. Just as chronic narcotic use can induce compensatory changes in opiate receptor activity, chronic stimulation of opiate receptors by endogenous opioids may also induce compensatory changes. Thus, if alcohol drinking also increases endorphin activity, alcohol may produce a drug dependence similar to narcotic addiction.

There are several reasons to suggest that alcohol increases endorphinergic activity. Alcohol and narcotics: (1) have similar pharmacological and behavioral effects, (2) show cross-tolerance (animals tolerant to the effects of alcohol are tolerant to some of the effects of morphine and vice versa), and (3) have many of their pharmacological effects reduced by drugs that block the opiate receptor. These relationships are illustrated in Table 14-1.

Subjectively, both alcohol and narcotics produce feelings of contentment and a calm euphoria. Indeed, both alcohol-dependent and narcotic-dependent people report that the reason they use alcohol or narcotics is to obtain

Alcohol drinking may produce a drug dependence similar to narcotic addiction.

Table 14-1 RELATIONSHIPS BETWEEN ALCOHOL AND OPIATES

	Alcohol	*Opiates*
Subjective effects	feel "high" blunts dysphoria	euphoria blunts dysphoria
Pharmacological effects	suppresses morphine withdrawal	suppresses alcohol withdrawal
	if become tolerant to alcohol, tolerant to morphine	if become tolerant to morphine, tolerant to alcohol
	effects blocked by opiate antagonists	effects blocked by opiate antagonists
	may interact with opioid receptors	interacts with opioid receptors

this "high" (Cohen, 1976). The use of alcohol and narcotics reduces physical and emotional pain. For example, a small dose of alcohol blunts the biochemical changes elicited by uncontrollable stress in animals.

Chronic use of alcohol and narcotics leads to tolerance. So, for example, an individual experienced with narcotic use will need a larger dose of narcotics to produce the same "high" as a new user of narcotics. If alcohol and narcotics have a common mechanism of action, then tolerance to narcotics should lead to tolerance to at least some of the effects of alcohol. Animal studies demonstrate cross-tolerance between alcohol and narcotics. Both alcohol and narcotics reduce core body temperature. After chronic use of morphine, alcohol is also less potent in reducing core temperature (Blum, Hamilton, and Wallace, 1977). This tolerance is also present for alcohol despite the fact that animal subjects have received morphine and not previously experienced alcohol. Pharmacological cross-tolerance is also demonstrated by the observations that morphine suppresses alcohol withdrawal symptoms in animals (Blum, Wallace, Schwertner, and Eubanks, 1976) and that alcohol suppresses morphine withdrawal (Jones and Spratto, 1977).

Opiate receptor blockers such as naltrexone or naloxone block many of the effects of alcohol and narcotics. For example, large doses of alcohol will induce sleep, coma, and eventually death in animals and humans. Research studies in animals show that naloxone decreases alcohol-induced sleep and mortality from a large dose of alcohol (Ho and Ho, 1979). Several anecdotal reports suggest that naloxone can reverse alcohol-induced coma in humans, although this finding remains controversial.

Alcohol drinking increases when opiate receptor activity is low

If alcohol stimulates endorphin activity, then alcohol drinking should increase during times when opiate receptor activity is low, and drinking should decrease when opiate receptor activity is high. This endorphin compensation hypothesis further suggests conditions in which people are more likely to become dependent on alcohol and conditions in which abstinent alcoholics will relapse. Substantial human and animal data support this inverse relationship between alcohol drinking and endorphin activity (see Sinclair, 1974; Genazzani et al., 1982).

Many patients participating in alcohol treatment state that alcohol drinking only became a problem after they stopped using narcotics. For ex-

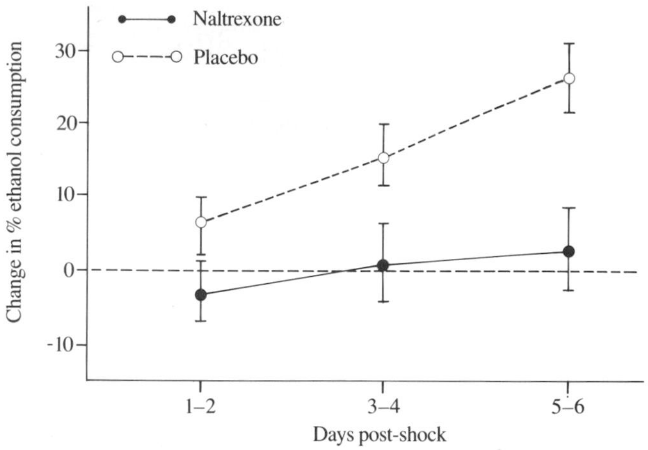

Figure 14-4
The effects on alcohol consumption of blocking opiate receptors with injections of an opiate antagonist, naltrexone.

ample, many heroin-dependent Vietnam veterans stopped narcotic use but became dependent on alcohol once they returned to the United States. Experimental studies in animals support these anecdotal reports (Volpicelli, 1987). Rats injected with low doses of morphine decreased alcohol preference. When the morphine injections stopped, a dramatic increase in alcohol preference was observed. In general, when opiate receptor activity is low (i.e., during morphine withdrawal), alcohol drinking increases, and when opiate receptor activity is high (i.e., during the acute administration of opiates), then alcohol drinking decreases.

The evidence presented above suggests that alcohol consumption compensates for deficiencies in opiate receptor activity. This deficiency can be brought about by prior use of narcotics (or alcohol), uncontrollable stress, or genetic predispositions. Therefore, by blocking opiate receptor activity with an opiate antagonist, alcohol consumption should no longer be effective in compensating for opiate receptor deficiencies, and alcohol drinking will decrease. Animals will reduce responding for alcohol if their opiate receptors are blocked with an opiate antagonist (Volpicelli, Davis and Olgin, 1986). For example, after having been exposed to the stress of electric shocks, the post-shock increase in alcohol drinking that typically occurs in rats is completely blocked by subcutaneous injections of naltrexone (see Figure 14-4).

MEDICAL AND SOCIAL COMPLICATIONS

Costs of alcohol use

The cost of our alcohol use is staggering. Alcohol dependence is one of the most common psychiatric diagnoses, with a lifetime prevalence rate of about 13 percent. As mentioned earlier, alcohol dependence cost the United States nearly $120 billion in 1983 in terms of lost productivity, health care, and legal costs. An alcohol-dependent individual loses about twelve years from his life-span. Alcoholism is the third leading public health problem in the United States, trailing only heart disease and cancer. About 40 percent of all hospital admissions are alcohol related. Alcohol is a poison to virtually every organ in the body, including the brain, peripheral nerves, heart, digestive system, and immune system. Alcohol intoxication is present in nearly half of all suicides, homicides, and accidental deaths. Severe complications from alcohol drinking result not only during the drinking episode but when alcohol is withdrawn.

INTOXICATION

Alcohol and disinhibition

In general, alcohol depresses central nervous system activity. At lower doses of alcohol, a paradoxical excitement or disinhibition is observed, since inhibitory brain centers are most easily depressed by alcohol. Alcohol's effect on sexual activity is a good example of this. At low doses of alcohol, one's sexual inhibitions are decreased, with alcohol stimulating sexual activity. At higher doses, alcohol depresses sexual responding and makes it more difficult to become aroused. As Shakespeare observed, ". . . it provokes the desire but it takes away the performance" (Macbeth). Other personality changes consistent with this disinhibition include increased expression of anger and decreased social anxiety. It is not clear to what extent alcohol pharmacologically produces these behavioral changes or if it simply gives one an excuse to do things that otherwise would produce conflict. When people believe they are drinking alcohol, but really drink a nonintoxicating placebo, there is more relief of social anxiety and increase in sexual arousal than in subjects who think they are drinking a nonintoxicating beverage but are actually drinking alcohol (Newlin, 1985). Clearly, one's expectations have important effects on behavior.

Alcohol in high doses, without doubt, interferes with coordination, and depresses motor and sensory functioning. At very high doses, alcohol can cause blackouts, unconsciousness, respiratory depression, and possibly death.

WITHDRAWAL

Some withdrawal effects

Everyone who has experienced a hangover following a bout of drinking has experienced alcohol withdrawal. Although for a non-alcohol-dependent person the thought of the resumption of drinking during a hangover may seem repugnant, alcohol will remove the withdrawal symptoms. This is known as "taking a hair of the dog that bit you." As we discussed earlier, using a substance to take away withdrawal from the substance sets up an addictive cycle that is characteristic of alcohol-dependent individuals. For someone who has been drinking heavily for several weeks, the withdrawal effects are more severe. If there is no drinking for twenty-four hours, the individual will experience increased sweating, shakes, poor appetite, difficulty sleeping, increased heart rate, and higher blood pressure. Emotionally, during this stage of alcohol withdrawal, a person will feel craving for alcohol and may feel depressed and anxious. Between twenty-four and forty-eight hours after the last drink, the central nervous system, which was previously depressed by the alcohol, exhibits irritability. At this stage, alcohol withdrawal seizures ("rum fits") occur. During the next two to seven days, one may experience hallucinations, usually visual and tactile. The most severe form of alcohol withdrawal symptoms is ***delirium tremens (DT's)***, where in addition to the symptoms described above, the individual experiences confusion, disordered memory, and disorientation. The following case history illustrates many of the adverse consequences of alcohol withdrawal:

A forty-three-year-old, divorced carpenter is examined in the hospital emergency observation ward. The patient's sister is available to provide some information. The sister reports that the patient has consumed large quantities of cheap wine daily for over five years. Evidently the patient had a reasonably stable home life and job record until his wife left him for another man five years previously. The sister indicates that the patient drinks more than a fifth of wine a day, and that this has been his unvarying pattern since the divorce. He often has had blackouts from drinking and has missed work; consequently, he has been fired from several jobs. Fortunately for him carpenters are in great demand, and he has been able to provide marginally for himself during these years. However, three days ago he ran out of money and wine and had to beg on the street to buy a meal. The patient has been poorly nourished, eating perhaps one meal a day and evidently relying on the wine as his prime source of nourishment.

The morning after his last day of drinking (three days ago), he felt increasingly tremulous, his hands shaking so grossly that it was difficult for him to light a cigarette. Accompanying this was an increasing sense of inner panic, which made him virtually unable to sleep. A neighbor became concerned about the patient when he seemed not to be making sense and clearly was unable to take care of himself. The neighbor contacted the sister, who brought him to the hospital.

On examination, the patient alternates between apprehension and chatty, superficial warmth. He is quite keyed up and talks almost constantly. At times he recognizes the doctor, but at other times he thinks the doctor is his older brother. Twice during the examination he calls the doctor by his older brother's name and asks when he arrived, evidently having lost track entirely of the interview up to that point. He has a gross hand tremor at rest, and there are periods when he picks at "bugs" he sees on the bed sheets. He is disoriented for time and thinks that he is in a supermarket parking lot rather than in a hospital. He indicates that he feels he is fighting against a terrifying sense that the world is ending in a holocaust. He is startled every few minutes by sounds and scenes of fiery car crashes (evidently provoked by the sound of rolling carts in the hall). Efforts at testing memory and calculation fail because his attention shifts too rapidly. (From DSM-III Casebook)

TREATMENT

Preventing relapse

A major concern of alcohol rehabilitation is to prevent relapse. In many programs, a thirty-day in-patient or day hospital program initiates the rehabilitation phase of treatment. Since many alcohol-dependent people often feel much better after alcohol treatment begins, issues of denial of alcohol-related problems must be confronted during this initial rehabilitation. Rehabilitation then continues with weekly or biweekly psychotherapy. Psychotherapy is often accomplished in groups, and some programs focus on relapse-prevention cognitive strategies to avoid situations that may put

The aim of alcohol rehabilitation is to prevent relapse by teaching coping behaviors in situations that could lead to relapse. In hospital programs as pictured here, patients go through alcohol counseling, both in group and individual sessions.

Box 14-2   AA'S TWELVE STEPS TO RECOVERY

Following are the twelve steps as they were originally presented in what is called the *Big Book, Alcoholics Anonymous.*

1. We admitted we were powerless over alcohol, that our lives had become unmanageable.

2. Came to believe that a Power greater than ourselves could restore us to sanity.

3. Made a decision to turn our will and our lives over to the care of God *as we understood Him.*

4. Made a searching and fearless moral inventory of ourselves.

5. Admitted to God, to ourselves, and to another human being the exact nature of our wrongs.

6. Were entirely ready to have God remove all these defects of character.

7. Humbly asked Him to remove our shortcomings.

8. Made a list of all persons we had harmed, and became willing to make amends to them all.

9. Made direct amends to such people wherever possible, except when to do so would injure them or others.

10. Continued to take personal inventory and when we were wrong promptly admitted it.

11. Sought through prayer and meditation to improve our conscious contact with God *as we understood Him,* praying only for knowledge of His will for us and the power to carry that out.

12. Having had a spiritual awakening as the result of these steps, we tried to carry this message to alcoholics, and to practice these principles in all our affairs.

Source: Alcoholics Anonymous. (1976).*The Big Book,* 3rd ed. New York: A. A. World Services, Inc. Reprinted with permission of Alcoholics Anonymous World Services, Inc.

---

one at risk for relapse. The goal is to teach patients alternative behaviors to cope with situations that lead to alcohol relapse. As discussed earlier, a return to environments associated with alcohol drinking can elicit subjective craving and signs of physiological withdrawal. Thus, returning to one's favorite bar or going to a party with some old drinking buddies may put a recovering alcohol-dependent person at risk for relapse. By monitoring moods and situations that are associated with alcohol craving, a person can learn to avoid these situations or substitute alternative behaviors. For example, during an argument with a spouse, the patient may learn to calmly assert herself rather than avoiding the confrontation and getting drunk. Thus, assertiveness training and relaxation therapy are often used to help patients.

Self-help groups   Self-help groups such as Alcoholics Anonymous have also been helpful for some people. This program was formed by two recovering alcohol-dependent men in 1935 and has become the world's largest self-help network and a model for other self-help groups. The philosophy of Alcoholics Anonymous is that one is powerless to control the disease of alcoholism without the help of a higher being and the fellowship of others in the program. Individuals are urged to admit their shortcomings and at meetings are encouraged to share their bad experiences that occurred while drinking. This philosophy is expressed in AA's twelve steps to recovery (see Box 14-2).

AIDS AND ALCOHOL

Alcohol drinking
and increased
risk for AIDS

The major public health concern of the 1980s is Acquired Immunodeficiency Syndrome (AIDS). As of December 1987, the number of reported AIDS cases worldwide is over 70,000 and the number of people infected with human immunodeficiency virus (HIV) is estimated to be between five and ten million. The U.S. Surgeon General has estimated that over one million people in the United States are infected with HIV.

The virus for AIDS is transmitted only by sharing blood or intimate sexual contact. Thus, people at risk for infection include needle sharing intravenous (IV) drug users, sexual partners of individuals who are infected with HIV, and the unborn fetus of a woman infected with the virus. Of the infected people, about 73 percent are homosexual men and 17 percent are intravenous drug users (Castro, Hardy, and Curran, 1986). The remaining high-risk groups include hemophiliacs, partners of IV drug users, and children of infected mothers.

Since there are no truly effective medications or vaccines, the only rational approach toward controlling the epidemic is by behavioral changes that limit exposure to the virus. Thus, it is important to educate people to avoid high-risk behaviors such as promiscuous sex and sharing dirty needles. In addition, it is important to identify factors that limit compliance with these guidelines. One such factor may be drug use, especially alcohol drinking.

ALCOHOL AND CELL-MEDIATED IMMUNITY

Impaired host
resistance factors

Exposure to the virus does not necessarily lead to infection. Moreover, once an individual is infected there are large individual differences in the disease progression. These data suggest that individual host resistance factors influence the rate of infection and disease progression. In addition to alcohol's effect of increasing exposure to the virus, alcohol may impair host resistance to fight the infection.

The part of the immune system responsible for fighting viral infections (cell-mediated immunity) is attacked by HIV. In this way, infection with HIV causes the slow deterioration of the immune system. The end result is the severe immunodeficiency state now known as AIDS. Since alcohol drinking impairs cell-mediated immunity (MacGregor, 1986), there is great concern that alcohol consumption may reduce the body's immune resistance to the initial infection by HIV and interfere with cell-mediated immune control of the infection once it is established. One recent report suggests that after four drinks one's resistance to HIV infection is 25 to 250 times less than that in someone who has not had any drinks (*New York Times,* May 5, 1988, p. B10).

ALCOHOL AND HIGH-RISK BEHAVIORS

There are several reasons to believe that alcohol use may not only decrease host resistance to the virus but it may also increase exposure to HIV and increase the spread of AIDS. First, clinicians treating alcohol-dependent patients observe that alcohol-dependent patients have a high incidence of behaviors that could put them at risk for infection. In a recent review, Daniel Flavin noted that:

> Apart from these direct biological effects [from alcohol] on the immune system, associated behavioral disinhibition resulting from the use of these substances may play a role in the acquisition and transmission of this disease. Activities such as engaging in high-risk sexual activity or sharing contaminated needles, which may be eschewed in a drug-free state, may occur in a drug-associated state or as a result of depression secondary to substance use. (Flavin and Frances, 1987, p. 24)

Flavin also observed in his alcohol treatment unit that three patients who were secondarily depressed from alcohol dependence actively sought to become infected with HIV. The patients stated that alcohol use "allowed each of them to distance themselves from their actions" and facilitated their contact with high-risk individuals.

Alcohol increases high-risk behavior

Experimental studies also show that alcohol increases high-risk behaviors. College women identified as problem drinkers engaged in more frequent sexual intercourse and were less likely to take measures to prevent conception (Zucker, Battistick, and Langer, 1981). Furthermore, in a recent survey of coed college freshman, people who engaged in indiscriminate sexual activity drank twice as much alcohol as those who did not engage in indiscriminate sexual activity (Smith et al., 1987).

To date, the only published study to examine alcohol and high-risk behavior for HIV infections is the recent study by Ron Stall and his colleagues (1986). Studying gay men, they compared the men's use of alcohol during sexual activity and compliance with safe sexual guidelines. Sexual behavior was assessed for high-risk activities, and people were characterized as being in no, medium, and high-risk groups. Among men who never drank alcohol just prior to sex (30 percent of the entire sample), 56 percent engaged in high-risk behaviors. In contrast, among people who drank alcohol prior to sex, 85 percent engaged in high-risk behaviors. These results suggest that alcohol leads to increased high-risk behaviors and therefore increased exposure to the virus.

If alcohol drinking is related to engaging in high-risk behaviors, then this has important implications. Among the high-risk groups for HIV infections, the rate of alcohol abuse is quite high (Lohrenz et al., 1978). If alcohol drinking decreases compliance with safe sexual and needle-sharing practices in people who are unaware of their HIV status, then alcohol drinking will facilitate the transmission of AIDS among the high-risk groups and into the non-IV drug-using heterosexual community. Currently, additional studies are underway to further assess the possible grave consequences of the effects of alcohol on HIV exposure and host resistance to HIV infection.

NARCOTICS

Opium

Narcotics, like alcohol, have been used since recorded history for their psychoactive effects. The word "opium" comes from the Greek word for juice. Indeed opium is derived from the juice of the seeds of the poppy plant. From opium, we derive several compounds, each of which has somewhat different pharmacological properties, such as duration and speed of action, but which all have similar affective and biological effects.

Morphine

Morphine (named after the Greek god for dreams) is a natural derivative of opium. It contains about 10 percent opium, and as its name suggests, when smoked or injected, it can produce a dreamlike state of calm euphoria. Another important opiate derivative is heroin, the generally preferred derivative of opiate abusers. This compound was synthesized in 1890, ironically, to treat morphine dependence. Because of its ability to cross the blood-brain barrier quickly, heroin produces a rapid, intense high that is followed by an unpleasant mood and narcotic craving four to six hours later. Not surprisingly, heroin users quickly learn that these withdrawal effects are quickly reversed by taking more heroin, thus establishing the addictive cycle.

PSYCHOPHARMACOLGY OF OPIATES

How do opiates produce their pharmacological effects? In contrast to alcohol, which has general effects on all membranes and nerve cells, opioid effects are specific to particular areas of membranes, opiate receptors, that attach specifically to one class of molecules, opioids. The opiates therefore produce their pharmacological effects by binding to opiate receptors. Opiate receptors are located in many parts of the body, including in the digestive tract and in white blood cells. Most importantly, there are large concentrations of opiate receptors in certain areas of the brain, particularly those areas that have to do with pain and feelings. Since opiates taken from external sources bind to these opiate receptors just as do endogenous opioids, we would expect opiate drugs to produce effects similar to naturally occurring opioids. Just as endogenous opioids such as beta-endorphins can block emotional and physical pain, drugs such as heroin or morphine can also blunt the emotional and physical consequences of pain. It is often remarked that with narcotics one can feel the pain sensation "but it doesn't hurt."

People may initially use narcotics to reduce emotional suffering or to produce a calm euphoria, but they may continue to use them to remove aversive withdrawal states.

The discussion above suggests that opiates may have an important physiological function and an important beneficial effect. Unfortunately, consistent with all psychoactive drugs of abuse, opposing processes produce affective tolerance and contrast. Frequent or prolonged use of opiates leads to less potent good effects when the drug is present and more severe aversive effects when the drug is withdrawn.

Initially, people who use opiates may start with an intravenous dose of heroin equivalent to 10 mg of morphine. This dose initially produces intense affective states of a profound calm, analgesia, and euphoria. It has been described as a state akin to being protected as a seven-month fetus in its mother's womb. With repeated use, however, people may need the equivalent of 100 times the original dose to get the same effect. This is a clear example of affective tolerance.

Withdrawal produces agitated dysphoria

Affective withdrawal is also present. In contrast to the calm euphoria produced by the presence of the drug, withdrawal from the drug produces an opposite state of agitated dysphoria. Physiologically, one experiences increased pain throughout the body, such as muscle pains and backaches. If no opiates are available, the individual may experience cramps, signs of increased anxiety such as sweating, fast heart rate, increased blood pressure, and stomach distress. These symptoms can easily be confused with the flu.

Reasons for using opiates

It is not clear why people start using narcotics. Since narcotics are illegal, expensive, and often injected into a vein, impulsive experimentation with narcotic use is not common. Only 5 percent of high school seniors have tried nonprescription opiates, in contrast to over 86 percent of seniors who have tried alcohol. Perhaps one reason people use narcotics is to reduce emotional suffering, just as endogenous opioids reduce emotional and physical pain. Apparently narcotics help individuals reduce feelings of loneliness and feelings of anger. Another reason people may use narcotics is to enjoy the euphoria produced by the drug. In any case, the reasons for starting opiate use may be different from the reasons for continuing to use opiates. As mentioned above, with prolonged use, the euphoria decreases and the withdrawal craving increases. If drugs are no longer available, a rebound deficiency in opioid activity occurs. This withdrawal reaction is reduced by retaking the drug. Consequently, an addictive cycle occurs so that the individual learns to depend on narcotic drugs in order to maintain normal opioid receptor functioning. Once use becomes motivated by the removal of aversive withdrawal states, then recreational use becomes drug dependence.

MEDICAL AND SOCIAL COMPLICATIONS

Few medical complications

In general, except for overdose, contaminants in narcotics, and unsterile techniques, there are few medical complications of narcotic use. In contrast to the theatrical portrayal of narcotic withdrawal and the assumed medical complications from narcotics, the actual complications from narcotics per se are minimal. The medical consequences from legal substances such as alcohol and cigarettes are far more severe.

Profound social consequences

The social consequences from narcotic dependence, however, are profound. Narcotics are expensive. It costs up to $100/day to obtain narcotics. To obtain money to purchase narcotics, many addicts engage in a variety of illegal activities, including robbery and prostitution.

Increased risk of AIDS from shared needles

In contrast to the mild consequences from the drug itself, the consequences from sharing needles among intravenous narcotic users are severe. It has been a social custom to share "works" as a sign of friendship. Unfortunately, this practice has facilitated the spread of serious diseases such as hepatitis and most recently, AIDS. About 60 percent of IV drug abusers in New York City and northern New Jersey test positive for the AIDS virus. Since the infection may not be apparent for several years, the narcotic user may unknowingly spread the virus by sharing needles or sexual activity. As mentioned above, one important way to pay for drugs is by prostitution. The primary spread of AIDS into the heterosexual community is via IV drug users.

TREATMENT FOR NARCOTIC DEPENDENCE

There are two general approaches to the treatment of opiate dependence. Given the few medical complications of narcotic use, some have suggested substitution therapy, that is, substituting street drugs with medically prescribed drugs that replace the pharmacological effects of the drug of abuse. A second approach is the various abstinence-oriented approaches that sug-

Narcotic dependence may be treated by substituting an oral dose of methadone for heroin. The patient on the left is taking her methadone at an outpatient treatment center. The men on the right are patients in a methadone maintenance program who are discussing what methadone will and will not do for them when they are out of the hospital and back in the community.

gest that the only effective treatment is to remain off all drugs. The advantages and disadvantages of each approach will now be considered.

SUBSTITUTION THERAPY

Substituting methadone for heroin

The substitution of intravenous narcotics with orally prescribed narcotics offers a safe and effective way to treat narcotic dependence. Usually, a long-acting opiate such as methadone is given once per day at a special outpatient drug dependence treatment center. The oral dose of methadone effectively relieves the withdrawal symptoms. In contrast to intravenous heroin, which has a pharmacological effect lasting only about four hours, oral methadone has a pharmacological effect lasting over twenty-four hours. In this way, one avoids the many episodes of drug high followed by drug withdrawal that typically occur several times each day with short-acting agents such as heroin. Thus, the repeated pairings of environmental cues associated with shooting up are no longer reinforced. Since the patient no longer experiences withdrawal symptoms, much of the motivation to use narcotics other than methadone is reduced. Furthermore, at high doses of methadone, intravenous heroin no longer produces a euphoric high. This further decreases the reinforcing properties of street drugs. With less intravenous drug use, the hazards of sharing needles and illegal activities are decreased. Methadone maintenance decreases intravenous drug use, crime, and needle sharing by about 50 percent (Ball et al., 1988).

The main disadvantage of methadone maintenance is that the patient remains dependent on narcotics. The patient needs to come to the clinic daily to receive his daily dose. In addition, the vials can be easily sold in the community, and this creates a black market to obtain methadone. Thus, the prescription of methadone to patients makes narcotics more available.

ABSTINENCE-ORIENTED THERAPY

Therapeutic communities

The second approach to treating narcotic dependence is abstinence-oriented therapy. Therapeutic communities demand complete abstinence from all psychotropic drugs. An implicit assumption is that drug users have an antisocial personality disorder, and that this is the main deterrent to treatment. Therefore, treatment is directed toward establishing an honest, open therapeutic relationship. At times, group therapy can be harsh, as encounters help patients face the effects of drug use. When effective, this approach helps patients learn appropriate social skills and fosters a sense of self-sufficiency. The main disadvantage of this treatment is the high drop-out rate. As estimated 75 percent of patients drop out of treatment in the first month. The high drop-out rate is thought to reflect poor patient motivation to abstain from drugs. From our general analysis of addictive behavior, however, we can see how behavioral factors such as drug reminder cues may stimulate withdrawal symptoms and lead to relapse.

INDIVIDUAL-BASED THERAPY

Matching patients to specific therapies

More recent therapeutic approaches have attempted to integrate medical and behavioral treatments based on the characteristics of the individual addict. The assumption here is that not all opiate-dependent patients are alike. Therefore, therapists attempt to match patients to specific therapies. For example, they give some patients antidepressant medications to improve their mood. Being less depressed, some patients then decrease drug use. For some very motivated patients, medications such as naltrexone are available to block opiate receptors and therefore block the pharmacological and reinforcing effects of narcotics. Patients with moderate amounts of emotional distress improve with individual psychotherapy provided by a trained therapist (McLellan et al., 1983).

STIMULANTS

There are two main types of stimulants, cocaine and amphetamines. Both of these drugs have the pharmacological effect of increasing subjective energy and producing affective states of euphoria and confidence. Both are subject to abuse, and cocaine especially may have lethal consequences. For example, Len Bias overdosed on cocaine on the day he was drafted by the Boston Celtics, and Richard Pryor nearly burned to death while smoking cocaine. Like many of the other psychoactive drugs discussed above, the use of stimulants has long been part of human experience, but serious medical problems have only recently been recognized.

Historical use of stimulants

For centuries, the Peruvian Indians have chewed coca leaves to obtain energy. In the 1880s, Freud used cocaine to decrease fatigue, depression, and boredom, stopping only after a bad experience with a friend who became psychotic from cocaine use. It is also of interest to note that cocaine was an ingredient in Coca-Cola until 1906 (it was the real thing indeed!).

Amphetamines have been used for centuries for medicinal purposes. The Chinese extracted amphetamines from the shrub mahuang for the relief of asthma. The alkaloid of this plant, ephedrine, helps in clearing up stuffy noses, overcoming depression, and suppressing appetites. Amphetamine, a synthetic substitute for ephedrine, was synthesized in 1927 and was much more potent. As is the case for cocaine, the more potent form of the drug is more liable to be abused.

PSYCHOPHARMACOLOGY OF STIMULANTS

COCAINE

When DSM-III was published in 1980, there was no category for cocaine dependence since no signs of physical withdrawal were known. Originally,

Popular means of using cocaine include nasal snorting and smoking, both of which promote rapid transportation of the drug to the brain.

Assessibility of cocaine

the very high cost of cocaine made the drug inaccessible to all except the affluent. In the 1980s, however, reports from affluent movie stars and athletes suggested that cocaine use was addicting and that it is associated with severe medical complications. With the introduction of crack, a particularly powerful yet inexpensive form of cocaine, the drug is now assessible to all segments of the population, and it is particularly popular among young adults. One in four young adults has tried cocaine, and about half of all cocaine users are between twelve and twenty-six (1985 National Household Survey on Drugs, National Institute on Drug Abuse).

Mode of use

The effects of cocaine in humans depend on mode of use. Popular means of using cocaine include injection, nasal snorting, and smoking. These modes promote rapid transportation to the brain and dramatic effects, including euphoria, increased self-confidence, increased sexual desire, increased sociability, decreased need for sleep, and increased energy. (These symptoms tend to mimic manic states described in Chapter 11, and since disrupted catecholamine activity may be the biological basis for bipolar disorder, this suggests that stimulants also affect catecholamines.)

Blocking reuptake of neurotransmitters

Cocaine is thought to produce its pharmacological effect by blocking the reuptake of such neurotransmitters as dopamine and norepinephrine, which are thought to be important in reward pathways and emotion. Recent evidence suggests that there are specific receptors for cocaine on neurons that contain dopamine. Furthermore, stimulation of these cocaine receptors inhibits the reuptake of dopamine into the presynaptic neuron (Ritz et al., 1987).

AMPHETAMINES

Effects of amphetamines

Amphetamines (speed), like cocaine, produce a rapid pleasurable state characterized by increased concentration, energy, and self-esteem. Affective and physiological tolerance is quickly produced, however. People will typically start with small oral doses, i.e., 20 to 30 mg, but to maintain the same euphoric state, they will increase the dose and change to an intravenous route of administration. Unlike cocaine, the amphetamine half-life is a few hours, and so marathon speed sessions can last three or four days, until the individual either collapses or runs out of amphetamines.

Except for the longer half-life, the pharmacological effects of amphetamines are similar to those of cocaine. Amphetamines are also thought to produce their psychoactive properties by inhibiting the reuptake of dopamine or norepinephrine from the presynaptic neuron, and thereby increasing the activity of the dopamine and norepinephrine system.

MEDICAL AND SOCIAL COMPLICATIONS

Paranoid
syndrome
produced

Stimulants have severe medical, emotional, and social consequences. While initially attention is increased by stimulants, with chronic high doses, the person's heightened awareness turns into hypervigilance for environmental stimuli. The chronic use of stimulants produces a paranoid syndrome that may be indistinguishable from schizophrenia. In a recent study by Michael Sherer (1988), paranoid feelings resulted from a single four-hour intravenous dose of cocaine as demonstrated by the following report from one of the subjects:

> At the beginning of the high cocaine-cocaine infusion, he reported that he experienced moderate degrees of the typical "rush" and "high" feelings. Uncharacteristically, he declined to leave the study room after the first thirty minutes of the infusion, and he began to be preoccupied with the IV needle and apparatus, expressing fear of "bubbles" that he felt could kill him. During the following hour, his concerns became more focused on the nursing staff, and he expressed fears that his pay was being stolen and that the research diet that he was receiving was a form of punishment. Three hours into the infusion, he emerged from the bathroom with shaving cream smeared all over his face, expressing a delusion that his face was disfigured, and he threatened to sue the staff for doing this. Examination of his face revealed no injury. (From Sherer et al., 1988)

Discharge in
sympathetic
activity

Not only do stimulants induce psychotic and paranoid states, but stimulants also produce dramatic increases in sweating, blood pressure, and heart rate, sometimes leading to irregular heart beats. This discharge in sympathetic activity can result in heart attack, strokes, and even death.

Behavioral and
emotional
withdrawal
symptoms

In contrast to the dramatic effects of stimulant intoxication, there are few physical signs of stimulant withdrawal. The lack of physical signs of stimulant withdrawal are misleading, however, since severe behavioral and emotional symptoms are present. As one might expect, since the effects of the drug initially produce such symptoms as increased energy, self-esteem, and euphoria, the withdrawal symptoms are opposite and resemble depression. The individual may complain of loss of energy, decreased interest in enjoyable activities, poor appetite, and disrupted sleep patterns. This crash after stimulant use can be alleviated by taking more cocaine or amphetamine, and thus the addictive cycle is created. As for narcotics and alcohol, this affective pattern fits an opponent-process model quite well. One important difference, however, is the time course to observe these effects. The withdrawal from narcotics and alcohol begins twelve to twenty-four hours after the last dose. In contrast, cocaine withdrawal can begin within minutes of the last dose, and amphetamine withdrawal begins within hours of its last dose. Thus, the addictive cycle of stimulant use is easily established. Rarely can an individual limit his use of cocaine while cocaine is available. Typically, once cocaine is purchased, it is entirely used in one sitting.

Special mention should be made of the recent cocaine epidemic. As cocaine has become more potent and available, the medical consequences have dramatically increased. For example, cocaine-related emergency room visits increased from 4,243 in 1982 to 18,202 in 1986. Similarly, cocaine-related deaths have increased five times in the past few years, from 217 deaths in 1982 to 1,080 deaths in 1986. Since the intravenous use of cocaine has gained popularity, we may expect IV cocaine use to contribute to the spread of AIDS during the next few years. Just as alcohol may increase high-risk behaviors such as promiscuous sex, the use of cocaine and amphetamine may also cloud one's judgment so that unsterile needles and promiscuous sex are no longer avoided.

The cocaine epidemic

TREATMENT

Use of dopamine blockers

To date, no truly effective treatments for stimulant dependence are known. Since chronic use of stimulants are thought to deplete the brain of catecholamines such as dopamine, it has been suggested that dopamine-like compounds can be used to decrease the withdrawal symptoms. Thus, clinicians have tried dopamine agonists such as Amantidine and Bromocriptine to reduce craving, but they have had limited success (Tennent and Tarver, 1988). Also, since the withdrawal symptoms resemble depression, clinicians have tried antidepressant medications to treat stimulant dependence (Tennent and Tarver, 1988). These studies have yielded conflicting reports of modest decreases in stimulant use. The use of dopamine blockers may be expected to block the reinforcing properties of stimulants, but these medications have been poorly tolerated in dependent patients.

Stimulant reminder cues

Just as situations associated with drug use can trigger craving in narcotic or alcohol-dependent subjects, stimulant reminder cues can trigger craving in stimulant-dependent subjects. Research conducted with cocaine-dependent patients showed that simply receiving a weekly paycheck could elicit craving. These experiments are attempting to decrease cocaine relapse by extinguishing cocaine reminder cues (Childress et al., 1988).

In summary, the recreational use of stimulants can quickly lead to an addictive cycle of dependence. This is especially true for cocaine, given cocaine's rapid half-life of action. Once initiated, this cycle is difficult to break, and thus far, treatment has had only modest success in breaking the cycle.

HALLUCINOGENS (MARIJUANA, PCP, LSD)

Historical use of hallucinogens

The use of hallucinogens for religious, mystical experiences has been prevalent for centuries. Mexican Indians have smoked or injested mescaline found in Peyote cactus to alter perceptions and obtain new mystical insights. This practice has been recently popularized by the writings of Carlos Castenada in his tetralogy of books describing the experiences of Don Juan.

The hallucinogens are so named because they cause perceptual changes and hallucinations. These compounds became of interest to modern scientists because of the similarities of the hallucinations caused by drugs and the hallucinations observed in specific mental disorders such as schizophrenia. Albert Hofmann, a Swiss researcher, accidentally swallowed a small amount of LSD and described the experience as follows:

I had a great difficulty in speaking coherently, my field of vision swayed before me, and objects appeared distorted like images in curved mirrors. I had the impression of being unable to move from the spot, although my assistant told me afterwards that we had cycled at a good pace. . . .

By the time the doctor arrived, the peak of the crisis had already passed. As far as I remember, the following were the most outstanding symptoms: vertigo, visual disturbances; the faces of those around me appeared as grotesque, colored masks; marked motor unrest, alternating with paresis; an intermittent heavy feeling in the head, limbs, and the entire body, as if they were filled with metal; cramps in the legs, coldness, and loss of feeling in the hands; a metallic taste on the tongue; dry, constricted sensation in the throat; feeling of choking; confusion alternating between clear recognition of my condition, in which state I sometimes observed, in the manner of an independent, neutral observer, that I shouted half insanely or babbled incoherent words. Occasionally I felt as if I were out of my body.

The doctor found a rather weak pulse but an otherwise normal circulation.

Six hours after ingestion of the LSD-25 my condition had already improved considerably. Only the visual disturbances were still pronounced. Everything seemed to sway and the proportions were distorted like the reflections in the surface of moving water. Moreover, all objects appeared in unpleasant, constantly changing colors, the predominant shades being sickly green and blue. When I closed by eyes, an unending series of colorful, very realistic and fantastic images surged in upon me. A remarkable feature was the manner in which all acoustic perceptions (e.g., the noise of a passing car) were transformed into optical effects, every sound causing a corresponding colored hallucination constantly changing in shape and color like pictures in a kaleidoscope. At about 1 o'clock I fell asleep and awakened the next morning somewhat tired but otherwise feeling perfectly well. (Hofmann, 1968, pp. 185–86)

Relationship of hallucinogens and schizophrenia not confirmed

Albert Hofmann was impressed that since a very small amount of LSD could produce profound visual hallucinations and perceptual changes, then perhaps small amounts of endogenous compounds could cause the psychotic episodes in mental disorders. His theory has not been confirmed. Additional studies have pointed out clear differences between the psychotic episodes observed in schizophrenia and those induced by drugs. For example, although many schizophrenic patients report auditory hallucinations, visual hallucinations are far less common. In contrast, common perceptual changes with hallucinogens include visual hallucinations: alterations in the size and shape of real objects, seeing vivid colors, and experiencing time distortions.

Phencyclidine (PCP) like LSD can cause perceptual changes, but it has more of a tranquilizing, disinhibiting effect on behavior. Initially, PCP was developed as an anesthetic, but because of the side effects of confusion and disorientation experienced during clinical trials, the drug was never marketed. Unfortunately, the drug has become popular in some circles for its hallucinogenic properties. Often mixed with marijuana, PCP is sold as superweed or known as angel dust.

PCP has several effects that depend on the dose of the drug. At low doses, PCP leads to a loss of inhibitions, poor psychomotor coordination, and a behavioral state that resembles that induced by alcohol intoxication. At higher doses, it produces distortions in body image as if one is not attached to one's body, that is, *depersonalization.* The person becomes sensitive to all sensory stimuli, and at high doses, PCP causes an agitated delirious state that is helped by removing all sensory input. Unfortunately for the PCP

To contain a PCP user, police often resort to shark nets.

user, the poor motor coordination induced by the drug often results in efforts by police or others to grab the user. This can lead to increased agitation and aggressive behavior from the PCP user. This, coupled with the fact that PCP produces analgesia and consequently users are not easily hurt, has given PCP the unfair reputation of causing wild, violent behavior.

Effects of
marijuana

Marijuana is obtained from the dried leaves and flowering tops of the hemp plant, which contains tetrahydrocannabinol (THC). Marijuana is usually smoked, whereby it is quickly absorbed into the lungs and THC is transported to the brain, producing an immediate rush. Marijuana, however, can also be taken by mouth, with the marijuana leaves brewed into a tea or baked into brownies, but then the psychoactive effects have a much slower onset. More concentrated THC can be obtained from the resin from the tops of the plants. This is called hashish; it can also be smoked or taken orally.

When marijuana was first brought to the United States, it was not used for its psychoactive properties. Indeed, originally marijuana plants were used to make ropes. The medicinal properties of marijuana were then touted, however, and marijuana was used to treat gout, depression, and neuralgia. Interestingly, the therapeutic effects of marijuana are again being promoted, as THC is effective in reducing the nausea and loss of appetite induced from chemotherapy for cancer.

Marijuana is usually smoked, whereby the THC can be quickly transported to the brain, producing an immediate rush.

The use of marijuana for its psychoactive properties began to increase in the United States in the 1920s with the prohibition of alcohol. In low doses, marijuana produces mild euphoria, increased appetite (the popular "munchies"), and perceptual distortions. It is thought to increase perception of auditory and visual stimuli, and was initially popular with musicians. At higher doses, marijuana can produce more profound perceptual changes, including hallucinations, depersonalization, time distortions, and panic reactions (Addiction Research Foundation, 1981).

PSYCHOPHARMACOLOGY

Long half-life of
marijuana

As discussed in previous sections, psychoactive drugs that produce dependence have in common affective tolerance and affective contrast. At first glance, the hallucinogens do not appear to be associated with these phenomena. For example, there does not appear to be tolerance to the effects of marijuana. Indeed, it has been suggested that marijuana smokers demonstrate reverse tolerance; that is, it takes smaller amounts of marijuana to get "high." While the other hallucinogens have not been studied systematically, a close examination of marijuana use remains consistent with general observations of the processes produced by psychoactive drugs. What appears to be reverse tolerance, or sensitization, is due to the long duration of Process A following marijuana use. Since marijuana is fat-soluble, it takes the body a long time to degrade marijuana, i.e., it has a long half-life. Traces of marijuana can be found in the urine *one month* following its last use. In contrast, alcohol is completely metabolized within one day of its use. Thus, someone who uses marijuana consistently during a month period will be experiencing the addictive effects of all the undegraded marijuana used during the entire month.

Tolerance to marijuana

Tolerance to marijuana can be demonstrated in chronic users. Tolerance was first shown by Vietnam veterans who regularly smoked concentrations of marijuana that were toxic to users in the United States. Controlled studies also show that there can be tolerance to marijuana (Nowlan and Cohen, 1977). Finally, withdrawal symptoms are observed following prolonged heavy use of marijuana. These symptoms include decreased appetite, irritability, nausea, and diarrhea. As we might expect, given the long duration of marijuana, it is relatively difficult for users to learn that one can overcome withdrawal craving by taking more marijuana. We would predict that dependence on marijuana would be difficult to obtain. Despite the high frequency of marijuana use in the late 1970s, it seems that users were able to stop using the drug without a great deal of difficulty. Similarly, there are few reports of tolerance, withdrawal, or dependence in the other hallucinogens. Cocaine use, with its short half-life, provides a good case in contrast, as drug treatment units are overwhelmed with cocaine-dependent patients.

MEDICAL AND SOCIAL COMPLICATIONS

Hallucinogens have important behavioral and cognitive complications. Marijuana, for example, decreases attention and vigilance. Experimental studies of marijuana intoxication reveal impairment in a variety of cognitive functions, including short-term memory and intellectual tasks. In addition, marijuana causes incoordination for psychomotor activities and can interfere with driving. Hallucinogens can also cause panic attacks during intoxication, and in some susceptible people, prolonged psychotic states following drug use. About one-third of regular marijuana users experience occasional episodes of acute panic, paranoid reaction, hallucinations, and distortions in body image. In addition, hallucinogens such as LSD have been associated with flashbacks (episodes resembling drug intoxication, which occur months or even years after drug use was discontinued). It is not clear what causes these flashbacks.

Medical complications from marijuana include impaired reproduction. In males, marijuana use is associated with low sperm counts; in females, menstrual cycles are impaired. Marijuana also crosses the placenta, and it can impair fetal development. Smoking marijuana cigarettes leads to high tar levels in the lungs similar to levels produced by tobacco cigarettes. The high tar levels can impair resistance to pulmonary infections and can lead to increased risk of lung cancer.

LSD produces perceptual changes and hallucinations, and may produce occasional episodes of acute panic.

CIGARETTE SMOKING AND NICOTINE

Historical use of tobacco

Tobacco was first used by American Indians. There is an old legend that tobacco was a gift from the gods.

> There was once a great famine across the land. There was no food to eat and the earth would yield no harvest. Finally, the Great Spirit sent a naked female messenger to replenish the lands and save his people. Where she touched the land with her left hand, the earth turned green with corn and the people were nourished.

Where she touched the land with her right hand, potatoes grew and the people's stomachs were full. Then she sat down; from her place of rest grew tobacco. (From Henningfield, 1984)

Apparently, the use of tobacco for its psychoactive properties was well known and valued by the Indians, as indicated by its placement alongside the important crops of corn and potatoes. It did not take long for the rest of the world to discover tobacco's pleasurable psychoactive properties. The use of tobacco spread quickly to Europe soon after Christopher Columbus brought back tobacco from the New World. In colonial times, tobacco was smoked in pipes, chewed, ground into small pieces and used as snuff. The cash value of tobacco was quite high, as an ounce of tobacco was exchanged for an ounce of silver. From these beginnings in the United States, it is not surprising that tobacco is now a $16 billion dollar industry that yields $8 billion in tax revenues per year. The commercial value of tobacco has clearly not been lost in the business community.

PSYCHOPHARMACOLOGY

Nicotine and tobacco dependence

Although the health consequences of cigarette smoking are well known, it is commonly assumed that tobacco is *not* in the same class as other psychoactive drugs of abuse. Ironically, some health providers continue to smoke while preaching abstinence from all drugs. It is remarked that cigarette smoking is simply a "bad habit." Or as Mark Twain quipped, "I can quit smoking if I wish; I've done it a thousand times." Empirical data clearly show that tobacco use leads to dependence just as does use of the other drugs discussed in this chapter. Tobacco dependence produces affective pleasure, tolerance, and withdrawal. The active ingredient in tobacco use that produces psychoactive effects is nicotine. The major reason people smoke cigarettes is to obtain the effects of nicotine. Consistent with people's self-report, it is quite easy to give up smoking (4 million quit each year), but 75 percent of these people relapse within one year. As shown in Figure 14-5 this relapse rate is very similar to that found with alcohol and heroin. Relapse is often precipitated by withdrawal symptoms. The familiar nicotine fits are characterized by sleep disruption, nausea, headaches, increased appetite, irritability, anxiety, poor concentration, increased heart rate, and hand tremor. Just as is the case for other psychoactive drugs, the withdrawal symptoms can be relieved by redosing on nicotine, for withdrawal symptoms are related to nicotine levels. Stanley Schachter (1977) manipulated urine acidity, which caused an increase in nicotine excretion. This in turn lead to increased cigarette smoking to bring up nicotine levels and prevent withdrawal symptoms. This may help explain the familiar observation that it is difficult to give up smoking during stressful times. During conditions of anxiety, there is increased urine acidity, with consequent increased nicotine excretion. Thus, the motivation to smoke cigarettes increases. If, however, the urine is made less acidic by the ingestion of bicarbonate, no increase in cigarette smoking with stress is observed.

Affective tolerance

Just as tobacco use is associated with affective withdrawal, there is also affective tolerance. As shown in Figure 14-6, with repeated nicotine use over time, the effect of nicotine diminishes. As one might expect, if the

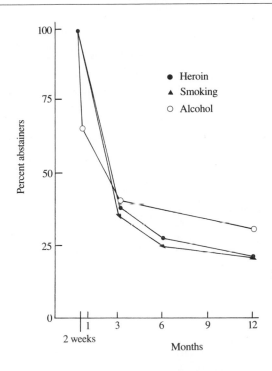

Figure 14-5
Relapse rates after achievement of abstinence from tobacco, alcohol, or heroin (Source: Hunt and Matarazzo, 1973).

pleasurable consequences of smoking are obtained from the nicotine content of cigarettes, then simply lowering the concentration of nicotine in cigarettes will elicit compensatory changes in smoking behavior. The results of several experiments demonstrate that as nicotine content is lowered, there are increases in smoking. Since people will increase smoking to compensate for lowered nicotine levels, there are thus no advantages to smoking low nicotine cigarettes.

Stimulation of nicotinic receptors

What is it about nicotine that produces its affective pleasure? Once nicotine enters the body, it directly stimulates a class of cholinergic receptors called the nicotinic receptors. The reinforcing properties of nicotine appear related to the stimulation of these nicotinic receptors since the blockade of the receptors with the drug mecamylamine will decrease the pleasure associated with smoking (see Figure 14-6).

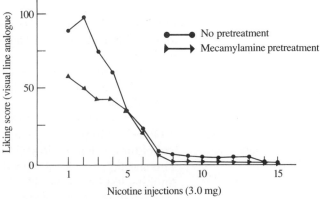

Figure 14-6
Ratings of "liking" one minute after nicotine injection (triangles indicate pretreatment with 10 mg mecamylamine) (Source: Henningfield, 1985)

MEDICAL AND SOCIAL CONSEQUENCES

Aversive
consequences of
smoking

Although the medical consequences from cigarette smoking have not always been known, it has been clear for the last decade that smoking has profound aversive consequences. In 1979, the Surgeon General stated that smoking is "the chief, single, preventable cause of death in our society, and the most important public health issue of our time" (U.S. Department of Health, Education, and Welfare, 1979). Every year, about 350,000 people die prematurely from smoking. While much deserved addition is being paid to the AIDS epidemic, it is important to note that for each person who has AIDS, there are about 10 people who die from cigarette smoking per year. The costs of cigarette smoking to society are staggering. Health costs alone account for $30 billion per year. This country loses 145 million extra days from work due to disability caused by smoking. Cigarette smoking shortens an individual's expected life span by eight years.

Tobacco use leads to dependence on nicotine, the active ingredient in tobacco. Whereas it is easy to give up smoking, 75 percent of those who give it up relapse within one year.

The medical complications from smoking come from three major sources: coronary heart disease, cancers, and chronic obstructive pulmonary disease. The effects of smoking on heart disease can be predicted from the pharmacological effects of nicotine. Nicotine binds to nicotinic receptors and causes increased blood pressure, more rapid heart rate, and increased work load on the heart. This causes increased oxygen consumption by the heart, and in certain people, it can produce heart attacks. In addition to the effects of nicotine, smoking also increases carbon monoxide levels in the blood. Carbon monoxide displaces oxygen from hemoglobin. In this way, not only do cigarettes increase the heart's need for oxygen, but they also decrease the ability of the body to deliver oxygen. Another hazard from tobacco smoking consists of the tars contained in cigarettes. These tars irritate the linings of the lungs and can cause chronic inflammation and cancers.

TREATMENT

Nicotine gum

Our understanding of the biochemical basis of cigarette smoking suggests several approaches to treatment. First, a chewing gum that releases nicotine can be substituted for the nicotine derived from smoking. Just as methadone does not remove the dependence on narcotics, this approach does not take away the dependence on nicotine. Nicotine gum, however, does remove withdrawal symptoms produced by a sudden termination of smoking, and it takes away the craving for cigarettes. Once maintained on the nicotine gum, it is presumably easier to then gradually taper the dose to eventually remove the dependence on nicotine. A second approach is the blockade of nicotine receptors. Although initially an individual may attempt to overcome the blockade by increasing his smoking, eventually the person will learn that smoking behavior is no longer effective in obtaining nicotine.

Behavioral
techniques

Other techniques to reduce or stop cigarette smoking include behavioral techniques such as rapid smoking so that one will become ill from smoking. This should pair illness with the behavior of smoking, and therefore make smoking less enjoyable. Hypnosis has also been used to pair smoking with aversive thoughts. In general, these techniques can usually produce an initial decrease in smoking, but long-term follow-up reports indicate a very high relapse rate.

SEDATIVES-TRANQUILIZERS (BARBITURATES, BENZODIAZEPINES)

Barbiturates and benzodiazepines are relatively new psychoactive drugs compared to the other drugs discussed in this chapter which have histories dating back thousands of years. The first barbiturate, barbital, was introduced in 1903. Since then, about 2,500 babiturates have been synthesized from the compound barbituric acid and about 50 specific compounds have been used clinically. The benzodiazepines were first synthesized in 1957; there are now eleven benzodiazepines available for clinical use in the United States. These drugs are widely used in the treatment of anxiety, insomnia, and seizure disorders. As is the case of other psychoactive drugs, however, they have also been abused.

Abuse of benzodiazepines

While abuse of barbiturates has decreased in recent years, the abuse of benzodiazepines has been increasingly recognized as a potential problem, particularly in people dependent on other drugs. The following example demonstrates many of the typical characteristics:

> Dr. C., a thirty-one year old, married, white physician, was referred for chemical dependency evaluation. Three years previously, he had a major depression with vegetative signs and symptoms and anxious features. The depressive symptoms responded to amoxapine, 100 mg/day, and chlordiazepoxide, 25 mg three times a day (t.i.d.). These were discontinued after three months.
>
> One year previously, he had a recurrence of depression with vegatative signs and symptoms. He placed himself on a regimen of amoxapine, up to 150 mg/day, and alprazolam (Xanax), 1 mg t.i.d. The depressive symptoms abated. Three months later, he began to see a psychiatrist, who continued the alprazolam, but changed the antidepressant to nortriptyline, 75 mg/day. Over the last years he had begun to drink 60 to 90 ml of alcohol two to three times a week and to smoke cannabis almost daily, using up to 15 g weekly.
>
> When Dr. C. attempted to taper his dose of alprazolam, his anxiety increased. He did not take more than the prescribed dose but became tolerant to its effects and saved doses during the day to permit a higher one-time dose for effect. He became increasingly preoccupied with his alprazolam use. His wife was concerned about his use of cannabis and alprazolam, and there were increasing arguments about his use of these drugs. His work attendance suffered, and he was placed on job probation.
>
> Three weeks before he sought medical assistance, Dr. C. had started an eight-day self-prescribed tapering of alprazolam. Thirty-six hours after his last dose, he suffered two grand mal seizures.
>
> Dr. C. had a history of cannabis abuse (up to seven "joints" daily) and alcohol abuse (binge drinking on weekends) in high school, with poor school performance and an arrest for possession of marijuana. In high school he had also used LSD, peyote, mescaline, and amphetamines—all fewer than five times. He had used cocaine approximately five times, the last time four years previously. After his mother died, when he was nineteen, he had cut down on his use of marijuana to two to three times monthly and did not continue his alcohol abuse, "pulling himself together" for college and medical school. His drug use had increased in the last year. (From Jeurgens and Morse, 1988)

Effects of
barbiturates

Barbiturates are depressants ("downers") for the central nervous system. Unlike other drugs discussed in this chapter, the barbiturates do not act specifically on a particular receptor or neurotransmitter system. Rather, barbiturates have a general effect on a variety of neurons to decrease neuronal activity. Barbiturates are similar in their pharmacological effects but differ widely in their potency and half-life. The differences in duration of action give each specific barbiturate a different therapeutic use. For example, the short-acting barbiturates are used primarily as a sleeping pill, whereas the longer-acting barbiturates are used to treat anxiety or prevent seizures. The differences in potency and duration of action also affect the abuse potential of the barbiturate. The short-acting barbiturates rapidly lead to affective and physiological tolerance. Also, the short-acting barbiturates make it easy to learn that by redosing on the drug one can decrease the withdrawal reactions.

In low doses, barbiturates can produce a pleasant dreamlike state of relaxation. In many respects, they produce an affective state similar to alcohol intoxication and opposite to the energetic "high" from stimulants ("uppers"). At higher doses, the inhibition of neurons becomes more complete, as the person experiences slurred speech, incoordination, poor judgment and concentration. Finally, consciousness is clouded, and the person may stop breathing. A particularly deadly combination results when barbiturates are taken with alcohol.

Withdrawal from
barbiturates

Withdrawal from barbiturates is particularly difficult. In contrast to the relatively mild physical symptoms of cocaine or narcotic withdrawal, the withdrawal from barbiturates is potentially life threatening. Withdrawal symptoms are similar to those from alcohol withdrawal and include tremors, increased heart rate, sweating, irritability, delirium, and convulsions. Just as during drug use the neurons become depressed, during drug withdrawal the neurons become hyperactive.

Effects of
benzodiazepines

Benzodiazepines are more specific in their pharmacological effects, acting on benzodiazepine receptors. Rather than having a general inhibiting effect on neuronal activity, evidence demonstrates that when benzodiazepines bind to benzodiazepine receptors, they increase the effectiveness of another neurotransmitter, GABA, the principal inhibitory neurotransmitter in the brain (Tallman et al., 1980). Since benzodiazepines are much more specific in their mechanism of action, these drugs are much safer than barbiturates.

PROGNOSIS FOR ENDING DRUG ABUSE

Cultural context

In this chapter, we have focused on the interaction of psychoactive drugs on individuals. This approach was taken because the basic assumption of abnormal psychology in general and DSM-III-R in particular is that psychopathology resides in the individual. But understanding of substance abuse is more complicated, since drug abuse, more than other mental or physical disorders, affects and is affected by the cultural context. Consider the following recent newspaper excerpt on drug-related deaths for the month:

There was a thirteen-year-old boy shot in the head because he hadn't sold enough crack for his bosses, and a sixty-four-year-old woman hacked to death because she refused to sell cocaine one night. One thirty-two-year-old man dropped dead on South Seventh Street, a bullet between his eyes, after he and another man shot at each other from about ten paces.

The dead include drug buyers and drug sellers: career criminals who lost control and conscience long ago, and innocents who had the wrong friends or happened to be in the wrong place at the wrong time.

Some sellers were killed by customers dissatisfied with the drugs they bought, others were killed in battles over price. One man lost his life fighting over $5 worth of cocaine, and two teenagers have been charged with knifing him to death.

For one fifteen-year-old boy, the end came in the middle of the night on a Friday in March.

In his last moments, he screamed in panic and begged for mercy, and then he took two bullets in the head. His body was found in a pile of trash and weeds in a swamp down by the airport.

Three days before, his thirteen-year-old brother had been found near train tracks along West River Drive. He, too, had been shot in the head, but he was still breathing when police got to him.

It took him a whole day to die. (*Philadelphia Inquirer*, July 24, 1988, p. 1)

While drug use has been part of society since recorded history, there has never been a time when drug use problems have imposed such a risk to society in the form of violence as described above and due to the spread of AIDS. What steps can we as a society take to stop drug dependence?

DRUG AVAILABILITY

Availability
affects drug use

One approach to stopping drug dependence is to limit drug availability. There can be no substance abuse if one never comes in contact with abusing substances. If alcohol was never available to a person prone to become dependent, then no alcohol problems would be observed. In general, as drugs become more available, drug use disorders increase. For example, populations that have access to psychoactive drugs are particularly at high risk for drug dependence. Health professionals such as doctors and nurses are particularly at risk for abusing narcotics, amphetamines, and tranquilizers, and professions such as bartending put people at risk for alcohol dependence.

During the past decade we have seen a naturalistic experiment that demonstrates that drug availability affects substance abuse. In the 1960s and 1970s, the legal drinking age was lowered from twenty-one to eighteen years of age in several states. During this time, there was a 20 to 50 percent increase in traffic fatalities for this age group. In contrast, between 1975 and 1984, twenty-six states raised the drinking age from eighteen to twenty-one. These states observed a 13 percent reduction in automobile fatalities. Since about half of all traffic fatalities occur when one of the drivers is intoxicated, these data suggest that decreased alcohol availability decreases alcohol-related problems. It is no accident that the period of lowest alcohol consumption in the United States was during Prohibition, a period (1919-1933) during which it was illegal to transport, manufacture, or sell alcoholic beverages.

Despite the apparent benefits of limiting drug availability, society maintains a curiously irrational attitude toward limiting drugs. It is not clear why alcohol and tobacco (our two most medically dangerous drugs) are legal and why drugs that have some medicinal value such as marijuana and narcotics are illegal. While cigarette smoking is now banned on domestic flights, we can still purchase cigarettes in the gift store at the airport. In some states, liquor is sold in state-sponsored stores presumably to control distribution of alcohol. How ironic, then, that in poor parts of these states frequented by "winos" it is cheaper, ounce per ounce, to buy a quart of Thunderbird wine than to buy a cup of coffee.

EDUCATION

Limiting demand through educating about adverse consequences

A second approach to control drug use disorders is to limit demand. Attempts to limit demand have usually centered on educating people to be aware of the adverse consequences of drugs. The success of an educational approach is apparent in attempts to decrease cigarette smoking. In the 1960s, advertising for cigarettes was banned from television and warnings were placed on cigarette cartons. The cultural stereotype of a sexy man lighting a cigarette to impress his female companion has been replaced by lawsuits crusading against greedy tobacco companies. This change in our attitudes is reflected in a 37 percent decrease during this decade in the number of adult Americans who smoke and a 10 percent decrease in sales of cigarettes. Still, our educational efforts are inconsistent. Cigarette ads are permitted in magazines, newspapers, and on billboards. Alcohol advertising is still permitted on television. Moreover it is ironic that while fatal traffic accidents related to alcohol drinking remain such an important problem, race cars are shown on television with beer labels plastered on the side of the cars.

Educational efforts directed at the use of marijuana and cocaine have been somewhat successful. In the late 1970s, stereotypes about marijuana use were quite unrealistic as presented in movies such as *Reefer Madness*. Among young people, marijuana was perceived as relatively harmless, and marijuana use was considered a quite fashionable way to express independence from a "misinformed" older generation. As shown in Figure 14-7, however, marijuana use peaked in 1978, when nearly 40 percent of all high school seniors reported using marijuana at least once during the past month. Starting in the early 1980s, however, a dramatic shift in the perceived harmfulness of daily marijuana use was observed. Correspondingly,

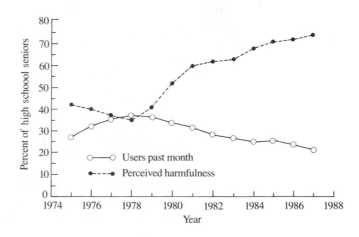

Figure 14-7
Perceived harmfulness and current use of marijuana

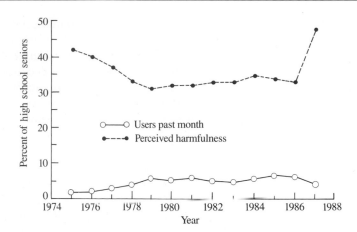

Figure 14-8
Perceived harmfulness and current use of cocaine

the use of marijuana steadily declined, so that in 1987 only 20 percent of high school seniors reported marijuana use in the past month.

Cocaine use also demonstrates how educational efforts can affect drug use. While cocaine use has been steadily increasing in recent years, there was a dramatic decrease in cocaine use in 1987. As Figure 14-8 shows, coincident with newspaper reports of the hazards of cocaine use, there was a dramatic increase in the number of high school seniors who perceived cocaine use to be harmful, from 34 percent in 1986 to 48 percent in 1987. There was also a related, dramatic decrease in current cocaine users, from 6.2 percent in 1986 to 4.3 percent in 1987.

TREATMENT

At the same time as government interventions to limit drug availability and demand have met with limited success, treatment for drug-dependent people remains woefully inadequate. It is difficult to blame any one group for the failure of many drug-dependent people to obtain adequate treatment. While about 40 percent of admissions to Veterans' Administration hospitals are related to substance abuse, health professionals often fail to diagnose and refer patients for substance abuse treatment. When patients are referred for treatment, they are not eligible for the same benefits offered to veterans with other medical or emotional disorders, since alcohol dependence and other drug dependencies are considered to be "willful misconduct." A recent Supreme Court decision reaffirmed the VA's claim that alcohol-dependent people are somehow uniquely responsible for their illness.

OUR SOCIETY AND DRUG USE AND ABUSE

Throughout this chapter, it has been clear that the use of psychoactive substances has a long history and that just as moderate controlled use can produce pleasant or even medicinal effects, for many people drug use cannot be controlled and this can lead to disastrous consequences. Some people "just *can't* say no" to drugs. Decreasing drug availability can decrease the number of people who experiment with drugs and will make it difficult for people to maintain their dependence. We have seen that both biological and behav-

Treatment of drug addicts is important to help in preventing relapse; unfortunately such treatment remains woefully inadequate.

ioral factors interact to make it difficult to quit drugs once a dependence has been established. While alcohol use decreased during the Prohibition period, organized crime prospered. As the 1990s approach, we are witnessing a similar increase in crime as drug-dependent people will risk jobs, relationships, and their lives to maintain a drug habit.

While there are no easy solutions to the drug problem, a mature policy based on scientific understanding about the cause and treatments of substance abuse is in order. People, through no fault of their own, may be born with biological predispositions to become dependent on certain substances. For others, environmental factors may conspire to place them at higher risk for drug dependence. For these individuals, we need empathy and effective treatments that are as readily available as the drugs they take. Claiming that these individuals lack willpower has no empirical validity and simply maintains the social stigma attached to drug dependence, making it more difficult to get individuals into treatment.

SUMMARY

1. Substance abuse is the leading health problem in the United States. Despite the severe medical and social consequences, society continues to have an ambivalent attitude about psychoactive drugs.

2. The diagnosis of substance dependence is made if a person exhibits: (1) loss of control over use of the substance, (2) psychosocial impairment because of substance use, and (3) evidence of affective or physiological adaptation to the drug.

3. The potency of a psychoactive drug depends on its ability to interact with neurotransmitters in the brain. Factors such as the route of administration of the drug, ability of the drug to cross the protective *blood-brain barrier,* and the drug's *half-life,* the rate at which a drug is degraded, all affect the ability of a drug to affect mood, perceptions, and behavior.

4. Substance dependence depends on factors within the individual (personality factors and biological vulnerability) and properties of certain classes of drugs.

5. Individuals with antisocial personality traits are more likely to try out different drugs and increase risk of dependence. Also, certain individuals are vulnerable to dependence because of inherited biological traits.

6. Drugs that produce pleasure and have the property of *affective tolerance* (less response to a specific dose of the drug), and *affective withdrawal* (opposite reactions to those felt when the drug was initially taken) lead to the addictive cycle. The addictive cycle occurs when an individual learns that by retaking the drug, affective withdrawal can be reduced or avoided.

7. Situations associated with drug use can trigger affective withdrawal and lead to drug use.

8. Alcohol dependence is the most common mental disorder, with a prevalence of 13 percent of the population. Alcohol intoxication results in impaired judgment and is associated with about half of all fatal car accidents and suicides. Alcohol withdrawal can produce seizures (rum fits), delirium tremens (DT's), and can result in death. The life expectancy of an alcohol-dependent person is reduced by twelve years.

9. The opiates produce their pharmacological effects by binding to opiate receptors. They blunt the emotional and physical consequences of pain, but larger and larger doses are required to achieve the same effect. Intravenous narcotic use is a major risk factor for infection with Human Immunodeficiency Virus (HIV) and primarily responsible for the transmission of AIDS into the heterosexual community.

10. Stimulant use, especially cocaine, has increased in recent years, and the introduction of more potent forms of cocaine (crack) has led to a dramatic increase in the incidence of medical and social problems from cocaine. These include psychosis and paranoia during chronic use and lack of energy and motivation during the crash from stimulants.

11. The hallucinogens produce perceptual changes and hallucinations. They may cause panic attacks during intoxication, and in some susceptible people, prolonged psychotic states follow drug use.

12. Most people smoke cigarettes to obtain the effects of nicotine, which stimulates a class of cholinergic receptors called the nicotinic receptors. It is easy for most people to give up smoking, but many people then relapse within one year. The costs of cigarette smoking to personal health and to society are staggering.

13. Abuse of barbiturates has decreased in recent years, but benzodiazepine abuse has been increasingly recognized as a potential problem. The barbiturates are depressants for the central nervous system, and they act generally to decrease neuronal activity. The benzodiazepines increase the effectiveness of GABA, the principal inhibitory neurotransmitter in the brain.

14. Drug abuse affects and is affected by cultural context. Society can try to stop drug dependence by limiting drug availability, limiting demand through education, and providing adequate treatment.

CHAPTER
15

Personality Disorders

How does one describe people who cheat needlessly and lie without reason in all kinds of contexts? Or people who are always suspicious of others' intentions? Or people who respond passively to all provocations? Such people are hardly psychotic, for they often have a good grip on reality. Nor are they necessarily dominated by unwarranted fears (see Chapter 8), sexual difficulties, addictions, and the like. Nevertheless, their behaviors strike observers as odd, as deviant, or as abnormal. Theirs seem to be a disorder of personality. Their characteristic ways of perceiving and thinking about themselves and their environment are inflexible, and a source of social and occupational maladjustment. In addition, their behaviors may well be a source of distress for themselves and others. Their disorders are called *personality disorders.*

Consider a young employee who is up for promotion. She knows she has done a good job, and that she probably deserves appropriate credit. But, she feels anxious, thinking perhaps that one of her colleagues is trying to undercut her achievements. When they learn of her fears, her friends call her "paranoid," pointing out that she is probably imagining the situation. Oddly reassured by that characterization, she is able to go about her business. Most of us have had similar concerns. Our worries are ones that grow out of specific situations. They are time-limited and easily dispelled. But some people's worries are not so easily relieved. Indeed, they spend much of their lives scanning the environment for cues that validate their paranoid feelings. Unlike the employee who has a few "paranoid" moments, individuals with the *paranoid personality disorder* are always suspicious of others' motives. While they are able to function and are not psychotic, they are continually troubled by deep distrust.

The personality disorders have provided a fascinating source of psychological study across the decades because they ascribe a stability and sturdiness to personality and behavior that extends across time and context. The personality disorders are fundamentally disorders of *traits,* that is, disorders that are reflected in the individual's tendency to perceive and respond to the environment in broad and maladaptive ways. Perhaps the most fascinating of these disorders is the *antisocial personality disorder.* Known also as *sociopathy* and *psychopathy,* this disorder has been studied extensively and is the best understood of the personality disorders.

THE ANTISOCIAL PERSONALITY DISORDER

Characteristics of the antisocial personality

People who suffer from the psychological disorders that were examined in earlier chapters create distress for their families and friends, but mainly they themselves are the ones who suffer. In contrast, the suffering in an individual with the antisocial personality disorder is muted. The hallmark of the disorder is a rapacious attitude toward others, a chronic insensitivity and indifference to the rights of other people that is marked by lying, stealing, cheating, and worse. Whereas those who suffer other psychological difficulties may be unpleasant, contact with antisocial personalities may be downright dangerous, for many of them are outright criminals. Because their numbers are not small, they constitute a major social and legal problem, as well as a psychological one.

DISORDERS OF WILL

The prevalence of the antisocial personality disorder is roughly 2 to 3 percent. Men are so diagnosed more than four times as often as women (Regier, Myers, Kramer, Robins, Blayer, Hough, Eaton, and Locke, 1984; Cadoret, 1986). But it is not only individuals with the antisocial personality disorder who steal and cheat. "Normal" people filch, forge, and embezzle. But when normal people steal and cheat we call them criminals and their acts, crime. Why should those who suffer the antisocial personality disorder be regarded any differently?

No control over criminal behavior

The fact is that for the longest time antisocial personalities were *not* thought about in psychological terms. Throughout most of history, criminals were criminals and the only distinctions that were made had to do with the severity of their crimes. But in the nineteenth century especially, the idea developed that certain kinds of criminal behavior might arise from conditions over which the individual had no control—that is, from social, psychological, or biological sources. Their crimes then were not acts of will, but rather the result of circumstances beyond their control. Much as noncriminal but clearly dysfunctional behaviors might be caused by psychological experiences over which the individual had little control, so too might criminal, antisocial ones.

In the nineteenth century, such antisocial people were said to be afflicted by *moral insanity.* This disorder was distinguished from other psychological disorders by the English psychiatrist J.C. Prichard (1837), who wrote:

Intellectual faculties appear to have sustained little or no injury, while the disorder is manifest principally or alone, in the state of the feelings, temper, or habits . . .

the moral and active principles of the mind are strangely perverted and depraved; the power of self-government is lost or greatly impaired; and the individual is found to be incapable, not of talking or reasoning upon any subject proposed to him, for this he will often do with great shrewdness and volubility, but of conducting himself with decency and propriety in the business of life. (Prichard, 1837, p. 15)

Moral insanity a disorder of will

Moral insanity then, was viewed as a disorder of the *will.* Although the term moral insanity has been displaced by "antisocial personality disorder" today, it continues to be viewed as a disorder of will. Whether for biological, social, or psychological reasons, these people are found "to be incapable . . . of conducting [themselves] with decency and propriety in the business of life." Where people are *capable* of exercising will and of conducting themselves properly, but simply *choose* not to do so, they continue to be called criminals.

How does a disorder of will develop? We are not yet certain, but there has been some interesting theoretical speculation. Robert Kegan (1986) suggests that people who have antisocial personality disorders most resemble ten-year-old children in their psychological makeup. Neither can handle responsibility, both have difficulty understanding others, and both are awfully concrete-minded. Some of the latter is represented in the following interchange between a reporter and the famous bank robber, Willy Sutton:

Why do you rob all these banks, Willy?
Because that's where they keep the money.

(Kegan, 1986)

There is often debate about whether or not a person is actually suffering a personality disorder, and that debate arises from the very nature of the disorder itself. The antisocial personality disorder is a disorder of will, and will is not an all-or-nothing matter. One does not either have or not have will. Rather, like most other psychological functions, will exists on a continuum: normal people have more or less of it, but those who suffer this disorder have even less. The line that divides those who suffer disorders from the rest of us is arbitrary. Because of this, we diagnose this disorder with caution.

Also, like anxiety, will is *inferred.* One does not see will. Rather, its presence is inferred from behaviors that are believed to reflect it. Unless one examines those specific behaviors, judging whether someone does or does not suffer a personality disorder can be hazardous. For that reason, DSM-III-R offers behavioral diagnostic criteria for the antisocial personality disorder.

CHARACTERIZING THE ANTISOCIAL PERSONALITY DISORDER

Criteria to diagnose antisocial personality disorder

Antisocial behavior alone is not sufficient for the diagnosis of antisocial personality disorder. Such behavior would merely qualify as "adult antisocial behavior," which in DSM-III-R is ruled out as a mental disorder. In order to qualify as a personality disorder, the antisocial behaviors must meet two primary criteria. First, the behavior has to be longstanding. Although the diagnosis cannot be applied to a person who is under eighteen, current diagnostic criteria require substantial evidence of antisocial behavior before the age of fifteen. Such evidence can include habitual lying, early and aggressive sexual behavior, excessive drinking, theft, vandalism, and chronic rule violation at home and at school. Second, the present antisocial behavior must be manifested in at least four classes of behavior, among which are: inconsistent work or school performance; irresponsible parenting; unlawful behaviors such as theft, pimping, prostitution, dealing drugs, or other felony convictions; inability to sustain a relationship with a sexual partner; repeated aggressiveness; recklessness that endangers others; repeated lying; and failure to honor financial obligations. The antisocial personality disorder then is defined by sustained antisocial behaviors that, having begun by adolescence, continue in a variety of areas during adulthood.

Three broad characteristics of antisocial personality

These behavioral criteria make clear who can be diagnosed as having an antisocial personality disorder and who cannot. What personality characteristics are reflected in such behaviors? Hervey Cleckley, a lifelong student of these behaviors and people, described some of their characteristics in *The Mask of Sanity* (1964). Cleckley lists sixteen features of the sociopath's personality. These sixteen characteristics can be reduced to three broad categories: inadequately motivated antisocial behavior, the absence of a conscience and sense of responsibility to others, and emotional poverty.

INADEQUATELY MOTIVATED ANTISOCIAL BEHAVIOR

Crimes as impulsive, not rational

Crime "makes sense" for normal criminals. We understand what they are doing and why, and so do they. They want to get rich—quick—and they may want status. These are motivations we can understand, however much we disapprove of the behaviors. But the crimes of sociopaths often seem aimless, random, and impulsive. We do not understand why they did what they did, and neither do they understand it. They seem not to be motivated by any rational purpose, but rather seem perversely impulsive.

If DSM-III-R had been available, convicted killer Gary Gilmore would have been diagnosed as having an antisocial personality disorder.

On October 7, 1976, Gary Gilmore was sentenced to death by a Utah court after a seemingly purposeless crime spree, and on January 7, 1977, he became the first person to be executed in the United States since 1966. During a psychological evaluation to determine whether Gilmore was competent to stand trial, it was determined that he suffered an antisocial personality disorder. Gilmore's activities provide an interesting example of crime without understandable motives.

Gilmore had been released from prison only six months earlier, after serving time for armed robbery. He promptly violated parole by leaving the state. His probation officer gave him another chance. But shortly thereafter, following a heated argument with his girlfriend, Gilmore stole a stereo. Once again, he persuaded the police not to bring charges. Gilmore himself described the next events: "I pulled up near a gas station. I told the service station guy to give me all his money. I then took him to the bathroom and told him to kneel down and then I shot him in the head twice. The guy didn't give me any trouble but I just felt like I had to do it."

The very next morning, Gilmore left his car at another service station for minor repairs and walked to a motel. "I went in and told the guy to give me the money. I told him to lay on the floor and then I shot him. I then walked out and was carrying the cash drawer with me. I took the money and threw the cash drawer in a bush and I tried to push the gun in the bush too. But as I was pushing it in the bush, it went off and that's how come I was shot in the arm. It seems like things have always gone bad for me. It seems like I've always done dumb things that just caused trouble for me."

ABSENCE OF A CONSCIENCE AND A SENSE OF RESPONSIBILITY TO OTHERS

Absence of remorse

The absence of shame or remorse for past misdeeds, of any sense of humiliation for egregious ones, is one of the most common characteristics of sociopaths. They lack conscience, and with it, any deep capacity to care about other people (Hare, 1980). Their relationships, therefore, tend to be quite shallow and exploitative. They lack a capacity for love and sustained attachment and are unresponsive to trust, kindness, or affection. They lie shamelessly and can mercilessly abuse those who have trusted them. Gary Gilmore did not have a serious relationship until several weeks before he committed the two murders. He was then thirty-six years old. Describing the affair, he said that it was "probably the first close relationship that I ever had with anyone. I just didn't know how to respond to her for any length of time. I was very insensitive to her . . . I was thoughtless in the way I treated her. . . . [H]er two children bugged me and sometimes I would get angry at them and slap them because they were so noisy."

EMOTIONAL POVERTY

Shallow emotions

One of the major differences between the normal person who is a criminal and the sociopath lies in the depth of experienced emotion. Ordinary criminals presumably experience the same emotions as other normal people. But sociopaths experience very shallow emotions. They seem to lack the capacity for sustained love, anger, grief, joy, or despair. During a psychiatric interview, Gilmore observed that "I don't remember any real emotional event in all my life. . . . When you're in the joint, you stay pretty even all the time . . . I'm not really excitable you know. I don't get emotional." Indeed, their incapacity to experience emotion may be significantly related to their lack of conscience and to the ease with which they violate the expectations of others.

THE SOURCES OF SOCIOPATHY

Personality disorders are long-lived. The antisocial personality disorder originates in childhood or early adolescence as a conduct disorder (see Chapter 16), and then continues into adulthood. Once again, Gary Gilmore is a case in point. Examining his childhood, we find that he had been suspended from school on several occasions for truancy and for alleged thefts from his classmates. When he was fourteen, he was sent to a correctional youth facility for auto theft. By the time of his last arrest, Gilmore had spent fifteen of his sixteen adult years behind bars.

Originates in childhood

What factors give rise to such continuously antisocial behavior? Four potential sources have been given considerable attention: (1) the family and social context, (2) defects in learning, (3) genetics, and (4) physiological dysfunctions in the central nervous system.

THE FAMILY AND SOCIAL CONTEXT

Because the sociopath seems not to have internalized the moral standards of the larger society, it is natural to examine the agents of socialization, particularly the family and social context, for clues about sociopathy. There is evidence, for example, that sociopaths who grew up in the lower social classes

Parental
deprivation in
negative
emotional climate

experienced more difficult childhoods than other people from those same social strata. A number of studies indicate that losing a parent through desertion, divorce, or separation (rather than through death or chronic hospitalization) is highly correlated with the later development of sociopathic behavior (Gregory, 1958; Greer, 1964; Oltman and Friedman, 1967). Moreover, the more severe the sociopathic behavior, the more likely it is that the sociopath experienced parental deprivation. Most writers believe, however, that it is not the parental deprivation per se that promotes sociopathy—otherwise the findings would include deprivation through death and hospitalization. Rather it is the emotional climate that precedes the divorce—the arguments and violent fights, the blatant promiscuity, alcoholism, parental instability, the neglectful father—which is implicated in socialization for sociopathy (Smith, 1978).

Similar but substantially enlarged findings emerged from a study of a large group of people who had been seen at a child guidance clinic between 1924 and 1929 (Robins, 1966). Fortunately, the clinic had maintained careful psychological and sociological records on the presenting problems and family circumstances of its clients. When these children grew up, they were carefully interviewed, along with a control group that had never been seen at the clinic. About 22 percent of the clinic referrals qualified for the adult diagnosis of sociopathic personality, while only 2 percent of the control group received that diagnosis.

What early experiences were correlated with the diagnosis of antisocial personality disorder in adulthood? First, as children, these sociopaths had been referred to that child guidance clinic for antisocial behaviors. Theft, truancy, and school discipline problems dot their clinic records. Second, they tended more often than the control group to come from impoverished homes and from homes that were broken by divorce or separation. Their fathers themselves were often antisocial persons who may well have served as sociopathic models for their children (Bandura and Walters, 1963), while simultaneously creating the marital discord that may spawn sociopathic development (Robins, 1966). Again taking Gary Gilmore's life as an example, we find that although Gilmore's parents were never formally separated, his father spent so much of his time away from home that Gilmore considered himself to have been raised by "a single parent." During some of that time, his father was in prison, serving eighteen months on a bad check charge. His mother was simultaneously overindulgent and neglectful: Gilmore was often left to fend for himself. Reflecting on his family, he described it as "typical" and noted that "there wasn't much closeness in it."

Juvenile offenses

The children who later became sociopaths were referred to juvenile court and were subsequently sent to correctional institutions much more often than other children. In such institutions, they very likely picked up some of the habits of their antisocial peers. These findings, however, should not be interpreted to mean that *all* punishment for juvenile offenses is necessarily harmful to the child. Indeed, one study revealed that children who were apprehended and *moderately* punished for juvenile crimes have a lower recidivism rate than those who were apprehended and released without punishment (McCord, 1980). In order for children to be deterred from further crime, they must be given a clear message that what they did was wrong. The message is clearest when it comes as punishment. *Too* clear a message —one that results in sending children to penal institutions—may teach that crime is wrong, but it may also put them in an environment where they can learn from their peers how to pursue a criminal career successfully.

Other longitudinal studies underscore the relationship of the home environment and subsequent criminality in delinquent boys. Once again, whether the father was absent or present was not a key determinant of subsequent criminality. The factors that did influence whether delinquent boys became criminal adults were maternal affection and self-esteem, parental supervision, harmony within the household, and the father's deviance. Indeed, separation and divorce do not lead to criminal behavior so long as the mother is affectionate and self-confident, the child is supervised, the level of discord between the parents is minimal, and the father is nondeviant (McCord, 1979).

DEFECTS IN LEARNING

Failure to learn from punishment

Many clinicians have been struck by the seeming inability of the sociopath to learn from experience. Prichard (1837) called them "moral imbeciles." Cleckley (1964) observed that they failed especially to learn from punishing experiences, and as a result, had poor judgment. But sociopaths are often "savvy" and intelligent. If they suffer a defect in learning, it must be a fairly subtle one. What form might such a defect take?

Chronic under-arousal

□ DEFICIENCIES IN AVOIDANCE LEARNING. Cleckley's observations, in particular, suggested that sociopaths were especially deficient in *avoidance* learning. Ordinary people rapidly learn to anticipate and avoid punitive situations. But sociopaths, perhaps because they are under-aroused and under-anxious, fail to do so. To examine this possibility, sociopaths and normal people were taken into the laboratory to test their ability to master a certain task (Lykken, 1957). The task involved learning to press a "correct" lever, but the idea was to find out which group learned to avoid punishment.

Participants sat in front of a panel that had four levers. Immediately above each lever was a red light and a green light (see Figure 15-1). The subject's task was to find and press the lever that turned on the green light on each of a series of twenty trials. Since the correct lever changed on each trial, the subjects had to remember their sequence of responses, from the first trial to the one they were now working on. A certain pattern had to be learned, and it was quite a complicated task, a veritable mental maze.

Figure 15-1
Apparatus for Lykken's (1957) study of avoidance learning in sociopaths. On any given trial, only one of the four levers is correct, and the correct lever changes from trial to trial. Subjects must learn a pattern of twenty correct lever-presses. A correct lever-press turns on a green light. Of the remaining three levers (each of which is wrong), two turn on red lights, while the third delivers electric shock.

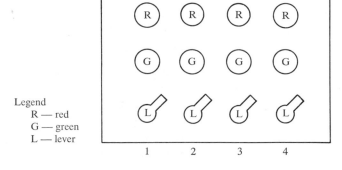

Legend
R — red
G — green
L — lever

On each trial, the subject had four choices, only one of which turned on the green light. Two of the levers turned on a red light—clearly a wrong response—while the third delivered electric shock. Having two kinds of wrong responses, one that simply says "wrong" and the other that delivers physical punishment, enabled the investigator to answer a telling question. Is it that sociopaths cannot learn from negative experience, or are there particular negative experiences, namely *avoidance* experiences, from which they cannot learn?

As expected, there were no differences in the total number of mistakes made by sociopaths and nonsociopaths. But whereas nonsociopaths quickly learned to avoid the electrified levers, the sociopaths made the most errors that led to shock, suggesting that their particular learning defect was an inability to learn from painful experiences (Lykken, 1957). In effect, punishment or threat of punishment does not seem to influence a sociopath's behavior.

Why should sociopaths be deficient in avoidance learning? One possibility is that sociopaths do not avoid shock because they do not find shock as noxious as do normal people, and they do not find shock as noxious because they are chronically *under-aroused.* Put differently, sociopaths may actually seek stimulation in order to elevate arousal to an optimal level. Indeed, it has often seemed to clinical observers that that is the case (Cleckley, 1964). Gary Gilmore, the sociopath who was described earlier, may well have experienced under-arousal and the need for stimulation as a child. Gilmore said, "I remember when I was a boy I would feel like I had to do things like sit on a railroad track until just before the train came and then I would dash off. Or I would put my finger over the end of a BB gun and pull the trigger to see if a BB was really in it. Sometimes I would stick my finger in water and then put my finger in a light socket to see if it would really shock me."

To examine the sociopath's possible need for stimulation, sociopathic and normal subjects were injected either with adrenaline, which heightens arousal, or with a placebo and tested on the "mental maze" described above. Once again, in both the adrenaline and placebo conditions, sociopaths made no more errors than normals. But sociopaths who received the placebo failed to learn to avoid shock. Only when they were given adrenaline was their characteristic under-arousal overcome. Being already aroused by the adrenaline, the sociopaths avoided the shocked lever just as the normals did in the placebo condition (Schachter and Latane, 1964).

Cleckley's observation that sociopaths are emotionally flat was confirmed in this experiment. Because they are under-aroused in general, the emotions that ordinarily inhibit criminal behavior are not sufficiently aroused in sociopaths. At the same time, the emotions that propel people into crimes of passion are also absent. Sociopaths are mainly responsible for "cool" crimes such as burglary, forgery, and con games. When they are involved in violence, as Gilmore was, it tends to be impulsive and irrational violence, and perverse because it so lacks in feeling.

Effects of different kinds of punishment

There are several kinds of punishment. There is *physical* punishment to which sociopaths do not respond as the above experiments suggest. But there is also *tangible* punishment such as the loss of money, and *social* punishment such as disapproval. Are sociopaths as unresponsive to the latter kinds of punishment as they are to physical punishment? The same "mental maze" was used to examine this question. But this time, if one of the wrong levers was pressed, the subject lost a quarter. If another was pressed, the subject received social disapproval, and the third wrong lever brought electric shock. Once again, sociopaths learned the task as quickly as nonsociopaths. And again, they were considerably less responsive to physical punishment than were normals. They were also less responsive to social disapproval. But they quickly learned to avoid the lever that would cost them a quarter. Indeed, they avoided this lever somewhat more than normals, indicating that sociopaths can learn to avoid punishment provided that the punishment is noxious to *them* (Schmauk, 1970).

☐ THE IMMEDIACY OF CONSEQUENCES.   The greater the interval between the time a behavior occurs and its consequences, the more difficult it is to learn the relationship between that behavior and its consequences. Some people generally have greater difficulty seeing a relationship between two events across time than do others. It may be that sociopaths have greater difficulty than most people. If this is the case, it would explain why sociopaths are not deterred from crime by the anticipation of punishment, since the punishment usually occurs long after the crime has been committed.

Low anxiety levels

An experiment was devised to determine whether individuals with antisocial personality disorders anticipated punishment in different ways than did normals. In this experiment, three groups of subjects were used: (1) criminals who had been diagnosed as sociopaths; (2) criminals who had been diagnosed as nonsociopaths; and (3) noncriminals. These subjects were presented with the numbers "1" through "12," one at a time and consecutively. They were told that they would receive an electric shock when the number "8" appeared. In order to determine the level of anxiety experienced, the galvanic skin response (GSR), which is one measure of experienced anxiety, was assessed for each subject throughout the experiment. Both normals and nonsociopathic criminals displayed fear of the anticipated electric shock from the start. Moreover, their anxiety, as measured by the GSR, mounted markedly as the number "8" drew closer, and it plummeted afterwards. In contrast, sociopathic subjects exhibited dramatically lower anxiety levels throughout the experiment, and their measured fear did not increase as the number "8" approached. Even when the shock was administered, their arousal and GSR activity levels were far lower than those in the other two groups (Hare, 1965).

When the data on avoidance learning are combined with those on family and social antecedents of sociopathy, an interesting picture emerges. The antisocial personality disorder does not arise simply from harsh circumstances. Nor is its development deterred by physical punishment or even by imprisonment. Neither poverty nor parental deprivation necessarily led to sociopathy. But affectionate parents and parental supervision can inhibit the development of sociopathy. So, too, can punishment when it is *felt* to be painful and abhorrent, rather than when it is merely automatically applied.

GENETICS AND CRIMINALITY

The possibility that sociopathy has a genetic basis has long been attractive. In the popular imagination, sociopathy and antisocial behavior have long been associated with the "bad seed," and particularly the bad seed that came from a family of bad seeds. That view, however, is hard to assess. The problems of sorting environmental from genetic influences are as difficult here as elsewhere. But the task here is further compounded by the fact that it is *criminals*—those who have been apprehended and convicted of a crime—who come to our attention, not those who have eluded apprehension. Not all criminals are sociopaths, of course, nor are all sociopaths criminals.

Strong roles of both genetics and environment

The data on the biology of sociopathy are fascinating for, though they are complex, they appear to indicate that both genetics and environment play strong roles in the development of sociopathy. We begin by considering twin and adoption studies, and then examine studies of men with an extra Y chromosome. But before doing so, one thing should be made clear. Most of these studies are concerned with the relations between biology and *criminality*. Criminality, as we indicated earlier, is not synonymous with sociopathy. Where the studies permit, we will distinguish between the two.

□ TWIN STUDIES.   One way to examine the relative influence of genetic and environmental factors in sociopathy is to study the concordance of sociopathic behavior in twins. Recall again that monozygotic or identical (MZ) twins each have exactly the same genetic heritage, while dizygotic (DZ) or fraternal twins are as genetically dissimilar as ordinary siblings (see Chapter 3). The environments of MZ and DZ twins are *nearly* the same. (These environments are nearly the same, rather than downright identical, because individuals contribute to their environments, and no two contributions are exactly the same.) This allows us to look at the other variable, genetics. If concordance for sociopathy or criminality is higher for MZ than for DZ twins, one can infer that genetic factors play a role.

Concordance for criminality greater in MZ than DZ twins

According to the series of studies that examine the rates of criminality among MZ and DZ twins, there is a strong relationship between zygosity and criminality. In a total of 216 MZ pairs and 214 same-sex DZ pairs, 69 percent of the MZ but only 33 percent of the DZ pairs were concordant for criminality (Christiansen, 1977). By themselves, these studies would strongly suggest that genetic influences are powerful in criminality.

There are two sources of evidence that suggest that such a conclusion would be premature. First, such high concordance for criminality among MZ twins was only marginally higher than for DZ twins (Dalgard and Kringlen, 1976). The latter finding can be explained by the fact that MZ twins share a more similar environment than DZ twins. Monozygotic twins, being identical, are more likely to be treated the same by parents and others than are dizygotic twins. Indeed, they are often confused for each other. Second, and even more interesting, are the data regarding *opposite-sex* DZ pairs. Opposite-sex twins are no different genetically than same-sex DZ twins, though patently they share different environments. If criminality is determined by heredity and heredity alone, the data for opposite-sex twins should be identical to the data for same-sex DZ twins. But they are not. The concordance for criminality among opposite-sex twins is only 16 percent, less than half of what it is for same-sex twins. This difference in concordance rates underscores the environmental influences on criminality (Cloninger, Christiansen, Reich, and Gottesman, 1978; Sigvardsson, Cloninger, Bohman, and von Knorring, 1982).

Table 15–1 CRIMINALITY OF ADOPTED SONS ACCORDING TO THE CRIMINALITY OF THEIR ADOPTIVE AND BIOLOGICAL FATHERS

Father		Percentage of sons who are criminal offenders	Number
Biological	*Adoptive*		
No registered offense	No registered offense	10.5	333
No registered offense	Criminal offense	11.5	52
Criminal offense	No registered offense	22.0	219
Criminal offense	Criminal offense	36.2	58
Total			662

SOURCE: Modified from Hutchings and Mednick, 1977, p. 132.

Comparing offspring's criminal record with those of adoptive and biological parents

□ ADOPTION STUDIES.   When children are raised by their natural parents, it is impossible to separate the effects of genetics from those of environment on their development. But studies of children who have been adopted at an early age allow these influences to be separated. These studies also provide evidence for the influence of heredity in both criminality and sociopathy. One study examined the criminal records of adopted persons in Denmark (Hutchings and Mednick, 1977; Mednick, Gabrielli and Hutchings, 1984). Their names were drawn from the Danish Population Register, which records the names of both the adoptive and the biological parents of these adoptees. Thus, it is possible to compare the criminal records of the adopted children with those of both sets of parents. These comparative data are shown in Table 15-1. The incidence of crime among these offspring was lowest when neither the biological nor the adoptive fathers had been convicted of a criminal offense. Nearly indistinguishable from that low rate was the rate among adoptees whose adoptive fathers had been convicted, but whose biological fathers were "clean." The incidence of criminal conviction among adoptees jumped dramatically, however, when the natural father had a criminal record, but the adoptive father had none, providing clear support for the view that the tendency to engage in criminal acts is hereditary. But highest of all was the incidence of criminality among adoptees when both their natural *and* adoptive fathers had criminal records, underscoring again the combined influence of heredity and environment on criminality. These individuals probably inherited a tendency toward criminality from their biological fathers and learned criminal behavior from their adoptive fathers (Cloninger and Gottesman, 1987). As we mentioned, however, criminality is not identical with sociopathy. But when a measure of sociopathy rather than criminality was used, similar findings were obtained (Schulsinger, 1972).

Men with an extra Y chromosome

□ XYY: AN EXTRA CHROMOSOME?   A person's sex is determined by a pair of chromosomes. Women have two X chromosomes (XX). Men have a single X and a single Y chromosome (XY). But some men have an extra Y chromosome (XYY). Since it is the Y chromosome that defines the male, the XYY is sometimes considered a "supermale." Such a person, for example, is especially tall—much taller than the ordinary male. It is also widely

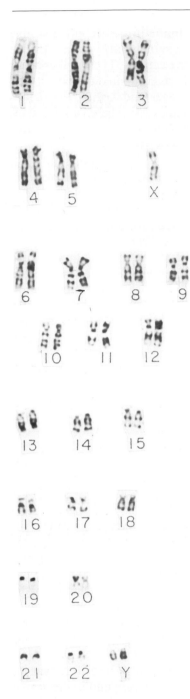

A karyotype of an XYY—a man with an extra chromosome. Generally, a man will have one X chromosome and one Y chromosome. An XYY may be prone to violent behavior.

believed that the XYY is especially violent and often prone toward criminal behavior.

These beliefs are difficult to verify. Not all tall men are XYY's. Nor, of course, are all criminals XYY's. Indeed, not more than 1.5 percent of criminals and delinquents who have been tested have this additional chromosome (Rosenthal, 1970b). Some of the studies take their evidence from a few or even single cases, and they often fail to include normal control groups. Until recently, a definite relationship between the XYY syndrome and violence could neither be demonstrated nor disconfirmed.

One study examined the criminal records of all men who were born in Copenhagen between 1944 and 1947 (Witkin et al., 1976). Once again, the Danish Population Register provides very complete data on Danish citizens, and therefore permits this kind of thorough study. The investigators began with a group of 31,436 men, of whom 4,591 were at least six feet tall. Since XYY's are tall, the latter group promised to produce the maximum number of XYY's. In that group, twelve XYY's were discovered, yielding a prevalence of 2.9 XYY's per thousand population. Of those twelve, five or 42 percent had been convicted of one or more criminal offenses, as against 9.3 percent of ordinary XY males who were six feet tall or more. While the data support the view that XYY men are more likely to be convicted of a crime, they do not confirm the view that XYY's engage in *violent* crime. Only one of the five committed an act of violence against another person, and that act was relatively mild. Otherwise, nearly all of the crimes involved property. Indeed, of the 149 offenses for which the five XYY's were convicted, fully 145 were against property—usually crimes of theft.

But while XYY's are not more violent, the evidence from this study indicates that they are convicted of crime much more frequently than are "normal" male criminals. Why should that be? One interesting bit of information that emerged from the above study is that, compared to XY criminals, XYY's have markedly lower intelligence. Conceivably, lower intelligence itself leads to criminal activity, perhaps because the less intelligent find it more difficult to get jobs or to resist temptations. Alternately, these findings may not reflect differences in the incidence of crime, but merely differences in *apprehension* and *conviction*. With lower intelligence, XYY's may stand a greater chance of being apprehended, convicted, and sentenced.

PHYSIOLOGICAL DYSFUNCTIONS

To whatever extent genetics is related to criminality and sociopathy, the relationship is not likely a direct one. One does not directly acquire from genes the skills and disposition to engage in crime. What then is it that *is* acquired genetically? What is passed down through the genes that makes one more likely to engage in sociopathic activities?

A number of investigators have sought to discover physiological differences between sociopaths and normal people. And a good number of such differences have been discovered. For example, a substantial proportion of sociopaths have abnormal electroencephalograms (EEG's). This is especially true of the most violent and aggressive sociopaths. The abnormalities are of two kinds. First, sociopaths show the slow brain waves that are characteristic of children and that suggest brain immaturity. Second, a sizable proportion of sociopaths show positive spiking in their brain waves. Positive spikes are sudden and brief bursts of brain wave activity. These spikes occur in the EEG's of 40 to 45 percent of sociopaths as compared to about 1 to 2 percent of the general population (Kurland, Yeager, and Arthur, 1963). Positive spiking is itself associated with impulsive, aggressive behavior. Most individuals who commit aggressive acts and who also manifest positive spiking report no guilt or anxiety about their actions.

Positive spiking in brain waves

These findings are of interest for several reasons. First, the possibility that sociopaths suffer cortical immaturity (Hare, 1978) suggests that as they get older (and their cortexes become more mature) sociopaths should engage in less antisocial behavior. That is precisely what has been found. Particularly between the ages of thirty and forty, a substantial proportion of sociopaths show marked behavioral improvements (Robins, 1966).

Dysfunction in brain's limbic system

Second, those positive spikes—the sudden and brief bursts of brain wave activity—appear to reflect a dysfunction in the brain's limbic system, precisely the system that controls emotion and motivation. And what emotion might be affected by this physiological dysfunction? Some theorists speculate that it is *fear,* the very emotion that is thought to be implicated in the phenomena of socialization and self-control (Cleckley, 1964). The sociopath's inability to inhibit behaviors and delay gratifications is generally thought to be similar to that of animals who have suffered lesions in the brain's septal region (Gorenstein and Newman, 1980). Thus, the sociopath's failure to learn from punishing experiences may be the product of faulty physiology. Biology, rather than malice, may be the wellspring of the antisocial personality disorder.

THE ANTISOCIAL PERSONALITY DISORDER: AN OVERVIEW

The sociopath has been given many different names over the decades, but the symptoms remain remarkably the same. Sociopathy originates in childhood, where it is characterized by such things as truancy, persistent lying, theft, and vandalism. Similar behaviors persist into adulthood, taking the forms of assaults against persons and property, defaulting on major debts and financial responsibilities, and involvement in the underworld. Sociopaths share a group of personality traits, which include the absence of a sense of shame or remorse, failure to learn from past experience, and impoverished emotions.

Thus, we come full circle. Clinical observations lead us to believe that sociopaths are deficient in the ability to experience emotion and in the degree to which conscience controls their behavior. These clinical observations are confirmed by laboratory studies, which indicate that physical punishment is particularly ineffective with sociopaths. Further studies suggest that physical punishment may be ineffective because sociopaths are under-aroused, a condition that may be due to aberrant limbic function. While the effects of environment are clearly evident in the development of sociopathy, there is evidence that genetics, too, plays a role. And speculation that genetic factors influence brain function, especially limbic function, is consistent with data that indicate that sociopaths are under-aroused.

OTHER PERSONALITY DISORDERS

The antisocial personality disorder is the best known and best studied of the personality disorders, but it is not the only one. People who are characteristically suspicious and distrustful, or passive, or inappropriately emotional, or overly dependent upon others, or enormously compulsive and orderly may also be suffering from a personality disorder.

Paranoid Personality Disorder

> After his wife died, Seymour moved to a retirement community in Florida. Healthy and attractive, he immediately joined a folk dancing group, a current events discussion group, and a ceramics class. Within six weeks, however, he had dropped out of all the programs, complaining to his children that other residents were talking about him behind his back, that he was unable to find a dancing partner, ignored in the current events group, and given improper instruction in ceramics.
>
> Before his retirement, Seymour had been a physicist. He had always been closed-mouthed about his work. His home study had always been locked. He had not permitted anyone to clean it, and he had become angry if anyone entered it without his permission. His son reported that his parents had been extremely close and affectionate, but that his father had had few other friends. He had been wary of new faces and concerned about the motives of strangers.
>
> A hard worker throughout his life, he was now gripped by fear. He spent much of his time overseeing his investments, fearful that his broker would give him poor advice, or neglect to tell him when to buy and when to sell.

Characteristics of paranoid personality disorder

The prominent characteristics of the ***paranoid personality disorder*** are a pervasive and longstanding distrust and suspiciousness of others; hypersensitivity to slight; and a tendency to scan the environment for, and to perceive selectively, cues that validate prejudicial ideas and attitudes. Those who suffer from the paranoid personality disorder are often argumentative, tense, and humorless. They seem ready to attack. They tend to exaggerate, to make mountains out of molehills, and to find hidden motives and special meanings in the innocuous behavior of others. They tend to blame others for whatever difficulties they experience, and they cannot themselves accept any blame or responsibility for failure. Recent evidence suggests that those with a paranoid personality disorder and those with a schizophrenic disorder share a common genetic structure (Kendler and Gruenberg, 1982).

Because such people tend to externalize blame and guilt, they are rarely seen in clinics or psychiatric hospitals. Thus, it is difficult to estimate how prevalent this problem is. Generally, however, it is felt to be a problem that tends to afflict men more than women (Kass, Spitzer, and Williams, 1983). As might be expected from their tendency to externalize, the prognosis for this disorder is guarded indeed.

Histrionic Personality Disorder

People who have long histories of drawing attention to themselves and of engaging in excited emotional displays that are caused by insignificant

Characteristics of histrionic personality disorder

In *Sunset Boulevard,* Gloria Swanson plays a faded movie star with a histrionic personality. She is self-absorbed and demanding, living amidst her old photographs and viewing her old films.

Characteristics of narcissistic personality disorder

events are captured in the diagnosis of *histrionic personality disorder.* Such people are apt to be superficially charming, warm, and gregarious, but they are often viewed by others as insincere and shallow. They seem to be seeking admiration by playing continually to unknown audiences. Once they form relationships, they become demanding and inconsiderate, egocentric, and self-absorbed. They can be enormously flirtatious or coquettish, yet their sexual adjustment is as often naive or frigid, suggesting that their flirtatious behavior serves the ends of attention-getting much more than those of sexuality. This disorder occurs more commonly among women (Kass, Spitzer, and Williams, 1983), but it is also seen among men and is then termed "machoism" (Chodoff, 1982).

At forty-two, Michael entered therapy after his second marriage failed. He strikes you as every bit the college professor: pipe-smoking, tweedy, facile with words, and somewhat theatrical. His difficulties are gripping, and they extend beyond his marriage. He has been the victim of muggings and robberies, of badly diagnosed ailments, and wrongly prescribed drugs. His scholarly papers are often rejected by journal editors, and his colleagues seem not to appreciate his genius. For all of this, he seems clearly a charming man, though one who is more interested in the therapist's reactions than in understanding his own plight.

Michael reports that he has an interesting social life, though he complains in passing that people often do not invite him to dinner a second time. Nor do they lend him money or allow him to borrow their car. Some probing reveals that Michael has frequently failed to repay loans, and that he has often been involved in accidents with other people's cars ("well, they're insured . . ."). He is prone to cancel social engagements at the last minute if something more interesting comes up. Indeed, he calls often to change his scheduled therapy sessions and is upset when those changes cannot be arranged.

NARCISSISTIC PERSONALITY DISORDER

The central feature of the *narcissistic personality disorder* is an outlandish sense of self-importance. It is characterized by continuous self-absorption, by fantasies of unlimited success, power and/or beauty, and by exhibitionistic needs for constant admiration. Criticism, the indifference of others, and threats to esteem characteristically receive exaggerated responses of rage, shame, humiliation, or emptiness. Of course, the near-total preoccupation with self massively disturbs interpersonal relationships in a variety of ways. Such people may simply lack the ability to recognize how others feel. They may have an exaggerated sense of "entitlement," expecting that the world owes them a living without assuming reciprocal responsibilities. They may simply be exploitative, taking advantage of others to indulge their own desires. When they are able to establish a relationship, they may vacillate between the extremes of overidealization and enormous devaluation of the other person.

There is reason to believe that, perhaps as a result of parental training, those who suffer the narcissistic personality disorder simply *expect* too much from others (Benjamin, 1987). And self theorists (see Chapter 4) would suggest that these expectations arise because empathic relationships with caretakers failed to develop (Kohut, 1978), resulting in a fragmented sense of self that is especially vulnerable to feelings of emptiness and low self-esteem, and the compensatory behaviors that these generate, as the following case illustrates.

> Marion is a bit player who, at twenty-four, has not had a major theatrical role since her high school play. She has just been turned down for the lead in a new musical. Plagued with self-doubt, she is simultaneously furious with the casting director, a man with whom she has studied acting for the past three years. In her view, she should have gotten the part—both because she was every bit as good as the young woman who ultimately did get it, and because she was owed the support of the director who encouraged her and took her money for years. Marion is certain that the other actress got the part because she slept with the director. But her own time will come, Marion believes, and when it does, her own name will be displayed on the theater marquee.
>
> Beyond her vocational difficulties, Marion also has difficulty in establishing and maintaining friendships. Slender, beautifully dressed, and seemingly self-assured, she has no trouble attracting men. At first, she enthusiastically envisions great times with them. But shortly thereafter she drops them, terming them "duds," "sexually unexciting," or "just plain boring." Women seem to fare no better. Marion gave a friend a ticket to see her in a play. Instead, her friend visited a hospitalized aunt. Marion fumed and viewed her friend's absence as a "betrayal."

A narcissistic personality is characterized by self-absorption, fantasies of unlimited success and beauty, exhibitionism, and a need for constant admiration.

Characteristics of avoidant personality disorder

AVOIDANT PERSONALITY DISORDER

At the core of the **avoidant personality disorder** is a *turning away:* from people, from new experiences, and even from old ones. The disorder often combines a fear of appearing foolish with an equally strong desire for acceptance and affection. Individuals who experience this disorder want very much to enter into social relationships or new activities, but they may find themselves unwilling to take even small risks unless they are given strong guarantees of uncritical acceptance. They are shy (Zimbardo, 1977). The slightest hint of disapproval by others and the slightest whiff of potential failure lead them to withdraw. They may interpret apparently innocuous events as ridicule. People suffering from this disorder are likely to be distressed by their relative inability to relate comfortably to others, which adds to their low self-esteem, which in turn makes them even more sensitive to criticism and humiliation—an especially vicious cycle.

This disorder is thought to be quite common. It restricts social relations, and it may also affect occupational functioning, especially where interaction with others is required. Although they seem psychologically similar to *social phobics* (Chapter 8), those who suffer from the avoidant personality disorder are distinguished from social phobics by their higher levels of anxiety in social situations, and their relatively inferior social skills (Turner, Beidel, Dancu, and Keys, 1986).

> Elaine became quite distraught when her co-worker and close friend left to train as a nurse-practitioner. Her replacement was "nice enough," but Elaine feared the new woman would find her boring. At twenty-one, Elaine has only one other friend, her married sister. But her sister is "too busy with her family right now," and so Elaine spends very little time with her. Her social life in high school was quite restricted, and at present, she has no social life at all. At work, she eats lunch alone and is viewed by other workers as unfriendly.

Characteristics of
the dependent
personality
disorder

Deference and fearfulness are characteristics of the dependent personality disorder.

DEPENDENT PERSONALITY DISORDER

The central characteristic of the ***dependent personality disorder*** involves allowing others to make the major decisions, to initiate the important actions, and to assume responsibility for significant areas of one's life. People with this disorder often defer to spouse, parent, or friend regarding where they should live, the kind of job they should have, and who their friends should be. They subordinate their own needs to the needs of the people upon whom they are dependent, feeling that any assertion of their own needs may jeopardize the relationship. Such people will often tolerate enormous physical and/or psychological abuse for fear that they will be abandoned. Correspondingly, when they are alone even for brief periods of time, they may experience intense discomfort and helplessness. Thus, they often seek companionship at great cost. They lack self-esteem, and they often refer to themselves as stupid or helpless. The dependent personality disorder occurs more frequently among women than among men (Kass, Spitzer, and Williams, 1983).

> The mother of two small children, Joyce was brought to the emergency room with multiple facial abrasions and a fractured jaw. She was no stranger to the hospital staff. Eight months earlier, she had been treated for two broken ribs and assorted bruises. Joyce was reluctant to give the details of her injuries. But the neighbor who brought her to the hospital reported that Joyce had been physically assaulted by her husband. According to the neighbor, Joyce's husband frequently abused her verbally and "slapped her around" on a number of occasions. Although Joyce feared for her own safety and that of her children, she was unresponsive to suggestions that she move out and separate from her husband.
>
> The middle child of three, Joyce was given neither great responsibility nor great attention during her childhood. Her father was a man of strong opinions and made all the decisions in the family. He believed adamantly that women belonged at home, and joked often and coarsely about "buns in the oven and bums in bed." He controlled the family finances, and delegated no responsibility in that area.
>
> Apart from a course in typing, Joyce learned no vocational skills in high school, and dropped out to get married. Indeed, other than baby-sitting and summer jobs as a mother's helper, Joyce had no work experience at all.
>
> During the five years of her marriage, Joyce left all decisions to her husband, even to the point of agreeing to the purchase of a sofa that she really disliked. Her husband was intensely jealous of her friendships, and she therefore abandoned all of them. Indeed, except for visits to her mother who lived in the neighborhood, she went nowhere without her husband.

This disorder is common, especially in women. It impairs occupational functioning if the nature of the job requires independent decision making. And social relations may be restricted to the few people upon whom the person is dependent.

OBSESSIVE-COMPULSIVE PERSONALITY DISORDER

The ***obsessive-compulsive personality disorder*** is characterized by a pervasive pattern of striving for perfection. Those with the disorder demand perfection in themselves as well as others. Nothing they do seems to please them, however excellent the outcome. And because they anticipate being

Characteristics of
the obsessive-
compulsive
personality
disorder

unable to meet their own unattainable standards, they often procrastinate in important matters, allocating their time poorly and leaving the things that mean most to them to the very last. While they prize work and productivity over pleasure and interpersonal relationships, they get overly involved in details, in lists and rules and schedules. They have great trouble making work-related decisions and are excellent at postponing pleasure-related ones. People who suffer this disorder tend to have difficulty expressing emotion, and they are often seen by others as formal, stiff, overly conscientious, and moralistic. The disorder is common among both sexes, but somewhat more frequent among men.

Laura and Steve began to see a marriage counselor because Steve insisted on it. He had become extremely distressed by Laura's unavailability and perfectionism. At thirty-seven, Laura was a partner in one of the nation's largest accounting firms. She worked long hours at the office, brought work home, was unwilling to go out more than once a week, and resisted taking vacations. At home, she snapped out orders to the children about housework and schoolwork. She could not tolerate an unwashed dish or a jacket on the sofa. She was critical and demanding of household help, and the cleaning staff changed frequently. Much of the time, Steve found her sexually unresponsive.

Laura did not believe she had a "marriage problem," though she freely acknowledged feeling harassed at work and at home. She attributed her long hours at work to the demands of her profession. Snapping at the children and nit-picking about domestic order were, she insisted, the result of being the person who had to clean up after everyone else. Laura did not consider herself sexually unresponsive, but she did think she was often tense and fatigued. The only child of upwardly striving immigrant parents, Laura had been encouraged to excel. She was valedictorian of her high school class and among the top ten of her college graduating class. The social milieu in which she grew up put great stress on the value of close family relationships. Laura never doubted that she would be a wife and mother, and she married soon after graduating college.

PASSIVE-AGGRESSIVE PERSONALITY DISORDER

Characteristics of
the passive-
aggressive
personality
disorder

The essential feature of the *passive-aggressive personality disorder* consists of a special kind of resistance to social and occupational performance demands. The resistance is not expressed directly or overtly, but rather emerges passively in the form of procrastination, dawdling, stubbornness, inefficiency, and forgetfulness that seems to border on the intentional. For example, when given an assignment by his boss, a worker will not directly express his unwillingness or inability to do the work by saying such things as "I'm really overloaded right now," "I have no skills in that area," or "That's really Bill's job, not mine." Rather he may simply misplace the work order, or delay doing the job because a hundred more important things suddenly need to be done, or forget the instruction altogether. Such indirect sabotage is called passive-aggressive because it is assumed that covert hostility is being expressed. As might be expected, both the passive resistance and the ways in which it is expressed, lead to longstanding social and occupational ineffectiveness.

Jeff, a thirty-year-old city planner, entered therapy when he learned that his contract would not be renewed. The city manager pointed to his chronic tardiness, his failure to keep up-to-date records, and his tendency to forget committee meetings and report deadlines. Jeff was very upset. He believed that he had performed quite well—better in fact, than might be expected, considering that budget cuts had eliminated a secretary and that his boss was carping and demanding. At the same time, Jeff recognized that this was a familiar scenario that had occurred often in the past with his bosses and teachers.

Jeff had been a "difficult" child. As a youngster, he had temper tantrums. Later, he would sulk or leave if other children played a game that he did not choose. His college record was spotty—very good grades mixed with awful ones in no apparent pattern. In one seminar, for example, he failed to prepare the oral report he was scheduled to present. Yet, he insisted that he had been treated unjustly when an excellent term paper did not suffice to yield the "A" he thought he deserved.

During the past three years, he has been living with Jennifer, but that relationship, too, is difficult. He is often sociable and fun to be with, but he is just as often uncooperative. He leaves the domestic work to Jennifer and neglects to do even the few tasks he has voluntarily accepted. When she makes her resentments known, he insists that she is nagging. They also seem unable to collaborate about how to use their free time. If Jennifer is firm about her preferences, Steve often simply refuses to join her. And when he does acquiesce, he makes his displeasure known through sullen silence and general lack of enthusiasm.

SCHIZOID PERSONALITY DISORDER

Characteristics of the schizoid personality disorder

The central feature of the *schizoid personality disorder* is a defect in the capacity to form social relationships, as reflected in the absence of desire for social involvements, indifference to both praise and criticism, insensitivity to the feelings of others, and/or lack of social skills. Such people have few, if any, close friends. They are withdrawn, reserved, and seclusive. Others see them as "in a fog" and absent-minded. In short, they are extreme introverts. Their feelings tend to be bland and constricted; they seem to lack warm feelings or the capacity for emotional display and are therefore perceived as cold, aloof, or distant. Sometimes, and especially in jobs that require a good deal of social isolation, these characteristics can be assets. But more often, the very poverty of social skills restricts occupational and social success.

A thirty-eight-year-old chemical engineer, Homer was forced into marriage counseling by his wife who complained of his failure to join in family activities or to take an interest in the children, his general lack of affection and responsiveness, and his disinterest in sex. His failure to relate socially to others extended also to his job, where colleagues characterized him as either shy and reticent, or as cold and aloof.

Homer's history revealed longstanding social indifference and little emotional responsiveness. He recalled that he was indifferent to the idea of marrying, but did so to please his parents. His wife tried repeatedly to arrange social situations that might be of interest to him, but to no avail.

SCHIZOTYPAL PERSONALITY DISORDER

Characteristics of the schizotypal personality disorder

The *schizotypal personality disorder* is described mainly by longstanding oddities in thinking, perceiving, communicating, and behaving—oddities that are severe enough to be noticed, but not serious enough to warrant the more serious diagnosis of schizophrenia (McGlashan, 1987). Odd thinking can be manifest in extreme superstitiousness, or in the sense that one is especially noticed by others. The latter sense, which is technically called an *idea of reference,* can also be a fertile breeding ground for suspiciousness and paranoia. Depersonalization—a sense of estrangement from oneself and from one's environment—may be present. Communication may be odd, but not downright peculiar. It may be tangential, digressive, vague, or overly elaborate, but it is not loose or incoherent. Finally, people suffering from this disorder may also experience constricted or inappropriate feelings, with the result that they are unable to maintain rapport in face-to-face interactions.

The schizotypal personality disorder seems genetically related to schizophrenia (Kety, 1974; Baron, Gruen, Kane, and Amis, 1985; Kendler and Gruenberg, 1984). Indeed, many of the disturbances described here are similar to those seen among chronic schizophrenics, but here the disturbances appear in milder forms. It is an error, however, to identify this disorder wholly with the schizophrenias because differences of degree are very important differences as far as psychological distress and prognosis are concerned (McGlashan, 1986b). As we do not confuse the poor and the rich, even though both have some money, so must the schizotypal personality disorder be distinguished from its more intense relatives, the schizophrenias.

At twenty-one, Mark complains that he feels "spaced out" and "creepy" much of the time. Unemployed, he lives with his parents and spends much of his time watching television or staring into space. He says that he often feels as if he is outside himself, watching himself through a TV screen, or running through a script that someone else has written. Mark has had several jobs, but none has lasted more than a month. He was fired from his last position as a toy salesman after several customers had complained that he had talked to them in vague terms about irrelevant things.

Mark is convinced that people do not like him, but he does not understand why. He is certain that people change their seats on buses to avoid sitting next to him. He is unhappy about his loneliness and isolation, but he has made no attempt to re-establish old relationships.

Several months ago, Mark learned that one of his parents' friends planned to open a chain of athletic shoe discount stores. Although he has no experience or training in business, Mark is "waiting" for an offer to manage one of these stores.

Borderline Personality Disorder

Characteristics of the borderline personality disorder

Borderline personality disorder is a very broad category whose essential feature is *instability* in a variety of personality areas, including interpersonal relationships, behavior, mood, and self-image. These areas are not necessarily related and, indeed, are themselves so broad that people with quite different problems are likely to be considered for this diagnosis.

Clearly, any diagnosis that is so broad and potentially inclusive runs the risk of becoming a "kitchen sink" diagnosis. In order to increase the validity of the borderline diagnosis, as well as limit its use to a restricted range of people, DSM-III-R requires that evidence for at least five of the following problems be present before the diagnosis can be made:

• Impulsivity or unpredictability in at least two potentially self-damaging areas, such as sex, gambling, drug or alcohol use, shoplifting, overeating, and physical self-damage.

• A pattern of unstable and intense interpersonal relationships marked by shifts of attitude, idealization, devaluation, or manipulation of others for one's own ends.

• Lack of control over anger.

• Identity problems, denoted by uncertainty about such matters as self-image, gender identity, long-term goals or career choice, friendship patterns, values, and loyalties.

• Affective instability, which involves marked shifts from normal mood to depression, irritability, or anxiety.

• Frantic efforts to avoid abandonment, real or imagined.

• Physically self-damaging acts, including suicidal gestures, self-mutilation, recurrent "accidents," or physical fights.

• Chronic feelings of emptiness and boredom.

Failed selfobject relationship in childhood

What causes the instability and unpredictability that is so characteristic of the borderline personality disorder? Modern self theorists (see Chapter 4, pp. 74–77) speculate that it is a failed selfobject relationship in childhood that leads to adult instability of this sort (Kohut, 1977). (Failed selfobject relationships in *adulthood* have only transitory effects. An unwanted ending of a love relationship, for example, may generate a variety of painful experiences such as loss of self-esteem, depression, and even some acting-out. But these behaviors and feelings commonly pass, and are therefore not characteristic of the personality disorders, which are made up of enduring problem behaviors.) In particular, the self is especially sensitive to failures in the growth of esteem during the development of the subjective self, as well as failures in the development of the sense of agency during the formative stages of the core or physical self. These result in protracted fragmentation of the self, and with it the sense that one is losing control or "coming apart." The following case illustrates some of the difficulties of the borderline personality.

Thomas Wolfe (1900–1938).

Thomas Wolfe was a writer whose first work was published in 1929 and who died less than ten years later, before he was forty. In that brief decade, he was a literary sensation, hailed by the greatest novelists of his time. He was enormously productive and driven. And he was painfully unhappy. Wolfe was described as nervous, surly, suspicious, given to brooding, to drinking, to violent outbursts, and sometimes even to fears that he was going mad. He was rude and dislikable. He said of himself that he was afraid of people and that he sometimes concealed his fear by being arrogant and by sneering magnificently.

It was hard for him to begin writing on any particular day, but once he began it was harder still for him to stop. The words would simply pour out of him. He would sleep late, gulp down cup after cup of black coffee, smoke innumerable cigarettes, pace up and down—and write endlessly. He would scrawl down the words on sheet after sheet of yellow paper, so hastily and hugely that the pages often contained only twenty words apiece, and those in abbreviated scrawl. At night, he would prowl the streets, drinking heavily, or spending hours in a phone booth, calling friends, and accusing them of having betrayed him. The next day, overcome with remorse, he would call again and apologize.

For all his writing, he had difficulty putting together a second book after *Look Homeward Angel*. Although he had written a million words, ten times that of an average novel, it still was not a book. He was fortunate to have as his editor Maxwell Perkins, who had discovered his talent and who cared to nurture it. Wolfe wrote: "I was sustained by one piece of inestimable good fortune. I had for a friend a man of immense wisdom and a gentle but unyielding fortitude. I think that if I was not destroyed at this time by the sense of hopelessness . . . it was largely because of . . . Perkins . . . I did not give in because he would not let me give in." Perkins recognized that Wolfe was a driven man, and feared that he would suffer either a psychological or physical breakdown, or both. He proposed to Wolfe that, having written a million words, his work was finished: it only remained for both of them to sit down and make a book out of his effort.

That collaboration was difficult. A million words do not automatically make a book. Wolfe was reluctant to cut. Most of the editing, therefore, fell to Perkins. And as Perkins slowly made a book out of Wolfe's words, Wolfe's resentment of Perkins increased. The work was not perfect, Wolfe felt. And it upset him to bring forth a book that did not meet his standards.

Until the book was published, Wolfe believed it would be a colossal failure. The reviews were magnificent, however. But although Wolfe was at first heartened by the reviews, he gradually began to feel again that the book was less than perfect, a matter for which he held Perkins responsible. His relationship with Perkins deteriorated. He became suspicious, even paranoid. Yet, apart from Perkins, he had no close friends. He became increasingly unpredictable, yielding easily to incensed anger, unable to control it. Ultimately, he broke with Perkins. Rosenthal (1979) has suggested that Wolfe's emotional liability, his inability to control his anger, the difficulties he had in being alone, his many self-damaging acts, as well as his identity problems point to the diagnosis of a borderline personality disorder. At the same time, Wolfe also had personality features that were consistent with the schizotypal personality disorder, especially his ideas of reference that made him so suspicious and paranoid.

THE PERSONALITY DISORDERS: AN EVALUATION

Documentation for disorders is anecdotal

Laboratory experiments, naturalistic studies, and longitudinal surveys all converge to support the existence of the antisocial personality disorder. On a variety of specific criteria, individuals with the disorder are demonstrably different from normal people. However, the legitimacy of the other personality disorders is far more problematic. No matter how convincing the descriptions of these disorders seem to be, the documentation for their existence as reliable and valid syndromes is, at bottom, anecdotal. It has grown out of clinical lore, and while it is not to be lightly dismissed for that reason, neither can it be easily accepted. For despite the effort that has gone into tightening the various categories of personality disorders they are still particularly prone to a variety of errors that easily erode their usefulness.

ALTERNATIVE VIEWS OF THE PERSONALITY DISORDERS

Misinterpreting lifelong behaviors due to missing context

Because personality disorders are characterized by the presence of enduring *traits* that often originate in childhood or early adolescence, evidence for their existence needs to be accumulated across a considerable period of time. As a result, distortions of memory and failure to obtain and properly assess facts are powerful potential sources of error for these diagnoses. Consider Seymour, who was held to be suffering from a paranoid personality disorder (p. 505). The behavioral facts relating to his difficulties were quite accurate. But subsequently, a careful investigation of the sources of his difficulties yielded a quite different picture. It turned out that Seymour had been experiencing a marked hearing loss. He had not mentioned it during his early interviews both because he underestimated its extent and because he dreaded wearing a hearing aid. He had difficulty getting dancing partners because, while he heard the music, he often missed the instructor's calls and was commonly out-of-step. In the discussion group, he often repeated comments that had already been made by others or, worse, misheard others' comments, such that his own were inappropriate and disruptive. Similar difficulties pervaded his experience in the ceramics class. Moreover, his seeming distrust of others, which had been manifested in the locking of his study and in not talking about his work, takes on a somewhat different meaning when one learns that as a physicist, he had spent his entire career working on classified military problems. In addition, like many professionals of the 1950s and 1960s, Seymour had moved a great deal. Making new friends in each new location required a heavy expenditure of time and energy. Precisely because he had a close relationship with his wife and because he was deeply involved in his work, Seymour was simply unwilling to invest himself in new, but transient, relationships.

Different therapies make different interpretations

Thus, the potential for misinterpreting lifelong behaviors is a potentially dangerous one because the contexts in which those behaviors developed may not be readily retrievable now. But even when considerable information *is* available, therapists of different theoretical persuasions may arrive at different diagnostic conclusions as far as the personality disorders are concerned. Consider Laura (p. 509) who appeared to have all of the characteristics of an obsessive-compulsive personality disorder. Might not a feminist therapist who is sensitive to the conflicts that arise from the competing demands of gender and work roles, see the case differently? Laura, who was traditional in her attitudes toward family and home, was simultaneously ambitious in her professional life. In attempting to fulfill both roles with excellence, she unwittingly aspired to the impossible: to be a "superwoman." She wanted her house neat, her children at the top of their class, and herself at the top of her male-dominated profession. Her carping and her insistence that the house be spotless reflected this competition between roles, for if the house was not spotless, to whom would it fall to clean it up? Similarly, in her refusal to take holidays and her long working hours, she was behaving like the ambitious men in her profession.

Do traits really exist?

Finally, there are theorists who question whether the traits that presumably underlie the personality disorders really exist and, therefore, whether the personality disorders themselves are real (Mischel, 1973; Mischel and Peake, 1982). Although the notion that traits exist is nearly as old as the notion of personality itself, it has proved quite difficult to obtain evidence that people are consistent in their dispositions and perceptions across different situations. To say that someone suffers a dependent personality disorder, for example, is to say that she manifests the traits of passivity and dependence in a variety of different contexts. Evidence for that assertion is, in fact, very hard to find. Nearly all studies that have attempted to verify the cross-situational assumptions behind the notion of traits have failed. If the notion of traits has little merit, then the personality disorders that are built upon them have shaky foundations indeed. It is no wonder then that, with the exception of the antisocial personality disorder, whose coefficient of reliability (see Chapter 6) ranges between .65 and .87, inter-judge reliability of the remaining personality disorders is uncertain, often plummeting as low as .26. Recent attempts to improve the reliability and validity of personality disorder diagnoses, however, are promising (Stangl, Pfohl, Zimmerman, Bowers, and Corenthal, 1985; Loranger, Susman, Oldham, and Russakoff, 1987).

SUMMARY

1. The personality disorders are fundamentally disorders of *traits,* that is, disorders that are reflected in the individual's tendency to perceive and respond to the environment in broad and maladaptive ways. The notion of a personality disorder assumes that people respond consistently across different kinds of situations.

2. Of all of the personality disorders, the *antisocial personality disorder* is the most widely studied. It is a disorder that is characterized clinically by inadequately motivated antisocial behavior, emotional poverty, and the apparent lack of conscience or shame.

3. The antisocial personality disorder originates in childhood or early adolescence, where it takes the form of truancy, petty thievery, and other rule-violating behavior. As children, those who suffer the disorder often come from emotionally deprived backgrounds and marginal economic circumstances. Moreover, there is evidence that their antisocial behaviors have a genetic basis that may be manifested in a constitutional brain defect. This defect makes them under-aroused emotionally, and therefore less able to learn from punishment or to control their impulses.

4. While severe punishment in childhood, such as sending a boy to a penal institution, increases the likelihood that the boy will subsequently engage in criminal activities, so too does no punishment at all. Moderate punishment—enough to make the boy take the consequences seriously, but not so much as to send him to places where he can learn to be a criminal—has a genuine deterrent effect.

5. The remaining personality disorders each center on a striking personality trait. *Paranoia, dependency, introversion, passive-aggressiveness,* and *obsessive-compulsiveness* are traits that have become so dominant that they merit the personality disorder designation. In addition, some personality disorders, such as *schizotypal,* reflect many of the symptoms that are found in the corresponding Axis I disorder, but in lesser degree and without the florid thought disorder.

6. With the exception of the antisocial personality disorder, there is genuine disagreement regarding whether the personality disorders truly and reliably exist. To some extent, the disagreement arises from the low reliability of the personality disorder diagnoses. But to a larger degree, the disagreement is rooted in the scientific debate about the existence of personality traits. If traits play a relatively minor role in personality organization, then the personality disorders cannot play a large role in abnormal psychology, for they are based on the notion of traits.

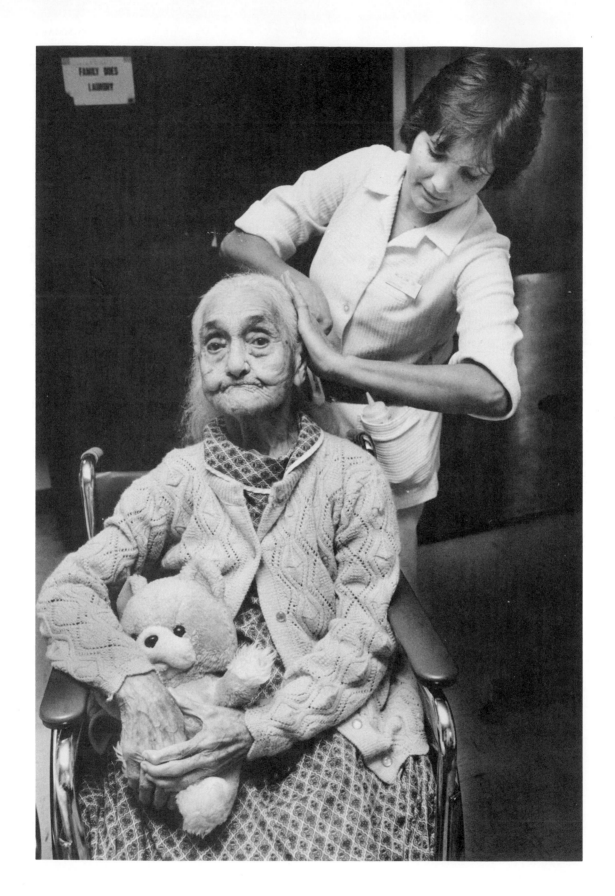

Part 7

ABNORMALITY ACROSS THE LIFESPAN

CHAPTER

16

Childhood Disorders and Mental Retardation

I N this chapter, we turn to the problems of children and adolescents— problems that, in many ways, are more difficult to understand than those of adults.

Varying rates of psychological development in different children

First, children's problems occur in the context of growing up, of psychological development. But normal psychological development proceeds at different rates for different children. As a result, it is often difficult to distinguish a genuine psychological problem that requires attention from one that merely reflects a developmental lag. For example, most children are toilet-trained by the time they are three years old. Of those who are not, some are merely developmental "laggards," while for others, continued bed-wetting reflects deeper emotional insecurities. Distinguishing problems that reflect the variability in rates of psychological development from those that suggest deep emotional difficulties is an issue one faces with children that is entirely absent among adults.

Adults may misinterpret children's behavior

Second, children often cannot communicate a problem directly through language. Instead, their distress is often manifested indirectly through maladaptive behaviors. Then it is up to parents and teachers to correctly identify behaviors in children that are indicative of severe problems. This is usually not a simple task. Often adults will mislabel a child's behavior as a "psychological problem" when it is merely something that will pass with time. At other times, adults will ignore children's problem behaviors, believing the child will grow out of these behaviors, when the child really does need adult intervention. One large study of children in the general population found that only 29 percent of those qualifying for some type of DSM-III diagnosis had ever been taken by their parents to a teacher or mental health professional for help (Anderson, Williams, McGee, and Silva, 1987). Because

Children often cannot communicate a problem directly through language; their distress is often manifested through maladaptive behaviors. This boy may simply be playing or he may be communicating an anger that he cannot express in words.

children are so dependent on adults' interpretations of their problems, we often know less about children with problems than we do about the adults who care for them.

Problems may be specific to a certain situation

Finally, children's problems are often quite specific to particular situations and contexts. Children may be aggressive at home, but not at school. Even overactivity—a common complaint of teachers—depends on the circumstances and situations. One study found that 75 percent of children who were allegedly overactive in school were not overactive at home or in the clinic (Klein and Gittelman-Klein, 1975).

Criteria for diagnosing psychological disorders in children

We will examine several kinds of children's problems. All are psychological disorders, not only because the child deviates from what is expected of a particular age and sociocultural context, but also for two other reasons: (1) the problem is persistent and severe, and (2) it impairs the child or others. Either the child must be suffering, as when a child with an animal phobia is paralyzed with fear, or the child is making others suffer, as when the child's aggression is turned on schoolmates or pets.

How common are DSM-type psychological disorders in children? Anderson et al. (1987) sought to answer this question by administering a clinical interview to 792 eleven-year-old children from the general population. On the basis of information from this clinical interview, the researchers diagnosed DSM-III disorders in 17.6 percent of the children. This is probably our best estimate to date of the prevalence of psychiatric disturbance in children.

What distinguishes a childhood disorder from normal variation of development is often only a matter of degree. With few exceptions, these disorders are not qualitatively different from normal, and minor variations of these problems can be found in many essentially normal children (Rutter, 1975). Thus, the temper tantrums that occur in most children once a month would hardly be labeled a psychological disorder. But if the tantrums were much more frequent, or if they occurred in peculiar circumstances or for a very long time, then the behavior might be considered abnormal. Before going into the specifics of any one disorder, let's look at the system by which all childhood disorders are broadly classified.

CLASSIFYING CHILDREN'S DISORDERS

Categories of childhood disorders

As a road map for viewing the scope of childhood disorders, consider Table 16-1. The disorders can be divided into five categories. *Disruptive behavior disorders* are characterized by symptoms such as hyperactivity, inattention, aggressiveness, destructiveness, and defiance of authorities. *Emotional disorders* are those in which symptoms of fear, anxiety, sadness, shyness, and overattachment predominate. *Habit and eating disorders* include a rather wide variety of disorders that are characterized by the repetitive acting out of maladaptive or nonfunctional behaviors. Examples include bed-wetting, stuttering, motor tics, and eating large quantities of food then forcing oneself to vomit. *Developmental disorders* are characterized by marked deficiencies in the child's development of important intellectual capabilities and social skills. This category includes the several levels of mental retardation as well as less severe learning disorders (such as developmental reading disorder). The category also includes autistic disorder, which is characterized by severe deficits in communication skills and social responsiveness. *Gender identity disorders,* the final category, includes very rare disorders in which a child is profoundly uncomfortable with his or her biological sex and desires to be the opposite sex. Because gender identity disorders are discussed in Chapter 13, they will not be discussed in this chapter. Note that one of the most severe of the adult disorders, schizophrenia, does not appear in Table 16-1. It is very rare for children to show signs of schizophrenia, although adolescents who will develop the disorder in adulthood sometimes

Table 16–1 MAJOR CLUSTERS OF CHILDHOOD DISORDERS	
Disruptive behavior disorders	Attention-deficit hyperactivity disorder Conduct disorder Oppositional defiant disorder
Emotional disorders	Separation anxiety disorder Avoidant disorder (shyness) Overanxious disorder Childhood depression Phobias
Habit and eating disorders	Elimination disorders (e.g., bed-wetting) Speech disorders (e.g., stuttering) Tic disorders Anorexia nervosa Bulimia nervosa
Developmental disorders	Mental retardation Learning disorders Autistic disorder
Gender identity disorders	Gender identity disorder Transsexualism

SOURCE: Adapted from DSM-III-R.

show the early symptoms of schizophrenia (social withdrawal, increasingly eccentric behavior, poor hygiene). When a young person is showing signs of schizophrenia, the criteria for the diagnosis of the disorder may be applied.

Similarly, the criteria for diagnosing depressive disorders in children are essentially the same as those for the adult diagnosis. Major depressive disorder is uncommon in children compared to adults. Milder forms of depression in children appear to be just as common as in adults, however (Nolen-Hoeksema, 1988).

Many children who receive one of the diagnoses listed in Table 16-1 will receive one or more other diagnoses as well. For example, in one study of children in the general population (Anderson et al., 1987), 55 percent of the disorders diagnosed occurred in combination with one or more other disorders. It was particularly common in this study for a child with a disruptive behavior disorder to also show an emotional disorder.

George, whose case is described below, qualifies for diagnoses of both major depressive disorder and conduct disorder.

> George is a sixteen-year-old who was admitted to the hospital from a juvenile detention center following a serious suicide attempt. He had, in some way, wrapped shoelaces and tape around his neck, causing respiratory impairment. When found, he was cyanotic and semiconscious. He had been admitted to the detention center earlier that day. It had been noted there that he was quite withdrawn.
>
> On admission, he was reluctant to speak, except to say that he would kill himself and nobody could stop him. He did, however, admit to a two-week history of depressed mood, difficulty sleeping, decreased appetite, decreased interest, guilt feelings, and suicidal ideation.
>
> According to his parents, George was without emotional difficulties until, at age 13, he became involved in drugs, primarily LSD, marijuana, and other non-opioid substances. His grades dropped drastically, he ran away from home on several occasions after arguments, and he made a suicide gesture by overdosing on aspirin. A year later he was expelled from school following an argument with the principal. Unable to control his behavior, his parents had him declared a child in need of assistance. He was then evaluated in a mental health clinic, and a recommendation was made for placement in a group home. He apparently did well in the group home, and his relationships with his parents improved immensely with family counseling. He was quite responsible in holding a job and attending school and was involved in no illegal activities, including use of drugs. However, six months ago he again became involved in drugs and, over a course of two weeks, engaged in ten breaking-and-enterings, all of which he did alone. He remembers being depressed at this time, but cannot recall whether the mood change was before or after reinvolvement with drugs. He was then sent to the juvenile detention center where he did well, so that he had been discharged to his parents' care three weeks ago. One day after returning home, he impulsively left with his buddies in a stolen car for a trip to Texas. His depression began shortly thereafter; and according to him, his guilt about what he had done to his parents led to his suicide attempt. (From Spitzer, Skodol, Gibbon, and Williams, 1981, pp. 129–30)

Combination of disorders

Although major depressive disorder is uncommon in children compared to adults, milder forms of depression appear to be as common in children as in adults.

DISRUPTIVE BEHAVIOR DISORDERS

There are three types of *disruptive behavior disorders. Conduct disorders* are characterized by persistent behaviors that seriously violate the rights of others and basic societal norms. Children with conduct disorders often get in trouble with the law and become career criminals. ***Attention-deficit hyperactivity disorder*** is characterized by marked impulsivity, inattention, and hyperactivity. Children with this disorder are often very disruptive at school and at home. A third disorder in this category is ***oppositional defiant disorder.*** Children with this disorder show a pattern of negativistic, hostile, and defiant behavior, but do not show the more serious violations of others' rights as do children with conduct disorders.

CONDUCT DISORDERS

Diagnosing a conduct disorder in a child

Most children, at one time or another, transgress important rules of conduct. A survey of 1425 British boys aged thirteen to sixteen years, from all socioeconomic groupings, found that 98 percent of them admitted to keeping something that did not belong to them (Belson, 1975). In only 40 percent of the instances were the goods worth more than two dollars, but even so the rate of childish dishonesty is quite high. Similar results are reported from other countries. In Norway and Sweden, 89 percent of children aged nine to fourteen confessed to petty illegal offenses (Elmhorn, 1965). For better or worse, it seems that stealing is a part of almost every child's development. But there are some children whose conduct persistently violates very basic norms for interpersonal behavior. These children are often physically aggressive and cruel to others. They will habitually lie and cheat. When adolescents, they may engage in muggings, armed robberies, and even rapes and homocides. When a child chronically shows such behavior, he or she may be diagnosed as having a *conduct disorder.* The following case is representative of a child with one type of conduct disorder:

Alan is the sort of teenager who makes all caring professionals despair. He has been in and out of trouble since he was six years old. At that early age, he truanted from school, and by the time he was twelve Alan had been excluded from ordinary schools and had been brought into juvenile court for persistent stealing. Within his neighborhood gang, he was popular with both boys and girls, and he

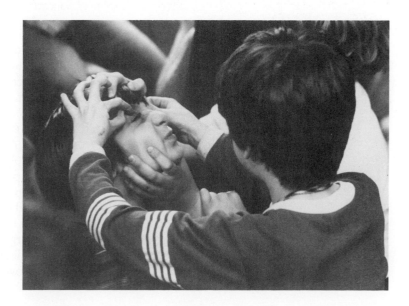

Children who chronically show behaviors that violate basic norms for interpersonal behaviors, such as frequently engaging in aggressive and cruel actions, may be diagnosed as having a conduct disorder.

was sexually active before he was fourteen. But he was quick to pick fights with boys who did not belong to his gang.

At fourteen his criminal career seemed set. He had been sentenced several times for stealing cars, and no end of this activity was in sight. His probation officer had the sense of standing by impotently until either maturation or a heavy prison sentence altered Alan's behavior.

Alan seemed to have all the cards stacked against him. He was the youngest of a large family. His father had himself been in and out of prison before finally deserting his mother when Alan was four. The mother struggled to keep the family together, but she frequently became depressed, during which times Alan spent long periods in foster homes. School was no refuge from these difficulties. Despite being of near-average ability, Alan had experienced considerable difficulty learning to read and spell. At fourteen, he could scarcely write a letter home.

Conduct disturbances stable

The persistence of antisocial and aggressive tendencies from childhood into early adulthood that Alan shows is common in children with conduct disorders (Olweus, 1979; Huesmann, Evon, Lefkowitz and Walder, 1984). Indeed, conduct disturbances and aggressivity are unusually stable characteristics across childhood and adolescence, particularly among boys (Fagot, 1984). Many children with conduct disorders develop antisocial personality disorders as adults. Alan's criminal behavior is also typical of children with conduct disorders. Many of these children are eventually classified as juvenile delinquents in adolescence. And over half of juvenile delinquents commit serious crimes by the age of twenty-five (Ross and Wirt, 1984).

Prevalence of conduct disorders

Fortunately, although many children will show minor, transient conduct disturbances, only about 3.4 percent will be as disturbed as Alan and will qualify for a diagnosis of conduct disorder (Anderson et al., 1987). The rate of conduct disorders rises in adolescence to about 8 percent (Gittelman, Mannuzza, Shenker, and Bonagura, 1985). The disorder is over three times more common in boys. Amazingly, only about 23 percent of children showing conduct disorders such as Alan's, or the less severe oppositional defiant disorder, appear to be referred for counseling (Anderson et al., 1987). Apparently, even when children are being extraordinarily disruptive, parents are reluctant to seek out mental health professionals.

POSSIBLE ORIGINS OF CONDUCT DISORDERS

What causes a child to develop patterns of aggressivity and criminal behavior? First we shall consider the influence of the social environment on the development of conduct disturbances. Then we shall investigate the possible genetic origins of these disorders.

Social environments

☐ SOCIAL SOURCES OF CONDUCT DISORDERS. Children with aggressive disorders often come from social environments that are unpleasant. Like Alan's family, their families tend to be those in which affection is lacking and discord is rampant; where discipline is either inconsistent, or extremely severe or lax; where the family has parted through divorce or separation; or where the children have been placed outside the home during times of family crisis (Rutter, 1975; Farrington, 1978; Hetherington and Martin, 1979). Often these children come from large families where there may be insufficient amounts of attention and affection to go around. Recent evidence suggests that many children who show conduct disturbances also have problems in maintaining attention (Quay, 1986; Anderson et al., 1987). Thus, they often do poorly in school, rendering them not only restless in the classroom during the long school day but also unavailable to the kinds of self-esteem socialization and feelings of competence that proper school performance engenders.

Family difficulties are augmented by poverty. Delinquency is particularly prevalent within inner cities. And even there, different schools, different housing areas, or different parts of town are associated with enormous variation in rates of conviction. Areas of high delinquency are characterized by high unemployment, poor housing, and poor schooling. Moreover, delinquency is highly related to indices of social pathology, such as illegitimate births, drug dependence, and venereal disease (West, 1976)

Genetic
influences

☐ GENETIC INFLUENCES ON THE DEVELOPMENT OF CONDUCT DISORDERS. While family and social factors strongly influence the development of agressive patterns in children, they are not wholly responsible. There seem to be genetic factors that play a role in determining which children have conduct problems and which do not. Studies have compared the criminal records (rather than the clinical diagnoses) of adopted children with those of their natural and adoptive fathers. If the incidence of criminality in the children is similar to that of the adoptive fathers, that would suggest that criminal habits are socially acquired. But if the offsprings' criminality resembles that of the biological parents, such data would strongly support a genetic influence. Studies have in fact demonstrated that the criminal records of adopted sons bear stronger resemblance to those of their biological fathers, with whom they never lived, than to the records of their adoptive fathers (Mednick, 1978).

Such evidence cannot be ignored, for it strongly suggests that biological endowment plays a part in determining who becomes delinquent. But how might that come about? Surely one does not inherit criminal *behaviors,* for those must be *learned.* What then is inherited?

Inheritance of
inability to
become
emotionally
aroused

What may be inherited and what may influence subsequent criminality is the failure to experience high emotional arousal (see Chapter 15). Because of such failure, boys with conduct disorders are less responsive than others to praise and encouragement (Patterson, 1975). Psychophysiologically they manifest low arousal and show a learning deficit in fear avoidance situations (Davies and Maliphant, 1971; Trasler, 1973)—precisely those situations that encourage socialization and that discourage social rule violation. It is this inability to become emotionally aroused that may be inherited and that may interfere with the ability to respond to the praises and punishments that encourage socialization. Conversely, genetic inheritance may account for the fact that some children from very difficult circumstances fail to become delinquents. Because they have inherited the capacity to be aroused by social stimuli, they avoid delinquency by becoming socialized.

TREATING THE CONDUCT DISORDERS

Historically, the conduct disorders have been difficult to treat; the success rate has been low. Heavy reliance has been placed on treatments that are derived from social learning theory. For example, where the conduct disorder appears to arise from communication difficulties within the family, the treatment attempts to restore communication and thereby eliminate the child's need to act out, as the following case illustrates:

> John was fourteen when he was referred to a treatment center because he had been stealing from his mother. He frequently stole large sums of money, often in excess of twenty dollars. His mother, however, knew precisely how much money she had, and there was no way in which John could pretend that his stealing would go unnoticed.
>
> Interestingly, during early discussions with the therapist, it became clear that John respected his parents, and that they loved him. The problem was that they could no longer discuss things together. John's stealing had driven a wedge of distrust between them, such that his parents could think of nothing else, yet John resented not being trusted.
>
> In fact, stealing was simply the most irritating of a group of problems that typically arise during adolescence and that neither John nor his parents knew how to discuss and resolve. Among these problems were conflicts over curfew, neatness, personal cleanliness, and table manners.
>
> Recognizing that these conflicts were by no means trivial irritants, the therapist arranged a series of contracts between John and his parents, whereby the rewards and penalties for meeting or violating explicit agreements were clear to both sides. In these contracts, John acknowledged that his lateness might be a source of great concern to his parents, while they recognized that his room was his own "space" which, subject only to fundamental rules of sanitation, was his to do with as he pleased. At the same time, the therapist encouraged John and his father to role-play how they might settle differences of opinion at home. After the first meeting, stealing was never discussed nor was it targeted as an area for contract or discussion. Nevertheless, it stopped altogether and long before the eight-week treatment terminated.

**Achievement
Place**

Where the fundamental problem seems not to be one of communication but rather of socialization, as is often the case among juvenile delinquents, the kind of treatment that is offered in such places as Achievement Place would appear to be quite promising. At Achievement Place, which began at the University of Kansas and is now in several locations around the country, two professionally trained "teaching parents" live together in a family-style arrangement with six to eight delinquent adolescent children who have been sent to Achievement Place by the local court. Often their homes are in the same community, and they can continue to attend their regular school and visit in their own homes.

The aim of Achievement Place is to teach prosocial behaviors. The teaching parents develop a mutually reinforcing relationship with their charges and model, role-play, and reinforce the kinds of social skills they want the children to acquire. They emphasize skills such as responding appropriately to criticism, as well as the academic skills that are necessary to make school interesting and to obtain employment afterwards. Moreover, Achievement Place emphasizes self-government, whereby the children take increasing responsibility for their own behavior and for helping their housemates (Wolf, Phillips, and Fixsen, 1975; Kirigin, Wolf, Braukmann, Fixsen, and Phillips, 1979).

How successful has the Achievement Place approach been? One measure of success is to look at what happens to adolescents during and after

Achievement Place compared to a similar group that spent time in a traditional facility. One such study found that the Achievement Place children showed greater improvement in conduct (Kirigin, Braukmann, Atwater, and Wolf, 1982). During the year of treatment, 56 percent of the boys and 47 percent of the girls assigned to Achievement Place were involved in a criminal offense, compared to 86 percent of the boys and 80 percent of the girls in more traditional institutions. One year following treatment, the Achievement Place children continued to be somewhat less likely to be in trouble with the law than the other children. One reason so many of the children in both types of treatment got into trouble when they were released was that many had to return to difficult home environments that may have undermined the effects of the treatment. Even so, the Achievement Place model remains the most effective type of intervention for children with conduct disorders. In addition, keeping a child at Achievement Place costs barely a third of what it would cost to send such a child to a state institution. Generally, then, both the efficacy and relative cost of behavioral resocialization programs generate optimism regarding the prognosis for delinquents.

ATTENTION-DEFICIT HYPERACTIVITY DISORDER (ADHD)

Characteristics of ADHD

Parents and teachers often complain that children are overactive and restless, that they won't sit still and cannot concentrate for long. What they usually mean is that the children won't concentrate for as long as the *adults* would like, forgetting that attention span and concentration increase with age. But there are cases in which children do show gross overactivity, both at home and at school, and these children can truly be regarded as having an ***attention-deficit hyperactivity disorder*** (ADHD). Their behavior is marked by developmentally inappropriate inattention, impulsiveness, and motor hyperactivity. In the classroom, their attentional difficulties are manifested in their inability to stay with a specific task. They have difficulty organizing and completing work. They often give the impression that they are not listening or that they have not heard what they have been told, and they seem unable to sit still. Similarly, at home they are described as failing to follow through on parental requests and instructions and failing to sustain activities, including play, for periods of time that are appropriate for their age. A good example of an attention-deficit hyperactivity disorder is provided in the following case:

> James was four years old when he was first admitted to a children's psychiatric ward as a day patient. Ever since infancy he had made life difficult for his elderly parents. As soon as he could crawl, he got into everything. He had no sense of danger. He slept very little at night and was difficult to pacify when upset. It was only because he was their only child and they could devote all of their time to him that his parents managed to maintain him at home.
>
> His problems were noticed by others just as soon as James began preschool at age three. He made no friends among the other children. Every interaction ended in trouble. He rushed around all day, and could not even sit still at story time. His flitting from one activity to another completely exhausted his teachers. After some eighteen months of trying, his teachers suggested that he be referred to the hospital for assessment and treatment.

On examination, no gross physical damage could be found in his central nervous system. Psychological examinations revealed that James had a nearly average intelligence. In the hospital, he was just as hyperactive as he had been in school and at home. He climbed dangerously to the top of the outdoor swings. He ran from one plaything to another and showed no consideration for other children who were using them. Left to his own devices, he was constantly on the move, tearing up paper, messing with paints—all in a nonconstructive manner.

James was placed in a highly structured classroom, with two teachers and five other children. There his behavior was gradually brought under control. He was given small tasks that were well within his ability, and he was carefully shown how to perform them. His successes were met with lavish praise. Moreover, patience and reward gradually increased the length of time he would spend seated at the table.

Ultimately, James was placed in a small, structured, residential school. By age sixteen, he had settled down a great deal. He was no longer physically overactive, but his conversation still flitted from one subject to another. He had no friends among his peers although he could relate reasonably well to adults. He showed little initiative in matters concerning his own life, and his prospects for gaining employment were not good.

Prevalence of
ADHD

James's behavior is typical of children with attention-deficit hyperactivity disorder. He is hyperactive, always on the go, with apparently boundless energy. He is impulsive, doing whatever comes to mind, often without regard to physical danger. And he has problems maintaining his attention on any one task without a great deal of support from teachers. As with James, children with ADHD often show these problems in very early childhood. The prevalence of attention-deficit disorders in preadolescents is about 6.7 percent, with over five times more boys than girls having this diagnosis (Anderson et al., 1987). Some children "grow out" of the symptoms, but as many as 50 to 80 percent continue to show symptoms into adolescence (Cantwell, 1985). Hyperactive children are also prone to conduct disturbances. In a follow-up study of 101 sixteen-year-olds who had ADHD in childhood, researchers found that 45 percent had a history of conduct disorders and drug abuse, compared to 16 percent of a control group of sixteen-year-olds (Gittelman et al., 1985). Not surprisingly, hyperactive children also tend to do very poorly in school, and as adults, they often do not attain occupations as high as do adults who were not hyperactive children (Thorley, 1984). Thus, hyperactive children seem to have quite a high risk of problems in adult life.

POSSIBLE CAUSES OF ATTENTION-DEFICIT HYPERACTIVITY DISORDER

Theories of
ADHD

Most theories of the etiology of attention-deficit hyperactivity disorder have focused on mechanisms in the central nervous system that control arousal (see Douglas, 1983). Some theorists argue that hyperactive children suffer from chronic over-arousal. This seems intuitively plausible, although the fact that hyperactive children actually are made more calm by stimulant drugs seems paradoxical from this viewpoint. More recently, theorists have suggested that hyperactive children suffer from chronic *under-arousal,* which makes it more difficult for them to maintain attention (Zentall and Zentall, 1983). Evidence supporting these and other theories of ADHD remains lacking, however.

TREATMENT

When very young, children with ADHD are very difficult to deal with. They quickly exhaust their teachers and parents, and they often cannot be taught in ordinary school classes. The two main therapeutic approaches are drug therapy and behavior management.

Treatment with stimulants

☐ **DRUG THERAPY.** Paradoxically, hyperactive children are made worse by tranquilizers. Instead, most hyperactive children show decreases in hyperactive behavior and increases in some types of simple school performance when given stimulant drugs (Pelham, Bender, Caddell, Booth, and Moorer, 1985). The most common stimulant is an amphetamine called methylphenidate (whose trade name is Ritalin). It is widely used in schools to control children's hyperactivity and to make the classroom more manageable. But unfortunately, there are dosage difficulties.

Let us return a moment to the profile of the hyperactive child. There are two major problems: (1) brief attention span, and (2) motor overactivity. It turns out that the attention problem is improved with relatively low dosages of Ritalin. Physical overactivity, however, is not reduced unless higher dosages are used. But with these higher dosages, the optimum conditions for learning are sacrificed (Sprague and Sleator, 1973; Sprague and Berger, 1980). Thus, it is quite difficult to control both the cognitive-attentional aspects of the disorder and the motor behaviors with the same drug regimen. Moreover, such gains that are achieved seem very short term. In the long run, children who receive these medications may be no better off than those who don't (Whalen and Henker, 1976). For these reasons, and because one should hesitate to medicate children when less risky treatment alternatives exist, clinicians have been increasingly advocating management methods.

Using operant conditioning techniques

☐ **BEHAVIOR MANAGEMENT.** Operant conditioning programs have been relatively effective in treating overactivity and its associated attentional deficits, particularly in the short run. Several investigators have used these techniques to extinguish the hyperactive child's problem behaviors—for example, distracting others—while simultaneously extending the amount of time the child attends. In one case, for example, after carefully establishing how overactive a nine-year-old boy was—that is, his base rate of overactive behavior—the boy was rewarded for sitting still. For every ten seconds that he sat quietly, he earned a penny. The first experimental session lasted only five minutes. But by the eighth session, the boy's overactivity had virtually ceased and, at follow-up four months later, his teacher reported that not only was he much quieter but he was also progressing in reading and making friends. Thus, the straightforward use of attention and tangible reinforcers can produce significant and rapid changes when they are systematically applied (Patterson, 1965; see also Ayllon and Rosenbaum, 1977).

These single case reports, while interesting, are not especially convincing in the long run, because there have been no studies of the long-term effects of behavioral treatments on hyperactive children. Short-term studies of these treatments seldom include control groups, so the effects of the treatment cannot be compared to the outcomes of children who receive no treatment. Even comparisons between drug and behavioral treatments are hard to come by. Some researchers (Gittelman-Klein, Klein, Abikoff, Katz, Gloisten, and Kates, 1976) find that drugs are more effective than behavioral treatments. Others (Wolraich, Drummond, Salomon, O'Brien, and Sivage, 1978; Kauffman and Hallahan, 1979) find that drugs and behavioral treatments are both effective, although only behavioral treatments affected children's academic performance. In any event, the studies that bear on the issue of comparative effectiveness are short-term studies, and these tell us nothing about the comparative effectiveness of the two treatments over longer durations. Drug treatments, however, may have serious side effects on children, such as weight loss, insomnia, and high blood pressure (Safer and Allen, 1976). Because behavioral treatments are less risky, they should usually be tried before drug treatments are applied (Heads, 1978).

EMOTIONAL DISORDERS

The rubric, *emotional disorders,* loosely describes those emotional abnormalities that are not accompanied by a loss in the sense of reality. Their symptomatology is frequently similar to that seen in adult emotional disorders (see Chapters 8, 9, and 10)—feelings of inferiority, self-consciousness, social withdrawal, shyness, fear, overattachment, chronic sadness, and the like. These complaints result in diagnoses that include anxiety states, depressive disorders, obsessive-compulsive conditions, phobias, and hypochondriasis (Hersov, 1976).

But there are several important differences between childhood emotional disorders and adult emotional disorders. First, adult emotional disorders are more common among women, while many childhood emotional disorders occur equally among boys and girls and only begin to be more common among girls with the onset of adolescence. Second, many childhood emotional disorders are age-specific, that is, they occur or terminate at particular ages. Animal phobias, for example, always begin in early childhood, while agoraphobia is rarely experienced before adulthood. Finally, children with emotional disorders do not necessarily grow up to be adults with emotional disorders. Untreated, many of the emotional disorders of childhood simply disappear by adulthood.

Because the emotional disorders of childhood do bear a strong resemblance to those of adulthood, we do not review all of the emotional disorders here. Rather, we shall discuss what appears to be the most common childhood emotional disorder, separation anxiety. We shall also examine one problem that afflicted all of us in childhood: fear. We will look at the kinds of troubles that fear can create when it gets out of hand.

SEPARATION ANXIETY DISORDER

Most of us can remember an incident sometime in our childhood in which we suddenly realized we had been separated from our parents and could not find them. We felt terror about being alone; we wondered if they would ever return. Eventually we were reunited with our parents, with great relief. For a short period after the incident, we were somewhat anxious about again

Chronic sadness in a child may be symptomatic of an emotional disorder.

Differences between emotional disorders in children and in adults being separated from our parents, and tried to stay close to them when in stores or other big places. But for the most part, the separation was an isolated incident that we soon forgot.

Continuous anxiety about separation

There are some children who live every minute of the day with terror that they might be separated from their families. They worry that terrible things will happen to their parents, siblings, or other loved ones. They refuse to be separated from loved ones, and become panicked if they must be separated. They have nightmares with themes of separation. They cling to loved ones and follow them around the house constantly. They may show continual physical symptoms of anxiety, such as headaches, stomach aches and nausea, particularly on days that they must be separated from parents (such as school days). Children who show such symptoms for at least two continuous weeks may be suffering from *separation anxiety.*

Prevalence of separation anxiety

Separation anxiety appears to be the most common of childhood emotional disorders, with a prevalence of 3.5 percent among preadolescents (Anderson et al., 1987). It is nearly twice as common in girls as in boys. In its severe form, separation anxiety can be incapacitating for children, preventing them from attending school or extracurricular activities. Also, these children often undergo repeated physical examinations as a result of their frequent complaints of aches and pains (APA, 1986). Episodes of separation anxiety often occur repeatedly over childhood and adolescence for children with this diagnosis.

A first episode of separation anxiety often occurs after some traumatic event in the child's life, such as the death of a relative or pet, being hospitalized, or moving to a new town. Children whose parents suffer from an anxiety disorder, particularly agoraphobia, are at an increased risk for separation anxiety (Gittelman and Klein, 1984). In addition, children with this disorder tend to come from very close-knit families (APA, 1986).

Treatment for separation anxiety

Imipramine, an antidepressant drug, appears to relieve the symptoms of anxiety and reduce complaints of physical symptoms in children with this disorder (Gittelman-Klein and Klein, 1980). These drugs can have severe side effects in children, however, sometimes leading to the child's death. Behavioral techniques are used more frequently than drugs. These techniques, especially systematic desensitization, are designed to help the child tolerate separations from parents. There are very few studies, however, on the effectiveness of different treatments for separation anxiety.

PHOBIAS

Fears common in childhood

Fears are very common throughout childhood, much more so than adults realize or remember from their own early years. Forty-three percent of children aged six to twelve years old have at least *seven* fears or worries at any one time (Lapouse and Monk, 1959). The nature of those fears often varies with age. Preschool children tend to be afraid of tangible objects, such as animals and insects. For example, Little Hans, you may recall from Chapter 8, developed his fear of horses at about age five. Tangible fears can continue throughout childhood and into adulthood, but they rarely begin after age five. As children grow older, so grow their fears of imaginary creatures, of disastrous events, and of the dark. Ghosts, murderers, and hidden dangers populate their imaginations. School-connected fears begin at age five or six when children are first enrolled in school, and they increase markedly between the ages of nine and twelve. From about age twelve and on through adolescence, children's fears begin to resemble those of adults, including fears about social relationships and anxieties about identity.

Fears become phobias when, as we saw in Chapter 8, the fear is out of proportion to the reality of the danger that an object presents (p. 196). The prevalence of simple phobias in preadolescents is about 2.4 percent, with twice as many girls as boys showing the disorder (Anderson et al., 1987). The following case demonstrates the transition of fear to phobia:

Transition of fear to phobia

Fears are very common throughout childhood, with the nature of those fears varying with age. Fears become phobias when they are out of proportion to the reality of the danger the object actually presents.

> Sometimes children's phobias develop in complex and unpredictable ways. Sara was referred for treatment of her phobias when she was thirteen. The referring physician indicated that the girl was afraid of airplanes and bees, but Sara, like so many such children, found it hard to put in words just what she was scared of. She acknowledged that, beyond airplanes and bees, she was also afraid of elevators, but nothing more. Yet, after she came to know and trust her therapist, it emerged that there was a fear that underlay and linked all the others: that was a fear of anesthesia. The link between airplanes, elevators, bees, and anesthesia was not immediately obvious, and it took some care to piece the following history together.
>
> A number of years earlier, Sara had to have a tooth extracted. The dentist used a general anesthetic. As she "went under," everything went black, but Sara could still hear voices and rushing noises. (In fact, this is an almost universal experience since, physiologically, the nerves controlling vision are affected seconds before the nerves controlling hearing.) Sara was not prepared for these sensations, and they terrified her. Ever since, she has studiously avoided putting herself in a situation where she *might* be injured and therefore might be rushed to a hospital, where she *might* be given an anesthetic. Airplanes crash. So do elevators. Bees sting. Any one of these might land her in the hospital.
>
> Like everyone else, Sara' parents did not understand the connection between her phobias and what gave rise to them. Rather, they tended to see her globally, simply as a fearful child. The therapist explained that what Sara had originally experienced, though unexpected and unpleasant, was hardly incomprehensible and very treatable. He then trained Sara in relaxation techniques that could be used in situations of high anxiety. By focusing on her fears of elevators, the therapist demonstrated to Sara that she could conquer one fear and could go on and conquer the others by herself. Within three months, Sara reported no more difficulties.

Behavioral treatments for phobias

Sara's shifting fears were complicated, but not unusual. In her case, a plausible traumatic event was easily identified. But such events are often more difficult to trace. In many children, phobias are often associated with general anxiety or emotional disturbance, and with having parents who are phobic (see Rutter and Garmezy, 1983). Phobias in children, like those in adults, respond best to behavioral treatments, especially modeling (Bandura, 1969; Gelfand, 1978; Rosenthal and Bandura, 1979). In these treatments, children are exposed to, and encouraged to imitate, models who are both attractive and relatively fearless. The use of such models enables children to quickly overcome their fear. Specific fears, such as fear of animals, respond best to such treatment. Phobias that are associated with more general emotional disturbance, such as agoraphobia and school phobia, have proven more difficult to treat (Rutter and Garmezy, 1983).

SCHOOL PHOBIA

Characteristics of children with school phobia

School phobia is a common childhood disorder that creates significant distress in both children and their parents. Not very long ago, it was assumed that all children who were absent from school, except those who were physically ill and could prove it, were playing hooky and were therefore truants. Yet, there seemed to be a subgroup of such absentees who differed markedly from the "real" truants who tended to be antisocial, underachieving children. In contrast, the subgroup tended to be children who were achieving very well at school, who said that they wanted to return to school, but who described all manner of anxiety symptoms whenever they set out to attend school. For example, they needed to go to the toilet frequently and they often felt sick and sweated profusely when the topic of school was brought up. Unlike the truants whose parents were often unaware that their offspring were not at school, these children stayed at home during their prolonged absences, and their parents knew exactly where they were. Consider the following case:

> Richard was a twelve-year-old who had been out of school almost continuously for five months. The previous summer he had won a scholarship to a well-known private school. He did exceedingly well in his first term. Then, just after the beginning of the second term, he contracted severe influenza which left him feeling very weak. He was worried that he would lose ground academically, and his anxious parents shared that concern. He tried to go back to school, but once in the classroom, he had a panic attack and ran home. Thereafter, he worried increasingly about what to say to the other boys and how to explain his flight and long absence. He was brought to a therapist for help in overcoming his fear.
> Richard was given some training in relaxation and was accompanied to his school in graded stages during the summer vacation. He and his therapist rehearsed what he would say to his friends when he returned in the fall. The therapist accompanied him to school for the first three mornings, but thereafter, he was on his own. Follow-up during the next two years revealed no further difficulty. (Yule, Hersov, and Treseder, 1980)

School phobia presents a serious challenge because it is so puzzling to teachers, to parents, and to the child who suffers from it. The situation is made more tragic by the fact that the child previously was a good attender and was doing well in school when, suddenly and for no apparent reason, he stopped going to school. Careful investigation often reveals many reasons for school refusal. In Richard's case and in most others, threats to self-esteem and an unrealistically high level of aspiration play significant roles in refusal. To a child who regularly receives straight A's, the threat of even a "B" can be highly aversive and anxiety-producing.

School refusal occurs at three points in children's school careers: at five to seven years, when children are first registered in school and separation anxiety is likely to be quite intense; at eleven to twelve years old, when children change schools and are fearful about their social or academic status; and at fourteen years old or older. In this oldest group, nonattendance may be the first sign of a more serious difficulty, such as adolescent depression or, more rarely, the early onset of schizophrenia. Whenever it occurs, school phobia requires careful attention, lest it fester into a more serious disorder (Yule, Hersov, and Treseder, 1980).

HABIT DISORDERS AND EATING DISORDERS

The **habit disorders** and **eating disorders** comprise a group of diagnoses that are united by a single fact: the troublesome behavior has a habitual physical component. They include the elimination disorders (enuresis and encopresis), speech disorders (stammering and stuttering), motor tics, and eating disorders (anorexia and bulimia). While the causes of these disorders are not entirely clear, their psychological consequences are dramatic. To be a bed wetter or much overweight in Western society is to be stigmatized and to have to deal regularly with the taunts of others and assaults on one's self-esteem. Below we shall discuss in detail one of the elimination disorders, enuresis, then stuttering, and then the eating disorders.

ENURESIS

Prevalence of enuresis

Enuresis is arbitrarily defined as involuntary voiding of urine at least twice a month for children between five and six, and once a month for those who are older. Most children gain bladder control between eighteen months and four years of age. Thereafter, the proportion of children who have difficulty containing urine, either during the day or while in bed, drops markedly. At age five, 7 percent of boys and 3 percent of girls are enuretic; at age ten, 3 percent of boys and 2 percent of girls are still having difficulty with continence. At age eighteen, 1 percent of boys continue to be enuretic and the disorder is nearly nonexistent for girls (DSM-III, 1980).

As with the other physical disorders, the problems of the enuretic are compounded by the social consequences of the disorder. Parents object to soiled clothes and bedding and commonly stigmatize the enuretic as immature. Schoolmates and friends are likely to tease the child who has an occasional "accident," the more so when those accidents are regular occurrences. Enuretics find it nearly impossible to accept overnight invitations from friends or to go to camp. These social consequences may create a fertile ground for other more serious psychological problems.

CAUSES OF ENURESIS

Genetic vulnerability to enuresis

The social consequences of enuresis are especially unfortunate because little is known about its causes. A distinction is made between primary enuresis, which is caused by a biological abnormality, and secondary enuresis, which has psychological causes such as anxiety. There is evidence that the predisposition to enuresis often is inherited. Approximately 75 percent of enuretic children have first-degree relatives who are or were enuretic, and the concordance for enuresis is higher in identical (MZ) than in fraternal (DZ) twins. That is, the more similar a person's genetic blueprint is to an enuretic's, the more likely the individual will also be enuretic (APA, 1980).

TREATMENT

Drug treatment

Some drugs, such as the amphetamines or imipramine, suppress bed-wetting temporarily. How these drugs work is not understood, and usually children begin to bed wet again once the drug is stopped. Even so, a few dry nights can be an enormous morale-booster to an enuretic child, particularly if it allows the child to visit friends overnight or go to camp without fear of embarrassment. Recall, however, that these drugs may have significant side effects that outweigh their usefulness, including toxic death (Rohner and Sanford, 1975).

Behavioral
treatments

There are two treatments in particular that have been quite successful with enuresis, far more successful than drug treatment. Both treatments are fundamentally behavioral. The first is a procedure that was first described nearly fifty years ago (Mowrer and Mowrer, 1938). The child sleeps in his or her own bed. Beneath the sheets is a special pad which, when moistened by urine, completes a harmless electric circuit that sounds a bell and awakens the child, who then goes to the toilet. A number of studies have shown that approximately 90 percent of children treated by the "bell and pad" method gain bladder control during the two-week treatment period. There is a relapse rate of up to 35 percent, but that can be reduced by giving a longer treatment period or by offering an additional "booster" dose of treatment (Lovibond and Coote, 1970; Shaffer, 1976; Doleys, 1979).

A more intense procedure amplifies this approach (Azrin, Sneed, and Foxx, 1974). About an hour before bedtime, a "trainer" tells the child and his or her parents about the "dry-bed" procedure. At this time, the child drinks a favorite beverage. Then, the trainer attempts to develop in the child the habit of rousing and urinating. With the lights out, the child lies on the bed and counts to fifty. Then, he or she rises slowly, heads for the bathroom and attempts to urinate. This procedure is repeated many times over the course of that night's treatment. Subsequently, the child is given more to drink, reminded of these procedures, and told that he or she will be awakened each hour to practice going to the toilet. If there is an "accident," the child will have to change the bedsheets and practice using the toilet several times. And, of course, if there is no accident during the hour, the child will be praised for that continence. This procedure is rather more intensive than the bell and pad treatment, and it is even more effective. After four nights of such treatment, all of the children were continent throughout the six-month follow-up period.

STUTTERING

Stuttering or stammering is a marked disorder in speech rhythm. While most children go through transient periods of hesitating over particular words, the dysrhythmia is both more pronounced and more prolonged in those who are regarded as stutterers. Often, it is the initial consonants in certain words, particularly explosive sounds, that cause real problems. "I d-d-d . . . don't know what to d-d-d-do!" is a typically problematic sentence that is often accompanied by a flushed or pained face.

Prevalence of
stuttering

About 1 percent of all children are stutterers, and another 4 to 5 percent experience transient stuttering for a period of up to six months. For unknown reasons, boys outnumber girls as stutterers by four to one.

The causes of stuttering are still unclear, but as in other physical disorders, the consequences are enormous. Stutterers tax the patience of other children and teachers. They are often taunted and ostracized by peers. Teachers may avoid calling on them in class, with the result that their academic interest and performance may flag.

TREATMENT

By the time a stutterer seeks help, he or she is likely experiencing considerable tension that both results from the speech problem and magnifies it. Consequently, most treatments of stuttering combine psychotherapeutic counseling with specific reeducational techniques. The latter serve to distract the stutterer from his own speech while training him to speak fluently.

Three techniques seem particularly promising. The first is called ***delayed auditory feedback*** and involves hearing one's own speech played back over earphones at about a .1 second delay. When fluent speakers hear their own speech delayed in this manner, they stutter enormously. But when stutterers receive delayed auditory feedback, they become nearly fluent. These paradoxical findings suggest that feedback from their own speech is what maintains stuttering, and that any interference in that feedback will reduce it. The problem, of course, is affecting feedback outside of the treatment situation. Delayed auditory feedback works quite well in the clinic but transfers hardly at all outside of the clinic.

Shadowing is a variant of the delayed auditory feedback technique. Here, the therapist reads from a book, and the stutterer repeats the therapist's words shortly after the latter has spoken them (and without reading the words). This requires the stutterer to concentrate carefully on what the therapist is saying, and in the process, to ignore his own stuttering. Several studies indicate that shadowing may be useful in alleviating stuttering (Cherry and Sayers, 1956; Kondas, 1967).

A third method, called ***syllable-timed speech,*** requires stutterers to speak in time to a metronome or bleeper that sounds in an earpiece. This procedure, too, may have the effect of distracting the stutterer from his own stuttering. Combined with a system of rewards for maintaining non-stuttering, this procedure has been found relatively effective in reducing stuttering (Meyer and Mair, 1963; Ingham, Andrews, and Winkler, 1972). None of these three techniques, however, can be described as more than "promising" for the treatment of stuttering.

Techniques for distracting stutterer from his own speech

ANOREXIA NERVOSA

The main symptoms of ***anorexia nervosa*** are substantial loss of body weight and deliberate restriction of calory intake. It is therefore sometimes called the "slimmer's disorder." The diagnosis is not accorded unless the individual has lost 25 percent of normal body weight (or, if the person is under eighteen, the actual weight loss and the weight that would have been gained as a result of ordinary maturation combine to meet the 25 percent criterion).

Prevalence of anorexia nervosa

A central feature of anorexia nervosa is an intense preoccupation with body size and a very distorted body image. Even when they are emaciated, individuals with this disorder feel fat. About 95 percent of those suffering from the disorder are women. Moreover, it prevalence appears to be rising (Bruch, 1978; Yule, 1980), such that as many as 1 in 100 females between the ages of twelve and eighteen succumb (APA, 1986). The average age of onset of the disorder is usually early to late adolescence. Often, the disorder is accompanied by a variety of other physical changes. ***Amenorrhea***—that is, loss of the menstrual period—is a common occurrence in women anorexics.

Anorexics are preoccupied with body size and image. An anorexic suffers substantial loss of body weight due to a deliberately restricted calorie intake. This is a painting made by an anorexic during the severest stage of her illness.

Blood pressure may be lowered; sleep patterns may be disturbed, with early morning insomnia common; there may be noticeable hyperactivity and a general loss of interest in sex. The salient symptom, however, remains the persistent determination not to eat, a determination that is so powerful that, in nearly a fifth of the cases, it results in death. The following case illustrates this disorder.

Physical changes in the anorexic

Frieda had always been a shy, sensitive girl who gave little cause for concern at home or in school. She was bright and did well academically, although she had few friends. In early adolescence, she had been somewhat overweight and had been teased by her family that she would never get a boyfriend unless she lost some weight. She reacted to this teasing by withdrawing and becoming very touchy. Her parents had to be careful about what they said. If offended, Frieda would throw a tantrum and march off to her room—hardly the behavior they expected from their bright and sensitive fifteen-year-old.

Frieda began dieting. Initially, her family was pleased, but gradually her parents sensed that all was not well. Mealtimes became battletimes. Frieda hardly ate at all. Under pressure, she would take her meals to her room and later, having said that she had eaten everything, her mother would find food hidden away untouched. When her mother caught her deliberately inducing vomiting after a meal, she insisted they go to the family physician. He found that Frieda had stopped menstruating a few months earlier. Not fooled by the loose, floppy clothes that Frieda was wearing, he insisted on carrying out a full physical examination. Her emaciated body told him as much as he needed to know, and he arranged for Frieda's immediate hospitalization.

THEORIES OF ANOREXIA NERVOSA

Pressure for women to be thin

Anorexia is much more common in the United States and other westernized cultures than in non-Western cultures. In addition, the incidence of anorexia appears to have risen sharply in the last few decades. These trends have led some psychologists to propose that anorexia is, at least in part, a result of the overwhelming pressure on women to be thin found in modern Western cultures (Garfinkel and Garner, 1982). There is no doubt that thinness is considered a virtue in our society, especially for females. The "ideal" shape for women, as indicated by television stars, models in women's magazines, and winners of beauty pageants, has become more and more thin over the last thirty years. Over the same time period, there has been an increase in the average weight of women due to improvement in nutrition. Thus, women are being told to become thin when it is becoming harder to do so.

Deficit in sense of autonomy

Most persons exposed to social pressures to be thin, however, do not become anorexic. Several theories of anorexia see it as the result of a deficit in the sense of autonomy (e.g., Bruch, 1982; Garfinkel and Garner, 1982; Minuchin, Rosman, and Baker, 1980). The person who becomes anorexic has not separated adequately from her family and feels no control over her life. Restricting her eating becomes a way of controlling at least one aspect of her life, perhaps while retaliating against an overbearing family. There has been some support for these claims (e.g., Strauss and Ryan, 1987), but they are in need of more research.

Possible physiological causes

Anorexia nervosa is such a powerful disorder, however, one that results in death in 15 to 21 percent of the cases (Halmi, 1978), that we are inevitably led to suspect that there is more than social pressure and a desire for control often at work here. Some suggest that there is a fundamental disorder in the hormonal and/or endocrine systems. Others postulate hypothalamic malfunctioning (Gelfand, Jenson, and Drew, 1982). Yet others believe that anorexics have not learned to label the hunger sensation and, as a result, simply do not eat (Agras, Barlow, Chapin, Abel, and Leitenberg, 1974).

TREATMENT

Contingency management as treatment

Quite often, hospitalization of the anorexic is recommended because the patient is dangerously ill and can be carefully monitored in the hospital. Even at the point where hospitalization is required, however, some anorexics will protest that they have no problem, that they are not ill. As many as 30 percent will refuse treatment (Crisp, 1980). A successful hospital treatment usually must include education about the dangers of anorexia, supportive counseling around issues of control, family counseling, and contingency management, which makes various privileges contingent on positive changes in eating habits and on weight gain (Hsu, 1986). Drugs have not proven consistently effective in the treatment of anorexia.

BULIMIA NERVOSA: THE GORGE/PURGE CYCLE

Prevalence of bulimia

Unlike anorexics, people with **bulimia nervosa** usually do not starve themselves for long periods of time. Instead, bulimics will gorge themselves on thousands of calories of food in one sitting. Then they will often induce vomiting in themselves or use laxatives to purge themselves of the food they have just eaten. Like anorexia, bulimia is much more common among women than men. Bulimia is estimated to affect between 1 percent and 5 percent of the female population in the United States and Britain (Cooper and Fairburn, 1983; Hart and Ollendick, 1985). It is particularly prevalent among people in their early twenties. One survey of 355 undergraduates at a college in New York found that 13 percent reported having all the major

Bulimics engage in a binge/ purge cycle because of their lack of control over their food intake combined with their inordinate concern with their body image and attractiveness.

symptoms of bulimia (Halmi, Falk, and Schwartz, 1981). Once again, the vast majority of these bulimics were women.

Like anorexics, bulimics are inordinately concerned with body image and attractiveness. Many bulimics begin purging as a way to control their weight. But unlike anorexics, who feel they can control their food intake, bulimics often cannot control their intake of food. One little taste of a "forbidden" food, such as a sweet, can set off hours of binging, which ends only when the bulimic begins to experience severe stomach pain, induces vomiting, or is interrupted by other people. The sense of shame, distress, and lack of control that follows such binges is often overwhelming. Not surprisingly, depression is a common problem for bulimics (Hinz and Williamson, 1987). In addition, many bulimics also have periods in which they are anorexic.

Although bulimia nervosa is not as deadly a disorder as anorexia nervosa, the frequent vomiting and other types of purging can lead to severe loss of body fluids and electrolytes, and the stomach acid vomited up can lead to severe dental decay (Herzog, 1982). Over half of bulimic women experience menstrual problems (Fairburn and Cooper, 1982).

TREATMENT

Several types of drug therapy have been used to treat bulimia, without much success. Anticonvulsant drugs have been used to prevent vomiting and appetite suppressants have been used to prevent the bulimic from feeling hungry. These drugs have proven ineffective, however (Stunkard and Stellar, 1984). Because bulimics are often depressed, some clinicians advocate prescribing antidepressants (Pope and Hudson, 1982). The side effects of these drugs can be particularly serious for bulimics, however. Tricyclic antidepressants often lead to weight gain and craving for carbohydrates, both of which would discourage a bulimic from taking the drugs. Monoamine oxidase inhibitors can be lethal when mixed with certain foods, many of which are exactly the foods bulimics like to binge on.

Effectiveness of cognitive- behavioral therapies

Cognitive-behavioral therapies administered individually or in a group setting have proven effective in several small studies (Schlesier-Stropp, 1984). Such therapies usually begin with helping the bulimic identify what situations and feelings often precipitate the desire to binge and to purge. Then, while maintaining a healthy diet, the client is taught problem-solving techniques for better coping with the negative moods that inspire binging and purging. The therapist also helps the client challenge her maladaptive beliefs about her body image and weight. Eventually, the client learns to incorporate foods she used to binge on into her diet in reasonable amounts, without succumbing to the desire to binge.

OBESITY

Strictly speaking, obesity is not a psychological disorder. It is not included in DSM-III-R, nor was it included in its predecessors. Yet, obesity afflicts such a large number of children, has such dire consequences on their social and physical lives, and has such grave psychological effects that it is difficult to discuss the problems of childhood and adolescence without mentioning obesity.

People become obese for constitutional and hereditary reasons, as well as for psychological ones. These children are exercising during a meeting of the Child Weight Control Program, a program aimed at curbing childhood obesity.

Defining obesity

Obesity is defined as excess fat on the body. But among *growing* children and adolescents, it is often difficult to know what is *excess* fat. A fairly common standard defines a child as obese if his or her weight is more than 20 percent higher than the median weight for children of the same height (Epstein and Wing, 1987). Given this definition of obesity, approximately 17 percent of American children can be said to be obese (Mack, 1978).

Consequences of obesity

Obesity in children is a major risk factor for the development of high blood pressure (Lauer, Anderson, Beaglehole, and Burns, 1983). Obese children very often grow into obese adults, and obesity in adults is associated with increased risk of cardiovascular disease (Stark, Atkins, Wolff, and Douglas, 1981). The immediate consequences of obesity in children, however, lie in others' reactions to them. Obese children are taunted, scorned, and rejected by others. For example, a variety of drawings of children were shown to groups of school children, who were asked to select the ones they liked best. The drawings included normal boys and girls, as well as children who were obese, children who had facial deformities, children who had had limb amputations, and the like. Consistently, obese children were least liked. This rejection is the major psychological consequence of obesity (Richardson, 1970).

CAUSES OF OBESITY

Constitutional causes of obesity

People become obese for constitutional and hereditary reasons, as well as for psychological ones. On the constitutional side, there appear to be vast differences in the size and number of fat cells that obese and normal children have. Normal people have around three billion fat cells, while obese people may have nearly twice that number. Obesity appears to develop during childhood and is likely to remain throughout a person's life. One explanation for this is that obese children develop a higher "set-point" for levels of fat in their bodies (Johnston and Keesey, 1980). A set-point is the weight that an individual's body is naturally predisposed to maintain. When attempts are made to bring body fat below that set-point, physiological and psychological mechanisms fight to maintain the obese person's high set-point. As a result, dieting often does not result in permanent weight loss. Indeed, the frustration of frequent, unsuccessful dieting may cause emotional problems in some obese people, and the stress on the body of dieting may cause physiological problems (Polivy and Herman, 1985). There is mixed support for this set-point hypothesis, but it is clear that many obese people have a very difficult time losing weight, even with severe restriction of intake (Bennett and Gurin, 1982).

Genetic propensity toward obesity

Genetics appear to play a part in the propensity toward obesity. Studies of obese adopted children show that these children's biological parents are much more likely to be obese than their adoptive parents (Stunkard, Sorensen, Hanis, Teasdale, Chakraborty, Schull, and Schulsinger, 1986).

The habit component

Eating, however, serves such significant psychological and social functions in most societies that it is difficult to overlook the habit component of this problem. Many families socially reinforce children for eating by reminding them of the importance of cleaning one's plate ("waste not, want not") or by tying eating to guilt and affection ("don't you like what daddy made for you?").

TREATMENT

Treatment of eating habits

Obesity in children as in adults is difficult to eliminate. A staggering variety of treatments have been tried over the years, with reasonable initial success that fades over the long term. The more promising treatments have emphasized the acquisition of self-control and *de-emphasized* weight loss per se as a goal of treatment (Jeffery, 1977; Stunkard, 1972, 1979). Overweight is merely considered the *outcome* of bad eating habits. These programs therefore concentrate on the eating habits themselves, and they encourage children to do such things as eating only at mealtimes, eating slowly, and expending more energy through exercise. It also appears to be important to get the parents of obese children involved in treatment (Epstein and Wing, 1987). When parents are trying to lose weight along with their children, they serve as role models for good eating habits, and they are less likely to encourage children to overeat or underexercise.

DEVELOPMENTAL DISORDERS

MENTAL RETARDATION

Prevalence of mental retardation

Mental retardation is a disorder that afflicts three out of every hundred children, two-thirds of them boys. Thus, it is a widely prevalent disorder, often heartbreaking in its emotional costs to families and in the lifelong economic burdens it imposes on them and on society. For all of its prevalence, however, and despite the fact that everyone feels they know what mental retardation is, it is a difficult disorder to define precisely and to diagnose accurately. In part, the difficulty arises from the stereotypes that people have about mental retardation. But in larger measure, the difficulty occurs be-

Defining mental
retardation

cause the notion of intelligence is at the heart of mental retardation, and intelligence is very difficult to define (Kamin, 1974; Gould, 1981).

The most comprehensive and detailed definition of mental retardation has been put forth by the American Association on Mental Deficiency: "Mental retardation refers to significantly subaverage general intellectual functioning existing concurrently with deficits in adaptive behavior, and manifested during the developmental period" (Grossman, 1973). "Subaverage intellectual functioning" refers to performance on individually administered intelligence tests that is minimally two standard deviations below the mean for that test. "Adaptive behavior" refers to the standards of personal independence and social responsibility expected for the person's age and cultural group. Finally, the "developmental period" is the period of time between birth and the eighteenth birthday. Persons are not classified as mentally retarded unless both their level of intellect and ability to adapt are below average (Grossman, 1983).

LEVELS OF RETARDATION

The various levels of mental retardation and their associated IQ scores on a standard test of intelligence are shown in Table 16-2. What do these levels of retardation mean?

Mild mental
retardation

□ MILD MENTAL RETARDATION.   The largest group of retarded children, about 75 percent of them, fall into this category. These children develop social and communication skills just like all others and at quite the same times. In fact, their retardation is often not noticed until they are in the third or fourth grade, when they begin to have academic difficulties. Without help, they can acquire academic skills through the sixth grade; with help, they can go beyond that level. In all other respects, their needs and abilities are indistinguishable from those of other children. Special education programs often enable these children to acquire the vocational skills that are necessary for minimal self-support. When under social or economic stress, they may need guidance and supervision, but otherwise they are able to function quite adequately in unskilled and semiskilled jobs.

□ MODERATE MENTAL RETARDATION.   Children in this category make up 20 percent of the mentally retarded. Like other children, they learn to talk and communicate during the preschool period. But unlike other children, the moderately retarded have difficulty learning social conventions. During the school-age period, they can profit from training in social and occupational skills, but they are unlikely to go beyond the second-grade level in academic subjects. Physically, they may be clumsy and occasionally they may

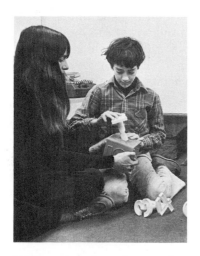

Mildly and moderately mentally retarded children can be taught numbers and eye-hand coordination.

Table 16-2	SEVERITY LEVELS OF MENTAL RETARDATION	
Level	*Percent of Retarded People*	*Weschler IQ*
Mild	75.0	55–69
Moderate	20.0	40–54
Severe	3.5	25–39
Profound	1.5	below 25

suffer from poor motor coordination. They may learn to travel alone in familiar places and can often contribute to their own support by working at semiskilled or unskilled tasks in protected settings.

Severe mental retardation

☐ SEVERE MENTAL RETARDATION. Before they are five, the severely retarded provide considerable evidence of poor motor development, and they develop little or no communicative speech. At special schools, they may learn to talk and can be trained in elementary hygiene. Generally, they are unable to profit from vocational training, though as adults, they may be able to perform simple and unskilled job tasks under supervision.

Profound mental retardation

☐ PROFOUND MENTAL RETARDATION. Children in this category are severely handicapped in adaptive behavior and are unable to master any but the simplest motor tasks during the preschool years. During the school years, some development in motor skills may occur, and the child may respond in a limited way to training in self-care. Severe physical deformity, central nervous system difficulties, and retarded growth are not uncommon. Health and resistance to disease are poor, and life expectancy is shorter than normal. These children require custodial care.

CAUSES OF MENTAL RETARDATION

There are two sources of mental retardation. The first is associated with *pathological physical conditions.* In this type, mental retardation arises as a secondary consequence of injury and disease. The second is called *cultural-familial retardation,* and it arises from genetic and environmental influences. Most mental retardates are from this group.

☐ RETARDATION ASSOCIATED WITH ILLNESS AND DISEASE. Some retardation arises from organic causes, such as illness, disease, and chromosomal abnormality. Two common forms of this kind of retardation are Down's syndrome and phenylketonuria.

Characteristics of Down's syndrome

About 1 in every 600 children born in the United States suffers from *Down's syndrome,* a form of moderate-to-severe mental retardation that is named after Langdon Down, who recognized it in 1886. Down's childrens' eyes are almond-shaped and slanted, and their round faces have an Oriental cast, so much so that this syndrome is often called *mongolism,* and the children mongoloids. (The similarity between these features and true Oriental ones is superficial at best. The condition is as easily recognizable among Oriental as Caucasian children.) Children suffering from this disorder also suffer from numerous physical anomalies, among them heart lesions and gastrointestinal difficulties. About one-fourth of these children do not survive the first few years of life. And because they are uncommonly friendly, cooperative, and cheerful, their early death touches parents and siblings very deeply.

Detecting Down's syndrome through amniocentesis

Down's syndrome arises because there are forty-seven chromosomes, rather than the usual forty-six, in the cells of these children. The disorder itself does not seem to be inherited, but the reason for this chromosomal abnormality is not presently known. Interestingly, while the risk for the disorder is about 1 in 1500 for children born to mothers in their twenties, it

Down's syndrome is a form of moderate to severe mental retardation.

increases to 1 in 40 when the mother is over the age of forty. It is now possible to detect a Down's syndrome fetus through *amniocentesis,* a painless test that is administered to the mother after the thirteenth week of pregnancy. In this procedure, a small amount of amniotic fluid (the fluid that surrounds the fetus) is drawn off and examined for the presence of the extra chromosome. When it is found, mothers have the option of continuing the pregnancy or undergoing an abortion.

PKU

There are a number of metabolic diseases that are associated with mental retardation, including Tay-Sachs disease, Nieman-Pick disease, and phenylketonuria (Carter, 1970). Phenylketonuria is the best understood of these diseases. PKU is a rare metabolic disease that occurs in roughly 1 out of 20,000 births. PKU results from the action of a recessive gene that is inherited from each parent. The infant cannot metabolize phenylalanine, an amino acid which is an essential component of proteins. As a result, phenylalanine and its derivative, phenyl pyruvic acid, build up in the body and rapidly poison the central nervous system, causing irreversible brain damage. About a third of such children cannot walk; nearly two-thirds never learn to talk; and more than half have IQs that are below 20.

Carriers of PKU can be identified through biochemical tests and receive genetic counseling (Stern, 1981). In addition, affected babies can be identified by a simple test of their urine about three weeks after birth. Provided they are kept on a diet that controls the level of phenylalanine in their system until age six, when the brain is nearly fully developed, their chances of surviving with good health and intelligence are fairly high.

☐ CULTURAL-FAMILIAL RETARDATION.   For approximately two-thirds of retardates, there is no clear injury or disease that caused their retardation. Rather, there seem to be factors in their genetic or environmental backgrounds that have contributed to their condition. These persons are said to have a cultural-familial retardation.

Cognitive ability (as measured by the IQ) appears, to some extent, to be passed through the genes. The IQs of identical (MZ) twins reared together

Intellectual ability influenced by genetics

correlate between .80 and .95, whereas the IQs of DZ twins correlate much lower, from .40 to .70 (Schwartz and Johnson, 1985). Even MZ twins reared apart have more similar IQs than DZ twins reared together (Scarr, 1975). The IQs of adopted children correlate more powerfully with the IQs of their biological parents (.48) than their adoptive parents (.19) (Munzinger, 1975). These data suggest that intelligence is partly inherited. Recent studies indicate that a wide range of disorders in intellectual functioning, including mental retardation and autism, co-occur in families at a high rate (Quay, Routh, and Shapiro, 1987). Thus, there may not be a genetic predisposition specifically to mental retardation. Rather, it may be intellectual ability in general that is partially influenced by genetics.

Influence of environment

Environment also appears to play an extremely important role in the development of intelligence. Frequently, retarded children come from poverty-stricken backgrounds and from broken families. While less than 3 percent of the general population is retarded, between 10 and 30 percent of the poor are retarded (Cytryn and Lourie, 1967). There are a number of reasons why socioeconomic class may be related to retardation. Wealth and social class powerfully determine the kind of stimulation children receive. Middle-class mothers tend to give children more verbal explanations of problem solutions, and more praise when the children have solved the problems, than do lower-class mothers (Hess and Shipman, 1965). Such training may increase children's verbal facility, while the praise augments their interest in such problems and their self-confidence in solving them.

Lower-class mothers are more likely to give birth to premature infants with low birth weights, and low birth weight is a risk factor for retardation (Kiely, Paneth, and Susser, 1981). In addition, children from lower-class families are more likely than upper-class children to be malnourished, to receive poor health care, and to suffer from a variety of illnesses across childhood. Such an environment inhibits the full development of the intellectual abilities a child does have.

TREATMENT

Training in language

Mentally retarded children often have defects in language skills that manifest themselves even before the child enters school. Training in language necessitates that the required sounds be demonstrated, and that the child be rewarded for closer and closer approximations to normal speech. Such training, whether conducted by professionals (Baer and Guess, 1971; Garcia, Guess, and Brynes, 1973), or by parents who have been trained to do such teaching (Cheseldine and McConkey, 1979), can be very useful in helping the child communicate more effectively. Behavioral training methods have also been used successfully to teach self-care skills to retardates (Watson and Uzzell, 1981).

The education of mentally retarded children

As we indicated earlier, many children, particularly those who are mildly handicapped, are not identified as requiring assistance until they enter school. There is considerable continuing controversy about the kind of remedial help they need once they are in school. One view holds that they should be educated with other school children, in the same classes and with the same teachers, since after all the vast majority of them will ultimately live with their "normal" peers. Another view holds that the needs of the retarded are so different that they need to be educated separately, with separate teaching methods and different schedules and curricula. According to this view, the education of mentally retarded children proceeds best when they are segregated in different institutions, or at least in separate classes. The fact is that neither *mainstreaming,* as integrated education programs are called, or segregation has proven particularly effective in training mentally retarded children (Cegelka and Tyler, 1970; MacMillan and Semmel, 1977). Segregation to special institutions, however, has other deleterious effects that arise from conditions within institutions for the retarded, and from the educational deficits that develop there and that prevent the children from living effectively outside the institution (Ohwaki and Stayton, 1978; Birenbaum and Rei, 1979; Chinn, Drew, and Logan, 1979). Generally, then, the issue of how the mentally retarded are best educated is unresolved. Many educators feel that until it becomes absolutely clear that the child cannot function in the normal classroom, she should remain there for humanistic as well as educational reasons.

SPECIFIC DEVELOPMENTAL DISORDERS

Tardy development

Much more common than mental retardation are the *specific developmental disorders,* difficulties that reflect enormous developmental tardiness. Such tardy development mainly affects the development of language and academic skills. Specific developmental disorders occur frequently in combination with other difficulties, and in fact, may spawn them.

To survive in adult life, people must be able to learn a language, to learn to read, and to do simple arithmetic. Because of this, most modern industrial societies make education compulsory for about ten years of a child's life. As in most developmental matters, children progress in their education at different speeds. A certain amount of lagging behind is to be expected of some children some of the time. But when a child is significantly below the expected level, as indexed by the child's schooling, age, and IQ, then the matter is viewed as a psychological problem. For children between the ages of eight and thirteen—the critical ages for the acquisition and implementation of academic skills—a significant problem may exist if a child is more than two years behind his or her age level.

READING DIFFICULTIES

Who has reading disabilities?

Of all the specific developmental disorders, reading difficulties have been studied most. As a group, poor readers were late in acquiring language, and they have more of a history of reading difficulty in their families. Most children who have reading difficulties also have trouble with other domains of learning. More than three times as many boys as girls suffer serious reading difficulties. Children with severe reading difficulties at age ten have an increased risk of other psychological disorders, particularly behavior disorders.

Treatment of reading disabilities

A combination of training in reading skills and behavior therapy designed to maintain a child's interest in learning has proven effective for many children with reading disabilities. This training must start early in a child's school career and be maintained throughout the school years for the child to sustain the gains that have been made and to continue to improve. Unfortunately, children's reading difficulties often are not detected until quite late in childhood.

The social implications of serious reading problems are alarming. Poor readers who are of average intelligence rarely read books or newspapers. They aspire to little that involves reading and, therefore, they often fail to graduate high school. Retarded readers emerge from the school system handicapped educationally, socially, and economically, in the sense that their employment opportunities have been significantly constricted (Yule and Rutter, 1976).

AN EDUCATIONAL OR PSYCHOLOGICAL DISORDER?

The specific developmental disorders are often correlated with, or give rise to, a host of distinctly psychological symptoms. It is mainly for this reason that these developmental disorders are considered *psychological,* rather than educational. But fundamentally, these are skills disabilities; they are in the domain of education rather than psychology and psychiatry. And many believe that they should continue to be viewed that way (cf. Garmezy, 1977a).

Problems of calling skills disabilities psychological disorders

The argument is not without merit. There is no evidence, for example, that psychological treatment or drugs have any positive effect on say, the developmental reading disorder. Calling the difficulty a *psychological* disorder in fact may lead teachers to believe that reading disability is outside of their sphere, leaving the child helped neither by the teacher nor by the psychologist. Moreover, terming reading retardation a psychological disorder may stigmatize the child without contributing a solution to the problem. Indeed, it may simply compound the difficulties. Consider the case of Nelson Rockefeller, former governor of New York and Vice President of the United States. Rockefeller had a severe reading difficulty that handicapped him from childhood through adulthood. Even as an undergraduate, friends and others had to read his textbooks to him. Throughout his career, he much preferred oral communications to written ones. His problems were difficult enough to deal with. Would his life have been made any easier if those difficulties had been described as a severe psychological disorder of childhood? Indeed, could he have been elected to high office if he had been so diagnosed?

PERVASIVE DEVELOPMENTAL DISORDERS: AUTISM

There may be some question about whether the specific developmental disorders are psychological disorders at all, but no such question attaches to pervasive developmental disorders. For the latter are all-encompassing, involving difficulties of such magnitude and across so many modalities—language, attention, responsiveness, perception, motor development—that little doubt remains about the psychological devastation they create. The primary type of pervasive developmental disorder is autism.

Lack of responsiveness

The essential feature of **autism** is that the child's ability to respond to others does not develop within the first thirty months of life. Even at that early age, gross impairment of communicative skills is already quite noticeable, as are the bizarre responses these children make to their environment. They lack interest in and responsiveness to people, and they fail to develop

An autistic boy.

normal attachments. In infancy, these characteristics are manifested by their failure to cuddle, by lack of eye contact, or downright aversion to physical contact and affection. These children may fail entirely to develop language, and if language is acquired, often it will be characterized by *echolalia*—the tendency to repeat or echo immediately or after a brief period precisely what one has just heard—or *pronominal reversals*—the tendency to use "I" where "you" is meant, and vice-versa. Such children also react very poorly to change, either in their routines or in their environments. These symptoms will be taken up at greater length momentarily. But first, some of the difficulties created by autism can be seen in the following case:

Looking at family photographs of John, one sees a good-looking, well-built, sandy-haired ten-year-old. He looks like thousands of other ten-year-olds—but he's not. If one saw a movie of John it would be immediately obvious that his *behavior* is far from normal. His social relationships seem peculiar. He seems distant, aloof. He seldom makes eye contact. He rarely plays with other children, and when he does, he plays like a three-year-old, not like someone who is ten.

Some things fascinate him, and his most recent fascination has been with shiny leather belts. He carries one around with him nearly always and at times whirls it furiously, becoming more and more excited in the process. At the height of his excitement, he lets out high-pitched, bird-like noises, jumps up and down on the spot, and flaps his hands at eye level. At other times, John appears to be living in a world of his own, entirely impervious to what is happening around him. A car can backfire near him, but he doesn't flinch. He stares into space, gazing at nothing in particular, occasionally flicking his fingers at something in the periphery of his vision.

In addition to the peculiar squeaks, John's speech is most unusual. He can follow a few simple instructions, but only if he is in familiar surroundings. He will say, "Do you want a drink?," and his parents will know that he means *he* wants a drink. Often, he will repeat complex phrases that he has heard a few days before; television commercials particularly feature in this sort of meaningless speech. At other times, he will echo back large chunks of his parents' speech, but they have realized that this is a signal that he has failed to understand them. He can ask for some things, but even simple requests come out muddled. When he fails to get his meaning across—and this can be several times a day—he will fly into temper tantrums that can become quite wild.

John's parents are both intelligent, articulate, professional people who, right from the early months after John was born, were convinced that something was wrong with him. But since John was their first child, they shrugged off their worries and attributed them to inexperience. So, too, did their family physician. But gradually, no amount of bland reassurance that John would soon "grow out of it" gave any comfort. John was still too good, too quiet, yet too little interested in them as people, and entirely unwilling to be cuddled.

Worried still, they brought John to child specialists. Again the opinions were reassuring. But as John approached age two and was not yet speaking, the experts' views began to change. Words like "slow," "backward," and "retarded" began to be used more frequently. Finally, John was formally tested by a psychologist, and a surprising fact emerged. Although he was grossly retarded in language development, he was advanced for his age on nonverbal puzzles. Difficulties with hearing were ruled out, and it was during these investigations that autism was first suggested.

Oddly, merely knowing that what was wrong with John had a name, provided his parents with some relief. But it was only momentary, for as they read popular accounts of autism, they found that many experts blamed the parents for the child's bizarre problems. Damning accounts of obsessional, emotionally remote parents—dramatized as "refrigerated mothers"—soon had them questioning whether they were fit parents. Their relationship to each other, as well as to John, was undermined.

John's parents managed to get him into a small class in a school for children with learning handicaps. The teacher took a special interest in John and, encouraged by his parents, she adopted a firm, structured approach to teaching him. To everyone's surprise, he took to some aspects of schoolwork readily. He loved counting things and could add, subtract, multiply, and divide by the time he was seven. Moreover, he learned to read fluently—except that he could not understand a single word of what he read. This was brought home to his parents when he picked up a foreign language journal of this father's and read a whole page in phonic French—without, of course, understanding a word! At about this time, he began talking. He referred to himself as "John," got his personal pronouns in a dreadful muddle, and learned to say "no." He used telegraphic sentences of a sort more appropriate to a boy many years younger than he, but at least he was beginning to make himself understood.

He seemed to cherish all kinds of monotonous routines. His diet consisted of a very restricted selection of foods, and he could not be induced to try new foods. He went to school by a prescribed and invariable route, watched television from the same armchair, and strenuously resisted change. Taking him outside was a nightmare, for there was no anticipating when he might throw an embarrassing tantrum. Try as she might, his mother could not help but be hurt by the glares and comments from passersby as she struggled to get John out of the supermarket or into their car. "If only he looked *abnormal*," she often said, "people would be more understanding."

SYMPTOMS OF AUTISM

Inability to relate

The central feature of autism, according to Leo Kanner, a child psychiatrist who was the first to recognize this disorder as a distinct syndrome, is the "inability to relate . . . in the ordinary way to people and situations . . . an *extreme autistic aloneness* that, whenever possible, disregards, ignores, shuts out anything that comes to the child from outside" (Kanner, 1943).

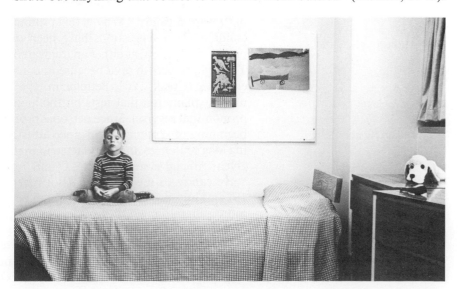

Autistic children shut out everything outside of themselves. They are thus characterized by extreme autistic aloneness.

This striking aloneness takes a variety of forms in the areas of language, behavior, intellectual and cognitive development, and in social relationships.

☐ LANGUAGE DEVELOPMENT.   One of the striking features of autistic children is how poorly their understanding and use of spoken language develops. Most parents report that the language of autistic children is delayed and deviant right from the beginning. Toward the end of the second year, when normal children are babbling in a characteristically varied way, autistic children frequently show decidedly abnormal and idiosyncratic patterns. Speech falters badly in these children because they fail to imitate or to initiate imaginative play, both of which are crucial for early language development. For example, they show little skill in such simple social imitations as "waving bye-bye." And their later use of small toys in imaginative play is severely limited if, indeed, it ever develops. Unlike deaf children, who understand the ideas of communication and who have developed nonverbal skills for communicating, autistic children do not use gestures and mime to make their needs known. They may point to objects they need, but if the object is not immediately present, their ability to communicate about it is very much restricted.

Restricted ability to communicate

It is in their very peculiar use of sounds and words that autistic children's difficulties are most noticeable. About half of the autistic children never learn to use even simple words. Those who do, show many characteristic abnormalities. In the early stages, the child often uses a high-pitched, bird-like squeaking voice, as John did. Again, like John, both immediate and delayed echolalia occur for long periods after speech develops. The child latches on to a phrase from, say, a television commercial, and echoes it for weeks on end.

When speech does develop, autistic children show many of the same sorts of grammatical errors that normal children do. But with autistic children, these errors are more long-lasting and peculiar. We will look at two of these errors; pronoun reversal and the misuse of the rule for adding *-ing*.

Pronoun reversal

Autistic children tend to reverse the pronouns *I* and *you*. For example, when the child wants a candy, he may say "Do *you* want a candy?" instead of "*I* want a candy." Why is this pronominal reversal so typical in autistic children? Two suggestions have been offered. Psychoanalysts have interpreted this reversal as either an unawareness or a denial of personal identity. The child refuses to say *I* because unconsciously he does not accept his own existence (Creak, 1961; Bettelheim, 1967). Others suggest a more parsimonious explanation that rests on the high correlation between echoing and pronominal reversal. Since personal pronouns occur more frequently at the beginning of sentences, and since autistic children have difficulty processing long sentences, they tend to echo the last few words only. When they are given artificial sentences with "I" and "me" placed at the end (for example, "give candy to me"), they do not reverse pronouns (Bartak and Rutter, 1974). Thus, pronominal reversal can be understood as an integral part of a more general language disorder, rather than as a symptom of emotional problems in identity formation.

Misuse of -ing rule

While both normal and autistic children misuse the *-ing* rule, autistic children are older when the errors arise and the errors persist long after the age when normal children learn the rule. One nine-year-old autistic girl described a man smoking a pipe as "Daddy piping," while a boy blowing bubbles was "boy bubbling" (Wing, 1976). Autistic children also often identify objects by their use, such as "make-a-cup-of-tea" for kettle, and "sweep-the-floor" for broom.

Language use
seems artificial

These are but two of the kinds of language errors made by autistic children. For many of these children, language development proceeds no further. Even the small proportion of autistic children who do learn to talk, continue to use language in a noticeably peculiar way. Often it is *too perfect, too* grammatical, rather like a person using a foreign language learned artificially. There is a lack of colloquialism. Conversation is stilted. These children can maintain a concrete question-and-answer interchange, but the subtleties of emotional tone are lost on them. They seem to know the formal rules of language, but they do not comprehend the idea of communication. This defect extends to the nonverbal aspects of communication as well.

Exaggerated
insistence on
sameness

☐ INSISTENCE ON SAMENESS. Many normal children react badly to changes in their environment, particularly if those changes are sudden. But for reasons that are not at all clear, autistic children show this trait in greatly exaggerated form. For example, some autistic children will have severe temper tantrums if the furniture in the house is moved around. Others insist on being driven to school over the same route every day. Parents find that what begins as a harmless routine becomes so rigid that it seriously interferes with everyday life.

Insistence on sameness is seen in other ways. Autistic children frequently use toys and other objects to make long lines or complex patterns. They seem more interested in the pattern than in the functional or imaginative play qualities of the objects. Frequently, these children become intensely attached to one or more objects. John, you recall, carried around a long belt and gyrated it. Other children may refuse to part from a grubby piece of toweling. These intense attachments interfere with normal development and everyday living in a number of ways. If the object is lost, life is made unbearable for the child and the rest of the family. If it is a large object, it prevents hand-eye coordination since the child's hands are not free to play with other objects. As can be seen in Box 16-1, however, it is possible to reduce these abnormal attachments and promote normal development (Marchant, Howlin, Yule, and Rutter, 1974).

Autistic children often have severe temper tantrums, particularly when their environment changes suddenly.

Failure to develop
social
attachments

☐ SOCIAL DEVELOPMENT. One other striking characteristic of the autistic child is aloofness, a physical and emotional distance from others that is especially troublesome to parents and quite noticeable by others. John was clearly aloof, and his mother particularly was troubled by it. This aloofness reflects a fundamental failure to develop social attachments. This is shown by the fact that when autistic children can choose where to spend their time, they will spend more time near a nonreacting adult than near an empty chair (Hermelin and O'Connor, 1970). Thus, active avoidance (which would have been shown by choosing to be near the empty chair) is not the case for autistic children. Recent evidence suggests that autistic children have fundamental problems in understanding expressions of emotions in others and in using their own faces, voices, and gestures to communicate their own emotions (Hobson, 1986).

Box 16-1   TREATING INSISTENCE ON SAMENESS

One of the less obvious consequences of many autistic children's insistence on sameness is the direct interference with their already limited cognitive development. Many children become compulsively attached to unusual objects. Some carry small stones clenched tightly in their fists; one child refused to be parted from a metal wire filing basket; and others carry discs they can spin. Any attempt by their parents or teachers to remove these objects is met with an immediate and violent temper tantrum. In these circumstances, adults often give in to the child's wishes. The result can be that the child wanders aimlessly around with his hands fully occupied by the object. In turn, this means that his hands are not free to pick up other things and generally to interact with his physical environment so as to allow hand-eye coordination to develop. Missing out on this stage of normal development may interfere with the development of later, more complex cognitive skills.

Some professionals have advised parents not to interfere with their child's unusual object attachment, in the belief that the object somehow represents the parent and that to intervene will mean damaging an already precarious relationship. In contrast, Marchant and her colleagues argue that these objects fulfill different functions from other attachment objects and that intervention is desirable to promote cognitive growth.

Marchant reports on the case of a five-year-old non-speaking autistic boy who constantly carried around a large (2 foot by 2 foot) blanket. This effectively meant that he had only one arm free for all activities. His mother attempted to prevent him from carrying the blanket everywhere, but to no avail.

It was decided to use a graded-change approach. His mother was asked to cut a small piece off the blanket each night and to increase the amount cut off. The blanket was quickly reduced from 4 square feet to a small bundle of five threads. At this point, the boy was able to abandon for awhile what was left of the blanket. Soon the boy took to carrying other objects. Where these were deemed inappropriate, they were dealt with in the same way. In fact, he appeared to enjoy watching them being cut up! Within four months, he carried a wider range of objects and his interest in any one of them was short-lived. Objects that were of play value were not destroyed, rather he was praised for playing with them appropriately. A year later, he spontaneously abandoned objects for long periods of time and, by then, his comprehension skills as well as his social behavior were improving markedly.

This case illustrates that a direct behavioral approach can be helpful in dealing with one of the major behavioral problems presented by many autistic children.

SOURCE: Based on Marchant, Howlin, Yule, and Rutter, 1974.

Many autistic children gradually improve in their social relationship beginning at about age five, provided that they have not been institutionalized in unstimulating surroundings. Ultimately, however, the relationships these children establish are difficult at best. Their social skills deficits show themselves in their lack of cooperative group play with other children, their failure to make personal friendships, and in the enormous difficulty they have in recognizing and responding appropriately to other people's feelings.

☐ INTELLECTUAL DEVELOPMENT.   While autistic children do poorly on tests that require verbal ability, they may perform far above average on tests

Islands of
intelligence

that involve rote memory or spatial tasks. Moreover, they may be quite talented in music or drawing. But despite evidence of islands of intelligence, autistic children function quite poorly in the cognitive domain. Only about one-quarter to one-third of them have IQ scores above 70, and those scores appear to be quite stable over a ten-year period. In fact, the child's measured IQ is one of the best predictors of later progress: those with higher IQ scores do better in a variety of educational and remedial settings (Mittler, Gillies, and Jukes, 1966; Gittleman and Birch, 1967; Lockyer and Rutter, 1969; DeMeyer, Barton, Alpern, Kimberlin, Allen, Yang, and Steel, 1974).

PREVALENCE OF AUTISM

Prevalence of
autism

Fortunately, the severe disorders of childhood are rare. Yet, the total number of children suffering from autism is considerable. It occurs in about 2 to 4 cases per 10,000, about as frequently as deafness occurs among children, and twice as commonly as blindness (Wing, Yeates, Brierly, and Gould, 1976; Steinhausen, Gobell, Breinlinger, and Wohlleben, 1986). With regard to sex differences, boys outnumber girls by about three to one. The disorder appears to be more common among children from the upper socioeconomic classes. This may be because upper-class, well-educated parents recognize the disorder earlier and can afford the expensive, long-term treatment for autism, thus their children show up in the epidemiological statistics.

CAUSES OF AUTISM

The sorts of behavior associated with autism are so far removed from people's expectations of normal development that most now believe that there must be some obscure form or forms of biological abnormality underlying the syndrome. The professional climate has not always been so biologically oriented, however. Those who first studied the disorder tended to focus on the parents and *their* abnormal traits (Kanner, 1943). By examining these traits, they hoped to come up with possible psychological causes of autism. Since the evidence on parental traits is now fairly clear, let us examine this first.

Parental
introversion?

□ PSYCHODYNAMIC THEORIES. To some psychodynamic theorists, the parents of autistic children seemed to be introverted, distant, intellectual, and meticulous. These children seemed to be reared under conditions of "emotional refrigeration." The introvertedness of the parents was reflected in their offspring: parental distance was seen in the child's aloofness, while parental meticulousness was mirrored in the child's repetitive behaviors. Even if one accepts the evidence, however, to conclude that the parents' behavior *caused* the child's disorder is not logical. It is equally plausible that, faced with such an unusual child, parental attitudes and behaviors became unusual. This alternative hypothesis was overlooked in the rush to demonstrate parental culpability.

The psychoanalyst Bruno Bettelheim (1967) offered a similar indictment of parents and family environments. He argued that, in their hopelessness and apathy, autistic children resemble inmates of concentration camps. In his view, the autistic child is one who actively withdraws from an increasingly hostile world, the hostility being relayed through his mother's insensitive handling. But there is little evidence to suggest that the parents of autistic children do behave very differently than the parents of normal children behave toward them. No confirmation of extremely damaging parental behavior exists. Few autistic children actually come from broken homes, and most have not experienced early family stresses. Their parents turn out not to be overly introverted or obsessional, nor do they show any excess of thought disorder. Most autistic children experience the normal range of parental attitudes and child-rearing practices (Cantwell, Baker, and Rutter, 1978).

Parents not strong reinforcing agents for infants

□ BEHAVIORAL THEORIES. Behavioral and particularly social learning views of autism are strikingly similar to the psychodynamic views that were just described. These behavioral theories suggest that the way parents interact with their infants interferes with the parents becoming strong reinforcing agents for the infants. That is, the parent does not attend to the infant and does not relate to the infant in the manner that normal parents do. In turn, this results in parents being much less influential in the developing child's behavior (Ferster, 1961).

□ BIOLOGICAL THEORIES. Because psychogenic theories have not been substantiated (Ornitz, 1978), and because many autistic children appear to also suffer from a variety of physiological deficits, increasing attention has been directed to the possible biological origins of autism. During adolescence, nearly 30 percent of autistic children develop epileptic seizures even though they had shown no clear evidence of neurological disorder when they were younger. Furthermore, electroencephalographic (EEG) studies—that is, studies that examine the electrical activity of the brain—reveal that autistic children have a higher rate of abnormal brain waves than do normal children. The types of abnormalities found so far, however, do not suggest any specific form of central nervous system dysfunction. Nevertheless, both kinds of data suggest biological involvement. Biological studies of autism have focused mainly on two areas: neurotransmission and genetics.

EEG studies reveal that autistic children have a higher rate of abnormal brain waves than do normal children. This suggests a biological component to infantile autism.

When neurotransmission is faulty, the brain is unable to pass messages efficiently from one neuron to another. As a result, both perception and learning are interfered with, and patchy cognitive development results. A variety of neurotransmitters could be at fault here, but the most promising leads concern the metabolism of a particular neurotransmitter called *serotonin* (Ritvo, Rabin, Yuwiler, Freeman, and Geller, 1978). Serotonin is involved in both perception and memory, and up to one-third of autistic children show abnormal serotonin levels (Campbell et al., 1975). Note, however, that the great majority of autistic children do not show neurotransmitter abnormalities. Also, such abnormalities are found in several other disorders. Thus, imbalances in serotonin levels may be one cause of autism, but there are clearly other causes, too.

Weak genetic transmission

Because autism is a relatively rare condition, it is difficult to gather extensive data on the genetics of the disorder. Available data indicate that there is a high incidence of many types of cognitive impairment in the families, and especially the identical twins, of autistic children (see Quay, Routh, and Shapiro, 1987), but that the specific syndrome of autism is only weakly transmitted genetically.

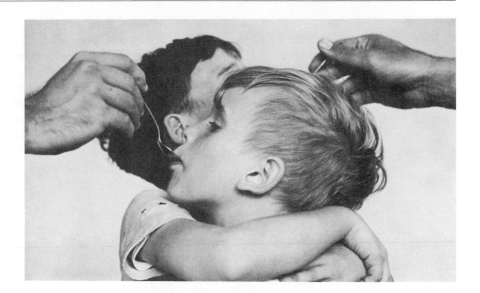

Behavioral techniques are used to treat specific deficits caused by autism. Here, these autistic children are being positively reinforced for hugging each other.

TREATING AUTISM

Behavioral
treatment

Insight-oriented treatments that arc derived from psychodynamic views of autism have not proven to be particularly effective (Rutter, 1968). Instead, current treatment efforts arise mainly from behavioral sources that focus on the specific deficits that are engendered by autism. Considerable effort, for example, has focused on language development, on the grounds that the inability to communicate properly is so central to this disorder. In these treatments, children's vocalizations are reinforced by the therapist until they occur very frequently. Next, the children are rewarded for imitating the sounds produced by the therapist, and simultaneously punished for producing meaningless sounds. When imitation is established, children are taught to label everyday objects. And finally, the same techniques are used to teach them to ask questions (Lovaas, 1966; Risley and Wolf, 1967). Early studies of the effectiveness of these methods engendered considerable optimism that these behavioral techniques might enable children to overcome the deficits associated with autism. But this optimism was tempered somewhat by the studies showing that gains made during treatment often disappear when the children are returned to institutional care (Lovaas, 1973). A recent study, however, suggests that if autistic children are given intensive behavioral treatment for a significant period of time (i.e., forty hours per week for at least two years) at an early age, long-term prognosis can be good (Lovaas, 1987). In this study, 47 percent of the autistic children receiving such intensive treatment achieved normal intellectual and educational functioning by age six to seven, compared to only 2 percent of autistic children who received minimal, institutional care. Furthermore, when parents participate in treatment programs, both their behaviors and those of the children undergo change. And the more the parents are involved in the treatment program, the more likely are the language gains to be maintained (Hemsley, Howlin, Berger, Hersov, Holbrook, Rutter, and Yule, 1978).

In conjunction with behavioral approaches, direct structured educational approaches have also proven beneficial to autistic children (Hung, Rotman,

Direct structured educational approaches

Consentino, and MacMillan, 1983). These approaches zero in on the specific cognitive, motor, and perceptual handicaps of these children. A carefully designed educational program minimizes the kinds of distractions that accompany ordinary teaching, making it possible for these children to concentrate. For example, when normal children are taught to read, some texts and teaching materials print vowels in one color and consonants in another. While this helps normal children differentiate between vowels and consonants, it confuses children with pervasive developmental difficulties (Schreibman, 1975). Generally, structured education aimed at overcoming the specific handicaps of the disorder seems to be the best method presently available for helping these children.

PROGNOSIS

Prognosis not favorable

Long-term follow-up studies of autistic children indicate that the prognosis for them is not favorable. Close to 60 percent will be unable to lead an independent life as adults. Only one in six will make a good enough adjustment to hold down a job, and even those will still be socially handicapped and will be considered odd in their interpersonal behavior (Lotter, 1978).

The IQ score turns out to be one of the most sensitive early indices of later outcome. In the main, the higher the autistic child's IQ, the better his prognosis. Another good prognostic indicator is the presence of some useful spoken language before the age of five. While the outlook for such children is slowly improving as treatment slowly improves, most autistic adolescents and young adults will still need access to residential facilities.

AREAS FOR FURTHER CONSIDERATION

Reclassifying childhood disorders

We have much yet to learn about the disorders discussed in this chapter. Throughout the chapter, we have pointed out gaps in our knowledge about each of the disorders. There are at least three broad sets of questions about childhood psychopathology in general that also need to be addressed over the next few years. First, does the current DSM-III-R classification system for childhood disorders accurately represent the breakdown of childhood syndromes? Children's problems are extremely difficult to translate into specific syndromes with clear-cut criteria for diagnosis. This is because the symptom configuration of any disorder may change with the child's development. Also, some symptoms, such as aggressive behavior, are associated with many different disorders. The classification of children's disorders is one area that experts expect to undergo much revision in future editions of the DSM.

Identifying children with disorders

The second question is related to the first: How can we better identify children who have serious psychological problems and how can we assess their particular problems? At the beginning of this chapter, we mentioned that we must rely on the adults in a troubled child's life to bring that child to the attention of clinicians. In addition, children's underdeveloped language skills make it difficult to obtain information from them about their condition. We need to know how to ask better questions of parents, teachers, and children that will provide the information clinicians need to assess children's psychological health.

Identifying and assessing problems in children is difficult because of children's underdevelopd language skills. Better questions and methods of assessment are needed to discover children's problems and then treat them. This child is using her doll to explain her problems to this therapist.

The final question is about the long-term prognosis for children who have a psychological problem. We mentioned that children with autism or a conduct disorder appear to be at high risk for psychological disturbance in adulthood. We know very little about the long-term prognosis of many of the other disorders, however. There have just been too few studies that follow children all the way into adulthood. We also know very little about the long-term effects of different types of therapy for children, especially drug therapies. What therapies are the most effective at helping a child to recover from a given problem and at preventing the recurrence of that problem in later years? Longitudinal studies of the outcome of children with different types of problems, who undergo different types of therapy, will be expensive, but the need for them is obvious.

SUMMARY

1. Children's psychological disorders are often difficult to distinguish from the relatively common problems of growing up because they occur in a developmental context, because children cannot communicate a problem directly through language, and because children's problems are often specific to particular situations and contexts.

2. On the whole, children's problems can be divided into five areas: disruptive behavior disorders, emotional disorders, habit and eating disorders, developmental disorders, and gender identity disorders.

3. The disruptive behavior disorders, including conduct disorder, oppositional defiant disorder, and attention-deficit hyperactivity disorder, appear to be quite persistent from childhood into adulthood. Children with these disorders often show criminal behavior, drug abuse, and low educational and occupational attainment.

4. The most common emotional disorder in children is separation anxiety disorder. Children with this disorder have a marked fear of separation from loved ones. Phobias, such as school phobia, are also common among children.

5. The habit disorders and eating disorders include bed-wetting, stuttering, tics, and two eating disorders, anorexia nervosa and bulimia nervosa. The prevalence of the two eating disorders appears to be increasing.

6. The developmental disorders range from learning disabilities in specific areas such as reading or math to various levels of mental retardation to autism. Autism is the most severe of these because it involves both intellectual retardation and severe disturbances in the abilities to have social and emotional experiences. The developmental disorders are more likely than any other class of disorders to persist into adulthood.

7. There is still much to be learned about childhood disorders, and especially about their treatment. Drug therapies have been used for some disorders, but there is great concern about the toxicity of drugs in children. Behavioral treatments seem effective for several disorders, including attention-deficit hyperactivity disorder, separation anxiety disorder, phobias, bed-wetting, stuttering, and some symptoms of autism. Many therapists also advocate involving a child's parents in therapy in order to facilitate a child's recovery from a disorder and to reverse any negative effects the parents might be having on the child.

Disorders of the Nervous System and Psychopathology

Morris Moscovitch and Paul Rozin

THE human brain is the most complex biological structure on earth. We may know more about the human brain, its anatomy and physiology, than about any other structure in the human body. But that is partly because there is so much to know. It is also true that there is more that we *don't* know about the human brain than about any other human structure.

Organic vs. functional syndromes

Most scientists believe that all of the phenomena of behavior and the mind, whether they are normal or abnormal, have a basis in the activities of the nervous system. Modern medicine, however, distinguishes between two broad classes of abnormal behaviors: ***organic syndromes,*** which are caused by known pathology in the structure or function of the nervous system, and ***functional syndromes,*** which are believed to be caused by abnormal experience imposed upon normal brain mechanisms. This split is generally represented by two branches of medicine, neurology and psychiatry. In psychology, there is a corresponding split between neuropsychology, devoted to studying organic syndromes, and clinical psychology, which is concerned more with functional syndromes. The distinction between these disciplines and the syndromes is not, however, hard and fast.

Type of diagnosis affects treatment and attitudes

Clinicians are often forced to make a determination of organic or functional disorder. This decision will have broad implications. It will determine the type of medical-psychological care that the patient receives, and the extent of insurance coverage for the costs of treatment and loss of income. It will also affect the way the patient views herself and the way others view her. Our judgment of a person's behavior is affected by whether we believe it is part of a neurological disorder or an aspect of the individual's personality. Let us briefly examine two cases to illustrate this point, and to show the overlap between neurology and psychiatry.

Organic
disorders that
may seem
functional

Before the onset of her disorder, a woman had worked for years as a fish-filleter. When the symptoms of damage to both parietal lobes appeared, she began to experience difficulty in doing her job. "She did not seem to know what to do with her knife. She would stick the point in the head of a fish, start the first stroke, then come to a stop. In her own mind, she knew how to fillet fish, but yet she could not execute the maneuver. The foreman accused her of being drunk and sent her home for mutilating fish." (Critchley, 1966, pp. 158–59)

As shown in this case, before the woman was diagnosed as having an organic syndrome—damage to both parietal lobes in her cortex—a functional syndrome had been suspected—drunkenness. The woman was treated as a drunk and sent home from work by her boss. Had an organic cause been clear, however, her boss might have solicitously taken her to a hospital.

Looking at her symptoms, one would ask: Did the woman really not want to work? Was she anxious about something and was it interfering with her work? Or was she actually *unable* to work? As it turned out, the woman was suffering from an **apraxia,** a basic disorder of movement, in the absence of muscle weakness or inability to perform any specific movement. Her symptoms had indicated the site of the damage, which was specific and localized to the parietal lobes.

Cases of this sort are typically caused by a stroke, that is, a critical reduction in the blood supply to the affected area. The diagnosis of a stroke is based on a careful case history, in which sudden onset and absence of other precipitating causes, including psychological causes, are critical features. The diagnosis is supported by a neurological examination that includes an expert assessment of mental status and sensory and motor abilities. In cases of doubt, the diagnosis can be confirmed by radiological brain-imaging techniques, measurement of the electrical activity in the brain, and other tests (see later section on diagnosis).

Not all cases are as easy to diagnose as this type of apraxia. Patients with slight damage to the right posterior parietal region (Figure 17-1A) also have no obvious physical symptoms; there is no paralysis, nor is there loss of sen-

Figure 17-1
Anatomy of the human brain.
(A) Photograph of the left hemisphere, showing the major lobes of the cerebral cortex. The front of the brain is at the left. (Courtesy The American Museum of Natural History.) (B) Diagram of the human brain cut on the mid-line (dividing the brain into equal left and right halves). (Modified from Keeton, 1980)

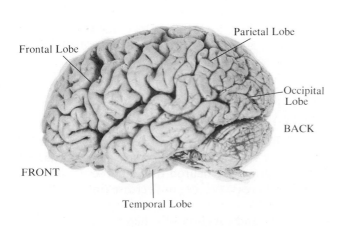

Frontal Lobe

Parietal Lobe

Occipital Lobe

BACK

FRONT

Temporal Lobe

A

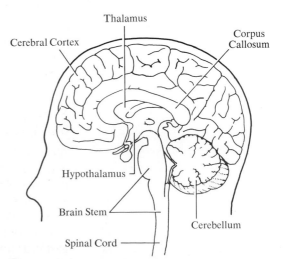

Thalamus

Cerebral Cortex

Corpus Callosum

Hypothalamus

Brain Stem

Cerebellum

Spinal Cord

B

sation, nor are there any gross defects in language or thinking. The patients' behavior, however, is often socially inappropriate. They are poor at expressing or interpreting emotional cues that are conveyed by tone of voice or by facial movement. They miss the point of stories and jokes. Nuances, which are fundamental to social interactions, escape them. Subtlety is not their suit. Patients exhibiting these symptoms may first be referred to psychiatrists. Only the presence of additional symptoms that have nothing to do with personality suggests to the clinician that there is a neurological disorder. These symptoms include deficient visuo-spatial abilities, such as difficulty in drawing even simple figures like cubes and clocks, and a peculiar failure to pay attention to events and stimuli that occur on the left side of the patient (see later discussion of the brain's front-back organization) (Ross, 1981, 1983).

Reclassifying functional disorders as neurological

The fact that it is difficult to determine whether some syndromes are organic or functional is only one reason why a person interested in psychopathology should know something about neurology. In the future, it is likely that once we understand more about their underlying pathology, some disorders now considered to be functional will be reclassified as neurological. This has already occurred for the case of the paralysis and dementia syndrome caused by syphilis (see Chapter 3), and it may also occur for some of the major psychoses. Furthermore, neurology is based on a body of knowledge about the structure and function of the nervous system, and uses a set of advanced diagnostic techniques that compare very favorably to what is available in many other branches of medicine. As a result, neurologists work with diagnostic tools that are sophisticated and precise, and a classificatory scheme that is more clear-cut than what psychologists and psychiatrists have available to them in DSM-III-R. Neurology provides an opportunity to view an advanced discipline that deals with phenomena similar to those that are the focus of abnormal psychology.

THE ORGANIZATION OF THE NERVOUS SYSTEM IN RELATION TO ORGANIC DISORDERS

In this section, we will show how some basic principles of the structure and function of the nervous system can account for a variety of disorders of mind and behavior.

STRUCTURAL AND FUNCTIONAL UNITS: NEURONS, GLIA, SYNAPSES, AND NEUROTRANSMITTERS

Defects in synapses as cause of some disorders

Neurons are the "units" of the nervous system (Figure 17-2A). Neurons communicate with one another by releasing neurotransmitter substances into the *synapse,* the gap separating one neuron from another (Figure 17-2B). These transmitters either increase (excite) or decrease (inhibit) the activity of other neurons.

Defects in the basic structure and function of synapses have been suggested as causes of some major mental illnesses. You will recall the catecholamine theory of depression, which holds that a deficiency in the

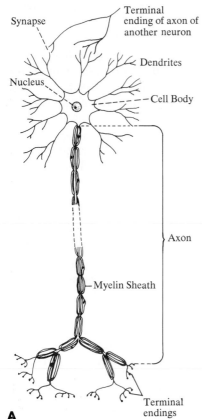

A

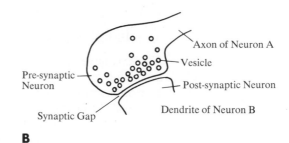

B

Figure 17-2
(A) Schematic diagram of the principal parts of a neuron. Neurons vary in form. The neuron pictured is a motor neuron from the spinal cord. The terminal endings of another pre-synaptic neuron are shown at the top, to illustrate synaptic endings. (Source: Modified from Katz, 1952) (B) Schematic diagram of a synapse. Neurotransmitters made in the presynaptic neuron are stored in vesicles in the ending of the pre-synaptic neuron. When a nerve impulse reaches the synaptic ending of the presynaptic cell, it causes release of the neurotransmitter into the synaptic gap. It diffuses across the gap, attaches to receptors on the membrane of the post-synaptic neuron, and produces electrical changes (excitation or inhibition) in the post-synaptic neuron. (Source: Modified from Gardner, 1975, p. 47)

neurotransmitter norepinephrine in certain parts of the brain is the cause of depression.

Some of the pathology of the nervous system derives from damage to the supportive tissue of the brain, particularly the glia cells that are dispersed throughout the brain and that are much more numerous than neurons (Figure 17-3). Many tumors and other disorders originate in the glia cells. Multiple sclerosis is a disorder of the glia cells that manufacture and maintain the myelin sheath that surrounds the axons of many neurons. The result is impaired function of neurons, often leading to weakness, loss of sensation, and even mental disorders.

Disorders of the glia cells

Figure 17-3
Photomicrograph (magnified about 60X) of motor neurons of the spinal cord. The numerous small dots are nuclei of glial cells, indicating the large number of glia with respect to neurons. (Source: Carolina Biological Supply)

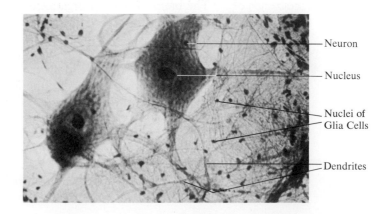

THE BIOCHEMICAL ORGANIZATION OF THE BRAIN

Biochemical
specificity of
neurons

Neurons have specific biochemical identities. They can be differentiated according to which chemicals are in their cell membranes and which neurotransmitters they produce. Neurons with similar biochemical properties tend to be located near one another, or in identifiable clusters of neurons running through the nervous system.

Depletion of
dopamine in
Parkinson's
disease

Parkinson's disease is a disorder of movement that has a biochemical basis. It is characterized by tremor of the hands, rigidity, and difficulty in initiating movement. It afflicts, in some degree, about 1 percent of the people over fifty in the United States. It is caused by degeneration of specific neurons, which causes a depletion of the neurotransmitter dopamine in certain structures in the brain. Although there is now no cure for the disease, its symptoms can be effectively relieved by administration of the drug L-DOPA, which is converted into dopamine in the brain (Adams and Victor, 1981). There is also evidence that schizophrenia is caused by an excess of dopamine in the brain. Given that Parkinson's disease and schizophrenia are associated with opposite disturbances in dopamine, it should not be surprising that treating Parkinson's disease patients with high levels of L-DOPA can induce the symptoms of schizophrenia, and treating schizophrenics with drugs that reduce dopamine activity can lead to the appearance of the symptoms of Parkinson's disease (Gilman, Goodman, Rall, and Murad, 1985).

Degeneration of
motor neurons in
ALS

Neurons serving the same function have certain biochemical similarities in their membranes. Because of this, toxins, certain infectious agents such as viruses, or other influences may specifically affect particular types of neurons. In amyotrophic lateral sclerosis, "Lou Gehrig's disease," there is selective degeneration of motor neurons, with progressive loss of movements in the limbs, body, and head (see Box 17-1; Figure 17-4). The cause of this disease is unknown, but since the damage is specific to motor neurons, there must be some specific and unique property of these cells that makes them more susceptible to a pathological agent.

THE SPATIAL ORGANIZATION OF THE BRAIN: LOCALIZATION OF FUNCTION

Localization of
function allows
diagnosis of the
site of damage

The brain is spatially organized; that is, neurons in different regions of the brain perform different functions. Furthermore, neurons close to one another are likely to perform related functions. This spatial organization of the nervous system (localization of function) allows a neurologist to determine the location of damage in the nervous system by just examining behavioral symptoms. Most damage to the nervous system affects a moderately well-defined area, as would clearly be the case for damage resulting from strokes, bullet wounds, or tumors.

Damage to
processing
centers or to their
connections

The nervous system contains areas in which nerve cell bodies are concentrated, called *gray matter,* and areas in which axons are concentrated into tracts, called *white matter,* because of the white myelin surrounding many axons. Tissue damage can occur in either or both regions. Functionally, we

Box 17-1   LOU GEHRIG: THE IRON HORSE OF BASEBALL STRICKEN BY AMYOTROPHIC LATERAL SCLEROSIS

It is ironic that the most durable of all baseball players, Yankee Lou Gehrig, who had a major league record of playing in 2130 consecutive games, was stricken by one of the most debilitating of all diseases, amyotrophic lateral sclerosis (ALS). The motor neuron degeneration that characterizes ALS produces weakness and a loss of the motor control that is especially necessary in athletics. In keeping with the specificity of this disease, Gehrig's first symptoms were a deterioration in batting performance. He played only the first eight games of 1939, batting only .143, an enormous drop for a consistent (lifetime .340 batting average) hitter. On May 2, 1939, Gehrig withdrew himself from the Yankee starting lineup, breaking his consecutive games' string, on the grounds of poor performance. In June, he went to the Mayo Clinic for diagnosis, and the following announcement was made to the startled press and public on June 21, 1939: "After a careful and complete examination, it was found that he is suffering from amyotrophic lateral sclerosis. This type of illness involves the motor pathways. . . . The nature of this trouble makes it such that Mr. Gehrig will be unable to continue his active participation as a baseball player. . . ." (Hubler, in Voigt, 1987, p. 185). Thus ended one of the greatest careers in baseball. Gehrig's uniform number, 4, was retired so that no other Yankee can ever wear it. In one of the most moving events in baseball history (Figure 17-4B), 60,000 fans turned out to honor him in Yankee Stadium on July 4, 1939. To say his goodbye, Gehrig shuffled to the microphone, with a gait already hampered by the affliction of ALS. His closing remarks were: "I may have been given a bad break, but I've an awful lot to live for. With all this, I consider myself the luckiest man on the face of the earth."

Gehrig took a job working for the Parole Board in New York City, and he continued at this until he was unable to function. As is characteristic of ALS, his mind remained clear, but he gradually lost his ability to walk or move in other ways, and he lost his ability to speak clearly. Gehrig died on June 2, 1941, about two years after diagnosis of the disease.

Figure 17-4
(A) Lou Gehrig connecting for a homer in 1938, his last full season. (B) Lou Gehrig being honored at Yankee Stadium on July 4, 1939, shortly after his retirement and affliction with ALS was announced.

A

B

can think of the gray matter as processing centers where neurons interact, and the white matter as tracts that connect areas of gray matter. Some disorders may result either from loss of a processing center (gray matter), and others from disconnection of processing centers as a result of damage to tracts. Consider a person who cannot move his left hand in response to a verbal command. This deficit could result from damage to the processing centers that deal with language or hand movement, or from the severing of the connection between language processing areas and hand movement areas.

Modular organization of brain and diagnosing site of damage

The current view is that the brain is organized into large functional systems made up of separate components or modules, each serving a different function. In other words, the organization of the brain is modular in much the same way that an audio system or computer is modular. Removing a module or altering or interfering with its function will affect the entire system. Areas of gray matter correspond to modules, and areas of white matter to the connections (equivalent to the wires in an audio system) between the modules. Modules can be more or less restricted in their domain of operation. Some operate over a wide domain, such as gathering or evaluating information that might be required for planning or problem solving. Other modules operate on only limited sensory information, such as those involved in processing speech sounds or faces. Based on observing abnormal behavior, neurologists can determine where malfunctions have occurred, and which modules of the brain have been affected.

There are three basic dimensions of spatial organization of the brain, corresponding to the three axes that describe any three-dimensional object: front-back, left-right, and up-down. We will consider the organizing principle of each axis, and the implications for organic pathology.

FRONT-BACK ORGANIZATION OF THE BRAIN

Motor functions in front; sensory functions in back

In general, both the brain and spinal cord are organized so that motor functions are in the front and sensory functions are in the back. Therefore, the damage involved in most sensory disorders occurs further back in the nervous system than that involved in motor disorders. As we ascend to the cerebral cortex, the motor-sensory distinction is preserved, but the scope of these terms is expanded.

Damage to the information-processing system

Alexander Luria (1973), the eminent Russian neuropsychologist, distinguished between two broad domains of the "higher" function of the human brain: information processing and planning-verification-action. The information-processing system corresponds to the expanded sensory system and is located in the back (posterior) portion of the cerebral cortex. It handles the representation of the inputs from each of the senses and the integration of information from the senses, in the service of building a useful representation of the world. Within the system are the primary projection areas, the parts of the brain that receive inputs from the skin, ears, eyes, nose, and mouth. These areas are located in the parietal, temporal, and occipital lobes (see Figure 17-1A); damage to them causes loss of sensation. Other parts of the parietal and temporal lobes receive input from these projection areas, which they process and integrate into higher-order perceptual units. Damage to these areas leads to such symptoms as poor representation of space, inability to recognize meaningful objects like combs and hammers (a disorder called *agnosia*), or inability to name objects (a disorder called *anomia*).

A particularly interesting syndrome, ***left-sided neglect,*** which involves disturbance of higher-order perceptual functions, results from damage to the right parietal area (Mesulam, 1981) (Figure 17-1A). Patients with this syndrome neglect the left half of their body and the left side of space in front of them. When dressing, they fail to put the left hand into their shirt sleeve, or the left leg into their pants. When writing, they may only use the right side of the page, and when copying a figure, they may omit the part on the left side (Figure 17-5).

Even when they shut their eyes and imagine a scene, say of a town square or of a particular room in their house, they describe what is to the right of the vantage point they have assumed, and they neglect the left side (Bisiach and Luzzatti, 1978). Posner and his colleagues (Posner, Walker, Friedrich, and Rafal, 1984) have suggested that the deficit in this neglect syndrome arises because patients have difficulty in disengaging their attention automatically from the right side, not because they cannot shift their attention voluntarily on the left. Thus, if told to attend to the left side of a page or an imagined scene, patients with neglect can usually do so. If, however, they are already attending to the right side, and something occurs on the left side, they cannot spontaneously redirect their attention to the left.

The expanded motor system, which corresponds to Luria's planning-verification-action system, is located in the front (anterior) part of the brain, in the frontal lobes. It is primarily involved in acting upon the world. It plans and executes action, and it verifies the outcome of the action. A particular higher-order function mediated by the frontal lobes is the transition from one action to another. After frontal damage, the isolated components are intact, but the smooth sequencing is disturbed. A striking clinical sign of this deficit is ***perseveration,*** a difficulty in making transitions between one action and the next, or in simply terminating a prepotent behavior or response. It is often expressed as excessive repetition. Perseveration appears at many levels of function. Frontal patients have a tendency to grasp objects and then to be unable to let go. Similarly, they may repeat an action over and over, and have great difficulty in alternating two actions. This problem can be graphically illustrated by looking at what these patients do when told to draw a sequence of alternating figures. Typically, they continue to draw the original figure, and they cannot shift (Figure 17-6). This perseverative tendency is also manifested at higher levels, in the planning and execution of strategies. Thus, frontal patients are particularly poor at abandoning a

Left-sided neglect

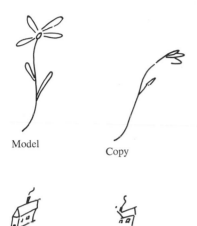

Model   Copy

Figure 17-5
Brain damage leading to unilateral neglect. These are copies of two drawings made by a patient with damage to the right hemisphere of the brain, showing the symptoms of neglect of the left side of space. (Source: Hecaen and Albert, 1978, p. 219)

Damage to the motor system

Figure 17-6
Drawings made by two patients with damage to the frontal lobes, in response to the instruction printed above each drawing. Each row represents the sequence of requests made to one patient. The tendency to repeat the previous response is called perseveration. (Source: Luria, 1970, p. 239)

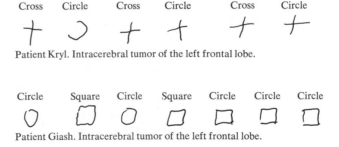

Cross	Circle	Cross	Circle	Cross	Circle

Patient Kryl. Intracerebral tumor of the left frontal lobe.

Circle	Square	Circle	Square	Circle	Circle	Circle

Patient Giash. Intracerebral tumor of the left frontal lobe.

strategy they have learned, even after it ceases to work. In a test of card sorting that requires formulating hypotheses and then changing them once they are no longer valid, patients with frontal damage manage to formulate an initial hypothesis, but find it difficult to abandon it once it is no longer useful (Milner, 1964). This "fixedness" or "inflexibility" in behavior has a clear neurological origin in damage to the frontal lobes. We can only wonder whether other examples of inflexibility, such as excessively repeated obsessional behavior, might share a common pathology, or at least, a common site of action.

Additional effects of frontal lobe damage are revealed by testing patients on laboratory or clinical tasks that are highly controlled yet that capture features of real-life situations. Patients with frontal damage are highly distracted by irrelevant stimuli when they are searching for a target among other alternatives. In a test that requires them to suppress powerful competing responses, such as naming the color in which a word is written rather than the word itself, frontal patients perform much more poorly than patients with damage to other cortical areas. In solving mazes, patients with frontal damage do not always plan their moves appropriately and end up in blind alleys. Even once they have learned to solve the maze, they will make impulsive mistakes, including breaking such rules as not touching the boundaries of the maze, or following new paths simply to find out where they lead rather than attempting to solve the puzzle (Milner, 1964; Stuss and Benson, 1986).

A classical case that gives the flavor of frontal damage on an entire personality is that of Phineas Gage (Figure 17-7).

> Phineas Gage was the twenty-five-year-old foreman of a group of men working on railroad track in Vermont in 1848. An explosion caused an iron bar, over an inch in diameter, to pass through the front of his skull, damaging a large part of the frontal area of his brain (see Figure 17-1A). Miraculously, Gage survived, with no more than a few moments of loss of consciousness. After recovery, he reapplied for his job as foreman. His contractors, who regarded him as the most efficient and capable foreman in their employ previous to his injury considered the change in his mind so marked that they could not give him his place again. The equilibrium or balance, so to speak, between his intellectual faculties and animal propensities, seems to have been destroyed. He is fitful, irreverent, indulging at times in the grossest profanity (which was not previously his custom), manifesting but little deference for his fellows, impatient of restraint or advice when it conflicts with his desires, at times perniciously obstinate, yet capricious and vacillating, devising many plans of future operations, which are no sooner arranged than they are abandoned in turn for others. . . . his mind is radically changed, so decidedly that his friends and acquaintances said he was "no longer Gage." (Harlow, 1868, pp. 339–40)

There are obvious similarities between the performance of frontal patients in the laboratory and clinic and the behavior of Phineas Gage. Like the frontal patients, Phineas was impulsive, easily distracted, and unable to follow through on plans or evaluate their consequences. The emotional and personality changes that he underwent may have similar causes. He could no more control, modulate, inhibit, or evaluate his emotional response than he could his actions.

Frontal damage and distracting stimuli

The case of Phineas Gage

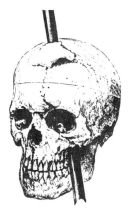

Figure 17-7
Skull of Phineas Gage, the patient described by Harlow (1868), showing the hole in the frontal bone made by the iron rod blown through his head. The bar entered below the left eye and passed through the skull. (Source: Harlow, 1868)

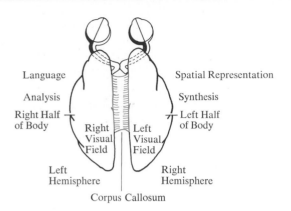

Figure 17-8
Schematic diagram of the human brain, as seen from above, to illustrate the corpus callosum and the specialized functions of each hemisphere. (Source: Modified from Levy, 1972, p. 163)

LEFT-RIGHT ORGANIZATION OF THE BRAIN

Left-right differentiation

The human brain, more than the brain of any other species, is differentiated on a left-right basis. Among all vertebrates, the left half of the brain receives most of the input from the right side of the body, and the left half controls action primarily on the right side. This "contralateral" projection is of powerful diagnostic value. In almost all cases, if weakness, paralysis, or loss of sensation on one side of the body results from damage to the brain, the damage is on the side of the brain opposite to the afflicted body part.

The split-brain syndrome

There is a qualitative difference in the functioning of the two human cerebral hemispheres. The full significance of this difference is best illustrated by the split-brain syndrome. (For the rest of this chapter, assume that all statements refer to right-handers, unless otherwise indicated. Left-handers are much less consistent than right-handers in hemispheric organization.)

Left brain and language; right brain and spatial abilities

The split-brain syndrome is a by-product of a surgical procedure (Bogen and Vogel, 1975) in which the corpus callosum (Figures 17-1B and 17-8) and other major connections between the hemispheres are cut to prevent the transmission of epileptic seizures (discussed later in the chapter) from one side of the brain to the other. As a result of the operation, the two hemispheres cannot communicate with each other; the patients appear to have two consciousnesses in one head. The left brain is the only half that can speak, and it has a much more sophisticated understanding of language. The right brain is superior to the left brain in tasks involving spatial abilities and the recognition of complex forms that are difficult to describe in words, such as faces (Gazzaniga, 1970; Levy, 1972, 1980; Sperry, 1974; Zaidel, 1978a, 1978b).

Left brain and analytic abilities; right brain and synthetic abilities

The differences between the hemispheres are well illustrated by the performance of the right hand (left hemisphere) and left hand (right hemisphere) in copying simple figures (Figure 17-9). The drawings of the right hand suggest a general deficit in the organization of the spatial world. The three-dimensional aspect of the figures is lost, whereas it is preserved in the drawings by the left hand. One way to summarize the hemispheric differences is to say that the left hemisphere is better at analyzing inputs and breaking inputs or outputs into sequences over time, while the right hemisphere is better at synthesizing components into wholes and making spatial representations (Levy, 1980; Bradshaw and Nettleton, 1981).

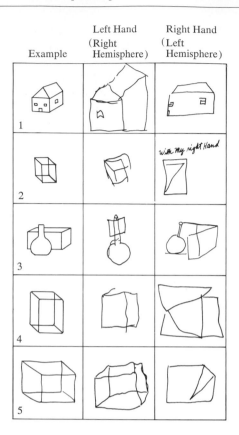

Figure 17-9
Split-brain patients were asked to make copies of various examples—one copy was made by the left hand (right hemisphere); the other by the right hand (left hemisphere). These results illustrate the superior spatial orientation capacity of the right hemisphere. Patients with damage to the right parietal lobe show, with either hand, the type of deficit seen in the right-hand drawings. (Source, Gazzaniga, 1970, p. 99)

These differences have many implications for psychopathology. Language disorders are much more common with left hemisphere damage (for right-handers), while disorders in getting around in space or recognizing faces and other complex configurations occur much more frequently with right hemisphere damage.

UP-DOWN (HIERARCHICAL) ORGANIZATION OF THE NERVOUS SYSTEM

Higher levels build on lower levels of the nervous system

The brain is organized vertically in a hierarchical structure. This means that particular functions (e.g., control of movement) are carried out at a number of different levels in the nervous system, from spinal cord to cerebral cortex. The higher levels are generally more abstract, cognitive, and voluntary. This basic idea was expressed forcefully and eloquently by the nineteenth-century British neurologist, John Hughlings Jackson (1884, in Taylor, 1958). The higher levels build on or modulate the lower levels, which represent the contract with the outside world, at the receptors or the action of the muscles. Jackson claimed that the higher levels are more vulnerable than the lower levels, and more often than not are the first systems to malfunction in general diseases of the whole nervous system. This is illustrated by a common sequence of symptoms seen in some old adults as senility progresses: first there is a loss of higher cortical functions that produces difficulty in dealing with new situations, chronological ordering of events, and loss of powers of narration with patchy memory. Subsequently, subcortical functions are compromised, leading to failures in the performance of bodily functions (modified from Barbizet, 1970).

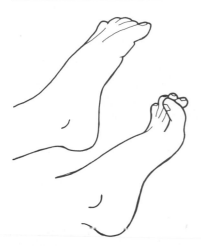

Figure 17-10
On the upper left is the normal response to scratching on the sole of the foot. On the lower right is the pathological Babinski response to this same stimulation. The Babinski response results from release of inhibition caused by damage to higher levels of the motor system. (Source: Gardner, 1975)

Higher levels of the nervous system often inhibit lower levels. When the higher levels are damaged, there is a *release* of inhibition. A particularly clear example of release is the ***Babinski sign,*** a reflex normally shown only by infants. When the bottom of the foot is irritated, the toes fan out (Figure 17-10). This reflex disappears early in life. The circuits that mediate it remain intact, however, inhibited by higher centers. Severe damage to higher motor centers releases this reflex; this is one of the cardinal signs of damage to the higher parts of the motor system.

Because of the neural hierarchy, damage at any number of levels can compromise function. The programming of action is a prime example of hierarchical organization. At the lower levels, the motor system operates with the unit of specific muscles. Damage to motor nerves or spinal motor centers that directly control movement usually leads to weakness or paralysis in particular muscles. At the higher levels, damage to some areas of the cortex, particularly in the frontal or parietal lobes, leads to defects in the planning or sequencing of movements, or defects in the linkage of movements with thought and language (Luria, 1973; Geschwind, 1975; Heilman, 1979; Kolb and Whishaw, 1980; Adams and Victor, 1981; Roy, 1982). Yet, each of the particular movements in the sequence may be executed normally (see, for example, the case history of the fish filleter on p. 559).

GENERAL ASPECTS OF DISEASES OF THE NERVOUS SYSTEM

In this section, we will discuss the causes of damage to the nervous system, the way that damage expresses itself as a symptom, and susceptibility and resistance to damage.

AGENTS OF DAMAGE TO THE NERVOUS SYSTEM

The agents of damage to the nervous system may produce acute or chronic symptoms. They may act locally, or throughout the body and nervous system. They may produce behavioral symptoms suddenly or gradually. We briefly review here the agents of disease.

Causes of widespread disorders

Widespread disorders often result from deficiencies in nutrients—minerals like calcium, vitamins, amino acids; from lack of oxygen—resulting from reduced blood supply caused by narrowing of the arteries, or atherosclerosis, or from suffocation. Ingested toxins, infections, trauma to the head, and general degeneration of neurons can also produce diffuse damage. Because of differing vulnerabilities, symptoms may appear only, or at first, in specific systems. Many general disorders of this type affect level of consciousness and memory. A clearly localized site of damage may also produce widespread symptoms. For example, a tumor may cause a build-up in pressure of cerebrospinal fluid, thus affecting the whole brain and causing symptoms like headache and drowsiness.

Causes of localized symptoms

More localized symptoms are often produced by tumors, disorders in blood supply produced by either ***stroke*** (occlusion of blood vessels) or ***hemorrhage*** (ruptured arteries that leak blood), localized infections, specific genetic malformations, or degeneration of cells in a specific area.

THE EXPRESSION OF DAMAGE IN THE NERVOUS SYSTEM

Positive and
negative
symptoms

The kinds of symptoms that may appear after nervous system damage can be positive or negative. Common sense suggests that damage should result in negative symptoms—loss or deficiency in the function that the damaged area serves. This is true much, but not all of the time. Sometimes, there are "positive" symptoms, which may occur for two reasons. First, damage can cause irritation and can increase the activity of neurons in the injured area. Second, if damage decreases the activity of an area that inhibits another area, there will be an increase of activity due to release from inhibition. In either case, the symptoms are positive in the sense that there is more activity in the nervous system and more behavior in the organism.

Epilepsy

Epilepsy is the best example of a disorder whose primary symptoms are "positive." Epilepsy is a common disorder that affects over one million Americans. Damage to neural tissue produced by any of a number of different agents of disease may leave the tissue irritable and may lead to increased synchronized activity because of damage to inhibitory systems or because the residue of the damage (e.g., scar tissue) excites neighboring neurons. The excessive synchronized activity (seizures) that is produced leads to an exaggerated expression of the function of the area. Seizures occur intermittently, with sudden discharge of neurons. These may be widespread, leading to muscle contraction throughout the body and loss of consciousness, or they may be much more localized. The part of the brain or type of mental event that appears first in the seizure is an indicator of the location of the primary damage in the brain. Depending on the location of the irritable tissue, the primary symptoms may be sensory (e.g., an hallucination), motor (e.g., twitches or larger muscle contractions), or emotional (e.g., fear or laughing). Sometimes, the initial events of the seizure produce an aura, or mild symptoms such as unusual sensations or feelings related to the site of damage. Some seizures spread progressively from the original site to other parts of the brain. Epilepsy can be treated by controlling the agent of disease that caused it, by use of drugs that reduce the irritability of neurons, or by surgery that excises the irritated nervous tissue (Adams and Victor, 1981).

SUSCEPTIBILITY TO DAMAGE: VULNERABLE SYSTEMS

Some parts of the
brain more
vulnerable than
others

Some functions of the brain are more vulnerable to damage than others. All parts of the body and brain are not equally resilient. The lower back is a weak spot in the human skeleton, causing more than its share of misery. The stomach and cardiovascular system both seem particularly susceptible to stress-related problems and psychosomatic effects (see Chapter 10). Similarly, there are vulnerable parts of the brain. A consequence of this is that general stress to the nervous system, by vitamin deficiencies, blows to the head, or toxins, can produce surprisingly specific symptoms.

Some neurons
more vulnerable
than others

A group of neurons may be more vulnerable because it has a relatively poor blood supply. Not all parts of the brain are equal in terms of blood supply (see an example in the section on language disorders). Some neurons, because they are especially large or active, have higher requirements for oxygen or nutrients. Thus, one of the earliest symptoms of vitamin B1 deficiency is deficits in sensation and motor control in the hands and feet (peripheral neuropathy). The vitamin deficiency affects all neurons. But the long axons of the neurons innervating the hands and feet place an extra load on the maintenance of these cells, making them more vulnerable. Other neurons are more vulnerable because they are located in a place where a stroke is more likely to occur. As we point out in the section on amnesia, the system that is involved in remembering is particularly vulnerable, and it is often selectively damaged by general trauma, such as blows to the head, or vitamin B1 deficiency. The cause of this vulnerability is unknown.

RESISTANCE TO DAMAGE: REDUNDANCY IN THE NERVOUS SYSTEM

Alternative pathways in the nervous system

Redundancy and the existence of alternative pathways are common in the nervous system. Redundancy, or overdetermination, occurs throughout vital biological systems. Humans can function well with only one kidney, one eye, or without a majority of their liver cells. To a lesser extent, this is true of the brain, as well.

Redundant neurons

Where more neurons are involved in a particular function than is absolutely necessary, the destruction of some of the cells, or moderate damage to all of them—as might happen with small wounds produced by bullets, or small strokes—may not produce any observable symptoms. For example, even though there is a steady degeneration (without replacement) of the cells that respond to odors, most people in their seventies are still able to detect and identify odors fairly well and some remain professional wine tasters or perfumers. All systems, however, do not show this type of redundancy.

Circumventing damage

Where there are alternative pathways that can accomplish the same end, damage to one pathway may be circumvented. Thus, although movement of the right side of the body is primarily handled by neurons originating in the left brain, there is a small pathway leading from the right brain that allows people with split brains, or people with left hemisphere damage, to exert some control over the right side of their body, but not over fine finger movements. Also, some functions, such as the control of eating or other basic bodily responses, are represented in equivalent form on both sides of the brain, so that damage to one side may not have a substantial effect.

Alternative strategies

The availability of alternative strategies also has the effect of reducing the symptoms resulting from tissue damage. For example, a person who has damage to the right hemisphere, which affects his ability to recognize faces, might be able to recognize faces by relying more on explicit, verbally described features of the face (wears glasses, has thin lips), rather than the more holistic representation that one normally gets from the right hemisphere. Alternative strategies can also be facilitated by cultural inventions. For a person who is unable to walk, crutches make the arms into organs of locomotion.

Finally, because of redundancy, it is common to see normal function in partially damaged systems when conditions are optimal. But as the environmental challenges become greater, as they do under stress or with fatigue, performance falls apart. Fatigue often brings on latent symptoms of diseases as varied as multiple sclerosis and senile dementia. For similar reasons, demented people often function better intellectually in the morning than later in the day. In general, more redundant systems are less vulnerable.

THE NEUROLOGICAL DIAGNOSIS

Determining
which disease
process causes
patient's
symptoms

Diagnosis is more advanced in neurology than in psychology because of extensive knowledge of the structure and function of the nervous system, and because it is possible to verify diagnoses objectively with sophisticated measurements of the living brain, or at autopsy. The first task of the neurologist is to determine whether the patient is indeed suffering from a disease of the nervous system. This may be extremely difficult, as we noted in the beginning of this chapter. Having some reason to believe that the symptoms are caused by a disease of the nervous system, the neurologist assumes that *one* disease process and/or *one* lesion can account for all of the symptoms. His problem is to determine what agent of disease, acting in what location, could produce the full pattern of symptoms, and *no other* symptoms. Thus, if a patient is paralyzed on the left side of the body, it is necessary to account both for this paralysis and the lack of any paralysis or other symptoms on the right side of the body.

The neurologist has three sources of information: the history of the symptoms as described by the patient and her family, the neurological examination, which consists of an interview and observation of the patient, and the use of special diagnostic techniques to gain direct information about events in the nervous system. The history and neurological examination may be sufficient to make a diagnosis; the special diagnostic tools may serve to confirm an almost certain diagnosis, or they may be of essential importance in determining the nature of the disease.

Our ability to find out what is going on inside the bony skull without going inside is quite remarkable. We briefly review some of these techniques here because they often play a central role in the determination of whether symptoms point to a neurological or psychological disturbance. Absence of evidence of damage to the nervous system makes it more likely that the symptoms have a psychological origin.

Samples of cerebrospinal fluid, taken from the base of the spine, can reveal evidence for internal bleeding, infection, and other sources of disease. Abnormal pressure of the fluid is suggestive of tumors or other obstructions. A whole family of techniques, including a dazzling array of computer hardware, allows visualization of what is going on in the living brain, from the outside. These techniques depend on the fact that abnormal brain tissue, e.g., a tumor, damaged or dead neurons or scar tissue, is different from normal tissue. Electrical differences are detected by the ***electroencephalogram (EEG),*** which records electrical events occurring in the brain by using wires taped to the surface of the head and scalp. This technique can often record the electrical changes that occur in particular parts of the brain during epileptic seizures, as well as other electrical changes in abnormal tissue (Figure 17-11).

The greatest advance in neurological diagnosis in recent years has been in the development of new brain-imaging techniques. The most widely used

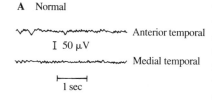

A Normal

I 50 μV

Anterior temporal

Medial temporal

1 sec

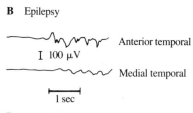

B Epilepsy

I 100 μV

Anterior temporal

Medial temporal

1 sec

Figure 17-11
Selections from (A) a normal EEG, and (B) an EEG from an epileptic patient. Note that the records from the epileptic patient use a smaller voltage scale. Thus, the difference in amplitude between normal and epileptic EEGs is even greater than it appears to be. (Source: Adams and Victor, 1981, pp. 19–20)

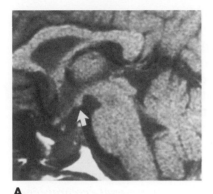 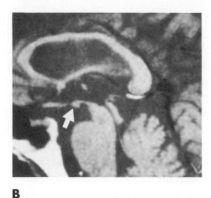 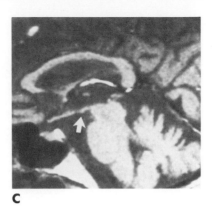

A   **B**   **C**

Figure 17-12
(A) MRI brain scan from a normal patient, (B) a patient with Alzheimer's disease, and (C) a patient with chronic Wernicke's encephalopathy. The brain image represents what might be seen in a saggital section of the brain, as in Figure 17-1B. The arrow indicates the mammillary bodies, a structure more or less intact in the Alzheimer's disease patient, but severely damaged on both sides in the Wernicke's encephalopathy patient. The latter patient, also described as suffering from Korsakoff's psychosis, typically shows a profound amnesia, often associated with damage to the mammillary bodies (see Figure 17-16, and the discussion on amnesia. The MRI scans in that figure come from the same patients as in the left and right panels in this figure). (Source: Charness and DeLa Paz, 1987)

method is known as *computer-assisted tomography,* which produces an X-ray image of the brain and is known as a *CAT scan.* It is based on the principle that abnormal tissue absorbs X rays to a different degree than bone or normal brain tissue. From a series of X rays of the brain taken at different angles, a three-dimensional representation of the brain can be constructed, with the aid of a computer, and abnormal tissue within the brain can be located.

MRI, or *magnetic resonance imaging,* is a new technique that is gaining in popularity because it is believed to be more sensitive than the CAT scan at detecting abnormalities. In MRI, a magnetic field is imposed on the brain and a pulsed radio frequency wave is applied that causes each atom of any particular element to behave as a tiny spinning magnet that resonates or wobbles at a frequency that is characteristic for that element. The signal emitted by the resonating atoms is detected by a sensor. The distribution of resonating atoms of any particular element is analyzed by computer and reconstructed as an image representing the concentration of that element in different parts of the brain (Figure 17-12). The images are usually based on the behavior of hydrogen, which is richly distributed in tissue in the nervous system. In contrast to the CAT scan, which reveals the density of the tissue, MRI shows the composition of cells and their surroundings. Damaged areas of the brain have a different concentration of the element than normal areas and appear differently in MRI. The quality of the image in MRI scans can be appreciated by comparing the saggital scans in Figure 17-12 with the schematic view of the medial saggital view of the brain in Figure 17-1B. In addition, Figure 17-16 shows a comparison of MRI scans with actual post-mortem brain sections of comparable patients with Korsakoff's psychosis. The MRI is strikingly similar to the actual brain section. The MRI scan is painless and harmless as far as we know.

Both the CAT scan and the MRI provide images of static brain structures without regard to whether these areas are functioning normally. Other techniques have been developed that can indicate something about the dynamic function of different brain regions. These techniques are sensitive to the metabolic activity of the brain. The more active a particular region, the greater its rate of metabolism. These techniques have been used with normal people to determine the regions that are involved in performing different tasks, such as reading. They have also been used with patients to determine which brain regions are not functioning normally. Abnormal brain tissue usually has a different rate of metabolism from normal tissue.

SPECT scan, rCBF, PET scan

At any moment, regions of the brain that are more active receive more blood flow. The flow is measured by many small detectors placed on the skull that are sensitive to emissions from inert radioactively labeled substances that the patient has inhaled or that are injected into the patient. The amount of blood flow to a brain region is measured by the amount of radioactivity detected in that region. The radioactivity of these substances is low, and the life of the substances in the body is very short, so that the risks of using these techniques are very small. Two techniques that are based on the measurement of cerebral blood flow are the ***SPECT scan,*** or ***single photon emission computerized tomography,*** and ***rCBF,*** or ***regional cerebral blood flow.*** These techniques are used to provide an indirect image of brain activity in different regions. The ***PET scan,*** or ***positron emission tomography,*** provides a more direct measure of brain activity. In the PET scan procedure, the radioactive substance, which is usually glucose or oxygen, is incorporated directly into the neuron in proportion to the neuron's metabolic rate. With the aid of computers, a representation of the metabolic rate in different brain regions is produced.

Exploratory neurosurgery

It is not always possible to assess the precise location and nature of damage, and hence to determine the most appropriate treatment. In such cases, it may be necessary, if the costs of inaction are serious enough, to examine the brain directly. Exploratory neurosurgery, often leading directly into explicit surgical intervention to deal with the problem, is then called for.

We illustrate the process of neurological diagnosis with one case history:

Sample diagnosis: case history

> This fifty-five-year-old, right-handed . . . housewife . . . while working in her garden at 10:00 A.M. on the day of admission suddenly developed a weakness of her right side and was unable to speak. Apparently, the right-sided weakness mainly affected her face and arm since she was still able to walk. Neurological examination revealed the following: The patient was alert. She had no spontaneous speech and could not use speech to answer questions and could not even use yes or no answers. She could not repeat words. The patient was, however, able to indicate answers to questions by nodding or shaking her head if questions were posed in a multiple-choice situation. In this manner, it was possible to determine that she was grossly oriented for time, place, and person. The patient was able to carry out spoken commands and simple written commands . . . Strength of voluntary movement: there was a marked deficit in the right upper extremity (arm). There was a minor degree of weakness involving the right lower extremity (leg). Sensation appeared normal. Brain X rays and EEGs showed no abnormality. [This was in 1969, when the more modern, computer-enhanced techniques were not generally available.] The patient showed recovery over the following days. A significant amount of strength returned to the right hand within twenty-four hours, and by forty-eight hours, she could speak single words, but there was still no spontaneous speech. Some weeks later, she still had an expressive problem: her speech was slow and labored. (Curtis, Jacobson, and Marcus, 1972, pp. 526–28)

Sample diagnosis: explanation

The above pattern of symptoms clearly suggests damage to the left hemisphere, since this is the hemisphere that contains speech centers in almost all right-handers. The weakness of the right side of the body suggests left-hemisphere damage, because of contralateral control. The greater weakness

Figure 17-13
CAT scan of a patient with Broca's aphasia. Note the darker area in the upper left (left frontal area) indicating brain damage. In describing a picture of a boy flying a kite, this patient says, "Waving and uh . . . the . . . oh dear . . . and the kite and boy and . . . and eeth . . . uh barking and a . . . a lil boy and a bigs. . . ." (Source: Kertesz, 1982, p. 35)

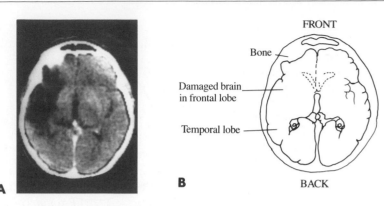

in the arm than the leg makes sense, because the areas innervating the arm are closer to the areas controlling speech than are the areas controlling the leg. The fact that all of the symptoms are in action, as opposed to sensation, suggests a forward location of the lesion, as does the fact that the language problem is in expression, rather than in comprehension of speech. Since the most striking and long-lasting symptom is the speech disturbance, it is reasonable to presume that the focus of damage is Broca's area in the left frontal lobe, since this is the center for speech production. The patient has an expressive (Broca's) aphasia (see next section), unconfirmed in this case by direct measurements on the nervous system. The source of the damage, given the sudden onset, is almost certainly a blockage of a blood vessel feeding this area; that is, a stroke. (A CAT scan from a typical, more recent case of Broca's aphasia, is shown in Figure 17-13.)

SOME SELECTED DISEASES OF THE NERVOUS SYSTEM

In the following section, we consider a few diseases of the nervous system in some detail. We selected these diseases because they are common and/or well studied. The first group of diseases, disorders of language, conveniently continues our discussion of Broca's aphasia from the last section on diagnosis.

DISORDERS OF LANGUAGE: THE APHASIAS

Language is a uniquely human activity, and of vital importance to thought, communication, and social life. Hence, disturbances in language are particularly upsetting. Most major disorders of language have a well-defined neurological basis, and are called aphasias. We will begin our discussion of the aphasias by presenting the classical view, widely held until the last decade or two.

THE CLASSICAL VIEW OF APHASIA

Expressive
aphasia

Aphasias illustrate particularly well the principles of spatial and left-right organization (see Geschwind, 1972; Marin, Saffran, and Schwartz, 1976; Adams and Victor, 1981, for general discussion of aphasia). We have already pointed out that most language functions are localized in the left

Figure 17-14
Schematic side view of the left hemisphere of the human brain, showing parts of the brain concerned with language. The tract connecting Wernicke's area to Broca's area is labeled A. When this tract is destroyed (as at A), the result is conduction aphasia. (Source: Modified from Geschwind, 1975, p. 189)

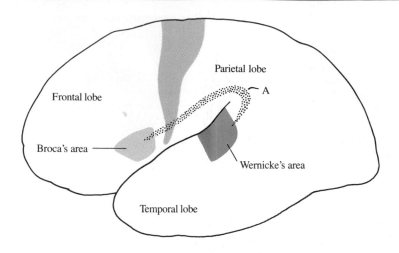

hemisphere of right-handers; hence, aphasias in right-handers are almost always the result of damage to the left hemisphere. Speech is controlled primarily by neurons located in the part of the frontal lobe designated Broca's area, in honor of the nineteenth-century neurologist, Paul Broca, who first described this syndrome (Figures 17-13 and 17-14). Damage in this area leads to difficulties in expression, as indicated in the case history in the last section. Perception and comprehension of language are often more or less intact, but speech is halting, labored, and ungrammatical. Many of the common small words are omitted. This pattern of symptoms is described as an *expressive aphasia*.

Receptive aphasia

The perception of speech is accomplished primarily in a part of the left temporal lobe called Wernicke's area (Figure 17-15). Damage to this area results in a *receptive aphasia,* often without any loss in ability to hear non-speech sounds. The patient has difficulties in perceiving and/or comprehending speech, and so has difficulty following instructions. Speech is also disordered in a manner that is consistent with a comprehension deficit. The speech disorder, in contrast to that of patients with damage to Broca's area, is characterized by fluent and grammatical speech that consists of many empty words, circumlocutions, paraphasias (word or sound substitutions), and neologisms (new, made-up words). The damage is usually caused by a stroke, that is, a critical reduction in the blood supply to Wernicke's area. Note that in accord with the motor-front, sensory-back principle, the speech production area is in front of the speech reception area. Consider the following case of Wernicke's aphasia:

Patient B.A. was admitted to the hospital because of a slight weakness in her hand. Her strength gradually returned, but a few days later, she suddenly developed severe comprehension problems. She was disoriented, yet she seemed strangely unconcerned about her condition. She was a native English speaker, but she was unable to comprehend the simplest words or sentences. When addressed, she responded with grammatically correct but meaningless sentences spoken in a pleasant manner with the intonation and inflection of someone recounting a story to friends over coffee. She was unaware that what she was saying was often gibberish, nor was she sensitive to the responses of the person to whom she addressed her remarks. For example, when asked to describe a picture, she replied,

"Yeh, about . . . mmmm . . . that is all. It's a bramblejite. I was at work at soler baks and baks. I did a lot of litins in England. . . . Well, kurly re retin han just the han junikin saddle. We'd nothin to sigh in England, tenah we'd come off the durlin a lot."

Her speech was no different during unstructured interviews. When one of us interviewed her, it was noted that her responses and reactions were unchanged when she was addressed in a foreign language that she did not understand or even when spoken to in a made-up gibberish. In fact, two such patients will happily exchange utterances with each other as if they are having a perfectly normal chat. (Case history courtesy of the Communication and Behavioral Neurology Department, Baycrest Hospital, Toronto, Ontario.)

Disconnection syndrome and conduction aphasia

Both Broca's and Wernicke's areas are connected to other parts of the brain that allow for the extraction of the meaning of language. There is also, however, a direct connection from Broca's area to Wernicke's area (Point A in Figure 17-14). Damage to this nerve tract, a classic example of a *disconnection syndrome,* leaves speech production, speech perception, and the comprehension of language more or less intact. But in the absence of the direct connection from speech perception to speech production, these patients cannot repeat, verbatim, a sentence that they hear, a condition called *conduction aphasia* (Geschwind, 1965). They are still able, however, to extract the meaning of the sentence, and thus they can follow verbal instructions.

Isolation of speech perception and production areas

There is another striking but rare aphasia that is just the opposite of conduction aphasia. In this disorder, Broca's area, Wernicke's area, and the connection between them are intact, but the speech perception and production unit that they make up is cut off from the rest of the brain, due to extensive brain damage. This damage occurs because the "ring" of brain tissue surrounding Broca's area, Wernicke's area, and their connection is relatively far from the main artery that supplies blood to it. This "ring" is therefore more vulnerable to the effects of low levels of oxygen or other nutrients which result from exposure to some toxins, lung disease, and other causes. These areas cannot survive on the more limited rations of oxygen and nutrients, and permanent damage results. The following case illustrates the symptoms that result in a person whose speech perception and production "unit" is isolated from most of the rest of her brain.

As a result of carbon monoxide poisoning, a twenty-two-year-old woman sustained the pattern of brain damage we have described. The result was an isolated speech system that functioned relatively well, in the absence of any ability to comprehend or spontaneously produce language. The patient could repeat sentences spoken to her, verbatim. But she could not understand anything that was said to her, and her very minimal spontaneous speech was of inappropriate and stereotyped expression (e.g., "Hi, daddy"). In short, she was much more compromised in language function than the conduction aphasic, because she could not really use language, although she could do the one thing conduction aphasics fail to do: repeat sentences verbatim. (Geschwind, Quadfasel, and Segarra, 1968)

NEUROPSYCHOLOGICAL ANALYSIS OF BROCA'S APHASIA

In the last decade or two, there has been an explosion of interest in the analysis of the nature of the cognitive deficit resulting from different types of brain damage. The rapidly developing disciplines of cognitive science and

Advances in
neurological
analysis of
language
disorders

neuroscience converge on this problem. Often, in the wake of these advances, old and clear distinctions become muddied, and the full complexity of phenomena is uncovered. This has happened in the study of the neurological aspects of language. We review here some of these advances, with respect to the classical syndrome of Broca's aphasia. This exercise will give us a sense of how neurologists and neuropsychologists attempt to understand a syndrome in terms of fundamental cognitive processes. A crucial aspect of this approach is the importance of showing what functions are preserved as well as what functions are impaired in any syndrome.

Broca's aphasia
not a motoric
disorder

First we ask whether Broca's aphasia is truly a linguistic disorder. Might the linguistic symptoms be explained by a nonlinguistic deficit? Broca's area lies close to the motor area of the tongue and other speech musculature. Perhaps the deficit is motoric rather than linguistic. Patients with Broca's aphasia, however, can move their lips and tongue with sufficient agility to speak. They sometimes can even sing quite well the very words that they cannot otherwise say. Moreover, patients with Broca's aphasia often have the same difficulty in writing that they do in speaking, indicating that the loss involves functions that are not confined to the speech musculature (Kertesz, 1982).

Broca's aphasia
not a generalized
intellectual
disorder

Can the disorder result from a generalized intellectual impairment? This is a little more difficult to discount, because language enters into so much of our thinking and reasoning, even when the problem does not appear to be verbal. Nonetheless, it has been shown that the performance of many Broca's aphasics (including the case illustrated in Figure 17-13) on tests of nonverbal intelligence and visuo-spatial problem solving is normal (Kertesz, 1982).

Broca's aphasia
affects all
expressive
domains

So far the evidence indicates that what is damaged is a module whose function is necessary for expressive language. We next ask whether Broca's aphasia is limited to speech, or whether it extends to other expressive domains. Writing may be as severely compromised as speaking (Kertesz, 1982). Deaf-mutes who use American sign language and suffer damage to the anterior region that includes Broca's area become aphasic in their use of signs in a manner that resembles the speech of Broca's aphasics (Poizner, Klima, and Bellugi, 1987). In light of these findings, we may conclude that the expressive deficit in Broca's aphasia affects all domains.

Syntactic disorder
part of Broca's
aphasia

For over a hundred years after Broca's discovery, it was generally believed that Broca's aphasia was primarily expressive. One strong impetus for this belief was that not all linguistic functions were equally compromised. In particular, language comprehension seemed to be intact. Recent work in linguistics, however, has suggested that the same processes are involved in comprehending grammatical utterances as in producing them. This has changed the focus of attention from linguistic expression in general to the poor grammatical structure of the utterances in Broca's aphasia. Is the agrammatism in Broca's aphasia better described as an expressive disorder or as a disorder that affects comprehension as well? The speech of Broca's aphasics is ungrammatical in the sense that function words such as articles and prepositions are absent or used inappropriately (Goodglass and Mayer, 1958). Recent studies have shown that Broca's aphasics have difficulty in comprehending sentences in which syntactic knowledge is essential for understanding. For example, to understand the sentence: "the woman drove the man home," requires syntactic knowledge in order to determine who did the driving. The same type of syntactic knowledge is needed to understand that "the man was driven home by the woman" has the same meaning. In contrast, a sentence like "The woman drove the truck home" can be understood without extensive syntactic knowledge. For example, if the sentence is scrambled into: "the truck woman home drove," one can still extract its basic meaning (Schwartz, Saffran, and Marin, 1980).

Matters are yet more complex. It has recently been shown that Broca's aphasics can judge whether sentences are grammatical or not, even though they cannot accurately comprehend them. Thus, they confuse "put the ball on the box" with "put the box on the ball," but they know that both are grammatical sentences, as opposed to "put the ball the box" (Linebarger, Schwartz, and Saffran, 1983). Hence, it appears that comprehension and production of syntactic utterances are defective in Broca's aphasia, but that judgments of grammaticality are preserved.

We have argued that a syntactic disorder is part of Broca's aphasia and that Broca's aphasia is at its core, linguistic. The linguistic deficit involves phonological as well as syntactic systems, with perhaps a greater emphasis on expressive than on receptive processes. Within the larger picture we have drawn of brain function, it is appropriate that Broca's area is part of the frontal lobes, which are generally involved in sequencing and planning. Both functions are central to syntactic processing.

Dyslexia

Learning disabilities are a common disorder of childhood. One subtype, ***developmental dyslexia,*** consists of a difficulty in learning to read that is out of proportion to the child's intellectual and emotional development. The incidence of dyslexia varies greatly as a function of both the precise definition employed and the country or locality in question. Estimates vary from about 1 percent to over 10 percent. About 75 percent of dyslexics are male (Rutter, 1978). Because literacy is so important in our society, a great deal of attention has been paid to this problem.

Acquired dyslexia is a disorder in reading that occurs in adults who once knew how to read well. As a result of a stroke or some other injury, they lose this ability. This loss may be quite specific; in one case, a patient awoke, got dressed, made breakfast without noticing anything was wrong. On picking up the newspaper, however, he discovered that he could make no sense of the letters in it (Dejerine, 1892, cited in Geschwind, 1972). Acquired dyslexia is much rarer than developmental dyslexia, but because it is usually associated with clear damage to the nervous system, it has been a major source of information about the neural control of reading. Its study has led to suggestions about possible causes of some cases of developmental dyslexia.

We must briefly consider the nature of the reading process, in order to understand its pathology (Gleitman and Rozin, 1977; Rozin and Gleitman, 1977; Coltheart, 1985). The natural route for language is from mouth to ear. Reading is a cultural invention that allows for representation of language in the visual modality. In alphabetic writing systems, a set of visual units or graphemes (called letters in English) corresponds to the individual sounds

Judgments of grammaticality preserved

Developmental dyslexia

Acquired dyslexia

The nature of the reading process

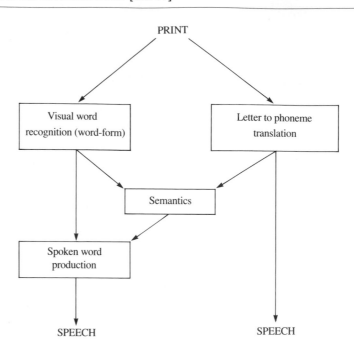

Figure 17-15
A gross architecture for the reading system. (Based on Coltheart, 1985)

(phonemes) that underly the stream of speech. For English, mastery of the mapping between twenty-six graphemes and their corresponding phonemes makes the full range of known spoken and heard words accessible through reading. The beginning reader sounds out a written word that he has never seen before, recognizes this sound as a familiar word, and then has access to all of its meanings. As the reader becomes more fluent, the sounding-out process seems to recede. Some common words are recognized directly by their overall shapes. More importantly, readers seem able to convert written letter sequences directly into meanings, as if they had created an internal dictionary (or lexicon). The lexicon has information about both the meaning and pronunciation of all letter sequences that are entered in it. Readers learn about regularities in the sequences of letters: *u* regularly follows *q, w* never follows *v.* Knowledge of these orthographic regularities allows for rapid perception of words. Sounding out cannot always produce the correct pronunciation of words, for example, "yacht" or "sword." These types of words have to be read at least in part by sight. In short, for the adult reader, there seem to be two routes from print to meaning: one via conversion to sound and then to meaning, and a second via direct conversion from letter sequence to meaning. Indeed, some children learn to read without going through direct training in sounding out words; they may directly learn the letter sequences that correspond to meanings, though they almost always also learn to sound out words even if they weren't so instructed. (The two reading pathways are diagrammed in Figure 17-15.) There are reading disorders corresponding to damage in either or both pathways. The principle of redundancy makes diagnosis of a reading disorder quite complex.

Phonological dyslexia

In ***phonological dyslexia,*** there is damage to the system involved in reading by sound, typically a result of a specific lesion in the posterior part of the left hemisphere. Because the visual route is available, such a patient may not make too many mistakes in reading aloud. But these patients are unable to pronounce a written word that they have never seen even if it corresponds to a spoken word they know. Lacking the ability to convert even familiar written words to their sound directly, that is, through grapheme-phoneme correspondence, such patients will also be unable to determine whether visually presented non-words rhyme with each other. Asked to choose which two of the following three words rhyme ("rite," "kight," and "rit") they are likely to guess that the first and third rhyme, because they resemble each other visually (Beauvais and Derouesne, 1979; Coltheart, 1985).

Surface dyslexia

As the model in Figure 17-15 predicts, there are patients who cannot read words by sight; they read the words only by sounding them out. Although they can sound out words they have never seen before, there are many familiar words that they cannot read correctly; these are the words that violate standard rules of pronunciation, such as "have," "yacht," "bread," "sew," and "sword." Such patients have *surface dyslexia,* and their lesion is usually in the posterior temporal/parietal region (Patterson, Marshall, and Coltheart, 1985).

Dyslexia and the reading of Japanese

Among people who read non-alphabetic languages, some of these reading disorders take on characteristically different forms. Japanese has two basic writing systems. One is a syllabary, in which each of about forty-eight symbols represents a different spoken syllable, for example, "ka" or "ta." Words are formed by combining the sounds of each of these syllables. Indeed, one of the two Japanese syllabaries is called Ka-ta-ka-na, expressed as four syllabic symbols. The other writing system, Kanji, is ideographic; each symbol stands for an entire word. Written Japanese text is a mixture of these two systems, both normally within the same sentence. In Japanese, phonological dyslexia is manifested by a severe impairment in reading the syllabic script but preserved ability in reading the ideographic one. The converse is true of Japanese surface dyslexics (Sasanuma and Fujimura, 1971).

Applying findings to developmental dyslexia

A number of investigators have tried to apply the findings from research on acquired dyslexia to children with developmental dyslexia. There is no doubt that at least a subset of dyslexic children show evidence of abnormal neuronal development in the posterior left hemisphere, where lesions have been shown to produce reading disorders in adults (Galaburda, Sherman, Rosen, and Geschwind, 1985). The underlying cause of the developmental disorder does not always correspond clearly to the cause of the acquired dyslexias. Some children behave like phonological dyslexics, in that they have severe deficits in sounding out words. Although at first one might be tempted to teach these children to read using only the sight method, such an approach would be limited in value, since there are just too many English words to learn to recognize. A better therapy might involve an intensive program of teaching the child how to parse words into their phonemic constituents, which would provide them with the foundation on which to apply rules for sounding out words (Rozin and Gleitman, 1977).

A DISORDER OF MEMORY: THE AMNESIC SYNDROME

We have considered the varieties of pathology that can cause disorders in language and reading. We now turn to one specific and common disorder, the amnesic syndrome.

We are now at what will be, in but a moment, a memory. It is this memory of our past experiences, the idea that it is "me" who has passed through all of these experiences, the yesterdays and years ago, that gives continuity to the self. Amnesia strikes at this junction between the present and the past (see Talland, 1965; Barbizet, 1970; Rozin, 1976; Butters and Cermak, 1980; Moscovitch, 1982a; Squire, 1987, for more detailed reviews of amnesia).

THE SYNDROME

Components of memory

The great nineteenth-century psychologist, William James, divided memory into two components: primary and secondary. He said that an object in primary memory "never was lost; its date was never cut off in consciousness from that of the immediately present moment. In fact it comes to us as belonging to the rearward portion of the present space of time, and not the genuine past." From what we can tell, primary memory (or short-term memory) is quite normal in amnesia. James continues: "Memory proper or secondary memory as it might be styled, is the knowledge of a former state of mind after it has already once dropped from consciousness; or rather it is the knowledge of an event, or fact, of which meantime we have not been thinking, with the additional consciousness that we have thought or experienced it before" (James, 1890, p. 648). This capacity is severely compromised in the amnesic syndrome, with respect to events that have occurred since the onset of the illness. Sergei Korsakoff (1889), one of the pioneers in the study of the pathology of memory described the amnesic syndrome in terms of two deficits: (1) the failure to recall events of the recent past, despite a more or less normal short-term (primary) memory, and (2) the loss of a feeling of familiarity or self-reference with respect to recent experiences that are either represented or happen to be recalled, as they occasionally are. To convey the character of this syndrome, we will describe two case histories. The first, H.M., is probably the most studied neurological case in history, and it is an example of as "pure" an amnesic syndrome as has ever been described. The second case is more representative.

The case of H.M.

H.M. was a blue-collar worker suffering from severe epileptic seizures. They became progressively worse, and by age twenty-seven he was unable to work. Neurosurgeons removed parts of both temporal lobes (the source of the seizures) to control the seizures in 1953 (Scoville and Milner, 1957). H.M. was carefully evaluated prior to the operation, and had a normal memory and an I.Q. of 112. On the return of consciousness following surgery, he could no longer recognize the hospital staff, apart from Dr. Scoville, whom he had known for many years. He could not remember or learn his way around the hospital. He could not remember important events that occurred in the few years before the surgery, such as the death of his uncle, but his early memories appeared clear and vivid. His short-term (primary) memory appeared normal, and he could carry on a normal conversation. However, he could not remember any events that occurred after the operation, once they passed out of his direct attention (short-term memory). He did the same puzzles day after day and reread the same newspapers and magazines. Each time he learned of the death of his uncle, he became very moved, treating it as a new occurrence. H.M. is still alive. His epilepsy is under control, but he still shows the same amnesic syndrome. He is dimly aware of his father's death, which occurred some years ago. He has aged normally in appearance, but is surprised whenever he sees himself in a mirror, since he remembers himself as he was at twenty-seven. (In 1988, he is now about sixty.) Remarkably, H.M.'s "intelligence" remained intact; over many years his IQ did not decrease. He has some realization that he has a memory deficit. He says: "Every day is alone in itself, whatever enjoyment I've had, and whatever sorrow I've had. . . . Right now, I'm wondering, have I done or said anything amiss? You see, at this moment everything looks clear to me, but what happened just before? That's what worries me. It's like waking from a dream. I just don't remember." As you might expect, H.M. is able to remember something if he can keep it "in mind." He can retain a number, say 584, by constantly repeating it to himself, or repeatedly adding up the three digits. However, after being interrupted with another task for less than a minute, he is unable to recall either the number or the fact that he had been rehearsing it for some minutes. (Adapted from Milner, 1970.)

A case of
Korsakoff's
syndrome

The second case illustrates a common type of amnesia, Korsakoff's syndrome, that results from chronic alcoholism.

The patient, aged sixty, was admitted to the hospital with a history of excessive alcohol consumption for many years. His memory had been deteriorating, and on admission he was amnesic and disoriented. Even though it was 1963, he said the year was 1956, and his age was fifty-two. He gave his present home address as one from which he had in fact moved five years previously. He retained practically nothing of his current experience, but otherwise (e.g., in conversation) behaved as a person of about average intelligence. He showed no appreciation of the fact that he had a memory deficit, and this deficit never improved. (Adapted from Zangwill, 1966.)

The syndrome is an extreme form of what we normally call a "bad memory," an inability to remember: to recognize people whom one has met, to remember definitions for multiple-choice tests, to remember appointments and the like.

CAUSES OF AMNESIA: A VULNERABLE SYSTEM

Pathological
agents that can
produce amnesia

The memory "systems" that when damaged cause the amnesic syndrome are *the* prime example of vulnerable systems. The range of pathological agents that can produce the syndrome is astounding. In addition to the usual causes of specific neurological syndromes such as strokes and tumors, a variety of generally harmful agents can cause amnesia. For example, infections can produce amnesia: when the herpes simplex virus attacks the nervous system, it seems to have a predilection for a few structures, including the hippocampus, an area critical for memory. Toxins and nutritional deficiencies can also cause amnesia. Chronic alcoholics get a good portion of their calories from alcohol, an essentially vitamin-free food source. They sometimes develop a deficiency in vitamin B1 (thiamine), a critical component of metabolic processes in all cells of the body. It is believed that, for some reason, a few groups of cells in the memory system are particularly vulnerable to this deficiency. They are the first to be destroyed, leading to the amnesia of Korsakoff's syndrome (Figure 17-16).

Blows to the skull
and amnesia

A concussion or other severe damage to the skull, as often happens in automobile accidents, and occasionally in sports and other activities, not infrequently produces an amnesic syndrome that is usually transient but can

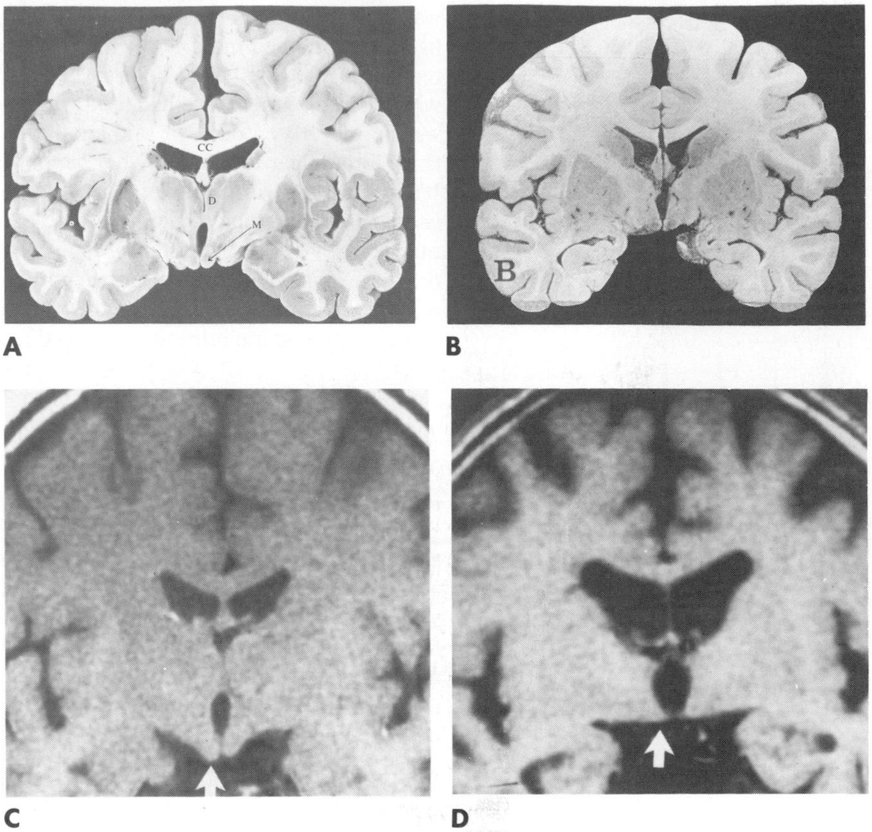

Korsakoff's
syndrome and
damaged
areas of brain

Figure 17-16
Damage to the mammillary bodies in Korsakoff's syndrome. The figure panels compare normal brains (A and C) with the brains of two patients with Korsakoff's syndrome. Panels A and B are stained sections from brains obtained after death. The brain sections are made in a plane that would separate the body into the front and back. (A) A section from a normal brain. The mammillary bodies are the two bumps located at the central base of the section (indicated with an arrow in Panel C). The dorsomedial nucleus of the thalamus, indicated with a D, is a structure frequently damaged in Korsakoff's psychosis. For purposes of orientation, the corpus callosum is also labeled (CC). (Source: Gluhbegovic and Williams, 1980). (B) A section from a Korsakoff brain. Notice the damage to the mammillary bodies in this patient (Source: Victor, Adams and Collins, 1971). (C) MRI image of a normal brain, with the same orientation as panels A and B. An arrow points to the mammillary bodies. Note that this image is made from a living, normal brain, through the non-invasive technique of magnetic resonance imaging. The correspondence to the section of the actual brain in Panel A is striking. (D) MRI of a patient with Korsakoff's psychosis. Note the virtual absence of mammillary bodies. The MRI scans in Panels C and D come from the same brains as the sagittal scans in Figure 17-12. (Source for Panels C and D: Charness and DeLa Paz, 1987)

last for years. Amnesia rarely occurs unless there was loss of consciousness. A similar, though usually shorter lasting syndrome is observed in the clinic in patients given electroconvulsive therapy for depression, a treatment that consists of passing an electric current across their skull, which throws their brain into a temporary seizure (Squire, Slater, and Miller, 1981; see Chapter 11).

The fact that head trauma and electric shocks to the head often produce an acute and fairly pure amnesia suggests extreme vulnerability. The most delicate system is what breaks when a piece of complicated equipment or a brain is jarred. We do not know the source of this vulnerability. It could be that memory "formation" is vulnerable because it requires rapid protein synthesis. Animal memory formation is specifically disrupted by drugs that interfere with protein synthesis in *all* cells. It could be that there is a "weak link" in the system, a point where everything comes together in the brain, that is poorly located in terms of blood supply, or subject to compression when the skull is struck.

THE ANATOMY OF THE AMNESIC SYNDROME

Although we don't understand the process of memory formation, there are clear relations between a set of interconnected brain structures that make up the limbic system and amnesic syndromes (Victor, Adams, and Collins, 1971; Mishkin and Appenzeller, 1987). In most cases of Korsakoff's syn-

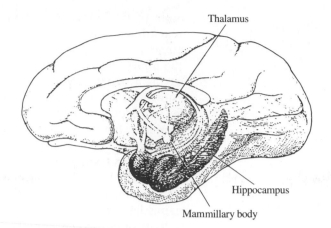

Thalamus

Hippocampus

Mammillary body

Figure 17-17
Schematic diagram of limbic system structures involved in memory. (Source: Mishkin and Appenzeller, 1987)

drome, there is bilateral (both sides) damage to the mammillary bodies and/or the dorsomedial nucleus of the thalamus (Figures 17-16 and 17-17). In cases resulting from surgery, viral attacks, and other sources, there is bilateral damage to the hippocampus, in the temporal lobe. Recent evidence indicates that damage to a layer of cells in the hippocampus is sufficient to produce a full-blown amnesic syndrome (Zola-Morgan, Squire, and Amaral, 1986). Most critically, in cases of damage to the temporal lobes in which memory loss is minimal, there is not bilateral damage to the hippocampus (Milner, 1972).

Damage to the hippocampus

Bilateral damage must occur to produce the full syndrome. That is why it is usually caused by general insults to the brain, such as traumatic accidents, poisoning, vitamin deficiencies, infections, or degenerative processes. In contrast, tumors, strokes, and externally induced wounds almost always occur in one continuous spatial location, and hence are likely to affect only one side.

Bilateral damage

Careful analysis of patients with unilateral damage (that is, damage on only one side) to the critical memory structures reveals a more limited memory deficit, of just the type one would predict given the specialized functions of the two hemispheres. Left temporal damage (in right-handers, of course) leads to a memory impairment primarily for verbal materials, and right temporal damage leads to deficits in memory for visual and other forms of "nonverbal" memory (Milner, 1972).

Unilateral damage

DESCRIPTION OF THE MEMORY DEFICIT

The nature of the memory defect in the amnesic syndrome has been explored in great detail (reviewed in Milner, 1972; Rozin, 1976; Moscovitch, 1982a, Squire, 1987). The basic features of the syndrome are:

1. More or less normal short-term memory. This is often measured as **digit span,** the number of digits a person can remember immediately after he hears them.

Basic features of the memory deficit

2. Severe deficits in recall and recognition of events experienced since the onset of the disease. This is called **anterograde amnesia.**

3. There is often loss of recall and recognition for events that occurred for a period of time *prior* to the onset of the syndrome. This is called a **retrograde amnesia.** The retrograde amnesia typically runs back in time from the

onset of the illness or accident, and covers recent events (days, months, years) but not early events of life. In most accident cases, the retrograde amnesia is eventually reduced to a period of seconds or minutes preceding the injury (Russell, 1959). The retrograde amnesia is crudely assessed by asking a patient about current events. For example, the patient may not know who the current president is; sometimes he will give the names of a few presidents back in time, and he will know all the presidents up to that president, but no further. One professional quarterback, following a head injury on the field, returned to the huddle and called plays that came from his previous team; he showed temporary retrograde amnesia for the period in which he had learned his new team's plays. Sometimes retrograde amnesia can extend for decades. Recently, detailed and standardized questionnaires have been devised that can be used to document the extent and severity of retrograde amnesia (Squire, Slater, and Miller, 1981).

Priming

4. A severely amnesic patient has no recall or recognition of events that occurred even a few minutes ago, but he has some type of record of them. That record can be revived if the patient is cued in particular ways and encouraged to respond without reflecting on the past. The procedure that elicits this performance is called **priming.** For example, when asked to remember a series of words, like "metal" or "carpet," after a brief delay, amnesics failed miserably. When prompted with partial cues (e.g., "met" or "car"), however, and encouraged to say the first word that came to mind, they guessed the words quite accurately, though claiming no sense of familiarity with the words they had uttered (Warrington and Weiskrantz, 1973; Diamond and Rozin, 1984).

Lack of a sense of familiarity

5. Lack of a sense of familiarity ("I've seen it before") when re-presented with recently experienced events.

Types of learning that are preserved in amnesics

6. Some specific types of learning and memory are preserved in amnesics (Moscovitch, 1984). Acquired skills are an example. Amnesics can be taught new skills, such as making drawings while looking in a mirror (Milner, 1972). There is also some evidence that they can retain the emotional component of an experience. In the classic case, an amnesic was pricked by a pin while shaking hands with his doctor (Claparède, 1911). On their subsequent meeting, the amnesic withdrew her hand when the doctor offered to shake it. The patient could not explain why she did this, but she felt a negative emotion, and she denied any familiarity with the situation.

THEORIES OF AMNESIA

Consolidation block theory

In the past, attempts were made to account for all the aspects of amnesia by a defect in a single process. The consolidation block theory held that the basic deficit was in the formation and storage of new long-term memories (Milner, 1966; Squire, Cohen, and Nadel, 1984). This view easily captures the salient symptoms of amnesia (see Table 17-1), but it has trouble explaining retrograde amnesia, priming, and skill acquisition. If no new memories are formed, how can performance be normal on priming and skill acquisition? If memories were consolidated long before the illness, why can't they be recalled?

Retrieval failure theory

The retrieval failure theory was another attempt to explain amnesia (Warrington and Weiskrantz, 1973). This theory held that new memories are formed normally (no consolidation block), but that there is a deficit in

Table 17-1 ASPECTS OF AMNESIA EXPLAINED BY THEORIES OF AMNESIA

Aspect of amnesia	Consolidation block	Retrieval defect	Explicit memory defect
1. Normal short-term memory	Yes	Yes	Yes
2. Anterograde amnesia	Yes	Yes	Yes
3. Retrograde amnesia	No	No	No
4. Priming	No	Yes	Yes
5. Lack of sense of familiarity	Yes	No	Yes
6. Preserved skill acquisition and emotional memories	No	Yes	Yes

the retrieval process. A defect in retrieval might explain why performance on priming tests and skill acquisition is normal. Both types of tests provide the patient with extensive cues to retrieve memories that are available but temporarily inaccessible. Retrieval theory, however, cannot account for the patient's lost sense of familiarity, even when memory performance is normal. Nor can it explain why some patients have only a very limited retrograde amnesia (Table 17-1). If retrieval is deficient, then all past memories should be compromised. If one assumes that both consolidation and retrieval defects occur, it is still not possible to account for the pattern of retrograde amnesia or the preserved skills.

Damage to some of components of long-term memory

The failure of single or combined process theories to account for all aspects of amnesia led investigators to propose that long-term memory is comprised of different components or subsystems that mediate performance on different types of memory tests. In amnesia, only some of these components are damaged, leading to severe memory impairment on some tests but preserved memory on others. In other words, instead of emphasizing defects in one or another phase of a general memory system that handles all memories, the emphasis is placed on defects in a system that handles a particular type of memory.

Explicit vs. implicit memory

The emerging consensus is that it is important to distinguish between at least two broad classes of memory and memory tests: ***explicit*** and ***implicit*** (Graf and Schacter, 1985; Schacter, 1987). Explicit tests of memory, such as recall and recognition, are those that require conscious recollection of past experiences. On implicit tests of memory, the subject is never asked to reflect on the past, but merely to perform. Memory for the past is inferred by changes in performance with experience or practice. Tests of priming and skill acquisition are implicit tests of memory. In amnesia, it is primarily performance on explicit tests of long-term memory, namely, recognition, recall, and the sense of familiarity that is impaired (Moscovitch, 1984).

Failure to record or retrieve spatio-temporal markers

The attribution of pastness or familiarity to an event depends on the individual's ability to recreate, at retrieval, critical aspects of the event that were encoded and consolidated when the event was first experienced. The event thus becomes a part of the continuing spatio-temporal flow of experiences that constitute one's past. Amnesia may result from the failure to record or retrieve these spatio-temporal markers (Rozin, 1976). These markers may be especially vulnerable because they are, by their nature, unique, one-time occurrences. The hippocampus and related limbic structures may be necessary for encoding the unique spatio-temporal aspects of events as they occur so that they can be retrieved at a later time, and thus they may be necessary for making newly acquired information available to conscious awareness. Without these spatio-temporal markers, conscious recollection would not be possible.

Implicit memory does not require conscious recollection

Conscious recollection is not a necessary component on *implicit* tests such as priming or skill learning. In implicit tests, performance is driven by a retrieval cue that reactivates, without our awareness, only that portion of a stored event that fits with the cue, and not the spatio-temporal context that locates the event in one's experience. As a result, the individual may emit the target word in response to a highly specific cue, or perform a task faster or more efficiently with practice, but he will have no sense of familiarity or pastness in doing so (Moscovitch, 1984, 1989).

This alternative explicit memory defect view can account for all of the basic features of the amnesic syndrome (Table 17-1), except for the occurrence of extensive retrograde amnesia in some patients. Because it is virtually absent in some cases, retrograde amnesia may have a different cause from anterograde amnesia, which is the core of the amnesic syndrome.

THE TREATMENT OF AMNESIA

Drugs and surgical treatment

The amnesias produced by head trauma typically recover completely, and the main function of medical treatment is to maintain the health of the patient in the acute phase of the illness. Occasional cases caused by tumors or infections may be treated surgically or with drugs, with possible alleviation of some symptoms. At this time, there is no treatment that will arrest or slow down the degeneration of neurons that causes the amnesias associated with senile dementia (see discussion of Alzheimer's disease, below).

Treatment using remaining intact structures

Although neural structures cannot be repaired, treatment programs can be designed that use the structures that remain intact. This is one of the forms of redundancy that we referred to earlier. Although this mode of treatment has been used for other disorders, few have used it to deal with memory disorders. At the Unit for Memory Disorders at the University of Toronto, a treatment was devised that capitalizes on the fact that amnesic patients perform well on implicit tests of memory (Glisky, Schacter, and Tulving, 1986). The technique used was the method of vanishing cues; it converts an explicit, conscious learning task into an implicit task. A response is elicited to a cue, and gradually more and more of the cue is removed, until only minimal cues are necessary for eliciting the appropriate response. By carefully linking a series of such cues, an entire behavioral repertoire can be taught. To test this technique, severely amnesic patients with no computer experience were taught to write simple programs on the computer. One patient, having demonstrated her ability on the laboratory task, was taught to enter data into a computer, a skill that is valued and for which she is now well paid. As with laboratory tests, performance on these real-life implicit tests is situation-specific. That is, learning does not transfer easily, if at all, to other situations. Moreover, after the patients had mastered their skill, they had little or no awareness of having acquired it and were unable to provide any but the most rudimentary description of what they had learned.

Adjustments in
living and use of
memory aids

Memory disorders can also be treated as problems in living. Family members can accommodate to and compensate for some of the problems. Adjustments in living and working conditions can be made. Sometimes, memory tricks such as simply writing notes on a pad can help. We must remember that there is a little memory loss in all of us. As we grow older, it becomes more severe in most people. Intelligent people compensate in their life-style and in the memory support or crutches they develop for themselves. This is graphically illustrated by a study that compared memory in sixty- to seventy-year-old University of Toronto alumni and current University of Toronto students (Moscovitch, 1982b). Subjects from each age group were told they were in a study of memory, and that the task was simply to remember to call a particular phone number on a particular day and at a particular time (some weeks ahead), simply leaving their name. All agreed to do it. About half of the students failed to call, whereas almost all of the older group remembered to call. It appears that at least part of the result is due to different approaches to remembering. The student subjects, interviewed after the study, said they were confident they would remember the task, and they made no special effort to remind themselves. The older people thought they would forget, wrote the date down in their date books, put notes by the phone, and so on. Old age would be a lot less tolerable if these compensations did not occur.

FUNCTIONAL AMNESIA

Distinguishing
functional and
organic amnesias

There are also functional amnesias, such as hysterical or dissociative amnesias, that occur in cases of multiple personalities or in fugue states in which the patient has lost all memory, including personal identity. In these cases, there is often a history of psychological disturbance, along with an absence in the history or clinical examination of any signs of neurological damage. In both organic and functional amnesias, learned skills tend to remain intact, and personal memories are most affected. The retrograde amnesia in functional amnesias, however, tends to extend back into childhood; people with the neurologically based amnesic syndrome rarely forget their childhood or their name, unless they are at the end of a long period of senile degeneration, in which they lose the ability for intelligent performance on any task.

DEMENTIA

Diffuse damage
resulting from
progressive
degenerative
disorders

Our concern so far has been to describe and understand the effects of focal (well-localized) lesions on behavior. Many neurological disorders result from damage that is widespread, affecting more than one region of the brain. Some progressive degenerative disorders are of this type. Sometimes the disorder begins in a localized area, as in Parkinson's disease (see p. 562), but its effects gradually spread. We can apply what we have learned from studying the effects of focal lesions to understanding the effects of diffuse damage. By noting the symptoms, we can determine which structures are damaged, and vice versa. If the diffuse damage, however, is of slow onset, compensatory neurological and psychological changes may mask the extent of the damage. Conversely, once the damage is severe and appears in behavior, the symptoms may be exaggerated in comparison to focal lesions of the same area because there is less healthy tissue, in a sense, less redundancy, to compensate for the damage. With these qualifications in mind, we will turn our attention to Alzheimer's disease, the most common of all degenerative disorders.

ALZHEIMER'S DISEASE

Incidence of Alzheimer's disease

Dementia is a progressive loss of a variety of higher mental functions usually occurring in old age. Whether or not Alzheimer's disease should be viewed as accelerated or pathological aging, it is a disease of major proportions. About 15 percent of adults over sixty-four years of age suffer from this disorder, and about one-third of these people are severely handicapped (Terry and Davies, 1980). The beginning of this decline is sometimes seen in people in their fifties. About half of all old people diagnosed as demented probably have Alzheimer's disease. There is accumulating evidence that some forms of Alzheimer's disease are inherited. The risk of Alzheimer's disease in first-degree relatives (immediate family) of patients with the disease converges on 50 percent by age ninety compared to a risk of about 25 percent in the population at large in this age range (Mohs, Breitner, Silverman, and Davis, 1987). Here is a case of Alzheimer's disease with early onset:

> A fifty-two-year-old taxi driver is admitted to the hospital because of progressive failing memory. He has been a taxi driver in Philadelphia for the past twenty years. Approximately nine months ago, he first noted some difficulty in remembering certain street names and localities. . . . Three months ago, he was unable to find his way to the airport. . . . The patient has also become easily confused in giving change to customers and in remembering routine tasks such as maintenance of his automobile. Occasionally he becomes withdrawn and seems depressed. . . . For the past two weeks, he has been unable to drive his taxi and remains home sitting in a chair. The family has brought him to the hospital because they can no longer handle him.
>
> In the hospital, he speaks only when spoken to and answers in single words or simple sentences. . . . The patient's attention span is very short, and he cannot recall three simple objects that are described to him after five minutes. (University of Pennsylvania Case Study, 1976)

Gradual onset of symptoms

Alzheimer's disease has a gradual onset. Its initial symptoms include loss of initiative, forgetfulness, naming disability, and spatial disorientation. Different symptoms predominate in different patients. In many patients, an amnesic syndrome will be the prominent symptom; in other patients, naming or spatial disorders are the primary symptoms (Schwartz, Baron, and Moscovitch, 1989). As the disease progresses, more and more severe deficits appear, in more and more systems. Over a period from a few to ten years, it leads to severe deterioration of intellectual and basic maintenance functions, and to death.

Malformed neurons and acetylcholine deficit

A distinctive brain pathology has been identified in Alzheimer patients: malformations of neurons and loss of cells in a number of areas of the nervous system (Figure 17-18). A biochemical deficit has also been identified: an abnormally low level of an enzyme that is critical in the synthesis of

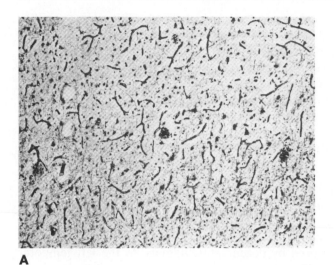

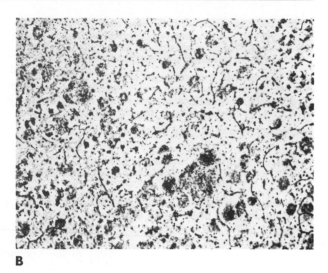

A

B

Figure 17-18

Photomicrograph of brain tissue from (A) the cortex of a normal patient, and (B) a patient with Alzheimer's disease. Note the small number of senile plaques (the darker areas) in the normal patient, and the larger number of plaques in the Alzheimer patient. (Source: Blessed, Tomlinsun, and Roth, 1968)

Increased levels of aluminum in Alzheimer brains

Inherited chromosomal abnormality

acetylcholine, a major brain neurotransmitter (Coyle, Price, and DeLong, 1983). The number of malformed neurons and the degree of the neurotransmitter deficit are related to the degree of dementia. To complete the link between neural damage and memory disorders in Alzheimer's disease, studies on both animals and humans have shown that brain deficits in acetylcholine are related to defective memory. This is, in part, because neurons using this transmitter have extensive terminals in the hippocampus. Furthermore, given that the early symptoms usually include memory and spatial constructive disorders, one can predict that the hippocampus and parietal lobes are particularly likely to be affected. Indeed, neural malformations in Alzheimer's patients are particularly common in the hippocampus (Hyman, Van Hocsen, Damasio, and Barnes, 1984). Recent studies of metabolic activity of the cortex in Alzheimer's patients show that the parietal lobe is one of the most severely affected cortical areas (Figure 17-19; Benson, Metter, Kuhl, and Phelps, 1983).

The causes of Alzheimer's disease are not known. One hypothesis is that it is caused by an increase in aluminum in the body, which concentrates in parts of the brain and causes the neural malformations that have been observed (Crapper, Karlik, and DeBoni, 1978). There are a number of reports of markedly increased levels of aluminum in Alzheimer brains, especially in those areas that are most affected. However, it is also known that heavy metals such as aluminum collect at sites of neural damage, so the question is whether high levels of aluminum in areas like the hippocampus in Alzheimer's patients are a cause or an effect of the disease. Since many people with high levels of exposure to aluminum do not get Alzheimer's disease, most investigators think that aluminum is an effect rather than a cause (Zatta et al., 1988).

Another hypothesis is that Alzheimer's disease is caused by an inherited chromosomal abnormality. All people with Down's syndrome (a form of mental deficiency) who live past forty-five years of age develop Alzheimer's disease. A recent study on patients with familial Alzheimer's disease found a defective gene that was located on the same region of the same chromosome that carries the defective gene for Down's syndrome (St. George-Hyslop et

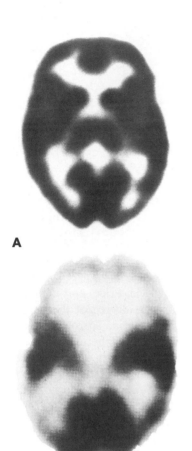

A

B

Figure 17-19
(A) PET scan of normal brain, and (B) PET scan of an Alzheimer patient's brain. Note the generally low level (light color) of metabolism in the Alzheimer brain. The only areas of normal metabolic rate are the primary motor and sensory areas, including the visual projection area in the occipital lobe at the bottom of the scan. (Source: Benson, Metter, Kuhl, and Phelps, 1983)

al., 1987). But although Alzheimer's disease runs in families to some extent, and there is evidence that there is a genetic basis for this, family histories of Alzheimer's disease are not present in the majority of cases.

It is possible that these hypotheses are complementary. For example, aluminum may cause the defective genetic program to be expressed, or the chromosomal defect may make neural tissue much more likely to incorporate aluminum.

PICK'S DISEASE: DEMENTIA OF FRONTAL LOBE TYPE

There are a significant number of patients with progressive dementia whose behavioral and neurological symptoms and brain pathology are not consistent with the diagnosis of Alzheimer's disease. Unlike patients with Alzheimer's disease, patients with Pick's disease show variable memory deficits and little or no visuo-spatial impairment. Some of these patients have a progressive aphasia caused by degenerative damage to the left temporal lobe. Others present with marked changes in personality, disinhibition, unconcern, language problems, and socially inappropriate behaviors that are probably caused by frontal lobe degeneration. The following case illustrates this condition:

A fifty-year-old shop manager suffered a gradually progressive change in his personality. He became outspoken, rude and callous, lacking in initiative, self-care, and responsibility towards his family. His mood would fluctuate between facetiousness and jocularity and negativism and irritability, with verbal and physical aggression, thought to be totally out of character. He was inattentive and forgetful, but no change in his speech nor in his vision had been noted. His mother died aged eighty-two years in a psychiatric hospital, having become demented in her middle fifties. Prior to death she was mute and had remained in an essentially vegetative state for the previous ten years. . . .

On examination he was free from neurological signs. He was generally courteous, although mildly disinhibited, talking excessively loudly, and giving frequent and inappropriate guffaws of laughter. In carrying out tests he was impulsive and unconcerned, failing to check his responses. He showed no insight. His speech was normal. There was no evidence of impaired comprehension, he was left/right oriented, and no word finding difficulty was evident. Repetition tasks elicited perseverations of previous responses. He could read and write, although spelling was poor. He showed substantial difficulty in calculating, failing to carry out the simplest mental subtraction and completing two figure written sums only by counting on his fingers. He had no difficulty in the perceptual identification of objects, line drawings and faces of celebrities. . . . He was fully oriented, and displayed preserved memory for day-to-day events. He recalled six of seven items from a name and address immediately following presentation, and again after a two-minute delay. He could not summarize a short story immediately after reading it aloud, although his ability to provide accurate answers to specific questions about the story indicated that information was available to him. His delayed recall performance, after one hour, provided no evidence of loss of information over time. . . .

Over a four-year follow-up period his behavior became increasingly rigid and inflexible, and violent outbursts were more common. He was inert and lacked initiative. Stereotyped mannerisms were increasingly evident. His cognitive performance remained qualitatively similar, although increasing impulsivity, carelessness and lack of attention to the task resulted in reduced performance accuracy. (From Neary, Snowden, Northen, and Goulding, 1988)

Brain areas
damaged in
Pick's disease

The patient's behavior is reminiscent of the behavior of Phineas Gage. Indeed, on neuropsychological testing, he performed poorly on all tests of frontal lobe function. The diagnosis of frontal lobe dysfunction in these patients is supported by SPECT scan studies showing abnormally decreased frontal lobe activity.

AIDS DEMENTIA

Pathological
changes in
nervous system of
AIDS patients

It is now recognized that clinically observable neurological disorders occur in about 40 percent of adult AIDS patients, and pathological changes in the nervous system have been noted in 80 to 90 percent of cases that have come to autopsy (Snyder, Simpson, Nielson et al., 1983). Some of the changes may be caused by tumors or bacterial infections that accompany AIDS. In a significant number of cases, however, there is a syndrome of acquired dementia, called AIDS dementia complex, that cannot be explained as secondary to tumor growth or bacterial infection.

Symptoms of
AIDS indicate
damage to
subcortical areas

The early symptoms of AIDS dementia complex include word-finding difficulty, verbal memory deficits, psychomotor slowing, impaired problem-solving ability, and poor fine motor control. AIDS was only first recognized as a syndrome in 1981, and the dementia that sometimes accompanies it was not noted until a few years later. It is therefore too early to know exactly which brain regions are affected. Judging from the symptoms and from brain-imaging evidence, however, the affected region is initially subcortical, including the basal ganglia, an area that is also affected in Parkinson's disease.

THE TREATMENT OF DISEASES OF THE NERVOUS SYSTEM

Prognosis varies

The prognosis and treatment of diseases of the nervous system are determined in large part by some of the basic principles we stated at the beginning of this chapter: the inability to make new neurons, the possibility for damaged neurons to recover, the principle of redundancy. The course and effectiveness of treatment depend on the nature of the disease process, the spatial extent of the pathology (generalized or highly localized), and the specific location of the pathology (whether it is accessible to surgery, for example) (Adams and Victor, 1981).

Intervention
possible where
neurons
damaged but not
destroyed

Many neurological symptoms are produced by damage to, but not destruction of neurons. Such reversible damage can be produced by lowered oxygen and nutrient supply resulting from atherosclerosis or lung disease, and by acute pressure produced by swelling of the brain after head trauma, infection, or a tumor that impedes circulation of cerebrospinal fluid. Since damaged or nutrient-deprived neurons can recover, intervention can produce a cure. This would be the case for infections, which can be treated with antibiotics, for acute cases of high intracranial pressure, which can be relieved by draining some of the fluid, or for certain tumors, which can be removed. Since the nervous system has some ability to repair itself, a large part of the treatment of some acute disorders consists in maintaining the patient's health, to allow his nervous system to recover from the shock of

A

Next Page of Words

naked	need	new	nor
name	negative	Newcastle	normal
napkin	neglect	newspaper	normally
nation	negligible	newton	north
national	neighbour	Newton's	nose
natural	neither	next	nostril
nature	nerve	nhs	not
	nervous	nice	notably
nearer	network	night	notation
nearest	neurone	no	note
nearly	neutrino	nobel	nothing
necessaril	neutron	noise	notice
necessary	never	non	now
neck	neverthele	none	nu

TALKING   70/69/360

It doesn't matter what the exact numbers
are. The point is there are ∎

B

Figure 17-20
(A) Stephen Hawking, a forty-six-year-old distinguished British physicist, suffers from amyotrophic lateral sclerosis and is almost completely paralyzed. (B) Even so, Hawking is able to produce scientific writings of major import through the use of a personal computer.

Lack of
significance
of many
"neurological"
symptoms

trauma. Partial recovery from strokes occurs for this reason. For most of the degenerative diseases, however, as well as many of the cases of stroke or hemorrhage, there is little that can be done that would constitute a cure.

A second line of treatment, when cure is impossible, is to take medical measures to contain the problem or to treat the symptoms. The use of L-DOPA to replace the deficiency in the transmitter in the basal ganglia in someone with Parkinson's disease is an example of this. The L-DOPA does not cure the disease, but it reduces symptoms such as tremor and rigidity.

The situation of many people with neurological damage can also be improved by restructuring their patterns of living, usually with the help of their family or those who care for them. Family members can compensate for deficits, by taking over or assisting in those functions that are compromised. It is sometimes possible to teach them ways around their deficit: Braille for the blind, memo pads for those with bad memories. And, more and more, specific devices, from wheelchairs to mini-computers, are becoming available that compensate for deficits (Figure 17-20).

When a patient is referred to a neurologist, he is often anxious, because he doesn't want to have a disease of the nervous system. A "psychological" disorder is preferable to most people. In fact, much of what neurologists do is to discover that common neurological symptoms, such as tingling of the fingers, muscle twitches, and headaches, are *not* indicative of diseases of the nervous system. Although they may be early signs of neurological disease, they are often either functional problems or minor disorders of unknown origin that will neither progress nor seriously compromise the life of the patient. In other words, some patients leave the care of the neurologist cured, some leave improved, some cannot be helped, and quite a few leave with the confidence that there is really nothing serious that is wrong with them, neurologically.

For the moment, the triumph of neurology is in diagnosis. It is a frustration to the neurologist that she can understand many disease processes, but she cannot cure them. Although neurologists know a lot about the nervous

Strength of
neurology in
diagnosis not
treatment

system, they still have only limited abilities to repair it, and none to replace it. Dramatic cures of neurological disorders can be produced by neurosurgery, and many symptoms can be relieved with drugs. It is much more common, however, to have understanding without successful treatment in neurology than in psychology. Our present ability to repair functional disorders is probably better than our ability to repair the nervous system.

Rapid advances
in understanding
promise more
successful
treatments in
future

Because of rapid advances in neuroscience, the prospects for successful treatment of more diseases of the nervous system are very good. The steady stream of important findings on neurotransmitters, and the operation of the immune system, as well as surgical innovations, have already made some impact on neurology. For example, research with rats has demonstrated that tissue from fetal brains or adrenal glands can be transplanted to the brain of adult rats, where it survives, forms viable connections, and releases neurotransmitters (Sladek and Shoulson, 1988). When introduced into a damaged area, the fetal transplants lead to recovery of function. Recently, similar procedures have been tried with human patients suffering from Parkinson's disease. Although initial reports are encouraging, it is too soon to pass judgment on this promising approach.

Psychotherapy
also helps those
with neurological
disorders

Much of the treatment of neurological disorders falls to psychiatrists and nonmedical health practitioners, such as psychologists, speech therapists, and physical therapists. As we noted in the case of treating patients with amnesia, the therapist's job involves helping the patient make maximum use of remaining abilities. Although functions can recover spontaneously, the evidence suggests that recovery is better following treatment, whether the disorder involves speech, movement, or attention.

Because neurological deficits are, by definition, diseases, people rarely pay attention to the functional syndromes that often accompany neurological disease. Many neurological patients suffer from depression, insecurity, or fear. Their feelings can exacerbate their neurological symptoms and prevent recovery. Psychotherapy can be valuable for these patients in this context.

THE VIRTUES AND LIMITATIONS OF THE NEUROLOGICAL APPROACH

Advances in the
neurosciences

The neurological approach shares with the biomedical model the promise of harnessing the greater knowledge and success of the more developed branches of medicine to the formidable task of understanding psychopathology. Surely the high science and art of diagnosis in neurology and the reasonably effective treatments of disorders such as Parkinson's disease are to be admired. The recent trend to account for more and more psychopathology in terms of neurotransmitter levels, altered levels of hormones, and brain abnormalities reflects a healthy advance in the neurosciences. In some cases, such as depression, these advances have led to new modalities of treatment.

Aim to
understand
normal function

The rapidly growing field of neuropsychology has as one of its principal aims the understanding of normal function. Just as pathology has been a powerful tool in the study of normal biological function in other areas, it can be used as a tool to understand normal behavior and mental function.

Thus, researchers study disorders of the nervous system, particularly in the areas of language, cognition, perception, and action, to understand normal function. Since the nervous system is organized in a meaningful way, damage often breaks complex systems apart at their "joints." Thus, the study of split brains has contributed to our understanding of different modes of thought, and the study of amnesics has contributed to our understanding of normal memory.

Neurological explanations for some functional disorders

There is a certain respectability that a psychopathological syndrome gains as a disease when it has a definite underlying neuropathology. Some definitions of disease include underlying biological pathology as a critical feature. Thus, the intrusion of neurological explanations into what were previously thought to be functional disorders dispels some of the lingering uncertainty we have about how to classify a variety of forms of mental illness. There is something to be said for this, but there are also serious intellectual and social problems raised by these advances. We devote our closing section to this problem.

Organic disorders may not be more serious than functional disorders

First, we must realize that a form of psychopathology is not more serious because it has a demonstrable or likely neurological basis. From the point of view of the individual or society, some of the most painful and debilitating disorders fall outside of the domain of neurology. Agoraphobia, a variety of addictions, anorexia nervosa, and the personality disorders are salient examples.

Discovery of a neurological cause may not improve treatment

Second, discovery of a neurological basis for psychopathology does not necessarily improve the chances for treatment. On the contrary, given the limited capacity of the nervous system to repair itself, the prospects for treatment are often discouraging. Psychotherapy for certain disorders, such as phobias, is probably much more successful than treatments for the great majority of organic disorders. Moreover, there is the danger that physicians and patients may become overzealous in their search for a quick neurological cure to a functional disorder. The disastrous history of frontal lobotomies as a treatment for frank psychiatric disorders should serve as a warning.

Role for cultural context in determining if there is disease

Third, the linkage between neurological damage and disease is weaker than one might imagine. Insofar as a notion of disease includes maladaptiveness, one must consider cultural context in determining whether a disease is present. Consider the case of reading disorders. Dyslexia is a crippling disorder in our literate society. Today, reading ability is almost a prerequisite to success. One hundred years ago, however, literacy was a capacity pretty much limited to an economically and culturally privileged few. At that time, society was not built around the assumption of literacy, as ours is today. A person with severe reading disorders resulting from pathologies in the linkages between the visual system and the language system would not have been considered sick one hundred years ago, nor would such a person be considered sick today in a primarily illiterate culture. Furthermore, as we indicated in our discussion of reading disorders, different writing systems, produced by different cultures, make different cognitive demands on the reader, and hence engage different brain mechanisms. The English alphabet is a system built on the sounds of speech, while the Chinese writing system is not. As a result, there is more reliance on phonological decoding mechanisms in reading English than in reading Chinese; brain damage that may have a small effect on a Chinese reader may seriously compromise a reader of English, and vice versa. Thus, cultural institutions increase the importance of certain skills and decrease the importance of others. Reading disability is devastating for most people in our society, and physical weakness is not. The reverse is true in some hunter-gatherer societies. It would not be surprising if the enormous influence of computers in modern life leads to realization of new deficits, perhaps with a neurological basis, that currently go unnoticed.

Effect of neurological disease on different individuals in same culture

The same issue arises with respect to the effect of neurological diseases on different individuals in the same culture. Consider the effect of amyotrophic lateral sclerosis (ALS) on two accomplished figures, baseball great Lou Gehrig (Figure 17-4) and theoretical physicist Stephen Hawking (Figure 17-20). The progressive muscular weakness that is the hallmark of ALS was absolutely devastating, even at early stages, to Lou Gehrig, a man whose accomplishments were based on physical strength and coordination. On the other hand, Hawking's purely mental efforts, the core of his professional accomplishments, have continued in the face of the extensive paralysis or weakness of the later stages of this disease.

Disorders without a basis in neuropathology

Fourth, and most critically, one should not expect too much from the neurological approach to psychopathology. There are some types of pathology that surely do not have a basis in neuropathology. A dog phobia, an obsessive concern with cleanliness, an inability to speak in public, these are disorders that surely result from the interaction of a particular set of experiences with a normal brain. They are no doubt represented in some way in brain circuitry, but not in any way that a neuroscientist would be able to detect. It is inconceivable that fearing versus liking dogs would be diagnosable with even the most sophisticated possible brain-scanning device.

Locating the pathology not sufficient to fully explain a disorder

Furthermore, even for cases where there is definable neuropathology, the identification of this pathology does not usually account for the psychopathology, in the sense that it fully explains its manifestations. Knowing that depression is "caused" by low levels of norepinephrine does not tell us what depression is like, nor that depressives have a characteristic attributional style. Neither the pain and frustration of having expressive deficits nor the precise structure of the grammatical breakdown in Broca's aphasia are explained by locating the lesion in the left frontal lobes.

Appropriate levels of explanation

Many human phenomena are most usefully explained or dealt with at the level of mental events or behavior. There may be a biochemical basis for mother love, but mother love is best described, for some purposes, as a mental state. In the same way, one can describe one's word-processing program in terms of machine language code, but terms such as "delete," "insert," and "search" seem much more appropriate for comprehending and using it.

Dangers of over- and under-neurologizing

In short, there are dangers of both over- and under-neurologizing. This alone is an important reason to have a chapter on neurology in a textbook on abnormal psychology. There are important neurological components in some types of psychopathology, and there is much to be learned from neurology as an advanced area of medicine. We hope this chapter has convinced you of that. It is also important that the neurological approach occupies only one or a few chapters, and not the whole book. We hope that this chapter, and the others in this book have convinced you of *that*.

SUMMARY

1. Although all mental illnesses are in some sense represented in the nervous system, one group of these illnesses can be traced to specific defects in the structure and function of the nervous system. This group, which can be thought of as organic disorders, falls in the domain of neurologists and neuropsychologists, while the remaining functional disorders fall in the domain of clinical psychologists and psychiatrists.

2. Basic principles of the structure and function of the nervous system can account for many organic syndromes.

3. Principles of synaptic physiology and the action of neurotransmitters account for a number of disorders, including some types of depression.

4. The spatial (modular) and biochemical organization of the nervous system account for the fact that damage at specific sites or by specific toxins produces specific and distinctive symptoms.

5. In the nervous system, in general, structures at the front represent motor functions, and those at the back represent sensory functions. In the cerebral cortex, this front-back distinction is represented in an expanded way. The parietal lobes, located toward the back of the brain, are involved in information processing, while the frontal lobes, located at the front, are involved in the organization of action. Damage to the parietal lobes produces inabilities to represent the world visuo-spatially and/or neglect (inattention to) certain parts of the world. Frontal damage leads to disruption of strategies or plans for action, problems in negotiating the transition from one action to another, and difficulties in impulse control.

6. The left-right organization of the brain explains why damage to the left hemisphere often produces verbal deficits, while damage to the right hemisphere often leads to disorders in spatial representation.

7. The up-down (hierarchical) organization of the nervous system explains how similar symptoms can be produced by damage at different levels of the nervous system. The fact that balance among various centers in the nervous system is produced by inhibition explains the appearance of symptoms by release of inhibition from a damaged area.

8. There are many causes of diseases of the nervous system, including nutrient deficiencies, strokes, degenerative diseases, and head trauma. The symptoms of damage can be negative (a deficit) or positive (an increase in activity), resulting from release of inhibition or irritability, as in the case of epilepsy.

9. Some parts of the nervous system, such as parts involved in the formation of memories, are particularly vulnerable to damage. As a result, specific symptoms may result from general trauma to the nervous system, as in exposure to toxins or blows to the head.

10. The principle of redundancy accounts for the paucity of symptoms and recovery of function following some kinds of brain damage.

11. The diagnosis of damage to the nervous system is a well-developed science and art, based on history of the disorder, current symptoms, and highly sophisticated electrophysiological and brain-imaging techniques that allow direct measurement of brain structures and metabolism.

12. According to the classical view, disorders of language can be subdivided in terms of whether reception, comprehension, or production of language is primarily affected. They illustrate two principles of spatial organization of the brain: (1) left-right specialization (language functions on the left), and (2) the front-back principle, since receptive aphasias result from lesions near the back of the brain and expressive aphasias result from lesions near the front.

13. The classical view has been modified by recent studies based on advances in cognitive psychology and linguistics. Thus, Broca's aphasia, traditionally considered as an expressive disorder, also comprises a grammatical disorder that affects both comprehension and production of language.

14. Acquired dyslexia is a disorder of reading caused by brain damage. The symptoms of dyslexia will vary depending on which reading processes are disturbed. Phonological dyslexics are impaired at sounding out words, whereas surface dyslexics have a deficit in identifying words by their visual form.

15. The most common disorder of memory, the amnesic syndrome, most frequently results from aging (senile dementia, such as Alzheimer's disease), head trauma, or chronic alcoholism (Korsakoff's psychosis). The symptoms result from damage to a few particularly vulnerable areas of the brain, on both sides. The major feature of the amnesic syndrome is the inability to recall or recognize recent events, although new information can be "acquired" and retained without any awareness of these new memories.

16. Parkinson's disease, Alzheimer's disease, and Pick's disease all represent degenerative disorders and are associated with old age. Alzheimer's disease, the principal form of senile dementia, is characterized by progressive loss of mental functions, with memory disorders and problems in spatial relations often the most prominent early symptoms. A distinctive pathology of neurons is associated with this disorder, especially in the hippocampus.

17. Because new neurons rarely, if ever, arise in adult humans, the prospects for treatment of neurological illness are limited. But recovery occurs because damaged neurons can recover. In addition, symptoms can be treated by drugs and by teaching the patient strategies that help him to minimize deficits. These strategies often involve enlisting the help of friends or family, and/or special devices such as wheelchairs or computers.

18. Diseases of the nervous system account for some instances of abnormal behavior or thought. In some cases, discovery of a neurological basis for psychopathology may improve prospects for treatment, but in other cases, it may not because of the limited ability of the nervous system to recover. The maladaptiveness of neurological syndromes depends on the cultural context and the individual life context within which they are manifested.

Part 8

ABNORMALITY, THE LAW, AND CHOOSING A PSYCHOTHERAPY

The Law and Politics of Abnormality

Society and the
mentally ill

PSYCHOLOGICAL distress can be examined from two perspectives. The first is the perspective of the individual who is suffering: how he or she might have acquired the disorder, what the present experience is like, and what remedies are available to ameliorate that condition. Until now, that has been the perspective of this book.

But there is another way to examine abnormality, and that is from the viewpoint of society. In this chapter, we examine the ways in which society protects its members from the consequences of psychological suffering. The conditions under which society moves to protect, and the forms that such protection takes, often involve options that are costly in terms of human rights as well as monetarily. In choosing between public protection and the civil liberties of the mentally ill, as exemplified in laws concerning civil and criminal commitment, society must make difficult and often painful choices (Steadman, 1981). Those choices concern us here.

In addition to the issues associated with involuntary and criminal commitment, we will discuss two kinds of abuse of abnormal psychology. First, we will look at how a state or government abuses what we know about psychology and psychiatry by removing dissident (but sane) individuals or groups from society, or controlling their behavior. Second, we will look at a more general problem: the stigma that is cast over an individual when that individual is labeled "mentally ill." In any profession, there are often conflicts between the requirements of practice and those of society. The practice of psychology and psychiatry is no exception.

INVOLUNTARY COMMITMENT AND TREATMENT

Involuntary commitment

No societal response to psychological suffering has received more attention during the past decade than has *involuntary commitment,* the process whereby the state hospitalizes people for their own good, and even over their vigorous protest. In effect, the state acts as parent to those who have "lost their senses," doing for them what they might do for themselves if they had their wits about them. Consider the following situations in which the state might seek to involuntarily commit an individual, and in which most people would agree that the state is right in doing so:

• As the result of a toxic psychosis, a young man wants to throw himself from the roof of a tall building. In twenty-four hours, both the impulse and the psychosis will have passed—if he is restrained now.

• A young man is despondent over the termination of his first love. To him, there is currently no alternative to suicide. A month from now, even sooner, he may think differently.

• An attorney is overcome by irrational guilt. She calls two of her clients and informs them that she has not handled their cases properly, and that she has stolen from them. Of course, this is untrue. She would have called the rest of her clients had the state, through her family, not intervened and hospitalized her against her will.

• Following the birth of two previous children, a woman suffered a post-partum depression, and attempted to murder the infants. She is about to give birth again, and is experiencing the same impulse. To protect those young lives, the state hospitalizes the mother involuntarily.

Difficulty in determining danger to self or others

For most people, these cases are compelling arguments for involuntary hospitalization. Where there is clear-cut danger to self or to others, most people agree that some kind of intervention is necessary. But most cases are not nearly so clear-cut as these. Indeed, many cases test the very meanings of normality and abnormality that were discussed in Chapter 1. Abnormal by whose standard? Recall that some people believe themselves depressed for good reason, but "society" finds them "mentally ill" and in need of treatment. Others enjoy the relaxation and "highs" conferred by recreational drugs, yet society views them as addicts who require psychiatric attention. Still others radically alter their life-styles on discovering a "true religion," but society may designate that discovery as psychotic and commit the discoverer to a psychiatric facility. *Mayock v. Martin** illustrated this issue well:

Mr. Mayock was hospitalized in July, 1944, after he had removed his right eye. He was subsequently diagnosed paranoid schizophrenic, eventually released on probation, and finally discharged three years later. Three days after discharge, Mayock removed his right hand, and was committed once again to the state hospital. At the time of trial, some twenty years later, Mayock was still confined involuntarily to the state hospital with the diagnosis of paranoid schizophrenia.

* Mayock v. Martin, 157 Conn, 56, 245 A.2d 574 (1968).

At his trial, Mayock insisted that there was nothing mysterious or crazy about his self-maimings. Rather, he is a deeply religious man who believes that society's attempts to establish peace by force are entirely misguided. God's way, he says, is to encourage peace through love. If society continues on its present path, many lives will be lost through war. Mayock believes that one man has been chosen to make a peace offering to God: that he, Mayock, is that man; and that it is better for one person to accept a message from God to sacrifice an eye or a hand than it is for society to suffer a great loss of human life.

During the twenty years that he had been hospitalized, Mayock had had complete freedom of the hospital grounds: He had not once maimed himself. Yet, he acknowledged that he would gladly do so again either as a significant freewill offering or in response to divine revelation.

Beyond this single symptom, there was no further evidence that Mayock was disturbed. He had risen to a position of considerable responsibility in the hospital, running the recreation center for parole-privileged patients, as well as the hospital news stand. There was ample evidence that he could handle financial matters and take care of himself in all other respects.

Psychiatrists at the hospital contended that his prophetic view of himself was "grandiose," that his religious beliefs were "grossly false," and that the diagnosis of paranoid schizophrenic was entirely warranted by the facts. Mayock contended that he is religious, not mentally ill, and that his First Amendment constitutional rights ("Congress shall make no law respecting an establishment of religion or prohibiting the free exercise thereof . . .") had been violated.

Mayock lost. Some will feel that he should have lost, for only the truly mad would gouge out their eyes and chop off their arms. Others will feel that Mayock's loss is tragic, for he was acting with courage upon deeply held religious beliefs and harming no one but himself. Perhaps the tragedy lies in that ambiguity, for Mayock can be seen as quite abnormal by some standards, and not abnormal at all by others. Given a large area of doubt, how did it happen that he was involuntarily hospitalized, and for so long? In order to understand Mayock's case, as well as literally thousands of other commitments that occur involuntarily, we need to know something about the laws that regulate commitment procedures. Our focus will be on laws in the United States.

PROCEDURES TO COMMIT

COMMITMENT REQUIREMENTS

In the movie *Frances*, Jessica Lange depicts Frances Farmer, whose involuntary commitment was based on "impaired judgment." Here Frances is being left in the sanitarium by her mother who has just committed her.

States differ enormously in the procedures that are used to commit people, and in the safeguards those procedures provide. All states require that the individual be suffering from a ***psychological disability,*** variously termed "mental illness," "mental disease," or "mental disability." But often these phrases are not specifically defined, leaving unclear which disabilities qualify and which do not.

In addition to psychological disability, all states stipulate that the individual must meet additional requirements. While these requirements vary from state to state, they require that one or more of the following "incapacitating conditions" must arise from the psychological disability: impaired judgments, need for treatment, dangerousness to self or others, and "grave disability." We will examine each in turn.

Impaired
judgment

☐ IMPAIRED JUDGMENT.　The person is so distressed that he does not recognize the need for hospitalization. Mayock could well have qualified for commitment under such a requirement since in the view of his psychiatrists, he was blind to his need for hospitalization.

Need for
treatment

☐ NEED FOR TREATMENT.　The need for treatment often serves to qualify what is meant by mental disability. Thus, the state of Virginia defines a committable person as "any person afflicted with mental disease to such an extent that . . . he requires care and treatment. . . ."*

But however humane the "need for treatment" statute may seem, experience with it has demonstrated that this approach can have some surprisingly untoward consequences, as the case of Emily Bronson reveals.

> Emily Bronson, a widow, suffered two delusions: The first, that the restaurant at which she frequently ate, poisoned her food; and the second, that men were constantly planning sexual assaults upon her. These delusions were mild and harmless, and she continued to eat at the same restaurant, and her behavior with men seemed unaffected by these concerns. Her friends knew of her delusions, but they seemed to cause them or her no difficulty.
>
> One day Mrs. Bronson fell and injured her hip. She was brought to the emergency ward of a nearby hospital where she remained for several days during which time she spoke of her delusions. In this wholly fortuitous manner she was perceived as a paranoid schizophrenic who needed treatment and was transferred to a psychiatric hospital just as soon as her hip improved. Subsequently, she was involuntarily committed to a county facility where she remained for five years before she saw an attorney. During that time, the hospital ordered her estate to pay for her psychiatric hospitalization. (Brooks, 1974, p. 655)

Dangerousness
to others

☐ DANGEROUSNESS TO OTHERS.　Many states require that there be some evidence that the individual is dangerous, either to himself or to others. And indeed, more involuntary hospitalizations are justified on these grounds than on any others. In some state statutes, the definition of dangerousness is vague. Alabama, for example, provides for commitment when a person "poses a real and present threat of substantial harm."† Florida, on the other hand, is more specific: a mentally disordered individual can be hospitalized if "[t]here is substantial likelihood that in the near future he will inflict serious bodily harm on himself or another person, as evidenced by recent behavior causing, attempting, or threatening such harm."‡

But regardless of how carefully or vaguely it is defined, two serious problems arise from the notion of dangerousness, one legal and the other scientific. The legal problem is straightforward. Incarcerating people because they are *predicted* to be dangerous creates a dilemma because Western legal traditions generally mandate the deprivation of liberty only *after* a crime has been commited, not before. The mere fact that someone is expected to violate law is not sufficient reason for incarceration.

This legal problem has painful ramifications, for involuntary commitments are not entirely unlike imprisonment insofar as deprivation of liberty

---

* Va. Code Ann. SS37.1-1, 37.1–67.1 (1984, Supp. 1986).
† Ala. Code SS22-52-1(a) (1977).
‡ West's Fla. Stats. Ann. SS394.467 (1986).

Many involuntary hospitalizations occur when an individual is judged to be dangerous to himself or others. Would this man be a candidate for involuntary commitment?

is concerned. Yet, few of the procedures that protect an alleged criminal defendant are available to the psychologically distressed who have been predicted to be violent. The latter can be involuntarily hospitalized on an emergency basis for as little as twenty-four hours (in Georgia) to as long as twenty-eight days (in Oklahoma), entirely without a trial or judge, and often on the allegation of a spouse or friend. In some jurisdictions, hospitalization can be extended indefinitely, simply on the word of a physician who deems the individual in need of further observation or treatment. And even when the matter is subjected to judicial review, the courts often rubber-stamp the physician's view, on the grounds that the hospitalization is being undertaken with the patient's best interests in mind. Thus, at many such judicial reviews, the patient need not be present, and commonly is not afforded an attorney. Many writers, and especially psychiatrist Thomas Szasz (1963), see in the involuntary commitment process an enormous and needless abuse of constitutional protection. Yet, no "plot" to deprive the patients of their rights to due process is intended in these procedures. Rather, because patients are held to be "sick," and because they are being sent to a hospital, the ordinary protections of criminal law are deemed unnecessary.

The scientific problems inherent in the prediction of dangerousness are as difficult as the legal problems. There is reason to doubt whether dangerousness can ever be predicted so precisely that only the dangerous will be hospitalized, while the not dangerous will not be. Psychological tests are just not as reliable as we would like. A variety of studies indicate that psychiatrists and psychologists are simply unable to predict dangerousness (Diamond, 1974; Ennis and Litwack, 1974; Stone, 1975; Monahan, 1976). One of the most interesting of these studies (Steadman and Keveles, 1972, 1978) arose out of the case of *Baxtrom* v. *Herold.**

> After serving more than two years for second-degree assault, Johnnie K. Baxtrom was certified as insane by a prison physician and transferred to a prison-hospital. Baxtrom's sentence was about to end, however, but because he was still in need of psychiatric care, the director of the prison-hospital petitioned that Baxtrom be committed involuntarily to an ordinary psychiatric hospital. That petition was denied for administrative reasons. Baxtrom, therefore, was forced to remain where he was.
>
> Baxtrom went to court with the following contention: If he was sane, he deserved to be discharged as soon as he completed his sentence. And if he was not sane, he should be transferred to an ordinary psychiatric hospital. Thus, he argued, his constitutional rights were being violated insofar as he was required to remain in prison beyond the termination of his sentence.

Operation Baxtrom

The United States Supreme Court agreed. And as a result, "Operation Baxtrom," which was designed to effect the rapid release of 967 similarly confined patients from New York State's prison-hospitals, was launched. These people were not merely predicted to be dangerous to others on the basis of their "insanity." They were also considered to be *criminally insane,* held to be violent now and in the future because they had been violent in the

* Baxtrom v. Herold, 383 U.S. 107 (1966).

past and because, additionally, they were psychologically distressed. Would those predictions hold up?

Operation Baxtrom afforded Henry Steadman and his colleagues an excellent opportunity to follow up on these patients and examine how accurate psychiatric predictions about dangerousness are. Precisely because most of these patients had been convicted of a dangerous act, one would expect predictions about their dangerousness to be quite accurate, since the past is the best predictor of the future. But that was not the case, for there were abundant false positives—individuals who did not act out violently—as well as false negatives—individuals released as nonviolent who later committed violent crimes. After four years, Steadman and Keveles (1972) reported that only 2.7 percent of these released patients had behaved dangerously and were either in a correctional facility or back in a hospital for the criminally insane. Careful examination of those who were dangerous revealed no "set of factors that could have selected these returnees from all the Baxtrom patients without a very large number of false positives" (Steadman, 1973, p. 318). Little if any progress has been made in the prediction of violent behavior since *Baxtrom* v. *Herold* (Steadman, 1983).

Dangerousness
to self

☐ DANGEROUSNESS TO SELF.   Still another criterion for involuntary commitment is dangerousness to self. The kinds of behaviors that are held to be dangerous are defined by informal social convention. Suicidal impulses qualify, but cigarette-smoking and drunk-driving do not.

In general, the use of involuntary hospitalization for people who are believed to be dangerous to themselves ought to be guided by the "thank you" test (Stone, 1975). This test asks: Will the person, once recovered, be grateful for that hospitalization, however much it was protested? That test would likely be passed by the people you read about earlier on page 604, and by others who are severely depressed and suicidal and who, once the depression has lifted, are simply grateful to be alive.

But the informal social conventions that regulate who should and who should not be hospitalized because they are dangerous to themselves are sometimes inconsistent and ambiguous. People who seem to be experiencing similar degrees of danger to themselves may be seen as good candidates for commitment in one case but not in another, as the following two cases demonstrate:

Case 1: Emma Lake. At sixty, Emma Lake was involuntarily committed to St. Elizabeth's Hospital after she was found wandering the streets of Washington, D.C. At the commitment hearing, two psychiatrists testified that she was unable to care adequately for herself. At a subsequent hearing, she was held to be suffering from "chronic brain syndrome with arteriosclerosis (hardening of the arteries) . . ." She was prone to "wandering away and being out exposed at night or any time that she is out." On one occasion, it was related, Mrs. Lake left the hospital and was missing for about thirty-two hours. She was brought back after midnight by a policeman who found her wandering the streets. She thought she had only been gone for a few hours, could not tell where she had been, and suffered a minor injury, that she attributed to having been chased by boys.

Mrs. Lake acknowledged that there were times when she lost track of things. Nevertheless, she felt able to be at liberty and willing to run the requisite risks. Her husband and sister were eager for her release and willing to provide a home for her. Moreover, she was willing to endure some form of confinement at home rather than the total confinement of a psychiatric hospital.

Ultimately the court concurred with her psychiatrists and required that she be hospitalized. She spent the last five years of her life in a psychiatric hospital, during the last year of which she received no visitors (Chambers, 1972). Often, families that would willingly provide a home for a patient are unable or unwilling to visit a psychiatric hospital regularly.

Case 2: Robert Jackson. At the age of sixty-two, Justice Robert Jackson suffered a severe heart attack while serving on the United States Supreme Court. The Court's work is arduous and taxing. His doctors gave him the choice between years of comparative (though not, by any means, total) inactivity off the Court, and the risk of death at any time by continuing his work on the Court. Jackson chose to remain on the Court. He suffered a fatal heart attack shortly thereafter.

No court interfered with the Justice's decision, nor was it ever suggested that he was dangerous to himself and therefore in need of psychiatric care. Quite the contrary: his decision to continue the work of the Court was widely praised. Many people would choose to do the same: take their chances with the things they enjoy doing rather than be cooped up, inactively, for the rest of their lives.

What distinguishes Mrs. Lake's case from Justice Jackson's? For both, the choices jeopardized their lives, Jackson's even more than Lake's. Why was Lake involuntarily committed and Jackson never questioned? The major difference between Mrs. Lake's case and Justice Jackson's is that Mrs. Lake's request to live out her years at home, and with people who loved her, was "psychiatrized." That is, her choice was believed to arise from mental illness ("chronic brain syndrome"), while Justice Jackson's was not. The fact that she suffered "chronic brain syndrome" obscured the similarities between her choice and that of others. Now, it is clearly the case that some psychologically distressed persons suffer thought disorders of such magnitude that they are rarely, if ever, lucid. But that was not the case with Mrs. Lake, nor is it the case for most psychiatric patients, all of whom enjoy long periods of clarity during which they are as capable as others of making significant choices between the risks of liberty and the security of incarceration (Dershowitz, 1968).

Grave disability

☐ GRAVE DISABILITY.   Many states permit commitment of mentally ill individuals when, as a result of their mental state, they are unable to adequately care for themselves. Again, recall from Chapter 1 Joyce Brown's plight. Because she *appeared* unable to care for herself, the City of New York placed her in Bellevue Hospital and held her there for treatment. Subsequently however, Ms. Brown demonstrated that she could care for herself and that being on the street was, for her, a matter of choice (and unemployment), not mental disorder.

California, defines "grave disability" as "a condition in which a person, as a result of mental disorder, is unable to provide for his basic personal needs for food, clothes, or shelter."* But where those needs can be met through the

* Cal. Welfare and Institutions Code SS5008.

willing assistance of relatives, as in the case of Emma Lake (on p. 608), should we deprive people of their liberty?

DUE PROCESS OF LAW

Rights and privileges of due process

If Mrs. Lake's case serves to teach anything, it is that once behavior is described or "explained" in terms of psychological abnormality, it encourages people to think of a different set of "solutions" than they would if it had been explained as the normal product of rational decision making. And because, as we have said, nothing less than deprivation of liberty is involved in involuntary commitment, it seems only reasonable to provide the psychologically distressed with the same privileges that are afforded to anyone whose liberty is threatened by state action—to criminal defendants, for example. These rights and privileges are collectively called "due process of law" and include:

- The right to be notified of trial in a timely manner
- The right to trial by jury
- The right to be present at one's own trial
- The right to legal counsel and the appointment of counsel in a timely manner
- The right to exclude unreliable evidence, such as hearsay evidence, from the testimony
- The right to challenge witnesses
- The privilege against self-incrimination
- The right to counsel at all interviews, including psychiatric interviews
- The right to know, with considerable precision, which laws one has violated and under which laws one stands accused.

Lessard case

In one case, *Lessard* v. *Schmidt,* Alberta Lessard complained that these very rights and privileges had been violated in her own involuntary commitment. Moreover, she argued that she had been detained without benefit of a hearing for better than three weeks, and could have been detained for as long as 145 days. The court held that Ms. Lessard's rights had been grossly violated and that all of her complaints were justified.* Commitment to a psychiatric hospital, the court held, may involve a serious restriction of individual rights. Those adjudged to be mentally ill, for example, like convicted felons, are unable to vote and may not serve on a jury. They may not drive a car. Their right to practice certain professions is restricted, as are their rights to make contracts, to sue, and to be sued. Those restrictions distinguish psychiatric from other kinds of medical care, and require that special attention be paid to due process issues.

In further support of its view that the psychologically distressed are entitled to due process, in the *Lessard* case, the court pointed out that psychiatric hospitalization may not be an entirely therapeutic experience.

---

* Lessard v. Schmidt, 349 F. Supp. 1078 (E.D. Wis. 1972). The Wisconsin court's judgment was vacated by the U.S. Supreme Court in 1974, on procedural rather than substantive grounds.

Perhaps the most serious possible effect of a decision to commit an individual lies in the statistics which indicate that an individual committed to a mental institution has a much greater chance of dying than if he were left at large. Data compiled in 1966 indicate that while the death rate per 1000 persons in the general population in the United States each year is only 9.5, the rate among resident mental patients is 91.8. . . . Figures for Wisconsin are similar. [One] study showed a death rate for the Wisconsin populace in general of 9.7 per 1000 population per year (or less than 1 percent) and a death rate in Wisconsin mental institutions of 85.1 per thousand (or 8.51 percent).

Although part of this difference may be accounted for by a large number of older persons in mental institutions, studies indicate that other factors also are involved. One factor is the smaller number of physicians per patient in public mental institutions in comparison to the ratio of doctors to individuals in the general population. . . . The damage done is not confined to a small number among the population. In 1963, 679,000 persons were confined in mental institutions in the United States; only 250,000 persons were incarcerated in all prisons administered by the states and federal government. . . . It would thus appear that the interests in avoiding civil commitments are at least as high as those of persons accused of criminal offenses.*

STANDARD OF PROOF

Three standards of proof

Throughout this section, we have emphasized that involuntary hospitalization involves a significant deprivation of liberty. The degree of deprivation may vary: some patients are permitted freedom on the hospital grounds, while others are locked into the ward, day and night. But even those in the former group experience a restriction on their liberty, in that they must be in the hospital rather than elsewhere. In order to so restrict a person's freedom one must prove that, in accord with the law, they belong in a psychiatric hospital. Mere allegation is insufficient. What standard of proof should be required? Generally speaking, three standards of proof are available in law: preponderance of evidence, beyond a reasonable doubt, and clear and convincing proof.

Often called the 51 percent standard, *the preponderance of evidence* standard requires just enough proof to shift the weight of evidence to one side. This is the standard used in civil cases, where penalties are often monetary and do not involve deprivation of liberty.

Beyond a reasonable doubt is the most severe standard of proof and requires that the evidence be so compelling as to convince a reasonable listener beyond a reasonable doubt. This standard is used in criminal law, where the presumption of a defendant's innocence is very strong, and the cost of wrongful incarceration of an innocent person high indeed. It is often termed the 90 percent or 99 percent standard, implying that the weight of evidence must be such that people would be willing to stake high odds on the guilt of the defendant.

Clear and convincing proof is an intermediate standard that is not quite so severe as that requiring proof beyond a reasonable doubt, but not as lenient as the 51 percent standard that requires the mere preponderance of evidence. Consider it the 75 percent standard.

Recalling what you have read here regarding the validity of predictions of dangerousness, and what you have learned in Chapter 7 on the reliability

* Ibid, p. 1089.

and validity of psychiatric diagnoses generally, what standard of proof should be invoked in order to commit a person involuntarily? In 1979, the matter was taken up by the Supreme Court in *Addington* v. *Texas*.*

Addington case

Frank O'Neal Addington had been hospitalized seven times between 1967 and 1975. His mother now petitioned the court to have him involuntarily committed because he was both dangerous to himself and dangerous to others. In accord with Texas law, a jury trial was held to determine if he required hospitalization. The judge instructed the jury to determine whether there was "clear, unequivocal and convincing evidence"—the 75 percent standard—that Addington was mentally ill and required hospitalization for his protection and for the safety of others. The jury so found, but Addington appealed the decision to the U.S. Supreme Court on the grounds that the appropriate standard of proof should have been a tougher one—beyond a reasonable doubt—the 90 percent standard.

The Supreme Court held that the 90 percent standard was simply too severe. Given the uncertainties of psychiatric diagnosis and prediction, requiring proof beyond a reasonable doubt would render the state unable to commit many truly distressed people who were much in need of treatment. The preponderance of evidence standard, on the other hand, was much too lenient. If the state wanted to deprive a person of liberty, it needed to bear a greater burden of proof than that implied in the 51 percent standard. The Supreme Court therefore upheld the original decision, maintaining that the presentation of clear and convincing evidence —roughly 75 percent certainty—is the minimum standard for involuntary commitment and that states may not commit below this minimum standard (though they are free to fix standards that are higher than this required minimum).

TREATMENT

THE RIGHT TO TREATMENT

Right to treatment after commitment

The *Lessard* and *Addington* cases dealt with the rights people can exercise and the standard of proof that is required before they can be involuntarily committed. What about after they have been committed? Is there a "right to treatment" for those who have been deprived of their liberty, presumably because they required psychiatric treatment? Oddly, and with few exceptions, the courts have been very cautious on this matter. They are understandably reluctant to invent new "rights." Yet, deprivation of liberty is a serious matter in a democratic society, and the courts have occasionally been responsive to cases in which hospitalization has occurred without the person receiving adequate treatment. Thus, in *Rouse* v. *Cameron*,† Judge David Bazelon clearly enunciated a right to treatment that was rooted in federal statute. He wrote:

Rouse case

The purpose of involuntary hospitalization is treatment, not punishment . . . absent treatment, the hospital is transform[ed] . . . into a penitentiary where one could be held indefinitely for no convicted offense. (*Rouse* v. *Cameron,* 1966, p. 453)

* Addington v. Texas, 99 S. Ct. 1804 (1979).
† Rouse v. Cameron, 373 F. 2d 451 (D.C. Cir. 1966).

Not all "treatments" count as treatment, however. Bazelon said:

> The hospital need not show that the treatment will cure or improve him but only that there is a bona fide effort to do so. This requires the hospital to show that initial and periodic inquiries are made into the needs and conditions of the patient with a view to providing suitable treatment for him. . . . Treatment that has therapeutic value for some may not have such value for others. For example, it may not be assumed that confinement in a hospital is beneficial "environment therapy" for all. (*Rouse* v. *Cameron,* 1966, p. 456)

Wyatt case

In *Wyatt* v. *Stickney,** Judge Frank Johnson insisted that the constitutional right to treatment is accorded to every person who has been involuntarily hospitalized. In his opinion, Johnson wrote:

> To deprive any citizen of his or her liberty upon the altruistic theory that the confinement is for humane therapeutic reasons and then fail to provide adequate treatment violates the very fundamentals of due process.

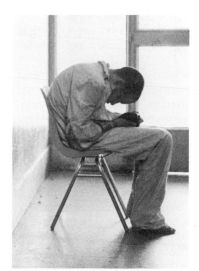

Conditions such as the starkness of this environment caused the courts to stipulate minimal objective standards of care in psychiatric hospitals.

In a later opinion,† Judge Johnson recognized that the absence of therapeutic regimens in the Alabama state hospitals was less a matter of simple neglect than it was one of personnel and facilities. He therefore stipulated minimal objective standards of care, standards, by the way, that were far below those recommended by the American Psychiatric Association. Thus, he required that for every 250 patients, there should be at least two psychiatrists, three additional physicians, twelve registered nurses, ninety attendants, four psychologists, and seven social workers. While these may seem a large number of personnel for every 250 patients, remember that patients are in the hospital twenty-four hours a day, seven days a week, and that personnel are needed to take care of them on a continuous basis.

In that same opinion, Judge Johnson made clear that patients have a right to privacy and dignity, to the least restrictive regimen necessary to achieve the purposes of commitment, and to freedom from unnecessary or excessive medication. He affirmed their right to send sealed mail and to use the telephone—privileges that are often denied patients on the grounds that they might say things that they would later have cause to regret. Finally, Johnson said that each patient was entitled to an individual treatment plan, and to periodic review of his or her plan and progress.

Judge Bazelon's and Judge Johnson's opinions have been hailed by civil libertarians and mental health professionals alike as major steps forward in the treatment of the psychologically distressed. Although other courts have not concurred that there is a right to treatment, these opinions have had far-reaching effects (see Box 18-1).

RELEASING MENTAL PATIENTS

Board and care facilities

Opinions written in such cases as *Rouse* v. *Cameron* and *Wyatt* v. *Stickney* have alerted people to the plight of psychiatric patients, and promise to improve their fate. But unfortunately, they have also had a major unintended consequence. Faced with the prospect of pouring more money into psychi-

* Wyatt v. Stickney, 325 F. Supp. 781 (M.D. Ala. 1971).
† Wyatt v. Stickney, 344 F. Supp. 343 (M.D. Ala. 1972).

Box 18-1   KENNETH DONALDSON'S SAGA

Perhaps Kenneth Donaldson needed treatment. But did he get it?

Kenneth Donaldson was already forty-eight years old when his parents, themselves in their seventies, petitioned for his commitment to Florida State Hospital at Chattahoochee. His life had not been an easy one until then, Donaldson frankly points out in his book, *Insanity Inside Out* (1976). He had had one psychiatric hospitalization of three-months' duration, some thirteen years earlier. It was a hospitalization that followed him, and marred his life subsequently. Afterwards, his marriage had failed, his relationship with his children had cooled, he had had difficulty holding a job, and sometimes he had felt that people were out to get him. But he was not dangerous to himself, had never been dangerous to others (although his father had alleged he was in order to get him committed), and he emphatically did not want to be committed to Chattahoochee. One hospitalization was more than enough.

The judge who committed Donaldson told him that he would be in the hospital for "a few weeks." A progress note written less than three months after he was admitted indicated that he appeared to be in remission. And because his first hospitalization had been brief, there was every reason to expect this one to be brief too. Nevertheless, Donaldson remained in Florida State Hospital for fourteen-and-a-half years.

Donaldson is a Christian Scientist. Medication and electric shock treatments were both offered to him, but he refused them on religious grounds. What care and treatment did he get then? None. He rarely saw Drs. O'Connor or Gumanis, his physicians, and then only briefly. Grounds privileges and occupational therapy were denied him during the first ten years of his hospitalization. Some six years after he had been hospitalized, Helping Hands, Inc., a reputable organization that operates halfway houses for mental patients, offered to care for Donaldson. But his psychiatrist, Dr. O'Connor, refused to release him to anyone but his parents. By this time, his parents were too old and infirm to accept that responsibility, and presumably Dr. O'Connor knew that. Finally, a college friend made four separate attempts to have Donaldson released in his custody. His requests were either refused outright or frustrated.

During this period, Donaldson smuggled letters out of the hospital to anyone who might help. Often, however, mail sent through hospital channels would be opened or simply thrown out. Donaldson's teenage daughter wrote "Daddy, I know you are not sick. But why don't you write?" "I was writing," Donaldson says.

atric care, many states have taken the least expensive route and have simply discharged patients from psychiatric hospitals, and closed the hospitals. During the seventies, for example, California closed a majority of its psychiatric hospitals and cut back severely on funding of mental health programs. Other states followed suit. As a result, thousands of people who were formerly housed in psychiatric hospitals have been shunted to "board and care" homes in local communities. Living conditions there are sometimes substandard. Treatment is minimal, and former patients have little to do but lie in bed or walk the streets. The new visibility of these people has frequently created a harsh and angry community reaction. The powerful stigma associated with those labeled mentally ill, and particularly the vio-

Kenneth Donaldson is pictured here after the Supreme Court ruled in his favor.

"Then her letters stopped." (Donaldson, 1976, p. 84). As a result, he acquired a reputation for being a difficult person. But he had much to be difficult about. Day after day was spent in a locked, crowded room with sixty other people, nearly one-third of whom had undergone criminal commitments. At night, some of the patients would have fits. It was frightening. Some of the beds in this crowded room were so close together that they touched. Donaldson lived in constant fear that someone would jump him during the night.

Donaldson sought the help of the Mental Health Law Project, a Washington, D.C., group of lawyers who serve the legal needs of the mentally distressed. And, finally, in 1971, Donaldson sued for his release and for damages from Drs. O'Connor and Gumanis, alleging "intentional, malicious, and reckless disregard of Donaldson's constitutional rights." The jury awarded Donaldson compensatory and punitive damages from both physicians. The physicians appealed, and the case went up to the Supreme Court, where many of the justices were simply outraged over Donaldson's incarceration (Woodward and Armstrong, 1979). On January 26, 1975, the Court unanimously wrote in *O'Connor v. Donaldson:**

A state cannot constitutionally confine . . . a nondangerous individual who is capable of surviving safely in freedom by himself or with the help of willing and responsible family members or friends.

* O'Connor v. Donaldson, 422 U.S. 563, 95 S.Ct 2486 (1975).

lence and unpredictability that is erroneously attributed to mental patients, creates enormous community fear and backlash.

Are patients better off in board and care facilities than in psychiatric hospitals? We don't yet know. Psychiatric hospitals have yet to establish their ability to substantially improve the lives of involuntarily committed patients (Kiesler, 1982a, 1982b). Moreover, informal conversations with these patients strongly indicate that they prefer being in the community to being warehoused in psychiatric hospitals, and there is evidence that they are no worse off in the community than in hospitals (Lamb, 1979). But neither are they as well off as they would like to be or should be. Many find employment difficult to procure, and social relationships difficult to establish.

They react strongly to community stereotypes about them. Given these facts, a policy that establishes and supports *community-based* treatment is clearly called for.

THE PATIENTS' RIGHTS MOVEMENT

Self-help organizations

The wholesale release of patients into the community has had some positive effects. In many communities, former psychiatric patients have established self-help organizations which, in addition to providing social networks and employment opportunities, also have given the mentally ill a political base. A Presidential Commission on Mental Health, appointed by President Carter in 1978, led to the passage of Section 501 of the Mental Health Systems Act of 1980, otherwise known as the Patients' Bill of Rights (see Box 18-2). While this law is only advisory in nature, most states provide at least some of those rights, and some states provide all of them.

Patients' rights advocates

To assure that the rights of the mentally ill are protected, former patients, their families, and others have joined to form a network of patients' rights advocates, such as NAMI (National Alliance for the Mentally Ill) or CAMI (California Alliance for the Mentally Ill). These advocates work for changes in state laws, monitor mental health facilities, and in some cases, provide legal representation for patients. Their efforts have resulted in considerable improvement in the conditions under which patients are housed and treated.

ABOLISH INVOLUNTARY HOSPITALIZATION?

Former mental patients who have been released from psychiatric hospitals often may end up walking the streets.

Involuntary commitment gives rise to serious problems. Coerced hospitalization and coercive treatment please no one and require that one ask whether involuntary hospitalization should be abolished altogether. The "ayes" have had their vigorous spokesmen, from the English philosopher John Stuart Mill of the last century to psychiatrist Thomas S. Szasz today. In *On Liberty* (1859), Mill wrote:

> The only freedom which deserves the name is that of pursuing our own good in our own way, so long as we do not attempt to deprive others of theirs, or impede their efforts to obtain it. Each is the proper guardian of his own health, whether bodily, or mental and spiritual. Mankind are greater gainers by suffering each other to live as seems good to themselves, than by compelling each to live as seems good to the rest. (Mill, 1859, p. 18)

Thomas Szasz is one of the most critical analysts of the nature of psychiatry and its role in society today. Szasz points out that mental illness is different from physical illness. There are no clear or generally accepted criteria of mental illness. "[L]ooking for evidence of such illness is like searching for evidence of heresy: Once the investigator gets into the proper frame of mind, anything may seem to him to be a symptom of mental illness" (Szasz, 1963, p. 225). As a result, Szasz believes that psychiatry has a great potential for social abuse, particularly as it lends itself, through involuntary commitment, to ridding society of all manner of deviants and eccentrics, all in the name of treating mental illness. Szasz is not opposed to voluntary hospital-

Box 18-2   SUMMARY OF THE PATIENTS' BILL OF RIGHTS

The right to appropriate treatment and related services in a setting which is most supportive and least restrictive of a person's liberty.

The right to an individualized, written treatment or service plan.

The right, consistent with one's capabilities, to participate in and receive a reasonable explanation of the care and treatment process.

The right not to receive treatment without informed, voluntary, written consent, except in a documented emergency or as permitted under applicable law for someone who has been civilly committed.

The right not to participate in experimentation in the absence of informed, voluntary, written consent.

The right to be free from restraint or seclusion except in an emergency situation pursuant to a contemporaneous written order by a responsible mental health professional.

The right to a humane treatment environment that affords reasonable protection from harm and appropriate privacy.

The right to confidentiality of personal records.

The right to have access to personal mental health records and have a lawyer or legal representative have reasonable access to records if the patient provides written authorization.

The right to private conversations, reasonable access to telephones and mail, and to visitation during regular visiting hours.

The right to timely and meaningful information about one's rights at the time of and after admission.

The right to assert grievances with regard to the infringement of rights.

The right to have a fair, timely, and impartial grievance procedure provided.

The right of access to, including private communications with, any available rights protection service or qualified advocate.

The right to exercise other rights without reprisal, including denial of appropriate treatment.

The right to referral as appropriate to other providers of mental health services upon discharge.

The right to confidentiality of and access to records continues following one's discharge.

The patient has a right that his attorney or legal representative has reasonable access to the patient/client, the facility at which the patient resides and, with written authorization, the patient's medical and service records.

SOURCE: Adapted from the Mental Health Systems Act, 1980.

izization, provided patients are frankly told whether or not they will receive the best treatment. But he believes involuntary hospitalization should be abolished.

Some critics of psychiatry oppose not only involuntary hospitalization, but involuntary treatment as well. Citing the adverse side effects of many

Opposition to
involuntary
treatment

antipsychotic medications, patients in a number of jurisdictions have sued to assert the right to refuse the "chemical straitjacket." Holding that medications may be administered to nonconsenting patients only in an emergency or after a full, fair adversary hearing, the Colorado Supreme Court recognized the risk involved in the use of antipsychotic drugs:

> Although the decision to forcibly medicate a patient with antipsychotic drugs undoubtedly involves an aspect of professional medical judgment in connection with psychiatric diagnosis and treatment alternatives, the fact remains that the decision itself directly implicates the patient's legal interests in personal autonomy and bodily integrity. Antipsychotic medications, either alone or in combination, can cause numerous and varied side effects and carry with them the risk of serious and possibly permanent disabilities in the patient. . . . The effects of these drugs can be far more debilitating to the patient than the physical restraint incident to the involuntary commitment process.*

CRIMINAL COMMITMENT

Defining criminal
commitment

Involuntary commitment is sometimes called *civil commitment,* the process used to hospitalize people who have committed no crime. *Criminal commitment,* on the other hand, refers to the coerced psychiatric hospitalization of people who have acted harmfully but are not legally responsible because they lack a "guilty mind" or *mens rea.* "Where there is no *mens* (i.e., mind) there can be no *mens rea*" the legal maxim goes (Fingarette and Hasse, 1979, p. 200). In the eyes of the law, such people are insane, and the legal defense used in their cases is called the *insanity defense.*

John Hinckley, Jr., successfully used the insanity defense when he was tried for the attempted assassination of former President Ronald Reagan.

THE INSANITY DEFENSE

The insanity defense requires that the defendant was wholly or partially irrational *when the crime took place,* and that this irrationality affected his or her behavior. The psychologist or psychiatrist who serves as an expert witness in this matter is required to reconstruct the defendant's state of mind as it was before and during the crime. This is not a simple task. If diagnostic opinions are often unreliable for *present* behavior, as we saw in Chapter 7, how much more unreliable are they for speculative reconstructions of the past? No wonder, then, that experts for the defense are often contradicted by equally capable experts for the prosecution, and that judges and jurors will disagree on the defendant's state of mind when he committed the crime.

USE OF THE INSANITY DEFENSE

Insanity defense
not widely used

Popular opinion notwithstanding, the insanity defense is not widely used. It is invoked in fewer than 1 out of 400 homicide cases that come to trial, even more rarely in nonhomicide trials. And it is successful in many fewer cases than that, mainly by agreement between the prosecutor and defense attorneys. Even when successful, the defense usually leads to long-term incarceration in an institution for the criminally insane, a fate sometimes worse than incarceration in prison (see Box 18-3). Nevertheless the role and

* People v. Medina, 705 P.2d 961, 968 (Colorado Supreme Court, 1985).

Box 18-3   IS A HOSPITAL FOR THE CRIMINALLY INSANE WORSE THAN A PRISON?

The word "hospital" and the phrase "treatment center" have such overwhelming kind and curative connotations that it is difficult to believe, as the text points out, that many people would prefer prison to these places. Yet, that is the case. Patients often resist being transferred to treatment centers because they restrict individual rights and are more punitive. Documentary filmmaker, Frederick Wiseman, in *Titticut Follies*, depicted life at Bridgewater, Massachusetts, Treatment Center. And a former inmate there, Donald McEwan, compared Bridgewater with the nearby state prison in a brief which was an appendix to *United States ex rel. Schuster v. Herold**** (cited in Brooks, 1974, p. 423). A portion of that appendix is excerpted here:

Item	Treatment Center	State Prison at Walpole
Punishment (lock-up)	No semblance of trial. Any guard may order.	Only disciplinary board (composed of deputy supt., a guard, and a civilian employee).
Rules and procedures	Different from night and day.	Same all the time.
Cells	No lockers; no control of light from inside; no lamps allowed. No smoking. Arrangements of furniture, blankets, etc. specified in detail. No glass objects or food allowed.	Wall locker provided; light switch inside; lamps allowed. Smoking allowed. No specification on arrangements. Glass objects and food allowed.
Sanitary facilities	Primitive, no running water in cell; showers available only at specified times; frequently only 1 toilet to entire population (100 +).	Modern toilet and basin in cell; showers available any free time.
Mail	Frequently delayed by being passed to various persons. Outgoing certified mail may take weeks. Supt. includes apology in all mail to public officials. Censor stamp used on all mail.	Prompt delivery both incoming and outgoing. No unauthorized missives enclosed. Censor stamp not ordinarily used.
Free time	Required to be either in yard or rec. room (no choice) or locked in cell.	Choice of yard, TV rooms, gym, chapel, own cell (which is open), other cell-block rec. areas.
Library	Cannot browse; no catalog available.	Open daily for browsing; catalog available.
Lawyer visit	In presence of guard.	Private.
Visiting	1 hour once a week across table with wire fence underneath.	All morning or afternoon (2½ hours) twice a week, in chairs side by side.

* United States ex rel. Schuster v. Herold, 410 F.2d 1071 (2d Cir. 1969).

meaning of the insanity defense is one of the most hotly debated issues in criminal law. Why should that be?

While the insanity defense is something of a bother in the criminal law, "we must put up with [it] . . . because to exclude it is to deprive the criminal law of its chief paradigm of free will" (Packer, 1968). Thus, the insanity defense is the exception that proves the rule: the notion that each of us is responsible for his or her behavior is strengthened by the recognition that some of us patently are not (Stone, 1975; Rosenhan, 1983). Below are three cases in which the insanity defense has been used (adapted from Livermore and Meehl, 1967). Is there *mens rea* in each of these defendants (see Table 18–1)?*

Case 1: The Pigtail Snipper. Victor Weiner, a hair fetishist, was charged with assault for snipping off a girl's pigtail while standing on a crowded bus. His experience before cutting off the pigtail (which was corroborated by psychiatric testimony and by an acquaintance with whom he had discussed this problem several days earlier) was one of mounting tension, accompanied by a feeling that was close to anxiety and erotic excitement. He made various efforts to distract himself and place himself in situations where he would be safe from performing this act, but finally he gave in to the impulse and boarded the bus with a pair of scissors in his pocket. Victor was diagnosed "sociopathic personality disturbance, sexual deviation, fetishism."

Case 2: The Axe-handle Murderer. Arthur Wolff, a fifteen-year-old, was charged with murdering his mother.† During the year preceding the crime, Wolff "spent a lot of time thinking about sex." He made a list of the names and addresses of seven girls in his community whom he planned to anesthetize and then either rape or photograph nude. One night, about three weeks before the murder, he took a container of ether and attempted to enter the house of one of these girls through the chimney. But he became wedged in and had to be rescued. In the ensuing weeks, Wolff apparently decided that he would have to bring the girls to his house to achieve his sexual purposes, and that it would therefore be necessary to get his mother (and possibly his brother) out of the way first.

On the Friday or Saturday before he murdered his mother, Wolff obtained an axe handle from the family garage and hid it under the mattress of his bed. On Sunday, he took the axe handle from its hiding place and approached his mother from behind, raising the weapon to strike her. She sensed his presence and asked him what he was doing; he answered that it was "nothing," and returned to his room and hid the axe handle under his mattress again. The following morning, Wolff ate the breakfast that his mother had prepared, went to his room, and took the axe handle from its hiding place. He returned to the kitchen, approached his mother from behind, and struck her on the back of the head. She turned around screaming. He hit her several more times, and they fell to the floor fighting. He got up to turn off the water running in the sink, and she fled through the dining room. He gave chase, caught her in the front room, and choked her to death with his hands.

Wolff then took off his shirt and hung it by the fire, washed the blood off his face and hands, read a few lines from the Bible or prayer book lying upon the dining room table, and walked down to the police station to turn himself in. He told

---

* 51 Minn L. Rev. 789, 833–55 (1967).
† People v. Wolff, 61 Cal. 2d 795, 800.

the desk officer, "I have something I wish to report . . . I just killed my mother with an axe handle." The officer testified that Wolff spoke in a quiet voice and that "his conversation was quite coherent in what he was saying and he answered everything I asked him right to a T."

At his trial, four expert witnesses testified that Arthur Wolff had been suffering from schizophrenia when he murdered his mother.

Case 3: The Delusional Informer. Calvin Ellery was a paranoid schizophrenic who experienced delusions and hallucinations, and who believed that the Masons were plotting to take over the government. He believed, moreover, that the Masons had learned that he was aware of their intentions, and that because he was a potential informer, the Masons had determined to do away with him.

As a result of delusional misinterpretation of certain things he had heard on a news broadcast, Ellery believed that "today is the day for his execution." When a salesman with a Masonic button on his lapel came to the front door, he was sure that the salesman had been sent to kill him. When the salesman reached into his pocket for his business card, Ellery was convinced that he was reaching for a revolver. Ellery drew his own weapon and shot first in self-defense.

TESTS FOR DETERMINING INSANITY

Three views to determine if the insanity defense can be used

What determines if the insanity defense can be used? When is a person considered to be so insane in the eyes of the law that the ordinary cannons of criminal law do not apply? Because the answer to these questions is crucial to the very meaning of criminal law, the questions themselves have generated hot dispute. Historically, there have been three views of the insanity defense: the M'Naghten rule, the Durham test, and the American Law Institute rule.

M'Naghten test

☐ M'NAGHTEN: THE "RIGHT-WRONG" TEST.   In 1843, Daniel M'Naghten, after whom the "right-wrong" test was named, murdered Drummond, the secretary to Sir Robert Peel, the British Prime Minister. Drummond, however, was not M'Naghten's intended victim; Peel was. A "voice of God" had instructed M'Naghten to kill the Prime Minister. Unfortunately for Drummond, Peel had been invited to travel in Queen Victoria's carriage. Drummond rode in the vehicle that normally would have been reserved for the Prime Minister, and was mistaken for him by M'Naghten.

The trial was remarkable in that M'Naghten's defense counsel relied heavily on *Medical Jurisprudence of Insanity* (1838), a recently published work by Dr. Isaac Ray. M'Naghten, the defense counsel argued, was clearly deranged, in that he suffered delusions of persecution (and, in modern terms, command hallucinations). It was one of the first times that psychiatric testimony had been permitted in a murder trial, and the judges were so impressed that the Lord Chief Justice practically directed a verdict for M'Naghten. Subsequently, the judges enunciated the ***M'Naghten rule,*** which holds that:

> It must be clearly proved that, at the time of the committing of the act, the party accused was laboring under such a defect of reason, from disease of the mind, as not to know the nature and quality of the act he was doing; or, if he did know it, that he did not know he was doing what was wrong.

The M'Naghten test is widely used in the United States. Nearly half of the states use it alone as the yardstick for insanity, while other states use the M'Naghten rule in conjunction with other rules. It is a relatively narrow test, which relies merely on what the accused knew and whether he knew it was wrong.

Under the M'Naghten rule, only Calvin Ellery, the delusional informer, would be acquitted, for only he clearly did not "know the nature and quality of the act he was doing," believing that he was acting in justifiable self-defense. The axe-handle murderer's behavior was clearly bizzare, yet because there was no evidence that he failed to distinguish right from wrong, he could not be acquitted according to the M'Naghten rule. Similarly, Weiner, the pigtail snipper, though clearly disturbed and seemingly caught up in an impulse that ultimately overcame his best efforts at suppression, could not be acquitted under the M'Naghten rule. He, too, knew right from wrong.

Durham test

□ DURHAM: "THE PRODUCT OF MENTAL DISEASE." In *Durham* v. *United States*,* Judge David Bazelon broadened the insanity defense to state that "an accused is not criminally responsible if his unlawful act was the product of mental disease or mental defect." Notice the difference between the Durham "mental disease" and the M'Naghten "right-wrong" test. In the ***Durham test,*** incapacitating conditions, such as the inability to tell right from wrong are not specified. One goes directly from "mental disease" to the act (Brooks, 1974), leaving it to advanced knowledge in psychiatry and psychology to determine whether the act was or was not a product of mental disease or mental defect. Under the Durham rule, the axe-handle murderer would probably have been acquitted on the grounds that, absent his schizophrenic condition, he would not have murdered his mother. Likewise, defining fetishism as a "mental disease," the pigtail snipper, too, would have been acquitted on the grounds that were he not a fetishist, he would not have had such a prurient interest in little girls' pigtails. And of course, Calvin Ellery, the delusional informer, would also have been acquitted under the "mental disease" test (he was paranoid schizophrenic), as well as under the M'Naghten "right-wrong" test.

As Justice Bazelon maintained, the Durham rule was an experiment, one that extended for some eighteen years, from 1954 until 1972, and during which time, a view of criminal responsibility and nonresponsibility was developed. Fundamentally, the Durham rule was withdrawn for two reasons: (1) it relied too heavily on the expert testimony of psychiatrists, rendering judge and jury wholly dependent upon psychiatric testimony for the determination of criminal responsibility, and (2) it was as difficult then as it is now to know and attain agreement about what constituted a "mental disease." The metaphor itself left much to be desired, implying a distinct and verifiable organic state. Moreover, one could never be sure which of the disorders listed in the *Diagnostic and Statistical Manual of Mental Disorders* qualified. Should stuttering, tobacco dependence, and sociopathy all be considered mental diseases that can produce unlawful acts? The seeming breadth of the Durham rule created problems that were difficult to adjudicate and that ultimately, led to its near demise. Only one state, New Hampshire, still uses the *Durham* test.

* Durham v. United States, 214 F. 2d 862 (D.C. Cir. 1954).

ALI rule

☐ THE AMERICAN LAW INSTITUTE (ALI) RULE: "APPRECIATE AND CONFORM." In *United States* v. *Brawner,** some eighteen years after the *Durham* case, the Durham mental disease test was succeeded by a modification of the insanity defense that had earlier been propounded by the American Law Institute. That rule is considerably more specific than the Durham rule, and yet not so narrow as the M'Naghten rule. It states:

1. A person is not responsible for criminal conduct if, at the time of such conduct, as a result of mental disease or defect, he lacks substantial capacity either to appreciate the criminality (wrongfulness) of his conduct or to conform his conduct to the requirements of law.

2. As used in the Article, the terms "mental disease or defect" do not include an abnormality manifested only by repeated criminal or otherwise antisocial conduct. (American Law Institute, 1985, p. 62).

In the *Brawner* case, the court tried to further narrow the meaning of "mental disease." Citing an earlier case,† it wrote:

[A] mental disease or defect includes any abnormal condition of the mind which substantially affects mental or emotional processes and substantially impairs behavior controls.

The ***ALI rule,*** as modified in the *Brawner* case, has been adopted by thirty state courts and is the standard in all federal courts of appeal. Under that standard, Calvin Ellery would, of course, be acquitted. Convinced that the Masons were both plotting to take over the government and assassinate him, Ellery clearly lacked "substantial capacity . . . to appreciate the criminality (wrongfulness) of his conduct." The verdict with regard to Victor Weiner, the pigtail snipper, would depend on whether the court was willing and able to assess the strength of Weiner's desire and, therefore, his ability "to conform his conduct to the requirements of law."

The outcome of the case of Arthur Wolff, who murdered his mother because she seemed in the way of his sexual schemes, depends wholly on how a jury would interpret the word *appreciate* in the section of the ALI rule that says ". . . he lacks substantial capacity . . . to appreciate the criminality (wrongfulness) of his conduct. . . ." Wolf "knew" he did wrong in killing his mother, for he confessed immediately at the police station. But did he really *appreciate* that this was wrong? Did he "feel it in his heart" affectively, or did he merely "know" cognitively? If the latter, he would be acquitted under the ALI rule. If the former, he would be convicted of murdering his mother.

GBMI verdict

☐ GUILTY BUT MENTALLY ILL (GBMI) Perhaps as the result of public perceptions that defendants are "beating the rap" by entering insanity pleas, some states have abolished the "not guilty by reason of insanity" verdict, replacing it with the verdict of "guilty but mentally ill" (GBMI). A finding that a defendant is guilty but mentally ill results in commitment to a mental institution rather than to a prison.‡

* United Stated v. Brawner, 471 F. 2d 969 (D.C. Dir. 1972).
† McDonald v. United States, 312 F. 3d 847 (D.C. Cir. 1962).
‡ Thirteen states had adopted this standard by 1985.

Table 18-1 ACQUITTAL UNDER THE VARIOUS INSANITY DEFENSES					
Case	Diagnosis	M'Naghten "right-wrong" test	Durham "product of mental disease" test	American Law Institute (ALI) "appreciate and conform" test	Guilty but mentally ill
Victor Weiner (Pigtail snipper)	Fetishist	Guilty—he knew it was wrong	Not guilty—fetishism is a mental disease according to DSM-III-R	Maybe—depends on court's assessment of his ability to conform his conduct to law.	Guilty
Arthur Wolff (Axe-handle murderer)	Schizophrenic	Guilty—he knew it was wrong.	Probably acquitted—if he were not schizophrenic, he probably would not have murdered.	Probably guilty if *affectively*, he knew murder was wrong.	Guilty
Calvin Ellery (Delusional informer)	Paranoid schizophrenic	Not guilty—he thought he was shooting in self-defense.	Not guilty—the killing was clearly the product of his delusions.	Not guilty—he could appreciate the criminality of his conduct.	Guilty

The GBMI verdict is an instance of a legislative rush to action, and it is mistaken on at least two counts. In the first place, the insanity defense is rarely invoked and much more rarely successful. The public impression of its usefulness arises nearly wholly from sensational news stories, not from accurate estimates of incidence. Moreover, the GBMI verdict is a contradiction in its own terms. In order to be guilty, one needs to have been able to form a morally coherent intent to harm (*mens rea*—see p. 618). But mental illness exonerates one precisely because one is held to be *unable* to form such an intent. How then can one be simultaneously guilty and mentally ill?

COMPETENCE TO STAND TRIAL

Defendants found incompetent to stand trial

For every defendant found not guilty by reason of insanity, at least a hundred defendants are found incompetent to stand trial and are sent to institutions for the criminally insane until they are able to be tried (Bacon, 1969). Being incompetent to stand trial augurs a long incarceration: the average confinement of people committed as incompetent was sixty-one months, and the average for those civilly committed (in Massachusetts at the time of the study) was fourteen months (McGarry and Bendt, 1969). It is not uncommon for people alleged to be incompetent to stand trial to be remanded to institutions for the criminally insane for decades, and simply forgotten. At one such institution, three people among those who were now fully able to stand trial but who had been "overlooked" had been incarcerated for forty-two, thirty-nine, and seventeen years respectively—this, before any determination of their guilt had been made! (McGarry and Bendt,

1969). Moreover, even when treatment is accorded, there is mounting evidence that neither the competency evaluations nor the treatments within psychiatric hospitals are worth much (Melton, Weithorn, and Slobogin, 1985). As a result, many states are turning toward community- rather than hospital-based competency evaluation and treatment.

Statutory definitions

What does "incompetent to stand trial" mean? Most statutory definitions are similar to New York's, which defines an "incompetent person" as one "who as a result of mental disease or defect lacks capacity to understand the proceedings against him or to assist in his own defense."* The intent of the statute is noble, growing out of the English common law tradition that forbids a trial in absentia. While the defendant may be physically present, when he is judged incompetent to stand trial, he is believed to be *psychologically absent,* and the trial is delayed until he can participate in his own defense.

Limits on duration of commitment

Until recently, there were no limits on *how long* people could be committed until judged competent to stand trial. What if they would *never* be competent to stand trial? Such a dilemma arose tragically in *Jackson* v. *Indiana*.†

> Theon Jackson was a mentally defective deaf-mute. He could not read, write, or otherwise communicate except through limited sign language. In May, 1968, at the age of twenty-seven, Jackson was charged with separate robberies of two women, both of which robberies were alleged to have occurred in the previous July. The first robbery involved a purse and its contents; the total value was four dollars. The second concerned five dollars in cash. Jackson entered a plea of not guilty through his attorney.
>
> Had he been convicted, Jackson would likely have received a sentence of sixty days. But he could not be tried because, in accord with Indiana law, Jackson was examined by two psychiatrists who found that he lacked the intellectual and communicative skills to participate in his own defense, and that the prognosis for acquiring them was dim indeed. Moreover, Jackson's interpreter testified that Indiana had no facilities that could help someone as badly off as Jackson to learn minimal communication skills. The trial court, therefore, found that Jackson "lack[ed] comprehension sufficient to make his defense," and ordered him committed until the Indiana Department of Mental Health certified that the "defendant is sane."
>
> Jackson's attorney filed for a new trial, contending that Jackson was not insane, but that because his mental retardation was so severe, he could never attain competence to stand trial. Jackson's commitment under these circumstances amounted to a life sentence without his ever having been convicted of a crime! By the time the case reached the U.S. Supreme Court, Jackson had already been "hospitalized" for three and a half years. Justice Blackmun, writing for a unanimous court, concurred with Jackson's attorney that Indiana's rule was unconstitutional. Jackson was freed.

Theon Jackson's case resolved one issue—that a person who would never be competent to stand trial could not be detained indefinitely. Many others are still unresolved. What of a person who might some day be competent to stand trial. How long may he or she be held? Some states set no limits.

---

* New York Criminal Code S730.10(1).
† Jackson v. Indiana, 406 U.S. 715 (1972).

Others, like New York, limit incarceration, depending upon the charge. Federal courts require release after eighteen months. But do even those limited periods violate a person's right to bail and to a speedy trial? And should they count against time served if convicted? Can a person be required to take medications against his or her will in order to be competent to stand trial? Practices in these matters vary enormously across states and are unlikely to be systematically resolved in the near future because such defendants, by definition, often lack the resources to press their claims vigorously.

As a result, some have urged that the notion of incompetence to stand trial be abolished on the grounds that even if impaired, the defendant is better off tried. "Withholding trial often results in an endless prolongation of the incompetent defendant's accused status, and his virtually automatic civil commitment. This is a cruelly ironic way by which to ensure that the permanently incompetent defendant is fairly treated" (Burt and Morris, 1972, p. 75). This view, however, violates the Supreme Court's dictum in *Pate* v. *Robinson* that "the conviction of an accused person while he is legally incompetent violated due process . . ."*

THE SOCIAL AND POLITICAL ABUSE OF ABNORMAL PSYCHOLOGY

Political abuse of diagnosis of abnormality

The ideal underlying clinical psychology and psychiatry is to help humankind, but in various societies at various times, these professions have been used toward political ends. In order to confine or control individuals holding dissident views, some political leaders have sanctioned abuses of personal liberties in the name of psychiatry. In large part, the potential for abuse arises from the very definition of abnormality that was discussed in Chapter 1. There we suggested that whether or not people are seen as abnormal depends on whether they possess a "family resemblance" to other abnormal people. There need not be an identity, or perfect match, between the behaviors of those people and the behaviors of abnormal people; so as long as *some* elements are similar, individuals might be considered abnormal by society. Among the behaviors or elements of abnormality are: whether the person produces discomfort in others, the degree to which his or her behavior is unconventional, and the degree to which the behavior violates idealized standards. If an individual's behavior triggers these criteria, he or she may be labeled abnormal, even though other criteria of abnormality, such as intense suffering, are absent. People who hold different views from those of a society's leaders might be seen (or made to be seen) as unconventional, or in violation of idealized standards. It is therefore easy to consider them abnormal and to overlook the fact that they fail to meet any of the other criteria for abnormality.

Potential for abuse arising from changing categories of abnormality

Beyond the political abuse that relies on the definitional ambiguities of abnormality, the potential for abuse arises from the fact that the meanings of abnormality change dramatically over time. For example, in DSM-II, which was approved by the American Psychiatric Association in 1968, homosexuality was listed as a mental disorder. But new information revealed

* Pate v. Robinson, 383 U.S. 375, 378 (1966).

that as many as 10 percent of the adult population practice homosexuality. The behavior, therefore, was no longer as unconventional as it had seemed, nor did it violate community standards as intensely as it had earlier. Consequently, in 1976, by a vote of its membership, the association decided that homosexuality was no longer a mental disorder. Similarly, in 1966, the American Association for Mental Deficiency reduced the IQ required for designating a person "mentally retarded" from 80 to 70, thereby releasing more than a million people from the retarded category (Bryan and Bryan, 1975).

The potential for abuse of clinical psychology and psychiatry was highlighted again with the publication of DSM-III-R. The task force that proposed that revision also proposed three additional diagnostic categories: *Late luteal phase dysphoric disorder,* a diagnostic mouthful that some of you recognize as "premenstrual syndrome," the physical and emotional changes that are associated with specific phases of the menstrual cycle; the *self-defeating personality disorder,* in which the person "may often avoid or undermine pleasurable experiences, be drawn to situations or relationships in which he or she will suffer, and prevent others from helping him or her"; and the *sadistic personality disorder,* whose essential feature is "a pervasive pattern of cruel, demeaning, and aggressive behavior directed toward other people" (DSM-III-R, pp. 367–74). The task force felt that there was sufficient research and clinical evidence to justify including these categories in the DSM-III-R. But critics felt that "these categories had such a high potential for misuse, particularly against women, that they should not be included" (pp. xxv–xxvi). The critics won. These three disorders are not listed in the formal classification of mental disorders. They are, however, included in the appendix to DSM-III-R in order to facilitate further research.

Changing attitudes of what is normal and what is abnormal

Attitudes toward work, sexuality, manners, the opposite sex, marriage, clothing—indeed, toward most of the significant aspects of social life—have changed over the decades and will continue to change. Canons of appropriate behavior and attitude are fundamental to judgments of normality and abnormality. As these canons change, so will change our notions of what is normal, and what is abnormal.

Power of the "experts"

Potential for abuse arises also from the fact that society endows psychologists and psychiatrists with enormous power. Perry London (1986) says they constitute a "secular priesthood"; Thomas Szasz (1963) sees (and decries) the rise of the "therapeutic state." But any general reservations we might have about psychiatry and psychology often dissolve when our own lives are touched by psychological distress. We tend to accept the views of "experts." Our personal reliance on a practitioner, and our vulnerability to the practitioner's judgments and recommendations, make all clients of psychiatry and psychology particularly vulnerable to abuse. Below we will distinguish broadly between two kinds of potential abuse: abuse by state and abuse by society.

ABUSE BY STATE

Psychiatric diagnosis, subsequent involuntary hospitalization and treatment with neuroleptic drugs have been used to stifle political dissent. Particularly during the past decade, it has been revealed that such political psychiatry is heavily relied upon in the Soviet Union. At least 210 cases of *sane* people who were interned in Soviet prison-hospitals for political reasons have been reported (Bloch and Reddaway, 1977). Others claim even higher figures (see Podrabenek, in Fireside, 1979). Anatoli Koryagin, a Soviet psychiatrist who recently emigrated to the West, has described the Soviet use of psychiatric hospitals and drugs to punish political activists.

How is this done? And how especially in the Soviet Union, where the legal safeguards against abuse of involuntary commitment procedures are clearly stronger than they are in many other countries? The Soviet code, for example, allows the individual's family to nominate one or more psychiatrists to the examining commission; it requires that the family be notified of the results of the examination; and it states that an individual cannot be held for more than three days. Nevertheless, considerable potential for abuse exists, as the experience of the Russian scientist Zhores A. Medvedev indicates.

Medvedev is a talented biologist whose interests run from gerontology (the science of aging), to the sociology and history of science. One of his manuscripts was confiscated by the Soviet secret police during a search of a colleague's apartment. There was nothing illegal about the manuscript, but it had been found amid a group of "samizdat," or underground publications. Medvedev, moreover, was known to be an outspoken scientist, who had been in "trouble" before. In fact, he had been unemployed for more than a year, having been relieved of his post in the Institute of Medical Radiology.

Medvedev was first tricked into a psychiatric interview, which was conducted under the guise of discussing his son. Subsequently, two psychiatrists, as well as several police, arrived at his home. Medvedev was interviewed under quite strained conditions and then forcibly removed to the local psychiatric hospital. He was seen subsequently by several other psychiatrists. He must have appeared generally quite robust to them, for the best they could say was that he had a "psychopathic personality" (the Soviet term for neurotic), "an exaggerated opinion of himself" and that he was "poorly adapted to his social environment." They noted that his writing in recent years was weaker than his earlier work, and observed as a further symptom that Medvedev had shown " 'excessively scrupulous' attention to detail in his general writings" (Medvedev and Medvedev, 1971).

The Soviet prison-hospital at Oryol, southwest of Moscow.

Left: Pyotr Grigorenko. *Right*: Zhores Medvedev.

Medvedev was held for nineteen days, a relatively brief period for these proceedings, and then released. Pyotr Grigorenko suffered a worse fate. Grigorenko was a distinguished general who had served in the Red Army for thirty-five years. At the age of fifty-four, he began to question the policies of the Communist Party of which he was a member. Ultimately, he was remanded for psychiatric examination at Moscow's Serbsky Institute, where his diagnosis read, "Paranoid development of the personality, with reformist ideas arising in the personality, with psychopathic features of the character and the presence of symptoms of arteriosclerosis of the brain." Shortly thereafter, he underwent an examination by a second group of psychiatrists who found him admirably sane and vigorous. But a third commission overruled the second. Grigorenko spent six years in three of the most difficult Soviet "psychoprisons" before he was permitted to emigrate to the United States. (Fireside, 1979)

While some of the psychiatrists who examined Medvedev and Grigorenko may well have subverted scientific knowledge to political expediency, many probably did not. Rather, they were well-known and highly regarded psychiatrists, both within and outside of the Soviet Union who truly believed that these people were ill. These psychiatrists would point out that one symptom of their "illness"—and not, by any means, the only one—was their unconventionality, which consisted in their open questioning and occasional defiance of the "system."

Use of psychiatry for political ends in the U.S.

The unwitting use of psychology and psychiatry for political ends is not a practice that is confined to the Soviet Union. They have also been used in the United States, as shown below:

When the Second World War was over, Ezra Pound, the eminent poet, was taken into custody by the American troops in Italy, returned to the United States, and charged with treason. Pound had lived in fascist Italy during the war and had supported Mussolini. It was alleged that the broadcasts that Pound made from Rome were treasonous. Pound denied the charge, but he never came to trial. Instead, the government and his attorneys agreed that he was incompetent to stand trial. He was therefore remanded to St. Elizabeth's Hospital in Washington, D.C., and effectively imprisoned without trial. Thirteen years later, in 1958, he was still considered "insane," incurably so, but not dangerous to others. He was therefore released.

Left: Ezra Pound was confined in St. Elizabeth's Hospital after being judged incompetent to stand trial for treason. *Right:* This is the section of St. Elizabeth's Hospital where Pound was confined.

All his life, Pound had been an eccentric: enormously conceited, flamboyant, sometimes downright outrageous. But he had never had a brush with the law, nor had he been remanded for psychiatric care. But because his politics were aversive, his eccentricities were invoked to indicate that he was not of sane mind and therefore that he could not stand trial (Torrey, 1983). As you saw in Chapter 7, relatively innocent behaviors change meaning drastically when observed in a diagnostic context. In Pound's case, conceit and flamboyance became "grandiosity of ideas and beliefs," contributing to the psychiatric impression that he was of unsound mind.

Abuse of psychology and psychiatry by the state occurs when the state is threatened by the actions of the individual. Fear underlies the state's abuse. It also underlies abuse by society, to which we now turn.

ABUSE BY SOCIETY

Society's stigma of those seeking psychiatric care

During the 1972 presidential campaign, George McGovern, the front-running Democratic nominee, proposed Senator Thomas Eagleton as his vice-presidential running mate. Eagleton apparently neglected to tell McGovern that he had been treated for depression, either because he viewed that as a private matter or because the stigma of such treatment might deprive him of the candidacy. In the latter, he was right: the press soon learned that Eagleton had undergone treatment and made a national story of it. After much pressure, McGovern took Eagleton off the ticket. There was no question of Eagleton's effectiveness: he had served splendidly as a senator from Missouri. Rather, there was considerable fear that he would weaken the ticket. He was, after all, stigmatized (Rosenhan, 1975; Reich, 1986).

Society stigmatizes ordinary people who have sought psychiatric care, often to the disadvantage of both the individual and society, as the following case indicates:

Myra Grossman had had a difficult childhood and adolescence. Yet she managed to survive well enough to graduate high school, enter college, and be at the very top of her class during her first two years. Conflicts with her parents, however, and a nagging depression continued unabated and, during her third year, she left school to seek treatment. She began seeing a psychotherapist and subsequently entered a private psychiatric hospital. During that year, Myra developed considerable ability to deal with her own distress and her family conflicts. She returned to college, continued to major in both chemistry and psychology, earned her Phi Beta Kappa in her junior year, and graduated magna cum laude.

During her senior year, she applied to medical school. Her Medical College Aptitude Test (MCAT) scores were extraordinarily high, and she had won a New York State Regent's Medical Scholarship. But she was rejected by all thirteen schools to which she had applied.

She consulted an attorney, and they jointly decided to concentrate on the "easiest" school that had rejected her. During the trial, it became known that fewer than 8 percent of those admitted to this school had won the Regent's Medical Scholarship, that none had been admitted to Phi Beta Kappa, and that she possibly had the highest MCAT scores of any applicant. She was an attractive person, obviously well motivated, clearly bright. Why then had she been rejected? Clearly, it was because of her prior psychiatric hospitalization.

Ms. Grossman and her attorney marshaled clear evidence that she was quite well integrated psychologically. Five psychiatrists and a psychologist testified in effect that she was the better for her prior troubles, and that they had no doubt that she could successfully complete medical school and become a first-rate doctor. She and her attorney successfully demolished the contention that she might still suffer from her prior "illness." But still, the judge ruled against her. Ms. Grossman might have appealed that decision, and might well have won her appeal had not a far better medical school admitted her when the ruling came down. (Ennis, 1972)

SUMMARY

1. The constitutional privileges that are available to ordinary citizens are not extended to the severely distressed, who can be deprived of liberty through *involuntary commitment,* often without trial.

2. Depending on the state in which they reside, individuals who are psychologically disabled can be hospitalized involuntarily, provided they either experience impaired judgment, are in need of treatment, are dangerous to themselves or others, or suffer from a "grave disability." The notion of dangerousness, especially, is rife with scientific, legal, and moral problems.

3. Involuntary commitment deprives a person of liberty. Before it occurs, *clear and convincing* evidence must be marshaled that indicates that the person requires hospitalization.

4. Several significant court decisions have held that those committed to psychiatric hospitals have a *right to treatment* that includes individual diagnosis and the preparation of a treatment plan that is periodically reviewed. One negative consequence of right-to-treatment decisions has been the decline in support for mental health programs, as the states often prefer to cut back their support for these programs rather than incurring the additional costs of implementing proper treatment. A positive result of deinstitutionalization, however, has been the growth of the patients' rights movement, including self-help organizations and patients' rights advocates.

5. *Criminal commitment* can occur either because a person was "insane" at the time of the crime, or because he or she is presently psychologically incompetent to stand trial.

6. The *insanity defense* requires that the defendant was wholly or partially irrational when the crime took place, and that this irrationality affected his or her behavior. While the insanity defense seemingly protects those who commit crimes while distressed, the fact is that such people are commonly sent to prison-hospitals, where care is worse than in prisons themselves, and incarceration longer. Because being indefinitely committed to a psychiatric hospital is often worse than going to prison, the insanity defense is rarely used.

7. Historically, there have been three views of the insanity defense: the M'Naghten "right-wrong" test, the Durham "product of mental disease test, and the American Law Institute (ALI) "appreciate and conform" rule. Another standard that has been adopted by some states is "guilty but mentally ill"; this standard, however, is a contradiction in terms. Today, there is no uniform insanity defense in Western countries, although in the United States an increasing number of states, as well as the federal courts, favor the American Law Institute formulation.

8. The notion of *competence to stand trial* is rooted in the right of every person to defend himself against accusations. A person judged incompetent to stand trial is sent to an institution for the criminally insane until he is able to be tried, which often means a long incarceration. The courts have recently decided that people who can never become competent to stand trial need not be "hospitalized" forever. But there is still no uniform practice regarding how long those who are treatably incompetent may be committed, and whether the time spent in such commitment is later to be subtracted from the defendant's sentence.

9. Psychiatry and psychology are particularly prone to social and political abuses. Both in the United States and the Soviet Union, people who should have been given their day in court have been summarily committed to psychiatric hospitals, there to languish, often for many years.

10. Considerable stigma attaches to seeking or requiring psychological care. That stigma may continue long after the psychological problem has been solved.

A Consumer's Guide to Psychological Treatment

W HAT does one do when psychological problems arise? The answer to that question has changed with the times. A century ago, people with problems might have been sent off to a good friend, a relative, or perhaps a clergyman who would have offered them sympathy, wisdom, and prayer. But today, as one writer observes, we have a "secular priesthood." a panoply of professional and nonprofessional counselors and therapists, all of whom stand ready to deal with the psychological troubles that were once the province of family and church (London, 1986). One in five people will seek the advice of these therapists sometime during their lives, fully half of them for problems that are quite serious and painful. How should they go about it? From the many available therapists and therapies, how should they choose the ones that are most likely to help, and help quickly?

In this chapter, we bring together a group of issues associated with treatment, often issues that have been remarked upon earlier. First, we describe those who treat psychological difficulties. We then consider the ingredients that all good therapies have in common, regardless of whether they are biological, psychodynamic, cognitive, behavioral, or humanistic, and regardless of whether they are practiced by highly trained professionals or by nonprofessionals. Understanding these ingredients should enable anyone to make a better choice of a therapist, and also to avoid the pitfalls of poorly practiced treatments (which are also described in this chapter). Subsequently, we recommend the best treatments for certain kinds of problems. Our recommendations are based on good evidence where that exists and on clinical wisdom where it does not. Finally, we discuss community psychological approaches that are concerned with prevention as much as treatment, and with social and economic remedies as much as psychological ones.

© 1966 United Feature Syndicate, Inc.

WHO TREATS?

Distinguishing
those who treat
psychological
difficulties

A large number of people and disciplines are concerned with treating psychological difficulties, and it is sometimes hard to distinguish among them. Some professional training takes many years to acquire, while training in other skills may require just a few months. Some therapists are certified and licensed in the states in which they reside. Others are not. A potential client is always entitled to inquire carefully about the training, licenses, certificates, and experience of anyone he or she consults. Do not be embarrassed to do this. It is equivalent to looking carefully at all the rooms in a house before purchasing or renting it. Professionals and nonprofessionals alike respect these questions; they spare all concerned from making costly mistakes.

Psychologists who offer psychological assessment and therapeutic services have obtained advanced graduate training in clinical, counseling, or school psychology. Usually, but not invariably, they hold a Ph.D. (Doctor of Philosophy) or a Psy.D. (Doctor of Psychology) degree. The former is a *scientific* degree. It emphasizes training in research, as well as clinical diagnosis and psychotherapy. The Psy.D. is an *applied* degree that certifies training mainly in diagnosis and treatment. Both degrees require a minimum of four or five years of study *beyond* the bachelor's degree, and include, or are immediately followed by, an extensive applied internship. In addition, nearly all states require psychologists to pass a licensing or certification examination.

Not all psychologists are qualified to assess and treat. Only those trained in clinical, counseling, or school psychology should be consulted. *Clinical psychologists* work mainly with people who suffer psychological difficulties, *counseling psychologists* deal with vocational problems as well, while *school psychologists* focus on academic difficulties, mainly with young people.

Psychiatrists are physicians who, after completing college, have earned a medical degree, and have completed a three-year residency in a mental health facility. Subsequently, many but not all psychiatrists take an examination in psychiatry and become board-certified. Psychiatrists are the only psychological professionals who can prescribe medications and administer such treatments as electroshock. Of course, psychiatrists often make use of psychological treatments as well.

Psychiatric social workers have completed a two-year postgraduate program in individual and group social work techniques, which includes extensive training in interviewing and in treatment.

Psychiatric nurses are centrally concerned with the care of hospitalized psychiatric patients. Beyond their basic courses in nursing, they receive training in psychiatry and psychology, as well as supervised experience on a

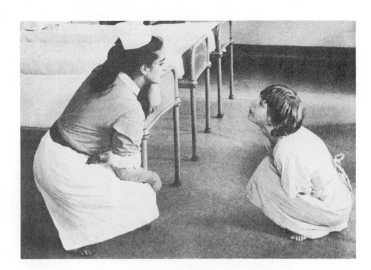

Psychiatric nurses are trained in psychiatry and psychology and care for hospitalized patients.

psychiatric unit. On any psychiatric ward, the nurse is usually the person in charge of ward management, housekeeping, and recreation, as well as the one who administers medication.

Psychoanalysts are fully trained mental health professionals—psychiatrists mainly, but also psychologists, social workers, and sometimes clergy —who have undertaken further training in a specific treatment approach, psychoanalysis and psychoanalytic psychotherapy. Such training is offered in psychoanalytic training institutes, and requires several years to complete. Psychoanalysts-in-training must undergo their own personal psychoanalysis, as well as treat several clients psychoanalytically, before they are considered fully accredited.

The *clergy,* that is, ministers, rabbis, and priests, are increasingly being trained to do personal counseling, not only with problems of a distinctly religious nature, but often with problems that go quite beyond those. While the quality of training in pastoral counseling, as it is sometimes called is highly variable, many clergy augment their seminary training in graduate departments of psychology or social work, and in postgraduate institutes.

Psychiatric attendants or *aides* are paraprofessionals who work exclusively in psychiatric hospitals. Their training can vary widely. Some are high school graduates. Others have attended community colleges, many of which train mental health paraprofessionals to work on psychiatric wards. Most attendants receive brief on-the-job training to work with the severely disturbed. From the viewpoint of hospitalized patients, the attendants are the most important people in their day-to-day lives. It is the attendants with whom they interact most, and who determine whether their experience in the hospital will be pleasant or unpleasant.

Skills therapists also work in psychiatric hospitals and have special abilities in the work-related, recreational, or artistic realms. These include occupational, art, and educational therapists, music and dance therapists, as well as recreational therapists of all kinds. These therapists enable patients to pass time pleasantly and constructively. They also provide a setting for developing psychosocial skills and for expressing personal problems. A dance therapist, for example, may enable a person to express through dance feelings that cannot otherwise be expressed verbally.

Marriage and family counselors deal with relationship problems that arise within the family. These therapists usually have postgraduate training, but commonly they do not possess doctoral degrees. The quality of their training is highly variable.

The provision of therapeutic services has become a big business that has spawned a host of nonprofessional therapists during the past decade or two. Massage therapists, hypnotherapists, primal therapists, Zen therapists, and bioenergetic therapists, are among those who, for want of a better term, we call *miscellaneous therapists.* Becoming one or another of these therapists may require little or much training. But it is not formal training at a recognized academic or medical institution. Commonly, the government neither licenses these therapists nor certifies their skills, nor are there professional organizations that control their activities. Finally, by and large what they offer has not been evaluated for therapeutic effectiveness. As a result, *caveat emptor*—client, beware!

Here a marriage counselor is treating a couple for problems in their relationship.

> A young man had been "tight and tense" for more than two years when he began to experience paranoid delusions and hallucinations. He was referred by a friend to a massage therapist, who treated the client with deep massage while encouraging him to recall "the memories that are stored in your muscles and bones." This treatment continued for eighteen months. The man's condition deteriorated until finally he became so discouraged and disordered that he required hospitalization. Had he been seen earlier by a trained therapist, there seems little doubt that a combination of drugs and counseling would have brought about improvement in short order.

Self-help groups

Several nonprofessional peer self-help groups exist to help overcome specific problems, and these groups appear to be quite effective. Alcoholics Anonymous (AA) is one such group; Weight Watchers and TOPS (Take Off Pounds Sensibly) are others. Similar problem-oriented groups, such as Daytop Village and Phoenix House, exist for drug addicts.

One type of self-help group deserves special note, and that is the consciousness raising (CR) or "rap" group. This form of self-help grew originally out of the political needs of minority groups, and it now extends to women, the elderly (e.g., The Gray Panthers), homosexuals (e.g., Gay Liberation), and a variety of mental patient groups. Fundamentally, such groups are political and intellectual. Through the common exploration of "personal" problems, group members come to understand that their difficulties are often shared by others. The recognition that painful individual problems are neither unique nor idiosyncratic encourages members to seek larger solutions to these problems, often through social and political action.

> Jane Williams experienced enormous discomfort at her office. Her boss continually put his arm around her and frequently suggested that they see each other after work. At first, Jane felt that she had somehow provoked his interest. Resolving to put an end to his advances, she dressed conservatively for work and kept a professional distance. To no avail. Finally, with great embarrassment, she mentioned the problem at a meeting of a women's group to which she belonged, and she was surprised to find that many of her friends had had the same experience. The fact that the problem was not idiosyncratic gave her considerable comfort, and subsequently, a diplomatic visit to the personnel office brought about a much-hoped-for transfer to another department.

THE COMMON INGREDIENTS OF THERAPY

Psychological therapy consists of a systematic series of interactions between a trained therapist who has been authorized by society to minister to psychological problems, and one or more clients who are troubled, or troubling others, because of such problems. The goal of psychological therapy is to produce cognitive, emotional, and behavioral changes that will alleviate those problems. While professional therapists are trained for the job, and paid as well, that should not blind us to the fact that there are strong similarities between the ways they function and the manner in which friends, relatives, and clergy dealt with those problems in earlier times and continue to deal with them today.

Need for a therapeutic relationship

In fact, it would be a serious mistake to identify treatment wholly with the training of the therapist and the nature of the treatment he or she dispenses, for there is much more to treatment than that. In order for treatment to be maximally effective, a therapeutic relationship needs to be established, one that is voluntary and cooperative and that maximally fulfills the expectations of each participant. Only rarely do clients enter treatment suddenly or lightly. The decision to seek professional help is commonly preceded by agonizing conflict, conflict that may last for months or years. To begin with, most people try to solve their problems by themselves. Then, they may seek out parents, teachers, ministers, and friends. But it is only when all else fails that they seek professional treatment. And then, they come with a headful of hopes, expectations, and information; some of it accurate, some inaccurate, and much of it likely to affect the course of treatment.

Unlike many other transactions, the effectiveness of the therapeutic relationship depends heavily for its success on the free choices, hopes, expectations, and relationships of the participants. You can have your shoes redone by the neighborhood cobbler and neither your personal view of him nor his of you matters for the success of that venture; only his cobbling skill counts. Not so in psychological treatment. There, a host of "common treatment factors" play a large role in determining outcome (Kazdin, 1979). The success of highly skilled therapists is augmented massively, or greatly reduced, by the interplay of such common treatment factors as the free choices of the client, his or her hopes and expectations, the personal qualities of the therapist, and the match between those qualities and the needs of the client. We begin with the matter of free choice because choice affects the therapeutic relationship from the very outset.

FREE CHOICE AND TREATMENT

Entering treatment willingly and fully informed

You can bring a horse to water, the saying goes, but you can't make it drink. That adage holds for psychological treatment, too. Clinical experience strongly suggests that children who are dragged unwillingly into treatment, spouses who enter marriage therapy under threat of divorce, and patients who are involuntarily committed to psychiatric hospitals, all suffer substantial deficits in motivation and understanding that make treatment less effective. Sometimes coercive encouragement is all that is available, but the best way to enter treatment is willingly and fully informed; any other way substantially diminishes the likelihood of successful outcome, regardless of the kind of therapy.

The role of choice and volition in therapeutic outcome was splendidly demonstrated by Devine and Fernald (1973). Clients who suffered snake phobias were shown films of four possible treatments. Some clients were permitted to choose the treatment they preferred; others were randomly assigned to treatment; and yet a third group was required to undergo a nonpreferred treatment. Those who received the treatment they preferred had the more successful therapeutic experience. In selecting their own treatment, clients were able to exercise control over a portion of the therapy process, and this sense of control (see Chapter 5) may well have influenced therapeutic outcome.

Clients who are forced into treatment likely will view it as a mere exercise in compliance, or a punishment. Unless time and effort are taken to convince them otherwise, treatment will fail. Conversely, those who enter treatment of their own free choice are more likely to benefit from it. Their hopes and expectations are themselves curative, greatly augmenting the effectiveness of any treatment. We therefore turn to the nature of hopes and expectations in therapy.

HOPES AND EXPECTATIONS

Role of future expectations on experiences and behaviors in present

A unique characteristic of humans is that their expectations about the future powerfully affect their experiences and behaviors in the present (Frank, 1978). The hope of eventual salvation has sustained countless people, enabling them to endure lifetimes of misery. For others, as we saw in Chapter 11, the belief that the future is hopeless has intensified their depression. In similar fashion, expectations strongly affect psychological treatment. "Expectation . . . coloured by hope and faith," Freud wrote, "is an effective force with which we have to reckon . . . in *all* our attempts at treatment and cure" (Freud, 1905/1976, p. 289).

MOLDING CLIENT EXPECTATIONS

Clients and therapists often have distorted expectations of each other that may impede therapeutic progress. Insight therapists, for example, expect clients to talk about their feelings, experiences, and often, their dreams. But clients, especially those from lower-class backgrounds, tend to talk about their psychological symptoms precisely as they might describe a sore throat to a physician. Their expectations about how therapists behave are frustrated when they are asked about feelings and dreams. Conversely, therapists gain the impression that clients will not profit from treatment when the clients persist in merely describing their ailments and when they continue to be reluctant to discuss feelings and dreams. One result of these jointly disappointed expectations is that lower-class clients drop out of insight therapy at a considerably higher rate than middle- and upper-class clients.

Role Induction Interview

To deal with this problem, Jerome Frank and his colleagues devised a Role Induction Interview, during which clients' expectations about treatment could be molded (Hoehn-Saric, Frank, Imber, Nash, Stone, and Battle, 1964; Nash, Hoehn-Saric, Battle, Stone, Imber, and Frank, 1965; Orne and Wender, 1968). In a controlled study, lower-class clients were interviewed briefly before entering treatment and told what they could expect. Psychotherapy, they were told, is a way of learning to deal more effectively with life's problems, but it takes time and practice to implement what is learned. They were told that four months would be needed before improvement was seen, and even then, that they would still have problems, though they would be coping more effectively. Further, they were told that the therapist would talk very little, but would listen carefully and try to understand the problems. They were advised that they were to talk freely, describe fantasies and daydreams, express feelings, and especially, feelings toward the therapist. The concept of resistance was explained in everyday language and was described to them as evidence that the client was approaching and dealing with issues that were both significant for progress and difficult to face. Such difficulties were to be viewed as a positive sign of progress. A second group of clients was given no information on what they might expect during treatment.

The therapeutic results for clients who participated in the brief interview were remarkable. First, their drop-out rate declined precipitously. Therapists were behaving the way they were supposed to behave, so clients experienced less need to terminate. Second, therapist ratings of clients' improvement were considerably higher for these clients than for the control group that had not gone through the Role Induction Interview. Finally, clients who had experienced the Role Induction Interview rated themselves as considerably more improved on their target complaints than did those who had not participated in the interview.

The Role Induction Interview may have brought client expectations in line with their therapists' expectations, led clients to behave in ways that increased therapist optimism about, and liking for them. These considerations correlate highly with clients' tendency to remain in therapy (Rosenzweig and Forman, 1974; Shapiro, 1974), and with therapist ratings of client improvement (Shapiro, Struening, Shapiro, and Barten, 1976).

Anticipatory socialization of the sort that is conveyed in such interviews has been found to affect clients and therapists in a wide variety of settings. Hospitalized lower-class patients benefit from it (Heitler, 1973), as do clients in group therapy (Yalom, Houts, Newell, and Rand, 1967). Moreover, films that portray therapy sessions, and even tape recordings of therapy sessions, work as well as informative interviews to prepare clients for treatment (Truax, Shapiro, and Wargo, 1968; Strupp and Bloxom, 1973). In short, any information that enables clients to develop reasonable expectations about treatment facilitates treatment.

While shared expectations of clients and therapists regarding the process of treatment clearly affect its outcome, so too do expectations regarding the outcome itself. Indeed, the belief that treatment will be effective is itself such a powerful treatment that the mere anticipation of cure often brings at least momentary relief and, not uncommonly, permanent gains. Such cures are termed "placebo effects."

THE PLACEBO EFFECT

In medicine, a placebo is a pharmacologically inert substance, and the *placebo effect* describes positive treatment outcomes that result from the administration of such substances. But placebo effects, as we have seen in

Chapter 6, occur with surprising regularity in a variety of settings and may be produced not only by inert substances but also by a patient's belief that treatment of any kind has been undertaken. Beecher (1961) reported that about 40 percent of patients who were suffering from a painful heart disease called angina pectoris experienced marked relief from their symptoms after merely undergoing a mock operation! In a later study, Ross found that 60 percent of patients who had undergone surgery to improve their blood circulation showed clinical improvement, even though the surgery may have left the blood supply to the heart unchanged and, in fact, may have reduced it (Ross, 1976, cited in Frank, 1978).

Powerful effects
of placebos

Placebos are sometimes as effective as psychotropic medications in treating psychological disorders, with their dosage curves showing similar characteristics. In the first part of a double-blind study, about 35 percent of patients who were given either drugs or placebos at a particular dosage level improved. Subsequently, the dosages of drugs and placebos were doubled in the second part of the study, and improvement rates jumped to 66 percent for patients on active drugs, and 76 percent for those on placebos (Lowinger and Dobie, 1969).

What is it that makes the placebo, a mere inert substance, so powerful? The power of the placebo resides in the expectation that positive results will accrue from a particular treatment (Cousins, 1979). So long as the client believes that the treatment works, it will likely have some positive effect. In no way are these effects shams or fakes, or merely the results of the gullibility of impressionable clients. Rather, they appear to be powerful treatments in themselves for reasons that are not yet fully understood. Current speculation suggests that placebos work on the immune system and that their effects are mediated through a group of enzymes called endorphins. Endorphins have been called "the brain's opiates." They affect how individuals subjectively experience pain and mood, and they may be produced when one expects to become well and able to cope.

Characteristics of Therapist-Client Interactions

Free choice, rational expectations, and effective hope are crucial for therapeutic success. But they are not sufficient. The therapist's personal characteristics, and how those characteristics fulfill the needs and expectations of the clients, are necessary ingredients for successful therapy. Not all characteristics play a central role in treatment, but some, such as empathy, warmth, and genuineness seem absolutely necessary. We turn to those characteristics now.

THERAPIST EMPATHY, WARMTH, AND GENUINENESS

Therapist
characteristics
positively
affecting
outcome

Therapist empathy, warmth, and personal genuineness facilitate the therapeutic relationship and, presumably, increase the likelihood of a positive outcome. *Empathy* describes the "ability of the therapist accurately and sensitively to understand experiences and feelings and their meaning to the client during the moment-to-moment encounter of psychotherapy" (Rogers and Truax, 1967, p. 104). *Warmth* is manifest in the therapeutic relationship when "the therapist communicates to his client a deep and genuine caring for him as a person with human potentialities, a caring

For treatment to be maximally effective, a therapeutic relationship must be established between therapist and client. Such a relationship is more likely to develop where there is therapist empathy, warmth, and personal genuineness, as shown here.

uncontaminated by evaluations of his thoughts, feelings, or behaviors" (Rogers and Truax, 1967, p. 102). Therapist *genuineness* means precisely that: the therapist avoids communicating in a phony, "professional," or defensive manner. He is "freely and deeply himself" (Truax and Carkhuff, 1967). Obviously, a therapist can neither be empathic nor warm if he or she is not being genuine. Obviously, too, when shopping for a therapist, genuineness may be one of the first things to look for.

It is generally believed that warmth, empathy, and genuineness are necessary preconditions for successful therapy, though they do not guarantee it (Gurman, 1977; Mitchell, Bozarth, and Krauft, 1977). These characteristics would seem to apply to all kinds of therapists, regardless of their orientation. For example, with regard to behavior therapy (which concentrates on changing immediate behavior rather than the exploration of feelings), Marks and Gelder (1966) have argued that the single most important ingredient in determining outcome is the relationship between client and therapist. Moreover, Morris and Suckerman (1974a, 1974b) have shown that "warm" therapists are far more effective than "cold" ones in utilizing the behavioral techniques of desensitization for snake phobias.

THERAPIST EXPERIENCE

The relationship between therapist experience and outcome

Beyond warmth, empathy, and genuineness, are there other therapist characteristics that facilitate treatment? There probably are, but their meaning is not entirely clear. Consider the matter of experience. Some studies find that experienced therapists promote greater improvement among their clients than do inexperienced ones (Myers and Auld, 1955; Katz, Lorr, and Rubinstein, 1958; Cartwright and Vogel, 1960; Barrett-Lennard, 1962; Strupp, Wallach, and Wogan, 1964; Scher, 1975). To the extent that empathy and genuineness are requisites for therapeutic progress, they are likely to be found in greater quantity among experienced therapists, if only because experience makes one more comfortable and competent in that role. Nonetheless, other studies have found no relationship between therapist experience and client outcome (Fiske, Cartwright, and Kirtner, 1964; Fiske and Goodman, 1965; Strupp, Fox, and Lessler, 1969; Auerbach and Johnson, 1977). Relatively inexperienced therapists may bring enormous enthusiasm to treatment, thereby compensating for the fact that they are relatively "green." Conversely, experienced therapists may become tired and less empathic with time. Experience, then, is no uniform guarantor of excellence in therapy, although there are no studies in which inexperienced therapists were more successful than experienced ones.

THE HELPING ALLIANCE

Shared goals of treatment

A powerfully significant determinant of the outcome of psychotherapy is the therapist's capacity to establish with the patient a ***therapeutic alliance,*** a joint sense of the goals of therapy and how they can best be achieved (Alexander and Luborsky, 1984; Luborsky, McLellan, Woody, O'Brien, and Auerbach, 1985). Regardless of therapeutic orientation, therapists who are able to engender such a cooperative spirit about the shared goals of treatment are much more likely to have successful outcomes.

OTHER CONCERNS

Matching therapist and client

Other factors that might possibly influence therapeutic outcome, such as gender, race, social class, sexual preference, religious involvement, and marital status, have not been fully investigated yet. Some studies have found that opposite-sex dyads communicate more effectively with each other (Cartwright and Lerner, 1963; Brooks, 1974; Jones and Zoppel, 1982); others (e.g., Mendelsohn and Geller, 1963) have suggested that this is not the case. These are matters where good sense is more important than research findings. A woman whose problems touch on matters of feminism, for example, may want to see a female therapist. But because all female therapists are not feminists nor even sympathetic to feminist concerns, a sensitive male therapist may be as effective (Rawlings and Carter, 1977). Gender alone is not a certain guide to insight and understanding.

A good therapist may well be sensitive to, and understanding of, a wide variety of concerns and issues that reach beyond the therapist's own gender, sexual orientation, religious preference, and the like. But if a particular type of therapist is wanted, demand may exceed supply. For example, female therapists are in short supply—about seven out of ten therapists are male, despite the fact that the majority of clients are female. Therapists come mainly from the upper middle class; clients from all classes. Nearly all therapists are white, but clients come in all colors. In a very large city, a black woman who wants to consult a black feminist therapist may be lucky enough to find one. But people in small cities and towns, where few qualified therapists practice, are not likely to be lucky enough to find therapists with all the desired characteristics, as the following case demonstrates:

> She is the intelligent, well-educated mother of two small children, wife of a popular internist in a small, remote town. Increasingly, she finds herself depressed. Worse, she finds herself jealous of her husband, who gets all of the community rewards ("Oh Dr. Barker—isn't he just wonderful . . .") while she gets the diapers. The very intensity of her feelings troubles her. With the passage of time, she hurts more and more and understands less and less. She tries to talk to her husband— really, her best friend—but he reacts guiltily and defensively. He really does love

his work and finds it hard to understand that his pleasure and success should cause her such pain.

What to do? Somehow, she feels this is a "woman's problem" and would prefer to see a woman. In fact, she would prefer to see a woman who is a feminist, one who understands something of the social and political aspects of womanhood, in addition to the psychological ones. Most of all, she wants someone to reassure her that though she is quite upset, she is not crazy, and that her feelings have some basis in reality.

There are two therapists in her town, both men, both colleagues of her husband. One of them is "fresh out" of his residency. She finds him too young. The other is well into his seventies. He seems too old. She has other concerns about these therapists as well, but already her dilemma is clear. There are no nonprofessional alternatives in town: no women's groups in which these matters could be discussed, no sympathetic clergy. What should she do?

Perhaps you can find a solution to her dilemma. We cannot. Some problems simply do not lend themselves to easy solutions, and this is one of them. She might try one of the psychiatrists in town, and begin by discussing her reservations and discomforts about working with him. He *might* be able to get her over these hurdles, but then again he might not. Alternately, she might wait until spring thaws the mountain snow, and travel some three hours to a larger city. Even then, there is no guarantee that the help she wants would be found. For some problems there are no easy solutions.

AVOIDING THE "PSYCHONOXIOUS" THERAPIST

Factors to beware of

Most therapists are professionals in whom one can trust. A few, however, are not. Whether from defects of training, character, or personality, they are unlikely to help and more likely to harm. In addition, there are therapists who, while useful to some, are harmful to others. Below follow some ways in which to detect such therapists (Segal, 1968; Haley, 1969).

☐ NEVER WORK WITH A THERAPIST WHOSE PERSONALITY IS DISTASTEFUL. If you find the therapist is aggressive, frequently angry or sadistic, impatient, challenging, or nasty, find another! Such therapists, regardless of their reputation, are unlikely to be able to do any good, and can often do considerable harm, as in the following case:

> One therapist spent two years mocking a client's passivity, appearing to retch every time she said something sweet. It was his conviction that this client needed to know how others felt about her, and he feigned retching in order to demonstrate. But the effects on the client were simply disastrous. Intimidated by him as she was by others, she became all the more sweetly passive, hoping thereby to avert yet another disaster. Only the insistence of friends made her terminate the treatment. While one ought not to expect a therapist to be constantly agreeable and protective, a therapist should appear to respect the client and to care for his or her well-being.

☐ BEWARE OF SEXUAL EXPLOITATION. A substantial minority of psychologists and psychiatrists acknowledge having had a sexual relationship with one or more clients (Keith-Spiegel, 1977). Occasionally, such relationships are rationalized by the therapists on the grounds that they teach clients to enjoy "intimacy" or simply to make love. But these practices have more to do with the needs of the therapists and their own psychological immaturity than any treatment goal. There is no evidence that physical intimacy with one's therapist works for the client's benefit. In fact, close to 20 percent of the malpractice suits against therapists, and nearly half of the payouts are occasioned by allegations of sexual impropriety (Bales, 1987). When intimacy is suggested, the client should terminate treatment.

☐ AVOID SUSPICIOUSLY HIGH FEES. One of the most self-serving myths among psychologists and psychiatrists is that the more the client pays, the more progress he or she makes in treatment. Pure nonsense! Some of the finest clinicians work in colleges and community clinics where fees are low or nonexistent. If you feel you are being overcharged, discuss the matter with your therapist. If you can't reach a comfortable understanding, seek help elsewhere.

☐ KNOW YOUR MEDICINES. If a psychiatrist has prescribed psychoactive drugs (and only a physician can prescribe such drugs), you deserve to know the names of the drugs that are being prescribed, what symptoms they are supposed to treat, how long it will be before effects are seen, how long you will have to take them, and what the short-term and long-term side effects of these drugs are. Discuss these matters carefully with the psychiatrist, and read about them in a current edition of a lay text on medication, such as *The Essential Guide to Prescription Drugs,* published by Consumers Union (Long, 1985). Anything less than a frank and open response to your inquiries by the therapist violates the requirements of effective treatment that were discussed earlier, and may be dangerous to your health besides.

☐ BE FREE TO QUESTION. Sometimes treatment bogs down. Clients, and often therapists, feel that insufficient progress is being made. If you feel that way, raise the matter openly with the therapist. Often progress is blocked because the client has hit a ***resistance:*** a transient inability to deal with a significant issue. Such resistances may seem insurmountable, but they are commonly signs that progress is about to be made. Talking about feelings openly often helps to overcome resistances.

But sometimes progress is blocked, not by resistance, but by the therapist's lack of skill. Not all therapists can help all clients all the time. A therapist may occasionally lack the ability to help the client surmount particular kinds of difficulties. Again, open discussion of the stalemate can yield insight and resolution. If it does not, ask for a consultation with another professional. An objective third party can frequently shed light on the causes of stalemate, enabling client and therapist to continue their progress.

If the therapist refuses a consultation, however, seek help elsewhere. And surely if at any time during treatment, the therapist forbids discussing treatment with anyone else, question the therapist carefully. Such admonitions, often given on the grounds that therapy is a private matter, are equally often self-serving. They may be designed to protect the therapist, not you.

☐ SPECIFY TREATMENT GOALS. The goals of treatment should be specified early in the treatment process. Otherwise, the treatment risks floundering. Many therapists arrive at an agreement with clients, not only regarding goals of treatment, but also how long treatment will last. That agreement is put in the form of a contract that serves to remind each party of their aims and obligations. Though not universal by any means, such contracts appear to hasten progress in treatment, especially when time seems to be running out. Then, clients really bend their energies toward getting the most out of what time is left. When a therapist cannot specify the goals of treatment fairly concretely, or when client and therapist do not share a common understanding of these matters, it may be wiser to seek help elsewhere.

Avoiding the wrong therapist reduces the probability of dissatisfaction and harm. And finding the right therapist, one who fulfills expectations and promotes effective hope, goes a long way toward ensuring therapeutic progress. But it does not guarantee such progress by any means. Beyond the personal qualities of the therapist are the techniques that he or she employs. Some of these techniques are highly effective for certain kinds of problems. Others are less effective.

THERAPEUTIC EFFECTIVENESS

Assessing effectiveness of treatment

Therapists vary in their effectiveness (Luborsky, Crits-Cristoph, McLellan, Woody, Piper, Liberman, Imber, and Pilkonis, 1986). Broadly speaking, there are three ways in which one can assess the effectiveness of therapy. First, one can collect opinions regarding satisfaction with treatment from the client, as well as from his or her family, friends, and employers. Second, one can examine changes on a variety of personality measures, some of which were discussed in Chapter 7. Third, one can look at target behaviors —the behaviors that brought the client into treatment and that treatment is supposed to change. In a proper evaluation study, several measures of each of these types will be used. But some of these measures seem weaker than others.

PERSONAL SATISFACTION

Client satisfaction

Consider satisfaction. The fact of the matter is that most clients express considerable satisfaction with treatment. Indeed, it is rare to encounter someone who says that his therapy did him or her no good. Yet, client satisfaction, while important, cannot be a significant criterion of effectiveness. People can be satisfied for a variety of reasons having little or nothing to do with whether they were changed in significant ways. They may be inclined to indicate that they were satisfied merely because they had spent a good deal of time and money on treatment. It would make them quite uncomfortable to believe that it had all been for nought. Because their investment is so large, they may be motivated to seek genuine reasons for satisfaction, such as "I learned a lot about myself," even though those reasons are unrelated to the ones that brought them into treatment in the first place.

PERSONALITY CHANGE

Global assessments of personality change

Global assessments of personality change are a second index of the effectiveness of treatment. Such measures are taken at the outset of therapy, often during therapy, and surely at the end of it, with "improvement" (or "deterioration") being attributed to the effects of the treatment.

There is often, however, a mismatch between what the patient wants to change and what therapy does change: people rarely enter treatment to have their personalities changed (London, 1986). Rather, they seek help because they suffer a particular problem: they find it difficult to find and hold a job, hard to sustain a loving relationship, uncomfortable to be in school. They present *problems,* and it is those problems that they want to eliminate. Were it demonstrable that their problems arose from underlying personality difficulties, much as fever arises from an underlying virus, one would have little to complain about. But the relationship between presenting problems and the global personality characteristics that are said to underlie them has yet to be demonstrated.

Even if a patient consciously did want to have his personality changed, this would be a difficult task. Rather, the therapist is better able to focus on treating behaviors or feelings, and this may indirectly lead to personality change. Thus, a person who is unassertive may also experience low self-esteem. Merely training him or her to be more assertive may have dramatically positive effects on self-esteem.

BEHAVIORS

Changed
behaviors

Examining the impact of treatment on target behaviors is one of the most effective ways to assess treatment outcome. This criterion involves a careful assessment of the problems the client presents at the outset of treatment, with further similar assessments during and at the end of treatment. These assessments may be conducted jointly by client and therapist, and they may also be conducted by outside "blind" evaluators. Their hallmark, however, is that they are precise and replicable, and they stay quite close to the client's initial complaints.

These kinds of assessments are the benchmark of the action therapies, and they are increasingly being used with the insight therapies. But these assessments are not entirely without hazards. Some behaviors are elusive and difficult to measure with precision and reliability. Problems of meaning are among these. Some complaints, moreover, are very complex and intertwined. The presence of multiple phobias, for example, which extend over a range of environments and stimuli, makes assessment complex and difficult. In the main, however, behavioral change, where it can be assessed, is the "kingpin" of measures of therapeutic effectiveness.

THE VARIETY OF TREATMENT

Growing number
of therapies

It has recently been estimated that clients can choose from among 130 different "brands" of therapy (Parloff, 1976). Each year the number of therapies grows. And, of course, each "therapy" has its loyal adherents who confidently proclaim its efficacy for a host of problems. Behavior modification, Rolfing, insight therapy, rebirthing, cognitive therapy, lithium, flooding—these and dozens more are possible choices. Unfortunately, it is extremely difficult to make informed choices. Claims for success are broad but the evidence is slim. Only a few controlled tests have been conducted to assess the effectiveness of particular therapies, and even fewer tests have been done to compare the relative efficacy of various treatments. Equally important, little is known about the possible harmful effects a therapy might have. There is no protection for the consumer of therapy analogous to the protection afforded the consumer of drugs. The Federal Drug Administration imposes stringent testing procedures on all new drugs *before* they can be marketed: they must be effective; they must be relatively harmless; side effects must be clearly stated. No governmental agency acts as watchdog in the case of psychotherapy. Claims can be made with no concern for evidence.

Nonetheless, choices have to be made. In the following section, we discuss some of the more prevalent forms of psychotherapy. After a description of the unique goals and methods of particular therapies, we turn to an examination of the kinds of problems that are best addressed by one or another treatment. Although not an encyclopedic guide to all existing therapies, this overview will provide familiarity with the issue to consider when a choice must be made.

SPECIFIC VS. GLOBAL THERAPIES

It is rare that clients enter psychotherapy solely to explore themselves. More likely, clients are brought to treatment by one or more painful problems with which they are unable to cope. Loneliness, anxiety, vague or specific fears, addictions, consuming anger, these and other problems drive people to seek therapeutic help. *All* therapies share the goal of ridding the client of distress. But all therapies do *not* share the belief that ridding the client of immediate distress is the exclusive, or even primary, goal of treatment.

Distinguishing specific therapies from insight therapies

Therapies may be divided into two broad categories: those that are designed to treat specific problems and those that seek to encourage personal insight. ***Specific therapies*** attempt to resolve psychological problems without altering underlying personality problems. ***Insight*** or ***global therapies*** are quite different. They treat presenting problems as the symptoms of underlying personality distress and therefore seek to change those deeper personality patterns. Obviously, there is often overlap between these approaches. The insight therapist who ignores the concrete problems that brought the client into therapy is likely to fail because the client will be impatient and dissatisfied (Haley, 1969). Similarly, the behavioral or cognitive therapist who ignores an underlying problem that spawns a host of behavioral difficulties reduces his or her chances of therapeutic success.

We have discussed the details of many global and specific therapies in earlier chapters. But in order to make our therapeutic recommendations clear and meaningful, it is useful to review the kinds of treatment that are available and useful. We will not describe *all* of the treatments that are presently offered: that would require a book in itself. Rather, we will restrict ourselves to those that have proven useful or are very popular.

SPECIFIC THERAPIES

Specific therapies for specific problems

Specific therapies deal with specific problems. Those problems can often be defined quite narrowly and precisely, such as a fear of heights. Or the specific problem may be a broad one, such as depression which, as discussed in Chapter 11, encompasses a heterogeneous group of symptoms, among them fatigue, loss of appetite, somatic concerns, and the like. The important thing about specific therapies is that they take one or more target problems and seek to resolve them without going deeply into other aspects of personality or unconscious processes.

There are two classes of specific therapies: biological treatments and specific psychological therapies. We examine these in turn.

BIOLOGICAL THERAPIES

Drug treatments

Among the biological therapies, drug treatments are by far the most popular. Psychoactive drugs are more often prescribed than others; among these, Valium is the second most commonly prescribed drug in the United States. Drug therapies have been successful with a variety of common disorders, including anxiety, unipolar and bipolar depression, and schizophrenia. They can often have quite specific effects. For example, certain drugs may affect schizophrenic thought, while others may influence schizophrenic emotion.

ECT

Another form of biological therapy is *electroconvulsive shock therapy,* or *ECT.* It consists of sending a pulse of electricity through the brain, thereby producing a minor convulsion. The treatment may be repeated six to ten times. As mentioned in Chapter 11, ECT is a fast and effective treatment for unipolar depression but it can have serious side effects.

Like all therapies, biological treatments are most effective with willing and cooperative clients. But unlike psychological treatments, many biological ones can be administered against the client's will and still have moderate effects. One of the major sources of failure in drug treatment, however, resides in the client's failure or refusal to take the prescribed medications. That failure often arises from the fact that the client is unwilling to take the treatment, fails to understand how it will help, or has not developed the helping alliance with the therapist that is necessary for successful treatment.

Biological therapies are designed to provide immediate relief for immediate problems. They cannot teach clients to alter their behaviors, to avoid stressful difficulties, or to cope better in the future. Nor do they try to bring about greater insight or understanding into the causes of personal difficulties. They affect biology, not learning. But in so doing, their effects are not at all trivial, for problems tend to breed further problems. In reducing current anxiety, arousal, or depression, biological treatments prevent additional troubles from arising.

SPECIFIC PSYCHOLOGICAL THERAPIES

Like biological therapies, the specific psychological therapies seek specific solutions to specifiable problems. These therapies, too, fall into two classes: behavioral treatment and cognitive restructuring.

Changing learned behavior

□ BEHAVIORAL TREATMENT.   The behavioral treatments see the roots of clients' distress, not in physiological processes gone awry, but in behavior itself (see Chapter 5). Distressing behavior is learned, and what is learned can be unlearned and replaced by more constructive modes of coping and adaptation. Behavior therapists therefore deal directly with the problem that the client is experiencing, and seek to resolve that specific difficulty (see Table 19-1).

Table 19-1 STRATEGIES OF BEHAVIOR THERAPY

Technique	Outcome
Contingency management	Altering the consequences of a behavior in order to change the frequency of the behavior.
Contingency contracting	Increasing desired behaviors, and decreasing undesired ones, by drawing up a contract that stipulates rewards and punishments for the relevant behaviors.
Stimulus control	Increasing the likelihood of a behavior by magnifying the stimuli that promote the desired behavior and eliminating the stimuli that undercut it.
Systematic desensitization	Training a person to engage in behavior that makes the unwanted behavior difficult or impossible to perform. Systematic desensitization eliminates anxiety, as it is difficult to experience anxiety during a state of relaxation.
Implosion	Extinguishing anxiety by inducing the client to imagine intensely anxiety-provoking scenes that, because they produce no harmful consequences, lose their power to induce fear.
Flooding	Extinguishing anxiety by exposing the clients to actual fear-producing situations that, because they produce no harmful consequences, lose their power to produce fear.
Modeling	Exposing clients to desired behavior that is modeled by another person, and rewarding the client for imitating that behavior.
Aversion therapy	Eliminating an unwanted behavior by pairing it with powerfully aversive consequences.
Covert sensitization	Inducing an aversion for an unwanted behavior by pairing that behavior with vividly imagined aversive consequences.
Time out	Suppressing an unwanted response by removing the client to a "neutral" environment when that response is manifested.

Although behavior treatments have become popular only in the past quarter century, many of them have their roots in an ageless folk wisdom. Consider the child who fears darkness. At first, parents will naturally accede to the child's demand that the bedroom remain lit. Over time, however, the overhead light will be replaced by a low-wattage night-light. And finally, that too will be extinguished. Used therapeutically, that process is one form of in vivo *systematic desensitization* (see Chapters 5 and 8). Introduced by Joseph Wolpe in 1958, it is used primarily to treat phobias and specific anxieties. The client is first reassured and relaxed, and then exposed to stimuli that are minimally anxiety producing. Because one cannot be relaxed and tense simultaneously, the anxiety dissipates, and gradually, the client is trained to remain relaxed in the presence of stimuli that were formerly associated with increasing anxiety. Over time and training, stimuli that formerly induced panic are now greeted with calm.

Flooding treats anxiety in quite the opposite manner (see Chapters 5 and 8). Instead of gradually approaching the anxiety-provoking stimulus, clients are encouraged to experience the full force of the anxiety storm. Because by definition phobias are irrational fears, they are unlikely to elicit reinforcement. Consequently, like any unreinforced behavior, they will extinguish.

Someone who is agoraphobic and afraid to leave home, for example, would be encouraged to spend an hour in the park, and thus be flooded with anxiety. Gradually, through the process of extinction, that anxiety would abate.

Modeling is yet another form of behavioral treatment that has helped clients to overcome fears and acquire new standards for their behaviors (see Chapters 5 and 8). Here, for example, a client who is painfully shy might observe and gradually imitate the behavior of a model who both enjoys being outgoing and is rewarded for it. Combined with graded rehearsal and practice, modeling treatments are quite effective in overcoming fears and inhibitions (Bandura, 1969).

Aversion therapy aims to rid a client of undesired behavior by pairing that behavior with aversive consequences (see Chapters 5 and 14). If alcohol is paired with a nausea-inducing drug, or a sexually deviant impulse is paired with electric shock, the expected result is that the client will avoid the undesired behavior.

Behavioral treatments often can be very effective in speedily eliminating sources of distress. As we will shortly see, they have been used quite successfully for a variety of psychological troubles. But their virtues are also their limitations, for they often fail to deal with the thoughts and feelings that promote irrational behaviors in the first place. For these thoughts and feelings, cognitive therapies are quite useful.

Changing
irrational thoughts

☐ COGNITIVE RESTRUCTURING. Treatments that involve cognitive restructuring are predicated on the assumption that irrational thoughts breed irrational behaviors. Such thoughts are by no means rare, for they commonly arise from the fundamental attribution errors that people make about their own behaviors (Nisbett and Ross, 1980). Consider the person who says "I have no friends because I am boring." That would be an irrational thought on the part of a young man newly arrived at a college campus, irrational because insufficient time had passed for him to meet people and test that belief. It would also be an irrational thought, but a different sort, by a rude and critical member of a typing pool. Cognitive therapies seek to illuminate these thoughts, to make clear their irrational basis, and thereby, to change them.

Rational-emotive therapy is one of the more effective and popular cognitive therapies (see Chapter 5). Developed by Albert Ellis (1962), it attacks the faulty philosophical assumptions that are made by individuals and that generate irrational behaviors. The notion, for example, that it is absolutely necessary for an adult to be loved by each and every significant person in his or her community, is a widely held irrational assumption. So, too, is the assumption that in order to consider oneself worthwhile, one needs to be thoroughly competent, adequate, and fully achieving in all possible respects. These and other assumptions are vigorously challenged and attacked in rational-emotive therapy, with the aim of laying bare and ultimately changing these cognitions and the behaviors they promote.

Cognitive therapy is quite similar to rational-emotive therapy and is used primarily in the treatment of depression and anxiety (Beck 1976; Beck and Emery, 1985). Beck emphasizes such negative cognitions as self-devaluation, a negative view of life experience, and a pessimistic view of the future as leading to depression (see Chapter 11).

Acquiring and maintaining realistic cognitions is no easy task. Cognitive restructuring therapies use graded tasks, often done as "homework" outside of the therapy session, to yield a succession of mastery and success experiences. Like biological and behavioral therapies, cognitive therapies seek to eliminate a specific problem, and to eliminate it quickly. They differ from those treatments, however, in the requirement that, in order to alleviate a particular problem, one needs to understand and change the thoughts that promote it. And they differ from the global therapies, to which we now turn, both in their insistence on staying "close" to the client's presenting problem, and because they find it unnecessary to explore why the relevant cognitions were distorted in the first place.

GLOBAL THERAPIES

Identifying and overcoming underlying conflicts

Cognitive and behavioral therapies are specific treatments for quite specific problems. Those therapies assume that the presenting problem *is* the problem that requires treatment, and that nothing else requires treatment. Global therapies, on the other hand, all assume that the presenting problem is merely the symptom of some larger, underlying disorder. Much as fever is not itself the entire illness but rather a symptom of a deeper malaise, so are psychological symptoms merely the outcropping of underlying conflicts and erroneous perceptions. It is the latter that require treatment because they tend to radiate a host of cognitive and behavioral difficulties.

Global therapies are mainly those that are derived from the psychodynamic approaches. Each of these therapies assumes that psychological distress arises because something is *fundamentally* wrong with the client's personality. They differ, as we will shortly see, in their view of precisely what is wrong and how it can best be remedied.

CLASSICAL PSYCHOANALYSIS

Making conscious unconscious impulses

As we saw in Chapter 4, the heartland of psychological distress in the psychoanalytic view lies in the anxiety and self-defeating postures that are generated by unacceptable impulses. These impulses are repressed and otherwise restrained from consciousness by the host of coping mechanisms that can be generated by an enormously creative and flexible mind. But ultimately, these defenses are costly, for they sap the strength of the ego and continue to leave residual anxieties that render individuals miserable. The solution for Freud, and for those who followed his tradition, was to make conscious the unconscious impulses so that acceptable means of gratifying them could be found.

With the help of the therapist, the client seeks to define his or her unconscious motivations. Classical psychoanalysts require their clients to lie on a couch in order to minimize their attention to the therapist, relax them, and enable them to engage in *free association.* Clients are instructed to say whatever comes to mind, regardless of how ridiculous or embarrassing it is, and without attempting to censor. The rationale behind this procedure is that the unconscious has a logic of its own that is manifested in these seemingly disconnected and meaningless associations. If the client associates freely, the unconscious motives and conflicts will reveal themselves through these disconnected verbal threads. The analysis of dreams proceeds in the same manner. There, the client associates to the content and theme of the dream and, in the process, uncovers its unconscious meaning.

Unconscious impulses and conflicts do not yield easily or readily to this form of exploration. As the client begins to confront a conflict, he or she is likely to resist going further. Such resistance can take many forms, such as changing the subject, starting an argument with the therapist, coming late, and even missing appointments. Trained not to take these matters personally, the therapist patiently interprets the resistance just as any other symptoms might be interpreted. These interpretations bring the client back to the "work of analysis."

As a psychoanalysis progresses, clients find themselves revealing things to their therapists that they had never revealed to anyone before, not even to themselves. Understandably, the relationship to the therapist becomes richly emotional and complex. And although the therapist remains impassive, clients react to him or her with intense love, dependency, biting anger, or rebellion, and often all at once. As we saw in Chapter 4, psychoanalysts view this behavior as the *transference* of conflicts and frustrations that were experienced with parents during early childhood, onto the therapist. The analysis of transference, because it is immediate and real, is a major opportunity for self-understanding and growth during psychoanalysis.

MODERN PSYCHODYNAMIC PSYCHOTHERAPIES

How modern psychodynamic therapies differ from classical psychoanalysis

Psychoanalysis is a time-consuming, costly, and cumbersome method of treatment. Moreover, as discussed in Chapter 4, not all therapists believe in all of its basic assumptions. As a result, a variety of psychodynamically oriented therapies have been developed. All of them retain the notion that unconscious impulses and conflicts spawn anxiety and other forms of human misery, and that insight into those conflicts is the goal of treatment. But the kinds of impulses that are examined, and the ways in which they can be made conscious, vary enormously from therapist to therapist. In general, modern psychodynamic therapies differ from classical psychoanalysis in three ways. First, the therapist is much more active, not merely in interpreting unconscious material, but also in offering advice and suggesting constructive options. Second, these therapies are more efficient and less time consuming. Whereas classical psychoanalysis required the client to lie on the couch five times a week for several years, modern psychodynamic therapies are conducted face-to-face, commonly no more than once or twice a week, and for a briefer duration. Third, perhaps because they are briefer, the newer psychodynamic therapies concentrate on the present rather than the past, and emphasize current social relationships rather than earlier ones.

The very content of these therapies may differ widely, according to the orientation of the therapist. Whereas classical psychoanalysis is concerned mainly with the dynamics of sexual and aggressive impulses. Jungian therapists take a larger view of the psyche and may, as we saw in Chapter 4, allude to a variety of archetypes, unconscious materials, and dynamics. Adlerian therapists stress the will to superiority, and Sullivanian therapists examine current social relationships. Many psychodynamic therapists are eclectic, meaning that they use insights from each school of treatment in accord with the needs of individual cases. These newer and briefer forms of treatment are among the most widely practiced and available today (Parloff, 1976).

EXISTENTIAL THERAPIES

Encouraging
clients to take
responsibility for
themselves

Existential therapists stress the importance of freedom and free choice. They believe that these are gradually acquired through the individual's struggles with responsibility. They encourage clients to view their psychological problems as being of their own making: individuals themselves are the source of their own difficulties. Viktor Frankl (1975) first described two techniques that are now increasingly used by existential therapists. The first is *paradoxical intervention,* wherein the therapist encourages clients to indulge in and even exaggerate their symptoms. For example, someone who "just can't resist ice cream" will be encouraged to eat massive amounts of it in order to be convinced that he really does control his intake. Paradoxical interventions, particularly those that accord positive connotations to symptoms ("you're mildly depressed because you're in touch with your feelings"), are especially effective with severe symptoms (Shoham-Salomon and Rosenthal, 1987). The second, *dereflection,* involves directing the client's attention away from his symptoms and pointing out how much he could be doing and enjoying if he were not so preoccupied with his troubles. As a result of taking responsibility for themselves, clients become more aware of their choices and values, and their lives and interpersonal relations become more open, honest, and meaningful.

Other therapies, such as encounter therapies, borrow heavily on these techniques and use them in an eclectic manner. But they are characterized by their intensity over a brief period of time. Encounter groups, for example, often meet on a weekend and provide very intense experiences that are directed toward heightening feelings and examining attitudes and beliefs. But because these and other "mod" therapies have undergone little evaluation, their overall effectiveness is yet unknown and, regardless of their popularity, we have nothing more to say about them.

COUPLES AND FAMILIES IN THERAPY

Until this point, our attention has been directed to individuals seen in therapy alone or in groups. But in the past two decades, people have been seen increasingly in therapy with *significant others,* either as couples or in families. The promise of such treatment arises from the notion that symptoms are not wholly the result of individual learning, nor do they inflict suffering on individuals alone. Rather, symptoms may themselves arise from, and be maintained by, the attitudes and behaviors of significant others. And they may well cause intense suffering to significant others. Indeed, it is difficult to imagine an unpleasant symptom that does not impinge directly on the lives of others, especially intimates. Depression affects individuals, but it also deeply affects children and spouses. Impotence affects partners. Anorexia and bulimia create painful problems in families. Moreover, the reciprocal interactions of family members may well spawn, and can surely maintain those symptoms. Thus, it seemed sensible to consider couples and families as the unit of treatment, rather than individuals alone.

Seen in this light, the family substitutes for the individual as the unit of analysis. The way the *family* functions, the way it organizes and maintains its own homeostasis and its habitual patterns of interaction become the focus of assessment. Changing that homeostasis and those patterns of interaction becomes the goal of treatment. What is called the "client" or the "patient" in individual therapy becomes in family therapy the "identified patient," the one whom the family system nominated for patienthood, and who perhaps has volunteered to carry the heaviest burdens of family homeostasis.

Some family therapists take seriously the notion that individual symptoms reflect something that has gone wrong in the family system. They seek to reduce individual malfunction and pain, while simultaneously changing the ways in which the family is organized and interacts (e.g., Minuchin, 1971; Nichols, 1984). They are best described as *systemic* family therapists. But others, who are often described as *strategic* family therapists (Nichols, 1984) bring families to the consulting room with a different view in mind. For them, couples and families are powerful instruments for effecting individual change. They often use techniques that were found to be effective in individual treatment in the family context. Thus, *behavioral* family therapists seek to bring the powerful array of behavioral treatment techniques to bear on individual problems that seem to occur in the family (e.g., Patterson, 1971; Jacobson, 1981). *Psychoanalytic* family therapists (e.g., Meissner, 1981) similarly seek to apply insights gained from individual psychoanalytic treatment to problems that occur in families.

Both the relative newness of family therapies and their diversity (perhaps especially within the strategic dimension) make studies of the effectiveness of these therapies difficult to conduct. Nevertheless, despite the relative paucity of research findings, a recent examination of nearly all of the research efforts suggests that family treatments are particularly effective in reducing the symptoms of the identified patient. And family therapy may also be effective in altering family interactions (Hazelrigg, Cooper, and Borduin, 1987).

With this brief overview of treatment modalities behind us, we now turn to the treatments that are especially useful for particular kinds of psychological problems.

Symptoms may arise from and be maintained by the attitudes and behaviors of significant others. Thus, family therapists believe that symptoms reflect something that has gone wrong in the family system and they seek to treat the whole family.

THE CHOICE OF TREATMENT

Importance of
careful defining
of problems

Some problems lend themselves easily to relatively clear definition. Fear of public speaking is one such problem. Compulsions are another. Although there are important exceptions, the more specific the problem, the greater the likelihood that it can be treated successfully. It is common, therefore, for therapists to encourage clients to define their problems as carefully as possible. Such definition unfortunately does not guarantee therapeutic success, but it surely increases the likelihood that the outcome of treatment will be positive.

SPECIFIC TREATMENTS

Once a problem is defined, it may become especially amenable to treatment by the specific behavioral and cognitive therapies, as well as biological ones. These therapies address symptoms primarily. But this is surely no shortcoming, for as we have seen earlier in this chapter, the symptoms often *are* the problem and, in any event, they are fully capable of breeding more intense and intractable problems. Symptoms treatments are, therefore, significant treatments, made all the more so by their comparative likelihood of succeeding. We turn to these first.

TREATMENTS FOR FEARS, PHOBIAS, AND ANXIETIES

Systematic
desensitization

There are three psychological treatments that are enormously effective in reducing fears and anxieties (see Chapter 8). Perhaps the oldest, and surely the most researched of these, is systematic desensitization, which is useful not only for simple animal phobias, but also for the more complex social anxieties, as well as for agoraphobias and even insomnia (Steinmark and Borkevic, 1974). It is, in fact, so successful that it has become the yardstick against which the effectiveness of new treatment techniques is measured (Kazdin and Wilson, 1978). Recent evidence, however, suggests that cognitive and cognitive-behavioral therapies are as effective as systematic desensitization (Miller and Berman, 1983).

Flooding

A second psychological treatment consists of flooding and reinforced practice. As discussed in Chapter 8, flooding consists of encouraging the client to remain in the presence of the feared object (Crowe, Marks, Agras, and Leitenberg, 1972; Leitenberg and Callahan, 1973). A variant of flooding, called *implosion,* requires clients to imagine fearful scenes (Stampfl and Levis, 1967; Levis and Carrera, 1967), and to examine the symbolic meaning of the anxiety-causing stimuli (Linden, 1981). Such imaginal exposure techniques have been shown to be somewhat less effective than real-life exposure situations (Linden, 1981; Klein, Zitrin, Woerner, and Ross, 1983). But they are promising nonetheless because imaginal techniques are intended to be practiced during non-therapy intervals, increasing the likelihood that the client would confront an anxiety-inducing stimulus in real life.

Modeling

The third psychological treatment that seems particularly effective with phobias is modeling, which consists in observing a nonfearful model perform the task that generates fear in the client (Bandura, Blanchard, and Ritter, 1969; Bandura, 1977b). Modeling appears to work as well as do desensitization and flooding in alleviating both mild and severe phobias (Rachman, 1978).

Drug treatments

Biological treatments, such as the administration of Valium and Miltown, are often useful for alleviating anxiety, especially anxiety that is manifest in body tensions. Untreated, such body tensions tend to accumulate and mount, rendering a person continually anxious. Moreover, antidepressants such as imipramine and phenelzine have been shown to alleviate phobic behavior. Unlike psychological treatments, however, these biological treatments do not teach people to *cope* with anxiety; they merely alleviate the symptoms that present circumstances have generated. If active coping techniques are not learned, new troubling circumstances will probably bring further anxiety symptoms and require further treatment. Biological treatments, therefore, are relatively transient and passive treatments that minimize present symptoms and prevent new ones from developing during a particular crisis.

TREATMENTS FOR COMPULSIONS AND OBSESSIONS

Therapies to alleviate compulsions

Until recently, compulsions and obsessions were refractory to every form of psychological and psychopharmacological treatment. Neither systematic desensitization, the various insight therapies, nor chemotherapy appeared to have much effect. Recently, however, new techniques based on participant modeling, in vivo exposure, and response prevention have shown enormous promise in alleviating compulsions. As discussed in Chapter 9, when a client interrupts his own compulsive rituals after watching a model demonstrate the technique, there is a marked decline in the incidence of that symptom (Marks, Rachman, and Hodgson, 1975; Roper, Rachman, and Marks, 1975). The effectiveness of participant modeling is augmented further by imaginal exposure (Steketee, Foa, and Grayson, 1982). The use of such techniques to alleviate *obsessions,* however, has not worked as dramatically as the technique has worked to relieve the compulsions. Thus, powerful techniques for dealing with the problem of obsessions have yet to be devised (Rachman and Hodgson, 1980).

TREATMENTS FOR DEPRESSION

There are several treatments for depression, and they are all quite powerful. Cognitive and psychodynamic therapies are especially useful in treating unipolar depression, as are three biological treatments: tricyclic antidepressants, monoamine oxidase inhibitors, and electroconvulsive shock therapy. In addition, lithium carbonate is an excellent treatment of bipolar or manic-depression.

Cognitive therapy for depression

Cognitive therapy, as described in Chapter 5, is based on the rationale that an individual's affect and behavior arise from the way he or she structures and perceives the world. The therapy encourages clients to identify the "cognitive triad": those thoughts that generate unrealistically negative views of *self,* the *world,* and the *future.* These are replaced by objectively more accurate cognitions in a context in which the therapist provides feedback and reinforcement for both cognitive and behavioral change. The effects of the treatment begin to be seen after about two weeks (Beck, Rush, Shaw, and Emery, 1979).

Interpersonal therapy

Psychodynamic psychotherapy, and particularly a version called interpersonal therapy (Klerman, Weissman, and Rounsaville, 1984), is also effective in alleviating depression. This therapy is based on the premise that depression occurs in an interpersonal context. Interpersonal therapists seek to clarify internal emotional states, as well as improve emotional communication. While psychodynamic therapies have not received as much research attention as the cognitive ones, recent evidence from a large-scale psychotherapy study indicates that they are as effective as cognitive therapies (Elkin, Shea, Imber, Pilkonis, Sotsky, Glass, Watkins, Leber, and Collins, 1986).

Tricyclic antidepressants

The tricyclic antidepressants are the most commonly used treatments against depression, and for good reason: they work quickly, and they are particularly effective against severe depression. They work by blocking the reuptake of norepinephrine and serotonin. One particular tricyclic, imipramine, was found to be more effective than cognitive or interpersonal therapy early in treatment, but after sixteen weeks those differences had disappeared, and biological and psychological approaches to depression seemed equally effective (Elkin et al., 1986). Tricyclics, however, also have limitations. They give rise to a variety of side effects: mild ones, such as dry mouth, blurred vision, and drowsiness, and rather serious ones among elderly clients and those with cardiovascular disease and urinary problems. Moreover, the relatively high dropout rates associated with tricyclic therapy (Kovacs, Rush, Beck, and Hollon, 1981), as well as the high relapse rate (Simons, Murphy, Levine, and Wetzel, 1986), further limit the usefulness of tricyclic treatments.

MAO inhibitors

Monoamine oxidase (MAO) inhibitors gradually prevent the breakdown of norepinephrine and serotonin, again over ten days to three weeks. They are prescribed less often than the tricyclics both because they are considerably less effective (Klerman, 1975) and because their side effects can be lethal. Taken with cheese, alcohol, or a variety of other medications, MAO inhibitors can actually kill. In some patients, however, they are the only drugs that work at all in overcoming depression.

Combining treatments

There is no reason to choose between the psychological and biological treatments for depression: one can use both. The combination of interpersonal psychotherapy and tricyclic treatment yields a better immediate outcome than either treatment alone (Weissman, Klerman, Prusoff, Sholomskas, and Padian, 1981). And while there are no similar short-term benefits from the combination of cognitive and tricyclic therapy, it is likely that any form of supportive psychotherapy will reduce the high dropout rate that is associated with drug treatment.

ECT

Although it is viewed with dread by some people, electroconvulsive shock therapy (ECT) is clearly a quick and effective treatment for severe unipolar depression. In fact, it may surpass the tricyclic antidepressants and MAOs in treatment efficacy (Janicak, Davis, Gibbons, Ericksen, Chang, and Gallagher, 1985). Half of the people who do not respond to the tricyclics or the MAO inhibitors respond favorably to ECT. ECT can be particularly effective with suicidal persons. ECT too, however, has powerful short-term side effects, which include memory loss and motivational changes, and occasional long-term memory loss as well. But these effects are neither as dramatic nor as long-lasting as the public imagines; they can be reduced, without sacrificing treatment efficacy, by using unilateral rather than bilateral ECT (Janicak et al., 1985), and by varying the placement of electrodes and intensity of shock (Weiner, 1984; Squire and Zouzounis, 1986).

Lithium

The treatment of choice for bipolar depression and for mania itself is lithium carbonate, a simple inorganic salt. The symptoms of 80 percent of bipolar depressives are either fully or partially remitted as a result of lithium administration (Depue and Monroe, 1979). Repeated administration to individuals who are predisposed to bipolar depression may prevent the occurrence of that disorder or alleviate its severity. Lithium, however, has serious side effects that can be lethal unless its administration is carefully supervised by a knowledgeable physician throughout the entire course of treatment. Moreover, because some people find the effects of lithium mildly annoying (it cuts out the joyous "highs" from the manic phase of the bipolar disorder), and therefore terminate the treatment quite prematurely, lithium treatment should always be accompanied by supportive psychotherapy.

TREATMENTS FOR SEXUAL DYSFUNCTION

Direct sexual therapy

For the host of problems that generate sexual dysfunction, including fear of sexuality, lack of sexual pleasure, and premature ejaculation, the treatments of choice, as we saw in Chapter 13, are those that are based on the work of Masters and Johnson (1970). Indeed, no psychological treatment program, with the exception of systematic desensitization for phobias, has been quite as successful as the Masters and Johnson therapy regimen. They have reported that better than 80 percent of nearly 800 people who entered their two-week treatment program were greatly improved, and that nearly 75 percent of them maintained that improvement after a five-year follow-up. Similar findings have been reported by other workers who have evaluated these techniques (Hartman and Fithian, 1972; Kaplan, 1974).

TREATMENTS FOR ADDICTIONS

Problems of dropout and relapse in treating addictions

The addictions—alcoholism, smoking, and drug dependence—are difficult to treat. The solid treatment techniques that are available for phobias, compulsions, depression, and sexual dysfunction are not yet available here. For the soul of addiction is temptation, rather than fear and incompetence, and temptation does not seem to yield to either the rational reasoning of cognitive therapies, the control of behavioral treatments, or the insight of global psychodynamic ones. Most treatment programs, whether conducted by professionals or nonprofessionals (such as Alcoholics Anonymous, Weight Watchers, TOPS, or Daytop Village for drug addicts), are subject to two overlapping problems: drop out and relapse. Those who drop out of a treatment program almost always fail to change. And those who go through a treatment program but then resume old habits often suffer slights to their sense of hope and efficacy. This corrosion of hope and self-efficacy makes them unavailable for further treatment for a considerable period of time. Thus, in this area, researchers have begun to describe their techniques as "*more* effective" rather than "*very* effective," their typical gains as "*modest* rather than impressive," and their outcomes as "variable rather than consistent" (Mahoney and Mahoney, 1976).

Alcoholics' Anonymous (AA) is one of several successful treatments for those whose lives are severely affected by alcoholism. The group stresses self-help and offers group support to help those who are struggling to control drinking.

Abstention

□ ALCOHOLISM.   The treatment of choice for most of the addictions is abstention. But unfortunately, abstention is more easily recommended than achieved and, as a result, a multiplicity of behavioral and cognitive approaches to the addictive disorders have been suggested.

AA

Treatments that evoke enthusiasm, hope, and commitment from participants are seen again in the help provided by Alcoholics Anonymous (AA). AA describes itself as "a fellowship of men and women who share their experiences, strength and hope with each other that they may solve their common problem and help others to recover from alcoholism." By the time an alcoholic makes first contact with AA, he or she has already acknowledged that alcohol is a problem—an enormous first step. Subsequently, two members of AA meet with the alcoholic and invite him or her to join the group. The group stresses self-help, underscoring that the alcoholic controls the drinking problem, and not vice versa. It offers group support during the struggle to control drinking, and hope—for after all, many of the other members of the group were once alcoholics and are now entirely abstinent. And while receiving support from others enables one to better control the urge to drink, *giving support* to people with similar problems serves much the same purpose. Indeed, in looking back over the AA experience, reformed alcoholics rate altruism and group cohesiveness as two of its most helpful aspects (Emrick, Lassen, and Edwards, 1977). Data on the effectiveness of AA, as well as the drop-out rate, are sparse and hard to come by, but what is available suggests that AA is better than no treatment at all (Emrick, Lassen, and Edwards, 1977).

□ SMOKING.   Smoking is no less a puzzle than alcoholism. Little is known about why people smoke in the first place or why smoking persists in being so popular (Jarvik, 1977). Unlike eating, it is difficult to know what is reinforcing in smoking behavior. But whatever reinforces smoking, it does so powerfully. The pack-a-day smoker who averages ten puffs to a cigarette will have taken some 70,000 shots of nicotine and tar in a year, a frequency unmatched by any other form of addiction (Russell, 1977).

Behavioral therapies

Unhooking the long-term smoker is no easy matter. The best procedures utilize a broad spectrum of behavioral strategies. One study, utilizing a combination of aversion therapy, contractual management, booster sessions, and group contact and support, resulted in a 76 percent abstinence rate six months after treatment (Lando, 1977). Unfortunately, such impressive long-term results are seldom replicated. Even rapid smoking, a most successful aversion therapy in the short term, results in high rates of relapse in the long run (Danaher, 1977; Hall, Rugg, Tunstall, and Jones, 1984).

Problem of relapse

In fact, as is the case for most addictions, relapse rates have been the bane of treatments for smoking. Within a year, 75 percent of reformed smokers can be expected to be puffing once again (Marlatt and Gordon, 1980). To combat relapse, cognitive and behavioral treatments aimed at relapse prevention have been added to successful short-term therapies. Oddly, these treatments have not fared well. Although they are associated with some long-term reduction in smoking, these relapse-prevention treatments fail to maintain meaningful abstinence levels (Danaher, 1977; Brown, Lichtenstein, McIntyre, and Harrington-Kostur, 1984; Hall et al., 1984).

Aversive techniques

□ DRUG ABUSE.   For drug abuse, and especially for heroin addiction, three forms of treatment have shown some modest success. The first pairs aversive stimulation, such as shock, with the client's verbal descriptions of his or her need for the drug and consumption of it. Such direct interference with the pleasures of the drug is often combined with relaxation training and systematic desensitization to reduce the tension that promotes drug taking in the first place. But aversive techniques such as these (which were popularized in Anthony Burgess's novel and film *A Clockwork Orange*) have serious shortcomings. In the first place, they often fail to generalize from the therapists' office to the social world in which the addict lives. Second, while the theory underlying aversive techniques indicates that when shock has been paired with desire, people should feel anxious, in fact they commonly feel merely neutral. Thus, the procedure does not evoke a response that is strong enough to resist the social and personal pressures that lead to drug addiction in the first place. Finally, there are ethical considerations. Often, drug addicts are required by law to undergo treatment. Is it really fair to force them to undergo such harsh treatment?

Methadone programs

Some of these concerns have led people to favor a second form of treatment for drug addiction, one that substitutes a different drug, methadone, for the heroin that is being consumed. Methadone is a synthetic narcotic that can be taken orally, does not cloud consciousness, lasts longer than heroin, and partially blocks the "rush" that comes if the addict resumes the heroin habit. Early results of methadone maintenance programs indicated that they reduced incarcerations by 98 percent and criminal activities (which support drug purchases) by 94 percent (Dole and Nyswander, 1965). Moreover, because methadone leaves the addict with a relatively clear consciousness, this study revealed that former addicts found new interest in life and were able to take and retain jobs.

The remarkable success of the early programs, however, was not maintained in later studies. Although present evidence indicates that at least 50 percent of enrolled addicts remain in the program for a year, relapse rates are high. Moreover, methadone itself is an addicting drug, for which a secondary black market now exists. It is also a dangerous drug; an increasing number of deaths from methadone overdose have been reported (Platt and

Labate, 1976). In addition, many heroin addicts who live in the ghettos and barrios feel that methadone is "establishment medicine," a palliative for the poverty that often leads people to seek the thrills of heroin, and an addicting way of controlling these people (Senay and Renault, 1972). Finally, the same ethical objection to aversive techniques applies here: Is it fair to require heroin addicts to become addicted to another drug, methadone?

Self-help, live-in programs

A third kind of treatment consists of self-help, live-in programs conducted by such groups as Odyssey House, Daytop Village, and Synanon. Admission to these therapeutic communities is voluntary and selective. Drugs are prohibited. Addicts are required to avoid former friends and family, to become involved in the social structure of the community, and to "begin at the bottom," performing menial labor at the outset and earning their way up the labor ladder with good performance and drug-free behavior. All residents participate in intensive group therapy, which can be very aggressive and confronting. Finally, therapeutic communities vary in their goals. Some, such as Synanon, require residents to remain within the community indefinitely. Others, such as Odyssey House, emphasize returning addicts to the community.

The therapeutic community approach to treatment has, however, serious limitations. Addicts often find the program unappealing, and the drop-out rate is therefore appallingly high. In one study, only 3.7 percent of those who were enrolled completed the program (New York Legislative Commission on Expenditure Review: Narcotics Drug Control, 1971). A more recent study found that residential treatment is about as effective as methadone maintenance for heroin addicts, and both are more effective than no treatment at all, especially for heavy heroin users (Simpson, Savage, and Sells, 1978).

TREATMENTS FOR EATING DISORDERS

☐ OBESITY. Obesity is an even more intractable problem than alcoholism. The simple fact is that it is quite easy to take off weight, but very difficult to keep it off (Schachtner and Rodin, 1974). Thus, many reports of diet and treatment "breakthroughs" prove to be premature when clients are followed up.

Appetite suppressants

Behavior therapy

The short- and long-term effects of therapies for obesity vary greatly. For example, appetite suppressants are moderately successful while they are being taken, but they lose their beneficial effects once treatment is terminated. Compared to such medication, behavior therapy produces equivalent short-term results. In the long-term, however, behavior therapy proves to be more efficacious than medication (Craighead, 1984). And although such therapy surpasses cognitive-behavioral therapy as well as cognitive therapy alone in the short-term treatment of obesity, in the long run these three therapies generate similar (and very modest) outcomes (Collins, Rothblum, and Wilson, 1986).

Diets and exercise

Low-calorie diets offer an immediate, accessible method of weight loss, but the results are temporary (Wadden and Stunkard, 1986). Moreover, such diets lower the body's resting metabolic rate to an energy-conserving level that thwarts further desirable weight loss. Perhaps the only way to avoid this problem is to exercise, which brings the resting metabolic rate to normal levels among dieters (Donahoe, Lin, Kirschenbaum, and Keesey, 1984). The addition of a behavioral component to a diet regimen also increases the likelihood of maintaining some of the initial weight loss (Wadden and Stunkard, 1986).

Social support

Social support seems to be an important component in the treatment of obesity. When parents participate in their child's weight-loss program by attending evening sessions, children lose more weight (Lansky and Vance, 1983). Adults in group therapy lose more weight than do those in individual therapy (Graham, Taylor, Hovell, and Siegel, 1983). Social support, moreover, seems to enable people to maintain their weight loss. Both the formation of "buddy groups" and post-therapy client-therapist contact via telephone and mail effectively enhance weight-loss maintenance (Perri, McAdoo, Spevak, and Newlin, 1984; Perri, Shapiro, Ludwig, Twentyman, and McAdoo, 1984).

Behavioral techniques

Modestly successful self-help programs for obese people, such as TOPS and Weight Watchers, have included behavioral techniques to augment their efficacy. Like AA, these programs provide members with information, in this case, about obesity and dieting. A "buddy" system is used for initially controlling temptation, and recognition is given to those members who successfully lose weight. Long-term studies of dieting programs have shown that members who had been trained to self-observe their eating, to control how and where they ate, and to substitute other behaviors for nonnecessary eating were more successful in losing weight and keeping it off. Moreover, such groups suffered less attrition through dropout than did the traditional, non-behavioral groups (Levitz and Stunkard, 1974; Stuart, 1980). The combination of these behavioral techniques in the context of a self-help group has proven more effective than pharmacological treatment (Ost and Gotestam, 1976), ordinary insight psychotherapy (Hall, Hall, DeBoer, and O'Kulitch, 1977), and social pressure (Kingsley and Wilson, 1977), although the superiority of the combined behavioral treatment is most apparent immediately after treatment, and tends to decline over time. Unfortunately, after five years, most people, regardless of treatment, have regained all the weight they had lost (Stunkard and Penick, 1979).

Treatment of anorexia

☐ ANOREXIA AND BULIMIA. Anorexia nervosa involves serious cognitive distortions about body image, as well as irrational beliefs about food and weight gain (see Chapter 16). The disorder is more than a compulsion to be thin. It demands minute-to-minute attention in order to achieve such near-death levels of food intake. Cognitive and behavioral therapies offer some promise in the treatment of anorexia. Techniques such as behavior rehearsal, scheduling of pleasant events, and modeling of proper eating make up the behavioral side of treatment. The cognitive approach concerns the evaluation of thoughts and beliefs and their underlying irrational assumptions, as well as the reinterpretation of body image (Garner and Bemis, 1982). Together, these techniques have helped anorexics to gain and maintain a reasonable weight; at follow-up, however, it appears that many "recovered anorexics" still maintain serious distortions of body image despite their weight gain.

Treatment of bulimia

Bulimia combines the morbid fear of obesity with an equally compelling passion for eating. Such competing urges cause the victim to fall into a relentless cycle of binging and purging, in a futile attempt to satisfy antagonistic desires. Therapists have found that the use of cognitive-behavioral techniques (that are similar to those used with compulsions) enables the individual to control the binge/purge cycle, while cognitive techniques help her gain a better understanding of body, food, and eating (Kirkley, Schneider, Agras, and Bachman, 1985; Ordman and Kirschenbaum, 1985).

TREATMENTS FOR THE SCHIZOPHRENIAS

Neuroleptics

The age of hope with regard to the schizophrenias began thirty years ago with the advent of the neuroleptics, a class of drugs that seemed to have dramatic calming effects on the symptoms of these disorders. Until then, individuals afflicted with these disorders were considered hopeless and warehoused in the back wards of psychiatric hospitals. But faith in neuroleptics has declined considerably in recent years, especially since it has been found that those so treated and released from hospitals are often shortly rehospitalized—the so-called "revolving door phenomenon." Neuroleptics seem only to control certain symptoms, mainly the positive symptoms of schizophrenia (see Chapter 12). They are not sufficient to remedy the broad array of cognitive, affective, and social symptoms that these disorders seem to generate. Each year brings a new generation of more focal and powerful neuroleptics to the market and with them renewed optimism. But it seems altogether clear that medications alone will not suffice for the schizophrenias. Indeed, as recently as the early 1980s, most researchers and clinicians continued to believe that improvement of those suffering from the schizophrenias, either through therapy or the natural course of the disorder, was highly unlikely. Studies clearly supported the notion that the schizophrenias were, in most cases, untreatable in the long run (e.g., May, Tuma, Dixon, Yale, Thiele, and Kraus, 1981).

Psychosocial treatments

Today, comprehensive psychosocial treatment may compliment these pharmacological treatments, offering hope to these suffering from the schizophrenias. These therapies apply a diathesis-stress model to the schizophrenias. They posit that socioenvironmental stressors exacerbate schizophrenic symptoms in individuals who are biologically predisposed to the schizophrenias (Falloon and Liberman, 1983). Indeed, a variety of studies have clearly linked stress, in the form of high tension levels in the family, with relapse into schizophrenia following successful maintenance on neuroleptics alone (Brown, Birley, and Wing, 1972; Vaughn and Leff, 1976) and on psychotherapy and neuroleptics (Doane, Falloon, Goldstein, and Mintz, 1985).

Behavioral family therapy

Based on such research findings, behavioral family therapy aims to reduce family tension by combining education, communication skills training, and problem-solving methods, along with stabilizing neuroleptic medication in long-term intervention (Falloon, Boyd, and McGill, 1984). Results have been heartening: those who receive family therapy function better socially and suffer fewer and much less major exacerbations of schizophrenic symptoms than do those treated with a more traditional individual-oriented approach (Falloon, Boyd, McGill, Williamson, Razani, Moss, Gilderman, and Simpson, 1985). In addition, it appears that the combination of social skills training and family therapy produces even more favorable effects than family therapy alone. In particular, the combination of these therapies appears to protect from relapse individuals who must continue to live in tension-filled homes (Hogarty, Anderson, Reiss, Kornblith, Greenwald, Javna, and Madonia, 1986). While these results are encouraging, we do not presently know whether the clinical gains afforded by these experimental therapies can be maintained once therapist-family contact has been terminated.

Because behavioral family therapy is conducted almost exclusively on an experimental basis in research studies, it is not as of now a widely available treatment for the schizophrenias. Rather, individual therapy and hospitalization are more commonly available treatments. The decision of whether or not to hospitalize an individual suffering from the schizophrenias should be made in close consultation with both the client and the therapist.

Hospitalization

Often enough, brief hospitalizations can be quite useful in that they allow a careful examination of the patient's difficulties, as well as prescription of psychotropic medication. Moreover, such hospitalizations often take the pressure off the patient and his or her family, affording the momentary relief that allows all parties to recoup strength and perspective. Longer periods of hospitalization may prove to be necessary for certain patients, but the longer the hospitalization the greater the probability of merely marginal adjustment after discharge.

If a decision is made to hospitalize, it is important for the patient's well-being that family and close friends establish regular contact with both the patient and the hospital staff. Too often, hospitalized psychiatric patients, especially long-term ones, are "warehoused" out of sight and, without malicious intent, forgotten. Regular contact with loved ones very likely accelerates progress in the hospital and increases the likelihood that post-hospital adjustment will be satisfactory.

Where long-term hospitalization is a prospect, consider first less restrictive alternatives, if they exist within or near the community. Supervised halfway houses are especially attractive as therapeutic alternatives because they minimally disrupt the contact between the patients and their social environment, and because, unlike psychiatric hospitals, they are so patently temporary residences. Day hospitals, which provide daytime care for patients and return them to their families in the evenings, are sometimes also alternatives to full hospitalization.

Specific treatments, where they exist, are the quickest and most effective way of treating specific problems. Unfortunately, however, there continue to be problems for which no specific treatment is really effective. Autism is one such problem, and some forms of schizophrenia are others. Such problems are presently untreatable, but the future holds promise for their treatment. Most of the specific biological and psychological treatments that were described here and in earlier chapters simply did not exist thirty years ago. Progress in this area has been explosive and likely will accelerate further in coming years.

GLOBAL TREATMENTS

Besides specific problems, there are also problems that are global and that resist specification. Among these are problems of meaning, where people ask about the purpose of their lives, and problems in loving. The latter, while specific enough, is an affective problem for which, unless it is promoted by fear, no specific treatment remedies exist. For global problems, global treatments may be the only remedy.

Global treatments include those that were discussed in Chapter 4: the psychodynamically oriented therapies, as well as the existential ones. These therapies seek to explore, strengthen, and change the *self*—not merely the individual's *image* of self, but the host of traits, abilities, beliefs, attitudes, and broad dispositions that give rise to self. They may even try to help people develop a sense of self, to know who they are, and what they believe. The goals of self-exploration and changing the self in accord with that knowledge are the goals of these global therapies.

THE SEARCH FOR SELF

Self-exploration

The problems of self—of the meaning of life and work, of loving, and of commitment—are fundamental problems that everyone faces, or avoids, throughout life. These problems need not be considered abnormal, for we are not put in this world with a script that tells us "what it's all about." Each of us discovers that for himself or herself. This process is often as complicated and painful as it is fascinating, and one simply may want a professional guide to lead one through the forests and around the dead ends.

Traditional vehicles for self-exploration have been Freudian or Jungian psychoanalysis and their many psychodynamic offshoots. These psychodynamic therapies are more than treatments for distress. They are methods of self-examination. In "Psychoanalysis: Terminable or Interminable," Freud (1905/1976) concluded that the process of self-exploration is an interminable one for which psychoanalysis can serve as a useful adjunct throughout life. In fact, the ideal psychoanalytic client is still captured by the acronym YAVIS—young, attractive, verbal, intelligent, and successful—someone who may have some problems but, on the spectrum of these matters, is surely experiencing no real desperation. The YAVIS client benefits from psychoanalysis to the extent that he or she develops deep understandings of self that, in turn, lead to greater change and self-fulfillment.

Effectiveness of global therapies

Do these therapies work? The answer to this question is complex. When global treatments are applied to specific problems, they seem to work less well than specific treatments (Kazdin and Wilson, 1978). Even so, however, they are more effective than no treatment at all. But when global treatments are used to facilitate the search for self, questions about effectiveness lose much of their meaning, for here, notions of "cure" and of "symptoms remission" are entirely inappropriate. To the extent that the question has any meaning at all, the answer must be a private one, entirely dependent upon whether the client *believes* it has been meaningful. When asked, close to 90 percent of such clients reported themselves satisfied with the outcomes of such treatment (Strupp, Fox, and Lessler, 1969).

The treatments that have been discussed in this section apply to problems that are full-grown. Such problems already will have taken their toll in human misery, long before they come to the attention of professional therapists. Once they do, moreover, treatment will be expensive and time-consuming, and outcomes will not always be optimistic. Can anything be done to prevent problems from arising in the first place? And if they do arise, can their effects be minimized and contained? Finally, are there alternatives to the kinds of treatment that have been discussed in this section, alternatives that utilize community rather than professional resources? Because, as an old adage tells us, it is the squeaky wheel that gets the oil, clinical psychology and psychiatry have attended mainly to those who are in need of treatment, often desperately in need of it. But plain common sense makes clear that the squeaky wheel principle is wrong. If problems were prevented in the first place, or minimized before they flowered, both human misery and the need for expensive professional treatment would be greatly reduced. In the next section, we turn to efforts to prevent and contain human distress, as well as alternative modes of treatment in the community.

OUTREACH AND PREVENTION: THE HOPES OF COMMUNITY PSYCHOLOGY

Community efforts to prevent and contain psychological disorders

Traditional psychological treatment suffers two major liabilities. First, as we have seen, it arrives only *after* a problem has entailed untold misery for the client. And second, there are simply not enough professional therapists to treat all those who are in need. As a result, psychologists and psychiatrists have become increasingly involved in *community* efforts to *prevent* and *contain* psychological disorders. Because they are allied with others, the efforts of psychologists can now influence the psychological well-being of a much larger proportion of the population than is possible through traditional treatment.

These collaborative efforts between psychologists and the community take place on three fronts: prevention, containment, and alternative modes of treatment and rehabilitation. We take these areas up in turn.

PREVENTION

An ounce of prevention is worth a pound of cure, we are told. And a review of the chapters that deal with anxiety, depression, crime and delinquency, and children's disorders, makes clear that many of the multiple causes of

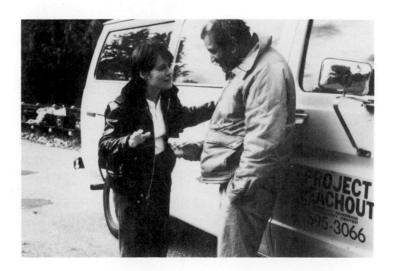

Community efforts to prevent and contain psychological disorders attempt to deal with problems before specific crises necessitate more drastic efforts.

these distresses could well have been prevented. Unfortunately, our society budgets much less for preventive efforts than for treatment, largely because of the squeaky-wheel principle. But it has chosen to invest resources in three areas that are significant for prevention: child-care facilities, preschool preparation, and job training.

CHILD-CARE

Child-care facilities

Imagine a mother raising three children, all of them under five. Worse yet, imagine her as a single parent, responsible for the economics, as well as the psychological welfare of her brood.

> I had to work at night, while the children slept. If one of them was sick and needed me, and the neighbor's kid wasn't free to baby-sit, I missed work and pay. There was one year when I was fired from four jobs because Julie and Richard were sick a lot and needed me. Finally, I just couldn't take it.

Such mothers are hardly rare in our society. In 1982, it was estimated that more than five million women maintained families while being employed (Monthly Labor Review, 1983). And they were not the only ones who needed child-care facilities. Often, in two-parent families, both adults have to work in order to make ends meet. Either their own needs, or those of their children, and commonly both, are neglected.

Child-care facilities provide a safe and healthy environment for young children, one that parents and children can count on. Not only do they reduce familial pressures, but often they provide children with experiences that simply could not be gotten at home, such as learning to socialize with other children and to respond to adults other than parents. These experiences are likely beneficial for children when they begin school.

PRESCHOOL INTERVENTIONS

Preschool preparation

The early school years are fertile ground for psychological problems. Once a child falls behind in work, fails to make friends, or becomes disruptive in the classroom or playground, the likelihood is high that these problems will endure and grow. Often, such problems develop because children are ill-prepared for the school experience, either intellectually or socially. Preschool programs, such as Operation Headstart are intended to encourage the development of cognitive and intellectual skills necessary for kindergarten and the early school grades.

JOB TRAINING AND RETRAINING

Job training

Poverty and unemployment take enormous tolls on people, and they probably spawn more social problems than any other cause. Simple economic need often drives people to crime and violence. Training the unemployed in the host of skills necessary to both find a job and keep it goes a long way toward preventing psychological problems.

It is important to note that psychologists do not usually establish or control child-care, preschool, or job-training facilities. Rather, their contribution is made through *consultation* and *collaboration* with members of the community who want to establish these centers in the first place. They often and successfully consult in schools to increase communication between teachers, students, and their families (Sarason, 1974). They may even consult with urban renewal organizations regarding creating new cities that are psychologically stimulating and that encourage neighborliness and conviviality (Lemkau, 1969). And often they consult with legislators, policymakers, and the courts on such issues as school desegregation and detention of juveniles, issues whose resolution can eventually prevent the development of psychological difficulties. By collaboration with other members of the community, the resources of psychologists can be utilized more broadly and effectively than would be possible in traditional professional roles.

How effective are these efforts at prevention? The evidence with regard to preschool programs such as Operation Headstart suggests that they are not as good as had earlier been hoped, but that they are surely better than no preschool training at all. Child-care facilities and job training, on the other hand, have not yet been evaluated for their impact on psychological distress. Undoubtedly, they are effective, but how effective is not yet clear. The entire area of prevention, however, is still in its infancy, still more of a hope than a reality (Cowen, 1977); it may yet be too early to expect full and careful evaluation of these efforts.

CONTAINMENT

Community
containment
services

Psychological crises often have immediate consequences. A heated argument may result in violence; a painful rejection, in suicide; an overwhelming impulse, in rape, murder, or drunkenness. **Containment services** are designed to limit the consequences of such crises, as they affect the individual, the potential or actual victim, and their families. In the main, these services are characterized by three features. First, treatment is delivered quickly. The potential Friday night suicide, for example, need not wait until Monday morning when the clinics open; by then, it may be too late. He or she can immediately go to a crisis intervention center, or phone a "hot-line" for counseling. Second, services are delivered to a broad range of people, including many who would never seek traditional psychological help. And third, they are located in the community and offered by the community,

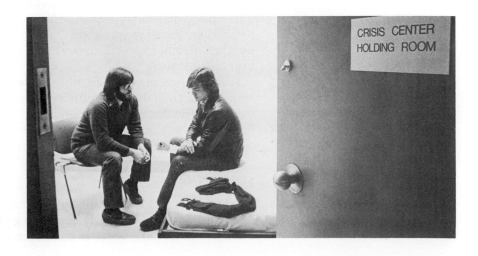

Containment services are designed to limit the consequences of crises. Here a person who has attempted to commit suicide is being counseled.

rather than through hospitals, clinics, or professionally trained therapists. Their very visibility and availability ensures their use.

"HOT-LINES"

Hot-lines

The telephone ***hot-line*** is a twenty-four-hour phone service for people who are undergoing deep distress. The first of these hot-lines was established in 1958 by Norman Farberow and Edwin Schneidman as part of the Los Angeles Suicide Prevention Center (Farberow, 1974). Presently, more than 200 communities have developed such centers.

In the main, hot-lines are staffed by carefully trained nonprofessional volunteers. The primary functions of the volunteer are to establish a sympathetic relationship with the caller, to help him clarify his problem, and to formulate a constructive plan that immediately mobilizes the individual's resources as well as those of family friends, and community. Volunteers will often attempt to assess the suicidal potential of their caller (see Chapter 11), as well as whether the suicide has already been attempted. This kind of work is exceedingly stressful for the volunteers, for they, too, are on the "hot seat." The results of their efforts often determine whether someone will continue to live, yet because callers often hang up without leaving their name or phone number, the volunteers rarely learn to what extent they have helped. As a result, volunteers often become discouraged on this job, and frequently burn out quickly.

Beyond offering instant counseling, hot-lines serve to educate callers about available treatment resources. Often, callers will be referred to a community mental health center, where the causes of the crisis can be explored and treated in greater depth. The emphasis, however, is not on long-term treatment, but on crisis intervention and speedy referral.

Such emergency treatment appears effective in reducing suicide rates. Among 8000 high-risk callers to the Suicide Prevention Center in Los Angeles, Farberow (1970) reports that fewer than 2 percent committed suicide, compared to the estimated 6 percent overall rate of suicide among such persons.

Hot-line services have been extended to people who are experiencing many different kinds of crises. For example, there are child-abuse hot-lines, which seek to cool parental rage before harm is done to children. Other hot-lines exist to defuse impulses to drink, gamble, and engage in violent behavior. Finally, there are yet others that have no particular focus or specialty, but that attempt to provide a listening ear and immediate counsel to whoever calls.

Hot-line users are often ashamed of their behavior and their lack of control. The fact that they are assured of anonymity encourages them to call in the first place; that may be one of the hot-line's greatest strengths. For while hot-line services neither cure nor provide long-term solutions, they diffuse crises and head off serious and immediate losses. That is no small virtue.

SHORT-TERM TREATMENT

Short-term crisis treatment

In many cases, distraught individuals may be unable to undertake long-term treatment, but they may be able to go for short-term ***crisis treatment.*** Such treatment rarely requires more than six sessions. In it, the therapist is

These women and their children are in a shelter for battered women.

extremely active, helping the client to focus on his or her problem, providing support and reassurance, and devising constructive solutions (Golan, 1978). Such crisis intervention often enables a person to resume her life without hospitalization or disruption of employment.

HELP FOR VICTIMS AND THEIR FAMILIES

Being the victim of brutality often has enormous psychological consequences that, if left unattended, can be long-lasting. Immediately after being raped, for example, women experience considerable psychological disorganization, including feelings of insecurity and loneliness and rampant fear, and they are subject to heightened influence by others. Depending on their prior experiences and background, these fears and insecurities can develop into stable patterns of avoidance (Burgess and Holmstrom, 1974). Their spouses and families, moreover, often experience changes in these women's attitude and affection that can be directly traced to these traumatic experiences (Bard and Sangrey, 1979). As described in Chapter 8, political hostages, too, have similar reactions to the trauma and humiliation that result from being held against their will (Sank, 1979). Short-term crisis interventions may range from support and counseling, to brief behavioral treatments that are useful in alleviating and containing these symptoms.

Help for battered women and children

Until recently, battered wives and children had no recourse except to "take it," or perhaps to turn to the police and courts. As their numbers have become known, however, concern for these victims has heightened and has led to the establishment of shelters for battered women. Such shelters provide temporary sanctuary for women and their children, enabling them to take some time out to recover from abuse and plan their futures. Staffed almost entirely by nonprofessionals, their central function is protection. Unfortunately, shelters are often dangerous and unhappy places—dangerous because of possible retaliation from still-angry husbands, and unhappy because these women are beset with doubts about themselves and their futures.

EARLY DETECTION OF PSYCHOLOGICAL DIFFICULTIES

Detecting
behavioral
problems in
school children

Several programs have been concerned with detecting behavioral problems in school children. Some programs train teachers to detect the early signs of maladjustment (Zax and Cowen, 1969; Levine and Graziano, 1972), while others use brief tests that can be easily scored (Cowen, 1973). Both types of programs seek to identify early signs of maladjustment so that children can be referred for remediation before their problems become relatively insurmountable.

CONSULTATION

Psychologists and psychiatrists are often consulted by a variety of other professionals and organizations. They may be consulted by teachers on how to increase children's motivation, or about how to handle a particular child's problem in the classroom rather than at the clinic. They will often be consulted by industry about how to make working conditions more pleasant, and how to reduce executive stress.

Training police to
intervene in family
quarrels

One ingenious example of consultation has arisen in the training of police who are often called to mediate family quarrels. Family quarrels are a major source of assaults and homicides. They are dangerous, not only for the participants, but also for those who intervene. Many police have been assaulted while attempting to calm family conflicts. In one New York City precinct, police were given extensive training by psychologists on how to intervene in these family quarrels, and then worked as family crisis-intervention teams in that precinct. In contrast to the police in the neighboring precinct, who were not given such training and who both suffered and witnessed the same amount of violence that is usually associated with such calls, the trained police fared much better. In the next 1388 calls to intervene in family crises, trained team members did not suffer an assault, did not witness a family homicide, and were able to markedly reduce the number of assaults on family members (Bard, 1970). The enormous success of this program in New York City has led to its wider adoption. The positive results strongly support the idea of providing psychological consultation for other service agencies.

Here a clinical psychologist is consulting police on how to handle hostage situations. He is providing them with psychological cues for police negotiations and actions in such situations.

REHABILITATION

Until quite recently, as we have seen, treatment and rehabilitation of those who were seriously distressed was in the hands of professional psychologists and psychiatrists and was conducted mainly in psychiatric hospitals. But partly because of shortages of fully qualified personnel, and partly because hospitals have serious shortcomings as treatment centers for the psychologically distressed, community psychologists have devised other settings in which such people and problems can be treated. They have trained nonprofessionals to deal with these problems. They have established alternative treatment centers such as halfway houses, residential treatment programs, and day and night hospitals. And they have encouraged patients and former patients to establish self-help groups, designed to find employment for and combat discrimination against, those who suffer or have suffered serious psychological distress.

TRAINING NONPROFESSIONALS

Training paraprofessionals

It takes a long time to become a psychologist, psychiatrist, or social worker. Not many people have the time or resources to undertake such training, and as a result, there are far too few trained people to meet current need. Recently, there have been increasing efforts to train paraprofessionals in this area. Whether through on-the-job training, or in undergraduate and junior colleges, these paraprofessionals are trained to take over some of the functions of the professional. Trained paraprofessionals can interview, test, make home visits, and often handle social and vocational rehabilitation under the supervision of psychologists or psychiatrists. They can serve as aides and attendants in psychiatric hospitals. And indeed, some studies have shown that paraprofessionals can be trained to be good therapists (Rioch, 1967). Though their training is narrower than that of fully qualified professionals, and though they can perform fewer tasks, a variety of studies have indicated that what they do, they do quite well (Rioch, 1967; Brown, 1974). Moreover, they vastly increase the number of people who can be treated, enabling professionals to reserve their skills for complicated problems, for consultation and supervision, and for training.

ALTERNATIVE TREATMENT CENTERS

Alternative settings for treatment

The search for alternatives to the traditional mental hospital is an ongoing one. Long-term patients in such hospitals tend to become habituated to that environment, and subsequently unable to function outside of it. Even short-term patients suffer enormously after discharge; they have difficulty finding adequate employment and establishing satisfying social lives. Alternative treatment centers have tried to overcome these problems by loosening the ties to the hospital, by maintaining patients in the community where they can often retain old friendships and establish new ones, and where they can be trained for job responsibilities.

Day and night hospitals are intended to serve as transition points for fully hospitalized patients, as well as treatment centers for those who were never hospitalized. In day hospitals, patients are treated during the day, and then permitted to join their families at night and over the weekend. Night hospi-

Halfway houses help patients to adjust to living outside the hospital before they return to the community and to living on their own.

tals are for patients who either have daytime employment, or families with whom they are comfortable and supported. Such patients return to the hospital in the evening to continue their treatment. Participation in day and night treatment is often brief, just long enough to enable the former patient to get his or her feet on the community ground.

Halfway houses or community lodges are also designed as transition experiences between hospital and community. Optimally, these residences house no more than twenty people. With only paraprofessionals in residence, and a psychologist or psychiatrist on call, halfway houses serve to train patients to govern themselves after they have been governed by the hospital. Here patients make decisions about running the house. They often establish small businesses to support themselves, and they receive training both in vocations and in the skills necessary for holding a job. Former patients who have resided in halfway houses before fully entering the community are less likely to be rehospitalized than those who have entered the community directly from the hospital.

Residential treatment centers attempt to avoid the hospital entirely. Here, distressed people are treated in the community, either by families who are willing to take them in (Stein, Test, and Marx, 1975; Polak and Kirby, 1976; Mosher and Menn, 1978), or in residences established for these purposes. Such treatment commonly takes more time than does traditional drug-oriented therapy. But its consequences are commonly more beneficial. People in these settings emerge without a "record" of psychiatric hospitalization, which enables them to find employment more easily and to establish social relationships with greater ease and less stigma. The evidence, moreover, suggests that residential treatment centers cost less to operate than traditional hospitals (Kiesler, 1982).

SELF-HELP GROUPS

Self-help groups

Funds for treating the psychologically distressed, which never were plentiful, are much less available today than a decade ago. Psychiatric hospitals are being closed. Patients are being discharged, often to "board and care" facilities that provide little more than a bed to sleep in and meals. One would expect that the closing of psychiatric hospitals would free funds for community treatment, but that has not been the case. Rather, patients have been thrown on their own resources—and have done some fairly remarkable things without much help from government and society.

One focus of self-help groups has been to establish a community where patients can associate with and help each other. Because they often reside in the marginal areas of cities, former patients have been plagued by poverty and dislocation in addition to their own psychological difficulties. Self-help groups have established cooperatives where members can obtain food and services at affordable prices. Using their political strength—for they now constitute a sizable voting minority in some neighborhoods—they have been able to locate community facilities in which to meet. Increasingly, they have turned to the law to remedy the abuses of discrimination that they face. Such groups as NAPA (Network Against Psychiatric Assault), moreover, have sought to correct what they perceive to be abuses in patient care. Increasingly, members of such groups are invited to the professional meetings of psychologists and psychiatrists, to "tell their story" and to alert professionals to the difficulties that present and former patients experience.

SUMMARY

1. The kinds of people who offer help for psychological problems, and the kinds of help they offer, are difficult to enumerate, and harder still to catalog properly. Most people are familiar with the names of one or two kinds of traditional therapists: psychologists, psychiatrists, psychiatric social workers, and psychiatric nurses. But the available help for psychological problems extends far beyond those narrow confines and includes friends, teachers, parents, clergy, and self-help groups, to name a few.

2. Psychotherapy, if it is anything, is an active collaborative process in which both therapist and client work to overcome the client's problems. While they clearly depend for their outcome on the competence of the therapist, they depend equally on the hopes and expectations of the client.

3. The therapeutic relationship is facilitated when the therapist shows empathy, warmth, and genuineness. It is also enhanced when the client feels free to question and when treatment goals are specified early in the treatment process.

4. The effectiveness of therapy can be assessed by considering the client's satisfaction with the treatment, by measuring the extent of the client's personality change, and by examining the impact of treatment on target behaviors.

5. After finding a therapist whom one likes, and avoiding poorly trained or simply immature therapists, one is ready to consider the type of treatment that will be most useful. Generally, the more specific the problem, the better the chance that it can be resolved through specific treatments. The less specific the problem, the more likely global treatment will be called upon.

6. There are psychological problems that are quite treatable today that could not be resolved a decade ago. Great strides have been made in behavioral treatment of fears, phobias, and compulsions, in cognitive treatment of depression, and in pharmacological treatment of bipolar depression. But some forms of schizophrenia, and many of the serious childhood disorders, such as autism, are still difficult problems to cope with.

7. Psychologists and psychiatrists have become increasingly involved in community efforts to prevent and contain psychological disorders. Three significant areas in which funds have been invested in an effort to prevent psychological disorders from developing are: child-care facilities, preschool interventions, and job training and retraining. Areas in which containment services have been designed to limit the consequences of psychological crises include hot-lines, short-term crisis treatment centers, and shelters for battered wives.

8. Because some treatments have powerful side effects, and because some treatment settings, such as hospitals, create undesired difficulties for patients, increasing effort has been directed toward finding treatment alternatives. Paraprofessionals are being trained to take on many of the tasks that were once the exclusive province of professionals. Residential treatment centers and halfway houses are increasingly coming to supplement and replace the traditional psychiatric hospital. And former patients are gradually collecting into self-help groups.

The Revised Diagnostic and Statistical Manual of Mental Disorders (DSM-III-R)

DSM-III-R is a revision of the third edition of the *Diagnostic and Statistical Manuals,* the first of which was published in 1952, the second in 1968. DSM-III, which emerged in 1980, constituted a major overhaul of the psychological diagnostic system, and it differed from its predecessors in many respects (see pp. 175–79). There were two major differences, however, that dwarfed all the others. First, DSM-III attempted to clearly delineate the psychological "elements" that went into a diagnosis, as well as their temporal parameters. Second, DSM-III emphasized *multi-axial classification.* Earlier versions of the *Diagnostic and Statistical Manual* had concentrated on psychological diagnoses alone. DSM-III, however, enlarged the diagnostic context by insisting that examiners search for "background" physical and psychological disorders that might amplify or otherwise affect diagnosis and treatment.

DSM-III-R is an interim revision of DSM-III. It was begun in 1983 and culminated in 1987 and reflects new understandings that have arisen since DSM-III was published in 1980. It is expected that DSM-III-R will itself be replaced by DSM-IV in 1992.

Like its predecessor, DSM-III-R relies heavily on multi-axial classification. Formal diagnoses should emerge in the following manner:

Axes I and II: the "traditional" clinical syndromes, personality disorders, and developmental disorders.

Axis III: Physical disorders and conditions that might affect psychological functioning and treatment.

Axis IV: The examiner's rating of the severity of psychosocial stressors.

Axis V: The examiner's estimate of the highest level of adaptive functioning.

Axes I and II from DSM-III-R are reprinted below. Axis II categories are in boxes; the rest of the diagnoses are Axis I categories. These are the traditional psychological nomenclature for such disorders. Axes III, IV, and V, of course, are not classifications, but rather, they deal more generally with the physical and psychosocial stressors that may affect an individual's psychological status. We include Axes IV and V, but Axis III cannot be included because it is mainly medical.

Axes I and II Categories and Codes*

DISORDERS USUALLY FIRST EVIDENT IN INFANCY, CHILDHOOD, OR ADOLESCENCE

DEVELOPMENTAL DISORDERS

Mental Retardation

317.00	Mild mental retardation
318.00	Moderate mental retardation
318.10	Severe mental retardation
318.20	Profound mental retardation
319.00	Unspecified mental retardation

Pervasive Developmental Disorders

299.00	Autistic disorder
	Specify if childhood onset
299.80	Pervasive developmental disorder

Specific Developmental Disorders

Academic skills disorders

315.10	Developmental arithmetic disorder
315.80	Developmental expressive writing disorder
315.00	Developmental reading disorder

Language and speech disorders

315.39	Developmental articulation disorder
315.31	Developmental expressive language disorder
315.31	Developmental receptive language disorder

Motor skills disorder

315.40	Developmental coordination disorder
315.90	Specific developmental disorder

Other Developmental Disorders

315.90	Developmental disorder

Disruptive Behavior Disorders

314.01	Attention-deficit hyperactivity disorder

Conduct disorder,

312.20	group type
312.00	solitary aggressive type
312.90	undifferentiated type
313.81	Oppositional defiant disorder

*Source: The American Psychiatric Association: *Diagnostic and Statistical Manual of Mental Disorders,* Third Edition, Revised, 1987. Reprinted by permission of the American Psychiatric Association, Washington, D.C.

Anxiety Disorders of Childhood or Adolescence

309.21   Separation anxiety disorder
313.21   Avoidant disorder of childhood or adolescence
313.00   Overanxious disorder

Eating Disorders

307.10   Anorexia nervosa
307.51   Bulimia nervosa
307.52   Pica
307.53   Rumination disorder of infancy
307.50   Eating disorder

Gender Identity Disorders

302.60   Gender identity disorder of childhood
302.50   Transsexualism
    Specify sexual history: asexual, homosexual, heterosexual, unspecified
302.85   Gender identity disorder of adolescence or adulthood, nontranssexual type
    Specify sexual history: asexual, homosexual, heterosexual, unspecified
302.85   Gender identity disorder

Tic Disorders

307.23   Tourette's disorder
307.22   Chronic motor or vocal tic disorder
307.21   Transient tic disorder
    Specify: single episode or recurrent
307.20   Tic disorder

Elimination Disorders

307.70   Functional encopresis
    Specify: primary or secondary type
307.60   Functional enuresis
    Specify: primary or secondary type
    Specify: nocturnal only, diurnal only, nocturnal and diurnal

Speech Disorders Not Elsewhere Classified

307.00   Cluttering
307.00   Stuttering

Other Disorders of Infancy, Childhood, or Adolescence

313.23   Elective mutism
313.82   Identity disorder
313.89   Reactive attachment disorder of infancy or early childhood
307.30   Stereotypy/habit disorder
314.00   Undifferentiated attention-deficit disorder

ORGANIC MENTAL DISORDERS

Dementias Arising in the Senium and Presenium

    Primary degenerative dementia of the Alzheimer type, senile onset
290.30   with delirium
290.20   with delusions
290.21   with depression
290.00   uncomplicated
    (Note: code 331.00 Alzheimer's disease on Axis III)
Code in fifth digit:
1 = with delirium, 2 = with delusions, 3 = with depression, 0 = uncomplicated
290.1x   Primary degenerative dementia of the Alzheimer type, presenile onset, _____
    (Note: code 331.00 Alzheimer's disease on Axis III)
290.4x   Multi-infarct dementia, _____
290.00   Senile dementia
    Specify etiology on Axis III if known
290.10   Presenile dementia
    Specify etiology on Axis III if known (e.g., Pick's disease, Jakob-Creutzfeldt disease)

Psychoactive Substance-Induced Organic Mental Disorders

    Alcohol
303.00   intoxication
291.40   idiosyncratic intoxication
291.80   uncomplicated alcohol withdrawal
291.00   withdrawal delirium
291.30   hallucinosis
291.10   amnestic disorder
291.20   dementia associated with alcoholism

    Amphetamine or similarly acting sympathomimetic
305.70   intoxication
292.00   withdrawal
292.81   delirium
292.11   delusional disorder

    Caffeine
305.90   intoxication

    Cannabis
305.20   intoxication
292.11   delusional disorder

Cocaine
305.60   intoxication
292.00   withdrawal
292.81   delirium
292.11   delusional disorder

Hallucinogen
305.30   hallucinosis
292.11   delusional disorder
292.84   mood disorder
292.89   posthallucinogen
          perception disorder

Inhalant
305.90   intoxication

Nicotine
292.00   withdrawal

Opioid
305.50   intoxication
292.00   withdrawal

Phencyclidine (PCP) or
similarly acting
arylcyclohexylamine
305.90   intoxication
292.81   delirium
292.11   delusional disorder
292.84   mood disorder
292.90   organic mental disorder

Sedative, hypnotic, or anxiolytic
305.40   intoxication
292.00   uncomplicated sedative, hypnotic, or
          anxiolytic withdrawal
292.00   withdrawal delirium
292.83   amnestic disorder

Other or unspecified psychoactive substance
305.90   intoxication
292.00   withdrawal
292.81   delirium
292.82   dementia
292.83   amnestic disorder
292.11   delusional disorder
292.12   hallucinosis
292.84   mood disorder
292.89   anxiety disorder
292.89   personality disorder
292.90   organic mental disorder

Organic Mental Disorders associated with Axis III physical disorders or conditions, or whose etiology is unknown
293.00   Delirium
294.10   Dementia
294.00   Amnestic disorder
293.81   Organic delusional disorder
293.82   Organic hallucinosis
293.83   Organic mood disorder
          Specify: manic, depressed, mixed
294.80   Organic anxiety disorder
310.10   Organic personality disorder
          Specify if explosive type
294.80   Organic mental disorder

PSYCHOACTIVE SUBSTANCE USE DISORDERS

Alcohol
303.90   dependence
305.00   abuse

Amphetamine or similarly acting
sympathomimetic
304.40   dependence
305.70   abuse

Cannabis
304.30   dependence
305.20   abuse

Cocaine
304.20   dependence
305.60   abuse

Hallucinogen
304.50   dependence
305.30   abuse

Inhalant
304.60   dependence
305.90   abuse

Nicotine
305.10   dependence

Opioid
304.00   dependence
305.50   abuse

Phencyclidine (PCP) or similarly acting
arylcyclohexylamine
304.50   dependence
305.90   abuse

Sedative, hypnotic, or anxiolytic
304.10   dependence
305.40   abuse

304.90   Polysubstance dependence
304.90   Psychoactive substance dependence
305.90   Psychoactive substance abuse

SCHIZOPHRENIA
Code in fifth digit: 1 = subchronic, 2 = chronic, 3 = subchronic with acute exacerbation, 4 = chronic with acute exacerbation, 5 = in remission, 0 = unspecified.

Schizophrenia,
295.2x   catatonic, _____
295.1x   disorganized, _____
295.3x   paranoid, _____
        Specify if stable type
295.9x   undifferentiated, _____
295.6x   residual, _____
        Specify if late onset

DELUSIONAL (PARANOID) DISORDER
297.10   Delusional (Paranoid) disorder
        Specify type: erotomanic
                 grandiose
                 jealous
                 persecutory
                 somatic
                 unspecified

PSYCHOTIC DISORDERS NOT ELSEWHERE CLASSIFIED
298.80   Brief reactive psychosis
295.40   Schizophreniform disorder
        Specify: without good prognostic features or with good prognostic features
295.70   Schizoaffective disorder
        Specify: bipolar type or depressive type
297.30   Induced psychotic disorder
298.90   Psychotic disorder
        (Atypical psychosis)

MOOD DISORDERS
Code current state of Major Depression and Bipolar Disorder in fifth digit:
1 = mild
2 = moderate

3 = severe, without psychotic features
4 = with psychotic features (specify mood-congruent or mood-incongruent)
5 = in partial remission
6 = in full remission
0 = unspecified
For major depressive episodes, specify if chronic and specify if melancholic type.
For Bipolar Disorder and Depressive Disorder, specify if seasonal pattern.

Bipolar Disorders
Bipolar disorder
296.6x   mixed, _____
296.4x   manic, _____
296.5x   depressed, _____
301.13   Cyclothymia
296.70   Bipolar disorder

Depressive Disorders
Major Depression
296.2x   single episode, _____
296.3x   recurrent, _____
300.40   Dysthymia (or Depressive neurosis)
        Specify: primary or secondary type
        Specify: early or late onset
311.00   Depressive disorder

ANXIETY DISORDERS (or Anxiety and Phobic Neuroses)
Panic disorder
300.21   with agoraphobia
        Specify current severity of agoraphobic avoidance
        Specify current severity of panic attacks
300.01   without agoraphobia
        Specify current severity of panic attacks
300.22   Agoraphobia without history of panic disorder
        Specify with or without limited symptom attacks
300.23   Social phobia
        Specify if generalized type
300.29   Simple phobia
300.30   Obsessive compulsive disorder (or Obsessive compulsive neurosis)
309.89   Post-traumatic stress disorder
        Specify if delayed onset
300.02   Generalized anxiety disorder
300.00   Anxiety disorder

SOMATOFORM DISORDERS
300.70 Body dysmorphic disorder
300.11 Conversion disorder (or Hysterical neurosis, conversion type)
    Specify: single episode or recurrent
300.70 Hypochondriasis (or Hypochondriacal neurosis)
300.81 Somatization disorder
307.80 Somatoform pain disorder
300.70 Undifferentiated somatoform disorder
300.70 Somatoform disorder

DISSOCIATIVE DISORDERS (or Hysterical Neuroses, Dissociative Type)
300.14 Multiple personality disorder
300.13 Psychogenic fugue
300.12 Psychogenic amnesia
300.60 Depersonalization disorder (or Depersonalization neurosis)
300.15 Dissociative disorder

SEXUAL DISORDERS

Paraphilias
302.40 Exhibitionism
302.81 Fetishism
302.89 Frotteurism
302.20 Pedophilia
    Specify: same sex, opposite sex, same and opposite sex
    Specify if limited to incest
    Specify: exclusive type or nonexclusive type
302.83 Sexual masochism
302.84 Sexual sadism
302.30 Transvestic fetishism
302.82 Voyeurism
302.90 Paraphilia

Sexual Dysfunctions
Specify: psychogenic only, or psychogenic and biogenic (Note: If biogenic only, code on Axis III)
Specify: lifelong or acquired
Specify: generalized or situational

    Sexual desire disorders
302.71 Hypoactive sexual desire disorder
302.79 Sexual aversion disorder

    Sexual arousal disorders
302.72 Female sexual arousal disorder

302.72 Male erectile disorder

    Orgasm disorders
302.73 Inhibited female orgasm
302.74 Inhibited male orgasm
302.75 Premature ejaculation

    Sexual pain disorders
302.76 Dyspareunia
306.51 Vaginismus

302.70 Sexual dysfunction

Other Sexual Disorders
302.90 Sexual disorder

SLEEP DISORDERS

Dyssomnias
    Insomnia disorder
307.42   related to another mental disorder (nonorganic)
780.50   related to known organic factor
307.42 Primary insomnia

    Hypersomnia disorder
307.44   related to another mental disorder (nonorganic)
780.50   related to a known organic factor
780.54 Primary hypersomnia
307.45 Sleep-wake schedule disorder
    Specify: advanced or delayed phase type, disorganized type, frequently changing type

    Other dyssomnias
307.40   Dyssomnia

Parasomnias
307.47 Dream anxiety disorder (Nightmare disorder)
307.46 Sleep terror disorder
307.46 Sleepwalking disorder
307.40 Parasomnia

FACTITIOUS DISORDERS
    Factitious disorder
301.51   with physical symptoms
300.16   with psychological symptoms
300.19 Factitious disorder

IMPULSE CONTROL DISORDERS NOT ELSEWHERE CLASSIFIED

312.34   Intermittent explosive disorder
312.32   Kleptomania
312.31   Pathological gambling
312.33   Pyromania
312.39   Trichotillomania
312.39   Impulse control disorder

ADJUSTMENT DISORDER

Adjustment disorder
309.24   with anxious mood
309.00   with depressed mood
309.30   with disturbance of conduct
309.40   with mixed disturbance of emotions and conduct
309.28   with mixed emotional features
309.82   with physical complaints
309.83   with withdrawal
309.23   with work (or academic) inhibition
309.90   Adjustment disorder

PSYCHOLOGICAL FACTORS AFFECTING PHYSICAL CONDITION

316.00   Psychological factors affecting physical condition
Specify physical condition on Axis III

PERSONALITY DISORDERS

Cluster A
301.00   Paranoid
301.20   Schizoid
301.22   Schizotypal

Cluster B
301.70   Antisocial
301.83   Borderline
301.50   Histrionic
301.81   Narcissistic

Cluster C
301.82   Avoidant
301.60   Dependent
301.40   Obsessive compulsive
301.84   Passive aggressive
301.90   Personality disorder

V CODES FOR CONDITIONS NOT ATTRIBUTABLE TO A MENTAL DISORDER THAT ARE A FOCUS OF ATTENTION OR TREATMENT

V62.30   Academic problem
V71.01   Adult antisocial behavior

V40.00   Borderline intellectual functioning *(Note: This is coded on Axis II.)*

V71.02   Childhood or adolescent antisocial behavior
V65.20   Malingering
V61.10   Marital problem
V15.81   Noncompliance with medical treatment
V62.20   Occupational problem
V61.20   Parent-child problem
V62.81   Other interpersonal problem
V61.80   Other specified family circumstances
V62.89   Phase of life problem or other life circumstance problem
V62.82   Uncomplicated bereavement

ADDITIONAL CODES

300.90   Unspecified mental disorder (nonpsychotic)
V71.09   No diagnosis or condition on Axis I
799.90   Diagnosis or condition deferred on Axis I

V71.09   No diagnosis or condition on Axis II
799.90   Diagnosis or condition deferred on Axis II

Axis IV—Severity of Psychosocial Stressors Scale: Adults

Code	Term	Examples of Stressors	
		Acute events	**Enduring circumstances**
1	None	No acute events that may be relevant to the disorder	No enduring circumstances that may be relevant to the disorder
2	Mild	Broke up with boyfriend or girlfriend; started or graduated from school; child left home	Family arguments; job disatisfaction; residence in high-crime neighborhood
3	Moderate	Marriage; marital separation; loss of job; retirement; miscarriage	Marital discord; serious financial problems; trouble with boss; being a single parent
4	Severe	Divorce; birth of first child	Unemployment; poverty
5	Extreme	Death of spouse; serious physical illness diagnosed; victim of rape	Serious chronic illness in self or child; ongoing physical or sexual abuse
6	Catastrophic	Death of child; suicide of spouse; devastating natural disaster	Captivity as hostage; concentration camp experience
0	Inadequate information, or no change in condition		

Axis IV—Severity of Psychosocial Stressors Scale: Children and Adolescents

Code	Term	Examples of Stressors	
		Acute events	**Enduring circumstances**
1	None	No acute events that may be relevant to the disorder	No enduring circumstances that may be relevant to the disorder
2	Mild	Broke up with boyfriend or girlfriend; change of school	Overcrowded living quarters; family arguments
3	Moderate	Expelled from school; birth of sibling	Chronic disabling illness in parent; chronic parental discord
4	Severe	Divorce of parents; unwanted pregnancy; arrest	Harsh or rejecting parents; chronic life-threatening illness in parent; multiple foster home placements
5	Extreme	Sexual or physical abuse; death of a parent	Recurrent sexual or physical abuse
6	Catastrophic	Death of both parents	Chronic life-threatening illness
0	Inadequate information, or no change in condition		

Axis V—Global Assessment of Functioning Scale (GAF Scale)

Consider psychological, social, and occupational functioning on a hypothetical continuum of mental health-illness. Do not include impairment in functioning due to physical (or environmental) limitations.

Note: Use intermediate codes when appropriate, e.g., 45, 68, 72.

Code

90
| **Absent or minimal symptoms** (e.g., mild anxiety before an exam), **good functioning in all areas, interested and involved in a wide range of activities, socially effective, generally satisfied with life, no more than everyday**
81 | **problems or concerns** (e.g., an occasional argument with family members).

80
| **If symptoms are present, they are transient and expectable reactions to psychosocial stressors** (e.g., difficulty concentrating after family argument);**no more than slight impairment in social, occupational, or school**
71 | **functioning** (e.g., temporarily falling behind in school work).

70
| **Some mild symptoms** (e.g., depressed mood and mild insomnia) **OR some difficulty in social, occupational, or school functioning** (e.g., occasional truancy, or theft within the household), **but generally functioning pretty**
61 | **well, has some meaningful interpersonal relationships.**

60
| **Moderate symptoms** (e.g., flat affect and circumstantial speech, occasional panic attacks) **OR moderate difficulty in social, occupational, or**
51 | **school functioning** (e.g., few friends, conflicts with co-workers).

50
| **Serious symptoms** (e.g., suicidal ideation, severe obsessional rituals, frequent shoplifting) **OR any serious impairment in social, occupational, or**
41 | **school functioning** (e.g., no friends, unable to keep a job).

40
| **Some impairment in reality testing or communication** (e.g., speech is at times illogical, obscure, or irrelevant) **OR major impairment in several areas, such as work or school, family relations, judgment, thinking, or mood** (e.g., depressed man avoids friends, neglects family, and is unable to work; child frequently beats up younger children, is defiant at home, and
31 | is failing at school).

30
| **Behavior is considerably influenced by delusions or hallucinations OR serious impairment in communication or judgment** (e.g., sometimes incoherent, acts grossly inappropriately, suicidal preoccupation) **OR inability to function in almost all areas** (e.g., stays in bed all day; no job, home, or
21 | friends).

20
| **Some danger of hurting self or others** (e.g., suicide attempts without clear expectation of death, frequently violent, manic excitement) **OR occasionally fails to maintain minimal personal hygiene** (e.g., smears feces) **OR**
11 | **gross impairment in communication** (e.g., largely incoherent or mute).

10
| **Persistent danger of severely hurting self or others** (e.g., recurrent violence) **OR persistent inability to maintain minimal personal hygiene OR**
1 | **serious suicidal act with clear expectation of death.**

Glossary

acquired dyslexia Difficulty in reading experienced by those who had been able to read well.

addiction Dependence on a drug, resulting in tolerance and withdrawal symptoms when the addict is deprived of the drug. *See also* tolerance and withdrawal.

adrenaline (or *epinephrine*) A hormone secreted by the adrenal glands, which causes increase in blood pressure, release of sugar by the liver, and a number of the other physiological reactions to threat.

adrenergic A descriptive term for the nerve cells that use adrenaline and noradrenaline as chemical transmitters. The sympathetic nervous system is an andrenergic system.

affective disorders A class of mental disorders characterized by a disturbance of mood. Includes unipolar depression, bipolar depression, and mania.

affective pleasure An effect of drug use in the opponent-process model of addiction. Affective pleasure is the pleasant emotional state that is the initial pharmacological effect produced by the drug.

affective tolerance An effect of drug use in the opponent-process model of addiction. With continued use, the addictive drug tends to lose its affective pleasure.

affective withdrawal An effect of drug use in the opponent-process model of addiction. The sudden termination of narcotic use often produces the opposite affective state of the initial pleasant one.

agnosia Inability to recognize meaningful objects.

agoraphobia An anxiety disorder characterized by fear of situations in which one might be trapped and unable to acquire help, especially in the event of a panic attack. Agoraphobics will avoid crowds, enclosed spaces (such as elevators and buses), or large open spaces. From the Greek "fear of the marketplace."

alexia Acquired inability to read resulting from brain damage, with vision intact.

alexithymia The word literally means "no words for feelings" and is used to describe people who have difficulty expressing their feelings.

altruistic suicide Suicide required by the society (as defined by Durkheim; for example, hari-kari).

Alzheimer's disease Degenerative disease of late middle or old age, in which mental functions deteriorate. An amnesic syndrome is often the major feature of this disorder. Its initial symptoms include loss of initiative, extreme forgetfulness, memory disability, and spatial disorders. It progresses to severe deteriorations of intellect and basic maintenance functions that lead to death.

amenorrhea Loss of the menstrual period. A common occurrence in women anorexics.

amnesia (or psychogenic amnesia) A dissociative disorder characterized by loss of memory of happenings during a certain time period, or loss of memory of personal identity. Includes retrograde amnesia, anterograde amnesia, and selective amnesia.

amnesic syndrome A disorder of memory, of organic origin, in which memory for recent events (events occurring after the brain damage) is very poor or completely absent.

amphetamine A stimulant that causes agitation, increase in energy and activity, hyper-responsiveness to the environment, euphoria, and a number of physiological signs of hyperactivation.

amyotrophic lateral sclerosis (ALS) Also known as Lou Gehrig's disease, this disorder is characterized by weakness and a loss of motor control produced by motor neuron degeneration, and by gradual loss of ability to move; it eventually leads to death.

anaclitic depression A depression experienced by some infants between the ages of six and eighteen months who have been separated from their mothers for prolonged periods. This disorder is characterized by apathy, listlessness, weight loss, susceptibility to illness, and sometimes death.

anal character traits Traits such as orderliness, stinginess, and stubbornness which, according to psychoanalytic theory, result from fixation during the anal stage of psychosexual development.

anal stage The second stage of psychosexual development whose principal foci, according to psychodynamic theorists, are pleasure and the parental control involved in toilet training.

androgen A hormone that is principally responsible for the morphological development of the external genitals of the male.

androgen insensitivity syndrome   A syndrome in which the fetus lacks the receptors for the sex hormone, androgen, and which produces neurological females in male fetuses.

anomia   Inability to name objects.

anomic suicide   Suicide precipitated by a shattering break in an individual's relationship to his society (as defined by Durkheim).

anorexia nervosa   A disorder in which the individual has an intense fear of becoming fat, eats far too little to sustain herself, and has a distorted body image.

anterograde amnesia   The principal feature of the amnesic syndrome: a failure to recall events that occurred since the onset of brain damage or trauma.

antigens   Invaders of the immune system.

anti-reductionism   A philosophy that holds that at least some psychological phenomena exist that cannot be reduced to biological phenomena.

anxiety   Fear, commonly inferred fear, characterized by the expectation of an unspecified danger, dread, terror, or apprehension, often leading to an emergency reaction and "flight or fight" behavior. As used in psychoanalytic theory, the psychic pain that results from conflicts among the various personality processes.

anxiety disorders   A class of mental disorders characterized by chronic and debilitating anxiety. Includes generalized anxiety disorder, panic disorder, phobias, and post-traumatic stress disorder.

aphasia   Disorders of language resulting from damage to certain areas of the cerebral cortex.

appraisal   Evaluation of short-term mental events, a target of cognitive therapy.

apraxia   A disorder of movement in the absence of muscle weakness or inability to perform any specific movement.

arbitrary inference   Reaching a conclusion for which there is little or no evidence. According to Beck, depressives are prone to making arbitrary inferences.

archetypes   As used by Jung, universal ideas about which we are knowledgeable even at birth.

assimilative projection   Attribution to another of beliefs, attitudes, or feelings that we are quite unaware of experiencing ourselves.

attention deficit hyperactivity disorder   A disorder characterized by marked impulsivity, inattention, and hyperactivity.

attribution   An assignment of cause for an event; a short-term mental event, and a target of cognitive therapy.

autism   A childhood disorder whose central feature is the failure to develop the ability to respond to others within the first thirty months of life.

automatic thoughts   Discrete sentences, negative in character, that a person says to himself, quickly and habitually. According to Beck, depressives typically engage in automatic thoughts.

autonomic nervous system   The system that regulates the internal environment of the body, including the heart, stomach, adrenals, and intestines. The autonomic nervous system is divided into the sympathetic and parasympathetic nervous systems.

aversion therapy   A behavior therapy that seeks to rid a client of undesired behavior by pairing that behavior with aversive consequences.

avoidance-approach conflict   A conflict between a desire to approach an object or situation that has some positive value, and a desire to avoid that object or situation because it has been associated with harm. According to traditional learning theory, this conflict is a root of anxiety.

avoidance responding   The act of getting out of a situation that has been previously associated with an aversive event, thereby preventing the aversive event. Differs from escape responding, which is getting out of the aversive event itself.

avoidant personality disorder   A disorder whose central feature is social withdrawal combined with hypersensitivity to rejection.

Babinski sign   A change in the reflex response to scratching of the bottom of the foot that indicates damage to upper levels of the motor system.

barbiturates   A class of drugs that depress the central nervous system, decreasing anxiety and blunting sensitivity to the environment. Includes phenobarbital, pentobarbital, secobarbital, and benzodiapines.

behavior therapy   A therapy that is rooted in the view that psychological distress results from learned behavior that can be unlearned; the therapy seeks to replace the distressing behavior with more constructive modes of coping and adaptation.

behavioral assessment   A record of behaviors and thoughts one wishes to change, including their time of occurrence, duration, and intensity.

behavioral disorder   A disorder in which something behavioral, rather than emotional, is amiss, such as hyperactivity, attentional problems, and aggressive, destructive, and dishonest behaviors.

behavioral school   The school of abnormal psychology that claims that behavior is shaped by the environment, and that behavior can be changed by changing the environment. According to the behavioral theorists, the symptomatic behavior of a mental disorder is the disorder, and is that which should be treated.

benzodiazepines   A group of mild tranquilizers that result in muscle relaxation, decreased anxiety, and sedation. Includes Librium, Valium, and Dalmane.

beta cells   Lymphocytes that come from bone marrow and that have receptors on their surface for specific antigens.

beta-endorphins   Large proteins that are produced in the body and that are opiate-like compounds.

biofeedback   Therapeutic technique in which the individual is given electronically amplified information on certain (somewhat) controllable physiological systems (such as heart rate and blood pressure) and trained to control that response system.

biomedical model of abnormality   The school of abnormal psychology that claims that mental disorders are illnesses of the body resulting from an underlying physiological pathology such as a virus, disordered biochemistry or genes, or a dysfunctional organ.

bipolar depression (or manic-depressive disorder)   An affective disorder characterized by alternating periods of depression and mania.

bisexuality   Desire for sexual relations with members of both sexes.

blood-brain barrier   A barrier in the brain composed of tiny capillaries that prevent many chemicals from going from the bloodstream to the brain cells.

borderline personality disorder A broad Axis-II diagnostic category that designates people whose salient characteristic is instability in a variety of personality areas, including interpersonal relationships, behavior, mood, and self-image.

Briquet's syndrome *See* somatization disorder.

bulimia nervosa (or bulimia) A disorder in which people alternately gorge themselves with enormous quantities of food, and then purge themselves of that food by vomiting, or using laxatives or diuretics.

bypassing Tuning out what turns you off during sexual activity and instead focusing on fantasy.

caffeine A drug that stimulates the central nervous system and the skeletal muscles, lengthening the time it takes to fall asleep, decreasing fatigue, and aiding the individual in doing physical work.

castration anxiety Fear of having one's penis removed or harmed; part of the basis for the Oedipus conflict.

catecholamines Hormones involved in neural transmission in the brain. Includes norepinephrine, epinephrine, and dopamine.

catharsis In psychoanalytic theory, the uncovering and reliving of early traumatic conflicts.

cathexis Charging of a neutral object with psychical energy, either positive or negative. Psychoanalytic basis of acquired fears and lusts.

central nervous system (CNS) That part of the nervous system that coordinates all of the activity of the nervous system. In vertebrates, the CNS is made up of the brain and the spinal cord. All sensory inputs are transmitted to the CNS and all motor impulses are transmitted from the CNS.

cerebral cortex The outermost layer (gray matter) of the cerebral hemispheres.

cerebrospinal fluid A clear fluid, like blood plasma, that accounts for some of the circulation in the brain and spinal cord.

cholinergic A descriptive term for the nerve cells that use acetylcholine as a chemical transmitter. The parasympathetic nervous system is a cholinergic system.

clang associations Associations produced by the rhyme of words. Commonly found in schizophrenics.

clinical case history The record of part of the life of an individual seen in therapy.

clitoris A small organ located forward of the vagina in females. It becomes erect upon sexual arousal and is involved in orgasm.

cocaine The psychoactive agent in the coca plant. Cocaine increases energy, combats fatigue and boredom, and enhances the individual's responsiveness to things in his environment.

cognitions Beliefs, thoughts, attitudes, expectations, and other mental events.

cognitive-behavioral therapy A therapeutic technique in which therapists attempt to alter both the maladaptive thoughts and maladaptive behaviors of a client through restructuring of maladaptive belief systems and re-training behavior.

cognitive model The school of abnormal psychology that claims that many disorders result from maladaptive beliefs or thought styles.

cognitive restructuring Treatments that are predicated on the assumption that irrational thoughts create irrational behaviors, which can be eliminated by changing the underlying thoughts.

cognitive therapy Used primarily in the treatment of depression, this therapy seeks to change the cognitive triad of (a) self-devaluation, (b) a negative view of life experience, and (c) the pessimistic view of the future, as the determining cognitions for depression.

cognitive triad A group of cognitions that, according to Beck, characterizes depressives. These cognitions include (a) negative thoughts about the self, (b) negative thoughts about ongoing experience, and (c) negative thoughts about the future.

collective unconscious As used by Jung, the memory traces of the experience of past generations.

compulsion A repetitive, stereotyped, and unwanted action that can be resisted only with difficulty. It is usually associated with obsessions.

compulsive personality disorder A disorder that is characterized by the long-term inability to express warm emotions, combined with an inappropriate preoccupation with trivial rules and details.

computer-assisted tomography (or CAT scan) An X-ray technique, used in neurological diagnosis, for constructing three-dimensional representations of the X-ray density of different areas of the brain.

concordant When both of two twins have a disorder such as schizophrenia, they are called concordant for that disorder. *See also* discordant.

conditioned cravings Drug cravings elicited by the settings formerly associated with using the substance.

conditioned response (CR) A response that is evoked by a certain stimulus (conditioned stimulus) once that stimulus has become associated with some other stimulus (unconditioned stimulus) that naturally evokes the unconditioned response. *See also* Pavlovian conditioning.

conditioned stimulus (CS) A stimulus that, because of its having been paired with another stimulus (unconditioned stimulus) that naturally provokes an unconditioned response, is eventually able to evoke that response. *See also* Pavlovian conditioning.

conduct disorders A cluster of children's behavioral disorders that consists mainly of aggressive and rule-breaking behaviors.

confound A factor other than the experimentally controlled independent variable that might produce an experimental effect.

consolidation block Failure to establish (consolidate) short-term memories. This is a mechanism proposed as an explanation of the amnesic syndrome.

contiguity Conjunction in time and place.

contingency A conditional relationship between two objects or events, describable by the probability of event A given event B, along with the probability of event A in the absence of event B. A positive contingency between A and B obtains when A is more likely in the presence of B than in the absence of B. *See also* Pavlovian conditioning.

continuous reinforcement Provision of reinforcement every time a subject makes a response. *See also* reinforcement.

control group A group of subjects similar to those in an experimental group, who experience everything the experimental group does, except the independent variable.

conversion *See* hysterical conversion.

coping strategies As used by psychoanalytic theorists, the process by which people alter the meaning and significance of troublesome drives and impulses in order to eliminate anxiety.

core self The self that develops first, between the second and sixth month of an infant's life. It embraces the infant's awareness that she and her caretaker are *physically separate.*

corpus callosum The largest tract in the brain, connecting corresponding areas of the two hemispheres.

correlation coefficient A statistic indicating the degree of contingency between two variables.

corticospinal tract A tract of axons from cell bodies in the motor cortex that innervates motor neurons in the spinal cord, and mediates (among other things) voluntary movements of the hands.

co-twin As used in psychological research, one of a pair of twins whose sibling is seen at a psychiatric clinic in order to diagnose a psychological problem.

counterbypassing A sexual therapy designed to broaden rather than narrow awareness during sexual arousal. This therapy aims to increase the awareness of suppressed negative thoughts and to encourage partners to talk to each other about such thoughts.

counterconditioning A therapeutic technique for phobias in which a phobic patient is helped to relax while imagining fear-provoking situations (usually at first the least fear-provoking situation, then gradually more and more fear-provoking situations). The relaxation response to the imagined situation is incompatible with the fear the patient has previously associated with the situation, and the fear is thus extinguished.

counterphobia The pursuit of precisely those activities that are deeply feared.

cross tolerance When tolerance to one drug produces tolerance to other drugs.

defense mechanisms *See* coping strategies.

delayed auditory feedback Used in the treatment of stuttering, this technique involves hearing one's own speech played back over earphones at about a one-second delay.

delirium tremens A dangerous syndrome of withdrawal from alcohol, which is characterized by psychomotor agitation, hyperactivity of the autonomic nervous system, anxiety, loss of appetite, delusions, amnesia, and convulsions.

delusions False beliefs that resist all argument and are sustained in the face of evidence that normally would be sufficient to destroy them.

delusions of control Beliefs that one's thoughts or behaviors are being controlled from without.

delusions of grandeur Unsubstantiable convictions that one is especially important.

delusions of persecution Groundless fears that individuals, groups, or the government have malevolent intentions and are "out to get me."

delusions of reference Incorrect beliefs that the casual remarks or behaviors of others apply to oneself.

demand characteristics Aspects of the experimental setting that induce the subject to invent and act on an hypothesis about how one should behave.

dementia A more or less general deterioration of mental function, found most commonly in old people. Alzheimer's disease is a common form of dementia.

denial As used in psychoanalytic theory, the process by which distressing external facts are eliminated.

dendrites A usually highly branched part of a neuron that is stimulated by neurotransmitters produced by receptors or other neurons.

dependent personality disorder A disorder wherein people allow others to make major decisions, to initiate important actions, and to assume responsibility for the significant areas of one's life.

dependent variable The factor that the experimenter expects will be affected by changes in the independent variable.

depersonalization A dissociative disorder in which the individual feels often cut off from or unsure of his or her identity.

depression An affective disorder characterized by (a) sad affect and loss of interest in usually satisfying activities, (b) a negative view of the self and hopelessness, (c) passivity, indecisiveness, and suicidal intentions, and (d) loss of appetite, weight loss, sleep disturbances, and other physical symptoms.

deprivation dwarfism A disorder marked by retarded bone age without evidence of primary medical disease in children. The disorder can be reversed by removing the child from her family environment and placing her in an emotionally supportive hospital setting.

dereflection Used by existential therapists, this technique involves directing the client's attention away from his symptoms and pointing out how much he could be doing and enjoying if he were not so preoccupied with his troubles.

developmental disorders A cluster of disorders of childhood that may consist of deficits in language comprehension, speech, and responses to others that can result in such serious disorders as autism or childhood schizophrenia.

developmental dyslexia Difficulty in learning to read out or proportion to intellectual and emotional development.

diathesis Physical vulnerability or predisposition to a particular disorder.

diathesis-stress model A general model of disorders that postulates that an individual develops a disorder when he both has some constitutional vulnerability (diathesis) and when he experiences psychological disturbance (stress).

direct sexual therapy A therapeutic method developed by Masters and Johnson, in which (a) sexual dysfunctions are clearly and simply defined, (b) clients explicitly practice sexual behavior under the systematic guidance of therapists, and (c) clients are treated as couples, not as individuals.

disconnection syndrome A disorder accounted for by severing of or damage to tracts connecting specific areas of the brain.

discordant When only one of two twins has a disorder such as schizophrenia, they are called discordant for that disorder. *See also* concordant.

discriminative stimulus A signal indicating that reinforcement is available if a certain operant response is made.

disinhibition An increase in some reaction resulting from release of inhibition.

disorganized schizophrenia A schizophrenic disorder whose most striking behavioral characteristic is apparent silliness and incoherence. Behavior is jovial but quite bizarre and absurd, suggesting extreme sensitivity to internal cues and extreme insensitivity to external ones, but without systematic delusions or hallucinations.

disowning projection A process whereby feelings and experiences that one personally denies having and that are usually repressed are attributed to others.

displacement A cognitive alteration of reality that involves replacing the true object of one's emotions with one that is more innocent and less threatening.

disruptive behavior disorders A cluster of disorders characterized by symptoms such as hyperactivity, inattention, aggressiveness, destructiveness, and defiance of authority.

dissociative disorders A group of mental disorders characterized by fragmentation of an individual's identity. Dissociative disorders include amnesia, fugue, multiple personality, and depersonalization disorder.

diversiform disorder A type of somatization disorder in which individuals have few back problems but tend to complain about the rest of the body.

dizygotic twins Fraternal twins, or twins who developed from separate eggs, and whose genes are no more alike than are any pair of non-identical-twin siblings.

dopamine A catecholamine that facilitates neural transmission.

dopamine hypothesis The theory that schizophrenia results from an excess of the neurotransmitter dopamine.

double-blind experiment An experiment in which both the subject and experimenter are blind as to whether the subject has received an experimental treatment or a placebo.

Down's syndrome (or **mongolism**) A disorder that results from the fact that an individual has forty-seven rather than the usual forty-six chromosomes in his or her cells.

drug dependence The regular use of drugs acting on the brain that leads to maladaptive behavioral changes that would be seen as maladaptive in any culture. Three criteria characterize the disorder: (a) a pattern of pathological use of a drug, (b) impairment in occupational, social, physical, or emotional functioning, and (c) evidence of affective or physical adaptation to the drug.

drug tolerance The need to use increased amounts of the drug to get the desired effect.

drug withdrawal Characteristic affective and physical symptoms that follow drug use after the drug is discontinued.

DSM-III-R Published in 1987, this is the interim revision of the third edition of the *Diagnostic and Statistical Manual of Mental Disorders* of the American Psychiatric Association.

Durham test A legal test for insanity which provides that an accused is not criminally responsible if his unlawful act was the product of mental disease or mental defect.

dysfunction Impairment of functioning.

dysphoria An unpleasant emotional state experienced during drug withdrawal; the opposite of ephoria.

efficacy expectation According to Bandura, a person's belief that he can successfully execute the behavior that will produce a desired outcome.

ego The self.

ego-dystonic homosexuality Homosexuality that is incongruent with the individual's desire for sexual preference, and which the individual wants to change.

ego-syntonic homosexuality Homosexuality that is congruent with the individual's desire for sexual preference, and which the individual does not want to change.

egoistic suicide Suicide resulting when the individual has too few ties to his fellow humans (as defined by Durkheim).

ejaculation The vigorous contraction of the muscles at the base of the penis, which causes sperm to be ejected from the penis. *See also* orgasm.

electroconvulsive shock treatment (ECT) A therapeutic treatment for depression, in which metal electrodes are taped to either side of the patient's head, and the patient is anesthetized. A high current is passed through the brain for a half second, followed by convulsions lasting almost one minute.

electroencephalogram (EEG) A record of the electrical activity of cells in the brain (primarily the cortex) obtained from wires placed on the skull, and used in neurological diagnosis.

emergency reaction A reaction to threat in which the sympathetic nervous system mobilizes the body for action. The blood pressure rises, heart rate increases, breathing becomes deeper, perspiration increases, and the liver releases sugar for use by the muscles.

emission Discharge of semen with contraction of the reproductive organs in the male.

emotional disorders A cluster of disorders found often among children, in which symptoms of fear, anxiety, inhibition, shyness, and overattachment predominate.

empiricism The school of philosophy that claims that all that people are and all that they know are the result of experiences.

endogenous depression A depression resulting from disordered biology. From the Greek "arising from within."

endorphins Endogenous morphine-like substances.

endorphin compensation hypothesis A hypothesis stating that drinking alcohol increases endogenous opioid activity and that the desire to drink alcohol increases during conditions of deficiencies in endorphin activity.

enkephalins Small amino acid compounds that are endogenous opioids.

enuresis (or **bed-wetting**) A disorder that is manifested by regular and involuntary voiding of urine.

environmentalist model of abnormality The cognitive-behavioral approach that maintains that organisms, including humans, are shaped by the environment and that abnormality is learned through conditioning or from disordered conscious thoughts.

epilepsy A disorder of the brain that expresses itself as excessive neuronal discharge (seizure) in some parts of the brain, with appropriate sensory, mental, or motor effects, and frequently some alteration in consciousness.

epinephrine *See* adrenaline.

epiphenomenon A process, which while not causal, reflects the underlying process, which is causal.

erectile dysfunction (or **impotence**) In males, recurrent inability to have or to maintain an erection for intercourse.

erogenous zones Pleasure centers.

erotic arousal Excitement of sexual desire.

escape responding The act of getting out of an ongoing harmful situation. *See also* avoidance responding.

etiology Causal description of the development of a disorder.

exhibitionism A psychosexual disorder in which the individual is sexually aroused primarily by exposing his genitals to unwitting strangers.

existential theory A theory that holds that mental disorders result when an individual fails to confront the basic questions of life successfully. Three issues are particularly important: fear of dying, personal responsibility, and will.

existential therapy A therapy that encourages clients to view their psychological problems as being of their own making.

exogenous depression A depression precipitated by a life stressor. Sometimes called reactive depression. From the Greek "arising from without."

expectations Cognitions that extrapolate the present to the anticipation of future events.

experiment A procedure in which an hypothesized cause (independent variable) is manipulated and the occurrence of an effect (dependent variable) is measured.

experimental artifact Experimental features other than the independent variable, which cause the experimental effect.

experimental effect The change in the dependent variable as a result of the manipulation of the independent variable.

experimental group A group of subjects who are given experience with an independent variable.

experimentalism The behaviorist view that experiments can reveal what aspects of the environment cause behavior.

experimenter bias The exertion of subtle influences by the experimenter on subjects' responses in an experiment.

experiments of nature Studies in which the experimenter observes the effects of an unusual natural event.

expressive aphasia A language disorder that manifests itself primarily as a deficit in speech or the organization of spoken language.

external attribution An assignment of cause for an event to a factor that is outside oneself (i.e., other people or circumstances).

extinction In Pavlovian conditioning, cessation of a previously conditioned response to a conditioned stimulus, due to having learned that the conditioned stimulus no longer signals the onset of an aversive or desirable event. In instrumental learning, cessation of acquired operant responses due to reinforcement being discontinued. Modern theorists believe that extinction occurs when there is a negative contingency between the conditioned stimulus and the unconditioned stimulus. *See also* contingency.

factitious disorder A mental disorder characterized by multiple hospitalizations and operations precipitated by the individual's having self-inflicted signs of illness.

false alarm In experimental analysis, accepting the hypothesis that independent and dependent variables are related, when they really are not. *See also* miss.

family therapy A group of diverse psychotherapies that treat the couple or family, rather than the individual alone.

fat solubility Ability of a substance to be stored in fat cells.

feeling substitution A process by which feelings that are stressful are unconsciously replaced by less painful feelings.

fetish A psychosexual disorder characterized by a need to have an inanimate object close by in order to become sexually aroused.

fixation Stagnation of psychological development.

flaccid A flabbiness or lack of firmness in muscles.

flooding A method used by behavioral therapists to treat phobias.

The phobic is exposed to the situations or objects most feared for an extended length of time without the opportunity to escape. *See also* response prevention.

free association A psychoanalytic instruction to say whatever comes to mind, regardless of how ridiculous or embarrassing it is, and without attempting to censor.

frequency distribution The number of observations in each given class observed.

frontal lobe A lobe in each cerebral hemisphere that includes control and organization of motor function.

fugue (or **psychogenic fugue**) A dissociative disorder in which an individual, in an amnesic state, travels away from home and assumes a new identity.

functional analysis A behavioral assessment that is accompanied by a description of the stimuli that are presumed either to increase or decrease the incidence of specified behaviors.

functional syndromes Abnormal behaviors believed to be caused by abnormal experience imposed upon normal brain mechanisms. Psychiatry and clinical psychology study these syndromes.

gender identity Awareness of being male or being female.

gender identity disorder A class of mental disorders in which the essential feature is an incongruence between anatomic sex and gender identity. Includes transsexualism.

gender role Public expression of gender identity; what an individual does and says to indicate that he is a man or she is a woman.

general adaptation syndrome According to Selye, a sequence of three stages that ensues when an individual is stressed: (a) the somatic emergency reaction is initiated, (b) the individual engages in defensive behaviors, and (c) eventually the individual's adaptive actions are exhausted.

general paresis A disorder characterized by mental deterioration, paralysis, then death. This disorder is caused by a spirochete involved in syphilis.

generalized anxiety disorder An anxiety disorder characterized by chronic tenseness and vigilance, beliefs that something bad will happen, mild emergency reactions, and feelings of wanting to run away.

genital stage In psychoanalytic theory, the fifth and final stage of psychosexual development during which the adolescent learns to channel sexual energy into love and work.

global attribution An individual's assignment of cause for an event to a factor that will affect a number of different areas of his life.

glove anesthesia A conversion symptom in which nothing can be felt in the hand and fingers, but sensation is intact from the wrist up.

Gestalt therapy A therapy that emphasizes taking responsibility for one's life by living in the present.

grave disability A legal phrase that describes an individual's psychological inability to provide food or shelter for herself, which places her in imminent danger.

gray matter That part of the central nervous system that is composed primarily of neurons and glia cell bodies.

growth hormone The pituitary gland regulates growth by the differential secretion of the growth hormone.

habit disorders A collection of childhood disorders in which the prominent symptoms include difficulties associated with eating, movement disorders, or tics. These disorders consist of a diverse group of problems with physical manifestations such as bed-wetting, stuttering, sleepwalking and epilepsy.

half-life The length of time it takes for the level of a drug in the blood to be decreased by 50 percent.

hallucination A perception that occurs in the absence of an identifiable stimulus.

hallucinogens Chemicals that cause perceptual disorientation, depersonalization, illusions, hallucinations, and physiological symptoms such as tachycardia, palpitations, and tremors. Includes marijuana, PCP, and LSD.

hemorrhage Bleeding or loss of blood resulting from rupture or leakage from a blood vessel.

hermaphrodites People born with ambiguous-looking genitals.

heterosexuality Preference for sexual partners of the opposite sex.

hierarchy A form of organization, characteristic of the nervous system, in which narrower "categories" or domains of "control" are subsumed under successively broader "nodes."

high frequency somatization disorder A disorder in which individuals have frequent stomach and back pains in conjunction with psychiatric problems.

homosexuality Preference for sexual partners of one's own sex.

hormones Genes that modulate physical growth, bodily differentiation, and psychological growth.

hypomanic personality A chronic form of mania involving an unbroken two-year-long manic state. *See also* mania.

hyposomnia Greatly lessened need for sleep.

hyperactivity A disorder that is marked by developmentally inappropriate impulsiveness, inattentiveness, and excessive motor behavior. *See also* attention-deficit hyperactivity disorder.

hypochondriasis The sustained conviction, in the absence of medical evidence, that one is ill or about to become ill.

hypothalamus A brain structure that lies under the cortex. The hypothalamus influences eating, drinking, and sexual behavior, and is involved in regulating fundamental bodily processes, including metabolism and water balance.

hysterical conversion A somatoform disorder characterized by the loss of functioning of some part of the body not due to any physical disorder, but apparently due to psychological conflicts. The loss is not under voluntary control.

id In psychoanalytic theory, the mental representation of biological drives.

identification As used by psychoanalytic theorists, the process by which the characteristics of others—their ideas, values, mannerisms, status, and power—are internalized.

immunocompetence The degree to which the immune system is able to efficiently protect the organism.

immunologic memory The factor that enables those T-cells and G-cells that initially combated an antigen to multiply more rapidly the second time the antigen is spotted, such that the immune system is able to do a better job of destroying the antigen than it did the first time.

incidence The rate of new cases of a disorder in a given time period.

independent variable The hypothesized cause of some effect, manipulated by the experimenter in an experiment.

index case In psychological research, one of a pair of twins who is first seen at a psychiatric clinic.

indoleamines Hormones involved in neural transmission. Indoleamines include serotonin and histamine.

inhibition An active process through which the excitability of a particular neuron or center (group of neurons) is decreased.

instrumental learning (or instrumental conditioning) A technique in which an organism must learn to perform some voluntary behavior in order to acquire a desired outcome, or to stop an undesirable event.

instrumental response A response whose probability can be modified by reinforcement; a response that an organism has learned will bring about a desired outcome, or will stop an undesired event. *See also* operant.

intellectualization A coping strategy that takes the form of repressing the emotional component of experience, and restating that experience as an abstract intellectual analysis.

intercourse The sexual act in which the male inserts his penis into the female's vagina and the two move toward ejaculation of semen by the male, and orgasm for the female.

internal attribution An individual's assignment of cause for an event to a factor that is an aspect of himself.

introcosm A metaphor that describes a person's internal world.

intromission Insertion of the penis into the vagina or other orifice.

isolation A coping strategy in which only the affective component of an unpleasant experience is repressed while the information is retained.

Kappa A statistic that attempts to describe the extent to which observers agree about a diagnosis by taking into consideration the likelihood that such an agreement might have arisen by coincidence.

Korsakoff's syndrome A particular form of the amnesic syndrome caused by alcoholism.

laboratory model The production, under controlled conditions, or phenomena analogous to naturally occurring mental disorders.

latency stage In psychoanalytic theory, the third stage of psychosexual development during which sexuality is repressed and attention is directed toward mastering social and cognitive skills.

learned helplessness A condition characterized by an expectation that bad events will occur, and that there is nothing one can do to prevent their occurrence. Results in passivity, cognitive deficits, and other symptoms that resemble depression.

left visual field The left half of one's visual world, that is, the part of the world that projects onto the right side of the retina and into the right hemisphere.

lesion Localized damage to (neural) tissue.

libido In psychoanalytic theory, psychic energy that can become associated with a host of pleasurable activities.

LSD (lysergic acid diethylamide) An hallucinogenic drug that causes changes in body sensations (dizziness, weakness, nausea), perception (distorted time sense), emotion, and cognitive processes.

lycanthropy   A disorder in which people believe they are wolves, and act accordingly.

lymphocytes   Cells in the immune system that recognize foreign cells.

macrophages   Cells in the immune system that "eat" antigens.

magnetic resonance imaging (MRI)   A brain-imaging technique in which each type of atom behaves like a tiny spinning magnet, wobbling at a characteristic frequency in the magnetic field. An MRI shows the elemental composition of cells and surrounding tissue. Damaged areas of the brain have a different concentration of elements than normal areas and appear differently on an MRI.

magnification   Overestimating the impact of a small bad event; error of logic made by those who are depressed.

malingering   A disorder in which the individual reports somatic symptoms, but these symptoms are under the individual's control, and the individual has an obvious motive for the somatic complaints. *See also* hysterical conversion.

mania   An affective disorder characterized by excessive elation, expansiveness, irritability, talkativeness, inflated self-esteem, and flight of ideas.

MAO (monoamine oxidase)   An enzyme that helps to break down catecholamines and indoleamines. MAO inhibitors are used to treat depression.

marijuana   A psychoactive drug that, when used chronically and heavily, causes impairment of ability to focus on a task, impulsive and compulsive behavior, delusions, sensory-perceptual distortions, and sometimes panic reactions.

masochism   A psychosexual disorder in which the individual prefers to become sexually aroused by having suffering or humiliation inflicted upon him.

masturbation   Self-stimulation of one's genitals for sexual arousal and orgasm.

mean   Average value of a set of values.

melancholia   Depression characterized chiefly by loss of pleasure in most activities and by somatic symptoms, including sleep loss and loss of appetite.

mental disorder   In DSM-III-R, a behavioral or psychological pattern that is genuinely dysfunctional and that either distresses or disables the individual in one or more significant areas of functioning.

methadone   A narcotic used in heroin treatment programs. Methadone acts as a substitute for heroin, and prevents the heroin addict from experiencing withdrawal.

Minnesota Multiphasic Personality Inventory (MMPI)   A widely used personality inventory consisting of 550 test items that inquire into a wide array of behaviors, thoughts, and feelings.

M'Naghten test   A legal test for insanity which provides that a person cannot be found guilty of a crime if, at the time of committing the offense, due to "disease of the mind," the individual did not know the nature and quality of the act or that the act was wrong.

minimization   Downplaying good events; an error of logic in depression.

miss   Rejecting an hypothesis that the independent variable and dependent variable are related, when they really are.

modeling   The observation and gradual imitation of a model who exhibits behavior that the client seeks to adopt in place of an undesirable behavior.

mongolism   *See* Down's syndrome.

moral anxiety   As used by psychoanalytic theorists, anxiety that arises when one anticipates that one's behavior will violate one's personal standards, or when that behavior has in fact violated those standards.

multiple personality   A dissociative disorder in which more than one distinct personality exists in the same individual, and each personality is relatively rich, integrated, and stable.

myelin   A fatty substance that surrounds many axons in the peripheral and central nervous system.

narcissistic personality disorder   A personality disorder whose salient characteristics are an outlandish sense of self-importance, continual self-absorption, fantasies of unlimited success, power and/or beauty, and needs for constant admiration.

narcotics   A class of psychoactive drugs that blocks emotional response to pain and produces euphoria, dysphoria, apathy, psychomotor retardation, drowsiness, slurred speech, and maladaptive behavior. Includes opium, morphine, heroin, and methadone.

natural killer cells   Cells in the immune system that lyse cells of a tumor.

nature-nurture issue   A major debate in psychology, concerning the relative roles of environment and heredity in the development of personality and behavior.

negative reinforcer   An event whose removal increases the probability of a response that precedes it. *See also* punishment.

neurology   The clinical discipline that studies the diseases of the nervous system.

neuron   A nerve cell; the basic unit of the nervous system.

neurosis   Formerly, a category for disorders in which the individual experienced (a) emotionally distressing symptoms, (b) an unwelcome psychological state, (c) reasonably good reality testing, and (d) behavior that was reasonably within social norms. A neurotic disorder was not considered a transient reaction to stress or the result of organic brain damage.

neurotic anxiety   As used in psychoanalytic theory, anxiety that arises from the possibility that one will be overwhelmed by one's impulses, especially unconscious sexual and aggressive impulses.

neurotransmitter   A chemical that facilitates the transmission of electrical impulses among nerve endings in the brain.

neutrophils   Cells in the immune system that "eat" an antigen-antibody complex.

niacin (nicotinic acid)   An essential vitamin, the deficiency of which results in pellagra, a disease marked by dermatitis, diarrhea, and dementia.

nicotine   The active ingredient in tobacco that produces psychoactive effects.

norepinephrine   A hormone involved in neural transmission. Disturbances of the availability of norepinephrine in the brain have been associated with affective disorders.

obsessions   Repetitive thoughts, images, or impulses that invade consciousness, are abhorrent, and are very difficult to dismiss or control; usually associated with compulsions.

obsessive-compulsive disorder   An anxiety disorder in which the individual is plagued with uncontrollable, repulsive thoughts (obsessions) and engages in seemingly senseless rituals (compulsive behaviors).

obsessive personality   A personality characterized by a rigid, methodical, moralistic personality. The individual with an obsessive personality is meticulous in dress and speech, pays much attention to detail, and often has problems making decisions.

occipital lobe   A lobe in each cerebral hemisphere which includes the visual projection area.

Oedipal conflict   The conflict between a boy's desire for his mother, and the fear of punishment by castration for that desire by the father.

operant   A response whose probability can be increased by positive reinforcement, or decreased by negative reinforcement.

operant conditioning   Training the organism to perform some instrumental response in order to escape punishment or gain reward.

operational definition   A set of observable and measurable conditions under which a phenomenon is defined to occur.

opioid   A class of drugs which, when taken, produce euphoria or dysphoria, apathy, psychomotor retardation, pupillary constriction, drowsiness, slurred speech, and impairment in attention and memory.

opponent-process model of addiction   A model developed by Richard Solomon which explains the increased motivation to use a drug which occurs with continued use of that drug. According to the model, all drugs that produce dependence have three properties: affective pleasure, affective tolerance, and affective withdrawal.

oral character traits   In psychoanalytic theory, traits such as dependency that result from fixation at the oral stage of psychosexual development and that persist into adulthood.

oral sex   Stimulation of a sexual partner's genitals using the mouth and tongue.

oral stage   In psychoanalytic theory, the earliest psychosexual stage of development during which pleasure arises from feeding.

organic syndromes   Abnormal behaviors caused by known pathology in structure or function of the nervous system. Neurology and neuropsychology concentrate on the study of these syndromes.

orgasm   The climax of sexual arousal. In males, orgasm consists of emission and ejaculation. In women, orgasm consists of a series of reflexive contractions of the muscles surrounding the vagina.

outcome expectation   A person's estimate that a given behavior will lead to the desired outcome. *See also* efficacy expectation.

overdetermination   Behaviors that are caused or determined by more than one psychological force and with more than the requisite psychic energy.

overgeneralization   Drawing global conclusions on the basis of a single fact; an error of logic made by those who are depressed.

panic disorder   An anxiety disorder characterized by severe attacks of panic, in which the person (a) is overwhelmed with intense apprehension, dread, or terror, (b) experiences an acute emergency reaction, (c) thinks he might go crazy or die, and (d) engages in fight or flight behavior.

paradoxical intention   A therapeutic technique that encourages clients to indulge and even exaggerate their symptoms in order to convince them that they really do control those symptoms.

paranoid schizophrenia   A form of schizophrenia in which delusions of persecution or grandeur are systematized and complex.

paraphilias   A group of psychosexual disorders in which bizarre sexual acts or imagery are needed to produce sexual arousal. Includes fetishes, masochism, exhibitionism, voyeurism, transvestism, sadism, zoophilia, and pedophilia.

parasympathetic nervous system (PNS)   That part of the autonomic nervous system which generally works to counteract arousal. *See also* sympathetic nervous system and autonomic nervous system.

parietal lobe   A lobe in each cerebral hemisphere which includes the somatosensory projection areas and is involved with many perceptual functions.

Parkinson's disease   Disorder of movement characterized by tremor of the hands, rigidity, and difficulty in initiating movement. It is caused by degeneration of specific neurons, which leads to decreased amounts of the neurotransmitter dopamine in certain structures in the brain.

partial reinforcement   Rewarding or punishing only some percentage of instrumental responses.

passive-aggressive personality disorder   A disorder that is characterized by resistance to social and occupational performance demands through procrastination, dawdling, stubbornness, inefficiency, and forgetfulness that seem to border on the intentional.

Pavlovian conditioning (or classical conditioning)   Training in which an organism is exposed to one neutral stimulus (conditioned stimulus) and a stimulus (unconditioned stimulus) that naturally provokes a certain response (unconditioned response). Through the learned association between the conditioned stimulus and the unconditioned stimulus, the conditioned stimulus is able to evoke the conditioned response. Modern theorists believe that acquisition occurs when there is a positive contingency between the conditioned stimulus and the unconditioned stimulus. *See also* contingency.

PCP (phencyclidine)   An hallucinogen that causes sensitization to all sensory inputs, depersonalization, diminished awareness of self and the environment, disorientation, muddled thinking, and impaired attention and memory.

pedophilia   A psychosexual disorder in which the individual needs to engage in sexual relations with children below the age of mature consent in order to be sexually aroused.

pellagra psychosis   The dementia that can develop from pellagra, a condition that results from a niacin deficiency.

penile erection   The condition of the penis of being rigid and elevated, as the vessels in the penis fill with blood.

penis envy   In psychoanalytic theory, girls' negative feelings associated with the absence of a penis and possible anger at their mothers for having created them incomplete and inferior.

peptic ulcer   A circumscribed erosion of the mucous membrane of the stomach or of the duodenum, the upper portion of the small intestine. The main symptom of a peptic ulcer is abdominal pain.

perceptual consciousness   As used by Freud, the first of three levels of consciousness that describes the small number of mental events to which the individual is presently attending.

perseveration   A tendency to repeat the same actions, and to have difficulty making transitions from one action (or idea or strategy) to another. Characteristic of frontal lobe damage.

personalization Incorrectly taking responsibility for bad events; an error of logic in those who are depressed.

phallic stage In psychoanalytic theory, the third stage of psychosexual development during which the libido focuses on phallic pleasures or masturbation.

pharmacology The study of drugs and their actions in cells and physiological processes.

phenylalanine An amino acid that is an essential component of proteins. Children with phenylketonuria cannot metabolize phenylalanine.

phenylketonuria (PKU) A rare metabolic disease that prevents digestion of an essential amino acid called phenylalanine. As a result of this disease, phenopyruvic acid, a derivative of phenylalanine, builds up in and poisons the nervous system, causing irreversible damage.

phobia An anxiety disorder characterized by (a) persistent fear of a specific situation out of proportion to the reality of the danger, (b) compelling desire to avoid and escape the situation, (c) recognition that the fear is unreasonably excessive, and (d) the fact that it is not due to any other disorder.

phonological dyslexia Inability to pronounce a written word that has never been seen before even if it corresponds to a known spoken word.

physiological Having to do with the body.

Pick's disease A disorder in which patients show variable memory deficits but little or no visuo-spatial impairments. Patients exhibit marked changes in personality, disinhibition, and socially inappropriate behavior.

placebo A neutral stimulus that produces some response because the subject believes it should produce that response.

placebo effect A positive treatment outcome that results from the administration of placebos.

pleasure principle As used in psychodynamic theory, biological drives that clamor for immediate gratification.

population The entire set of potential observations.

positive reinforcer An event that increases the probability of a response when made contingent upon it. *See also* operant, discriminative stimulus, and instrumental learning.

positron emission tomography (PET) scan A brain-imaging technique that produces a three-dimensional image of the brain. A radioactive substance, usually glucose or oxygen, is incorporated directly into the neuron in proportion to the metabolic rate. With the aid of a computer, a representation of metabolic rate in different brain regions can be shown.

post-traumatic stress disorder An anxiety disorder resulting from experience with a catastrophic event beyond the normal range of human suffering, and characterized by (a) numbness to the world, (b) reliving of the trauma in dreams and memories, and (c) symptoms of anxiety.

pre-conscious \ As used by Freud, the second of three levels of consciousness, consisting of information and impulses that are not at the center of attention, but that can be retrieved relatively easily.

premature ejaculation The recurrent inability to exert any control over ejaculation, resulting in rapid ejaculation after penetration.

prepared conditioning In learning theory, the concept of the organism as being biologically predisposed to learning about relationships between certain stimuli, and therefore learning the relationship very easily.

prevalence The percentage of a population having a certain disorder at a given time.

primary erectile dysfunction A disorder in which the male has never been able to achieve or maintain an erection sufficient for intercourse.

proband *See* index case.

prognosis Outlook for the future of a disorder.

projection Attributing private understandings and meanings to others; substituting "you" for "I."

psychalgia *See* somatoform pain disorder.

psychoactive drugs Drugs that affect consciousness, mood, and behavior.

psychoanalysis The psychological theory that claims that disorders are the result of intrapsychic conflicts, usually sexual or aggressive in nature, stemming from childhood fixations. Psychoanalysis is also a therapeutic method in which the therapist helps the patient gain insight into those intrapsychic conflicts behind his or her symptoms.

psychodynamic Dealing with the psychological forces that influence mind and behavior.

psychodynamic model of abnormality A model whose theorists believe that abnormality is driven by hidden conflicts within the personality.

psychomotor retardation Slowing down of movement and speech; prominent in severe depression.

psychoneuroimmunology The study of how mental state and behavior influence the immune system.

psychopharmacology That branch of pharmacology that studies drug effects on the cells of the brain and drug actions affecting consciousness, mood, and behavior.

psychosexual Concerning the relationship between the mind and pleasure.

psychosexual disorders A class of mental disorders in which psychological factors impair sexual functioning.

psychosis A mental state characterized by profound disturbances in reality testing, thought, and emotion. *See also* schizophrenia.

psychosomatic disorders A group of disorders in which actual physical illness is caused or influenced by psychological factors. The diagnosis of a psychosomatic disorder requires that the physical symptoms represent a known physical pathology and that psychologically meaningful events preceded and are judged to have contributed to the onset or worsening of the physical disorder.

punishment In psychology experiments, inflicting aversive stimuli on an organism, which reduces the probability of recurrence of certain behaviors by that organism. *See also* negative reinforcement.

Q-sort A personality inventory consisting of a large number of cards, each of which contains a statement such as "is an assertive person," "evades responsibility," or "is sensitive." The person being tested must place each statement in one of nine categories according to whether the statement is more or less characteristic of him. The number of items permitted in each category is ranged in accord with the bell-shaped normal distribution.

random assignment   Assigning subjects to groups in an experiment such that each subject has an equal chance of being assigned to each group.

rational-emotive therapy   A therapy in which the therapist challenges the irrational beliefs of the client, and encourages the client to engage in behavior that will counteract his irrational beliefs.

rationalization   The process of assigning to behavior socially desirable motives, which an impartial analysis would not substantiate.

reaction formation   The process of substituting an opposite reaction for a given impulse.

realistic anxiety   As used in psychoanalytic theory, the fear that arises from the expectation that real world events may be harmful to the self.

reality principle   In psychodynamic theory, the way in which the ego expresses and gratifies the desires of the id in accordance with the requirements of reality.

receptive aphasia   An aphasia (disorder of language) where the primary deficit is in the perception of speech.

reductionism   A philosophy that holds that all psychological phenomena can be explained by and reduced to biological phenomena.

regional cerebral blood flow (rCBF)   A brain-imaging technique that uses xenon, an inert, radioactively labeled substance that the patient has inhaled or been injected with, to detect the region of the brain receiving the most blood flow, and which as such is most active and therefore involved in performance of a task.

reinforcement   An event which, when made contingent on a response, increases its probability. A reward or punishment.

relaxation response   Physiological response regulated by the parasympathetic nervous system (PNS), which counteracts the emergency reaction to threat. In the relaxation response, the PNS inhibits heart action, constricts respiratory passages, and causes secretion of digestive fluids.

release from inhibition   Disinhibition or removal of inhibition.

repeatability   The chance that, if an experimental manipulation is repeated, it will produce similar results.

repression   A coping strategy by which the individual forces unwanted thoughts or prohibited desires out of consciousness and into the unconscious mind.

reserpine   A powerful sedative given to lower high blood pressure. Reserpine occasionally induces depression.

residual schizophrenia   A form of schizophrenia characterized by the absence of such prominent symptoms as delusions, hallucinations, incoherence or grossly disorganized behavior, but in which there is continuing evidence of the presence of two or more relatively minor but distressing symptoms.

response prevention   A therapeutic technique in which a therapist prevents the individual from engaging in a behavior that the therapist wishes to extinguish. *See also* flooding.

retarded ejaculation   In men, great difficulty reaching orgasm during sexual intercourse.

retrograde amnesia   Loss of memory of events predating some disease or trauma. The loss is often confined to a period seconds or minutes prior to a trauma.

reward   In psychology experiments, giving the organism positive stimuli, which increases the probability of recurrence of certain behaviors by the organism. *See also* positive reinforcement.

right visual field   The right half of one's visual world, that is, the part of the world that projects onto the left side of the retina and into the left hemisphere.

role construct repertory test (Rep test)   A personality inventory that examines the constructs that a person uses in interpreting significant events.

Rorschach test   A personality test consisting of ten bilaterally symmetrical "inkblots," some in color, some in black, gray, and white, each on an individual card. The respondent is shown each card separately and asked to name everything the inkblot could resemble. The test is supposed to elicit unconscious conflicts, latent fears, sexual and aggressive impulses, and hidden anxieties.

sadism   A psychosexual disorder in which the individual becomes sexually aroused only by inflicting physical and psychological suffering and humiliation on another human being.

sample   A selection of items or people, from the entire population of similar items or people.

schizoid personality disorder   A disorder that is manifested by the inability to form social relationships, the absence of desire for social involvements, indifference to both praise and criticism, insensitivity to feelings of others, and by lack of social skills.

schizophrenia   A group of disorders characterized by incoherence of speech and thought, hallucinations, delusions, blunted or inappropriate emotion, deterioration in social and occupational functioning, and lack of self-care.

schizophrenogenic families   Families that seem to foster schizophrenia in one or more family members.

school of thought   In abnormal psychology, a theory-driven common focus on specific types of causes, cures, and prevention methods for abnormality. Among these are biomedical, psychodynamic, behavioral, and cognitive schools of thought.

school phobia   A persistent and irrational fear of going to school.

seasonal affective disorder (SAD)   Characterized by depression beginning each year in the fall and remitting or switching to mania in the spring.

secondary erectile dysfunction   Loss of the ability in a male to achieve or maintain an erection.

selective abstraction   Focusing on one insignificant detail while ignoring the more important features of a situation; an error of logic in those who are depressed.

selective amnesia   Loss of memory of all events related to a particular theme.

selective positive reinforcement   Therapeutic technique in which the therapist delivers positive reinforcement contingent on the occurrence of one particular behavior.

selective punishment   Therapeutic technique in which the therapist negatively reinforces a certain target event, causing it to decrease in probability.

selfobject   Those people and things that are critically significant for personality cohesiveness.

self theory   A personality theory that addresses the fact that people feel *whole* and *unified* rather than fragmented into ego, superego, behaviors, etc. Wholeness is thought to be endowed by the *self.*

sensate focus   A strategy of direct sexual therapy that involves (a) a "pleasuring" phase during which the couple engages in nongenital erotic activity, but restrains from intercourse, then (b) a phase of "genital stimulation" in which the couple engages in genital play, but without intercourse, then (c) the phase of "nondemand intercourse" in which the couple engages in intercourse, but without making demands on each other.

separation anxiety disorder A disorder characterized by a very strong fear of being separated from one's family. Childen with this disorder become panicked if they must separate from loved ones, and they often show continual physical symptoms of anxiety.

set-point theory The theory that an individual's body is naturally predisposed to maintain a certain weight.

sexual dysfunction Disorders in which adequate sexual arousal, desire, or orgasm are inhibited.

sexual object choice The types of persons, parts of the body, and situations that are the objects of sexual fantasies, arousal, and preferences.

sexual unresponsiveness (or frigidity) In women, lack of sexual desire and impairment of physical excitement in appropriate situations.

shadowing A technique used in treating stuttering which entails repeating the therapist's words shortly after the latter has spoken them.

single-blind experiment An experiment in which the subject, but not the experimenter, is blind as to whether the subject has received an experimental treatment or a placebo.

single photon emission computerized tomography (SPECT) scan A brain-imaging technique that measures cerebral blood flow by measuring the concentration of a radioactive substance, injected in nonharmful amounts, into the brain.

social phobias Unreasonable fear of and desire to avoid situations in which one might be humiliated in front of other people.

somatic Having to do with the body

somatization disorder (Briquet's syndrome) A somatoform disorder characterized by the experience of a large number and variety of physical symptoms, for which there are no medical explanations. These symptoms are not under the voluntary control of the individual.

somatoform disorders A group of mental disorders characterized by (a) loss or alteration in physical functioning, for which there is no physiological explanation, (b) evidence that psychological factors have caused the physical symptoms, (c) lack of voluntary control over physical symptoms, and (d) indifference by the patient to the physical loss. Includes conversion, somatization disorder, and somatoform pain disorder.

somatoform pain disorder (psychalgia) A somatoform disorder in which the individual experiences pain, not attributable to a physical cause, but to psychological conflict.

spastic Overactive muscles, more contracted (tense and rigid) than is normal, with increased muscle tone spasms.

specific attribution An individual's assignment of cause for an event to a factor that is relevant only to that situation.

specific phobias There are three classes of specific phobias: animal phobias are unreasonable fears of and desires to avoid or escape specific animals. Illness and injury phobias (nosophobias) are unreasonable fears of and desires to avoid or escape a specific illness or injury. Inanimate objects phobias are unreasonable fears of and desires to avoid certain situations or objects other than social situations, crowds, animals, illness, or injuries.

stable attribution An individual's assignment of cause for an event to a factor that persists in time.

statistical inferences Procedures used to decide whether a sample or a set of observations is truly representative of the population.

statistically significant effect An effect that is highly unlikely (typically less than one time in twenty) to occur solely by chance.

stigmata Marks on the skin, usually bleeding or bruises, and often of high religious or personal significance, brought on by an emotional state.

stimulants A class of psychoactive drugs that induces psychomotor agitation, physiological hyperactivity, elation, grandiosity, loquacity, and hypervigilance. Includes amphetamines and cocaine.

stroke Damage to the nervous system caused by loss or severe reduction in the supply of nutrients and oxygen, resulting from damage to blood vessels (e.g., hemorrhage or occlusion by a blood clot).

subject Participant in an experiment.

subject bias The influence of a subject's beliefs about what he is expected to do in an experiment on his responses in the experiment.

subjective self The second sense of self, which develops between the age of seven and nine months. It gives rise to the sense that we understand each others' feelings and intentions.

sublimation In psychoanalytic theory, the transfer of libidinal energies from relatively narcissistic gratifications to those which gratify others and are highly socialized. More generally, the process of rechanneling psychic energy from socially undesirable goals to constructive and socially desirable ones.

superego Those psychological processes that are "above the self," i.e., conscience, ideals, and morals.

surface dyslexia Someone with surface dyslexia can only read words by sounding them out.

syllable-timed speech Used in treating stuttering, this technique requires stutterers to speak in time to a metronome.

sympathetic nervous system (SNS) That part of the autonomic nervous system which mobilizes the body's reaction to stress. *See also* parasympathetic nervous system and autonomic nervous system.

symptom A sign of disorder.

synapse The junction between neurons. Excitation or inhibition is transmitted from one neuron to another by diffusion of neurotransmitters across the synaptic gap.

syndrome A set of symptoms that tend to co-occur.

systematic desensitization A behavior therapy primarily used to treat phobias and specific anxieties. The phobic is first given training in deep muscle relaxation and is then progressively exposed to increasingly anxiety-evoking situations (real or imagined). Because relaxation and fear are mutually exclusive, stimuli that formerly induced panic are now greeted calmly.

T cells Cells in the immune system that are produced in the thymus gland. They have receptors on their surfaces for specific antigens.

tarantism A dancing mania that occurred in Italy and was thought to have been brought on by a tarantula's bite.

tardive dyskinesia A nonreversible neurological side effect of antipsychotic drug treatment, whose symptoms consist of sucking, lip smacking, and peculiar tongue movements.

temporal lobe A lobe in each cerebral hemisphere that includes the auditory projection area and is particularly involved in memory.

tension reduction hypothesis A hypothesis that states that people drink alcohol to reduce tension.

Thematic Apperception Test (TAT) A personality test that consists of a series of pictures that are not as ambiguous as Rorschach cards, but not as clear as photographs either. Respondents look at each picture and make up a story about it. The test is supposed to elicit underlying psychological dynamics.

tolerance The state of drug addiction in which, after repeated use of a drug, the addict needs more and more of the drug to produce the desired reaction, and there is great diminution of the effect of a given dose.

transsexuality A psychosexual disorder characterized by the belief that one is a woman trapped in the body of a man, or a man trapped in the body of a woman.

transvestism (or transvestitism) A psychosexual disorder in which a man often dresses in the clothes of a woman in order to achieve sexual arousal.

tricyclic antidepressants Antidepressant drugs that block uptake of norepinephrine, thus increasing the availability of norepinephrine.

tumor An abnormal tissue that grows by cell multiplication more rapidly than is normal.

Type A behavior pattern A personality type characterized by (a) an exaggerated sense of time urgency, (b) competitiveness and ambition, and (c) aggressiveness and hostility when thwarted.

unconditioned stimulus (US) A stimulus that will provoke an unconditioned response without training. For example, a loud noise will naturally provoke a startle response in humans.

unconscious In psychoanalytic theory, the third level of consciousness consisting of the large mass of hidden memories, experiences, and impulses.

undifferentiated schizophrenia A category of schizophrenia used to describe disturbed individuals who present evidence of thought disorder, as well as behavioral and affective anomalies, but who are not classifiable under the other subtypes.

unipolar depression A disorder characterized by depression, in the absence of a history of mania.

unstable attribution An individual's assignment of cause for an event to a factor that is transient.

vagina The sheathlike female genital canal that leads from the uterus to the external opening.

validity The extent to which a test of something is actually measuring that something.

venereal disease A disease contracted through sexual intercourse.

verbal self The third sense of self, which develops between fifteen and eighteen months of age. It is the verbal and symbolic storehouse of experience and knowledge.

voyeurism A psychosexual disorder in which the individual habitually gains sexual arousal only by observing the naked body, the disrobing, or the sexual activity of an unsuspecting victim.

white matter Those parts of the central nervous system composed primarily of myelinated axons. The myelin imparts a white color to these areas.

withdrawal A substance-specific syndrome that follows cessation of the intake of a substance that has been regularly used by the individual to induce intoxication.

xenon The radioactive gas that in minute and harmless quantities is used to trace the blood flow in the brain in regional cerebral blood flow.

yoking An experimental procedure in which both experimental and control groups receive exactly the same physical events, but only the experimental group influences these events by its responding.

zoophilia (or bestiality) A psychosexual disorder in which the individual habitually engages in sexual relations with animals in order to be sexually aroused.

References

Abrams, R., Taylor, M., Faber, R., Ts'o, T., Williams, R., & Almy, G. (1983). Bilateral vs. unilateral electroconvulsive therapy: Efficacy and melancholia. *American Journal of Psychiatry, 140,* 463–65.

Abramson, L. Y. (1978). Universal versus personal helplessness. Unpublished doctoral dissertation, University of Pennsylvania.

Abramson, L. Y., Garber, J., Edwards, N., & Seligman, M. E. P. (1978). Expectancy change in depression and schizophrenia. *Journal of Abnormal Psychology, 87,* 165–79.

Abramson, L. Y., Seligman, M. E. P., & Teasdale, J. (1978). Learned helplessness in humans: Critique and reformulation. *Journal of Abnormal Psychology, 87,* 32–48.

Acosta, T. X. (1975). Etiology and treatment of homosexuality: A review. *Archives of Sexual Behavior,* pp. 9–29.

Adams, H. E., & Sturgis, E. T. (1977). Status of behavioral reorientation techniques in the modification of homosexuality: A review. *Psychological Bulletin, 84,* 1171–88.

Adams, R. D., & Victor, M. (1981). *Principles of neurology* (2nd ed.). New York: McGraw-Hill.

Addiction Research Foundation. (1981). Report of an ARF/WHO Scientific Meeting on Adverse Health and Behavioral Consequences of *Cannabis* Use. Toronto: Author.

Agras, W. S., Barlow, T. H., Chapin, H. N., Abel, G. G., & Leitenberg, H. (1974). Behavior modification of anorexia nervosa. *Archives of General Psychiatry, 30,* 343–52.

Akhter, S., Wig. N. N., Varma, V. K., Pershard, D., & Verma, S. K. (1975). A phenomenological analysis of symptoms in the obsessive-compulsive neurosis. *British Journal of Psychiatry, 127,* 342–48.

Akiskal, H. S. (1979). A biobehavioral model of depression. In R. A. Depue (Ed.), *The psychobiology of depressive disorders: Implications for the effects of stress.* New York: Academic Press.

Akiskal, H. S., & McKinney, W. T. (1973). Depressive disorders: Toward a unified hypothesis. *Science, 182,* 20–29.

Akiskal, H. S., & McKinney, W. T. (1975). Overview of recent research in depression. *Archives of General Psychiatry, 32,* 285–305.

Aleksandrowicz, D. R. (1961). Fire and its aftermath on a geriatric ward. *Bulletin of the Menninger Clinic, 25,* 23–32.

Alexander, F. (1950). *Psychosomatic medicine.* New York: Norton.

Alexander, F., French, T. M., & Pollack, G. H. (1968). *Psychosomatic specificity: Experimental study and results.* Chicago: University of Chicago Press.

Alexander, L., & Luborsky, L. (1984). Research on the helping alliance. In L. Greenberg & W. Pinsof (Eds.), *The psychotherapeutic process: A research handbook.* New York: Guilford Press.

Allen, M.G. (1976). Twin studies of affective illness. *Archives of General Psychiatry, 33.* 1476–78.

Alloy, L. B., & Abramson, L. Y. (1979). Judgment of contingency in depressed and nondepressed students: Sadder but wiser? *Journal of Experimental Psychology: General, 108,* 441–85.

Allport, G. W. (1937). *Personality: A psychological interpretation.* New York: Henry Holt.

American Psychiatric Association (1980). *Diagnostic and Statistical Manual of Mental Disorders* (DSM-III), Washington, DC: Author.

American Psychiatric Association (1987). *Diagnostic and statistical manual of mental disorders,* (3rd ed., revised) (DSM-III-R). Washington, DC: Author.

Andersen, B. L. (1983). Primary orgasmic dysfunction: Diagnostic conditions and review of treatment. *Psychological Bulletin, 93,* 105–36.

Anderson, J. C., Williams, S., McGee, R., & Silva, P. A. (1987). DSM-III: Disorders in preadolescent children. *Archives of General Psychiatry, 44,* 69–76.

Anderson, J. R., & Bower, G. H. (1973). *Human associative memory.* Washington, DC: Winston.

Andreasen, N. C., Nasrallah, H. A., Dunn, V., Olson, S. C., Grove, W. M., Ehrhardt, J. C., Coffman, J. A., & Crossett, J. H. (1986). Structural abnormalities in the frontal system in schizophrenia: A magnetic resonance imaging study. *Archives of General Psychiatry, 43* (2), 136–44.

Andreasen, N. C., Olsen, S. A., Dennert, J. W., & Smith, M. R. (1982). Ventricular enlargement in schizophrenia: Relationship to positive and negative symptoms. *American Journal of Psychiatry, 139* (3), 297–302.

Andreasen, N. C., Scheftner, W., Reich, T., Hirschfeld, R. M. A., Endicott, J., & Keller, M. B. (1986). The validation of the concept of endogenous depression. *Archives of General Psychiatry, 43,* 246–51.

Angst, J., Baastrup, P., Grof, P., Hippius, H., Poldinger, W., & Weis, P. (1973). The course of monopolar depression and bipolar psychoses. *Psykiotrika, Neurologika and Neurochirurgia, 76,* 489–500.

Anisman, H. (1978). Aversively motivated behavior as a tool in psychopharmacological analysis. In H. Anisman & G. Binami (Eds.), *Psychopharmacology of aversively motivated behavior.* New York: Plenum.

Annau, Z., & Kamin, L. J. (1961). The conditional emotional response as a function of intensity of the US. *Journal of Comparative and Physiological Psychology, 54,* 428–32.

Ansbacher, H. L., & Ansbacher, R. (1956). *The individual psychology of Alfred Adler.* New York: Basic Books.

Anthony, J. C., Folstein, M., Romanoski, A. J., Von Korff, M. R., Nestadt, G. R., Chahal, R., Merchant, A., Brown, C. H., Shapiro, S., Kramer, M., & Gruenberg, E. M. (1985). Comparison of the lay Diagnostic Interview Schedule and a standardized psychiatric diagnosis. *Archives of General Psychiatry, 42,* 667–75.

Apfelbaum, B. (1980). The diagnosis and treatment of retarded ejaculation. In S. A. Leiblum & L. A. Pervin (Eds.), *Principles and practice of sex therapy* (pp. 236–96). New York: Guilford Press.

Apfelbaum, B. (1983). Expanding the boundaries of sex therapy (2nd ed.). Berkeley, CA: Berkeley Sex Therapy Group.

Apfelbaum, B., & Apfelbaum, C. (1984). The ego-analytic approach to sexual apathy. In D.C. Goldberg (Ed.), *Contemporary marriage handbook.* New York: Dorsey Press.

Archibald, H. C., & Tuddenham, R. D. (1965). Persistent stress reaction after combat. *Archives of General Psychiatry, 12,* 475–81.

Arendt, H. (1978). *The life of the mind.* New York: Harcourt Brace Jovanovich.

Arieti, S. (1974). *Interpretation of schizophrenia.* New York: Basic Books.

Arieti, S. (1979). New views on psychodynamics of phobias. *American Journal of Psychotherapy, 33,* 82–95.

Arieti, S., & Bemporad, J. (1978). *Severe and mild depression.* New York: Basic Books.

Aronow, E., & Reznikoff, M. (1976). *Rorschach content interpretation.* New York: Grune & Stratton.

Aronow, E., Reznikoff M., & Rauchway, A. (1979). Some old and new directions in Rorschach testing. *Journal of Personality Testing, 43,* 227–34.

Asberg, M., Traskman, L., & Thoren, P. (1976). 5-HIAA in the cerebrospinal fluid. *Archives of General Psychiatry, 33,* 1193–97.

Asch, S. E. (1951). Effects of group pressure on the modification and distortion of judgments. In H. Guetzkow (Ed.), *Groups, leadership and men: Research in human relations.* Pittsburgh, PA: Carnegie Press.

Ashcroft, G., Crawford, T. B. B., Eccleston, D., Sharman, D. F., MacDougall, E. J., Stanton, J. B., & Binns, J. K. (1966). 5-hydroxylindole compounds in the cerebrospinal fluid of patients with psychiatric or neurological diseases. *Lancet, 2,* 1049–52.

Assad, G., & Shapiro, B. (1986). Hallucinations: Theoretical and clinical overview. *American Journal of Psychiatry, 143* (9), 1088–97.

Atkinson, J. W. (1958). *Motives in fantasy, action and society.* Princeton: Van Nostrand.

Auerbach, A. H., & Johnson, M. (1977). Research on the therapist's level of experience. In A. S. Gurman & A. M. Razin (Eds.), *Effective psychotherapy.* New York: Pergamon.

Averill, J. R., & Rosenn, M. (1972). Vigilant and non-vigilant coping strategies and psychophysiological stress reactions during the anticipation of an electric shock. *Journal of Personality and Social Psychology, 23,* 128–41.

Ax, A. F. (1953). The physiological differentiation between fear and anger in humans. *Psychosomatic Medicine, 15,* 433–42.

Ayllon, T., & Michael, J. (1959). The psychiatric nurse as a behavioral engineer. *Journal of the Experimental Analysis of Behavior, 2,* 323–34.

Ayllon, T., & Rosenbaum, M. S. (1977). The behavioral treatment of disruption and hyperactivity in school settings. In B. B. Lahey & A. E. Kazdin (Eds.), *Advances in clinical child psychology* (Vol. 1). New York: Plenum.

Azrin, N. H., Sneed, T. J., & Foxx, R. M. (1974). Dry-bed training: Rapid elimination of childhood enuresis. *Behavior Research and Therapy, 11* (4), 147–56.

Bacon, D. L. (1969). Incompetency to stand trial; commitment to an inclusive test. *Southern California Law Review, 42,* 444.

Baer, D. M., & Guess, D. (1971). Receptive training of adjectival inflections in mental retardates. *Journal of Applied Behavior Analysis, 4,* 129–39.

Baker, T. B., & Cannon, D. S. (1979). Taste aversion therapy with alcoholics: Techniques and evidence of a conditional response. *Behavior Research and Therapy, 17,* 229–42.

Bales, J. (1987). A few smart habits cut malpractice risk. *The APA Monitor, 18* (8), 39.

Ball, J., Corty, E., Bond, H., Myers, C., & Tommasello,A. (1988). The reduction of intravenous heroin use, non-opiate abuse and crime during methadone maintenance treatment: Further findings. *NIDA Research Monographs, 81,* 224–30.

Ballenger, J. C. (1986). Pharmacotherapy of the panic disorders. *Journal of Clinical Psychiatry, 47* (suppl), 27–32.

Baltes, P. B., Reese, H. W., & Lipsitt, L. P. (1980). Life-span developmental psychology. *Annual Review of Psychology, 31,* 65–110.

Ban, T. A., Choi, S. M., Lamonn, H. E., & Adamo, E. (1966). Conditional reflex studies in depression. *Canadian Psychiatric Association Journal, 11,* 98–105.

Bandura, A. (1969). *Principles of behavior modification.* New York: Holt, Rinehart & Winston.

Bandura, A. (1977a). Self efficacy: Toward a unifying theory of behavioral change. *Psychological Review, 84,* 191–215.

Bandura, A. (1977b). *Social learning theory.* Englewood Cliffs, NJ: Prentice-Hall.

Bandura, A. (1978). The self system in reciprocal determinism. *American Psychologist, 33,* 344–58.

Bandura, A. (1982). Self-efficacy mechanism in human agency. *American Psychologist, 37,* 122–47.

Bandura, A. (1986). Fearful expectations and avoidant actions as coeffects of personal self-inefficacy. *American Psychologist, 41* (12), 1389–91.

Bandura, A., & Adams, N. E. (1977). Analysis of self-efficacy theory of behavioral changes. *Cognitive Therapy and Research, 1,* 287–310.

Bandura, A., Adams, N. E., & Beyer, J. (1977). Cognitive processes mediating behavioral change. *Journal of Personality and Social Psychology, 35,* 125–39.

Bandura, A., Blanchard, E. B., & Ritter, B. (1969). Relative efficacy of desensitization and modelling approaches for inducing behavioral, affective, and attitudinal change. *Journal of Personality and Social Psychology, 13,* 173–99.

Bandura, A., & Walters, R. H. (1959). *Adolescent aggression.* New York: Ronald Press.

Bandura, A., & Walters, R. H. (1963). *Social learning and personality development.* New York: Holt, Rinehart & Winston.

Barbizet, J. (1970). *Human memory and its pathology.* (D. K. Jardine, Trans.) San Francisco: Freeman.

Bard, M. (1970). *Training police as specialists in family crisis intervention.* Washington, DC: U.S. Government Printing Office.

Bard, M., & Sangrey, D. (1979). *The crime victim's book.* New York: Basic Books.

Bardhan, K. D. (1980). Cimetidinea in duodenal ulcer: The present position. In A. Torsoli, P. E. Lucchelli, & R. W. Brimbelcombe (Eds.), *H2 antagonists.* Amsterdam: Excerpta Medica.

Barefoot, J. C., Dahlstrom, W. G., & Williams, R. B. (1983). Hostility, CHD incidence, and total mortality: A 25-year follow-up study of 255 physicians. *Psychosomatic Medicine, 45* (1), 59–63.

Barlow, D. H. (1986). The classification of anxiety disorders. In G. L. Tischler (Ed.), *Diagnoses and classification in psychiatry: A critical appraisal of DSM-III* (pp. 223–42). Cambridge: Cambridge University Press.

Barlow, D. H. (1988). *Anxiety and its disorders: The nature and treatment of anxiety and panic.* New York: Guilford Press.

Barlow, D. H., Abel, G. G., & Blanchard, E. B. (1979). Gender identity change in transsexuals. *Archives of General Psychiatry, 36,* 1001–1007.

Barnes, G. E., & Prosen, H. (1985). Parental death and depression. *Journal of Abnormal Psychology, 94,* 64–69.

Barnes, T. R. E., & Braude, W. M. (1985). Akathisia variants and tardive dyskinesia. *Archives of General Psychiatry, 42,* 874–78.

Baron, M., Gruen, R., Kane, J., & Amis, L. (1985). Modern research criteria and the genetics of schizophrenia. *American Journal of Psychiatry, 142,* 697–701.

Barrett-Lennard, G. T. (1962). Dimensions of therapist response as causal factors in therapeutic change. *Psychological Monographs, 76,* (43, Whole No. 562).

Barsky, A. J., Wyshak, G., & Klerman, G. L. (1986). Hypochondriasis, an evaluation of the DSM-III criteria in medical outpatients. *Archives of General Psychiatry, 43,* 493–500.

Bartak, L., & Rutter, M. (1974). Use of personal pronouns by autistic children. *Journal of Autistic Children and Schizophrenia, 4,* 217–22.

Barlett, D. L., & Steele, J. B. (1979). *Empire: The life, legend, and madness of Howard Hughes.* New York: Norton.

Bartrop, R. W., Luckhurst, E., Lazarus, L., Kiloh, L. G., & Penny, R. (1977). Depressed lymphocyte function after bereavement. *The Lancet, I,* April 16, 834–36.

Bateson, G., Jackson, D. D., Haley, J., & Weakland, J. (1956). Toward a theory of schizophrenia. *Behavioral Science, 1,* 251–64.

Baum, M. (1969). Extinction of an avoidance response following response prevention: Some parametric investigations. *Canadian Journal of Psychology, 23,* 1–10.

Baumgold, J. (1977, December 4). Agoraphobia: Life ruled by panic. *New York Times Magazine,* p. 46.

Baxter, L. R., Phelps, M. E., Mazziotta, J. C., Guze, B. H., Schwartz, J. M., & Selin, C. E. (1987). Local cerebral glucose metabolic rates in obsessive-compulsive disorder: A comparison with rates in unipolar depression and normal controls. *Archives of General Psychiatry, 44,* 211–18.

Bazelon, D. (1971). New gods for old: "Efficient" courts in a democratic society. *New York University Law Review, 46,* 653, 658–60.

Beauvais, M. F., & Derouesne, J. (1979). Phonological alexia: The dissociations. *Journal of Neurology, Neurosurgery, and Psychiatry, 42,* 1115–24.

Beck, A. T. (1967). *Depression: Clinical, experimental, and theoretical aspects.* New York: Hoeber.

Beck, A. T. (1973). *The diagnosis and management of depression.* Philadelphia: University of Pennsylvania Press.

Beck, A. T. (1976). *Cognitive therapy and the emotional disorders.* New York: International Universities Press.

Beck, A. T. (1988). Cognitive approaches to panic disorder: Theory and therapy. In S. Rachman & J. D. Maser (Eds.), *Panic: Psychological perspectives.* Hillsdale, NJ: Erlbaum.

Beck, A. T., & Emery, G. (1985). *Anxiety disorders and phobias: A cognitive perspective.* New York: Basic Books.

Beck, A. T., & Horvich, M. J. (1959). Psychological correlates of depression. *Psychosomatic Medicine, 21,* 50–55.

Beck, A. T., Kovacs, M., & Weissman, A. (1975). Hopelessness and suicidal behavior: An overview. *Journal of the American Medical Association, 234,* 1146–49.

Beck, A. T., Rush, A. J., Shaw, B. F., & Emery, G. (1979). *Cognitive therapy of depression.* New York: Guilford Press.

Beck, A. T., Ward, C. H., Mendelson, M., Mock, J. E., & Erbaugh, J. K. (1962). Reliability of psychiatric diagnoses II: A study of consistency of clinical judgments and ratings. *American Journal of Psychiatry, 119,* 351–57.

Beck, T. R. (1811). An inaugural dissertation on insanity. Cited in A. Deutsch, *The mentally ill in America.* New York: Columbia University Press, 1949.

Beech, H. R., & Vaughan, M. (1979). *Behavioural treatment of obsessional states.* Chichester: Wiley.

Beecher, H. K. (1959). *Measurement of subjective responses: Quantitative effects of drugs.* New York: Oxford University Press.

Beecher, H. K. (1961). Surgery as placebo. *Journal of the American Medical Association, 176,* 1102–1107.

Begleiter, H., Porjesz, B., Bihari, & Kissin,B. (1984). Event-related brain potentials in children at risk for alcoholism. *Science, 255,* 1493–96.

Bell, A. P., & Weinberg, M. S. (1978). *Homosexualities: A study of the diversity among men and women.* New York: Simon & Schuster.

Bell, A. P., Weinberg, M. S., & Hammersmith, S. K. (1981). *Sexual preference: Its development in men and women.* Bloomington, IN: Indiana University Press.

Belson, R. (1975). The importance of the second interview in marriage counseling. *Counseling Psychologist, 5*(3), 27–31.

Benes, F. M., Davidson, J., & Bird, E. D. (1986). Quantitative cytoarchitectural studies of the cerebral cortex of schizophrenics. *Archives of General Psychiatry, 42,* 874–78.

Benjamin, H. (1966). *The transsexual phenomenon.* New York: Julian Press.

Benjamin, L. S. (1987). The use of the SASB dimensional model to develop treatment plans for personality disorders. I: Narcissism. *Journal of Personality Disorders, 1* (1), 43–70.

Bennett, W., & Gurin, J. (1982). *The dieter's dilemma: Eating less and weighing more.* New York: Basic Books.

Benson, D. F., Metter, J. E., Kuhl, D. E., & Phelps, M. E., (1983). Positron computed tomography in neurobehavioral problems. In A. Kertesz (Ed.), *Localization in neuropsychology.* New York: Academic Press.

Berenbaum, H., Gottesman, I. I. & Oltmanns, T. F. (1985). Formal thought disorder in schizophrenics and their twins. *Journal of Abnormal Psychology, 94* (1), 3–16.

Bergin, A. E. (1966). Some implications of psychotherapy research for therapeutic practice. *Journal of Abnormal Psychology, 71,* 235–46.

Bergin, A. E. (1971). The evaluation of therapeutic outcomes. In A. E. Bergin & S. L. Garfield (Eds.), *Handbook of psychotherapy and behavior change* (pp. 217–70). New York: Wiley.

Bergler, E. (1949). *The basic neurosis: Oral regression and psychic masochism.* New York: Grune & Stratton.

Berkman, L. F. (1984). Assessing the physical health effects of social networks and social support. *Annual Review of Public Health, 5,* 413–32.

Berkman, L. F. (1986). Social networks, support, and health: Taking the next step forward. *American Journal of Epidemiology, 123,* 559–62.

Berman, J. S., & Norton, N. C. (1985). Does professional training make a therapist more effective? *Psychological Bulletin, 98.*

Bernheim (1886). In F. A. Pattie, A brief history of hypnotism. In J. E. Gordon (Ed.), *Handbook of clinical and experimental hypnosis.* New York: Macmillan, 1967.

Bettelheim, B. (1943). Individual and mass behavior in extreme situations. *Journal of Abnormal and Social Psychology, 38,* 417–52.

Bettelheim, B. (1967). *The empty fortress.* New York: The Free Press.

Bexton, W. H., Heron, W., & Scott, T. H. (1954). Effects of decreased variation in the sensory environment. *Canadian Journal of Psychology, 8,* 70–76.

Bibring, E. (1953). The mechanism of depression. In P. Greenacre (Ed.), *Affective disorders.* New York: International Universities Press.

Binstock, J. (1974). Choosing to die. The decline of aggression and the rise of suicide. *The Luterost, 8,* 68–71.

Biran, M., & Wilson, G. T. (1981). Treatment of phobic disorders using cognitive and exposure methods: A self-efficacy analysis. *Journal of Consulting and Clinical Psychology, 48,* 886–87.

Bird J. (1979). The behavioural treatment of hysteria. *British Journal of Psychiatry, 134,* 129–37.

Birenbaum, A., & Rei, M. A. (1979). Resettling mentally retarded adults in the community—almost 4 years later. *American Journal of Mental Deficiency, 83,* 323–29.

Bisiach, E., & Luzzatti, C. (1978). Unilateral neglect of representational space. *Cortex, 14,* 129–33.

Black, A. (1974). The natural history of obsessional neuroses. In H. R. Beech (Ed.), *Obsessional states.* London: Methuen.

Blair, C. D., & Lanyon, R. I. (1981). Exhibitionism: A critical review of the etiology and treatment. *Psychological Bulletin, 89,* 439–63.

Blakemore, C. (1977). *Mechanics of the mind.* Cambridge, Eng.: Cambridge University Press.

Blashfield, R. K. (1984). *The classification of psychopathology: NeoKraeplinian and quantitative approaches.* New York: Plenum.

Blashfield, R. K., & Draguns, J. G. (1976). Evaluative criteria for psychiatric classification. *Journal of Abnormal Psychology, 85,* 40–150.

Blessed, G., Tomlinsun, B. E., & Roth, M. (1968). The association between quantitative measures of dementia and of senile change in the cerebral gray matter of elderly subjects. *British Journal of Psychiatry, 114,* 797–811.

Bleuler, E. (1924). *Textbook of psychiatry.* New York: Macmillan.

Bleuler, M. (1984). Different forms of childhood stress and patterns of adult psychiatric outcome. In W. F. Watt, E. J. Anthony, L. C. Wynne, & J. E. Rolf (Eds.), *Children at risk for schizophrenia: A longitudinal perspective* (pp. 537–42). Cambridge: Cambridge University Press.

Bliss, E. L. (1980). Multiple personalities: Report of fourteen cases with implications for schizophrenia and hysteria. *Archives of General Psychiatry, 37,* 1388–97.

Bliss, E. L., & Jeppsen, A. (1985). Prevalence of multiple personality among inpatients and outpatients. *American Journal of Psychiatry, 142,* 250–51.

Bloch, S., & Reddaway, P. (1977). *Psychiatric terror: How Soviet psychiatry is used to suppress dissent.* New York: Basic Books.

Blum, K., Hamilton, M. L., & Wallace, J. E. (1977). Alcohol and opiates: A review of common neurochemical and behavioral mechanisms. In K. Blum (Ed.), *Alcohol and opiates: Neurochemical and behavioral mechanisms.* New York: Academic Press.

Blum, K., Wallace, J. E., Schwertner, H. A., & Eubanks, J. D. (1976). Morphine suppression of ethanol withdrawal in mice. *Experimentia, 32,* 79–82.

Blumberg, S. H., & Izard, C. E. (1985). Affective and cognitive characteristics of depression in 10- and 11-year-old children. *Journal of Personality and Social Psychology, 49,* 194–202.

Boehnlein, J. K., Kinzie, J. D., Ben, R., & Fleck, J. (1985). One-year follow-up study of posttraumatic stress disorder among survivors of Cambodian concentration camps. *American Journal of Psychiatry, 142,* 956–59.

Bogen, J. E., & Vogel, P. J. (1975). Neurological status in the long term following complete cerebral commisurotomy. In F. Michel & B. Schott (Eds.), Les syndromes de disconnexion calleuse chez l'homme. Lyons: Hôpital Neurologique.

Bootzin, R. R. (1975). *Behavior modification and therapy: An introduction.* Cambridge, MA: Winthrop.

Borysenko, M. (1987). The immune system: An overview. *Annals of Behavioral Medicine, 9,* 3–10.

Bourne, H. R., Bunney, W. E., Colburn, R. W., Davis, J. M., Davis, J. N., Shaw, D. M., & Loppen, A. J. (1968). Noradrenalin, 5-hydroxytryptamine and 5-hydroxyindoleacidic in hind brains of suicidal patients. *Lancet, 2,* 805–808.

Bowlby, J. (1960). Grief and mourning in infancy and early childhood. *The Psychoanalytic Study of the Child, 15,* 9–52.

Bowlby, J, (1969). *Attachment.* New York: Basic Books.

Bradshaw, J. L., & Nettleton, N. C. (1981), The nature of hemispheric specialization in man with commentary. *The Behavioral and Brain Sciences 4,* 51–92.

Brady, J. P. (1958). Ulcers in "executive" monkeys. *Scientific American, 199,* 95–100.

Brady, J. P., & Lind D. L. (1961). Experimental analysis of hysterical blindness: Operant conditioning techniques. *Archives of General Psychiatry, 4,* 331–39.

Brady, J. P., Porter, R. W., Conrad, D. G., & Mason, J. W. (1958). Avoidance behavior and the development of gastroduodenal ulcers. *Journal of Experimental Analysis of Behavior, 1,* 69–73.

Braff, D. L., & Saccuzzo, D. P. (1985). The time course of information-processing deficits in schizophrenia. *American Journal of Psychiatry, 142* (2), 170–74.

Bregman E. O. (1934). An attempt to modify the emotional attitudes of infants by the conditioned response technique. *Journal of Genetic Psychology, 45,* 169–98.

Brehm, S. S., & Brehm, J. W. (1981). *Psychological reactance: A theory of freedom and control.* New York: Academic Press.

Breier, A., Charney, D. S., & Heninger, G. R. (1984). Major depression in patients with agoraphobia and panic disorder. *Archives of General Psychiatry, 41* (12), 1129–35.

Breier, A., Charney, D. S., & Heninger, G. R. (1985). The diagnostic validity of anxiety disorders and their relationship to depressive illness. *The American Journal of Psychiatry, 142,* 787–97.

Breier, A., Charney, D. S., & Heninger, G. R. (1986). Agoraphobia with panic attacks: Development, diagnostic stability, and course of illness. *Archives of General Psychiatry, 43,* 1029–36.

Breslau, N. & Davis, G. C. (1986). Chronic stress and major depression. *Archives of General Psychiatry, 43,* 309–14.

Breslau, N., & Davis, G. C. (1987). Posttraumatic stress disorder: The etiologic specificity of wartime stressors. *American Journal of Psychiatry, 144,* 578–83.

Brett, C. W., Burling, T. A., & Pavlik, W. B. (1981). Electroconvulsive shock and learned helplessness in rats. *Animal Learning and Behavior, 9,* 38–44.

Broadbent, D. E. (1958). *Perception of communication,* London: Pergamon.

Broadbent, D. E. (1971). *Decision and stress.* New York: Academic Press.

Brodie, H. K. H., & Leff, M. J. (1971). Bipolar depression: A comparative study of patient characteristics. *American Journal of Psychiatry, 127,* 1086–90.

Broen, W. E., Jr. (1968). *Schizophrenia: Research and theory.* New York: Academic Press.

Brooks, A. D. (1974a). *Law, psychiatry and the mental health system.* Boston: Little, Brown.

Brooks, L. (1974b). Interactive effects of sex and status on self-disclosure. *Journal of Counseling Psychology, 21,* 469–74.

Brooks-Gunn, J. (1986). Differentiating premenstrual symptoms and syndromes [editorial]. *Psychosomatic Medicine, 48,* 385–87.

Brown, G. W., Birley, J. L. T., & Wing, J. K. (1972). Influence of family life on the course of schizophrenic disorders: A replication. *British Journal of Psychiatry, 121,* 241–58.

Brown, G. W., & Harris, T. (1978). *Social origins of depression.* London: Tavistock.

Brown, R., Colter,N., Corsellis, J. A., Crow, T. J., Frith, C. D., Jagoe, R., Johnstone, E. C., & Marsh, L. (1986). Postmortem evidence of structural brain changes in schizophrenia. Differences in brain weight, temporal horn area, and parahippocampal gyrus compared with affective disorder. *Archives of General Psychiatry, 43* (1), 36–42.

Brown, R. A., & Cutter, H. S. G. (1977). Alcohol, customary drinking behavior, and pain. *Journal of Abnormal Psychology, 86,* 179–88.

Brown, R., & Herrnstein, R. J. (1975). *Psychology.* Boston: Little, Brown.

Brown, R. A., Lichtenstein, E., McIntyre, K. O., & Harrington-Kostur, J. (1984). Effects of nicotine fading and relapse prevention on smoking sensation. *Journal of Consulting and Clinical Psychology, 52,* 307–308.

Brown, W. F. (1974). Effectiveness and paraprofessionals: The evidence. *Personnel and Guidance Journal. 53,* 257–63.

Bruch. H. (1978). *The golden cage: The enigma of anorexia nervosa.* Cambridge, MA: Harvard University Press.

Bruch, H. (1982). Anorexia nervosa: Therapy and theory. *American Journal of Psychiatry, 139,* 1531–38.

Bryan, T. H., & Bryan, J. H. (1975). *Understanding learning disabilities.* New York: Alfred Publishing Co.

Buchwald, A. M., Coyne, J. C., & Cole, C. S. (1978) A critical evaluation of the learned helplessness model of depression. *Journal of Abnormal Psychology, 87,* 180–93.

Budzynski, T. H., Stoyva, J. M., Adler, C. S., & Mullaney, D. M. (1973). EMG biofeedback and tension headache: A controlled outcome study. *Psychosomatic Medicine, 35,* 484–96.

Bunney, W. E., Murphy, D. L., Goodwin, F. K., & Borge, G. L. (1972). The switch process in manic depressive illness. *Archives of General Psychiatry, 27,* 295.

Bunney, W. E., & Murphy, D. L. (1974). Switch processes in psychiatric illness. In N. S. Kline (Ed.), *Factors in depression.* New York: Raven Press.

Burgess, A. W., & Holstrom, L. L. (1974). *Rape: Victims of crisis.* Bowie, MD: Robert J. Brady Co.

Burgess, A., & Holmstrom, L. (1979). Adaptive strategies and recovery from rape. *American Journal of Psychiatry, 136,* 1278–82.

Burnett, K. F., Taylor, C. B., & Agras, W. S. (1985). Ambulatory computer assisted therapy for obesity: A new frontier for behavior therapy. *Journal of Consulting and Clinical Psychology, 53,* 698–703.

Burns, B., & Reyher, J. (1976). Activating posthypnotic conflict: Emergent, uncovering, psychopathology, repression and psychopathology. *Journal of Personality Assessment, 40,* 492–501.

Burns, D., & Mendels, J. (1977). Biogenic amine precursors and affective illness. In W. Fann, I. Karacan, A. Pikorny, & R. Williams (Eds.), *Phenomenology and a treatment of depression.* New York: Spectrum.

Burt, R. A., & Morris, N. (1972). A proposal for the abolition of the incompetency plea. *Chicago Law Review, 40,* 66–80.

Buss, A. H., & Lang, P. J. (1965). Psychological deficit in schizophrenia: Affect reinforcement and concept attainment. *Journal of Abnormal Psychology, 70,* 2–24.

Butcher, J. N. (1969). *MMPI: Research developments and clinical applications.* New York: McGraw-Hill.

Butterfield, E. C. (1964). Locus of control, test anxiety, reaction to frustration, and achievement attitudes. *Journal of Personality, 32,* 298–311.

Butterfield, F. (1986, June 5). Judge backs discipline at institute for autistic. *New York Times.*

Butters, N., & Cermak, L. S. (1980). Alcoholic Korsakoff syndrome: An information-processing approach to amnesia. New York: Academic Press.

Bynum, W. F., Jr. (1981). Rationales for therapy in British psychiatry, 1780–1835. In A. Scull (Ed.), *Madhouses, mad-doctors, and madmen: The social history of psychiatry in the Victorian era* (pp. 35–57). Philadelphia: University of Pennsylvania Press.

Cade, J. F. J. (1949). Lithium salts in the treatment of psychotic excitement. *Medical Journal of Australia, 36,* 349–52.

Cadoret, R. (1986). Epidemiology of antisocial personality. In W. H. Reid, D. Dorr, J. I. Walker, & J. W. Bonner, III (Eds.), *Unmasking the psychopath: Antisocial personality and related syndromes* (pp. 28–44). New York: Norton.

Cameron, N. (1938). Reasoning, regression and communication in schizophrenia. *Psychological Monographs, 50* (Whole No. 221).

Cameron, N. (1947). *The psychology of behavior disorders.* Boston: Houghton Mifflin.

Campbell, M., Friedman, E., Green, W. H., Collins, P. J., Small, A. M., & Breuer, H. (1975). Blood serotonin in schizophrenic children: A preliminary study. *International Pharmacopsychiatry, 10,* 213–21.

Cantor, N., Smith, E., French, R. de S., & Mezzich, J. (1980). Psychiatric diagnosis as prototype categorization. *Journal of Abnormal Psychology, 89,* 181–93.

Cantwell, D. P. (1985). Hyperactive children have grown up. *Archives of General Psychiatry, 42,* 1026–28.

Cantwell, D. P., Baker, L., & Rutter, M. (1978). Family factors in the syndrome of infantile autism. In M. Rutter & E. Schopler (Eds.), *Autism: A reappraisal of concepts and treatment.* New York: Plenum.

Carey, G. (1982). Genetic influences on anxiety neurosis and agoraphobia. In R. J. Mathew (Ed.), *Biology of anxiety* (pp. 37–50). New York: Brunner-Mazel.

Carey, G., & Gottesman, I. I. (1978). Reliability and validity in binary ratings: Areas of common misunderstandings in diagnosis and symptom ratings. *Archives of General Psychiatry, 35,* 1454–59.

Carey, G., & Gottesman, I. I. (1981). Twin and family studies of anxiety, phobic, and obsessive disorders. In D. F. Klein & J. Rabkin (Eds.), *Anxiety: New research and changing concepts* (pp. 117–36). New York: Raven Press.

Carkesse, J. (1679). Lucida intetvalla. Quoted in R. Hunter and I. Macalpine, *Three hundred years of psychiatry: 1535–1860.* London: Oxford University Press, 1963.

Carlson, G. A., Kotin, J., Davenport, Y. B., & Adland, M. (1974). Followup of 53 bipolar manic depressive patients. *British Journal of Psychiatry, 124,* 134–39.

Carpenter, W. T., Jr., Strauss, J. S., & Bartko, J. J. (1973). Flexible system for the diagnosis of schizophrenia: Report from the WHO International Pilot Study of Schizophrenia. *Science, 182,* 1275–78.

Carpenter, W., Strauss, J., & Bartko, J. (1974). Use of signs and symptoms for the identification of schizophrenic patients. *Schizophrenia Bulletin, 11,* 37–49.

Carrington, R. (1959). *Elephants.* New York: Basic Books.

Carter, A. B. (1949). The prognosis of certain hysterical symptoms. *British Medical Journal, 1,* 1076–80.

Carter, C. H. (1970). *Handbook of mental retardation syndromes.* Springfield, IL: Charles C. Thomas.

Carter, R. B. (1853). *On the pathology and treatment of hysteria.* London: John Churchill.

Cartwright, R. D., & Lerner, B. (1963). Empathy, need to change, and improvement with psychotherapy. *Journal of Consulting Psychology, 27,* 138–44.

Cartwright, R., & Vogel, J. (1960). A comparison of changes in psychoneurotic patients during matched periods of therapy and no therapy. *Journal of Consulting Psychology, 24,* 121–27.

Casey, J. F., Bennett, I. F., Lindley, C. J., Hollister, L. E., Gordon, M. H., & Springer, N. N. (1960). Drug therapy and schizophrenia: A controlled study of the effectiveness of chlorpromazine, promazine, phenobarbitol and placebo. *Archives of General Psychiatry, 2,* 210–20.

Casey, R. J., & Berman, J. S. (1985). The outcome of psychotherapy with children. *Psychological Bulletin, 98* (2), 388–400.

Castro, K. G., Hardy, A. A., & Curran, J. W. (1986). The acquired immunodeficiency syndrome: Epidemiology and risk factors for transmission. *Medical Clinic of North America, 70.*

Cautela, J. R. (1967). Covert sensitization. *Psychological Reports, 20,* 459–68.

Cegelka, W. J., & Tyler, J. L. (1970). The efficacy of special class placement for the mentally retarded in proper perspective. *Training School Bulletin, 67,* 33–68.

Chambers, D. L. (1972). Alternatives to civil commitment of the mentally ill: Practical guides and constitutional imperatives. *Michigan Law Review, 70B,* 1107–1200.

Chapman, L. J., & Chapman, D. T. (1969). Illusory correlations as an obstacle to the use of valid psychodiagnostic signs. *Journal of Abnormal Psychology, 74,* 271–80.

Chapman, L. J., & Chapman, J. P. (1973). *Disordered thought in schizophrenia.* New York: Appleton-Century-Crofts.

Chapman, L. J., & Taylor, J. A. (1957). Breadth of deviate concepts used by schizophrenics. *Journal of Abnormal Social Psychology, 54,* 118–23.

Chappell, M. N., & Stevenson, T. I. (1936). Group psychological training in some organic conditions. *Mental Hygiene, 20,* 588–97.

Charness, M. E., & DeLa Paz, R. L. (1987). Mammillary body atrophy in Wernicke's encephalopathy: Antemortem identification using magnetic resonance imagery. *Annals of Neurology, 22,* 595–600.

Charney, D. S., & Heninger, G. R. (1985). Noradrenergic function and the mechanism of action of antianxiety treatment: The effect of long-term imipramine treatment. *Archives of General Psychiatry, 42,* 473–81.

Cherry, C., & Sayers, B. McA. (1956). Experiments upon the total inhibition of stammering by external control and some clinical results. *Journal of Psychosomatic Research, 1,* 233.

Cheseldine, S., & McConkey, R. (1979). Parental speech to young Down's syndrome children: An intervention study. *American Journal of Mental Deficiency, 83,* 612–20.

Childress, A., Ehrman, R., McLellan, A. T., & O'Brien, C. P. (1988). Conditioned craving and arousal in cocaine addiction: A preliminary report. *NIDA Research Monographs, 81,* 74–80.

Chinn, P. C., Drew, C. J., & Logan, D. R. (1979). *Mental retardation: A life cycle approach* (2d. ed.). St. Louis: Mosby.

Chodoff, P. (1963). Late effect of the concentration camp syndrome. *Archives of General Psychiatry, 8,* 323–33.

Chodoff, P. (1973). The depressive personality: A critical review. *International Journal of Psychiatry, 11,* 196–217.

Chodoff, P. (1974). The diagnosis of hysteria: An overview. *American Journal of Psychiatry, 131,* 1073–78.

Chodoff, P. (1982). Hysteria and women. *American Journal of Psychiatry, 139,* 545–51.

Christiansen, K. O. (1977). A review of studies of criminality among twins. In S. A. Mednick & K. O. Christiansen (Eds.),

Biosocial bases of criminal behavior. New York: Gardner Press.

Christodoulou, G. N., Gergoulas, A., Paploukas, A., Marinopoulou, A., & Sideris, E. (1977). Primary peptic ulcer in childhood. *Acta Psychiatrica Scandinavia, 56,* 215–22.

Cicero, J. J., Myers, R. D., & Black, W. C. (1968). Increase in volitional ethanol consumption following interference with a learned avoidance response. *Physiology and Behavior, 3,* 657–60.

Claparède, E. (1911). Recognition and "me-ness." In D. Rapaport (Ed.), *Organization and pathology of thought.* New York: Columbia University Press, 1951. (Reprinted from Recognition et moiite. *Archives de Psychologie,* 1911, *11,* 79–90).

Clark, D. M. (1986). A cognitive approach to panic. *Behaviour Research and Therapy, 24,* 461–70.

Clark, D. M. (1988). A cognitive model of panic attacks. In S. Rachman & J. D. Maser (Eds.), *Panic: Psychological perspectives.* Hillsdale, NJ: Erlbaum.

Clark, R. E. (1948). The relationship of schizophrenia to occupational income and occupational prestige. *American Sociological Review, 13,* 325–30.

Clarke-Stewart, K. A. (1973). Interactions between mothers and their young children: Characteristics and consequences. *Monographs of the Society for Research in Child Development, 37,* 153.

Clausen, J. A., & Kohn, M. L. (1959). Relation of schizophrenia to the social structure of a small city. In B. Pasamanick (Ed.), *Epidemiology of mental disorder.* Washington, DC: American Association for the Advancement of Science.

Cleckley, H. (1964). *The mask of sanity.* St. Louis: Mosby.

Cloninger, C. R., Bohman, M., Sigvardsson, S., & von Knorring, A. L. (1985). Psychopathology in adopted-out children of alcoholics: The Stockholm Adoption Study. In M. Galanter (Ed.), *Recent developments in alcoholism.* New York: Plenum Press.

Cloninger, C. R., Christiansen, K. O., Reich, T., Gottesman, I. I. (1978). Implications of sex differences in the prevalences of antisocial personality, alcoholism, and criminality for familial transmission. *Archives of General Psychiatry, 35,* 941–51.

Cloninger, C. R., & Gottesman, I. I. (1987). Genetic and environmental factors in antisocial behavior disorders. In S. Mednick, T. Moffitt, & S. Strack (Eds.), *The causes of crime: New biological approaches.* Cambridge: Cambridge University Press.

Cloninger, C. R., Sigvardsson, S., von Knorring, A., & Bohman, M. (1984). An adoption study of somatoform disorders: II. Identification of two discrete somatoform disorders. *Archives of General Psychiatry, 41,* 863–71.

Cobb, S., & Rose, R. M. (1973). Hypertension, peptic ulcer and diabetes and the traffic controllers. *Journal of the American Medical Association, 224,* 489–92.

Cohen, A. (1976). Alcohol and heroin: Structural comparison of reasons for use between drug addicts and alcoholics. *Annals of the New York Academy of Sciences, 273,* 605–12.

Cohen, B. M. (1977). Genetics of psychiatric disorders. *McLean Hospital Lecture Series.* Tape recording reproduced by Endo Laboratories, Garden City, N.Y.

Cohen, J. A. (1960). A coefficient of agreement for nominal scales. *Educational and Psychological Measurement, 20,* 37–46.

Cohen, J. B., & Reed, D. (1985). The Type A behavior pattern and coronary heart disease among Japanese men in Hawaii. *Journal of Behavioral Medicine, 8* (4), 343–52.

Cohen, N. B., Baker, G., Cohen, R. A., Fromm-Reichmann, F., & Weigert, E. B. (1954). An intensive study of 12 cases of manic-depressive psychosis. *Psychiatry, 17,* 103–37.

Cohn, N.R.C. (1975). *Europe's inner demons: An enquiry inspired by the great witch-hunt.* Chatto, Eng.: Heinemann for Sussex University Press.

Collins, R. L., Rothblum, E. D., & Wilson, G. T. (1986). The comparative efficacy of cognitive and behavioral approaches to the treatment of obesity. *Cognitive Therapy and Research, 10,* 299–318.

Coltheart, M. (1985). Cognitive neuropsychology and the study of reading. In M. I. Posner & O. S. M. Marin (Eds.), *Attention and Performance XI.* Hillsdale, NJ: Erlbaum.

Cook, W. W., & Medley, D. M. (1954). Proposed hostility and pharisaic-virtue scales for the MMPI. *Journal of Applied Psychology, 38,* 414–18.

Cooke, G., Johnston, N., & Pogany, E. (1973). Factors affecting referral to determine competency to stand trial. *American Journal of Psychiatry, 130*(8), 870.

Cooper, A. F., Garside, R. F., & Kay, D. W. (1976). A comparison of deaf and non-deaf patients with paranoid and affective psychoses. *British Journal of Psychiatry, 129,* 532–38.

Cooper, A. F., & Porter, R. (1976). Visual acuity and ocular pathology in the paranoid and affective psychoses. *British Journal of Psychiatry, 129,* 532–38.

Cooper, A. J. (1978). Aetiology of homosexuality. In J. A. Loraine (Ed.), *Understanding homosexuality* (pp. 1–23). New York: Elsevier.

Cooper, P.J., & Fairburn, C. G. (1983). Binge-eating and self-induced vomiting in the community: A preliminary study. *British Journal of Psychiatry, 142,* 139–44.

Coppersmith, S., & Woodrow, K. (1967). Basal conductance levels of normals and alcoholics. *Quarterly Journal of Studies on Alcohol, 17,* 296–305.

Coppen, A., Prange, A. J., Whybrow, P., & Noguera, R. (1972). Abnormalities of indoleamines and affective disorders. *Archives of General Psychiatry, 26,* 474–78.

Coryell, W., & Norten, S. (1981). Briquet's Syndrome and primary depression: Comparison of background and outcome. *Comprehensive Psychiatry, 22,* 249–56.

Costello, C. G. (1972). Depression: Loss of reinforcers or loss of reinforcer effectiveness. *Behavior Therapy, 3,* 240–47.

Cousins, N. (1979). *Anatomy of an illness: As perceived by the patient.* New York: Norton.

Cowen, E. L. (1973). Social and community interventions. *Annual Review of Psychology, 24,* 423–72.

Cowen, E. L. (1977a). Baby steps toward primary prevention. *American Journal of Community Psychology, 5,* 1–22.

Cowen, E. L. (1977b). Psychologists in primary prevention: Blowing the cover story. An editorial. *American Journal of Community Psychology, 5,* 481–90.

Cowen, E. L., & Zax, M. (1968). Early detection and prevention of emotional disorder: Conceptualizations and programming. In J. W. Carter (Ed.), *Research contributions from psychology to community mental health.* New York: Behavioral Publications.

Cox, P., Hallam, R., O'Connor, K., & Rachman, S. (1983). An experimental analysis of fearlessness and courage. *British Journal of Psychology, 74,* 107–17.

Coyle, J. T., Price, D. L., & DeLong, M. R. (1983). Alzheimer's disease: A disorder of cortical cholinergic innervation. *Science, 219,* 1184–90.

Craighead, L. W. (1984). Sequencing of behavior therapy and pharmacotherapy for obesity. *Journal of Consulting and Clinical Psychology, 52,* 190–99.

Craighead, W. E., Kazdin, A. E., & Mahoney, M. J. (1976). *Behavior modification: Principles, issues and applications.* Boston: Houghton Mifflin.

Crapper, D. R., Karlik, S., & De Boni, U. (1978). Aluminum and other metals in senile (Alzheimer) dementia. In R. Katzman, R. D. Terry, K. L. Bick, *Alzheimer's disease: Senile dementia and relaxed disorders* (Aging, Vol. 7) (pp. 471–85). New York: Raven Press.

Craske, M. G., Sanderson, W. C., Barlow, D. H. (1987). The relationships among panic, fear, and avoidance. *Journal of Anxiety Disorders, 1* (2), 153–60.

Creak, M. (1961). Schizophrenia syndrome in childhood: Progress report of a working party. *Cerebral Palsy Bulletin, 3,* 501–504.

Crisp, A. H. (1980). *Anorexia nervosa—Let me be.* London: Plenum.

Critchley, M. (1966). *The parietal lobes.* New York: Hafner.

Crocetti, G. M., & Lemkau, P. V. (1967). Schizophrenia: II. Epidemiology. In A. M. Freeman & H. I. Kaplan (Eds.), *Comprehensive textbook of psychiatry.* Baltimore: Williams & Wilkins.

Cronbach, L. J., Gleser, G. C., Nanda, H., & Rajaratnam, N. (1972). *The dependability of behavioral measurements: Theory of generalizability for scores and profiles.* New York: Wiley.

Crow, T. J. (1980). Molecular pathology of schizophrenia: More than one disease process? *British Medical Journal,* 66–68.

Crow, T. J. (1982). Two dimensions of pathology in schizophrenia: Dopaminergic and non-dopaminergic. *Psychopharmacology Bulletin, 18,* 22–29.

Crow, T. J. (1985). The two-syndrome concept: Origins and current status. *Schizophrenia Bulletin, 11* (3), 471–85.

Crowe, M. J., Marks, I. M., Agras, W. S., & Leitenberg, H. (1972). Time limited desensitization, implosion and shaping for phobic patients: A crossover study. *Behavior Research & Therapy, 10*(4), 319–28.

Cullen, 1808. In A. Scull, moral treatment reconsidered: Some sociological comments on an episode in the history of British psychiatry. In A. Scull (Ed.), *Madhouses, mad-doctors and madmen: The social history of psychiatry in the Victorian era* (pp. 105–18). Philadelphia: University of Pennsylvania Press, 1981.

Currie, E. P. (1968). Crimes without criminals: Witchcraft and its controls in Renaissance Europe. *Law and Society Review, 3,* 7–32.

Curtis, B. A., Jacobson, S., & Marcus, E. M. (1972). *An introduction to the neurosciences.* Philadelphia: Saunders.

Cushing, H. (1932). Peptic ulcers and the interbrain. *Surgery, Gynecology and Obstetrics, 55,* 1–34.

Cytryn, L., & Lourie, R. D. (1967). Mental retardation. In A. M. Freedman & H. I. Kaplan (Eds.), *Comprehensive textbook of psychiatry.* Baltimore: Williams & Wilkins.

Cytryn, L., & McKnew, D. H. (1972). Proposed classification of childhood depression. *American Journal of Psychiatry, 129,* 149–55.

Dalgard, O. S., & Kringlen, E. (1976). A Norwegian twin study of criminality. *British Journal of Criminality, 16,* 213–32.

Danaher, B. G. (1977). Rapid smoking and self-control in the modification of smoking behavior. *Journal of Consulting and Clinical Psychology, 45,* 1068–75.

Datey, K. K., Deshmuck, S. N., Dalvi, C. P., & Vinekarsl (1969). "Shavasan": A Yogic exercise in the management of hypertension. *Angiology, 20,* 325–33.

Davenport, H. W. (1972). Why the stomach does not digest itself. *Scientific American, 226,* 86–92.

Davenport, W. (1965). Sexual patterns and their regulation in a society in the Southwest Pacific. In F. A. Beach (ed.), *Sex and behavior* (pp. 164–209). New York: Wiley.

Davidson, L. M., & Baum, A. (1986). Chronic stress and post-traumatic stress disorders. *Journal of Consulting and Clinical Psychology, 54,* 303–308.

Davidson, R. J., Schaffer, C. E., & Saron, C. (1985). Effects of lateralized presentations of faces on self-reports of emotion and EEG asymmetry in depressed and non-depressed subjects. *Psychophysiology, 22* (3), 353–64.

Davies, J. C. V., & Maliphant, R. (1971). Autonomic responses of male adolescents exhibiting refractory behavior in school. *Journal of Child Psychology and Psychiatry, 12,* 115–27.

Davies, R. (1978). *One half of Robertson Davies.* New York: Penguin.

Davis, J., & Miller, N. (1963). Fear and pain: Their effect on self-injection of ambarbitol sodium by rats. *Science, 141,* 1286–87.

Davis, P. H., & Osherson, A. (1977). The current treatment of a multiple-personality woman and her son. *American Journal of Psychotherapy. 31,* 504–15.

Davis, P. J., & Schwartz, G. E. (1987). Repression and the inaccessibility of affective memories. *Journal of Personality and Social Psychology, 51* (1), 155–62.

Davison, G. C. (1976). Homosexuality: The ethical challenge. *Journal of Counseling and Clinical Psychology, 44,* 157–62.

Davison, G. C. (1978). Not can but ought: The treatment of homosexuality. *Journal of Consulting and Clinical Psychology, 46,* 170–72.

Davison, G. C., & Wilson, G. T. (1972). Critique of "Desensitization: Social and cognitive factors underlying the effectiveness of Wolpe's procedure." *Psychological Bulletin, 78*(1), 28–31.

Dekker, E., Pelse, H., & Groen, J. (1957). Conditioning as a cause of asthmatic attacks: A laboratory study. *Journal of Psychosomatic Research, 2,* 97–108.

DeMeyer, M. K., Barton, S., Alpern, G. D., Kimberlin, C., Allen, J., Yang, E., & Steel, R. (1974). The measured intelligence of autistic children. *Journal of Autistic Children and Schizophrenia, 4,* 42–60.

Department of International Economic and Social Affairs. (1985). Demographic Yearbook (37th ed.). New York: United Nations.

Depue, R. (1979). *The psychobiology of the depressive disorders: Implications for the effect of stress.* New York: Academic Press.

Depue, R. H., & Monroe, S. (1978). The unipolar-bipolar distinction in depressive disorders. *Psychological Bulletin, 85,* 1001–29.

Depue, R. A., & Monroe, S. M. (1986). Conceptualization and measurement of human disorder in life stress research: The problem of chronic disturbance. *Psychological Bulletin, 99,* 36–51.

Dershowitz, A. M. (1968). Psychiatry in the legal process: "A knife that cuts both ways." *Trial, 4,* 29.

De Sade, Marquis. (1791). *Justine, Philosophy in the Bedroom, and Other Writings.* (Richard Seaver & Austryn Wainhouse, Trans.). New York: Grove, 1965.

De Silva, P., Rachman, S., & Seligman, M. E. P. (1977). Prepared phobias and obsessions: Therapeutic outcome. *Behaviour Research and Therapy, 15*(1), 65–77.

Deutsch, A. (1949). *The mentally ill in America.* New York: Columbia University Press.

Devine, P. A., & Fernald, P. S. (1973). Outcome effects of receiving a preferred randomly assigned or nonpreferred therapy. *Journal of Consulting and Clinical Psychology, 41*(1), 104–107.

Diamond, B. L. (1974). Psychiatric prediction of dangerousness. *University of Pennsylvania Law Review, 123,* 439–52.

Diamond, E. L. (1982). The role of anger and hostility in essential hypertension and coronary heart disease. *Psychological Bulletin, 92,* 410–33.

Diamond, R. G., & Rozin, P. (1984). Activation of existing memories in anterograde amnesia. *Journal of Abnormal Psychology, 93,* 98–105.

Diggory, J. C. (1976). United States suicide rates, 1933–1968: An analysis of some trends. In E. S. Shneidman (Ed.), *Suicidology: Contemporary Developments.* New York: Grune & Stratton.

Dimsdale, J. E., Pierce, C., Schoenfeld, D., Brown, A., Zusman, R., & Graham, R. (1986). Suppressed anger and blood pressure: The effects of race, sex, social class, obesity, and age. *Psychosomatic Medicine, 48,* 430–36.

DiPalma, J. R. (1971). Introduction: Brief history. In J. R. DiPalma (Ed.), *Drill's pharmacology in medicine.* New York: McGraw-Hill.

Doane, J. A., Falloon, I. R. H., Goldstein, M. J., & Mintz, J. (1985). Parental affective style and the treatment of schizophrenia: Predicting the course of illness and social functioning. *Archives of General Psychiatry, 42,* 34–42.

Dohrenwend, B. P., & Shrout, P. E. (1985). "Hassles" in the conceptualization and measurement of life stress variables. *American Psychologist, 40,* 780–85.

Dohrenwend, B. S., & Dohrenwend, B. P. (Eds.). (1974). *Stressful life events: Their nature and effects.* New York: Wiley.

Dohrenwend, B. S., & Martin, J. L. (1978, February). Personal vs. situational determination of anticipation and control of the occurrence of stressful life events. Paper presented at the annual meeting of AAAS, Washington, D.C.

Dole, V. P., & Nyswander, M. E. (1965). Heroin addiction—a metabolic disease. *Archives of Internal Medicine, 120,* 19–24.

Doleys, D. M. (1979). Assessment and treatment of childhood enuresis. In A. J. Finch, Jr., & P. C. Kendall (Eds.), *Clinical treatment and research in child psychopathology* (pp. 207–33). New York: Spectrum.

Donahoe, C. P., Jr., Lin, D. H., Kirschenbaum, D. S., & Keesey, R. F. (1984). Metabolic consequences of dieting and exercise in the treatment of obesity. *Journal of Consulting and Clinical Psychology, 52,* 827–36.

Donaldson, D. (1976). *Insanity inside out.* New York: Crown.

Dorner, G., Schenk, B., Schmiedel, B., & Ahrens, L. (1983). Stressful events in prenatal life of bi- and homosexual men. *Experimental and Clinical Endocrinology, 81,* 83–87.

Dorsey, M. F., Iwata, B. A., Ong, P., & McSween, T. (1980). Treatment of self-injurious behavior using a water mist: Initial response suppression and generalization. *Journal of Applied Behavior Analysis, 13,* 343–53.

Dorworth, T. R. (1971). The effect of electroconvulsive shock on "helplessness" in dogs. Unpublished doctoral dissertation, University of Minnesota.

Dostoyevsky, D. (1864). *Notes from the underground.* New York: Dell, 1960.

Douglas, M. (Ed.). (1970). *Witchcraft: Confessions and accusations.* London: Tavistock.

Douglas, V. I. (1983). Attentional and cognitive problems. In M. Rutter (Ed.), *Developmental neuropsychiatry* (pp. 280–329). New York: Guilford Press.

Drossman, D. A. (1982). Patients with psychogenic abdominal pain: Six years' observation in the medical setting. *American Journal of Psychiatry, 139,* 1549–57.

Drummond. (1875). In R. Carrington, *Elephants.* New York: Basic Books, 1959.

Dunbar, H. F., & Arlow, J. (1944). Criteria for therapy in psychosomatic disorders. *Psychosomatic Medicine, 6,* 283–86.

Dunner, D. L., Gershom, E. S., & Goodwin, F. K. (1976). Heritable factors in the severity of affective illness. *Biological Psychiatry, 11,* 31–42.

Early, L. S., & Lisschutz, J. E. (1974). A case of stigmata. *Archives of General Psychiatry, 30,* 197–200.

Eberhard, G. (1968). Personality in peptic ulcer: Preliminary report of a twin study. *Acta Psychiatrica Scandinavia, 203,* 131.

Egeland, J. A., Gerhard, D. S., Pauls, D. L., Sussex, J. N., Kidd, K. K., Allen, C. R., Hostetter, A. M., & Housman, D. E. (1987). Bipolar affective disorders linked to DNA markers on chromosome 11. *Nature, 325,* 783–87.

Egeland, J. A., & Hostetter, A. M. (1983). Amish study, I: Affective disorders among the Amish, 1976–1980. *American Journal of Psychiatry, 140,* 56–61.

Egeland, J. A., & Sussex, J. N. (1985). Suicide and family loading for affective disorders. *Journal of the American Medical Association, 254,* 915–18.

Eidelson, J. I. (1977). Perceived control and psychopathology. Unpublished doctoral dissertation, Duke University.

Eisenberg, L. (1956). The autistic child in adolescence. *American Journal of Psychiatry, 112,* 607–12.

Eisenberg, L. (1977). Psychiatry and society: A sociobiological synthesis. *New England Journal of Medicine. 29,* 903–10.

Ekman, P., & Friesen, W. V. (1975). *Unmasking the face.* Englewood Cliffs, NJ: Prentice-Hall.

Ekman, P., Friesen, W. V., & Ellsworth, P. (1972). *Emotion in the human face.* New York: Pergamon.

Elashoff, J. D., & Grossman, M. I. (1980). Trends in hospital admissions and death rates for peptic ulcer in the United States from 1970 to 1978. *Gastroenterology, 78,* 280–85.

Elkin, I., Shea, T., Imber, S., Pilkonis, P., Sotsky, S., Glass, D., Watkins, J., Leber, W., & Collins, J. (1986). NIMH treatment of depression collaborative research program: Initial outcome findings. Paper presented at meetings of the American Association for the Advancement of Science, May 1986.

Ellenberger, H. F. (1970). *The discovery of the unconscious: The history and evolution of dynamic psychiatry.* New York: Basic Books.

Ellis, A. (1962). *Reason and emotion in psychotherapy.* New York: Lyle Stuart.

Ellis, L., & Ames, M. A. (1987). Neurohormonal functioning and sexual orientation: A theory of homosexuality-heterosexuality. *Psychological Bulletin, 101* (2), 233–58.

Ellis, L., Ames, M. A., Peckham, W., & Burke, D. (1988). Sexual orientation of human offspring may be altered by severe maternal stress during pregnancy. *Journal of Sex Research, 25* (1), 152–57.

Ellis, A., & Harper, R. A. (1975). *A new guide to rational living.* Englewood Cliffs, NJ: Prentice-Hall.

Ellison, G. D. (1977). Animal models of psychopathology. *American Psychologist, 32,* 1036–55.

Ellsworth, P. C., & Carlsmith, M. J. (1968). Effects of eye contact and verbal content on affective response to dyadic interactions. *Journal of Personality and Social Psychology, 10,* 15–20.

Elmhorn, K. (1965). Study in self-reported delinquency among school children. In *Scandinavian studies in criminology.* London: Tavistock.

Emmelkamp, P., & Kuipers, A. (1979). Agoraphobia: a follow-up study four years after treatment. *British Journal of Psychiatry, 134,* 352–55.

Emrick, C. D., Lassen, C. L., & Edwards, M. T. (1977). Nonprofessional peers as therapeutic agents. In A. S. Gurman & A. M. Razin (Eds.), *Effective psychotherapy.* New York: Pergamon Press.

Endicott, J., & Spitzer, R. L. (1978). A diagnostic interview: The schedule for affective disorders and schizophrenia. *Archives of General Psychiatry, 35,* 837–44.

Endler, N. S., Magnusson, D., Ekehammar, B., & Okada, M. O. (1975). The multidimensionality of state and trait anxiety. Reports from the Department of Psychology, University of Stockholm.

Ennis, B. J. (1972). *Prisoners of psychiatry: Mental patients, psychiatrists, and the law.* New York: Harcourt Brace Jovanovich.

Ennis, B. J., & Litwack, T. R. (1974). Psychiatry and the presumption of expertise: Flipping coins in the courtroom. *California Law Review, 62,* 693.

Ennis, B., & Siegel, L. (1973). *The rights of mental patients: The basic ACLU guide to a mental patient's rights.* New York: Discus Books.

Epstein, L. H., & Wing, R. R. (1987). Behavioral treatment of childhood obesity. *Psychological Bulletin, 101,* 331–442.

Erikson, K. (1976). *Everything in its path: Destruction of community in the Buffalo Creek flood.* New York: Simon & Schuster.

Evans, M. D., Hollon, S. D., De Rubeis, R. J., Piajeck, J., Grove, W. M., & Tuason, V. B. (1989). Differential relapse following treatment for depression: IV. A two-year follow-up at the cognitive-pharmacotherapy project. In press.

Exline, R., & Winters, L. C. (1965). Affective relations and mutual glances in dyads. In S. Tomkins & C. E. Izard (Eds.), *Affect, cognition and personality.* New York: Springer.

Exner, J. E. (1974). *The Rorschach: A comprehensive system.* New York: Wiley.

Exner, J. E. (1978). *The Rorschach: A comprehensive system: Vol. 2. Current research and advanced interpretation.* New York: Wiley.

Eysenck, H. J. (1952). The effects of psychotherapy: An evaluation. *Journal of Consulting Psychology, 16,* 319–24.

Eysenck, H. J. (1961). The effects of psychotherapy. In H. J. Eysenck (Ed.), *Handbook of abnormal psychology: An experimental approach* (pp. 697–725). New York: Basic Books.

Eysenck, H. J. (1979). The conditioning model of neurosis. *Communications in Behavioral Biology, 2,* 155–99.

Fagot, B. I. (1984). The consequences of problem behavior in toddler children. *Journal of Abnormal Child Psychology, 12,* 385–96.

Fairburn, C. G., & Cooper, P. J. (1982). Self-induced vomiting and bulimia nervosa: An undetected problem. *British Journal of Medicine, 284,* 1153–55.

Fairweather, G. W., Sanders, D. H. Cressler, D. L., & Maynard, H. (1969). *Community life for the mentally ill.* Chicago: Alpine.

Falloon, I. R. H., Boyd, J. L., & McGill, C. W. (1984). *Family care of schizophrenia: A problem-solving approach to the treatment of mental illness.* New York: Guilford Press.

Falloon, I. R. H., Boyd, J. L., McGill, C. W., Williamson, M., Razani, J., Moss, H. B., Gilderman, A. M., & Simpson, G. M. (1985). Family management in the prevention of morbidity in schizophrenia. *Archives of General Psychiatry, 42,* 887–96.

Falloon, I. R. H., & Liberman, R. P. (1983). Interactions between drug and psychosocial therapy in schizophrenia. *Schizophrenia Bulletin, 9,* 543–55.

Fancher, R. (1973). *Psychoanalytic psychology: The development of Freud's thought.* New York: Norton.

Farber, L. H. (1966). *The ways of the will: Essays toward a psychology and psychopathology of will.* New York: Basic Books.

Farberow, N. L. (1970). Ten years of suicide prevention—past and future. *Bulletin of Suicidology, 6,* 6–11.

Farberow, N. L. (1974). *Suicide.* Morristown, NJ: General Learning Press.

Faris, R. E. L., & Dunham, H. W. (1939). *Mental disorders in urban areas.* Chicago: University of Chicago Press.

Farrington, D. P. (1978). The family background of aggressive youths. In L. A. Hersov & D. Shaffer (Eds.), *Aggression and antisocial behavior in childhood and adolescence.* New York: Pergamon.

Fawcett, J., Maas, J., & Dekirmenjian, H. (1972). Depression and MHPG excretion: Response to dextroamphetamine and tricyclic antidepressants. *Archives of General Psychiatry, 26,* 246–51.

Feinberg, I. (1962). A comparison of the visual hallucinations in schizophrenics with those induced by mescaline and LSD. In L. J. West (Ed.), *Hallucinations.* New York: Grune & Stratton.

Feinberg, T. E., Rifkin, A., Schaffer, C., & Walker, E. (1986). Facial discrimination and emotional recognition in schizophrenia and affective disorders. *Archives of General Psychiatry, 43,* 276–79.

Feldman, M. P., & MacCulloch, M. J. (1971). *Homosexual behaviour: Theory and assessment.* Oxford: Pergamon.

Fenichel, O. (1945). *The psychoanalytic theory of neurosis.* New York: Norton.

Ferster, C. B. (1961). Positive reinforcement and the behavioral deficits of autistic children. *Child Development, 32,* 437–56.

Ferster, C. B. (1974). Behavioral approaches to depression. In R. J. Friedman & M. M. Katz (Eds.), *The psychology of depression: Contemporary theory and research.* Washington, DC: Winston.

Fieve, R. R. (1975). *Mood swing.* New York: Morrow.

Fingarette, H., & Hasse, A. (1979). *Mental disabilities and criminal responsibility.* Berkeley: University of California Press.

Fink, M. (1979). *Convulsive therapy: Therapy and practice.* New York: Raven Press.

Fireside, H. (1979). *Soviet psychoprisons.* New York: Norton.

Fisher, J., Epstein, L. J., & Harris, M. R. (1967). Validity of the psychiatric interview: Predicting the effectiveness of the first Peace Corps volunteers in Ghana. *Archives of General Psychiatry, 17,* 744–50.

Fisher, S., & Greenberg, R. P. (1977). *The scientific credibility of Freud's theories and therapy.* New York: Basic Books.

Fiske, D., Cartwright, D., & Kirtner, W. (1964). Are psychotherapeutic changes predictable? *Journal of Abnormal and Social Psychology, 69,* 418–26.

Fiske, D., & Goodman, G. (1965). The post-therapy period. *Journal of Abnormal Psychology, 70,* 169–70.

Flavell, J. H. 1977, *Cognitive development.* Englewood Cliffs, NJ: Prentice-Hall.

Flavin, D. K., & Frances, R. J. (1987). Risk taking behavior, substance abuse disorders, and acquired immune deficiency syndrome. *Advances in Alcohol and Substance Abuse, 6,* 23–32.

Fleiss, J. L. (1971). Measuring nominal scale agreement among many raters. *Psychological Bulletin, 76,* 378–82.

Flood, R., & Seager, C. (1968). A retrospective examination of psychiatric case records of patients who subsequently commit suicide. *British Journal of Psychiatry, 114,* 443–50.

Foa, D. B., & Kozak, M. J. (1986). Emotional processing of fear: Exposure to corrective information. *Psychological Bulletin, 99,* 20–35.

Fodor, O., Vestea, S., & Urcan, S. (1968). Hydrochloric acid secretion capacity of the stomach as an inherited factor in the pathogenesis of duodenal ulcer. *American Journal of Digestive Diseases, 13,* 260.

Ford, C. S., & Beach, F. A. (1951). *Pattern of sexual behavior.* New York: Harper.

Foster, D. W., & Wilson, J. D. (Eds.). (1985). *William's textbook of endocrinology* (7th ed.). Philadelphia: Saunders.

Foucault, M. (1965). *Madness and civilization: A history of insanity in the age of reason.* New York: Random House.

Fowler, R. D. (1986). Howard Hughes: A psychological autopsy. *Psychology Today, 20,* 22–33.

Fowles, D. C., & Gersh, F. (1979). Neurotic depression: The endogenous-neurotic distinction. In R. A. Depue (Ed.), *The psychobiology of the depressive disorders: Implications for the effects of stress.* New York: Academic Press.

Fox, R. (1976). The recent rise of suicide in Britain: The role of the samaritan suicide prevention movement. In E. S. Shneidman (Ed.), *Suicidology: Contemporary developments.* New York: Grune & Stratton.

Frank, E., Anderson, C., & Rubenstein D. (1978). Frequency of sexual dysfunction in "normal" couples. *New England Journal of Medicine, 299,* 111–15.

Frank, J. D. (1978). Expectation and therapeutic outcome—The placebo effect and the role induction interview. In J. D. Frank, R. Hoehn-Saric, S. D. Imber, B. L. Liberman, & A. R. Stone (Eds.), *Effective ingredients of successful psychotherapy.* New York: Brunner/Mazel.

Frankl, V. E. (1975). Paradoxical intention and dereflection. *Psychotherapy: Theory, Research and Practice, 12,* 226–37.

Frederick, C. J. (1973). Suicide, homicide and alcoholism among American Indians. (DHEW Publication No. ADM 24–42). Washington, DC: U.S. Government Printing Office.

Frederick C. J. (1978). Current trends in suicidal behavior in the United States. *American Journal of Psychotherapy, 32,* 172–200.

Freud, A. (1936). *The ego and mechanisms of defense* (rev. ed.). New York: International Universities Press, 1967.

Freud, S. (1884). Letter to his fiancée. In N. Taylor, *Flight from reality.* New York: Duell, Sloan, & Pearce, 1949.

Freud, S. (1894). The neuro-psychoses of defense. In J. Strachey (Ed. and Trans.), *The complete psychological works* (Vol. 3). New York: Norton, 1976.

Freud, S. (1905). Psychical (or mental) treatment. In J. Strachey (Ed. and Trans.), *The complete psychological works* (Vol. 7). New York: Norton, 1976.

Freud, S. (1909). Some general remarks on hysterical attacks. In J. Strachey (Ed. and Trans.), *The complete psychological works* (Vol. 9). New York: Norton, 1976.

Freud, S. (1909). Notes upon a case of obsessional neurosis. In J. Strachey (Ed. and Trans.), *The complete psychological works* (Vol. 10). New York: Norton, 1976.

Freud, S. (1917). Introductory lectures on psychoanalysis, Part III. In J. Strachey (Ed. and Trans.), *The complete pschological works* (Vol. 16). New York: Norton, 1976.

Freud, S. (1923). The ego and the id. In J. Strachey (Ed. and Trans.), *The complete psychological works* (Vol. 19). New York: Norton, 1976.

Freud, S. (1933). New introductory lectures on psychoanalysis. In J. Strachey (Ed. and Trans.), *The complete psychological works* (Vol. 22). New York: Norton, 1976.

Freud, S. (1936). A disturbance of memory on the Acropolis. In J. Strachey (Ed. and Trans.), *The complete psychological works* (Vol. 22). New York: Norton, 1976.

Freud, S. (1937). Analysis terminable and interminable. In J. Strachey (Ed. and Trans.), *The complete psychological works* (Vol. 23). New York: Norton, 1976.

Friedman, M., & Rosenman, R. H. (1974). *Type A behavior.* New York: Knopf.

Friedman, M., Thoresen, C. E., Gill, J. J., Powell, L. H., Ulmer, D., Thompson, L., Price, V. A., Rabin, D. D., Breall, W. S., Dixon, T., Levy, R., & Bourg, E. (1984). Alteration of Type A behavior and reduction in cardiac recurrences in postmyocardial infarction patients. *American Heart Journal, 108,* 237–48.

Frumkin, K., Nathan, R., Prout, M., & Cohen, M. (1978). Nonpharmacologic control of essential hypertension in men: A critical review of the experimental literature. *Psychosomatic Medicine, 40,* 294–320.

Fuche, C. Z., & Rehm, L. P. (1977). A self-control behavior therapy program for depression. *Journal of Consulting and Clinical Psychology, 45,* 206–15.

Furstenburg, F., Moore, K. A., & Peterson, J. L. (1986). Sex education and sexual experience among adolescents. *American Journal of Public Health, 75* (11), 1331–32.

Gadpaille, W. J. (1972). Research into the physiology of maleness and femaleness: Its contributions to the etiology and understanding of homosexuality. *Archives of General Psychiatry, 26,* 193–206.

Gagnon, J. H. (1977). *Human sexuality.* Chicago: Scott, Foresman.

Galen. In Veith, I. *Hysteria: The history of a disease.* Chicago: University of Chicago Press, 1965.

Galaburda, A. M., Sherman, G. F., Rosen, G. D., & Geschwind, N. (1985). Developmental dyslexia: Four consecutive cases with cortical anomalies. *Annals of Neurology, 18,* 222–33.

Garcia, J., Ervin, F. R., & Koelling, R. A. (1967). Toxicity of serum from irradiated donors. *Nature, 213,* 682–83.

Garcia, E., Guess, D., & Brynes, J. (1973). Development of syntax in a retarded girl using procedures of imitation, reinforcement, and modelling. *Journal of Applied Behavior Analysis, 6,* 299–310.

Garcia, J., & Koelling, R. A. (1966). Relation of cue to consequence in avoidance learning. *Psychonomic Science, 4,* 123–24.

Gardner, E. (1975). *Fundamentals of neurology: A psychophysiological approach* (6th ed.). Philadelphia: Saunders.

Gardner, H. (1974). *The shattered mind.* New York: Vintage.

Garfinkel, P. E., & Garner, D. M. (1982). *Anorexia nervosa: A multidimensional perspective.* New York: Brunner/Mazel.

Garmezy, N. (1971). Vulnerability research and the issue of primary prevention. *American Journal of Orthopsychiatry, 41,* 101–16.

Garmezy, N. (1974). Children at risk: The search for the antecedents of schizophrenia: Part II. Ongoing research programs, issues, and intervention. *Schizophrenia Bulletin, 9,* 55–125.

Garmezy, N. (1977a). DSM III: Never mind the psychologists—Is it good for the children? *The Clinical Psychologist, 31,* 3–4.

Garmezy, N. (1977b). The psychology and psychopathology of Allenhead. *Schizophrenia Bulletin, 3,* 360–69.

Garner, D. M., & Bemis, K. M. (1982). A cognitive-behavioral approach to anorexia nervosa. *Cognitive Therapy and Research, 6,* 123–50.

Garrity, T. F., Somes, G. W., & Marx, M. B. (1977). Personality factors in resistance to illness after recent life changes. *Journal of Psychosomatic Research, 21,* 23–32.

Gay, P. (1988). *Freud: A life for our time.* New York: Norton.

Gazzaniga, M. (1970). *The bisected brain.* New York: Appleton-Century-Crofts.

Gebhard, P. H., Gagnon, J. H., Pomeroy, W. B., & Christenson, C. V. (1965). *Sex offenders.* New York: Harper & Row.

Gelenberg, A. J., & Klerman, G. L. (1978). Maintenance drug therapy in long-term treatment of depression. In J. P. Brady & H. K. H. Brodie (Eds.), *Controversy in psychiatry.* Philadelphia: Saunders.

Gelfand, D. M. (1978). Social withdrawal and negative emotional states: Behavioral treatment. In B. B. Wolman, J. Egan, & A. O. Ross (Eds.), *Handbook of treatment of mental disorders in childhood and adolescence.* Englewood Cliffs, NJ: Prentice-Hall.

Gelfand, D. M., Jenson, W. R., & Drew, C. J. (1982). *Understanding child behavior disorders.* New York: Holt, Rinehart & Winston.

Genazzani, A. R., Nappi, G., Eacchinetti, F., Mezzella, G. L., Parrini, D., Sinforiani, E., Petraglia, F., & Savoldi, F. (1982). Central deficiency of beta-endorphin in alcohol addicts. *Journal of Clinical Endocrinology and Metabolism, 55,* 583–86.

Gergen, K. J. (1982). *Toward transformation in social knowledge.* New York: Springer Verlag.

Gershon, E. S. (1983). The genetics of affective disorders. In L. Grinspoon (Ed.), *Psychiatry update* (pp. 434–538). Washington, DC: American Psychiatric Press, Inc.

Geschwind, N. (1962). The anatomy of acquired disorders of reading. In J. Money (Ed.), *Reading disability* (pp. 115–30). Baltimore: Johns Hopkins University Press.

Geschwind, N. (1965). Disconnection syndromes in animals and man. *Brain, 88,* 237–94, 585–640.

Geschwind, N. (1972). Language and the brain. *Scientific American, 226,* 76–83.

Geschwind, N. (1975). The apraxias: Neural mechanisms of disorders of learned movement. *American Scientist, 188,* 188–95.

Geschwind, N. Quadfasel, F. A., & Segarra, J. M. (1968). Isolation of the speech area. *Neuropsychologia, 6,* 327–40.

Gilberstadt, H., & Duker, J. (1965). A handbook for clinical and actuarial MMPI interpretations. Philadelphia: Saunders.

Gill, J. J., Price, V. A., Friedman, M., Thoresen, C. E., Powell, L. H., Ulmer, D., Brown, B., & Drews, F. R. (1985). Reduction in Type A behavior in healthy middle-aged American military officers. *American Heart Journal, 110,* 503–14.

Gilman, A. G., Goodman, L. S., Rall, T. W., & Murad, F. (Eds.). (1985). In Goodman & Gilman, *The pharmacological basis of therapeutics.* New York: Macmillan.

Gittelman-Klein, R., Klein, D. F., Abikoff, H., Katz, S., Gloisten, A. C., & Kates, W. (1976). Relative efficacy of methylphenidate and behavior modification in hyperkinetic children: An interim report. *Journal of Abnormal Child Psychology, 4,* 361–79.

Gittelman-Klein, R., & Klein, D. F. (1980). Separation anxiety in school refusal and its treatment with drugs. In B. Hersov (Ed.), *Out of school* (pp. 321–41). London: Wiley.

Gittelman, R., & Klein, D. F. (1984). Relationship between separation anxiety and panic and agoraphobic disorders. *Psychopathology, 17,* 56–65.

Gittelman, R., Mannuzza, S., Shenker, R., & Bonagura, N. (1985). Hyperactive boys almost grown up. *Archives of General Psychiatry, 42,* 937–47.

Gittleman, M., & Birch, H. G. (1967). Childhood schizophrenia: Intellect, neurologic status, perinatal risk, prognosis and family pathology. *Archives of General Psychiatry, 17,* 16–25.

Gittleson, N. L. (1966). Depressive psychosis in the obsessional neurotic. *British Journal of Psychiatry, 122,* 883–87.

Glazer, H. I., & Weiss, J. M. (1976). Long-term interference effect: An alternative to "learned helplessness." *Journal of Experimental Psychology: Animal Behavior Processes, 2,* 202–13.

Glass, D. C. (1977). *Behavior pattern stress in coronary disease.* Hillsdale, NJ: Erlbaum.

Gleitman, H. (1981). *Psychology.* New York: Norton.

Gleitman, L. R., & Rozin, P. (1977). The structure and acquisition of reading: I. Relations between orthographics and the structure of language. In A. S. Reber & D. Scarborough (Eds.), *Toward a psychology of reading* (1–53). Potomac, MD: Erlbaum.

Gleser, G. C., Green, B. L., & Winget, C. (1981). *Prolonged psychosocial effects of disaster.* New York: Academic Press.

Glisky, E. L., Schacter, D. L. & Tulving, E. (1986). Computer learning by memory-impaired patients: acquisition and retention of complex knowledge. *Neuropsychologia, 24,* 313–28.

Gluhbegovic, N., & Williams, T. H. (1980). *The human brain: A photographic guide.* Hagerstown, MD.: Harper & Row.

Golan, N. (1978). *Treatment in crisis situations.* New York: The Free Press.

Goldfried, M. R., & Davison, G. C. (1976). *Clinical behavior therapy.* New York: Holt, Rinehart & Winston.

Goldfried, M. R., Decenteceo, E., & Wineburg, L. (1974). Systematic rational restructuring as a self-control technique. *Behavior Therapy, 3,* 398–416.

Goldfried, M. R., Linehan, M. M., & Smith, J. L. (1978). Reduction of test anxiety through cognitive restructuring. *Journal of Consulting and Clinical Psychology, 46,* 32–39.

Goldstein, K. (1939). *The organism.* New York: American Book Company.

Goodglass, H., & Mayer, J. (1958). Agrammatism in aphasus. *Journal of Speech and Hearing Disorders, 23,* 99–111.

Goodman, L., & Gilman, A. (1941). *The pharmacological basis of therapeutics.* New York: Macmillan.

Goodwin, D. W. W., Schulsinger, F., Hermansen, L., Guze, S. B.,

& Winokur, G. (1973). Alcohol problems in adoptees raised apart from alcoholic biological parents. *Archives of General Psychiatry, 28,* 238–43.

Goodwin, F., Brodie, H., Murphy, D., et al. (1970). L-dopa, catecholamines and behavior: A clinical and biochemical study in depressed patients. *Biological Psychiatry, 2,* 341–66.

Gorenstein, E. E., & Newman, J. P. (1980). Disinhibitory psychopathology: A new perspective and a model for research. *Psychological Review, 87,* 301–15.

Gottesman, I. I., & Shields, J. (1972). *Schizophrenia and genetics: A twin study vantage point.* New York: Academic Press.

Gottesman, I. I., & Shields, J. (1982). *Schizophrenia: The epigenetic puzzle* (pp. xiii and 258). Cambridge: Cambridge University Press.

Gould, S. J. (1981). *The mismeasure of man.* New York: Norton.

Gove, W. R. (1975). Labelling and mental illness: A critique. In W. R. Gove (Ed.), *The labelling of deviance: Evaluating a perspective.* New York: Sage.

Grace, W. J., & Graham, D. T. (1952). Relationship of specific attitudes and emotions to certain bodily disease. *Psychosomatic Medicine, 14,* 243–51.

Graf, P., & Schacter, D. L. (1985). Implicit and explicit memory for new associations in normal and amnesic subjects. *Journal of Experimental Psychology: Learning, Memory, and Cognition, 11,* 501–18.

Graham, L. E. II, Taylor, C. B., Hovell, M. F., & Siegel, W. (1983). Five-year follow-up to a behavioral weight-loss program. *Journal of Consulting and Clinical Psychology, 51,* 332–33.

Granville-Grossman, K. L. (1968). The early environment and affective disorder. In A. Coppen & A. Walk (Eds.), *Recent developments in affective disorders. British Journal of Psychiatry.* (Special Publication No. 2).

Green, R. (1985). Gender identity in childhood and later sexual orientation: Follow-up of 78 males. *American Journal of Psychiatry, 142,* 339–41.

Greenspoon, J. (1955). The reinforcing effect of two spoken sounds on the frequency of two responses. *American Journal of Psychology, 68,* 409–16.

Greer, S. (1964). Study of parental loss in neurotics and sociopaths. *Archives of General Psychiatry, 11,* 177–80.

Greer, S., Morris, T., & Pettingale, K. W. (1979). Psychological response to breast cancer: Effect on outcome. *The Lancet, II,* October 13, 785–87.

Gregory, I. (1958). Studies on parental deprivation in psychiatric patients. *American Journal of Psychiatry, 115,* 432–42.

Gregor, T. (1985). *Anxious pleasures: The sexual lives of an Amazonian people.* Chicago: University of Chicago Press.

Grimshaw, L. (1964). Obsessional disorder and neurological illness. *Journal of Neurology, Neurosurgery and Psychiatry, 27,* 229–31.

Gross, H. J., & Zimmerman, J. (1965). Experimental analysis of hysterical blindness: A follow-up report and new experimental data. *Archives of General Psychiatry, 13,* 255–60.

Grossman, H. J. (Ed.) (1973). *Manual on terminology and classification in mental retardation.* Washington, DC: American Association of Mental Deficiency. (Special Publication Series, No. 2).

Grossman, H. J. (Ed.). (1983). *Manual on terminology and classification in mental retardation.* Washington, DC: American Association of Mental Deficiency.

Grove, W. M., & Andreasen, N. C. (1985). Language and thinking in psychosis. *Archives of General Psychiatry, 42,* 26–32.

Grunbaum, A. (1984). *The foundations of psychoanalysis: A philosophical critique.* Berkeley: University of California Press.

Gunderson, J. G., & Mosher, L. R. (1975). The cost of schizophrenia. *American Journal of Psychiatry, 132,* 901–906.

Gur, R. E., Gur, R. C., Skolnick, B. E., Caroff, S., Obrist, W. D., Resnick, S., & Reivich, M. (1985). Brain function in psychiatric disorders: III. Regional cerebral blood flow in unmediated schizophrenia. *Archives of General Psychiatry, 42,* 329–34.

Gurman, A. S. (1973a). Instability of therapeutic conditions in psychotherapy. *Journal of Counseling Psychology, 20,* 16–24.

Gurman, A. S. (1973b). The effects and effectiveness of marital therapy: A review of outcome research. *Family Process, 12,* 145–70.

Gurman, A. S. (1977). Therapist and patient factors influencing the patient's perception of facilitative therapeutic conditions. *Psychiatry, 40,* 218–31.

Guze, S. B., & Robins, E. (1970). Suicide and primary affective disorders. *British Journal of Psychiatry, 17,* 437.

Hackmann, A., & McLean, C. (1975). A comparison of flooding and thought-stopping treatment. *Behavior Research and Therapy, 13,* 263–69.

Halbreich, U., Endicott, J., & Nee, J. (1983). Premenstrual depressive changes. *Archives of General Psychiatry, 40,* 535–42.

Haley, J. (1969). *The power tactics of Jesus Christ.* New York: Grossman.

Hall, C. S., & Lindzey, G. (1970). *Theories of personality.* New York: Wiley.

Hall, R. V., Fox, R., Willard, D., Goldsmith, I., Emerson, M., Owen, M., Davis, T., & Porcia, E. (1971). The teacher as observer and experimenter in the modification of disputing and talking-out behaviors. *Journal of Applied Behavior Analysis, 4,* 141–49.

Hall, S. M., Hall, R. G., DeBoer, G., & O'Kulitch, P. (1977). Self and external management compared with psychotherapy in the control of obesity. *Behavior Research and Therapy, 15*(1), 89–95.

Hall, S. M., Rugg, D., Tunstall, C. & Jones, R. T. (1984). Preventing relapse to cigarette smoking by behavioral skill. *Journal of Consulting and Clinical Psychology, 52,* 372–82.

Halmi, K. A. (1978). Anorexia nervosa: Recent investigations. *Annual Review of Medicine, 29,* 37–149.

Halmi, K. A., Falk, J. R., & Schwartz, E. (1981). Binge-eating and vomiting: A survey of a college population. *Psychological Medicine, 11,* 697–706.

Halpern, J. (1977). Projection: A test of the psychoanalytic hypothesis. *Journal of Abnormal Psychology, 86,* 536–42.

Hamilton, J. W. (1973). Voyeurism: Some therapeutic considerations. *International Journal of Psychotherapy, 2,* 77–91.

Hammen, C. L. & Glass, D. R. (1975). Expression, activity, and evaluation of reinforcement. *Journal of Abnormal Psychology, 84,* 718–21.

Hammen, D. L., & Padesky, C. A. (1977). Sex differences in the expression of depressive responses on the Beck Depression Inventory. *Journal of Abnormal Psychology, 86,* 609–14.

Hannum, R. D., Rosellini, R. A., & Seligman, M. E. P. (1976). Retention of learned helplessness and immunization in the rat from weaning to adulthood. *Developmental Psychology, 12,* 449–54.

Harburg, E., Erfurt, J. C., Hauenstein, L. S., Chape, C., Schull, W. J., & Schork, M. A. (1973). Socio-ecological stress, suppressed hostility, skin color, and black-white male blood pressure: Detroit. *Psychosomatic Medicine, 35,* 276.

Hare, R. D. (1965). Temporal gradient of fear arousal in psychopaths. *Journal of Abnormal Psychology, 70,* 442–45.

Hare, R. (1970). *Psychopathy: Theory and research.* New York: Wiley.

Hare, R. D. (1978). Electrodermal and cardiovascular correlates of sociopathy. In R. D. Hare & D. Schalling (Eds.), *Psychopathic behavior: Approaches to research.* New York: Wiley.

Hare, R. D. (1980). A research scale for the assessment of psychopathy in criminal populations. *Personality and Individual Differences, 1,* 111–19.

Harlow, J. M. (1868). Recovery from the passage of an iron bar through the head. *Publications of the Massachusetts Medical Society, 2,* 327.

Harris, B. (1979). Whatever happened to little Albert? *American Psychologist, 34,* 151–60.

Harris, E. L., Noyes, R., Crowe, R. R., & Chaudry, D. R. (1983). Family study of agoraphobia. *Archives of General Psychiatry, 40,* 1061–64.

Harrison, R. (1965). Thematic apperceptive methods. In B. B. Wolman (Ed.), *Handbook of clinical psychology.* New York: Wiley.

Hart, K. J., & Ollendick, T. H. (1985). Prevalence of bulimia in working and university women. *American Journal of Psychiatry, 142,* 851–54.

Hartman, W. E., & Fithian, M. A. (1972). *Treatment of sexual dysfunction.* New York: Jason Aronson.

Hartmann, H. (1958). *Ego psychology and the problem of adaptation.* New York: International Universities Press.

Hasin, D. S., & Grant, B. F. (1987). Assessment of specific drug disorders in a sample of substance abuse patients: A comparison of the DIS and the DADS-L procedures. *Drug and Alcohol Dependence, 19,* 165–76.

Hathaway, S. R., & McKinley, J. C. (1943). *MMPI manual.* New York: Psychological Corporation.

Haynes, S. G., Feinleib, M., & Kannel, W. B. (1980). The relationship of psychosocial factors to coronary heart disease in the Framingham study: III. Eight years incidence in coronary heart disease. *American Journal of Epidemiology, 3,* 37–85.

Hazelrigg, M. D., Cooper, H. M., & Borduin, C. M. (1987). Evaluating the effectiveness of family therapies: An integrative review and analysis. *Psychological Bulletin, 101* (3), 428–42.

Heads, T. B. (1978). Ethical and legal considerations in behavior therapy. In D. Margolin (Ed.), *Child behavior therapy.* New York: Gardner Press.

Hecaen, H., & Albert, M. L. (1978). *Human neuropsychology.* New York: Wiley.

Hegedus, A. M., Tarter, R. E., Hill, S. Y., Jacob, T., & Winsten, N. E. (1984). Static ataxia: A possible marker for alcoholism. *Alcoholism: Clinical and Experimental Research, 8,* 580–82.

Heider, F. (1958). *The psychology of interpersonal relationships.* New York: Wiley.

Heilman, K. M. (1979). The neuropsychological basis of skilled movement in man. In M. Gazzaniga (Ed.), *Handbook of behavioral neurobiology: Vol. 2. Neuropsychology* (pp. 447–61). New York: Plenum.

Heiman, J. R., & LoPiccolo, J. (1983). Clinical outcome of sex therapy. *Archives of General Psychiatry, 40,* 443–49.

Heinicke, C. M. (1973). Parental deprivation in early childhood: A predisposition to later depression. In J. P. Scott & E. C. Senay (Eds.), *Separation and depreciation.* Washington, DC: American Association for the Advancement of Science.

Heitler, J. (1973). Preparation of lower class patients for expressive group psychotherapy. *Journal of Consulting and Clinical Psychology, 41,* 260–61.

Hellekson, C. J., Kline, J. A., & Rosenthal, N. E. (1986). Phototherapy for seasonal affective disorder in Alaska. *American Journal of Psychiatry, 143,* 1035–37.

Helsing, K. J., Szklo, M., & Comstock, G. W. (1981). Factors associated with mortality after widowhood. *American Journal of Public Health, 71,* 802–809.

Hemsley, R., Howlin, P., Berger, M., Hersov, L., Holbrook, D., Rutter, M., & Yule, W. (1978). Treating autistic children in a family context. In M. Rutter & E. Schopler (Eds.), *Autism: A reappraisal of concepts and treatment.* New York: Plenum.

Hendin, H. (1969). Black suicide. *Archives of General Psychiatry, 21,* 407–22.

Henningfield, J. E. (1984). Pharmacological basis and treatment of cigarette smoking. *Journal of Clinical Psychiatry, 45,* 24–34.

Henningfield, J. E. (1985). Behavioral pharmacology of cigarette smoking. In T. Thompson & D. P. Dews (Eds.), *Advances in behavioral pharmacology* (Vol. IV). New York: Academic Press.

Hermelin, B., & O'Connor, N. (1970). *Psychological experiments with autistic children.* Oxford: Pergamon.

Herrnstein, R. (1969). Method and theory in the study of avoidance. *Psychological Review, 76,* 49–69.

Herson, M., Eisler, R. M., Alford, G. S., & Agras, W. S. (1973). Effects of token economy on neurotic depression: An experimental analysis. *Behavior Therapy, 4,* 392–97.

Hersov, L. (1976). Emotional disorders. In M. Rutter & L. Hersov (Eds.), *Child psychiatry: Modern approaches.* Oxford: Blackwell.

Herzog, D. B. (1982). Bulimia: The secretive syndrome. *Psychosomatics, 23,* 481–84.

Hess, R. D., & Shipman, V. C. (1965). Early experiences and the socialization of cognitive modes in children. *Child Development, 36,* 869–86.

Heston, L. L. (1966). Psychiatric disorders in foster home reared children of schizophrenic mothers. *British Journal of Psychiatry, 112,* 819–25.

Heston, L. L. (1970). The genetics of schizophrenia and schizoid disease. *Science, 167,* 249–56.

Heston, L. L., & Denney, D. (1968). Interactions between early life experience and biological factors in schizophrenia. In D. Rosenthal & S. S. Kety (Eds.), *The transmission of schizophrenia* (pp. 363–76). New York: Pergamon.

Hetherington, E. M., & Martin, B. (1979). Family interaction. In H. C. Quay & J. S. Werry (Eds.), *Psychopathological disorders of childhood.* New York: Wiley.

Hilgard, E. R. (1965). *Hypnotic susceptibility.* New York: Harcourt Brace Jovanovich.

Hilgard, E. R. (1977). *Divided consciousness: Multiple controls in human thought and action.* New York: Wiley.

Hill, P. O. (1972). Latent aggression and drug-abuse: An investigation of adolescent personality factors using an original cartoon-o-graphic aggressive tendencies test. *Dissertation Abstracts International, 33,* 1765.

Hinz, L. D., & Williamson, D. A. (1987). Bulimia and depression: A review of the affective variant hypothesis. *Psychological Bulletin, 102,* 105–58.

Hiroto, D. S. (1974). Locus of control and learned helplessness. *Journal of Experimental Psychology, 102,* 187–93.

Hirst, W. (1982). The amnesic syndrome: Descriptions and explanations. *Psychology Bulletin, 91,* 1480–83.

Hirota, D. S. & Seligman, M. E. P. (1975). Generality of learned helplessness in man. *Journal of Personality and Social Psychology, 31,* 311–27.

Ho, A. K., & Ho, C. C. (1979). Toxic interactions of ethanol with other central depressants: Antagonism by naloxone to narcosis and lethality. *Pharmacology, Biochemistry, and Behavior, 11,* 111–14.

Hobson, R. P. (1986). The autistic child's appraisal of expressions of emotion. *Journal of Childhood Psychology and Psychiatry, 27,* 321–42.

Hodgson, R., Rachman, S., & Marks, I. (1972). The treatment of chronic obsessive-compulsive neurosis. *Behavior Research and Therapy, 10,* 181–89.

Hoehn-Saric, R., Frank, J. D., Imber, S. D., Nash, E. H., Stone, A. R., & Battle, C. C. (1964). Systematic preparation of patients for psychotherapy I. Effects on therapy behavior and outcome. *Journal of Psychiatric Research, 2,* 267–81.

Hoenig, J., & Kenna, J. C. (1974). The nosological position of transsexualism. *Archives of Sexual Behavior, 3,* 273–87.

Hofmann, A. (1968). Psychotomimetic agents. In A. Burger (Ed.), *Drugs affecting the central nervous system* (Vol. 2). New York: Marcel Dekker.

Hogarty, G. E., Anderson, C. M., Reiss, D. J., Kornblith, S. J., Greenwald, D. P., Javna, C. D., & Madonia, M. J. (1986). Family psychoeducation, social skills training and maintenance chemotherapy in the aftercare treatment of schizophrenia: I. One-year effects of a controlled study on relapse and expressed emotion. *Archives of General Psychiatry, 43,* 633–42.

Hokanson, J. E. (1961). The effects of frustration and anxiety on aggression. *Journal of Abnormal and Social Psychology, 62,* 346.

Hokanson, J. E., & Burgess, M. (1962). The effects of three types of aggression on vascular processes. *Journal of Abnormal and Social Psychology, 65,* 446–49.

Hokanson, J. E., Willers, K. R., & Koropsak, E. (1968). Modification of autonomic responses during aggressive interchange. *Journal of Personality, 36,* 386–404.

Holden, C. (1986a). Manic-depression and creativity. *Science, 233,* 725.

Holden,C. (1986b). Youth suicide: New research focuses on a growing social problem. *Science, 233,* 839–41.

Hollingshead, A. B., & Redlich, F. C. (1958). *Social class and mental illness: A community study.* New York: Wiley.

Hollister, L. E. (1962). Drug-induced psychoses and schizophrenic reactions: A critical comparison. *Annals of the New York Academy of Sciences, 96,* 80–89.

Hollister L. E. (1973). *Clinical uses of psychotherapeutic drugs.* Springfield, IL: Charles C. Thomas.

Hollon, S. D., DuRubeis, R. J., Evans, M. D., Weimer, M. J., Garvey, M. J., Grove, W. M., & Tuason, V. B. (1988). Cognitive therapy, pharmacotherapy, and combined cognitive-pharmacotherapy in the treatment of depression: I. Differential outcome in the C.P.T. project. Manuscript submitted for publication.

Hollon, S. D., & Kendall, P. C. (1980). Cognitive self-statements in depression: Development of an automatic thoughts questionnaire. *Cognitive Therapy and Research, 4,* 383–95.

Hollon, S. D., Kendall, P. C., & Lumry, A. (1986). Specificity of depressotypic cognitions in clinical depression. *Journal of Abnormal Psychology, 95,* 52–59.

Holmes, G. (1935). Treatment of syphilis of the nervous system. *British Medical Journal, 3909,* 1111–14.

Holmes, T. H., & Rahe, R. H. (1967). The social readjustment ratings scale. *Journal of Psychosomatic Research, 11,* 213–18.

Holtzman, W. H. (1961). *Inkblot perception and personality: Holtzman Inkblot Technique.* Austin: University of Texas Press.

Hope, H., Jonas, J., & Jones, B. (1982). Factitious psychosis: Phenomenology, family history, and long-term outcome of nine patients. *American Journal of Psychiatry, 139,* 1480–83.

Horne, A. S., & Snyder, S. H. (1971). Chlorpromazine and dopamine: Conformational similarities that correlate with the antischizophrenic activity of phenothiazine drugs. *Proceedings of the National Academy of Sciences, 68,* 2325–28.

Horne, R. L., & Picard, R. S. (1979). Psychosocial risk factors for lung cancer. *Psychosomatic Medicine, 41,* 503–14.

Horney, K. (1945). *Our inner conflicts: A constructive theory of neurosis.* New York: Norton.

Horowitz, L. M., Post, D. L., French, R. de S., Wallis, K. D., & Seigelman, E. Y. (1981). The prototype as a construct in abnormal psychology: 2. Clarifying disagreement in psychiatric judgments. *Journal of Abnormal Psychology, 90,* 568–74.

Horowitz, M. (1975). Intrusive and repetitive thoughts after experimental stress. *Archives of General Psychiatry. 32,* 1457–63.

Hsu, L. K. G. (1986). The treatment of anorexia nervosa. *American Journal of Psychiatry, 143,* 5.

Huesmann, L. R., Eron, L. D., Lefkowitz, M. M., & Walder, L. O. (1984). Stability of aggression over time and generations. *Developmental Psychology, 20,* 1120–34.

Hugdahl, K., & Ohman, A. (1977). Effects of instruction on acquisition and extinction of electrodermal response to fear-relevant stimuli. *Journal of Experimental Psychology: Human Learning and Memory, 3*(5), 608–18.

Hung, D. W., Rotman, Z., Consentino, A., & MacMillan, M. (1983). Cost and effectiveness of an educational program for autistic children using a systems approach. *Education and Treatment of Children, 6* (1), 47–68.

Hunt, D. D., & Hampson, J. L. (1980). Transsexualism: A standardized psychosocial rating format for the evaluation of results of sex reassignment surgery. *Archives of Sexual Behavior, 9,* 225–63.

Hunt, J. McV., & Cofer, C. N. (1944). Psychological deficit. In J. McV. Hunt & C. N. Cofer (Eds.), *Personality and the behavior disorders* (Vol. 2) (pp. 971–1032). New York: Ronald.

Hunt, M. (1974). *Sexual behavior in the 1970's.* New York: Dell.

Hunt, W. A., & Matarazzo, J. D. (1973). Three years later: Recent developments in the experimental modification of smoking behavior. *Journal of Abnormal Psychology, 81,* 107–14.

Hunter, R., & McAlpine, I. (1963). *Three hundred years of psychiatry.* London: Hogarth Press.

Hutchings, B., & Mednick, S. A. (1977). Criminality in adoptees and their adoptive and biological parents: A pilot study. In S. A. Mednick & K. O. Christiansen (Eds.), *Biosocial bases of criminal behavior* (pp. 127–41). New York: Gardner Press.

Hygge, S., & Ohman, A. (1978). Modeling processes in the acquisition of fear: Vicarious electrodermal conditioning to fear-relevant stimuli. *Journal of Personal and Social Psychology, 36* (3), 271–79.

Hyler, S. E., & Spitzer, R. T. (1978). Hysteria split asunder. *American Journal of Psychiatry, 135,* 1500–1504.

Hyman, B. T., Van Hoesen, G. W., Damasio, A. R., & Barnes, C. L. (1984). Alzheimer's disease: Cell-specific pathology isolates the hippocampal formation. *Science, 225,* 1168–70.

Ickes, W. J., & Leyden, M. A. (1978). Attributional styles. In J. H. Harvey, W. J. Ickes, & R. F. Kidd (Eds.), *New directions in attribution research* (Vol. 2). Hillsdale, NJ: Erlbaum.

Imboden, J. B., Cantor, A., & Cluff, L. E. (1961). Convalescence from influenza: The study of the psychological and clinical determinants. *Archives of Internal Medicine, 108,* 393–99.

Imperato-McGinley, J., Peterson, R. E., Goutier, T., & Sturla, E. (1979). Androgens and the evolution of male-gender identity among male pseudohermaphrodites with 5-α-reductase deficiency. *New England Journal of Medicine, 300,* 1233–39.

Ingham, R. J., Andrews, G., & Winkler, R. (1972). Stuttering: A comparative evaluation of the short-term effectiveness of four treatment techniques. *Journal of Communicative Disorders, 5,* 91–117.

Irwin, M., Daniels, M., Bloom, E. T., Smith, T. L., & Weiner, H. (1987). Life events, depressive symptoms, and immune function. *American Journal of Psychiatry, 144,* 437–41.

Ishii, N., & Nishihara Y. (1985). Pellagra encephalopathy among tuberculous patients: Its relation to isoniazid therapy. *Journal of Neurology, Neurosurgery, and Psychiatry, 48,* 628–38.

Iverson, S. D., & Iverson, L. L. (1975). *Behavorial pharmacology.* New York: Oxford University Press.

Jacobs, W. J., & Nadel, L. (1985). Stress-induced recovery of fears and phobias. *Psychological Review, 92,* 512–31.

Jacobson, E. (1971). *Depression: Comparative studies of normal, neurotic and psychotic conditions.* New York: International Universities Press.

Jacobson, N. S. (1981). Behavioral marital therapy. In A. S. Gurman & D. P. Kniskern (Eds.), *Handbook of family therapy.* New York: Brunner/Mazel.

Jackson, J. H. (1884). Croonian lectures on evolution and dissolution of the nervous system. *British Medical Journal, 1,* 591.

Jahoda, M. (1958). *Current concepts of positive mental health.* New York: Basic Books.

James, W. (1890). *The principles of psychology.* New York: Henry Holt.

Janicak, P. G., Davis, J. M., Gibbons, R. D., Ericksen,S., Chang, S., & Gallagher, P. (1985). Efficacy of ECT: A meta-analysis. *American Journal of Psychiatry, 142,* 297–302.

Jarvik, M. F. (1979). Biological influences on cigarette smoking. In N. A. Krasnegor (Ed.), *The behavioral aspects of smoking.* Washington, DC: National Institute on Drug Abuse.

Jaynes, J. (1977). *The origin of consciousness in the breakdown of the bicameral mind.* Boston: Houghton Mifflin.

Jeffery, D. B. (1977). Introduction: Self control techniques. In J. P. Foreyt, *Behavioral treatments of obesity.* Oxford: Pergamon.

Jenkins, C. D. (1982). Psychosocial risk factors for coronary heart disease. *Acta Medica Scandinavia Supplimentum, 660,* 123–36.

Jenkins, C. D., Rosenman, R. H., & Friedman, M. (1967). Development of an objective psychological test for the determination of the coronary prone behavior pattern in employed men. *Journal of Chronic Disease, 20,* 371–79.

Jens, K. S., & Evans, H. I. (1983, April). The diagnosis and treatment of multiple personality clients. Workshop presented at the Rocky Mountain Psychological Association, Snowbird, Utah.

Jerome, J. (1880). Intern's syndrome. In *Three men in a boat, not to mention the dog.*

Jerome, J. (1979, January 14). Catching them before suicide. *The New York Times Magazine.*

Jeurgens, S. M., & Morse, R. M. (1988). Alprazolam dependence in seven patients. *American Journal of Psychiatry, 145,* 625–27.

Johnston, F. E., & Keesey, R. E. (1980). A set-point analysis of the regulation of body weight. In A. J. Stunkard (Ed.), *Obesity.* Philadelphia: Saunders.

Jones. (1955). In W. F. Bynum, Jr., Rationales for therapy in British psychiatry, 1780–1835. In A Scull (Ed.), *Madhouses, mad-doctors, and madmen: The social history of psychiatry in the Victorian era* (pp. 35–57). Philadelphia: University of Pennsylvania Press.

Jones, E. E., & Zoppel, C. L. (1982). Impact of client and therapist gender on psychotherapy process and outcome. *Journal of Consulting and Clinical Psychology, 50,* 259–72.

Jones, M. A., & Spratto, S. R. (1977). Ethanol suppression of naloxone-induced withdrawal in morphine-dependent rats, *Life Sciences, 20,* 1549–56.

Jourard, S. M. (1974). *Healthy personality: An approach from the viewpoint of humanistic psychology.* New York: Macmillan.

Kaffman, M. (1986). The Israeli high-risk study: Some critical remarks. *Schizophrenia Bulletin, 12,* 151–57.

Kahn, M. (1973). Social class and schizophrenia: A critical review and a reformulation. *Schizophrenia Bulletin, 1,* 60–74.

Kahoe, M., & Ironside, W. (1963). Studies on the experimental evocation of depressive responses under hypnosis. II. The influence of depressive responses on the secretion of gastric acid. *Psychosomatic Medicine, 25,* 403.

Kamen, L., Rodin, J., Seligman, M. E. P., & Dwyer, C. (1988). Pessimism and cell-mediated immunity. Manuscript submitted for publication.

Kamin, L. J. (1974). *The science and politics of IQ.* Potomac, MD: Erlbaum.

Kanfer, F. H., & Grimm, L. G. (1976). The future of behavior modification. In W. E. Craighead, A. E. Kazdin, & M. J. Mahoney (Eds.), *Behavior modification: Principles, issues and applications.* Boston: Houghton Mifflin.

Kanfer, F. H., & Karoly, P. (1972). Self-control. A behavioristic excursion into the lion's den. *Behavior Therapy, 3,* 398–416.

Kanfer, F. H., & Saslow, G. (1969). Behavioral analysis. In C. M. Franks (Ed.), *Behavior therapy: Appraisal and status.* New York: McGraw-Hill.

Kanner, A. D., Coyne, J. C., Schaefer, C., & Lazarus, R. S. (1981). Comparison of two modes of stress measurement: Minor daily hassles and uplifts vs. major life events. *Journal of Behavioral Medicine, 4,* 1–39.

Kanner, L. (1943). Autistic disturbances of affective contact. *Nervous Child, 2,* 217–50.

Kaplan, H. S. (1974). *The new sex therapy.* New York: Brunner/Mazel.

Kaplan, R. F., Cooney, N. L., Baker, L. H., Gillespie, R. A., Meyer, R. E., & Pomerleau, O. F. (1985). Reactivity to alcohol-related cues: Physiological and subjective responses in alcoholics and non-problem drinkers. *Journal of Studies on Alcohol, 46,* 267–72.

Kaplan, S. M., Gottschalk, L. A., Magliocco, D., Rohobit, D., & Ross, W. D. (1960). Hostility in hypnotic "dreams" of hypertensive patients. (Comparisons between hypertensive and normotensive groups and within hypertensive individuals.) *Psychosomatic Medicine, 22,* 320.

Karasek, R., Baker, D., Marxer, F., Ahlbom, A., & Theorell, T. (1981). Job decision latitude, job demand, and cardiovascular disease: A prospective study of Swedish men. *American Journal of Public Health, 71,* 694–705.

Karlsson, J. L. (1972). An Icelandic family study of schizophrenia. In A. R. Kaplan (Ed.), *Genetic factors in schizophrenia* (pp. 246–55). Springfield, IL: Charles C. Thomas.

Kasl, S. V. (1983). Pursuing the link between stressful life experiences and disease: A time for reappraisal. In C. L. Cooper (Ed.), *Stress research: Issues for the eighties.* New York: Wiley.

Kasl, S. V., & Cob, S. (1979). Blood pressure changes in men undergoing job loss: A preliminary report. *Psychosomatic Medicine, 32,* 19–38.

Kaslow, N. J., Tannenbaum, R. L., Abramson, L. Y., Peterson, C., & Seligman, M. E. P. (1983). Problem solving deficits and depressive symptoms among children. *Journal of Abnormal Child Psychology.*

Kass, F., Spitzer, R. L., & Williams, J. B. W. (1983). An empirical study of the issue of sex bias in the diagnostic criteria of DSM-III axis II personality disorders. *American Psychologist, 38,* 799–801.

Katchadourian, H. A., & Lunde, D. T. (1972). *Fundamentals of human sexuality.* New York: Holt, Rinehart & Winston.

Katz, B. (1952). The nerve impulse. *Scientific American, 187,* 55–64.

Katz, M., Lorr, M., & Rubinstein, E. (1958). Remainder patient attributes and their relation to subsequent improvement in psychotherapy. *Journal of Consulting Psychology, 22,* 411–13.

Kaufman, I. C., & Rosenblum, L. A. (1967). Depression in infant monkeys separated from their mothers. *Science, 155,* 1030–31.

Kauffman, J. M., & Hallahan, D. P. (1979). Learning disability and hyperactivity (with comments on minimal brain dysfunction). In B. B. Lahey & A. E. Kazdin (Ed.), *Advances in child clinical psychology* (Vol. 2). New York: Plenum.

Kazdin, A. E. (1979). Nonspecific treatment factors in psychotherapy outcome research. *Journal of Consulting and Clinical Psychology, 47,* 846–51.

Kazdin, A. E., & Wilcoxon, L. A. (1976). Systematic desensitization and nonspecific treatment effects: A methodological evaluation. *Psychological Bulletin, 83*(5), 729–58.

Kazdin, A. E., & Wilson, G. T. (1978). *Evaluation of behavior therapy: Issues, evidence, and research strategies.* Cambridge, MA: Ballinger.

Keefe, J. A., & Magaro, P. A. (1980). Creativity and schizophrenia: An equivalence of cognitive processing. *Journal of Abnormal Psychology, 89,* 390–98.

Keeton, W. T. (1980). *Biological science* (3rd ed.). New York: Norton.

Kegan, R. (1986). Pathology in moral development. In W. H. Reid, D. Dorr, J. I. Walker, & J. W. Bonner, III (Eds.), *Unmasking the psychopath: Antisocial personality and related syndromes.* New York: Norton

Kehoe, M., & Ironside W. (1963). Studies on the experimental evocation of, depressive responses using hypnosis: II. The influence upon the secretion of gastric acid. *Psychosomatic Medicine, 25,* 403–19.

Keith, S. J., Gunderson, J. G., Reifman, A., Buchsbaum, S., & Mosher, L. R. (1976). Special report: Schizophrenia, 1976. *Schizophrenia Bulletin, 2,* 510–65.

Keith-Spiegel, P. (1977). Violation of ethical principles due to ignorance or poor professional judgment versus willful disregard. *Professional Psychology, 8,* 288–96.

Keller, M. B., Beardslee, W. R., Dorer, D. J., Lavori, P. W., Samuelson, H., & Klerman, G. R. (1986). Impact of severity and chronicity of parental affective illness on adaptive functioning and psychopathology in children. *Archives of General Psychiatry, 43,* 930–37.

Kelley, H. H. (1967). Attribution theory in social psychology. In D. Levine (Ed.), *Nebraska Symposium on Motivation* (pp. 192–240). Lincoln: Dot Nebraska Press.

Kelly, G. A. (1955). *The psychology of personal constructs* (Vols. 1 & 2). New York: Norton.

Kendall, P., Williams, L., Pechacek, T., Graham, L., Shisslac, C., & Hertzoff, N. (1979). Cognitive, behavioral and patient education interventions in cardiac catheterization procedures: The Palo Alto medical psychology project. *Journal of Consulting and Clinical Psychology, 47,* 49–58.

Kendler, K. S., & Gruenberg, A. M. (1982). Genetic relationship between paranoid personality disorder and the "schizophrenic spectrum" disorders. *American Journal of Psychiatry, 139,* 1185–86.

Kendler, K. S., & Gruenberg, A. M. (1984). An independent analysis of the Danish adoption study of schizophrenia: VI. The relationship between psychiatric disorders as defined by DSM-III in the relatives and adoptees. *Archives of General Psychiatry, 41,* 555–64.

Kenyon, F. E. (1965). Hypochondriasis: A survey of some historical, clinical and social aspects. *British Journal of Psychiatry, 38,* 117.

Kerr, T. A., Roth, M., Schapira, K., & Gurney, C. (1972). The assessment and prediction of outcome in affective disorders. *British Journal of Psychiatry, 121,* 167.

Kertesz, A. (1982). Two case studies: Broca's brain and Wernicke's aphasia. In M. A. Arbib, D. Caplan, & J. C. Marshall (Eds.), *Neural models of language processes.* New York: Academic Press.

Kety, J. (1974). Biochemical and neurochemical effects of electroconvulsive shock. In M. Fink, S. Kety, & J. McGough (Eds.), *Psychology of convulsive therapy.* Washington, DC: Winston.

Kety, S. S. (1974). From rationalization to reason. *American Journal of Psychiatry, 131,* 957–63.

Kety, S., Rosenthal, D., Wender, P. H., & Schulsinger, F. (1968). The types and prevalence of mental illness in the biological and adoptive families of adopted schizophrenics. In D. Rosenthal & S. S. Kety (Eds.), *The transmission of schizophrenia.* New York: Pergamon Press.

Kiecolt-Glaser, J. K., Garner, W., Speicher, C., Penn, G. M., Holliday, J., & Glaser, R. (1984). Psychosocial modifiers of immunocompetence in medical students. *Psychosomatic Medicine, 46,* 7–14.

Kiecolt-Glaser, J. K., & Glaser, R. (1987). Psychosocial moderators of immune function. *Annals of Behavioral Medicine, 9,* 16–20.

Kiely, J. L., Paneth, N., & Susser, M. (1981). Low birthweight, neonatal care and cerebral palsy: An epidemiological review. In P. J. Mittler & J. M. deJong (Eds.), *Frontiers in mental retardation: II: Biomedical aspects.* Baltimore, MD: University Park Press.

Kiesler, C. A. (1980). Mental health policy as a field of inquiry for psychology. *American Psychologist, 35,* 1066–80.

Kiesler, C. A. (1982a). Mental hospitals and alternative care: Noninstitutionalization as potential public policy for mental patients. *American Psychologist, 37,* 349–60.

Kiesler, C. A. (1982b). Public and professional myths about mental hospitalization: An empirical reassessment of policy-related beliefs. *American Psychologist, 37,* 1323–39.

King, S., & Phillips, S. (1985). Problem-solving characteristics of process and reactive schizophrenics and affective-disordered patients. *Journal of Abnormal Psychology, 94* (1), 17–29.

Kingsley, R. G., & Wilson, G. T. (1977). Behavior therapy for obesity: A comparative investigation of long-term efficacy. *Journal of Consulting & Clinical Psychology, 45*(2), 288–98.

Kinsey, A. C., Pomeroy, W. D., & Martin, C. E. (1948). *Sexual behavior in the human male.* Philadelphia: Saunders.

Kinsey, A. C., Pomeroy, W. D., Martin, C. E., & Gebhard, P. H. (1953). *Sexual behavior in the human female.* Philadelphia: Saunders.

Kinzie, J. D., Fredrickson, R. H., Ben, R., Fleck, J., & Karls, W. (1984). Post-traumatic stress disorder among survivors of Cambodian concentration camps. *American Journal of Psychiatry, 141,* 645–50.

Kirigin, K., Wolf, M. M., Braukman, C. J., Fixsen, D. L., & Phillips, E. L. (1979). Achievement Place: A preliminary outcome evaluation. In J. S. Stumphauzer (Ed.), *Progress in behavior therapy with delinquents.* Springfield, IL: Charles C. Thomas.

Kirigin, K. A., Braukmann, C. J., Atwater, J. D., & Wolf, M. M. (1982). An evaluation of teaching-family (Achievement Place) group homes for juvenile offenders. *Journal of Applied Behavior Analysis, 15,* 1–16.

Kirkley, B. G., Schneider, J. A., Agras, W. S., & Bachman, J. A. (1985). Comparison of two group treatments for bulimia. *Journal of Consulting and Clinical Psychology, 53,* 43–48.

Kittel, F., Kornitzer, M., de Backer, G., & Dramaix, M. (1982). Metrological study of psychological questionnaires with reference to social variables: The Belgian Heart Disease Prevention Project (BHDPP). *Journal of Behavioral Medicine, 5*(1), 9–35.

Klein, D. F. (1980). Anxiety reconceptualized. In Klein, D. F. & Rabkin, J. G. (Eds.), *Anxiety revisited.* New York: Raven Press.

Klein, D. F. (1984). Psychopharmacologic treatment of panic disorder. University of California, Los Angeles, Department of Psychiatry and Biobehavioral Sciences at the 137th Annual Meeting of the American Psychiatric Association: Panic disorders: Clinical update 1984. Los Angeles, CA.

Klein, D. F., & Davis, J. M. (1969). *Diagnosis and drug treatment of psychiatric disorders.* Baltimore: Williams & Wilkins.

Klein, D. N., Depue, R. A., & Slater, J. F. (1985). Cyclothymia in the adolescent offspring of parents with bipolar affective disorder. *Journal of Abnormal Psychology, 94,* 115–27.

Klein, D. F., & Gittelman-Klein, R. (1975). Are behavioral and psychometric changes related in methylphenidate treated, hyperactive children? *International Journal of Mental Health, 14*(1–2), 182–98.

Klein, D. F., Ross, D. C., & Cohen, P. (1987). Panic and avoidance in agoraphobia, application of path analysis to treatment studies. *Archives of General Psychiatry, 44,* 377–85.

Klein, D. F., Zitrin, C. M., Woerner, M. G., & Ross, D. C. (1983). Treatment of phobias: II. Behavior therapy and supportive psychotherapy: Are there any specific ingredients? *Archives of General Psychiatry, 40,* 139–45.

Klerman, G. L. (1975). Drug therapy of clinical depressions—Current status and implications for research on neuropharmacology of the affective disorders. In D. F. Klein & R. Gittleman-Klein (Eds.), *Progress in psychiatric drug treatment.* New York: Brunner/Mazel.

Klerman, G. L., Endicott, J., Spitzer, R., & Hirschfeld, R. (1979). Neurotic depressions: A systematic analysis of multiple criteria and meanings. *American Journal of Psychiatry, 136,* 57–61.

Klerman, G. L., Lavori, P. W., & Rice, J., et al. (1985). Birth cohort trends in rates of major depressive disorder among relatives of patients with affective disorder. *Archives of General Psychiatry, 42* (7), 689–93.

Klerman, G. L., Rounsaville, B., Chevron, E., Neu, C., & Weissman, M. M. (1979). Manual for short-term interpersonal therapy (IPT) of depression (fourth draft preliminary). New Haven-Boston Collaborative Depression Project.

Klerman, G. L., Schildkraut, J., & Hassenbush, J. (1963). Clinical experience with dihydroxyphrenylalanine (dopa) in depression. *Journal of Psychiatric Research, 1,* 289–97.

Klerman, G. L., Weissman, M. M., & Rounsaville, E. S. (1984). *Interpersonal psychotherapy of depression.* New York: Basic.

Kluft, R. P. (1987). An update on multiple personality disorder. *Hospital and Community Psychiatry, 38,* 363–73.

Kluznik, J. C., Speed, N., Van Valkenberg, C., & Magraw, R. (1986). Forty-year follow-up of United States prisoners of war. *American Journal of Psychiatry, 143,* 1443–46.

Kobasa, S. C. (1979). Stressful life events, personality, and health: An inquiry into hardiness. *Journal of Personality and Social Psychology, 37,* 1–11.

Koh, S. D., & Peterson, R. A. (1974). Perceptual memory for numerousness in "nonpsychotic schizophrenics." *Journal of Abnormal Psychology, 83,* 215–26.

Kohn, M. L. (1973). Social class and schizophrenia: A critical review and a reformulation. *Schizophrenia Bulletin, 7,* 60–79.

Kohut, H. (1971). *The analysis of the self.* New York: International Universities Press.

Kohut, H. (1977). *The restoration of the self.* New York: International Universities Press.

Kohut, H. (1978). *The search for self.* New York: International Universities Press.

Kohut, H. (1984). How does analysis cure? In A. Goldberg & P. E. Stepansky (Eds.). Chicago: University of Chicago Press.

Kolb, B., & Whishaw, I. Q. (1980). *Fundamentals of human neuropsychology.* San Francisco: Freeman.

Kondas, O. (1967). The treatment of stammering in children by the shadowing method. *Behavior Research and Therapy, 5*(4), 325–29.

Korchin, S. J. (1976). *Modern clinical psychology: Principles of intervention in the clinic and the community.* New York: Basic Books.

Korsakoff, S. S. (1889). Etude medicopsychologique sur une forme des maladies de la memoire. *Revue Philosophique, 5,* 501–30.

Kotsopoulos, S., & Snow, B. (1986). Conversion disorders in children: A study of clinical outcome. *Psychiatric Journal of the University of Ottawa, 11,* 134–39.

Kovacs, M., & Beck, A. T. (1977). An empirical-clinical approach towards a definition of childhood depression. In J. G. Schulterbrand & A. Raven (Ed.), *Depression in childhood: Diagnosis, treatment, and conceptual models.* New York: Raven Press.

Kovacs, M., Rush, A. J., Beck, A. T., & Hollon, S. D. (1981). Depressed outpatient treatment with cognitive therapy or pharmaco therapy: A one year follow-up. *Archives of General Psychiatry, 38,* 33–39.

Kraepelin, E. (1919). *Dementia praecox and paraphrenia.* New York: Robert E. Krieger.

Krafft-Ebing, R. von. (1931). *Psychopathia sexualis.* New York: Physicians & Surgeons Book Co.

Kraupl Taylor, F. (1966). *Psychopathology: Its causes and symptoms.* London: Butler Wells.

Kriegman, D., & Solomon, L. (1985). Cult groups and the narcissistic personality: The offer to heal defects in the self. *International Journal of Group Psychotherapy, 35* (2), 239–61.

Kringlen, E. (1965). Obsessional neurotics. A long-term follow-up. *British Journal of Psychiatry, 111,* 709–22.

Krystal, H. (1968). *Massive psychic trauma.* New York: International Universities Press.

Kugelmass, S., Marcus, J., & Schmueli, J. (1985). Psychophysiological activity in high-risk children. *Schizophrenia Bulletin, 11,* 66–73.

Kupfer, D. J., Berger, P. A., Conger, J. J., Endicott, J., Gergen, J. A., Guze, S. B., Hollister, L. E., Keller, M. B., Laska, E. M., Prior, R. E., Robbins, H. H., Rush, A. J., & Schorr, L. B. (1984). Mood disorders: Pharmacologic prevention of recurrences. *NIH Consensus Development Conference Consensus Statement, 5* (4).

Kurland, H. D., Yeager, C. T., & Arthur, R. J. (1963). Psychophysiologic aspects of severe behavior disorders. *Archives of General Psychiatry, 8,* 599–604.

Kutchins, H., & Kirk, S. A. (1986). The reliability of DSM-III: A critical review. *Social Work Research and Abstracts,* 3–12.

Lacey, J. I. (1950). Individual differences in somatic response patterns. *Journal of Comparative and Physiological Psychology, 43,* 338–50.

Lachman, S. J. (1972). *Psychosomatic disorders: Behavioristic interpretations.* New York: Wiley.

Laing, R. D. (1965a). Mystification, confusion and conflict. In I. Boszormeny-Nagy & J. L. Framo (Ed.), *Intensive family therapy.* New York: Hueber Medical Division, Harper & Row.

Laing, R. D. (1965b). *The divided self.* Baltimore: Penguin.

Laing, R. D. (1967). *The politics of experience.* New York: Pantheon Books.

Laing, R. D. (1970). *Knots.* New York: Pantheon Books.

Laing, R. D., & Esterson, A. (1964). *Sanity, madness, and the family.* London: Tavistock.

Lamb, H. R. (1979). The new asylums in the community. *Archives of General Psychiatry, 36,* 129–34.

Lambert, M. J., Bergin, A. E., & Collins, J. L. (1970). Therapist-induced deterioration in psychotherapy. In A. S. Gurman & A. M. Razin (Eds.), *Effective psychotherapy: A handbook of research.* New York: Pergamon.

Lamiell, J. T. (1987). *The psychology of personality: An epidemiological inquire.* New York: Columbia University Press.

Lamontagne, Y., & Lesage, A. (1986). Private exposure and covert sensitization in the treatment of exhibitionism. *Journal of Behavior Therapy and Experimental Psychiatry, 17* (3), 197–201.

Lamy, R. E. (1966). Social consequences of mental illness. *Journal of Consulting Psychology, 30,* 450–55.

Lando, H. A. (1977). Successful treatment of smokers with a broad-spectrum behavioral approach. *Journal of Consulting and Clinical Psychology, 45,* 361–66.

Lang, P. (1967). Fear reduction and fear behavior. In J. Schlein (Ed.), *Research in psychotherapy.* Washington DC: American Psychological Association.

Lang, P. J. (1977). Imagery in therapy: An information processing analysis of fear. *Behavior Therapy, 8* (5), 862–86.

Lang, P. J. (1979). A bio-informational theory of emotional imagery. *Psychophysiology, 92* (3), 276–306.

Langer, E. J., & Abelson, R. P. (1974). A patient by any other name . . .: Clinician group difference in labelling bias. *Journal of Consulting and Clinical Psychology, 42,* 4–9.

Langer, E. J., Janis, I., & Wolfer, J. (1975). Effects of a cognitive coping device and preparatory information on psychological stress in surgical patients. *Journal of Experimental Social Psychology, 11,* 155–65.

Langer, E. J., & Rodin, J. (1976). Effects of choice and enhanced personal responsibility for the aged: A field experiment in an institutional setting. *Journal of Personality and Social Psychology, 34,* 191–99.

Langman, M. (1974). The changing nature of the duodenal ulcer diathesis. In C. Waspell (Ed.), *Westminister Hospital Symposium on chronic duodenal ulcer* (pp. 3–12). London: Butterworth.

Lansky, D., & Vance, M. A. (1983). School-based intervention for adolescent obesity: Analysis of treatment, randomly selected control, and self-selected control subjects. *Journal of Consulting and Clinical Psychology, 51,* 147–48.

Lanzetta, J. T., & Orr, S. P. (1980). Influence of facial expressions on the classical conditioning of fear. *Journal of Personality and Social Psychology, 39,* 1081–87.

LaPouse, R., & Monk, M. (1959). Fears and worries in a representative sample of children. *American Journal of Orthopsychiatry, 29,* 803–18.

Laudenslager, M. L., Ryan, S. M., Drugan, R. C., Hyson, R. L., & Maier, S. F. (1983). Coping and immunosuppression: Inescapable but not escapable shock suppresses lymphocyte proliferation. *Science, 221,* 568–70.

Lauer, R. M., Anderson, A. R., Beaglehole, R., & Burns, T. L., (1983). Factors related to tracking of blood pressure in children: U.S. National Center for Health Statistics Health Examination Surveys Cycles II and III. *Hypertension, 6,* 307–14.

Laughlin, H. P. (1967). *The neuroses.* Washington, DC: Butterworth.

Lazarus, A. A. (1971). *Behavior therapy and beyond.* New York: McGraw-Hill.

Lazarus, A. A. (1976). *Multimodal behavior therapy.* New York: Springer.

Leff, J. P. (1976). Schizophrenia and sensitivity to the family environment. *Schizophrenia Bulletin, 2,* 566–74.

Leff, M. J., Roatch, J. F., & Bunney, W. E. (1970). Environmental factors preceding the onset of severe depressions. *Psychiatry, 33,* 293–311.

Lehman, D. R., Wortman, C. B., & Williams, A. F. (1987). Long-term effects of losing a spouse or child in a motor vehicle crash. *Journal of Personality and Social Psychology, 52,* 218–31.

Leiberman, M. A., Yalom, I. D., & Miles, M. B. (1973). *Encounter groups: First facts.* New York: Basic Books.

Leitenberg, H., & Callahan, E. J. (1973). Reinforced practice and reduction of different kinds of fears in adults and children. *Behavior Research & Therapy, 11*(1), 19–30.

Lemkau, P. V. (1969). The planning project for Columbia. In M. F. Shore & F. V. Mannino (Ed.), *Mental health and the community: Problems, programs and strategies.* New York: Behavioral Publications.

Leopold, R. L., & Dillon, H. (1963). Psychoanatomy of a disaster: A long-term study of post-traumatic neurosis in survivors of a marine explosion. *American Journal of Psychiatry, 119,* 913–21.

Lesser, I. M. (1985). Current concepts in psychiatry: Alexithymia. *New England Journal of Medicine, 312,* 690–92.

Lester, D. (1977). Multiple personality: A review. *Psychology, 14,* 54–59.

Levenson, R. W., Sher, K. J., Grossman, L. M., Newman, J., & Newlin, D. B. (1980). Alcohol and stress response dampening: Pharmacological effects, expectancy, and tension reduction. *Journal of Abnormal Psychology, 89,* 528–38.

Levine, M., & Graziano, A. M. (1971). Intervention programs in elementary schools. In S. E. Golann & C. Eisdorfer (Eds.), *Handbook of community psychology.* New York: Appleton-Century-Crofts.

Levis, D. J., & Carrera, R. (1967). Effects of 10 hours of implosive therapy in the treatment of outpatients. *Journal of Abnormal Psychology, 72,* 504–508.

Levitz, L. S., & Stunkard, A. J. (1974). A therapeutic coalition for obesity: Behavior modification and patient self-help. *American Journal of Psychiatry, 131,* 423–27.

Levy, J. (1972). Lateral specialization of the human brain. Behavioral manifestations and possible evolutionary basis. In J. A. Kiger, Jr. (Ed.), *The biology of behavior* (pp. 159–80). Corvallis, OR: Oregon State University Press.

Levy, J. (1980). Cerebral asymmetry and man and the psychology of man. In M. Wittrock (Ed.), *The brain and psychology.* New York: Academic Press.

Levy, S., Morrow, L., Bagley, C., & Lippman, M. (1989). Survival hazards analysis in first recurrent breast cancer patients: Seven-year follow-up. *Psychosomatic Medicine,* in press.

Lewine, R. R. J. (1981). Sex differences in schizophrenia: Timing or subtypes. *Psychological Bulletin, 90,* 432–44.

Lewinsohn, P. M. (1975). Engagement in pleasant activities and depression level. *Journal of Abnormal Psychology, 84,* 718–21.

Lewinsohn, P. M. (1977). The behavioral study and treatment of depression. In M. Hersen, R. M. Eisler, & P. M. Miller (Eds.), *Progress in behavior modification.* New York: Academic Press.

Lewinsohn, P. M., Mischel, W., Chaplin, W., & Barton, R. (1980). Social competence and depression: The role of illusory self-perceptions. *Journal of Abnormal Psychology, 89,* 203–12.

Lewis, J. M., Rodnick, E. H., & Goldstein, M. J. (1981). Interfamilial interactive behavior, parental communication deviance, and risk for schizophrenia. *Journal of Abnormal Psychology, 90,* 448–57.

Lewy, A. J., Sack, L., Miller, S., & Hoban, T. M. (1987). Antidepressant and circadian phase-shifting effects of light. *Science, 235,* 352–54.

Liberman, R. P., Mueser, K. T., & Wallace, C. J. (1986). Social skills training for schizophrenic individuals at risk for relapse. *American Journal of Psychiatry, 143* (4), 523–26.

Lichtenstein, E., et al. (1973). Comparison of rapid smoking, warm smoky air, and attention placebo in the modification of smoking behavior. *Journal of Consulting and Clinical Psychology, 40,* 92–98.

Lick, J., & Bootzin, R. (1975). Expectancy factors in the treatment of fear: Methodological and theoretical issues. *Psychological Bulletin, 82,* 917–31.

Lidz, T. (1975). *The origin and treatment of schizophrenic disorders.* London: Hutchinson.

Liebowitz, M. R., Fyer, A. J., Gorman, J. M., Dillon, D., Davies, S., Stein, J. M., Cohen, B. S., & Klein, D. F. (1985). Specificity of lactate infusions in social phobia versus panic disorders. *American Journal of Psychiatry, 142,* 947–50.

Liebowitz, M. R., Gorman, J. M., Fyer, A. J., Levitt, M., Dillon, D., Levy, G., Appleby, I. L., Anderson, S., Palij, M., Davies, S. O., & Klein, D. F. (1985). Lactate provocation of panic attacks: II. Biochemical and physiological findings. *Archives of General Psychiatry, 42,* 709–19.

Linden, L. L., & Breed, W. (1976). The demographic epidemiology of suicide. In E. S. Shneidman (Ed.), *Suicidology: Contemporary developments.* New York: Grune & Stratton.

Linden, W. (1981). Exposure treatments for focal phobias: A review. *Archives of General Psychiatry, 42,* 602–11.

Lineberger, M., Schwartz, M. F., & Saffran, E. M. (1983). Sensitivity to grammatical structure in so-called agrammatic aphasics. *Cognition, 13,* 361–92.

Linsky, A. S., Straus, M. A., & Colby, J. P. (1985). Stressful events, stressful conditions, and alcohol problems in the United States, a partial test of Bale's Theory. *Journal of Studies on Alcohol, 33,* 979–89.

Lippold, S., & Claiborn, J. M. (1983). Comparison of the Wechsler Adult Intelligence Scale and the Wechsler Adult Intelligence Scale–Revised. *Journal of Consulting and Clinical Psychology, 51,* 315.

Littlefield, C. H., & Rushton, J. P. (1986). When a child dies: The Socio-biology of bereavement. *Journal of Personality and Social Psychology, 51,* 797–802.

Livermore, J. M., & Meehl, P. E. (1967). The virtues of M'Naghten. *Minnesota Law Review. 51,* 789–856.

Lockyer, L., & Rutter, M. (1969). A five-to fifteen-year follow-up study of infantile psychosis. *British Journal of Psychiatry, 115,* 865–82.

Logue, C. M., & Moos, R. H. (1986). Premenstrual symptoms: Prevalence and risk factors. *Psychosomatic Medicine, 48,* 388–414.

Lohrenz, L. J., Connelly, L. C., Coyne, L., & Spare, K. E. (1978). Alcohol problems in several midwestern homosexual communities. *Journal of Studies on Alcoholism, 39,* 1959–63.

London, P. (1969). *Behavior control.* New York: Harper & Row.

London, P. (1986). *The modes and morals of psychotherapy.* New York: Hemisphere.

London, P., & Rosenhan, D. L. (1968). Mental health: The promise of behavior science. In P. London & D. L. Rosenhan (Eds.), *Foundations of abnormal psychology* (pp. 599–619). New York: Holt, Rinehart & Winston.

Long, J. W. (1985). *The essential guide to prescription drugs.* Mount Vernon, NY: Consumers Union.

Looney, J. G., Lipp, M. G., & Spitzer R. L. (1978). A new method of classification for psychophysiological disorders. *American Journal of Psychiatry, 135,* 304–308.

Loranger, A., & Levine, P. (1978). Age of onset of bipolar affective illness. *Archives of General Psychiatry, 35,* 1345–48.

Loranger, A. W., Susman, V. L., Oldham, J. M., & Russakoff, L. M. (1987). The personality disorder examination: A preliminary report. *Journal of Personality Disorders, 1* (1), 1–13.

Losonczy, M. F., Song, I. S., Mohs, R. C., Mathe, A. A., Davidson, M., Davis, B. M., & Davis, K. L. (1986). Correlates of lateral ventricular size in chronic schizophrenia: II. Biological measures. *American Journal of Psychiatry, 143*(9), 1113–17.

Lotter, V. (1978). Follow-up studies. In M. Rutter & E. Schopler (Eds.), *Autism: A reappraisal of concepts and treatment.* New York: Plenum.

Lovaas, O. I. (1966). A program for the establishment of speech in psychotic children. In J. K. Wing (Ed.), *Early childhood autism.* New York: Pergamon.

Lovaas, O. I. (1973). *Behavioral treatment of autistic children.* Morristown, NJ: General Learning Press.

Lovaas, O. I. (1987). Behavioral treatment and abnormal education and intellectual functioning in young autistic children. *Journal of Consulting and Clinical Psychology, 55,* 3–9.

Lovaas, O. I., & Simmons, J. Q. (1969). Manipulation of self-destruction in three retarded children. *Journal of Applied Behavior Analysis, 2,* 143–57.

Lovibond, S. H., & Coote, M. A. (1970). Enuresis. In C. G. Costello (Ed.), *Symptoms of psychopathology.* New York: Wiley.

Lowinger, P., & Dobie, S. (1969). What makes the placebo work? A study of placebo response rates. *Archives of General Psychiatry, 20,* 84–88.

Luborsky, L. (1972). Another reply to Eysenck. *Psychological Bulletin, 78,* 406–408.

Luborsky. L. (1984). *Principles of psychoanalytic theory: A manual for supportive expressive treatment.* New York: Basic Books.

Luborsky, L., Crits-Cristoph, P., McLellan, A. T., Woody, G.,

Piper, W., Liberman, B., Imber, S., & Pilkonis, P. (1986). Do therapists vary much in their success? Findings from four outcome studies. *American Journal of Orthopsychiatry, 56* (4), 501–12.

Luborsky, L., McLellan, A. T., Woody, G. E., O'Brien, C. P., & Auerbach, A. (1985). Therapist success and its determinants. *Archives of General Psychiatry, 42* (6), 602–11.

Luborsky, L., Singer, B., & Luborsky, L. (1975). Comparative studies of psychotherapies. *Archives of General Psychiatry, 32,* 995–1008.

Luria, A. (1970). The functional organization of the brain. *Scientific American, 222,* 66–78.

Luria, A. (1973). *The working brain.* New York: Basic Books.

Lykken, D. T. (1957). A study of anxiety in the sociopathic personality. *Journal of Abnormal and Social Psychology, 55,* 6–10.

Maas, J. W. (1975). Biogenic amines and depression. *Archives of General Psychiatry, 32,* 1357–61.

MacDonald, M. *Mystical bedlam: Madness and healing in seventeenth-century England.* Unpublished doctoral dissertation, Stanford University.

MacDonald, N. (1960). Living with schizophrenia. *Canadian Medical Association Journal, 82,* 218–21.

MacFarland, J. W., Allen, L., & Honzik, N. P. (1954). *A developmental study of the behavior problems of normal children between 21 months and 14 years.* Berkeley and Los Angeles: University of California Press.

McGregor, R. R. (1986). Alcohol and immune defense. *Journal of the American Medical Association, 256,* 1474–79.

Mack R. W. (1978). Obesity in urban black adolescents of high and low relative weight at 1 year of age. *American Journal of Diseases of Children, 132,* 862–64.

Mackay, A. V. P. (1980). Positive and negative schizophrenic symptoms and the role of dopamine. *British Journal of Psychiatry, 137,* 379–86.

MacMillan, D. L., & Semmel, M. I. (1977). Evaluation of mainstreaming programs. *Focus on Exceptional Children, 6* (4), 8–14.

Magaro, P. A. (1981). The paranoid and the schizophrenic: The case for distinct cognitive style. *Schizophrenia Bulletin, 7,* 632–61.

Maher, B. A. (1966). *Principles of psychopathology: An experimental approach.* New York: McGraw-Hill.

Maher, B. A. (1971). The language of schizophrenia: A review and interpretation. *British Journal of Psychiatry, 120,* 3–17.

Maher, B. A. (1974). Delusional thinking and cognitive disorder. In H. London & R. E. Nisbett (Eds.), *Thought and feeling: Cognitive alteration of feeling states.* Chicago: Aldine.

Maher, W. B., & Maher, B. (1982). The ship of fools: *Stultifera Navis* or *Ignis Fantuus? American Psychiatrist, 37,* 756–61.

Mahler, M. (1979). *The selected papers of Margaret Mahler* (Vol. 1, 2, 3). New York: Jason Aronson.

Mahoney, M. J. (1971). The self-management of covert behavior: A case study. *Behavior Therapy, 2,* 575–78.

Mahoney, M. J. (1974). *Cognition and behavior modification.* Cambridge, MA.: Ballinger.

Mahoney, M. J., & Mahoney, K. (1976). *Permanent weight control: A total solution to the dieter's dilemma.* New York: Norton.

Mahoney, M. J., & Thoresen, C. E. (1974). *Self-control: Power to the person.* Belmont, CA: Brooks/Cole.

Mai, F., & Mersky, H. (1980). Briquet's treatise on hysteria. *Archives of General Psychiatry, 37,* 1401–1405.

Maier, S. F., Laudenslager, M., & Ryan, S. M. (1985). Stressor controllability, immune function, and endogenous opiates. In F. Bush & J. B. Overmier (Eds.), *Affect, conditioning, and cognition.* Hillside. NJ: Erlbaum.

Maier, S. F., & Seligman, M. E. P. (1976). Learned helplessness: Theory and evidence. *Journal of Experimental Psychology, 105* (1), 3–46.

Maier, S. F., Seligman, M. E. P., & Solomon, R. L. (1969). Pavlovian fear conditioning and learned helplessness: Effects on escape and avoidance behavior of (a) the CS-US contingency and (b) the independence of the US and voluntary responding. In Campbell & Church (Eds.), *Punishment and aversive behavior.* New York: Appleton.

Maletzky, B. M. (1974). "Assisted" covert sensitization in the treatment of exhibitionism. *Journal of Consulting and Clinical Psychology, 42,* 34–40.

Malitz, S., Wilkens, B., & Escover, H. (1962). A comparison of drug induced hallucinations with those seen in spontaneously occurring psychoses. In L. J. West (Ed.), *Hallucinations.* New York: Grune & Stratton.

Malitz, S., et al., (1984). Low dosage ECT: Electrode placement and acute physiological and cognitive effects. Special Issue: Electroconvulsive therapy. *American Journal of Social Psychiatry, 4* (4), 47–53.

Malmo, R. B., & Shagass, C. (1949). Physiological study of symptom mechanism in psychiatric patients under stress. *Psychosomatic Medicine, 11,* 25–29.

Marchant, R., Howlin, P., Yule, W., & Rutter, M. (1974). Graded change in the treatment of the behavior of autistic children. *Journal of Child Psychology & Psychiatry, 15,* 221–27.

Marciano, T. D. (1982). Four marriage and family texts: A brief (but telling) array. *Contemporary Sociology, 11,* 150–53.

Margraf, J., Ehlers, A., & Roth, W. T. (1986). Sodium lactate infusions and panic attacks: A review and critique. *Psychosomatic Medicine, 48,* 23–51.

Marin, O. S. M., Saffran, E., & Schwartz, M. (1976). Dissociation of language in aphasia: Implications for normal function. *Annals of the New York Academy of Science, 280,* 868–84.

Marks, I. M. (1969). *Fears and phobias.* New York: Academic Press.

Marks, I. M. (1976). The current status of behavioral psychotherapy: Theory and practice. *American Journal of Psychiatry, 133,* 253–61.

Marks, I. (1977). Phobias and obsessions: Clinical phenomena in search of laboratory models. In J. Maser & M. E. P. Seligman (Eds.), *Psychopathology: Experimental models.* San Francisco: Freeman.

Marks, I. M. (1981). Review of behavioral psychotherapy: II. Sexual disorders. *American Journal of Psychiatry, 138,* 750–56.

Marks, I. M. (1986a). Epidemiology of anxiety. *Social Psychiatry, 21,* 167–71.

Marks, I. M. (1986b). Genetics of fear and anxiety disorders. *British Journal of Psychiatry, 149,* 406–18.

Marks, I., Boulougouris, J., & Marset, P. (1971). Flooding versus desensitization in the treatment of phobic patients: A crossover study. *British Journal of Psychiatry, 119,* 353–75.

Marks, I. M., & Gelder, M. G. (1966). Common ground between behavior therapy and psychodynamic methods. *British Journal of Medical Psychology, 39,* 11–23.

Marks, I. M., Gray, S., Cohen, D., Hill, R., Mawson, D., Ramm, E., & Stern, R. S. (1983). Imipramine and brief therapist-aided exposure in agoraphobics having self-exposure homework. *Archives of General Psychiatry, 40,* 153–62.

Marks, I. M., & Rachman, S. J. (1978). Interim report to the Medical Research Council.

Marks, I. M., Rachman, S., & Hodgson, R. (1975). Treatment of chronic obsessive-compulsive neurosis by in-vivo exposure: A two-year follow-up and issues in treatment. *British Journal of Psychiatry, 127,* 349–64.

Marlatt, G. A. (1983). The controlled drinking controversy: A commentary. *American Psychologist, 38,* 1097–1110.

Marlatt, G. A., & Gordon, J. R. (1980). Determinants of relapse: Implications for the maintenance of behavior change. In P. O. Davison & S. M. Davidson (Eds.), *Behavioral medicine: Changing health lifestyles.* New York: Brunner/Mazel.

Marsella, A. J. (1982). Culture and mental health: An overview. In A. J. Marsella & G. M. White (Eds.) *Cultural conceptions of mental health and therapy* (pp. 359–88). Dordecht, Holland: D. Reidel.

Marshall, C. D. (1976). The affective consequences of "inadequately explained" physiological arousal. Unpublished doctoral dissertation, Stanford University.

Marshall, E. (1980). Psychotherapy faces test of worth. *Science, 207,* 35–36.

Martin, B. (1977). *Abnormal psychology.* New York: Holt, Rinehart & Winston.

Marx, M. B., Garrady, T. F., & Bowens, F. R. (1975). The influence of recent life experience on the life of college freshmen. *Journal of Psychosomatic Research, 19,* 87–98.

Maslow, A. H. (1954). *Motivation and personality.* New York: Harper & Row.

Maslow, A. H. (1971). *The farther reaches of human nature.* New York: Viking.

Mason, J. W. (1971). A re-evaluation of the concept of "non-specificity" in stress theory. *Journal of Psychiatric Research, 8,* 323–33.

Mason, J. W. (1975). A historical view of the stress field, Part I. *Journal of Human Stress, 1,* 6–12.

Masters, W. H., & Johnson, V. E. (1970). *Human sexual inadequacy.* Boston: Little, Brown.

Matarazzo, J. D. (1983). The reliability of psychiatric and psychological diagnosis. *Clinical Psychology Review, 3,* 103–45.

Matthews, A., & MacLeod, C. (1986). Discrimination of threat cues without awareness in anxiety states. *Journal of Abnormal Psychology, 95,* 131–38.

Matthews, K. A. (1981). Psychological perspectives on the Type A behavior pattern. *Psychological Bulletin, 90,* 293–323.

Matthews, K. A., & Haynes, S. G. (1986). Type A behavior pattern and coronary disease risk: Update and critical evaluation. *American Journal of Epidemiology, 123,* 923–60.

Matthews, K. A., Stoney, C. M., Rakaszky, C. J., & Jamison, W. (1986). Family characteristics and school achievements of Type A children. *Health Psychology, 5,* 453–67.

Matthysse, S. (1973). Antipsychotic drug actions: A clue to the neuropathology of the schizophrenias. *Federation Proceedings, 32,* 200–205.

Matthysse, S. (1977). The role of dopamine in schizophrenia. In E. Usdin, D. A. Homburg, & J. D. Barkus (Eds.), *Neuroregulators and psychiatric disorders* (pp. 3–13). New York: Oxford University Press.

Mavissakalian, M., Perel, J., Bowler, K., & Dealy, R. (1987). Trazodone in the treatment of panic disorder and agoraphobia with panic attacks. *American Journal of Psychiatry, 144,* 785–91.

May, P. R. A., Tuma, A. H., Dixon, W. J., Yale, C., Thiele, D. A., & Kraus, W. H. (1981). Schizophrenia: A follow-up study of the results of five forms of treatment. *Archives of General Psychiatry, 38,* 776–84.

May, R. (1953). *Man's search for himself.* New York: Norton.

McCary, J. L. (1978). Human sexuality: Past present and future. *Journal of Marriage and Family Counseling, 4,* 3–12.

McClearn, G. E. (1968). Genetics and motivation of the mouse. In W. J. Arnold (Ed.), *Nebraska Symposium on Motivation.* Lincoln: University of Nebraska Press.

McClelland, D.C. (1979). Inhibited power motivation and high blood pressure in men. *Journal of Abnormal Psychology, 88,* 182–90.

McClelland, D. C., Alexander, C., & Marks, E. (1982). The need for power, stress, immune function, and illness among male prisoners. *Journal of Abnormal Psychology, 91,* 61–70.

McClelland, D. C., Atkinson, J. W., Clark, R. A., & Lowell, E. L. (1953). *The achievement motive.* New York: Appleton.

McConaghy, N. (1969). Subjective and penil plethysmograph response following aversion-relief and apomorphine aversion therapy for homosexual impulses. *British Journal of Psychiatry, 115,* 723–30.

McConnell, R. B. (1966). *Genetics of gastro-intestinal disorders.* London: Oxford University Press.

McCord, J. (1979). Some child-rearing antecedents of criminal behavior in adult men. *Journal of Personality and Social Psychology, 37,* 1477–86.

McCord, J. (1980, November 5–8). Myths and realities about criminal sanctions. Paper presented at the annual meetings of the American Society of Criminology, San Francisco, CA.

McFarlane, A. (1970). *Witchcraft in Tudor and Stuart England; A regional and comparative study.* New York: Harper & Row.

McGarry, A. L., & Bendt, R. H. (1969). Criminal vs. civil commitment of psychotic offenders: A seven year follow-up. *American Journal of Psychiatry, 125,* 1387–94.

McGhie, A. (1969). *Pathology of attention.* London: Penguin.

McGhie, A., & Chapman, J. S. (1961). Disorders of attention and perception in early schizophrenia. *British Journal of Medical Psychology, 34,* 103–16.

McGlashan, T. H. (1986a). Predictors of shorter-, medium-, and longer-term outcome in schizophrenia. *American Journal of Psychiatry, 142* (10), 50–55.

McGlashan, T. H. (1986b). Schizotypal personality disorder. Chestnut Lodge follow-up study: VI. Long-term follow-up perspectives. *Archives of General Psychiatry, 43,* 329–34.

McGlashan, T. H. (1987). Testing DSM-III symptom criteria for schizoptypal and borderline personality disorders. *Archives of General Psychiatry, 44,* 143–48.

McGue, M., Gottesman, I. I., & Rao, D. C. (1985). Resolving genetic models for the transmission of schizophrenia. *Genetic Epidemiology, 2,* 99–110.

McGuire, R. J., Carlisle, J. M., & Young, B. G. (1965). Sexual deviation as conditioned behavior. *Behavior Research and Therapy, 2,* 185–90.

McKinney, W. T., Suomi, S. J., & Harlow, H. F. (1972). Repetitive peer separations of juvenile age Rhesus monkeys. *Archives of General Psychiatry, 27,* 200–203.

McKnew, D. H., Jr., Cytryn, L., & Yahraes, H. (1983). *Why isn't Johnny crying?* New York: Norton.

McLellan, A. T., Luborsky, L., Woody, G. E., O'Brien, C. P., & Druley, K. A. (1983). Predicting response to alcohol and drug abuse treatments: Role of psychiatric severity. *Archives of General Psychiatry, 40,* 620–25.

McMillan, M. J., & Pihl, R. O. (1987). Premenstrual depression: A distinct entity. *Journal of Abnormal Psychology, 96,* 149–54.

McNally, R. J. (1987). Preparedness and phobias: A review. *Psychological Bulletin, 101,* 283–303.

McNeal, E. T., & Cimbolic, P. (1986). Antidepressants and biochemical theories of depression. *Psychological Bulletin, 99* (3), 361–74.

Medley, E. S. (1978). Peptic ulcer disease in children. *Journal of Family Practice, 7,* 281–84.

Mednick, B. R. (1973). Breakdown in high-risk subjects: Familial and early environmental factors. *Journal of Abnormal Psychology, 82,* 469–75.

Mednick, S. A. (1978). Berkou's fallacy and high risk research. In L. C. Wynne, R. L. Cromwell, & S. Matthysse (Eds.), *The Nature of schizophrenia.* New York: Wiley.

Mednick, S. A., Cudeck, R., Griffith, J. J., Talovic, S. A., & Schulsinger, F. (1984). The Danish high-risk project: Recent methods and findings. In N. F. Watt, E. J. Anthony, L. C.

Wynne, & J. E. Rolf (Eds.), *Children at risk for schizophrenia: A longitudinal perspective* (pp. 21–42). Cambridge: Cambridge University Press.

Mednick, S. A., Gabrielli, W. F., & Hutchings, B. (1984). Genetic influences in criminal convictions: Evidence from an adoption cohort. *Science, 224,* 891–94.

Mednick, S. A., Parnas, J., & Schulsinger, F. (1987). The Copenhagen high-risk project, 1962–1986. *Schizophrenic Bulletin, 13,* 485–95.

Mednick, S. A., & Schulsinger, F. (1968). Some premorbid characteristics related to breakdown in children with schizophrenic mothers. In D. Rosenthal & S. S. Kety (Eds.), *The transmission of schizophrenia.* Elmsford, NY: Pergamon.

Medvedev, Z. A., & Medvedev, R. A. (1971). *A question of madness.* New York: Knopf.

Meehl, P. E. (1986). Diagnostic taxa as open concepts: Meta-theoretical and statistical questions about reliability and construct validity in the grand strategy of nosological revision. In T. Millon & G. L. Klerman (Eds.), *Contemporary directions in psychopathology: Toward the DSM-IV* (pp. 215–31). New York: Guilford Press.

Meichenbaum, D. (1977). *Cognitive-behavior modification.* New York: Plenum.

Meissner, W. W. (1978). The conceptualization of marriage and family dynamics from a psychoanalytic perspective. In T. J. Paolino & B. S. McCrady (Eds.), *Marriage and marital therapy.* New York: Brunner/Mazel.

Mellsop, F. & Varghese, F. (1983). An Australian study reflecting on the reliability and validity of Axis II. In R. Spitzer, J. Williams, & A. Skodal (Eds.), *International perspectives on DSM-III.* Washington, DC: American Psychiatric Press.

Melton, G. B., Weithorn, L. A., & Slobogin, C. (1985). *Community mental health centers and the courts.* Lincoln, NE: University of Nebraska Press.

Melzack, R. (1973). *The puzzle of pain.* New York: Basic Books.

Mendels, J. (1970). *Concepts of depression.* New York: Wiley.

Mendels, J., & Cochran, C. (1968). The nosology of depression: The endogenous-reactive concept. *American Journal of Psychiatry, 124,* Supplement 1–11.

Mendelsohn, F., & Ross, M. (1959). An analysis of 133 homosexuals seen at a university health service. *Diseases of the Nervous System, 20,* 246–50.

Mendelsohn, G. A., & Geller, M. H. (1963). Effects of counselor-client similarity on the outcome of counseling. *Journal of Counseling Psychology, 10,* 71–77.

Mendelsohn, G. A., & Geller, M. H. (1967). Similarity, missed sessions, and early termination. *Journal of Counseling Psychology, 14,* 210–15.

Merbaum, M. (1971). Some personality characteristics of soldiers exposed to extreme war stress: A follow-up study of post-hospital adjustment. *Journal of Clinical Psychology, 32,* 558–62.

Merikangas, K. R., Leckman, J. F., Prusoff, B. A., Pauls, D. L., & Weissman, M. M. (1985). Familial transmission of depression and alcoholism. *Archives of General Psychiatry, 42,* 367–72.

Merton, R. K. (1957). *Social theory and social structure.* Glencoe, IL: Free Press.

Mesulam, M. M. (1981). A cortical network for directed attention and unilateral neglect. *Annals of Neurology, 10,* 309–24.

Metalsky, G. I., Halberstadt, L. J., Abramson, L. Y. (1987). Vulnerability to depressive mood reactions: Toward a more powerful test of the diathesis-stress and causal mediation components of the reformulated theory of depression. *Journal of Personality and Social Psychology, 52* (2), 386–93.

Meyer, C. B., & Taylor, S. E. (1986). Adjustment to rape. *Journal of Personality and Social Psychology, 50,* 1226–34.

Meyer, V. (1966). Modification of expectations in cases with obsessional rituals. *Behaviour Research and Therapy, 4,* 273–80.

Meyer, V., & Mair, J. M. M. (1963). A new technique to control stammering: A preliminary report. *Behavior Research Therapy, 1,* 251–54.

Midelfort, H. C. E. (1972). Witch-hunting in Southwestern Germany, 1562–1684. Stanford, CA: Stanford University Press.

Miklowitz, D. J., Strachan, A. M., Goldstein, M. J., Doane, J. A., Snyder, K. S., Hogarty, G. E., & Falloon, I. R. H. (1986). Expressed emotion and communication deviance in the families of schizophrenics. *Journal of Abnormal Psychology, 95* (1), 60–66.

Mill, J. S. (1859). *On liberty: The subjugation of women.* New York: Henry Holt.

Miller, D., & Dawson, W. H. (1965). Effects of stigma on re-employment of ex-mental patients. *Mental Hygiene, 49,* 281–87.

Miller, L. (1986, June). Talking or signing ups blood pressure. *Psychology Today,* p. 18.

Miller, N. E. (1969). Learning of visceral and glandular responses. *Science, 163,* 434.

Miller, N. E. (1985). The value of behavioral research on animals. *American Psychologist, 40,* 423–40.

Miller, R. C., & Berman, J. S. (1983). The efficacy of cognitive behavioral therapies: A quantitative review of the research. *Psychological Bulletin, 94,* 39–53.

Miller, S. M. (1978). Controllability in human stress. In M. E. P. Seligman & J. G. Garber (Eds.), *Human helplessness: Theory and application.* New York: Academic Press.

Miller, W. R., & Seligman, M. E. P. (1975). Depression and learned helplessness in man. *Journal of Abnormal Psychology, 84,* 228–38.

Miller, W. R., & Seligman, M. E. P. (1976). Learned helplessness, depression, and the perception of reinforcement. *Behavior Research and Therapy, 14,* 7–17.

Milner, B. (1964). Some effects of frontal lobectomy in man. In J. M. Warren & K. Akert (Eds.), *The frontal granular cortex and behavior.* New York: McGraw-Hill.

Milner, B. (1966). Amnesia following operation on the temporal lobes. In C. W. M. Whitty & O. L. Zangwill (Eds.), *Amnesia.* London: Butterworth.

Milner, B. (1970). Memory and the medial temporal regions of the brain. In K. H. Pribram & D. E. Broadbent (Eds.), *Biology of memory.* New York: Academic Press.

Milner, B. (1972). Disorders of learning and memory after temporal lobe lesions in man. *Clinical Neurosurgery, 19,* 421–46.

Mineka, S. (1985). Animal models of anxiety-based disorders: Their usefulness and limitations. In A. H. Tuma & J. D. Maser (Eds.), *Anxiety and the anxiety disorders* (pp. 199–244). Hillsdale, NJ: Erlbaum.

Mineka, S., Davidson, M., Cook, M., & Keir, R. (1984). Observational conditioning of snake fear in rhesus monkeys. *Journal of Abnormal Psychology, 93* (4), 355–72.

Minuchin, S. (1974). *Families and family therapy.* Cambridge, MA: Harvard University Press.

Minuchin, S., Rosman, B. L., & Baker, L. (1980). *Psychosomatic families: Anorexia nervosa in context.* Cambridge: Harvard University Press.

Mirsky, A. F., & Duncan-Johnson, C. (1984). Nature versus nurture in schizophrenia—the struggle continues. *Integrative Psychiatry, 2,* 137–48.

Mirsky, A. F., Silberman, E. K., Latz, A., & Nagler, S. (1985). Adult outcomes of high-risk children: Differential effects of town and kibbutz rearing. *Schizophrenia Bulletin, 11,* 150–54.

Mirsky, I. A. (1958). Physiologic, psychologic, and social determinants of the etiology of duodenal ulcer. *American Journal of Digestive Diseases, 3,* 285–314.

Mirsky, I. A., Futterman, P., & Kaplan, S. (1952). Blood plasma pepsinogen. II. The activity of the plasma from "normal" subjects, patients with duodenal ulcer and patients with pernicious anemia. *Journal of Laboratory and Clinical Medicine, 40,* 198–99.

Mischel, H. N., & Mischel, W. (1973). *Readings in personality.* New York: Holt, Rinehart & Winston.

Mischel, W. (1968). *Personality and assessment.* New York: Wiley.

Mischel, W. (1973). Toward a cognitive social learning reconceptualization of personality. *Psychological Review, 80,* 252–83.

Mischel, W. (1976). *Introduction to personality* (2nd ed.). New York: Holt, Rinehart & Winston.

Mischel, W., & Baker, N. (1975). Cognitive transformations of reward objects through instructions. *Journal of Personality and Social Psychology, 31,* 254–61.

Mischel, W., & Ebbesen, E. (1970). Attention in delay of gratification. *Journal of Personality and Social Psychology, 16,* 329–37.

Mischel, W., Ebbesen, E., & Zeiss, A. R. (1972). Cognitive and attentional mechanisms in delay of gratification. *Journal of Personality and Social Psychology, 21,* 204–18.

Mischel, W., & Peake, P. K. (1982). Beyond deja vu in the search for cross-situational consistency. *Psychological Review, 89,* 730–55.

Mishkin, M., & Appenzeller, T. (1987). The anatomy of memory. *Scientific American, 256* (6), 80–89.

Mishra, S. P., & Brown, K. H. (1983). The comparability of WAIS and WAIS-R IQs and subtest scores. *Journal of Clinical Psychology, 39,* 754–57.

Mitchell, K. M., Bozarth, J. D., & Krauft, C. C. (1977). A reappraisal of the therapeutic effectiveness of accurate empathy, nonpossessive warmth, and genuineness. In A. S. Gurman & A. M. Razin (Eds.), *Effective psychotherapy: A handbook of research.* New York: Pergamon.

Mittelmann, B., Wolff, H. G., & Scharf, M. (1942). Emotions in gastroduodenal functions. *Psychosomatic Medicine, 4,* 5–61.

Mittler, P., Gillies, S., & Jukes, E. (1966). Prognosis in psychotic children. Report of follow-up study. *Journal of Mental Deficiency Research, 10,* 73–83.

Model Penal Code and Commentaries, Sec. 4.01 (Part I). (1962). Philadelphia, PA: American Law Institute, 1980.

Modell, W. (1967). Mass catastrophes and the roles of science and technology. *Science, 156,* 346–51.

Mohler, H., & Okada, T. (1977). Properties of 3H-diazepam binding to benzodiazepine receptors in rat cerebral cortex. *Life Science, 20,* 2101–10.

Mohs, R. D., Breitner, J. C. S., Silverman, J. M., & Davis, K. L. (1987). Alzheimer's disease: Morbid risk among first-degree relatives approximates fifty percent by ninety years of age. *Archives of General Psychiatry, 44,* 405–408.

Monahan, J. (1976). *Community mental health and the criminal justice system.* New York: Pergamon.

Monahan, J., & Wexler, D. (1978). A definite maybe: Proofs and probability in civil commitment. *Law and Human Behavior, 2,* 37–42.

Money, J., & Ambinder, R. (1978). Two-year, real-life diagnostic test: Rehabilitation vs. cure. In J. P. Brady & H. K. H. Brodie (Eds.), *Controversy in psychiatry.* Philadelphia: Saunders.

Money, J., & Ehrhardt, A. A. (1972). *Man and woman, boy and girl.* Baltimore: The John Hopkins University Press.

Money, J., Schwartz, M., & Lewis, V. G. (1983, June). Adult erotosexual status and fetal hormonal masculinization and demasculinization: 46XX congenital virilizing adrenal hyperplasia (CVAH), and 46XY androgen insensitivity syndrome (AIS) compared. Paper presented at the 14th International Congress of the International Society of Psychoneuroendocrinology, New York.

Monthly Labor Review. (1983, July). Washington, DC: U.S. Department of Labor, Bureau of Labor Statistics, p. 54.

Moody, R. L. (1946). Bodily changes during abreaction. *The Lancet, 2,* 934–35.

Morris, R. J., & Suckerman, K. R. (1974a). The importance of the therapeutic relationship to systematic desensitization. *Journal of Consulting and Clinical Psychology, 42,* 142.

Morris, R. J., & Suckerman, K. R. (1974b). Therapist warmth as a factor in automated systematic desensitization. *Journal of Consulting and Clinical Psychology, 42,* 244–50.

Moscovitch, M. (1982a). Multiple dissociations of function in amnesia. In L. S. Cermak (Ed.), *Human memory and amnesia.* Hillsdale, NJ: Erlbaum.

Moscovitch, M. (1982b). A neuropsychological approach to perception and memory in normal and pathological aging. In F. I. M. Craik & S. Trehub (Eds.), *Aging and cognitive processes.* New York: Plenum.

Moscovitch, M. (1984). The sufficient conditions for demonstrating preserved memory in amnesia: A task analysis. In L. R. Squire & N. Butters (Eds.), *Neuropsychology of memory.* New York: Guilford Press.

Moscovitch, M. (1989). Confabulation and the frontal lobes: Strategic vs. associative retrieval in neuropsychological theories of memory. In H. L. Roediger III & F. I. M. Craik (Eds.), *Varieties of memory and consciousness: Essays in Honor of Endel Tulving* (pp. 133–60), Hillsdale, NJ: Erlbaum.

Mosher, L. R., & Menn, A. Z. (1978). Community residential treatment for schizophrenia: Two year follow-up. *Hospital and Community Psychiatry, 29,* 715–23.

Mosher, L. R., Menn, A., & Matthews, S. (1975). Soteria: Evaluation of a home-based treatment for schizophrenia. *American Journal of Orthopsychiatry 45,* 455–67.

Mowrer, O. H. (1947). On the dual nature of learning—A re-interpretation of "conditioning" and "problem-solving." *Harvard Educational Review, 17,* 102–50.

Mowrer, O. H. (1948). Learning theory and the neurotic paradox. *American Journal of Orthopsychiatry, 18,* 571–610.

Mowrer, O. H., & Mowrer, W. M. (1938). Enuresis: A method for its study and treatment. *American Journal of Orthopsychiatry, 8,* 436–59.

Mullaney, J. A., & Trippett, C. J. (1982). Alcohol dependence and phobias: Clinical description and relevance. *British Journal of Psychiatry, 135,* 565–73.

Munzinger, H. (1975). The adopted child's IQ: A critical review. *Psychological Bulletin, 80,* 623–29.

Murray, H. A. (1951). Forward. In H. H. Anderson & G. L. Anderson (Eds.), *An introduction to projective techniques.* Englewood Cliffs, NJ: Prentice-Hall.

Murphy, D., Brodie, K., Goodwin, F., & Bunney, W. E. (1971). Regular induction of hypomania by L-dopa in "bipolar" manic-depressive patients. *Nature, 229,* 135–36.

Murphy, J. M., Sobol, A. M., Neff, R. K., Olivier, D. C., & Leighton, A. H. (1984). Stability of prevalence: Depression and anxiety disorders. *Archives of General Psychiatry, 41,* 990–97.

Murstein, B. I. (1965). New thoughts about ambiguity and the TAT. *Journal of Projective Techniques and Personality Assessment, 29,* 219–25.

Myers, J., & Auld, F. (1955). Some variables related to outcome of psychotherapy. *Journal of Clinical Psychology, 11,* 51–54.

Myers, J. K., Weissman, M. M., Tischler, G. L., Holzer, C. E., Leaf, P. J., Orvaschel, H., Anthony, J. C., Boyd, J. H., Burke, J. D., Kramer, M., & Stolzman, R. (1984). Six-month prevalence of psychiatric disorders in three communities: 1980 to 1982. *Archives of General Psychiatry, 41,* 959–67.

Nagler, S., & Glueck, Z. (1985). The clinical interview. *Schizophrenia Bulletin, 11,* 38–47.

Nagoshi, C. T., & Wilson, J. R. (1987). Influence of family alcoholism history on alcohol metabolism, sensitivity, and tolerance. *Alcoholism: Clinical and Experimental Research, 11,* 392–98.

Nash, E. H., Hoehn-Saric, R., Battle, C. C., Stone, A. R., Imber, S. D., & Frank, J. D. (1965). Systematic preparation of patients for short-term psychotherapy. II. Relation to characteristics of patient, therapist and the psychotherapeutic process. *Journal of Nervous and Mental Disorders, 140,* 374–83.

Nasrallah, H. A., Schroeder, D., & Petty, F. (1982). Alcoholism secondary to essential tremor. *Journal of Clinical Psychiatry, 43,* 163–64.

Nathan, P. E. (1988). The addictive personality is the behavior of the addict. *Journal of Consulting and Clinical Psychology, 56,* 183–88.

Neary, D., Snowden, J. S., Northern, B., & Goulding, P. (1988). Dementia of frontal lobe type. *Journal of Neurology, Neurosurgery and Psychiatry, 51,* 353–61.

Nemiah, J. C. (1971). The psychophysiologic management: A treatment of patients with peptic ulcer. *Advances in Psychosomatic Medicine, 6,* 169–85.

Nesse, F. M., Cameron, O. G., Curtis, G. C., McCann, D. S., & Huber-Smith, M. J. (1984). Adrenergic function in patients with panic anxiety. *Archives of General Psychiatry, 41,* 771–76.

Nestel, P. J. (1969). Blood pressure in catecholamine excretion after mental stress in labile hypertension. *Lancet, 1*(2), 692–94.

Newlin, D. B. The antagonistic placebo response to alcohol cues. *Alcoholism: Clinical and Experimental Research, 9,* 411–16.

Nichols, M. (1984). *Family therapy: Concepts and methods.* New York: Gardner.

Nicol, S. E., & Gottesman, I. I. (1983). Clues to the genetics and neurobiology of schizophrenia. *American Scientist, 71,* 398–404.

Nisbett, R., & Ross, L. (1980). *Human inference: Strategies and shortcomings of social judgment.* Englewood Cliffs, NJ: Prentice-Hall.

Noel, N. E., & Lisman, S. A. (1980). Alcohol consumption by college women following exposure to unsolvable problems: Learned helplessness or stress-induced drinking? *Behavior Research and Therapy, 18,* 429–40.

Nolen-Hoeksema, S. (1988). Life-span views on depression. In P. B. Baltes, D. L. Featherman, & R. M. Lerner (Eds.), *Life span development and behavior* (Vol. 9). New York: Erlbaum.

Nolen-Hoeksema, S., Girgus, J., & Seligman, M. E. P. (1986). Learned helplessness in children: A longitudinal study of depression, achievement, and explanatory style. *Journal of Personality and Social Psychology, 51,* 435–42.

Nowlan, R., & Cohen, S. (1977). Tolerance to marijuana: Heart rate and subjective "high." *Clinical Pharmacology and Therapeutics, 22,* 123–32.

O'Brien, C. P., Testa, T., O'Brien, T. J., Brady, J. P., & Wells, B. (1977). Conditioning narcotic withdrawal in humans. *Science, 195,* 1000–1002.

Odier, C. (1956). *Anxiety and magical thinking.* New York: International Universities Press.

Ohman, A. (1979). Fear relevance, autonomic conditioning and phobias: A laboratory model. In S. Bates, W. K. Dockens, K. G. Blotesharm, L. Melin, & P. O. Sjoden (Eds.), *Trends in behavior therapy.* New York: Academic Press.

Ohman, A., Anders, E., & Olafson, C. (1975). One trial learning and superior resistance to extinction of autonomic responses conditioned to potentially phobic stimuli. *Journal of Comparative and Physiological Psychology, 88* (88), 619–27.

Ohman, A., Fredrikson, M., & Hugdahl, K. (1978). Orienting and defensive responding in the electrodermal system: Palmardorsal differences and recovery rate during conditioning to potentially phobic stimuli. *Psychophysiology, 2,* 93–102.

Ohman, A., Fredrikson, M., Hugdahl, K. & Per-Arne, R. (1974). A dimension of preparedness in human learning: The effect of potentially phobic stimuli as CS's in electro-dermal conditioning. *Biological Psychology, 2,* 85–93.

Ohman, A., Fredrikson, M., Hugdahl, K., & Rimmo, P. (1976). The premise of equipotentiality in human classical conditioning: Conditioned electrodermal responses to potentially phobic stimuli. *Journal of Experimental Psychology-General, 105* (4), 313–37.

Ohman, A., Nordby, H., & d'Elia, G. (1986). Orienting and schizophrenia: Stimulus significance, attention, and distraction in a signaled reaction time task. *Journal of Abnormal Psychology, 95* (4), 326–34.

Ohwaki, S., & Stayton, S. E. (1978). The relation of length of institutionalization to the intellectual functioning of the profoundly retarded. *Child Development, 49,* 105–109.

Oi, M., Oshida, K., & Sugimura, A. (1959). Location of the gastric ulcer. *Gastroenterology, 36,* 45–56.

O'Leary, S. G., & Pelham, W. E. (1978). Behavior therapy and withdrawal of stimulant medication in hyperactive children. *Pediatrics, 61,* 211–17.

Oltman, J., & Friedman, S. (1967). Parental deprivation in psychiatric conditions. *Diseases of the Nervous System, 28,* 298–303.

Olweus, D. (1979). Stability of aggressive reaction patterns in males: A review. *Psychological Bulletin, 86,* 852–75.

Ordman, A. M., & Kirschenbaum, D. S. (1985). Cognitive behavioral therapy for bulimia: An initial outcome study. *Journal of Consulting and Clinical Psychology, 53,* 305–13.

Orgel, S. (1958). Effects of psychoanalysis on the course of peptic ulcer. *Psychosomatic Medicine, 20,* 117–23.

Orne, M. T. (1962). On the social psychology of the psychological experiment: With particular reference to demand characteristics and their implications. *American Psychologist, 17,* 776–83.

Orne, M. T., Dinges, D. F., & Orne, E. C. (1984). On the differential diagnosis of multiple personality in the forensic context. *International Journal of Clinical and Experimental Hypnosis, 32,* 118–69.

Orne, M. T., & Wender, P. H. (1968). Anticipatory socialization for psychotherapy. *American Journal of Psychiatry, 124,* 1202–11.

Ornitz, E. M. (1973). Childhood autism: A review of the clinical and experimental literature. *California Medicine, 117,* 21–47.

Ornitz, E. M. (1978). Biological homogeneity or heterogeneity? In M. Rutter & E. Schopler (Eds.), *Autism: A reappraisal of concepts and treatment.* New York: Plenum.

Osler, W. (1897). *Lectures on angina pectoris and allied states.* New York: D. Appleton and Company.

Osmond, H., & Smythies, J. R. (1952). Schizophrenia: A new approach. *Journal of Mental Science, 98,* 309–15.

Ost, L., & Gotestam, K. (1976). Behavioral and pharmacological treatments for obesity: An experimental comparison. *Addictive Behaviors, 1,* 331–38.

Ost, L. G., & Hugdahl, K. (1981). Acquisition of phobias and anxiety response patterns in clinical patients. *Behaviour Research and Therapy, 19,* 439–48.

Overholser, J. C., & Beck, S. (1986). Multimethod assessment of rapists, child molesters, and three control groups on behavioral and psychological measures. *Journal of Consulting and Clinical Psychology, 54* (5), 682–87.

Overmier, J. B., & Seligman, M. E. P. (1967). Effects of inescapable shock upon subsequent escape and avoidance learning. *Journal of Comparative and Physiological Psychology, 63,* 23–33.

Packer, H. (1968). *The limits of the criminal sanction.* Stanford: Stanford University Press.

Palmer, R. L. (1980). *Anorexia nervosa.* New York: Penguin.

Parloff, M. B. (1976, February). Shopping for the right therapy. *Saturday Review, 21,* 14–20.

Parloff, M. B. (1979). Can psychotherapy research guide the policymaker? A little knowledge may be a dangerous thing. *American Psychologist, 34,* 296–306.

Parloff, M. B. (1982). Psychotherapy research evidence and reimbursement decisions: Bambi meets Godzilla. *American Journal of Psychiatry, 139,* 718–27.

Parloff, M. B., Waskow, I. E., & Wolfe, B. E. (1978). Research on therapist variables in relation to process and outcome. In S. L. Garfield & A. E. Bergin (Eds.), *Handbook of psychotherapy and behavior change: An empirical analysis* (2nd ed.). New York: Wiley.

Parkes, M. C. (1964). Recent bereavement as a cause of mental illness. *British Journal of Psychiatry, 110,* 194–204.

Parkes, M. C., Benjamin, B., & Fitzgerald, R. G. (1969). Broken heart: A statistical study of increased mortality among widowers. *British Medical Journal, 1,* 740–43.

Pasner, M. I., Walker, J. A., Friedrich, F. J., & Rafal, R. D. (1984). Effects of parietal lobe injury on covert orienting of visual attention. *Journal of Neuroscience, 4,* 1863–74.

Patterson, E. M. (1965). Treatment of alcoholic families with nurse home visits. *Family Process, 4,* 75–94.

Patterson, G. R. (1971). *Families: Applications of social learning theory to family life.* Champaign, IL: Research Press.

Patterson, G. R. (1973). Reprogramming the families of aggressive boys. In C. Thoreson (Ed.), *Behavior modification in education: 72nd Year Book, Part I.* Chicago: University of Chicago Press.

Patterson, G. R. (1975). *Families: Applications of social learning theory to family life.* Champaign, IL: Research Press.

Patterson, G. R., Weiss, R. L., & Hops, H. (1976). Training of marital skills: Some problems of concepts. In H. Leitenberg (Ed.), *Handbook of behavior modification and behavior therapy.* Englewood Cliffs, NJ: Prentice-Hall.

Patterson, K., Marshall, J. C., & Coltheart, M. (Eds.). (1985). Surface dyslexia: *Cognitive and neuropsychological studies of phonological reading.* Hillsdale, NJ: Erlbaum.

Patterson, T., Spohn, H. E., Bogia, D. P., & Hayes, K. (1986). Thought disorder in schizophrenia: Cognitive and neuroscience approaches. *Schizophrenia Bulletin, 12* (3), 460–72.

Pattie, F. A. (1967). A brief history of hypnotism. In J. E. Gordon (Ed.), *Handbook of clinical and experimental hypnosis.* New York: Macmillan.

Paul, G. L. (1966). Insight vs. desensitization in psychotherapy. Stanford: Stanford University Press.

Paul, G. L. (1967). Insight vs. desensitization in psychotherapy two years after termination. *Journal of Consulting Psychology, 31* (4), 333–48.

Pauly, I. B. (1969). Adult manifestation of male transsexualism. In R. Green & J. Money (Eds.), *Transsexualism and sex reassignment.* Baltimore: The Johns Hopkins Press.

Pauly, I. B. (1974). Female transsexualism. *Archives of Sexual Behavior, 3,* 487–526.

Paykel, E. S. (1973). Life events and acute depression. In J. P. Scott & E. C. Senay (Eds.), *Separation and depression.* AAAS.

Paykel, E. S. (1974a). Recent life events and clinical depression. In E. K. E. Gunderson & R. H. Rahe (Eds.), *Life stress and illness* (pp. 150–51). Springfield, IL: Charles C. Thomas.

Paykel, E. S. (1974b). Life stress and psychiatric disorder: Application of the clinical approach. In B. P. Dohrenwend & B. S. Dohrenwend (Eds.), *Stressful life events: Their nature and effects* (pp. 135–49). New York: Wiley.

Paykel, E. S., Meyers, J. K., Dienelt, M. N., Klerman, J. L., Lindenthal, J. J., & Peffer, M. P. (1969). Life events and depression. *Archives of General Psychiatry, 21,* 753–60.

Payne, R. W. (1966). The measurement and significance of over-inclusive thinking and retardation in schizophrenic patients. In P. H. Hoch & J. Zubin (Eds.), *Psychopathology of schizophrenia* (pp. 77–79). New York: Grune & Stratton.

Payne, R. W., & Hewlett, J. H. G. (1960). Thought disorder in psychotic patients. In H. J. Eysenck (Ed.), *Experiments in personality* (Vol. 2) (pp. 3–104). London: Routledge & Kegan Paul.

Pelham, W. E., Bender, M. E., Caddell, J., Booth, S., & Moorer, S. H. (1985). Methylphenidate and children with attention deficit disorder. *Archives of General Psychiatry, 42,* 948–52.

Pennebaker, J. W. (1985). Traumatic experience and psychosomatic disease: Exploring the roles of behavioural inhibition, obsession, and confiding. *Canadian Psychology, 26,* 82–95.

Perkins, K. A., & Reyher, J. (1971). Repression, psychopathology and drive representation: An experimental hypnotic investigation of impulse inhibition. *American Journal of Clinical Hypnosis, 13,* 249–58.

Perls, F. S. (1970). *Gestalt therapy now.* Palo Alto, CA: Science & Behavior Books.

Perly, M. J., & Guze, S. B. (1962). Hysteria: The stability and usefulness of clinical criteria. *New England Journal of Medicine, 266,* 421–26.

Perri, M. G., McAdoo, W. G., Spevak, P. A., & Newlin, D. B. (1984). Effect of a multicomponent maintenance program on long-term weight loss. *Journal of Consulting and Clinical Psychology, 52,* 480–81.

Perri, M. G., Shapiro, R. M., Ludwig, W. W., Twentyman, C. T., & McAdoo, W. G. (1984). Maintenance strategies for the treatment of obesity: An evaluation of relapse prevention training and post-treatment contact by mail and telephone. *Journal of Consulting and Clinical Psychology, 52,* 404–13.

Perris, C. (1968). The course of depressive psychosis. *Acta Psychiatrica Scandinavica, 44,* 238–48.

Persons, J. B. (1986). The advantages of studying psychological phenomena rather than psychiatric diagnoses. *American Psychologist, 41,* 1252–60.

Peterson, C., Luborsky, L., & Seligman, M. E. P. (1983). Attributions and depressive mood shifts: A case study using the symptom-context method. *Journal of Abnormal Psychology, 92,* 96–103.

Peterson, C., & Seligman, M. E. P. (1984). Explanatory style and depression: Theory and evidence. *Psychological Review.*

Peterson, C., & Seligman, M. E. P. (1987). Explanatory style and illness. Special Issue: Personality and physical health. *Journal of Personality, 55* (2), 237–65.

Peterson, C., Seligman, M. E. P. & Vaillant, G. (1988). Pessimistic explanatory style as a risk factor for physical illness: A 35-year longitudinal study. *Journal of Personality and Social Psychology, 55,* 23–27.

Peterson, D. R. (1978). *The clinical study of social behavior.* New York: Appleton.

Petzel, T. P., & Johnson, J. E. (1972). Time estimation by process and reactive schizophrenics under crowded and uncrowded conditions. *Journal of Clinical Psychology, 28*(3), 345–47.

Phares, E. J. (1976). *Locus of control in personality.* Morristown, NJ: General Learning Press.

Phares, E. J., Wilson, K. G., & Klyrer, N. W. (1971). Internal-external control and the attribution of blame under neutral and distractive conditions. *Journal of Personality and Social Psychology, 18,* 286–88.

Place, E. J. S., & Gilmore, G. C. (1980). Perceptual organization in schizophrenia. *Journal of Abnormal Psychology, 89,* 409–18.

Platt, J. J., & Labate, C. (1976). *Heroin addiction.* New York: Wiley.

Poizner, H., Klima, E. S., & Bellugi, U. (1987). *What the hands reveal about the brain.* Cambridge, MA: MIT/Bradford Books.

Pokorny, A. D. (1964). Suicide rates and various psychiatric disorders. *Journal of Nervous and Mental Diseases, 139,* 499–506.

Polak, P. R., & Kirby, M. W. (1976). A model to replace psychiatric hospitals. *Journal of Nervous & Mental Diseases, 162,* 13–22.

Polivy, J., & Herman, C. P. (1985). Dieting and binging: A causal analysis. *American Psychologist, 40,* 193–201.

Pollack, J. M. (1979). Obsessive-compulsive personality: A review. *Psychological Bulletin, 86,* 225–41.

Pollit, J. D. (1960). Natural history studies in mental illness: A discussion based on a pilot study of obsessional states. *Journal of Mental Science, 106,* 93–113.

Pomerleau, O. F., & Pomerleau, C. S. (1984). Neuroregulators and the reinforcement of smoking: Towards a biobehavioral explanation. *Neuroscience and Biobehavioral Reviews, 8,* 503–13.

Pope, Jr., H. G., & Hudson, J. I. (1982). Treatment of bulimia with antidepressants. *Psychopharmacology, 78,* 176–79.

Pope, H. G., Jonas, J. M., & Jones, B. (1982). Factitious psychosis: Phenomenology, family history, and long-term outcome of nine patients. *American Journal of Psychiatry, 139,* 1480–83.

Porsolt, R. D., Anton, G., Blavet, N., & Jalfre, M. (1978). Behavioral despair in rats: A new model sensitive to antidepressant treatments. *European Journal of Pharmacology, 47,* 379–91.

Posner, M. I., Walker, J. A., Friedrich, F. J., & Rafal, R. D. (1984). Effects of parietal lobe injury on covert orienting of visual attention. *Journal of Neuroscience, 4,* 1863–74.

Post, R., Kotin, J., Goodwin, F. K., & Gordon, E. K. (1973). Psychomotor activity and cerebrospinal fluid amine metabolites in affective illness. *American Journal of Psychiatry, 130,* 67–72.

Powell, K. E., Thompson, P. D., Caspersen, C. J., & Kendrick, J. S. (1987). Physical activity and the incidence of coronary heart disease. *Annual Review of Public Health, 8,* 253–87.

Prange, A. J., Wilsan, J. C., Knox, A., McClane, T. K., & Lipton, M. A. (1970). Enhancement of imipramine by thyroid stimulating hormone: Clinical and theoretical implications. *American Journal of Psychiatry, 127,* 191–99.

Premack, D. (1959). Toward empirical behavior laws: I. Positive reinforcement. *Psychological Review, 66,* 219–33.

Price, K. P., Tryon, W. W., & Raps, C. S. (1978). Learned helplessness and depression in a clinical population: A test of two behavioral hypotheses. *Journal of Abnormal Psychology, 87,* 113–21.

Prichard, J. C. (1837). *Treatise on insanity and other disorders affecting the mind.* Philadelphia: Haswell, Barrington & Haswell.

Propping, P., Kruger, J., & Mark, N. (1981). Genetic predisposition to alcoholism. An EEG study in alcoholics and relatives. *Human Genetics, 59,* 51–59.

Purcell, D., Brady, K., Chai, H., Muser, J., Molk, L., Gordon, N., & Means, J. (1969). The effect of asthma in children during experimental separation from the family. *Psychosomatic Medicine, 31,* 144–64.

Putnam, F. W., Guroff, J. J., & Silberman, E. K., et al. (1986). The clinical phenomenology of multiple personality disorder: Review of 100 recent cases. *Journal of Clinical Psychiatry, 47* (6), 285–93.

Quade, H. C. (1986). A critical analysis of DSM-III as a taxonomy of psychopathology in childhood and adolescence. In T. Millon & G. L. Klerman (Eds.), *Contemporary directions in psychopathology: Toward the DSM-IV* (pp. 151–66). New York: Guilford Press.

Quay, H. C. (1986). Conduct disorders. In H. C. Quay & J. S. Werry (Eds.), *Psychopathological disorders of childhood* (pp. 35–62). New York: Wiley.

Quay, H. C., Routh, D. K., & Shapiro, S. K. (1987). Psychopathology of childhood: From description to validation. *Annual Review of Psychology, 38,* 491–532.

Rabavilos, A. D., Boulougouris, J. C., & Stefanis, C. (1976). Duration of flooding session in the treatment of obsessive-compulsive patients. *Behavior Research and Therapy, 14,* 349–55.

Rachman, S. J. (1965). Aversion therapy: Chemical or electrical? *Behaviour Research Therapy, 2,* 289–99.

Rachman, S. J. (1971). *The effects of psychotherapy.* Oxford: Pergamon.

Rachman, S. J. (1976). Therapeutic modeling. In M. Felman & A. Broadhurst (Ed.), *Theoretical and experimental bases of behavior therapy.* Chichester. Wiley.

Rachman, S. J. (1978). *Fear and courage.* New York: Freeman.

Rachman, S. J., Cobb, J., Grey, S., MacDonald, B., Mauson, C., Sartory, G., & Stern, R. (1979). The behavioral treatment of obsessive-compulsive disorders, with and without domipramine. *Behavior Research and Therapy, 17,* 467–78.

Rachman, S. J., & Hodgson, R. J. (1968). Experimentally induced "sexual fetishism": Replication and development. *Psychological Records, 18,* 25–27.

Rachman, S. J., & Hodgson, R. J. (1980). *Obsessions and compulsions.* Englewood Cliffs, NJ: Prentice-Hall.

Rachman, S. J., Hodgson, R., & Marks, I. M. (1971). The treatment of chronic obsessional neurosis. *Behaviour Research and Therapy, 9,* 237–47.

Rachman, S. J., Marks, I., & Hodgson, R. (1973). The treatment of chronic obsessive compulsive neurosis by modeling and flooding in vivo. *Behaviour Research and Therapy, 11,* 463–71.

Rachman, S. J., & Wilson, G. T. (1979). *The effects of psychotherapy.* Oxford: Pergamon.

Rack, P. (1977). Clinical experience in the treatment of obsessional states. *Journal of International Medical Research, 5,* 81–91.

Radloff, L. S. (1975). Sex differences in depression: The effects of occupation and marital status. *Sex Roles, 1,* 249–65.

Rado, S. (1928). Psychodynamics of depression from the etiological point of view. In W. Galen (Ed.), *The meaning of despair.* New York: Science House.

Raps, C. S., Peterson, C., Reinhard, K. E., Abramson, L. Y., & Seligman, M. E. P. (1982). Attributional style among depressed patients. *Journal of Abnormal Psychology, 91,* 102–103.

Raps, C. S., Reinhard, K. E., & Seligman, M.E.P. (1980). Reversal of cognitive and affective deficits associated with depression and learned helplessness by mood elevation in patients. *Journal of Abnormal Psychology, 89,* 342–49.

Raskin, A., Crook, T. H., & Herman, K. D. (1975). The psychiatric history and symptom differences in black and white depressed patients. *Journal of Consulting and Clinical Psychology, 43,* 73–80.

Raskind, M. A. (1976). Helping the elderly psychiatric patient in crisis. *Geriatrics, 31,* 51–56.

Rattan, R. B., & Chapman, L. J. (1973). Associative intrusions in schizophrenic verbal behavior. *Journal of Abnormal Psychology, 82,* 169–73.

Rawlings, E. I., & Carter, D. K. (1977). *Psychotherapy for women.* Springfield, IL: Charles C. Thomas.

Ray, W. J., & Katahn, M. (1968). Relation of anxiety to locus of control. *Psychological Reports, 23,* 1196.

Redmond, D. E., Maas, J. W., Kling, A., & DeKirmenjian, H. (1971). Changes in private school behavior after treatment with alpha-methyl-para-tyrosine. *Psychosomatic Medicine, 33,* 97–113.

Reiger, D., Myers, J., Kramer, M., Robins, L., Blayer, D., Hough, R., Eaton, W., & Locke, B. (1984). The NIMH epidemiological catchment area program: Historical context, major objectives, and study population characteristics. *Archives of General Psychiatry, 41,* 934–41.

Rehm, L. (1977). A self-control model of depression. *Behavior Therapy, 8,* 787–804.

Rehm, L. P. (1978). Mood pleasant events, and unpleasant events: Two pilot studies. *Journal of Consulting and Clinical Psychology, 46,* 854–59.

Rehyer, J., & Smyth, L. (1971). Suggestibility during the execution of a posthypnotic suggestion. *Journal of Abnormal Psychology, 78,* 258–65.

Reich, L. H., Davies, R. K., & Himmelhoch, J. M. (1974). Excessive alcohol use in manic-depressive illness. *American Journal of Psychiatry, 131*(1), 83–86.

Reich, W. (1986). Diagnostic ethics: The uses and limits of psychiatric explanation. In L. Tancredi (Ed.), *Ethical issues in epidemiological research.* New Brunswick, NJ: Rutgers University Press.

Reid, W. H., Dorr, D., Walker, J. I., & Bonner, III, J. W. (Eds.). (1986). *Unmasking the psychopath: Antisocial personality and related syndromes.* New York: Norton.

Reisen, M. F., Brust, A. A., & Farris, E. B. (1951). Life situations, emotions, and the course of patients with arterial hypertension. *Psychosomatic Medicine, 13,* 133.

Reisenger, J. J. (1972). The treatment of "anxiety-depression" via positive reinforcement and response. *Journal of Applied Behavior Analysis, 5,* 125–30.

Reiss, S., Peterson, R. A., Erron, L. D., & Reiss, N. M. (1977). *Abnormality: Experimental and clinical approaches.* New York: Macmillan.

Rennie, M. A., & Wollensheim, J. P. (1979). Cognitive therapy, stress management training and the Type A behavior pattern. *Cognitive Therapy and Research, 3*(1), 61–73.

Rescorla R. A., & Solomon, R. L. (1967). Two-process learning theory: Relationship between Pavlovian conditioning and instrumental learning. *Psychological Review, 74,* 151–82.

Rescorla, R. A., & Wagner, A. R. (1972). A theory of Pavlovian conditioning: Variations in the effectiveness of reinforcement and nonreinforcement. In A. Black & W. F. Prokasy (Eds.), *Classical conditioning II.* New York: Appleton-Century-Crofts.

Resick, P., & Ellis, E. (1982). Victims of rape: Repeated assessment of depressive symptoms. *Journal of Consulting and Clinical Psychology, 50,* 96–102.

Reynolds, W. M., & Coats, K. I. (1986). A comparison of cognitive-behavioral therapy and relaxation training for the treatment of depression in adolescents. *Journal of Consulting and Clinical Psychology, 54,* 653–60.

Rice, J., Reich, T., Andreasen, N. C., Endicott, J., Van Eerdewegh, M., Fishman, R., Hirschfeld, R. M. A., & Klerman, G. L. (1987). The familial transmission of bipolar illness. *Archives of General Psychiatry, 44,* 441–47.

Richardson, S. A. (1970). Age and sex differences in values towards physical handicaps. *Journal of Health and Social Behavior, 11,* 207–14.

Richter, C. P. (1957a). Hormones and rhythms in man and animals. *Recent Progress in Hormone Research, 13.*

Richter, C. P. (1957b). On the phenomenon of sudden death in animals and men. *Psychosomatic Medicine, 19,* 191–98.

Ricks, D. F. (1974). Supershrink: Methods of a therapist judged successful on the basis of adult outcome of adolescent patients. In D. Ricks, M. Roff, & A. Thomas (Eds.), *Life history research in psychopathology* (Vol. 3). Minneapolis: University of Minnesota Press.

Rimm, D. C., & Masters, J. C. (1974). *Behavior therapy: Techniques and empirical findings.* New York: Academic Press.

Rioch, M. J. (1967). Pilot projects in training mental health counselors. In E. L. Cowen, E. A. Gardner, & M. Zax (Eds.),

Emerging approaches to mental health problems. New York: Appleton-Century-Crofts.

Risley, T., & Wolf, M. (1967). Establishing functional speech in echolalic children. *Behavior Research and Therapy, 5,* 73–88.

Rittenhouse, J. D. (1976). Selected themes of discussion. In J. D. Rittenhouse (Ed.), *The epidemiology of heroin and other narcotics.* Menlo Park, CA: Stanford Research Institute.

Ritvo, E. R., Rabin, K., Yuwiler, A., Freeman, B. J., & Geller, E. (1978). Biochemical and hematogic studies: A critical review. In M. Rutter & E. Schopler (Eds.), *Autism: A reappraisal of concepts and treatment.* New York: Plenum.

Ritz, M. C., Lamb, R. J., Goldberg, S. R., Kumar, M. J. (1987). Cocaine receptors on dopamine transporters are related to self-administration of cocaine. *Science, 237,* 1219–23.

Roberts, M., & Hanaway, J. (1970). *Atlas of the human brain in section.* Philadelphia: Lea & Febiger.

Robins, E., & Guze, S. B. (1972). Classification of affective disorders: The primary-secondary, the endogenous-reactive, and the neurotic-psychotic concepts. In T. A. Williams, M. M. Katz, & J. A. Shields (Eds.), *Recent advances in the psychobiology of the depressive illnesses* (pp. 283–93). Washington, DC: U.S. Government Printing Office.

Robins, L. N. (1966). *Deviant children grow up.* Baltimore: Williams & Wilkins.

Robins, L. N. (1985). Epidemiology: Reflections on testing the validity of psychiatric interviews. *Archives of General Psychiatry, 42,* 918–24.

Robins, L. N., & Helzer, J. E. (1986). Diagnosis and clinical assessment: The current state of psychiatric diagnosis. *Annual Review of Psychology, 37,* 409–32.

Robins, L. N., Helzer, J. E., Croughan, J., & Ratcliff, K. S. (1981). National Institute of Mental Health Diagnostic Interview Schedule. *Archives of General Psychiatry, 21,* 75–80.

Robins, L. N., Helzer, J. E., Weissman, M. M., Orvaschel, H., Gruenberg, E., Burke, J. D., & Regier, D. A. (1984). Lifetime prevalence of specific psychiatric disorders in three sites. *Archives of General Psychiatry, 41,* 949–58.

Robinson, D. S., Davis, J., Nies, A., Ravaris, C., & Sylvester, D. (1971). Relation of sex in aging to monoamine oxidase activity in human brain, plasma, and platelets. *Archives of General Psychiatry, 24,* 536.

Rodin, J., & Langer, E. J. (1977). Long-term effects of control intervention with the institutionalized patient. *Journal of Personality and Social Psychology, 12,* 897–902.

Rodnick, E. H., Goldstein, M. J., Lewis, J. M., & Doane, J. A. (1984). Parental communication style, affect, and role as precursors of offspring schizophrenia-spectrum disorders. In N. F. Watt, E. J. Anthony, L. C. Wynne, & J. E. Rolf (Eds.), *Children at risk for schizophrenia: A longitudinal perspective* (pp. 81–92). Cambridge: Cambridge University Press.

Roff, J. D., & Knight, R. (1981). Family characteristics, childhood symptoms, and adult outcomes in schizophrenia. *Journal of Abnormal Psychology, 90,* 510–20.

Rogers, C. (1951). *Client-centered therapy.* Boston: Houghton-Mifflin.

Rogers, C. R. (1959). A theory of therapy personality, and interpersonal relationships as developed in the client-centered framework. In S. Koch (Ed.), *Psychology: A study of science* (Vol. 3) (pp. 184–256). New York: McGraw-Hill.

Rogers, C. (1961). *On becoming a person.* Boston: Houghton Mifflin.

Rogers, C. (1977). *Carl Rogers on personal power.* New York: Delacorte.

Rogers, C. R., & Dymond, R. (Eds.). (1954). *Psychotherapy and personality change.* Chicago: University of Chicago Press.

Rogers, C. R., & Truax, C. B. (1967). The therapeutic conditions antecedent to change: A theoretical view. In C. R. Rogers

(Ed.), *The therapeutic relationship and its impact: A study of psychotherapy with schizophrenics.* Madison: University of Wisconsin Press.

Rogerson, H. L. (1951). Venerophobia in the male. *British Journal of Venereal Disease, 27,* 158–59.

Rohner, J. J., & Sanford, E. J. (1975). Imipramine toxicity. *Journal of Urology, 114,* 402–403.

Rooth, F. G., & Marks, I. M. (1974). Persistent exhibitionism: Short-term responses to aversion, self-regulation, and relaxation treatment. *Archives of Sexual Behavior, 3,* 227–48.

Roper, G., Rachman, S., & Marks, I. M. (1975). Passive and participant modeling in exposure treatment of obsessive compulsive neurotics. *Behavior Research and Therapy, 13,* 271–79.

Rosellini, R. A., Binik, Y. M., & Seligman, M. E. P. (1976). Sudden death in the laboratory rat. *Psychosomatic Medicine, 38,* 55–58.

Rosenberg, C. M. (1967). Personality and obsessional neurosis. *British Journal of Psychiatry, 133,* 471–77.

Rosenhan, D. L. (1969). Some origins of concern for others. In P. Mussen, J. Langer, & M. Covington (Eds.), *Trends and issues in developmental psychology* (pp. 132–53). New York: Holt, Rinehart & Winston.

Rosenhan, D. L. (1970). The natural socialization of altruistic social autonomy. In J. Macaulay & L. Berkowitz (Eds.), *Altruism and helping behavior* (pp. 251–68). New York: Academic Press.

Rosenhan, D. L. (1973). On being sane in insane places. *Science, 179,* 250–58.

Rosenhan, D. L. (1975). The contextual nature of psychiatric diagnosis. *Journal of Abnormal Psychology, 84,* 462–74.

Rosenhan, D. L. (1983). Psychological abnormality and law. In C. J. Scheirer & B. L. Hammonds (Eds.), *Psychology and the law* (pp. 89–118). Washington, DC: American Psychological Association.

Rosenman, R. H., Brand, R. J., Jenkins, C. D., Friedman, M., Straus, R., & Wurm, M. (1975). Coronary heart disease in the western collaborative group study: Final follow-up experience at 8½ years. *Journal of the American Medical Association, 233,* 872–77.

Rosenthal, D. (1970a). Genetic research in the schizophrenic syndrome. In R. Cancro (Ed.), *The schizophrenic reactions* (pp. 245–58). New York: Brunner/Mazel.

Rosenthal, D. (1970b). *Genetic theory and abnormal behavior.* New York: McGraw-Hill.

Rosenthal, D. (1974). Issues in high risk studies of schizophrenia. In D. F. Ricks, A. Thomas, & M. Roff (Eds.), *Life history research in psychopathology* (Vol. 3) (pp. 25–41). Minneapolis: University of Minnesota Press.

Rosenthal, D. (1979). Was Thomas Wolfe a borderline? *Schizophrenia Bulletin, 5,* 87–94.

Rosenthal, D., Lawlor, W. G., Zahn, T. P., & Shakow, D. (1960). The relationship of some aspects of mental set to degree of schizophrenic disorganization. *Journal of Personality, 28,* 26–38.

Rosenthal, N. E., Carpenter, C. J., James, S. P., Parry, B. L., Rogers, S. L. B., & Wehr, T. A. (1986). Seasonal affective disorder in children and adolescents. *American Journal of Psychiatry, 143,* 356–86.

Rosenthal, N. E., Sack, D. A., Gillin, J. C., Lewy, A. J., Goodwin, F. K., Davenport, Y., Mueller, P. S., Newsome, D. A., & Wehr, T. A. (1984). Seasonal affective disorder: A description of the syndrome and preliminary findings with light therapy. *Archives of General Psychiatry, 41,* 72–80.

Rosenthal, P. A., & Rosenthal, S. (1984). Suicidal behavior by preschool children. *American Journal of Psychiatry, 141,* 520–25.

Rosenthal, T. L., & Bandura, A. (1979). Psychological modeling: Theory and practice. In A. Bergin & S. Garfield (Eds.), *Hand-*

book of psychotherapy and behavior change. New York: Wiley.

Rosenzweig, S. P., & Forman, R. (1974). Patient and therapist variables affecting premature termination in group psychotherapy. *Psychotherapy: Theory, research and practice, 11,* 76–79.

Rosman, B., Minuchin, S., Liebman, R., & Baker, Y. (1976). Input and outcome of family therapy in anorexia nervosa. In J. L. Claghorn (Ed.), *Successful therapy.* New York: Brunner/Mazel.

Ross, E. D. (1981). The aprosodias: Functional-anatomic organization of the affective components of language in the right hemisphere. *Archives of Neurology, 38,* 561–69.

Ross, E. D. (1983). Right-hemisphere lesions in disorders of affective language. In A. Kertesz, *Localization in neuropsychology.* New York: Academic Press.

Ross, J. D., & Wirt, R. D. (1984). Childhood aggression and social adjustment as antecedents of delinquency. *Journal of Abnormal Child Psychology, 12*(1), 111–26.

Ross, L. (1977). The intuitive psychologist and his shortcomings: Distortions in the attribution process. In L. Berkowitz (Ed.), *Advances in experimental social psychology* (Vol. 10). New York: Academic Press.

Ross, L., Greene, D., & House, P. (1977). The false consensus phenomenon: An attributional bias in self perception and social perception processes. *Journal of Experimental Social Psychology, 13,* 279–301.

Rothaus, P., Hanson, P. G., Cleveland, S. E., & Johnson, D. L. (1963). Describing psychiatric hospitalization: A dilemma. *American Psychologist, 18,* 85–89.

Rothbaum, F., Weisz, J. R., & Snyder, S. S. (1982). Changing the world and changing the self: A two-process model of perceived control. *Journal of Personality and Social Psychology, 42,* 5–37.

Rothblum, E. D., Solomon, L. J., & Albee, G. W. (1986). A sociopolitical perspective of DSM-III. In T. Millon & G. L. Klerman (Ed.), *Contemporary direction in psychopathology: Toward the DSM-IV* (pp. 167–89). New York: Guilford Press.

Rothman, D. (1971). *The discovery of the asylum.* New York: Harper & Row.

Rotter, J. (1954). *Social learning and clinical psychology.* Englewood Cliffs, NJ: Prentice-Hall.

Rotter, J. B. (1966). Generalized expectancies for internal versus external control of reinforcement. *Psychological Monographs, 80*(1).

Rotter, J. B., Chance, J. E., & Phares, E. J. (1972). *Applications of a social learning theory of personality.* New York: Holt, Rinehart & Winston.

Roy, E. A. (1982). Action and performance. In A. Ellis (Ed.), *Normality and pathology in cognitive function* (pp. 265–98). London: Academic Press.

Roy-Byrne, P. P., Geraci, M., & Uhde T. W. (1986). Life events and the onset of panic disorder. *American Journal of Psychiatry, 143,* 1424–27.

Rozin, P. (1976). The psychobiological approach to human memory. In M. R. Rosenzweig & E. L. Bennett (Eds.), *Neural mechanisms of learning and memory* (pp. 3–46). Cambridge, MA: MIT Press.

Rozin, P. (1978). *Personal communication.* Based on data collected in the introductory course of psychology at the University of Pennsylvania.

Rozin, P. (1981). *Personal communication.* Based on data collected in the introductory course of psychology at the University of Pennsylvania.

Rozin, P., & Gleitman, L. R., (1977). The structure and acquisition of reading: II. The reading process and the acquisition of the alphabetic principle. In A. S. Reber & D. Scarborough (Eds.), *Toward a psychology of reading* (pp. 55–141). Potomac, MD: Erlbaum.

Rozin, P., & Kalat, J. (1971). Specific hungers and poison avoidance as adaptive specializations of learning. *Psychological Review, 78,* 459–86.

Rush, H. A., Beck, A. T., Kovacs, M., & Hollon, S. (1977). Comparative efficacy of cognitive therapy and pharmacotherapy in the treatment of depressed outpatients. *Cognitive Research and Therapy, 1,* 17–37.

Ruskin, A., Beard, O. W., & Schaffer, R. L. (1948). "Last hypertension": Elevated arterial pressure in victims of the Texas City disaster. *American Journal of Medicine, 4,* 228.

Russell, M. (1977). Smoking problems: An overview. In M. Jarvik, J. Cullen, E. Gritz, T. Vogt, & L. West (Eds.), *Research on smoking behavior.* (NIDA Research Monograph No. 17). Rockville, MD: National Institute on Drug Abuse.

Russell, W. R. (1959). *Brain, memory, learning: A neurologist's view.* Oxford, England: Oxford University Press.

Rutter, M. (1968). Concepts of autism: A review of research. *Journal of Child Psychology and Psychiatry, 9,* 1–25.

Rutter, M. (1975). *Helping troubled children.* New York: Plenum.

Rutter, M. (1978). Prevalence and types of dyslexia. In A. L. Benton & D. Pearl, *Dyslexia: An appraisal of current knowledge.* New York: Oxford University Press.

Rutter, M., & Garmezy, N. (1983). Developmental psychopathology. In P. H. Mussen (Ed.), *Handbook of child psychology, Vol. 4: Socialization, personality, and social development.* New York: Wiley.

Saccuzzo, D. P., & Braff, D. L. (1986). Information processing abnormalities: Trait- and state-dependent components. *Schizophrenia Bulletin, 12* (3), 447–59.

Sackheim, H. A., Greenberg, M. S., Weiman, A. L., Gur, R. C., Hunger-Buhler, J. P., & Geschwind, N. (1982). Hemispheric asymmetry in the expression of positive and negative emotions: Neurological evidence. *Archives of Neurology, 39,* 210–18.

Sackeim, H. A., Nordlie, J. W., & Gur R. C. (1979). A model of hysterical and hypnotic blindness: Cognitions, motivation and awareness. *Journal of Abnormal Psychology, 88,* 474–89.

Safer, D. J., & Allen, R. P. (1976). *Hyperactive children: Diagnosis and management.* Baltimore: University Park Press.

St. George-Hyslop, et al., (1987). The genetic defect causing familiar Alzheimer's disease maps on chromosome 21. *Science, 235,* 885–90.

Sakai, T. (1967). Clinico-genetic study on obsessive compulsive neurosis. *Bulletin of Osaka Medical School,* Supplement XII, 323–31.

Salzman, L., & Thaler, F. (1981). Obsessive-compulsive disorders: A review of the literature. *American Journal of Psychiatry, 138,* 286–96.

Sanchez-Craig, M., Annis, H. M., Bornet, A. R., & MacDonald, K. R. (1984). Random assignment to abstinence and controlled drinking: Evaluation of a cognitive-behavior program for problem drinkers. *Journal of Clinical and Consulting Psychology, 52,* 390–403.

Sandler, J., & Hazari, A. (1960). The "obsessional": On the psychological classification of obsessional character traits and symptoms. *British Journal of Medical Psychology, 33,* 113–22.

Sank, L. I. (1979). Community disasters: Primary prevention and treatment in a health maintenance organization. *American Psychologist, 34,* 334–38.

Sank, L. (1982, February). Personal communication.

Sarason, S. B. (1974). *The psychological sense of community: Prospects for a community psychology.* San Francisco: Jossey-Bass.

Sartorius, N., Jablensky, A., Korten, A., Ernberg, G., Anker, M., Coaper, J. E., & Day, R. (1986). Early manifestations and first-contact incidence of schizophrenia in different cultures. *Psychological Medicine, 16,* 909–28.

Sasanuma, S., & Fujimura, O. (1971). Selective impairment of phonetic nonphonetic transcription of words in Japanese aphasic patients: Kana versus Kanji in visual recognition and writing. *Cortex, 7,* 1–18.

Sawrey, W. L., Conger, J. J., & Turrell, E. S. (1956). An experimental investigation of the role of psychological factors in the production of gastric ulcers in rats. *Journal of Comparative and Physiological Psychology, 49,* 457–61.

Sawrey, W. L., & Weiss, J. D. (1956). An experimental method of producing gastric ulcers. *Journal of Comparative and Physiological Psychology, 49,* 269.

Scarr, S. (1975). Genetics and the development of intelligence. In F. D. Horowitz (Ed.), *Child development research* (Vol. 4). Chicago: University of Chicago Press.

Schacter, D. L. (1987). Implicit memory: History and current status. *Journal of Experimental Psychology: Learning, Memory and Cognition, 13,* 501–18.

Schacter, S., Kozlowski, L. T., & Silverstein, B. (1977). Effects of urinary pH on cigarette smoking. *Journal of Experimental Psychology: General, 106,* 13–19.

Schachter, S., & Latane, B. T. (1964). Crime, cognition, and the autonomic nervous system. In D. Levine (Ed.), *Nebraska Symposium on Motivation.* Lincoln: University of Nebraska Press.

Schachter, S., & Rodin, J. (Eds.). (1974). *Obese humans and rats.* Washington, DC: Erlbaum.

Schachter, S., Silverstein, B., Kozlowski, L. T., Perlick, D., Herman, C. P., & Liebling, B. (1977). Studies of the interaction of psychological and pharmacological determinants of smoking. *Journal of Experimental Psychology—General, 106,* 3–40.

Schachter, S., & Singer, J. E. (1962). Cognitive, social and physiological determinants of emotional state. *Psychological Review, 69,* 379–99.

Schaefer, H., & Martin, P. (1977). *Behavioral therapy* (2nd ed.). New York: McGraw-Hill.

Scheff, T. J. (1966). *Being mentally ill: A sociologial theory.* Chicago: Aldine.

Scher, M. (1975). Verbal activity, sex counselor experience and success in counseling. *Journal of Counseling Psychology, 22,* 97–101.

Schiavi, R. C., et al. (1984). Pituitary-gonadal function during sleep in men with erectile impotence and normal controls. *Psychosomatic Medicine, 46* (3), 239–54.

Schildkraut, J. J. (1965). The catecholamine hypothesis of affective disorders: A review of supporting evidence. *American Journal of Psychiatry, 122,* 509–22.

Schildkraut, J. J., & Kety, S. S. (1967). Biogenic amines and emotion. *Science, 156,* 21–30.

Schlesier-Stropp, B. (1984). Bulimia: A review of the literature. *Psychological Bulletin, 95,* 247–57.

Schlichting, U. U., Goldberg, S. R., Wuttke, W., & Hoffmeister, F. (1970). D-amphetamine self-administration by Rhesus monkeys with different self-administration histories. *Proceedings of the European Society for the Study of Drug Toxicity, 220,* 62–69.

Schmale A., & Iker, H. (1966). The psychological setting of uterine cervical cancer. *Annals of the N.Y. Academy of Sciences, 125,* 807–13.

Schmauk, F. J. (1970). Punishment, arousal, and avoidance learning in sociopaths. *Journal of Abnormal Psychology, 76,* 443–53.

Schneider, R. A., & Zangori, V. N. (1951). Variations in clotting time, relative viscosity and other physiochemical properties of the blood accompanying physical and emotional stress in the normotensive and hypertensive subject. *Psychosomatic Medicine, 13,* 289–303.

Schreiber, F. R. (1974). *Sybil.* New York: Warner Books.

Schreibman, L. (1975). Effects of within-stimulus and extra-stimulus prompting on discrimination learning in autistic children. *Journal of Applied Behavioral Analysis, 8,* 91–112.

Schuckit, M. A. (1987). Biological vulnerability to alcoholism. *Journal of Consulting and Clinical Psychology, 55,* 301–309.

Schulsinger, F. (1972). Psychopathy, heredity and environment. *International Journal of Mental Health, 1,* 190–206.

Schulterbrand, J. G., & Raven, A. (Eds.). (1977). *Depression in childhood: Diagnosis, treatment, and conceptual models.* New York: Raven Press.

Schuyler, D. (1974). The evaluation of the suicidal patient. In J. R. Novello (Ed.), *Practical handbook of psychiatry.* Springfield, IL: Charles C. Thomas.

Schuyler, D., & Katz, M. M. (1973). The depressive illnesses: A major public health problem. Washington, DC: U.S. Government Printing Office.

Schwab, J. J., Bialow, M., Holzer, C. E., Brown, J. M., & Stevenson, B. E. (1967). Socio-cultural aspects of depression in medical inpatients. *Archives of General Psychiatry, 17,* 533–43.

Schwartz, B. (1983). *Psychology of learning and behavior* (2nd ed.). New York: Norton.

Schwartz, G. E. (1973). Biofeedback as therapy. Some theoretical and practical issues. *American Psychologist, 29,* 633–73.

Schwartz, G., & Weiss, S. M. (1977). What is behavioral medicine? *Psychosomatic Medicine, 39,* 377–81.

Schwartz, M. F., Baron, J., & Moscovitch, M. (1989). Symptomatology of Alzheimer-type dementia: Report on a survey-by-mail. In M. Schwartz (Ed.), *degenerative dementia and the neuro-cognitive modules of mind.* Cambridge, MA: MIT/Bradford Press.

Schwartz, M. F., & Masters, W. H. (1984). The Masters and Johnson treatment program for dissatisfied homosexual men. *American Journal of Psychiatry, 141* (2), 173–81.

Schwartz, M. F., Saffran, E. M., & Marin, O.S.M. (1980). The word order problem agrammatism: I. Comprehension. *Brain and Language, 10,* 249–62.

Schwartz, S., & Johnson J. H. (1985). *Psychopathology of childhood: A clinical-experimental approach.* New York: Pergamon.

Scott, R. A. (1985). *Rational uses of irrationality: Insanity as a resource for coping in total institutions.* Unpublished manuscript.

Scovern, A. W., & Killman, P. R. (1980). Status of electroconvulsive therapy: Review of the outcome literature. *Psychological Bulletin, 87,* 260–303.

Scoville, W. B., & Milner, B. (1957). Loss of recent memory after bilateral hippocampal lesions. *Journal of Neurology, Neurosurgery and Psychiatry, 20,* 11–21.

Scull, A. (1981). Moral treatment reconsidered: Some sociological comments on an episode in the history of British psychiatry. In A. Scull (Ed.), *Madhouses, mad-doctors and madmen: The social history of psychiatry in the Victorian era* (pp. 105–18). Philadelphia: University of Pennsylvania Press.

Searles, H. F. (1959). The effort to drive the other person crazy! An element in the aetiology and psychotherapy of schizophrenia. *British Journal of Medical Psychology, 32,* 1–18.

Searles, J. (1988). The role of genetics in the pathogenesis of alcoholism. *Journal of Abnormal Psychology, 97,* 153–67.

Sears, R. R. (1936). Experimental studies of projection: I. Attribution of traits. *Journal of Social Psychology, 7,* 151–63.

Secunda, S., Katz, M. M., & Friedman, R. (1973). "The depressive disorders in 1973." National Institute of Mental Health. Washington, DC: U.S. Government Printing Office.

Seeman, P., Lee, T., Chau-Wong, M., & Wong, K. (1976). Antipsychotic drug doses and neuroleptic/dopamine receptors. *Nature, 261,* 717–19.

Segal, J. (1968). Finding the right therapy for you. *Cosmopolitan, 304,* 262–77.

Seligman, M. E. P. (1968). Chronic fear produced by unpredictable shock. *Journal of Comparative and Physiological Psychology, 66,* 402–11.

Seligman, M. E. P. (1970). On the generality of the laws of learning. *Psychological Review, 77,* 406–18.

Seligman, M. E. P. (1975). *Helplessness: On depression, development, and death.* San Francisco: Freeman.

Seligman, M. E. P. (1978). Comment and integration. *Journal of Abnormal Psychology, 87,* 165–79.

Seligman, M. E. P. (1980). Harris on selected misrepresentation: The selected misrepresentation of Seligman. *American Psychologist, 35,* 214–15.

Seligman, M. E. P., Abramson, L. Y., Semmel, A., & von Baeyer, C. (1979). Depressive attributional style. *Journal of Abnormal Psychology, 88,* 242–47.

Seligman, M. E. P., & Binik, Y. M. (1977). The safety signal hypothesis. In H. Davis & H. Hurwitz (Eds.), *Pavlovian operant interactions.* Hillsdale, NJ: Erlbaum.

Seligman, M. E. P., & Hager, J. (Eds.). (1972). *Biological boundaries of learning.* New York: Appleton-Century-Crofts.

Seligman, M. E. P., & Johnston, J. C. (1973). A cognitive theory of avoidance learning. In F. J. McGuigan, & D. B. Lumsden (Eds.), *Contemporary approaches to conditioning and learning.* Washington, DC: Winston.

Seligman, M. E. P., & Maier, S. F. (1967). Failure to escape traumatic shock. *Journal of Experimental Psychology, 74,* 1–9.

Selye, H. (1956). *The stress of life.* New York: McGraw-Hill.

Selye, H. (1975). Confusion and controversy in the stress field. *Journal of Human Stress, 1,* 37–44.

Semans, J. H. (1956). Premature ejaculation: A new approach. *Southern Medical Journal, 49,* 353–58.

Senay, E. C., & Renault, P. F. (1972). Treatment methods for heroin addicts. In D. E. Smith & G. R. Gay (Eds.), *It's so good, don't even try it once.* Englewood Cliffs, NJ: Prentice-Hall.

Serling, R. J. (1986). Curing a fear of flying. *USAIR,* 12–19.

Shaffer, D. (1976). Enuresis. In M. Rutter & L. Hersov (Eds.), *Child psychiatry: Modern approaches.* Oxford: Blackwell.

Shah, D. R., Pandey, S. K., & Rathi, R. (1972). Psychiatric manifestation in pellagra. *Journal of Association of Physicians of India, 20,* 573–78.

Shapiro, A. K., Struening, E., Shapiro, E., & Barten, H. (1976). Prognostic correlates of psychotherapy in psychiatric outpatients. *American Journal of Psychiatry, 133,* 802–808.

Shapiro, D. (1965). *Neurotic styles.* New York: Basic Books.

Shapiro, D. A., & Shapiro, D. (1982). Meta-analysis of comparative therapy outcome studies: A replication and refinement. *Psychological Bulletin, 92,* 581–604.

Shapiro, D. A., & Shapiro, D. (1983). Comparative therapy outcome research: Methodological implications of meta-analysis. *Journal of Consulting and Clinical Psychology, 51,* 42–53.

Shapiro, R. J. (1974). Therapist attitudes and premature termination in family and individual therapy. *Journal of Nervous and Mental Diseases, 159,* 101–107.

Shavit, Y., & Martin, F. C. (1987). Opiates, stress, and immunity: Animal studies. *Annals of Behavioral Medicine, 9,* 11–15.

Sheehan, D. V. (1984). Delineation of anxiety and phobic disorders responsive to monoamine oxidase inhibitors: Implications for classification. *Journal of Clinical Psychiatry, 45* (7), 29–36.

Sheehan, D. V. (1985). Monoamine oxidase inhibitors and alprazolam in the treatment of panic disorder and agoraphobia. *Psychiatric Clinics of North America, 8* (1), 49–82.

Shekelle, R. B., Gale, M., Ostfeld, A. M., & Paul, O. (1983). Hostility, risk of coronary heart disease, and mortality. *Psychosomatic Medicine, 45* (2) 109–14.

Shekelle, R. B., Hulley, S. B., & Neaton, J. D., et al. (1985). The MRFIT behavior study. Type A behavior and incidence of coronary heart disease. *American Journal of Epidemiology, 122,* 559–70.

Sher, K. J., Mann, B., & Frost, R. O. (1984). Cognitive dysfunction in compulsive checkers: Further explorations. *Behavior Research and Therapy, 22,* 493–502.

Sherer, M. A., Kumor, K. M., Cone, E. J., & Jaffe, J. (1988). Suspiciousness induced by four-hour intravenous infusions of cocaine: Preliminary findings. *Archives of General Psychiatry, 45,* 673–77.

Sherman, A. D., & Petty, F. (1980). Neurochemical basis of the action of antidepressants on learned helplessness. *Behavioral and Neurological Biology, 30,* 119–34.

Sherman, A. D., & Petty, F. (1982). Additivity of neurochemical changes in learned helplessness and imipramine. *Behavioral and Neurological Biology, 35* (4), 344–53.

Shields, J. (1972). *Monozygotic twins brought up apart and brought up together.* Oxford: Oxford University Press.

Shneidman, E. (1976). *Suicidology: Contemporary developments.* New York: Grune & Stratton.

Shoham-Salomon, V., & Rosenthal, R. (1987). Paradoxical interventions: A meta-analysis. *Journal of Consulting and Clinical Psychology, 55* (1), 22–28.

Shore, J. E., Tatum, E. L., & Vollmer, W. M. (1986). Psychiatric reaction to disaster: The Mount St. Helens experience. *American Journal of Psychiatry, 143* (5), 590–95.

Siegel, D., & Wissler, T. (1986). Family environment as a predictor of psychiatric rehospitalization. *American Journal of Psychiatry, 143*(1), 56–60.

Siegel, S. (1977). Morphine tolerance as an associative process. *Journal of Experimental Psychology: Animal Behavior Processes, 3,* 1–13.

Siegal, S. (1979). The role of conditioning in drug tolerance and addiction. In J. D. Keehn (Ed.), *Psychopathology in animals: Research and treatment implications.* New York: Academic Press.

Sifneos, P. E. (1973). The prevalence of "alexithymic" characteristics in psychosomatic patients. *Psychotherapy and Psychosomatics, 22,* 255–62.

Sigvardsson, S., Cloninger, C. R., Bohman, M., & von Knorring, A. L. (1982). Predisposition to petty criminality in Swedish adoptees. III: Sex differences and validation of the male typology. *Archives of General Psychiatry, 39,* 1248–53.

Silverman, J. (1964). The problem of attention in research and theory in schizophrenia. *Psychological Review, 71,* 352–79.

Silverman, L. H. (1976). Psychoanalytic theory: The reports of my death are greatly exaggerated. *American Psychologist, 31*(9), 621–37.

Silverstone, J. T., & Salkind, M. R. (1973). Controlled evaluation of intravenous drugs in the specific desensitization of phobias. *Canadian Psychiatric Association Journal, 18*(1), 848–50.

Simons, A. D., Murphy, G. E., Levine, J. L., & Wetzel, R. D. (1986). Cognitive therapy and pharmacotherapy for depression: Sustained improvement over one year. *Archives of General Psychiatry, 43,* 43–48.

Simpson, D. D., Savage, L. J., & Sells, S. B. (1978). *Data book on drug treatment outcomes.* Fort Worth: Institute of Behavioral Research.

Sinclair, J. D. (1974). Morphine suppresses alcohol drinking regardless of prior alcohol access duration. *Pharmacology, Biochemistry, and Behavior, 2,* 409–12.

Skinner, B. F. (1971). *Beyond freedom and dignity.* New York: Knopf.

Sklar, L. S., & Anisman, H. (1979). Stress and coping factors influence tumor growth. *Science, 205,* 513–15.

Sladek, J. K., Jr., & Shoulson, I. (1988). Neural transplantation: A call for patience rather than patients. *Science, 240,* 1386–88.

Sloane, R. B., Cristol, A. H., Pepernik, M. C., & Staples, F. R. (1970). Role preparation and expectation of improvement in psychotherapy. *Journal of Nervous and Mental Diseases, 150,* 18–26.

Sloane, R. B., Staples, F. R., Cristol, A. H., Yorkston, N. J., & Whipple, K. (1975). *Psychoanalysis versus behavior therapy.* Cambridge: Harvard University Press.

Smith, D. S., Collins, M., Kreisberg, J. P., Volpicelli, J. R., & Alterman, A. I. (1987). Screening for problem drinking in college freshman. *Journal of American College Health, 36,* 89–94.

Smith, J. C., Glass, G. V., & Miller, T. I. (1980). *The benefits of psychotherapy.* Baltimore: The Johns Hopkins Press.

Smith, M. L., & Glass, G. V. (1977). Meta-analysis of psychotherapy outcome studies. *American Psychologist, 32,* 752–60.

Smith, R. E., Sarason, I. G., & Sarason, B. R. (1982). *Psychology: The frontiers of behavior.* New York: Harper & Row.

Smith, R. J. (1978). *The psychopath in society.* New York: Academic Press.

Snyder, S. H. (1974a). Catecholamines as mediators of drug effects in schizophrenia. In F. O. Schmitt & F. G. Worden (Eds.), *The neurosciences: Third study program.* Cambridge, MA: MIT Press.

Snyder, S. H. (1974b). *Madness and the brain.* New York: McGraw-Hill.

Snyder, S. H. (1977). Opiate receptors and internal opiates. *Scientific American, 236,* 44–56.

Snyder, S. H. (1981). Dopamine receptors, neuroleptics and schizophrenia. *American Journal of Psychiatry, 138,* 460–64.

Snyder, S. H., Banerjee, S. P., Yamamura, H. I., & Greenberg, D. (1974). Neurotransmitters and schizophrenia. *Science, 184,* 1243–53.

Snyder, W. D., Simpson, D. M., Nielson, S., et. al., (1983). Neurological complications of Acquired Immune Deficiency Syndrome: Analysis of 50 patients. *Annals of Neurology, 14,* 403–18.

Sohlberg, S. C., & Yaniv, S. (1985). Social adjustment and cognitive performance of high-risk children. *Schizophrenia Bulletin, 11,* 61–64.

Solomon, R. L. (1977). An opponent process theory of acquired motivation: The affective dynamics of addiction. In J. Maser & M. Seligman (Eds.), *Psychopathology: Experimental models.* San Francisco: Freeman.

Solomon, R. L., & Corbit, J. D. (1974). An opponent process theory of motivation. *Psychological Reviews, 81*(2), 119–45.

Solomon, R. L., Kamin, L. J., & Wynne, L. C. (1953). Traumatic avoidance learning: The outcomes of several extinction procedures with dogs. *Journal of Abnormal Social Psychology, 48,* 291–302.

Sontag, S. (1978). Disease as political metaphor. *New York Review of Books, 25,* 33.

Southard, D. R., Coates, T. J., Kolodner, K., Parker, F. C., Padgett, N. E., & Kennedy, H. L. (1986). Relationship between mood and blood pressure in the natural environment: An adolescent population. *Health Psychology, 5,* 469–80.

Spanos, N. P., Weekes, J. R., & Bertrand, L. D. (1985). Multiple personality: A social psychological perspective. *Journal of Abnormal Psychology, 94,* 362–76.

Spark, R. F., White, R. A., & Connelly, P. B. (1980). Impotence is not always psychogenic. *Journal of the American Medical Association, 243,* 750–55.

Sperry, R. W. (1974). Lateral specialization in the surgically separated hemispheres. In F. O. Schmitt & F. G. Worden (Eds.), *The neurosciences: Third study program.* Cambridge, MA: MIT Press.

Spielberger, C. D., Gorsuch, R. C., & Lushene, R. E. (1970). *Manual for the state-trait anxiety inventory.* Palo Alto, CA: Consulting Psychologists Press.

Spiegel, D. (1984). Multiple personality as a post-traumatic stress disorder. *Psychiatric Clinics of North America, 7,* 101–10.

Spies, T. D., Aring, C. D., Gelperin, J., & Bean, W. B. (1938). The mental symptoms of pellagra. Their relief with nicotinic acid. *American Journal of the Medical Sciences, 196,* 461–75.

Spitz, R. A. (1946). Anaclitic depression. *The Psychoanalytic Study of the Child, 2,* 313–47.

Spitzer, R., Forman, J., & Nee, J. (1979). DSM-III field trials: I. Initial inter-rater diagnostic reliability. *American Journal of Psychiatry, 136,* 815–17.

Spitzer, R. L. (1975). On pseudoscience in science, logic in remission and psychiatric diagnosis: A critique of Rosenhan's "On being sane in insane places." *Journal of Abnormal Psychology, 84,* 442–52.

Spitzer, R. L., & Endicott, J. (1969). Diagno II: Further developments in a computer program for psychiatric diagnosis. *American Journal of Psychiatry, 125,* 12–21.

Spitzer, R. L., Endicott, J., Robins, E., Kuriansky, J., & Gurland, B. (1975). Preliminary report of the reliability of research diagnostic criteria applied to psychiatric case records. In A. Sudilofsky, B. Beer, & S. Gershon (Eds.), *Prediction in psychopharmacology.* New York: Raven Press.

Spitzer, R. L., & Fleiss, J. L. (1974). A reanalysis of the reliability of psychiatric diagnosis. *British Journal of Psychiatry, 125,* 341–47.

Spitzer, R. L., Skodol, A. E., Gibbon, M., & Williams, J. B. W. (1981). *DSM–III casebook.* Washington, DC: American Psychiatric Association.

Spitzer, R. L., & Wilson, P. T. (1975). Nosology and the official psychiatric nomenclature. In A. Freedman & H. Kaplan (Eds.), *Comprehensive textbook of psychiatry.* New York: Williams & Wilkins.

Sprague, R. L., & Berger, B. D. (1980). Drug effects on learning performance: Relevance of animal research to pediatric psychopharmacology. In R. M. Knights & D. J. Bakker (Eds.), *Treatment of hyperactive and learning disabled children.* Baltimore: University Park Press.

Sprague, R., & Sleator, E. (1973). Effects of psychopharmacologic agents on learning disorders. *Pediatrics Clinicians of North America, 20,* 719–35.

Squire, L. R. (1982). The neuropsychology of memory. *Annual Review of Neuroscience, 5,* 241–73.

Squire, L. R. (1986). Memory functions as affected by electroconvulsive therapy. *Annals of the New York Academy of Sciences, 462,* 307–14.

Squire, L. R., (1987). *Memory and brain.* New York: Oxford University Press.

Squire, L. R., Cohen, N. J., & Nadel, L. (1984). The medial temporal region and memory consolidation: A new hypothesis. In H. Weingarten & E. Parker (Eds.), *Memory consolidation: Towards a psychobiology of cognition* (pp. 185–210). Hillsdale, NJ: Erlbaum.

Squire, L. R., Slater, P. C., & Miller, P. L. (1981). Retrograde amnesia and bilateral electroconvulsive therapy: Long-term follow-up. *Archives of General Psychiatry, 38,* 89–95.

Squire, L. R., & Zouzounis, J. A. (1986). ECT and memory: Brief pulse versus sine wave. *American Journal of Psychiatry, 143,* 596–601.

Srole, L., Langner, T. S., Michael, S. T., Opler, M. K., & Rennie T. A. (1962). *Mental health in the metropolis: The midtown Manhattan study.* New York: McGraw-Hill.

Staats, A. W. (1978). *Child learning intelligence and personality* (rev. ed.). Kalamazoo, MI: Behaviordela.

Stall, R., McKukusick, L., Wiley, J., Coates, T. J., & Ostrow, G. G.

(1986). Alcohol and drug use during sexual activity and compliance with safe sex guidelines for AIDS: The AIDS Behavioral Research Project. *Health Education Quarterly, 13,* 359–71.

Stampfl, T. G. (1967). Implosive therapy. In S. G. Armitage (Ed.), *Behavior modification techniques in the treatment of emotional disorders.* Battle Creek, MI.: V.A. Publication.

Stampfl, T. G., & Levis, D. J. (1967). Essentials of implosive therapy: A learning-theory-based psychodynamic behavioral therapy. *Journal of Abnormal Psychology, 72,* 496–503.

Stangl, D., Pfohl, B., Zimmerman, M., Bowers, W., & Corenthal, R, (1985). A structured interview for the DSM–III personality disorders: A preliminary report. *Archives of General Psychiatry, 42,* 591–96.

Stark, O., Atkins, E., Wolff, O. H., & Douglas, J. W. B. (1981). Longitudinal study of obesity in the National Survey of Health and Development. *British Medical Journal, 283,* 13–17.

Steadman, H. J. (1973). Follow-up on Baxtrom patients returned to hospitals for the criminally insane. *American Journal of Psychiatry, 3,* 317–19.

Steadman, H. J. (1981). The statistical prediction of violent behavior: Measuring the costs of a public protectionist versus a civil libertarian model. *Law and Human Behavior, 5,* 263–74.

Steadman, H. J. (1983). Predicting dangerousness among the mentally ill: Art, magic, and science. *International Journal of Law and Psychiatry, 6,* 381–90.

Steadman, H. J., & Keveles, G. (1972). The community adjustment and criminal activity of the Baxtrom patients: 1966–1970. *American Journal of Psychiatry, 129,* 304–10.

Steadman, H., & Keveles, C. (1978). The community adjustment and criminal activity of Baxtrom patients. *American Journal of Psychiatry, 135,* 1218–20.

Stein, L. (1968). Chemistry of reward and punishment. In D. Efron (Ed.), *Psychopharmacology: Review of progress, 1957–1967* (pp. 105–23). Washington, DC: U.S. Government Printing Office.

Stein, L. I., Test, M. A., & Marx, A. J. (1975). Alternative to the hospital: A controlled study. *American Journal of Psychiatry, 132,* 517–21.

Steinberg, L. (1986). Stability and instability of Type A behavior from childhood to young adulthood. *Developmental Psychology, 22,* 393–401.

Steinhausen, H. C., Göbel, D., Breinlinger, M., & Wohlleben, B. (1986). A community survey of infantile autism. *Journal of the American Academy of Child Psychiatry, 25,* 186–89.

Steinmark, W. W., & Borkevic, T. D. (1974). Active and placebo treatment effects on moderate insomnia under counter-demand and positive demand instructions. *Journal of Abnormal Psychology, 83,* 157–63.

Steketee, G.,Foa, E. B., & Grayson, J. B. (1982). Recent advances in the behavioral treatment of obsessive-compulsives. *Archives of General Psychiatry, 39,* 1365–71.

Stern, D. (1985). *The interpersonal world of the infant.* New York: Basic Books.

Stern, J. (1981). Brain dysfunction in some hereditary disorders of amino acid metabolism. In P. J. Mittler, & J. M. deJong (Eds.), *Frontiers of knowledge in mental retardation: Vol II. Biomedical aspects.* Baltimore, MD: University Park Press.

Stinnett, J. (1978). Personal communication.

Stoller, R. J. (1969). Parental influences in male transsexualism. In R. Green & J. Money (Eds.), *Transsexualism and sex reassignment.* Baltimore: The Johns Hopkins Press.

Stoller, R. J. (1976). *Sexual gender—the transsexual experiment* (Vol. II). New York: Jason Aronson.

Stone, A. A. (1975). *Mental health and law: A system in transition.* Rockville, MD.: National Institute of Mental Health, Center for Studies of Crime and Delinquency.

Stone, G. C., Weiss, S. M., Matarazzo, J. D., Miller, N. E., Rodin, J., Belar, C. K., Fullick, M., & Singer, J. E. (Eds.). (1987). *Health Psychology: A discipline and a profession.* Chicago: University of Chicago Press.

Storms, M. D. (1981). A theory of erotic orientation development. *Psychological Review, 88,* 340–53.

Strauss, J., & Ryan, R. M. (1987). Autonomy disturbances in subtypes of anorexia nervosa. *Journal of Abnormal Psychology, 96,* 254–58.

Strauss, M. E., Foureman, W. C., & Parwatikar, S. D. (1974). Schizophrenics' size estimations of thematic stimuli. *Journal of Abnormal Psychology, 83*(2), 117–23.

Strupp, H. H. (1963). The outcome problem in psychotherapy revisited. *Psychotherapy. Theory, Research and Practice, 1,* 1–13.

Strupp, H. H., & Bloxom, A. (1973). Preparing lower-class patients for group psychotherapy: Development and evaluation of a role induction film. *Journal of Consulting and Clinical Psychology, 41,* 373–84.

Strupp, H. H., Fox, R., & Lessler, K. (1969). *Patients view their psychotherapy.* Baltimore: The Johns Hopkins Press.

Strupp, H. H., Hadley, S. W., & Gomes-Schwartz, B. (1977). *Psychotherapy for better or worse: An analysis of the problem of negative effects.* New York: Jason Aronson.

Strupp, H. H., Wallach, M., & Wogan, M. (1964). Psychotherapy experience in retrospect: Questionnaire survey of former patients and their therapists. *Psychological Monographs, 78* (11, Whole No. 588).

Stuart, R. B. (1969). Operant-interpersonal treatment for marital discord. *Journal of Consulting and Clinical Psychology, 33,* 675–82.

Stuart, R. B. (1980). *Helping couples change: A social learning approach to marital therapy.* New York: Guilford Press.

Stunkard, A. J. (1972). New therapies for eating disorders. *Archives of General Psychiatry, 26,* 391–98.

Stunkard, A. J. (1976). Anorexia nervosa. In J. P. Sanford (Ed.), *The science and practice of clinical medicine* (pp. 361–63). New York: Grune & Stratton.

Stunkard, A. J. (1979). Behavioral medicine and beyond: The example of obesity. In O. F. Pomerleau & J. P. Brady (Eds.), *Behavioral medicine: Theory and practice* (pp. 279–98). Baltimore: Williams & Wilkins.

Stunkard, A. J., & Penick, S. B. (1979). Behavior modification and treatment of obesity. *Archives of General Psychiatry, 36,* 801–11.

Stunkard, A. J., Sorensen, T. I. A., Hanis, C., Teasdale, T. W., Chakraborty, R., Schull, W. J., & Schulsinger, F. (1986). An adoption study of human obesity. *New England Journal of Medicine,* 193–98.

Stunkard, A. J., & Stellar, E. (Eds.). *Eating and its disorders.* New York: Raven Press.

Sturdevant, R. A. L. (1976). Epidemiology of peptic ulcer: Report of a conference. *American Journal of Epidemiology, 104,* 9–14.

Stuss, D. T., & Benson, D. F. (1986). *The frontal lobes.* New York: Raven Press.

Suarez, J. M., & Pittluck, A. T. (1976). Global amnesia: Organic and functional considerations. *Bulletin of the American Academy of Psychiatric Law, 3,* 17–24.

Summers, M. (1971). *Witchcraft and black magic.* New York: Grand River Books.

Susser, M. (1967). Causes of peptic ulcer: A selective epidemiological review. *Journal of Chronic Disabilities, 20,* 435–56.

Swanson, D. W. (1968). Adult sexual abuse of children: The man and circumstances. *Diseases of the Nervous System, 29*(10), 677–83.

Swanson, W. C., & Breed, W. (1976). Black suicide in New Orleans. In E. S. Shneidman (Ed.), *Suicidology: Contemporary developments.* New York: Grune & Stratton.

Sweeney, P. O., Anderson, K., Bailey, S. (1986). Attributional style in depression: A meta-analytic review. *Journal of Personality and Social Psychology, 50* (5), 974–91.

Szasz, T. S. (1961). *The myth of mental illness.* New York: Dell.

Szasz, T. S. (1963). *Law, liberty and psychiatry: An inquiry into the social uses of mental health practices.* New York: Macmillan.

Szasz, T. S. (1970). *The manufacture of madness.* New York: Dell.

Szasz, T. S. (1974). The ethics of suicide. *Bulletin of Suicidology* (Vol. 9). Philadelphia: Charles Press.

Tagiuri, R., Bruner, J. S., & Blake, R. R. (1958). On the relation between feelings and the perception of feelings among members of small groups. In E. E. Maccoby, T. M. Newcomb, & E. L. Hartley (Eds.), *Readings in social psychology* (pp. 110–16). New York: Holt, Rinehart & Winston.

Talland, G. (1965). *Deranged memory.* New York: Academic Press.

Tallman, J. F., Paul, S. M., Skolnick, P., & Gallager, D. W. (1980). Receptors for the age of anxiety: Pharmacology of the benzodiazapines. *Science, 207,* 274–81.

Talovic, S. A., Mednick, S. A., Schulsinger, F., & Falloon, I. R. H. (1981). Schizophrenia in high-risk subjects: Prognostic maternal characteristics. *Journal of Abnormal Psychology, 89,* 501–504.

Tarter, R. E., Alterman, A. I., & Edwards, K. L. (1985). Vulnerability to alcoholism in men: A behavior-genetic perspective. *Journal of Studies on Alcoholism, 46,* 329–56.

Tarter, R. E., Hegedus, A. M., Goldstein, G., Shelly, C., & Alterman, A. I. (1984). Adolescent sons of alcoholics: Neuropsychological and personality characteristics. *Alcoholism: Clinical and Experimental Research, 8,* 216–22.

Taube, C. A. (1976). Readmissions to inpatient services of state and county hospitals 1972. Statistical note 110. (DHEW Publications No. ADM 76–308). Rockville, MD: National Institute of Mental Health.

Taubee, E. S., & Wright, H. W. (1971). A psychosocial behavioral model for therapeutic intervention. In C. D. Spielberger (Ed.), *Current topics in clinical and community psychology* (Vol. 3). New York: Academic Press.

Taylor, J. A. (1951). The relationship of anxiety to the conditioned eyelid responses. *Journal of Experimental Psychology, 41,* 81–92.

Taylor, J. A. (1953). A personality scale of manifest anxiety. *Journal of Abnormal and Social Psychology, 48,* 285–90.

Taylor, J. (Ed.). (1958). *Selected writings of John Hughlings Jackson.* New York: Basic Books.

Taylor, W. S., & Martin M. F. (1944). Multiple personality. *Journal of Abnormal and Social Psychology, 39,* 281–300.

Teasdale, J. D. (1985). Psychological treatments for depression: How do they work? *Behavior Research and Therapy, 23,* 157–65.

Teasdale, J. D., & Rezin, V. (1978). The effect of reducing frequency of negative thoughts on the mood of depressed patients: Test of a cognitive model of depression. *British Journal of Social and Clinical Psychology, 17,* 65–74.

Telch, M. J. (1988). Combined pharmacological and psychological treatments for panic sufferers. In S. Rachman & J. D. Maser (Eds.), *Panic: Psychological perspectives.* Hillsdale, NJ: Erlbaum.

Temerlin, M. K. (1970). Diagnostic bias in community mental health. *Community Mental Health Journal, 6,* 110–17.

Tennant, C. C., Goulston, K. J., & Dent, O. F. (1986). The psycho-logical effects of being a prisoner of war: Forty years after release. *American Journal of Psychiatry, 143,* 618–21.

Tennent, F., & Tarver, A. (1988). Step-wise withdrawal from cocaine dependence: Outcome of 106 consecutive patients. *NIDA Research Monographs, 81,* 317.

Terenius, L. (1978). Endogenous peptides and analgesia. *Annual Review of Pharmacology and Toxicology, 18,* 189–204.

Terry, R. D., & Davies, P. (1980). Dementia of the Alzheimer type. *Annual Review of Neuroscience, 3,* 77–95.

Teuber, H. L., & Powers, E. (1953). Evaluating therapy in a delinquency prevention program. *Psychiatric Treatment, 21,* 138–47.

Theodor, L. H., & Mandelcorn, M. S. (1978). Hysterical blindness: A case report and study using a modern psychophysical technique. *Journal of Abnormal Psychology, 82,* 552–53.

Theorell, T., & Rahe, R. H. (1971). Psychosocial factors in myocardial infarction. I. An inpatient study in Sweden. *Journal of Psychosomatic Research, 15,* 25–31.

Thigpen C. H., & Cleckley, H. (1954). A case of multiple personality. *Journal of Abnormal and Social Psychology, 49,* 135–51.

Thomas, K. (1971). *Religion and the decline of magic.* New York: Charles Scribner's Sons.

Thompson, T., & Dews, P. B. (1985). *Advances in behavioral pharmacology* (Vol. IV). New York: Academic Press.

Thorley, G. (1984). Review of follow-up and follow-back studies of childhood hyperactivity. *Psychological Bulletin, 96,* 116–32.

Tizard, J., & Venables, P. H. (1956). Reaction time responses by schizophrenics, mental defectives, and normal adults. *American Journal of Psychiatry, 112,* 803–807.

Tobias, L. L., & MacDonald, M. L. (1974). Withdrawal of maintenance drugs with long-term hospitalized schizophrenics: A critical review. *Psychological Bulletin, 81,* 107–25.

Tomes, N. (1984). *A generous confidence.* London: Cambridge University Press.

Tonks, C. M., Paykel, E. S., & Klerman, J. L. (1970). Clinical depressions among Negroes. *American Journal of Psychiatry, 127,* 329–35.

Torgersen, S. (1983). Genetic factors in anxiety disorders. *Archives of General Psychiatry, 40,* 1085–89.

Torgersen, S. (1986a). Genetic factors in moderately severe and mild affective disorders. *Archives of General Psychiatry, 43,* 222–26.

Torgersen, S. (1986b). Genetics of somatoform disorders. *Archives of General Psychiatry, 43,* 502–505.

Torrey, E. F. (1983). *The roots of treason: Ezra Pound and the secret of St. Elizabeth's.* New York: McGraw-Hill.

Tourney, G. (1967). A history of therapeutic fashions in psychiatry, 1800–1966. *American Journal of Psychiatry, 124,* 784–96.

Trasler, G. (1973). Criminal behavior. In H. J. Eysenck (Ed.), *Handbook of abnormal psychology.* London: Pitman Medical.

Trevor-Roper, H. (1970). *The European witch-craze of the sixteenth and seventeenth centuries.* New York: Harper & Row.

Trotter, R. J. (1986, May). The making of a Type A. *Psychology Today,* p. 12.

Truax, C. B., & Carkhuff, R. R. (1967). *Toward effective counseling and psychotherapy: Training and practice.* Chicago: Aldine.

Truax, C. B., & Mitchell, K. M. (1971). Research on certain therapist interpersonal skills in relation to process and outcome. In A. E. Bergin & S. L. Garfield (Eds.), *Handbook of psychotherapy and behavior change.* New York: Wiley.

Truax, C. B., Shapiro, J. G., & Wargo, D. G. (1968). Effects of alternate sessions and vicarious therapy pretraining on group psychotherapy. *International Journal of Group Psychotherapy, 18,* 186–98.

Tryon, W. W. (1976). Models of behavior disorder. *American Psychologist, 31,* 509–18.

Tuke, S. (1813). Description of the Retreat, an institution near York for insane persons of the Society of Friends. Cited in Foucault, M., *Madness and civilization: A history of insanity in the age of reason.* New York: Random House, 1965.

Tulving, E. (1985). How many memory systems are there? *American Psychologist, 40,* 385–98.

Turner, R. J., & Wagenfeld, M. O. (1967). Occupational mobility and schizophrenia. *American Sociological Review, 32,* 104–13.

Turner, S. M., Beidel, D. C., Dancu, C. V., & Keys, D. J. (1986). Psychopathology of social phobia and comparison to avoidant personality disorder. *Journal of Abnormal Psychology, 95,* 389–94.

Turner, S. M., Beidel, D. C., & Nathan, R. S. (1985). Biological factors in obsessive compulsive disorders. *Psychological Bulletin, 97,* 430–50.

Ullman, L. P., & Krasner, L. (1965). *Case studies in behavior modification.* New York: Holt, Rinehart & Winston.

Understedt, V. (1971). Stereotoxic mapping of the monoamine pathways in the rat brain. *Acta Psychiatrica Scandinavica, 10,* 1–48.

Upham, Charles W. (1867). Salem witchcraft. Cited in A. Deutsch, *The mentally ill in America.* New York: Columbia University Press, 1949.

Urbina, S. P., Golden, C. J., & Ariel, R. N. (1982). WAIS/WAIS-R: Initial comparisons. *Clinical Neuropsychology, 4,* 145–46.

U.S. Department of Health and Human Services. (1987). Vital Statistics of the United States, 1984. Volume II-Mortality. National Center for Health Statistics, Hyattsville, MD.

Vaillant, G. E. (1977). *Adaptation to life.* Boston: Little, Brown.

Vaillant, G. E. (1978). Natural history of male psychological health: IV. What kinds of men do not get psychosomatic illness. *Psychosomatic Medicine, 40,* 420–31.

Vaillant, G. (1986). *Empirical studies of ego mechanisms of defense.* Washington, DC: American Psychiatric Press.

Vaillant, G. E., Bond, M., & Vaillant, C. O. (1986). An empirically validated hierarchy of defense mechanisms. *Archives of General Psychiatry, 43,* 786–94.

Valentine, C. W. (1930). The innate bases of fear. *Journal of Genetic Psychology, 37,* 394–419.

Valins, S., & Nisbett, R. E. (1976). Attribution processes in the development and treatment of emotional disorders. In J. T. Spence, R. C. Carson, & J. W. Thibaut (Eds.), *Behavioral approaches to therapy.* Morristown, NJ: General Learning Press.

VandenBos, G. R., & Karon, B. P. (1971). Pathogenesis: A new therapist personality dimension related to therapeutic effectiveness. *Journal of Personality Assessment, 35,* 252–60.

Van Dyke, C., Zilberg, N. J., & McKinnon, J. A. (1985). Post-traumatic stress disorder: A thirty-year delay in a World War II veteran. *American Journal of Psychiatry, 142,* 1070–73.

Van Praag, H., Korf, J., & Sheet, D. (1973). Cerebral monoamines and depression: An investigation with the probenecid technique. *Archives of General Psychiatry, 28,* 827–31.

Vaughn, C. E., & Leff, J. P. (1976). The influence of family and social factors on the course of psychiatric illness: A comparison of schizophrenic and depressive-neurotic patients. *British Journal of Psychiatry, 129,* 127–37.

Vaughn, C. E., Snyder, K. S., Jones, S., Freeman, W. B., & Falloon, I. R. H. (1984). Family factors in schizophrenic relapse: Replication in California of British research on expressed emotion. *Archives of General Psychiatry, 41,* 1169–77.

Veith, I. (1965). *Hysteria: The history of a disease.* Chicago: University of Chicago Press.

Venables, P. (1964). Input dysfunction in schizophrenia. In B. A. Maher (Ed.), *Progress in experimental personality research.* New York: Academic Press.

Victor, M., Adams, R. D., & Collins, G. H. (1971). *The Wernicke-Korsakoff syndrome. A clinical and pathological study of 245 patients, 82 with post-mortem examinations.* Philadelphia: Davis.

Videnbech, T. (1975). A study of genetic factors, childhood bereavement, and premorbid personality traits in patients with anancastic endogenous depression. *Acta Psychiatrica Scandinavica, 52,* 178–222.

Visintainer, M., Volpicelli, J. R., & Seligman, M. E. P. (1982). Tumor rejection in rats after inescapable or escapable shock. *Science, 216,* 437–39.

Vogel, G. W. (1975). A review of REM sleep deprivation. *Archives of General Psychiatry, 32,* 96–97.

Voigt, D. Q. (1987). *Baseball: An illustrated history.* University Park, PA: Pennsylvania State University Press.

Volpicelli, J. R. (1987). Uncontrollable events and alcohol drinking. *British Journal of Addiction, 82,* 381–92.

Volpicelli, J. R., Davis, M. A., & Olgin, J. E. (1986). Naltrexone blocks the post-shock increase of ethanol consumption. *Life Sciences, 38,* 841–47.

Volpicelli, J. R., Tiven, J., & Kimmel, S. C. (1982). The relationship between tension reduction and ethanol consumption in rats. *Physiological Psychology, 10,* 114–16.

Wadden, T. A., & Stunkard, A. J. (1986). Controlled trial of very low calorie diet, behavior therapy, and their combination in the treatment of obesity. *Journal of Consulting and Clinical Psychology, 54,* 482–88.

Walker, E., Hoppes, E., Emory, E., Mednick. S., & Schulsinger, F. (1981). Environmental factors related to schizophrenia in psychophysiologically high-risk males. *Journal of Abnormal Psychology, 90(4),* 313–20.

Wallerstein, J. S., & Kelly, J. B. (1980). California children of divorce. *Psychology Today, 13.*

Walinder, J. (1967). *Transsexualism.* Goteburg: Scandinavian University Books.

Ward, C. H., Beck, A. T., Mendelson, M., Mock, J. E., & Erbaugh, J. K. (1962). The psychiatric nomenclature: Reasons for diagnostic disagreement. *Archives of General Psychiatry, 7,* 198–205.

Warheit, G., Holzer, C., & Schwab, J. (1973). An analysis of social class and racial differences in depressive symptom etiology: The community study. *Journal of Health and Social Behavior, 4,* 921–99.

Warrington, E. K., & Weiskrantz, L. (1973). An analysis of short-term and long-term memory defects in man. In J. A. Deutsch (Ed.), *The physiological basis of memory* (pp. 365–96). New York: Academic Press.

Watkins, G. (1960). The incidence of chronic peptic ulcer sounded necropsy: The study of 20,000 examinations performed in Leeds in 1930 to 1949 and in England and Scotland in 1956. *Gut, 1,* 14.

Watson, J. B., & Rayner, R. (1920). Conditioned emotional reactions. *Journal of Experimental Psychology, 3,* 1–14.

Watson, C. G., & Buranen, C. (1979). The frequency of conversion reaction. *Journal of Abnormal Psychology, 88,* 209–11.

Watson, L. S. (1973). *Child behavior modification: A manual for teachers, nurses, and parents.* New York: Pergamon.

Watson, L. S., & Uzzell, R. (1981). *Handbook of behavior modification with the mentally retarded.* New York: Plenum.

Watt, N. F., Anthony, E. J., Wynne, L. C., & Rolf, J. E. (Eds.). (1984). *Children at risk for schizophrenia: A longitudinal perspective.* Cambridge: Cambridge University Press.

Watts, F. N., McKenna, F. P., Sharrock, R., & Trezise, L. (1986). Colour naming of phobia-related words. *British Journal of Psychology, 77,* 97–108.

Watzlawick, P., Beavin, J. H., & Jackson, D. D. (1967). *Pragmatics of human communication.* New York: Norton.

Wegner, J. T., Catalano, F., Gibralter, J., & Kane, J. M. (1985). Schizophrenics with tardive dyskinesia. *Archives of General Psychiatry, 42,* 860–65.

Wehr, T. A., Sack, D. A., & Rosenthal, N. E. (1987). Sleep reduction as a final common pathway in the genesis of mania. *American Journal of Psychiatry, 144,* 201–204.

Weinberg, M., & Williams, C. J. (1974). *Male homosexuals: Their problems and adaptations in three societies.* New York: Oxford University Press.

Weinberger, D. R., Berman, K. F., & Zec, R. F. (1986). Physiologic dysfunction of dorsolateral prefrontal cortex in schizophrenia. I. Regional cerebral blood flow evidence. *Archives of General Psychiatry, 43* (2), 114–24.

Weiner, B. (1972). *Theories of motivation: From mechanism to cognition.* Chicago: Rand McNally.

Weiner, B. (Ed.) (1974). *Achievement motivation and attribution theory.* Morristown, NJ: General Learning Press.

Weiner, H. M. (1977). *Psychology and human disease.* New York: Elsevier.

Weiner, H., Failer, M., Reiser, M. F., & Mirsky, I. A. (1957). Ideology of duodenal ulcer. I. Rise in specific psychological characteristics to rate of gastric secretion (serum pepsinogen). *Psychosomatic Medicine, 19,* 1.

Weiner, I. (1969). Effectiveness of a suicide prevention program. *Mental Hygiene, 53,* 357.

Weiner, R. D. (1984). Convulsive therapy: 50 years later. *American Journal of Psychiatry, 141,* 1078–79.

Weiskrantz, L., Warrington, E. K., Sanders M.D., & Marshall, J. (1974). Visual capacity of the hemianopic field following a restricted occipital ablation. *Brain, 97,* 709–28.

Weisman, A. D. (1956). A study of the psychodynamics of duodenal ulcer exacerbations. *Psychosomatic Medicine, 18,* 2–42.

Weiss, J. M. (1968). Effects of predictable and unpredictable shock on the development of gastrointestinal lesion in rats. *Proceedings of the 76th Annual Convention of the American Psychological Association, 3,* 263–64.

Weiss, J. M. (1970). Somatic effects of predictable and unpredictable shock. *Psychosomatic Medicine, 32,* 397–409.

Weiss, J. M. (1971). Effects of coping behavior in different warning signaled conditions on stress pathology in rats. *Journal of Comparative and Physiological Psychology, 77,* 1–13.

Weiss, J. M., Glazer, H. I., & Pohoresky, L. A. (1976). Coping behavior and neurochemical change in rats: An alternative explanation for the original "learned helplessness" experiments. In G. Serban & A. King (Eds.), *Animal models in human psychobiology.* New York: Plenum.

Weiss, J. M., Pohoresky, L. A., Salman, S., & Gruenthal, M. (1976). Attenuation of gastric lesions by psychological aspects of aggression in rats. *Journal of Comparative Physiological Psychology, 90,* 252–59.

Weiss, J., et al. (1981). Behavioral depression produced by an uncontrollable stressor: Relationship to norepinephrine, dopamine, and serotonin levels in various regions of the rat brain. *Brain Research Reviews, 3,* 167–205.

Weiss, J. M., Simson, P. G., Ambrose, M. J., Webster, A., & Hoffman, L. J. (1985). Neurochemical basis of behavioral depression. *Advances in Behavioral Medicine, 1,* 253–75.

Weissman, M. M., Kidd, K. K., & Prusoff, B. A. (1982). Variability in rates of affective disorders in relatives of depressed and normal probands. *Archives of General Psychiatry, 39,* 1397–1403.

Weissman, M. M., Klerman, G. L., Prusoff, B. A., Sholomskas, D., & Padian, N. (1981). Depressed patients: Results one year after treatment with drugs and/or interpersonal psychotherapy. *Archives of General Psychiatry, 38,* 51–55.

Weissman, M. M., & Paykel, E. S. (1974). *The depressed woman: A study of social relationships.* Evanston: University of Chicago Press.

Welgan, P. R. (1974). Learned control of gastric acid secretions in ulcer patients. *Psychosomatic Medicine, 5,* 411–19.

Wender, P. H., Kety, S. S., Rosenthal, D., Schulsinger, F., Ortmann, J., & Lunde, I. (1986). Psychiatric disorders in the biological and adoptive families of adopted individuals with affective disorders. *Archives of General Psychiatry, 43,* 923–29.

Werner, P. D., & Pervin, L. A. (1986). The content of personality inventory items. *Journal of Personality and Social Psychology, 51,* 622–28.

Werry, J. S., Methven, J., Fitzpatrick, J., & Dixon, H. (1983). The inter-rater reliability of DSM-III in children. *Journal of Abnormal Child Psychology, 11,* 341–54.

Wertheimer, M. (1978). Humanistic psychology and the humane and tough-minded psychologist. *American Psychologist, 33,* 631–47.

West, D. J. (1976). Delinquency. In M. Rutter & L. Hersov (Eds.), *Child psychiatry: Modern approaches.* Oxford: Blackwell.

Whalen, C. K., & Henker, B. (1976). Psychostimulants and children: A review and analysis. *Psychological Bulletin, 83,* 1113–30.

White, R. W. (1959). Motivation reconsidered: The concept of competence. *Psychological Review, 66,* 297–333.

White, R. W. (1963). Ego and reality in psychoanalytic theory: A proposal regarding independent ego energies. *Psychological Issues, 3,* 1–210.

Whiting, B. B., & Whiting, J. W. (1974). *Children of six cultures: A psycho-cultural analysis.* Cambridge, MA: Harvard University Press.

Wikler, A. (1948). Recent progress in research on the neurophysiologic basis of morphine addiction. *American Journal of Psychiatry, 105,* 329–88.

Wilkins, M. A. (1971). Comparisons of attitudes toward childrearing of parents of certain exceptional and normal children. *Dissertation Abstracts International, 31* (11-A), 5894.

Wilkins, W. (1979). Expectancies in therapy research: Discriminating among heterogeneous nonspecifics. *Journal of Consulting and Clinical Psychology, 47,* 837–45.

Williams, P., & Smith, M. (1980). Interview in "The First Question." London: British Broadcasting System, Sciences and Features Department Film, 1979. Cited in Diamond, M., & Karlen, A. (Eds.), *Sexual decisions.* Boston: Little, Brown.

Williams, R. B., Barefoot, J. C., & Shekelle, R. B. (1985). The health consequences of hostility. In M. Chesbney & R. Rosenman (Eds.), *Anger and hostility in cardiovascular and behavioral disorders.* New York: McGraw-Hill/Hemisphere.

Willis, M. H., & Blaney, P. H. (1978). Three tests of the learned helplessness model of depression. *Journal of Abnormal Psychology, 87,* 131–36.

Willner, A. G., Brankman, C. J., Kirigan, K. A., & Wolf, M. M. (1978). Achievement Place: A community treatment model for youths in trouble. In D. Marholin (Ed.), *Child behavior therapy.* New York: Gardner Press.

Wilner, A., Reich, T., Robins, I., Fishman, R., & van Doren, T. (1976). Obsessive-compulsive neurosis. *Comprehensive Psychiatry, 17,* 527–39.

Wilson, P. H., Goldin, J. C., & Charbonneau-Powis, M. (1983). Comparative efficacy of behavioral and cognitive treatments of depression. *Cognitive Therapy and Research, 7,* 111–24.

Wing, J. K., & Hailey, A. M. (Eds.). (1972). *Evaluating a community psychiatric service.* London: Oxford University Press.

Wing, L. (1976). *Diagnosis, clinical description and prognosis.* Oxford: Pergamon.

Wing, L., Yeates, S. R., Brierly, L. M., & Gould, J. (1976). The prevalence of early childhood autism: Comparison of administrative and epidemiological studies. *Psychological Medicine, 6,* 89–100.

Winnicott, D. W. (1971). *Playing and reality.* New York: International Universities Press.

Winokur, G. (1972). Family history studies VIII: Secondary depression is alive and well and . . . . *Diseases of the Nervous System, 33,* 94–99.

Winokur, G., & Tanna, V. L. (1969). Possible role of X-link dominant factor in manic-depressive disease. *Diseases of the Nervous System, 30,* 89.

Witkin, H. A., Mednick. S. A., Schulsinger, F., Bakkestrom, E., Christiansen, K. O., Goodenough, D. R., Hirschhorn, K., Lundsteen, C., Owen, D. R., Philip, J., Rubin, D. B., & Stocking, M. (1976). Criminality in XYY and XXY men: The elevated crime rate of XYY males is not related to aggression. *Science, 193,* 547–55.

Witkin, M. J. (1981). Provisional patient movement and selective administrative data, state and county mental hospitals, by state: United States, 1977. Mental Health Statistical Note No. 156. United States Department of Health and Human Services, Public Health Service, Alcohol, Drug Abuse and Mental Health Administration, National Institute of Mental Health.

Wittgenstein, L. (1953). *Philosophical investigations.* New York: Macmillan.

Wolf, M. M., Phillips, E. L., & Fixsen, D.C. (1975). *Achievement Place, phase II: Final report.* Kansas: Department of Human Development, University of Kansas.

Wolf, S. (1965). *The stomach.* New York: Oxford University Press.

Wolf, S., Cardon, P. V., Shepard, E. M., & Wolff, H. G. (1955). *Life stress and essential hypertension.* Baltimore: Williams & Wilkins.

Wolf, S., & Wolff, H. G. (1947). *Human gastric function.* New York: Oxford University Press.

Wollheim, R. (1974). *Freud: A collection of critical essays.* Garden City, NY: Anchor/Doubleday.

Wolpe, J. (1958). *Psychotherapy by reciprocal inhibition.* Stanford: Stanford University Press.

Wolpe, J. (1969). Basic principles and practices of behavior therapy of neuroses. *American Journal of Psychiatry, 125*(5), 1242–47.

Wolpe, J. (1971). Neurotic depression: Experimental analogue, clinical syndromes and treatment. *American Journal of Psychotherapy, 25,* 362–68.

Wolpe, J., & Lazarus, A. A. (1969). *The practice of behavior therapy.* New York: Pergamon.

Wolpe, J., & Rachman, S. (1960). Psychoanalytic "evidence": A critique based on Freud's case of Little Hans. *Journal of Nervous and Mental Disease, 131,* 135–47.

Wolraich, M., Drummond, T., Salomon, M. K., O'Brien, M. L., & Sivage, C. (1978). Effects of methylphenidate alone and in combination with behavior modification procedures on the behavior and academic performance of hyperactive children. *Journal of Abnormal Child Psychology, 6,* 149–61.

Wong, D. F., Wagner, H. N., Tune, L. E., Dannals, R. F., Pearlson, G. D., Links, J. M., Tamminga, C. A., Broussolle, E. P., Ravert, H. T., Wilson, A. A., Toung, J. K. T., Malat, J., Williams, J. A., O'Tuama, L. A., Snyder, S. H., Kuhar, M. J., & Gjedde, A. (1986). Positron emission tomography reveals elevated D_2 dopamine receptors in drug-naive schizophrenics. *Science, 234,* 1558–63.

Woodruff, R. A., Clayton, P. J., & Guze, S. B. (1971). Hysteria: Studies of diagnosis, outcome and prevalence. *Journal of the American Medical Association, 215,* 425–28.

Woodruff, R. A., Goodwin, D. W., & Guze, S. B. (1974). *Psychiatric diagnosis.* New York: Oxford University Press.

Woodward, B., & Armstrong, A. (1979). *The brethren: Inside the Supreme Court.* New York: Simon & Schuster.

Wrobel, T. A., & Locher, D. (1982). Validity of the Wiener subtle and obvious scales for the MMPI: Another example of the importance of inventory-item content. *Journal of Consulting and Clinical Psychology, 50,* 469–70.

Wynne, L. C. (1970). Communication disorders and the quest for relatedness in families of schizophrenics. *American Journal of Psychoanalysis, 30,* 100–14.

Wynne, L. C. (1972). *Psychotherapy of schizophrenia.* Amsterdam: Excerpta Medica Foundation.

Wynne, L. C., Rykoff, I. M., Day, J., & Hirsch, S. I. (1958). Pseudo mutuality in the family relations of schizophrenics. *Psychiatry, 21,* 205–20.

Wynne, L. C. Singer, M. T., Bartko, J. J., & Toohey, M. I. (1977). Schizophrenics and their families: Recent research on parental communication. In J. M. Tanner (Ed.), *Developments in psychiatric research.* London: Hodder & Stoughton.

Yalom, I. D. (1980). *Existential psychotherapy.* New York: Basic Books.

Yalom, I. D., Houts, P. S., Newell, G., & Rand, K. H. (1967). Preparation of patients for group therapy. *Archives of General Psychiatry, 17,* 416–27.

Yates, A. (1966). *Theory and practice in behavior therapy* (2nd ed.). New York: Wiley.

Youkilis, H. D., & DeWolfe, A. S. (1975). The regression hypothesis and scales classification in schizophrenia. *Journal of Abnormal Psychology, 84,* 36–40.

Yule, W. (1980). The epidemiology of child psychopathology. In B. B. Lahey & A. E. Kazdin (Eds.), *Advances in child clinical psychology* (Vol. 4) (pp. 1–51). New York: Plenum.

Yule, W., Hersov, L., & Treseder, J. (1980). Behavioral treatments of school refusal. In L. Hersov & I. Berg (Eds.), *Out of school: Modern perspectives in truancy and school refusal.* New York: Wiley.

Yule, W., & Rutter, M. (1976). Epidemiology and social implication of specific reading retardation. In R. M. Knights & D. J. Bakker (Eds.), *The neuropsychology of learning disorders.* Baltimore: University Park Press.

Zafiropoulou, M., & McPherson, F. M. (1986). "Preparedness" and the severity and outcomes of clinical phobias. *Behavior Research and Therapy, 24,* 221–22.

Zahn, T. P., & Rosenthal, D. (1965). Preparatory set in acute schizophrenia. *Journal of Nervous and Mental Disease, 141,* 352–58.

Zaidel, E. (1978a). Auditory language comprehension in the right hemisphere following cerebral commisurotomy and hemispherectomy: A comparison with child language and aphasia. In A. Caramazza & E. B. Zurif (Eds.), *Language acquisition and language breakdown: Parallels and divergences.* Baltimore, MD: Johns Hopkins University Press.

Zaidel, E. (1978b). Lexical organization in the right hemisphere. In P. Buser & A. Rougeul-Buser (Eds.), *Cerebral correlates of conscious experience.* Amsterdam: Elsevier.

Zangwill, O. L. (1966). The amnesic syndrome. In C. W. M. Whitty & O. L. Zangwill (Eds.), *Amnesia.* London: Butterworth.

Zatta, P., et al. (1988). Alzheimer's dementia and the aluminum hypothesis. *Medical Hypotheses, 26,* 139–42.

Zax, M., & Cowen, E. L. (1969). Research on early detection and prevention of emotional dysfunction in young school children. In C. D. Spielberger (Ed.), *Current topics in clinical and community psychology* (Vol. 1) (pp. 67–108). New York: Academic Press.

Zentall, S. S., & Zentall, T. R. Optimal stimulation: A model of disordered activity and performance in normal and deviant children. *Psychological Bulletin, 94,* 446–71.

Ziegler, F. J., & Imboden, J. B. (1962). Contemporary conversion reactions: II. A conceptual model. *Archives of General Psychiatry, 6,* 279–87.

Ziegler, F. J., Imboden, J. B., & Meyer, E. (1960). Contemporary conversion reactions: A clinical study. *American Journal of Psychiatry, 116,* 901–10.

Ziegler, D. K., & Paul, N. (1954). Hysteria. *Diseases of the Nervous System, 15,* 30.

Zigler, E., & Levine, J. (1981). Age on first hospitalization of schizophrenics: A developmental approach. *Journal of Abnormal Psychology, 90,* 458–67.

Zigler, E., & Phillips, L. (1961). Psychiatric diagnosis and symptomatology. *Journal of Abnormal and Social Psychology, 63,* 69–75.

Zilbergeld, B., & Evans, M. (1980). The inadequacy of Masters and Johnson. *Psychology Today, 14,* 28–43.

Zilboorg, G., & Henry, G. W. (1941). *A history of medical psychology.* New York: Norton.

Zimbardo, P. G. (1977). Shy murderers. *Psychology Today, 148,* 66–76.

Zimbardo, P. G., Andersen, S. M., & Kabat, L. G. (1981). Induced hearing deficit generates experimental paranoia. *Science, 212,* 1529–31.

Zitrin, C. M., Klein, D. F., Woerner, M. G., & Ross, D.C. (1983). Treatment of phobias I. Comparison of imipramine hydrochloride and placebo. *Archives of General Psychiatry, 40,* 125–38.

Zola-Morgan, S., Squire, L. R., & Amaral, D. (1986). Human amnesia and the medial temporal region: Enduring memory impairment following a bilateral lesion limited to the CA 1 field of the hippocampus. *Journal of Neuroscience, 6,* 2950–67.

Zubin, J., Eron, L. D., & Schumer, F. (1965). *An experimental approach to projective techniques.* New York: Wiley.

Zubin, J. E., & Spring, B. (1977). Vulnerability: A new view of schizophrenia. *Journal of Abnormal Psychology, 86,* 103–26.

Zuckerman, M., & Lubin, B. (1965). *Manual for the Multiple Affect Adjective Check List.* San Diego, CA: Educational and Industrial Testing Service.

Zucker, R. A., Battistich, V. A., & Langer, G. B. (1981). Sexual behavior, sex-role adaptation, and drinking in young women. *Journal of the Studies on Alcohol, 42,* 457–65.

Zullow, H., & Seligman, M. E. P. (1985). Pessimistic ruminations predict increase in depressive symptoms: A process model and longitudinal study. Unpublished manuscript.

Name Index

Abel, G. G., 448, 538
Abelson, R. P., 182
Abikoff, H., 530
Abraham, K., 329
Abrams, R., 329
Abramson, L. Y., 123, 152, 310–11, 313, 320, 337, 338, 339, 340, 343, 345
Acosta, T. X., 440
Adams, H. E., 443
Adams, N. E., 121, 212
Adams, R. D., 562, 569, 570, 572, 575, 584, 593
Addington, F. O., 612
Adland, M., 351
Adler, A. A., 71, 72
Adler, C. S., 173
Agras, W. S., 212, 538, 656, 664
Ahlbom, A., 287
Ahrens, L., 442
Akhtar, S., 237
Akiskal, H. S., 347
Albert, M. L., 565
Alexander, F., 280–81, 284, 294, 298
Alexander, L., 643
Allen, C. R., 57
Allen, J., 553
Allen, L., 206
Allen, M. G., 57, 325, 352
Allen, R. P., 530
Alloy, L. B., 310–11
Allport, G. W., 19
Almy, G., 329
Alpern, G. D., 553
Alterman, A. I., 462
Amaral, D., 585
Ambinder, R., 448, 449
Ambrose, M. J., 152, 153
Ames, M. A., 427, 442
Amis, L., 511
Andersen, B. L., 418, 424
Andersen, S. M., 379
Anderson, A. R., 540
Anderson, C. M., 403, 404, 422, 665

Anderson, J. C., 519, 520, 522, 524, 525, 528, 531, 532
Anderson, J. R., 78–79
Anderson, K., 345
Anderson, S., 230
Andreasen, N. C., 316, 352, 375, 395
Andrews, G., 536
Angst, J., 351
Anisman, H., 293, 346
Anker, M., 369
Annau, Z., 208
Ansbacher, H. L., 72
Ansbacher, R., 72
Anthony, W. A., 161, 389
Apfelbaum, B., 418, 419, 424
Appenzeller, T., 584, 585
Appleby, I. L., 230
Archibald, H. C., 223, 224, 225
Arendt, H., 91
Argyll, D. M., 51
Ariel, R. N., 169
Arieti, S., 204, 206, 331, 380, 382
Armstrong, A., 615
Aronow, E., 168
Arthur, R. J., 504
Asberg, M., 357
Asch, S. E., 181
Assad, G., 373
Atkins, E., 540
Atkinson, J. W., 169
Atwater, J. D., 527
Auerbach, A. H., 643
Auld, F., 642
Ayllon, T., 117, 529
Azrin, N. H., 535

Baastrup, P., 351
Bachman, J. A., 664
Bacon, D. L., 624
Baer, D. M., 545
Bagley, C., 291
Bailey, S., 345
Bailly, J.-S., 32

Baker, D., 287
Baker, L., 538, 554
Baker, T. B., 108
Bales, J., 645
Ball, J., 474
Ballenger, J. C., 213
Baltes, P. B., 151
Bandura, A., 20, 120–21, 212, 217, 291, 497, 532, 651, 657
Barbizet, J., 568, 582
Bard, M., 671, 672
Bardhan, K., D., 281
Barefoot, J. C., 159, 285
Barlow, D. H., 229, 448
Barlow, T. H., 538
Barnes, C. L., 591
Barnes, G. E., 322
Barnes, T. R. E., 403
Baron, J., 590
Baron, M., 511
Barrett-Lennard, G. T., 642
Barsky, A. J., 203
Bartak, L., 550
Barten, H., 640
Bartko, J. J., 380, 396
Barlett, D. L., 238
Barton, R., 311
Barton, S., 553
Bartrop, R. W., 293
Bateson, G., 389, 396
Battistick, V. A., 471
Battle, C. C., 639
Baum, M., 209, 211, 220
Baumgold, J., 199
Baxter, L. R., 241
Baxtrom, J. K., 607, 608
Bayle, A. L. J., 50, 52
Bazelon, D., 612–13, 622
Beach, F., 412, 426
Beaglehole, R., 540
Bear, 248–49, 253–54, 255
Beardslee, W. R., 325
Beauvais, M. F., 581

Beck, A. T., 121, 122, 124, 125, 175, 230, 231, 309, 310–12, 313, 314, 315, 320, 323, 328, 332–36, 346, 358, 360, 361, 362, 436, 651, 658
Beck, R., 42
Beech, H. R., 239, 246
Beecher, H. K., 141, 641
Beethoven, L. van, 355
Begleiter, H., 462
Beidel, D. C., 241, 507
Belar, C. K., 271
Bell, A. P., 426, 442
Bellugi, U., 578
Belson, R., 523
Bemis, K. M., 663
Bemporad, J., 331
Ben, R., 228
Bender, M. E., 529
Bendt, R. H., 624, 625
Benes, F. M., 395
Benjamin, B., 290
Benjamin, H., 430
Benjamin, L. S., 506
Bennett, I. F., 402
Bennett, W., 541
Benson, D. F., 566, 591, 592
Berger, B. D., 529
Berger, M., 555
Berkman, L. F., 302
Berman, J. S., 656
Berman, K. F., 395
Bernheim, H., 33, 35
Bertrand, L. D., 268
Bettelheim, B., 81–82, 550, 553–54
Bexton, W. H., 141
Beyer, J., 212
Bialow, M., 322
Bianchi, K., 267–68
Bias, L., 475
Bibring, E., 331
Bihari, 462
Binet, A., 169
Binik, Y. M., 278
Biran, M., 121
Birch, H. G., 553
Bird, E. D., 395
Bird, J., 257
Birenbaum, A., 546
Birley, J. L. T., 664
Bisiach, E., 565
Blackmun, H. A., 625
Blair, C. D., 438
Blake, R. R., 82
Blanchard, E. B., 448, 657
Blaney, P. H., 347
Blashfield, R. K., 159, 180
Blayer, D., 493
Blessed, G., 591
Bleuler, E., 175, 365, 366, 374, 376
Bliss, E., 261, 263, 264–66
Block, S., 628
Bloom, E. T., 293
Bloxom, A., 640
Blum, K., 465
Blumberg, S. H., 320
Boehnlein, J. K., 228
Bogen, J., 567

Bogia, D. P., 375
Bohman, M., 249, 253, 501
Bonagura, N., 524
Bond, M., 85
Booth, S., 529
Borge, G. L., 352
Borkevic, T. D., 656
Borysenko, M., 292
Boulougouris, J. C., 212, 246
Bower, G. H., 79
Bowers, W., 515
Bowlby, J., 320
Bowler, K., 213
Boyd, J. L., 664
Bozarth, J. D., 642
Bradshaw, J. L., 567
Brady, J. P., 256, 257
Brady, J. V., 140, 279
Brady, K., 296
Braff, D. L., 375
Brand, R. J., 283
Braude, W. M., 403
Braukmann, C. J., 526–27
Breed, W., 357, 358
Bregman, E. O., 214
Brehm, J. W., 10
Brehm, S. S., 10
Breier, A., 200, 230, 232
Breinlinger, M., 553
Breitner, J. C. S., 590
Breslau, N., 223, 323
Brett, C. W., 344
Breuer, J., 35–36, 248
Bridgman, P., 360
Brierly, L. M., 553
Broadbent, D. E., 374
Broca, P., 576, 578
Brodie, H. K. H., 351
Bronson, E., 606
Brooks, A. D., 606, 622
Brooks, L., 643
Brown, A., 285
Brown, C. H., 161
Brown, G. W., 322, 323, 345, 664
Brown, J. M., 3–5, 10, 12, 17, 322, 609
Brown, K. H., 169
Brown, R. A., 395, 463, 661
Brown, W. F., 673
Bruch, H., 536, 538
Bruner, J. S., 82
Bryan, J. H., 627
Bryan, T. H., 627
Brynes, J., 545
Buchsbaum, S., 403
Buchwald, A. M., 346
Budzynski, T. H., 173
Bunney, W. E., 316, 323, 352, 353
Bunyan, J., 237
Buranen, C., 250, 256
Burgess, A. W., 222, 671
Burgess, M., 284
Burling, T. A., 344
Burns, B., 78
Burns, T. L., 540
Burt, R. A., 626
Burton, R., 200
Butcher, J. N., 163

Butters, N., 582
Bynum, W. F., Jr., 39

Caddell, J., 529
Cade, J., 58, 353
Cadoret, R., 493
Callahan, E. J., 656
Cameron, N., 9, 230, 375
Campbell, M., 554
Cannon, D. S., 108
Cantor, A., 315
Cantor, N., 15
Cantwell, D. P., 528, 554
Cardon, P. V., 284
Carey, G., 159, 198, 217, 239
Carkesse, J., 30, 41
Carkhuff, R. R., 642
Carlisle, J. M., 437
Carlsmith, J. M., 159
Carlson, G. A., 351
Caroff, S., 55
Carpenter, C. J., 355
Carpenter, W. T., Jr., 380
Carrera, R., 656
Carrier, M., 28
Carrier, S., 28
Carter, A. B., 257
Carter, C. H., 544
Carter, D. K., 643
Carter, J., 616
Cartwright, R. D., 642, 643
Casey, J. F., 402
Caspersen, C. J., 287
Castro, K. G., 470
Catalano, F., 402
Cautela, J. R., 438
Cegelka, W. J., 546
Cermak, L. S., 582
Chahal, R., 161
Chai, H., 296
Chakraborty, R., 541
Chang, S., 658–59
Chapin, H. N., 538
Chaplin, W., 311
Chapman, D. T., 168, 374, 377
Chapman, J. S., 374
Chapman, L. J., 168, 374, 375, 377
Charcot, J. M., 33, 36, 247–48, 255, 258
Charness, M. E., 573, 584
Charney, D. S., 200, 213, 230, 232
Chaudry, D. R., 200
Cherry, C., 536
Cheseldine, S., 545
Chiarugi, V., 40
Childress, A., 478
Chinn, P. C., 546
Chodoff, P., 225, 248, 253, 256, 506
Christenson, C. V., 432, 435
Christiansen, K. O., 501
Christodoulou, G. N., 276
Churchill, R., 52
Churchill, W., 52, 352
Cimbolic, 326
Claiborn, J. M., 169
Claparède, E., 586
Clark, D. M., 230, 231
Clark, R. E., 398

Clarke-Stewart, K. A., 71
Clausen, J. A., 398
Clayton, P. J., 252, 253
Cleckley, H., 261, 495, 498, 499, 504
Cloninger, C. R., 249, 253, 462, 501, 502
Cluff, L. E., 315
Coaper, J. E., 369
Coates, T. J., 287
Coats, K. I., 346
Cobb, J., 246
Cobb, S., 277
Cochran, C., 316
Coffman, J. A., 395
Cohen, A., 465
Cohen, D., 213
Cohen, J. B., 284
Cohen, N. J., 586
Cohen, S., 481
Cohn, N. R. C., 24
Colby, J. P., 463
Cole, C. S., 346
Collins, G. H., 584
Collins, J., 345, 658
Collins, R. L., 662
Colter, N., 395
Coltheart, M., 579, 580, 581
Comstock, G. W., 290
Conger, J. J., 278
Connolly, P. B., 420
Consentino, A., 556
Cook, M., 217
Cook, W. W., 285
Cooper, A. F., 379
Cooper, A. J., 442
Cooper, P. J., 539
Coopersmith, S., 462
Coote, M. A., 535
Corbit, J. D., 352
Corenthal, R., 515
Corsellis, J. A., 395
Coryell, W., 253
Costello, C. G., 346–47
Cousins, N., 641
Couthon, 41
Cowen, E. L., 669, 672
Cox, P., 196
Coyle, J. T., 591
Coyne, J. C., 300, 346
Craighead, L. W., 662
Creak, M., 550
Crisp, A. H., 538
Critchley, M., 559
Crits-Cristoph, P., 646
Crocetti, G. M., 369
Cronbach, L. J., 158
Crook, T. H., 322
Crossett, J. H., 395
Croughan, J., 161
Crow, T. J., 384, 394, 395, 402
Crowe, M. J., 212, 656
Crowe, R. R., 200
Cudeck, R., 389
Cullen, W., 39
Curran, J. W., 470
Currie, E. P., 25
Curtis, B. A., 574
Curtis, G. C., 230

Cutter, H. S. G., 463
Cytryn, L., 320, 545

Dacquin, J., 40
Dahlstrom, W. G., 285
Dalgard, O. S., 501
Damasio, A. R., 591
Danaher, B. G., 661
Dancu, C. V., 507
Daniels, M., 293
Darwin, C., 101
Davenport, H. W., 275
Davenport, W., 442
Davenport, Y. B., 351
Davidson, J., 395
Davidson, L. M., 220
Davidson, M., 217
Davidson, R. J., 328
Davies, J. C. V., 525
Davies, P., 590
Davies, R. K., 351
Davies, S. O., 230
Davis, G. C., 223, 323
Davis, J. M., 59, 319, 658–59
Davis, K. L., 590
Davis, M. A., 466
Davis, P. H., 261–63
Davis, P. J., 78
Davison, G. C., 170, 441
Day, R., 369
Dealy, R., 213
DeBacker, G., 284
DeBoer, G., 663
Dejerine, 579
Dekker, E., 298
DeLa Paz, R. L., 573, 584
Delay, J., 58, 401
d'Elia, G., 375
DeLong, M. R., 591
DeMeyer, M. K., 553
Deniker, P., 58, 401
Denney, D., 391
Dent, O. F., 223
Depue, R. H., 58, 300, 346, 351, 354, 659
Derouesne, J., 581
Dershowitz, A. M., 609
Descartes, R., 105
De Silva, P., 215
Deutsch, A., 28, 38, 41, 42
Devine, P. A., 639
Dews, P. B., 483
Diamond, B. L., 282, 284, 607
Diamond, R. G., 586
Dienelt, M. N., 300, 316
Diggory, J. C., 357
Dillon, H., 225, 230
Dimsdale, J. E., 285
Dinges, D. F., 268
Dixon, H., 178
Dixon, W. J., 664
Doane, J. A., 396, 405, 664
Dobie, S., 641
Dohrenwend, B. P., 300, 369
Dohrenwend, B. S., 300, 369
Dole, V. P., 661
Doleys, D. M., 535
Donahoe, C. P., Jr., 663

Donaldson, K., 614–15
Dorer, D. J., 325
Dorner, G., 442
Dorsey, M. F., 116
Dorworth, T. R., 344
Dostoyevsky, F., 78
Douglas, J. W. B., 540
Douglas, M., 25
Douglas, V. I., 528
Down, L., 543
Draguns, J. G., 180
Dramaix, M., 284
Drew, C. J., 538, 546
Drossman, D. A., 250
Drugan, R. C., 293
Drummond, T., 530, 621
Duker, J., 165
Duncan-Johnson, C., 390
Dunham, H. W., 398
Dunn, V., 395
Dunner, D. L., 351
Durkheim, E., 360
DuRubeis, R. J., 341
Dwyer, C., 293

Eagleton, T., 630
Eaton, W., 493
Eberhard, G., 276
Eddy, M. B., 32
Eddy, T., 42
Edwards, K. L., 462
Edwards, M. T., 660
Edwards, N., 313, 343
Egeland, J. A., 57, 319, 353, 357
Ehlers, A., 230
Ehrhardt, A. A., 427, 444, 446, 447
Ehrhardt, J. C., 395
Ehrlich, P., 52, 53
Eidelson, J. I., 344
Eisenberg, L., 52
Ekehammar, B., 232, 233
Ekman, P., 159, 194
Elashoff, J. D., 275, 276
Elkin, I., 345, 658
Ellenberger, H. F., 25, 33
Ellery, C., 621, 622, 623, 624
Ellis, A., 124–25, 332, 651, 336
Ellis, E., 222
Ellis, L., 427, 442
Ellsworth, P. C., 159
Elmhorn, K., 523
Emery, G., 230, 334, 362, 651, 658
Emmelkamp, P., 212
Emrick, C. D., 660
Endicott, J., 161, 316, 320, 352
Endler, N., 232, 233
Ennis, B. J., 607, 631
Epstein, L. H., 540, 541
Epstein, L. J., 160
Erdelyi, 71
Ericksen, S., 658–59
Erikson, E. H., 73, 97
Erikson, K., 150, 218
Ernberg, G., 369
Eron, L. D., 168
Ervin, F. R., 217
Escover, H., 373

Esquirol, J., 50
Esterson, A., 396, 397
Eubanks, J. D., 465
Evans, H. I., 264
Evans, M. D., 341, 424
Evon, L. D., 524
Exline, R., 159
Exner, J. E., 166, 168
Eysenck, H., 71, 214, 216

Faber, R., 329
Fagot, B. I., 524
Fairburn, C. G., 538, 539
Fairweather, G., 405–6
Falk, J. R., 539
Falloon, I. R. H., 390, 396, 405, 664
Fancher, R., 331
Farberow, N., 670
Faris, R. E. L., 398
Farrington, D. P., 524
Feinberg, 372
Feinleib, M., 283
Feldman, M. P., 442
Fenichel, O., 245, 331
Fernald, P. S., 639
Ferster, C. B., 554
Fieve, R. R., 349, 350
Fingarette, H., 618
Fink, M., 328
Fireside, H., 628
Fisher, J., 160
Fisher, S., 102
Fishman, R., 239, 352
Fiske, D., 642
Fithian, M. A., 659
Fitzgerald, R. G., 290
Fitzpatrick, J., 178
Fixsen, D. C., 526
Flavell, J. H., 71
Flavin, D., 471
Fleck, S., 228
Fleiss, J. L., 159, 177
Flood, R., 357
Foa, D. B., 191, 213, 657
Fodor, O., 276
Follick, M., 271
Folstein, S., 161
Ford, C. S., 4, 12, 426
Forman, R., 640
Foster, D. W., 60
Foucault, M., 29, 34, 37, 38, 41, 42
Foureman, W. C., 372
Fournier, A., 51
Fowler, R. D., 238
Fowles, D. C., 309, 316
Fox, R., 362, 643, 666
Foxx, R. M., 535
Frances, R. J., 471
Frank, E., 422
Frank, J. D., 639, 641
Frankl, V., 100, 654
Franklin, B., 32, 38
Frederick, C. J., 358
Fredrickson, R. H., 228
Fredrikson, M., 215
Freeman, B. J., 554
Freeman, W. B., 405

French, R., 15
French, T. M., 281, 284
Freud, A., 82
Freud, S., 33, 36, 62–74, 77–84, 93, 94–98,
    101–4, 134, 204–6, 211, 244, 248,
    253–54, 255, 256, 257, 258, 329, 330,
    420, 436–37, 475, 639, 652, 666
Friedman, M., 283, 288
Friedman, S., 497
Friedrich, F. J., 565
Friesen, W. V., 159, 194
Frith, C. D., 395
Fromm, E., 73
Fujimura, O., 581
Furstenberg, F., 426
Fyer, A., 230

Gabrielli, W. F., 502
Gadpaille, W. J., 442
Gage, P., 566, 593
Gagnon, J. H., 426, 431, 432, 433, 435,
    436
Galaburda, A. M., 581
Gale, M., 285
Galen, 29, 30–31
Gallagher, P., 658–59
Garber, J., 313, 343
Garcia, E., 545
Garcia, J., 214, 216, 217
Gardner, E., 561, 569
Garfinkel, P. E., 538
Garmezy, N., 374, 532, 547
Garner, D. M., 538, 663
Garner, W., 293
Garrity, T. F., 302
Garside, R. F., 379
Gautier, T., 427
Gay, P., 101
Gazzaniga, M., 567, 568
Gebhard, P. H., 432, 435
Gehrig, L., 563, 597
Gelder, M. G., 642
Gelenberg, A. J., 328
Gelfand, D. M., 532, 538
Geller, E., 554
Geller, M. H., 643
Genazzani, A. R., 465
George III, King of England, 39
Geraci, M., 230
Gergen, K. J., 181
Gergoulas, A., 276
Gerhard, D. S., 57
Gersh, F., 309, 316
Gershom, E. S., 351
Gershon, E. S., 57
Geschwind, N., 569, 575, 576, 577, 579,
    581
Gibbon, M., 522
Gibbons, R. D., 658–59
Gibralter, J., 402
Gilberstadt, H., 165
Gilderman, 664
Gill, J. J., 288
Gillies, S., 553
Gillin, J. C., 355
Gilman, A. G., 562
Gilmore, G. C., 374, 495, 496, 497, 499

Girgus, J., 340
Gittelman, M., 531, 553
Gittelman, R., 524, 528
Gittelman-Klein, R., 520, 530, 531
Gittleson, N. L., 239
Glaser, R., 293
Glass, D. C., 283, 285–86, 345, 658
Glass, D. R., 149
Glass, G. V., 101, 139
Glazer, H. I., 343, 346
Gleitman, H., 166, 192
Gleitman, L. R., 579, 581
Gleser, G. C., 218
Glisky, E. L., 588
Gloisten, A. C., 530
Glueck, Z., 390
Gluhbegovic, N., 584
Göbell, D., 553
Golan, N., 671
Golden, C. J., 169
Goldfried, M. R., 122, 170
Goldstein, A., 19
Goldstein, M. J., 396, 400, 405, 664
Goodglass, H., 578
Goodman, G., 643
Goodman, L. S., 562
Goodwin, D. W., 256, 462
Goodwin, F. K., 351, 352
Gordon, J. R., 463, 661
Gordon, M. H., 402
Gordon, N., 296
Gorenstein, E. E., 504
Gorman, J. M., 230
Gorsuch, R. C., 232
Gotestam, K., 663
Gottesman, I. I., 54, 159, 198, 239,
    385–87, 501, 502
Gottschalk, L. A., 284
Gould, J., 553
Gould, S. J., 542
Goulding, P., 592
Goulston, K. J., 223
Grace, W., 299
Graf, P., 587
Graham, D., 299
Graham, L. E., II, 663
Graham, R., 285
Grant, B. F., 159
Gray, S., 213
Grayson, J. B., 657
Graziano, A. M., 672
Green, B. L., 218
Green, R., 445
Greenberg, M. S., 328
Greenberg, R. P., 102
Greene, D., 10
Greenspoon, J., 141
Greenwald, D. P., 403, 404, 665
Greer, S., 290, 497
Gregor, T., 26
Gregory, I., 497
Greisinger, W., 50, 51
Grey, S., 246
Griffith, J. J., 389
Grigorenko, P., 629
Grimshaw, L., 245
Groen, J., 298

Grof, P., 351
Gross, H. J., 256, 257
Grossman, H. J., 542
Grossman, L. M., 463
Grossman, M. I., 275, 276, 630–31
Grove, W. M., 375, 395
Gruen, R., 511
Gruenberg, A. M., 505, 511
Gruenberg, E. M., 161
Grunbaum, A., 71
Guess, D., 545
Gumanis, Dr., 614, 615
Gunderson, J. G., 403
Gur, R. C., 55, 256
Gur, R. E., 55
Gurin, J., 541
Gurman, A. S., 642
Gurney, C., 324
Guroff, J. J., 261, 264
Guze, S. B., 241, 252, 253, 256, 323, 357, 462

Hackmann, A., 246
Hager, J., 216
Halberstadt, L. J., 341
Halbreich, U., 320
Haley, J., 396, 644, 648
Hall, C. S., 71
Hall, R. G., 663
Hall, R. V., 145
Hall, S. M., 661, 663
Hallahan, D. P., 530
Hallam, R., 196
Halmi, K. A., 538, 539
Hapern, J., 80
Hamilton, M. L., 465
Hammen, C. L., 149, 315
Hammersmith, S. K., 442
Hampson, J. L., 448
Hanis, C., 541
Hannum, R. D., 345
Harcourt, Countess, 39
Hardy, A. A., 470
Hare, R. D., 496, 500, 504
Harlow, H. F., 320
Harlow, J. M., 566
Harrington-Kostur, J., 661
Harris, B., 208
Harris, E.L., 200
Harris, M. R., 160
Harris, T., 320, 323, 345
Harrison,R., 169
Hart, K. J., 538
Hartman, W. E., 659
Hasin, D. S., 159
Hasse, A., 618
Hathaway, S. R., 162
Hawking, S., 594, 597
Hayes, K., 375
Haynes, S. G., 284, 285
Hazari, A., 240, 241
Heads, T. B., 530
Hecaen, H., 565
Hegedus, A. M., 462
Heider, F., 123
Heilman, K. M., 569
Heiman, J. R., 424

Heitler, J., 640
Hellekson, C. J., 355
Helsing, K. J., 290
Helzer, J. E., 161, 180
Hemsley, R., 555
Hendin, H., 358
Heninger, G. R., 200, 213, 230, 232
Henker, B., 529
Hennigfield, J. E., 482
Henry VIII, King of England, 52
Herman, C. P., 541
Herman, K. D., 322
Hermansen, L., 462
Hermelin, B., 551
Heron, W., 141
Hersov, L., 530, 533, 555
Herzog, D. B., 539
Hess, R.D., 545
Heston, L., 369, 388–89, 391
Hetherington, E. M., 524
Hilgard, E. R., 83, 256
Hill, P. O., 168
Hill, R., 213
Himmelhoch, J. M., 351
Hinckley, J., Jr. 618
Hinz, L. D., 539
Hippius, H., 351
Hippocrates, 200
Hiroto, D.S., 152, 338
Hirschfeld, R. M. A., 316, 352
Hirst, W., 260
Ho, A. K., 465
Ho, C. C., 465
Hoban, T. M., 355
Hobson, R. P., 551
Hodgson, R. J., 114, 236, 237, 239, 240, 241, 242, 246, 255, 438, 657
Hoehn-Saric, R., 639
Hoenig, J., 445
Hoffman, L. J., 152, 153
Hofmann, A., 478–79
Hogarty, G. E., 396, 403, 404, 665
Hokanson, J. E., 284, 285
Holbrook, D., 555
Holden, C., 352, 360
Holliday, J., 293
Hollingshead, A. B., 398
Hollister, L. E., 402
Hollon, S. D., 122, 341, 346, 658
Holmes, G., 206
Holmes, T., 150, 300, 301
Holmstrom, L. L., 222, 668, 671
Holtzman, W. H., 168
Holzer, C. E., 322
Honzik, C. E., 322
Honzik, N. P., 206
Horne, R. L., 290
Horney, K., 72
Horowitz, M., 242
Hostetter, A. M., 57, 319
Hough, R., 493
House, P., 10
Housman, D. E., 57
Houts, P. S., 640
Hovell, M. F., 663
Howlin, P., 551, 552, 555
Hsu, L. K. G., 538

Huber-Smith, M. J., 230
Hubler, 563
Hudson, J. I., 539
Huesmann, L. R., 524
Hugdahl, K., 202, 215, 216
Hughes, H., 237–38
Hulley, S. B., 284
Hume, D., 106
Hung, D. W., 555–56
Hunt, 41
Hunt, M., 412, 425, 431, 448
Hunt, W. A., 483
Hunter, R., 237
Hutchings, B., 502
Hyde, E., 430
Hygge, S., 217
Hyler, S. E., 252
Hyman, B. T., 591
Hyson, R. L., 293

Ickes, W. J., 124
Iker, H., 290
Imber, S. D., 345, 639, 646, 658
Imboden, J. B., 253, 255, 315
Imperato McGinley, J., 427
Ingham, R. J., 536
Ironside, W., 277
Irwin, M., 293
Ishii, N., 60
Iwata, E. A., 116
Izard, C. E., 320

Jablensky, A., 369
Jackson, D. D., 396
Jackson, J. H., 568–69
Jackson, R., 609
Jackson, T., 625
Jacobs, W. J., 215
Jacobson, S., 574
Jagoe, R., 395
Jahoda, M., 19
James, S. P., 355
James, W., 582
Jamison, W., 288
Janah, 462
Janet, P., 248
Janicak, P. G., 658–59
Janis, I., 122
Jarvik, M. F., 660
Javna, C. D., 403, 404, 665
Jaynes, J., 74
Jeffrey, D. B., 541
Jenkins, C. D., 283, 287
Jens, K. S., 264
Jenson, W. R., 538
Jeppsen, A., 261
Jerome, J., 21, 359
Jeurgens, S. M., 485
Johnson, F., 613
Johnson, J. E., 372
Johnson, J. H., 545
Johnson, M., 643
Johnson, V., 413, 417, 420, 422–23, 424, 659
Johnson, W., 170
Johnston, F. E., 541

Johnston, J. C., 209, 246
Johnstone, E. C., 395
Jonas, J. M., 251
Jones, 39
Jones, B., 251
Jones, E. E., 643
Jones, M. A., 465
Jones, R. T., 661
Jones, S., 405
Jourard, S. M., 160
Jukes, E., 553
Jung, C., 71–72

Kabat, L. G., 379
Kaffman, M., 390
Kalat, J., 216
Kamen, L., 293
Kamin, L. J., 208, 542
Kane, J. M., 402, 511
Kanfer, F. H., 122
Kannel, W. B., 284
Kanner, A. D., 300
Kanner, L., 549, 553
Kaplan, H. S., 416, 418, 420, 422, 423,
    433, 659
Kaplan, R., 460–61
Kaplan, S. M., 284
Karasek, R., 287
Karls, W., 228
Karlsson, J. L., 391
Karoly, P., 122
Kasl, S. V., 302
Kaslow, N. J., 320
Kass, F., 505, 506, 508
Katchadourian, H. A., 432, 433
Kates, W., 530
Katz, B., 561
Katz, M., 642
Katz, S., 530
Kauffman, J. M., 530
Kaufman, I. C., 320
Kay, D. W., 379
Kazdin, A. E., 211, 638, 656, 666
Keefe, J. A., 391
Keesey, R. F., 541, 663
Keeton, W. T., 559
Kegan, R., 494
Kehoe, M., 277
Keir, R., 217
Keith, S. J., 403
Keith-Spiegel, P., 644
Kekor, 25
Keller, M. B., 316, 325
Kelley, H. H., 123
Kellogg, J. H., 425
Kelly, G. A., 165
Kelly, J. B., 321
Kendall, P. C., 122
Kendler, K. S., 505, 511
Kendrick, J. S., 287
Kenna, J. C., 445
Kennedy, H. L., 287
Kerr, T. A., 324
Kertesz, A., 575, 578
Kety, S. S., 325, 389, 511
Keveles, G., 608

Keys, D. J., 507
Kidd, K. K., 57, 325
Kiecolt-Glaser, J. K., 293
Kiely, J. L.,545
Kiesler, C. A., 406, 615, 674
Killman, P. R., 329
Kiloh, L. G., 293
Kimberlin, C., 553
Kimmel, S. C., 463
Kingsley, R. G., 663
Kinsey, A. C., 412, 425, 426, 430–31, 435
Kinzie, J. D., 228
Kirby, M. W., 674
Kirigin, K., 526, 527
Kirk, S. A., 178
Kirkley, B. G., 664
Kirschenbaum, D. S., 663, 664
Kirtner, W., 642
Kisson, B., 462
Kittel, F., 284
Klein, D. F., 59, 200, 213, 230, 232, 520,
    530, 531, 656
Klerman, G. L., 203, 300, 316, 318, 320,
    328, 345, 352, 658
Klerman, G. R., 325
Klima, E. S., 578
Kline, J. A., 355
Kluft, R. P., 266, 267
Kluznik, J. C., 223
Knight, R., 400
Knorring, A. L. von, 249, 253, 501
Kobasa, S. C., 300
Koch, E., 3–5, 12, 17
Koelling, R. A., 214, 216, 217
Koh, S. D., 369
Kohn, M. L., 398, 399
Kohut, H., 74, 76, 77, 506, 512
Kolb, B., 569
Kolodner, K., 287
Kondas, O., 536
Korchin, S. J., 165
Kornblith, S. J., 403, 404, 665
Kornitzer, M., 284
Koropsak, E., 285
Korsakoff, S., 582
Korten, A., 369
Koragin, A., 628
Kotin, J., 351
Kotsopoulos, S., 252
Kovacs, M., 320, 346, 658
Kozak, M. J., 191, 213
Kraemer, H., 26
Kraepelin, E., 175, 366, 367, 374
Krafft-Ebing, R. von, 51–52, 429
Kramer, M., 161, 493
Krasner, L., 115
Krauft, C. C., 642
Kraus, W. H., 664
Kretschmer, E., 175
Kringlen, E., 245, 501
Kruger, J. 462
Krystal, H., 221
Kugelmass, 390
Kuhl, D. E., 591, 592
Kuipers, A., 212
Kurland, H. D., 504
Kutchins, H., 178

Labate, C., 661–62
Laborit, H., 401
Lacey, J. I., 296
Lachman, S. J., 275, 282
Laing, R. D., 382, 396, 397, 399
Lake, E., 608–609, 610
Lamb, H. R., 615
Lamiell, J. T., 71
LaMontagne, Y., 438
Lando, H. A., 661
Lang, P., 191, 213
Langer, E. J., 122, 182, 291
Langer, G. B., 471
Langman, M., 276
Langner, T. S., 398
Lansky, D., 663
Lanyon, R. I., 438
Lanzetta, J. T., 192
LaPouse, R., 531
Lassen, C. L., 660
Latane, B. T., 499
Latz, A., 390
Laudenslager, M. L., 292, 293
Lauer, R. M., 540
Laughlin, H. P., 203, 206, 228, 229, 231,
    238, 245, 246, 250, 252, 254, 256,
    257, 259
Lavoisier, A. L., 32
Lavori, P. W., 318, 325
Lazarus, A., 122, 125, 216, 226, 232
Lazarus, L., 293
Lazarus, R. S., 300
Leber, W., 345, 658
Leckman, J. F., 325
Leff, J. P., 403, 404
Leff, M. J., 316, 323, 351, 664
Lefkowitz, M. M., 524
Lehman,D. R., 223
Leitenberg, H., 212, 538, 656
Lemkau, P. V., 369, 669
Leopold, R. L., 225
Lerner, B., 643
LeSage, A., 438
Lesser, I. M., 255
Lessler, K., 643, 666
Lester, D., 264
Levenson, R. W., 463
Levine, J. L., 369, 658
Levine, M., 672
Levine, P., 351
Levis, D. J., 211, 656
Levitz, L. S., 663
Levy, G., 230
Levy, J., 567
Levy, S., 291
Lewine, R. R. J., 369
Lewinsohn, P. M., 147, 311
Lewis, J. M., 396, 400
Lewis, V. G., 446
Lewy, A. J., 355
Leyden, M. A., 124
Liberman, B., 646
Liberman, R. P., 404, 664
Lichtenstein, E., 661
Lidz, T., 397
Liebowitz, M. R., 230

Lin, D. H., 663
Lincoln, A., 352
Lind, D. L., 256, 257
Linden, L. L., 357, 358
Linden, W., 656
Lindenthal, J. J., 300, 316
Lindley, C. J., 402
Lindzey, G., 71
Linebarger, 579
Linehan, M. M., 122
Linsky, A. S., 463
Lipp, M. G., 273
Lippman, M., 291
Lippold, S., 169
Lipsitt, L. P., 151
Little Albert B., 207–208, 214
Littlefield, C. H., 323
Little Hans, 204–206, 207, 420
Litwack, T. R., 607
Livermore, J. M., 620
Lochar, D., 162
Locke, B., 493
Locke, J., 105–106
Lockyer, L., 553
Logan, D.R., 546
Logue, C. M., 320
Lohrenz, L. J., 471
London, P., 10, 627, 633, 647
Long, J. W., 645
Looney, J. G., 273
LoPiccolo, J., 424
Loranger, A. W., 351, 515
Lorr, M., 642
Losonczy, M. F., 395
Lotter, V., 556
Louis XVI, King of France, 32
Lourie, R. D., 545
Lovaas, O. I., 116, 555
Lovibond, S. H., 535
Lowinger, P., 641
Lubin, B., 232
Luborsky, L., 126, 340, 643, 646
Luckhurst, E., 293
Ludwig, W. W., 663
Lumry, A., 122
Lunde, D.T., 432, 433
Lunde, I., 325
Luria, A., 564–65, 569
Lushene, R. E., 232
Luzzatti, C., 565
Lykken, D. T., 498, 499

Maas, J. W., 326
McAdoo, W. G., 663
MacAlpine, I., 237
McCann, D. S., 230
McCary, J. L., 418, 420, 423, 425, 426, 427, 430, 431, 433, 434, 435
McClelland, D. C., 169, 286, 294
McConaghy, N., 435, 439
McConkey, R., 545
McConnell, R. B., 275, 276
McCord, J., 497, 498
MacCulloch, M. J., 442
MacDonald, B., 246
MacDonald, N., 375
McEwan, D., 619

MacFarland, J. W., 206
McFarlane, A., 26
McGarry, A. L., 624
McGee, R., 519, 520, 522, 524, 525, 528, 531, 532
McGhie, A., 374
McGill, C. W., 664
McGlashan, T. H., 400, 510, 511
McGovern, G., 630
MacGregor, R. R., 470
McGue, M., 54
McGuire, R. J., 437, 438
McIntyre, K. O., 661
Mack, R. W., 540
Mackay, A. V. P., 394
McKinley, J. C., 162
McKinncy, W. T., 320, 347
McKinnon, J. A., 218
McKnew, D. H., 320
McLean, 246
McLellan, A. T., 475, 643, 646
MacLeod, C., 242
MacMillan, D. L., 546
MacMillan, M., 320, 556
McNally, C. F., 215, 217
McNeal, 326
McNitt, P. C., 347
McPherson, F. M., 215
McSween, T., 116
Madonia, M. J., 403, 404, 665
Magaro, P. A., 391
Magliocco, D., 284
Magnusson, D., 232, 233
Magraw, R., 223
Maher, B. A., 34, 371, 379
Maher, W. B., 34
Mahler, M., 74
Mahoney, K., 659
Mahoney, M. J., 122, 125, 171, 659
Mai, F., 249
Maier, S. F., 152, 292, 293, 337, 338
Mair, J. M. M., 536
Maletzky, B. M., 433, 438, 439
Maliphant, R., 525
Malitz, S., 328, 373
Malmo, R. B., 296
Mandelcorn, M. S., 256
Mannuzza, S., 524
Marchant, R., 551, 552
Marciano, T.D., 442
Marcus, J., 390
Marcus, M., 574
Margraf, J., 230
Marin, O. S. M., 575, 579
Marinopoulou, A., 276
Mark, N., 462
Marks, I. M., 197, 198, 199, 200, 201, 203, 212, 213, 216, 245, 246, 294, 424, 433, 438, 642, 656, 657
Marlatt, G. A., 463, 661
Marset, P., 212
Marsh, L., 395
Marshall, J. C., 256, 581
Martin, B., 376, 524
Martin, F. C., 293
Martin, J. L., 300
Martin, M. F., 261, 264

Marx, A. J., 674
Marx, K., 101
Marx, M. B., 302
Marxer, F., 287
Maslow, A. H., 19
Mason, W., 298
Masters, W. H., 413, 417, 420, 422–23, 424, 442, 659
Matarazzo, J. D., 161, 271, 483
Mather, C., 28
Mathews, A., 242
Matthews, K. A., 285, 288
Matthews, S., 406
Matthysse, S., 55
Mavissakalian, M., 213
Mawson, D., 213, 246
May, P. R. A., 664
May, R., 21
Mayer, J., 578
Mayock, Mr., 604–605
Mazziotta, J. C., 241
Means, J., 296
Medley, E. S., 276, 285
Mednick, S. A., 151, 389, 390, 502, 525
Medvedev, R. A., 628
Medvedev, Z. A., 628–29
Meehl, P.E., 159, 620
Meichenbaum, D., 119, 122, 125
Mellsop, F., 178
Melton, G. B., 625
Melzack, R., 141
Mendels, J., 316, 358
Mendelsohn, F., 442
Mendelsohn, G. A., 643
Menn, A. Z., 406, 674
Merbaum, M., 225
Merchant, A., 161
Merikangas, K. R., 325
Mersky, H., 249
Mesmer, F. A., 31–32, 35
Mesulam, M. M., 565
Metalsky, G. I., 341
Metcalfe, 171
Methuen, J., 178
Metter, J. E., 591, 592
Meyer, A., 175, 366–67
Meyer, C. B., 222
Meyer, E., 253
Meyer, V., 246, 536
Meyers, J. K., 300, 316
Mezzich, J., 15
Michael, S. T., 398
Michel, J., 117
Midelfort, H. C. E., 26
Miklowitz, D. J., 396
Mill, J. S., 616
Miller, J. S., 616
Miller, N. E., 146, 153, 271
Miller, P. L., 584, 586
Miller, R. C., 656
Miller, S., 355
Miller, T. I., 101
Miller, W. R., 315, 343
Mills, H., 41
Milner, B., 566, 582, 583, 585, 586
Milton, J., 77
Mineka, S., 214, 217

Mintz, J., 405, 664
Minuchin, S., 538
Mirsky, A. A., 276
Mirsky, A. F., 390
Mischel, W., 71, 168, 171, 311, 514
Mishkin, M., 584, 585
Mishra, S. P., 169
Mitchell, K. M., 642
Mittelmann, B., 277
Mittler, P., 553
M'Naghten, D., 621–22
Mohs, R. C., 590
Molk, L., 296
Monahan, J., 607
Money, J., 427, 444, 446–47, 448, 449
Monk, M., 531
Monroe, S., 300, 346, 351, 659
Moody, R. L., 272
Moore, K. A., 426
Moorer, S. H., 529
Moos, R. H., 320
Morris, N., 626
Morris, R. J., 642
Morris,T., 290
Morrow, L., 291
Morse, R. M., 485
Morton, 38
Moscovitch, M., 588, 589
Mosher, L. R., 403, 406, 674
Moss, H. B., 664
Mowrer, O. H., 117, 535
Mowrer, W. M., 535
Mueser, K. T., 404
Mullaney, D. M., 173
Mullaney, J. A., 463
Munzinger, H., 545
Murad, F., 562
Murphy, D. L., 352, 353
Murphy, G. E., 658
Murray, H. A., 166
Murstein, B. I., 169
Muser, J., 296
Myers, J. K., 229, 317, 321, 493, 642

Nadel, L., 215, 586
Nagler, S., 390
Nagoshi, C. T., 463
Nash, E. H., 639
Nasrallah, H. A., 395, 462
Nathan, P. E., 241, 454
Neary, D., 592
Neaton, J. D., 284
Nee, J., 320
Nesse, F. M., 230
Nestadt, G. R., 161
Nettleton, N. C., 567
Newell, G., 640
Newlin, D. B., 463,
    467, 633
Newman, B., 463
Newman, J. P., 504
Nielson, S., 593
Nies, A., 319
Nisbett, R., 73, 79, 167, 379, 651
Nishihara, Y., 60
Nolen-Hoeksema, S., 319, 320, 340, 522
Nordby, H., 375

Nordlie, J. W., 256
Norris, W., 40
Norten, S., 253
Northen, B., 592
Nowlan, R., 481
Noyes, R., 200
Nyswander, M. E., 661

O'Brien, C. P., 461, 643
O'Brien, M. L., 530
Obrist, W. D., 55
O'Connor, Dr., 614, 615
O'Connor, K., 196
O'Connor, N., 551
Odier, C., 204
Öhman, A., 215, 216, 217, 375
Ohwaki, S., 546
Oi, M., 273
Okada, M. O., 232, 233
O'Kulitch, P., 663
Oldham, J. M., 515
Olgin, J. E., 466
Ollendick, T. H., 538
Olsen, S. C., 395
Oltman, J., 497
Olweus, D., 524
Ong, P., 116
Opler, M. K., 398
Ordman, A. M., 664
Orgel, S., 282
Orne, M. T., 142, 267, 268, 639
Ornitz, E. M., 554
Orr, S. P., 192
Ortmann, J., 325
Osherson, A., 261–63
Oshiba, K., 273
Osler, Sir W., 282
Öst, L. G., 202, 663
Ostfeld, A. M., 285
Overholser, J. C., 436
Overmier, B., 337, 338

Packer, H., 620
Padesky, C. A., 315
Padgett, N. E., 287
Padian, N., 658
Palij, M., 230
Paneth, N., 545
Paploukas, A., 276
Parker, F. C., 287
Parkes, M. C., 290
Parloff, M. B., 647, 653
Parnas, J., 151
Parwatikar, S. D., 372
Patterson, G. R., 525, 529
Patterson, K., 581
Patterson, T., 375
Pattie, F. A., 32, 35
Paul, G. L., 171, 172, 211
Paul, N., 253
Paul, O., 285
Pauls, D. L., 57, 325
Pauly, I. B., 444, 445
Pavlik, W. B., 344
Pavlov, I., 107–12, 117–18, 214, 337, 437
Paykel, E. S., 300, 316, 319, 322, 323
Payne, R. W., 375

Peake, P. K., 514
Pearson, K., 149
Peel, R., 621
Peffer, M. P., 300
Pelham, W. E., 529
Pelse, H., 298
Penick, S.B., 127, 663
Penn, G. M., 293
Pennebaker, J. W., 255
Penny, R., 293
Pepys, S., 30
Perel, J., 213
Perkins, K. A., 78
Perkins, M., 512–13
Perley, M. J., 253
Perls, F., 99–100
Perri, M. G., 663
Perris, C., 324
Pershard, D., 237
Persons, J., 184
Pervin, L. A., 164
Peterson, C., 291, 320, 340, 344, 347
Peterson, D.R., 168
Peterson, J. L., 426
Peterson, R. A., 369
Peterson, R.E., 427
Pettingale, K. W., 290
Petty, F., 153, 462
Petzel, T. P., 372
Pfefer, 316
Pfohl, B., 515
Phelps, M. E., 241, 591, 592
Phillips, E. L., 526
Phillips, L., 180, 382
Picard, R. S., 290
Pierce, C., 285
Pihl, 320
Pilkonis, P., 345, 646, 658
Pinel, P., 40–41, 175
Piper, W., 646
Pittluck, A. T., 260
Place, E.J. S., 374
Platt, J. J., 661
Podrabenek, 628
Pohoresky, L. A., 343, 346
Poizner, H., 578
Pokorny, A. D., 357
Polak, P. R., 674
Poldinger, W., 351
Polivy, J., 541
Pollack, G.H., 281, 284
Pollack, J. M., 240, 241
Pollit, J. D., 245
Pomerleau, C. S., 302
Pomerleau, O. F., 302
Pomeroy, W. D., 432, 435
Pope, H. G., Jr., 251, 539
Porjesz, B., 462
Porsolt, R. D., 344
Porter, R.W., 379
Posner, M. I., 565
Pound, E., 629–30
Powell, K. E., 287
Premack, D., 115
Price, D.L., 591
Price, K.P., 315, 343
Price, V. A., 288

Prichard, J. C., 493–94, 498
Propping, P., 462
Prosin, H., 322
Prusoff, B. A., 325, 658
Pryor, R., 475
Puig-Antich, J., 358–59
Purcell, D., 296
Putnam, F. W., 261, 264

Quadfasel, F. A., 577
Quay, H. C., 525, 545, 554

Rabavilos, A. D., 246
Rabin, K., 554
Rachman, S. J., 114, 191, 196, 207, 212,
    215, 236, 237, 239, 240, 241, 242,
    245, 246, 253, 255, 438, 657
Rack, P., 241
Radloff, L. S., 319
Rado, S., 331
Rafal, R. D., 565
Rahe, R., 150, 300, 301
Rakaczky, C.J., 288
Rall, T. W., 562
Ramm, E., 213
Rand, K. H., 640
Rao, D. C., 54
Raps, C. S., 315, 343, 344
Raskin, D. E., 321
Raskin, R., 443
Ratcliff, K. S., 161
Rat Man, 244
Rattan, R. B., 377
Ravaris, C., 319
Raven, A., 320
Rawlings, E. I., 643
Ray, I., 621
Rayner, R., 146, 207–208, 214
Razani, J., 664
Reagan, R., 618
Reddaway, P., 628
Redlich, F.C., 398
Reed, D., 284
Reese, H. W., 151
Rehm, L. P., 122, 334
Rei, M. A., 546
Reich, L. H., 351
Reich, T., 239, 316, 352, 501
Reich, W., 630
Reifman, A., 403
Reiger, D., 493
Reinhard, K. E., 344
Reiss, D.J., 403, 404, 665
Reivich, M., 55
Renault, P. F., 662
Rennie, T. A. C., 398
Rescorla, R. A., 117, 209, 216
Resick, P., 222
Resnick, S., 55
Reyher, J., 78
Reynolds, W. M., 346
Rezin, V., 239
Reznikoff, M., 168
Rhazes, 257
Rice, J., 318, 352
Richards, R., 443
Richardson, S. A., 540

Richter, C., 289–90
Rifkin, A., 372
Rimmo, P., 215
Rioch, M. J., 673
Risley, T., 555
Ritter, B., 657
Ritvo, E. R., 554
Ritz, M. C., 476
Roatch, J. F., 316, 323
Robins, E., 323, 357
Robins, I., 239
Robins, L. N., 159, 161, 180, 198, 229,
    317, 318, 321, 350, 493, 497, 504
Robinson, D. S., 319
Rockefeller, N., 547
Rodin, J., 271, 291, 293, 662
Rodnick, E. H., 396, 400
Roff, J. D., 400
Rogers, C., 19, 77, 98–99, 165, 641, 642
Rogerson, H.L., 203
Rohner, J. J., 535
Rohobit, D., 284
Rolf, J. E., 389
Romanoski, A. J., 161
Roosevelt, E., 19
Roosevelt, T., 351, 352
Rooth, F. G., 433, 438
Roper, G., 246, 657
Rorschach, H., 166–68, 169
Rose, R. M., 277
Rosellini, R. A., 345
Rosenbaum, M. S., 529
Rosenberg, C. M., 241
Rosenblum, L. A., 320
Rosenhan, D. L., 10, 19, 159, 175, 182,
    183, 184–85, 620, 630
Rosenman, R. H., 283
Rosenthal, D., 325, 387, 389, 391, 392,
    503, 513
Rosenthal, N. E., 352, 354, 355
Rosenthal, P. A., 358
Rosenthal, R., 654
Rosenthal, S., 358
Rosenthal, T. L., 532
Rosenzweig, S. P., 640
Rosman, B., 538
Ross, 541
Ross, D. C., 200, 213
Ross, E. D., 560
Ross, J. D., 524
Ross, L., 10, 73, 79, 167, 379, 651, 656
Ross, M., 442
Ross, W. D., 284
Roth, M., 324, 591
Roth, W. T., 230
Rothbaum, F., 10
Rothblum, E. D., 662
Rothman, D., 42
Rotman, Z., 555–56
Rotter, J. B., 10, 121, 122
Rounsaville, E. S., 345, 658
Routh, D. K., 545, 554
Roy, E. A., 569
Roy-Byrne, P. P., 230
Rozin, P., 216, 412, 425, 426
Rubenstein, D., 422

Rubinstein, E., 255, 642
Rugg, D., 661
Rush, A. J., 334, 346, 362, 658
Rushton, J. P., 323
Russakoff, L. M., 515
Russell, M., 660
Russell, W.R., 586
Rutter, M., 520, 524, 532, 547, 550, 551,
    552, 553, 554, 555
Ryan, R. M., 538
Ryan, S. M., 292, 293

Saccuzzo, D.P., 375
Sacher-Masoch, L., 431
Sack, D.A., 352, 355
Sackheim, H. A., 256, 328
Sade, Marquis de, 431
Safer, D.J., 530
Saffran, E., 575, 579
St. George-Hyslop, 591–92
Sakai, T., 239
Salomon, M. K., 530
Salzman, L., 246
Samuelson, H., 325
Sanders, M. D., 256
Sandler, J., 240, 241
Sanford, E.J., 535
Sangrey, D., 671
Sank, L. I., 226, 227, 671
Sarason, S. B., 669
Saron, C., 328
Sartorius, N., 369
Sartory, G., 246
Sasanuma, S., 581
Savage, L. J., 662
Sawrey, W. L., 278
Sayers, B., 536
Scarr, S., 545
Schachter, S., 482, 499–662
Schacter, D. L., 587, 588
Schaefer, C., 300
Schaffer, C. E., 328, 372
Schapira, K., 324
Scharf, M., 277
Scheff, T. J., 11
Scheftner, W., 316
Schenk, B., 442
Scher, M., 642
Schiavi, R., C., 419
Schildkraut, J. J., 326
Schlesier-Stropp, B., 539
Schmale, A., 290
Schmauk, F. J., 500
Schmiedel, B., 442
Schmueli, J., 390
Schneider, J. A., 664
Schneidman, E., 670
Schoenfeld, D., 285
Schreiber, F., 261
Schreibman, L., 556
Schroeder, D., 462
Schuckit, M. A., 462, 463
Schull, W. J., 541
Schulsinger, F., 151, 325, 390, 462, 502,
    541
Schulterbrandt, J. G., 320
Schumer, F., 168

Schuyler, D., 324, 325, 329, 357, 362
Schwab, J. J., 322
Schwartz, 579
Schwartz, E., 539
Schwartz, G. E., 78
Schwartz, J. M., 241
Schwartz, M. F., 113, 442, 446, 575, 590
Schwartz, S., 545
Schwertner, H. A., 465
Scott, T. H., 141
Scovern, A. W., 329
Scoville, W. B., 582–83
Scull, A., 39, 42
Seager, C., 357
Searles, H. F., 396
Searles, J., 463
Sears, R. R., 80
Segal, J., 644
Segal, S., 460
Segarra, J. M., 577
Seligman, M. E. P., 10, 123, 152, 208, 209,
    214, 215, 216, 242, 246, 278, 279,
    291, 293, 307, 312, 313, 315, 319, 320,
    332, 337, 338, 340, 342, 343, 344, 347
Selin, C. E., 241
Sells, S. B., 345, 662
Selye, H., 297
Semmel, A., 345
Semmel, M. I., 546
Senay, E. C., 662
Seneca, M., 355
Serling, R. J., 211
Shaffer, D., 359, 535
Shafi, M., 359
Shagass, C., 296
Shapiro, A. K., 640
Shapiro, B., 373
Shapiro, D., 240, 241
Shapiro, J. G., 640
Shapiro, R. J., 640
Shapiro, R. M., 663
Shapiro, S. K., 161, 545, 554
Shavit, V., 293
Shaw, B. F., 362, 658
Shaw, D. W., 334
Shea, T., 345, 658
Sheehan, D. V., 230
Shekelle, R. B., 159, 284, 285
Shenker, R., 524
Shepard, E. M., 284
Sher, K. J., 463, 464
Sherer, M., 477
Sherman, A.D., 153
Sherman, G. F., 581
Shields, J., 190, 386–87
Shipman, V. C., 545
Shneidman, E., 356, 358, 360, 361
Shoham-Salomon, V., 654
Sholomskas, D., 658
Shore, J. E., 220
Shoulson, I., 595
Shrout, P. E., 300
Sideris, E., 276
Siegel, W., 663
Sifneos, P. E., 255
Sigvardsson, S., 249, 253, 501
Silberman, E. K., 261, 264, 390

Silva, P. A., 519, 520, 522, 524, 525, 528,
    531, 532
Silverman, J. M., 590
Silverman, L. H., 78
Simmons, J. Q., 116
Simons, A. D., 658
Simpson, D. D., 662
Simpson, D. M., 593
Simpson, G. M., 664
Simson, P. G., 152, 153, 342
Sinclair, J. D., 465
Singer, J. E., 271
Singer, M. T., 396
Sivage, C., 530
Sizemore, C., 262
Skinner, B. F., 112–17
Sklar, L. S., 293
Skodol, A. E., 522
Skolnick, B. E., 55
Sladek, J. K., Jr., 595
Slater, P. C., 584, 586
Sleator, E., 529
Slobogin, C., 625
Smith, D. S., 471
Smith, E. E., 15
Smith, J. C., 101
Smith, J. L., 122
Smith, M. L., 44, 139
Smith, R. J., 497
Smith, T. L., 293
Smyth, L., 78
Sneed, T.J., 535
Snow, B., 252
Snowden, J. S., 592
Snyder, K. S., 396, 405
Snyder,S.H., 392, 394, 402
Snyder, S.S., 10
Snyder,W. D., 593
Sohlberg, S. C., 390
Solomon, R. L., 117, 209, 337, 352, 458
Somes, G.W., 302
Soranus, 29
Sorensen, T. I. A., 541
Sotsky, S., 345, 658
Southard, D. R., 287
Spanos, N. P., 268
Spark, R. F., 420
Speed, N., 223
Speicher, C., 293
Spence, J. T., 232
Sperry, R., 567
Spevak, P. A., 663
Spiegel, D., 264
Spielberger, C., 232
Spitz, R. A., 320
Spitzer, R. L., 159, 161, 175, 177, 252,
    273, 505, 506, 508, 522
Spohn, H. E., 375
Sprague, R. L., 529
Spratto, S. R., 465
Sprenger, J., 26
Spring, B., 384
Springer, N. N., 402
Squire, L. R., 329, 584, 585, 586, 659
Srole, L., 275, 398
Staats, A.W., 121
Stall, R., 471

Stampfl, T. G., 211, 656
Stangl, D., 515
Stark, O., 540
Stayton, S. E., 546
Steadman, H., 603, 608
Steel, R., 553
Steele, J. B., 238
Stefanis, C., 246
Stein, L., 326, 674
Steinberg, L., 283
Steinhausen, H.-C., 553
Steinmark, W. W., 656
Steketee, G., 657
Stellar, E., 539
Stern, D., 71, 74
Stern, J., 544
Stern, R.S., 213, 246
Stevenson, B. E., 322
Stinnett, J., 135, 249
Stoller,R.J., 429, 444, 449
Stone, A. A., 607, 608, 620
Stone, A. R., 639
Stone, G. C., 271
Stoney, C. M., 288
Storms, M. D., 437, 441
Stoyva, J. M., 173
Strachan, A.M., 396
Straus, M. A., 463
Straus, R., 283
Strauss, J., 380, 538
Strauss, M. E., 372
Struening, E., 640
Strupp, H. H., 640, 642, 643, 666
Stuart, R.B., 663
Stunkard, A. J., 116, 127, 539, 541, 662,
    663
Sturdevant, R. A. L., 276
Sturgis, E. T., 443
Sturla, E., 427
Stuss, D. T., 566
Suarez, J. M., 260
Suckerman, K. R., 642
Sugimura, A., 273
Sullivan, H. S., 72–73
Summers, M., 26
Suomi, S. J., 320
Susman, V. L., 515
Susser, M., 276, 545
Sussex, J. N., 57, 357
Sutton, W., 494
Swanson, D. W., 435
Swanson, W.C., 358
Sweeney, P. O., 345
Sylvester, D., 319
Szasz, T. S., 60, 355, 373, 607, 616–17,
    627
Szklo, M., 290

Taguiri, R., 82
Talland, G., 582
Tallman, J. F., 486
Talovic, S. A., 389, 390
Tanenbaum, R. L., 320
Tarter, R. E., 462
Tarver, A., 478
Tatum, E. L., 220
Taube, C. A., 403

Zimbardo, P. G., 379, 507
Zimmerman, J., 256, 257
Zimmerman, M., 515
Zitrin, C. M., 200, 213, 656
Zola-Morgan, S., 585
Zoppel, C. L., 643
Zouzounis, J. A., 659
Zubin, J. E., 168, 384
Zucker, R. A., 471
Zuckerman, M., 232
Zullow, H., 319, 340
Zusman, R., 285

., 10
L. A., 625
R., 282
H., 325, 389, 639
D., 164
., 178
, 525
D., 658
. K., 529
I. Q., 569
A., 420
B. B., 426
J. W., 426
J., 237
., 460
, L. A., 211
B., 373
. R., 285
, T. H., 584
, A. F., 223
, C. J., 441
, J. B. W., 505, 506, 508, 522, 637
, P., 447
, R. B., 60, 159, 285, 329
, S., 519, 520, 522, 524, 525, 528,
, 532
son, D. A., 539
son, M., 664
.H., 347
., 50
A., 239
G. T., 121, 253, 656, 662, 663, 666
, J. D., 60
, J. R., 463
.K., 664
L., 551, 553
R. R., 540, 541
, C., 218
er, R., 536
cott, D. W., 74
tur, G., 319, 462
rs, L. C. 159
R. D., 524
nan, F., 619
in, H. A., 503
in, M., 401
rner, M. G., 200, 213, 656
zan, M., 642
nlleben, B., 553
ff, M. M., 526, 527, 555
f, S., 284
fe, T., 512–513
fer, J., 122
ff, A., 620–21, 623, 624
ff, H. G., 277, 284
ff, O. H., 540
pe, J., 112, 207, 209–11, 232, 650
raich, M., 530
odrow, K., 462
odruff, R. A., 252, 253, 256
odward, B., 615
ody, G. E., 643, 646
rtman, C. B., 223
bel, T. A., 162
rm, M., 283
nne, L. C., 389, 396, 397
shak, G., 203

Yale, C., 664
Yalom, I. D., 74, 88, 90, 91, 640
Yang, E., 553
Yaniv, S., 390
Yates, A., 375
Yeager, C. T., 504
Yeates, S. R., 553
Young, B. G., 437
Yule, W., 533, 536, 547, 551, 552, 555
Yuwiler, A., 554

Zafiropoulou, M., 215

Zaidel, E., 567
Zangwill, O. L., 583
Zatta, P., 591
Zax, M., 672
Zec, R. F., 395
Zentall, S. S., 528
Zentall, T. R., 528
Ziegler, F.J., 253, 255
Zigler, E., 180, 369, 382
Zilberg, N. J., 218
Zilbergeld, B., 424
Zilboorg, G., 35

Subject Index

abnormality:
  assessment methods for, 156–73
  defining of, 5–7
  diagnosing of, 3–5, 15–17, 49–50,
    156–85
  elements of, 7–15
  family resemblance approach to, 7,
    13–15, 15–16, 626
  history of approaches to, 23–37
  investigating of, 133–55
  linguistic conventions for, 11–12
  models of, 47–49; *see also* behavioral
    model; biomedical model; cognitive
    model; existential model; psychody-
    namic model
  normality vs., 5, 17–19, 68, 101, 107,
    626–27
  organic-functional distinction in,
    558–69
  as social judgment, 9, 10, 12–13, 16,
    23–24, 593–94, 626–27
  societal stigma and, 603, 630–31
  see also specific disorders
abnormal psychology, social and political
  abuses of, 603, 626–31
acetylcholine, 47, 193, 590–91
Achievement Place, 526–27
acquisition phenomena, 109, 113–14, 194,
  207–209, 214–16
ACTH (adrenocorticotrophic hormone),
  297
action-orientation, 319
activity raising, 334
addictions, *see* alcohol dependence; drug
  dependence; obesity
Addington v. *Texas,* 601
Adlerian therapy, 653
adoption studies:
  on alcohol dependence, 461–62
  on antisocial personality disorder, 501,
    502
  on criminality, 525
  on depression, 325

on IQs, 545
on manic-depression, 57
on schizophrenia, 388–89
adrenaline (epinephrine), 193, 499
adrenergic system, 193, 230
adrenocorticotrophic hormone (ACTH),
  297, 456
Affect Adjective Checklist, 232
affective disorders, 59, 227, 308–63
  see also depression, bipolar; depression,
    unipolar; mania
age:
  and depression, 307, 317–18, 320–21
  and schizophrenia, 389
  and suicide, 358–60
aggressiveness, 283, 284, 286
agnosia, 565
agoraphobia, 9, 199–200, 201, 530, 531,
  596
  panic attacks in, 198–200, 213–14, 229,
    230
  treatment of, 212, 532, 656
AIDS (Acquired Immunodeficiency
  Syndrome), 450, 470, 473, 478, 484,
  487
  and alcohol, 470–71
  dementia complex, 593
air traffic controllers, 277
akathesia, 402
alarm reaction, 297
alcohol, 450, 451, 460, 461–71, 473, 482,
  488, 583, 660
  and cell-mediated immunity, 470
  dependence on, 461–66
  and high-risk behaviors, 470–71
  intoxication, 466, 467, 479, 487
  tolerance of, 481
  withdrawal, 465–66, 467–68, 477
alcohol dependence, 175, 321, 351,
  361–71, 452, 453, 454, 461–66, 478,
  489, 660
  AIDS and, 470–71, 478
  amnesia resulting from, 260

DT's and, 467
endorphin compensation hypothesis in,
  464–66
genetics and, 455, 461–63, 466
medical and social complications in,
  466–68
and society, 450, 451, 460, 461
tension reduction hypothesis in, 463–64
treatment of, 108–109, 118, 468–69, 660
Alcoholics Anonymous (AA), 469, 660
alexithymia, 255
ALI (American Law Institute) rule, 623
altruism, 66, 84, 87
Alzheimer's disease, 588, 590–92
  aluminum and, 591, 592
amenorrhea, 536
American Law Institute (ALI) rule, 623
Amish:
  manic-depression study among, 47,
    56–58, 352–53
  unipolar depression among, 317, 318–19
amnesia, 235, 581–89, 595
  and Alzheimer's disease, 588, 590–92
  anatomy of, 584–85
  anterograde, 260, 585, 588
  causes of, 259, 260–61, 571, 583–84
  consolidation block theory of, 586
  description of, 585–86
  digit span in, 585
  functional, 589
  global (generalized), 259
  Korsakoff's syndrome, 573, 583, 584–85
  in multiple personality, 263, 589
  nature of memory defect in, 260, 585–86,
    590–93, 594
  neurologically based, 260, 581–89
  psychogenic, 259–61, 269, 273
  retrieval failure theory of, 586–88
  retrograde, 259–60, 585–86, 587, 588,
    589
  selective (categorical), 260
  syndrome of, 582–83, 584–85
  treatment of, 586, 588–89

amniocentesis, 544
amphetamine psychosis, 392, 394
amphetamines, 392, 457, 476–78, 487
    disorders treated with, 529, 534–35
amyotrophic lateral sclerosis (ALS), 562,
    563, 597
anal character traits, 64
anal stage, 63–64
androgen, 442, 446–47
androgen-insensitivity syndrome, 442
anger, 80, 277
    in depression, 329–31
    hostility and, 284–85
animalism, 29–30, 38, 39, 40
animal magnetism, 32, 35
animal phobia, 121, 196, 198, 199,
    201–202, 597
    among children, 206, 530, 532
    irrationality of, 216
    Little Albert experiment and, 146,
        207–208
    Little Hans case and, 204–206
    selectivity of, 214–16
    therapy for, 93–94, 212–13
animal possession, 24, 25
animism, 24–25, 26, 28
animistic approach, 24–30, 34
    treatment in, 24, 25, 27, 34
anomia, 565
anorexia nervosa, 115–16, 534, 536–39,
    596, 663
anticonvulsant drugs, 539
antidepressant drugs, 138, 213–14, 226,
    230, 316, 325, 328, 344, 475, 478, 531,
    539, 657, 658
antigens, 292, 293
anti-hypertensive drugs, 288
anti-mentalism, 107
antipsychotic drugs, 616
anti-reductionists vs. reductionsts, 60–61
antisocial personality disorder (psychopa-
    thy; sociopathy), 9, 49, 128, 268,
    493–504, 513, 514, 524
    causes of, 496–504
    chronic under-arousal in, 499, 504, 525
    conscience and responsibility lacking in,
        495, 496
    criminality linked to, 493–94, 500–503
    diagnosing of, 494–95
    as disorder of will, 493–94
    and drug abuse, 454–55, 461, 462, 474
    emotional poverty in, 495, 496, 499
    family and social context in, 496–98
    genetic basis for, 496, 500–503, 504, 525
    inadequately motivated behaviors in,
        495
    learning defects in, 496, 498–500, 525
    personality characteristics of, 494–96
    physiological dysfunctions in, 496,
        503–504
anxiety, 9, 63, 77, 189–234, 235–70,
    271–303, 482
    and alcohol, 463
    aleviation of, 77; *see also* coping
        strategies
    castration, 65, 102, 204, 205, 207, 420
    cognitive therapy for, 120, 121–22

components of, 195
    about death, 88–90, 203, 261, 300
    drug treatment for, 58, 226–28, 230,
        656–57
    in Freudian theory, 70–71
    gastric secretions and, 276–78, 282
    physiological correlates of, 172–73
    in post-traumatic stress disorder, 218,
        219
    questionnaires on, 232, 233
    as realistic, neurotic, or moral, 70
    separation, 531, 533
    in sexual dysfunction, 420–21, 423
    as social experience, 72
    state vs. trait distinction, 232
anxiety disorders, 150, 189–90, 226, 228,
    268, 269
    experience class of, 189–234
    generalized, 195, 228, 231–32, 233, 268
    inferred class of, 235–70; *see also*
        dissociative disorders; obsessive-com-
        pulsive disorders; somatoform pain
        disorders
    panic disorder, 195, 228–31, 268
    treatment of, 227, 232, 656–57; *see also*
        phobia; post-traumatic stress disorder
aphasias (language disorders), 55, 462
    conduction, 577
    expressive, 576
    receptive, 576
appraisals, 121–22, 124
apraxia, 559–60
arbitrary inference, 333
arousal level, 499, 525
arteriosclerosis, 282
ASQ (Attributional Style Questionnaire),
    340, 341
assertiveness training, 126, 334, 344
assessment, *see* psychological assessment
assimilative projection, 79
asthma, 58, 295, 298, 452, 475
atherosclerosis, 569, 593
at-risk studies, on schizophrenia, 388,
    389–90
attentional deficits, 462
    in schizophrenics, 374–75, 376
attention-deficit hyperactivity disorder
    (ADHD), 521, 523, 527–30
attention disorders, in children, 523,
    527–30
attention withdrawal, 78
attributions:
    in cognitive therapy, 122–24, 334,
        335–36
    of depressives, 338–42, 343, 345, 347
    global-specific dimension in, 123,
        339–42, 345
    internal vs. external, 122, 123, 339–42,
        345
    stable-unstable dimension in, 122–23,
        339–42, 345
    therapy and, 123–24, 125–26, 334–36,
        344
authenticity, 90
autism, 547–56
    behavioral therapy for, 115, 116,
        127–28, 552, 555

causes of, 553–55
    insistence on sameness in, 549, 551, 552
    intellectual development in, 545,
        552–53
    language development in, 547, 550–51,
        555–56
    prevalence of, 553
    prognosis for, 556, 557
    social development in, 551–52
    symptoms of, 547–48, 549–53
automatic thoughts, 121–22, 127, 334–35,
    344
autonomic nervous system (ANS), 192
autonomy, 20, 538
aversion therapy, 438–39, 442, 651, 661
avoidance-approach conflicts, 278
avoidance responding, 117–18, 194
    extinction of, 208–209, 246
    learned helplessness and, 337–38
    sociopaths deficient in, 498–500, 525
avoidant personality disorder, 507
axons, 564, 571

Babinski reflex, 569
barbiturates, 402, 485–86
basal ganglia system, 241, 593, 594
BASIC ID technique, 125–26
battered women, shelters for, 671
Baxtrom v. *Herold,* 607–608
B-cells, 292
BDI (Beck Depression Inventory), 340
bed wetting (enuresis), 534–35
behavioral assessment, 170–72
    therapeutic effectiveness measured by,
        647
behavioral disorders, in children, 522–30
behavioral medicine, 271
behavioral model, 48, 105–29, 165
    amnesia as viewed in, 261
    assumptions of, 107
    autism as viewed in, 554
    avoidance learning in, 117–18
    cognitive model vs., 118–19, 126–27
    empiricism and, 105–106
    and erectile dysfunction, 421
    evaluation of, 127–28, 268, 269
    existential psychology vs., 91
    normal vs. abnormal behavior in, 107
    obsessive-compulsive disorders as
        viewed in, 242–44, 268
    operant conditioning in, 107, 112–17
    paraphilia as viewed in, 436, 437–38
    Pavlovian conditioning in, 107–12
    phobia as viewed in, 110, 205, 206–17,
        268
    psychosomatic disorders as viewed in,
        295, 298–300
    sexual dysfunction as viewed in, 421
behavioral therapy, 649–51
    for alcoholism, 108–109, 118, 660
    for anorexia nervosa, 115–16, 663
    assessment of, 102–103, 127–28
    assumptions of, 106–107
    for autism, 116, 127, 552, 555–56
    avoidance learning in, 118
    for bulimia nervosa, 539, 664
    client-therapist relationship in, 642

cognitive-, 125–27, 226, 227
for depression, 657
for enuresis, 535
for homosexuality, 442–43
for hyperactivity, 529–30
for obesity, 127, 662, 663
for obsessive-compulsive disorders, 118, 245–46
operant conditioning in, 114–17
for paraphilias, 438–39
Pavlovian conditioning in, 109–12, 209–14
for phobia, 111–12, 205, 209–14, 532, 650–51
for reading disabilities, 546–47
for schizophrenia, 664–65
for separation anxiety disorder, 531
for smoking, 660–61
behaviorism, 106–107
beliefs, 120, 121, 124
and depressions, 312–13
irrational and illogical, 124–25
benzodiazepines, 58, 485, 486
bereavement:
depression after, 82–83, 300, 322, 330–31
normal vs. depressive reaction to, 330
and stress, 293, 299–303
sudden death and, 289–91
beta-endorphins, 456, 472
biochemistry, as etiology, 48, 49, 54–55, 56–58
biofeedback, 172–73, 282
biogenic amines, 325–28, 329, 347
biomedical model, 28–30, 47–61, 156–57, 595
assessment of, 59–60
assumptions of, 49–58
autism as viewed in, 554
biochemistry as etiology in, 48, 49, 54–55, 56–58
depression as viewed in, 315, 325–29, 347–48, 350
genetics as etiology in, 49, 53–54
germs as etiology in, 49, 50–53
juvenile delinquency as viewed in, 525
and phobias, 213
psychosomatic disorders as viewed in, 295–98
schizophrenia as viewed in, 384–95
sociopathy as viewed in, 500–504
transsexualism as viewed in, 446–47
biomedical treatment:
behavioral therapy vs., 111
cognitive therapy vs., 229–31
drawbacks of, 60
for general paresis, 53, 60
methodology of, 49, 58–59
neuroanatomy as etiology in, 55–56
see also drug treatment
bisexuality, 426–27
blacks, depression among, 321–22
blame, irrational, 336
blanchophobia, 198, 202–203
blindness, hysterical, 134–35, 136–38, 256–57, 258
blood-brain barrier, 455–56, 472

blood pressure:
in emergency reaction, 193, 297
see also high blood pressure
borderline personality disorder, 511–13
brain, 193
anatomy of, 559, 562–68
biochemical organization of, 383, 562
biomedical model and, 56–58
blood supply to, 574
diagnostic techniques for, 572–75, 594, 595
disordered, 55–56
dopamine in, 54–55, 326, 383, 392–95, 400, 402, 476, 477, 478, 562
drug use and, 450, 454, 455–57, 462, 466, 467, 472, 486
dysfunctions of, in sociopaths, 503–504
front-back organization of, 564–66
hierarchical organization of, 568–69
information-processing system in, 564
language center in, 567, 575–76
lateral organization of, 567–68, 574–75
left-right organization of, 567–68
movement center in, 564–66, 568–69, 571
planning-verification-action system in, 564, 569
in schizophrenics, 392–95
seizures in, 554, 567, 570, 572, 584
spatial organization of, 395, 562–69, 571
surgery on, 595
tumors in, 562, 569, 572, 583, 585, 588, 593
see also nervous system; neurons
brain damage, 170, 544, 577, 596–97
to left vs. right hemisphere, 328, 567–68, 571, 574–75, 575–76, 581, 585
movement after, 564–66
personality changes after, 566
recovery of function after, 593, 595
redundancy and, 571–72, 593, 596
systems vulnerable to, 570–71
unilateral neglect and, 565, 585
see also nervous system disorders
brain waves, abnormal, 554
brief psychotherapy, 93–98
Briquet's syndrome, 248, 249, 253
Broca's area, 575, 576, 577–78, 597
bulimia nervosa, 521, 534, 538–39, 663–64
bypassing, 418

caffeine, 454
CAMI (California Alliance for the Mentally Ill), 616
cancer, 289, 480, 481, 484
susceptibility to, 290–91, 294
cannabis, see marijuana
case histories, see clinical case histories
castration anxiety, 65, 71, 102
in erectile dysfunction, 420
in phobia, 204, 205, 207
catatonic schizophrenia, 370, 371
catecholamines, 57–58, 294, 295, 325–27, 353, 476, 478, 560–61
catharsis, 36, 96
cathexis, 436–37, 438, 441

cat phobia, 196–97, 208, 218
CAT scan, 573, 575
causality, see etiology
cell-mediated immunity, 470
central nervous system (CNS), 58, 192, 467, 486, 528, 544
cerebral cortex, 241, 559, 564, 568
cerebrospinal fluid, 569, 572, 593
childhood disorders, 519–57
adult-life related to, 521–22, 524, 528, 531, 540, 557
anorexia nervosa, 115–16, 534, 536–39, 663
attention-deficit hyperactivity disorder (ADHD), 521, 523, 527–30
autism, 116, 127, 521, 545, 547–56, 557
behavioral, 521, 522–30
bulimia nervosa, 521, 534, 538–39, 663–64
classifying of, 521–22, 556
conduct, 496, 522–27, 557
developmental, 520–21, 541–57
disruptive behavior, 521, 522–23
eating, 521, 534
emotional, 522, 530–34
encopresis, 534
enuresis, 521, 534–35
gender identity, 521
habit (physical), 521, 534–41
identifying, 556
intellectual (mental retardation), 521, 541–46
obesity, 539–41
oppositional defiant, 523
parental agency and, 519–20, 556
phobia, 205–206, 530–33
prognosis for, 557
reading difficulties, 521, 546–47
separation anxiety, 530–31, 533
situational-specificity of, 520
stuttering (stammering), 521, 534, 535–36
suicide among, 358–59
child molestation (pedophilia), 428, 434–35, 435–36
cholinergic receptors, 483
cholinergic system, 193
chromosomes, 11, 57, 58, 61, 352
abnormal, in Down's syndrome, 543–44, 591, 592
antisocial personality disorder and, 500–501, 502–503
chronic hypomanic disorder, 348
cigarette smoking, see smoking
civil commitment, see involuntary commitment
clang associations in schizophrenia, 374
classical conditioning, see Pavlovian conditioning
client-centered therapy, 98–99, 654, 666
clinical case histories, 133, 134–37
evaluation of, as method, 135–36, 153–54
example of, 134–35
psychodynamic theory based on, 101–103, 106
clinical interviews, 159–61

clinical psychologists, 635
cocaine, 451, 452, 454, 457, 458, 475–76, 477, 478, 481, 488, 489
cognitive ability, 544–45
cognitive-behavioral therapy, 125–26, 226, 227
cognitive deficits:
 cognitive (selective) filter, 374, 375, 376
 in depression, 313–15, 342, 343
 in learned helplessness, 338, 343
cognitive model, 48, 107, 118–28
 behavioral model vs., 118–19
 depression as viewed in, 324, 332–48, 349–50
 evaluation of, 127–28
 obsessive-compulsive disorders as viewed in, 241–44
 psychosomatic disorders as viewed in, 295, 298–99
 sexual dysfunction as viewed in, 421
cognitive processes, 120–25
 appraisals, 121–22
 attributions, 122–24
 beliefs, 124–25, 312–13
 expectations, 120–21
cognitive therapy, 651–52
 for anorexia nervosa, 663
 for anxiety, 120, 121–22
 assessments of, 127–28, 334
 for bulimia nervosa, 539, 664
 for depression, 119–20, 334–37, 341, 345–48, 651–52, 657–58
 focus of, 119, 125
 for obesity, 662
 for phobia, 121
 for PNI, 295
 psychodynamic therapy vs., 126–27, 334
 rational-emotive therapy, 124–25
cognitive treatment
 biomedical therapy vs., 229–31
cognitive triad, 332–33, 657
cohort trends, 318, 320
collective unconscious, 72
color obsession, 238–39, 243, 247
combat fatigue, 223–24
commitment, see criminal commitment; involuntary commitment
communication:
 in autism, 547–48, 550–51
 difficulties in, between parents and children, 396, 526–27, 538
 schizophrenics' attempts at, 381–82
 in schizophrenogenic family, 396–97
communicaion deviance, 396
competence, in optimal living, 19, 20
competitiveness, 283, 284, 285, 288, 289
compulsions:
 anxiety neutralized by, 238–39, 242–44, 246–47
 cleaning rituals, 236, 237–38
 defined, 236
 see also obsessive-compulsive disorders
compulsive personality disorder, 508–509, 514
computer-assisted tomography (CAT scan), 573, 575
concealment of meaning, 396, 397

concentration camps, 81–82, 82–83, 100
 survivors of, post-traumatic stress disorder among, 218, 221, 223, 226–28
conditioned responses (CR), 108–10, 194, 207–11, 213
conditioned stimulus (CS), 108–10, 194, 207–11, 213, 214
conditioning, see operant conditioning; Pavlovian conditioning
conduct disorders, 496, 522–27
 genetic influences on, 525
 juvenile delinquency and, 522–23, 524–25
 prognosis for, 521–22, 557
 treatment of, 525–27
conflict, 62, 63, 77, 93, 140, 345
 anxiety caused by, 70–71
 avoidance-approach, 278
 Oedipal, 65, 68–69, 102, 204–206
 repressed in unconscious, 69–70, 78–79
 between self-image and memory, 78
conformity, 399
confounds, 140–42
 demand characteristics, 140, 141–42
 experimenter bias, 140, 141
 nonrandom assignment, 140
 subject bias, 140, 141
conscious experience, 86–87
consciousness, 69–70, 73, 107, 569
 defenses and, 77–87
consciousness raising (CR), 637
containment services, 669–72
 hot-lines, 670
contamination obsession, 236, 237–38, 243, 245–46
continual emergency reaction, 287
continuous reinforcement (CRF), 114
control, 100, 285–86, 538
 and CHD, 285–86
 and environment, 291
 flexible, 10
 loss of, 7, 10, 14
 parental, 64
 sense of, 75
control groups, 139, 140, 141, 142, 144
conversions, see hysteria; somatoform pain disorders
Cook-Medley hostility score, 285
coping strategies (defense mechanisms), 63, 72, 77–87, 93, 95
 denial, 82, 84
 displacement, 81, 84, 244
 editing processes, 79
 fusion, 88, 89–90
 identification, 81–82
 intellectualization, 83, 84
 isolation, 82–83, 84
 maturational hierarchy of, 84–86
 in obsessive-compulsive disorders, 244–45
 projection, 79–80, 81, 84
 rationalization, 83–84
 reaction formation, 80
 repression, 77–78, 82–83, 84
 specialness, 88–89, 90
 sublimation, 84

core conflictual relationship theme (CCRT), 126–27
coronary heart disease (CHD), 484
 risk factors for, 282–83
 studies of, 283–84, 285, 287
 and Type A personality, 282–88
corpus callosum, 567
corpus stratum, 393, 394
correlational studies, 133, 147–50
 causality unclear in, 149–50
 evaluation of, 150, 153–54
 example of, 147–50
 relationships in, 147
correlation coefficient (r), 149
counseling psychologists, 635
counterbypassing, 423–24
counterphobia, 81
counter shock, 297
crack, 476
creativity, of schizophrenics, 391–92
criminal commitment, 603, 618–26
 incompetence to stand trial and, 624–26
 insanity defense and, 619–23
criminal insanity, 607–608
criminality:
 childhood conduct disorders and, 522, 523
 genetic factors in, 525
 see also antisocial personality disorder
crisis interventions, 669–72
cross tolerance, 465
cultural differences:
 and attitudes toward sex, 425–26
 and drug abuse, 451, 486
 and suicide, 358

dancing manias, 25
dangerousness:
 to others, 606–608
 prediction of, 607–608
 to self, 606, 608–609
death, 302
 fear of, 88–90
 of spouse, 255, 290–91, 293, 294, 300
 sudden, 289–92
death phobia, 198, 203
decision making, difficulty in, 315
defense mechanisms, see coping strategies
delayed auditory feedback, 536
delinquency, see juvenile delinquency
delirium tremens (DT's), 467
delusions, 87, 368
 of control, 377, 378
 of grandeur, 50, 370, 377, 379
 normal cognitive processes and, 378–80
 of persecution, 370, 377–78, 379, 606, 621
 of reference, 377, 378, 379
 in schizophrenia, 368, 370, 377–80, 383, 395
demand characteristics, 140, 141–42
dementia, 175, 589–93
dementia praecox, 366, 367
demonic possession, 24, 34
denial, 82, 84, 87, 450
 of meaning, 396, 397

dependence, in ulcer-prone personality, 280–81
dependent personality disorder, 508, 514
dependent variables, 137
depersonalization, 258, 479–80
depressants, barbiturates as, 402, 485–86
depression, 175, 307–55
    as element of abnormality, 9, 11
    normal vs. clinical, 307–308
    suicide as outcome of, 308, 351, 355, 357, 360
    treatments for, 657–58
depression, bipolar (manic-depression), 47, 48–49, 61, 308, 348–54
    among Amish, 47, 56–58, 352–53
    cause of, 352–53, 476
    characteristics of, 350–52
    depressive component of, 348–49, 350–51
    genetic vulnerability to, 352–53
    manic component of, 56, 349–50
    symptoms of, 349–50, 354, 355
    treatment of, 58, 308, 353–54, 659
    unipolar depression vs., 308
depression, unipolar, 47–48, 308–48, 355, 471
    age factors in, 307, 317–18, 320–21
    agoraphobia and, 200
    among Amish, 317, 318–19
    anaclitic, 320
    as anger turned upon self, 329–31
    animal model of, 152–53
    attributional style in, 343, 345, 347
    behavioral therapy for, 657
    biological model of, 47–48, 324–29, 346, 347
    bipolar depression vs., 308
    among blacks, 321–22
    bulimia nervosa and, 539
    childhood or recent losses and, 82, 322–23, 344, 345, 347
    in children, 320–21, 522
    cognitive deficit in, 313–15, 343
    cognitive models of, 48, 324, 332–47
    cognitive therapy for, 119–20, 334–37, 341, 345–48, 651–52, 657–58
    course of, 324, 347–48
    dream deprivation and, 138–39, 344
    and drugs, 471, 478
    drug treatment for, 58, 138, 153, 316, 325, 327–28, 344, 657, 658
    electroconvulsive shock treatment for, 59, 316, 325, 328–29, 344, 657, 658–59
    endogenous vs. exogenous, 316
    episodic vs. chronic, 315–16
    explanatory style and, 339–42
    genetics and, 318, 325
    helplessness perceived in, 329, 331
    integration of theories and therapies for, 347
    lack of pleasant events, 147–50
    learned helplessness model of, 332, 337–45, 346–47
    measuring symptoms of, 314
    modernity studies of, 317–19
    mood and emotional symptoms of, 308, 309, 314, 333, 343

    motivational deficit in, 308, 313–15, 325–27, 337, 342
    neuroanatomical basis of, 328
    neurochemical basis of, 325–27, 560–61, 597
    obsessions linked, 239, 242
    physical symptoms of, 308, 315, 333, 343, 346
    PNI and, 293, 294, 295
    premenstrual, 319–20
    psychodynamic model of, 324, 329–32
    psychodynamic therapy for, 316, 331–32, 657, 658
    self-esteem problems in, 310–12, 329, 331, 332–33, 343, 512
    social class and, 321–22
    sudden death and, 290
    symptoms of, 308–15
    thought symptoms of, 308, 309–13, 332–36, 343
    vulnerability to, 317–23, 344–45, 347
    among women vs. men, 317, 319–20
depressive personality, 331
depressogenic assumptions, changing of, 334, 336
deprivation dwarfism, 60, 61
dereflection, 100, 654
desire, lack of, 418, 424
developmental disorders, 520–21, 541–57
    pervasive, 547–56; see also autism
    specific, 546–47
diagnosis, 156–57, 173–85
    in biomedical model, 50
    cluster and specific, 178–79
    context factor in, 181–83
    diagnostician's expectations and, 181, 183
    DSM-III in, 15, 175–81, 184
    evaluation of, 184
    historical origins of, 174–75
    psychological vs. medical, 175, 181
    reasons for, 174
    research vs. clinical, 184–85
    self-, 21–22
    source credibility and, 181, 183–84
Diagnostic Interview Schedule (DIS), 161
diatheses, genetics and, 275, 276, 282, 295–98
diathesis-stress models, 273, 295
    behavioral view of, 298, 299–302
    of peptic ulcers, 276–81, 282
    psychodynamic view of, 298
    of schizophrenia, 664
diets, and exercise, 662–63
direct sexual therapy, 421, 422–23
disconnection syndromes, 577
discriminative stimuli, 112, 113
disinhibition, 467
disorganized schizophrenia, 370
disowning projection, 79–80
displacement, 81, 84
    in obsessive-compulsive disorders, 244
disruptive behavior, 521, 522–30
dissidents, political psychiatry and, 603, 626, 627–30
dissociative disorders, 235, 258–68
    amnesia, 235, 259–61, 268, 269, 273

    anxiety component of, 235–36, 259, 261, 268, 269
    multiple personality, 235, 259, 261–68, 269
divorce, childhood depression and, 320–21
dopamine, 326, 383, 392–95, 476, 477, 478
    Parkinson's disease and, 402, 562
    schizophrenia and, 54–55, 400
dopamine hypothesis, 392, 393, 394, 395
double-binds, 389, 396
double-blind experiments, 141
Down's syndrome, 543–44, 591
dream deprivation, 138–39, 344
dreaming:
    physiological signs of, 138
    sexual excitement during, 420
dreams:
    in Gestalt therapy, 99–100
    traumas relived in, 218, 219, 221
    unconscious revealed in, 69
drug dependence, 450–91
    alcohol, 461–71
    amphetamines, 476–77
    and availability, 487–88
    barbiturates, 485–86
    cocaine, 475–76
    dependence and vulnerability in, 454–55
    diagnosing, 451–54
    drug effectiveness and, 455–61
    education and, 488–89
    emotional and financial costs of, 450, 454
    hallucinogens, 478–81
    IV, 450, 470, 471, 473, 474, 478
    LSD, 478–79, 481
    marijuana, 480, 487–89
    narcotics, 471–75
    PCP, 479–80
    prognosis for, 486–90
    sedatives-tranquilizers, 485–86
    smoking and nicotine, 481–85
    society and, 450, 451, 460, 461, 486–87, 489–91
    stimulants, 475–78
    treatment of, 468–69, 473–75, 478, 484–85, 489, 659, 661–62
drug reminder cues, 460–61, 475, 478
drugs, 49, 450–91
    acquired motivation of, 457–60
    addiction to, 451, 457–60
    affective properties of, 458–60, 472, 476
    antipsychotic, 55
    availability of, 487–88
    basic effects of, 455–61
    brain functions and, 450, 454, 455–57, 462, 466, 467, 472, 486
    conditioned craving for, 460–61
    dose-response relationship of, 458–59
    effectiveness of, 455–56
    half-life of, 456, 457, 460, 476–77, 478, 480, 486
    historical use of, 451, 461, 470–72, 475, 478, 481–82, 485
    intoxication of, 456, 466, 467
    pleasure of, 458, 459–60
    potency of, 455–56

drugs *(continued)*
  rate of deactivation of, 456
  side effects of, 58–59
  tolerance to, 453, 454, 458, 459
  vulnerability to, 455
  withdrawal from, 451, 453–54, 456, 458,
    459–60
  see also alcohol; depressants; hallucino-
    gens; marijuana; narcotics; stimulants
drug treatment, 485, 645, 649
  for anxiety disorders, 232, 657
  in biomedical model, 49, 54–55, 58–59,
    60
  for bulimia nervosa, 539
  for childhood disorders, 557
  for drug abuse, 661–62
  for enuresis, 534–35
  for hyperactivity, 529–30
  for manic-depression, 58, 308, 353–54,
    659
  for nervous system disorders, 588, 595
  for panic attacks, 230
  for peptic ulcers, 281
  for phobia, 213
  placebo effect in, 141
  for PNI, 295
  for post-traumatic stress disorder,
    226–28
  for schizophrenia, 58, 59, 60, 174, 392,
    394, 395, 402–404, 406, 664–65
  for separation anxiety disorder, 531
  for unipolar depression, 138, 316, 325,
    327–28, 341–42, 344, 345–46, 657,
    658
DSM-I *(Diagnostic and Statistical Manual
    of Mental Disorders,* First Edition),
    175, 180
DSM-II *(Diagnostic and Statistical
    Manual of Mental Disorders,* Second
    Edition), 175, 180, 626–27
  DSM-III vs., 176, 177–78
  reliability of, 175, 176, 177
DSM-III *(Diagnostic and Statistical
    Manual of Mental Disorders,* Third
    Edition)
  childhood disorders in, 519, 520, 534
  depression in, 315–16
  drug abuse in, 475
  DSM-II vs., 176, 177–78
  homosexuality in, 426
  multiple axes approach in, 176–77
  post-traumatic stress disorder in, 224
  reliability of, 177–79
  schizophrenia in, 369
  somatoform disorders in, 248
  validity of, 180–81
DSM-III-R *(Diagnostic and Statistical
    Manual of Mental Disorders,* Third
    Edition—Revised), 175–81
  antisocial personality disorder in, 494
  borderline personality disorder in, 511
  categories in, 627
  childhood disorders in, 556
  depression in, 152, 316
  and diagnosis, 15, 184, 273, 539
  drug abuse in, 451–54, 486
  DSM-II vs., 176

homosexuality in, 426
mental disorder defined in, 175–76
multiple axes approach in, 176–77
neurology and, 560
neurosis defined in, 268–69
premenstrual depression in, 320
reliability of, 177–78
schizophrenia in, 367, 382
somatoform disorders in, 248
validity of, 180–81
Durham test, 622, 624
Durham v. *United States,* 622
dysfunction, 175–76
dyslexia, 579–81, 596–97
  acquired, 579, 581
  Chinese and, 596–97
  developmental, 579, 581
  English and, 596–97
  Japanese and, 581
  phonological, 580–81
  surface, 581

eating disorders, 521, 534
  anorexia nervosa, 115–16, 534, 536–38,
    663
  bulimia nervosa, 521, 534, 538–39,
    663–64
  obesity, 127, 539–41
  treatments for, 662–64
echolalia, 548, 550
efficacy expectation, 121
ego, 67, 68, 70, 72, 74, 96, 97
ego-dystonic homosexuality, 426, 439–43
  treatment of, 442–43
ego-syntonic homosexuality, 439–40
ejaculation, 432
  physiology of, 414–15
  premature, 416, 419, 424
  retarded, 416, 419
electroconvulsive shock therapy (ECT), 59,
    316, 325, 328–29, 344, 649, 657,
    658–59
electroencephalograms (EEG's), 503–504,
    554, 572
electromyagraphs (EMG's), 173
elimination disorders, 521, 534–35
emergency reaction, 192–93, 195, 230,
    231, 238
  blood pressure and, 193, 297
  evolution and, 297
  general adaptation syndrome and,
    297–98
  and Type A personality, 283, 284,
    286–87, 288
emotional arousal, chronic deficit in, 499,
    525
emotional catharsis, 36, 96
emotions:
  core self and, 74–75
  and environment, 404–405
  expressed, 396
  Pavlovian conditioning and, 110–11,
    112
  of sociopaths, 495, 496, 499
empathy, 75, 77, 98
empiricism, 105–106, 107
encopresis, 534

encounter therapies, 654
endogenous morphine and opioids, 456,
    464, 472, 473
endorphins, 294, 295, 456–57, 464–66,
    641
enkephalins, 456
enuresis, 521, 534–35
environment, 151, 404–405, 544–45
environmental competence, 19, 20
environmentalism, 106, 107
environmental model, *see* behavioral
    model; cognitive model
enzymes, 58, 319, 451, 590
epidemiological evidence, 51
epilepsy, 554, 567, 570, 572
epinephrine (adrenaline), 193, 326, 499
erectile dysfunction, 416, 417, 419, 429
  of physical vs. psychological origin, 420
  primary vs. secondary, 417
  psychological causes of, 420
  situation specific vs. global, 417
  therapy for, 421, 424
erection, penile, 414, 415, 420
erogenous zones, 63
erotic arousal:
  impairment of, 415–16, 416–18, 420–21
  physiology of, 414–15
  therapy for, 422–24
errors in logic, 332, 333–34
escape responding, 194–95
etiology (causality), 133
  biochemistry as, 48, 49, 54–55, 56–58
  in biomedical model, 49, 229–31
  in clinical case histories, 134, 136, 137
  in cognitive model, 229–31
  in correlation studies, 149–50
  in experiments of nature, 151
  genetics as, 49, 53–54, 56–58
  germs as, 49, 50–53
  neuroanatomy as, 55–56
  in scientific experimentation, 137–40,
    145, 153
  suggested by diagnosis, 174
executive monkey study, 140, 279–80
exercise
  and CHD, 283, 287, 288
  diets and, 662–63
exhibitionism, 428, 432–33, 439
exhortative will, 91, 93
existential model, 88–93
existential psychology, 88–93
  fear of dying and, 88–90
  responsibility central to, 90–91
  will concept in, 91–93
existential therapy, 48, 654–55, 666
  client-centered therapy, 98–99
  Gestalt therapy, 99–100
  logotherapy, 100
  philosophical beliefs in, 98
exorcism, 34, 448
expectations, 120–21, 124
experimental effects, 137–38
experimental groups, 139, 141, 142, 144
experimentalism, 106, 107
experimental method, 106
experimental studies, *see* scientific
    experimentation

experimenter bias, 139, 141
experimenter-blind design, 141
experiments of nature, 133, 150–52,
 340–41, 342
 evaluation of, 151–52, 153, 154
 prospective, 151
explanatory style
 and depression, 339–42
 pessimistic and optimistic, 291–92, 293,
 294, 340
extinction:
 of avoidance responding, 208–209, 246
 obsessive-compulsive disorders and,
 246–47
 as operant phenomenon, 113–14
 as operant therapy, 116–17
 partial reinforcement and, 114
 as Pavlovian phenomenon, 109
 in phobia therapies, 111–12, 209–14
 see also flooding; modeling therapy;
 response prevention; systematic
 desensitization
extinction trials, 208–209

factitious disorders, 250, 251–52
family:
 communication within, 396, 526–27,
 538
 counseling, 636, 654–55
 schismatic (divided), 397
 schizophrenia relapse rate and, 404,
 664–65
 schizophrenogenic, 384, 389–90,
 395–97, 399–400
family resemblance approach:
 abnormality recognized by, 7, 13–15
 hazards of, 15–17, 626
family therapy, 636, 654–55
fear, 189–95, 269, 463
 as conditioned response, 109, 110, 194,
 207–208
 of death, 88–90
 degree of, 195
 elements of, 190–95
 instrumental responses to, 194
 normal vs. phobic, 195, 196, 206–207,
 532
 in panic attacks, 231
 as treatment for reason, 38–39
fear disorders, 189–90, 226, 228
 see also phobia; post-traumatic stress
 disorder
feelings:
 confronted in existential therapies,
 98–100
 somatoform pain disorder and, 255
feeling substitution, 80–81
fetal hormones, 441–42, 446–47, 447–48
fetishes, 428–29, 430, 432
 conditioning of, 437–38
flat affect, 383, 395
flooding, 111, 650–51
 obsessive-compulsive disorders and,
 245–46
 phobia and, 111, 209, 211–12, 656
foot fetishists, 429, 437–38
free association, 93, 97, 334, 652–53

frequency distribution, 143
frigidity, see sexual unresponsiveness
fugue states, 259, 260, 589
functional analyses, 171
fusion, 88, 89–90

galvanic skin response (GSR), 500
gastric secretions, 275, 276–78, 282, 295,
 298
gender identity, 427
gender identity disorders, 521
gender role, 427
general adaptation syndrome, 297–98
generalized anxiety disorder, 190, 195, 228,
 231–32, 268
general paresis, 61, 184
 eradication of, 53, 60, 156
 syndrome of, 50
 syphilis linked to, 50–53, 60
genetics:
 alcoholism and, 455, 461–63, 466
 Alzheimer's disease and, 590, 591–92
 antisocial personality disorder and, 496,
 500–503, 504, 525
 autism and, 554
 cultural-familial retardation and,
 544–45
 depression and, 308, 319, 325, 352–53
 diathesis and, 275, 276, 282, 295–98
 and drug dependence, 455
 enuresis and, 534
 as etiology, 49, 53–54, 56–58
 homosexuality and, 441–42
 juvenile delinquency and, 523–25
 mental retardation and, 543
 obesity and, 541
 panic attacks and, 230
 PKU and, 544
 schizophrenia and, 53–54, 384–92,
 395–96, 400
 see also adoption studies; twin studies
genital plethysmographs, 173
genital stage, 63, 66–67
genital stimulation, 423
germs, as etiology, 49, 50–53
Gestalt therapy, 99–100
glia cells, 561
glove anesthesia, 251, 255
goal-directed will, 91–93
graded task assignment, 334
graphemes, 579, 580
grave disability, 609–10
growth:
 and existential model, 88–93
 in optimal living, 19–21
 see also personality development
guilt, 217–18, 220, 221
guilty but mentally ill (GBMI) verdict,
 623–24

habit disorders, 521, 534–41
hallucinogens, 478–81
 LSD, 478–79, 481
 marijuana, 456, 479, 480, 481, 487,
 488–89
 medical and social complications of, 481
 PCP, 479–80

psychopharmacology of, 480–81
 tolerance of, 480–81
 withdrawal from, 481
hallucinations, 59, 60, 368–69, 570
 hallucinogens and, 478, 479, 480, 481
 in schizophrenia, 161, 368, 372–73, 375,
 383, 395
 sensory deprivation and, 141–42
haloperidol, 59, 393–94, 402
hashish, 480
headaches, biofeedback and, 173
head trauma, 593
 amnesia caused by, 260, 583–84, 585,
 588
health psychology, 271–303
heart attacks, 477
 hypertension and, 282, 284, 286, 288
 among Type A vs. Type B persons, 283,
 284, 285, 286, 288, 300
 uncontrollable life events and, 286, 300
helplessness:
 attributional model of, 338–42
 immune system and, 292–94, 295
 perceived in depression, 329, 331
 sudden death and, 289–91
 and Type A personality, 284, 285–86,
 288
 see also learned helplessness
hermaphrodites, 446–47
heroin, 456, 457, 458, 466, 472, 474, 482
 methadone programs and, 661–62
high blood pressure (hypertension), 297,
 540
 personality traits and, 284–85, 286, 287,
 299
 treatment of, 325–327
hippocampus, 583, 585, 587–88, 591
histrionic personality disorder, 505–506
HIV (human immunodeficiency virus),
 470, 471
homosexuality, 426–27, 430, 439–43
 causes of, 441–42
 changeability of, 442–43
 ego-dystonic, 426, 439–43
 ego-syntonic, 439–40
 exclusive, 426
 societal attitudes toward, 425, 426–27,
 441
 transsexuality and, 445
hopelessness:
 in depression, 312–13, 332–33
 immune system and, 292–94
 sudden death and, 289–91
 and suicide, 362
hormones, 60, 441–42, 446–47, 447–48,
 595
hospitals:
 insane segregated at, 37–39
 rise of, 36–37
 see also psychiatric hospitals
hostages, post-traumatic stress disorders
 of, 227
hostility, 283, 284–85, 288, 289
hot-lines, 362, 670
Huntington's chorea, 593
hyperactivity, 454, 521, 523, 527–30
 behavior management for, 529–30

hyperactivity *(continued)*
  drug therapy for, 529
hypersensitivity tests, 292, 294
hypertension, *see* high blood pressure
hyperventilation, 231
hypnosis, 32–34, 83–84
  catharsis under, 35–36
  Charcot's study of, 33–34, 35
  mesmerism as precursor of, 32–33, 35
  self-, 265, 266, 267–68
  in treatment of hysteria, 32–34, 35,
    247–48, 258
  in treatment of multiple personality, 266
  in treatment of smoking, 484
hypochondriasis, 84, 87, 203–204
hypomanic personality, 348–352
hypothalamus, 193
hypotheses, in clinical case histories,
  135–36, 137
hysteria:
  Galen's investigation of, 29, 30–31
  historical view of, 29–34, 49
  hypnosis in treatment of, 32–34, 35,
    134–35, 247–48, 258
  prevalence of, in historical periods, 23*n*
  see also somatoform pain disorders

id, 67–68, 69–70, 72, 74
ideal standards, violation of, 7, 12, 14, 16
ideas:
  associations between, 105–106
  flight of, 350
  of reference, 377, 511, 513
identification:
  with aggressor, 81–82
  as coping strategy, 82
  with same-sex parent, 66, 427
identity, gender, 427
illnesses, *see* physical illnesses
illness phobia, 198, 203, 218
imagery, 227
imipramine, 213, 531, 534–35, 658
immune system, 289, 290–95, 595
immunization, 292
immunocompetence, 292–94
immunoglobulin, 292, 294
immunologic memory, 292
impaired judgment, 606
implosion, 656
impotence, *see* erectile dysfunction
inanimate object phobia, 198, 202–203
inauthenticity, 90
incest, 66
incidence, 198
incomplete penetrance, 57, 58
incompetence to stand trial, 623–26
incomprehensibility, 7, 9, 14
independent variable, 137, 147
indoleamines, 326
infanticide obsession, 244, 245, 247
infantile autism, 547–56. *See also* autism
injection of meaning, 396–97
injury phobia, 198, 203
insanity defense, 618–24
  "appreciate and conform" test in, 623
  debate over, 432, 618, 621
  GBMI verdict in, 623–24

mental disease test in, 622, 623
  "right-wrong" test in, 621–22, 623
instrumental conditioning, *see* operant
  conditioning
instrumental responses, 194
intellectualization, 83, 84, 87
Intelligence Quotient (IQ), 169–70
  developmental disorders and, 546, 553,
    556
  genetic factors in, 462, 543
  mental retardation and, 170, 542, 544,
    627
intelligence tests, 162, 169–70, 542
inter-judge reliability, 157, 159
"intern's syndrome," 21–22
interpersonal relationships, 227, 523
  positive, in optimal living, 19, 20–21
interpersonal therapy (IPT), 345, 346, 658
intersubjectivity, 75
interviews, 159–61
interview schedule, 160–61
intravenous (IV) drug users, 450, 470, 471,
  473, 474, 478
introcosm, 74
introspection, 107
involuntary (civil) commitment, 603,
  604–18
  abolishment of, 616–18
  as deprivation of liberty, 606–607
  due process of law in, 606–607, 610–11
  release from, 613–16
  requirements for, 605–10
  right to treatment in, 612–13
  standard or proof in, 611–12
  see also criminal commitment
irrationality, 7, 9, 14
isolation, 72, 302
  as coping strategy, 82–83, 84

Jackson v. *Indiana,* 625
job training programs, 668–69
Jungian therapy, 653, 666
juvenile delinquency, 521, 523
  genetic factors in, 525–27
  socialized vs. unsocialized, 523–24
  social sources of, 524–25
  treatment of, 526–27

Kappa statistic *(K),* 159, 179
Korsakoff's syndrome, 573, 583, 584–85

laboratory models, 133, 152–53
  see also animal studies
language, 75–76, 91, 102
language deficits, in autism, 547, 550–51,
  555–56
language disorders, *see* aphasias
latency stage, 63, 66
law, and abnormality, 603–26
law of effect, 112
L-DOPA, 393, 562, 594
learned helplessness, 319, 337–45, 456
  assessment of, 346–47
  attributional dimensions in, 338–39,
    343, 345
  cause of, 344

cognitive deficit in, 338, 343
  experimental discovery of, 337–38
  in humans, 338, 346–47
  norepinephrine depletion in, 343
  passivity deficit in, 152, 337–38, 342–43
  prevention of, 344–45
  therapy for, 152–53, 344, 346–47
  unipolar depression compared with,
    152, 339–45
learning:
  avoidance, 117–18
  defects in, sociopathy and, 496, 498–500
  by operant conditioning, 112–15
  by Pavlovian conditioning, 107–11
  vicarious, 121
left-sided neglect, 565
Lessard v. *Schmidt,* 610–11, 612
libido, 63, 64, 67
life events:
  and alcohol, 463
  depression and, 293, 294, 322–23
  psychosomatic disorders and, 299–302
  stress and, 293–94, 300, 463
lifespan, and stress, 296–97
lithium carbonate, 57, 58, 308, 353–54,
  657, 659
Little Albert experiment, 146, 207–208,
  214
Little Hans case:
  behavioral analysis of, 207
  psychodynamic analysis of, 204–206
lobotomies, 596
logical errors, 332, 333–34
logotherapy, 100
loneliness, fusion and, 89–90
longitudinal studies, 151
Lou Gehrig's disease, 562, 563, 597
lycanthropy, 25
lymphocytes, 292
lysergic acid diethylamide (LSD), 478–79,
  481
lysing, 292, 293, 294

macrophages, 292
magnetic resonance imaging (MRI), 573
magnification, 333, 334
mainlining, 455
mainstreaming, 546
maladaptiveness, 7, 8–9, 14
malingering, 250–51, 252
Malleus Maleficarum, 26
mammillary bodies, 585
mania, 81, 175, 308, 348, 349–50, 476
manias, dancing, 25
manic-depression, *see* depression, bipolar
Manifest Anxiety Scale, 232
MAO (monoamine oxidase) inhibitors,
  138, 325, 327–28, 344, 539, 657, 658
marijuana, 456, 479, 480, 481, 487,
  488–89
marriage counselors, 636
masochism, 430–31
masturbation, 65, 419, 432, 433, 434, 438,
  441
  fetishes in, 429, 430, 437, 438
  Kinsey's data on, 412
  normality of, 18, 425, 427

Maudsley Obsessive-Compulsive Disorder Inventory, 240–41
Mayock v, *Martin,* 604–605
mean, in statistical inference, 143
meaning, communication distortions and, 396–97
medial forebrain bundle (MFB), 326
melancholia, 30, 175, 330
  age of, 316, 317–19
  depression with vs. without, 316
memory, 581–89
  aging and, 588–89, 590–93
  collective unconscious and, 72
  components of, 582–83
  deficit, 585–86
  digit span in, 585
  explicit vs. implicit, 587–88
  familiarity in, 586, 587, 588
  loss of, 59, 258–61, 329, 658
  priming in, 586, 587, 588
  reconstruction of, 78–79
  repressed, 69, 77–79
  short-term vs. long-term, 585–86, 587
  skill acquisition in, 586, 587, 588
  vulnerability of, 583–84
  see also amnesia
mens rea, 618, 620, 624
  see also insanity defense
menstrual cycles, 481, 539
mental disorder, DSM-III-R definition of, 175–76
mental inhibition, 78
mental retardation, 170, 541–46
  cultural-familial, 543, 544–45
  definition of, 542
  Down's syndrome, 543–44
  IQ and, 170, 542, 544, 627
  levels of, 542–43
  phenylketonuria and, 543, 544
  treatment of, 545–46
mesmerism, 32–33, 35, 265, 266
meta-analysis, 139–40
methadone, 456, 474, 484
methadone maintenance programs, 661–62
milieu therapy, 404–406
minimization, 334
Minnesota Multiphasic Personality Inventory (MMPI), 162–65, 285
M'Naghten rule, 621–22, 623
modeling therapy, 651
  for obsessive-compulsive disorders, 245, 657
  for phobia, 121, 209, 212–13, 532, 656–57
models of abnormality, 48–49
  see also behavioral model; cognitive model; existential model; psychodynamic model
modernity, and depression, 317–19
mongolism (Down's syndrome), 543–44
monoamine oxidase (MAO) inhibitors, 138, 325, 327–28, 344, 658
moral anxiety, 70
moral insanity, 493–94
moral standards, violation of, 7, 12–13, 14
moral treatment, 42–43

morphine, 456, 460, 465, 466, 472
motivational deficits:
  behavioral view of, 331–32
  as depression symptoms, 308, 313–15, 325–27, 337, 342
  neurochemical basis for, 328–29
  passivity deficit and, 337–38, 342
motor tics, 521, 534
movement disorders:
  damage to frontal or parietal lobes in, 564–66
  lower motor neuron damage and, 568–69
  upper motor neuron damage and, 568
  see also paralysis
MRFIT (Multiple Risk Factor Intervention Trial), 284
multi-modal therapy, 48–49, 125–26, 226, 227
multiple personality, 78, 235, 259, 261–68, 589
  etiology of, 265–66
  faking, 267–68
  incidence of, 261–62
  psychological health of individual personalities in, 264
  psychotherapy for, 266–67
  schizophrenia vs., 264, 365
Münchhausen syndrome (factitious disorders), 250, 251–52
mystification, 396

naloxone, 457, 465
naltrexone, 457, 465, 466, 475
NAMI (National Alliance for the Mentally Ill), 616
narcissism, 89
narcissistic personality disorder, 506–507
narcotics, 453, 458, 460, 471–75, 478, 487
  addiction to, 472
  alcohol and, 461, 464, 465–66
  heroin, 456–58, 466, 472, 474, 482, 661–62
  medical and social complications of, 473
  methadone, 474, 661–62
  morphine, 456, 460, 465, 466, 472
  opium, 471–72
  psychopharmocology of, 472–73
  tolerance to, 472
  treatment for, 473–75
  withdrawal from, 472, 473, 474, 475, 477
narrenschiffen, 34
National Institutes of Mental Health (NIMH), 345
Natural Killer (NK) cells, 292, 293, 294
negative appraisals, 121–22
negative correlation, between depression and pleasant activities, 147–49
negative reinforcement, 112
  selective, 116–17
negativism, in catatonic schizophrenia, 371
Neo-Freudians, 62, 71–73
neologism, 374, 576
nervous system:
  central (CNS), 192
  gray vs. white matter in, 562–64

  hierarchical organization, 568–69
  inhibition-excitation balance in, 569
  movement controlled by, 564–66, 568–69, 571
  organization of, 560–69
  parasympathetic (PNS), 193, 414, 415, 421
  recovery of function in, 593, 595
  redundancy in, 571–72, 593, 596
  structure and function of, 560–61, 562–69
  sympathetic (SNS), 193, 414
  vulnerable areas in, 569, 570–71
  see also brain; neurons
nervous system, diseases of, 558–99
  abnormal behaviors based in, 596
  agents of damage in, 569
  cultural values and, 596–97
  diagnosing of, 594–95
  of language (aphasias), 564, 568, 574–75, 575–81, 596–97
  of memory, 260, 568, 569, 581–89
  of movement, 564–66, 568–69, 571
  of reading, 579–81, 596, 597
  symptoms of, 564–65, 569–70, 571–72, 574–75, 594–95
  treatment of, 593–97
nervous system disorders:
  functional syndromes in, 558, 560
  organic syndromes in, 558–59, 560
neuroanatomy, 49
  as etiology, 55–56
neuroleptics, 383, 392, 395, 401, 627–28, 664
neurology:
  domain of, 560, 572–75, 594–95
  virtues and limitations of, 595–97
neurons:
  anatomy of, 560–61
  axons of, 564, 571
  biochemistry of, 562
  degeneration or damage of, 562, 569, 570, 571, 574, 576, 581, 588, 590–91, 593
  glia cells and, 561
  in gray matter, 562
  recovery of, 593, 595
  redundancy and, 571, 593, 596
  synapses and, 560
  vulnerability of, 569, 570–71
neurosis:
  adult vs. childhood disorders, 521–22, 524, 528, 531, 540, 557
  anxiety and, 189, 235–36, 268–69
  see also anxiety disorders; dissociative disorders; obsessive-compulsive disorders; phobia; post-traumatic stress disorder; somatoform pain disorders
neurosurgery, 595
neurotic anxiety, 70
neurotransmitters, 47, 57, 230, 294, 383, 392–93, 394, 395
  brain, 590–91, 594, 595
  deficits in, 560–61, 562
  psychoactive drugs interact with, 450, 455, 457, 463, 476, 486
  see also dopamine

neutrophils, 292
nicotine, 457, 482–83, 484
nicotine receptors, 483, 484
Nieman-Pick disease, 544
nocturnal emission, 441
norepinephrine (noradrenaline; NE):
  depression and, 326–28, 329, 347, 560–
    61, 597, 658
  in emergency reaction, 193
  learned helplessness and, 343
  stimulants and, 476, 477
normality:
  abnormality vs., 5, 17–19, 68, 101, 107,
    626–27
  definition of, 17–18
nosophobia, 203–204
nuclear medicine, and schizophrenia, 55
nutrient deficiencies, 569, 571, 583, 585,
    593

obesity:
  in children, 539–41
  treatment of, 127, 662–63
observations, 159, 170–73
observer disagreement, 16–17
  observer discomfort, 7, 11–12, 14, 15
observers, actors' disagreements with,
    16–17
obsessions, 128, 566
  content of, 244–45, 247
  defined, 236
  depression linked to, 239, 242
  harmless vs. clinical, 236–37
  social context of, 237–38
obsessive-compulsive disorders, 200, 235,
    236–47
  anxiety component of, 235–36, 238–39,
    242–45, 246–47
  cognitive-behavioral view of, 242–44,
    268
  psychodynamic view of, 244–45, 269
  treatment of, 118, 245–46, 657
  vulnerability to, 239–41, 244
  see also compulsions
obsessive personality, 239–41
O'Connor v. Donaldson, 614–15
Odyssey House, 662
Oedipus complex, 65–66, 68, 71, 102
  in erectile dysfunction, 420
  in phobia, 204–206
operant (instrumental) conditioning, 107,
    112–17
  acquisition and extinction phenomena
    in, 113–14
  in avoidance situation, 117–18
  basic concepts of, 112–13
operant therapies, 114–17
  extinction, 113–14, 116–17
  for hyperactivity, 529–30
  principls of, 114–15
  selective positive reinforcement, 115–16
  selective punishment, 116–17
operational definitions, 137
opiates, 456, 457, 460, 463, 472–73
opioid receptors, 457, 464, 465, 466, 472,
    475
opium, 471–72

opponent-process model of addiction,
    457–60
oppositional defiant disorder, 523
optimal living, 19–21
optimism, 106–107, 291–92, 293
oral character traits, 63
oral-dependent personality disorder, 454
oral stage, 63, 64, 102
organ vulnerability, 295–97, 298
orgasm, 416
  dysfunctions of, 416, 418–19, 421
  physiology of, 414, 415
  after sex-change operations, 448
ostracism, 34
outcome expectations, 121
overdetermined behaviors, 101–102
overgeneralization, 334
overinclusiveness, in schizophrenia, 375,
    379

panic attacks, 58, 228–31, 232, 481
  in agoraphobia, 198–200, 213–14, 229,
    230
  fear elements in, 228–29
  spontaneous, 213, 218
panic disorder, 190, 195, 200, 228–31,
    232, 268, 200
  etiology and therapy in, 229–31
paradoxical intention technique, 100, 654
paralysis:
  hysterical, 33, 247, 248–49, 254, 255,
    258, 261
  malingering and, 250
  see also movement disorders
"paralysis of will," 313
paranoia, 174
paranoid personality disorder, 492, 505,
    513–14
paranoid schizophrenia, 4, 370, 384,
    604–605
  delusions of persecution in, 377–78,
    606, 621
  drug use and, 392, 394, 477, 481
  treatment of, 174
paraphasias, 576
paraphilias, 411, 428–43
  behavioral view of, 436, 437–38
  causes of, 436–39
  ego-dystonic homosexuality, 426,
    439–43
  exhibitionism, 428, 431, 432–33, 439
  fetishes, 428–29, 430, 432, 437–38
  pedophilia, 428, 431, 432, 435–36
  psychodynamic view of, 436–37
  sadomasochism, 428, 431
  transvestism, 428, 429–30
  treatment of, 438–39
  voyeurism, 428, 431, 432, 433–35
parasympathetic nervous system (PNS),
    193, 414, 415, 421
parental control, 64, 519–20
Parkinson's disease, 392, 393, 402, 562,
    589, 593, 594, 595
partial reinforcement extinction effect, 114
passive-aggressive personality disorder, 87,
    509–10
passivity deficit, 337–38, 342

pastoral counseling, 636
Pate v. Robinson, 626
patients' rights movement, 616, 617
Pavlovian (classical) conditioning, 107–12
  acquisition and extinction phenomena
    in, 109
  in avoidance situation, 117–18, 208–209
  conditioned response in, 108–109
  emotional states acquired by, 110, 112,
    194, 207–208, 214–16, 216–17
  of paraphilias, 437–38
  of phobia, 110, 206–209, 437–38
  prepared, 215–16, 438, 441
Pavlovian therapies, 111–12
  for alcoholism, 108
  for phobia, 111–12, 209–14
pedophilia (child molesting), 428, 431,
    432, 435–36
pellagra psychosis, 60–61
penile erection, 414, 416, 420
  see also erectile dysfunction
penis:
  for hermaphrodites, 446
  sex-change operations and, 448
penis envy, 65, 102
pepsin, 273, 275
peptic ulcers, 271, 272, 273–82
  animal models of, 278–80
  cognitions and, 299
  description of, 273
  diathesis-stress model of, 276–81, 282
  emotional states and, 274, 276–81, 282
  general adaptation syndrome and,
    297–98
  personality factors in, 280–81, 298
  physiological development of, 275
  prevalence of, 273, 275–76
  susceptibility to, 275–76
  symptoms of, 274–75
  treatment of, 281–82
perception, 77
  reconstruction of, 78–79
  responsibility for, 90
perceptual consciousness, 69, 70
perceptual deficits:
  in schizophrenia, 372–73, 379–80, 397
peripheral neuropathy, 571
periventricular system (PVS), 326
perseveration, 565–66
personality, 48, 102
  depressive, 331
  Freudian view of, 67–71
  hypertensive, 298
  hypomanic, 348
  illness and, 301–302
  multiple, 78, 235, 259, 261–68
  obsessive, 239–41
  psychodynamic view of, 73–87
  and self, 74–77
  Type A vs. Type B, 283–87
  ulcer-prone, 280–81, 299
personality alterations:
  as measure of therapeutic
    effectiveness, 646–47
  in psychodynamic treatment, 96–98
personality development:
  conflict resolution in, 63

psychosexual stages of (Freud), 63–67
psychosocial stages of (Erikson), 73, 96
personality disorders, 76, 492–515, 596
　avoidant, 507
　borderline, 511–13
　compulsive, 508–509, 514
　dependent, 508, 514
　histrionic, 505–506
　interpretation discrepancies in, 514
　narcissistic, 506–507
　oral-dependent, 454
　paranoid, 492, 505, 513–14
　passive-aggressive, 508–10
　sadistic, 627
　schizoid, 390, 510–11
　schizotypal, 510–11, 513
　self-defeating, 627
　underlying traits in, 493, 513, 514–15
　see also antisocial personality disorder
personalization, 334
pessimism, 291–92, 293, 294
PET (position emission tomography) scan,
　241, 393, 394, 574, 592
phallic stage, 63, 64–66, 95
phencyclidine (PCP), 455, 479–80
phenothiazines, 392, 393, 394, 395, 402,
　404
phenylalanine, 544
phenylketonuria (PKU), 543, 544
phobia, 128, 189, 195, 196–218, 226, 228,
　463, 596, 597
　behavioral analysis of, 110, 111–12, 205,
　206–17, 268
　in childhood, 205–206, 530–33
　among concentration camp survivors,
　221
　defined, 196–98
　diagnosing of, 196, 197
　drug treatment for, 58, 213
　irrationality of, 214, 216
　Little Albert experiment and, 146,
　207–208, 214
　Little Hans case and, 204–206, 207
　non-traumatic, 211, 216–17
　normal fear vs., 195, 196, 206–207, 532
　panic attacks in, 198–99, 213–14, 218,
　231
　persistence of, 208–209, 212, 437
　in post-traumatic stress disorder, 218
　prevalence of, 198
　psychoanalytic analysis of, 204–209, 211
　in rape trauma syndrome, 222
　selectivity of, 214–16
　self-efficacy expectations and, 121
　societal judgment and, 197–98
　susceptibility to, 217
　symptom substitution in, 211
　therapies for, 111–12, 204, 205–206,
　209–14, 532, 650–51, 656–57
　types of, 198–204
physical approach, 28–30, 47
　animalism and, 29–30
　hysteria and, 29, 35
　treatment in, 30, 34, 35, 49
　see also biomedical model
physical excitement:
　impairment of, 415–16, 419–20

physiology of, 414–15, 416
　therapy for, 422–24
physical illnesses:
　from life events and personality,
　301–302
　phobia of, 198, 203
　PNI and, 289–95
　susceptibility to, 315
　undiagnosed, 249, 252
　see also nervous system disorders;
　psychosomatic disorders; somatoform
　pain disorders
physiological correlates of, 172, 192–93
Pick's disease, 592–93
placebo effect, 141, 345, 346, 641
pleasure principle, 67–68
"pleasuring," 423
political psychiatry, 5, 627–30
population, statistical inferences and,
　142–43
positive correlation, 147
positive reinforcement, 112
　selective, 115–16
positive symptoms of schizophrenia, 664
posthypnotic suggestion, 83–84
post-traumatic stress disorder, 189, 195,
　217–28, 268
　course of, 222–24
　as experiment in nature, 150
　after manmade catastrophes, 218,
　220–21, 223, 225–26, 227
　after naturally occurring disasters, 150,
　218–20, 224, 225–26
　rape trauma syndrome, 218, 221–22
　symptoms of, 218, 224
　treatment and prevention of, 225–28
poverty of speech, 383, 395
precipitating incidents, 347–48
pre-consciousness, 69, 70
premarital intercourse, 425, 426, 427
premenstrual depression, 319–20
premenstrual syndrome (PMS), 627
prepared classical conditioning, 214–15,
　216, 438
preschool interventions, 668
presynaptic neuron, 476, 477
prevalence, 198
prevention efforts, 362, 667–69
prisoners-of-war, post-traumatic stress
　disorders of, 223
problems in living, 60
Prohibition, 487, 490
projection, 79–80, 81, 84, 87
projective tests, 162, 166–69, 286
　Rorschach Test, 166–68
　Thematic Apperception Test, 166,
　168–69, 286
prospective studies, 151
pseudopatients, diagnosis of, 181–82
psychalgia, 248, 249–50, 251, 253
psychiatric attendants (aides), 636
psychiatric hospitals, 5, 36–43, 608–9, 665
　animalism and, 29–30, 39, 40
　board and care facilities vs., 613–16, 674
　confinement as purpose of, 36–37,
　40–41
　day or night care at, 673–74

death rate at, 611
English religious reforms at, 41–42
humane treatment introduced in, 39–43
insane abused at, 37–39
moral treatment at, 42–43
prison vs. punitive measures at, 619
rise of, 36–43
shackles and chains at, 38, 39, 40–41
psychiatric nurses, as therapists, 635–36
psychiatric social workers, as therapists,
　635
psychiatrists, as therapists, 627, 635
psychic energy, 62–63, 84, 93, 96
　in id, ego, and superego processes, 67, 68
　transformed in psychosexual develop-
　ment, 63–67
　transmuted into somatic loss, 253
psychoactive substance use disorders, 450–
　91
psychoanalysis, 62
　classical, 48, 652–53, 666
　see also psychodynamic therapies
psychoanalysts, as therapists, 636
psychodynamic (psychoanalytic) model,
　48, 62–104, 111, 166
　amnesia as viewed in, 260
　anorexia nervosa as viewed in, 537
　anxiety role in, 70–71, 72, 93, 253–54
　assessment of, 101–103, 268–69
　autism as viewed in, 550, 553–54, 555
　clinical cases as basis for, 101, 102, 106
　comprehensiveness of, 101
　coping strategies in, 77–84, 92, 93, 95
　depression as viewed in, 324, 329–32,
　347
　existential psychology vs., 91
　faults of, 71
　hostility in, 284
　neo-Freudians' criticisms of, 71–73
　normal vs. abnormal behavior in,
　68–69, 101
　obsessive-compulsive disorders as
　viewed in, 244–45, 269
　paraphilia as viewed in, 436–37
　personality development in, 63–67,
　72–73, 96
　personality processes in, 67–69, 69–70,
　72; see also ego; id; superego
　phobia as viewed in, 204–206, 211
　problems of proof in, 101–103
　psychosomatic disorders as viewed in,
　295, 298
　scientific evidence lacking in, 101, 102
　self in, 74–77
　sexual dysfunction as viewed in, 420–21
　situation and context underestimated in,
　101, 102–103
　unconscious forces in, 69–70, 72
psychodynamic (psychoanalytic) therapies,
　652–53, 665–67
　assessment of, 101–103
　behavioral therapy vs., 110–11, 126–27
　case study in, 93–98
　catharsis in, 96
　classical psychoanalysis, 652–53, 666
　cognitive therapy vs., 126–27, 334
　for conversion disorders, 257–58

psychodynamic therapies *(continued)*
  for depression, 316, 331–32, 657, 658
  focus of, 93
  free association in, 93, 97, 334
  for multiple personality, 266–67
  for obsessive-compulsive disorders, 245
  for peptic ulcers, 281–82
  personality altered in, 95–98
  for phobia, 204, 205–207
  transference in, 96–97
  varied orientations of, 653
psychogenic approach, 30–34
  Charcot's hypnosis studies and, 33–34, 35
  Galen's theory of, 30–31
  Mesmer's cures and, 31–32, 35
  treatment based on, 34, 35–36
  see also psychodynamic model
psychological assessment, 156–73
  clinical interviews in, 159–61
  MMPI, 162–65
  observation in, 159, 170–73
  psychological inventories, 162–66
  psychological testing in, 159, 161–70
  Q-sort, 162, 165
  reliability of, 157–59, 173
  Rep Test, 162, 165–66
psychological disability, 605
psychological states, 292–94
psychological testing, 159, 161–70
  intelligence tests, 162, 169–70
  projective tests, 162, 166–69
  psychological inventories, 162–66
  reliability of, 157–59, 168
psychologists, as therapists, 627, 635
psychomotor retardation, 313, 316
psychoneuroimmunology (PNI), 61, 271, 289–95
psychopathology, 49, 55, 558–99
psychopathy, *see* antisocial personality disorder
psychopharmacology, 450, 454, 456
  of hallucinogens, 480–81
  of opiates, 472–73
  of smoking, 482–83
  of stimulants, 475–77
psychophysiological assessment, 172–73
psychophysiological disorders, *see* psychosomatic disorders
psychoses, 368
  neuroses vs., 189
  see also schizophrenia
psychosexual development:
  neo-Freudians' disagreements with, 71–73
  stages of, 63–67
psychosocial development, 73, 96
psychosocial treatments, 664
psychosomatic disorders, 249, 251, 271–303, 390, 570
  behavioral model of, 295, 298–300
  biomedical model of, 295–98
  cognitive model of, 295, 298–99
  diagnosing of, 273
  evolution and, 297
  general adaptation syndrome and, 297
  life events and, 299–302

psychodynamic model of, 295, 298
somatoform disorders vs., 250, 251, 273
stigmata, 271–72, 273
sudden death, 289–91
  see also high blood pressure; peptic ulcers
psychotropic medication, 665
psychotropics, 401
punishment, 112
  anticipation of, 500
  as physical, tangible or social, 499–500
  selective, 116
  sociopaths' responses to, 498–500

Q-sort, 162, 165
questionnaires. *see* psychological testing

random assignment, 140
rape, 432
rape trauma syndrome, 221–22, 671
rational-emotive therapy, 124–25, 651
rationalism, 105
rationalization, 83–84
Rat Man case, 244
rCBF (regional cerebral blood flow) technique, 55, 574
reaction formation, 80, 87
reaction time (RT) studies, 376
reactive crisis, 382
reading deficits, 521, 546–47
realistic anxiety, 70
reality:
  accurate perception of, 19, 20
  depressed people's perception of, 310–11
reality principle, 68
reality testing:
  by depressives, 335
  by phobics, 208–209, 211–12
  by schizophrenics, 367–68
reason, loss of, 38–39
reattribution training, 334, 335–36
reductionism, 60–61
reductionists vs. anti-reductionists, 60–61
regional cerebral blood flow (rCBF) technique, 55, 574
reinforcement:
  continuous (CRF), 114
  negative, 112, 116–17
  partial (intermittent), 114
  positive, 112, 155–16
relaxation, in systematic desensitization, 112, 209–11
reliability, 157–59, 173
  acceptable degree of, 159
  of DSM-III and DSM-III-R, 177–79
  high vs. low, 158
  inter-judge, 157, 159
  test-retest, 57–58, 159
Renard Diagnostic Interview (RDI), 161
repeatability, as methodological concern, 136, 144, 145, 150
repression, 66
  as coping strategy, 77–78, 82–83, 84, 87
  unconscious level and, 69
research diagnoses, 184
resemblance principle, 106
reserpine, 325, 327

residual rules, 11
resistances, in therapy, 645
resistance stage, 297
response initiation, lack of, 313
response prevention, 246
  obsessive-compulsive disorders and, 246–47
responsibility, 88, 102–103
  avoidance of, 91
  in existential view, 90–91
  for feelings, 99–100
retrospective studies, 151
reuptake process, 327
Ritalin, 529
Role Construct Repertory Test (Rep Test), 162, 165–66
Role Induction Interviews, 639–40
Rorschach Test, 166–69
  interpreting of, 167–68
  reliability and validity of, 168
Rouse v. *Cameron*, 612–13

sadism, 268, 430–31, 432, 443
sadistic personality disorder, 627
sadness, as symptom of depression, 309
sadomasochism, 428, 431
samples, statistical inference and, 142
Satanistic forces, 26–28
Schedule for Affective Disorders and Schizophrenia (SADS), 161
schizoid personality disorder, 510–11
schizophrenia, 5, 23, 128, 313, 364–407, 533
  acute vs. chronic, 382–83, 384, 392, 394
  affective disturbances in, 380–81
  attentional deficits in, 374–75, 376
  biological basis of, 54–55, 366–67, 392–97
  brain structure in, 395
  catatonic, 370, 371
  causes of, 53–55, 366–67, 384–400
  and children, 151, 388–91, 395–97, 521–22
  cognitive distractibility in, 376–77
  communication attempts in, 381–82
  course of, 365, 366–67
  creativity and, 391–92
  dangerous behavior associated with, 365
  defining of, 367–69
  delusions in, 368, 370, 377–80, 606, 621
  dimensions of, 382–84
  disorganized, 370, 384
  drug or alcohol abuse and, 477, 478, 479
  drug therapy for, 58, 59, 60, 174, 402–404, 406, 664–65
  genetic factors in, 53–54, 384–92, 395–96, 400
  hallucinations in, 368, 372–73, 375
  historical survey of views on, 366–67
  hospitalization decision in, 382–83, 665
  milieu therapy and therapeutic communities for, 404–406
  multi-modal therapy for, 125–26
  multiple personality vs., 264, 365
  myths about, 364–65
  negative and positive symptoms of, 383, 395, 402

neurochemical basis of, 58, 384, 392–95, 400, 562
nuclear medicine and, 55
overinclusiveness in, 375, 379
perceptual difficulties in, 372–73, 379–80, 397
prevalence and incidence of, 369
prospective studies on, 151
pseudopatients diagnosed as, 182, 183
"revolving-door" phenomenon in, 403–404, 406, 664
SADS in diagnosis of, 161
schizotypal personality disorder and, 510–11
societal factors in, 320–21, 398–400, 484
symptoms of, 55, 372–82, 383, 392, 395
thought disorder in, 9, 373–80, 396–97
treatments for, 664–65
two-self view of, 382
types of, 370–72, 383–84, 392, 395
undifferentiated, 370, 372
see also paranoid schizophrenia
schizophrenogenic family, 384, 389–90, 395–97, 399–400
communication distortions in, 396–97
schizotypal personality disorder, 510–11, 513
school phobia (refusal), 532, 533
school psychologists, 635
scientific experimentation, 133, 137–47
basic method in, 137
causality in correlation studies and, 149–50
confounds in, 139, 140–42
ethical issues in, 133, 137–38, 146–47
evaluation of, as investigative method, 146–47, 153
example of, 138–40
indirect methods of, 133, 147–53
meta-analysis in, 139–40
repeatability and generality in, 144–45
with single subject, 144–45
statistical inferences in, 142–44
scientific method, origin of, 31
seasonal affective disorder (SAD), 354–55
secondary gains, 225, 250–51
sedatives, 485–86
selective abstraction, 333
selective (cognitive) filter, 374, 375, 376
selective positive reinforcement, 115–16
selective punishment, 116
self, 48, 73, 74–77, 102, 512
Adler's view of, 72
care, 74–75
false, 76
search for, 666–67
significance of, 77
subjective, 75, 77
verbal, 75–76, 77
self-actualization, 19
self-coherence, 74
self-defeating personality disorder, 627
self-diagnosis, 21–22
self-esteem, low, 310–12, 329, 331, 332–33, 343, 512
self-help groups, 469, 616, 637, 663, 674
self-hypnosis, 265, 266

self-image, repression and, 78
selfobjects, 76, 512
senile dementia, 588–89
senility, 174–75
sensate focus, 423
sensory deficits, 227, 564
sensory deprivation experiments, 141–42
separation anxiety, 531, 533
separation anxiety disorder, 530–31
serotonin, 326, 554, 658
set-point, 540–41
sex-change operations, 444, 448–49
sex differences:
in depression, 317, 319–20
and schizophrenia, 369
and suicide, 357–58
sex drive, maturation of, 441
sex-role behavior, 446–47
sexual activity, 222, 467, 471, 473, 478
sexual apathy, 424
sexual behavior, 411–15
physiology of, 414–15
scientific study, 412–13
societal norms and, 411, 425–27, 441
see also homosexuality; masturbation
sexual crimes, 432, 432–33, 434, 435
sexual disorders, 411, 424–49
see also ego-dystonic homosexuality; paraphilias; transsexuality
sexual dysfunctions, 128, 315, 411, 415–24, 429
in erotic arousal and excitement, 415–18, 420–21
in orgasm, 416, 418–19, 421
partner's responses to, 416–17, 418–19
physical causes of, 419–20
physiological correlates of, 172, 173
psychological causes of, 420–21
treatment of, 421, 422–24, 659
sexual energy, 63
libido, 63, 64, 67
sexual identity, 427–28
disorders of, *see* transsexuality
sexual intercourse, 10
nondemand, 423
premarital, 425, 426, 427
sexual object choice, 427–28
disorder in, *see* paraphilias
sexual unresponsiveness, 416–17, 420
therapy for, 422–24
shadowing, 536
shamans, 25, 34
single-blind experiments, 141
single photon emission computerized tomography (SPECT scan), 574, 593
single-subject experiments, 144–45
skills therapists, 636
sleep disturbance, 315, 316
smoking, 282, 284, 287, 288, 451, 452, 454, 473, 487–88, 481–85, 659, 660–61
affective properties of, 482, 484
medical and social consequences of, 484
psychopharmocology of, 482–83
treatment of, 484–85
snake phobia, 121, 212, 215–16, 217
snow phobia, 198, 202–203

social deviance, 175–76
social phobia, 198, 200–201, 209
Social Readjustment Rating Scale, 300–301
social skills training, 439, 520–21, 552
social support, 302, 663
society:
abnormality as judgment of, 5, 9, 10, 12–13, 16, 23–24, 593–94, 603, 626–27, 630–31
and drug use and abuse, 450, 451, 460, 461, 486–87, 489–91
stigma of mental illness and, 603, 630–31
well-being of, 8, 9
sociopathy, *see* antisocial personality disorder
sodium lactate, 230
somatic therapies, 58–59
somatization disorder (Briquet's syndrome), 248, 249, 253
somatoform pain disorders (hysterical conversions), 235, 247–58, 268–69, 462
anxiety component of, 235–36, 253–57, 259, 268–69
Briquet's syndrome, 248, 249, 253
communicative model of, 254–56
course of, 253
diagnosing of, 250–52
etiology of, 253–57, 260–61
historical trends in, 255–56
hysterical blindness, 134–35, 136–38, 256–57, 258
hysterical paralysis, 33, 247, 248–49, 254, 255, 258, 261
percept blocking model of, 256–57
psychalgia, 248, 249–50, 251, 263
psychodynamic view of, 253–54
psychosomatic disorders vs., 250, 251, 273
symptoms of, 248, 249, 252, 254, 255
treatment of, 257–58
vulnerability to, 252–53
see also hysteria
Soteria House, 406
Soviet Union, psychiatric abuses in, 627–30
specialness, 88–89, 90
speech anxiety:
behavioral assessment and, 171–72
behavioral vs. cognitive view of, 120
cognitive therapy for, 120, 121–22
spider phobia, 215, 217
spinal cord, 565, 568, 572
spirits, possession by, 25, 34
split-brain syndrome, 567–68, 571, 596
stammering, 128, 521, 534, 535
Stanford-Binet Intelligence Test for Children, 169
state-orientation, 319
State-Trait Anxiety Inventory, 232
statistical inference, 142–44
statistical significance, 143, 149
stigmata, 61, 271–72, 273
stimulants, 475–78
addiction to, 477, 478

stimulants *(continued)*
  amphetamines, 392, 476–77, 529, 534–35
  caffeine, 454
  cocaine, 475–76
  intoxication, 477
  medical and social complications of, 477–78
  psychopharmacology of, 475–77
  tolerance of, 476
  treatment of, 478
  withdrawal, 477, 478
straitjackets, 42
stress, 215, 220, 570
  and alcohol, 463–65, 466
  defined, 276
  general adaptation syndrome and, 297
  life events and, 293–94, 300
  lifespan and, 296–97
  of modern living, 399–400
  see also diathesis-stress models
strokes, 477
  amnesia and, 260
  neural damage and, 559, 562, 569, 571, 575, 576, 583, 585, 594
  Type A personality and, 288
structured interviews, 160–61
stuttering, 128, 521, 534, 535
subject bias, 140, 141
sublimation, 67, 84, 87
substance abuse, *see* drug dependence
substitution, 80–81
  in obsessive-compulsive disorder, 244
sudden death, 282, 289–91
  animal models of, 289–91
  after death of spouse, 290–91
  hopelessness and helplessness in, 289–91
  process of, 289
suffering, as element of abnormality, 7–8, 14
suicide, 56, 308, 327, 330, 355–62, 450, 466
  altruistic, 360
  anomic, 360
  in Briquet's syndrome, 249
  among children, 358–59
  cultural differences and, 358
  egoistic, 360
  hot-lines and, 670
  involuntary commitment and, 608
  manipulative, 360–62
  motivations for, 57, 360–62
  among older people, 360
  prevention and treatment of, 362
  statistics on, 356–57
  surcease as goal of, 360, 362
  surviving relatives and, 362
  among women vs. men, 357–58
  among young people, 359–60
Sullivanian therapy, 653
superego, 67, 68–69, 69–70, 74
suppression, 78
survival guilt, 217–18, 220, 221
sympathetic nervous system (SNS), 193, 414
symptoms:
  diagnosis based on, 174, 175, 176, 180

disorders equated with, 110–11
  in logotherapy, 100
  organized into syndromes, 49, 50
  see also specific disorders
symptoms substitution, in phobia, 211
Synanon, 662
syndromes, 49, 50
syntactic knowledge, 578–79
syphilis, 61, 426, 560
  general paresis linked to, 50–53, 60
syphilophobia, 203
systematic desensitization, 112, 121, 650
  phobia and, 112, 140, 209–11, 213, 226, 656
  for separation anxiety disorder, 531
  for sexual dysfunction, 424

tarantism, 25
tardive dyskinesia, 402–403
target behaviors, 115
taste aversions, 217
TAT (Thematic Apperception Test), 166, 168–69, 286
Tay-Sachs disease, 544
T-cells, 292, 293, 294
tension, 77, 172, 173, 463–64
test anxiety, 122
testing, *see* psychological testing
tetrahydrocannabinol (THC), 456, 480
thalamus, 585
Thematic Apperception Test (TAT), 166, 168–69, 286
therapeutic alliance, 643
therapeutic communities:
  for drug or alcohol abusers, 474, 662
  for schizophrenics, 404–406
therapies, *see* treatments
therapists:
  defects in, 627, 644–46
  empathy, warmth, and genuineness of, 642
  experience of, 642–43
  gender and race of, 643–44
  paraprofessionals, 673
  therapeutic alliance with, 643
  types of, 634–37
therapy outcome studies, 139
Thorazine, 402
thought disorders, 9, 55, 59, 383, 395
thymus gland, 292, 297
time urgency, 283, 284, 285, 288
tobacco dependence, *see* smoking
Tofranil (imipramine), 213, 534–35
toilet training, 64, 519
toxins, neurological effects of, 577, 583
tranquilizers, 485–86, 487
tranquilizing agents, 58–59, 232, 401, 529
transference, 96, 653
transsexuality, 411, 430, 433–49
  etiology of, 445–48
  as homosexual, heterosexual, or asexual, 445
  sex-change operations for, 444, 448–49
  typical life history of, 444–45
transvestism, 428, 429–30, 444
trauma, *see* post-traumatic stress disorder

treatments (therapies):
  alternative centers for, 616, 673–74
  animistic, 24, 25, 27, 34
  assessing effectiveness of, 646–47
  behavioral assessment in, 171
  choice of, 656–67
  classical, 93–100
  common ingredients of, 638–47
  consumer's guide to, 633–75
  containment services and, 669–72
  free choice and, 638–39
  global, 665–67
  goals set in, 645–46
  hopes and expectations in, 639–41
  physical approach to, 30, 34, 35, 49
  preventive efforts and, 667–69
  psychogenic, rise of, 34, 35–36
  short-term, 670–71
  specific vs. insight (global), 648
  suggested by diagnosis, 172–74, 181
  types of, 648–55
  see also behavioral therapy; biomedical treatment; cognitive therapy; drug treatment; existential therapy; psychiatric hospitals; psychodynamic therapies; therapists; *specific disorders*
trephining, 25, 29
tricyclics, 138, 325, 327, 328, 341, 344, 345–46, 539, 657, 658
tuberculosis, 58, 60, 327
tumors, 293, 294
twins:
  identical, maturation and upbringing of, 388, 390–91
  identical (monozygotic; MA) vs. fraternal (dizygotic; DZ), 53–54, 384–87
twin studies:
  on antisocial personality disorder, 501
  on autism, 554
  concordance vs. discordance in, 54, 384–85
  on diatheses, 276, 295
  index case (proband) vs. co-twin in, 386
  on IQs, 544–45
  logic of, 54, 384–85
  on manic-depression, 57, 325, 352
  on obsessive-compulsive disorder, 239
  on panic attacks, 230
  on schizophrenia, 53–54, 384–87, 388, 400
  on unipolar depression, 325
Type A personality, 282–88
  assessment of, 284–87
  changing behavior of, 288
  CHD and, 282–88
  defining of, 283
  emergency reaction and, 283, 284, 286–87, 288
  helplessness and, 284, 285–86, 288
  hostility and, 284–85, 288
  at risk for CHD, 283–84
Type B personality, 283–87

ulcer-prone personality, 280–81, 298
ulcers, *see* peptic ulcers

unconditional positive regard, 98
unconditioned response (UR), 108–109, 110, 194, 207–11, 213
unconditioned stimulus (US), 108–10, 194, 207–11, 213, 214
unconscious, 69–70
  collective, 72
  explored in classical psychoanalysis, 652–53
uncontrollability:
  in learned helplessness, 152, 286, 337–38, 456
  psychosomatic events and, 278–80
unconventionality, 7, 10–11, 12, 16
uncorrelated events, 147
undifferentiated schizophrenia, 370, 372
United States v. *Brawner,* 623
unpredictability:
  as element of abnormality, 7, 10, 14
  ulcers and, 278–79, 280
unstructured interviews, 160
uterus:
  malfunctions of, hysteria caused by, 29, 31
  wandering, hysteria caused by, 29, 35, 49, 252

vagina:
  of hermaphrodites, 446
  sex-change operations and, 448
vaginal lubrication, 420
  dysfunctions of, 416
  physiology of, 415, 416
validity, 157, 168, 179–81
  descriptive, 180
  predictive (outcome), 180–81
Valium, 649, 657
values acquired from experience, introjected values vs., 77, 100
variables:
  in correlation studies, 147
  dependent and independent, 137, 147
variances, occasion and information, 159
veterans:
  combat fatigue among, 223–24
  drug abuse among, 460, 481, 489
victims, counseling for, 671
vividness, 7, 10–11, 12, 14, 16
volition, loss of, 383, 395
voyeurism, 428, 431, 432, 433–35

Weshsler Adult Intelligence Scale (WAIS), 169

Wechsler Adult Intelligence Scale—Revised (WAIS-R), 169
Wechsler Intelligence Scale for Children (WISC), 169
Wechsler Preschool and Primary Scale of Intelligence (WPPSI), 169
weight loss, 315, 662–63
well-being:
  individual, 8, 9
  societal, 8, 9
Wernicke's area, 576–77
will, 88
  disorders of, 92–93, 493–94
  exhortative, 91, 93
  goal-directed, 91–93
  wishing, willing and, 92–93
witchcraft, 23
  abnormal behavior attributed to, 25, 26–28
  tests for, 27
work:
  sexual energy channeled into, 66, 84
  therapeutic value of, 42
workaholics, 89
work ethic, 37, 42
Wyatt v. *Stickney,* 613, 615

Acknowledgments and Copyrights

Excerpts

Pages 86–87: Vaillant, G., *Empirical studies of ego mechanisms of defense.* Washington, D.C.: American Psychiatric Press, 1986. Adapted by permission. *Pages 124–25:* Ellis, A., *Reason and emotion in psychotherapy.* Copyright © 1962 by Institute for Rational Living. Published by arrangement with Lyle Stuart. *Pages 134–35, 248–49:* Personal communications from Dr. James Stinnett, 1978, Hospital of the University of Pennsylvania. *Pages 202–203, 206, 228, 229, 231, 238, 244–45, 250, 259:* From Laughlin, H.P., *The neuroses,* Woburn: Butterworth Publishers, 1967. Excerpted by permission of the publisher. *Pages 219–20:* From Erikson, K., *Everything in its path: Destruction of community in the Buffalo Creek flood.* New York: Simon & Schuster, 1976. Reprinted by permission of Simon & Schuster. *Pages 236, 238 and 239:* From Rachman, S.J., & Hodgson, R.J., *Obsessions and compulsions.* © 1980. Reprinted by permission of Prentice-Hall, Inc., Englewood Cliffs, N.J. *Pages 237–38:* From Bartlett, D.L., & Steele, J.B., *Empire: The life, legend, and madness of Howard Hughes.* New York: W.W. Norton and Company, Inc., 1979. Copyright © 1979 by W.W. Norton and Company. Reprinted by permission. *Pages 248–49.* From Stinnett, J., 1978. By permission. *Pages 262–63:* From Davis, P.H., & Osherson. A., The current treatment of a multiple-personality woman and her son. *American Journal of Psychotherapy,* 1977, 31, 304–515. Copyright 1977. Adapted by permission of the Association for the Advancement of Psychotherapy. *Page 265:* Writing samples courtesy of Dr. Eugene L. Bliss. *Page 272:* Moody, R.L., Bodily changes during abreaction. *The Lancet,* 1946, 2: 934–35. Reprinted by permission. *Page 274:* Weisman, A.D., A study of the psychodynamics of duodenal ulcer exacerbations. *Psychosomatic Medicine,* 1956, 18: 2–42. Copyright 1956 by the American Psychosomatic Society. *Pages 310–12, 313, 315, 333, 335, and 336:* From Beck, A.T., Rush, A.J., Shaw, B.F., & Emery, G., *Cognitive therapy of depression.* New York: Guildford Press, 1979. Reprinted by permission. *Pages 330–31:* From Fancher, R., *Psychoanalytic psychology: The development of Freud's thought.* New York: W.W. Norton & Company, Inc., 1973. Copyright 1973 by W.W. Norton & Company. Reprinted by permission. *Pages 348–49 and 350:* From Fieve, R.R., *Mood swing.* New York: Morrow, 1975. Reprinted by permission. *Pages 358–59:* Jerome, J., Catching them before suicide. *The New York Times Magazine,* January 11, 1979. Copyright © 1979 by the New York Times Company. Reprinted by permission. *Page 429:* Stoller, R.J., Parental influences in male transsexualism. In R. Green & J. Money (Eds.), Transsexualism and sex reassignment. Baltimore: Johns Hopkins Press, 1969. Copyright 1969 by Johns Hopkins University Press. Reprinted by permission. *Page 444:* Pauly, I.B., Adult manifestations of male transsexualism. In R. Green & J. Money (Eds.), *Transsexualism and sex reassignment.* Baltimore: The Johns Hopkins University Press, 1969. Copyright 1969 by Johns Hopkins University Press. Adapted by permission. *Page 447:* Money, J., & Ehrhardt, A., *Man and woman, boy and girl.* Baltimore: The Johns Hopkins University Press, 1972. Copyright 1972 by Johns Hopkins University Press. Reprinted by permission. *Pages 468 and 522:* Spitzer, R.L., Skodol, A.E., Gibbon, M., &

Williams, J.B.W., *DSM-III casebook.* Washington, D.C.: American Psychiatric Association, 1981. Reprinted by permission of the American Psychiatric Association. *Page 479:* From Hofmann, A., Psychotomimetic agents. In A. Burger (Ed.), *Drugs affecting the central nervous system* (Vol. 2). New York: Marcel Dekker, Inc., 1968. Reprinted by permission. *Page 485:* Jeurgens, S.M., & Morse, R.M., Alprazolam dependence in seven patients. *American Journal of Psychiatry,* 1988, 145: 625–27. Reprinted by permission. *Pages 486–87:* Except from *Philadelphia Inquirer,* July 24, 1988. Reprinted by permission. *Pages 576–77:* Courtesy of the Communication and Behavioral Neurology Department, Baycrest Hospital, Toronto, Ontario. *Pages 582–83:* Milner, B., Memory and the medial temporal regions of the brain. In K.H. Pribram & D.E. Broadbent (Eds.), *Biology of memory.* New York: Academic Press, 1970. Reprinted by permission. *Page 592:* Neary, D., Snowden, J.S., Northern, B., & Goulding, P., Dementia of frontal lobe type. *Journal of Neurology, Neurosurgery and Psychiatry,* 1988, 51: 353–61. *Page 628:* Medvedev, Z.A., & Medvedev, R.A., *A question of madness.* (Ellen de Kadt, Trans.). New York: Knopf, 1971. Reprinted by permission. *Page 629:* Fireside, H., *Soviet psychoprisons.* New York: W.W. Norton and Company, Inc., 1979. Copyright © 1979 by W.W. Norton and Company, Inc. Reprinted by permission. *Pages 630–31:* Excerpt from *Prisoners of psychiatry: Mental patients, psychiatrists, and the law,* copyright © 1972 by Bruce J. Ennis, reprinted by permission of Harcourt Brace Jovanovich, Inc.

Figures

Figure 4-1: Data from Sears, R.R., Experimental studies of projection: I. Attribution of traits. *Journal of Social Psychology,* 1936, 7: 151–63. Reprinted with permission of the Helen Dwight Reid Educational Foundation. Published by Heldref Publications. *Figure 4-2:* Vaillant, G.E., Bond, M., & Vaillant, C.O., An empirically validated hierarchy of defense mechanisms. *Archives of General Psychiatry,* 1986, 43: 786–94. Copyright 1986. Adapted by permission of the American Medical Association. *Figure 5-1:* Schwartz, B., *Psychology of learning and behavior,* 2nd ed. New York: W.W. Norton and Company Inc., 1984. Copyright © 1984 by W.W. Norton and Company, Inc. Reprinted by permission. *Figure 6-2:* Hall, R.V., Fox, R., Williard, D., Goldsmith, L., Emerson, M., Owen, M., Davis, T., & Porcia, E., The teacher as observer and experimenter in the modification of disputing and talking-out behaviors. *Journal of Applied Behavior Analysis,* 1971, 4: 143. Adapted by permission of the society for Experimental Analysis of Behavior Inc. *Figure 7-2A:* Gleitman, H., *Psychology.* New York: W.W. Norton and Company, Inc., 1981. Copyright © 1981 by W.W. Norton & Company, Inc. Reprinted by permission. *Figure 7-2B:* Specimen of the Minnesota Report. Professional Assessment Services, A Division of National Computer Systems, Inc. *Figure 7-3:* Gleitman, H., *Psychology.* New York: W.W. Norton and Company, Inc., 1981. Copyright © 1981 by W.W. Norton and Company, Inc. Reprinted by permission. *Figure 7-4:* Reprinted from *Insight vs. desensitization in psychotherapy* by Gordon L. Paul with the permission of the publishers. Stanford University

Press. © 1966 by the Board of Trustees of the Leland Stanford Junior University. *Figure 7-5:* Langer, E.J., & Abelson, R.P., A patient by any other name...: Clinician group difference in labelling bias. *Journal of Consulting and Clinical Psychology,* 1974, 42: 4–9. Reprinted by permission. *Figure 8-1:* Ekman, P., & Friesen, W., *Unmasking the face.* Englewood-Cliffs, N.J., 1975. Reprinted by permission of the author. *Figure 8-3:* Shore, J.E., Tatum, E.L., & Vollmer, W.M., Psychiatric reactions to diaster: The Mount St. Helens experience. *American Journal of Psychiatry,* 1986, 143 (5): 590–95. Copyright 1986, the American Psychiatric Association. Reprinted by permission. *Figure 8-4:* Archibald, H.C., & Tuddenham, R.D , Persistent stress reaction after combat. *Archives of General Psychiatry,* 1965, 12: 475–81. Copyright 1965, American Medical Association. Reprinted by permission. *Figure 10-1:* Moody, R.L. Bodily changes during abreaction. *The Lancet,* 1946, 2: 934–35. Reprinted by permission. *Figure 10-3:* Reprinted by permission of Elsevier Science Publishing Co., Inc., from Barefoot, J.C., Dahlstrom, W.G., & Williams, R.B., Hostility, CHD incidence, and total mortality: A 25-year follow-up study of 255 physicians. *Psychosomatic Medicine,* 1983, 45 (1): 59–63. Copyright 1983 by the American Psychosomatic Society, Inc. *Figure 10-4:* Karasek, R., Baker, D., Marxer, F., Ahlbom, A., & Theorell, T., Job decision latitude, job demand, and cardiovascular disease: A prospective study of Swedish men. *American Journal of Public Health,* 1981, 71: 694–705. Reprinted by permission. *Figure 10-6:* Selye, H., *The Stress of Life.* New York: McGraw-Hill, 1956. Reprinted by permission. *Figure 11-1:* Klerman, G.L., Lavori, P.W., & Rice, J., et al., Birth cohort trends in rates of major depressive disorder among relatives of patients with affective disorder. *Archives of General Psychiatry,* 1985, 42 (7): 689–93. Copyright 1985. Reprinted by permission of the American Medical Association. *Figure 11-4:* Maier, S.F., Seligman, M.E.P., & Solomon, R.L., Pavlovian fear conditioning and learned helplessness: Effects on escape and avoidance behavior of (a) the CS-US contingency and (b) the independence of the US and voluntary responding. *Punishment and Aversive Behavior.* Edited by Campbell and Church. © 1969, p. 328. Adapted by permission of Prentice-Hall, Inc., Englewood Cliffs, N.J. *Figure 11-5:* Peterson, C., Luborsky, L., & Seligman, M.E.P., Attributions and depressive mood shifts: A case study using the symptom-context method. *Journal of Abnormal Psychology,* 1983, 92: 96–103. Copyright © 1983 by the American Psychological Association. Reprinted by permission. *Figure 11-6:* Bunney, W.E., & Murphy, D.L., Switch processes in psychiatric illness. In N.S. Kline (Ed.), *Factors in depression.* New York: Raven Press, 1974. Reprinted by permission. *Figure 11-7:* Rosenthal, N.E., Sack, D.A., Gillin, J.C., Lewy, A.J., Goodwin, F.K., Davenport, Y., Mueller, P.S., Newsome, D.A., & Wehr, T.A., Seasonal affective disorder: A description of the syndrome and preliminary findings with light therapy. *Archives of General Psychiatry,* 1984, 41: 72–80. Copyright 1984. Reprinted by permission of the American Medical Association. *Figure 11-8:* Jerome, J., Catching them before suicide. *The New York Times Magazine.* January 11, 1979. Copyright © 1979 by the New York Times Company. Reprinted by permission. *Figure 12-1:* Nicol, S.E., & Gottesman, I.I., Clues to the genetics and neurobiology of schizophrenia. *American Scientist,* 1983, 71: 398–404. Reprinted by permission. *Figure 12-2:* Courtesy Johns Hopkins Medical Institutions/Divisions of Nuclear Medicine and Radiation Health Sciences. At request of Dr. Henry N. Wagner. *Figure 12-4:* From Gleitman, H., *Psychology:* New York: W.W. Norton, 1981. Adapted from Faris, R.E.L., & Dunham, H.W., Mental disorders in urban areas. Chicago: University of Chicago Press, 1939. Adapted by permission of the authors. *Figure 12-5:* Keith, S.J., Gunderson, J.G., Reifman, A., Buschbaum, S., & Mosher, L.R., Special report: Schizophrenia, 1976. *Schizophrenia Bulletin,* 1976, 2: 510–65. Adapted by permission of the National Institute of

Mental Health. *Figure 12-6:* Vaughn, C.E., & Leff, J.P., The influence of family and social factors on the course of psychiatric illness: A comparison of schizophrenic and depressive-neurotic patients. *British Journal of Psychiatry,* 1976, *129,* 127–37. Adapted by permission. *Figure 13-1:* Money, J., & Ehrhardt, A.A., *Man and woman, boy and girl.* Baltimore: The Johns Hopkins University Press, 1972. Reprinted by permission of Johns Hopkins University Press and the authors. *Figure 14-5:* Hunt, W.A., & Matarazzo, J.D., Three years later: Recent developments in the experimental modification of smoking behavior. *Journal of Abnormal Psychology,* 1973, *81:* 107–14. Copyright 1973 by the American Psychological Association. Reprinted by permission. *Figure 14-6:* Henningfield, J.E., Behavioral pharmacology of cigarette smoking. In T. Thompson & P.B. Dews (Eds.), *Advances in behavioral pharmacology,* Vol. IV. New York: Academic Press, 1985. Reprinted by permission. *Figure 15-1:* Based on Lykken, D.T., A study of anxiety in the sociopathic personality. *Journal of Abnormal and Social Psychology,* 1957, *55,* 6—10. Adapted by permission of the American Psychological Association. 17-1A: Courtesy The American Museum of Natural History. *Figure 17-1B:* Modified from Keeton, W.T., *Biological Science,* 3rd ed. New York: W.W. Norton and Company, 1980. Copyright 1980, 1979, 1972, 1967 by W.W. Norton and Company Inc. *Figure 17-2A:* Modified from Katz, B., The nerve impulse. *Scientific American,* November 1952, *187:* 164–65. Copyright © 1952 by Scientific American Inc. All rights reserved. *Figure 17-2B and Figure 17-10:* From *Fundamentals of neurology: A psychological approach,* 6th ed., by Ernest Gardner, M.D. Copyright © 1975 by W.B. Saunders Company. Reprinted by permission. *Figure 17-3:* Supplied by Carolina Biological Supply Company. *Figure 17-4A:* AP/Wide World Photos. *Figure 17-4B:* Bettmann Archives. *Figure 17-5:* Hecaen, M., & Albert, M.L., Human neuropsychology. New York: John Wiley and Sons, Inc. Copyright © 1978 by John Wiley and Sons, Inc. *Figure 17-6:* Adapted from Luria, A., The functional organization of the brain. *Scientific American,* 1970, *222:* 66–78. Copyright © 1970 by Scientific American Inc. All rights reserved. *Figure 17-8:* Modified from Levy, J., Lateral specialization of the human brain. Behavioral manifestations and possible evolutionary basis. In J.A. Krieger, Jr. (Ed.), The biology of behavior. Corvallis, Oregon: Oregon State University Press, 1972. Copyright © 1972 by Oregon State University Press. Reprinted by permission. *Figure 17-9:* Gazzaniga, M., *The bisected brain,* New York: Plenum Publishing Corporation, 1970, p. 47. Copyright © 1970 by Plenum Publishing Corporation. Reprinted by permission. *Figure 17-11:* Adams, R.D., & Victor, M., *Principles of neurology,* 2nd ed. New York: McGraw-Hill, 1981. Adapted by permission of McGraw-Hill Book Company. *Figure 17-12 A,B,C and Figure 17-16C,D:* Charness, M.E., & DeLa Paz, R.L., Mammillary body atrophy in Wernicke's encephalopathy: Antemortem identification using magnetic resonance imagery. *Annals of Neurology,* 1987, 22: 595–600. Reprinted by permission of Little, Brown and the authors. *Figure 17-13:* Kertesz, A., Two case studies: Broca's and Wernicke's aphasia. In M.A. Arbib, D. Caplan, J.C. Marshall (Eds.), *Neural models of language processes.* New York: Academic Press, 1982. Reprinted by permission of Academic Press and the author. *Figure 17-14:* Modified from Geschwind, N. The apraxias: Neural mechanisms of disorders of learned movement. *American Scientist,* 1975, *188:* 189. Reprinted by permission. *Figure 17-16A,B:* Gluhbegovic, N., & Williams, T.H., *The human brain: A photographic guide.* Hagerstown, Md.: Lippincott/Harper and Row, 1980. Copyright © 1980 by Lippincott/Harper and Row. Reprinted by permission. *Figure 17-17:* Mishkin, M., & Appenzeller, T. The anatomy of memory. *Scientific American,* 1987, *256* (6): 80–89. Copyright © 1987 by Scientific American, Inc. All rights reserved. *Figure 17-18:* Blessed, G., Tomlinson, B.E., & Roth, M. The association between quantitative measures of dementia and of senile change in the cerebral gray matter of elderly subjects. *British Journal of Psychiatry,* 1968, *114:* 797–811. Reprinted by permission. *Figure 17-19:* Benson, D.F., Metter, E.J., Kuhl, D.E., & Phelps, M.E. Positron-computed tomography in neurobehavioral problems. In A. Kertesz (Ed.), *Localization in neuropsychology.* New York: Academic Press, 1983. Reprinted by permission of Academic Press and the authors. *Figure 17-20A,B:* © 1987 Stephen Shames/Visions.

Tables
Table 4-1: Valliant, G.E., *Adaptation to life.* Boston: Little, Brown, 1977. Adapted by permission. *Table 5-1:* Abramson, L.T., Seligman, M.E.P., & Teasdale, J., Learned helplessness in humans; Critique and reformulation. *Journal of Abnormal Psychology.* 1978, *87:* 32–48. Copyright © 1978 by the American Psychological Association. Reprinted by permission of the author. *Table 5-2:* Lazarus, A.A., *Multimodal behavior therapy.* Copyright © 1976 by Springer Publishing Company, Inc., New York. Used by permission. *Table 7-1:* Butcher, J.N., *MMPI: Research developments and clinical applications.* Copyright © 1969. Used with permission of McGraw-Hill Book Company. *Table 7-2:* Data from Diagnostic and Statistical Manual of Mental Disorders, 3rd ed., rev. (DSM-III-R). Adapted by permission of The American Psychiatric Association. *Table 8-3:* Marks, I.M., *Fears and phobias.* New York: Academic Press, 1969. Adapted by permission. *Table 8-5:* Sank, L.I., Psychology in action: Community disasters. Primary prevention and treatment in a health maintenance organization, *American Psychologist, 1979, 34:* 334–38. Copyright © 1979 by the American Psychological Association. Reprinted by permission of the author. *Table 9-1:* Rachman, S.J., & Hodgson, R.J., *Obsessions and compulsions.* © 1980, pp. 406–407. Adapted by permission of Prentice-Hall, Inc., Englewood Cliffs, N.J. *Table 9-2:* Hyler, S.E., & Spitzer, R.T., Hysteria split asunder. *American Journal of Psychiatry.* 1978, *135* (12): 1500–4. Copyright, 1978, the American Psychiatric Association. Reprinted by permission. *Table 10-1:* Weiss, J.M., Effects of coping behavior in different warning signaled conditions on stress pathology in rats. *Journal of Comparative and Physiological Psychology.* 1971, *77:* 1–13. Copyright © 1971 by the American Psychological Association. Reprinted by permission of the author. *Table 10-2:* Adapted by permission of Elsevier Science Publishing Co., Inc., from Grace, W.J., & Graham, D.T., Relationship of specific attitudes and emotions to certain bodily disease. *Psychosomatic Medicine.* 1952, *14:* 243–51. Copyright 1952 by the American Psychosomatic Society, Inc. *Table 10-3:* Holmes, T.H., & Rahe, R.H., The Social Readjustment Ratings Scale. *Journal of Psychosomatic Research,* 1967, *11:* 213–18. Reprinted with permission from the *Journal of Psychosomatic Research.* Copyright 1967. Pergamon Press, Ltd. *Table 11-1:* Robins, L.N., Helzer, J.E., Weissman, M.M., Orvaschel, H., Gruenberg, E., Burke, J.D., & Regier, D.A., Lifetime prevalence of specific psychiatric disorders in three sites. *Archives of General Psychiatry,* 1984, *41,* 949–58. Copyright 1984. Adapted by permission of the American Medical Association. *Table 11-3:* Shneidman, E., Introduction: Current Overview of Suicide. In E.S. Shneidman (Ed.), *Suicidology: Contemporary developments,* pages 16–17. New York: Grune & Stratton, 1976. Adapted by permission of The Psychological Corporation, and Edwin Shneidman. *Table 12-1:* Gottesman, I.I., & Shields, J., *Schizophrenia: The epigenetic puzzle.* Cambridge: Cambridge University Press, 1982. Adapted by permission. *Table 15-1:* Hutchings, B., & Mednick, S.A., Criminality in adoptees and their adoptive and biological parents: A pilot study. In S.A. Mednick & K.O. Christiansen (Eds.), *Biosocial bases of criminal behavior.* New York: Gardner Press, 1977. Modified with permission.

Boxes
Box 7-1: Diagnostic and Statistical Manual of Mental Disorders, 3rd ed., rev. (DSM-III-R), 1987. Reprinted by permission of The American Psychiatric Association. *Box 8-1:* Diagram from H. Gleitman, *Psychology.* New York: W.W. Norton & Co., 1981. Adapted by permission of Hawthorne Properties, Elsevier-Dutton Publishing Co., Inc., from *Bodily changes in pain, hunger, fear and rage* by W.B. Cannon. Copyright © 1929 by Appleton-Century Co.; 1957 by W.B. Cannon. *Box 8-2:* Endler, N.S., Magnusson, D., Ekehammar, B., & Okada, M.O., The multidimensionality of state and trait anxiety. Reports from the Department of Psychology, University of Stockholm, 1975. Adapted by permission of the authors. *Box 11-1:* Diagram from Alloy, L.B., & Abramson, L.Y., Judgment of contingency in depressed and nondepressed students. Sadder but wiser? *Journal of Experimental Psychology, General,* 1979, *108:* 441–85. Copyright © 1979 by the American Psychological Association. Reprinted by permission of the author. *Box 11-2:* Beck Depression Inventory, from Beck, A.T., *Depression: Clinical, experimental, and theoretical aspects.* New York: Hoeber, 1967. Reprinted by permission of the author. *Box 11-3:* Shneidman, E., Suicide Notes Reconsidered. In E.S. Shneidman (Ed.), *Suicidology: Contemporary developments,* pages 257, 269–71. New York: Grune & Stratton, 1976. Adapted by permission of The Psychological Corporation and Edwin Shneidman. *Box 14-1:* Diagnostic and Statistical Manual of Mental Disorders, 3rd ed., rev. (DSM-III-R), 1987. Reprinted by permission of The American Psychiatric Association. *Box 14-2:* Alcoholics Anonymous, *The Big Book,* 3rd ed. New York: A.A. World Services, Inc., 1976. Reprinted by permission of Alcoholics Anonymous World Services, Inc.

Photos
Part Opener 1: Photograph by Arthur Tress. *Page 4:* (left) Thomas Mclaular/*New York Post.* (right) Adam Scoll/Globe Photos. *Page 6:* ©Robin Laurance/Photo Researchers, Inc. *Page 8:* Courtesy The Phillips Collection. *Page 9:* ©Ira Berger 1982/Woodfin Camp. *Page 11:* ©Jim Anderson 1980/Woodfin Camp. *Page 12:* Photograph by Joan Roth. *Page 14:* Copyright © 1975, Fantasy Films and United Artists Corporation. *Page 17:* Dennis Brack/Black Star. *Page 19:* (top) Barbara Docktor/Leo de Wys, Inc. (bottom) Courtesy of The Warder Collection. *Page 20:* (left) © Michael Hayman 1982/Black Star. (right) Wide World Photos. *Page 24:* Courtesy The Warder Collection. *Page 25:* University Museum, University of Pennsylvania. *Page 26:* The New York Public Library, Astor, Lenox and Tilden Foundations. *Page 27:* Copyright Bodleian Library, Oxford, U.K. *Page 29:* Courtesy National Library of Medicine. *Page 31:* Courtesy The Mansell Collection. *Page 33:* (top) Courtesy National Library of Medicine. (bottom) Austrian Information Service. *Page 34:* Courtesy National Library of Medicine. *Page 36:* Courtesy Ernest Freud. *Page 38:* Courtesy National Library of Medicine. *Page 39:* Courtesy Bethlem Royal Hospital and The Maudsley Hospital Authority. Photos by permission of the Victoria and Albert Museum. *Page 40:* (top) Courtesy Clements Fry Collection, Yale University. (bottom) Courtesy National Library of Medicine. *Page 41:* Courtesy The Warder Collection. *Part Opener 2 (page 44):* Paul Klee, *Figure of the Oriental Theater,* 1934. Oil on fabric mounted on plywood panel, 20½ x 15½ in. The Phillips Collection, Washington, D.C. *Page 48:* Courtesy Johns Hopkins Medical Institutions/Division of Nuclear Medicine and Radiation Health Sciences. At request of Dr. Henry N. Wagner, Jr., M.D. *Page 49:* Courtesy Museo del Prado, Madrid. *Page 51:* Courtesy National Library of Medicine. *Page 52:* Courtesy The Bettmann Archive. *Page 53:* ©Bob Sacha, 1987/©Discover Publications. *Page 54:* Courtesy Henry N. Wagner, Jr., M.D., Division of Nuclear Medicine and Radiation Health Science, The Johns Hopkins Medical Institutions. *Page 57:* Svat Macha/Leo de Wys, Inc. *Page 59:* ©Will McIntyre/Photo Researchers, Inc. *Page 62:* Courtesy National Library of Medicine. *Page 63:* Copyright John Blaustein 1982/Woodfin Camp. *Page 64:* Photograph by Suzanne Szasz. *Page 65:* (left) Photograph by Suzanne Szasz. (right) Photograph by Frostie 1981/Woodfin Camp.

Page 66: ©Michael Hardy 1980/Woodfin Camp. *Page 67:* (both) Photographs by Suzanne Szasz. *Page 68:* Photograph by Suzanne Szasz. *Page 70:* Photograph by Suzanne Szasz. *Page 72:* (top) Courtesy The Bettmann Archive. (center) Courtesy Alexandra Adler. (bottom left) Courtesy National Library of Medicine. (bottom right) Courtesy The Warder Collection. *Page 73:* (left) Photograph by Jon Erikson. (right) Wide World Photos. *Page 74:* (top) The Warder Collection. (bottom) ©Stan Goldblatt/Photo Researchers, Inc. *Page 75:* Photograph by Suzanne Szasz. *Page 76:* (top) ©Michael Heron 1985/Woodfin Camp. (bottom left) Photograph by Suzanne Szasz. (bottom right) ©Rhoda Sidney/Leo de Wys, Inc. *Page 78:* Dorka Raynor/Leo de Wys, Inc. *Page 83:* Erika Stone/Photo Researchers, Inc. *Page 88:* Wide World Photos. *Page 89:* Wide World Photos. *Page 90:* (left) Photograph by Suzanne Szasz. (right) Jay Hoops/Leo de Wys, Inc. *Page 92:* Barton Silverman/Leo de Wys, Inc. *Page 96:* ©1982 Susan Rosenberg/Photo Researchers, Inc. *Page 98:* Photograph by Nozizwe S. *Page 99:* Courtesy Mrs. Frederick Perls. *Page 100:* Copyright Ernst Kaincrstorfer. *Page 105:* Photograph by Arthur Tress. *Page 108:* Courtesy Sovfoto. *Page 110:* (left) Courtesy Leo de Wys, Inc. (right) Photograph by Suzanne Szasz. *Page 111:* (all) © Erika Stone 1983. *Page 112:* (top) Courtesy National Library of Medicine. (bottom) Photograph by Christopher S. Johnson. *Page 113:* Photograph by R.E. Burdick/Leo de Wys, Inc. *Page 114:* ©Vivienne della Grotta 1979/Photo Researchers, Inc. *Page 115:* (top) Allan Grant. (bottom) Setri Hman/Gamma/Liaison. *Page 117:* ©Sylvia Johnson 1980/Woodfin Camp. *Page 119:* (top) Courtesy The Mayfield and George Arents Research Libraries, Syracuse University. (bottom) © Jerome Friar, 1987/Black Star. *Page 121:* (left) ©Time, Timothy Eagan 1978/Woodfin Camp. (right) Photograph by Suzanne Szasz. *Page 122:* (top) Phil Velasquez, ©*Chicago Sun-Times.* (bottom) Calvin Horn/United Press International. *Page 124:* Courtesy Institute for Rational Living. *Part Opener 3 (page 130):* ©Sepp Seitz 1982/Woodfin Camp. *Page 134:* Source unknown. *Page 138:* (both) The Warder Collection. *Page 140:* Courtesy Dr. Joseph Brady. *Page 142:* Yale Joel, *Life Magazine,* ©1958, Time Inc. *Page 151:* Wide World Photos. *Page 159:* ©Bettye Lane/Photo Researchers, Inc. *Page 160:* ©David M. Grossman/Photo Researchers, Inc. *Page 162:* Photograph by Jeffrey Grosscup. *Page 167:* Copyright Sepp Seitz 1982/Woodfin Camp. *Page 169:* ©Van Bucher, 1971, Photo Researchers, Inc. *Page 170:* ©Suzanne Szasz, 1981, Photo Researchers, Inc. *Page 173:* Courtesy Dr. Steve Wolf, Emory University. *Page 175:* Courtesy National Library of Medicine. *Part Opener 4 (page 186):* Photograph by Arthur Tress. *Page 190:* Courtesy The Warder Collection. *Page 193:* Courtesy The Museum of Modern Art/Film Stills Archive. *Page 197:* (left) Copyright Hope Alexander, 1980/Woodfin Camp. (center) ©Ray Ellis/Photo Researchers, Inc. (right) Wide World Photos. *Page 200:* ©1984 Ed Lettau/Photo Researchers, Inc. *Page 201:* Frostie 1982/Woodfin Camp. *Page 202:* Courtesy The Mayfield and George Arents Research Libraries, Syracuse University. *Page 207:* Leo de Wys, Inc. *Page 208:* Courtesy The Bettmann Archive. *Page 209:* Courtesy The Mayfield and George Arents Research Libraries, Syracuse University. *Page 210:* Courtesy Dr. Joseph Wolpe. *Page 211:* ©Tim Kelly, 1980/Black Star. *Page 212:* (both) ©1982 Susan Rosenberg/Photo Researchers, Inc. Snake Courtesy of Academy of Natural Sciences of Philadelphia. *Page 215:* (top) Pauline Lubens, *Detroit Free Press.* (bottom) Photograph by Suzanne Szasz. *Page 218:* (left) Wide World Photos. (right) Wide World Photos. *Page 220:* Wide World Photos. *Page 221:* Courtesy The Warder Collection. *Page 222:* Photograph by Jeffrey Grosscup. *Page 223:* UPI Photo by Kyoichi Sawada/UPI/Bettmann Newsphotos. *Page 225:* Wide World Photos. *Page 229:* Rocky Weldon/Leo de Wys, Inc. *Page 237:* Wide World Photos. *Page 240:* Courtesy The Museum of Modern Art/Film Stills Archive. *Page 242:* Courtesy S. J. Rachman. *Page 247:* Courtesy The Warder Collection. *Page 258:* Courtesy The Museum of Modern Art/Film Stills Archive. *Page 262:*

Staff photo by Gerald Marineau, *The Washington Post. Page 265:* Courtesy Dr. Eugene L. Bliss. *Page 267:* Wide World Photos. *Page 277:* (top) ©Leonard Freed/Magnum. (bottom) Herlinde Koelbl/Leo de Wys, Inc. *Page 278:* ©Ulrike Welsch 1988/Photo Researchers, Inc. *Page 279:* ©1976 Yan Lukas/Photo Researchers, Inc. *Page 280:* ©1981 Andy Sachs/Black Star. *Page 285:* Courtesy Leo de Wys, Inc. *Page 286:* Henri Cartier-Bresson/Magnum. *Page 287:* ©Stephen L. Feldman/Photo Researchers, Inc. *Page 289:* Courtesy Dr. Curt Richter. *Page 290:* Dan McCoy/Black Star. *Page 291:* Photograph by Judy Griesedieck, *San José Mercury News. Page 297:* National Archives of Canada Neg. #PA116671. *Page 300:* (top) Charles Moore/Black Star. (center) ©1981 Andy Sachs/Black Star. (bottom) ©1978 Thom O'Connor/Black Star. *Part Opener 5 (page 304):* ©1983 Stephen Shames/Black Star. *Page 307:* Vincent van Gogh Foundation/National Museum Vincent van Gogh, Amsterdam. *Page 309.* Copyright Christina Thomson 1982/Woodfin Camp. *Page 313:* Photograph by Arthur Tress. *Page 319:* Howard Dratch/Leo de Wys, Inc. *Page 321:* ©David M. Grossman/Photo Researchers, Inc. *Page 323:* ©Ed Lettau/Photo Researchers, Inc. *Page 329:* ©Thomas S. England, 1980/Photo Researchers, Inc. *Page 330:* Copyright by Harry Bleyenberg/Freelance Photographer's Guild. *Page 333:* The Warder Collection. *Page 344:* Copyright Bill Strode 1980/Woodfin Camp. *Page 345:* Photograph by Jeffrey Grosscup. *Page 351:* (left) Collections of the Library of Congress. (right) The National Archives. *Page 355:* Wide World Photos. *Page 356:* United Press International Photo. *Page 357:* Photograph by Joyce Marshall, *The Fort Worth Star-Telegram. Page 360:* United Press International Photo. *Page 364:* Charles Bell's "Madness" from his *Essays on the Anatomy of Expression in Painting,* 1806. *Page 365:* Courtesy National Library of Medicine. *Page 366:* Courtesy National Library of Medicine. *Page 367:* Drawing by Carl Lange, Copyright Prinzhorn-Sammlung, Universität Heidelberg, Foto Klinger Kunsthist, Institute. *Page 368:* Private Collection. *Page 371:* (left) Jerry Cooke/Photo Researchers, Inc. (right) Bill Bridges/Globe Photos. *Page 373:* From *Jugend,* Munich. *Page 375:* Courtesy Prinzhorn-Sammlung, Universität Heidelberg. *Page 376:* August Klett (Klotz), Courtesy Prinzhorn-Sammlung, Universität Heidelberg, Foto Zentsch. *Page 378:* Courtesy Dr. Otto Billig. *Page 381:* (left) Courtesy Dr. Otto Billig. (right) Edvard Munch's *Despair,* source unknown. *Page 383:* Courtesy Dr. Otto Billig. *Page 391:* (left) Courtesy Lessing J. Rosenwald, Library of Congress, Washington, D.C. (right) Courtesy Sotheby Parke Bernet. *Page 400:* ©Jerry Cooke 1979/Photo Researchers, Inc. *Page 403:* Photograph by Eugene Gordon. *Part Opener 6 (page 408):* Richard Laird/Leo de Wys, Inc. *Page 412:* Photograph by Wallace Kirkland. *Life Magazine* ©1948 Time Inc. *Page 413:* Photograph by Scott F. Johnson. *Page 414:* Courtesy The Rodin Museum: Gift of Jules E. Mastbaum. Photographed by Philadelphia Museum of Art. *Page 418:* Richard Laird/Leo de Wys, Inc. *Page 425:* OHANIA: Or The Heinous Sin of Self-Pollution and Its Frightful Consequences in Both Sexes,... By N. Crouch, London, 1725. *Page 426:* Courtesy The Metropolitan Museum of Art. Kennedy Fund, 1910. *Page 429:* Jason Laure/Woodfin Camp. *Page 430:* Courtesy of the New York Historical Society, New York City. *Page 434:* Courtesy The Museum of Modern Art/Film Stills Archive. *Page 435:* Courtesy The Museum of Modern Art/Film Stills Archive. *Page 439:* Photograph by Ernie Hearion, *The New York Times. Page 440:* ©Alon Reininger 1981/Woodfin Camp. *Page 443:* (both) Wide World Photos. *Page 445:* Chris Steel Perkins/Magnum. *Page 451:* ©1984 John Devisser/Black Star. *Page 452:* ©David M. Grossman/Photo Researchers, Inc. *Page 455:* ©Copyright 1987 by Ulrike Welsch/Photo Researchers, Inc. *Page 457:* (left) Dan McCoy/Black Star. (right) Archie Lieberman/Black Star. *Page 460:* ©Stephen L. Feldman/Photo Researchers, Inc. *Page 461:* ©Arthur Tress 1981/Woodfin Camp. *Page 463:* ©Arthur Tress 1978/Woodfin Camp. *Page 464:* Werner Wolff/Black Star. *Page 468:* ©M. M. Mamano

1977/Photo Researchers, Inc. *Page 472:* John Collier/Black Star. *Page 474:* (left) ©Robert Goldstein, 1982/Photo Researchers, Inc. (right) Wide World Photos. *Page 476:* (left) ©Ken Lone 1979/ Black Star. (right) ©Michel Ducille 1988/Black Star. *Page 479:* Courtesy Sygma. *Page 480:* Richard Lawrence Stack/Black Star. *Page 481:* Photo by Laurence Schiller, ©1976 The New Ingot Co./ Photo Researchers, Inc. *Page 484:* ©Michael Hayman/Photo Researchers, Inc. *Page 489:* Photo by Lou Moore/Black Star. *Page 495:* Courtesy *The Salt Lake Tribune. Page 501:* Courtesy Dr. Kurt Hirschhorn. *Page 506:* Courtesy The Museum of Modern Art/ Film Stills Archive. *Page 507:* Photograph by Yemima Rabin. *Page 508:* Courtesy Mrs. James Thurber. *Page 512:* Courtesy The Warder Collection. *Part Opener 7 (page 516):* Photograph by Judy Griesedieck, *San José Mercury News. Page 520:* ©Alice Kandell/ Photo Researchers, Inc. *Page 522;* Jeff Persons/New England Stock Photo. *Page 523:* ©Alice Kandell/Photo Researchers, Inc. *Page 530:* Photograph by Rhoda Sidney/Leo de Wys, Inc. *Page 532:* Photo by Erika/Photo Researchers, Inc. *Page 537:* ©1982 Susan Rosenberg, Photo Researchers, Inc. *Page 539:* ©1980 Susan Rosenberg, Photo Researchers, Inc. *Page 540:* Wide World Photos. *Page 542:* Photograph by Alan Carey/The Image Works. *Page 544:* (left) Photograph by Nancy Kaye/Leo de Wys, Inc. (right) Photograph by Alan Carey/The Image Works. *Page 548:* Photograph by Alan Carey/The Image Works. *Page 549:* Photograph by Allan Grant. *Page 551:* Photograph by Allan Grant. *Page 554:* Photograph by Allan Grant. *Page 555:* Photograph by Allan Grant. *Page 557:* ©Jan Lukas/Photo Researchers, Inc. *Page 600:* Photograph by G.M.S. *Page 605:* Courtesy The Museum of Modern Art/Film Stills Archive. *Page 607:* Photograph by Charles Gatewood. *Page 613:* Photograph by Raymond Depardon/Magnum. *Page 615:* Wide World Photos. *Page 616:* Photographs by Michael O'Brien. *Page 618:* Wide World Photos. *Page 628:* ©Peter Reddaway. *Page 629:* (left) Courtesy The Warder Collection. (right) ©M. J. Tatham, National Institute for Medical Research, London. *Page 630:* United Press International Photos. *Page 635:* Picture Collection, The Branch Libraries, The New York Public Library. *Page 637:* Photograph by Ann Chwatsky/Leo de Wys, Inc. *Page 642:* Photograph by Harry Benton. *Page 655:* Don Cunningham for American Psychological Association. *Page 660:* Photograph by Jeffrey Grosscup. *Page 667:* Ricki Rosen/Picture Group, Inc. *Page 669:* Photograph by Jeffrey Grosscup. *Page 671:* Photograph by Ann Chwatsky/Leo de Wys, Inc. *Page 672:* Courtesy Don Cunningham for American Psychological Association. *Page 674:* Photograph by Jeffrey Grosscup.

pertiment